The advantages and limitations of diagnosis: Like other scientific fields, abnormal psychology relies on a system of categories for classifying its subject matter. These diagnostic systems have the advantages of facilitating treatment, research, and teaching in abnormal psychology. But diagnostic systems in abnormal psychology also have important limitations; they can oversimplify complex problems, and a diagnosis of mental illness can be stigmatizing and demoralizing to the person being diagnosed.

The principle of multiple causality: Mental disorders can result from a wide variety of causes: some predisposing, some precipitating; some psychological, some biological; some internal to the person in distress, and some external or environmental. Most disorders involve multiple, interacting causes. In addition, several different theoretical perspectives co-exist within the field of abnormal psychology. Each theoretical perspective has something important to contribute, and the field of abnormal psychology is increasingly moving towards explanations and treatments that combine *components* from various theories.

The connection between mind and body: A thorough understanding of psychopathology requires an appreciation of the connection between mind and body. We know that brain abnormalities can cause emotional symptoms, and, conversely, that emotional distress can cause physical symptoms. As a result, it is important to attend to the interrelationships between a person's psychological and physical functioning in order to explain and treat abnormal behavior.

Are you interested in incorporating the latest technology in your classroom, but are unsure of your skills or how to get started? The Faculty Resource Network is composed of a group of specially trained college professors who are currently teaching and successfully using technology in their psychology classes. These professors offer one-on-one assistance to adopters interested in incorporating online course management tools and specific software packages. They also provide innovative classroom techniques and methods for tailoring the technology experience to the specific needs of your course. For more information, go to www.FacultyResourceNetwork.com.

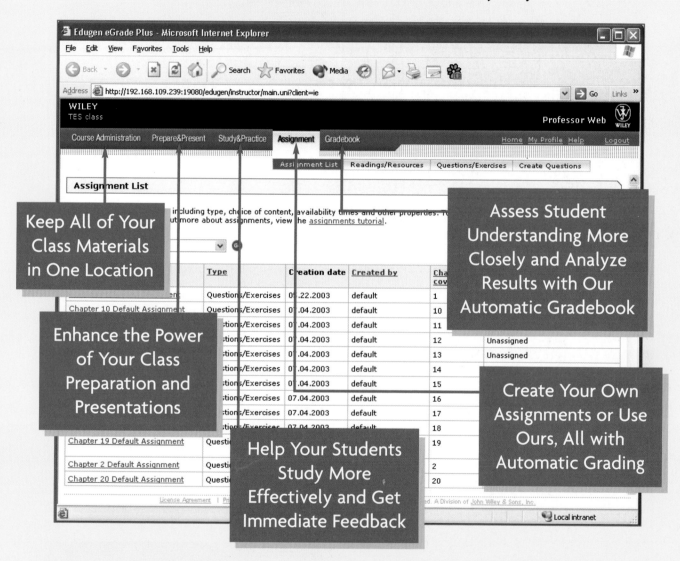

Students,
eGrade Plus Allows You to:

Study More Effectively

Get Immediate Feedback When You Practice on Your Own

eGrade Plus problems link directly to relevant sections of the **electronic book content,** so that you can review the text while you study and complete homework online. Additional resources include **vidoe clips, practice tests, study guide** and other tutorial resources.

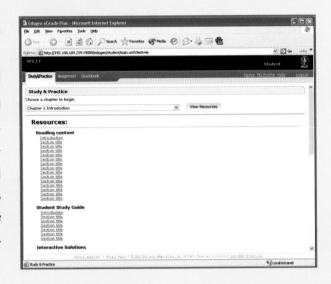

Complete Assignments / Get Help with Problem Solving

An **Assignment** area keeps all your assigned work in one location, making it easy for you to stay "on task." In addition, many homework problems contain a **link** to the relevant section of the **multimedia book,** providing you with a text explanation to help you conquer problem-solving obstacles as they arise. You will have access to a variety of **content enrichment resources,** as well as other tools for building your confidence and understanding.

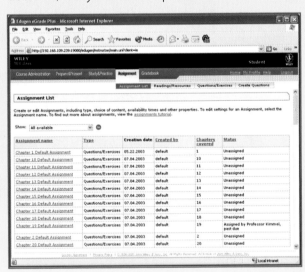

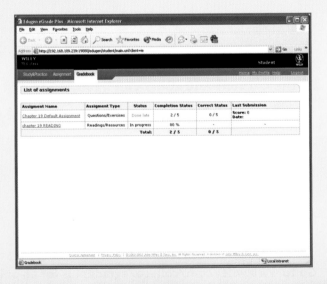

Keep Track of How You're Doing

A **Personal Gradebook** allows you to view your results from past assignments at any time.

ABNORMAL PSYCHOLOGY

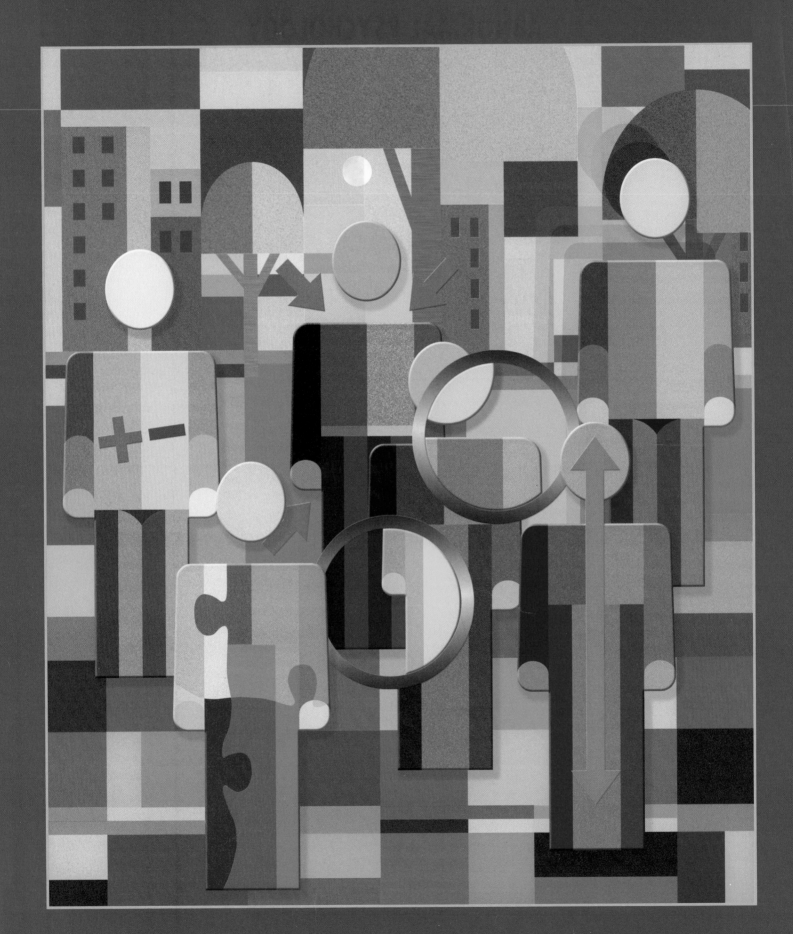

Abnormal Psychology

James Hansell & Lisa Damour

University of Michigan   **John Carroll University**

WILEY

John Wiley & Sons, Inc.

Executive Editor	Ryan Flahive
Senior Developmental Editor	Suzanne Thibodeau
Marketing Manager	Kate Stewart
Media Editor	Thomas Kulesa
Associate Editor	Lili DeGrasse
Editorial Assistant	Deepa Chungi
Senior Production Editor	Norine Pigliucci
Senior Designer	Karin Gerdes Kincheloe
Illustration Editor	Sandra Rigby
Senior Photo Editor	Sara Wight
Photo Researchers	Alexandra Truitt and Jerry Marshall
Production Management Services	Hermitage Publishing Services
Cover Illustration	Carol C. Grobe

This book was set in Times by Hermitage Publishing Services and printed and bound by Von Hoffmann Press. The cover was printed by Von Hoffmann Press.

This book is printed on acid free paper. ∞

To order books or for customer service please, call 1-800-CALL WILEY (225-5945).

ISBN 0-471-38982-X
WIE ISBN 0471-65821-9

Printed in the United States of America

10 9 8 7 6 5 4 3 2 1

James Hansell received a B.A. in Philosophy from Amherst College in 1979 and a Ph.D. in Clinical Psychology from the University of Michigan in 1988. He also completed a post-Doctoral fellowship at the University of Michigan Psychological Clinic and psychoanalytic training at the Michigan Psychoanalytic Institute. Since 1989, Jim has been teaching at the University of Michigan and seeing clients in his private practice in Ann Arbor. He has won several awards for his teaching and writing. Jim's teaching, research, and writing have focused on abnormal psychology, psychotherapy process and outcome, the therapeutic alliance, gender and sexual identity, and psychoanalytic theory. Jim is also a licensed soccer coach (who still plays occasionally, joints permitting) and co-chair of the Committee on Psychoanalysis and Sport of the American Psychoanalytic Association. He enjoys coaching his two teenagers' sports teams, traveling with his family, and playing guitar in The Shrunken Heads and The Spaceheaters, two rock bands composed of fellow psychologists.

Lisa Damour received her B.A. from Yale in 1992, and her Ph.D. in Clinical Psychology from the University of Michigan in 1997. She completed a post-Doctoral fellowship at the University of Michigan Psychological Clinic and now maintains a private psychotherapy practice working with adults, children, and families. Lisa taught at University of Michigan for several years before moving to the Cleveland area where she now teaches in the Department of Psychology at John Carroll University and is affiliated with the Hanna Perkins Center for Child Development. She is the co-author (with Anne Curzan) of *First Day to Final Grade: A graduate student's guide to teaching.* Lisa and Anne have also developed a consulting practice in which they visit universities to train graduate teaching assistants. When not practicing, teaching, writing, or consulting, Lisa likes to cook, knit, play sports, and hang out with her husband and daughter.

This book grew out of our enthusiasm for the fascinating subject of abnormal psychology, and our experiences of sharing this enthusiasm with our students at the University of Michigan and John Carroll University over the past 15 years. We are convinced that an abnormal psychology textbook can be informative and current yet remain as intriguing and lively as the field itself. In addition, we see the need for a more contemporary approach to the teaching of abnormal psychology. Most textbooks, in an effort to remain consistent with 1990s psychiatry, use the DSM-IV-TR as the backbone of their content and organization. In our view, this focus misses what is most important and interesting about the field. We have found that our students learn the most when they focus on the core concepts and controversies in the field rather than on fine diagnostic distinctions and details. While our book thoroughly covers the DSM system and the current DSM-IV-TR categories, *core concepts in abnormal psychology* form the backbone of the text.

A brief vignette about teaching may help communicate our vision for this book. At some point in every semester we are approached by students who have heard about someone (an acquaintance, a movie character, a figure in the news) struggling with emotional or behavioral symptoms and ask, "So, what's his/her diagnosis?" We usually try to explain that a diagnostic label, while important, is not the most interesting, helpful, or complete way to think about this person. We pose some other questions. How did the person come to have these symptoms and how might the person be helped? Are the symptoms severe enough that they should be considered pathological? What contextual factors, such as family and cultural background, can help us understand this person? These questions relate to our core concepts approach and help students to see the complex contextual issues that make the study of psychopathology interesting, humane, and relevant.

THE CORE CONCEPTS APPROACH

The field of abnormal psychology focuses on three related questions:

- How do we distinguish normal behavior from abnormal behavior? (*defining* abnormality)

- How are abnormal behaviors categorized and diagnosed? (*classifying* abnormality)

- How can abnormal behaviors be understood and changed? (*explaining and treating* abnormality)

To address these questions, we have organized our book around six core concepts in abnormal psychology. These concepts are introduced in Chapter 1, and the core concepts are emphasized in every chapter. They are highlighted visually with icons and boldface italic blue type. The six core concepts are:

The importance of context in defining and understanding abnormality: We can only identify a behavior as abnormal if we consider the situational context in which it occurs; behaviors that are normal in one context may be abnormal in another. Furthermore, abnormal behavior is usually most understandable when viewed in the context of life history and life events. Finally, demographic context variables such as age, gender, culture, and class influence the definition, classification, explanation, and treatment of abnormal behaviors.

The continuum between normal and abnormal behavior: Emotional and behavioral symptoms occur along a continuum that ranges from mild to severe, and many forms of abnormality are exaggerated versions of normal feelings and behaviors. The dividing line between normal and abnormal behavior is never entirely clear, but the field of abnormal psychology has developed criteria that help us make this distinction.

Cultural and historical relativism in defining and classifying abnormality: Definitions and classifications of abnormal behavior vary considerably across different cultures and across different historical periods. As a result, we cannot make absolute, universal statements about what constitutes abnormal behavior, and we always need to be mindful of the cultural and historical lenses through which we view the concept of abnormality.

The advantages and limitations of diagnosis: Like other scientific fields, abnormal psychology relies on a system of categories for classifying its subject matter. These diagnostic systems have the advantages of facilitating treatment, research, and teaching in abnormal psychology. But diagnostic systems in abnormal psychology also have important limitations; they can oversimplify complex problems, and a diagnosis of mental illness can be stigmatizing and demoralizing to the person being diagnosed.

The principle of multiple causality: Mental disorders can result from a wide variety of causes; some predisposing, some precipitating; some psychological, some biological; some internal to the person in distress, and some external or environmental. Most disorders involve multiple, interacting causes. In addition, several different theoretical perspectives co-exist within the field of abnormal psychology. Each theoretical perspective has something important to contribute, and the field of abnormal psychology is increasingly moving towards explanations and treatments that combine components from various theories.

The connection between mind and body: A thorough understanding of psychopathology requires an appreciation of the connection between mind and body. We know that brain abnormalities can cause emotional symptoms, and, conversely, that emotional distress can cause physical symptoms. As a result, it is important to attend to the interrelationships between a person's psychological and physical functioning in order to explain and treat abnormal behavior.

These six core concepts provide students with a sophisticated framework for learning about psychopathology. The concepts contextualize abnormal behavior in a way that helps students understand, remember, and integrate the material they cover in this course. Finally, these concepts promote students' critical thinking and class discussions of controversies in the field.

AN INTEGRATED APPROACH TO THE THEORETICAL PERSPECTIVES IN ABNORMAL PSYCHOLOGY

Most abnormal psychology texts still focus on the differences among the traditional theoretical perspectives, and teach them as distinct, competing approaches to explaining and treating psychopathology (for example, behavioral versus psychodynamic explanations of phobias). In our view, this approach misleads students. In contemporary practice, the integration of multiple theoretical perspectives is increasingly commonplace. In this book, we describe the differences among theoretical perspectives, but we also focus on how they overlap and complement each other. Accordingly, we describe the various theoretical perspectives as *components* that can be combined to explain and treat psychopathology. We have seen undergraduates benefit from this approach even in introductory courses aimed at providing a clear, basic understanding of the field.

A CLINICAL CASE FOCUS

We include several case examples per chapter, and we make clinical material a central focus of the book. As practicing clinicians, we use the numerous case examples at our disposal to illustrate the core concepts and to make the text lively and compelling. We use case examples that illustrate the ways psychopathology usually presents in the real world: mixed symptom pictures which call for multi-modal treatment strategies, rather than contrived cases that conform precisely to DSM-IV-TR categories. Using multiple case examples also allows us to show students the subtypes of various disorders. Chapter openers that describe famous artists who suffered from psychological symptoms provide additional case material while demonstrating that psychopathology often exists alongside other normal, and sometimes exceptional, aspects of functioning. Often, students say that this case focus is their favorite part of our courses.

THE PEDAGOGICAL FRAMEWORK

Our book aims to be accessible to the student and easy to use for the instructor. This book contains a number of innovative features designed to enhance its pedagogy, accessibility, and appeal.

Streamlined Table of Contents

We have streamlined the traditional table of contents of abnormal psychology texts to a 14-chapter book by integrating certain topics throughout the book rather than placing them in separate chapters. For example, research methods are discussed throughout the text, social and legal issues are addressed in the chapters where they are most relevant, and treatment is covered in every chapter, not in a separate chapter on psychotherapy. We feel that a 14-chapter format is more appropriate than the traditional 16-20 chapter text given that the typical semester is 12–14 weeks long. With 14 chapters, students can read 1 chapter per week and feel that they have used most of the book that they have purchased.

Consistent Chapter Format

To help students master complex material, we use a consistent format in Chapters 5 through 14, which cover the various categories of disorders. The disorders presented in each chapter are addressed under the major headings <u>Defining</u>, <u>Classifying</u>, and <u>Explaining and Treating</u>. The core concepts are included under these major headings where they are naturally relevant. We have found that students quickly become familiar with this format, and then find it easier to assimilate new material. Instructors can also use this format as a template for their lectures and organization of the course. This is the typical outline for Chapters 5 through 14:

Case Vignettes: Brief, compelling narratives to give a picture of the disorders in the chapter.

Defining the category (e.g., Mood Disorders)
    The importance of *context* in defining and understanding abnormality
    The *continuum* between normal and abnormal behavior

Classifying the disorders in this category
    Cultural and historical relativism in classifying the disorders
    The DSM-IV-TR categories
    Classification in demographic *context* (gender, age, class, and culture)
    The *advantages and limitations* of diagnoses in this category

Explaining and Treating the disorders in this category
    Relevant theoretical components (behavioral, cognitive, psychodynamic, biological, etc.)
    The principle of *multiple causality*
    The *connection between mind and body* in these disorders

Case Vignettes: Treatment strategies for the opening cases

Chapter Summary

ADDITIONAL CHAPTER FEATURES

Each chapter has several "extra" features:

- Multiple boxes on issues relevant to the chapter topic (such as the recovered memory debate, prevention, confidentiality, managed care, mental health parity, duty to warn, competency to stand trial, the terrorist attacks of September 11, 2001, etc.)

- Tables and figures illustrating chapter content.

- Discussion of well-known books and films related to the chapter topic.

- Frequent interim summaries that enable students to spot-check their comprehension of the material.

- Critical thinking questions throughout each chapter to stimulate students' reflection, review, and test preparation.

- Definitions of all key terms in the margin near their discussion in the text.

- A chapter summary that focuses on the core concepts presented in the chapter.

We feel that we have something innovative and timely to offer with our book, based on our experiences teaching abnormal psychology to thousands of students over the past 15 years. We hope that you and your students agree!

TEACHING AND LEARNING SUPPLEMENTS

Abnormal Psychology offers a full line of teaching and learning resources to enhance the instructor's use of the text and encourage students' active reading and learning.

Resources for the Instructor

Videos. We have created three distinct DVD, VHS, and streaming video resources to support *Abnormal Psychology.* Each resource provides short lecture-launching video clips that can be used to introduce new topics, enhance your presentations, and stimulate classroom discussions. Our topical video clips are organized to support the textbook's table of contents. Our thematic video clips support the six core concepts that run throughout the text. Our third video resource presents topics from current news headlines that are relevant to the study of abnormal psychology. To help you integrate these video clips into your syllabus, we have developed a comprehensive library of teaching resources, study questions, and assignments.

PowerPoint Presentations, created by each of the text's authors:

- James Hansell has created a set of PowerPoint presentations that support the table of contents. Each chapter will have slide files containing (1) lecture outlines and (2) the chapter line illustrations.
- Lisa Damour has created a set of PowerPoints that support the core concepts that run throughout the text. These concepts are introduced in Chapter 1, and the core concepts are emphasized in every chapter where they are highlighted visually with an icon and boldface italic blue type.

Animation of the Core Concepts. The textbook authors have created an animated walkthrough of the text's core concepts, using a case example, for presentation on the first day of class; the animation is available at: www.wiley.com/college/hansell.

Image Gallery. We provide online electronic files for the line illustrations in the text, which the instructor can customize for presenting in class (for example, in handouts, overhead transparencies, or PowerPoints).

Wiley Faculty Resource Network is a peer-to-peer network of faculty ready to support your use of online course management tools and discipline-specific software/learning systems in the classroom. The Faculty Resource Network will help you apply innovative classroom techniques, implement software packages, tailor the technology experience to the needs of each individual class, and provide you with virtual training sessions led by faculty for faculty.

TA Training. While many universities rely on graduate students to teach undergraduates, few universities provide adequate training or support for their graduate teaching assistants. To aid graduate student instructors and the departments in which they teach, Lisa Damour has teamed up with Wiley to develop resources to help teaching assistants succeed. The resources described below provide classroom-tested advice for the new instructor and specific, practical answers to questions that arise throughout the semester.

Using the Wiley Faculty Resource Network, Lisa Damour will offer live on-line training that addresses issues unique to graduate student instructors. She will focus on the "how to's" of teaching, such as setting up a lesson plan, running a discussion, and grading, as well as issues specific to the teaching assistant's unique role as both student and teacher, such as establishing authority, working effectively with the course professor, and balancing teaching with graduate studies. If you would like to participate in one of these sessions, or to arrange a training session for your teaching assistants, please contact your local Wiley representative, or visit our website: www.FacultyResourceNetwork.com.

Lisa Damour and Anne Curzan (University of Michigan) provide on-site teaching assistant training to a variety of universities throughout the United States. We have made relevant video clips from their TA training sessions available on the *Abnormal Psychology* Instructor Website. These clips offer useful advice that ranges from the broad (how to lead discussions, how to evaluate student learning) to the specific yet nevertheless important (how to dress, how to respond to student emails). To register for access to these video clips, please visit our website: www.wiley.com/college/hansell.

For a comprehensive guide to all aspects of teaching as a graduate assistant, please order a copy of Lisa and Anne's book from the University of Michigan Press: Curzan, A. & Damour, L. (2000). First day to final grade: A graduate student's guide to teaching.

Instructor's Manual, prepared by Gayle E. Pitman of Sacramento City College, includes chapter learning objectives, lecture outlines, lecture extensions, and classroom activities and discussion topics.

Test Bank, written by Kristine Jacquin of Mississippi State University, contains over 750 questions, offering multiple choice, true/false, fill-in-the-blank, matching, and essay questions for each chapter. The Test Bank is available in printed form as well as online, where it can be downloaded into individual word processing programs.

Computerized Test Bank. For the instructor's convenience, the test bank questions are available on CD-ROM or online, with software from Brownstone Research Group that allows the instructor the flexibility to create and customize exams (for example, by scrambling the order of questions, adding new questions, or editing existing ones). The test engine for PC computers is Diploma, and the test engine for Mac computers is Exam.

Assignment Questions. Over 200 multiple choice, true/false, and essay questions written by Laurie MacKenzie of San Diego Mesa College, for use in content management systems, for online homework, or for use in classroom response systems.

Resources for the Student

Study Guide, prepared for students by Shannon M. Lynch of Western Illinois University. Each chapter contains learning objectives, key terms with page numbers, and practice questions that include conceptual, multiple-choice (with answers), fill-ins (with answers), and short-answer essay questions.

Online Flash Cards offer the opportunity to drill and practice the glossary terms.

Online Self Tests for each chapter, written by Laurie MacKenzie of San Diego Mesa College, offer students immediate feedback on their answers to multiple choice, matching, and fill-in questions.

Annotated Web Links direct students to articles related to specific disorders and explain how the web links relate to the chapter content. We also provide questions to frame the students' web exploration.

eGrade Plus
Helping Teachers Teach and Students Learn
(www.wiley.com/college/hansell)

Abnormal Psychology is available with eGrade Plus, a powerful online tool that provides instructors and students with an integrated suite of teaching and learning resources in one easy-to-use website. eGrade Plus is organized around the essential activities you and your students perform in class:

For Instructors

- **Prepare and Present:** Create class presentations using a wealth of Wiley-provided resources such as an online version of the textbook, PowerPoint slides, and interactive simulations, making your preparation time more efficient. You may easily adapt, customize, and add to this content to meet the needs of your course.

- **Create Assignments:** Automate the assigning and grading of homework or quizzes by using Wiley-provided question banks or by writing your own. Student results will be automatically graded and recorded in your gradebook. eGrade Plus can link homework problems to the relevant section of the online text, providing students with context-sensitive help.

- **Track Student Progress:** Keep track of your students' progress via an instructor's gradebook, which allows you to analyze individual and overall class results to determine their progress and level of understanding

- **Administer Your Course:** eGrade Plus can easily be integrated with another course management system, gradebook, or other resources you are using in your class, providing you with the flexibility to build your course, your way.

For Students

Wiley's eGrade Plus provides immediate feedback on student assignments and a wealth of support materials. This powerful study tool will help your students develop their conceptual understanding of the class material and increase their ability to solve problems.

- **A "Study and Practice"** area links directly to text content, allowing students to review the text while they study and complete homework assignments. Additional resources can include interactive simulations, study guides and solutions manual material, and other problem-solving resources.

- **An "Assignment"** area keeps all of the work that you want your students to complete in one location, making it easy for them to stay "on task." Students will have access to a variety of interactive problem-solving tools, as well as other resources for building their confidence and understanding. In addition, many homework problems contain a link to the relevant section of the multimedia book, providing students with context-sensitive help that allows them to conquer problem-solving obstacles as they arise.

- **A Personal Gradebook** for each student will allow students to view their results from past assignments at any time.

Please view our online demo at www.wiley.com/college/egradeplus. Here you will find additional information about the features and benefits of eGrade Plus, how to request a "test drive" of eGrade Plus for *Abnormal Psychology*, and how to adopt it for class use.

ACKNOWLEDGMENTS

We would like to thank all of the reviewers who helped us to shape and refine this book. We have received and carefully considered well over 100 reviews of different parts of the manuscript over the 4 years of its development. These thoughtful and insightful comments from our knowledgeable colleagues have been invaluable in taking our vision for this book and making it a reality. We would like to extend our warm thanks to:

John Allen *University of Arizona*
Jay Alperson *Palomar College*
Diana Anson *Community College of Southern Nevada*
Carol Austad *Central Connecticut State University*
Amy Badura *Creighton University*
Keith Beard *Marshall University*
Michael Becker *York College*
Sarah Bing *University of Maryland, Eastern Shore*
Ann Brandt-Williams *Glendale Community College*
Joanne Brewster *James Madison University*
Jeannie Buchanan *Palomar College*
James Calhoun, *University of Georgia*
Glenn Callaghan *San Jose State University*
Etzel Cardena *University of Texas, Pan American*
Richard Cluff, *Missouri Western State College*
Lee Cohen *Texas Tech University*
Patti Connor-Greene *Clemson University*
Jennifer Connor-Smith *Oregon State University*
Judith Crothers-Flamming, *Georgia Institute of Technology*
Eric Dahlen *University of Southern Mississippi*
James O. Davis, *Southwestern Missouri State University*
Joseph A. Davis *San Diego State University; University of California, San Diego*
Lenore Defonso *Indiana-Purdue University, Fort Wayne*
Joan Doolittle *Anne Arundel Community College*
Susann Doyle *Gainesville College*
Michael Ellison *Texas Wesleyan University*
Carrie Elrod *Georgia State University*
Michael J. Eltz *Pennsylvania State University*
William Flack *Bucknell University*
Natalie C. Frank *George Washington University*
William Fremouw *West Virginia University*
Steven Funk *Northern Arizona University*
Robert Gallen *Indiana University of Pennsylvania*
Brian Garavaglia *Macomb Community College*
Cathy Hall *East Carolina University*
Marjorie Hanft-Martone *Eastern Illinois University*
Ben Hankin *University of Illinois at Chicago*
David Hargrove *University of Mississippi*
Morton Harmatz *University of Massachusetts*
Charlyn Harper Browne *Clark Atlanta University*
Richard Heath *St. Thomas Aquinas College*
JWP Heuchert *Allegheny College*
Joyce Hopkins *Illinois Institute of Technology*
Joseph Hovey *University of Toledo*

Robert Intrieri *Western Illinois University*
Kristine Jacquin *Mississippi State University*
Gregory Jarvie *Georgia College & State University*
Cynthia Jenkins *Creighton University*
Richard Kandus *Mt. San Jacinto College*
Sandra Kerr *West Chester University*
Bonnie Kin *Georgia State University*
Elise Labbe *University of South Alabama*
Karl Laves *Western Kentucky University*
Thad Leffingwell *Oklahoma State University*
Penny Leisring *Quinnipiac University*
Erica Lilleleht *Seattle University*
Laura Liljequist *Murray State University*
Shannon M. Lynch *Western Illinois University*
Michael MacLean *Buffalo State College*
William McCown *University of Louisiana at Monroe*
Howard Markowitz *Hawaii Pacific University*
Brian Marx *Temple University*
Kevin Masters *Utah State University*
Dorothy Mercer *Eastern Kentucky University*
Chelley Merrell *Tidewater Community College*
Michelle Merwin *Univesity of Tennessee*
Bjorn Meyer *University of Surrey, Roehampton*
Joni L. Mihura *University of Toledo*
Christine Molnar *Medical University of South Carolina*
Pamela Mulder *Marshall University*
Alan Nagamoto *University of California Los Angeles*
Paul Neunuebel *Sam Houston State University*
Gayle Norbury *University of Wisconsin, Milwaukee*
Patricia Owen *St. Mary's University*
Irene Ozbek *University of Tennessee at Chattanooga*
Ju Hui Park *University of Utah*
Leanne Parker *Lewis-Clark State College*
Ramona Parrish *Guilford Technical Community College*
Linda Petroff *Central Community College, Nebraska*
Gayle E. Pitman *Sacramento City College*
Cynthia Pury *Clemson University*
Stuart Quirk *Central Michigan University*
David Reitman *Louisiana State University*
Paul Rhoads *Williams College*
Michael Rose *Georgia College & State University*
Michael Sakuma *Dowling College*
Peggy Saltz *University of Central Arkansas*
Joanna Salapska-Gelleri *University of Nevada*
Stephen Saunders *Marquette University*
Robert Seifer *Nova Southeastern University*
Richard Siegel *University of Massachusetts, Lowell*
Rebecca Simms *Barat College of DePaul University*
Susan Simonian *College of Charleston*
Norman Simonson *University of Massachusetts, Amherst*
Arthur Skibbe *Appalachian State University*
Denise Sloan *Temple University*
Patricia Slocum *College of DuPage*

Valerie Smead *Western Illinois University*
Michael Southam-Gerow *Virginia Commonwealth University*
Richard Spates *Western Michigan University*
Joanne Stohs *California State University, Fullerton*
Carla Strassle *York College of Pennsylvania*
Jaine Strauss *Macalester College*
Brian Sullivan *College of Charleston*
Carol Terry *University of Oklahoma*
Irving Tucker *Shepherd College*
Michael Villaneuva *University of New Mexico*
Teraesa Vinson *University of Florida*
Susan Waldman *San Francisco State*
Nathan Weed *Central Michigan University*
Sandra Wilcox *California State University, Dominguez Hills*
Lester Wright, Jr. *Western Michigan University*
Zakhour Youssef *Eastern Michigan University*
Robert Zettle *Wichita State University*

Several publishing houses were interested in our prospectus for this book, but we knew from our initial contacts with John Wiley & Sons that Wiley was the right place for us. We couldn't be happier with our decision. Ellen Schatz, our initial acquisitions editor, and Anne Smith, Vice-President and Publisher, not only "got" what we were talking about immediately, but showed us how well our vision fit with Wiley's tradition of quality and innovation. Suzanne Thibodeau, Senior Development Editor, who has been with us from the start, deserves as much credit for this book as anyone. She has patiently and skillfully guided us through every stage of the process, and her belief in our vision, which she helped shape, has been invaluable. Ellen Schatz moved on to motherhood during the writing of the book but remains a valued friend, and we have since been fortunate to have the help of two other talented psychology editors, Tim Vertovec and Ryan Flahive. Ryan has been a recent addition to the team, but we already feel that he has made a substantial contribution to the project. On the marketing side, we had the benefit of Kevin Molloy's sage advice and good humor until his recent promotion, and since then we have been thrilled to be working with Kate Stewart who is full of great ideas and enthusiasm.

Several other members of the Wiley team deserve special thanks for their major helping roles. Lili DeGrasse, associate editor, and Deepa Chungi, editorial assistant, have helped enormously with the overwhelming number of details on such a big project. During the production process, we have worked with so many dedicated and talented professionals at Wiley: photo manager Hilary Newman; production editors Norine Pigliucci and Barbara Russiello; illustration coordinator Sandra Rigby; and photo editor Sara Wight. Senior designer Karin Kincheloe worked closely with us to make sure that the look of the book supported our goals and vision. Tom Kulesa has been tremendously creative and helpful in working on our video supplements and other media aspects of the project. Several outside consultants have also been terrific, especially Jerry Marshall of Marshall and Truitt, on photos; Jo-Anne Naples on permissions; Chris Coberly at Content Connections for the online reviewing program; and Larry Meyer and the staff at Hermitage Publishing Services for production services.

We would also like to thank the numerous colleagues, research assistants, and graduate student instructors who contributed to the book. Kirk Brower, Robert Cohen, and Roger Lauer went above and beyond the call of duty in reading sections of the manuscript and offering valuable suggestions. While graduate students, Lauren Kachorek and Jen Kittler provided immense help with the writing and referencing of several chapters, and Chris Barton made sure that Chapter 10 was well-written and fully referenced. We are also indebted to several excellent undergraduate research assistants: Beth Kibort, Shannon Dudley, Nance Rominger, Lorraine Darrow, Jill Dixon, and Daniel Munoz.

The Psychology Departments at the University of Michigan and John Carroll University have been wonderful home bases. We have been privileged to serve under supportive chairs such as Al Cain, Pat Gurin, Rich Gonzalez, Chris Peterson, Sheryl Olson, Nick Santilli, and Beth Martin; all have provided welcome support for our teaching and writing. We also deeply appreciate the support of Robert Hatcher, Kim Leary, Denia Barrett, and Deborah Paris in our other institutional "homes" over the past several years.

Finally, and most importantly, we would like to thank our students, our therapy clients, and our friends and families. Our students, with their curiosity, their questions, and their enthusiasm for learning, have inspired us to write this book. Our clients have given us the privilege of learning from and with them about the human condition and the process of change, whether it fit our theories or not. Our friends and families have provided support, love, advice, and, when needed, relief from this project; without them there would be no book. Our deepest gratitude is to Darren, Ellen, Andy, Julie, and Adam, who encouraged us even while tolerating our long hours of writing. We dedicate this book to you.

James Hansell
Lisa Damour

Core concepts in abnormal psychology provide an organizing framework to help students approach abnormal behavior in a way that helps them understand, remember, and integrate the material. The concepts are highlighted visually with an icon and boldface blue italic type.

and diagnosable eating disorders? To answer that question, we return to two core concepts: the *continuum between normality and abnormality* and the *importance of context in defining and understanding abnormality.*

The Continuum Between Normal and Abnormal Eating

While up to 6% of American women may suffer from anorexia or bulimia, many more suffer from "subclinical" eating disorders (meaning that they have some but not all of the symptoms of an eating disorder) and half of all American women are dieting at any given time (Brownell, 1995). On the *continuum between normal and abnormal* eating, we could place people who are at a healthy weight and have no concerns about their weight at one end, and people who are severely anorexic or bulimic at the other. Between these two

guidelines for defining how much weight loss, and how much bingeing and purging is necessary for a diagnosis of anorexia or bulimia. Although these diagnoses reflect an extreme version of behaviors that are quite common, they are still potentially problematic even in much milder forms.

The Importance of Context in Defining Abnormal Eating

In addition to considering the *continuum,* we must also consider *context* issues in order to define abnormal eating. In some subcultures, eating disordered behavior is the norm. For example, the fashion and entertainment industries are widely populated by women who weigh less than 85% of what is considered normal for their heights—one of the main diagnostic criteria for anorexia. Professional dancers and competitive gymnasts also commonly maintain very low body weights, and wrestlers, jockeys, and boxers

An integrated approach: the various theoretical perspectives in abnormal psychology are described as *components* that can be combined to explain and treat psychopathology.

EXPLAINING AND TREATING MOOD DISORDERS

All of the major theoretical perspectives in abnormal psychology have contributed to our understanding of mood disorders and their treatment. We'll review the explanatory concepts and treatment interventions associated with each perspective and then highlight areas in which they overlap or complement each ciple of *multiple causality.* As before, the term "dep both major depressive disorder and dysthymic disorde used to refer to bipolar I, bipolar II, and cyclothymic d ration of the explanations and treatments of mood dis logical components, since recent major breakthroug biology of mood disorders has brought the biological into prominence.

Biological components

Biological contributions to depression factors. Evidence from all three of adoption, and twin studies—demons depression can be inherited. For exam

Cognitive Components

The cognitive perspective has become one of the most influential approaches to explaining and treating mood disorders, particularly depression. One of the founders of this perspective, Aaron Beck, noticed that many of his depressed patients shared certain cognitive patterns that seemed to contribute to their depression. Specifically, he noted that they seemed to hold irrationally negative views of *themselves,* their *worlds,* and their *futures* (which he called the **negative cognitive triad**) (Beck, 1967; 1987;

Behavioral Components

B. F. Skinner, one of the founders of behaviorism, proposed many years ago that depression results from the interruption of *reinforcements* (rewards) from the environment (Skinner, 1953). This view has been elaborated and modified over the past five decades. For example, the next generation of behavioral theorists added that increased frequency of *punishments* (negative consequences) or the decreased *effectiveness* of reinforcements contribute to depression, as expressed by a decrease in adaptive behaviors (Costello, 1972; Ferster, 1966). In other words, a student who has worked hard with good results in the past may slack off if he starts to receive some negative feedback or becomes less encouraged by positive feedback.

A clinical case focus: numerous case examples that illustrate how psychopathology presents in the real world: complex symptom pictures that call for multimodal treatment strategies.

agoraphobia, and some people, such as Bill (described below), suffer from agoraphobia without a history of panic attacks.

Case Illustration Just over a year ago Bill, age 28, heard about a mugging in his neighborhood, which was overall quite safe. At first, Bill began to feel nervous in crowded places. Soon, Bill was getting uneasy in any public place, and he felt increasingly reluctant to leave the safety of his apartment. He decided to quit his job as a mechanic and to try working from home as ~~~~~~~~~. Rather than leaving his apartment to go shopping he began ~~~~~~~~ over the phone or over the Internet. On the occasio~~~~~~~~ leaving the house, such as when he needed to go to ~~~~~~~ sister to accompany him.

The third type of phobia, **specific phobia**, refers ~~~~~ social phobia or agoraphobia. Most often, specific pho~~~~~~

Specific pho~~~~~~
phobia or ag~~~~~~

ple who suffer from specific phobias, like Jenny (described below), usually recognize that their fears are excessive. However, they are usually unable to talk themselves out of being afraid and persistently avoid the feared object or situation.

Case Illustration Jenny, a high school sophomore who enjoys a wide variety of activities and plays for her high school's field hockey team, is deathly afraid of hypodermic needles. She does not mind the sight of blood—indeed she sees blood regularly when she or a teammate is injured—but she cannot stand the sight, or even thought, of syringes. When Jenny's father was hospitalized with cancer she was reluctant to visit him for fear that she would accidentally see or come into contact with a hypodermic needle. Jenny finally got up the courage to visit her father but passed out immediately when a nurse came into her father's room carrying a syringe.

Case Vignettes

- **Defining Eating Disorders**
  - The Continuum Between Normal and Abnormal Eating
  - The Importance of Context in Defining Abnormal Eating

- **Classifying Eating Disorders**
  - The DSM-IV-TR Categories
  - Classification in Demographic Context
  - Cultural Relativism in Defining and Classifying Eating Disorders
  - The Advantages and Limitations of the DSM-IV-TR Eating Disorder Diagnoses

- **Explaining and Treating Eating Disorders**
  - Psychodynamic Components
  - Family Systems Components
  - Cognitive-Behavioral Components
  - Sociocultural Components
  - Biological Components
  - The Connection Between Mind and Body in Eating Disorders
  - The Multiple Causality of Eating Disorders

Case Vignettes - **Treatments**

Consistent chapter format to help students master the material.

Edvard Munch, Seascape, 1899.
©Francis G. Meyer/Corbis©2004. The Munch Museum/The Munch-Ellingston Group/Artists Rights Society (ARS), New York

■ Edvard Munch (1863-1944), a Norwegian artist most famous for his painting "The Scream" (1893), endured a lifetime of tragedy. Munch's mother died when he was five, his sister, only a year his elder, died soon after his mother, and his father died while Munch was a young adult. Though Munch's ......continues on page 112

Chapter openers that feature famous artists: each chapter opener describes an artist's place in the art world and the artist's personal struggles. These chapter openers demonstrate how psychological suffering or impairment can exist alongside enormous talent, creativity, and skill.

edvard munch

chapter seven

DISSOCIATION AND THE DISSOCIATIVE DISORDERS

Case Vignettes

John, a college sophomore, came for a walk-in appointment at his university counseling center because he was worried that his tendency to "space out" was getting in the way of his schoolwork. Though he had experienced what he called "spacey" episodes off and on since his senior year in high school, they had increased in intensity and duration around the time of his most recent midterm exams, sometimes happening while he was in the middle of taking a test. John had been able to continue working through the exams when this happened, but his academic performance was dropping and he was sure that spacing out during exams wasn't helping. When the counselor asked if anything important had occurred in John's life around the time the episodes began John explained that his father died shortly after being diagnosed with lung cancer in the summer before John's freshman year of college. However, John felt that his father's surprising death was unrelated to the spacey episodes because he and his family were able to say their good-byes to their father and everyone handled the loss "very well." Further, John explained that when he felt spacey he didn't feel sad, or like he missed his father; he just felt nothing at all.

Margaret, a clerical worker at a manufacturing company, was contacted by the staff assistance program of her division due to her excessive absences. Though she did not feel comfortable giving the details of her many absences to the counselor. Margaret explained that she had been having "mental problems" and accepted a referral to a local psychologist. The psychologist was struck by Margaret's description of a typical week. On Mondays, she often awoke feeling miserable from the weekend's activities, though she could rarely remember what had occurred. Margaret was almost always terribly hungover and unable to go to work. Occasionally, she would find a strange man in her bed or would receive phone calls from men she had never met who

Case Vignettes

- **Defining Dissociation and the Dissociative Disorders**
  - The Importance of Context in Defining

Opening case vignettes give a brief, compelling picture of the disorders covered in the chapter. **Treatment discussions** for the opening cases at the end of the chapter illustrate multi-modal treatment strategies.

---

222 | *chapter seven* | Dissociation and the Dissociative Disorders

Case Vignettes | **Treatment**

John | **Depersonalization Disorder**

John sought help at his college counseling center because he was often feeling disconnected from his environment in a way that interfered with his schoolwork. After an evaluation, the psychologist recommended therapy and noted that John's otherwise lively manner seemed to go flat when he talked about his father and the time around his father's death. The psychologist suggested that perhaps John had more feelings about his father than he felt comfortable letting himself know. John asserted that he had already dealt with his father's death, especially since he had "two entire months of sadness" between the time of his father's cancer diagnosis and the time when he died.

However, in the next session, John reported the following dream: "I spent most of the evening at my own bachelor party, but it was never clear who I was marrying. Though I was at least 25, at the end of the evening I returned to my current dorm room where I found my father was sitting at my desk. When I told him that I missed him at the party he said that I should stop yelling at him, and he abruptly left the room." The

dream helped John to recognize that he did continue to have a lot of thoughts and feelings about his father, specifically, that he felt his father was missing out on important events in his life (such as a future marriage) and that he felt abandoned and angered by his father's death.

Over time, John was able to talk with his therapist in a heartfelt way about how he wished he could tell his father about his college life, and how sad he was that his father would not see him graduate from college. John began to cry during some sessions, especially when he talked about the enormous amount of physical pain his father had endured in the last months of his life and how difficult it had been to see his previously powerful father reduced to such a helpless state. Around the same time, John found that he was no longer experiencing depersonalization and became convinced that his "spacing out" had been a way to avoid his grief. By "spacing out" from time to time, John didn't have to feel sad about the loss, or have to experience the guilt-inducing anger he also felt toward his father.

Case Discussion | **Depersonalization Disorder**

John was able to benefit from psychodynamic interventions aimed at understanding the root causes of his depersonalization symptoms. As John became increasingly comfortable with and aware of the painful and contradictory feelings he

had about his father's death he no longer needed to use dissociation as a defense mechanism to block out distressing emotions.

Margaret | **Dissociative Identity Disorder**

As noted earlier, Margaret and her therapist soon learned that mild-mannered Margaret had two additional personalities: the promiscuous Janie, and the terrified young girl named Suzie. Margaret spent a great deal of time in therapy trying to understand the roles that each personality played. It became clear that by becoming Janie, Margaret could act out impulses that she could not otherwise tolerate, and that Suzie served the function of containing all of the painful memories from the past that Margaret did not wish to recall. As the therapy progressed, Margaret would turn into Suzie frequently during the sessions. The therapist observed that this seemed to happen most often when Margaret spoke of about her unstable father, who had raised her alone after her mother died when she was five. Margaret began to describe strange memories, starting just after her mother's death, of "games" with her father in which he would pretend she was "mommy" and he would teach her "how to make a baby." Then he would get mad, hit her, and

leave, sometimes for days. Margaret began to understand that she had inexplicably "forgotten" so much of her childhood in an effort to forget how betrayed, debased, and damaged she felt by the sexual abuse and neglect she'd suffered.

As Margaret recalled more and more of what had happened to her when she was growing up, she became extremely depressed. She had difficulty sleeping, often missed work, was at risk of losing her job, and was frequently suicidal. Margaret's therapist suggested that perhaps Margaret would be better able to function if she were to begin a course of antidepressant medication. The antidepressants did help, and Margaret and her therapist returned to the task of working through the painful memories from Margaret's childhood. As Margaret remembered what had happened when she was young, Suzie made fewer appearances in the therapy. In time, Margaret was able to accept some of her own "darker" parts and many aspects of Janie were also integrated into Margaret's personality.

Occasionally, Margaret would "forget" to attend several sessions in a row. Together, Margaret and her therapist understood that Margaret would skip sessions when she was feeling afraid of what she might remember or discover about herself. At other times, Margaret would forget her appointments because she felt that her therapist was being "pushy" and making her feel bad in a way that felt uncomfortably familiar. They talked about how old feelings of being mistreated and manipulated had made their way into the therapy relationship. Margaret agreed that she would let the therapist know when she did not want to talk about certain things so that she would-

n't feel pushed or have to [whelmed.]

Margaret remained she used the therapy to ta ences with her father, and pist's advice on how to a self-destructive manner. connected from her surro triggered, she was much her emotions and no long feel safe.

Case Discussion | **Dissociative Identity Disorder**

Margaret's therapist employed the multi-modal, stage approach to treat dissociative identity disorder (DID), as described earlier in the chapter. Her therapist used psychodynamic methods to explore unconscious traumatic memories and to address transference feelings when they arose in the therapy relationship. Cognitive-behavioral techniques were

used to "coach" Margaret in her life. A biological i garet's depressive sympto function in her life, work fering from DID, Margar that lasted many years.

Ch

- *Dissociation* is the term used to describe significant, psychologically based alterations in consciousness, memory, sense of identity, or any combination of the three.
- Dissociation can be adaptive or maladaptive depending on the **context** in which it occurs and on how severe it is on the **continuum between normality and abnormality.**
- The DSM-IV-TR describes four main dissociative disorders: depersonalization disorder, dissociative amnesia, dissociative fugue, and dissociative identity disorder (DID).
- The description and definition of dissociative disorders are **culturally and historically relative.** For example, dissociative phenomena take different forms in different parts of the world and classification of dissociative disorders has changed substantially over the past century.
- The major controversy concerning the **advantages and limitations** of the DSM-IV-TR dissociative disorder diagnoses centers on whether DID is a valid diagnostic entity or whether it is a diagnostic fad in which symptoms are iatrogenically created in suggestible individuals.
- Clinicians from most theoretical perspectives agree that trauma is the major causal factor in most dissociative disorders, yet each theoretical approach offers its own way of understanding how and why traumatic experiences contribute to dissociative phenomena.
- The various theoretical components provide complementary accounts of the processes underlying dissociative disorders, in keeping with the principle of *multiple causality.* An integrated multi-modal approach is particularly useful when attempting to conceptualize and treat a complex disorder like DID.

Multiple boxes on issues relevant to the chapter content.

BOX 7.2   Life as a Multiple

"My Guys"

In a book titled *First Person Plural: My Life as a Multiple,* Cameron West, Ph.D., describes suffering from dissociative identity disorder, recovering lost memories of having been sexually abused as a child, being treated for his disorder, and, ultimately, becoming a psychologist. He begins his book with a description of his 24 alternate personalities. Here are a few of his descriptions:

> *Soul* is an ageless alter who emerged early on and whose job it was to give me hope so I could survive. His presence is still felt but he rarely comes out, even in therapy.
>
> *Sharky* is a private alter who at first couldn't form words at all. He would grunt and swing his head from side to side and bite things, like tables and clothes and plants. One of the other alters drew a picture of him as a limbless being with a huge toothy mouth. Sharky has learned to talk and eat with his hands or a fork. He doesn't come out too often, but he likes to share treats with the others.
>
> *Davy* is four. He is sweet and sad. He was the first to emerge, but he doesn't come out much anymore.

> *Anna* and *Trudi* are four-year-old twins. Anna is doe-eyed and happy, with a smile so big it makes my face hurt. She remembers her abuse, but feels no anger, no sadness. She loves a good cookie. Trudi is dark and brooding, a kid in the corner. She remembers, too, but only the pain and sadness and horror. Anna shares her cookies with her. Anna is a member of the core group of alters who come out most frequently…
>
> *Switch* is eight years old. He held incredible rage for being abused, but he also felt a powerful allegiance to one of our abusers and turned that rage toward me and some of the others. Switch harmed my body many times. He is not so angry anymore and he has been accepted by everyone in the system. Switch has his own sheriff's badge now, which he likes to wear around. He is a member of the core group…

West, 1999 (pp. vii–viii)

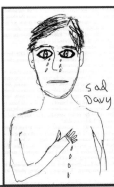

Cameron West's alter "Davy" Davy made this drawing on his first day "out."
From West, 1999, p. 51

Frequent interim summaries enable students to spot-check their comprehension of the material.

believer in the validity of the DID diagnosis—has reported that he has also seen cases of DID that were created iatrogenically by irresponsible therapists employing poor therapeutic technique (Ross, 1997).

Brief Summary

- Recent research suggests that dissociative disorders also occur in children and adolescents, but may have different clinical features than those usually seen in adults.

- Women are disproportionately represented among those diagnosed with dissociative identity disorder (DID), though the disorder is probably underdiagnosed in men.

- The diagnosis of dissociative disorders is *culturally relative* insofar as dissociative phenomena take different forms in various parts of the world.

- The definition and classification of dissociative symptoms has changed substantially over the last century, an example of *historical relativism*.

- Experts continue to debate the *advantages and limitations* of the DID diagnosis. The main controversy centers on whether DID is a valid disorder usually caused by childhood trauma, or a recent diagnostic fad supported by iatrogenically produced cases.

Critical Thinking Question   **Do you think a therapist who was skeptical of the DID diagnosis could work effectively with a person who believed that he or she had the disorder?**

Critical thinking questions throughout each chapter stimulate students' reflection, review, and test preparation.

> *Critical*
> *Thinking*
> *Question*
>
> **A**ttempts to be culturally sensitive to the various presentations of anxiety disorders risk engaging in cultural stereotyping. Does specifying cultural patterns (such as that Asian individuals tend to express anxiety through physical symptoms) seem helpful, to be an example of stereotyping, or both?

Definitions of all key terms in the margin near their discussion in the text.

Hysteria A term used for centuries to describe a syndrome of symptoms that appear to be neurological but do not have a neurological cause; now classified as **conversion disorder.**

Somatoform disorders Disorders in which physical symptoms are caused by psychological factors.

Posttraumatic model A theory of dissociative identity disorder that argues that the disorder results from traumatic childhood experiences.

Sociocognitive model A theory of dissociative identity disorder that argues that the disorder is iatrogenic and/or that it results from socially reinforced multiple role enactments.

Iatrogenic A disorder unintentionally caused by a treatment.

nents of the **posttraumatic model** (PTM) who argue that DID is a real disorder which can result from overwhelming childhood experiences such as severe abuse. According to this model, a dissociative response served as a survival strategy that helped the child cope with the overwhelming trauma (Gleaves, 1996). In other words, people develop alternative identities as a way of escaping severe physical or sexual abuse. Colin Ross, a psychiatrist who is an expert in the field of dissociative disorders states that DID develops from "a little girl imagining that the abuse is happening to someone else" (Ross, 1997).

On the other side of the debate stand the proponents of the **sociocognitive model** (SCM) of DID. According to these theorists, the diagnosis of DID is an unfortunate contemporary fad which is fueled by naive or overzealous therapists and the media. For example, one expert describes DID as "a syndrome that consists of rule-governed and goal-directed experiences and displays of multiple role enactments that have been created, legitimized, and maintained by social reinforcement. Patients with DID synthesize these role enactments by drawing on a wide variety of sources of information, including the print and broadcast media, cues provided by therapists, personal experiences, and observations of individuals who have enacted multiple identities" (Lilienfeld et al., 1999, pp. 507–508). In other words, proponents of the sociocognitive model believe that DID is an **iatrogenic** (eye-at-row-GEN-ick) disorder, which translates from Greek to mean "doctor borne." They propose that the disorder is created in suggestible individuals by clinicians who encourage clients, sometimes under hypnosis, to see their complex and opposing traits as independently operating personalities, or who unwittingly communicate this view through various cues.

A chapter summary that focuses on the core concepts presented in the chapter.

Chapter Summary

- Pathological anxiety is defined as anxiety that occurs in an inappropriate *context* or is toward the extreme end of the *continuum between normal and abnormal* anxiety.

- The DSM-IV-TR recognizes six different anxiety disorders: generalized anxiety disorder, panic disorder, phobias, obsessive-compulsive disorder, posttraumatic stress disorder, and acute stress disorder.

- The DSM-IV-TR anxiety diagnoses have important *advantages and limitations*. While the reliability and validity of the DSM-IV-TR anxiety diagnoses are relatively high, the DSM-IV-TR anxiety disorders are also highly comorbid, meaning that clients often meet criteria for more than one diagnosis.

- Demographic factors, such as age, gender, and social class, affect the features and prevalence and presentation of anxiety disorders.

- Various cultures and historical periods define and classify anxiety problems differently, highlighting with the core concept of *cultural and historical relativism.*

- All of the major theoretical perspectives in abnormal psychology offer concepts relevant to the explanation and treatment of anxiety disorders. Further, the different theoretical perspectives on anxiety often interact, overlap, or complement each other, highlighting the *principle of multiple causality*.

- Changes in brain structure and function resulting from traumatic emotional experiences and from psychotherapy are two illustrations of the *connection between mind and body* in anxiety disorders.

BRIEF CONTENTS

CONTENTS

LIST OF BOXES

ABNORMAL PSYCHOLOGY

Alice Neel, *Mrs. Paul Gardner and Sam*, 1967. ©Estate of Alice Neel. Courtesy Robert Miller Gallery, New York.

■ Alice Neel (1900-1984), known for her unflinching portraits of the poor and homeless as well as the rich and famous, is considered one of the most significant American artists of the twentieth century. Though she achieved professional success during her lifetime, Neel's personal life was touched by great sadness *...continues on page 4*

alice neel

chapter one

ABNORMAL

PSYCHOLOGY
THE CORE CONCEPTS

Case Vignette

Charlotte overcame an impoverished and emotionally deprived childhood and went on to become a successful writer. But when she was 25 years old, recently married, and had just given birth to a healthy daughter, she became, in her words, "a mental wreck." Charlotte lost her energy and drive, and grew increasingly sad and lethargic. She described her suffering vividly: "A sort of gray fog drifted across my mind, a cloud that grew and darkened…there was a constant dragging weariness…absolute incapacity. Absolute misery." Charlotte could not take care of herself or her baby. "I lay on that lounge and cried all day. The tears ran down into my ears on either side. I went to bed crying, woke in the night crying, sat on the edge of bed in the morning and cried—from sheer continuous pain… The baby?…I would hold her close—that lovely child!—and instead of love and happiness, feel only pain. The tears ran down on my breast… Nothing was more utterly bitter than this, that even motherhood brought no joy."

Charlotte's story, which we will return to shortly, is the kind most people associate with the topic of "abnormal psychology." This is a textbook about abnormal psychology—about how abnormal behavior can be *defined, classified, explained,* and *treated.* These topics will be covered in detail in later chapters, but first, in order to introduce the subject of abnormal psychology, we would like to make a general point about this field and about this book.

Abnormal psychology has experienced tremendous change, progress, and controversy over the roughly 100 years that it has existed as a field of study. But throughout this time, several concepts have remained at the heart of the subject. We call these concepts the ***core concepts*** in abnormal psychology because they have always been central to the field even as our knowledge has grown and changed, and they are receiving renewed attention as the field now enters its second century. Accordingly, we have made these concepts central to the organization of this book.

Before we present our six core concepts in abnormal psychology, consider the following brief examples of "abnormality." Examples like these are familiar to everyone, and they provide a background for our introduction to the core concepts. As you read them, consider the following questions:

- Do you think this person's behavior is abnormal?
- If so, what, specifically, seems abnormal about his or her behavior?
- How do you think the abnormality could be explained?
- How do you think it could be treated?

...continued from page 2

when her first child died of diptheria in 1926. Neel's depression in the wake of her child's death highlights some of the core concepts described in this chapter and addressed throughout the textbook. For example, we cannot understand Neel's depression, or any other complex human behavior, without taking into account the surrounding *context*, the *continuum between normal and abnormal behavior*, and a host of other considerations.

Dennis Rodman Rodman, the former NBA star, is well known for his outrageous behavior, such as wearing women's makeup and dressing up as a bride. Should he be considered "abnormal?"

Case Illustration Megan looks great, and she appears to be happy and successful in college. But she has gotten awfully thin. At meals she barely eats, and she, like several of her friends, occasionally makes herself vomit after drinking or eating a lot. When asked about having lost so much weight, Megan broke down crying and said that she still felt fat. She said that her life feels out of control and that she doesn't know what to do about it.

Case Illustration Dennis Rodman, the former NBA rebounding star, liked to make a splash. He frequently appeared in public wearing women's clothing, and claimed that he would like to play in an NBA game naked. Rodman could not be counted on to get to practice on time, and he was released from several teams because of his outlandish behavior. Rodman also admitted to heavy alcohol use, but he claimed that he was happy with himself and that his only problem was with society's intolerance of his lifestyle.

Case Illustration Seven year-old Yosef, the eldest child of immigrant parents who do not speak English, is having trouble in school. He cannot seem to sit still or pay attention for more than a minute. Yosef is continually fidgeting and getting out of his chair. As a result of these behaviors, he is already significantly behind the other students in his class. Yosef's home life seems stable, and his parents have not expressed concern, but his teacher is troubled by his behavior and lack of progress.

Case Illustration Ted Kaczynski entered Harvard at age 16 as a mathematics prodigy. He later earned his Ph.D. in mathematics from the University of Michigan and became a professor at the University of California, Berkeley. Almost 30 years later, he was taken into custody by federal agents who raided the tiny cabin in the Montana wilderness where he had been living in isolation for years. They had concluded that Kaczynski was the notorious Unabomber, responsible for two decades of lethal bombings motivated by his extreme anti-technology ideology.

Each of these examples raises questions about how we decide who is abnormal, what kind of abnormality is involved, what causes it, and how it can be treated. Our six core concepts will assist us in exploring and answering these questions (see Table 1.1).

Theodore Kaczynski, the "Unabomber" Kaczynski, a former mathematics professor at the University of California, has claimed that he is not mentally ill and was rationally motivated by his anti-technology political ideology. Kaczynski is shown at the University of California, Berkeley (left) and following his arrest (right).

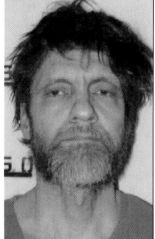

Six Core Concepts in Abnormal Psychology	Table 1.1

- The importance of context in defining and understanding abnormality
- The continuum between normal and abnormal behavior
- Cultural and historical relativism in defining and classifying abnormality
- The advantages and limitations of diagnosis
- The principle of multiple causality
- The connection between mind and body

THE CORE CONCEPTS

The Importance of Context in Defining and Understanding Abnormality

The *context* in which abnormal behavior occurs requires consideration for three crucial reasons. First, understanding the circumstances surrounding any behavior is essential to *defining* whether or not the behavior is abnormal. For example, if Charlotte's baby had just died, we would consider her symptoms (intense sadness, lethargy, inability to function) to be part of normal grief; it is only in the absence of any such tragedy that her symptoms seem abnormal. Similarly, experiencing intense fear in a dangerous situation such as wartime combat is normal, but the same kind of fear in a benign context—say, while out shopping—is not.

Second, the context in which abnormality occurs can help us to understand and *explain* it. As we will see, the fact that Charlotte's trouble began after childbirth indicates some of the psychological and biological causes of her symptoms. Third, abnormal behavior is profoundly influenced by demographic context categories such as gender, age, class, and culture. For example, Yosef's problems (inattention and impulsivity) are far more common among boys than girls, while Megan's problem (excessive dieting) occurs much more frequently in women than in men. In addition, attention to demographic contexts can help us to be aware of cultural, racial, and gender biases that influence the field of abnormal psychology just as they affect other fields. For instance, would Dennis Rodman's behavior be viewed differently if he were Caucasian? In each chapter, we will address these *context* issues as they influence the definitions, classifications, explanations, and treatments of various disorders.

The Continuum Between Normal and Abnormal Behavior

Even when the context suggests that a certain behavior is abnormal, we cannot define the behavior as abnormal without considering the *continuum* between normality and abnormality. How much weight does Megan have to lose before she is considered to have an eating disorder—10 pounds, 20 pounds, or some undefined amount? How outrageous does Dennis Rodman's behavior have to become before it stops being "eccentric" and starts being "pathological?" Since most 7-year-old boys are active and distractable, how inattentive and impulsive must Yosef be for his behavior to be considered abnormal? Many forms of abnormality can be seen as exaggerations of normal feelings and behaviors: everyone has felt a little depressed or anxious at times. One implication of this is that we should be mindful that people suffering from mental disorders are people much like ourselves, not "freaks" who are fundamentally foreign. The idea that normality and abnormality are on a continuum may seem unsettling at first, but it actually makes abnormality more understandable since the potential for abnormal behavior is part of our common humanity. At the same time, it means that the dividing line between normal and abnormal behavior is never entirely clear-cut. We discuss the problems with defining abnormality, and the field's solutions to these problems, in Chapter 2.

Cultural and Historical Relativism in Defining and Classifying Abnormality

You will probably not be surprised to hear that definitions of abnormality have changed dramatically over time and vary widely across cultures (Chapter 2). For instance, in some cultures talking to dead relatives is considered normal; in others it could be considered a sign of mental illness. In the United States, homosexuality was classified as a mental illness until 1973; today experts consider homosexuality a normal variant of human sexuality. Consequently, we cannot make absolute, universal statements about what constitutes abnormal behavior. Perhaps Yosef's parents are not concerned about his behavior because it does not seem unusual within their culture. And perhaps 30 years ago, before attention-deficit disorder and Ritalin were household terms, a boy like Yosef would be seen merely as an energetic or undisciplined boy, not as someone with a "disorder." As we cover different types of mental disorders in this book, we will frequently encounter important questions about their cultural and historical relativity.

The Advantages and Limitations of Diagnosis

Like all scientific and professional fields, abnormal psychology relies on categories for classifying its subject matter. Clinicians and researchers need diagnostic categories to help them study and treat mental illness and to communicate with other professionals. But categorizing mental disorders is a tricky business; the field of abnormal psychology has struggled to develop categories that consistently and accurately classify mental disorders. For example, if Ted Kaczynski is diagnosed with schizophrenia (see Chapter 12) by one psychologist (as indeed he was), would a second psychologist agree? And even if they do concur, how can we be sure that the diagnosis is correct? These questions relate to the scientific issues of **reliability** (the consistency with which a diagnostic category is applied) and **validity** (the accuracy of a diagnostic category), which we discuss in Chapter 4. In order to be useful, classification systems must be reasonably reliable and valid. The complexity of abnormal behavior has made it especially challenging to develop reliable and valid diagnostic categories for mental disorders.

In addition, too much emphasis on classifying disorders can oversimplify complex problems and keep us from fully understanding the people behind the diagnostic labels. Also, given the fears and prejudices about mental illness in our culture, diagnoses of mental disorders can be highly stigmatizing and demoralizing to the people diagnosed. For example, Yosef's parents might argue that giving him a psychological diagnosis would stigmatize him as "abnormal" and the diagnostic label could become a self-fulfilling prophecy that exacerbates his problematic behavior. Thus, the scientific and clinical advantages of classifying different kinds of abnormal behavior always have to be weighed against the imperfections of any diagnostic system and its potentially negative effects.

Reliability The consistency of a test, measurement, or category system.

Validity The accuracy of a test, measurement, or category system.

Precipitating causes The immediate trigger or precipitant of an event.

Predisposing causes The underlying processes that create conditions making it possible for a precipitating cause to trigger an event.

The Principle of Multiple Causality

In Chapter 3, we focus on how to *explain* (that is, identify the causes of) abnormal behavior. Abnormal behavior is always complex, and it is important not to oversimplify its causes. For example, mental disorders usually involve both **precipitating** (triggering) and **predisposing** (underlying) **causes**. The precipitating cause of Charlotte's depression may be the birth of her daughter, but the predisposing causes, as we will see, probably lie in traumatic childhood experiences and biological vulnerabilities that made her prone to depression. In addition, many different theoretical perspectives—psychodynamic, cognitive, behavioral, humanistic, biological, and more—coexist in the field of abnormal psychology, offering different explanations and treatments for mental disorders. Each theoretical perspective has something important to contribute, and the field of abnormal psychology is increasingly moving toward explanations and treatments that combine *components* from several theories. In the past, explanations and treatments of disorders often relied too heavily on just one theory or concept to explain disorders, a problem known as **reductionism**. Imagine, for instance, that Charlotte's doctor *only* considered her family situation and neglected to consider the biological components of her depression. Such a narrow approach would compromise the understanding and treatment of her disorder. In Chapter 3, we will review all of the major theoretical perspectives in the field of abnormal psychology and discuss how modern clinicians are combining and integrating these perspectives to explain and treat mental disorders.

Reductionism Explaining a disorder or other complex phenomenon using only a single idea or perspective.

The Connection Between Mind and Body

Contrary to popular belief, psychological and biological perspectives on mental disorders are not entirely distinct. We now know that the mind and brain are not unrelated realms as the philosophical "dualists" once believed. Emotional experiences can alter brain chemistry, and brain chemistry is in turn the basis of emotional experiences. For example, Charlotte's depression may be linked to profound hormonal changes of the postpartum period, but these changes themselves could be influenced by the personal meaning for Charlotte of becoming a mother. Megan's distorted thoughts about her body could be partially due to cognitive impairment resulting from her state of physical starvation. Throughout the book, we examine how the connection between the mind and body must always be taken into account in our efforts to explain and treat abnormal behavior.

| Critical Thinking Question | **Of** the four brief case examples (Megan, Dennis Rodman, Yosef, and Ted Kaczynski) which is the hardest to define as normal or abnormal? Which do you think would be the hardest to classify, explain, and treat? |

THE CORE CONCEPTS: A VIEW FROM THE PAST

Among other things, the six core concepts remind us that while abnormal psychology involves the study of disorders and diagnoses, the field is ultimately about *people* and *ideas*. To illustrate, let's return to the case of Charlotte.

Charlotte is actually Charlotte Perkins Gilman, an early feminist writer and lecturer, who was born in 1860. She is the author of *The Yellow Wallpaper,* an autobiographical novella about her "breakdown" at age 25. To help us illustrate just how enduring the core concepts have been, here is the rest of her story.

As mentioned previously, Charlotte had a difficult childhood. She was the middle of three children born in three years; the oldest died, and after the birth of the youngest, her father abandoned the family. The family suffered through poverty and instability, moving 19 times in 18 years. Most difficult of all for Charlotte was the absence of physical affection from her mother. Mrs. Perkins refused to touch her daughter because she believed that lack of physical contact would toughen Charlotte and prepare her (helpfully, in her mother's view!) not to expect affection from others. Despite these

Charlotte Perkins Gilman Gilman's fascinating life is recounted in her autobiography, *The Living of Charlotte Perkins Gilman,* and in several biographies.

S. Weir Mitchell Dr. Mitchell prescribed the "rest cure" for Charlotte Perkins Gilman and many other patients, but changed in his mind about the rest cure after reading *The Yellow Wallpaper.*

obstacles, Charlotte managed to pursue higher education—no small feat for a woman in her day—and to become an art teacher, governess, and poet as a young adult.

After her marriage, childbirth, and breakdown, Charlotte sought treatment from the leading "nerve specialist" of her day, Dr. S. Weir Mitchell of Philadelphia (he had previously treated some of her relatives in the famous Beecher family; Harriet Beecher Stowe, the author of *Uncle Tom's Cabin,* was Charlotte's great-aunt). Dr. Mitchell diagnosed Charlotte as having "hysterical nervous prostration" (also known then as "neurasthenia," although neither term is used today), a condition believed to be caused in men by overwork and in women by exhaustion from too much social, family, or intellectual work. He prescribed his famous "rest cure," which consisted of months of complete bed rest, seclusion, a diet of red meat and milk, massage, and electrical stimulation to prevent muscle atrophy (Bard, 1996; Golden, 1992). Charlotte reports in her autobiography that Dr. Mitchell gave her the following instructions: "Live as domestic a life as possible. Have your child with you at all times… Have but two hours' intellectual life a day. And never touch pen, brush, or pencil as long as you live" (Gilman, 1935).

Many patients apparently improved after the "rest cure," but Charlotte did not. In fact, she became worse and felt she almost lost her mind completely—not surprising, considering how important her intellectual life was to her. Eventually, Charlotte decided to leave her husband and child, recovered from her breakdown, and went on to become a prominent feminist and intellectual. She wrote *The Yellow Wallpaper*—which describes how the "rest cure" drives a fictional character literally insane—in order to show Dr. Mitchell the dangers of his treatment. Charlotte later heard that he changed his ideas as a result of her book, and she happily wrote in response that "[*The Yellow Wallpaper*] was not intended to drive people crazy, but to save them from being driven crazy. And it worked" (Gilman, 1913).

Most of the core concepts we have described are evident in the case of Charlotte Perkins Gilman. For instance, we can see the *importance of context* in the origin of her symptoms (for example, their onset after childbirth); the issues of *cultural and historical relativism* in her 19th century cultural setting that blamed depression in women on too much intellectual activity; and the questionable validity (accuracy) and other *limitations* of Dr. Mitchell's diagnosis. In addition, the case illustrates the interplay of *multiple causes* (such as her traumatic early childhood combined with postpartum hormonal and psychological changes) and of the connection between *mind and body* in her symptoms, which were not sufficiently appreciated by Dr. Mitchell in light of the limited theories of his day.

Fortunately, we are vastly more knowledgeable about mental disorders today, and psychologists would classify, explain, and treat a contemporary Charlotte very differently. She would probably be diagnosed as suffering from a postpartum major depressive disorder (Chapter 6), which would be explained with modern psychological, sociocultural, and biological concepts, and she would probably be treated with a combination of psychotherapy and antidepressant medication. But we would still encounter all of the core concepts in trying to define, classify, explain, and treat a contemporary Charlotte's problems. When someone with Charlotte's symptoms consults a psychologist today, the clinician must consider the ***continuum between normal and abnormal behavior*** and ***the importance of context*** in *defining* her behavior as abnormal; ***cultural and historical relativism*** and the ***advantages and limitations of diagnosis*** in *classifying* her abnormal behavior; and the issues of ***multiple causality*** and the connection between ***mind and body*** in *explaining* and *treating* her problems. Because modern clinicians have a more sophisticated understanding of the core concepts than Dr. Mitchell did, a contemporary Charlotte can count on a better understanding of her problems and more effective care. Future Charlottes will benefit from even more sophisticated knowledge.

As you will see in the following chapters, the core concepts are always present in the study of abnormal psychology, and they are part of what makes the field so fascinating and challenging. We will highlight them, with text and icons, as continuous themes throughout the book. In Chapter 2, we focus on the core concepts that inform the question of how to *define* abnormal behavior.

Postpartum depression This woman, like Charlotte Perkins Gilman, may be suffering from a postpartum depression. Temporary postpartum "blues" are very common after childbirth; full-fledged postpartum depressions, fortunately, are much less common (see Chapter 6 for more detail).

Critical Thinking Question	Imagine that Charlotte Perkins Gilman is being treated today and is prescribed an antidepressant medication such as Prozac by her doctor. How might an abnormal psychology textbook in the year 2100 evaluate this treatment? Could it seem as odd to people in the future as Charlotte's treatment by Dr. Mitchell does today?

Chapter Summary

- The field of abnormal psychology addresses how abnormal behavior is defined, classified, explained, and treated.
- The field of abnormal psychology is about 100 years old. Throughout its history, decisions about how to define, classify, explain, and treat abnormal behavior have revolved around certain concepts. We discuss six core concepts that continue to shape the field of abnormal psychology:
  - The importance of *context* in defining and understanding abnormality
  - The ***continuum between normal and abnormal behavior***
  - *Cultural and historical relativism* in defining and classifying abnormality
  - The ***advantages and limitations of diagnosis***
  - The principle of ***multiple causality***
  - The ***connection between mind and body***
- Every case of abnormal behavior touches on these core concepts—whether it is a case of a contemporary college student suffering from an eating disorder or of an historical figure like Charlotte Perkins Gilman with severe depression. While the field of psychopathology has made enormous advances, the core concepts remind us that there are still as many questions as answers in this field and that our understanding of abnormal behavior will continue to evolve.

Emil Nolde, *Still Life with Masks*, 1911.
© Private Collection/Bridgeman Art
Library International Ltd.

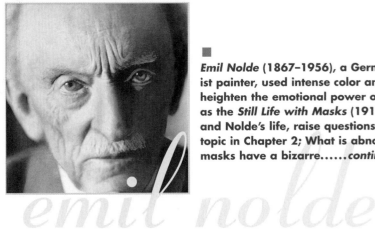

■ *Emil Nolde* (1867–1956), a German Expressionist painter, used intense color and patterns to
heighten the emotional power of his works, such
as the *Still Life with Masks* (1911). This painting,
and Nolde's life, raise questions relevant to our
topic in Chapter 2; What is abnormality? The
masks have a bizarre......*continues on page 12*

emil nolde

chapter two

DEFINING
ABNORMALITY
WHAT IS
PSYCHOPATHOLOGY?

The field of **abnormal psychology**, which is also called **psychopathology**, naturally interests most people. People often wonder: What is "mental illness" and what causes it—bad life experiences, or chemical imbalances in the brain? How many people suffer from mental disorders? Does psychopathology include common experiences like being shy or feeling "down" occasionally, or is it something altogether different? These and other interesting questions make courses in abnormal psychology popular at many colleges and universities. This book will focus on such questions.

In addition to being a fascinating area of study, abnormal psychology is also a controversial one. As you have seen in Chapter 1, there are no simple answers to some of the basic questions in the field of abnormal psychology. This can make a course in abnormal psychology challenging, but we think it is also part of what makes the study of abnormal psychology so interesting and worthwhile.

In this chapter we address the most basic question in the field: how do we *define* abnormal behavior? This seems like an obvious place to start. A definition of abnormality, after all, would seem like a prerequisite for research, teaching, and treatment. In light of this, you may be surprised to learn that there is no universally agreed upon or precise definition of *abnormal behavior, mental illness,* or *psychopathology* (these terms are roughly interchangeable). Yet, we will also explain how the field has come up with approximate, or *working,* definitions that serve reasonably well in most practical circumstances, so that research, teaching, and treatment can be usefully conducted.

In order to understand why there is no universally accepted definition of mental illness, we must take a look at the strengths and limitations of various approaches to defining abnormal behavior. Let's begin by considering an example: the case of a young man we'll call Dave. (All of the cases in this book are based on actual cases, but they have been modified and disguised to protect the privacy of the people involved.) As you read this case, ask yourself whether you think Dave's behavior is abnormal or not. Be aware of what factors you consider when addressing this question. For example, do you focus on whether he seems bizarre, or whether he is impaired by his problems? The factors you employ are technically known as *criteria* (singular: *criterion*). Following the case, we will review the commonly used criteria for defining psychopathology.

Abnormal psychology/Psychopathology The subfield of psychology devoted to the study of mental disorders.

Case Vignette Is This Person Abnormal?

Dave is a 20-year-old sophomore at a large East Coast university. He considers himself a happy person, and he has mostly fond memories of growing up in a comfortable suburban town. Dave looked forward to going to college

...continued from page 10

appearance—is that a useful marker of abnormality? Some look distressed—can distress help us define and identify abnormality? We will also consider the question of who defines abnormality. Nolde joined the Nazi Party along with millions of other Germans; ironically, the Nazis later banned Nolde's work (and that of many other artists) as "degenerate" and forbade him to paint. As we will see, Nazi Germany exemplifies the danger of defining abnormality in relation to social or cultural norms, since these norms can themselves become destructive and abnormal.

and was pleased to be accepted by one of his top choices. During his first year, he found it exciting to be on campus and quickly made a number of friends. Dave found his course work difficult but manageable. All in all, he seemed to be making a good adjustment to college life despite some mild anxiety about whether he could be academically and socially successful.

During the fall of Dave's sophomore year, however, his anxiety intensified. He began to worry about what everybody thought of him and became especially insecure about whether any woman could find him attractive. He felt self-conscious and shy, even around his good friends, and always anticipated that he would be left out or rejected. As a result, Dave became more withdrawn and quiet. He began to avoid parties, the dining hall, and other large social settings in which he knew he would feel uncomfortable. Dave kept his concerns to himself and was able to hide his discomfort from his friends, making excuses when he wanted to be alone. He was able to keep up with his work, and his grades remained high. Dave told himself he was just having a "sophomore slump." He tried to maintain hope that things would return to normal next semester.

COMMONLY USED CRITERIA FOR DEFINING ABNORMALITY

Is Dave a "normal" person simply experiencing a stressful time, or is his situation "abnormal?" Could Dave's condition be diagnosed as a mental disorder? To answer these questions, let us consider five commonly used criteria for determining whether behavior is normal or abnormal (see Table 2.1). All of these criteria are widely used by both lay people and mental health professionals. Nonetheless, they all have limitations. We begin with the least satisfactory criterion and proceed to those that are more helpful.

Help Seeking

This criterion suggests that we can identify abnormality simply by seeing who seeks treatment for emotional problems. Using this criterion assumes that people who seek mental health treatment services must have mental disorders, and that those who do not are "normal." While sometimes true, as a single criterion for defining psychopathology "help seeking" is quite inaccurate. Actually, most people with significant emotional disorders never seek treatment, and, further, many people seek psychotherapy for help with "normal" life stresses. Nevertheless, this criterion cannot

Table 2.1 | **Five Commonly Used Criteria for Defining Abnormality (Acronym: HIDES)**

1. **H**elp seeking
2. **I**rrationality/Dangerousness
3. **D**eviance
4. **E**motional distress
5. **S**ignificant impairment

Psychiatric Hospitals A patient walks down a corridor of a modern psychiatric hospital in California. In 1998, psychiatric hospitals in the United States alone processed over 2 million patient admissions.

be easily dismissed because it plays a large role in laypeople's attitudes about mental illness, and even mental health professionals sometimes mistakenly use this criterion.

In one of the most famous research studies in the field of abnormal psychology, David Rosenhan, a Stanford University psychologist, and several of his colleagues and friends were mistakenly diagnosed as mentally ill by doctors at several hospitals (see Box 2.1). In Rosenhan's (1973) study, each of the "pseudopatients" arrived at a hospital claiming, falsely, to have heard a hallucinated voice. In all other respects they acted normally. All eight of the pseudopatients were admitted to the psychiatric wards of the hospitals and all but one were given the diagnosis of schizophrenia (the other was diagnosed with manic-depressive psychosis—Chapter 6). After being admitted, the pseudopatients acted normally and said they had stopped hearing the voices. Yet they were kept in the hospital (their stays ranged from 7 to 52 days) and not one was detected as "normal" by the staff. During their hospital stays, the researchers were appalled by what they considered to be the dehumanizing experience of being a psychiatric inpatient. They felt that patients were routinely ignored and treated dismissively by the hospital staff.

Rosenhan used this experiment primarily to emphasize the dangers of diagnostic labeling. But the study also highlights the misleading use, in this instance by trained professionals, of the "help seeking" criterion for defining abnormality. The fact that the pseudopatients arrived at psychiatric facilities seeking help apparently caused the evaluating doctors to *assume* that the experimenters were mentally ill. So, even though we can easily see the limitations of this criterion as an indicator of psychopathology, we should not underestimate its influence.

Irrationality/Dangerousness

People often equate mental illness with irrational, dangerous, or out-of-control behavior. We have all been exposed to stereotypes of psychiatric patients as deranged, homicidal maniacs. Every time a mentally ill individual commits a violent crime, this unfortunate prejudice is reinforced. In truth, while some people with mental disorders do behave in a highly irrational or dangerous manner, most do not (Monahan, 1992; 1993). Similarly, self-destructive behaviors, such as suicidality or extreme recklessness, are associated only with a few mental disorders.

BOX 2.1   The Rosenhan Study and Controversy

On Being Sane in Insane Places

David Rosenhan's (1973) bold attempt to demonstrate that "insanity" is a problematic concept, was both highly influential and very controversial. His experiment was conducted as follows: Rosenhan and 7 confederates gained admission to the psychiatric units of a total of 12 hospitals by claiming, falsely, that they had heard hallucinated voices. After being admitted, they stated that their symptoms had ceased and acted as normally as possible. Yet they were never detected as fakes by hospital staff, and were kept in the respective hospitals for an average of 19 days.

Rosenhan hoped that his study would make two major points. The first and most widely noticed point was that the label "mental illness" is misleading because it cannot be accurately identified (a *validity* issue) even by professionals. Rosenhan is a social psychologist, a discipline that emphasizes social (or *situational*) rather than internal (or *dispositional*) causes of people's behavior. Accordingly, he argued that mentally ill behavior is largely caused by the expectations and influences of a person's social environment (such as a psychiatric hospital) rather than some true internal condition of mental illness.

His second major point, related to the first, was that the social environment in mental hospitals seemed to unwittingly encourage the very behaviors that they were trying to eliminate. For example, the "pseudopatients" felt that these hospitals were dehumanizing environments in which little attention was paid to patients, and that being labeled as "mentally ill" contributed to the patients' problems and to impersonal treatment by the staff.

Rosenhan received much acclaim but also some harsh criticism for his conclusions. The most prominent critic was Robert Spitzer, a leading research psychiatrist and one of the main authors of the American Psychiatric Association's *Diagnostic and Statistical Manual of Mental Disorders* (DSM), the official diagnostic manual for classifying mental disorders. Spitzer (1975) viewed the Rosenhan study as seductive but logically faulty and misleading. In particular, Spitzer argued that Rosenhan's study did not actually prove what Rosenhan claimed, namely that mental illness cannot be accurately identified. While Spitzer admitted that there were many problems with the state of psychiatric diagnosis, he argued that this is no different from other areas of medicine. Rosenhan's study, in Spitzer's view, only proved that these pseudopatients were not detected as faking mental illness, which is a far cry from proving Rosenhan's much more general claim that mental illness is only in the eye of the beholder. Here is Spitzer's (1975) conclusion to his rebuttal article "On Pseudoscience, Logic in Remission, and Psychiatric Diagnosis: A Critique of Rosenhan's 'On Being Sane in Insane Places.'"

In conclusion, there are serious problems with psychiatric diagnosis, as there are with other medical diagnoses. Recent developments indicate that the reliability of psychiatric diagnoses can be considerably improved. However, even with the poor reliability of current psychiatric diagnoses, it is not so poor that it cannot aid in the treatment of the seriously disturbed psychiatric patient. Rosenhan's study, "On Being Sane in Insane Places," proves that pseudopatients are not detected as having simulated signs of mental illness. This rather unremarkable finding is not relevant to the real problems of the reliability and validity of psychiatric diagnoses and only serves to obscure them… In the setting of a psychiatric hospital, psychiatrists are remarkably able to distinguish the "sane" from the "insane." (p. 451)

There are several other limitations of this criterion. First, irrational and dangerous behavior can occur for many reasons that have nothing to do with mental illness. For example, in the proper **context,** such as on a battlefield or a football field, reckless, out-of-control aggression can be considered appropriate or even heroic, not abnormal! Second, to equate irrationality or lack of control with mental illness might imply that their opposites—extreme rationality and control—are the essence of mental health. The capacity for rational, controlled behavior is obviously important, but it can be taken to an extreme that is just as pathological as extreme irrationality. In fact, there is a mental disorder characterized by the traits of hyper-rationality and a need for control taken to a pathological extreme. This disorder is called *obsessive-compulsive personality disorder* and it will be discussed in Chapter 11.

Finally, equating rationality with sanity and irrationality with insanity is a **culturally relative** assumption that tends to be particularly characteristic of Anglo-American and Northern European cultures (Arrington, 1979; Fabrega, 1982/1984; Ngcobo & Edwards, 1998; Pichot, 1997). For example, Gabriel Garcia Marquez, the Columbian

Nobel Prize-winning author, has pointed out that in Latin cultures the experience of falling in love is often described as a state of irrationality, danger, and loss of control— yet falling "madly" in love is a peak human experience, not a sign of pathology. Even within Anglo-European culture, the assumption that rationality is healthier than irrationality frequently comes into question. For example, in Peter Shaffer's fascinating play *Equus* (later made into a movie), a hyper-rational psychiatrist treats a teenage boy who has committed the bizarre, irrational, and dangerous act of blinding several horses in a stable. By the end of the play, the rational but passionless psychiatrist (and the audience) has begun to believe that the boy is healthier than he is, because the boy at least has love and passion in his life. In summary, then, irrationality and dangerousness, like help seeking, can sometimes be *markers* of abnormality, but they are potentially misleading as criteria for defining it.

Deviance

Deviance refers to differentness—behavior or feelings that are extreme or statistically unusual. Deviance is often used as a criterion for defining abnormality in the sense that people who are considered "strange," "weird," or "bizarre" are often assumed to be mentally ill. It is true that some forms of mental illness do involve extreme or rare behaviors such as suicide attempts or hallucinations. But deviance has some important limitations as a criterion for psychopathology (Blackburn, 1995; Fields, 1996; Leifer, 1966; Szasz, 1973; Szasz, Reiman, & Chamblis, 1995).

First, not all mental illness involves extreme behaviors. People with mild anxiety disorders or mild depression may not seem noticeably "different," yet these are diagnosable disorders that affect hundreds of millions of people worldwide. Even people with more unusual and severe disorders like schizophrenia may not behave in any obviously strange way much of the time. Second, deviance is not necessarily a sign of mental illness. Many people who are eccentric or who behave in extreme ways are emotionally healthy. In fact, many respected leaders, artists, athletes, and entrepreneurs are deviant in the sense that their behavior is highly unusual, yet it is highly con-

Deviants? Mahatma Gandhi and Albert Einstein were certainly "outliers" among the general population, yet they were models of greatness, not pathology.

Dr. Thomas Szasz Szasz has been one of the most influential critics of "deviance" as a criterion for abnormality.

Emotional distress Emotional distress is one of the more useful criteria for abnormality, but in some circumstances emotional distress is entirely normal. This distressed woman, for example, is searching for her fiancé after the terrorist attacks of September 11, 2001.

structive and creative (think of Shakespeare, Gandhi, Einstein, and Tiger Woods, all statistically "deviant" geniuses).

Conversely, it would clearly be a mistake to equate mental health with conformity and conventionality; that would make for a dull society indeed! Consider the case of Oscar Schindler, the hero immortalized in Steven Speilberg's movie about the Holocaust, *Schindler's List.* Schindler, who saved hundreds of Jews from extermination by employing them in his factory, was certainly deviant in Nazi Germany. Yet, in his case, we would say that his deviance represented sanity and that the norms of Nazi society were pathological.

In any society, people who express unconventional views or act in unconventional ways are easily targeted. Thus, a serious potential danger of using deviance as a criterion for mental illness is that people who are socially, politically, or culturally different may be persecuted and stigmatized with the label "mentally ill" when in fact they may be simply expressing legitimate views that fall outside the mainstream. In the former Soviet Union, for instance, political enemies of the government were at times detained in mental institutions with the groundless accusation that they were mentally ill (Bonnie, 1990; Goldstein, 1975).

The psychiatrist Thomas Szasz is the best-known critic of the deviance criterion. In numerous articles and books, Szasz argues that the very concept of mental illness is a "myth" used by authorities to enforce compliance with social norms (Szasz, 1960; 1975; 1994). The movie *One Flew Over the Cuckoo's Nest,* based on Ken Kesey's novel, also powerfully expresses this view (see Box 2.2). While most experts disagree with Szasz's extreme (deviant?) perspective, Szasz's general distrust of the use of deviance as a criterion has been very influential. A balanced appraisal would suggest that deviance, like help seeking and irrationality/dangerousness, can sometimes serve as a marker for abnormality, but has serious limits as a defining criterion for it.

Emotional Distress

Emotional distress in some form—such as sadness or anxiety—is associated with most forms of psychopathology, making it a more useful criterion for defining and identifying mental illness than those we have considered so far. When we think of the most common forms of mental illness—such as depression and anxiety disorders—emotional suffering is clearly a central feature of these conditions. In fact, it is hard to think of examples of psychopathology in which significant emotional distress is not present. Yet emotional distress has two important limitations as a defining criterion for mental illness.

First, in a few mental disorders emotional distress can be a relatively minor factor. For example, one interesting class of disorders, called the *personality disorders* (to be discussed in Chapter 11), involve personality traits so extreme and rigid that they are considered abnormal. Some individuals with personality disorders report little or no emotional distress. They may cause distress for the people around them, because of their extreme and rigid personalities, but they often do not recognize their own problems, and typically do not seek treatment. For example, people with *antisocial personality disorder* lack a normal conscience, violate social rules without remorse, and exploit others (Hare, 1999; Lykken, 1995; Richardson, 2000; Walsh, 1999). They rarely report emotional distress, yet they clearly exhibit abnormal behavior.

An even bigger problem for the "emotional distress" criterion is that many forms of emotional distress are normal and not indicative of psychopathology. Consider the *grieving* process. It is entirely normal to feel intense emotional distress after a significant loss (Danforth, 2000; Liiceanu, 2000; Sacks, 1999) and, in fact, it may be unhealthy and even pathological *not* to experience grief under these circumstances

BOX 2.2   Abnormal Psychology and Film

One Flew Over the Cuckoo's Nest

This 1975 movie starring Jack Nicholson, based on the novel of the same name by Ken Kesey, is one of the most powerful critiques of the mental health establishment ever filmed. A brilliant dark comedy about a rebellious hooligan (Nicholson) who is locked up in a mental hospital, *Cuckoo's Nest* won five Academy Awards including Best Picture. The plot of the film focuses on Nicholson's character, Randle Patrick McMurphy, who has been sent to the hospital for a psychiatric evaluation because of his aggressive behavior while incarcerated for various crimes. McMurphy is appalled by the passivity and submissiveness of the other patients on his hospital ward, most of whom seem to live in fear of Nurse Ratched, who runs the unit with an iron grip. McMurphy tries to rouse the men in rebellion, insisting that they are no crazier than anybody else and are simply hiding from life. One character, the huge "Chief," a Native American who does not seem to speak or hear, watches the drama from afar. At one point, however, the Chief comes to McMurphy's aid in a fight with the orderlies, and the two of them are punished with electroconvulsive therapy (ECT is discussed in Chapter 6).

McMurphy and the Chief later decide to escape from the hospital, but during a final illicit party on the ward their plans go awry. McMurphy has arranged for a shy, stuttering young patient named Billy to lose his virginity with a prostitute who has come to the party at McMurphy's invitation. Everyone passes out from drinking, and Nurse Ratched arrives the next morning to find the ward in a shambles. Billy is discovered with the prostitute, and when confronted about it by Nurse Ratched, he falls apart. McMurphy, enraged, attacks Nurse Ratched and nearly kills her. The story then moves to a dramatic climax, which we don't want to give away for those who haven't read the book or seen the movie!

The film, like Kesey's novel, tries to make the point that the label "mentally ill" is simply a convenient way for authorities to try to control people who are perceived as being too unconventional. "Treatment" is a euphemism for coercive efforts to make such people conform to social norms. In this sense, the film is a critique of the criterion of *deviance* for defining mental illness, and *Cuckoo's Nest* has a good deal in common with the work of Thomas Szasz in that respect. At the same time, the film obviously caricatures mental hospitals and treatments rather than presenting an accurate view of them. While the film may be a valid critique of some of the excesses of the mental health establishment, it presents the extreme view that there is really no such thing as mental illness, and that "treatment" is just a form of social control.

One Flew Over the Cuckoo's Nest The film version of Ken Kesey's novel is widely considered a classic. In this scene, McMurphy (Nicholson) is trying to instigate fellow inmates to revolt against the tyranny of Nurse Ratched.

(Edelstein et al., 1999; Worden, 1991). Thus, in some situations, the presence of emotional distress is more normal than its absence.

However, situations like grieving are exceptions to the general rule that significant emotional distress is a relatively good marker of psychopathology. This general rule works most of the time, and clinicians rely on it, in conjunction with other criteria, as a useful tool for identifying psychopathology. In sum, while emotional distress should be considered a partial rather than an absolute marker of psychopathology, it remains one of the most useful criteria.

Significant Impairment

Finally, let's consider the criterion of impairment in the ability to function. Many experts in the field view significant impairment in functioning as the hallmark of psychopathology and the best defining criterion for it. After all, most forms of psychopathology involve some form of impairment, such as decreased energy (in depression), avoidance behaviors (in anxiety), and pervasive problems in daily living (in severe disorders like schizophrenia). But with this criterion, too, we find some exceptions and limitations.

First, impairments in psychological functions (for example, memory or social skills) are sometimes caused by physical injuries or diseases, such as head injuries or strokes, not by psychopathology. Second, while it is difficult to think of emotional disorders that do not involve impairments of some kind, there are certain disorders—minor mood disorders, for example—in which functional impairments are relatively slight and certainly not the central features of the condition. A third limitation of this criterion is that "impairment in functioning" turns out to be almost as hard to define as "abnormality." After all, determining what constitutes an "impairment" in functioning requires a definition of "normal" functioning, and distinguishing between normal and abnormal is, as we have seen, no simple matter. In this sense, "impaired" is more like a synonym of "abnormal" than a criterion of it, a problem logicians refer to as a "circular definition."

Nonetheless, "impairment" can be a generally useful criterion for identifying psychopathology. After all, when we want to know whether someone's emotional problems are "pathological," we often begin by asking the question: "How much are these problems interfering with his or her life?" Thus, like emotional distress, significant impairment is one of the most useful, if imperfect, criteria for defining abnormality.

Let's consider the five criteria that we have just discussed by returning to the case of Dave. Do the criteria help us determine whether Dave's behavior is normal or abnormal? Dave does not seem to meet the first two criteria. He has not sought help, and he does not seem to be particularly irrational or dangerous, although his anxiety may be jeopardizing his overall health to some degree. Dave might meet the criterion of deviance since he is beginning to avoid people and activities in a somewhat unusual way, but his behavior is certainly not bizarre. However, he certainly meets the criteria of emotional distress and significant impairment in functioning. As we will see, the distress and impairment criteria form the basis of the current official definition of mental disorders. In fact, Dave's symptoms match a disorder that is formally recognized in current practice: *social phobia,* a significant fear and avoidance of social situations (this disorder will be discussed in detail in Chapter 5). Thus, despite their limitations, these last two criteria, especially when used together, do seem to help us define abnormality.

Brief Summary

- The case of Dave illustrates that it is difficult to precisely define abnormality.
- People use various criteria to try to define and identify abnormality; many of these are useful, but none work perfectly. Five widely used criteria are included in the acronym HIDES:
  - **H**elp seeking
  - **I**rrationality/dangerousness
  - **D**eviance
  - **E**motional distress
  - **S**ignificant impairment

- The first three criteria are sometimes markers of psychopathology but often they are not; as criteria for abnormality they are frequently misleading.

- Distress and impairment are more useful markers of psychopathology.

Critical Thinking Question	**C**an you think of an example of psychopathology that fits all five of the commonly used criteria for defining abnormality? Can you think of an example of psychopathology that involves only one of the criteria for defining abnormality?

CORE CONCEPTS IN DEFINING ABNORMALITY

We have determined that Dave's behavior fits the HIDES criteria well enough to be considered abnormal. But we are still faced with the broader question of how to define abnormality in general. Our review of the HIDES criteria demonstrates the complexity of defining psychopathology. This complexity stems from two core concepts in abnormal psychology: *cultural and historical relativism* and the *continuum between normal and abnormal behavior.*

Cultural and Historical Relativism

Relativism refers to the fact that what is considered normal and abnormal differs widely across cultures and over time (Fabrega, 1995; Leff, 1988; Lopez & Guarnaccia, 2000). Thus, there can be no *universal* definition of abnormality. Any definition will be *relative* to (that is, limited to) the cultural, social, and historical context in which it exists (Alarcon, Foulks, & Vakkur, 1998; Cohen, 1998; Comunian & Gielen, 2000; Kagitcibasi, 2000; Kim, 2000). In our society, for example, an individual who believes that he is possessed by a spirit which causes him to shout, laugh uncontrollably, and bang his head would certainly be considered abnormal. However, in certain North African and Middle Eastern cultures this experience has a name ("zar"; see Table 2.2 for other "culture-bound" syndromes) and is *not* considered pathological (Grisaru, Budowski, & Witztum, 1997; Mallery, 1999).

In contrast to *cultural relativism, historical relativism* refers to changes over time in a particular culture's views of abnormality. Perhaps one of the clearest examples concerns homosexuality. Until 1973, homosexuality was included as a mental disorder in the official diagnostic manual of the American Psychiatric Association. Individuals "diagnosed" with homosexuality were prescribed "treatments" intended to change their sexual orientation, usually with unsuccessful and unhappy results (Bullough & Bullough, 1997; King & Bartlett, 1999; Rottnek, 1999). In 1973, the diagnosis of homosexuality was removed from the diagnostic manual as a result of complex social, political, and scientific changes (the history of these changes is described in detail in Chapter 10). Most mental health professionals now consider homosexuality to be one variation of normal sexual functioning.

To summarize, ideas about what is normal and abnormal vary over time and across cultures so that we can never define psychopathology in a universal, timeless way. *Relativism* even affects our understanding of a person like Dave and makes it impossible to say in absolute terms whether he is normal or abnormal. Our evaluation of his behavior only applies to the social and historical context in which he lives. For example, on a contemporary American college campus, Dave's social iso-

Table 2.2	**Culture-Bound Syndromes**
(Adapted from DSM-IV by The New York Times)	

This chart describes unusual behavioral syndromes found in specific parts of the world. Some are considered normal within their cultural context, although they would be considered abnormal elsewhere, highlighting the core concept of *cultural relativism.*

BEHAVIORAL SYNDROME	WHERE RECOGNIZED	DESCRIPTION
Amok	Malaysia; similar patterns elsewhere	Brooding followed by a violent outburst; often precipitated by a slight or insult; seems to be prevalent only among men.
Ataque de nervios ("attack of nerves")	Latin America and Mediterranean	An episode of uncontrollable shouting, crying, trembling, heat in chest rising to the head; verbal or physical aggression.
Bills, colera, or muina	Many Latin groups	Rage perceived as disturbing bodily balances, causing nervous tension, headache, trembling, screaming, etc.
Boufée delirante	East Africa and Haiti	Sudden outburst of agitated and aggressive behavior, confusion, and mental and physical excitement.
Brain fag	West Africa; similar symptoms elsewhere	"Brain tiredness," a mental and physical reaction to the challenges of schooling.
Dhat	India; also in Sri Lanka and China	Severe anxiety and hypochondria associated with discharge of semen and feelings of exhaustion.
Falling out or blacking out	Southern United States and Caribbean	Sudden collapse; eyes remain open but sightless; the victim hears but feels unable to move.
Ghost sickness	American Indian tribes	Preoccupation with death and the dead, with bad dreams, fainting, appetite loss, fear, hallucinations, etc.
Hwa-byung	Korea	Symptoms attributed to suppression of anger, including insomnia, fatigue, panic, fear of death, depression, indigestion, etc.
Koro	Malaysia; related conditions in East Asia	Sudden intense anxiety that sexual organs will recede into body and cause death; occasional epidemics.

lation seems somewhat unusual and problematic. But in another time and place—a medieval monastery, for example—it might well have been considered typical and normal.

The Continuum Between Normal and Abnormal Behavior

The second general issue affecting definitions of abnormality is the fact that normal and abnormal behavior are not completely distinct but lie on a *continuum.* Abnormal behaviors and feelings are very often exaggerations of normal states. In other words, normality gradually shades into abnormality. Therefore, we cannot say exactly where to locate the cut-off between normal and abnormal behavior. Any decision about where to draw that line must be somewhat arbitrary.

BEHAVIORAL SYNDROME	WHERE RECOGNIZED	DESCRIPTION
Latah	Malaysia, Indonesia, Japan, Thailand	Hypersensitivity to sudden fright, often with nonsense mimicking of others, trancelike behavior.
Locura	United States and Latin America	Psychosis tied to inherited vulnerability and/or life difficulties; incoherence, agitation, hallucinations, and possibly violence.
Mal de ojo ("evil eye")	Mediterranean and elsewhere	Sufferers, mostly children, are believed to be under influence of "evil eye," causing fitful sleep, crying, sickness, fever.
Pibloktoq	Arctic and subarctic Eskimo communities	Extreme excitement, physical and verbal violence for up to 30 minutes, then convulsions and short coma.
Qi-gong, psychotic reaction	China	A short episode of mental symptoms after engaging in Chinese folk practice of qi-gong, or "exercise of vital energy."
Shen-k'uei or shenkui	Taiwan and China	Marked anxiety or panic symptoms with bodily complaints attributed to life-threatening loss of semen.
Sin-byung	Korea	Syndrome of anxiety and bodily complaints followed by dissociation and possession by ancestral spirits.
Spell	Southern United States	A trance in which individuals communicate with decreased relatives or spirits; not perceived as a medical event.
Susto ("fright" or "soul loss")	Latin groups in U.S. and Caribbean	Illness tied to a frightening event that makes the soul leave the body, causing unhappiness and sickness.
Taijin kyofusho	Japan	An intense fear that the body—its parts or functions—displease, embarrass, or are offensive to others.
Zar	North Africa and Middle East	Belief in possession by a spirit, causing shouting, laughing, head banging, etc.; not considered pathological.

Consider the case of Dave again. If Dave were so anxious that he could not leave his room, and he avoided all of his classes and friends for months, it would be easy to classify his behavior as abnormal. But when behavior is closer to the middle of the continuum, as in Dave's case, even experts within the same cultural and historical context will sometimes disagree about whether the behavior is normal or abnormal.

The continuum between normal and abnormal behavior has an implication specifically relevant to students taking courses in abnormal psychology. The fact that normality and abnormality lie on a continuum means that every human being experiences feelings and behaviors, like sadness or social anxiety, that are milder versions of the more extreme states found in mental disorders. For some, this can be a disturbing realization. Students of abnormal psychology may experience a form of *medical student syndrome,* a phenomenon that takes its name from a condition known among medical interns, who sometimes become alarmed by every minor headache or rash they experience while learning about exotic diseases (Hardy & Calhoun, 1997; Klamen, Grossman, & Kopacz, 1999). We can reassure students of abnormal psychology that in most cases such experiences are no cause for alarm and simply reflect the continuum between normal and abnormal states that is part of being human. In fact, the continuum between normality and abnormality can be an advantage in the study of abnormal psychology because we all can have some intuitive understanding of mental disorders by imagining exaggerations of our own experiences. Of course, some people may also become legitimately concerned about their mental health as they learn about psychopathology. We encourage people to speak with their instructor or to seek out a mental health professional on campus or in the community if they do experience such concerns.

Brief Summary

- The complexity of the HIDES criteria for defining abnormality relates to two core concepts in abnormal psychology: *cultural and historical relativism* and the *continuum between normal and abnormal behavior.*

- *Relativism* refers to the fact that all definitions of abnormality are limited to their specific cultural and historical context.

- The *continuum between normal and abnormal behavior* means that the distinction between normality and abnormality will always be somewhat arbitrary. This contributes to the difficulty of precisely defining abnormality, but it is helpful for understanding abnormal behavior.

Critical Thinking Question	**C**an you think of any examples of psychopathology that might be easy to define and identify as abnormal regardless of the issue of *relativism* and the *continuum between normal and abnormal behavior?*

DEFINING ABNORMALITY: PRACTICAL SOLUTIONS

From our discussion of the complexity of precisely defining abnormality, a natural question arises: How big a *practical* problem is this? How can one study and treat something that is so hard to define? In fact, the challenges of defining abnormality do create some practical problems, such as the risk of labeling as mentally ill, and even persecuting, people who are simply different. Even when clinicians are well intentioned, their misdiagnoses can adversely affect people in profound ways. If we could be more precise in identifying abnormality, what happened to David Rosenhan and his colleagues might not have happened, and other people might be spared similar experiences. So we cannot escape the fact that the problems in defining abnormality are not just academic or theoretical. They have real, and often very negative, consequences for people who are incorrectly or unfairly diagnosed.

On the other side of issue, there are several reasons to think that the practical problems of defining abnormality are not as serious as some critics contend. First of all, the psychiatrist Robert Spitzer points out in his critique of Rosenhan's study (see Box 2.1: The Rosenhan Study and Controversy) that in the world of everyday decision making about psychopathology, clinicians are rarely in the position of having to answer the question "Is this person sane or insane?" Rather, clinicians are usually concerned with questions such as: "This person is feeling distressed: how can I help him?"

or "This person is clearly mentally ill; what kind of disorder is she suffering from?" (Blechner, 2001; Kahn, 2001; O'Brien & Houston, 2000; Spitzer, 1975). Sanity and insanity are, in fact, legal terms rather than psychiatric ones. Only certain unusual circumstances, such as a court proceeding to determine if a person is "not guilty by reason of insanity" of a crime, require a legal determination (and therefore definition) of insanity (see Box 12.5). It is true that clinicians often diagnose clients with specific mental disorders as part of standard treatment and research procedures, and in so doing they implicitly define their clients' behaviors as "abnormal." However, in making diagnoses, clinicians can rely on *working definitions* of abnormality embedded in official diagnostic manuals, and therefore the lack of a precise definition is not an everyday practical problem.

What are these "working definitions" and how well do they work? In order to answer this question, let's briefly consider the concept of definition more generally. Many scientific terms and categories suffer from the same definitional problems that we have discussed regarding the terms "abnormality," "psychopathology," and "mental illness." For example, if you think about medical terms such as "disease" and "pain" it becomes clear that they, too, are somewhat vague and difficult to precisely define. Cognitive psychologists have argued that the definitions of many common, everyday concepts lack precise boundaries or specifications, and hence they have coined the terms *fuzzy* or **natural categories** (Massaro, 1987; McCloskey & Glucksberg, 1978). They also argue that fuzzy categories usually work reasonably well in everyday use, despite lacking precision (Rosch & Mervis, 1975). To demonstrate, consider the following situation. Imagine that someone set up a series of metal coils in a row. At the far left end, the coils are freezing cold, but as they progress to the right, each coil is one degree hotter until at the far right end the coils are burning hot. Now, imagine having to precisely define the (fuzzy) term "hot" and to identify precisely where the "hot" coils begin. With such a gradual **continuum** between the coils, this would be impossible; you could only make an arbitrary distinction about where to draw the imaginary line between "hot" and "warm." But imagine that someone asked you simply to identify a hot coil—a more typical categorization task. This would be easy, because you could point to the right end of the row.

Psychopathology, like the hot coils, is impossible to define *precisely*. But because psychopathology usually falls toward the extreme end of the continuum of behavior, it is still relatively easy to *identify* in most cases. The task of identifying abnormality becomes more challenging only in a case such as Dave's when the behavior in question falls in the fuzzy area at the boundary between normality and abnormality. To summarize, there are two main reasons why the lack of a precise definition of psychopathology is not as problematic as it might seem. First, clinicians rarely need to precisely define abnormality in typical clinical situations. Second, fuzzy, rather than precise, definitions are common in everyday and scientific contexts, and work reasonably well most of the time.

Working Definitions of Psychopathology

So far, we have reviewed the HIDES criteria that help us define and identify abnormal behavior. We have also considered the challenges of precisely defining psychopathology and recognized that such a definition is rarely necessary. However, we must address one last question. When a definition of psychopathology *is* necessary, what definition, fuzzy though it may be, should be used? As we will see, there are a variety of possibilities, including an "official" definition which, though controversial, is widely used in the field for identifying and diagnosing psychopathology. The following definitions can be

Natural categories Categories that usually work reasonably well in everyday use, despite their lack of precision.

thought of as working, or *operational,* definitions; they are designed to be useful in practical or research situations, even though they are subject to many of the limitations we have been discussing.

Some of the pioneers in the field of psychopathology were content with very simple working definitions. Sigmund Freud, for example, once defined normality as the capacity "to love and to work," so his implicit definition of abnormality could be stated as "impairments in the capacity to love and work." Freud's definition has the advantages of simplicity and directness, but it has the disadvantages of being very general and vague. Over time, mental health professionals have sought more detailed working definitions of mental illness. In fact, the recent trend has been toward increased emphasis on precise definitions of mental illness and specific mental disorders, as we will discuss in Chapter 4.

This detailed approach has become the hallmark of the recent editions of the "official" psychiatric manual for diagnosing mental disorders, a book called the *Diagnostic and Statistical Manual of Mental Disorders* published by the American Psychiatric Association. This book, currently in its fourth revised edition (generally referred to by its abbreviated name, the DSM-IV-TR) (APA, 2000), lists several hundred different mental disorders and provides instructions on how to identify them. The DSM-IV-TR definition of psychopathology is the currently accepted standard for diagnostic practice in the United States and many other countries. (We will discuss the development of the DSM system, how it is used in clinical practice, and its advantages and limitations in Chapter 4.)

The DSM-IV-TR includes an introductory chapter with a section entitled "Definition of Mental Disorder." This section discusses some of the problems we have been describing concerning the difficulties in defining the term "mental disorder." The authors state:

> …although this manual provides a classification of mental disorders, it must be admitted that no definition adequately specifies precise boundaries for the concept of "mental disorder." The concept of "mental disorder," like many other concepts in medicine and science, lacks a consistent operational definition that covers all situations. (APA, 2000, p. xxx)

The authors of DSM-IV-TR then proceed to offer their working definition of the term "mental disorder." As you will see, it is a long and complicated one, testifying to the definitional challenges we have been discussing:

> In DSM-IV, each of the mental disorders is conceptualized as a clinically significant behavioral or psychological syndrome or pattern that occurs in an individual and that is associated with present distress (e.g., a painful symptom) or disability (i.e., impairment in one or more important areas of functioning) or with a significantly increased risk of suffering death, pain, disability, or an important loss of freedom. In addition, this syndrome or pattern must not be merely an expectable and culturally sanctioned response to a particular event, for example, the death of a loved one. Whatever its original cause, it must currently be considered a manifestation of a behavioral, psychological, or biological dysfunction in the individual. Neither deviant behavior (e.g., political, religious, or sexual) nor conflicts that are primarily between the individual and society are mental disorders unless the deviance or conflict is a symptom of dysfunction in the individual, as described above. (APA, 2000, pp. xxxi)

We would like to emphasize four aspects of this definition. First, the DSM-IV-TR definition contains many qualifications and undefined phrases (for example, "clinically significant" and "behavioral, psychological, or biological dysfunction")

BOX 2.3 Defining Abnormality

The "Harmful Dysfunction" Debate

We have emphasized that no one has been able to come up with a fully acceptable definition of mental illness, but this hasn't kept people from trying! In fact, an entire issue of the *Journal of Abnormal Psychology* (APA, 1999) was devoted to just this effort. Jerome Wakefield, a clinical psychologist, had proposed in an earlier article that the term "mental disorder" should be defined as a "harmful dysfunction"; that is, any breakdown in an evolutionarily based human mental function that has harmful consequences. Here is an excerpt in which Wakefield (1999) outlines his position.

> In a recent series of articles, I proposed that *disorder* means *harmful dysfunction,* where dysfunctions are failures of internal mechanisms to perform naturally selected [i.e., evolutionarily adaptive] functions. The harmful dysfunction (HD) analysis rejects both the view that disorder is just a value concept referring to undesirable or harmful conditions [e.g., the impairment criterion] and the view that disorder is purely a scientific concept. Rather, the HD analysis proposes that a disorder attribution [i.e., a decision that someone has a disorder] requires both a scientific judgment that there exists a failure of designed function and a value judgment that the design failure harms the individual. (p. 374)

Roughly half of the commentaries on Wakefield's article argued in favor of Wakefield's definition; the other half argued against it. Here is an excerpt from Robert Spitzer (1999), the same psychiatrist who rebutted Rosenhan's study. In the summary of his article, he praises Wakefield's definition.

Physicians, including psychiatrists, give a lot of thought in their everyday work to answer the question of whether or not a particular patient has a disorder; they rarely give much thought to the broader issue of what constitutes a disorder. Remarkably, and consistent with the harmful dysfunction (HD) analysis, there is a broad consensus in both the general public and the medical and health professions as to what conditions are disorders—even though there is no consensus definition of disorder. The HD analysis is a substantial advance over previous attempts to define disorder… (p. 430)

On the other hand, some critics argued that Wakefield's definition amounts to "biological reductionism" which underestimates the complexity and "fuzziness" of the concept of a disorder. Here is an excerpt from one critical response (Kimayer & Young, 1999).

> The evolutionary theory of the concept of mental disorder as harmful dysfunction that J.C. Wakefield proposed (a) does not correspond to how the term *disorder* is used in psychiatric nosology [diagnosis] or in clinicians' everyday practice; (b) does not cover the territory to which the term *reasonably* could be applied; and (c) is not especially useful for research, clinical, or social purposes. The broad concept of disorder is a polythetic [multiple], not a monothetic [single], concept. As such, there need be no essential characteristic, criterion, or single prototype of disorder… (p. 446)

Jerome Wakefield

that highlight the fuzziness of the term "mental disorder." Second, it focuses mostly on the criteria of distress and impairment, which, as we discussed earlier, are generally considered more useful than the criteria of seeking help, irrationality/dangerousness, and deviance. Third, this definition is close, though not identical to, a simpler definition of mental illness as a *harmful dysfunction* proposed by Wakefield (1997; 1999) and discussed in Box 2.3.

Finally, as defined in the DSM-IV-TR, "mental disorder" is a broad concept that applies to a great many people. In fact, according to a recent authoritative study of the prevalence of mental disorders in the United States based on the DSM definition and guidelines, 48% of Americans experience at least one mental disorder during their lifetimes (Kessler, McGonagle, Zhao, Nelson et al., 1994). (See Figure 2.1 for the lifetime prevalence of common mental disorders in the United States.)

Figure 2.1 Lifetime prevalence of common mental disorders in the United States
Based on DSM-IV criteria, mental disorders are very common, as shown by these figures.
(Adapted from Kessler et al., 1994)

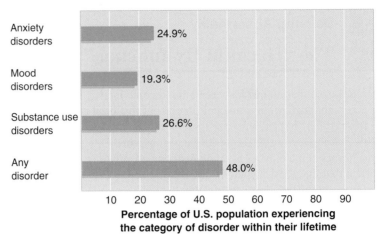

Percentage of U.S. population experiencing the category of disorder within their lifetime

Brief Summary

● The difficulty of precisely defining abnormality creates certain practical problems. For example, the Rosenhan study demonstrates that people can be mistakenly labeled as mentally ill, leading to potentially serious consequences.

● On the other hand, clinicians rarely need to precisely define abnormality. In most circumstances, they can do their jobs without a precise definition.

● Abnormality is a "fuzzy" concept. Like other fuzzy concepts, it works reasonably well in clinical practice despite its lack of precision.

● Experts in the field have developed a working definition of psychopathology described in the American Psychiatric Association's *Diagnostic and Statistical Manual of Mental Disorders*. It serves as the official definition of the concept "mental disorder," although it is somewhat fuzzy and quite broad.

Critical Thinking Question | **Does the lack of a precise definition of psychopathology seem to you to be a significant problem? Why or why not?**

The issues surrounding the definition and identification of psychopathology are part of what make the field of abnormal psychology so interesting and controversial. We revisit these issues many times throughout the book, and introduce you to several others as well. In the next chapter we take up another challenging and enduring issue in the field: how to *explain* abnormal behavior.

Chapter Summary

● The case of Dave highlights many of the complex issues involved in defining the terms "abnormality," "mental illness," and "psychopathology."

● It is never possible to universally and precisely define abnormality because of the core concepts of ***cultural and historical relativism*** and ***the continuum between normal and abnormal behavior.***

- While these core concepts can make it difficult to define abnormality and to decide whether an individual has a mental disorder, the degree of difficulty in doing so depends on certain circumstances. For example, the issue of *relativism* is lessened if we restrict our task to identifying abnormality within the limits of a given cultural and historical context, such as contemporary American society.

- In cases like Dave's, which are near the middle of the continuum between *normal and abnormal behavior,* it can still be difficult to identify abnormality because it is a fuzzy concept without clear-cut boundaries.

- Fortunately, the fuzziness of the category "abnormality" is not a significant problem in most everyday clinical decisions about identifying and treating psychopathology.

- Working definitions of psychopathology, like the one provided in the DSM-IV-TR, offer an official definition when one is needed.

Arshile Gorky, *The Artist and His Mother,* ca. 1926–1936. Oil on canvas (60 × 50 in.). Photo by Geoffrey Clement. Gift of Julien Levy for Maro and Natasha Gorky in memory of their father. ©1998: Whitney Museum of American Art, New York. ©2004 Artists Rights Society (ARS), New York.

■ *Arshile Gorky* (1904–1948) came to New York City in 1920 after escaping the massacre of Armenians and watching his mother die of starvation in his homeland of Turkey. He is credited with having developed a painting style that combined European Modernism with American Abstract Expressionism. ...*continues on page 30*

arshile gorky

chapter three

EXPLAINING

ABNORMALITY
WHAT CAUSES
PSYCHOPATHOLOGY?

In Chapter 2, we focused on the challenges of identifying and *defining* psychopathology—on how one might tell whether a person's behavior is "abnormal" or not. In this chapter we take up a second important issue in the study of abnormal psychology. Once a mental disorder has been identified, how can we understand and explain what causes it? Let's think back for a moment to the case of Dave—the college sophomore suffering from severe anxiety in social situations—and approach it from the perspective of *explanation*. What are the causes of his social anxiety? At this point, we'll add a bit more background information about Dave to help us think about the causes of his anxiety and his increasing social isolation.

Case Vignette

Despite Dave's hopes that he would feel less anxious during the second semester of his sophomore year, his troubles intensified to the point that he decided to seek help at the college clinic. During his first two sessions, Dave told his therapist about his problems and his life. Here is a summary of that information. Dave is the younger of two children in an upper-middle class family; his father is a successful physician and his mother is a teacher. Dave's older brother, Thomas, has had a difficult life, suffering for many years from severe anxiety which has made it hard for him to do well academically and socially. As a result, Dave feels that the family pressure to succeed has fallen increasingly on him. Dave has handled this pressure well, as his general success thus far in life would indicate, but he does occasionally lapse into an apprehensive, pessimistic attitude when the pressure feels too great. Dave's father is devoted to his family, but his job has always required him to work long hours, sometimes leading to marital tension. Dave's mother is loving and sensitive most of the time, but when she feels stressed by her work, family, and marriage, she tends to become anxious and withdrawn.

Dave occasionally feels that he gets "taken for granted" when he is doing well, since both of his parents are so busy and caught up in the demands of their own lives. Also, Dave's family seems to have a pattern of providing more attention and support to family members who are having trouble, like Dave's brother. For the most part, however, the family enjoys being together and gets along well despite these patterns and tensions. Everyone is in good physical health, although Dave has been diagnosed with a mild heart condition that causes him to experience occasional palpitations and shortness of breath.

With this brief description in mind, let's turn to the general issues of explaining abnormality. We will periodically return to the case of Dave to illustrate various points that come up along the way.

Case Vignette

- **Explaining Abnormality: The Core Concepts**
  - Cultural and Historical Relativism
  - The Principle of Multiple Causality
  - The Connection Between Mind and Body
- **The Theoretical Perspectives**
  - Psychodynamic Perspectives
  - Humanistic and Existential Perspectives
  - Behavioral Perspectives
  - Cognitive Perspectives
  - Sociocultural and Family Systems Perspectives
  - Biological Perspectives

Case Vignette - **Explanation and Treatment**

...continued from page 28

While professionally successful, Gorky experienced a number of tragic personal events including a fire in his studio, a bout of cancer, and the failure of his marriage. At age 44, he took his own life. How do we explain Gorky's suicide? Was it due to events in his early life, his later life, to biological abnormalities in his mood regulation, or to a complex mix of these and other factors? In this chapter we consider the issue of explaining abnormal behavior.

Animism Belief in the existence and power of a spirit world.

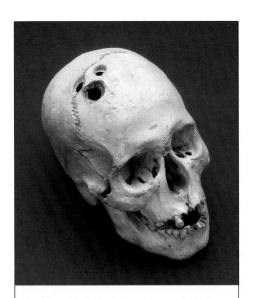

Trephinated skull This trephinated skull was excavated from Jericho. The individual survived the procedure as indicated by the bone growth around the holes.

EXPLAINING ABNORMALITY: THE CORE CONCEPTS

You may already be familiar with some of the theories that are most often used to explain psychopathology. Currently, the most widely used theories in the field are *psychological* theories, such as *psychodynamic, behavioral,* and *cognitive* theories, which focus on an individual's mental processes, and *biological* theories, which focus on biochemical influences on behavior. Before we present these theories and others in detail, we need to consider three core concepts in abnormal psychology: the issue of **cultural and historical relativism** that we encountered in Chapter 2; **the principle of multiple causality;** and **the connection between mind and body.**

Cultural and Historical Relativism

Many forms of mental illness have been present throughout recorded history. We can find stories in the Bible, for example, which describe people suffering from what today would be called depression and schizophrenia (Bark, 1988; Kahn, 1975). The history of humanity's ever-changing ways of identifying, classifying, and treating the mentally ill is a fascinating story in its own right (see Box 3.1). Every society develops ways of trying to understand and manage people who seem abnormal. Let's consider two distinct historical examples in order to illustrate the wide range of possible approaches to explaining abnormal behavior.

"Primitive" Explanations: Animism and Spiritual Theories

According to anthropological and archeological evidence, in so-called "primitive" or "pre-modern" societies, the typical approach to explaining abnormal behavior was a form of **animism** (Esper, 1964). Animism, in general, refers to the belief in the existence and power of a spirit world. According to an animistic worldview, a person afflicted with a mental disturbance has been possessed by a spirit, usually an evil or malevolent one.

Archeological evidence of a practice known as *trephination* provides one interesting indication of animistic beliefs. Trephination consisted of cutting an opening in the skull of a living person in the belief that this would allow the evil spirit causing abnormal behavior to escape. Apparently, techniques of trephination were refined enough that some "patients" survived; archeologists have found skulls with new bone growth around the holes! While there is some debate among historians about whether trephination was a common practice, there is little doubt that such animistic theories were widespread in many early societies (Selling, 1940; Tylor, 1958).

A second method of "treatment" related to the animistic views of abnormal behavior is a more familiar practice known as *exorcism.* Exorcism is a ritual, usually carried out by religious authorities, in which evil spirits thought to be causing pathological behavior are "cast out" of the suffering person.

Our point in describing these animistic belief systems is not only to illustrate the great variety of historical and cultural approaches to explaining mental disorders, but also to highlight that animistic theories that sound strange and unscientific today had a coherence that made them seem plausible to the people who believed in them. If the world seems populated by spirits, it is only logical to assume that strange behavior might be caused by evil spiritual forces. And if evil spirits have possessed a person's mind, then it follows logically that "treatment" might involve finding ways to expel those spirits. These beliefs were part of a coherent worldview that seems odd to us mainly because it is a worldview we do not share.

BOX 3.1 Cruelty and Compassion

A Brief History of the Treatment of Mental Illness

For centuries, the seriously mentally ill were sent to *asylums,* institutions where they were housed and treated. The history of such institutions and treatments is a varied and often horrifying one. The word "asylum" comes from the Greek word for "inviolable;" asylums are meant to be places of sanctuary and refuge that cannot be violated. Indeed, the ancient Greeks and Romans had relatively enlightened views of mental illness, and patients were often treated with baths, exercise, and emotional support. Following the Greek and Roman eras, however, mental institutions were generally not places of safety and inviolability for patients. The mentally ill were sometimes treated with compassion, but more often with cruelty, such as beatings and bloodletting. Attitudes toward the mentally ill are certainly more compassionate today than at most times in the past, but we have a long way to go before compassionate treatment becomes the standard rather than a historical novelty.

For many centuries, most asylums were run by religious institutions. Beginning in the Renaissance, the care of the mentally ill shifted increasingly to state and private institutions. For example, in 1547, King Henry VIII of England established an asylum called St. Mary of Bethlehem, from which came the word "bedlam," the local pronunciation of Bethlehem. This asylum became infamous as a tourist attraction where patients were exhibited to the public like creatures in a human zoo. During the Middle Ages and the Renaissance people could be locked up in asylums, without legal recourse, by family members or even by creditors. Conditions were usually more like unsanitary and abusive prisons than hospitals, and treatment was almost nonexistent.

In the eighteenth and nineteenth centuries, numerous reformers worked valiantly to improve conditions for the mentally ill. One of the most well known was the French reformer Philippe Pinel (1745–1826), a physician who was also known for his early work on psychiatric diagnosis and schizophrenia (Pinel's work is further discussed in Chapters 4 and 12). Together with like-minded colleagues, Pinel pursued what came to be known as *moral treatment,* the philosophy that mental patients should be

(continues)

An artistic depiction of an "insane asylum." Note the detailed portrayal of the partients' emotional expressions.

BOX 3.1   (continued)

treated humanely as sick individuals rather than as freaks, criminals, or animals. He freed many of the patients in La Saltpetrière, a famous hospital in Paris, and provided moral treatment to those who remained, removing their chains and encouraging exposure to fresh air and exercise.

In the United States, other reformers were advocating for more enlightened treatment practices similar to those advanced by Pinel. Dorthea Dix (1802–1887), a schoolteacher, campaigned tirelessly for improved conditions in asylums. She was appalled by the common practice of beating patients, tying them with ropes, and shackling them with balls and chains. Dix raised millions of dollars to establish state mental hospitals offering improved conditions.

But conditions deteriorated again in the first half of the twentieth-century. Huge increases in the number of hospitalized patients made it difficult to implement the principles of moral treatment. Many mental hospitals offered custodial care at best, and abusive maltreatment at worst.

The most recent chapter in this story is known as the **deinstitutionalization** movement (see Chapter 12). Beginning in the 1960s, the number of patients in psychiatric hospitals in the United States radically decreased—from over 500,000 in 1960 to

approximately 150,000 in 1980 (Willerman & Cohen, 1990)—and conditions for those who continued to be hospitalized improved dramatically. Similar trends occurred in the United Kingdom (Jamieson et al., 2000) and Greece (Madianos, Zacharakis, & Tsitsa, 2000), although psychiatric populations have been increasing in Russia (Ruchkin, 2000). In part, deinstitutionalization and improvements in hospital care were brought about by the development of new psychiatric medications during the 1950s which helped most hospitalized patients and allowed many to function outside of a hospital setting. Deinstitutionalization was also driven by economic forces as the cost of hospitalization increased. Overall, deinstitutionalization has had mixed results. It has allowed more patients to live freer lives, but it has also been blamed for contributing to the homeless population because, in many cases, people have been released from hospitals without the availability of adequate community support and treatment.

Deinstitutionalization The social policy, beginning in the 1960s, of discharging large numbers of hospitalized psychiatric patients into the community.

From cruelty to compassion Not long ago, people with mental disorders were treated like criminals or animals, as seen in this drawing (at left) of an 18th century mental asylum. While there are still many problems with our treatment of the mentally ill, conditions have become much more humane in psychiatric hospitals, as indicated by this photograph of an art therapy class.

Hippocrates Hippocrates lived from about 470–377 B.C.E. in Greece. These four medieval illustrations portray the temperaments associated with the four humours described by Hippocrates. For example, the upper left picture depicts an aggressive temperment thought to be caused by excessive yellow bile; the lower left illustration shows a melancholic temperment due to black bile.

The Ancient Greeks: Early Biological Theories

A very different way of explaining mental disorders arose among the physicians of ancient Greece and Rome as part of the development of a less animistic, more biological and scientific, worldview in these cultures. Two examples of these early biological theories of mental illness may help to illustrate this mode of explanation. First is the well-known theory of Hippocrates (460–377 B.C.E.), the great Greek philosopher and physician. Hippocrates believed that all diseases, including mental disorders, were caused by an imbalance among the four fluids, or **humours**, that were thought to circulate in the body. For example, among the four humours, too much *blood* was thought to cause moodiness; too much *phlegm* to cause lethargy; too much *black bile* to cause melancholia (depression), and too much *yellow bile* to cause aggressiveness and anxiety. In accordance with this theory of the causes of mental disorders, Hippocrates advocated treatments based on reestablishing proper balance among the four humours through dietary and behavioral changes. We can see how different this explanatory and treatment approach—with its emphasis on *biological* forces—is from an animistic one that emphasizes *spiritual* forces. It is also interesting to note how much more closely Hippocrates' theory resembles aspects of current biological explanations of mental illness with their emphasis on chemical imbalances in the brain.

A second example of an early biological theory developed by the ancient Greeks relates to a fascinating disorder known as **hysteria**. Hysteria has a special place in the history of the field of abnormal psychology. As we will explain later on in this chapter, it played a central role in the development of psychoanalysis many centuries after the Greek physicians theorized about it (see Box 3.2). Hysteria involves the develop-

Humours Four bodily fluids believed, by Hippocrates and Greek doctors, to control health and disease.

Hysteria A term used for centuries to describe a syndrome of symptoms that appear to be neurological, but do not have a neurological cause; now classified as *conversion disorder*.

Woman with hysteria This famous painting depicts a demonstration of the use of hypnosis to treat a woman suffering from hysteria. The lecturer is the great nineteenth century neurologist Jean Charcot who is teaching medical colleagues in Paris. Charcot's writings and demonstrations greatly influenced Sigmund Freud (pg. 41).

Suggestion The physical and psychological effects of mental states such as belief, confidence, submission to authority, and hope.

Paradigms Overall scientific worldviews, which radically shift at various points in history, according to philosopher of science Thomas Kuhn.

ment of various symptoms that are usually caused by neurological (brain) damage or disease—symptoms such as paralysis, loss of sensation, confusion, and various physical pains and ailments—when these symptoms occur *without* any neurological basis. This syndrome was common in ancient Greece, and Greek physicians developed a theory of its cause based on their medical observations. First, they noted that hysteria was found almost exclusively in women. Second, they observed that the symptoms of hysteria tended to be temporary and to move around to different parts of the body. Thus, a typical case of hysteria might consist of a paralysis of the arm lasting two days, followed by loss of sensation in the legs for a week, followed by pains in the feet. The Greek doctors put these observations together with their view of female anatomy, which included the belief that the uterus was not stationary in the abdomen, but actually traveled through the body in search of pleasant aromas. (In fact, the term "hysteria" is derived from the Greek word "hystera," which means uterus.) Not surprisingly, they developed the theory that hysteria resulted from the uterus getting stuck in various parts of the body, causing a temporary symptom wherever the blockage occurred (Willerman & Cohen, 1990). Based on this reasoning, the Greek physicians developed an ingenious treatment for hysteria: they tried to lure the uterus back to its home base in the abdomen by placing a bouquet of sweet smelling flowers there!

What is most interesting about this "treatment" is how often it apparently worked. Its success was undoubtedly due to the power of **suggestion**; that is, the profound physical and psychological effects of mental states such as belief, confidence, submission to authority, and hope. But our main point in using the example of hysteria is to highlight again the diversity of historical approaches to explaining mental disorders. For the Greek physicians, a biological way of thinking—though flawed in terms of current knowledge—logically tied together their beliefs and observations.

Obviously, approaches to explaining psychopathology have changed dramatically over time and across cultures. These changes are not limited to modifications of particular theories, but involve shifts in overall worldviews or **paradigms**. Explanatory paradigms for mental illness have shifted back and forth over many centuries among the spiritual, biological, and the psychological realms. These profound changes in

BOX 3.2 Modern Hysteria

New Forms for an Old Disorder?

It is often claimed that hysteria—the strange disorder that launched Freud's psychoanalytic theory—has all but disappeared in modern times. The DSM-IV-TR does not include hysteria by that name, although it does include a similar collection of symptoms under the name *conversion disorder*. Conversion disorder is defined much as Freud and his colleagues defined hysteria: symptoms affecting voluntary motor or sensory function that suggest a neurological or medical condition but have a psychological rather than a medical cause. The DSM-IV-TR states that the prevalence rate of conversion disorder is less than 0.3% of the general population (APA, 2000).

Some theorists, however, have argued that hysteria is actually much more common today than the DSM-IV-TR would suggest. Their view is that hysteria appears in different forms in different cultural and historical settings depending on which kinds of physical symptoms are considered "legitimate." Thus the essence of hysteria—psychologically based physical symptoms—remains the same across time and place. But the nature and focus of the physical symptoms of hysteria change across time and place because patients need to believe that their symptoms are "real," and to do so they unconsciously mimic common syndromes in their culture.

One such theorist, Elaine Showalter, a professor of humanities and English at Princeton University, goes so far as to argue that many recent media-hyped disease "fads" are essentially modern epidemics of hysteria. She includes chronic fatigue syndrome, Gulf War syndrome, alien abduction, satanic ritual abuse, and multiple personality disorder (Chapter 7) as examples of such hysterical epidemics. Here is an excerpt from her 1997 book *Hystories*.

> Just as scientists prematurely proclaimed infectious diseases to be dead, so too psychiatrists prematurely announced the death of hysteria. In her 1965 study, Ilza Veith marveled at the "nearly total disappearance" of the disorder. "Where has all the hysteria gone?" psychologist Roberta Satow asked a decade later. Some doctors explained that the diagnostic

tools of modern medicine had conquered hysteria by identifying it as unrecognized organic illness. A number of historians and sociologists argued that hysteria was really a Victorian disorder, a female reaction to sexual repression and limited opportunities, which diminished with the advent of modern feminism. Many psychiatrists believed that widespread awareness of Freudian psychoanalysis had made somatic conversion hysterias like limps and paralysis unfeasible as expressions of anxiety. According to the British analyst Harold Mersky in *The Analysis of Hysteria* (1978), conversion hysterias occur only in psychoanalytically unsophisticated areas such as East Africa, South Korea, Sri Lanka, or Nigeria. Whatever the cause, "hysteria is dead, that is certain," wrote the French medical historian Etienne Trillat, "and it has taken its secrets with it to the grave."

> But hysteria has not died. It has simply been relabeled for a new era. While Ebola virus and Lassa fever remain potential, psychological plagues at the end of the twentieth century are all too real. In the 1990s, the United States has become the hot zone of psychogenic diseases, new and mutating forms of hysteria amplified by modern communications and *fin de siecle* anxiety. Contemporary hysterical patients blame external sources—a virus, sexual molestation, chemical warfare, satanic conspiracy, alien infiltration—for psychic problems. A century after Freud, many people still reject psychological explanations for symptoms; they believe psychosomatic disorders are illegitimate and search for physical evidence that firmly places cause and cure outside the self. (p. 4)

Showalter's view is controversial, but it provides an interesting historical perspective on a number of contemporary medical and psychological syndromes.

Elaine Showalter

explanatory approach provide a caution against assuming that any particular explanations are "right" in some ultimate sense. How we explain psychopathology is always dependent on, or *relative* to, our cultural and historical context. These shifts may also tell us something surprising about the nature of scientific progress. Some philosophers of science describe scientific progress as a series of radical *paradigm shifts* (Kuhn, 1962) rather than as the gradual accumulation of knowledge that is generally assumed to characterize scientific advances (see Box 3.3). If this is so, we must be prepared to see our own current paradigms for explaining abnormal behavior change dramatically

---

BOX 3.3   Paradigm Shifts

Thomas Kuhn's *The Structure of Scientific Revolutions*

The historian and philosopher of science Thomas Kuhn (1922–1996) is best known for his influential 1962 book *The Structure of Scientific Revolutions.* In this book, Kuhn developed the argument that science does not proceed, as was commonly thought, by the steady accumulation of new observations and facts. Rather, scientists work within a framework of accepted assumptions, a *paradigm,* which is periodically revised and replaced by a new paradigm. Thus science progresses by "revolution" as opposed to orderly evolution, and the boundary between scientific "fact" and unscientific "superstitions" is blurrier than we often like to think. Here is an excerpt from Kuhn's introductory chapter in which he begins to question traditional views of science and how it progresses. Note the similarity of his argument to our discussion of the core concept of *historical relativism* and his implication that current "facts" in science (including abnormal psychology) will one day be regarded as superstitious "myths."

> If science is the constellation of facts, theories, and methods collected in current texts, then scientists are the men [*sic*] who successfully or not, have striven to contribute one or another element to that particular constellation. Scientific development becomes the piecemeal process by which these items have been added, singly and in combination, to the ever growing stockpile that constitutes scientific technique and knowledge. And history of science becomes the discipline that chronicles both these successive increments and the obstacles that have inhibited their accumulation...
>
> In recent years, however, a few historians of science have been finding it more and more difficult to fulfill the functions that the concept of development-by-accumulation assigns to them. As chroniclers of an incremental process, they discover that additional research makes it harder, not easier, to answer questions like: When was oxygen discovered? Who first conceived of energy conservation? Increasingly, a few of them suspect that these are simply the wrong sorts of questions to ask. Perhaps science does not develop by the accumulation of individual discoveries and inventions. Simultaneously, these same historians confront growing difficulties in distinguishing the "scientific" component of past observation and belief from what their predecessors had readily labeled "error" and "superstition." The more carefully they study, say, Aristotelian dynamics, phlogistic chemistry, or caloric thermodynamics, the more certain they feel that those once current views of nature were, as a whole, neither less scientific, nor more the product of human idiosyncrasy than those current today. If these out-to-date beliefs are to be called myths, then myths can be produced by the same sorts of methods and held for the same sorts of reasons that now lead to scientific knowledge. If, on the other hand, they are to be called science, then science has included bodies of belief quite incompatible with the ones we hold today. (pp. 1–2)

To illustrate Kuhn's point in regard to abnormal psychology, recall the animistic theories and Greek medical beliefs reviewed earlier. Kuhn would regard the change from animistic to medical explanations as a major paradigm shift.

Thomas Kuhn

---

in the future. We hope that this historical tour has served as a reminder of the issues of *cultural and historical relativism.* Having visited these historical examples, we now turn to another core concept relevant to explaining mental illness, the principle of *multiple causality.*

The Principle of Multiple Causality

Explaining psychopathology is also complicated by the number of different theoretical perspectives in abnormal psychology; students often wonder how to choose among or reconcile them (Valenstein, 1980). This theoretical pluralism can lead to a temptation to choose one favorite theory to explain all aspects of psychopathology, a prob-

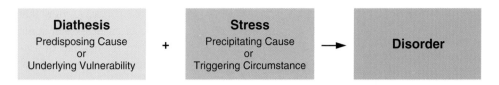

Figure 3.1 The diathesis-stress model: Predisposing and precipitating causes

lem known as **reductionism**. The old saying that "If the only tool you have is a hammer, everything starts to look like a nail" describes reductionism well. The problem with reductionism is that most mental disorders do not have a single, simple explanation. Rather, they have multiple causes and are often best explained by a combination of theoretical perspectives.

One particularly important example of the principle of multiple causality is the interaction of **precipitating causes** and **predisposing causes**. A precipitating cause is the immediate trigger or precipitant of an event, such as a sudden shift in the earth's tectonic plates triggering an earthquake. A predisposing cause is the underlying process that sets the stage for the event, such as the slow movement of the tectonic plates for years preceding the earthquake. This distinction is especially important in explaining psychopathology, because mental disorders like depression, anorexia, or Dave's social anxiety usually have both precipitating (immediate) and predisposing (underlying) causes. This point of view is also sometimes referred to as the **diathesis-stress** model of psychopathology (Lewinsohn, Joiner, & Rohde, 2001; Meehl, 1962). The diathesis-stress model posits that the development of a disorder requires the interaction of a diathesis (predisposition) and a stressor (precipitant) (see Figure 3.1).

A rather gruesome example of the importance of the distinction between diathesis/predisposing causes and stress/precipitating causes occurred in a notorious legal case in the 1980s. On December 23, 1985, Raymond Belknap, 18, and James Vance, 20, were listening to the music of their favorite band, Judas Priest. While doing so, they made a suicide pact and took a shotgun to a nearby playground to carry out the pact. Belknap died immediately and Vance was horribly disfigured but survived for several years. Later, the boys' families sued Judas Priest and their record company, claiming that suicidal hints in the lyrics of the songs (which the families claimed were *subliminal,* meaning below the threshold for conscious perception yet unconsciously perceived) had driven the boys to their fateful pact. Ultimately, the band and the record company were not held responsible on the grounds that even if the lyrics might have been a precipitating cause of the suicide pact, the predisposing cause lay in the serious emotional problems each young man had exhibited for years (Litman & Farberow, 1994). It is generally true that precipitating causes by themselves are not enough to cause a disorder even though they are often more obvious and therefore easy to seize upon as an explanation, as the families in the Vance case tried to do.

The Connection Between Mind and Body

It is often stated that there are currently two major paradigms for explaining mental disorders, the *psychological* paradigm and the *biological* paradigm. Remember that a paradigm is broader than a theory—it is a general way of thinking about the world that contains many specific and different theories within it. For example, included within the psychological paradigm are many distinct theoretical perspectives such as the psychodynamic, humanistic, cognitive, and behavioral perspectives. Similarly, the biological paradigm includes all theories that focus on physical causes of mental disorders. It involves a wide range of factors such as genetics, neurochemistry, and neuroanatomy.

Reductionism Explaining a disorder or other complex phenomenon using only a single idea or perspective.

Precipitating cause The immediate trigger or precipitant of an event.

Predisposing cause The underlying processes that create the conditions making it possible for a precipitating cause to trigger an event.

Diathesis-stress model The view that the development of a disorder requires the interaction of a diathesis (predisposing cause) and a stress (precipitating cause).

Judas Priest and James Vance Vance claimed that subliminal messages in the music of Judas Priest caused him to make a suicide pact with his friend, but the court found that the causes were more complex.

A major problem in the field of abnormal psychology is the pervasive view that these two paradigms are mutually exclusive. For example, one often hears that some mental disorders, such as depression, are "brain diseases," implying the absence of psychological causes. Such an approach can be misleading for two important reasons. First, while it is true that some disorders have either a primary psychological or a primary biological origin, most disorders involve both psychological and biological causes (Engel, 1977; Nolen-Hoeksema, 1998; Seligman, Walker, & Rosenhan, 2001). Second, and more fundamentally, separating the psychological and biological realms is misleading because the ***mind and body*** are complexly interconnected.

Most everyone now believes in the close interdependence of mind and body, a view known as *monism* in contrast to the *dualism* (mind and body as distinct realms) associated with the philosopher René Descartes (1596–1650). However, understanding the complex relationship between mind and body continues to be a challenge, especially in abnormal psychology, where mental disorders can result from such a wide variety of causes. As noted, some mental disorders have a clear biological cause, which can lead people to assume that the same might be true for *all* mental disorders. However, other mental disorders involve symptoms with clear psychological causes. In some cases, dramatic *physical* symptoms can result from psychological causes. Let's look at some examples.

General paresis, a disease that was common among men in the nineteenth century, consists of severe mental and physical symptoms, including psychosis and paralysis, leading eventually to death (the Chicago gangster Al Capone died of the disease in 1947). For many years the cause of paresis was unknown, until the German neurologist Richard von Kraft-Ebing (1840–1902) proved in 1897 that paresis resulted from a prior syphilis infection, which, untreated, later attacks the brain. His discovery had a profound effect on people interested in the causes of mental disorders. They reasoned that if a disorder with severe mental symptoms could be caused by a clear biological process (and cured by treating the infection), then perhaps all mental disorders had not-yet-discovered physical causes. Indeed, this perspective underlies a good deal of modern research on mental illness.

However, other disorders seem to suggest just the opposite conclusion about the relationship between mind and body—that mental processes can cause profound physical symptoms. For example, **psychosocial dwarfism** is a rare but dramatic disorder in which children who are severely emotionally deprived literally stop growing despite receiving physical and nutritional care (Ackerman et al., 1999; Mayes, 1992). Severe emotional deprivation, such as might occur in an abusive home or a substandard orphanage, can cause massive changes in the child's hormonal functioning and result in the cessation of normal physical growth. When children with psychosocial dwarfism are removed from emotionally depriving environments and given adequate emotional care, they typically recover, with hormonal functioning, physical growth, and mental age returning to normal (Gardner et al., 1999; Money, 1992; Nieves-Rivera, Gonzalez de Pijem, & Mirabal, 1998). Here we see an example of *psychological* forces causing profound *physical* changes. Yet, here too we must remain wary of reductionistic generalizations such as the assumption that many other physical disorders might also have psychological causes.

We must also be careful not to confound (mix up) questions about what *causes* psychopathology with questions about what can *treat* it. These are separate issues. Some disorders may have a primary psychological cause, yet they may be effectively treated with medication. Other disorders may have a primary biological cause yet be treatable with psychotherapy. We have to make sure that when we think about the *causes* of disorders we do not make unwarranted assumptions based on the *treatments* for these disorders (Huyse et al., 2001; Levy, 2000; Valenstein, 1980).

General paresis A disease, due to a syphilis infection, that can cause psychosis, paralysis, and death.

Psychosocial dwarfism A rare disorder in which the physical growth of children deprived of emotional care is stunted.

How to integrate the psychological and the biological paradigms is a complex issue. The current state-of-the-art for thinking about the ***connection between mind and body*** in abnormal psychology involves three principles.

1. The causes of mental disorders are not all the same: some disorders have a primary psychological cause, some a primary biological cause, and some a mix of the two.

2. Even in those disorders in which there is a primary biological or psychological cause, both biology and psychology (as well as cultural and social factors) are always involved in the manifestation and form of the disorder. This principle of *multiple causality*—sometimes referred to as the **biopsychosocial model** of psychopathology to emphasize the integration of different perspectives—will be illustrated in the case example at the end of this chapter (Dilts, 2001; Engel, 1977; Sperry, 2001).

3. Every emotion and behavior has both a psychological and a biological aspect (Brenner, 2000; Hansell, 2002). As a result, every mental disorder has both psychological and biological **correlates**, or associated processes. The research principle that "correlation does not imply causation" is especially relevant here; we must keep in mind that what *accompanies* a disorder does not necessarily *cause* the disorder (Levy, 2000). For instance, pessimistic thinking correlates with depression and is often described as a *cause* of depression, but pessimism can also be a manifestation or *result* of depression. Only noncorrelational research, such as **longitudinal** studies which follow subjects over time, can clarify the causal sequence of events in psychopathology.

We will now turn to the different theoretical perspectives that are most often used to explain and treat mental disorders. As we review these perspectives, keep in mind that they are most helpful in explaining abnormal behavior when used in combination, or complementarily, rather than being used singly and reductionistically.

Biopsychosocial model A perspective in abnormal psychology that integrates biological, psychological, and social components.

Correlation A statistical term for a systematic association between variables.

Longitudinal Research that studies subjects over time.

Brief Summary

- Explanations of abnormal behavior are influenced by several core concepts in the field. First, paradigms for explaining abnormal behavior have changed profoundly over the course of history *(historical relativism)* and undoubtedly will continue to do so. Second, we must take into account the principle of *multiple causality*, and the problem of reducing causal explanations to a single theory or idea (reductionism). For example, it is important to distinguish between predisposing (underlying) and precipitating (immediate) causes of abnormal behavior, a principle sometimes referred to as the diathesis-stress model.

- Currently, the two major paradigms for explaining abnormality are the psychological paradigm and the biological paradigm. Contrary to the common assumption that these are competing or contradictory paradigms, the mind (psychology) and body (biology) are closely interrelated. The ***connection between mind and body*** must be taken into account in explaining any abnormal behavior.

| *Critical Thinking Question* | Charlotte Perkins Gilman's doctor, Weir Mitchell, believed that Charlotte's depression was caused by her insistence on writing rather than devoting herself to motherhood (Chapter 1). How would you critique this explanation on the basis of the core concepts described in this chapter? |

THE THEORETICAL PERSPECTIVES

Scientific research in any field consists of the process of comparing ideas, and predictions generated by these ideas, with observations. Ideas are organized into *theories,* which are useful tools for generating predictions and creating conceptual "maps" of a phenomenon which can then be compared with observations and revised as necessary to improve the theory (Stiles, 2003). In abnormal psychology, unlike some other scientific fields, several different theoretical perspectives have been developed and continue to exist side-by-side.

In some respects, the specific theoretical perspectives (for example, cognitive, biological, psychodynamic, sociocultural, etc.) that we will describe diverge in their assumptions so that they may seem incompatible with one another. But in most ways they complement each other, as each perspective focuses on an important *component* of the complex phenomena of psychopathology. In this respect, the different perspectives are akin to the proverbial blind men describing the elephant, each one claiming to know what an elephant is while, in fact, each one is simply describing the part of the elephant he is touching. In our view, the different theoretical perspectives are too often presented as if they are competing and contradictory when, in fact, they often overlap and complement each other. Indeed, the field of abnormal psychology is increasingly moving toward an integration of theoretical perspectives which considers the behavioral, cognitive, psychodynamic, sociocultural, and biological components of emotional problems such as Dave's anxiety.

After describing each theoretical perspective, we will return to the case of Dave in order to see how that perspective would address the cause (or *etiology*) of his problems. Along the way, we will point out how the perspectives overlap or complement each other in explaining Dave's symptoms. In later chapters, we will describe these perspectives as different *components* that can be combined to explain and treat disorders in accord with the core concept of ***multiple causality***.

Psychodynamic Perspectives

Psychodynamic The theoretical perspective which began with Freud's work and is associated with emphasis on unconscious mental processes, emotional conflict, and the influence of childhood on adult life.

Psychodynamic theory is a large and still evolving school of thought. While it is most closely associated with Sigmund Freud (1856–1939), the founder of psychoanalysis, much of today's psychodynamic theory differs vastly from Freud's original ideas. (The terms *psychodynamic* and *psychoanalytic* are sometimes used interchangeably, but we will abide by the usual distinction: *psychoanalytic* refers more narrowly to Freudian theory, while **psychodynamic** is the broader term encompassing all the theories derived from Freud's work.) Despite frequent criticism of psychoanalysis as unempirical or unproven (Bauer, 2000; Gruenbaum, 1996; Haaken, 1995; Popper, 1959, 1986; Senf, 1995), it continues to be a popular and influential theory of explanation and treatment, and it has a particular place of importance in the field of abnormal psychology as the first comprehensive theory of psychopathology.

Freud's Early Model

The best way to explain psychodynamic theory is to put ourselves back in Freud's shoes as he was trying to help his patients with *hysteria* in 1880s Vienna. As you recall, hysteria consists of physical symptoms (such as paralyses, loss of sensation, tics, and physical pains) that would normally be associated with neurological (brain) disorders but occur in the absence of any neurological problem. Freud was impressed by the work of the French physicians Jean Charcot (1825–1893) and Pierre Janet (1859–1947) who were using hypnosis to treat hysteria. Many of their patients were cured simply by having the doctor use the power of suggestion to tell them, while they were hypnotized, that they would be fine when they awoke. This technique was known as *hypnotic suggestion.*

Freud was also influenced by a case described to him by his colleague Josef Breuer (1842–1925) (Freud, 1895). "Anna O." (whose real name was Bertha Poppenheim) had a number of serious symptoms of hysteria, and the hypnotic suggestion method was not working to cure them. One day, Anna O. developed a new, dangerous symptom—a fear of water *(hydrophobia)* that prevented her from drinking. In desperation, Breuer tried something new. He hypnotized Anna as usual, but this time, instead of *telling her* she would be fine (the hypnotic suggestion method) he asked *her to tell him* as much as possible about the circumstances which had led up to her new symptom. To Breuer's amazement, Anna O., under hypnosis, was able to tell him something that clearly explained the symptom, but which she had previously been unable to remember. Just before the fear of drinking began, she had seen a dog drink out of a glass during a party. She had been disgusted, but had squelched her feeling at the time because she was busy behaving properly at the party. Amazingly, immediately after telling Breuer this story under hypnosis she asked for water and guzzled it down—the symptom had disappeared!

From this example and similar experiences with his patients, Freud came to the conclusion that there must be a division within the mind, since these patients were unaware of some of the memories, thoughts, and feelings that emerged under hypnosis. Furthermore, it seemed to Freud that the condition of being unaware of such memories (which were invariably unpleasant) was connected to having pathological symptoms, and that when these memories and feelings were verbally expressed and brought into conscious awareness, the symptoms disappeared. Freud's idea that the mind is divided into an "acceptable" (usually conscious) part and an "unacceptable" (usually nonconscious) part, and that certain tensions or conflicts between these two parts can cause mental symptoms, is the core of the psychodynamic theory of explanation. This core theory has been revised and expanded in many ways, beginning with many revisions by Freud himself. We will track the progression from Freud's original theory to the contemporary psychodynamic perspective.

For most of his career, Freud focused his attention on understanding the contents of the **unconscious**—the part of the mind that seemed to be unacceptable to the conscious mind, and was therefore pushed out of conscious awareness through a process called **repression** (which means "motivated forgetting"). As he studied the unconscious, Freud expanded his view of it. At first, Freud thought that the unconscious just contained memories of recent unpleasant experiences like the one that Anna O. had repressed. Later, after listening to numerous female patients describe memories of sexual abuse in childhood, he briefly believed that it was mainly traumatic *childhood* sexual experiences, like sexual abuse, that were repressed. But as he worked with more patients and studied his own dreams, Freud began to believe that it was not just memories of painful actual events that were in the unconscious, but also a whole range of desires, feelings, and fantasies that were considered unacceptable by the person. For a long time, Freud believed that most of these unacceptable feelings were related to sexual desires (known as *libido* or *Eros*) originating in childhood, and he developed a model of *psychosexual development* according to which children went through a variety of normal stages in the development of their libido (see Table 3.1). Later in his career, Freud came to believe that there was a second general category of commonly repressed, unacceptable desires in the unconscious—aggressive and sadistic wishes that Freud later linked to his concept of *Thanatos,* a destructive instinct.

Unconscious Descriptively, mental contents that are outside of awareness; also, the irrational, instinctual part of the mind in Freud's topographic theory.

Repression A defense mechanism consisting of the forgetting of painful or unacceptable mental content.

Table 3.1 | **Psychodynamic Terms and Concepts**

Models of the Mind

Topographic Unconscious, preconscious, conscious
Structural Id, ego, superego

Motivational Drives

Libido or Eros Sexual drive
Thanatos Aggressive or destructive drive
Attachment Affectionate ties with others

Psychosexual Developmental Phases

Oral phase 0–18 months; issues of feeding and security
Anal phase 18–36 months; issues of control and autonomy
Phallic-Oedipal phase 3–6 years; issues of competence, competition, and gender identity
Latency phase 7–11 years; increasing influence of ego and superego
Adolescence 12–18 years; reworking of conflicts and consolidation of identity

Common Defense Mechanisms (self-protective, automatic, unconscious mental acts)

Repression Motivated forgetting
Denial/minimization Ignoring or minimizing particular facts
Projection Attributing one's own feelings to someone else
Rationalization A false but personally acceptable explanation for one's behavior
Displacement Transferring a feeling about one situation onto another situation
Reaction-formation Turning an unacceptable feeling into its opposite
Isolation of affect/emotion Avoiding painful feelings by focusing only on ideas
Compartmentalization Keeping different parts of one's emotional life separate
Undoing Using ritualized behavior to create an illusion of control
Dissociation Trancelike detachment
Withdrawal/avoidance Emotional or behavioral flight from painful situations
Fixation Clinging to a particular developmental phase
Regression Returning to an earlier developmental phase
Turning against the self Redirecting an unacceptable hostile impulse towards oneself
Sublimation Finding a constructive outlet for an unacceptable wish

Psychodynamic Treatment

Free association Talking as freely and openly as possible to the therapist or analyst
Resistance The use of defense mechanisms during therapy sessions
Transference The client's feelings about the therapist, especially those displaced from earlier relationships
Countertransference The therapist's feelings about the client
Interpretation Comments by the therapist about his or her client's emotional conflicts
Working through The client's gradual mastery over emotional conflicts resulting from discussion in therapy of these conflicts

The other major development in the early part of Freud's career was his discovery, made partly through studying dreams, jokes, art, and other phenomena, that the split in the mind between the unacceptable, unconscious part and the acceptable, conscious part existed in everyone, not just people with mental disorders. In this sense, Freud's view is very much in keeping with the core concept of the ***continuum between*** *normality and abnormality*, which we discussed in Chapter 2. He thought that most mental disorders were exaggerations of mental conflicts that all people experience, and that pathology results only when a person has not found a good solution to inevitable emotional conflicts.

Freud's Later Model

Toward the end of his career, Freud made a major revision in his theory of the mind. He became dissatisfied, for a number of reasons, with his original model of the mind as divided between the unconscious, childish, irrational part full of repressed, unacceptable desires, and the **conscious**, adult, rational part. (This model was known as the **topographic theory**, and it also included the **preconscious**, which contains thoughts that are not the focus of conscious attention at any given moment but are not unacceptable and therefore not repressed.) Freud became increasingly dissatisfied with the topographic theory as he realized that the repressing forces in the mind were also unconscious (people usually aren't aware that they are repressing something). In addition, he noticed that the repressing forces themselves were often irrational and contained harsh and distorted childish ideas about what was unacceptable and therefore required repression. For example, Anna O.'s horror at her feeling of disgust at the party (which necessitated the repression) may have been more irrational than the disgust itself. To account for these observations, Freud developed a new theory known as the **structural model** of the mind (Freud, 1923). In the structural model, the mind is divided into three parts: the **id** (consisting of childhood sexual and aggressive desires and general pleasure seeking, similar to the topographic unconscious), the **superego** (the realm of moral judgments, sometimes extreme and irrational, which determine what is acceptable and unacceptable), and the **ego** (the part of the mind that is oriented to reality and the external world and has to reconcile the demands of the id and superego while developing the skills and abilities necessary to function effectively in the world).

The structural model allowed Freud and his followers to develop a much more sophisticated understanding of how the mind could become divided in reaction to conflict over unacceptable or intolerable feelings. Freud's daughter Anna (1895–1982), herself an eminent psychoanalyst, and other analysts, clarified that the mind uses many **defense mechanisms** (see Table 3.1), in addition to repression, to cope with unacceptable thoughts and feelings (Freud, 1937). For example, sometimes people will be intellectually aware of an unacceptable wish or idea, but they will detach themselves from experiencing any feelings about it, a defense mechanism known as *isolation of affect* ("affect" is a synonym for emotion) or *intellectualization.* For instance, a 25-year-old man who was unable to tolerate feelings of grief after his father suddenly died talked to his friends for weeks, in an emotionless tone, about the history of burial traditions.

In *projection,* another defense mechanism, an intolerably painful feeling is unconsciously externalized and attributed to someone else, such as when a child struggling with learning problems and feelings of inadequacy calls his classmates "stupid." This example also illustrates that defense mechanisms are a part of everyone's mental functioning; they are not just found in mental disorders. Many experts believe that the defense mechanism of projection plays a central role in the development of prejudices, such as racism, anti-Semitism, sexism, and homophobia. For example, people who are especially uncomfortable with their own affectionate feelings toward members of the same sex may be inclined to accuse others of homosexuality and even to persecute them. Similarly, many scholars have noted that racism involves a majority group projection of unacceptable traits (such as laziness, greediness, hypersexuality) onto minority groups (Leary, 2000; Young-Bruehl, 1996).

Conscious Descriptively, mental contents that are within awareness; also, the rational part of the mind in Freud's topographic theory.

Topographic theory Freud's first model of the mind, divided into the unconscious, conscious, and preconscious parts.

Preconscious In Freud's topographic model, mental contents that are not the focus of conscious attention but are accessible because they are not repressed.

Structural model Freud's final model of the mind, divided into the id, the ego, and the superego.

Id In Freud's structural theory, the part of the mind containing instinctual urges.

Superego In Freud's structural theory, the part of the mind that contains moral judgments and evaluates the self.

Ego In Freud's structural theory, the part of the mind that is oriented to the external world and mediates the demands of the id and superego.

Defense mechanisms Unconscious, automatic mental processes that reduce anxiety by warding off unacceptable thoughts and feelings.

All of the defense mechanisms are automatic mental processes, executed by the unconscious part of the ego, in an effort to reduce anxiety caused by emotional conflict. Defense mechanisms are not necessarily pathological; they are just one of the ego's strategies for managing tensions among the id, the ego, the superego, and reality. For example, in the defense mechanism called *sublimation,* the ego finds a socially and personally acceptable outlet for otherwise unacceptable feelings. Becoming a police officer, for instance, might reflect someone's sublimation of aggressive impulses in a way that satisfies the id, the superego, and the ego's need to adapt to reality. (In fact, this is one of the reasons that so many children fantasize about becoming police officers!) Or, to use another example of the "healthy" use of a defense mechanism, *denial* (fooling oneself by ignoring upsetting feelings) might be temporarily adaptive in an emergency situation, such as fighting a fire, in which acknowledging fear might be more dangerous than denying it.

In summary, according to the structural theory, psychopathology results when conflicts involving the id, the ego, the superego, and reality are not successfully negotiated by adaptive defense mechanisms and coping strategies. For example, a child's hostile feelings toward a younger sibling might conflict with his or her strict superego idea that aggressive wishes are bad and dangerous. If the ego were unable to find an adaptive solution to this conflict the child might experience psychological symptoms, either during childhood when the conflict first arose, or later in adulthood when an event (for example, the hiring of a new, younger coworker) revived this childhood conflict.

Contemporary Psychodynamic Perspectives

In contemporary psychoanalysis, several distinct schools of thought coexist with Freud's theories, though most retain an emphasis on emotional conflict, unconscious processes, and the continuing, repetitive influence of experiences from childhood and adolescence on adult life (Maxwell, 2000; Mitchell, 2000; Pine, 1990; Weiss, 2001; Young, 2001). These other schools can, for the most part, be viewed as either having revised some of Freud's ideas or having focused on a particular part of Freud's theory.

The *Kleinian* school of psychoanalysis, named after Melanie Klein (1882–1960), a contemporary of Anna Freud's, focuses on the sexual and aggressive wishes and conflicts of early childhood, with less emphasis on the ego and Freud's structural model of the mind (Aguayo, 2000; Caper, 2000; Klein & Riviere, 1937/1967; Likierman, 2001; Schafer, 1997). Another school of psychodynamic thought, the *object-relational* perspective, emphasizes problems in the child's primary relationship *attachments* to his or her early caregivers as the source of later pathology (Aron, 1996; Bergner, 2000; Brink, 2000; Bowlby, 1982; Greenberg & Mitchell, 1983; Kernberg, 1995; Kernberg, 2001; Mahler, 1975). The object-relational school picks up on two elements of Freud's theory that he never fully developed. One is the idea that the superego and the ego are largely formed as a result of *identifications* with early caregivers (the "objects" in the child's environment). In other words, parents and other loved figures are crucial role models for the moral ideals of the child's developing superego and for the coping and defensive style of the ego. The second idea is that children develop mental models of how relationships work based on their experiences with their family members. For example, a child raised in a relaxed and happy atmosphere learns to feel relaxed and happy in relationships and seeks out such relationships later in life. On the other hand, a child raised by anxious or depressed parents will be prone to internalize an anxious or depressive view of relationships that may contribute to relationship problems in later life. (We will see later on how this view overlaps considerably with certain behavioral and family systems explanations of psychopathology.)

Self-psychology, another contemporary school of psychoanalysis which rests on similar assumptions about early relational attachments, is based on the work of Heinz Kohut (1913–1981). Kohut began his psychoanalytic career as a close follower of Sigmund Freud and Anna Freud, but he gradually came to believe that the most important cause of psychopathology was not emotional conflict but unempathic (that is, cold, harsh, or emotionally misattuned) parenting, which interfered with the development of healthy self-esteem. (We will see a similar view in the humanistic theory of Carl Rogers.) Kohut felt that the kinds of mental conflict Freud described could all be traced to empathic failures in the parent-child relationship (Kohut, 1977; Maxwell, 2000).

Psychodynamic Treatment Interventions

What follows is an overview of some of the basic concepts of psychodynamic therapy; psychodynamic interventions for particular disorders will be discussed in later chapters. While the techniques of psychodynamic therapy have changed significantly as psychodynamic theory has developed and diversified (Busch, 1999; Gurman & Messer, 1995), some central principles have remained constant. First, the goal of psychodynamic interventions is to help the client achieve a better mastery of his or her emotional conflicts, so that maladaptive defense mechanisms can be replaced by healthier ones, and self-defeating patterns can be shifted in a more constructive direction. Most psychodynamic theorists believe that therapeutic change is achieved through *insight,* in which the client learns to understand more about themselves and their unconscious emotional conflicts, and the *therapeutic relationship,* which is intended to feel safe, supportive, and conducive to the development of insight and new, healthier ways of relating to others.

In order to facilitate self-exploration and insight, the client is encouraged to *free associate,* or talk as freely and openly as possible about his or her emotional life. Naturally, when clients do so they eventually come to uncomfortable topics, and defense mechanisms, such as repression or intellectualization, inevitably begin to interfere with their openness. This is sometimes referred to as *resistance,* an important part of the therapy process in which clients use defense mechanisms during sessions as they approach disturbing emotional conflicts—the same emotional conflicts that have contributed to their symptoms. For example, a client might be thinking about a painful experience and then suddenly find himself switching topics or "drawing a blank." Resistance can also appear in the form of *transference,* in which the client unconsciously transfers experiences from earlier relationships onto the relationship with the therapist (for example, experiencing the therapist as a critical mother or a bossy older brother). The therapist's feelings about the client are referred to as *countertransference,* which the therapist must carefully monitor both for information about the client and to insure that the therapist's own emotional conflicts do not interfere with the therapy.

As an example of resistance and transference, a 25-year-old depressed woman felt that she could not talk to her male therapist about her anger toward a coworker because she feared that the therapist would disapprove of and reject her. In this case, the transference was the client's experience of the therapist as a feared, rejecting figure. Usually, transference feelings can be traced to difficult childhood experiences (especially those involving psychodynamically important issues such as attachment, sexuality, and aggression), such as this client's childhood fear of her disapproving father whose rejections contributed to her depression. The therapist may make an *interpretation*

Psychoanalysis In psychoanalysis, the client and analyst meet frequently and the client may lie on a couch rather than sit face to face. The aim of these arrangements is a deep, thorough exploration and resolution of the client's emotional conflicts.

about connections of this sort, or clients may be able to make such connections on their own with the help of the therapist's input. In this way, talking about resistances and transferences becomes an important part of the therapy process and facilitates the client's expanding self-awareness and self-acceptance, a process known as *working-through.*

Let's return now to the case of Dave, and apply psychodynamic explanatory concepts to his symptoms of social anxiety, loss of confidence, and social withdrawal.

> **Case Illustration** **Many psychodynamic hypotheses could be developed about the source of Dave's symptoms. From a psychodynamic conflict perspective, Dave's problems might result from emotional conflicts about success and failure. On one hand, Dave may fear that he can never live up to his father's successes or his parents' expectations. At the same time, Dave may also unconsciously worry that through his achievements he is competing with his father and his brother, which would make him feel guilty. Thus, a conflict exists between the id and the superego that the ego is unable to master, leading to symptoms of anxiety. From an object-relational standpoint, Dave's anxiety may involve an identification with his mother, who becomes anxious and withdrawn when she feels stressed. Dave's symptoms, which he knows upset his parents, might also represent an unconscious expression of anger at them due to his feeling that they have sometimes been unempathic. In this scenario, Dave's anger would be unconscious, and indirectly expressed, because it feels unacceptable to Dave and thereby causes emotional conflict.**

Humanistic and Existential Perspectives

Humanistic The theoretical perspective that emphasizes the importance of self-actualization in human life and unconditional positive regard in relationships.

Self-actualization In humanistic theory, the pursuit of one's true self and needs.

Unconditional positive regard In humanistic theory, the provision of unconditional love, empathy, and acceptance in relationships.

Existential The theoretical perspective that emphasizes individual responsibility for creating meaning in life in the face of universal anxiety about death.

Humanistic and **existential** theories in psychology, which became especially popular during the 1950s and 1960s, emphasize the importance of interpersonal connection, human freedom, and personal choice for emotional well-being. Generally speaking, humanistic and existential theories offer more specific ideas about the *treatment* of mental disorders than they do about the *causes* of them. Yet, the humanistic and existential traditions do offer some important views on the causes of emotional problems which we will review here.

The humanistic and existential traditions are in many ways related to the psychodynamic tradition, although they developed, in part, in reaction to the reductionistic aspects of early psychodynamic theory, which viewed all psychological symptoms as derived from sexual conflicts. Like psychodynamic theories, humanistic and existential approaches look at psychopathology as something that is rooted in an individual's overall personality and approach to living. In this sense, humanistic and existential theories view psychological symptoms as just that—symptoms of an underlying problem. The humanistic and existential schools each focus on a particular kind of underlying problem that they see as being at the root of many psychological symptoms.

Humanistic Explanations and Treatment Interventions

From the humanistic perspective, emotional health depends on the pursuit of **self-actualization**, a freedom to be true to oneself that depends upon receiving **unconditional positive regard** (unconditional love, empathy, and acceptance) from others (Raskin & Rogers, 2000). Correspondingly, psychopathology is thought to result from a lack of self-esteem and self-regard stemming from the failure of parents and others to provide warm, consistent support and validation. (You may have noted the substantial overlap here with Kohut's psychodynamic self-psychology). Carl Rogers (1902–1987), Abraham Maslow (1908–1970), and other humanistic theorists emphasize that without unconditional positive regard in childhood, people may develop a distorted and false self in an effort to be valued or appreciated by their loved ones. Unspoken but powerful *conditions of worth* (that is, parental standards that must be met in order to be loved or valued) are believed to cause feelings of inadequacy and to lead to various kinds of emotional problems (Maslow & Mittelman, 1951; Rogers, 1961).

Based upon the principles described above, humanistic therapists have developed a number of therapeutic techniques: *active listening, empathy,* and unconditional positive regard (see Table 3.2 for a list of humanistic terms and techniques) (Kuhn, 2001; Plante, 1999). These techniques are used in an effort to build clients' self-esteem and encourage self-actualization, a process Rogers calls **client-centered therapy** (Rogers, 1987; see Box 3.4 for a transcript of Carl Rogers' therapy technique). Often these techniques are incorporated into other theoretical approaches to treatment. For example, Keijsers, Schapp, and Hoogduin (2000) found that cognitive-behavioral therapists who showed warmth, positive regard, and genuineness achieved improved results.

Existential Explanations and Treatment Interventions

Existential theorists, borrowing from the existential tradition in philosophy (Sartre, 1953, 1956), emphasize a somewhat different source of psychopathology. From an existential perspective, everyone is faced with the stressful facts that life has no inherent meaning and that death is inescapable. As a result, each of us must confront the frightening reality that we are solely responsible for our lives. Existentialists view emotional health as the ability to face these facts and to create a meaningful life by accepting this responsibility. Conversely, emotional disorders are seen as rooted in people's failure to accept these facts, leading them to be anxious, *inauthentic* (not true to themselves), and depressed (May, 1961, 1967).

Existential therapists such as Frankl (1980), Yalom (1967), and Verhofstadt-Deneve (2000) have developed techniques to help clients improve their lives by confronting, rather than avoiding, these existential dilemmas. Common principles in existential therapy techniques include encouraging clients to face painful truths and to develop courage in the face of life's inevitable difficulties. As with humanistic therapies, existential principles are often incorporated into other modes of therapy (Protter, 2001).

Let's return again to Dave and apply humanistic and existential principles to his case.

Unconditional positive regard Humanistic theorists emphasize the importance of unconditional acceptance for healthy childhood development and in psychotherapy.

Client-centered therapy A humanistic treatment approach developed by Carl Rogers

Humanistic Terms and Techniques	Table 3.2
Self-actualization ■ Movement toward growth and fulfillment of one's potential.	*Adapted from Plante, 1999*
Unconditional positive regard ■ Fully accepting a person as they are.	
Conditions of worth ■ Parental standards that must be met in order to feel valued and loved.	
Active listening ■ Intense listening to the client, expressed in paraphrasing, reflecting back, and summarizing clients' comments.	
Empathy ■ Emotional understanding of and sympathetic attitude toward others feelings.	

BOX 3.4   Client-Centered Therapy

Transcript of Carl Rogers' Technique

Note the use of humanistic techniques (Table 3.2) by Dr. Rogers in this session. Asterisks indicate words that could not be made out in the transcription (T = Therapist; C = Client).

T-1:   OK, I think I'm ready. And you…ready?

C-1:   Yes.

T-2:   I don't know what you might want to talk about, but I'm very ready to hear. We have half an hour, and I hope that in that half an hour we can get to know each other as deeply as possible, but we don't need to strive for anything. I guess that's my feeling. Do you want to tell me whatever is on your mind?

C-2:   I'm having a lot of problems dealing with my daughter. She's 20 years old; she's in college; I'm having a lot of trouble letting her go… And I have a lot of guilt feeling about her; I have a read need to hang on to her.

T-3:   A need to hang on so you can kind of make up for the things you feel guilty about—is that part of it?

C-3:   There's a lot of that…Also, she's been a real friend to me, and filled my life…And it's very hard*** a lot of empty places now that she's not with me.

T-4:   The old vacuum, sort of, when she's not there.

C-4:   Yes. Yes. I also would like to be the kind of mother that could be strong and say, you know, "Go and have a good life," and this is really hard for me to do that.

T-5:   It's very hard to give up something that's been so precious in your life, but also something that I guess has caused you pain when you mentioned guilt.

C-5:   Yeah, and I'm aware that I have some anger toward her that I don't always get what I want. I have needs that are not met. And, uh, I don't feel I have a right to those needs. You know…She's a daughter; she's not my mother—though sometimes I feel as if I'd like her to mother me…It's very difficult for me to ask for that and have a right to it.

T-6:   So it may be unreasonable, but still, when she doesn't meet your needs, it makes you mad.

C-6:   Yeah, I get very angry, very angry with her.

[PAUSE]

T-7:   You're also feeling a little tension at this point, I guess.

C-7:   Yeah. Yeah. A lot of conflict…

T-8:   Umm-hmm…

C-8:   A lot of pain.

T-9:   A lot of pain. Can you say anything more what that's about?

C-9:   [Sigh.] I reach out for her, and she moves away from me. And she steps back and pulls back…And then I feel like a really bad person. Like some kind of monster, that she doesn't want me to touch her and told her like I did when she was a little girl…

T-10:   It sounds like a very double feeling there. Part of it is, "Damn it, I want you close." The other part of it is, "Oh my God, what a monster I am to not let you go."

C-10:   Umm-hmm. Yeah. I should be stronger. I should be a grown woman and allow this to happen.

T-11:   But instead, sometimes you feel like her daughter.

C-11:   Umm-hmm. Yeah. Sometimes when I cuddle her, I feel I'm being cuddled.

T-12:   Umm-hmm.

[PAUSE]

But you place a lot of expectations on yourself: "I should be different."

C-12:   Yeah. I should be more mature. I should have my needs met so that I don't have to get anything from her.

T-13:   You should find other ways and other sources to meet your needs, but somehow that doesn't seem to be happening?

C-13:   Well, I feel I get a lot of my needs met, but the need from her is very strong—it's the need from a woman really, I think…It doesn't quite make up the needs I get from men*****…

T-14:   There are some things that you just want from her.

C-14:   Umm-hmm. Yeah. Just from her. [Sigh.]

T-15:   When she pulls back, that's a very painful experience.

C-15:   Yeah, that really hurts. That really hurts. [Big sigh.]

[PAUSE]

T-16:   It looks like you're feeling some of that hurt right now.

C-16:   Yeah, I can really feel her stepping back.

(From Raskin & Rogers in Corsini & Wedding, 2000, pp. 149–150)

Case Illustration   Humanistic theorists would assume that Dave's problems are rooted in his relationship with his parents. They would hypothesize that he did not receive the unconditional positive regard from them necessary to develop strong self-regard and self-confidence, and they would probably consider Dave's father's absences and his mother's occasional withdrawal in this light. Existential theorists would be more likely to emphasize Dave's struggle handling the increased freedom and independence associated with going to college. They would point to Dave's anxiety and withdrawal as indications that he has not successfully confronted the daunting reality of his increased independence.

Behavioral Perspectives

Like the psychodynamic tradition, the behavioral perspective has a long and complex history covering much of the 20th century. In many respects, **behaviorism** developed as an alternative to the psychodynamic model, because behaviorism emphasizes overt, rather than hidden, causes of behavior; it rejects any explanatory concepts that cannot be directly observed and measured (Watson, 1914; Wolpe, 1990). In other respects, however, the two traditions overlap, since both emphasize that behavior, including abnormal behavior, is highly determined by prior life experiences (Hayes et al., 1994; Kohlenberg & Tsai, 1992).

The behavioral perspective can be summarized by an overarching principle: most behavior is *learned*. When applied to the explanation of abnormal behavior the principle is the same: abnormal behavior is learned. Behaviorists have identified and studied three primary types of learning that affect behavior, and all three are relevant to explaining abnormal behavior. These three types are: *classical conditioning, operant conditioning,* and *modeling* or *social learning.*

Classical Conditioning

Classical (or *respondent*) **conditioning** refers to the process of learning through *automatic associations* that the mind establishes between events that happen together in time. In particular, the theory focuses on the connection that is formed when an automatic emotional or behavioral reaction to a stimulus (known as a *reflex,* such as the fear reflex to a sudden flash of lightning) becomes associated with a *"neutral" stimulus* (any object, such as a window) that happens to be present simultaneously. Many animals (including humans) will subsequently associate the automatic (fear) reaction that occurred with the neutral stimulus, and the next time a window is passed it may trigger fear all by itself.

This form of learning was accidentally discovered and then studied by Ivan Pavlov (1849–1936), a Russian scientist; as a result, classical conditioning is sometimes referred to as *Pavlovian conditioning.* Pavlov's experiments involved teaching hungry dogs to associate salivation to meat powder, an unconditioned response, with a neutral stimulus, a sound produced by Pavlov. After repeatedly exposing the dogs to the two events together, Pavlov found that the dogs would begin to salivate just by hearing the sound alone. They had learned a behavior—salivation in response to the cue of sound—based on the automatic association between two stimuli that had happened to occur together in time (sometimes referred to as **temporal contiguity**). (See Figure 3.2.)

Classical conditioning theory uses the following terms to describe this learning process. A stimulus (such as meat powder) that automatically elicits a response (such as salivation) is known as an **unconditioned stimulus (UCS)**, because it causes the response by itself, without any conditioning. The automatic reflex response to the unconditioned stimulus (the salivation to the meat powder) is called the **unconditioned response (UCR)**, again because it happens naturally without any conditioning. A previously neutral stimulus (such as the sound) becomes known as a **conditioned stimulus (CS)** once it elicits a response (such as salivation) by itself due to pairings with the unconditioned stimulus (UCS). The response that a conditioned stimulus (CS) elicits is known as the **conditioned response (CR)**. Thus, when Pavlov's dogs salivated in response to the meat powder it was an unconditioned response (UCR); when they salivated in response to the sound it was a conditioned response (CR).

How is this relevant to explaining abnormal behavior? Recall the example given previously—feeling scared by a bright flash of lightning while standing next to a window. If classical conditioning occurred in this scenario, the unlucky person could

Behaviorism The theoretical perspective that emphasizes with the influence of learning—through classical conditioning, operant conditioning, and modeling—on behavior.

Classical conditioning Learning that takes place through automatic associations between neutral stimuli and unconditioned stimuli.

Temporal contiguity Two events occurring closely together in time.

Unconditioned stimulus A stimulus that automatically elicits a response through a natural reflex.

Unconditioned response The natural reflex response elicited by an unconditioned stimulus.

Conditioned stimulus A previously neutral stimulus that acquires the ability to elicit a response through classical conditioning.

Conditioned response The response elicited by a conditioned stimulus.

Figure 3.2 Classical or Pavlovian conditioning Schematic diagram of the acquisition of a conditioned response by a dog.

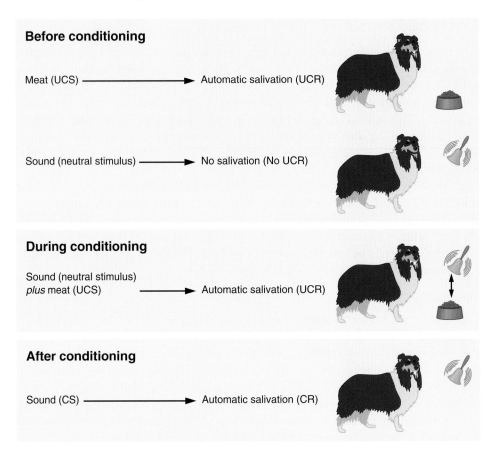

Before conditioning

Meat (UCS) ⟶ Automatic salivation (UCR)

Sound (neutral stimulus) ⟶ No salivation (No UCR)

During conditioning

Sound (neutral stimulus) *plus* meat (UCS) ⟶ Automatic salivation (UCR)

After conditioning

Sound (CS) ⟶ Automatic salivation (CR)

Phobia An intense, persistant, and irrational fear of a specific object or situation.

Operant conditioning A form of learning in which behaviors are shaped through rewards and punishments.

Reinforcement In operant conditioning theory, any environmental response to a behavior that increases the probability that the behavior will be repeated.

Punishment In operant conditioning theory, any environmental response to a behavior that decreases the probability that the behavior will be repeated.

develop a learned fear of windows—very much like the mental disorder known as a **phobia,** an irrational fear and avoidance of a nondangerous object or situation (Chapter 5). In fact, John B. Watson, in a famous experiment (Watson & Rayner, 1920), attempted to create a phobia of rats in a one-year-old boy ("Little Albert") by pairing a rat with a frightening noise. While the experiment has received much scientific and ethical criticism (Harris, 1979), Watson viewed it as a demonstration of a classically conditioned phobia (Watson & Rayner, 1920). Behaviorists have applied the principles of classical conditioning to many other kinds of mental disorders, arguing that these disorders, too, can be classically conditioned (Wagner & Brandon, 2001; Wolpe, 1990; Wolpe & Reyna, 1976). Reactions like fear or sexual arousal can become attached to "inappropriate," neutral stimuli through classical conditioning, creating problems ranging from anxiety disorders (Chapter 5) to certain sexual disorders (Chapter 10).

Operant Conditioning

Operant conditioning, also known as *instrumental conditioning,* is a theory most closely associated with B. F. Skinner (1904–1990). It addresses a different kind of learning—learning that occurs based on **reinforcements** and **punishments**. Reinforcements can be positive (pleasurable) or negative (the removal of something pleasurable) and always *increase* the probability that a behavior will be repeated. Punishments, or aversive consequences, *decrease* the likelihood that behaviors will be repeated.

Edward Thorndike (1874–1949) is often cited as a pioneer in the study of operant conditioning. In his efforts to study animal intelligence, Thorndike built various puz-

Operant conditioning Animal trainer Doug Seus uses operant conditioning principles to train Tank, a five-year-old grizzly bear, for a movie role.

zle boxes with levers, strings, and shelves for testing learning processes in cats. By observing hungry cats as they navigated their way around puzzle boxes to find food, Thorndike discovered that the cats gradually memorized the fastest routes to the food. Thorndike called this the **law of effect**: behaviors that are followed by pleasurable, or *rewarding,* consequences tend to be repeated, while behaviors that are followed by unpleasant, or *aversive,* consequences, tend to decrease. Skinner later applied this principle to real-life settings and to other animals, examining the *environmental contingencies* (that is, the reinforcements and punishments) that influence, or even determine, behavior (Skinner, 1953). Animal trainers, for example, rely on operant conditioning principles of rewards and punishments to elicit complex behaviors such as those that amaze audiences at Sea World.

When applied to explanations of abnormal behavior, operant conditioning theory proposes that abnormal behavior is learned when it has been reinforced in some way, or when normal behavior has been punished. Consider, for example, a young child who receives attention from a normally inattentive father only when the child is sad. A behaviorist (as well as a psychodynamic clinician; this is an area in which the theories overlap) would see this as a breeding ground for depression, because the child has learned that sad behavior will be reinforced with attention. As you might guess, the treatment of abnormal behaviors using operant conditioning theory focuses on eliminating reinforcements for abnormal or unhealthy behaviors, replacing reinforcements with aversive consequences (punishment), and adding reinforcements for adaptive behavior.

Law of effect Thorndike's principle that behaviors followed by pleasurable consequences are likely to be repeated while behaviors followed by aversive consequences are not.

Modeling (social/observational learning) Learning based on observing and imitating the behavior of others.

Modeling/Social Learning

The third form of learning described by behaviorists is called **modeling** or **social/observational learning**. Modeling, also referred to as *vicarious conditioning,* describes learning that occurs by observing and imitating others' behavior. Any observer of children knows how common this phenomenon is, but people do not often think of it as a way to explain abnormal behavior. Behaviorists, however, cite experimental evidence that suggests that abnormal, as well as normal, behaviors can be learned through modeling. For example, in a famous study, Albert Bandura and his colleagues (Bandura, Ross, & Ross, 1963) demonstrated that children who watched an adult act aggressively toward a large doll later acted aggressively toward the doll themselves, while other children who watched an adult play calmly with the same doll imitated the calm adult's behavior. Clearly, modeling can contribute to aggression, as well as many other potentially problematic behaviors.

Behavioral Treatment Interventions

Just as learning is the common element in behavioral *explanations* of psychopathology, unlearning is the common element in behavioral *treatment* interventions. A wide variety of behavioral treatment strategies for unlearning abnormal behaviors, sometimes referred to as *behavior therapies,* have been developed by behavioral researchers (Wolpe, 1990). Classical (or Pavlovian) conditioning interventions focus on breaking pathological conditioned associations through a process called **extinction,** the opposite of the acquisition of conditioned responses. Extinction is accomplished by repeatedly presenting a conditioned stimulus to the client without presenting the unconditioned stimulus, thereby breaking the contingency between the two. Techniques such as **exposure** and **systematic desensitization** (gradual exposure plus relaxation exercises) can help phobic clients by slowly exposing them to stimuli to which they have developed a conditioned fear. Through such exposure, the client unlearns (or extinguishes) the accidental connection between a conditioned stimulus and the unconditioned stimulus that caused the original fear (Nelissen, Muris, & Merckelbach, 1995; Wolpe, 1969). For example, if a child developed a fear of dogs barking (CS) after being bitten by a dog (UCS), exposing the child to barking dogs that do not bite should reduce the child's fear. Exposure, as the key to extinction, is the central technique in most classical conditioning based behavioral treatments.

Classical conditioning principles have also been used in a controversial behavioral therapy known as **aversion therapy** (Axelrod & Apshe, 1983; Hadley, 1985). In this technique, an unwanted behavior or impulse is paired with an aversive stimulus, such as a mild electric shock, in order to classically condition a connection between the two. Aversion therapies have been applied to behaviors such as problem drinking (Chapter 9) and deviant sexual arousal (Chapter 10), but ethical concerns have limited their use.

Operant, or instrumental, behavioral interventions use positive and negative reinforcements and punishments to reshape abnormal behaviors in more adaptive directions, a process known as **contingency management**. For instance, Linehan's (1992) *dialectical behavior therapy* uses operant conditioning principles to address suicidal and other self-destructive behaviors in clients with borderline personality disorder (Chapter 11). Therapists using Linehan's approach, which also integrates cognitive and psychodynamic principles, are more supportive of their clients when they control self-destructive behavior and less supportive when they do not. Similarly, **token economies** use coinlike tokens as rewards that can be exchanged for special privileges in order to reinforce appropriate behavior in individuals with schizophrenia (Chapter 12). **Social skills training**, based on reinforcement and modeling of appropriate social behavior, is used to treat a variety of disorders in which social functioning is impaired (McFall, 1990). Social skills training may focus on general behavioral skills like assertiveness, or address specific problem areas such as inappropriate sexual behavior in individuals with sexual disorders.

Many contemporary behavioral theorists emphasize the importance of understanding the client's unique psychological characteristics when using behavioral treatment techniques. For example, emotional and cognitive factors such as a particular client's attitudes and personality traits (sometimes referred to as "second order" fac-

---

Extinction The weakening of a connection between a conditioned stimulus and a conditioned response.

Exposure Technique of deliberately confronting a conditioned stimulus (such as a feared object) in order to promote **extinction.**

Systematic desensitization Technique of gradually increased exposure to a conditioned stimulus (such as a feared object) while practicing relaxation techniques.

Aversion therapy Behavioral technique involving pairing an unwanted behavior with an aversive stimulus in order to classically condition a connection between them.

Contingency management The use of reinforcements and punishments to shape behavior.

Token economies The systematic use of coinlike tokens as rewards in an operant conditioning treatment program.

Social skills training The use of operant conditioning techniques and modeling in order to improve social skills.

tors) must be taken into account in designing appropriate interventions for that client. In addition, techniques borrowed from Eastern religious traditions such as the "mindfulness" meditative techniques—which can help clients detach from distressing thoughts or emotions—have been integrated with behavioral interventions (Hayes et al., 1994; Linehan, 1992)

Some contemporary behavioral therapies also focus on empathically addressing abnormal behavior as it is exhibited during therapy sessions—a focus that overlaps with psychodynamic and humanistic principles. For example, Kohlenberg and Tsai's (1992) *functional analytic psychotherapy* emphasizes applying behavioral techniques to problematic behaviors expressed within the therapy relationship. A client who has been expressing intense angry feelings about the therapist in inappropriate ways might be rewarded with praise when he finds a more appropriate manner of communicating his feelings.

Let's now return to the case of Dave and look at it through the lens of the behavioral perspective.

Case Illustration **Behavioral theorists would focus on the environmental contingencies in Dave's life, looking for examples of operant conditioning and social learning which might be responsible for some of his symptoms. For instance, being distressed and upset in Dave's family is rewarded with attention and sympathy, while doing well leads to "being taken for granted," an aversive outcome that discourages good functioning. In addition, Dave's mother has modeled becoming anxious and withdrawn when under stress. A behavioral clinician would also look for evidence that Dave's anxiety at college might be a classically conditioned response to particular stimuli at school that have accidentally become paired with Dave's fear reflex. For example, it may be that Dave's preexisting anxiety has become associated with certain students or campus buildings, so that simply being near them automatically elicits anxiety. Behavioral explanations of Dave's problems focus on Dave's symptoms as learned behaviors based on classical conditioning, operant conditioning, and modeling/social learning.**

Cognitive The theoretical perspective that focuses on the influence of thoughts on behavior.

Cognitive schemas Mental models of the world used to organize information.

Cognitive Perspectives

The **cognitive** perspective on abnormal psychology developed during the "cognitive revolution" which swept through the field of psychology beginning in the 1950s. The cognitive perspective focuses on *thoughts* and *beliefs* that influence feelings and behaviors. Cognitive theorists emphasize that human beings fundamentally differ from other animals because we *interpret* the world, rather than simply react to it. In this sense, cognitive theorists echo the philosophy of the Stoic philosopher Epictetus (50–138 C.E.), who said: *"neither death, nor exile, nor pain, nor anything of this kind is the real cause of our doing or not doing any action, but our inward principles and opinions"* (*Discourses*, Chapter XI). To a cognitive theorist, human behavior, including pathological behavior, is always rooted in the particular beliefs, assumptions, and **cognitive schemas** (mental models of the world) that color reality for a given individual (Beck, 1987; Markus, 1977). Accordingly, we can understand why different people often react differentially to the same stimulus. For example, two students might receive the same low grade on an exam, but one becomes depressed while the other reacts with determination to improve.

This emphasis on the role of subjectivity and internal mental life may sound similar to the psychodynamic perspective, and in many respects the two perspectives do overlap, as theorists within both traditions are increasingly recognizing today (Erdelyi, 1985; Mahoney, 1993). However, the cognitive perspective actually developed largely as an alternative to, and a reaction against, both psychodynamic and behavioral perspectives. In fact, many of the founders of the cognitive approach were clinicians, such as Aaron Beck and Albert Ellis, who were originally trained in the psychody-

Aaron Beck Dr. Beck has been one of the most important figures in the development of the cognitive perspective in abnormal psychology. He is pictured here working with a couple on the maladaptive cognitions that are interfering in their relationship.

Cognitive restructuring Therapy techniques that focus on changing irrational and problematic thoughts.

Attributions People's beliefs about the causes of events.

Explanatory styles The patterned ways (such as pessimism) in which people perceive and explain the causes of life events.

Cognitive-behavioral Approaches that combine cognitive and behavioral principles.

Cognitive distortions Irrational beliefs and thinking processes.

Negative automatic thoughts Negative thoughts generated by negative cognitive schemas.

Cognitive triad In cognitive theory, the triad consisting of one's self, one's future, and one's world.

namic tradition but came to believe that changing their clients' maladaptive schemas and beliefs was sufficiently therapeutic. They rejected the psychodynamic assumption that therapeutic change required focusing on the deeper causes of emotional problems, such as childhood experiences. As a result, cognitive treatments focus on techniques for changing irrational and problematic beliefs and thoughts (such as extreme pessimism) into more rational attitudes. This therapeutic approach is often referred to as **cognitive restructuring**.

Cognitive theorists also reject behaviorists' primary focus on *external* influences (stimuli) on behavior, and they dispute the behaviorists' claim that *internal* processes (such as beliefs or motives) are irrelevant and unmeasurable. Historically, cognitive theory began as an exploration of the various mental factors, especially beliefs, that *mediate* (or influence) the relationship between stimuli and responses. For example, social psychologists discovered that **attributions**—people's beliefs about the causes of events—play a large role in determining their responses to social interactions (Fiske & Taylor, 1991; Heider, 1958). Most people, for instance, are more sympathetic to a criminal defendant if they *attribute* the criminal behavior to severe mental illness rather than to willful malevolence.

Recently, attribution theory has focused on the concept of **explanatory styles**—the patterned ways in which people perceive and explain the causes of life events. This approach has been used to understand how people react to stress (Major, Mueller, & Hildenbrandt, 1985), test failure (Ritchie, 2000; Williams & Brewin, 1984), physical injury or disease (Abrams & Finesinger, 1953; Peterson & Bossio, 1991), depression (Nolen-Hoeksema, Girgus, & Seligman, 1986; Peterson & Seligman, 1984; Seligman et al., 1979), learning challenges (Vermetten, Lodewijks, & Vermunt, 2001), difficult tasks that require persistence (Peterson, Maier, & Seligman, 1993), and more (Chang, 2001). For example, studies have shown that a *pessimistic* explanatory style regarding life events increases vulnerability to feelings of hopelessness and helplessness, key emotions in depression. A pessimistic style is defined as the tendency to explain negative events by assuming that they will generalize to other areas (*global* explanation), continue to happen (*stable* explanation), and are one's own fault (*internal* explanation).

After many years of seeming like rival traditions, cognitive and behavioral approaches to psychopathology have now become so well integrated that they are often referred to as a single, unified school: the **cognitive-behavioral** approach. This approach combines an emphasis on behavioral learning (such as stimulus-response connections) with attention to an individual's cognitive processes (such as attributions). This combination illustrates our general emphasis on the complementarity of various perspectives in abnormal psychology.

A few cognitive theorists have been especially influential in developing cognitive explanations of psychopathology. For example, Albert Ellis focuses on the role of *irrational assumptions and beliefs* in causing emotional distress. In particular, he cites irrational assumptions, like the idea that one must be "perfect" in order to be happy, as a frequent cause of depression and general unhappiness (Ellis, 1962; 1996; see also Kendall et al., 1995). Aaron Beck (1976, 1999) focuses on the role of **cognitive distortions** in the origin and maintenance of various disorders. Common pathological cognitive distortions include *magnification* (making mountains out of molehills), *overgeneralization* (inferring a general pattern from a single negative event), and *selective abstraction* (focusing on the negative; seeing the hole instead of the doughnut). For example, a student who thinks he is a terrible, hopeless student after doing poorly on one quiz while doing well on major tests would be exhibiting all three of these distortions. These cognitive distortions produce **negative automatic thoughts** concerning one's self, one's future, and one's world—three areas referred to as the **cognitive triad**. Researchers have established that negative automatic thoughts are

BOX 3.5 Changing Negative Thinking

Cognitive Restructuring in a Therapy Session

Note the therapist's techniques of using logical reasoning and rational explanations to counter the client's fear of fainting during a panic attack. P = Patient; T = Therapist.

P: In the middle of a panic attack, I usually think I am going to faint or collapse…

T: Have you ever fainted in an attack?

P: No.

T: What is it then that makes you think you might faint?

P: I feel faint, and the feeling can be very strong.

T: So, to summarize, your evidence that you are going to faint is the fact that you feel faint?

P: Yes.

T: How can you then account for the fact that you have felt faint many hundreds of times and have not yet fainted?

P: So far, the attacks have always stopped just in time or I have managed to hold onto something to stop myself from collapsing.

T: Right. So one explanation of the fact that you have frequently felt faint, had the thought that you would faint, but have not actually fainted, is that you have always done something to save yourself just in time. However, an alternative explanation is that the feeling of faintness that you get in a panic attack will never lead to you collapsing, even if you don't control it.

P: Yes, I suppose.

T: In order to decide which of these two possibilities is correct, we need to know what has to happen to your body for you to actually faint. Do you know?

P: No.

T: Your blood pressure needs to drop. Do you know what happens to your blood pressure during a panic attack?

P: Well, my pulse is racing. I guess my blood pressure must be up.

T: That's right. In anxiety, heart rate and blood pressure tend to go together. So you are actually less likely to faint when you are anxious than when you are not.

P: That's very interesting and helpful to know. However, if it's true, why do I feel so faint?

T: Your feeling of faintness is a sign that your body is reacting in a normal way to the perception of danger. Most of the bodily reactions you are experiencing when anxious were probably designed to deal with the threats experienced by primitive people, such as being approached by a hungry tiger. What would be the best thing to do in that situation?

P: Run away as fast as you can.

T: That's right. And in order to help you run, you need the maximum amount of energy in your muscles. This is achieved by sending more of your blood to your muscles and relatively less to the brain. This means that there is a small drop in oxygen to the brain and that is why you feel faint. However, this feeling is misleading because your overall blood pressure is up, not down.

P: That's very clear. So next time I feel faint, I can check out whether I am going to faint by taking my pulse. If it is normal, or quicker than normal, I know I won't faint.

(From Clark, 1989, pp. 76–77; in Wilson, 2000, p. 221)

---

usually very specific ideas that, despite their distortions, seem highly reasonable to the person who is thinking them (Beck, Steer, & Epstein, 1992). Cognitive therapists challenge both the negative schemas that produce negative automatic thoughts and the automatic thoughts themselves.

Cognitive Treatment Interventions

Cognitive interventions are based on the premise that modifying negative cognitions can alter problematic emotions and behaviors, such as depression or anxiety (Macleod & Cropley, 1995; see Box 3.5 for an example of cognitive restructuring in a therapy session). For example, Beck's cognitive therapy approach encourages clients to evaluate and question their maladaptive assumptions (Beck, 1976), and Beck and his colleagues have developed cognitive therapies for substance use disorders, personality disorders, and other conditions besides depression and anxiety (Beck & Freeman, 1990).

Other influential cognitively oriented approaches include Ellis's (1962; 1996) *rational-emotive therapy,* which disputes irrational beliefs (see Figure 3.3 for an example of a rational-emotive behavior therapy self-help form), and Donald Meichenbaum's (1997) *self-instructional training* which teaches clients to answer their overly negative *self-talk* with more realistic and positive self-statements. Albert Bandura (1977; 1986) believes that cognitive interventions work by improving clients' *efficacy expectations,* or *self-efficacy.* Self-efficacy refers to confidence that one can behave so as to successfully achieve desired outcomes, and researchers have shown that higher levels of self-efficacy reduce the amount of strain people experience in stressful situations (Jex et al., 2001). (The effectiveness of cognitive treatment interventions, and of other psychotherapy in general, is discussed in Box 3.6. Social issues regarding access to mental health treatment are discussed in Box 3.7.)

Figure 3.3 Rational emotive behavior therapy self-help form This self-help form is typically given to clients to fill out regarding disturbing events that occur in their daily lives between therapy sessions; it is then reviewed in the next therapy session.

(From Ellis in Corsini & Wedding, 2000, p. 194)

A (ACTIVATING EVENTS OR ADVERSITIES)

• Briefly summarize the situation you are disturbed about (what would a camera see?)

• An *A* can be *internal* or *external, real* or *imagined.*

• An *A* can be an event in the *past, present,* or *future.*

IBs (IRRATIONAL BELIEFS)

D (DISPUTING IBs)

To identify IBs, look for:

• Dogmatic Demands
(musts, absolutes, shoulds)

• Awfulizing
(It's awful, terrible, horrible)

• Low Frustration Tolerance
(I can't stand it)

• Self/Other Rating
(I'm/he/she is bad, worthless)

To dispute ask yourself:

• Where is holding this belief getting me? Is it *helpful* or *self-defeating*?

• Where is the evidence to support the existence of my irrational belief? Is it *consistent with social reality*?

• Is my belief *logical*? Does it follow from my preferences?

• Is it really *awful* (as bad as it could be)?

• Can I really not *stand* it?

BOX 3.6 Does Therapy Help?

The Effectiveness of Psychotherapy

For several decades now, researchers have been studying the effectiveness of psychotherapy. This is no easy task, since more than 100 varieties of psychotherapy exist. In addition, it is difficult to develop reliable and valid measures of the complex process of psychotherapy and its long-term results. As a result, the quality of psychotherapy studies is uneven. One landmark report summarized the results of 375 psychotherapy studies, finding that in 75% of cases therapy provided some benefit when compared to no treatment (Smith, Glass, & Miller, 1980). In addition, these researchers found that there were no significant differences in the effectiveness of various theoretical approaches. More recent studies have tended to confirm that psychotherapy is usually helpful, and that different treatment approaches produce similar results (for example, Lambert & Bergin, 1994; Lambert, Weber, & Sykes, 1993; Luborsky, Diguer, Luborsky, & Schmidt, 1999; Stiles, Shapiro, & Elliott, 1986).

In the early 1990s, *Consumer Reports* magazine used a controversial methodology to assess the effectiveness of psychotherapy, asking consumers about their experiences in psychotherapy rather than conducting a traditional controlled study. The results, based on thousands of responses, confirmed the findings that psychotherapy is generally effective, and that different approaches seem to work equally well (*Consumer Reports,* 1995; Seligman, 1995). However, therapy with psychiatrists, psychologists, and social workers was rated as more effective than therapy with marriage counselors, who typically have less formal training. In addition, the study indicated that the longer a person stayed in therapy the greater the benefit. This last finding was especially striking because it raised questions about the recent trend toward shorter therapies in response to pressures from insurance companies and employers to reduce costs.

Psychotherapy has also been compared with drug treatments for mental disorders. For example, a landmark study of treatments for depression conducted by the National Institute for Mental Health showed that cognitive-behavioral therapy, interpersonal therapy (a psychodynamic/humanistic blend), and antidepressant medication were about equally effective over a 16-week period (Hollon, 1996). However, the psychotherapies had some advantages over medication in the long run as they seemed to prevent recurrences of depression.

Since so many studies have shown little difference in effectiveness among various therapies, many researchers have shifted their attention to finding the common variables that account for therapeutic improvement in all treatments. The variable that has emerged as the best predictor thus far of good therapy outcome is known as the **therapeutic alliance**, which refers to a positive, collaborative partnership between the client and therapist (Hatcher et al., 1995; Horvath, 1994; Lambert & Bergin, 1994; Luborsky &

Crits-Cristoph, 1990; Strupp, 1995). As a result, therapists across all of the theoretical models now emphasize the importance of establishing and maintaining a good working relationship with their clients.

Researchers have also explored the possibility that some therapies may work better than others for specific disorders. For example, a controversial current movement in the field advocates the recognition of **empirically supported treatments (ESTs)** – specific forms of therapy that have been proven to work for specific disorders (Chambless, 1996; Crits-Cristoph, 1996). These treatments, such as the cognitive-behavioral and interpersonal therapies for depression, have been *standardized* in treatment manuals for therapists. However, some critics have questioned the claim that these therapies have greater, proven effectiveness. For example, Westen and Morrison (2002) summarized the results of 34 recent studies of manualized therapies and found that clients' initial improvements were often not maintained at follow-up, and that clients selected for and completing these studies may not be a representative sample of clients in the "real world" of typical clinical practice. Other researchers have argued that the standardization of these therapies in a therapy manual can interfere with a therapist's flexibility and responsiveness, which can be necessary to maintain a positive therapeutic alliance and to respond to the unique needs of each client (Garfield, 1996).

In addition, recent research has shown that the idea that manualized therapies can be usefully distinguished by "brand names" (for example, cognitive, behavioral, psychodynamic) may be misleading. In examining the detailed process of tape-recorded therapies described as either "cognitive-behavioral" or "psychodynamic," Jones and Pulos (1993) discovered that therapists in both groups actually used both cognitive-behavioral and psychodynamic strategies and interventions during sessions. In their study, for example, good outcomes were associated with the use of psychodynamic interventions by therapists in both the cognitive-behavioral and psychodynamic groups. This use of multiple, eclectic strategies even in "brand-name" therapies reflects the growing trend toward the *integration* of theoretical perspectives in psychotherapy—a trend consistent with the core concept of **multiple causality.** Integrated approaches and combined treatments (such as psychotherapy plus medication) are increasingly the norm (Hayes et al., 1994; Luborsky et al., 1999).

Therapeutic alliance A positive, collaborative partnership between client and therapist.

Empirically supported treatments (ESTs) Specific forms of therapy that have been shown, by certain standards, to be helpful for specific disorders.

FOCUS ON PSYCHOLOGY IN SOCIETY

BOX 3.7 Discrimination in Health Care

The Mental Health Parity Movement

As the effectiveness of psychotherapy has become clearer, public health experts have emphasized the importance of making psychotherapy widely available and reducing the stigma of mental health treatment. Their efforts have been reinforced by research findings that psychotherapy is not only effective in treating mental disorders but can also be useful in addressing some medical problems. It is estimated that up to 70% of visits to primary care physicians are for complaints that are mainly due to psychological factors (VandenBos & DeLeon, 1988). In addition, over half of all deaths in the United States are due to behavioral lifestyle factors, such as poor eating habits, smoking, lack of exercise, and substance misuse, which can be addressed in psychotherapy (Taylor, 1995). As a result, some experts have argued that expenditures for mental health treatment actually *reduce* overall health care expenses over the long run (Thompson et al., 1998).

Despite these findings, recent pressures from insurers, employers, and the government to cut escalating health care costs have resulted in a general reduction in insurance coverage for psychotherapy over the past decade. *Fee-for-service* health care plans that reimburse clients for medical expenses (including psychotherapy) have been disappearing, and they have been replaced by *managed care* plans which now cover a majority of Americans with health insurance. Most managed care plans tightly regulate the use of psychotherapy by subscribers. Typically, they offer a limit of 20 sessions or fewer per year, require clients to see therapists associated with the plan, and involve an authorization process to approve treatment. Problems with managed mental health care, such as denials of needed care and requests by insurers for information about the private content of therapies, have recently led to a backlash by clients and therapists against the

managed care approach (Phelps, Eisman, & Kohut, 1998). Many clients who can afford to do so simply choose to pay for psychotherapy "out of pocket," preserving their privacy and freedom of choice and bypassing insurance involvement. But for the millions of Americans who do not have the resources to pay out of pocket, other solutions are needed. One such effort is the **mental health parity** movement. This movement argues that health insurers routinely discriminate against those needing mental health treatment by providing lower levels of coverage for mental disorders than for physical disorders. For example, there are usually limits on the number of visits allowed to see a therapist for depression while there are no such limits on the number of visits to a doctor for medical diseases—even though depression is more treatable than many physical illnesses. Parity advocates have demonstrated that, contrary to insurers' fears, expanded mental health coverage causes, at most, minimal increases in costs (National Institute of Mental Health, 1998).

The parity movement has had mixed legislative success. The federal government passed a weak parity law in 1996, but a more meaningful law was defeated in 2001 after heavy lobbying by the insurance industry. At the state level, 31 states currently have parity laws, which are generally stronger than the federal law. However, in states with strong parity laws, managed care has actually become *more* pervasive since strict control over whether to authorize treatment at all (parity laws generally do not address this issue) has become a way for insurers to control costs in a parity environment. As a result, some mental health advocates have argued that the parity movement may be backfiring, and that it cannot succeed without addressing the problem of managed care (Hansell, 1997; Miller, 1997). They propose other solutions, such as encouraging insurers to generously subsidize *outpatient* psychotherapy, while focusing cost containment efforts on excessive *inpatient* treatment, which was the real source of runaway costs in the past. As noted above, generous benefits for outpatient psychotherapy may actually reduce overall health care expenditures in the long run as a result of the overall benefits of healthier lifestyles.

> **Mental health parity** A political movement advocating that mental disorders should be covered by health insurance on par with physical disorders.

Mental health parity Tipper Gore, shown here at the start of the 1999 White House Conference on Mental Health, has been a strong advocate of the mental health parity movement. Ms. Gore, the wife of former vice president Al Gore, has acknowledged her own struggle with depression.

Case Illustration Looking at Dave's symptoms through the lens of the cognitive perspective, we would focus on Dave's assumptions, explanatory style, automatic thoughts, self-talk, and efficacy expectations. For example, Dave becomes apprehensive and pessimistic when stressed. He starts to falsely assume that people do not like him and he has automatic self-critical thoughts; these cognitions lead to anxiety and withdrawal. Furthermore, Dave seems to believe that he must be perfectly successful in order to satisfy himself and his parents. He also assumes that if he is successful he will not receive as much attention as he does when struggling. This hypothesis overlaps with the behavioral focus on the reinforcement of sadness in his family, and with the psychodynamic hypothesis that Dave has ambivalent (or mixed) feelings about being successful. However, the unique focus of the cognitive approach is on the role of Dave's negative beliefs as the immediate, precipitating cause of his anxiety symptoms.

Brief Summary

- Psychodynamic explanations of psychopathology focus on motives, thoughts, and feelings that are outside awareness (unconscious), emotional conflicts, and the ongoing influence of childhood experiences. Psychodynamic interventions help clients gain insight and mastery over these conflicts and repetitive patterns.

- Humanistic explanations of psychopathology focus on the role of problems with self-regard that result from unempathic relationships. Humanistic interventions center on restoring positive self-regard through an empathic relationship with the therapist.

- Existential perspectives explain psychopathology as a form of inauthenticity based on the inability to accept responsibility for creating one's own meaning in life. In existential interventions, clients are encouraged to face this responsibility and to become more authentic and less avoidant.

- Behavioral perspectives are based on the principle that most behavior is learned. Behaviorists focus on three types of learning that can account for normal and abnormal behavior: classical conditioning (learning based on automatic mental associations), operant conditioning (learning based on what is reinforced and punished), and modeling/social learning (learning based on observation and imitation). Behavioral interventions involve unlearning maladaptive, abnormal behaviors, and learning new and more adaptive behaviors through the use of conditioning and modeling techniques.

- Cognitive theorists focus on thoughts and beliefs as the immediate cause of many feelings and behaviors, including abnormal behaviors. Cognitive therapists emphasize changing maladaptive thoughts and beliefs into more realistic and constructive thinking.

Critical Thinking Question Consider the psychodynamic, humanistic/existential, behavioral, and cognitive approaches to the case of Dave. In what ways do they seem to overlap? In what ways do they seem to diverge?

Sociocultural and Family Systems Perspectives

The **sociocultural** and **family systems** perspectives focus on how social, cultural, and familial environments contribute to mental disorders. As such, they overlap with other perspectives, especially the behavioral focus on environmental reinforcements and the psychodynamic focus on family influences. The sociocultural and family systems approaches are unique, however, in their primary emphasis on social forces that shape normal and abnormal behavior.

Sociocultural The theoretical perspective that focuses on the influence of large social and cultural forces on individual functioning.

Family systems The theoretical perspective that focuses on the importance of family dynamics in understanding and treating psychopathology.

Sociocultural factors The sociocultural perspective emphasizes the connections between sociocultural stressors and mental disorders. For example, rates of many mental disorders are higher among the urban poor, like these people waiting at a soup kitchen, than they are for other groups.

Anorexia nervosa A disorder involving extreme thinness, often achieved through self-starvation.

Sociocultural Perspectives

The sociocultural perspective draws on the intellectual traditions of sociology, the study of social organizations, and anthropology, the study of culture. We have already seen several examples of the relevance of the sociocultural perspective in abnormal psychology, especially in the core concept of *cultural and historical relativism*. For example, we focused in Chapter 2 on how it is virtually impossible to define "abnormality" without referring to a specific cultural and historical setting because every society has different ideas about what is normal and abnormal. Sometimes these ideas are so different from one another that they account for the "culture-bound syndromes" discussed in Chapter 2 (Table 2.1). On a related note, you may also recall from Chapter 2 that Thomas Szasz (1960) makes the extreme argument that the very idea of "mental disorders" is something invented by societies in order to control the behavior of their citizens (for a counterargument, see Zigmond, 1999, and Chapter 12, Box 12.1: The Politics of Psychosis: Mark Vonnegut and *The Eden Express*). Most sociocultural theorists do not go this far; rather, they see mental disorders as real, but influenced by social institutions, pressures, or stresses. For example, some sociocultural theorists have emphasized the role of unemployment, poverty, discrimination, and the prison system in causing and maintaining criminal behavior (for example, Kessler et al., 1994).

For the most part, sociocultural theorists believe that social forces contribute to mental disorders through *learning* (this is obviously an area of overlap with behaviorism). Individuals learn to adopt behaviors—normal and abnormal—on the basis of the social and cultural role models, ideals, pressures, and stresses that they encounter. These social and cultural roles and stresses vary a great deal by social class, culture, gender, and ethnicity. As a result, sociocultural theorists often focus on categories like socioeconomic status (SES), gender, and ethnicity in their explanations of mental illness. As evidence for their point of view, sociocultural theorists point to the fact that the prevalence of many mental disorders correlates with sociocultural variables. For example, depression is more common in women than in men; self-reported quality of life is lower for African Americans than whites, and schizophrenia is significantly more common among the poor than the wealthy (Keith, Regier, & Rae, 1991; Nolen-Hoeksema, 1990). While such correlations never prove causation, as we have discussed, they do point to the relevance of sociocultural factors in mental disorders.

An excellent example of this perspective is the sociocultural explanation of **anorexia nervosa** (Chapter 8), a view rooted in feminist theories about the disorder. Anorexia, a disorder involving self-starvation, is primarily found in a specific sociocultural group—contemporary, young, white, affluent women in Western, industrialized societies. Sociocultural theorists argue that the female beauty ideals, communicated through media images, along with complex sex role stresses facing young women in this sociocultural group, are direct causes of anorexia (Thompson et al., 1999). As we will see in Chapter 8, this kind of sociocultural theory, like most theories, is more useful in combination with other models than by itself. For example, since most young, affluent, white women in contemporary Western cultures do *not* develop eating disorders, looking only at the sociocultural causes of these disorders would be reductionistic. At the same time, the complete explanation of any mental disorder should include an understanding of sociocultural factors.

Because they focus on broader social forces, sociocultural theorists often view individual treatment for mental disorders with some skepticism. They tend to believe that social change, such as reducing unemployment, poverty, and discrimination, is the key to improving psychological well-being for the greatest number of people. We will consider sociocultural interventions in more detail in chapters that address disorders strongly influenced by sociocultural factors (for example, Chapter 8 on eating disorders and Chapter 12 on schizophrenia).

Family Systems Perspectives

Family systems theorists focus specifically on *family dynamics* rather than the broader social environment to explain emotional disorders. They emphasize that families are complex *systems* and consider the family as a unit rather than focusing on individuals within the family. The family systems approach is based on concepts and principles that apply to other kinds of complex systems. For example, family systems tend to maintain a certain stability, or **homeostasis**. Thus, a change in any part of a family will tend to cause disruption throughout the family system and trigger a counter-reaction to reestablish familiar patterns (Alexander & Waxman, 2000; Steinglass, 1987). Consider a family in which the parents anxiously focus on one of their children's learning problems in order to avoid dealing with problems in their marriage. When the child starts to be successful at school, the parents may find themselves focusing on another child's problems. These patterns can be described in terms of the interpersonal *boundaries* within a family (an **enmeshed** family has few boundaries between members and intrusive relationships, while a **disengaged** family has distant, detached relationships), and the *roles* within a family (for example, family power dynamics, responsibilities, alliances, and scapegoating of members) (Bermann, 1973; Minuchin, 1974; Steinglass, 1987). (See Table 3.3 for a list of family systems concepts and techniques.) Family therapists typically construct a **genogram** of families they work with—a complex diagram of the extended family system (see Figure 3.4). Genograms highlight the family systems principle that it is not individuals who have disorders, but families.

The family systems approach was pioneered in the 1950s by Gregory Bateson and Jay Haley, who conducted studies of family communication patterns. They focused on family communication problems such as *double-bind* communications, in which a child is given contradictory messages by other family members. Early family systems theorists believed that double-bind communications from parents, such as "Be independent!" but "Never leave us!" could lead to severe disturbances, such as schizophrenia, in a targeted child, although this view is now seen as extreme and unsupported. Later, Haley joined with Salvador Minuchin to develop *structural family therapy*, which focuses on identifying and reshaping family roles and boundaries

Homeostasis The tendency of systems, such as family systems, to maintain stable patterns.

Enmeshed families Families in which boundaries between members are weak and relationships tend to be intrusive.

Disengaged families Families in which relationships tend to be distant and unemotional.

Genogram Diagram of the structure of a family.

Some Family Systems Concepts and Techniques	Table 3.3
	Adapted from Plante, 1999

Homeostasis ▪ The tendency of a system to return to its usual equilibrium.

Enmeshment ▪ Maladaptive over-involvement among family members in the family system.

Disengagement ▪ Maladaptive over-detachment among family members in the family system.

Double-bind communication ▪ Confusing mixed messages that have a "damned if you do, damned if you don't" quality.

Identified patient ▪ The member of the family singled out by the family as "ill."

Paradoxical intervention ▪ A family therapy technique in which the therapist encourages the family to maintain their maladaptive patterns, assuming that this will motivate the family to change.

Figure 3.4 A sample family genogram In this genogram, relationships between members of the Pasadeno and Brown families, joined by the marriage of Michael and Judy, are diagrammed along with the dates of family transition events and notations on the individuals within the families.

(From Kaslow & Celano in Gurman & Messner, p. 369)

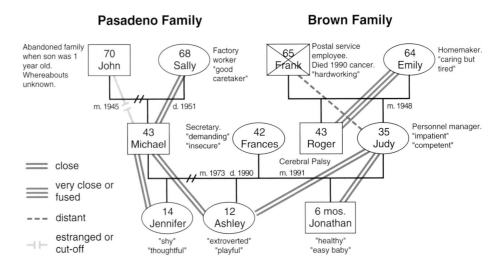

Family therapy In family therapy, the entire family typically meets with a therapist so that the family's interpersonal dynamics can be addressed.

Identified patient The member of the family identified by the family as having problems; family systems theorists see this as a manifestation of a problem in the family system, not in an individual member.

(Minuchin, 1974). Haley also developed *strategic family therapy,* a method for dealing with resistance in family therapy by using *paradoxical* techniques such as "prescribing the symptom"—a kind of "reverse psychology" in which the family is told to *increase* their problematic behavior, with the idea that this will mobilize the family to do just the opposite (Haley, 1987).

When an individual within a family develops emotional problems, family systems therapists understand this as an indication of difficulty within the broader family system. The person with the emotional problems is described by family systems theorists as the **identified patient**, in order to emphasize that the "real" patient is the entire family. For example, an eight-year-old girl developed tantrums and refused to eat shortly after the birth of a baby brother with minor medical problems. In this case, family therapy focused on helping the parents to see that their excessive anxiety about the baby had disrupted the family system, leading to their daughter's attention-getting symptoms. This example highlights the overlap between family systems and psychodynamic explanations because they share an emphasis on the central role of family relationships in an individual's emotional life. What distinguishes the family systems approach is its concern with treating the family as a unit. To this end, family therapy usually involves meeting with the whole family. The therapist offers comments and suggestions, and assigns homework designed to help the family system react in more constructive ways to changes and conflicts, such as encouraging the parents in the family just described to reconsider their excessive worry about their son and focus more on their daughter's needs. When the family is functioning more constructively as a unit, the pathological pressures on the individual members are relieved.

Case Illustration Looking at Dave's problems through the lens of the sociocultural perspective, we see some new possible explanations. Sociocultural theorists would focus on the social and cultural context of Dave's problems, such as the upper-middle class, professional expectations and pressures that might be contributing to Dave's anxiety in college. In addition, they would highlight the stresses associated with Dave's attendance at a prestigious university, and in particular the current historical context in which college students feel more competitive pressure than ever to succeed.

Family systems theorists would focus more specifically on Dave's family dynamics. They might hypothesize that Dave's problems erupted recently as a result of growing tension between his parents over Dave's father's work hours. Alternatively, family theorists might assume that Dave's departure for college has destabilized the family homeostasis because he is no longer present to compensate for his brother's problems with his own successes. Dave's symptoms could be an attempt to return to a familiar homeostasis by keeping him more connected to his family even though he has left home. Finally, family theorists would probably agree with the psychodynamic and behavioral hypotheses that Dave's symptoms are partially caused by the fact that his family reinforces distress with concern and care taking, while independence and self-reliance tend to lead to "being taken for granted."

Biological Perspectives

Biological explanations of mental disorders have a long history, as we have already seen. Even before the causes of diseases like *general paresis* (see page 38) were discovered, it was known that many physical illnesses, defects, or injuries could produce emotional symptoms. Accordingly, the biological perspective focuses on physical structures and biochemical functions in the body that contribute to abnormal behavior. In particular, contemporary biological researchers in abnormal psychology study the structure and function of the brain. In this section we will look at the major physical structures and biochemical functions of the brain that have been implicated in mental disorders.

As our understanding of the brain has grown dramatically in recent years, the biological perspective has become increasingly influential within the field of abnormal psychology. Indeed, the 1990s were often described in psychology as the "decade of the brain," and it has become commonplace to hear of exciting new discoveries relating mental illnesses to abnormal brain chemistry, abnormal brain structure, or brain disease and injury. In addition, there have recently been exciting discoveries regarding the role that *genetics* play in mental disorders.

The Central Nervous System

The nervous system is a vast electrochemical network that transmits information and impulses throughout the body. The **central nervous system,** consisting of the *brain* and the *spinal cord,* forms the hub of this network—its headquarters, so to speak (see Figure 3.5). In considering the biological bases of abnormal behavior, we will address both the *structure* of the brain, and the biochemical activities, or *functions* that take place there. The brain is made up of approximately 100 billion nerve cells, or **neurons,** as well as more than 10 times as many *glial cells,* support cells that hold the neurons together. The neurons and glial cells are organized into two general regions within the brain, the *hindbrain* and the *forebrain,* each of which is further divided into additional regions and structures (see Figure 3.6). The hindbrain is the most *caudal* part of our brains, that is, the portion closest to our spinal cord. It is relatively small in humans and is comprised of structures, such as the *pons,* the *cerebellum,* and the *medulla,* that we share with other vertebrates. These portions of the brain are thought of as more "primitive," in that they control functions that are not under conscious control, such as motor reflexes and the maintenance of balance (Nakamagoe, Iwamoto, & Yoshida, 2000; Smock, 1999).

In contrast to the hindbrain, the human forebrain is quite large, making up most of our brain mass. It includes the two *cerebral hemispheres* and is divided into the **cortex** (the folded matter on the outside of the brain that we generally associate with the brain's appearance), and the subcortical structures that are buried within the cortex. The cortex can be further divided into four *lobes,* or regions: the *frontal, occipital, parietal,* and *temporal lobes.* Humans' advanced cognitive operations, including reading, speaking, and reasoning, are controlled by different regions of the cortex. The *subcortical structures* include the **thalamus** (a relay station for routing and filtering

Central nervous system The control center for transmitting information and impulses throughout the body, consisting of the brain and the spinal cord.

Neuron An individual nerve cell.

Thalamus A subcortical brain structure involved in routing and filtering sensory input.

Figure 3.5 The nervous system This chart and the accompanying diagrams show the divisions of the human nervous system.

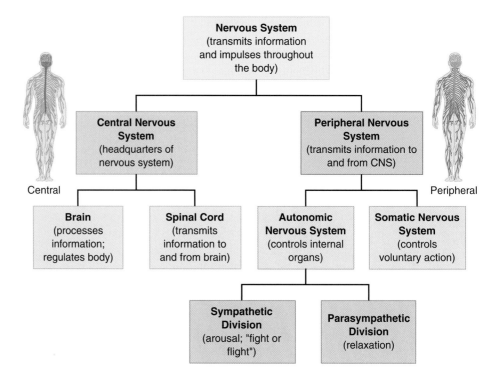

Hypothalamus A subcortical brain structure that controls the endocrine, or hormonal, system.

Basal ganglia A subcortical brain structure involved in the regulation of movement.

sensory input), the **hypothalamus** (the center of the endocrine, or hormonal, system), and **basal ganglia** (an area especially involved in the regulation of movement). These structures also appear to be important in regulating emotional processes, such as reactions to stress (Smock, 1999).

Abnormalities in brain structure, which may either be inherited genetically or result from injury or illness, can play a role in some types of abnormal behavior. Head injuries, for example, can cause brain damage which may cause behavioral changes. An example of an illness-related change in brain structure is *Huntington's disease.* This degenerative disorder, in which individuals suffer from odd and involuntary body movements, angry outbursts, loss of memory, and other cognitive disturbances, has been associated with a loss of nerve cells in the basal ganglia. Another well-known illness that causes brain changes is *Alzheimer's disease* (Chapter 13), in which neural damage leads to dramatic cognitive and behavioral changes. Some brain-altering dis-

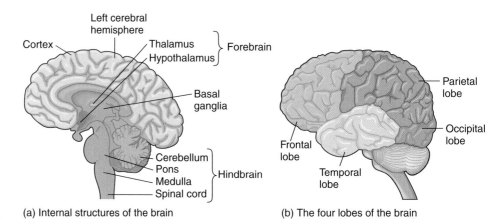

Figure 3.6 The human brain (a) Internal structures of the brain   (b) The four lobes of the brain

eases can be prevented, such as *Korsakoff's syndrome,* which is caused by chronic alcohol consumption (Chapter 9).

Another example of the link between abnormal brain structure and mental disorders is found in schizophrenia (Chapter 12). Some of the symptoms of schizophrenia may be associated with the presence of enlarged *ventricles,* the fluid-filled cavities in the brain (Allen et al., 2000). Modern imaging techniques such as *computerized axial tomography* (CAT scans), *positron emission tomography* (PET scans), and *magnetic resonance imagining* (MRI) can produce photographs of the living brain that document these structural changes.

Some mental disorders have been linked to disturbances in neurochemical functioning, rather than to structural abnormalities in the brain. Research in this area focuses on the role of **neurotransmitters**, chemicals that allow neurons in the brain to communicate with one another. As noted, the brain is comprised of an enormous number of neurons, or nerve cells, which connect with each other at **synapses** (see Figure 3.7). Each neuron is composed of a *cell body* (the main part of the nerve cell), an *axon* (a long extension from the cell body ending in *terminal buttons*), and many *dendrites* (branchlike receptors extending from the cell body). Information passes from one neuron to the next through electrical impulses. When an electrical impulse reaches the end of the axon, it triggers the neuron to release a neurotransmitter into the **synaptic cleft**, a tiny gap between one neuron and the next. The neurotransmitter then crosses the synaptic cleft and is picked up by **receptors** (composed of proteins) on the dendrites of the next neuron, where it converts into an electrical impulse, thus continuing the process. However, not all of the neurotransmitters that are released get taken into the adjacent neuron. Leftover neurotransmitters linger in the synaptic cleft, until they are either broken down by special enzymes in a process called *degradation* or reabsorbed by the presynaptic neuron in a process called *reuptake.* (Sometimes leftover neurotransmitters become less concentrated through *diffusion* as the neurotransmitters mix in with other neighboring substances.) These processes have a direct connection to the symptoms and treatment of many mental disorders. For example, **selective serotonin reuptake inhibitors** (SSRIs), widely used in the treatment of depression and other conditions, block the reuptake of the neurotransmitter serotonin, allowing more serotonin to move across the synapse.

There are hundreds of known neurotransmitters, with more being discovered all the time. Some of the key neurotransmitters are the *catecholamines* (dopamine, epinephrine, and norepinephrine), *serotonin,* the *amino acids* (glutamate, gamma-aminobutyric acid [GABA]), and *acetylocholine.* A few of these chemicals have been linked with specific mental disorders, such as serotonin and norepinephrine with depression (Chapter 6; Delgado & Moreno, 2000), norepinephrine and GABA with anxiety (Chapter 5; Antoni et al., 2000; Ninan, 1999), and dopamine with schizophrenia (Chapter 12; Owen, Crow, & Poulter, 1987; Taber, Lewis, & Hurley, 2001; Zaleman, 1995), and opiate and alcohol dependence (Chapter 9; Schmidt et al., 2001).

In talking about the role of neurotransmission in mental disorders we must be mindful of the ***connection between mind and body.*** Strictly speaking, we can only say that abnormal neurotransmission *correlates* with certain mental disorders. As with all correlations, it is often difficult to tell whether these chemical factors are the *cause* or the *result* of the disorders. Regardless, no explanation of a mental disorder can be complete today without considering the role of neurotransmitters.

The Peripheral Nervous System

The **peripheral nervous system (PNS)** is a network of nerves throughout the body that carry information to and from the central nervous system (see Figure 3.5). The

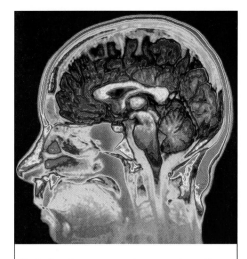

Brain imaging New techniques that offer images of the structure and functioning of the living brain are invigorating the biological perspective on abnormality.

Neurotransmitters Chemicals that allow neurons in the brain to communicate by traveling between them.

Synapse Point of connection between neurons.

Synaptic cleft The tiny gap between one neuron and the next at a synapse.

Receptors The areas of a neuron that receive neurotransmitters from adjacent neurons.

Selective serotonin reuptake inhibitors (SSRIs) Medications that block the reuptake of serotonin from the synapse; used in the treatment of depression and other disorders.

Peripheral nervous system (PNS) Network of nerves throughout the body that carries information and impulses to and from the CNS.

Figure 3.7 Nerve cells and neurotransmission This diagram shows the structure of a nerve cell and the path of a nerve impulse from one neuron to the next.

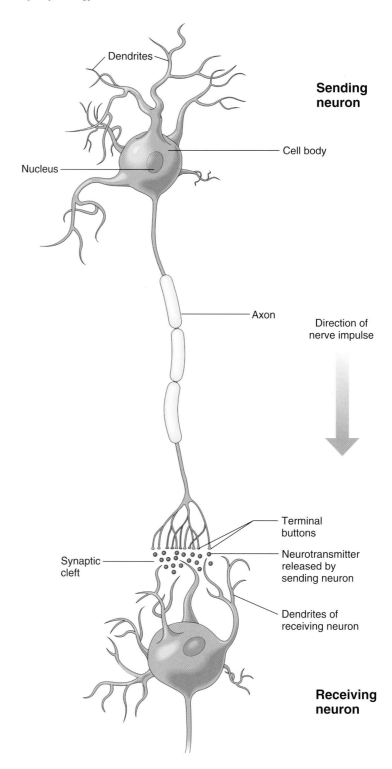

Dendrites

Sending neuron

Cell body

Nucleus

Axon

Direction of nerve impulse

Terminal buttons

Neurotransmitter released by sending neuron

Synaptic cleft

Dendrites of receiving neuron

Receiving neuron

Somatic nervous system Connects the CNS with the sensory organs and skeletal muscles.

Autonomic nervous system (ANS) Connects the CNS with the body's internal organs.

PNS has two parts—the **somatic nervous system** and the **autonomic nervous system**. The somatic system connects the central nervous system (CNS) with the sensory organs and skeletal muscles, carrying information and commands back and forth. Thus, the somatic system controls most voluntary actions, such as bringing visual information to the brain that one is about to walk into chair, and sending the command back to the muscles to stop walking and sit down.

The **autonomic nervous system (ANS)**, by contrast, is a network of nerves controlling the body's internal organs, which are generally not under voluntary control. The functioning of the heart, lungs, glands, and smooth muscles are all regulated by autonomic nerves. The ANS is in turn divided into two parts, the **sympathetic division** and the **parasympathetic division**. The sympathetic branch of the ANS consists of nerves that help the body respond to emergencies by increasing energy, arousal, and activity. When the sympathetic nerves are activated, adrenaline is released into the bloodstream, the heart rate and respiration increase, and a person experiences the subjective signs of anxiety and arousal—the "fight or flight" response. Accordingly, the sympathetic nervous system is especially relevant to the understanding of anxiety and stress-related disorders (Chapter 5). The parasympathetic division of the ANS has the opposite function, that of calming and relaxing the body and conserving energy. Parasympathetic nerves slow down respiration, heart rate, and other autonomic functions.

The Endocrine System

In addition to the nervous system, biological researchers have examined the role of the **endocrine system** in abnormal behavior. Endocrine glands release **hormones,** chemicals that play an important role in the regulation of sexual behavior, metabolism, emotion, physical maturation, and growth. Hormonal deficiencies or imbalances can cause a variety of symptoms similar to those seen in mood, anxiety, eating, and some personality disorders. For example, some hormones, such as *adrenaline* and *cortisol,* stimulate greater energy and activity, helping people to deal with situations of psychological and physical stress and danger. However, an excess of these hormones can result in aggressive and abusive behavior, like that of a person abusing anabolic steroids (Chapter 9). Abnormal levels of cortisol have also been associated with certain mood and anxiety disorders.

Genetics

The other major focus of biological explanations of mental disorders involves genetics and evolution. Just as many physical diseases are either partially or completely genetic in origin, biological researchers are learning that many mental disorders have a genetic component. It has been established that some mental disorders (including bipolar disorder, mental retardation, and schizophrenia) have a partially genetic basis (Cadoret et al., 1995; Gershon & Nurnberger, 1995; Gottesman, 1991; Kendler & Diehle, 1993; Winokur et al., 1995), although efforts to isolate the location of the particular genetic flaws (on one of the 23 pairs of chromosomes) or to specify precisely how they might contribute to the development of the disorder (for example, by impairing neurotransmission) are still in their elementary stages. One complication is that genetically influenced mental disorders appear to be polygenic (involving multiple genes) rather than related to a single gene. The *Human Genome Project,* which began in the 1980s and completed the initial sequencing of the human genome in 2001, will undoubtedly further our understanding of the genetic contribution to mental disorders (Marteau & Lerman, 2001).

Biological researchers use several strategies to determine whether genes contribute to mental disorders—the same strategies that are used to examine the genetic basis of any trait or disease. They begin with **family pedigree studies** to see whether the disorder runs in families, as genetic diseases and traits obviously do. However, even if a disorder is found to run in families, this by itself does not indicate that it has a genetic basis, since genetic similarity is confounded (mixed together) with *environmental* similarity (living in the same psychological, social, and biological environment) in families. As a result, researchers turn to two other strategies to separate genetic from environmental influences.

Sympathetic division Network of nerves within the ANS that regulate the body's response to emergency and arousal situations.

Parasympathetic division Network of nerves within the ANS that regulate the body's calming and energy-conserving functions.

Endocrine system The system of glands that controls the production and release of hormones.

Hormones Chemicals released by the endocrine system that regulate sexual behavior, metabolism, and physical growth.

Family pedigree studies Studies designed to investigate whether a disorder runs in families.

Identical twins Twin studies are one of the most important strategies for determining the role of genetics in the development of mental disorders.

Twin studies Studies designed to compare concordance rates for a given disorder between identical versus non-identical twins.

Concordance Situation in which two twins both have the same disorder.

Concordance rate In a group of twins, the percentage that both have the same disorder.

Adoption studies Studies designed to compare the concordance rates for a given disorder of biological versus nonbiological parent-child pairs.

Genetic linkage Studies looking for the specific genetic material that may be responsible for the genetic influence on particular disorders.

Natural selection The evolutionary theory and process by which organisms, over generations, tend to change and develop traits and behaviors that enhance survival and reproduction.

The first strategy is **twin studies**. In twin studies, the **concordance** (both twins having the same disorder or trait) **rates** of *monozygotic* (MZ), or identical, twins are compared to the concordance rates for *dizygotic* (DZ), or fraternal twins. Since MZ twins are genetic carbon copies, having 100% of their genes in common, compared to DZ twins, who have on average 50% of their genes in common (like ordinary siblings), MZ twins should show significantly higher concordance rates for genetically influenced disorders. For example, in looking at approximately 200 pairs of twins, McGuffin and colleagues (1996) found a concordance rate for depression of 46% for monozygotic (MZ) twins compared to a concordance rate of 20% for dizygotic (DZ) twins (Hyman & Moldin, 2001). Even though environmental confounds (for example, identical [MZ] twins are treated more similarly than nonidentical [DZ] twins) could account for some of this difference, these data do suggest a genetic role in depression. However, it is clearly a partial role, since if depression were entirely genetic in origin the MZ concordance rate would be 100%.

The second strategy for looking at genetic etiology involves **adoption studies**. In adoption studies, researchers try to separate genetic from environmental causes by studying the biological families of adopted children with mental illness or by studying the adopted-out children of parents with mental illnesses. Here, too, environmental confounds can creep in because the *prenatal* environment, and the family environment up until the adoption, are still shared between the child and the biological parent. Nonetheless, significantly elevated concordance rates of a mental disorder between adoptees and their biological families provide evidence of a genetic contribution to the disorder. Once it has been established that a disorder is genetically influenced, researchers begin to hunt for the specific genes involved. **Genetic linkage** studies analyze genetic material from families with high rates of a disorder to identify genetic discrepancies between family members with and without the disorder.

A second interesting area of research on the relationship between heredity and psychopathology involves the relatively new field of *evolutionary psychology*. Evolutionary psychologists examine human behavior, including abnormal behavior, through the lens of **natural selection**—the process by which organisms, over countless generations, tend to develop behaviors that enhance their ability to survive and reproduce. When looked at this way, many behaviors that might at first seem maladaptive or abnormal can be seen as having evolved for a useful purpose. In physical illnesses, for example, fever is usually regarded as an annoying symptom that should be reduced with medicine. But some evidence suggests that fever is an evolved mechanism for killing off pathogens by heating the blood; thus, the fever is not a part of the disorder but a part of a self-healing process (Hart, 1988). Similarly, some theorists (for example, Nesse, 1998) argue that mental disorders, like depression, may have evolved because they actually serve a useful purpose—depression, for instance, may be useful for causing one to stop and rethink an unproductive life strategy. If this is so, then rushing to alleviate the symptoms could be counterproductive. In this sense, the evolutionary perspective can have the radical implication that what we think of as disorders may actually be useful behaviors, which should be left alone rather than treated. Partly because of these radical implications, evolutionary approaches to explaining psychopathology are controversial, but they certainly have a place in explaining some disorders (for example, see Chapter 5 on the "prepared" conditioning theory, which argues that naturally evolved fears of archaic dangers such as darkness and open spaces play a role in the development of phobias).

Biological Treatment Interventions

Biological treatments for mental illness have a long and varied history, as we have already seen (Chapter 2). Some biological treatments thought at one time to be helpful (for example, **prefrontal lobotomy**, the surgical destruction of brain tissue connecting the prefrontal lobes with other areas of the brain, and **insulin coma** therapy, the practice of inducing seizures and coma by reducing patients' blood sugar with insulin) have now been discredited as harmful and even barbaric (Valenstein, 1986). Psychosurgery of any type is now rare and considered experimental, but induced seizures still have a role in the treatment of severe depression through **electroconvulsive therapy** (ECT; Chapter 6). ECT involves briefly passing an electric current through the brain, usually in a series of treatments over a period of weeks. Despite evidence of its high rate of effectiveness in treating severe depression, ECT is controversial because of concerns about its effects on memory and the fact that the mechanism by which it works remains unclear (Wilkinson, 1993).

For the most part, biological treatment of mental disorders today involves the use of **psychotropic** (mind-affecting) medications, and there are many medications available that target specific disorders such as depression, anxiety, and schizophrenia. The four major classes of psychotropic medications are *antianxiety* (or anxiolytic), *antidepressant, antipsychotic,* and *mood-stabilizing* drugs. These medications generally treat disorders by targeting their associated neurotransmitter systems, either increasing or decreasing the amount of neurotransmission. Drugs that increase neurotransmission are called drug **agonists**. Drug **antagonists** reduce neurotransmission by impeding synthesis of neurotransmitters or by blocking postsynaptic receptors. We will discuss each of these biological treatments in detail in subsequent chapters on specific disorders.

Prefrontal lobotomy The surgical destruction of certain brain tissue as a treatment for a mental disorder.

Insulin coma The deliberate induction of a seizure and coma using insulin; formerly used to treat certain mental disorders.

Electroconvulsive therapy The deliberate induction of a seizure by passing electrical current through the brain; currently used to treat severe depression in some circumstances.

Psychotropic Medications designed to affect mental functioning.

Agonists Drugs that increase neurotransmission.

Antagonists Drugs that reduce or block neurotransmission.

Case Illustration **Explaining Dave's symptoms using the biological perspective is very different from what we have considered thus far. All of the other perspectives have focused on psychological and social forces, while the biological approach looks at Dave's genetic, physical, and biochemical makeup. Biological theorists, for example, would be particularly interested in Dave's family medical and psychiatric history. Since Dave's brother and mother also have a history of anxiety problems, they would suspect that Dave's anxiety might have a genetic basis. (Of course, a family history of anxiety would not prove that it has a genetic cause, since it could also be caused by environmental factors.) Biological theorists would certainly be interested in Dave's neurochemical and hormonal functioning—in particular whether the neurotransmitters known to be associated with anxiety disorders, such as GABA and norepinephrine, are functioning normally. Finally, they would be very interested in Dave's minor heart condition. Heart palpitations and shortness of breath from this condition could be contributing to Dave's anxiety, particularly if he is cognitively misinterpreting them as signs of a more serious disorder. In summary, any or all of these biological factors could be contributing causes of Dave's anxiety.**

Brief Summary

- Sociocultural perspectives focus on the role of social pressures (such as advertising), social stressors (such as poverty), and cultural institutions (such as the prison system) in causing abnormal behavior. As a result, sociocultural theorists emphasize social change as the most effective solution to many mental health problems.

- Family systems perspectives emphasize maladaptive family dynamics as a major cause of psychopathology. When an individual develops emotional problems, family theorists use systems theories to explain the individual's difficulties in terms of a problem within the overall family system. Family therapists typically meet with the entire family in an effort to readjust the family dynamics so as to relieve the pathological pressures on the symptomatic member of the family.

- Biological perspectives on psychopathology focus on abnormal physical structures or abnormal biochemical functioning of the body, especially the brain. Bio-

Psychotic Out of contact with reality, such as experiencing hallucinations or delusions.

Delusions Fixed, false, and often bizarre beliefs.

Hallucinations Abnormal sensory experiences, such as hearing or seeing nonexistent things.

logical causes of these abnormalities include both genetic influences and environmental factors, such as diseases and injuries. Biological treatment approaches include any intervention of a physical nature, but usually involve medications that directly affect brain functions (especially neurotransmission).

Critical Thinking Question | **Thinking about the case of Dave, can you develop an explanation of his anxiety symptoms that combines sociocultural, family systems, and biological principles?**

In closing this chapter on explaining mental disorders, let's look at another clinical case example that can help us to review the central concepts.

Case Vignette | **Explanation and Treatment**

Marcus, a 13-year-old seventh grader in Texas, was admitted to a hospital for tests after his pediatrician could not find an explanation for a puzzling collection of symptoms he had been experiencing for several weeks. Marcus had been frequently complaining of not feeling well physically. He was exhausted much of the time and occasionally appeared to be mentally foggy and confused. His parents noticed that he seemed very anxious. When these symptoms did not clear up over time, Marcus's pediatrician suggested a brief hospitalization for a full diagnostic workup.

While in the hospital, Marcus's behavior became increasingly strange. He was often found pacing nervously in his room, talking to himself. He kept telling the doctors that he was dying, but he could not explain his concerns coherently. As a result, his doctors called in the hospital's pediatric psychologist, Dr. Robinson, to consult on the case. After being briefed, she first arranged to meet with Marcus's parents to learn about his medical and psychosocial history. They told Dr. Robinson that Marcus had never had any significant medical problems as a child, but that he had suffered from some emotional difficulties. They described Marcus, the youngest of their five children, as having always been quite shy and fearful, which they had attributed to his insecurity over being very small for his age and surrounded by older siblings. They had never been concerned about his fearfulness until recently. But during the past year, as Marcus had started going through puberty, he had become even more anxious, needing constant reassurance from them that the changes in his body were normal. He worried, for example, that he was too small, that his voice was too high, and that he was developing too slowly. Marcus's parents also revealed that, to their surprise, he had even spoken to them about his worries about masturbation. They told Dr. Robinson that they were a devoutly religious family and Marcus had been taught that masturbation was a

sin. He had come to them in tears, terrified that he would go to Hell since he had started masturbating. It was in the midst of all this that Marcus had started complaining about not feeling well, leading to his current medical situation.

Dr. Robinson then went to speak with Marcus. She found him pacing nervously in his room, and very eager to talk to her. In fact, Marcus practically pulled her into his room, shut the door, and pleaded with her to help him. Marcus then began to tell Dr. Robinson a bizarre story. He explained that since he had begun masturbating a few months ago, he had discovered that his penis was gradually shrinking. He knew that this was a punishment from God and he was certain that his penis would not only soon disappear, but that he would die as a result. Dr. Robinson could tell from the terror in Marcus's eyes that he believed every word of this. He also said that he had been hearing the voice of God condemning him, and hearing everyone in the hospital talking about him and his punishment from God.

Dr. Robinson knew immediately that Marcus was **psychotic**—a clinical term which refers to the condition of being out of touch with reality, usually in the form of **delusions** (false, bizarre beliefs) and **hallucinations** (aberrant sensory perceptions). Marcus clearly had both. Dr. Robinson began to think about Marcus's overall situation—the lifelong preoccupation with his physical inadequacy; the recent crisis with puberty; the current unexplained symptoms of tiredness, confusion, and now psychosis. As she headed toward her meeting with the medical team following her strange interview with Marcus, Dr. Robinson began considering whether Marcus's entire symptom picture might be due to a mental illness and psychological factors rather than to a medical condition. In particular she wondered to herself whether Marcus was suffering from an early adolescent onset of schizophrenia, the mental disorder most often associated with psychosis (Chapter 12).

Fortunately, before deciding on this diagnosis, Dr. Robinson checked with the medical team to see if any new test results had come in. Sure enough, the results of a spinal tap conducted days earlier had just arrived—and they indicated that Marcus was suffering from viral encephalitis (an infectious inflammation of the brain). Encephalitis, like general paresis and other infections that reach the brain, can cause psychosis, as well as all of the other symptoms that Marcus had been experiencing. So the diagnosis was not schizophrenia after all, but acute encephalitis. Marcus was treated with antiviral medications, and his psychosis cleared up quickly. However, emotionally he remained as he had been before the infection—anxious, guilty, and conflicted about his identity, his body, and his emerging sexuality. As a result, Dr. Robinson continued to work with Marcus and his family in therapy to help him overcome his emotional problems.

Case Discussion

The case of Marcus can help us summarize this chapter by reviewing two of the core concepts surrounding explanations of psychopathology: the principle of *multiple causality* and the *connection between mind and body*. Clearly, one has to include both biological *and* psychological perspectives in order to understand Marcus's symptoms. In his case, the major cause of his symptoms was biological—the encephalitis. But Marcus's psychological makeup was responsible for the way these symptoms appeared. For example, it was Marcus's preexisting preoccupation with his physical inadequacies and the belief he had committed sexual sins that determined the *content* of his delusions, such as the idea that his penis was disappearing.

At several points in the case, Marcus's doctors could have taken a *reductionistic* approach, but fortunately they did not. For example, Marcus's pediatrician suggested the medical workup, suspecting a biological cause, but he also encouraged the psychological consultation with Dr. Robinson. Dr. Robinson had almost decided that the symptoms reflected a mental disorder, but she waited to see the medical test results. The hospital team initiated antiviral treatment, but they also recommended psychotherapy to help Marcus and his family address his emotional problems. In short, these professionals were able to embrace *the principle of multiple causality* and avoid the problem of *reductionism* by seeing Marcus as a whole person rather than reducing his symptoms to a single cause. In addition, the case highlights the *connection between mind and body* in that Marcus' complex symptoms were caused by both biological and psychological factors.

Having discussed the many important issues surrounding explanations and treatments of psychopathology, we now turn to our last introductory topic: how is psychopathology *classified?* In Chapter 4, we will look at the many different ways that mental disorders can be categorized, as well as at the core concepts that affect these classifications.

Chapter Summary

- In explaining abnormality, three core concepts are especially relevant: *cultural and historical relativism*; the *connection between mind and body*; and the *principle of multiple causality*.

- Because explanations of abnormal behavior vary so widely across time and place, we must be mindful that any explanation is relative to its *cultural and historical* context.

- Despite the common view that abnormal behavior has either biological or psychological causes, these two realms are, in fact, mutually influencing and interdependent, in keeping with the core concept of *the connection between mind and body.*

- The various theoretical perspectives in abnormal psychology overlap in some respects. For example, the psychological perspectives all emphasize the importance of the therapeutic relationship in treatment. In other respects, the perspectives diverge and emphasize different causal processes. Each perspective has something to contribute, and even when they diverge they often complement each other by addressing different aspects of the *multiple causes* of abnormal behavior.

Gabriele Münter, *Sinnende,* 1917. Courtesy Städtische
Galerie im Lenbachhaus, Munich

Gabriele Münter (1877-1962), a German
Expressionist painter who counted Franz Marc
and Wassily Kandinsky among her colleagues,
emphasized simplified shapes and darkly outlined colors in her works. The title of *Sinnende*
meaning meditation (1917) suggests that the
woman in the painting ...*continues on page 74*

gabriele münter

chapter four

CLASSIFYING ABNORMALITY
DIAGNOSIS AND ASSESSMENT

In Chapter 2, we examined the question of how to *define* abnormal behavior and distinguish it from normal behavior. In Chapter 3, we reviewed different ways of *explaining* and *treating* abnormal behavior. In this chapter, we focus on how abnormal behavior can be categorized and *classified*. The different categories of psychopathology, like the different categories of medical diseases, are technically known as **diagnoses**. The word diagnosis is derived from the Greek roots *dia,* meaning "apart," and *gnosis,* meaning, "to know." Thus, to diagnose is to distinguish different *syndromes*—clusters of symptoms that form a distinctive pattern and follow a particular course over time—from each other. The process of gathering information about a client in order to make a diagnosis is technically known as **assessment**. We will discuss both diagnosis and assessment in this chapter, and we will see that classifying abnormality is as complex and interesting as defining, explaining, and treating it.

THE ADVANTAGES AND LIMITATIONS OF DIAGNOSIS

We begin with a question: Why should we want to categorize and classify different forms of abnormal behavior? The answer may seem obvious, and for most professionals in this field the advantages of having a classification system are clear-cut. But there are actually many sides to this complex issue, as suggested by the core concept of the ***advantages and limitations of diagnosis.*** Let's begin with the advantages. These include:

1. Classification allows clinicians, researchers, and teachers to communicate more effectively about their work.
2. Classification facilitates research on the causes of disorders.
3. Classification facilitates decisions about which treatments are most likely to be helpful for particular disorders.

In this sense, the arguments in favor of having a classification system for psychopathology are very similar to the arguments in favor of any scientific classification system, especially those in the field of medicine. However, a classification or diagnostic system (sometimes referred to as a *taxonomy*) is only useful when the categories in the diagnostic system consistently and accurately fit the phenomena being classified. It wouldn't be of much use, for example, to use the categories "black" and "white" to classify the colors of the rainbow. As it turns out, the professions that deal with mental disorders (see Box 4.1) have struggled for decades to come up with diag-

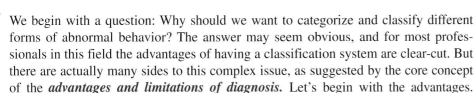

- **The Advantages and Limitations of Diagnosis**
  - Reliability
  - Validity
- **The History of Diagnostic Systems for Psychopathology**
  - The DSM-III Revolution and Controversy
  - Advantages of the Modern DSM Approach
  - Limitations of the Modern DSM Approach
- **Using the DSM-IV-TR: Making a Multiaxial Diagnosis**
  - Axis I and Axis II
  - Axes III, IV, and V
  - A Complete DSM-IV-TR Diagnosis
- **Assessment**
  - Interviews
  - Tests
  - Behavioral Observation
- **Diagnosis and Assessment in Perspective: Classifying and Understanding Dave**
  - Interview with Dave
  - Dave's Test Results
  - Behavioral Observations of Dave
- **The Advantages and Limitations of the Diagnosis of Dave**

Diagnoses Categories of disorders or diseases according to a classification system.

Assessment The process of gathering information in order to make a diagnosis.

BOX 4.1 Clinical Degrees and Disciplines

The Major Professions in the Field of Psychopathology

TITLE	DEGREES	ACADEMIC DISCIPLINE
Clinical Psychologist	M.A., Ph.D., or Psy.D	Psychology
Psychiatrist	M.D.	Medicine
	D.O.	Osteopathic Medicine
Clinical Social Worker	M.S.W (Master's)	Social Work
	D.S.W. (Doctorate)	
Psychiatric Nurse	R.N.	Nursing

Professionals with different degrees from several different disciplines work in the field of psychopathology. Indeed, there is considerable overlap in the activities of these professions, and the boundaries between them are in flux. For example, *clinical psychologists* in many states are currently seeking the right, with proper training, to prescribe medications for treating mental disorders, an area that has traditionally been the province of *psychiatrists*. Similarly, clinicians from any mental health discipline may now seek advanced training to become *psychoanalysts*—practitioners of psychoanalysis, the most intensive form of psychodynamic therapy (Chapter 3)—whereas this also used to be limited, in the United States, primarily to psychiatrists. Despite the overlap among them, each profession has its own code of ethics covering the appropriate scope and standards of practice for its members. In addition to these ethical guidelines, state and federal governments regulate these professions to some extent.

...continued from page 72

is deep in thought, yet the look on her face is hard to interpret. Is she pleased, sad, calm, or tense? In this chapter we turn our attention to questions of assessment and diagnosis. How do mental health professionals evaluate, describe, and classify psychopathology?

DSM The Diagnostic and Statistical Manual of Mental Disorders published by the American Psychiatric Association, currently in its 4th revised edition (DSM-IV-TR).

Reliability The consistency of a test, measurement, or category system.

nostic systems that are reasonably consistent and accurate. While this might seem surprising at first, think about the cases of Dave and Marcus discussed in Chapters 2 and 3. Both of them have complex emotional problems that in many respects are as unique as their personalities, although we would also expect that some aspects of their problems might well overlap with problems experienced by other people.

Indeed, a vigorous debate exists about the best way to classify psychopathology—and even over whether the disadvantages of classification outweigh the advantages. Some critics (most notably Thomas Szasz and theorists from the humanistic perspective) argue that attempts to categorize psychopathology actually do more harm than good because no diagnostic system can do justice to the uniqueness of individuals' emotional problems. Furthermore, such systems have the potential to dehumanize people with oversimplified and stigmatizing "labels" (Kramer & Buck, 1997; Szasz, 1960, 1975; Winthrop, 1964). Yet the mainstream opinion is that diagnostic classification of abnormal behavior is possible and useful, despite continuing debate over which diagnostic system works best.

One particular diagnostic system, developed over many decades by the American Psychiatric Association, has become the standard classification system for psychopathology; we will focus on explaining how it works. This system is usually referred to as the **"DSM"** system, because DSM is the abbreviation for the name of the manual (*The Diagnostic and Statistical Manual of Mental Disorders;* APA, 2000) which describes the system and how to use it. But before we discuss the DSM system, we must first consider more fully how to evaluate whether a diagnostic system is useful. This is done by examining two criteria that tell us how well the diagnostic system's categories "fit" the disorders being classified. These criteria are **reliability**, which assesses the *consistency* of the diagnostic categories, and **validity**, which assesses the *accuracy* of the diagnostic categories.

Validity The accuracy of a test, measurement, or category system.

Reliability

In order for any classification system to be useful, it must have reasonably good **reliability**—a statistical term referring to the stability and consistency of categorization decisions based on the system. For example, when a child is taken to a pediatrician with a sore throat, fever, and rash, the child may well be given a "strep" test (a swab in the throat to test for the presence of *Streptococcus* bacteria) in order to classify the child as "positive" for strep or "negative" for strep. Unless this test gives relatively consistent results—for example, a child given two consecutive tests should get the same result—it isn't very useful. Keep in mind that we are not yet concerned with the question of whether the strep test *accurately* detects strep throat; that is a question of validity. For the moment, we are only concerned that the test gives relatively *consistent* results, because if it doesn't, then the accuracy of the test hardly matters because the stability of the results cannot be trusted.

As you might guess, it is much harder to reliably diagnose mental disorders than to reliably diagnose strep throat, partly because there are no objective biological markers of most mental disorders. The diagnosis of mental disorders usually rests on the judgment of a clinical interviewer, sometimes in conjunction with the results of various diagnostic questionnaires (described in the Assessment section later in the chapter). The crucial question is whether the interviewers and questionnaires are *consistent* in their classification decisions. This consistency can be measured in different ways. The two most common ways are **interjudge** (or interrater) **reliability**, which refers to the agreement between two or more different interviewers or raters, and **test-retest reliability**, which refers to results produced by a test given more than once. To illustrate, let's consider the case of a patient with the eating disorder known as anorexia nervosa (Chapter 8). This patient receives a diagnostic interview from two different psychologists who are not aware of her diagnosis beforehand, and she is given a diagnostic questionnaire about anorexia to fill out twice with a one-day interval in between. If both psychologists independently come to the same diagnostic conclusion—regardless of whether they are correct—this is evidence for the *interjudge reliability* of the diagnostic interview for anorexia. If both questionnaire results are consistent—again, regardless of accuracy—then this is evidence for the *test-retest reliability* of the anorexia questionnaire (see Table 4.1). Reliability is typically studied

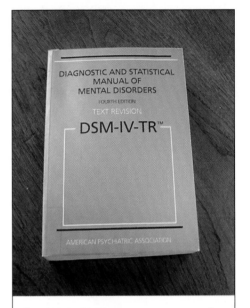

The DSM-IV-TR This diagnostic manual, published by the American Psychiatric Association, currently dominates diagnostic practice in the United States and many other countries despite some controversy about its utility.

Interjudge reliability Consistency or agreement between multiple interviewers or raters.

Test-retest reliability Consistency or agreement between multiple administrations of the same test.

Reliability		Table 4.1
Interjudge reliability		
Client has interview with Clinician 1	Diagnosis:	anorexia
Same client has interview with Clinician 2	Diagnosis:	anorexia
Diagnostic interview is reliable.		
Test-retest reliability		
Client given diagnostic anorexia test time 1	Result:	anorexia
Same client given same anorexia test time 2 (one day later)	Result:	no anorexia
Diagnostic test is not reliable.		

Reliability Judges' disagreements in categorization decisions are technically known as problems of reliability.

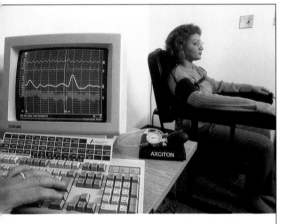

Validity of lie detector tests The validity, or accuracy, of lie detector tests is questionable enough that many jurisdictions forbid their use as evidence in court.

with large groups of patients and measured numerically by looking at the statistical **correlation** between judges or between test and retest results. The higher the correlation, the greater the reliability.

Validity

Once it has been established that a diagnostic category or test is reliable, then we can consider our other important question—is the category or test also *accurate?* (see Table 4.2). Keep in mind that strep tests and psychologists could be consistent but wrong, in which case they would be reliable but not valid. In fact, there are many examples of tests that are highly reliable but have questionable validity (Kaplan & Saccuzzio, 1993). IQ tests are perhaps the most notorious example; the consistency (reliability) of their results is rarely disputed, but many experts question whether they truly measure intelligence, as opposed to measuring something else like cultural competence and test-taking ability (Gould, 1981/1993; Suzuki & Valencia, 1997). Lie detector tests, similarly, have reasonably good reliability but generally weak validity, which is why they are not admissible as evidence in many legal proceedings (Brooks, 1985; Iancono & Patrick, 1997; Saxe & Ben-Shakhar, 1999).

Obviously, the goal of a diagnostic system is to have good reliability *and* good validity. We want the two psychologists and the two anorexia questionnaires not only to agree with each other but to be accurate as well. Unfortunately, when dealing with a subject matter as complex, multifaceted, and ambiguous as human behavior, it is not easy to achieve good reliability and validity at the same time. In fact, there can be a trade-off between reliability and validity when it comes to classifying abnormal behavior; in order to *increase* reliability, diagnoses must be simplified, which can *decrease* validity through oversimplification (Barron, 1998; McHugh, 1999; Wakefield, 1992). For example, let's imagine that researchers are trying to improve the reliability of the diagnostic category we referred to previously: anorexia. To do so, they might decide to be very specific about what qualifies as anorexia, so that different interviewers can agree on the diagnosis. This is just what the authors of the DSM have done, so that one of the current criteria for the diagnosis of anorexia is a body weight of 15% or more below the normal weight for a given person. But in defining anorexia so precisely, validity could be compromised if, for example, the actual phenomenon of anorexia includes people who are only 5% or 10% below normal body weight but still have other characteristics of the disorder. Since many, perhaps even most, of the people who seek mental health treatment fall into this "gray area" in which they have some but not all of the symptoms of a mental disorder (a situation sometimes referred to as a *forme fruste,* or incomplete expression of a disorder), this is a real practical consideration for clinicians (Eaton et al., 1989; Kramer, 1993; Ratey & Johnson, 1997).

Table 4.2	Validity	
Client's actual disorder:	anorexia	
Client's anorexia diagnostic test result:	anorexia	
Test is valid.		
Subject's actual behavior:	lying	
Subject's lie detector test result:	truthful	
Test is not valid.		

As you can probably tell, some of the challenges of developing a reliable and valid classification system for abnormal behavior relate to the core concept of the *continuum between normal and abnormal behavior*. In fact, some psychologists argue that abnormal behavior would be better classified by a **dimensional system** (that is, one that asks *to what degree* a person exhibits characteristics of a disorder on a continuum) rather than by the DSM's **categorical approach** (which asks *whether or not* a person has a specific disorder, and therefore has to establish a somewhat arbitrary cut-off for saying yes or no) (Nathan & Lagenbucher, 1999; Oldham & Skodol, 2000; Widiger, 1993; Widiger & Trull, 1991). In any case, the trade-off between reliability, which improves with more concrete, precise, and descriptive criteria, and validity, which improves with more complex and nuanced criteria, is one of the major challenges to researchers interested in improving diagnostic systems for psychopathology.

Dimensional system A diagnostic system in which individuals are rated for the degree to which they exhibit traits along certain dimensions.

Categorical approach A diagnostic system, like the DSM system, in which individuals are diagnosed according to whether or not they fit certain defined categories.

THE HISTORY OF DIAGNOSTIC SYSTEMS FOR PSYCHOPATHOLOGY

Numerous attempts have been made throughout history to classify abnormal behavior using some kind of diagnostic category system. In general, such attempts have progressed from systems that listed only a few different syndromes to much more detailed contemporary systems, such as the DSM-IV-TR, listing hundreds of different disorders.

One of the first modern diagnostic systems for abnormal behavior was developed by the famous French psychiatrist Philippe Pinel (1745–1826). Pinel is best known for his work to humanize and liberalize the treatment of psychiatric patients in French hospitals; his "moral treatment" movement was one of the humanitarian reforms in psychiatry during the late 18th and 19th centuries (see Box 3.1). Pinel also developed a diagnostic system consisting of four different types of mental abnormality: melancholia (depression), mania (extreme excitability), idiocy (mental retardation), and dementia (mental confusion) (Pinel, 1802/1803; Riese, 1969). Nearly a century later, the German physician Emil Kraepelin (1856–1926), often referred to as the father of modern psychiatric diagnosis, proposed a diagnostic system including 13 disorders

Philippe Pinel Pinel orders the chains removed from an asylum patient as part of his reform movement. Pinel's "moral treatment" movement was one of the great humanitarian reforms in the history of mental health care.

based on his extensive studies of hundreds of case histories of hospitalized patients (Berrios & Hauser, 1988; Jablensky, 1995; Kraepelin, 1899, 1904).

We can trace the development of increasingly complex diagnostic systems in the United States by examining census questionnaires, which used to include questions about mental illness. In the 1840 census, only one category of mental illness was identified: "idiocy/insanity." By the 1880 census, seven categories were identified: mania, melancholia, dementia, monomania (obsession with a single idea), paresis (Chapter 2), dipsomania (alcoholism), and epilepsy (at that time considered a psychiatric disorder) (American Psychiatric Association, 1994).

In the 20th century, the proliferation of diagnostic categories escalated, as interest in and research on mental illness increased. In 1952, the American Psychiatric Association (APA) published the first edition of the DSM. The DSM-I was a refinement of the psychiatric section of a medical diagnostic system developed by the World Health Organization (WHO) known as the International Classification of Diseases (ICD). The ICD at that time listed 26 mental disorders; the DSM-I, expanding on these categories, listed 108. Each subsequent edition of the DSM has included a larger number of diagnostic categories. The DSM-II (published in 1968) listed 182 disorders, the DSM-III (1980) included 265, and the DSM-IV-TR (2000), the current edition, has almost 300 separate disorders.

This ever-increasing number of officially identified mental disorders reflects, in part, our vastly increased knowledge about psychopathology, which allows us to differentiate distinct syndromes of psychological symptoms. However, some critics have argued that the proliferation of new diagnoses reflects the "invention" rather than the "discovery" of new disorders (Follette & Houts, 1996; Rothblum, Solomon, & Albee, 1986). For example, the DSM-IV-TR includes a category called "attention-deficit/hyperactivity disorder" (Chapter 13) which applies to children who are particularly impulsive and inattentive. Critics contend that such behavior is normal in many children, but it is now being pathologized as the mental health profession creates diagnostic categories which encroach on territory that has traditionally been considered within the bounds of normality (McHugh, 1999; Searight & McLaren, 1998). Box 4.2 discusses this controversy.

Brief Summary

- To diagnose means to identify different syndromes according to a classification system, or taxonomy.

- Assessment is the process of gathering information about a client in order to make a diagnosis.

- In order to be useful, diagnostic classification systems must have two statistical properties: reliability and validity. Reliability refers to the consistency of classification decisions. Validity refers to the accuracy of classification decisions.

- Diagnostic classification systems for psychopathology have grown increasingly detailed over time. The current official system in the United States, the DSM system, currently lists over 300 separate disorders in the DSM-IV-TR.

Critical Thinking Question | **Why do you think it has been so difficult to develop reliable and valid diagnostic systems in the field of abnormal psychology?**

The DSM-III Revolution and Controversy

The history of diagnostic systems described above may give the impression of a smooth progression toward more complete and comprehensive systems as researchers

BOX 4.2   Too Many Diagnoses?

A Critic Looks at the Pathologizing of Everyday Life

In December 1999, *Commentary* magazine published an article by Paul R. McHugh, M.D., the psychiatrist-in-chief at the Johns Hopkins Hospital in Baltimore and an influential writer about issues in psychiatry. The article, titled "How Psychiatry Lost Its Way," was a scathing attack on the DSM-IV. Coming from someone so prominent and sympathetic to contemporary biological psychiatry, the article stirred considerable controversy. McHugh's criticisms of the DSM-IV and how it has been used will remind you of many of the issues discussed in this chapter. Here is an excerpt from McHugh's article (pp. 32–33).

With help from the popular media, home-brewed psychiatric diagnoses have proliferated in recent years, preoccupying the worried imaginations of the American public. Restless, impatient people are convinced that they have attention deficit disorder (ADD); anxious, vigilant people that they suffer from post-traumatic stress disorder (PTSD); stubborn, orderly, perfectionistic people that they are afflicted with obsessive-compulsive disorder (OCD); shy, sensitive people that they manifest avoidant personality disorder (APD), or social phobia. All have been persuaded that what are really matters of their individuality are, instead, medical problems, and as such are to be solved with drugs. Those drugs will relieve the features of temperament that are burdensome, replacing them with features that please. The motto of this movement (with apologies to the DuPont corporation) might be: better living through pharmacology.

And—most worrisome of all—wherever they look, such people find psychiatrists willing, even eager, to accommodate them. Worse: in many cases, it is psychiatrists who are leading the charge. But the exact role of the psychiatric profession in our current proliferation of disorders and in the thoughtless prescription of medication for them is no simple tale to tell.

When it comes to diagnosing mental disorders, psychiatry has undergone a sea change over the last two decades. The stages of that change can be traced in successive editions of the *Diagnostic and Statistical Manual of Mental Disorders* (DSM), the official tome of American psychiatry published and promoted by the American Psychiatric Association (APA). But historically its impetus derives—inadertently—from a salutary effort begun in the early 1970's at the medical school of Washington University in St. Louis to redress the dearth of research in American psychiatry.

The St. Louis scholars were looking into a limited number of well-established disorders. Among them was schizophrenia, an affliction that can manifest itself in diverse ways. What the investigators were striving for was to isolate clear and distinct symptoms that separated indubitable cases of schizophrenia from less certain ones. By creating a set of such "research diagnostic criteria," their hope was to permit study to proceed across and among laboratories, free of the concern that erroneous conclusions might arise from the investigation of different types of patients in different medical centers.

With these criteria, the St. Louis group did not claim to have found the specific *features* of schizophrenia—a matter, scientifically speaking, of "validity." Rather, they were identifying certain markers or signs that would enable comparative study of the disease at multiple research sites—a matter of "reliability." But this very useful effort had baleful consequences when, in planning DSM-III (1980), the third edition of its *Diagnostic and Statistical Manual,* the APA picked up on the need for reliability and out of it

forged a bid for scientific validity. In both DSM-III and DSM-IV (1994), what had been developed at St. Louis as a tool of scholarly research into only a few established disorders became subtly transformed, emerging as a clinical method of diagnosis (and, presumably, treatment) of psychiatric states and conditions of all kinds, across the board. The signs and markers—the presenting symptoms—became the official guide to the identification of mental disorders, and the list of such disorders served in turn to certify their existence in categorical form.

The significance of this turn to classifying mental disorders by their appearances cannot be under-estimated. In physical medicine, doctors have long been aware that appearances, either as the identifying marks of disorder or as the targets of therapy, are untrustworthy. For one thing, it is sometimes difficult to distinguish symptoms of illness from normal variations in human life. For another, identical symptoms can be the products of totally different causal mechanisms and thus call for quite different treatments. For still another, descriptions of appearances are limitless, as limitless as the number of individuals presenting them; if medical classifications were to be built upon such descriptions, the enumerating of diseases would never end....

The new DSM approach of using experts and descriptive criteria in identifying psychiatric diseases has encouraged a productive industry. If you can describe it, you can name it; and if you can name it, then you can claim that it exists as a distinct "entity" with, eventually, a direct treatment tied to it. Proposals for new psychiatric disorders have multiplied so feverishly that the DSM itself has grown from a mere 119 pages in 1968 to 886 pages in the latest edition; a new and enlarged edition, DSM-V, is already in the planning stages. Embedded within these hundreds of pages are some categories of disorder that are real; some that are dubious, in the sense that they are more like the normal responses of sensitive people than psychiatric "entities"; and some that are purely the inventions of their proponents.

Why are psychiatrists not more like other doctors—differentiating among patients by the causes of their illnesses and offering treatments specifically linked to the mechanisms of these illnesses? One reason is that they cannot be. In contrast to cardiologists, dermatologists, ophthalmologists, and other medical practitioners, physicians who study and treat disorders of mind and behavior are unable to demonstrate how symptoms emerge directly from activity in, or changes of, the organ that generates them—namely, the brain. Indeed, many of the profession's troubles, especially the false starts and misdirections that have plagued it from the beginning, stem from the brain-mind problem, the most critical issue in the natural sciences and a fundamental obstacle to all students of consciousness.

have been able to identify additional syndromes of psychopathology. In fact, the progression has been anything but smooth. Rather, an enormous upheaval shook the field in the 1970s as the DSM-III was being developed. The reasons for this upheaval go back to our discussions of reliability and validity. Up until the 1960s, the mental health field in the United States was dominated by the psychodynamic perspective. Recall that the psychodynamic perspective focuses on the deeper, usually unconscious, roots of mental disorders, and therefore focuses on *syndromes of unconscious conflict* rather than on *syndromes of observable symptoms* in classifying disorders. As a result, the categories listed in DSM-I and DSM-II tended to rely on abstract psychodynamic concepts like the term *neurosis,* which was loosely defined as any mild to moderate mental disorder involving symptoms caused by unconscious emotional conflict. As you might guess, the reliability of the DSM-I and DSM-II systems tended to be quite poor because of the vagueness of such categories (Beck et al., 1962; Tarter, Templer, & Hardy, 1975). In addition, many researchers became frustrated with the psychodynamic concepts built into the DSM-I and DSM-II as clinicians and researchers became interested in other theoretical perspectives.

For these reasons, the APA decided to approach the DSM-III in a new way, with two primary aims in mind. First, in order to improve the reliability and validity of the diagnostic system, the APA hoped to make the diagnostic criteria (that is, the guidelines for making a particular diagnosis) in DSM-III as simple, descriptive, and clear as possible. This aim tied in with the second objective, which was to make the DSM-III diagnoses as *atheoretical* (not based on any theoretical perspective) as possible, which represented a radical change from the psychodynamic assumptions of the DSM-II. In short, the authors of the DSM-III hoped that creating a more detailed and purely descriptive diagnostic manual would produce more reliable and valid diagnoses and reduce theoretical squabbling (APA, 1994) (Table 4.3 compares DSM-II and DSM-III).

Table 4.3	**Comparing DSM-II and DSM-III**
APA, 1980	This table illustrates the revolutionary shift from DSM-II to DSM-III. The DSM-II diagnosis "Depressive neurosis" was divided into four separate diagnoses in the DSM-III in the hope that more precise and specific diagnostic categories would improve their reliability.

DSM-II CATEGORY	**DSM-III CATEGORIES**
	Major depression, single episode, without melancholia
Depressive neurosis (300.4)	Major depression, recurrent, without melancholia
	Dysthymia (minor depression)
	Adjustment disorder with depressed mood

In the DSM-III, the changes from DSM-II shown above are explained as follows:

The DSM-II category [Depressive neurosis] was defined merely as "an excessive reaction of depression due to an internal conflict or to an identifiable event...." For this reason, it was applied to a heterogeneous group of conditions. The ... major conditions to which it was applied have each been described descriptively [in DSM-III] without reference to etiology [cause].

DSM-IV-TR Criteria for Attention Deficit/Hyperactivity Disorder	Table 4.4

APA, 2000

DIAGNOSTIC CRITERIA FOR ATTENTION-DEFICIT/HYPERACTIVITY DISORDER

A. Either (1) or (2):

1. six (or more) of the following symptoms of **inattention** have persisted for at least 6 months to a degree that is maladaptive and inconsistent with developmental level:

Inattention
   a. often fails to give close attention to details or makes careless mistakes in schoolwork, work, or other activities
   b. often has difficulty sustaining attention in tasks or play activities
   c. often does not seem to listen when spoken to directly
   d. often does not follow through on instructions and fails to finish schoolwork, chores, or duties in the workplace (not due to oppositional behavior or failure to understand instructions)
   e. often has difficulty organizing tasks and activities
   f. often avoids, dislikes, or is reluctant to engage in tasks that require sustained mental effort (such as schoolwork or homework)
   g. often loses things necessary for tasks or activities (e.g., toys, school assignments, pencils, books, or tools)
   h. is often easily distracted by extraneous stimuli
   i. is often forgetful in daily activities

2. six (or more) of the following symptoms of **hyperactivity-impulsivity** have persisted for at least 6 months to a degree that is maladaptive and inconsistent with developmental level:

Hyperactivity
   a. often fidgets with hands or feet or squirms in seat
   b. often leaves seat in classroom or in other situations in which remaining seated is expected
   c. often runs about or climbs excessively in situations in which it is inappropriate (in adolescents or adults, may be limited to subjective feelings of restlessness)
   d. often has difficulty playing or engaging in leisure activities quietly
   e. is often "on the go" or often acts as if "driven by a motor"
   f. often talks excessively

Impulsivity
   g. often blurts out answers before questions have been completed
   h. often has difficulty awaiting turn
   i. often interrupts or intrudes on others (e.g., butts into conversations or games)

B. Some hyperactive-impulsive or inattentive symptoms that caused impairment were present before age 7 years.

C. Some impairment from the symptoms is present in two or more settings (e.g., at school [or work] and at home).

D. There must be clear evidence of clinically significant impairment in social, academic, or occupational functioning.

E. The symptoms do not occur exclusively during the course of a Pervasive Developmental Disorder, Schizophrenia, or other Psychotic Disorder and are not better accounted for by another mental disorder (e.g., Mood Disorder. Anxiety Disorder, Dissociative Disorder, or a Personality Disorder).

Code based on type:
   314.01 **Attention-Deficit/Hyperactivity Disorder, Combined Type:** if both Criteria A1 and A2 are met for the past 6 months
   314.00 **Attention-Deficit/Hyperactivity Disorder, Predominantly Inattentive Type:** if Criterion A1 is met but Criterion A2 is not met for the past 6 months
   314.01 **Attention-Deficit/Hyperactivity Disorder, Predominantly Hyperactive-Impulsive Type:** if Criterion A2 is met but Criterion A1 is not met for the past 6 months

Coding note: For individuals (especially adolescents and adults) who currently have symptoms that no longer meet full criteria, "In Partial Remission" should be specified.

To illustrate further, let's take a look at the criteria for the disorder mentioned earlier—attention-deficit/hyperactivity disorder—as they are listed in the DSM-IV-TR, which follows in the spirit of the DSM-III revolution (see Table 4.4). Note how detailed and specific the criteria are, with the aim of good reliability. The emphasis on detail and specificity highlights the changes brought about by the "DSM-III revolution."

Advantages of the Modern DSM Approach

Because it represented a significant change with implications for treatment, research, and training, the DSM-III was extremely controversial at the time that it was published in 1980. Although the DSM-III approach—carried forward in all subsequent editions of the DSM—has become the standard diagnostic system in the United States, it has remained controversial. Accordingly, we will review some of the achievements and advantages of this new system, followed by a discussion of the critics of the modern DSM approach and their views of its limitations. In so doing, we provide another overview of a core concept in abnormal psychology: ***the advantages and limitations of diagnosis***.

Advantage 1: Improved Reliability and Validity

The greatest advantage of the modern DSM approach has been the partial achievement of its primary goal—improved reliability and validity of diagnoses of psychopathology (Malt, 1986; Spitzer, Forman, & Nee, 1979). This is of enormous importance, since, as we have seen, diagnostic systems are useless without adequate reliability and validity, and research, treatment, and teaching in the field of abnormal psychology are facilitated by a sound diagnostic system (Malt, 1986; Spitzer, Williams, & Skodol, 1980). Even though the reliability and validity of the modern DSM system still leave much to be desired (Barron, 1998; Kirk & Kutchins, 1992; Wakefield, 1992), the new system represents a milestone as the first diagnostic system for psychopathology ever to approximate the goal of adequate reliability and validity (see Table 4.5).

Table 4.5	**Reliability of DSM-III Diagnoses**	

Adapted from DSM-III, APA 1980, pp. 470–471

This table shows the results of two phases of reliability testing for the DSM-III; the first phase involved 339 patients and the second phase 331. The *kappa coefficients*—a way of measuring reliability—reported in the table range from –.003 to 1.0. A coefficient of 1.0 represents perfect agreement or consistency; coefficients in the .60 to .70 range or better are usually considered to indicate adequate reliability. As you can see, the reliability for Axis I diagnoses is better than for Axis II, although both improved in phase two.

	KAPPA—PHASE ONE (N=339)	**KAPPA—PHASE TWO (N=331)**
Axis I		
Substance Use Disorders	.86	.82
Schizophrenic Disorders	.81	.81
Paranoid Disorders	.66	.75
Affective [Mood] Disorders	.69	.83
Anxiety Disorders	.63	.72
Overall Kappa for Axis I	*.68*	*.72*
Axis II		
Personality Disorders	.56	.65
Overall Kappa for Axis II	*.56*	*.64*

Advantage 2: Increased Emphasis on Diagnosis

A second advantage of the modern DSM approach is that it has increased clinicians' awareness of the importance of diagnosis. This increased attention to issues of classification has helped make the field of abnormal psychology more scientifically rigorous and precise (Malt, 1986). A related advantage is that the DSM provides a common language for clinicians and researchers. In this sense, the specific details of the modern DSM system may be ultimately less important than the principle it represents: that classification systems for mental disorders can and should be improved.

Limitations of the Modern DSM Approach

Despite its overwhelming acceptance, the modern DSM approach has also had many critics. A summary of their main concerns follows.

Limitation 1: Remaining Reliability and Validity Problems

Many critics focus on what they see as the DSM's failure to adequately achieve its own primary goal of achieving acceptable reliability and validity (Kirk & Kutchins, 1992, 1994). Some critics even contend that the new system has actually *decreased* the validity of diagnoses (Barron, 1998; Wakefield, 1992). As noted above, some say that the DSM has invented rather than discovered disorders, thereby inaccurately pathologizing many normal behaviors (Follette & Houts, 1996; McHugh, 1999; Rothblum et al., 1986) (see Box 4.2). Concerns about the stigma associated with the diagnosis of a mental disorder add urgency to this argument. (Being labeled with a psychiatric diagnosis can lead to discrimination and shame, which is all the more tragic if the diagnosis may not even be valid!) Others say that the new DSM system decreases validity because it classifies disorders solely based on observable, descriptive criteria. The critics contend that this has led to a superficial approach to diagnosis that overlooks complexity and the need for depth in understanding abnormal behavior (Jensen & Hoagwood, 1997).

In essence, these criticisms relate to the trade-off between reliability and validity discussed earlier; many critics see the current DSM system as having sacrificed too much validity in the pursuit of greater reliability. Their argument recalls the old joke about the drunken man searching one night for his lost keys under a lamppost. When a friend asks him if he had, in fact, dropped them there, the drunken man replies "No, I dropped them way over yonder, but this is where the light is!" According to the critics, the current DSM system only "finds" what it can see by the light of readily observable, descriptive criteria, and may lose sight of whatever exists outside of that light.

Some clinicians—particularly those associated with the humanistic and psychodynamic perspectives—consider the DSM-IV-TR generally misguided and may use it only when required to do so by a third-party such as an insurance company or professional regulatory agency. Humanistic clinicians, as noted earlier, tend to see any form of diagnosis as potentially restricting one's view of the whole, complex person behind the diagnosis. In this sense, the humanistic model includes an important critique of diagnosis in general by claiming that *classifying* is not the same as *understanding*— and can sometimes interfere with it (Winthrop, 1964). Psychodynamic clinicians, on the other hand, have developed their own diagnostic systems based on psychodynamic concepts such as defense mechanisms and ego functioning (see Box 4.3), which they consider more relevant than descriptive symptoms for classifying disorders (McWilliams, 1994). Often psychodynamic diagnoses are used by clinicians in combination with a DSM-IV-TR diagnosis in order to address both descriptive symptoms

BOX 4.3   An Alternate Classification System

Psychodynamic Diagnosis

Many psychodynamic therapists find the DSM-IV-TR diagnostic system to be at odds with their ways of thinking about diagnosis. In general, psychodynamic therapists tend to feel that diagnosis should be based not only on the client's symptoms but also on underlying conditions such as the client's personality organization, defense mechanisms, developmental fixations, and degree of ego strength. While psychodynamic therapists have not developed a comprehensive diagnostic manual as an alternative

to the DSM-IV-TR, some theorists have offered psychodynamic classification systems that can be used in conjunction with or instead of the DSM-IV-TR. Here is one such taxonomy, developed by Nancy McWilliams in her book, *Psychoanalytic Diagnosis*. Using this taxonomy, Dave would probably be classified as neurotic-to-healthy on the developmental dimension and obsessive-compulsive on the personality typological dimension.

Personality Typological Dimension

Developmental/Severity Dimension	Psychopathic	Narcissistic	Schizoid	Paranoid	Depressive	Masochistic	Obsessive Compulsive	Hysterical	Dissociative	Other
Neurotic-to-healthy level							Dave			
Borderline level										
Psychotic level										

(Adapted from McWilliams, 1994, p. 92)

and underlying psychodynamics when making a diagnosis (Jacobson & Cooper, 1993).

Limitation 2: Theoretical Bias

A second area of criticism of the modern DSM approach is that despite its stated intention to provide an atheoretical approach to diagnosis, the DSM, in fact, has a hidden theoretical bias in favor of the biological perspective. While the DSM-IV-TR makes no explicit claims about the etiology (cause) of, or most appropriate treatment for, the disorders it lists, many critics note that the DSM-IV-TR contains an implicit assumption that mental disorders are akin to medical disorders, with probable biological causes even if they are not yet known (Barron, 1998; McHugh, 1999; Nathan, 1995). To the extent that the DSM-IV-TR does implicitly prioritize biological factors, it can be criticized as biased or reductionistic.

Limitation 3: Cultural Bias

Finally, the current DSM system has been criticized for being culturally biased (Rogler, 1993). As we have noted, forms of psychopathology vary a great deal across different cultural and historical contexts (the core concept of **cultural and historical relativism**), and as a result there is always a danger of either pathologizing something normal or normalizing something pathological because of cultural, racial, class, or gender stereotypes. For example, anthropologists interested in psychopathology have pointed out that talking to dead relatives is considered normal in many cultures, yet it could easily be misinterpreted as a pathological psychotic hallucination by a clinician from a different cultural background (Liester, 1998). Because this concern was raised about the DSM-III (Kleinman, 1987, 1996), the DSM-IV-TR explicitly discusses cultural variations in psychopathology, with descriptions of "culture-bound syndromes" (see Table 2.2) and suggestions for helping clinicians consider cultural context when making diagnoses (APA, 2000).

Brief Summary

- The DSM system underwent a significant revolution with the introduction of the DSM-III in 1980. In an effort to improve the reliability and validity of previous systems, the DSM-III adopted a new approach emphasizing more specific, descriptive, and atheoretical criteria for diagnosing mental disorders.

- The DSM-III revolution remains controversial, yet the modern DSM approach has been widely adopted. The advantages of the new system have been improved reliability and validity, and an increased emphasis on the importance of diagnosis. Criticism of the new system focuses on remaining problems with reliability and validity, and concerns about theoretical and cultural bias.

Critical Thinking Question	**O**verall, does the "DSM-III Revolution" seem to you to have been a major step forward in the field, a minor step forward, or a step in the wrong direction?

USING THE DSM-IV-TR: MAKING A MULTIAXIAL DIAGNOSIS

Despite the concerns of the critics, the DSM-IV-TR is the current standard for diagnosing psychopathology. Accordingly, we will review in detail exactly how the DSM diagnostic system works and how it is used by clinicians to make diagnoses. The first important point is that the DSM-IV-TR is a *multiaxial* diagnostic system, meaning that a complete diagnosis involves several (five, to be exact) different dimensions or areas. However, the first two *axes* or dimensions contain all of the mental disorders listed in the DSM-IV-TR; the remaining three axes record supplemental information.

Axis I and Axis II

Probably the most difficult and confusing part of the DSM-IV-TR, even for experienced clinicians, is the distinction between Axis I and Axis II (see Table 4.6). This distinction is based on the long-established convention that mental disorders can be broken down into two basic types. The first type, far more common and familiar, are **symptom disorders**, characterized by the onset of unpleasant and unwanted emotional distress or impairments in functioning. This broad category includes everything from phobias to schizophrenia in the DSM-IV-TR, and these are all listed on Axis I. The second category, less common and familiar, are **personality disorders** (Chapter 11), characterized by certain personality *traits* that have become so extreme and rigid that they cause impairments in functioning. For example, "dependent personality disorder" is a diagnosis for individuals who are so dependent upon others that they are unable to make decisions for themselves, assert themselves, and act independently.

Symptom disorders Disorders characterized by the unpleasant and unwanted forms of distress and/or impairment.

Personality disorders Disorders characterized by extreme and rigid personality traits that cause impairment.

Table 4.6 | **General Differences Between Axis I and Axis II Disorders in DSM-IV-TR**

	AXIS I: SYMPTOM DISORDERS	AXIS II: PERSONALITY DISORDERS
Scope of problem	Often limited/specific	Pervasive
Course over time	Often episodic/acute	Persistent/chronic
Subjective experience	More ego-dystonic	More ego-syntonic

Comorbidity The presence of two or more disorders in one person, or a general association between two or more different disorders.

Ego-dystonic Behaviors, thoughts, or feelings that are experienced by an individual as distressing and unwelcome.

Ego-syntonic Behavior, thoughts, or feelings that are experienced by an individual as consistent with his or her sense of self.

There are 10 such personality disorders listed in the DSM-IV-TR (covered in Chapter 11), and they, along with the diagnosis of mental retardation, are the only disorders listed on Axis II.

One of the first decisions a clinician must make in diagnosing a client is whether his or her disorder seems to be a *symptom disorder* or a *personality disorder* (it is also possible for a person to have multiple diagnoses, a situation known as **comorbidity**). There are certain rules of thumb for distinguishing between symptom and personality disorders, although it is important to keep in mind that the distinction is not entirely clear-cut (and partly for that reason has been controversial) and that these rules of thumb have many exceptions.

The first rule of thumb is that personality disorders tend to be long-term and *chronic,* because personality, by definition, consists of a group of traits and patterns of functioning that are relatively stable over time. Most Axis I disorders, by contrast, tend to be more episodic and *acute,* although chronic disorders like schizophrenia and some forms of depression and anxiety are important exceptions to this rule.

The second rule of thumb is that personality disorders tend to have *pervasive* effects throughout the individual's life, because personality comes into play in everything one does. By contrast, many Axis I disorders have a more *specific* focus, and are limited to a particular area of functioning, such as a fear of public speaking. (Again, though, some Axis I disorders can be devastatingly pervasive, as anyone who has known someone with severe depression or schizophrenia can attest.)

The third rule of thumb is that the subjective attitude of the client toward his or her disorder is usually quite different in symptom disorders than in personality disorders. In symptom disorders, individuals usually feel that their problems, whatever they may be, are distressing, unwelcome, and puzzling. This situation is technically described as one in which the problems are **ego-dystonic**. ("Ego" here is a synonym for "self", and dystonic means "inconsistent," so that to say that a disorder is "ego-dystonic" means that the afflicted individual feels that the symptoms are inconsistent with his or her usual sense of self.)

By contrast, personality disorders are more **ego-syntonic**, meaning that the individual with the disorder may not feel that anything is wrong. While it may seem surprising that someone could have an extreme, rigid, pathological personality and not know or be bothered by it, keep in mind that most people take for granted and value their personality traits, even if extreme. However, this does have some serious implications for treatment, as you might guess. Because personality disorders tend to be ego-syntonic, individuals with personality disorders are less motivated and less likely to seek treatment than individuals with Axis I disorders, and when they do seek treatment it is often at the urging of others who are adversely affected by their extreme personalities (Oldham, 1994). But here, too, there are exceptions, so that in some cases an individual with a personality disorder may be quite aware of, distressed by, and motivated to change his or her extreme traits, while an individual with an Axis I disorder like anorexia may appear superficially concerned about her symptoms and appear motivated to change, but the anorexia may be more ego-syntonic under the surface.

Axes III, IV, and V

After a clinician has identified all of the DSM-IV-TR mental disorders that the client is experiencing and listed them on Axes I and II, the DSM-IV-TR includes three additional axes for listing relevant supplemental information.

Axis III is where a clinician lists any medical conditions "that are potentially relevant to the understanding or management of the individual's mental disorder" (APA, 2000). For example, a client suffering from schizophrenia might also, coincidentally, suffer from severe asthma that requires substantial self-monitoring and self-care. Obviously, the clinician treating this client needs to be aware that schizophrenic symptoms can interfere with effective self-monitoring of asthma. Another example in which an Axis III listing would be appropriate would be the case of a patient diagnosed with a mental disorder—let's say depression in this instance—for which medication might be recommended as part of the treatment. If this client also suffers from any medical conditions that require medication—arthritis, for example—a clinician would have to consider the possibility of medication interactions should antidepressants be prescribed, and therefore arthritis would be listed on Axis III. Finally, certain medical conditions can be relevant to understanding mental disorders if the mental disorder is a psychological reaction to the medical problem. For instance, someone may develop depressive symptoms after being diagnosed with AIDS. In this case, the DSM-IV-TR diagnosis, on Axis I, would probably be a disorder called "adjustment disorder with depressed mood" (adjustment disorders are symptomatic reactions to stressful life events) while AIDS would be listed on Axis III.

Axis IV is used for reporting current or recent stressors in an individual's life, which may affect the diagnosis, *prognosis* (expected course over time), or treatment of the disorders diagnosed on Axes I and II. The DSM-IV-TR provides a list of "Psychosocial and Environmental Problems" which could be relevant to the individual's condition (APA, 2000). As you can see from Table 4.7, this list focuses on common areas of life stress such as relationship stresses, financial stresses, work stresses, and so on. How can this information be relevant to the "diagnosis, prognosis, or treatment" of mental disorders? Consider the case of a woman with mild depressive symptoms who, it turns out, has just been left by her husband of 40 years and has had to move out of her home and lower her standard of living. Knowing about the divorce, and all of the psychosocial stressors it involves, may help the clinician to correctly diagnose the woman with an adjustment disorder rather than with a mood disorder. This information would also be relevant to prognosis and treatment, since an adjustment disorder has different prognostic and treatment implications than a mood disorder (Chapter 6).

Axis V is for "reporting the clinician's judgment of the individual's overall level of functioning" (APA, 2000). The DSM-IV-TR provides a rating scale to assist the clinician in making this judgment. This scale, known as the **Global Assessment of Functioning Scale (GAF)**, ranges from 100 (excellent functioning, no problems or symptoms) to 1 (extremely impaired functioning); it is shown in Table 4.8.

The Axis V rating can be useful to the clinician in several ways. First, it provides an overall indication of how severely the individual is affected by his or her problems. Secondly, the Axis V ratings can be used to monitor clients' progress in

Axis IV: Psychosocial and Environmental Stressors Axis IV of the DSM-IV-TR multiaxial system is used to describe stressful events or situations that may be associated with a mental disorder. This 10-year-old boy was rescued by three policemen from a rain-swollen river in Australia in 1996. If he subsequently developed an anxiety or adjustment disorder, the incident would belong on Axis IV.

Global Assessment of Functioning (GAF) A scale rating an individual's level of functioning used for Axis V of the DSM-IV-TR.

Table 4.7	Axis IV of DSM-IV-TR: Psychosocial and Environmental Problems
APA, 2000	**AXIS IV** **PSYCHOSOCIAL AND ENVIRONMENTAL PROBLEMS**

Problems with primary support group

Problems related to the social environment

Educational problems

Occupational problems

Housing problems

Economic problems

Problems with access to health care services

Problems related to interaction with the legal system/crime

Other psychosocial and environmental problems

- **Problems with primary support group**—e.g., death of a family member; health problems in family; disruption of family by separation, divorce, or estrangement; removal from the home; remarriage of parent; sexual or physical abuse; parental overprotection; neglect of child; inadequate discipline; discord with siblings; birth of a sibling.
- **Problems related to the social environment**—e.g., death or loss of friend; inadequate social support; living alone; difficulty with acculturation; discrimination; adjustment to life-cycle transition (such as retirement).
- **Educational problems**—e.g., illiteracy; academic problems; discord with teachers or classmates; inadequate school environment.
- **Occupational problems**—e.g., unemployment; threat of job loss; stressful work schedule; difficult work conditions; job dissatisfaction; job change; discord with boss or co-workers.
- **Housing problems**—e.g., homelessness; inadequate housing; unsafe neighborhood; discord with neighbors or landlord.
- **Economic problems**—e.g., extreme poverty; inadequate finances; insufficient welfare support.
- **Problems with access to health care services**—e.g., inadequate health care services; transportation to health care facilities unavailable; inadequate health insurance.
- **Problems related to interaction with the legal system/crime**—e.g., arrest; incarceration; litigation; victim of crime.
- **Other psychosocial and environmental problems**—e.g., exposure to disasters, war, other hostilities; discord with nonfamily caregivers such as counselor, social worker, or physician; unavailability of social service agencies.

treatment, as the client's GAF score can be assessed periodically during treatment. Finally, Axis V ratings can, in certain situations, provide crucial diagnostic information. For example, one of the characteristics of schizophrenia is a decline over time in an individual's ability to function; this, along with symptoms of psychosis, is a hallmark of the disorder (APA, 2000). GAF ratings of the client's prior levels of

GLOBAL ASSESSMENT OF FUNCTIONING (GAF) SCALE

APA, 2000

Consider psychological, social, and occupational functioning on a hypothetical continuum of mental health-illness. Do not include impairment in functioning due to physical (or environmental) limitations.

Code[1]

100 Superior functioning in a wide range of activities, life's problems never seem to get
 | out of hand, is sought out by others because of his or her many positive qualities. No
91 symptoms.

90 Absent or minimal symptoms (e.g., mild anxiety before an exam), good functioning in all
 | areas, interested and involved in a wide range of activities, socially effective, generally
 | satisfied with life, no more than everyday problems or concerns (e.g., an occasional argument
81 with family members).

80 If symptoms are present, they are transient and expectable reactions to psychosocial stressors
 | (e.g., difficulty concentrating after family argument); no more than slight impairment in
71 social, occupational, or school functioning (e.g., temporarily falling behind in schoolwork).

70 Some mild symptoms (e.g., depressed mood and mild insomnia) OR some difficulty in social,
 | occupational, or school functioning (e.g., occasional truancy, or theft within the household),
61 but generally functioning pretty well, has some meaningful interpersonal relationships.

60 Moderate symptoms (e.g., flat affect and circumstantial speech, occasional panic attacks) OR
 | moderate difficulty in social, occupational, or school functioning (e.g., few friends, conflicts
51 with peers or co-workers).

50 Serious symptoms (e.g., suicidal ideation, severe obsessional rituals, frequent shoplifting) OR
 | any serious impariment in social, occupational, or school functioning (e.g., no friends, unable
41 to keep a job).

40 Some impairment in reality testing or communication (e.g., speech is at times illogical,
 | obscure, or irrelevant) OR major impairment in several areas, such as work or school, family
 | relations, judgment, thinking, or mood (e.g., depressed man avoids friends, neglects family,
 | and is unable to work; child frequently beats up younger children, is defiant at home, and is
31 failing at school).

30 Behavior is considerably influenced by delusions or hallucinations OR serious impairment in
 | communication or judgment (e.g., sometimes incoherent, acts grossly inappropriately, suicidal
 | preoccupation) OR inability to function in almost all areas (e.g., stays in bed all day: no job,
21 home, or friends).

20 Some danger of hurting self or others (e.g., suicide attempts without clear expectation of
 | death; frequently violent; manic excitement) OR occasionally fails to maintain minimal
 | personal hygiene (e.g., smears feces) OR gross impairment in communication (e.g., largely
11 incoherent or mute).

10 Persistent danger of severely hurting self or others (e.g., recurrent violence) OR persistent
 | inability to maintain minimal personal hygiene OR serious suicidal act with clear expectation
1   of death.

0   Inadequate information.

[1] **Note:** Use intermediate codes when appropriate, e.g., 45, 68, 72.

functioning (based on the client's or family members' retrospective reports) can be compared with a current GAF score when diagnosing schizophrenia.

A Complete DSM-IV-TR Diagnosis

Now that we have described the multiaxial system and the specific purposes of Axes I through V, let's see what a complete DSM-IV-TR diagnosis might look like for a hypothetical client with multiple problems. You will note that each diagnosis has a code number in addition to a descriptive title.

Axis I: Social phobia (DSM-IV-TR code number 300.23)
            Alcohol abuse (code number 305.00)
Axis II: Dependent personality disorder (code number 301.6)
Axis III: Asthma (code number 493.90)
Axis IV: Unemployment
Axis V: 50

Now let's consider a familiar case—the case of Dave, presented in Chapters 2 and 3. As you recall, Dave attends an elite college; he is a successful student and has generally considered himself happy and well-adjusted despite some family stresses and his occasional lapses into a pessimistic frame of mind. However, during his sophomore year, Dave became increasingly anxious and insecure. He was so self-conscious and fearful of rejection that he began to avoid his friends and usual activities. Despite these problems, Dave was able to maintain good grades. Let's look at how Dave's situation would translate into a complete DSM-IV-TR diagnosis.

Axis I: Social phobia; 300.23 (Dave's social anxiety and fear of rejection are all characteristic of the anxiety disorder classified as social phobia; Chapter 5.)
Axis II: No diagnosis (Dave shows no evidence of a personality disorder or mental retardation.)
Axis III: Cardiac dysrhythmia; 427.9 (This is probably not a serious medical problem, but it could be relevant to Dave's treatment since it consists of heart palpitations similar to those that can occur when a person is anxious.)
Axis IV: Problems in primary support group (There are stresses in Dave's family associated with Dave's brother's problems and the discord between Dave's parents.)
Axis V: 65 (Moderate symptoms.)

Now that you have had a chance to see what a diagnosis might look like for a person whose story is familiar to you, you can better evaluate the ***advantages and limitations of diagnosis.*** Clearly, assigning a DSM-IV-TR diagnosis to Dave does help to classify his problems (telling us *what kind* of problem he has). But it is also clear that the diagnosis, by itself, tells us little about Dave as a person. At the end of the chapter, we will return to this issue of the advantages and limitations of diagnosis—including the difference between *classifying* and *understanding* a person with emotional problems, like Dave.

Brief Summary

● The current DSM system is a multiaxial system; a complete diagnosis includes five axes, or dimensions.

● Axis I lists all of the mental disorders except the personality disorders and mental retardation, which are listed on Axis II. Axes III, IV, and V contain supplemental information on relevant medical conditions, psychosocial and environmental problems, and a global assessment of functioning (GAF), respectively.

Critical Thinking Question The DSM system is increasingly being used around the world. What kinds of problems might clinicians encounter in using the DSM-IV-TR in other cultures?

ASSESSMENT

Assessment refers to the process of gathering information for the purpose of making a diagnosis and arriving at an understanding of a client. As you might expect, clinicians can use numerous methods to gather such information. For convenience, we will divide these data-gathering methods into three general categories: (1) *interviews,* (2) *tests,* and (3) *observations.*

Interviews

The term "interview" simply refers to the process of gathering information about a person by talking with him or her. Just as a company looking to hire an employee, or a medical doctor trying to diagnose a patient, usually begins by talking with the person, clinical psychologists also typically start with a clinical interview (Nietzel, Bernstein, & Milich, 1994). In general, there are two types of clinical interviews, *structured* and *unstructured* interviews, although they are on a continuum and are often combined in actual practice (Barker, Pistrang, & Elliott, 1994; Nietzel et al., 1994). In a structured interview, the clinician follows a script, which prompts him or her to ask the client about certain content areas. For example, the Structured Clinical Interview for DSM-IV Axis I Disorders (known as the SCID) (First, Spitzer, Gibbon, & Williams, 1997) is a structured interview designed to cover the DSM-IV Axis I diagnostic categories. Structured interviews are used in both clinical and research settings. For example, a clinician might use the SCID interview in a research study on schizophrenia in order to select subjects who clearly meet the criteria for the disorder.

Another important structured interview, and a much briefer one, is the **Mental Status Exam** (MSE). The Mental Status Exam consists of a series of questions designed to assess whether a client is experiencing any major problems with basic cognitive functions and orientation to reality (Trzepacz & Baker, 1993). For example, during an MSE clients are asked if they know where they are, what year it is, if they can count backward from 100 by sevens, and other questions which allow the clinician to assess whether cognitive functions have been disrupted by a physical (for example, head injury) or a mental (for example, schizophrenic psychosis) disorder.

Unstructured interviews, by contrast, focus less on obtaining answers to specific questions and more on gathering information about a client by facilitating a wide-ranging exploration of the client's situation. The ultimate aim of an unstructured interview is similar to that of a structured interview—arriving at a diagnosis and an understanding of the client—but in an unstructured interview the clinician uses different strategies for gathering information. First, the clinician allows the client to choose the topics of discussion and to elaborate on problems and concerns. Usually this is accomplished by asking nondirective questions such as "How have things

Clinical interviewing The clinical interview is the most important method for assessment of mental disorders. Here a clinician conducts an unstructured interview with a teenaged girl about her depression.

Mental Status Exam A series of questions designed to assess whether a client has major problems with cognitive functions and orientation to reality.

been going for you?" or "Could you tell me more about your difficulties at work?" rather than following a prescribed format. Also, the clinician gathers information not just about *what* the client says, but also about *how, when,* and *why* he or she says it. For example, in an unstructured interview, a clinician might discover that a particular client waits until near the end of the session to mention a major sexual problem. This might help the clinician understand that the client is feeling embarrassed or ashamed about the problem, a fact that might not have come out if the clinician had followed a structured interview format which included questions about sexual problems early on.

Clearly, in both structured and unstructured interviews the clinician must be skilled at making clients feel safe and comfortable enough to talk about difficult personal matters. In fact, interviewing technique is one of the most important topics clinicians study during their graduate training. Clinicians must learn how to create a climate of trust, caring, confidentiality, and professionalism in order to establish the conditions under which clients can provide the information necessary for a good assessment process (Nietzel et al., 1994).

Advantages and Limitations of Interviews

The difference between structured and unstructured interviews brings us back to the issue of *reliability*. The major advantage of structured interviews is that their consistent format improves their reliability. Numerous studies have shown that unstructured interviews are highly problematic when it comes to reliability, and it is more likely that two clinicians will arrive at the same diagnosis using a structured interview than an unstructured one (Harris, 1989; Kaplan & Saccuzzo, 1993). On the other hand, as we have seen before, a consistent structure that improves reliability can compromise validity if it narrows the range and depth of the questions asked. When it comes to interviewing as an assessment method, most clinicians find that they can have the best of both worlds by using both structured and unstructured techniques to interview clients. Sometimes these two methods can be alternated during various parts of a clinical interview, and sometimes they can be combined in a halfway structured format known as a *semi-structured* interview (Wiens, 1976).

Tests

There are literally hundreds of tests available to clinicians for the purpose of assessing psychopathology (Kaplan & Saccuzzo, 1993). Tests are not always used as part of the assessment process, but they can be especially helpful for answering particular diagnostic questions or assessing specific areas of functioning. In order to be useful, tests must go through a rigorous development process to establish standard administration techniques, reliability and validity, and statistical norms for various demographic groups—a process known as *standardization*. We will divide assessment tests into four general categories: (1) *symptom and personality questionnaires;* (2) *projective tests;* (3) *cognitive tests;* and (4) *biological tests.*

Symptom and Personality Questionnaires

Symptom and personality questionnaires
Tests designed to measure symptoms or personality traits based on clients' responses to structured questions.

Symptom and personality questionnaires are designed to measure psychological symptoms or personality traits based on clients' responses to questions administered either on paper or at a computer terminal. There are many such questionnaires available, though only a few are widely used. We will describe two of these tests, one symptom questionnaire and one personality questionnaire, in order to provide examples of what these kinds of tests look like and how they work.

Sample Items and Instructins from the Beck Depression Inventory-II (BDI-II) Table 4.9

Beck, 1997

Date: _____

Name: _____ Birth Date: _____

On this questionnaire are groups of statements. Please read each group of statements carefully. Then pick out the one statement in each group which best describes the way you have been feeling the PAST WEEK, INCLUDING TODAY. Circle the number beside the statement you picked. If several statements in the group seem to apply equally well, circle each one. <u>Be sure to read all the statements in each group before making your choice.</u>

Item 1. Sadness

    0   I do not feel sad.

    1   I feel sad much of the time.

    2   I am sad all the time.

    3   I am so sad or unhappy that I can't stand it.

Item 2. Pessimism

    0   I am not discouraged about my future.

    1   I feel more discouraged about my future than I used to be.

    2   I do not expect things to work out for me.

    3   I feel my future is hopeless and will only get worse.

The **Beck Depression Inventory-II (BDI-II)**, assesses symptoms of depression. As you can see in Table 4.9, the BDI-II is a simple questionnaire (the full questionnaire has 21 items) about depressive symptoms, which are rated by the client on a scale from 0 to 3. A total score above a certain level indicates that the client is clinically depressed (Beck et al., 1961; Beck, 1996). However, the BDI-II can do more than just provide a standardized, valid assessment of whether a person is "clinically depressed." It can also be used to gather information about the particular pattern of a client's depressive symptoms, and to track changes in depressive symptoms over the course of treatment (Maruish, 1999).

Personality questionnaires (or *inventories*) have a similar format but focus on broader personality traits rather than specific symptoms. The most widely used personality questionnaire is the **Minnesota Multiphasic Personality Inventory** (MMPI) currently in its second, revised edition known as the **MMPI-2** (Butcher et al., 1989; Hathaway & McKinley, 1989). This test, developed and standardized over many decades at the University of Minnesota, consists of 567 "true or false" questions that tend to differentiate between people with and without various mental disorders. Responses to these questions yield scores on 10 clinical scales of the MMPI-2, shown in Table 4.10.

Beck Depression Inventory-II (BDI-II) A widely used depression symptom questionnaire.

Minnesota Multiphasic Personality Inventory-2 (MMPI-2) A widely used personality questionnaire.

Table 4.10	**The 10 Clinical Scales of the Minnesota Multiphasic Personality Inventory-2 (MMPI-2)**
Butcher, 1999	1. **Hs** ▪ Hypochondriasis (anxiety related to bodily functioning) 2. **D** ▪ Depression (depressive traits and symptoms) 3. **Hy** ▪ Conversion Hysteria (expression of emotional distress through physical symptoms) 4. **Pd** ▪ Psychopathic Deviance (exploitive and irresponsible traits) 5. **Mf** ▪ Masculinity-Femininity (traits usually associated with the opposite sex) 6. **Pa** ▪ Paranoia (extreme suspiciousness) 7. **Pt** ▪ Psychasthenia (overanxious and self-doubting traits) 8. **Sc** ▪ Schizophrenia (bizarre and psychotic traits) 9. **Ma** ▪ Hypomania (grandiose and overexcited traits) 10. **Si** ▪ Social Introversion (shy, insecure, and easily embarrassed)

The MMPI-2 also contains scales that assess whether the client may be responding in a dishonest, careless, or defensive manner, which must be taken into account when interpreting the test. Dave's MMPI-2 scores—described later in the chapter—include results for all of the MMPI scales. The scale scores are plotted on a graph that provides a *profile* of the individual's overall personality. Trained MMPI interpreters (and various computerized scoring programs) can make additional diagnostic judgments based on specific scores and patterns among the scales. The MMPI and the MMPI-2 have been shown to have good reliability and moderate validity (Graham, 1987; Hiller et al., 1999; Johnson, Jones, & Brems, 1996).

Advantages and Limitations of Symptom and Personality Questionnaires The chief advantage of symptom and personality questionnaires is the relative ease with which they produce reliable and valid measures of psychological variables. Of course, no questionnaire has perfect reliability or validity, and the *psychometric* (that is, psychological measurement) properties and limitations of each individual questionnaire have to be taken into account by clinicians who use them. As we have seen, the major disadvantage of highly standardized assessment tools, such as questionnaires, is that standardization sacrifices flexibility in the collection of information.

Projective Tests

Projective tests Tests designed to measure client characteristics based on clients' responses to and interpretations of ambiguous stimuli.

Projective tests are based on the *projective hypothesis,* which holds that people's responses to and interpretations of ambiguous stimuli reveal a great deal about how their personalities operate in general (Exner, 1976; Frank, 1939). We all remember the game of looking up at cumulus clouds on a summer afternoon and deciding what they look like. According to the projective hypothesis, when three people look at the same cloud and one sees a violent fist-fight, the next sees a sad-looking child, and the third sees a couple tenderly kissing, each is revealing something about his or her own inner world and personality tendencies.

As implied in this description, projective tests are generally used to assess global issues such as personality traits rather than specific symptoms. However, they differ from personality questionnaires in that they are less structured. In a projective test, the client may be asked to say what an inkblot looks like (the *Rorschach test*) or to make up a story about a picture (the *Thematic Apperception Test*) rather than to answer a yes-no or numerical question. If the difference between personality questionnaires and projective tests sounds similar to you to the difference described earlier between structured and unstructured interviews, you are exactly right. The rationale, advantages, and limitations of projective personality tests are precisely the same as those of unstructured interviews. That is, projective testing is most commonly used when clinicians want to assess a client's internal world in more depth than a personality questionnaire can do (Exner, 1976; Kaplan & Saccuzzo, 1993). Projective tests gather tailor-made information about a client, but often at the expense of reliability and validity (Lanyon, 1984). This is not because projective tests cannot be standardized; in fact, most projective tests have elaborate standardized instructions for administration and scoring. But whenever clinicians are dealing with unstructured responses from clients (sometimes referred to as *qualitative* data) it is harder to convert them into highly reliable, *quantitative* data (Kaplan & Saccuzzo, 1993; Little & Schneidman, 1959).

We will discuss three widely used projective tests: the Rorschach test, the Thematic Apperception Test (TAT), and projective drawing tests. Most people have heard of the Rorschach test, and in fact the term "rorschach" has come into colloquial use to refer to any ambiguous situation which tends to elicit widely varying reactions in people. The actual test was developed by the Swiss psychoanalyst Hermann Rorschach (1884–1922). The **Rorschach test** consists of a series of 10 symmetrical inkblots on pieces of cardboard about the size of this textbook page. Clients are asked to tell the clinician what the inkblots look like to them. Later, clients are asked to explain exactly how they mentally constructed the image, because most Rorschach interpreters consider the *form* of the response (for example, which part of the inkblot is used or the exact sequence of responses) to be as important as the *content* of the response. The Rorschach is used primarily to assess personality structure and unconscious emotional conflicts (Allison, Blatt, & Zimet, 1968). There are numerous standardized systems for scoring Rorschach responses (including databases of common response profiles by various diagnostic groups), and some of these systems have shown moderate-to-good reliability and validity (Exner, 1995; Hiller et al., 1999). However, there has been much debate about the relative merits of various Rorschach scoring systems, and about the reliability and validity of the Rorschach in general (Aronow, Reznikoff, & Rauchway, 1979; Blatt, 1990; Kaplan & Saccuzzo, 1993; Wood et al., 2003).

Another popular and influential projective test, the **Thematic Apperception Test (TAT)**, was developed by the Harvard psychologist Henry Murray in 1935. Murray designed a series of pictures of people in ambiguous situations about which clients are asked to "make up a story." Typically, a clinician will ask a client to make up stories for 10 to 20 cards. Murray believed, in keeping with the projective hypothesis, that the stories made up about the picture would reveal a great deal about the client's basic needs, feelings, motives, and interpersonal patterns (Morgan & Murray, 1935; Murray, 1938, 1943). (See Box 4.4 for TAT stories of non-depressed versus depressed subjects.)

Clinicians follow a set of standardized instructions for administering the TAT, which include asking the client to make up a story with a beginning, middle, and end, and to describe what the characters are thinking and feeling. Numerous scoring systems for the TAT have been developed, but, as with the Rorschach, it has been a chal-

The Rorschach test This psychologist is administering a Rorschach type inkblot test. The client tells the psychologist what the inkblot looks like to her. Later, the client may be asked to explain how she mentally constructed the image.

Rorschach test A projective test in which clients' responses to inkblots are interpreted and scored.

Thematic Apperception Test (TAT) A projective test in which clients are asked to make up stories about pictures of people in ambiguous situations.

BOX 4.4	Projective Testing

TAT Stories of Nondepressed Versus Depressed Subjects

Card 1 of the TAT shows a young boy sitting at a table, looking at an ambiguous object that appears to be a violin. Note the difference in both the story content and the speech process of the nondepressed versus the depressed subject.

Story Told by a Nondepressed 24-Year-Old Male Subject

This boy, he looks at eight or nine...he's been studying the violin for a few months, and he's wondering how far he wants to go with it. He likes playing it, and his lessons have been going well, but sometimes he feels bored and wants to play outside. His parents have said it's up to him. It's a hard decision because he feels like if he keeps practicing he could get really good, but he might miss out on other things and he likes sports a lot, too. So he thinks about it for a while, and eventually decides to practice every day but for a shorter time, so he can have time for other things. And it turns out to be a good decision, because he ends up playing for many years and getting lots of enjoyment from his musical ability.

Story Told by a Depressed 30-Year-Old Male Subject

This kid looks really sad...I don't know why. (Long pause) I'd say he feels that nothing he does works out. He tried learning to play the violin and he couldn't do it. (Long pause) He feels...worn out. Tired. Discouraged. Disappointed in himself. (Long pause) Doesn't know what to do. So he sits there, waiting for something to happen. Unfortunately, he's all alone, so nothing really changes. That's the end.

Draw-A-Person Test (DAP) A projective test in which clients are asked to draw pictures of themselves and other people.

lenge to develop reliable and valid scoring systems because of the difficulty of translating complex stories into categories which can be quantitatively compared and analyzed (Kaplan & Saccuzzo, 1993; Westen et al., 1994).

Projective drawing tests work on the assumption that people's drawings reveal a great deal about their inner emotional worlds. In the **Draw-A-Person Test (DAP)**, a popular projective drawing test, a client is asked to draw a picture of a person, then a picture of a person of the opposite sex, and then a self-portrait (Machover, 1949). Although some standardized scoring systems have been devised for interpreting the DAP and other projective drawing tests for adults and children, their reliability and validity is not impressive, and clinicians usually rely on clinical intuition in interpreting them (Attkinson et al., 1974; Trevisan, 1996; Watson, Felling, & Maceachern, 1967). For example, drawings that appear bleak and without animation may indicate a depressive state, and drawings of only the head and face may reveal detachment from feelings and a tendency toward intellectualization.

Advantages and Limitations of Projective Tests There are numerous other projective tests available to clinicians; we have chosen to describe three of the most commonly used tests in order to illustrate the principles and techniques of projective testing. All projective tests share a similar set of advantages and disadvantages, which should be familiar by now. The major advantage of projective tests is that they assess clients' deeper, less easily observable emotional and personality patterns. These data may be helpful in diagnosing a client, although they are likely to be more useful for developing a psychological *understanding* of the client, which, as we have seen, is an important supplement to a diagnostic classification.

Unfortunately, projective methods have the same built-in limitations as most methods devoted to more in-depth, "tailor-made" assessment tools, namely that it is difficult to standardize projective methods so as to achieve adequate reliability and validity (Kaplan & Saccuzzo, 1993; Wood et al., 2003). Nonetheless, many clinicians still find projective tests very useful because they have developed a sophisticated clinical intuition from many years' experience in "reading" Rorschachs or TATs, just as experienced radiologists develop sophisticated clinical intuition in reading X-rays.

Cognitive Tests

Cognitive tests, which are used to assess cognitive abilities and deficits, are among the most commonly used tests by psychologists. They can subdivided into three groups: (1) intelligence tests; (2) achievement tests; and (3) neuropsychological tests. While cognitive tests are often administered for reasons other than the assessment of psychopathology—such as for school placement or educational assessment—they can also be useful for clinical purposes, as we will describe.

Intelligence Tests The two most widely used intelligence tests today (Aiken, 1987) are the *Stanford-Binet, Fourth Edition* (Thorndike, Hagen, & Sattler, 1986) and the *Wechsler Adult Intelligence Scale—Third Edition (WAIS-III)* (Wechsler, 1997). The **Stanford-Binet** was developed in 1916 and is based on the pioneering work of the French psychologist Alfred Binet (1857–1911), who was asked by French authorities to develop a method to assess individual differences in intellectual ability among French schoolchildren for educational tracking purposes. Binet's test consisted of a series of verbal and nonverbal tasks, geared to the age level of the subject, which tapped reasoning, communication, arithmetic, and memory skills. The Stanford psychologist Louis Terman (1877–1956) modified Binet's test (hence, Stanford-Binet), and coined the phrase **intelligence quotient,** or **IQ,** which is still used as the term for the final result of intelligence tests, a general score representing overall intellectual ability. (Keep in mind that intellectual ability is different from academic *achievement,* which is assessed by *achievement tests;* however, intelligence tests are relatively good predictors of academic achievement, which is an indication of their *validity.*)

The **Wechsler Adult Intelligence Scale (WAIS)** was first developed by the psychologist David Wechsler in 1936, and it has surpassed the Stanford-Binet in popularity. Like the Stanford-Binet, the WAIS has been continually revised over the years and subject to extensive and rigorous standardization. The current version, the WAIS-III-R (Wechsler, 1997) consists of seven "verbal" subscales (assessing skills such as reasoning and memory) and seven "performance" subscales (assessing skills such as spatial ability and visual problem solving). The test yields a verbal IQ score, a performance IQ score, and an overall IQ score. Alternate versions of the test are available for children (the Wechsler Intelligence Scale for Children–Fourth Edition, or WISC-IV) and for preschoolers (the Wechsler Preschool and Primary Scales of Intelligence–Revised, or WPPSI-R; Wechsler, 1989).

Why would a clinical psychologist want to administer an intelligence test as part of an assessment of psychopathology? First, there is one specific disorder listed in the DSM-IV-TR that is defined, in part, by very low intelligence—mental retardation. Second, intelligence tests can sometimes provide information about other disorders. For example, intelligence tests and achievement tests together can provide the data necessary to diagnose learning disabilities (see Achievement Tests, below). Third, intelligence tests are sometimes administered during a general psychological evaluation because it is helpful to have a sense of a client's intellectual ability and functioning as part of an overall understanding of his or her life situation and problems (Iverson, Turner, & Green, 1999; Sattler, 1988).

Achievement Tests Achievement tests are used to measure what a person (usually a child) has actually learned or achieved in a particular subject area such as mathematics or reading. Achievement tests are used primarily by educators to evaluate students

Intelligence testing This six-year-old girl is taking an IQ test.

Stanford-Binet The first widely used intelligence test.

Intelligence quotient (IQ) A measurement of overall intellectual ability obtained by intelligence tests.

Wechsler Adult Intelligence Test (WAIS) Currently, the most widely used intelligence test.

and programs. Their use in clinical psychology is mostly related to the diagnosis of learning disabilities, which are defined as a level of academic achievement (as measured by achievement tests) in reading, writing, mathematics, or another area which is "substantially below" what would be expected on the basis of a child's intellectual ability (as measured by an intelligence test). Many different achievement tests are available for these purposes, such as the widely used *Wechsler Individual Achievement Test (WIAT)* (Wechsler, 1992) and the *Woodcock-Johnson* test (Woodcock, 1977).

Neuropsychological Tests As their name suggests, neuropsychological tests are designed to assess neurological (brain) deficits as they affect psychological functions such as perception, attention, memory, and problem solving (Lezak, 1976). Because the focus of these tests is on assessing neurological deficits and their effects, they are often used in medical settings, for example to assess and treat victims of strokes and head injuries. Neuropsychological tests can also play a role in the assessment of several forms of psychopathology, usually in one of two ways. First, neuropsychological assessment can help a clinician determine whether a client's symptoms might be due to neurological deficits rather than psychological factors, which would obviously have implications for treatment. For example, a significantly lower score on the WAIS-III-R performance subtests than on the verbal subtests could be indicative of depression, which sometimes slows down motor performance (Iverson et al., 1999; Sattler, 1988). However, the performance deficit could also be a result of a learning disability or other neurological problem, which could be systematically assessed with neuropsychological tests (Cornoldi et al., 1999; Rourke, 1989). In fact, the WAIS-III-R is sometimes used as a screening device for neurological problems; if general cognitive deficits show up on the WAIS, then neuropsychological testing might be recommended to pinpoint the deficits and assist in treatment planning (Gregory, 1999; Goldstein & Hersen, 1990).

A second area in which neuropsychological tests are sometimes used in the assessment of psychopathology involves a few disorders in the DSM-IV-TR which are characterized by neuropsychological symptoms (Franzen & Smith-Seemiller, 1998; Kathol, Carter, & Yates, 1990; Weiner, 1991). The most prominent example of such a disorder is attention deficit/hyperactivity disorder (ADHD); many of the primary cognitive and behavioral symptoms of ADHD (for example, inattentiveness and impulsivity) can be assessed with neuropsychological tests (Doyle et al., 2000; Franzen & Smith-Seemiller, 1998; Rosen, 1990). However, ADHD can also be assessed using symptom questionnaires and through behavioral observations (see below) so that neuropsychological tests are generally necessary only in complex cases (Barkley, 1998).

The administration and interpretation of neuropsychological tests is a subspecialty within clinical psychology requiring specialized training. Neuropsychologists can choose from among dozens of different neuropsychological tests to assess clients, depending on the particular diagnostic questions. When neuropsychologists want to do an extensive neuropsychological assessment of a client they typically use a complete *battery* of cognitive, memory, and motor tests, which may require a full day to administer. The two most widely used neuropsychological test batteries are the *Halstead-Reitan Neuropsychological Battery* (Reitan & Wolfson, 1986) and the *Luria-Nebraska Neuropsychological Battery* (Golden, 1989), each of which includes a number of different tests measuring a wide range of neuropsychological functions. When a full battery of tests is not necessary, neuropsychologists can assemble a group of tests specifically designed to assess the cognitive functions in question.

Biological Tests

Despite the recent prominence of the biological perspective within the field of abnormal psychology, at present few biological tests are helpful in the assessment of men-

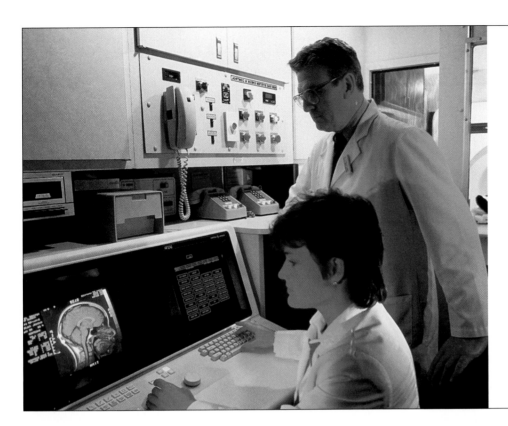

Brain imaging and assessment Brain imaging has great potential as an assessment tool for psychopathology, but it is still in its early stages.

tal disorders. Thus far, most efforts to find biological data which could serve as reliable and valid indicators of specific mental disorders have proved disappointing. For example, in the 1980s researchers began experimenting with a test of cortisol functioning known as the *Dexamethasone Suppression Test (DST)* which, it was hoped, would help diagnose a particular form of depression (Andreason, 1984; Carroll et al., 1980). (Abnormal levels of cortisol, a hormone sometimes referred to as the "stress hormone" because it is released by the adrenal glands at times of stress, appear to be related to depression; see Chapter 6.) However, on further investigation the DST did not prove adequately valid, and it is no longer used (Valenstein, 1998).

New brain scanning (*computerized axial tomography,* or *CAT*) and imaging (*positron emission tomography,* or *PET,* and *magnetic resonance imaging,* or *MRI*) techniques provide fascinating pictures of the physical structure and functioning metabolism of the brain. Accordingly, researchers are increasingly able to find brain abnormalities associated with particular mental disorders, such as neurotransmission changes in depression and schizophrenia (see Box 4.5). But, such findings are generally not yet sufficiently reliable or valid to serve as assessment tools because of the vast complexity of the brain, and the relative newness of these methods (Filipek, 1999). At present, brain scanning and imaging techniques are used mostly for research, not for clinical diagnostic purposes. In fact, even when it comes to assessing brain damage (such as might result from severe alcoholism, a head injury, or a stroke) neuropsychological tests still provide more subtle and useful assessment than brain scans or imaging (Rao, 2000). However, as the sophistication of these brain assessment techniques increases they are certain to play a larger role in the diagnosis of psychopathology.

Other biological tests can play a role in the assessment of specific disorders. For example, *psychophysiological tests,* which measure aspects of physiological arousal, can be helpful in the assessment of anxiety and sexual disorders, both of which involve

BOX 4.5	Brain Scanning and Imaging

An Assessment Tool of the Future? *by Erica Goode. The New York Times, December 11, 2002*

Researchers have been using brain imaging techniques for some time now to explore structural and functional changes associated with mental disorders. Until recently, these imaging techniques had little to offer as assessment tools. This situation may be on the verge of changing. This article by Erica Goode describes a recent study that suggests that brain imaging may soon be a useful assessment tool in the diagnosis of early schizophrenia.

Brain Imaging May Detect Schizophrenia in Early Stages

Scientists have known for some time that people who suffer from schizophrenia show abnormalities in the structure of their brains.

But in a new study, researchers for the first time have detected similar abnormalities in brain scans of people who were considered at high risk for schizophrenia or other psychotic illnesses but who did not yet have full-blown symptoms. Those abnormalities, the study found, became even more marked once the illness was diagnosed.

The subjects in the study who went on to develop psychoses had less gray matter in brain areas involved in attention and higher mental processes like planning, emotion and memory, the researchers found.

Experts said the study's results, reported yesterday in an online version of *The Lancet,* the medical journal, offered the possiblity that imaging techniques might eventually be used to predict who will develop schizophrenia, a devastating illness that affects more than 2.8 million Americans. Doctors could then offer treatment while the disease was still in its earliest stages, possibly preventing further damage to the brain.

But Dr. Christos Pantelis, an associate professor of psychiatry at the University of Melbourne and the lead author of the report, cautioned that much more research was needed before magnetic resonance imaging, the method used in the study, could serve as a diagnostic tool for individual people with schizophrenia.

"I think it's still too early to say how helpful it will be," Dr. Pantelis said.

Still, other researchers called the study's findings exciting and said that the areas of the brain in which the abnormalities were found would now be an active focus for study.

"This is a terrific first step," said Dr. Paul Thompson, a professor of neurology at the University of California at Los Angeles and an expert on brain imaging and schizophrenia.

Dr. Herbert Y. Meltzer, a professor of psychiatry at Vanderbilt University and an expert on schizophrenia, said, "It proves that the psychosis is almost a late stage in the evolution of the disease process."

He added, "The key message is that this is a neurodevelopmental disorder and that changes in memory, learning, attention and executive decision-making precede the experience of the psychosis."

People who suffer from schizophrenia typically experience auditory hallucinations and have blunted emotional responses and difficulty with activities that require planning or other higher-level processes.

Some studies have suggested that the earlier the illness is treated with antipsychotic drugs the better the prognosis. At least two research groups, one led by Dr. Patrick McGorry, an author of the *Lancet* report, and another at Yale, are conducting studies in which young people who are experiencing some symptoms but have not yet developed schizophrenia are treated with antipsychotic drugs. But the studies have been controversial because it is not yet clear which symptoms predict later illness.

In the new study, the researchers used magnetic resonance imaging to scan the brains of 75 people who were deemed "at high risk" for psychosis because they had a strong family history of severe mental illness or had other risk factors, including transient or mild symptoms of mental disturbance or a decline in mental functioning.

Over the next 12 months, 23 of the subjects developed a full-blown psychosis and 52 did not fall ill, the researchers found.

A comparison of the brain scans from the two groups

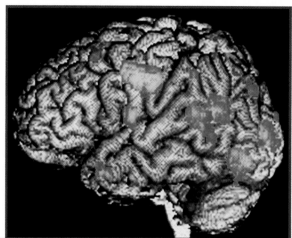

revealed significant differences in the volume of gray matter in areas of the frontal and temporal lobes and the cingulate gyrus. All three regions have been linked to schizophrenia by previous research, Dr. Pantelis said.

When the researchers conducted additional brain scans on some subjects who developed psychoses, they found further reductions in gray matter not seen in the scans taken before the illnesses were diagnosed.

abnormalities in states of physical arousal. In assessing anxiety disorders, *electromyographs (EMG),* which measure muscle tension, or recordings of pulse and blood pressure, are sometimes used to objectively determine the level of a client's anxiety. While interviews and symptom inventories are usually adequate to diagnose an anxiety disorder, biological tests can provide useful detail about the precise nature and extent of a client's anxiety, and they can be helpful in designing psychophysiological treatments for anxiety such as *biofeedback* (Chapter 14) (Blanchard, 1994; Stoyva & Budzynski, 1993).

Similarly, certain sexual disorders (Chapter 10) can be assessed using psychophysiological tests to provide an objective measure of sexual arousal. The *penile plethysmograph* is a mercury-filled rubber tube placed around the penis while the subject watches erotic videos; the expansion of the mercury in the tube can be measured, assessing sexual arousal (Gaither & Plaud, 1997). Similarly, the *vaginal pletysmograph,* a tampon-like probe that indirectly measures blood flow in the vagina, can be used to objectively assess female sexual arousal (Wincze & Lange, 1981; Sintchak & Geer, 1975).

A final area of biological assessment involves genetic tests. As we saw in Chapter 3, many mental disorders have a genetic component, and researchers are in hot pursuit of the specific genetic markers for these disorders. However, *genetic linkage* efforts are mostly still in the exploratory stage. Several studies have identified particular genes that seem to be linked to mental disorders in a sample population, but such findings have typically not been replicated in later studies with different populations. Nonetheless, it will undoubtedly be possible at some point in the near future to test for genetic vulnerability to some mental disorders—just as it is currently possible to test for genetic vulnerability to certain medical disorders.

Behavioral Observation

The third general method of assessment, in addition to interviews and tests, is direct observation of clients. Of course, some direct observation of clients naturally occurs when clinicians interview or test them; clinicians may notice anxiety symptoms, or emotional reactions to certain topics, which can help in assessment. But we are referring here to *systematic* observation strategies that can be used in the assessment

Observational assessment Clinicians will sometimes gather diagnostic information by observing a client's behavior.

process. These systematic observation strategies can be divided into those conducted by clients themselves, known as *self-monitoring,* and those conducted by someone else, usually a clinician, or, in the case of a child, a parent or teacher.

When an outside observer is used, observation of the client can be done in a *controlled setting,* such as a research laboratory, or a *naturalistic setting,* such as at home, work, or school (Aiken, 1999). There are certain situations in which behavioral observation can be essential for DSM-IV-TR classification purposes. For example, as noted previously, the diagnosis of childhood attention-deficit/hyperactivity disorder (ADHD) indicates that the child exhibits symptoms of inattention, impulsivity, and hyperactivity (APA, 2000). Various behavior rating scales, such as the *Conners' Rating Scale* (Conners, 1997), have been developed to help clinicians, parents, and teachers systematically observe and record these symptoms at home or at school (see Table 4.11).

Clinicians within the behavioral tradition are especially interested in systematic observations of clients' behaviors and environments. For example, a behavioral assessment might include asking parents to observe and record a child's problematic behaviors (such as excessive tantrums) and the events occurring just before and after the tantrums. This is not so much because it helps the clinician classify the child's problem using the DSM-IV-TR, but because it helps in understanding the symptom using the behavioral perspective with its focus on observable behavior and the reinforcements that shape it. Many behavioral therapists stress the importance of conducting a *functional analysis*—a thorough individualized analysis of the behavioral context of problematic behaviors—that can then be used as a basis for a treatment plan (Haynes & O'Brien, 1990; Scotti et al., 1996).

Self-observation is used in some cases when it is helpful to have clients monitor their own behavior as part of an assessment process. For example, a client seeking help for a drinking problem may be asked to observe and record his or her alcohol consumption over a period of time. This can help the clinician develop a more complete

---

Table 4.11 | **The Conners' Rating Scale: A Behavioral Observation Assessment Method—Instructions and Sample Items of the Teacher Version**

Conners, 1997

Instructions   Below are a number of common problems that children have in school. Please rate each item according to how much of a problem it has been in the last month. For each item, ask yourself "How much of a problem has this been in the last month?" and circle the best answer for each one. If none, not at all, seldom, or very infrequently, you would circle 0. If very much true, or it occurs very often or frequently, you would circle 3. You would circle 1 or 2 for ratings in between. Please respond to all the items.

		NOT TRUE AT ALL (Never, Seldom)	JUST A LITTLE TRUE (Occasionally)	PRETTY MUCH TRUE (Often, Quite a Bit)	VERY MUCH TRUE (Very Often, Very Frequent)
1.	Defiant	0	1	2	3
2.	Restless in the "squirmy" sense	0	1	2	3
3.	Forgets things he/she has already learned	0	1	2	3
	⋮				
7.	Temper outbursts; explosive, unpredictable behavior	0	1	2	3
8.	Excitable, impulsive	0	1	2	3
9.	Fails to give close attention to details or makes careless mistakes in schoolwork, work, or other activities	0	1	2	3

picture of the client's drinking than would be possible from interviews and tests alone (Watson, 1999).

Advantages and Limitations of Behavioral Observation

Systematic behavioral observations offer another potentially rich source of data for the clinician and can be especially important when the behaviors requiring assessment cannot be accessed in an interview or test situation (Stricker & Trierweiler, 1995). The major limitation of systematic behavioral observations relates to the possible biases of the observer, which can compromise reliability and validity (Goodwin, 1995).

Brief Summary

- Clinicians rely on three data-gathering methods for assessing clients: (1) clinical interviews; (2) tests; and (3) observations.

- Clinical interviews may be structured, unstructured, or semi-structured. Structured interviews are more systematic and reliable, while unstructured interviews offer the advantage of greater flexibility.

- Tests used in the assessment of psychopathology can be divided into four types: (1) symptom and personality questionnaires; (2) projective tests; (3) cognitive tests; and (4) biological tests.

- Symptom and personality questionnaires are lists of questions that yield measures of psychological symptoms and personality profiles. The Beck Depression Inventory-II (BDI-II) is an example of a widely used symptom inventory; the Minnesota Multiphasic Personality Inventory-2 (MMPI-2) is an example of a widely used personality inventory.

- Projective tests are based on the projective hypothesis which holds that individuals' interpretations of ambiguous stimuli reveal a great deal about their mental and emotional functioning. Examples of such tests are the Rorschach, which asks clients to describe what a series of inkblots looks like to them, the Thematic Apperception Test (TAT), which asks clients to make up stories about a series of ambiguous pictures, and the Draw-A-Person Test (DAP), which asks clients to draw pictures of various people. Researchers have had mixed success in developing reliable and valid scoring systems for projective tests. Their chief advantage is the possibility of obtaining more in-depth information about clients.

- Cognitive tests are typically used for educational purposes, but they also have applications in clinical psychology. Cognitive tests can be subdivided into three groups: (1) intelligence tests; (2) achievement tests; and (3) neuropsychological tests. Intelligence tests are designed to measure intellectual ability, while achievement tests measure academic achievement in various subjects. Both can be useful for identifying certain disorders with primarily cognitive symptoms such as learning disabilities, or for developing a full understanding of a person with other mental disorders. Neuropsychological tests are designed to assess neurological (brain) deficits affecting perception, attention, memory, and problem solving; these tests, too, can be helpful in diagnosing and understanding some forms of psychopathology.

- Biological tests are designed to identify biological markers of mental disorders, using techniques ranging from brain imaging to physiological tests which measure arousal. At present, only a few biological tests have proven useful in the assessment of psychopathology, but this is likely to change as research on the biological aspects of mental illness continues to progress.

● Behavioral observation refers to assessing clients through systematic monitoring of their behavior, either by a clinician, parent, or teacher, or by the individual client through self-monitoring. Observing, recording, and analyzing behavior patterns over time can be helpful in assessing and understanding certain disorders.

Critical Thinking Question	**W**hich assessment techniques seem most useful for classifying/diagnosing clients? Which seem most helpful for understanding clients? Do some seem especially useful for both?

DIAGNOSIS AND ASSESSMENT IN PERSPECTIVE: CLASSIFYING AND UNDERSTANDING DAVE

Having considered many of the assessment methods available to clinicians, we may have given the impression that most or all of these methods are used in a typical clinical evaluation. In fact, in most outpatient evaluations the assessment process consists simply of one or two clinical interviews, perhaps with the administration of some symptom or personality questionnaires. Occasionally, in situations such as an inpatient evaluation of a diagnostically complex client, or when there are specific diagnostic questions to be answered, more extensive interviewing, testing, or behavioral observations may be added.

In order to illustrate the use of the assessment methods we have covered, we'll describe the assessment of Dave, who happened to have a thorough evaluation when he sought help at the college counseling center. Because Dave was seeking mental health treatment for the first time, he and the psychologist evaluating him decided that a complete assessment, including interviews, tests, and some behavioral observation should be undertaken. We will review the results of this evaluation, which highlight the use of several assessment methods, and illustrate the difference between *classifying* and *understanding* Dave's problems. As you will see, some of the assessment methods provide data that help to *classify* Dave's problems (his DSM-IV-TR diagnosis, social phobia, was described earlier in the chapter), some methods provide data that help to *understand* Dave's problems, and some methods provide both.

Interview with Dave

The following is an excerpt from the *unstructured* portion of the evaluation interview with Dr. Ramirez.

Dr. R: Please sit down. Where would you like to start?

Dave: (Looking tense and near tears) I've been having a hard time this year… with anxiety… I don't know what's wrong, but I feel so tense all the time… I'm a perfectionist and a bit of a control freak; I think I have to be perfect and in control all the time and I'm not… I can't be with people, I just freak out… I don't really know where to start. (Ten second pause) I feel embarrassed to talk about this—I've never seen a psychologist before. (Brief pause) My brother has problems but I never have. (Dave's tone changes to an unemotional, factual mode) He has an anxiety disorder resulting from my family dynamic patterns—I've done quite a lot of reading on it. He's become the focus of our family; he uses it to get attention. Maybe I'm just whining, maybe nothing's really wrong—it's probably just a sophomore slump.

Dr. R: It sounds like it's not easy for you to come here, that you feel that you shouldn't have any problems. Is that right?

Dave: (Seeming more emotional again) Yeah, I'm supposed to be the strong one in the family. And I don't see any other kids here having problems like I do. They all seem confident and secure, and I don't know if I can measure up here—the competition is a lot tougher than in high school. My parents have been through so much with my brother. If my dad knew I was having problems too he'd … well, I know he'd be there for me, but it might be too much for them! (Five second pause) There's so much to tell. This anxiety has been building up for a long time—I've just been keeping it inside as much as possible. Should I tell you about what's going on now, or where it all started?

Dr. R: Whichever you'd like. We'll have time to get to everything.

Dave: Well, the main thing is I feel really anxious in public, especially at social events. I can't talk, I can't think… That's why I'm here. There's a long story behind it…

Interpretation/Commentary

Dr. Ramirez begins by trying to make Dave comfortable and by assessing the content and process of Dave's thoughts at the start of their session. Even in this initial segment of the interview, it becomes apparent that Dave's problems probably "fit" the DSM-IV-TR diagnostic category called social phobia, an excessive anxiety about social performance (Chapter 5). But this unstructured portion of the interview does not only focus on *classifying* Dave's problems. Dr. Ramirez also gathers data that will lead to an initial *understanding* of Dave's problems, such as Dave's tendency to feel extreme shame and embarrassment, to compare himself to his family and peers, and to feel that he is responsible for keeping his family together by being the "strong one." Also, Dave seemed to suddenly use the defense mechanism of intellectualization when he talked about his brother, suggesting that this is a particularly troublesome topic for him.

Understanding Dave's problems includes developing some initial hypotheses about their causes. For example, the unstructured interview data suggest that Dave's anxiety problem may be related to the reinforcement of anxiety within his family, to his perfectionistic thinking, and to his emotional conflicts over competition and achievement. It is also important to note that Dave seemed to respond positively to the initial empathic comments of Dr. Ramirez, which may bode well for a therapeutic relationship.

The following is an excerpt from the *structured* portion of interview with Dr. Ramirez (Mental Status Exam).

Dr. R: Dave, I want to ask you some questions just as part of our evaluation of how you're doing overall. Can you tell me where we are?

Dave: Sure, we're at the Counseling Center.

Dr. R: And what year is it?

Dave: It's 2004.

Dr. R. Okay, and could you count backwards for me from 100 by 7's.

Dave: 100, 93, 86, 79, 72…

Dr. R: Fine.

Interpretation/Commentary

Dr. Ramirez conducts a standard mental status exam, which Dave "passes;" there are no indications that Dave has any severe impairments in his thinking such as would be present in a psychotic disorder.

Dave's Test Results

Beck Depression Inventory-II (BDI-II)

Score: 10 out of a possible 63.

Interpretation/Commentary

This score is indicative of very mild depressive symptoms. Depression is unlikely to be the primary diagnosis with this score.

MMPI-2

Score/Profile: (Elevations reported are in comparison to sample of "normal" subjects.)

Validity Scales

Lie ("L" scale: Denial of problems; trying to look good): **Moderately elevated**

Carelessness ("F" scale: Symptom exaggeration or faking): **Not elevated**

Defensiveness ("K" scale: Evasiveness or guardedness): **Not elevated**

Clinical Scales

Hypochondriasis ("Hs" scale: Anxiety related to bodily functions): **Not elevated**

Depression ("D" scale: Depressive traits and symptoms): **Moderately elevated**

Conversion Hysteria ("Hy" scale: Expression of emotional distress through physical symptoms): **Not elevated**

Psychopathic Deviance: ("Pd" scale: Exploitative and irresponsible traits): **Not elevated**

Masculinity-Femininity: ("Mf" scale: For male subjects, stereotypically feminine traits): **Moderately elevated**

Paranoia: ("Pa" scale: Extreme suspiciousness): **Not elevated**

Psychasthenia: ("Pt" scale: Overanxious and self-doubting): **Highly elevated**

Schizophrenia: ("Sc" scale: Bizarre and psychotic traits): **Not elevated**

Hypomania: ("Ma" scale: Grandiose and over-excited traits): **Not elevated**

Social Introversion: ("Si" scale: Shy, insecure, easily embarrassed): **Moderately elevated**

Interpretation/Commentary

The validity scales indicate that Dave answered the test questions relatively honestly, and that the results can be trusted. He is able to be somewhat open in acknowledging personal problems, although he has a tendency to minimize them as seen on the "L" scale. The clinical scales indicate that Dave is not suffering from any severe psychopathology since only a few of the scale scores are elevated (the moderate elevation on the Masculinity-Femininity scale is typical of male college students, who tend to be relatively tolerant, sensitive, and intelligent). The significant elevations in the Depression, Psychasthenia, and Social Introversion scales indicate that Dave tends to be anxious, lacking in confidence, conventional, controlled, shy, and insecure. On the positive side, he is a conscientious and reflective person, and this may bode well for psychological treatment.

Wechsler Adult Intelligence Scale (WAIS)

Scores: Verbal IQ = 118; Performance IQ = 111; Full Scale IQ = 115.

Interpretation/Commentary

Dave's scores indicate intellectual ability in the high average range. This is consistent with Dave's high level of academic achievement. Individual subtest scores were also consistently in the high average range. There is no evidence of cognitive deficits and no need for further cognitive evaluation with achievement or neuropsychological tests.

Thematic Apperception Test (TAT)

(Card 1: This card shows a boy sitting with an object that is often seen as a violin on a table in front of him: see Box 4.4.)

Dave's Response: This kid looks pretty worried. His parents have pushed him to play the violin since he was five years old, and he has a big competition coming up. He's not mad at his parents for all the pressure, he just wonders if he can handle it. He's always been a star, but now the competition is getting tougher. The biggest problem is that he's holding it all inside. He thinks his nervousness could ruin his performance, and his parents would be worried about him. But he goes to the competition and does great. He realizes that anxiety is just a misfiring of neurons in his brain. The nervousness goes away and everybody is happy. That's all.

Interpretation/Commentary

Dave's intense anxiety about competition and performance come across strongly in this response. He also clearly conveys his feeling of pressure from the family to perform and excel. Dave's response also shows his use of defense mechanisms such as denial, intellectualization, and minimization at the end when he attempts to cover over the anxiety and the anger at the parents with a sugar-coated ending to the story.

Rorschach

(Card 1: This card has a symmetrical black inkblot, which is frequently seen as resembling a butterfly or bat.)

Dave's Response: It looks like a butterfly, based on the overall shape and configuration...one of those specimens you see in a museum. They prepare them carefully and mount them on a wall—it doesn't hurt the butterfly of course because it's deceased. The specimen appears to be shaking a little bit, as though there's a breeze in the room. The white spaces could be where the wings got damaged during the process. Somebody screwed up. That's all I see in the card.

Interpretation/Commentary

Dave's general response—a butterfly—is a common one, suggesting a conventional tendency in his personality. His tendency to feel ashamed, exposed, inadequate, and anxious come across in seeing the butterfly as a "specimen," and a damaged one at that. This may also reflect his anxiety about his psychological evaluation, in which he feels like a specimen. The movement Dave sees in the card is often considered a sign of anxiety as well (Weiner, 1998), particularly in this case because it is described as "shaking." Use of the white spaces inside the inkblot is often interpreted as indicating an oppositional or defiant tendency (Weiner, 1998), which, if also seen on other cards, could suggest that underneath Dave's conventional and compliant personality he struggles with rebellious feelings. Finally, Dave's tendency to use the defense mechanisms of intellectualization and denial are seen in his use of scientific language and the museum concepts.

It is important to note that in clinical practice the TAT and the Rorschach are only interpreted when the complete test, a sequence of several cards, is administered; our interpretation of one TAT and one Rorschach card alone is intended only to illustrate the interpretive process. The hypotheses about Dave's responses to this card would have to be balanced against hypotheses based on responses to additional cards. Further, the responses on all the cards would typically be scored using a standardized scoring system and compared to established norms for various diagnostic groups.

Behavioral Observations of Dave

Dr. Ramirez asked Dave to monitor his anxiety for one week after their appointment by keeping a daily journal and by rating his anxiety on a scale of 1 to 10 each time he felt anxious. Dave's journal entries described his preoccupation with being seen as unattractive and inferior to others. He compared himself unfavorably with his friends, his brother, and his father. Dave's anxiety ratings were in the 7- to 9-range several times each day, especially when he had to be in social situations.

Interpretation/Commentary

Dave's journal entries and self-ratings of anxiety are indicative of pronounced social anxiety and suggest that this is linked to feelings of inadequacy in comparison to others. The intensity of Dave's daily anxiety ratings alerts Dr. Ramirez to the urgency of providing Dave with some rapid relief from his high level of distress.

THE ADVANTAGES AND LIMITATIONS OF THE DIAGNOSIS OF DAVE

The data from this overall assessment of Dave allow us to both *classify* and *understand* Dave and his problems. Diagnostically, Dave's anxiety problem can be classified as a social phobia (Chapter 5), a persistent, irrational fear and avoidance of social situations, according to the DSM-IV-TR (see Dave's complete DSM-IV-TR diagnosis on page 90). But this diagnostic classification, while important, is not the same as *understanding* Dave and his problems. Many people have the same diagnosis as Dave and yet are vastly different as people, with different life histories and different causes of their problems. In short, the case of Dave highlights the core concept at the heart of this chapter: *the advantages and limitations of diagnosis.* While diagnosing a client is an important goal of the assessment process, it is equally important to develop an understanding of the client. Fortunately, the assessment process can also offer information that can help us understand clients and their problems. For example, the interviews, tests, and observations converge in showing that Dave's anxiety symptoms are related to his perfectionistic thinking and expectations, to the pressures from his family to be successful, to his feelings of competitive inadequacy, and to his emotional conflicts about anger. This initial understanding of Dave cannot be reduced to a diagnosis, but it is crucial to helping Dave. In fact, Dave began psychotherapy at his college's psychological clinic, and addressing these cognitive, behavioral, psychodynamic, and family themes helped him to overcome his anxiety. In sum, classification and understanding complement each other in any complete assessment and treatment of psychopathology.

Chapter Summary

- To diagnose means to identify different syndromes of psychopathology according to a classification system, or taxonomy. Assessment is the process of gathering information about a client in order to make a diagnosis.

- In order to be useful, diagnostic classification systems must have two statistical properties: reliability and validity. Reliability refers to the consistency of classification decisions using a certain system; validity refers to the accuracy of classification decisions.

- Diagnostic classification systems for psychopathology have grown increasingly detailed over time. The current official system in the United States, the DSM system, lists over 300 separate disorders in the DSM-IV-TR.

- Clinicians rely on three data gathering methods for assessing clients: (1) clinical interviews; (2) tests; and (3) observations.

- The purpose of an assessment process is to both classify (diagnose) and to understand (that is, develop an explanation of) a client's problems. Both goals are important, and different assessment methods contribute to each.

- The case of Dave illustrates *the advantages and limitations of diagnosis*, and the importance of both diagnosing and understanding a client in order to help the client in treatment.

Edvard Munch, *Seascape*, 1899.
©Francis G. Meyer/Corbis©2004. The Munch
Museum/The Munch-Ellingston Group/Artists
Rights Society (ARS), New York

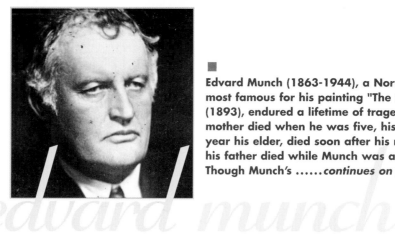

■ Edvard Munch (1863-1944), a Norwegian artist most famous for his painting "The Scream" (1893), endured a lifetime of tragedy. Munch's mother died when he was five, his sister, only a year his elder, died soon after his mother, and his father died while Munch was a young adult. Though Munch's ......*continues on page 112*

chapter five

ANXIETY AND THE
ANXIETY DISORDERS

Case Vignettes

Arthur, a 22-year-old engineering student, visited his primary care physician complaining that he had been experiencing occasional "spells" over the past two months. During the episodes he felt anxious, dizzy, nauseous, had intense headaches, and sometimes had difficulty breathing. After having a "spell" Arthur worried about when the next one would occur. A thorough medical exam and a series of laboratory tests found that nothing was physically wrong with Arthur. The physician suspected that Arthur was suffering from panic attacks and asked if he had been experiencing increased stress in recent weeks. Arthur acknowledged that he was somewhat anxious about graduating from college in a month, however, he doubted that his "spells" could have an emotional basis since the symptoms were mostly physical. Arthur was the first person in his family ever to have to gone to college and he had done very well in school despite being in a difficult engineering program. He had already been hired by a prestigious bioengineering firm near his hometown and was nervous about beginning his professional life. Arthur explained that his parents were extremely proud of his success and that his entire extended family was planning to attend his graduation.

Greg, a successful 35-year-old corporate attorney, decided to seek psychological help when his wife and children could no longer stand his cleaning habits. Greg had always been compulsive about straightening up his own possessions, but in recent years he had become increasingly picky about maintaining order in the entire house. Greg became agitated if the glasses in the kitchen cabinet were arranged in uneven rows, or if the throw pillows on the couch were not perfectly aligned with the couch's striped pattern. When stray hairs were left in the bathroom he flew into a panic and insisted that the offender clean the area immediately. Greg also felt, superstitiously, that he had to repeatedly check, double-check, and triple-check that everything was clean. Greg acknowledged that these were "over-reactions" but said that he could not control them and feared that something terrible would happen if he did not have everything in proper order. Greg's 7-year-old son stopped inviting friends over to the house because he knew that their play would irritate Greg, and his 12-year-old daughter reached the point where she would not follow any of her father's cleaning rules because she found them so ridiculous.

Case Vignettes

- **Defining Anxiety and Anxiety Disorders**
  - The Importance of Context in Defining Anxiety Disorders
  - The Continuum Between Normal and Abnormal Anxiety
- **Classifying Anxiety Disorders**
  - The DSM-IV-TR Categories
  - The Advantages and Limitations of the DSM-IV-TR Anxiety Disorder Diagnoses
  - Classification in Demographic Context
  - Cultural and Historical Relativism in Defining and Classifying Anxiety Disorders
- **Explaining and Treating Anxiety and Anxiety Disorders**
  - Behavioral Components
  - Cognitive Components
  - Biological Components
  - Psychodynamic Components
  - The Multiple Causality of Anxiety Disorders
  - The Connection Between Mind and Body in Anxiety Disorders

Case Vignettes - Treatment

DEFINING ANXIETY AND ANXIETY DISORDERS

All of us know what it is like to feel anxious or scared. Anxiety and its close relative, fear, are normal parts of everyday life. **Anxiety** is usually defined as an unpleasant emotion associated with a general sense of danger—the feeling that

Anxiety An unpleasant emotion characterized by a general sense of danger, dread, and physiological arousal.

...continued from page 110

paintings tend to reflect themes of emotional pain and brooding introspection, he was not able to channel all of his distress into his artwork. In 1908, Munch was hospitalized for anxiety and treated with electroshock therapy. Despite his emotional troubles, Munch produced many significant paintings until the time of his death and played an instrumental role in the development of German Expressionism.

something bad is going to happen. In *fear,* the danger is more specific. Most of us have felt anxiety and fear when we've been in a minor car accident, or had a near miss. You may have worried for a split-second that you would be seriously hurt. Perhaps you momentarily "froze" and felt unable to act quickly and appropriately. Whether or not you were aware of it, your pupils probably dilated, and your mouth may have become dry as a small burst of adrenaline was released into your bloodstream. After the danger passed, you may have noticed that your heart was pounding or that you had broken out in a sweat. In sum, the experience of anxiety is not just emotional, but involves cognitive, behavioral, and physical components as well (see Table 5.1).

Fear and anxiety are normal human responses to threatening or dangerous situations. Indeed, the capacity for a hearty fear response is an evolutionary gift from our ancestors (Nesse, 1998). The cave dwellers who didn't react to the presence of a saber-toothed tiger either by freezing (and thereby hiding themselves) or making an adrenaline-boosted sprint probably don't have too many descendents walking around today! But if fear and anxiety are normal and evolutionarily adaptive, on what basis do we decide that someone suffers from an anxiety *disorder?* When it comes to defining anxiety disorders, two core concepts are critical: the **context** in which the anxiety occurs, and the severity of the anxiety along the **continuum** from mild to severe.

The Importance of Context in Defining Anxiety Disorders

People with anxiety disorders experience anxiety and fear in **contexts** that do not justify such feelings. Unlike the cave dwellers described above, people with anxiety disorders feel anxious or even terrified in the face of a minor threat or when no threat is present at all. For example, a person with an intense, persistent, and irrational fear of snakes (a *phobia,* which will be discussed in detail later in the chapter), might shake with fear and break out in a sweat when seeing a small garter snake in the woods. Even though the snake presents a miniscule threat, the person with the phobia experiences the danger as intense. Some people with anxiety disorders experience anxiety when *no* danger exists at all. For example, the phenomenon known as a *flashback* is a common symptom in *posttraumatic stress disorder* (also discussed in detail later in the chapter). During a flashback, people with posttraumatic stress disorder recall a previous traumatic experience with such intensity that they feel as if they are reexperiencing the event. For example, when a rape survivor experiences a flashback she may feel as if she is being attacked again and experiences all of the terror she felt during the original attack, even if she is actually alone and in a safe place.

Table 5.1	**Common Components of Anxiety**			
	EMOTIONAL	**COGNITIVE**	**BEHAVIORAL**	**PHYSICAL**
	Fright	Hypervigilance	"Fight or flight" response[1]	Muscle tension
	Nervousness	Poor concentration	Freezing up	Pounding heart
	Irritability	Rumination	Avoidant behavior	Dry mouth

[1] An extreme sympathetic nervous system arousal that prepares humans to flee or attack when faced with danger (see Chapter 3).

The Continuum Between Normal and Abnormal Anxiety

In addition to matters of context, anxiety disorders are also defined by the intensity of the anxiety. In other words, the *continuum between normal and abnormal behavior* has to be considered in order to define pathological anxiety. Though everyone experiences anxiety at times, some people feel anxious rarely and mildly while others feel anxious often and intensely. The continuum between low and high levels of anxiety applies to two kinds of anxiety studied by psychologists: *trait* and *state* anxiety (Endler & Kocovski, 2001). **Trait anxiety** reflects an individual's predisposition to respond to a wide variety of situations with more or less anxiety. People with high levels of trait anxiety feel anxious most of the time, regardless of external circumstances. In contrast, people low in trait anxiety rarely feel anxious, even when anxiety would be an expected response (see Box 5.1).

State anxiety is typically defined as an individual's level of anxiety in response to a specific situation (an impending exam, going to a job interview). Like trait anxiety, state anxiety occurs along a continuum. Imagine, for example, various levels of being afraid of snakes. One person might feel a little nervous around snakes, but still be intrigued by the idea of seeing them at the zoo. Indeed, part of the fun of going to the zoo is getting to see potentially dangerous animals in a safe setting. Another person may decide to skip her visit to the snake house and agree to wait outside while her friends go in. A third person may feel so frightened of snakes that he refuses to go to the zoo with his friends and feels sorry that he missed the outing. The first two people share a mild fear of snakes, but the level of their anxiety does not appear to interfere with their functioning. The third person's state of anxiety can be considered pathological because his irrational fear of snakes causes intense distress and significantly impairs his ability to function.

Everyday anxiety Anxiety, seen on this girl's face as she waits for an amusement park ride to begin, is a part of everyday life.

Trait anxiety An individual's tendency to respond to a variety of situations with more or less anxiety.

State anxiety An individual's level of anxiety at a specific time.

Brief Summary

● Fear and anxiety are normal emotions which have evolved to help animals respond to danger.

● Pathological anxiety is defined as anxiety that occurs in an inappropriate *context* or is overly intense on the *continuum* between mild and extreme anxiety.

Critical Thinking Question | **W**e have suggested that abnormal anxiety can be defined as anxiety that is relatively intense or inappropriate to its context. With this definition in mind, which of Greg's reactions (described at the beginning of the chapter) seem to be unusually intense? Does any of his anxiety seem to be appropriate to its context?

CLASSIFYING ANXIETY DISORDERS

Anxiety is a part of many different mental disorders, but the DSM-IV-TR category called "anxiety disorders" includes only those disorders in which anxiety is the *main symptom*, in keeping with the DSM-IV-TR descriptive classification philosophy explained in Chapter 4. Anxiety disorders are some the most common mental disorders among the U.S. population, affecting at least 15% of Americans in any given

Just for the thrill of it Activities such as bungee-jumping are terrifying for some, but highly enjoyable and exhilarating for others.

BOX 5.1   High Risk Takers

Too Little Anxiety?

Ask a group of individuals how they would feel if they were hanging off the side of Mount Everest or chasing an armed criminal, and the majority would probably admit that they would feel scared or anxious. For a small percentage of individuals, however, these activities might be more exhilarating than anxiety provoking. Sometimes referred to as "high-risk takers," such individuals fall on the other end of the "anxiety continuum" from those suffering from the disorders discussed in this chapter. Rather than experiencing uncomfortably high levels of anxiety, high-risk takers may experience levels of anxiety that are actually lower than normal.

Compared to those who experience high levels of anxiety and are uncomfortable taking risks, risk takers are drawn to jobs in which they place themselves or others in physical jeopardy, are more likely to engage in physically risky sports, and are less likely to experience fear in typically frightening situations, such as being exposed to a spider or left alone in the dark (Breivik, 1996; Zuckerman, 1991). Such individuals may also not *anticipate* feeling anxious in situations, such as those described above, which would generally be expected to produce anxiety (Lykken, 1957; Zuckerman, 1991).

But can a person experience too little anxiety? From an evolutionary perspective, the answer appears to be "yes." As discussed earlier in the chapter, anxiety serves an important adaptive function (Nesse, 1998). While sometimes uncomfortable, the sensations associated with anxiety helped prepare our ancestors to fight in or flee from dangerous situations, thus promoting survival. And though most of us no longer need to protect ourselves from actual predators, the experience (or even the anticipation) of anxiety can help prepare us for situations that are potentially harmful. Because risk takers are less likely to experience or anticipate anxiety in dangerous situations, they are more prone to hurt themselves. For example, they are more likely to suffer injuries, engage in potentially risky sexual practices, smoke cigarettes, and abuse illegal drugs (Zuckerman, 1991).

Some experts have also argued that anxiety actually *helps* most people learn socially appropriate behavior: we behave appropriately partly in order to reduce the anxiety caused by the disapproval of others. Interestingly, low levels of anxiety and high levels of risk taking have been linked to antisocial personality disorder (APD), a disorder marked by chronic, pervasive impulsivity, deceitfulness, and lack of concern for the rights of others (Chapter 11). The low levels of anxiety exhibited by those with APD may make it difficult for them to learn to behave in socially acceptable ways. Indeed, one classic study showed that individuals with this disorder had difficulty learning to avoid incorrect responses to a laboratory game, even when these responses were paired with anxiety-producing stimuli, such as an electric shock (Lykken, 1957). If the experience of anxiety can be a useful teacher, those with APD appear to be at a learning disadvantage without it.

However, individuals with APD are not the only ones who exhibit low levels of anxiety. While studies have found that those with APD, and convicted criminals, do exhibit low levels of anxiety (Buikhuisen et al., 1984; Lykken, 1957), others have found similarly low levels of anxiety among those training to be police officers (Lorr & Strack, 1994). This appears to be one trait that police officers and criminals share.

So how does one become a high-risk taker with "too little anxiety?" Human beings may have a built-in optimal level of arousal: a moderate amount that is high enough to maintain focused attention, but low enough to maintain comfort. While the majority of individuals may be naturally close to this optimal level, risk takers appear to be chronically "under-aroused" (Zuckerman, 1991). Their low levels of anxiety and chronic under-arousal may lead them to seek out risky, highly stimulating situations which would be uncomfortably anxiety-provoking for most people, but serve to bring risk takers closer to the optimal state of arousal.

In other words, risk takers might be drawn to activities like mountain climbing as a corrective to their baseline under-arousal. For those of us who do not experience chronically low levels of arousal and anxiety, it will probably be stimulating enough to watch such activities on TV!

The DSM-IV-TR Anxiety Disorders	Table 5.2
Generalized anxiety disorder ■ Chronic, debilitating nervousness (lifetime prevalence estimate: 5% of the population). **Panic disorder** ■ Episodes of acute terror in the absence of real danger (lifetime prevalence estimate: between 1%–2%). **Phobias** ■ Persistent, irrational fear and avoidance of particular objects or situations (lifetime prevalence estimate: between 9%–24%). **Obsessive-compulsive disorder** ■ Anxiety producing, unwanted thoughts, usually leading to compulsive rituals (lifetime prevalence estimate: 1%–2.5%). **Posttraumatic stress disorder and acute stress disorder** ■ Persistent, debilitating anxiety symptoms occurring in the wake of a traumatic experience (lifetime prevalence estimate: over 8%).	*Adapted from the DSM-IV-TR, APA, 2000*

year and a much higher percentage over their lifetimes (Kessler et al., 1994; see Table 5.2). We'll begin with a description of the DSM-IV-TR anxiety disorders and then turn our attention to the core concepts of the ***advantages and limitations*** of the DSM-IV-TR anxiety disorder diagnoses and the issues of ***cultural and historical relativism*** in classifying anxiety disorders.

The DSM-IV-TR Categories

The DSM-IV-TR identifies six main anxiety disorders: *generalized anxiety disorder, panic disorder, phobias, obsessive-compulsive disorder, posttraumatic stress disorder,* and *acute stress disorder.* We will now describe each of these disorders in detail.

Generalized Anxiety Disorder

People with **generalized anxiety disorder** (GAD) experience chronic and pervasive anxiety. They feel tense and worried most of the time, which causes them distress and interferes with their functioning (Table 5.3).

Generalized anxiety disorder Chronic, pervasive, and debilitating nervousness.

Diagnostic Criteria for Generalized Anxiety Disorder (GAD)	Table 5.3
• Chronic, pervasive anxiety for at least six months. • Difficulty controlling the anxiety. • The anxiety includes three or more of the following symptoms: restlessness, fatigue, difficulty concentrating, irritability, muscle tension, sleep disturbance. • The anxiety, worry, or physical symptoms cause significant distress or impairment in normal functioning and are not due to the effects of a medication, drug, or medical condition.	*Adapted from DSM-IV-TR, APA, 2000*

Case Illustration Sharon had always considered herself to be a "worrier," but when she took a position as a bank teller she felt for the first time that her anxiety was really interfering with her life. Sharon felt tense most of the time that she was at work because she worried that she'd be caught in a bank robbery. When she wasn't at work, Sharon worried that she would be mugged or that someone would hack into the bank's computers and drain her personal accounts. She also constantly worried that her aging mother would experience a stroke or a heart attack and be unable to call for help. Sharon worried so much that even when she was very tired it took hours for her to fall asleep because she would lie in bed ruminating about her financial security, her mother's health, or her own future. After beginning her job at the bank, Sharon began to experience painful tension headaches that made it difficult for her to concentrate and caused her to miss several days of work. Not surprisingly, she became worried that she would be fired because of her absences. These concerns only increased her general anxiety and contributed to more frequent headaches.

Sharon experiences many of the symptoms commonly found in GAD. She feels anxious most of the time, worries about almost everything, and has trouble sleeping. Her anxiety is not limited to a specific situation—it pervades most aspects of her life. For Sharon, the physical symptoms of anxiety (her tension headaches) have begun to interfere with her ability to go to work. Other people with GAD find that their constant worrying can contribute to a wide variety of physical symptoms (such as dry mouth, nausea, or sweating) that may prevent them from pursuing or enjoying social relationships and new experiences (Noyes & Hoehn-Saric, 1998).

Panic Disorder

Panic disorder Panic attacks that cause ongoing distress or impairment.

Panic attack Discrete episode of acute terror in the absence of real danger.

People with **panic disorder** (PD) experience discrete episodes of intense terror—known as **panic attacks**—in which they feel overwhelmed by anxiety and have a strong urge to escape or get help. In contrast to generalized anxiety disorder (GAD), which involves *chronic* but milder anxiety, people with PD experience *acute* bursts of extreme anxiety (Table 5.4).

Case Illustration While on an airplane flight for a business trip, Simon began to feel like he was having a heart attack even though he could not understand how this was possible, given that he was a healthy 25-year-old man. He felt an enormous sense of dread and doom, his heart began to pound, he broke out in a sweat, and his throat felt like it was closing. The other passengers did not seem to notice his intense distress, but Simon was sure that he was going to die if he did not receive immediate medical

Table 5.4	Diagnostic Criteria for Panic Disorder (PD)

Adapted from the DSM-IV-TR, APA, 2000

- Episodes of intense panic *(panic attacks)*, including at least four of the following symptoms: pounding heart, sweating, shaking, shortness of breath, feeling of choking, chest pain, nausea, dizziness, fear of losing control, fear of dying, numbness or tingling, chills or hot flashes.
- Persistent concern about having additional attacks, worry about consequences of an attack, or changes in behavior because of the attack.
- The panic attacks are not due to the direct physiological effects of a drug, medication, or medical condition.

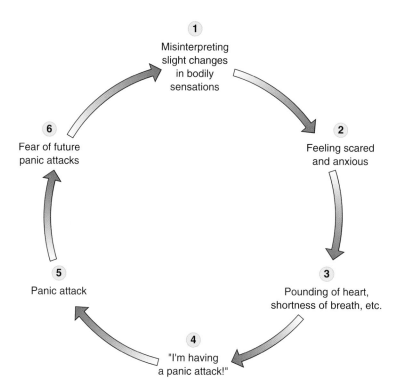

1 Misinterpreting slight changes in bodily sensations

2 Feeling scared and anxious

3 Pounding of heart, shortness of breath, etc.

4 "I'm having a panic attack!"

5 Panic attack

6 Fear of future panic attacks

Figure 5.1 A panic attack cycle Here we see how fear of having a panic attack can actually contribute to future panic attacks. Unfortunately, the more scared people become of future panic attacks, the more likely they are to experience intensifying physical symptoms such as quickening heart beat and difficulty breathing, that lead to further attacks.

(Based on Wells, 1997, p. 105)

attention. Yet, 20 minutes later while still on the plane, Simon felt better and decided that he probably didn't need to go to the emergency room. In the next few weeks, Simon had similar episodes of excruciating, short-lived anxiety while at work, in his car, and grocery shopping. Simon's girlfriend finally insisted that he consult a doctor when he started making excuses not to go out of his apartment for fear that he would have another attack.

Panic disorder is defined by the presence of panic attacks which lead to behavioral changes or worry about having future attacks. Panic attacks often seem to happen "out of the blue," but they may also be triggered by stressful circumstances (Craske, 1999). Regardless of what triggers a panic attack, the attacks themselves usually come on quickly, are experienced by their sufferers as terrifying and overwhelming, and last less than half an hour. After having had a panic attack, many people become preoccupied with the possibility of having future attacks and may find themselves in a distressing cycle of fearing fear itself (see Figure 5.1). Some people become so fearful of future panic attacks that they become housebound, a condition known as *agoraphobia*. Agoraphobia, a type of phobia that is a frequent consequence of panic disorder, is discussed in detail later in the chapter.

Panic attack sufferers often report feeling such intense anxiety and physical discomfort during the attacks that they are sure they are dying. In fact, one study estimated that between 16% to 25% of all people who come to hospital emergency rooms complaining of severe chest pain are actually experiencing a panic attack (Fleet et al., 1996).

Phobias

Phobias, the most common of the DSM-IV-TR anxiety disorders, are persistent and exaggerated fears of particular objects or situations (Table 5.5). Most people with phobias go out of their way to avoid the thing they fear, even if such avoidance is

What agoraphobics fear People suffering from agoraphobia avoid crowded places, like this New York subway platform, due to the fear that they would feel trapped or helpless if they were to experience a panic attack while surrounded by a large crowd.

Phobia An intense, persistent, and irrational fear and avoidance of a specific object or situation.

Table 5.5	Diagnostic Criteria for Phobias
Adapted from the DSM-IV-TR, APA, 2000	• Persistent, irrational fear of a specific object or situation. • Exposure to the feared object or situation usually provokes an intense anxiety reaction. • The person recognizes that the fear is excessive or unreasonable. • The phobic object or situation is avoided or else endured with intense anxiety or distress. • The avoidance, anxious anticipation, or worry about the feared object or situation interferes significantly with normal everyday functioning or there is substantial distress about having the phobia.

Social phobia A phobia in which fears are focused on social situations or other activities where there is a possibility of being observed and judged.

Agoraphobia A fear of wide open spaces or crowded places.

Creepy crawlies Almost half of all children experience phobias at one time or another, the most common fears being of the animal or natural environment type.

inconvenient and disruptive. The DSM-IV-TR distinguishes among three subtypes of phobias:

- *Social phobia*
- *Agoraphobia*
- *Specific phobia*

In **social phobia,** fears are focused on social situations or other activities where there is a possibility of being observed and judged, such as speaking in public or meeting new people. People who suffer from social phobia feel sure that other people are watching them closely and looking for signs of inadequacy. They often recognize that their fears are excessive, and yet their worries interfere with their daily functioning and/or cause considerable emotional distress.

People with social phobia often worry that they will humiliate or embarrass themselves and they tend to be "rejection sensitive." Often, their worries center on bodily functions, such as a fear of sweating or having one's stomach growl in public, which they fear will lead to humiliation or rejection. Those with fears of public speaking may anticipate being criticized by others if their hands shake or their voices tremble (Pollard & Henderson, 1988). As a result of their fears, people who suffer from social phobia may avoid speaking, eating, or drinking in public and may refuse to use public restrooms. When faced with a feared situation, people with social phobia may become so anxious that they experience a panic attack (APA, 2000). They often avoid social situations even at considerable economic or emotional expense.

Case Illustration Manuel, a first-year law student, came to a college counseling center when he could no longer tolerate his fear of speaking in class. Manuel had never been comfortable with public speaking, but he spent his college years at a large university where he was rarely expected to talk in front of his peers. Now, while sitting in class, Manuel worried that his mind would go blank, that his voice would waver, or that his classmates would think that he was stupid. Manuel's fear that he would be called on interfered with his ability to take notes and listen to his classmate's questions. Increasingly he found that he preferred to get class notes from his roommate rather than putting himself through the torture of attending class.

The second subtype of phobia is known as **agoraphobia,** which comes from the Greek for "fear (phobia) of the marketplace (agora)." People who suffer from agoraphobia are afraid of wide-open or crowded places and are often reluctant to leave their own homes. As we mentioned earlier in discussing panic disorder, agoraphobia frequently develops after a person has experienced panic attacks. In general, people suffering from agoraphobia are not afraid of public places per se, but of having a panic attack in a public place where it might be difficult to escape or get help (Noyes & Hoehn-Saric, 1998). For example, a woman who experiences a panic attack in a clothing store might develop an aversion to clothing stores and then soon find herself avoiding stores of any kind. Before long, she may feel uncomfortable in all public places. In this way, agoraphobia has a tendency to build over time until a person refuses to leave his or her own home or will only go out in public while in the company of a trusted companion. However, not all people who suffer from panic disorder develop agoraphobia, and some people, such as Bill (described below), suffer from agoraphobia without a history of panic attacks.

Case Illustration **Just over a year ago Bill, age 28, heard about a mugging in his neighborhood, which was overall quite safe. At first, Bill began to feel nervous in crowded places. Soon, Bill was getting uneasy in any public place, and he felt increasingly reluctant to leave the safety of his apartment. He decided to quit his job as a mechanic and to try working from home as a telephone salesman. Rather than leaving his apartment to go shopping he began to order the things he needed over the phone or over the Internet. On the occasions when Bill could not avoid leaving the house, such as when he needed to go to the dentist, he asked his older sister to accompany him.**

The third type of phobia, **specific phobia,** refers to any phobia that is not a social phobia or agoraphobia. Most often, specific phobias (formerly called *simple phobias*) fall into one of four common types described by the DSM-IV-TR: animal type (fear of spiders, snakes, dogs, etc.), natural environment type (heights, tornadoes, water), blood-injection-injury type (needles, injuries, the sight of blood), and situational type (enclosed spaces, flying in airplanes, elevators) (see Box 5.2). People who suffer from specific phobias, like Jenny (described below), usually recognize that their fears are excessive. However, they are usually unable to talk themselves out of being afraid and persistently avoid the feared object or situation.

Case Illustration **Jenny, a high school sophomore who enjoys a wide variety of activities and plays for her high school's field hockey team, is deathly afraid of hypodermic needles. She does not mind the sight of blood—indeed she sees blood regularly when she or a teammate is injured—but she cannot stand the sight, or even thought, of syringes. When Jenny's father was hospitalized with cancer she was reluctant to visit him for fear that she would accidentally see or come into contact with a hypodermic needle. Jenny finally got up the courage to visit her father but passed out immediately when a nurse came into her father's room carrying a syringe.**

Obsessive-Compulsive Disorder

Obsessive-compulsive disorder (OCD) is a condition involving repetitive, unwanted, anxiety-producing thoughts and compulsive rituals intended to protect against anxiety. (See Box 5.3 for one person's struggle with OCD.) The terms **obsession** and **compulsion** have specific technical definitions here that are different from their colloquial uses: obsessions are defined as unwanted and upsetting thoughts or impulses, while compulsions are defined as irrational rituals that are repeated over and over again in an effort to control or neutralize the anxiety brought on by the obsessions (Table 5.6).

Specific phobia Any phobia that is not a social phobia or agoraphobia.

Obsessive-compulsive disorder An anxiety disorder in which distressing and unwanted thoughts lead to compulsive rituals that significantly interfere with daily functioning.

Obsessions Unwanted and upsetting thoughts or impulses.

Compulsions Irrational rituals that are repeated in an effort to control or neutralize the anxiety brought on by obsessional thoughts.

Anxiety goes Hollywood In the movie *As Good as it Gets* (1997), Jack Nicholson's character has obsessive-compulsive anxieties and rituals. He also demonstrates many symptoms of *obsessive-compulsive personality disorder,* a disorder described in detail in Chapter 11.

BOX 5.2   **Excessive Fears**

Some Not So Common Phobias

People develop phobias to a wide variety of objects or situations. Some phobias, like claustrophobia (the fear of confined spaces), are relatively common, while other phobias are highly idiosyncratic and occur very rarely. Consider the following list of unusual phobias:

- Ablutophobia—Fear of washing or bathing
- Botanophobia—Fear of plants
- Chaetophobia—Fear of hair
- Dromophobia—Fear of crossing streets
- Ereuthrophobia—Fear of blushing
- Francophobia—Fear of France, French culture
- Genuphobia—Fear of knees
- Hippophobia—Fear of horses
- Illyngophobia—Fear of vertigo or feeling dizzy when looking down
- Keraunophobia—Fear of thunder and lightning
- Linonophobia—Fear of string
- Melanophobia—Fear of the color black
- Numerophobia—Fear of numbers
- Ornithophobia—Fear of birds
- Peladophobia—Fear of bald people

- Rupophobia—Fear of dirt
- Scoptophobia—Fear of being seen or stared at
- Thalassophobia—Fear of the sea
- Vestiphobia—Fear of clothing
- Xerophobia—Fear of dryness
- Zelophobia—Fear of jealousy

(From www.phobialist.com)

Table 5.6	Diagnostic Criteria for Obsessive-Compulsive Disorder (OCD)
Adapted from the DSM-IV-TR (APA, 2000)	<ul><li>The presence of obsessions and/or compulsions.</li></ul>**Obsessions**<ul><li>Are recurrent, anxiety-producing thoughts, impulses, or images that are intrusive, unwanted, and inappropriate to the current context.</li><li>Cause the sufferer to attempt to ignore or suppress the obsessional thoughts, impulses or images, or to neutralize them with some other thought or action.</li></ul>**Compulsions**<ul><li>Are ritualized behaviors (for example, hand-washing) or mental acts (such as counting) that the person feels driven to perform in response to an obsession, or according to rules that must be applied rigidly.</li><li>Are intended to magically prevent some dreaded event or situation.</li></ul><ul><li>At some point in the disorder, the person has recognized that the obsessions or compulsions are excessive or unreasonable.</li><li>The obsessions and compulsions cause significant distress, are time-consuming, and/or interfere with the person's normal routine.</li><li>The obsessions or compulsions are not due to the effects of a medication, drug, or medical condition.</li></ul>

BOX 5.3 Living with OCD

Passing for Normal

In her book, *Passing for Normal: A Memoir of Compulsion,* Amy Wilensky describes her struggles with obsessive-compulsive disorder. In addition to OCD, Ms. Wilensky also suffers from Tourette's syndrome, a disorder characterized by multiple motor tics (involuntary movements such as eye blinking or grimacing) and one or more vocal tics (such as making sounds, clicks, or grunts). Tourette's disorder co-occurs in about 5% to 7% of people with OCD (APA, 2000).

CASE My senior year of high school my parents planned a family trip to Maui for us and my grandmother over Christmas vacation … I've rarely been as convinced of anything as that I was doomed to die in that plane [to Hawaii]. I offered to stay home by myself, told my parents—and meant it—that I'd rather walk to California in bare feet and swim the Pacific Ocean than get on [the plane]. But my parents had little tolerance for my newfound fear of flying and even less for a child so spoiled as to be ungrateful for such an extravagant trip… As the date for our departure neared, the rituals that had become an integral part of my daily routine tripled. Like fractals, old ones spawned new ones, especially designed to prevent the plane from crashing, to keep me alive until I'd landed safely back in Boston. At first, I was not allowed to touch any (ground) cover—floor, carpet, grass—with my bare feet. After a few days I amended this and decided that I could not *have* bare feet, so I slept in my sneakers and socks; the sneakers were for insurance. I washed my hair in the bathtub faucet and my body with a washcloth so I wouldn't have to shower or bathe with my shoes or socks on. Through it all, I twitched more than ever, as if I'd stuck my finger in an electrical socket and was holding it there. Then, one afternoon a week before we were scheduled to leave, when I was absentmindedly chewing a piece of gum, it struck me that chewing gum until the plane landed safely would be another terrific insurance policy against a crash. For the next week I kept that same piece of gum in my mouth, tucking it between my gum and the inside of my cheek whenever I had to eat or drink.

The truth is, even as I followed through with the most bizarre of these rituals—sweating in bed at night in my heavy wool socks, praying that I wouldn't choke on my gum in my sleep—I wasn't truly convinced they would have the intended protective effect. Today, when I occasionally tap the threshold of my apartment door twice each time I leave and enter, I know more than ever how unconnected the ritual is with anything at all, let alone my personal safety or happiness or success.

(Wilensky, 1999, pp. 88–91)

Case Illustration Jackson constantly imagines that his wife will be killed in a gruesome car accident. This thought seems to "pop" into his head when he is trying to get work done at his office. Jackson knows that his fear is irrational—his wife is a good driver who has never had an accident—yet he feels very anxious when he imagines her fatal car accident. Jackson has found that he can reduce his anxiety about his wife's safety if he walks around his office in a particular pattern, touching certain pieces of furniture as he goes. He often has to repeat the pattern several times until it feels "right" before he can go back to doing his work. At home, Jackson feels anxiously compelled to perform a number of "checking" rituals, such as continually rechecking to make sure that the stove is turned off and that the doors are locked. On some days, Jackson must repeat his rituals several times in a row throughout the day in order to keep his anxiety under control.

Interestingly, obsessions usually focus on a few specific areas, such as fears of contamination, disarray, or aggressive/destructive, sexual, or socially inappropriate behavior (Pato, Pato, & Gunn, 1998; Akhtar et al., 1975). For example, people with OCD may worry that they will contract a horrible disease from touching a doorknob (contamination), feel extremely uncomfortable if the books on their shelves are not perfectly aligned (disarray), fear that they have accidentally poisoned a loved one (aggression), or worry that they will blurt out obscene words in front of a boss (sexually or socially inappropriate). Obsessions may also take the form of repeated doubts, such as worrying that one has forgotten to turn off a stove or an iron. A person with OCD might check an iron repeatedly, unplug it from the wall, or even move it away from any electrical outlet and yet still have concerns that the iron has not been properly turned off.

The compulsive behaviors associated with OCD can involve seemingly logical, though irrationally excessive, attempts to reduce the anxiety associated with obsessive thoughts, such as when people with fears of contamination wash their hands several times after touching a doorknob. However, some compulsive behaviors lack any apparent connection with the obsessions they are designed to counteract. For example, people with OCD may have elaborate rituals such as counting to one hundred by fours, or reciting a meaningless phrase in order to "undo" an obsessional thought about harm coming to a loved one.

Posttraumatic Stress Disorder and Acute Stress Disorder

In everyday conversation, we often use the term *trauma* to describe any stressful or upsetting event, but for the purpose of diagnosing stress disorders a **trauma** is defined as an emotionally overwhelming experience in which there is a possibility of death or serious injury to oneself or a loved one (APA, 2000). Following a traumatic experience, some people experience the symptoms described in Table 5.7. If these symptoms last more than two days, but less than a month, are accompanied by dissociative symptoms (a change in state of consciousness, such as feeling detached from one's body; described in detail in Chapter 7), and cause significant distress or impairment, a diagnosis of **acute stress disorder** (ASD) is indicated according to the DSM-IV-TR. If stress symptoms continue for more than one month, or begin more than a month after the trauma, the diagnosis of **posttraumatic stress disorder** (PTSD) applies. The DSM-IV-TR distinguishes among three types of PTSD: *acute,* when symptoms last for less than three months, *chronic,* when symptoms last for more than three months, and *with delayed onset,* when at least six months pass between the traumatic event and the onset of symptoms.

Much of what we know about stress disorders comes from research on survivors of war trauma, but there are many different kinds of events that can be traumatic, including natural disasters (such as earthquakes, tornadoes, and floods) and human-made disasters besides war (such as domestic violence and rape). Everyday events such as car accidents or the death of a loved one may be considered traumatic if they are accompanied by terror, horror, or helplessness. PTSD and ASD may also develop after witnessing a traumatic event, such as a parent who watches his or her child being hit by a car, or in bystanders who see horrible events like those who witnessed the collapse of the World Trade Center in the attacks of September 11, 2001. The likelihood of developing a stress disorder following a traumatic experience is increased by the length and intensity of the exposure to danger, by preexisting emotional problems, by a history of prior traumas, by guilt over surviving the trauma, and/or by a lack of social support. It has been estimated that as many as 90% of rape victims, prisoners of war, and concentration camp survivors (such as during the Holocaust) develop stress disorders; by contrast, 5% to 10% of people develop a stress disorder following a serious car accident. Initial studies indicated that about 20% of the residents of lower Manhattan experienced stress disorders in the wake of the September 11, 2001 attacks (Goode, 2002).

Trauma An emotionally overwhelming experience in which there is a possibility of death or serious injury to onself or a loved one.

Acute stress disorder Significant posttraumatic anxiety symptoms that occur within one month of a traumatic experience.

Posttraumatic stress disorder Significant posttraumatic anxiety symptoms occurring more than one month after a traumatic experience.

Written on their faces These children of the Hema ethnic group in northeastern Congo watched as members of their tribe were massacred during intertribal warfare for land and other resources. Their faces show the intense psychological distress associated with traumatic experiences.

Case Illustration Mary, a 37-year-old mother of three, began to take business classes at her local community college once her youngest child started attending preschool. One day, while walking to her car after class, Mary was attacked by a stranger and pulled into an alley where she was raped. After the attack, Mary had the presence of mind to go to an emergency room where she was medically treated and then interviewed by the police. Later in the same week she was able to pick her attacker out of a book of pho-

Diagnostic Criteria for Posttraumatic Stress Disorder (PTSD)	Table 5.7

Adapted from DSM-IV-TR (APA, 2000)

- The person experienced a traumatic event involving the possibility of death or serious injury *and* the person's response involved intense fear, helplessness, or horror.
- The traumatic event is persistently reexperienced in one or more of the following ways:
  - Recurrent, intrusive, and distressing memories of the event.
  - Recurrent distressing dreams about the event.
  - Acting or feeling as if the traumatic event is recurring ("flashbacks").
  - Intense psychological distress when exposed to internal or external cues that symbolize or resemble an aspect of the traumatic event.
  - Physiological reactivity (for example, heart pounding, sweating) when exposed to internal or external cues that symbolize or resemble an aspect of the traumatic event.
- The person avoids reminders of the trauma and experiences a numbing of general responsiveness as indicated by three or more of the following:
  - Efforts to avoid thoughts, feelings, or conversations associated with the trauma.
  - Efforts to avoid activities, places, or people that arouse recollections of the trauma.
  - Inability to recall important aspects of the trauma.
  - Markedly diminished interest or participation in significant activities.
  - Feeling detached or estranged from others.
  - Restricted range of affect (such as dulled emotions, lack of certain feelings).
  - Sense of a foreshortened future.
- The person experiences persistent symptoms of increased arousal as indicated by at least two of the following:
  - Difficulty falling or staying asleep.
  - Irritability or outbursts of anger.
  - Difficulty concentrating.
  - Hypervigilance.
  - Exaggerated startle response.
- The disturbance causes significant distress or impairment in normal functioning.

tographs at the police station, and he was soon arrested and jailed. Though Mary's attacker was in jail, she could not seem to recover emotionally. For months following the attack, Mary had nightmares in which she was running away from a faceless man. She could not discuss the rape with anyone and she quickly changed the subject if a friend or family member asked her how she was doing. Mary stopped taking her business classes because she lost interest in her studies and felt uncomfortable going back to the area where she was attacked. Even in the safety of her own home she could not concentrate and felt nervous and edgy. As time wore on, Mary's husband grew increasingly concerned about his wife and urged her to seek therapy.

Treating the traumatized Immediate response to disaster victims, such as the support offered by this New York City police officer on September 11, 2001, can help prevent or reduce the long-term effects of traumatization.

Flashback A vivid and often overwhelming recollection of a past traumatic experience.

Posttraumatic repetitive play Children who have been traumatized, such as these boys who live in the war-torn region of Bosnia and Herzegovina, often repeat the traumatic experiences through their play. Some theorists suggest that by doing so, children hope to gain mastery over situations that left them feeling helpless and overwhelmed.

Mary has all of the major symptoms associated with PTSD: reexperiencing the trauma in her mind (her nightmares), avoidance of events related to the trauma (stopping attending classes, not discussing the rape), emotional numbing (loss of interest in her business studies, difficulty feeling a range of emotions), and increased arousal (her nervousness and edginess).

While Mary reexperiences her attack through her nightmares, traumatic experiences can also be reexperienced in the form of intrusive thoughts that occur while awake, or by becoming very upset when reminded of the trauma. One of the most extreme forms of reexperiencing a traumatic event is the phenomenon known as a **flashback.** During a flashback, a person feels as if they are reliving the actual trauma, even if he or she is in a safe and familiar environment. For example, a walk through the woods on a particularly humid day may trigger a flashback for a Vietnam veteran reminded of the smell and feel of being in a Vietnamese jungle. Even though he is perfectly safe, he may believe that he is again under fire in Vietnam and relive all of the terror of that experience.

Most people with PTSD will try to avoid experiences, thoughts, and feelings associated with the traumatic experience. Just as Mary decided to stop taking her business classes after the rape, a war veteran might avoid discussing traumatic events from the war, or a survivor of a flood might begin to avoid water. Unfortunately, such efforts to avoid the thoughts and feelings associated with a past traumatic event often contribute to general feelings of emotional numbness and disengagement. Many trauma survivors report a loss of their "zest" for life and of their interest in relationships and the future. Paradoxically, many people who have experienced a trauma also feel overly aroused, irritable, edgy, or tense even while they are feeling emotionally numb. They may feel that they are constantly on guard, and often develop a strong startle response that causes them to jump or flinch at the slightest surprise. They may have difficulty managing frustrations and can become chronically irritable or explosively angry.

Studies have found that large-scale disasters such as earthquakes or major industrial accidents can lead to epidemics of PTSD affecting entire communities (Goenjian et al., 1994; Prince-Embury & Rooney, 1988). In response to these findings, the American Psychological Association and the American Red Cross teamed up to create the Disaster Response Network in 1991. The Network sends groups of volunteer psychologists and relief workers to disaster sites—from natural disasters such as floods and hurricanes, to human-made disasters such as the attack on the World Trade Center or the Columbine High School shooting. Short-term disaster response interventions that provide immediate psychological services and arrange for ongoing social support have been found to reduce long-term psychological distress (Gersons & Carlier, 1993).

Traumatic situations are not always single events; trauma can also be chronic, such as the experience of living in extreme poverty or in a dangerous neighborhood (Aneshensel & Sucoff, 1996). Stress disorders are extremely prevalent in areas where many people are chronically exposed to traumatic events, such as in a war-torn country or in a violent inner-city neighborhood.

Brief Summary

- The DSM-IV-TR recognizes six main anxiety disorders: generalized anxiety disorder, panic disorder, phobias (specific phobia, social phobia, and agoraphobia), obsessive-compulsive disorder, posttraumatic stress disorder, and acute stress disorder.

- Generalized anxiety disorder (GAD) involves chronic and pervasive nervousness.

- Panic disorder (PD) involves episodes of acute terror, known as panic attacks, which lead to worry about experiencing future panic attacks.

- Phobias are persistent and unreasonable fears of particular objects or situations.

- Obsessive-compulsive disorder (OCD) involves anxiety-producing, unwanted thoughts or impulses (obsessions) and/or uncontrollable rituals meant to decrease anxiety (compulsions).

- Posttraumatic stress disorder and acute stress disorder involve a variety of anxiety symptoms that occur in the wake of a traumatic experience.

> *Critical Thinking Question* | **W**hich anxiety disorders do Arthur and Greg, described at the beginning of the chapter, appear to suffer from?

The Advantages and Limitations of the DSM-IV-TR Anxiety Disorder Diagnoses

There are a number of *advantages and limitations* of the DSM-IV-TR anxiety disorder diagnoses. One major advantage is that the reliability and validity of the DSM-IV-TR anxiety diagnoses are relatively good (Brown, 1996). In other words, two different clinicians are likely to apply the same DSM-IV-TR diagnosis to the same client (reliability), and the diagnosis is likely to be accurate (validity). However, the DSM-IV-TR anxiety disorders are also highly **comorbid** with other DSM-IV-TR diagnoses; clients often meet criteria for more than one disorder. Indeed, one study found that half of all people with one anxiety disorder were diagnosed with at least one other anxiety or mood disorder (anxiety and mood disorders have especially high rates of comorbidity). As you can see in Figure 5.2, 82% of the research participants with GAD were also assigned another DSM-IV-TR diagnosis. While it may be that these people simply had multiple disorders, such findings also highlight the possibility that the DSM-IV-TR diagnostic categories artificially divide complex clinical conditions. In accord with this, clinicians frequently find that many clients with anxiety symptoms do not neatly fit into any of the DSM-IV-TR categories, and some experts generally oppose the descriptive DSM system for classifying anxiety disorders. They argue that since anxiety is present in almost all mental disorders it is arbitrary to classify some as anxiety disorders just because certain clients may emphasize their anxiety symptoms.

Comorbidity The presence of two or more disorders in one person, or a general association between two or more different disorders.

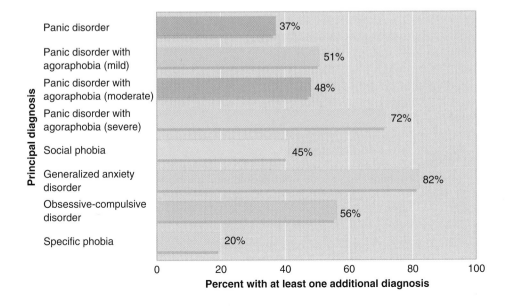

Figure 5.2 Comorbidity rates for DSM-IV-TR diagnoses A high percentage of individuals diagnosed with an anxiety disorder also warrant at least one other DSM-IV-TR diagnosis.

(Adapted from Brown, 1996, p. 26)

Classification in Demographic Context

While we have described the general features of anxiety disorders, we should be mindful that anxiety disorders occur in specific individuals, and that every individual is unique. Demographic factors such as an individual's age, gender, and social class are among the variables that significantly influence how anxiety disorders are manifested.

Age

Everyone experiences anxiety from time to time, but people of different ages tend to experience anxiety differently (Albano, Chorpita, & Barlow, 1996). Adults often describe their anxiety in terms of their emotional experience (feeling nervous, tense, or on edge), cognitive experience (mind going blank, thoughts racing) or physiological reactions (heart beating faster, palms sweating). Children, on the other hand, may not be able to verbalize their experience of anxiety and instead may express fear and anxiety behaviorally by crying, having tantrums, freezing up, or clinging to a caretaker. Children may also experience and express anxiety through physical complaints such as stomachaches and headaches. In addition, children may not be distressed by their own anxious behavior (Geller et al., 1998; Silverman & Nelles, 1990). For example, children who have OCD are often not bothered by their repetitive rituals. Indeed, they may see them as "solutions" to the problem of otherwise uncontrollable anxiety. While adults who suffer from phobias are often distressed by the very fact of having a phobia, children rarely appreciate that their phobic fears are excessive. In fact, childhood phobias are common and usually transitory. Almost half of all children experience a phobia at one time or another, with the most common childhood phobias being of the animal or natural environment type (Bell-Dolan, Last, & Strauss, 1990).

Young children with PTSD often reexperience traumatic events through their play. Lenore Terr (1983; 1990; 1991) has written extensively about the repetitive, joyless, and solitary play often seen in children who have been traumatized. For example, she described the play of several children who survived the harrowing experience of having their school bus hijacked and then buried in a cave. For months after surviving the kidnapping, a number of the children repeatedly played out scenes in which toy buses and cars were "stolen" and buried away.

Most of the anxiety disorders described in this chapter can occur at any age. The major exception to this is panic disorder, which is rarely found in children (Ollendick, Mattis, & King, 1994). Panic disorder generally begins sometime between late adolescence and the mid-30s. In contrast, nearly a third (30%) of all people who are diagnosed with generalized anxiety disorder report that their disorder began at some time in childhood or during their teenage years (Noyes & Hoehn-Saric, 1998).

Anxiety disorders are believed to be widely underdiagnosed among older adults despite the general recognition that declining health, monetary resources, personal relationships, and mental capacities contribute to heightened anxiety (Blazer, 1997). Research suggests that geriatric anxiety disorders are especially associated with negative life events (such as the death of a spouse), difficulties with daily living, and comorbid depression (Flint & Rifat, 2002).

Critical Thinking Question | **G**iven that transitory phobias are quite common among young children, how might you decide when a childhood phobia warrants concern and treatment?

Gender

One of the most striking demographic facts about anxiety disorders is that they occur disproportionately in women. Generalized anxiety disorder, panic disorder (with or without agoraphobia), specific phobias, and PTSD are all two to three times more common in women than they are in men (Fredrikson et al., 1996; Yonkers & Gurguis, 1995). Epidemiological studies also indicate that social phobia occurs somewhat more often in women, but men tend to seek treatment for social phobia more often than women do (Weinstock, 1999). Of all the DSM-IV-TR anxiety disorders, only OCD occurs equally in men and women (Douglass et al., 1995).

Sociocultural explanations have been offered to account for the disproportionate rates of anxiety disorders in women. Fodor (1974) suggests that women are not generally taught to be assertive and self-sufficient—skills that are important for overcoming anxiety. Support for this hypothesis has come from studies in which the severity of agoraphobia in women was found to be inversely correlated with their scores on measures of stereotypically "masculine" traits such as independence and leadership (Chambless & Mason, 1986). In other words, the more independent the woman, the less likely it is that she will have severe agoraphobia.

Gender differences in panic disorder have been linked to genetic and hormonal differences between men and women. Among first-degree relatives of people with panic disorder (children, parents, and siblings), women are three times more likely than men to also develop panic disorder, while men are more likely to suffer from alcoholism (which may be an effort to "self-medicate" undiagnosed anxiety symptoms) (Crowe et al., 1983). Further evidence for a genetic basis of panic disorder in women comes from studies finding that panic disorder tends to co-occur with two medical disorders that are more common in women than they are in men: mitral valve prolapse (in which the mitral valve in the heart fails to close completely causing blood to back-flow into the left ventricle) and hyperthyroidism (elevations of the hormones produced by the thyroid gland) (Zaubler & Katon, 1996). These medical conditions may contribute to panic disorder by producing physical and psychological symptoms associated with anxiety.

Fluctuating hormonal levels in menstruating women have also been found to influence neurotransmitter balances and other physiological systems associated with the onset of panic symptoms (Perna et al., 1995; Weinstock, 1999). Some empirical evidence supports the hypothesis that women are more vulnerable to panic at specific stages of their menstrual cycle (Cameron et al., 1988; Sigmon et al., 2000).

Though OCD occurs at equal rates in men and women, the disorder appears to manifest itself somewhat differently in each sex. Females tend to develop OCD later in life (between ages 26–35) than males do (between age 5–15), and they are more likely to experience depression along with OCD symptoms. Also, while men are more likely to engage in compulsive checking rituals, cleaning rituals are found predominantly among women (Noshirvani et al., 1991; Rasmussen & Eisen, 1990).

PTSD occurs twice as often in women as in men (Kessler et al., 1994). This may be due to fact that women are more likely than men to be victims of violence, especially three kinds of violence that are often highly traumatic: childhood sexual abuse, sexual assault in adulthood, and domestic violence. Surveys have found that girls are sexually abused two to three times more often than boys and that one out of every six or seven American women has been a victim of a rape (Gorey & Leslie, 1997; Koss, 1998; Spitzberg, 1999). One study found that 94% of rape victims met diagnostic criteria for ASD within two weeks following the rape and that as many as half of rape survivors qualify for a diagnosis of PTSD three months after the rape (Rothbaum et al., 1992). Similarly alarming statistics exist concerning the prevalence and effects of domestic violence. One third of all women experience domestic violence at some point in their lives, and up to 60% of these suffer from posttraumatic stress symptoms as a result (American Medical Association, 1992; Saunders, 1994).

A universal language The experience of intense anxiety is often accompanied by muscle tension and a fearful facial expression.

Women not only experience more traumatic events from men, but they are also more likely to develop PTSD when traumatized (Breslau et al., 1999; Breslau, Davis, & Andreski, 1995). For example, a study of 122 men and women who experienced a serious motor vehicle accident found that women were 4.7 times more likely to experience avoidance and numbing and 3.8 times more likely to experience increased arousal (for example, hypervigilance, startle response) than men (Fullerton et al., 2001). Gender differences in the rates of PTSD after exposure to trauma seem to be related to rates of preexisting anxiety or depression, and possibly to some of the hormonal differences described above (Breslau et al., 1997; Wong & Yehuda, 2002).

Studies have also found that generalized anxiety disorder (GAD) is twice as common in women as it is in men. While some of the sociocultural and biological factors described above may contribute to this difference, less is known about the disparity between men and women with regard to GAD (Wittchen et al., 1994).

Class

People living in poor urban environments are at increased risk for developing PTSD. There are at least two reasons for this: (1) they are more likely to have traumatic experiences than people living in other environments, and (2) they are more likely to experience additional psychological and sociocultural risk factors for PTSD (Buka et al., 2001). For example, inner-city residents witness more violence (gun fights, murders, etc.) than their middle-class counterparts, and they are also more likely to be the victims of violent crime (Hien & Bukszpan, 1999; Warner & Weist, 1996). A large community-based study of adolescents in Los Angeles found that the more dangerous the neighborhood, the more likely its teens were to report anxiety symptoms (Aneshensel & Sucoff, 1996). In addition, researchers have found that high levels of psychological stress prior to a trauma and a lack of social support afterward significantly increase the likelihood of developing a stress disorder in the wake of a traumatic experience (Shalev et al., 1996). Unfortunately, chronic psychological stress and inadequate social support are more often the rule than the exception in poor urban communities. For instance, one study found that urban, ethnic minority males with high levels of family conflict and low levels of family support were at greatest risk for developing PTSD when exposed to community violence (Buka et al., 2001). Evidence of heightened levels of anxiety among poor minority populations extends beyond elevated rates of PTSD. For example, the highest rates of GAD are found among the members of racial minorities who are living in poverty and likely have good reasons for feeling anxious given the inherently stressful nature of being poor (Blazer et al., 1991; Horwath & Weissman, 1997).

Nervios A term used by Latino populations in Latin America and in the United States to describe a range of symptoms of nervous distress.

Cultural and Historical Relativism in Defining and Classifying Anxiety Disorders

The core concept of *cultural and historical relativism* highlights some additional challenges for the DSM-IV-TR system of classifying anxiety disorders. Anxiety disorders do not have universally agreed upon features; different cultures experience, define, and classify anxiety problems differently (Lopez & Guarnaccia, 2000; Guarnaccia, 1997; Tseng et al., 1986). For example, Latino populations in Latin America and in the United States frequently use the term **nervios** (NER-vee-ose) to describe a range of symptoms of nervous distress similar to those listed in the DSM-IV-TR diagnosis of GAD (APA, 2000). Nervios may be characterized by headaches, irritability, stomachaches, and difficulty sleeping or concentrating. In some cases, it is accompanied by feelings of being nervous, but nervios may also involve subjective feelings of depression or dissociation (Chapter 7).

The phrase **ataque de nervios** (ah-TAH-kay duh NER-vee-ose) is also used in some Latino cultures to describe an episode of intense anxiety similar to a panic attack (APA, 2000). Symptoms associated with an ataque de nervios include a feeling of being out of control, shaking, unrestrained shouting or crying, heat in the chest rising into the head, and aggressive verbal or physical behavior. Such ataques may also include feelings of faintness, dissociation, or suicidal thoughts and gestures. Unlike panic attacks which tend to occur "out of the blue," ataques de nervios are usually associated with an upsetting precipitating event (such as learning about the death of a loved one). Also, they do not typically involve the dread of experiencing another such attack, which is one of the diagnostic criteria for panic disorder.

The Chinese Classification of Mental Disorders recognizes a syndrome known as **shenjing shuairuo** (shen-jing shwai-row) which shares similarities with the DSM-IV-TR descriptions of both anxiety and mood disorders (APA, 2000). Symptoms of shenjing shuairuo include difficulty sleeping and concentrating, physical or mental exhaustion, physical pains, and neurological symptoms such as dizziness, headaches, and memory loss. The Japanese diagnostic system includes a disorder known as **taijin kyofusho** (TIE-jean kyo-FOO-show) which is characterized by anxiety that one's body or aspects of one's body will be displeasing or offensive to others in terms of appearance, smell, or physical movement. This disorder has much in common with social phobia, although taijin kyofusho focuses specifically on concerns about bodily appearance or functioning.

As you may have already noted, members of Latino and Asian cultures often experience and describe anxiety mainly in terms of physical, not emotional, distress. This is related to the fact that emotional distress is highly stigmatized in some cultures and the expression of such distress to anyone outside of the immediate family is discouraged (Tseng et al., 1986). Thus, in working with people from different cultures, clinicians need to be aware that anxiety is experienced and expressed differently in clients from different cultural contexts.

As with cultural diversity, historical changes in the classification of anxiety disorders suggest that classification systems are always limited by the knowledge, values, and concerns of their particular historical settings. For example, the diagnosis of PTSD was not included in the DSM until 1980 with the publication of the DSM-III (APA, 1980) in spite of the fact that posttraumatic stress symptoms were commonly recognized in soldiers fighting in the American Civil War and both World Wars (see Figure 5.3). During these wars, posttraumatic combat stress was often viewed as a sign of malingering and cowardice rather than as a legitimate disorder, and the soldiers were often punished rather than given treatment. The addition of the PTSD diagnosis to the DSM-III was prompted by clinicians who specialized in the treatment of Vietnam War veterans. These clinicians argued that the psychological effects of war trauma were genuine, common, severe, and persistent. In fact, studies have found that 29% of Vietnam War veterans experienced significant PTSD symptoms, and 15% continued to have symptoms for at least 15 years after returning from the war (Friedman, Schnurr, & McDonagh-Coyle, 1994; Weiss et al., 1992).

Few questions remain about whether PTSD is a legitimate diagnosis, but much controversy remains about whether PTSD is best classified as an anxiety disorder. While there are compelling arguments that anxiety is the major symptom of PTSD (Barlow & Cerny, 1988), some experts argue that PTSD would be better classified as a dissociative disorder (Chapter 7) since it often involves significant changes in states of consciousness (such as flashbacks and extreme emotional detachment) (Brett, 1996; Davidson & Foa, 1991; Insel, Zahn, & Murphy, 1985).

Ataque de nervios A term used in some Latino cultures to describe an episode of intense anxiety.

Shenjing shuairuo An anxiety syndrome recognized in China including symptoms of physical or mental exhaustion, difficulty sleeping and concentrating, physical pains, dizziness, headaches, and memory loss.

Taijin kyofusho An anxiety disorder recognized in Japan characterized by worry that one's body or aspects of one's body will be displeasing or offensive to others.

Learning from experience Studies of Vietnam War veterans have contributed significantly to our modern understanding of posttraumatic stress disorder (PTSD) and played a crucial role in the inclusion of PTSD as a diagnosis in the DSM-III in 1980.

Figure 5.3 PTSD: Evolution of a diagnosis
The current form of the diagnosis of PTSD evolved over many decades. As you can see, advances in the understanding of the disorder have often occurred at times of war when clinicians are able to observe large numbers of traumatized veterans and civilians.

(Adapted from Goode, 2001, p. D1)

1871	Jacob Mendes Da Costa, an Army surgeon in the Civil War describes "irritable heart" in soldiers, characterized by shortness of breath, chest pains, dizziness, disturbed sleep, irritability and depression.
1883	Herbert Page, and English physician, asserts that "railway spine," the wide array of symptoms displayed by some train accident survivors, is a result of "nervous shock."
1895	Sigmund Freud and Josef Breuer publish "Studies on Hysteria," arguing that mental disorders are sometimes rooted in psychological traumas.
World War I	In 1919, Sir Thomas Lewis, a British cardiologist, notes "soldier's heart" in World War I veterans, with symptoms similar to those described by Da Costa.
	Other World War I surgeons identify "shell shock," blaming it on concussions from exploding shells. The symptoms – breakdown in battle, a dazed or detached manner, severe anxiety and an exaggerated startle response – are now considered hallmarks of PTSD.
	Dr. William Rivers, a psychiatrist at a military hospital in Scotland, becomes one of the first doctors to treat returning veterans by having them recall traumatic events. The poet and war hero Siegfried Sassoon was one of his patients.
World War II	In 1941, Abraham Kardiner, an American psychologist, suggests that "war neurosis" or "battle fatigue" has a physiological as well as a psychological basis.
	Twenty-five percent of evacuations from the front during World War II are for psychiatric reasons. Doctors find that soldiers treated promptly and near their combat units are better able to return to battle.
Korean War	Psychiatric casualties are often treated near the battlefield. In some cases, sodium amytal, or "truth serum," is used to aid recall of trauma.
1960s	Studies of Holocaust and Hiroshima survivors by Dr. Robert Jay Lifton and others document the impact of trauma on civilians.
Vietnam War	Troops frequently rotated in tours of duty often lack the bonds of earlier veterans, whose units were kept together. Many develop "post-Vietnam syndrome," the diagnostic forerunner to PTSD.
Late 1970s, 1980s	Pesearchers recognize that survivors of rape, earthquakes, and other nonmilitary traumas show many of the same symptoms as traumatized combat veterans.
1980	Post-traumatic stress disorder first appears in the American Psychiatric Association's Diagnostic and Statistical Manual.

Brief Summary

- There are important advantages and limitations of the DSM-IV-TR anxiety disorder diagnoses. While the reliability and validity of the DSM-IV-TR diagnoses are relatively high, anxiety disorders often co-occur, and they are also highly comorbid with disorders in other diagnostic categories.

- Children tend to express anxiety behaviorally (for example, crying, clinging) or in the form of physical complaints (stomachaches, headaches) and may be less bothered than adults by compulsive rituals or phobic behavior.

- Panic disorder is extremely rare in children, while generalized anxiety disorder (GAD) often begins in childhood or adolescence. Anxiety disorders are widely underdiagnosed among older adults.

- With the exception of OCD (which occurs equally in men and women) anxiety disorders are two to three times more common in females than in males.

- The gender differences in the rates of anxiety disorders may be explained by: sociocultural factors (for example, women are taught to be less assertive and self-sufficient), hormonal factors (panic attacks appear to be linked to hormonal fluctuations), and genetic factors (panic disorder is linked to mitral valve prolapse and hyperthyroidism which are found more frequently in women).

● People who live in poor and violent neighborhoods are more likely to experience posttraumatic and acute stress disorders. Economically disadvantaged racial minorities have been found to have the highest rates of GAD.

● The core concept of *cultural and historical relativism* highlights some additional challenges for the DSM-IV-TR system of classifying anxiety disorders. Anxiety disorders do not have universally agreed upon features; different cultures experience, define, and classify anxiety problems differently. Further, the classification of anxiety disorders has changed substantially over time, as in the relatively recent inclusion of PTSD in the DSM.

Critical Thinking Question	**Attempts to be culturally sensitive to the various presentations of anxiety disorders risk engaging in cultural stereotyping. Does specifying cultural patterns (such as that Asian individuals tend to express anxiety through physical symptoms) seem helpful, to be an example of stereotyping, or both?**

EXPLAINING AND TREATING ANXIETY AND ANXIETY DISORDERS

All of the major theoretical perspectives in abnormal psychology offer concepts relevant to the explanation and treatment of anxiety disorders. We'll begin by describing behavioral, cognitive, biological, and psychodynamic components of the etiology (causes) and treatment of anxiety disorders. Then, we'll turn our attention to the core concepts of the principle of *multiple causality* and the *connection between mind and body* to emphasize the ways in which theoretical components complement, interact, and overlap with each other.

Behavioral Components

Behavioral approaches to anxiety disorders draw on the three forms of learning described in Chapter 3:

● **Classical conditioning:** learning based on automatic mental associations

● **Operant conditioning:** learning based on reinforcement

● **Modeling:** learning based on observation of others

We will focus on the behavioral explanation of phobias, since it best illustrates the use of behavioral concepts to explain an anxiety disorder. According to classical conditioning theory, an irrational fear (a phobia) can be created when a neutral stimulus that does not usually cause fear happens to be present during a strong fear response to a naturally frightening stimulus. As you recall from Chapter 3, this theory was tested in John Watson's famous "Little Albert" experiment in which an 11-month-old infant boy was taught to fear a white rat that he had initially liked (Watson & Raynor, 1920). To do this, Watson and his assistant presented the rat (a neutral stimulus) to Little Albert and waited until Albert expressed interest in playing with the animal. When Albert eagerly reached for the rat, the experimenters banged a metal bar with a hammer, terrifying the boy with the loud noise. (To review, the noise is known as an unconditioned stimulus—UCS—because it auto-

Classical conditioning Learning that takes place via automatic associations between neutral stimuli and unconditioned stimuli.

Operant conditioning A form of learning in which behaviors are shaped through rewards and punishments.

Modeling Learning based on observing and imitating the behavior of others; see also **social/observational learning**.

matically elicits a fear reflex without any conditioning.) The procedure was repeated several times and before long Little Albert became frightened of the rat by itself (now, the conditioned stimulus—CS—since conditioning was necessary to make the rat elicit fear). Little Albert had automatically associated the rat and the noise because they were present together in time, a situation known as **temporal contiguity.** In addition, Watson demonstrated that Little Albert generalized this fear to other similar-looking objects including a rabbit, a fur coat, and a Santa Claus beard. Although Watson's treatment of Little Albert is highly unethical by modern research standards (Harris, 1979), the experiment provides a vivid example of the original classical conditioning explanation of phobias.

Interestingly, operant conditioning also plays an important role in behavioral explanations. Once people develop a phobic response, they tend to avoid what they fear. According to the principles of operant conditioning theory, this avoidance behavior is **negatively reinforced** because it removes people from feared unpleasant situations. People feel better when they avoid the feared objects and therefore they become more and more likely to continue their avoidance. Unfortunately, avoidance reduces the opportunity for **extinction** (that is, deconditioning, or unlearning) of the phobia. In other words, a person who develops a dog phobia after being bitten (UCS) by a dog (CS) may actively avoid all dogs and never come into contact with warm and friendly hounds that might help counteract the phobia. Modeling, or *vicarious conditioning* (learning by watching others), is another possible behavioral mechanism for the acquisition of phobias. For example, the son of a father with a dog phobia who sees his father panic at the sight of dogs might soon develop a fear of dogs.

Empirical support for behavioral explanations of phobia acquisition has been mixed. On the positive side, one study of people with blood-injection-injury-type phobias found that 76% of the research participants reported that the phobia developed in reaction to a prior, frightening experience in which the feared stimuli were present (such as a bad injury or a painful blood-draw), and 20% reported that their phobia developed through a modeling experience (Kleinknecht, 1994). In contrast, a study of water phobic children found that 56% of the children were afraid of water on their very first encounter (Menzies & Clark, 1993).

Modern behavioral theorists have noted that some phobias are acquired much more easily than others, possibly due to our genetic heritage (Oehman & Mineka, 2001). You may recall that most phobias involve potentially dangerous animals, or potentially risky natural situations, such as elevated or enclosed spaces, while few people have gun or knife phobias, even though guns are certainly more dangerous than spiders. Such observations lead to a theory of **prepared conditioning,** a modern revision of the original classical conditioning model (Seligman, 1971). According to this approach, humans may have a genetic predisposition to fear once-dangerous objects and situations such as snakes and heights because our ancestors who shared such fears are more likely to have survived to contribute to the gene pool. This could explain why phobias to these "prepared" stimuli can sometimes develop after a single conditioning experience without requiring repeated pairings of the UCS and CS.

Behavioral Interventions

Behavioral interventions are designed to extinguish (or unlearn) learned abnormal anxiety reactions. Although there are a number of behavioral approaches to treating anxiety, all rely on the principle that people must be *exposed* to the objects or situations that they fear in order to overcome their fears. In this way, fears can be unlearned in the same way they were learned in the first place.

Temporal contiguity Two events occuring closely together in time.

Negative reinforcement Increasing the probability of a behavior by removing an unpleasant stimuli when the behavior occurs.

Extinction The weakening of a connection between a conditioned stimulus and a conditioned response.

Prepared conditioning Classical conditioning based on an evolutionarily derived sensitivity to certain stimuli that were dangerous in an ancestral environment.

Phobias One of the most widely used interventions for phobias, **systematic desensitization** (Craske, 1999; Wolpe, 1958; 1969), involves two critical components: **relaxation training** and the construction of a **fear hierarchy**. First, clients are taught to relax themselves by focusing on their breathing and on flexing and relaxing their muscles in a predetermined sequence. With practice, many clients develop the ability to achieve a deep state of relaxation very quickly. Next, the therapist and client work together to develop a fear hierarchy in which they rank frightening situations from least to most terrifying. For example, a woman with a spider phobia might create a fear hierarchy that ranges from looking at a picture of a spider in a magazine, to holding a jar containing a spider, to touching a spider, to allowing several spiders to crawl on her arm. Eventually, she would participate in each of these activities in sequence while using her relaxation training to keep her feelings of anxiety at bay. For example, when able to feel relaxed while looking at a picture of a spider in a magazine, she would move on to holding a jar containing a spider, and so forth. If **in vivo desensitization** (actual physical exposure to the feared object) is not possible or desired, **covert desensitization** can also be considered. In covert desensitization the client *imagines* the frightening object or situation, such as being trapped in a room full of spiders, while using relaxation techniques to combat anxiety.

Flooding is another form of exposure therapy in which clients are directly confronted with the object or situation that they fear, but without working through a fear hierarchy first. Ideally, such exposure extinguishes the phobia because the experience proves that the pairing of the UCS and CS was merely accidental and the phobic object is not dangerous by itself. For example, one young man had an intense fear of the noise made by a popping balloon and avoided all situations in which he might possibly come into contact with balloons. In three flooding sessions on three consecutive days he participated in the popping of hundreds of balloons and soon after reported that his balloon phobia was substantially diminished (Houlihan et al., 1993). While flooding can be an effective and efficient treatment for phobias, few clients (not surprisingly) will agree to it and there are ethical concerns about recommending it given that it has the potential to make some clients more anxious.

Modeling can be used as a form of vicarious exposure therapy in which the therapist demonstrates for the client that his or her fears are unrealistic (Marks, 1990). For example, a therapist treating a client with a germ phobia might drop a cookie on the floor and then pick it up and eat it. In the treatment of a client with social phobia, the therapist might model the behavior of striking up a conversation with a stranger to demonstrate that no horrible consequence ensues. Ultimately, the therapist would try to help the client to imitate the modeled behavior.

Empirical research has found exposure-based therapies to be generally effective in the treatment of phobias (Barlow, Raffa, & Cohen, 2002). For example, a study evaluating the effectiveness of exposure interventions for people suffering from claustrophobia (fear of enclosed spaces) compared intensive exposure (similar to flooding), gradual exposure (like systematic desensitization), and interventions that drew on both cognitive and behavioral techniques (CBT) (Ost et al., 2001). Eighty percent of the participants who underwent a single 3-hour session of intensive exposure (containment in an enclosed space) reported significant improvement, as did 81% of the participants in the gradual (5-session) exposure group, and 79% of the participants in the CBT group. One year later, 100% (intensive exposure), 81% (gradual exposure), and 93% (CBT) of the participants reported that the improvement had been maintained.

Panic Disorder Systematic desensitization can also be used to address panic disorder. Clients construct a hierarchy of situations in which they feel they are most likely to have a panic attack and then use in vivo or covert desensitization to expose them-

Systematic desensitization Intervention involving gradually increasing exposure to a conditioned stimulus (such as a feared object) while practicing relaxation techniques.

Relaxation training Technique for teaching people to calm themselves by regulating their breathing and attending to bodily sensations.

Fear hierarchy In systematic desensitization, a list of feared situations ranging from least to most terrifying.

In vivo desensitization Behavioral desensitization training in which the client is actually confronted with the feared stimulus.

Covert desensitization Behavioral desensitization intervention for phobias in which the client practices relaxation techniques while imagining being confronted with the feared stimulus.

Flooding Intensive exposure to a feared stimulus.

Interoceptive exposure Deliberate induction of the physiological sensations typically associated with a panic attack.

Exposure and response prevention A behavioral intervention in which clients are encouraged to confront a frightening thought or situation and then prevented from engaging in anxiety-reducing behaviors.

Covert response prevention Exposure and response prevention in obsessive-compulsive disorder for clients whose compulsions are mental processes (not behaviors).

Prolonged imaginal exposure A behavioral intervention in which clients suffering from posttraumatic stress disorder are encouraged to describe the traumatizing experience(s) in detail.

selves to such situations while remaining relaxed. People suffering from panic disorder can also be helped by exposure to the bodily sensations typically associated with panic attacks. In a technique known as **interoceptive exposure** clients are encouraged to run up and down stairs to increase their heart rates, spin themselves in chairs until they feel dizzy, or hyperventilate until they feel numb and tingly. They are then encouraged to resist the impulse to over-react to their bodily sensations, and consequently learn that the feared bodily sensations are normal and do not necessarily herald a panic attack (Otto & Deckersbach, 1998). Interoceptive exposure can be combined with cognitive interventions designed to correct panic-inducing, catastrophic misinterpretations of normal bodily sensations.

Obsessive-Compulsive Disorder According to behavioral theory, OCD develops when a compulsive ritual happens to reduce anxiety caused by a disturbing thought, thereby reinforcing the ritual behavior (Foa & Kozak, 1996). Thus, in the leading behavioral intervention for OCD, clients are encouraged to entertain disturbing thoughts while they are prevented from carrying out their anxiety-reducing compulsive rituals—a process known as **exposure and response prevention.** For example, a man who feels compelled to constantly sort, clean, and organize in order to calm his disturbing thoughts that he will otherwise "lose control" of himself might be given the following instructions:

- Do not sort through the mail on the day it arrives—allow it to sit on the kitchen counter for two days.
- Do not make your bed for an entire week.
- Do not put your clothes away in the evening, lay them on your bedroom chair instead.

This intervention addresses both the compulsions and the obsessions. It interrupts the compulsive rituals and therefore keeps them from being reinforced by a reduction in anxiety. It also gives the client the chance to see that his anxiety (about losing control) is unfounded and tolerable, because he does not lose control. When both the obsessions and compulsions are mental processes—for example, an intrusive urge (obsession) to swear out loud in church countered by the ritual (compulsion) of silently reciting the Hail Mary exactly 55 times—**covert response prevention** may be used to break into the cycle. Such a person would be told to prevent herself from reciting the 55 Hail Marys after having the urge to swear out loud in church in order to create exposure to the anxiety and lead to its extinction. Exposure and response prevention therapy has been found to be a relatively effective intervention for the treatment of OCD (Franklin et al., 2000).

Posttraumatic Stress Disorder Behavioral explanations of PTSD assume that posttraumatic anxiety is maintained by the persistent avoidance of everything associated with the traumatic experience, which prevents exposure to the conditioned stimulus (CS) that could lead to extinction of the anxiety. In a technique known as **prolonged imaginal exposure,** clients are assisted in recounting all of the events surrounding the traumatic experience, and to describe the trauma as if it were happening all over again. By exposing themselves to their own memories of the traumatic event, clients learn that remembering the event is not the same as reliving it, and the link between the actual trauma and stimuli which evoke anxiety because they were associated with the trauma, is weakened (Craske, 1999). Training in relaxation techniques and the development of adequate coping mechanisms can help clients tolerate the anxiety that often accompanies the exposure process.

Consider how behavioral techniques were used to help a woman suffering from PTSD after the World Trade Center attacks:

Case Illustration Normally buoyant and filled with energy, Ms. Mendez, who worked as a security guard at the World Trade Center, has been disabled by the horrors she experienced on Sept. 11.

She feels dizzy and has heart palpitations. Plagued by insomnia she hardly sleeps; when she does, she has terrible nightmares. She is afraid of crowded places, startles at any loud noise and is reluctant to leave her apartment in Queens. Most upsetting, any reminder of the terrorist attacks sets off a cascade of terrifying mental images, like a movie she cannot turn off...

In mid-October, Ms. Mendez, 59, sought help at a medical clinic in Midtown Manhattan and was referred to Dr. Jaime Carcamo, a psychologist in private practice who is also a researcher at Columbia University.

"The first session, she wasn't able to talk about what happened to her," Dr. Carcamo said. "She was very brief in what she talked about and there were a lot of things she didn't remember."

But on her second visit, Ms. Mendez was able to tell her story in great detail, how she had been standing on the plaza when the planes hit, how she ran through a dark cloud of dust and debris, how she sat on a fire hydrant on Varick Street, weeping as she watched the towers collapse.

At the end of that session, "she was actually very relieved," Dr. Carcamo said.

In future sessions, he said, he will ask Ms. Mendez to recount her experience over and over in the present tense, periodically asking her to rate her anxiety level on a scale from 0 to 100. He will also teach her relaxation techniques to use when she becomes frightened, and give her assignments, like watching the news for one hour or telling a relative about her experience. At some point, he said, he may accompany her to a crowded place or some other situation she fears.

(Goode, 2001, pp. D1, D6)

Critical Thinking Question How might a clinician design a systematic desensitization treatment to help Ms. Mendez combat her fear of crowded places?

Facing one's fears Using systematic desensitization, a therapist can help a client to feel relaxed in the presence of what had been a terrifying stimulus.

Cognitive Components

People with anxiety disorders tend to misinterpret events in three important ways: they fixate on perceived dangers and threats, they over-estimate the severity of the perceived danger or threat, and they drastically under-estimate their ability to cope with the dangers and threats they perceive (Wells, 1997). People are especially likely to misinterpret events when maladaptive beliefs and assumptions influence their thinking (Brown & Beck, 2002). Maladaptive beliefs are global negative statements about the self or the world that go unquestioned by the person who holds the belief (for example, "I'm dumb," or "I'm unlovable"). Maladaptive assumptions are negative expectations about the relationship between behaviors and outcomes (for example, "Unless I do things perfectly, people will think I'm an idiot") (Ellis, 1979; 1997).

Beliefs and assumptions are part of general thought patterns known as **cognitive schemas** (Beck & Clark, 1997). Dysfunctional cognitive schemas are more rigid, simplistic, and negative than healthy cognitive schemas. For example, when someone who is an adequate but reluctant public speaker is asked to speak in front of an audience, a dysfunctional cognitive schema might be: "I'm a totally incompetent public speaker. I'll stutter while I talk and people will think I'm a fool." In contrast, the same

Cognitive schemas Mental models of the world that are used to organize information.

hypothetical person with a more adaptive cognitive schema might think "I don't like speaking in public, but I will do my best and get through it just fine." As you can see, the dysfunctional cognitive schema rests on maladaptive beliefs and assumptions that fixate on the threat ("I can't stop thinking about that speech I have to give"), over-estimate the threat involved ("people will think I'm a fool"), and under-estimate the individual's ability to cope with the threat ("I'm a totally incompetent public speaker"), all of which contribute to anxiety.

Dysfunctional cognitive schemas give rise to negative automatic thoughts that create a constant background of insecurity (Beck, 1976). On the day of her presentation, the reluctant public speaker described above might experience a barrage of negative automatic thoughts that only exacerbate her anxiety:

- "I've flubbed my introduction, there's no point in continuing."
- "This talk is a total disaster!"
- "I'm such a fool."
- "That person looks distracted, she hates my presentation."

Cognitive theorists have identified several maladaptive cognitive schemas that contribute to specific anxiety disorders (see Table 5.8).

Cognitive theories of anxiety focus both on the *content* of anxious thinking—dysfunctional cognitive schemas and negative automatic thoughts—and on the thought *processes* that generate anxiety-provoking themes. Cognitive theorists have identified several common **cognitive distortions,** or biased thought processes, that contribute to the maladaptive interpretation of events (see Table 5.9). If we return to our public speaker's negative automatic thoughts, we can see how each results from a cognitive distortion.

- "I've flubbed my introduction, there's no point in continuing." **Dichotomous reasoning**
- "This talk is a total disaster!" **Catastrophizing**
- "I'm such a fool." **Labeling**
- "That person looks distracted, she hates my presentation." **Personalization**

Unfortunately, anxiety-producing thoughts interfere with optimal functioning, creating a vicious cycle. Returning once again to our public speaker, we can see how her negative automatic thoughts might interfere with her ability to give a good speech. Rather than thinking about her presentation, she's worrying about what the audience is thinking about her. When the presentation goes poorly, she will be even more convinced of her incompetence as a public speaker. While other people might understand that being anxious makes it hard to give a good speech, the cognitive distortions that shape our speaker's thinking may prevent her from considering that possibility.

As described in the section on Behavioral Components, an individual's anxious thoughts can lead to avoidance behaviors which prevent the extinction of anxiety and maintain anxious thinking (France & Robson, 1997). Consider, for example, a man who avoids elevators because he fears that the elevator will get stuck causing him to experience a humiliating panic attack in front of his colleagues. Since he always takes the stairs, he never has experiences that could contradict his maladaptive beliefs that: (1) elevators are likely to get stuck, (2) his racing heartbeat while in a stuck elevator will cause a panic attack, and (3) if he has a panic attack in front of his colleagues, they will think less of him.

Cognitive distortions Irrational beliefs and thinking processes.

Dichotomous reasoning A cognitive distortion involving thinking in terms of extremes and absolutes.

Catastrophizing A cognitive distortion involving the tendency to view minor problems as major catastrophes.

Labeling A cognitive distortion in which people or situations are characterized on the basis of global, not specific, features.

Personalization A cognitive distortion in which one wrongly assumes that he or she is the cause of a particular event.

DISORDER	MALADAPTIVE COGNITIVE SCHEMAS	TYPICAL NEGATIVE AUTOMATIC THOUGHTS
Generalized anxiety disorder	• Overestimates dangerousness of situations • Doubts coping abilities	• "I forgot to lock the window—I'll certainly be robbed." • "If my boyfriend breaks up with me, I'll fall apart."
Panic disorder	• Acute "fear of fear"—fearing that benign bodily sensations herald a panic attack	• "My heart is beating quickly. Oh no! I'm about to have a panic attack!"
Specific phobia	• Overestimates dangerousness of feared object or situation • Overestimates likelihood of negative outcomes in relation to feared object or situation	• "All dogs are vicious." • "If I am in a high place, I will certainly fall."
Social phobia	• Fears performance failure • Fears negative evaluation • Self-focuses attention	• "My mind will go blank if someone asks me a question." • "I can tell that he already hates me." • "Everyone can see that I'm sweating."
Agoraphobia	• Generalizes anxiety associated with having a panic attack to all external situations	• "If I go to the mall, I'll have a panic attack."
Obsessive-compulsive disorder	• Exaggerates risk appraisals • Holds maladaptive beliefs about the unacceptability of certain types of thoughts	• "If I handle money, I might contract AIDS." • "Only a horrible person would have thoughts about hurting a child."
Posttraumatic and acute stress disorders	• Exaggerates risk appraisals • Over-generalizes emotional response	• "I can't keep myself safe." • "If I feel scared, I must be in danger."

Maladaptive Cognitive Schemas Associated with Specific Anxiety Disorders

Table 5.8

Adapted from Caballo, 1998; Leahy, 1997; and Wells, 1997

Empirical evidence supports several aspects of the cognitive explanation of anxiety disorders. To test whether highly anxious people do, in fact, focus their attention on dangerous situations, one research team presented research participants, some with generalized anxiety disorder (GAD) and some without GAD, with pictures of four kinds of faces: threatening, happy, sad, and neutral. They found that the participants

Table 5.9	Common Cognitive Distortions

Information from Freeman et al. 1990, p. 5.

Dichotomous reasoning ■ Seeing things in terms of two mutually exclusive categories with no "shades of gray" in between. Example: believing that one is *either* a success *or* a failure and that anything short of a perfect performance is a total failure.

Over-generalization ■ Seeing a specific event as being characteristic of life in general rather than as one event among many. Example: concluding that an inconsiderate response from one's spouse shows that she doesn't care despite her having showed consideration on other occasions.

Selective abstraction ■ Focusing on one aspect of a complex situation and ignoring other relevant aspects of the situation. Example: focusing on the one negative comment in a performance evaluation received at work and overlooking a number of positive comments.

Disqualifying the positive ■ Discounting positive experiences that would conflict with the individual's negative views by declaring that they "don't count." Example: disbelieving positive feedback from friends and colleagues and thinking "They're only saying that to be nice."

Mind reading ■ Assuming that others are reacting negatively without evidence that this is the case. Example: thinking "I just *know* he thought I was an idiot!" despite the other person's polite behavior.

Fortune-telling ■ Reacting as though one's negative expectations about future events are established facts. Example: thinking "He'll leave me, I just know it!" and acting as though this is definitely true.

Catastrophizing ■ Treating negative events that might occur as intolerable catastrophes rather than being seen in perspective. Example: thinking "Oh my God, what if I faint?" without considering that, while fainting may be unpleasant or embarrassing, it is not terribly dangerous.

Minimization ■ Treating positive characteristics or experiences as insignificant. Example: thinking, "Sure I'm good at my job, but so what?"

Emotional reasoning ■ Assuming that emotional reactions necessarily reflect the truth. Example: deciding that because one feels hopeless, the situation must really be hopeless.

"Should" statements ■ Using *should* and *have-to* statements. Example: thinking "I *shouldn't* feel aggravated. She's my mother, I *have-to* listen to her."

Labeling ■ Attaching a global label to oneself rather than referring to specific events or actions. Example: thinking "I'm a failure!" rather than "Boy, I really blew that one!"

Personalization ■ Assuming that one is the cause of a particular external event when, in fact, other factors are responsible. Example: taking a supervisor's lack of friendliness personally rather than realizing that the supervisor is upset about something else.

with GAD were more likely to look at the threatening faces first, and that, compared to the control group, they shifted their gaze quickly *toward* the threatening face rather than quickly *away* from it (Mogg, Millar, & Bradley, 2000). Some studies have also found that in comparison to nonanxious controls, anxious people recall more of the threatening words on a list that also includes positive and neutral words (Cloitre & Liebowitz, 1991), although other studies have not confirmed these results (Rapee, 1994).

Cognitive Interventions

Cognitive interventions for anxiety disorders are generally goal-oriented and highly structured; cognitive therapists take an active, directive stance toward the client and his or her problems (Leahy, 1997). Early sessions are spent formulating goals and introducing the client to the idea that anxious feelings arise from problematic thoughts and maladaptive thought processes. Next, the therapist usually helps the client to:

Using reason to conquer anxiety In cognitive interventions for anxiety, clients are helped to evaluate the evidence for and against negative automatic thoughts and anxiety-provoking schemas. Therapists and fellow members of a therapy group can help anxious individuals to identify and challenge cognitive distortions.

- Identify negative automatic thoughts and the cognitive schemas that underlie such thoughts
- Evaluate the evidence for and against the negative automatic thoughts and schemas
- Identify cognitive distortions (dichotomous thinking, mind reading, minimization, etc.) that cause the client to interpret information in anxiety-provoking ways.

Consider the following conversation between a cognitive therapist (T) and a patient (P) suffering from a social phobia:

T: When you say that you might act foolish, what do you mean by that?

P: People will think I'm foolish.

T: What will happen to make people think that?

P: I will do something and draw attention to myself.

T: What will you do?

P: I will get my words wrong and I won't know what to say.

T: So your negative thought is that you will get your words wrong and people will think that you're foolish?

P: Yes, I don't want people to think that.

T: Do you have evidence that this will happen?

P: It's happened before when I've been anxious in situations. I don't know what to say and my mind goes blank.

T: It's true that your mind goes blank sometimes, but what makes you think that people see you as foolish?

P: Well, I don't know for sure.

T: How would people react to you if they thought you were foolish?

P: I suppose they wouldn't talk to me and they would ridicule me.

T: Is there any evidence that people do that to you?

P: No. Some people might, but people usually don't do that.

T: So it sounds as if there might be some counter-evidence, some evidence that people don't think you're foolish?

P: Yes, I suppose there is when you look at it like that.

T: What is the evidence that people don't think you're foolish?

P: I have a couple of good friends and I get on well with people at work.

T: What do you mean by getting on well with people at work?

P: Some people ask my advice about jobs they are working on.

T: Is that evidence that they think you are foolish?

P: No, quite the opposite.

(From Wells, 1997, pp. 69–70)

Once clients have been taught to identify and challenge their own negative automatic thoughts, they are instructed to continue to do so on their own, using homework sheets like the one shown in Table 5.10.

Sometimes clients are given a "prescription" to collect information about the validity of their negative automatic thoughts (Freeman et al., 1990). For example, the treatment of a person with a dog phobia who believes that all dogs are vicious might involve asking other people about their beliefs about dogs. Though the client may still feel nervous about dogs, she will be hard-pressed to maintain her belief that they are always dangerous.

A number of studies have found cognitive interventions to be effective in the treatment of anxiety disorders (Borkovec & Costello, 1993; Power et al., 1990). Cognitive techniques appear to be especially useful in the treatment of panic disorder; one study found that 94% of panic disorder clients were panic-free after only 12 weeks of treatment (Beck et al., 1992). In general, outcome studies for the treatment of GAD, OCD, social phobia, specific phobia, and panic disorder have found that cognitive interventions are most effective when used in combination with behavioral techniques such as relaxation exercises and exposure and response prevention techniques (Nathan & Gorman, 2002).

Brief Summary

- Behavioral explanations of anxiety disorders are based on the principles of classical conditioning, operant conditioning, and modeling.

- According to the theory of prepared conditioning, common phobias may have an evolutionary basis. Humans may have a genetic predisposition to fear dangerous animals and situations because our ancestors who had such fears are more likely to have survived and contributed to the gene pool.

- Behavioral interventions attempt to extinguish abnormal anxiety by providing exposure to the feared object or situation and preventing avoidance. Exposure

Table 5.10	**Homework for Challenging Negative Automatic Thoughts**			
Situation	Initial level of anxiety; rate on scale of 0–100	Negative automatic thought	Alternative thought	Subsequent level of anxiety
Touched the doorknob in a public restroom	75—felt panicked, started sweating	"I've touched horrible germs; I'm going to contract meningitis."	"There probably aren't meningitis germs on the doorknob. My immune system is healthy and capable of fighting off disease."	40—heart rate nearing normal, more relaxed

may involve in vivo desensitization (actual exposure to the feared object or situation) or covert desensitization (imagined exposure), be modeled (watching therapists expose themselves to the feared object or situation), or it may occur in a massive dose, as in flooding.

- According to the cognitive perspective, anxiety disorders result from negatively distorted thinking. People with anxiety disorders tend to misinterpret events in three important ways: they fixate on perceived dangers and threats, they over-estimate the severity of the perceived danger or threat, and they drastically under-estimate their ability to cope with the dangers and threats they perceive.

- Cognitive interventions for anxiety involve two key components: (1) the identification of dysfunctional cognitive schemas and negative automatic thoughts and (2) the use of a collaborative logical approach (between therapist and client) to evaluate and challenge anxiety-producing assumptions, beliefs, and thoughts.

Critical Thinking Question | **The cognitive model proposes that thoughts determine feelings. How might this be true for Arthur, the man described at the beginning of the chapter?**

Biological Components

For all of us, the experience of anxiety involves important physiological reactions. As we discussed at the beginning of this chapter, the human body has an extensive set of reactions to danger situations. It should come as no surprise, then, that the biological perspective has much to contribute to the explanation and treatment of anxiety disorders.

The Autonomic Nervous System

The experience of fear and anxiety, whether pathological or normal, is almost always accompanied by the mobilization of the **autonomic nervous system** (which regulates involuntary bodily systems) (see Figure 3.5 in Chapter 3, p. 64) and its two divisions: the **sympathetic** and **parasympathetic systems**. The sympathetic division activates survival responses to perceived threats. Under the direction of the sympathetic nervous system, the adrenal glands secrete stress hormones (adrenaline, cortisol, epinephrine, and norepinephrine), the heart beats faster, pupils dilate, muscles tense, and breathing speeds up and deepens. An extreme version of sympathetic nervous system arousal is known as the **fight-or-flight response,** which prepares animals to flee or attack when faced with danger. The existence of the fight-or-flight response reminds us that anxiety reactions are primitive and evolutionarily based. When the danger has passed, the parasympathetic system reverses the work of the sympathetic nervous system and returns the body to its resting, pre-anxiety state.

From a biological perspective, panic attacks can be viewed as an activation of the fight-or-flight response that occurs in the absence of any real threat. In other words, people who repeatedly experience panic attacks suffer from a fight-or-flight response that is triggered inappropriately. Researchers have shown that when the sympathetic nervous system is artificially stimulated (for example, by asking research participants to deliberately hyperventilate), people who have previously experienced panic attacks will often develop a full-blown panic attack while people with no history of panic attacks will not (Nardi et al., 2001).

Autonomic nervous system (ANS) The part of the central nervous system that regulates involuntary bodily systems, such as breathing and heart rate; it is made up of the sympathetic and parasympathetic nervous systems.

Sympathetic nervous system The part of the autonomic nervous system that activates the body's response to emergency and arousal situations.

Parasympathetic nervous system The part of the autonomic nervous system that regulates the body's calming and energy-conserving functions.

Fight-or-flight response Extreme sympathetic nervous system arousal that prepares animals to flee or attack when faced with danger.

A threatened mountain lion The fight-or-flight response is an adaptive, primitive reflex shared by all animals, humans included.

Limbic system A group of subcortical structures involved in the experience and expression of emotions and the formation of memories.

Amygdala A brain structure which registers the emotional significance of sensory signals and contributes to the expression of emotion.

Hippocampus A brain structure involved in the formation of memories.

Hypothalamus A subcortical brain structure that controls the endocrine, or hormonal, system.

Gamma-aminobutyric acid (GABA) A neurotransmitter that inhibits nervous system activity.

Norepinephrine A neurotransmitter associated with the activation of the sympathetic nervous system; involved in depression and panic attacks.

Locus coeruleus A part of the brain stem associated with activation of the sympathetic nervous system.

The Limbic System

Located beneath the cerebral cortex, the **limbic system** includes the **amygdala** (uh-MIG-duh-la), **hippocampus,** and **hypothalamus** (see Figure 5.4). The limbic system plays an integral part in emotional reactions (such as anxiety), motivation, learning, and certain aspects of memory. The amydala registers the emotional significance of the sensory signals it receives from the cortex (Noyes & Hoehn-Saric, 1998), and researchers have found that the formation of memories involves changes in the neural pathways of the amygdala and hippocampus (Davis, Rainnie, & Cassell, 1994). The amygdala sends information along to the hypothalamus, an area of the brain believed to play an important role in the development of conditioned emotional responses. When a person with a spider phobia sees a spider, the relevant sensory information (the visual image of the spider) is processed by the amygdala which works in concert with the hippocampus to remember the emotional significance of the spider, and then send a signal to the hypothalamus saying "Danger! Activate emergency responses!"

Neurotransmission

The neurotransmitter **gamma-aminobutyric acid (GABA)** serves an inhibitory function in the central nervous system, meaning that it works to suppress nervous system activity. The limbic system is particularly rich with GABA receptors, and researchers believe that GABA works to calm the limbic system when it becomes overly excited (Sibille et al., 2000). For reasons that are not well understood, GABA does not seem to work effectively in the brains of people who suffer from high levels of chronic anxiety (as in GAD). It remains unclear whether highly anxious people have insufficient levels of the neurotransmitter, whether other neurochemicals interfere with GABA functioning, or whether they have problems with their GABA receptors. Substances such as Valium (a benzodiazapine) and alcohol are known to exert their relaxing effects by binding to GABA receptors.

Norepinephrine, another neurotransmitter, plays an active role in the functioning of the **locus coeruleus** (LO-cus sew-REEL-yus), a part of the brain stem associated with activation of the sympathetic nervous system (Figure 5.5). The locus coeruleus helps regulate arousal: monkeys with underactivated neurons in the locus coeruleus seem inattentive and drowsy, while monkeys with excessive neural firing in the locus coeruleus are distracted and disorganized (Noyes & Hoehn-Saric, 1998). Once conditioned to a fear response, the neurons in the locus coeruleus become hypersensitive,

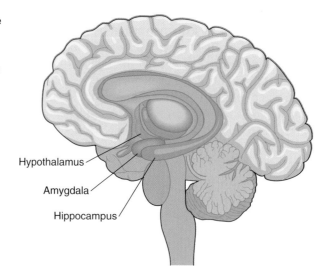

Figure 5.4 The limbic system The limbic system, located near the center of the brain, includes the amygdala, hippocampus, and parts of the hypothalamus. The amygdala, in particular, plays a crucial role in recognizing the emotional significance of a stimulus.

Hypothalamus

Amygdala

Hippocampus

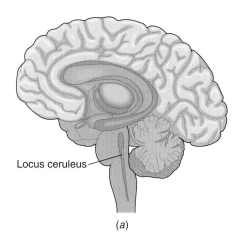
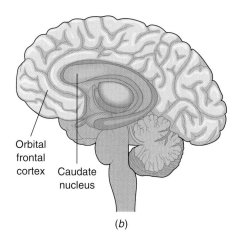

Locus ceruleus

(a)

Orbital frontal cortex   Caudate nucleus

(b)

Figure 5.5 Brain structures involved in panic attacks, PTSD, and OCD Hypersensitive norepinephrine pathways in the locus coereleus (Part *a*), a brain structure that regulates physiological arousal, appear to play a role in the generation of anxiety symptoms associated with panic attacks and PTSD. Overactive primitive brain structures, such as the caudate nucleus and the orbital frontal cortex (Part *b*), have been implicated in the intrusive, unwanted thoughts associated with OCD.

firing even with minimal stimulation. Hypersensitive norepinephrine pathways in the locus coereleus seem to be involved in panic attacks and PTSD (Shekhar et al., 2002; Southwick et al., 1993). Norepinephrine has been found at unusually high levels in people who have experienced extreme stress, and it appears that chronic exposure to uncontrollable stress may increase the sensitivity of norepinephrine receptors in the brain (Southwick et al., 1999).

Serotonin, like GABA, can serve an inhibitory function within the brain. When serotonin receptors are artificially blocked with metergoline (an antagonist to the serotonin system) people experience heightened levels of anxiety (Ben-Zion et al., 1999). People who suffer from repeated panic attacks may have depleted serotonin levels in their limbic system and other brain regions associated with the fight-or-flight response (Deakin & Graeff, 1991). As a result, the fight-or-flight systems in the brain may be chronically over-stimulated and ready to fire at the slightest provocation. Serotonin has also been implicated in OCD although the relationship between the two is not well understood (Micallef & Blin, 2001). The link between serotonin and obsessive-compulsive symptoms was discovered when clients with OCD who were taking serotonin-stimulating drugs for other reasons (primarily depression) reported a reduction in their obsessions and compulsions.

Another interesting line of speculation about the biological basis of OCD (which overlaps with psychodynamic explanations) suggests that we all have constant sexual or violent urges in the "primitive" part of our brains, but these impulses normally do not "break through" to consciousness and are therefore not usually problematic. There is evidence that primitive brain structures (for example, the caudate nuclei and the orbital frontal cortex; Figure 5.5) that may give rise to such "forbidden" impulses are overly active in people who suffer from OCD, causing unwanted and disturbing thoughts to make their way into consciousness (Rapoport, 1991; Salloway & Cummings, 1996).

Serotonin A neurotransmitter associated with depression and anxiety.

Genetic Factors

Genetic vulnerabilities appear to play a role in most of the anxiety disorders. Concordance rates in monozygotic (identical) versus dyzygotic (fraternal) twins for the presence of any anxiety disorder have been reported to be 63.6% and 43.5%, respectively, suggesting a substantial genetic contribution (Andrews et al., 1990). However, the amount of genetic influence varies considerably among the different DSM-IV-TR disorders. Panic disorder appears to be significantly heritable (Noyes et al., 1987); lifetime rates of panic disorder among the first-degree relatives of people known to have the disorder range between 7.7% and 17.3% compared to a range from 0.8% to 4.2% among first-degree relatives of people who do not have panic disorder (Noyes & Hoehn-Saric, 1998). Genetic factors also play a significant role in OCD and in specific and social phobias (Fyer et al., 1993; Kendler et al., 1992). However, studies have not consistently found a genetic component in GAD and PTSD (MacKinnon & Foley, 1996).

Biological Interventions

Researchers discovered in the 1960s that certain antidepressant drugs could reduce or eliminate panic attacks—even in clients who were not depressed—although the same drugs did not generally help with other anxiety disorders (Klein, 1964). This evidence led to the hypothesis that the biological basis of panic might be different from that of other forms of anxiety, a hypothesis that remains a focus of research. In any case, antidepressant medications are the leading biological treatment for panic disorder. Antidepressants, especially **SSRIs** (selective serotonin reuptake inhibitors such as Prozac, Zoloft, Paxil) and **tricyclic antidepressants** (such as Tofranil, Elavil, Sinequan), affect levels of key neurotransmitters such as serotonin and norepinephrine (Chapter 6). These medications are a very effective treatment for panic disorder. Nearly 90% of clients in one study reported relief from panic attacks while taking antidepressants (Black, Wesner, & Bowers, 1993). Unfortunately, most clients taking antidepressants for panic attacks relapse when they stop taking the medication. The SSRIs are also widely prescribed to reduce OCD symptoms and to decrease the frequency of intrusive thoughts in PTSD (Yehuda et al., 2002).

Barbiturates, powerful sedating drugs such as Amytal, were widely used to treat anxiety symptoms until the 1950s when it became apparent that they were dangerously addictive (Chapter 9). **Benzodiazepines** (such as Valium, Xanax, Ativan), which enhance the functioning of the inhibitory neurotransmitter GABA, seemed at first to be a much safer alternative to barbiturates. However, it has since been recognized that the benzodiazepines are also physically addictive, often have undesirable side effects (such as drowsiness and loss of coordination), and do not provide long-term relief from anxiety. Further, the benzodiazepines heighten the effects of other depressant drugs, such as alcohol, and are potentially lethal when taken in combination with other depressants. However, benzodiazepines are widely and safely used for the short-term treatment of anxiety. **Beta-blockers** (such as Inderal) which decrease the activity of norepinephrine, and **azaspirones** (such as BuSpar) which help regulate serotonin, are relatively new medications for anxiety. Beta-blockers can be an effective intervention for social phobia, and azaspirones for GAD (Den Boer, van Vliet, & Westnberg, 1996). Both appear to have many of the positive effects of the barbiturates and benzodiazepines, with fewer side effects.

Psychodynamic Components

Freud proposed two theories about the causes of anxiety. Early in his career, Freud was struck by the coexistence of anxiety symptoms and sexual abstinence or frustration among his clients. He developed a theory that the energy of repressed sexual urges transforms into anxiety (Freud, 1895). Later on, he decided that this first theory had it backward—that anxiety is actually the *cause* of **repression**, not the *result* of it. Specifically, Freud's second theory argued that anxiety is the ego's reaction to perceived dangers (from the id, the superego, or reality), very much in keeping with the common sense view of anxiety as a form of fear. For example, anxiety can be an indication that unacceptable impulses are on the verge of being expressed, and the anxiety is a "signal" to initiate defense mechanisms such as repressing these impulses (Freud, 1926).

Selective serotonin reuptake inhibitors (SSRIs) A "second generation" class of antidepressant medications that block the reuptake of serotonin from the synapse; used in the treatment of depression and other disorders.

Tricyclic antidepressants A "first generation" class of antidepressant medications which increases the availability of both serotonin and norepinephrine.

Barbiturates Sedative drugs sometimes used to treat anxiety.

Benzodiazepines Sedative drugs that treat anxiety by increasing the activity of gamma-aminobutyric acid (GABA).

Beta-blockers Drugs that treat anxiety by decreasing the activity of norepinephrine.

Azaspirones Drugs that treat anxiety by regulating serotonin.

Repression A defense mechanism consisting of the forgetting of painful or unacceptable mental content.

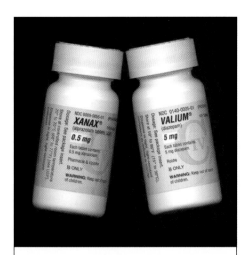

Medicating anxiety Benzodiazepines, such as Xanax and Valium, can be useful in the treatment of anxiety. However, because they are highly addictive, benzodiazepines should only be used to treat anxiety on a temporary basis.

Later psychodynamic theorists expanded on Freud's view of the internal and external dangers that can cause extreme anxiety. Their ideas generally focus on traumatic childhood situations, such as losses or empathic failures in important relationships, abuse, and overstimulation (Greenberg & Mitchell, 1983; Kohut, 1977; Winnicott, 1965). Psychodynamic theorists propose specific explanations for different types of anxiety symptoms based on the defense mechanisms associated with them. We will illustrate this approach by focusing on two anxiety disorders—phobias and obsessive-compulsive disorder (OCD).

Phobias

Freud proposed that phobias result when the defense mechanism of **displacement** causes perceptions of danger to shift from a threatening situation onto a neutral object in an effort to reduce anxiety. Freud's approach to phobias was outlined in his famous case study, "Little Hans" (1909). Interestingly, Freud never worked directly with this five-year-old boy, but he communicated regularly with Hans' father who acted as the therapist to his own son. Little Hans developed a severe phobia of horses after seeing an accident involving a horse. (Needless to say, having a horse phobia in Vienna in 1909 caused a great deal of trouble since horses were everywhere!) Based on Hans' father's reports, Freud speculated that Little Hans' fear of horses was a displacement of a fear of his father. The background for Freud's hypothesis was this: the horse phobia developed around the time that Hans was struggling with wishes to have an exclusive loving relationship with his mother. (Freud called this scenario, which he believed was a universal developmental stage occurring around ages 4 to 6, the **Oedipus complex**, after the Greek myth in which Oedipus kills his father and marries his mother.) Freud believed that Hans, thinking like a five-year-old, began to fear that his father would be angered by his desire to monopolize his mother's affections. But, to be scared of his father, who was big and powerful and whom he loved and needed, caused Hans even more anxiety. A defense mechanism, displacement, "solved" this problem. Rather than being afraid of his father, Hans' fear was displaced to horses. Freud theorized that horses became the focus of the displaced fear because Hans often played "horsey" with his father, and because he associated horses' muzzles with his father's moustache.

Subsequent psychodynamic theorists have also emphasized the role of the defense mechanism called **projection** in phobias. In projection, an internal feeling that seems dangerous or unacceptable is attributed to someone or something else (Chapter 3). For example, Hans was also very uncomfortable about his competitive anger toward his father. To reduce this discomfort, Hans projected his hostile feelings onto horses, perceiving horses to be dangerous and aggressive (he feared they would bite him). Then, by avoiding horses (his horse phobia), Hans could also "solve" the problem of his anger toward his father.

This theory highlights the *continuum between normal and abnormal behavior*. Hans was experiencing a more extreme version of the same process that often causes young children to become temporarily afraid of angry robbers or mean ghosts just after they have had an angry tantrum. The much loved children's book *Where The Wild Things Are* by Maurice Sendak, in which a child imagines and then tames angry monsters after receiving a scolding and having a tantrum, beautifully illustrates the processes of displacing fears and projecting angry feelings. In summary, the psychodynamic explanation of phobias emphasizes that phobias result when feelings are shifted from one situation or person to another through the defense mechanisms of displacement and projection.

Obsessive-Compulsive Disorder

Freud argued that obsessive-compulsive symptoms are based on the defense mechanisms called **isolation of affect** and **undoing** when they are used to manage anxiety-

Displacement A defense mechanism in which feelings about someone or something are unconsciously shifted to someone or something else.

Oedipus complex A phase during normal development when children desire an exclusive loving relationship with the parent of the opposite sex.

Projection A defense mechanism in which an individual attributes his or her own unacceptable emotions to someone or something else.

Isolation of affect A defense mechanism in which thoughts occur without associated feelings.

Undoing A defense mechanism in which one action or thought is used to "cancel out" another action or thought.

provoking thoughts and impulses. Through *isolation of affect*, unwanted thoughts and impulses are treated as if they were not connected to one's actual feelings and past experiences, but are simply disturbing intrusions. *Undoing*, the magical use of ritualized action to "undo" a troublesome thought or impulse, relates to the compulsions of OCD. For example, a person is employing the defense mechanism of undoing when he compulsively cleans his desk each afternoon, thinking that this will "undo" or cancel out his unacceptable angry thoughts about his boss.

Another of Freud's case studies, the "Rat Man" (1909), helped Freud formulate his theory of OCD-like symptoms. The Rat Man came to Freud for help with disturbing thoughts (that his fiancée and father were being tortured by rats), and the compulsive rituals (such as having to neatly arrange rocks on the roadside) he used to magically counteract these thoughts. Freud discovered that the Rat Man was unconsciously enraged at his fiancée and his father, and that his anxiety about his fury led to the use of the defense mechanisms of isolation of affect and undoing. The isolation of affect transformed the unacceptable rage into abstract thoughts of torture which the Rat Man could disavow, though his thoughts still caused enough anxiety to also require undoing rituals.

Other Sources of Anxiety

In addition to focusing on the role of defense mechanisms in the specific forms of anxiety described above, psychodynamic theorists believe that high levels of anxiety often result from disrupted or inadequate early parent-child relationships. Parents have the important job of helping their children learn how to manage normal, but sometimes disturbing, wishes and feelings. If parents are too harsh in response to id-based childhood behaviors, their child may grow to feel anxious about some of his or her own natural feelings. If parents protect and gratify a child too much, the child may not develop adequate defense mechanisms for dealing with id impulses (A. Freud, 1936).

For example, imagine a five-year-old child who is always hungry a half-hour before dinnertime. If his parents tend to get very angry with him for whining about being hungry, he may grow up to feel quite uneasy with his wishes for satisfaction. He may begin to repress such wishes before they reach consciousness. If repressed too forcefully, he may lose awareness of his wants and desires and feel anxious whenever they are unconsciously aroused. At the other extreme, a parent may respond immediately to the child's request for food (or for anything else) to the point that the child fails to develop good skills for dealing with frustration, delayed gratification, or disappointment. As an adult, such a person may feel ill-equipped to manage his or her own powerful impulses and become quite anxious when faced with the frustration or disappointment of his or her desires.

Psychodynamic Interventions

Since psychodynamic therapists focus on pathological anxiety that arises from unconscious emotional conflicts, they tend to use basic psychodynamic techniques to address most anxiety disorders (Abend, 1996). Clients in psychodynamic therapy are encouraged to speak as freely as possible and to attend, with the therapist, to uncovering the roots of their anxieties. This includes exploring how the underlying emotional conflicts emerge in the form of resistance (for example, topics the client feels reluctant to explore) and transference (feelings from past relationships that are transferred into present relationships, including the relationship with the therapist) during the therapy process. The goal of psychodynamic therapy is to help clients understand the roots of their symptoms, gain greater self-acceptance, develop better solutions to emotional conflicts, and decrease needs for problematic defense mechanisms. Consider the following description by a psychoanalyst of a case involving a phobia:

Case Illustration A divorced woman in her early thirties, a successful junior executive in a multinational corporate enterprise, sought treatment because a flying phobia threatened to limit her career advancement… Despite many difficulties in immersing herself freely in the treatment, the patient's persistent and conscientious work gradually permitted a progressive unfolding of the many levels of meaning of her phobia, accompanied by relief to the point of full recovery…

The first level of understanding to emerge was that the patient used her anxiety before and during flights as a way of tormenting and punishing herself unmercifully. This punishment came to be seen as related to her career ambitions, which she imagined would necessarily involve intense and deadly competition, especially with men. As this configuration became clearer, the patient became able to report a more precise description of her anxiety about flying. She was terrified that in the course of a flight her discomfort would grow so intense that she would lose control of herself and become hysterical. Such an outburst would be intensely humiliating to her, especially if it were to occur in the company of a male co-worker. Eventually she was able to elaborate her view that such a hysterical loss of control as she imagined, and dreaded, would characterize her as a weak, contemptible female, destroying the image of the competent, firm, rational, and composed person (qualities she attributed to men) that she wished to present to the world. This disgrace would be a fit punishment for her ruthlessly defeating the males she competed with, which she imagined humiliated them terribly. In time it also became clear how these conflicts resonated with issues in her childhood relationship to her father, a successful businessman.

(Abend, 1996, pp. 407–408)

As you can see, the psychodynamic approach assumes that once the meaning of the anxiety symptoms can be articulated and understood, the symptoms will diminish. Research on the effectiveness of psychodynamic interventions for anxiety is mixed. Some researchers suggest that other theoretical approaches offer quicker and more consistently positive results, but numerous case reports and many systematic studies support the effectiveness of psychodynamic interventions (Crits-Cristoph et al., 1996).

The Multiple Causality of Anxiety Disorders

As you can tell from our review of the different theoretical perspectives on anxiety, the principle of *multiple causality* is highly relevant to anxiety disorders. Because the experience of anxiety involves emotional, behavioral, cognitive, and physical components, various perspectives can be combined in the explanation and treatment of anxiety disorders.

Cognitive and behavioral approaches can be integrated to explain and treat some anxiety disorders. For example, maladaptive cognitions ("I'm certain I'll have a panic attack if I leave the house!") are often reinforced by maladaptive behaviors (experiencing a reduction in anxiety by staying home). Though we presented the cognitive and behavioral components separately for the sake of clarity, the two approaches are almost always combined in the contemporary treatment of anxiety disorders. For instance, interventions for OCD often combine the correction of cognitive distortions that underlie obsessions with behavioral techniques that address the accompanying compulsions (exposure and response prevention). David Barlow and his colleague (Barlow & Cerny, 1988) have developed an extensive cognitive-behavioral technique for treating panic attacks that draws upon training in relaxation, planned exposure to anxiety-provoking situations, and cognitive interventions. This program has been found to be at least as effective as antidepressant medications in the treatment of panic, and to produce longer-lasting benefits.

HPA axis A brain system involving the hypothalamus, pituitary gland, and adrenal cortex that regulates the release of stress hormones into the bloodstream.

Other theoretical perspectives can also be combined in explaining or treating anxiety disorders. Imagine, for example, a person who was frequently mistreated and humiliated by his family throughout his childhood and as an adult exhibits the symptoms of social phobia. Psychotherapy aimed at working through his childhood experiences and addressing maladaptive cognitions and behaviors might help, but he may feel so anxious in social situations that he cannot consider the possibility of discussing personal difficulties with a stranger (such as a therapist). In this case, it might be appropriate to use an anti-anxiety medication to reduce the man's anxiety so that he can engage in a psychotherapy. In everyday clinical practice, a variety of interventions are often combined in this fashion to treat anxiety disorders.

The various theoretical models of anxiety not only complement each other, but they often overlap. For example, despite their differences, the psychodynamic, behavioral, and cognitive perspectives all share the common belief that clients must face their fears in order to overcome them. Even some approaches that seem to be at odds with each other share common origins. John Watson's behavioral view of phobias was originally sparked by his interest in psychodynamic explanations of how fears could be shifted or displaced from one object to another, as is often the case with phobias (Rilling, 2000).

The Connection Between Mind and Body in Anxiety Disorders

In addition to noting the complementarity and overlap among the various theoretical perspectives, it is important to highlight how profoundly the psychological and biological realms influence each other in anxiety disorders. For example, there is considerable evidence that emotionally traumatic experiences can alter the functioning of components of the nervous system. The **HPA** (hypothalamic-pituitary-adrenal) **axis** responds to stressful experiences by releasing stress hormones such as adrenaline and cortisol into the bloodstream (see Figure 5.6). These stress hormones elevate emotional arousal and help prepare animals to fight or flee. Ideally, the response of the HPA axis is commensurate with the level of threat and, when the threat ends, the HPA axis returns to its proper resting state. But, some researchers suggest that sustained stress during critical periods of development may permanently damage the cells regulating the functioning of the HPA axis. One study compared HPA axis activity in women with and without histories of childhood abuse by measuring stress hormone levels while the research participants engaged in a mildly stressful activity (such as speaking in front of a group). Women who had been abused as children released more than six times as many stress hormones as women who had not been abused (Heim et al., 2000). In other words, extremely stressful events such as early childhood traumas may predispose an individual to lifelong hyperactivity of the HPA axis and subsequent chronic anxiety (Bremner & Vermetten, 2001). This finding provides a powerful example of the core concept of the *connection between mind and body* insofar as emotional experiences have the potential to shape the structure and functioning of systems within the body.

Similarly, studies have shown that PTSD is associated with a reduction in the volume of the right hippocampus affecting both verbal memory and performance on neuropsychological tests (Bremner, 1999). In addition, when people with PTSD experience flashbacks, the part of the brain responsible for using language to communicate past experiences (known as Broca's area) appears to be "turned off" (Van der Kolk, 1996). Based on these findings, researchers believe that the brain stores memories of traumatic events differently than most other memories; this may partially account for the fact that traumatic memories are often reexperienced as flashbacks, rather than simply remembered.

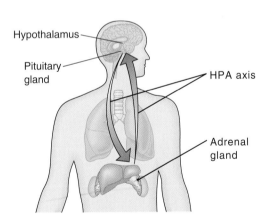

Hypothalamus

Pituitary gland

HPA axis

Adrenal gland

Figure 5.6 The HPA axis The HPA (hypothalamic-pituitary-adrenal) axis is believed to play a key role in the transformation of psychological stress into a physiological response. Emotional experiences, as processed by the hypothalamus, activate the pituitary gland, which activates the adrenal gland, causing it to secrete adrenocortical hormones, such as adrenaline and cortisol. The release of adrenaline and cortisol causes subjective feelings of arousal and anxiety.

Finally, with the advent of brain imaging techniques, researchers have been able to show that psychotherapies affect and change brain functioning. For example, Baxter and his colleagues (1992) demonstrated with positron emission tomography (PET) scans that successful exposure plus response prevention therapy for OCD led to reduced activity levels in the right caudate nucleus after the therapy was completed. These changes were similar to those seen in OCD clients successfully treated with Prozac.

Brief Summary

- The biological perspective emphasizes the role of the autonomic nervous system, the limbic system, neurotransmitters, and genetic factors in anxiety disorders.

- Presently, the major biological treatments for panic attacks are the SSRI antidepressants and the tricyclic antidepressants, both of which inhibit the reuptake of certain neurotransmitters. The SSRI antidepressants are also helpful in treating the intrusive thoughts in OCD and PTSD. Beta-blockers and azaspirones are alternatives to habit-forming barbiturates and benzodiazepines in the treatment of some anxiety disorders.

- Freud developed two different explanatory models for anxiety. Originally, he proposed that anxiety is produced by the energy of repressed sexual impulses. Later, he concluded that anxiety is the ego's reaction to perceived internal or external dangers. Modern psychodynamic theorists also propose that high levels of anxiety often result from disrupted or inadequate early parent-child relationships. Psychodynamic treatment interventions focus on improved mastery of anxiety-causing psychological conflicts.

- The various theoretical approaches to anxiety often overlap or complement each other, highlighting the principle of *multiple causality*. Cognitive and behavioral techniques are often combined in interventions for anxiety disorders, and anti-anxiety medications are often used in combination with psychotherapies. In addition, changes in brain structure and function resulting from traumatic emotional experiences and from psychotherapy illustrate *the connection between mind and body* in anxiety disorders.

> **Critical Thinking Question** | **W**hich combination of theoretical components seems most useful to you for explaining Arthur's and Greg's anxiety disorders?

Case Vignettes | Treatment
Arthur | Panic Disorder

Arthur, the 22-year-old engineering student suffering from anxiety "spells" followed up on his physician's referral to a psychologist. In his first meeting with the psychologist, Arthur made it clear that he was doubtful that his physical symptoms had a psychological basis. The therapist noted Arthur's skepticism, and offered him some information about the kinds of physical symptoms that often accompany panic attacks. Arthur was surprised to hear the therapist describe many of the symp-

toms he had experienced, and relieved to learn that something could be done to reduce his distress. By the end of the first session, Arthur agreed to try a cognitive-behavioral program for his panic attacks.

Over the next several sessions, the psychologist taught Arthur relaxation techniques, and Arthur practiced the techniques at home several times a week. Before long, Arthur was able to get his body into a deep state of relaxation in only a few minutes. Two weeks after he had started therapy Arthur felt like he was going to have a panic attack while standing in line at the grocery store. He immediately started to concentrate on his breathing and to tense and relax his muscles. His anxiety passed without ever developing into a full-blown panic attack. Arthur and his psychologist created a hierarchy of anxiety-provoking situations (such as studying for a final exam, or being caught in a large crowd of people) and Arthur practiced controlling his anxiety by using relaxation while he placed himself in increasingly difficult situations.

Next, Arthur and his psychologist worked on uncovering the thoughts that accompanied Arthur's panic attacks. Arthur kept a record of all the things that went through his mind when he felt like he was about to have a panic attack. Among his thoughts were the statements that he was sure he was going to die, and that this would be especially tragic since things in his life were going so well. Arthur and his psychologist evaluated his fearful thoughts that he would die and challenged them with the facts that Arthur was healthy and had already survived numerous panic attacks.

Within a few months of starting therapy, Arthur's panic attacks were well under control. Arthur's psychologist took this opportunity to point out how much success Arthur had had in understanding how his mind worked and suggested that Arthur might now want to explore what caused the panic

attacks to begin when they did. Arthur agreed that he was curious about what had brought on his troubles, and decided to continue therapy, but with a new focus on gaining insight into the roots of his anxiety.

Arthur began speaking to his psychologist about how much pressure he felt from his family to succeed academically. Even though he welcomed his family's constant support, he hated feeling like it was his job to be the family "success story." He talked about being jealous of his classmates who came from families where everyone had gone to college, and about how he worried that his family would make a scene at his graduation because it was such a big deal for them. Arthur also recognized that his continuing success would leave him feeling more and more distant from his family. He worried that his potential earning power would lead him to develop tastes that they didn't approve of or understand. At the same time, he worried that it would be obvious to his employers and new colleagues that his background was very different from theirs. Arthur and his psychologist both noticed how much calmer he became as he allowed himself to explore these feelings. Arthur told the therapist that he had felt like a "bad person" for resenting his loving family, and that it was a relief to realize that he could continue to have an appreciation for his family even if he did feel angry and disappointed with them at times.

Case Discussion | Panic Disorder

Arthur's symptoms closely correspond with the DSM-IV-TR definition of panic attacks, but he never developed the behavior changes based on a fear of future attacks that can sometimes be part of the DSM-IV-TR criteria for panic disorder. Fortunately, he also never developed agoraphobia in reaction to his attacks.

Arthur initially doubted that psychotherapy could be helpful to him. As a result, the psychologist began with *psycho-*

education—meaning that he informed Arthur that his physical symptoms could result from an anxiety disorder. This helped Arthur to accept a psychological treatment, one that focused at first on controlling his panic attacks, not exploring their meaning. The therapy then proceeded to a psychodynamic exploration of how previously "unacceptable" thoughts had contributed to the onset of Arthur's anxiety.

Greg | Obsessive-Compulsive Disorder (OCD)

Greg, the 40-year-old attorney, and his wife happened to see a news program on OCD. Afterward, Greg's wife suggested that he seek treatment and he agreed with her suggestion. A social worker met with Greg and his wife, and heard from both of them about how Greg's "habits" had been causing problems at home. The social worker concurred that Greg likely suffered from OCD and referred Greg to a psychiatrist who prescribed Prozac. Greg was initially reluctant to consider medication for

his problem, but his wife insisted that he try it "for the family." Greg was reassured by the social worker that it would probably help Greg to feel more in control of his worries about keeping the house clean. Within a few weeks, Greg and his family noticed that he was much more "laid back" about keeping order around the house. Even though Greg still liked things to be neat, he did not become upset when his son left his coat on a chair or when dishes sat in the sink. Greg's social worker recommended that Greg also consider beginning an exposure and response prevention therapy. She assisted Greg in gradually increasing his exposure to anxiety-producing situations, like dirt and messiness, without responding with clean-ing and checking rituals. One year later, on a lower dose of Prozac and having occasional therapy sessions, Greg was described by his wife as "90% better."

Case Discussion | Obsessive-Compulsive Disorder

Initially, Prozac, which increases the availability of serotonin in the nervous system, was used to help bring Greg's obsessive-compulsive symptoms under control. Greg's social worker also suggested some cognitive-behavioral techniques to help Greg make further progress. Through exposure and response prevention, Greg was helped to tolerate situations that had previously made him extremely anxious and to resist his impulse to clean or to badger the offending family member. Over time, the cognitive-behavioral interventions helped Greg to adapt to normal levels of disarray and he was able to reduce his dose of Prozac while maintaining his improvement.

Chapter Summary

- Pathological anxiety is defined as anxiety that occurs in an inappropriate *context* or is toward the extreme end of the *continuum between normal and abnormal* anxiety.

- The DSM-IV-TR identifies six different anxiety disorders: generalized anxiety disorder, panic disorder, phobias, obsessive-compulsive disorder, posttraumatic stress disorder, and acute stress disorder.

- The DSM-IV-TR anxiety disorder diagnoses have important *advantages and limitations*. While the reliability and validity of the DSM-IV-TR anxiety diagnoses are relatively high, the DSM-IV-TR anxiety disorders are also highly comorbid, meaning that clients often meet criteria for more than one diagnosis.

- Demographic factors, such as age, gender, and social class, affect the prevalence and manifestation presentation of anxiety disorders.

- Various cultures and historical periods define and classify anxiety problems differently, highlighting with the core concept of *cultural and historical relativism.*

- All of the major theoretical perspectives in abnormal psychology offer concepts relevant to the explanation and treatment of anxiety disorders. Further, the different theoretical perspectives on anxiety often interact, overlap, or complement each other, highlighting the *principle of multiple causality.*

- Changes in brain structure and function resulting from traumatic emotional experiences and from psychotherapy are two illustrations of the *connection between mind and body* in anxiety disorders.

Emily Carr, *Forest, British Columbia*, 1932, oil on canvas, Vancouver Art Gallery, Emily Carr Trust, VAG 42.3.9 (Photo: Trevor Mills)

In the years since her death, Emily Carr (1871–1945) has been recognized as one of Canada's most important painters. Carr's innovative post-Impressionist style brought a vibrant energy to her paintings of the trees and landscapes of British Columbia. Known for her independent spirit, ...*continues on page 154*

emily carr

chapter six

MOOD AND THE MOOD DISORDERS

Case Vignettes

Tamara, age 37, asked her family physician for the name of a good psychologist three months after her husband abruptly moved out of their house and announced that he was planning to file for divorce. Tamara was devastated by the news at the time and felt so sad and hopeless that even death seemed a preferable alternative. As time went on, Tamara felt less sad and more angry about her soon-to-be-ex-husband's behavior. Though she no longer felt suicidal, she found it impossible to feel good or even "okay." She continued to go to work and spend time with friends but always had the sense she was just going through the motions of her life. Her two children, ages 7 and 10, were equally shocked and upset by the separation. Tamara knew that her children were suffering, but felt powerless to help them given how badly she was feeling herself. She decided to seek help when her worries about her children became more than she could bear.

Most of Tamara's first meeting with the psychologist was spent explaining her divorce proceedings and her concerns about her children. Though Tamara described the poignant situation of her husband leaving abruptly, the psychologist noted that Tamara seemed to be almost completely devoid of feelings. Tamara did become teary when explaining her concerns about her children, but described herself as only feeling "empty."

In the second session Tamara described the time since her husband left. She explained that she had felt intensely sad, occasionally suicidal, and had found it difficult to feel excited or happy about anything. When asked about eating and sleeping Tamara explained that she went through a period when she woke up at 3:00 each morning and was unable to go back to sleep, but that had ended after a few weeks. She had, however, lost 20 pounds since her husband left and had yet to regain her appetite.

Mark, age 33, was taken by his wife to the hospital emergency room late one night after he climbed onto the roof of the family house, declared himself "the happiest man in the world," and refused to come down for hours. The doctors at the E.R. gave Mark medications to help calm him and arranged for Mark to have a full psychiatric evaluation. A few days later, Mark and his wife met with a psychiatrist. They reported that he often experienced periods when he was extremely excited, talked very quickly, and slept very little. Mark was accustomed to his strange moods, but his wife admitted to the psychiatrist that she had been worrying about their finances since Mark started using credit cards to buy expensive and unnecessary electronic equipment when he was in an excited mood. Six months prior, Mark had come home with two digital video players, three large screen televisions, and a $5,000 sound system with the plan of transforming the family basement into the "ultimate entertainment center." Mark stayed in the basement for several days setting up his new system but then suddenly abandoned the project.

...continued from page 152

cantankerous personality, and disregard for the restrictive Victorian values of the time, Carr also experienced periodic episodes of severe depression.

Mark's wife also explained that he experienced periods when he was extremely "mellow and sad"—even to the point of not getting out of bed for days at a time. Mark recalled feeling periodically depressed since he was in college, but he told the psychiatrist that his "down times" seemed to be lasting longer and feeling more intense as he got older. Mark's wife added that she felt like there were "three Marks: excited Mark, sad Mark, and regular Mark."

DEFINING MOOD AND MOOD DISORDERS

Fluctuations in *mood* are part of everyday life. Everyone goes through periods of being unusually happy or somewhat sad, and each individual has a mood baseline from which he or she typically operates. Some people are generally in a good mood and only feel "down" in the face of a major negative life event, such as the death of a loved one, while other people tend to feel a little gloomy much of the time and need significantly good news to put a spring in their step. Whether or not we tune into our own feelings and those of the people around us, mood and its normal variations permeate every aspect of daily life. In fact, psychologists define mood as much more than just an *emotional* (feeling) state. They regard mood as a state that also includes *cognitive* (thinking), *motivational* (behavioral), and even *physical* (bodily) aspects. In other words, mood not only influences how we feel, but also how we think, act, sleep, eat, and live.

While most people experience normal ups and downs in their mood, moods can become pathologically low (**depression**) or pathologically high (**mania**). (Later on in this chapter we will explain how it is that mood can be *pathologically* high, which may seem like an odd idea!) The fact that everyone knows what it is like to feel "up" or "down" makes understanding mood disorders easier in some ways, but harder in others. Because we are all familiar with mood fluctuation, the mood disorders make more intuitive sense than disorders like schizophrenia (Chapter 12) that are outside the realm of experience for most people. On the other hand, our familiarity with mood changes raises some difficult questions. What is the difference between a brief case of the blues and a clinical depression, or between feeling "up" and being manic? The answers to these questions lie in two of the core concepts in abnormal psychology: the

Depression A state of abnormally low mood, with emotional, cognitive, motivational, and/or physical features.

Mania A state of abnormally high mood, with emotional, cognitive, motivational, and/or physical features.

Mood Moods range from elated to depressed and include cognitive, motivational, and physical components in addition to feeling states.

importance of context in defining and understanding abnormality and the *continuum between normal and abnormal behavior.*

The Importance of Context in Defining Mood Disorders

Variations in mood often occur in response to life events. Winning the lottery or acing an exam usually puts a person in a very good mood, while being fired from a job or dumped by a girlfriend typically causes feelings of sadness. Within the context of such events, mood variation is expectable and normal, and the *absence* of joy or sadness may be more abnormal than their presence. Even intense changes in mood are considered normal in certain contexts; the death of a family member often evokes intense grief, but we would hardly consider such a reaction to be a sign of a mental disorder. In contrast, *pathological* changes in mood sometimes seem to occur "out of the blue," without a significant event that might explain the onset or intensity of euphoria or sadness. This is not to say that mood changes are only pathological when no precipitating factor can be found. Indeed, even grieving can become pathological when it crosses certain thresholds of duration or intensity. But, in general, pathological mood states can be defined as emotional extremes that do not seem appropriate to the person's *context* or circumstances.

The Continuum Between Normal and Abnormal Mood

As we just noted, mood disorders also differ from normal mood variations in terms of their duration and intensity. While we would expect someone to be very sad for several months after the death of a spouse, parent, or child, we would be surprised if mourning continued uninterrupted for years. Similarly, even a minor case of the blues warrants concern if it is present for an extended period of time. As for intensity, depression and mania do not always last very long, but they can be so intense that they seriously interfere with functioning and may even be life-threatening. For example, people who are severely depressed often have trouble working, maintaining relationships, caring for their own hygiene, or feeling that life is worth living.

Of course, the line between "normal" and "abnormal" mood will always be somewhat blurry and arbitrary. For example, we cannot say with certainty that it is "normal" to take to bed for two days after a bad breakup, but not for four. One useful way to think about the difference between normal and pathological moods is to compare mood to physical health. Healthy people still get sick, but their bodies are capable of fighting off many infections, and their illnesses usually do not develop into serious conditions. Similarly, it is normal to feel sad occasionally, but some people do not recover easily from periods of sadness and instead spiral into severe, immobilizing depressions. In sum, pathological mood states are also defined by being at the extreme ends of the mood *continuum.*

Brief Summary
- Moods include emotional, cognitive, motivational, and even physical components.
- Fluctuations in mood are normal and expectable reactions to life events.
- Mood disorders are characterized by moods of extreme intensity or duration that are debilitating and often seem "out of context."

Critical Thinking Question | **W**ould you say that it is *context* or *continuum* issues, or both, that define Mark's moods, described at the beginning of the chapter, as abnormal?

CLASSIFYING MOOD DISORDERS

Fluctuations in mood occur in many forms of psychopathology where mood disturbance is not the central feature. For example, people with *personality disorders* (Chapter 11), *eating disorders* (Chapter 8), *anxiety disorders* (Chapter 5), *sexual problems* (Chapter 10), *schizophrenia* (Chapter 12), or *substance use problems* (Chapter 9) often become depressed. This chapter, however, will focus on the classification, explanation, and treatment of disorders in which significant disruption in mood is the *central* symptom—the group of disorders currently classified in the DSM-IV-TR as the Mood Disorders.

Historical Relativism in Classifying Mood Disorders

The evolution of the DSM-IV-TR classification of mood disorders is worth noting because it highlights the core concept of ***historical relativism.*** The concept of pathological alterations of mood is hardly new; some of the earliest references to depression as a mental disorder come from Sumerian and Egyptian documents dating back to 2600 B.C.E. (Stefanis & Stefanis, 1999). Biblical descriptions of depression also abound. King David, overwhelmed with guilt for having committed adultery explains, "I am troubled; I am bowed down greatly; I go mourning all the day long…I am feeble and sore broken…My heart panteth, my strength faileth me: as for the light of mine eyes, it also is gone from me" (*Psalms* 38:6,8,10). The Greek physician Hippocrates (460–357 B.C.E.) attributed **melancholia** (an old term for depression) to an imbalance of the four bodily fluids or *humors*—in particular to the presence of too much *black bile* (Chapter 3). In a book from the Middle Ages titled *Anatomy of Melancholy* (1621) Robert Burton, an English scholar, writer, and clergyman, provides an historical summary and description of mood disturbances along with an extensive list of the possible causes of depression: the position of Saturn, melancholy parents, intense love, a ruddy complexion, and so on.

At the end of the 19th century, Emil Kraepelin (the "father of modern psychiatry") made a significant advance in the classification of mood disorders by separating *bipolar disorder* (then known as *manic-depression*) from *schizophrenia* (Chapter 12); these disorders had previously been lumped together since both can involve hallucinations and delusions. Another major step forward in the classification of mood disorders came in 1957 when Karl Leonhard, a German psychiatrist, argued that **unipolar** mood disorders, in which people experience only abnormally low moods, and **bipolar** mood disorders, in which people experience *both* abnormally low *and* high moods, were two distinct syndromes. As you will see in the upcoming description of the DSM-IV-TR mood disorder categories, the differentiation of unipolar and bipolar mood disorders has been retained as an important diagnostic distinction. Even the name of this category of disorders has changed over time. Early editions of the DSM used the term *affective disorders* for the category now known as mood disorders (*affect* is still sometimes used as a synonym for mood or emotion).

Brief Summary

- Classification systems for mood disorders have changed significantly over time, highlighting the core concept of ***historical relativism.***
- The separation of bipolar mood disorders from schizophrenia (by Emil Kraepelin) and the recognition of unipolar and bipolar mood disorders as distinct syndromes (by Karl Leonhard) are two significant milestones in the history of classifying mood disorders.

Melancholia An earlier historical term for depression.

Bipolar disorders Mood disorders in which an individual experiences both abnormally low and high moods.

Unipolar disorder Mood disorders in which an individual experiences only abnormally low moods.

Critical Thinking Question Scientists in every historical period view depression through currently available paradigms for understanding mental distress. Hippocrates explained depression in terms of an imbalance in the bodily humors. Burton's explanation involved a misalignment of the planets. Do we have any good reason to believe that our "modern" views of depression won't seem equally ridiculous to abnormal psychology students in the year 2200?

The DSM-IV-TR Categories

The DSM-IV-TR recognizes five main mood disorders: *major depressive disorder; dysthymic disorder* (sometimes referred to as "minor depression"); *bipolar I disorder; bipolar II disorder;* and *cyclothymic disorder.* These disorders are based on various combinations of **mood episodes,** which are the "building blocks" of mood disorders. There are three different mood episodes listed in the DSM-IV-TR: *major depressive episode, manic episode,* and *hypomanic episode* (Table 6.1).

Mood Episodes

We'll begin our description of the DSM-IV-TR mood *disorders* by presenting the mood *episodes* from which they are built. Once you are familiar with the DSM-IV-TR mood episodes we will turn our attention to how they occur, repeat, or combine to create full-blown mood disorders.

Major Depressive Episode People who are in the midst of a **major depressive episode** are overwhelmed by feelings of sadness or emptiness. A major depressive episode also typically disrupts thinking, activity, energy levels, and sleep; in short, most aspects of life (Table 6.2). Sylvia Plath, a writer who ultimately committed suicide, provided this description of a depressive episode in her autobiographical novel, *The Bell Jar.*

> I was still wearing Betsy's white blouse and dirndl skirt. They drooped a bit now, as I hadn't washed them in my three weeks at home. The sweaty cotton gave off a sour but friendly smell.
>
> I hadn't washed my hair for three weeks, either.
>
> I hadn't slept for seven nights.
>
> My mother told me that I must have slept, it was impossible not to sleep in all that time, but if I slept, it was with my eyes wide open, for I had followed the green, luminous course of the second hand and the minute hand and the hour hand of the bedside clock through their circles and semicircles, every night for seven nights, without missing a second, or a minute, or even an hour.

Mood episodes Periods of abnormal mood that are the building blocks of the DSM-IV-TR mood disorders.

Major depressive episode A two-week or longer period of depressed mood along with several other significant depressive symptoms.

Sylvia Path Plath (1932–1963) is recognized as one of the great poets of the 20th century despite her untimely death by suicide at the age of 30.

The Three Primary DSM-IV-TR Mood Episodes	Table 6.1

Adapted from APA, 2000

Major depressive episode ▪ Severe depression lasting at least 2 weeks, including several emotional, cognitive, motivational, or physical symptoms.

Manic episode ▪ Abnormally elevated, expansive, or irritable mood that lasts at least 1 week and impairs social and occupational functioning.

Hypomanic episode ▪ A less severe version of a manic episode, lasting 4 days or more, that does not impair functioning.

Table 6.2	Diagnostic Criteria for Major Depressive Episode
Adapted from DSM-IV-TR (APA, 2000)	A minimum of five of the following symptoms must be present for at least 2 weeks. Depressed mood or loss of interest or pleasure must be one of them. • Depressed mood most of the day, nearly every day. • Diminished interest or pleasure in all or almost all activities nearly every day. • Significant weight loss or weight gain. • Insomnia or hypersomnia (excessive sleeping) nearly every day. • Restlessness or lethargy nearly every day. • Frequent fatigue or loss of energy. • Feelings of worthlessness or inappropriate guilt. • Difficulty thinking, concentrating, or making decisions. • Recurrent thoughts of death or suicide, planning for suicide, or suicide attempt.

The reason I hadn't washed my clothes or my hair was because it seemed so silly.

I saw the days of the year stretching ahead like a series of bright, white boxes, and separating one box from another was sleep, like a black shade. Only for me, the long perspective of shades that set off one box from the next had suddenly snapped up, and I could see day after day after day glaring ahead of me like a white, broad, infinitely desolate avenue.

It seemed silly to wash one day when I would only have to wash again the next.

It made me tired just to think of it.

I wanted to do everything once and for all and be through with it.

(Plath, 1966, pp. 142–143)

Plath's description highlights several emotional, cognitive, motivational, and physical symptoms of severe depression. Emotionally, Plath describes feeling completely empty—experiencing neither pleasure nor pain. In contrast, other people who experience a major depressive episode feel extremely sad and may cry for days, often without being able to pinpoint the source of their pain.

Cognitive distortions are also prominent in depression. For example, Plath cannot see the point of doing anything, even things as simple as washing her hair or changing her clothes. Such dramatic loss of perspective can also include an inability to concentrate, make plans, or imagine the future. Andrew Soloman (1998), a writer who, like Plath, has struggled with many depressive episodes explains: "When you are depressed, the past and future are absorbed entirely by the present, as in the world of a three-year-old. You can neither remember feeling better nor imagine that you will feel better. Being upset, even profoundly upset, is a temporal experience, whereas depression is atemporal. Depression means that you have no point of view." People who experience extreme or frequent depressive episodes may come to the conclusion that they are worthless, a burden on their loved ones, and that their depression will never end (Plath's "broad, infinitely desolate avenue").

Depression also interferes with motivation. People who are depressed often have difficulty getting out of bed in the morning, going to work, spending time with friends, or attending to the duties of daily life. Plath describes feeling tired just *thinking* about washing her hair. Unfortunately, such loss of motivation often exacerbates the cognitive distortions common in depression. When unable to motivate themselves to do even simple things, people who are depressed are prone to feeling guilty and worthless and may quickly lose sight of the fact that their diminished motivation is a symptom of depression, not a reflection of personal inadequacy.

Depressive episodes often affect aspects of physical functioning such as sleeping, eating, and energy level. Some people who are depressed develop insomnia (like Plath) while others sleep all the time (hypersomnia). Weight loss from lack of appetite is common, but so is constant eating and accompanying weight gain. People who are depressed may also feel extremely lethargic and fatigued, or be tormented by an irritating restlessness.

Major depressive symptoms often build up slowly before reaching the levels of intensity described by Sylvia Plath and in Box 6.1. The DSM-IV-TR criteria define a major depressive episode as lasting for at least two weeks, but in most cases an untreated major depressive episode persists for at least six months. As many as 5% to 10% of people who meet diagnostic criteria for a major depressive episode continue to do so for two years or more (APA, 2000).

One of the most important and serious symptoms of depression, and of mood disorders generally, is *suicidality.* The emotional pain and feelings of hopelessness associated with a major depressive episode can be enough to make people feel that death would be preferable to their suffering (see Box 6.1). Though not all individuals who attempt suicide are depressed, mood disorders, including bipolar disorders, are an enormous risk factor for suicide. As you can see in Figure 6.1, the risk of suicide is greatly increased in individuals with mood disorders, and it is also high in people suf-

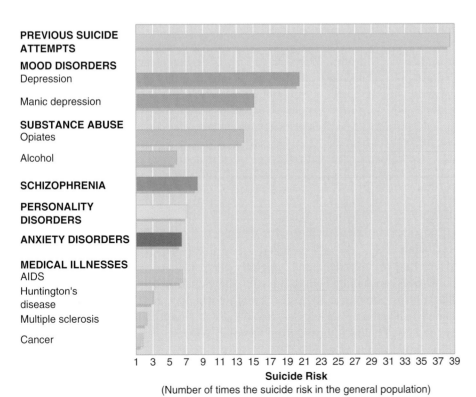

PREVIOUS SUICIDE ATTEMPTS

MOOD DISORDERS
Depression

Manic depression

SUBSTANCE ABUSE
Opiates

Alcohol

SCHIZOPHRENIA

PERSONALITY DISORDERS

ANXIETY DISORDERS

MEDICAL ILLNESSES
AIDS
Huntington's disease
Multiple sclerosis
Cancer

1 3 5 7 9 11 13 15 17 19 21 23 25 27 29 31 33 35 37 39
Suicide Risk
(Number of times the suicide risk in the general population)

Figure 6.1 Suicide risk in selected psychiatric and medical conditions This graph shows the increased risk for suicide associated with various psychiatric and medical conditions. As you can see, the greatest risk for suicide is a history of previous suicide attempts—such individuals are almost 39 times more likely than the general population to commit suicide. Among the psychiatric and medical disorders, mood disorders are by far the biggest risk factors for suicide.

(Adapted from Jamison, 1999b, p. 101)

BOX 6.1 **Suicide: The Loss of Hope**

Kay Redfield Jamison, a psychologist and leading expert in the area of mood disorders, suffers from bipolar disorder and has written extensively about the personal and scientific aspects of depression, mania, and suicide. In *Night Falls Fast: Understanding Suicide.* Dr. Jamison describes the final days of a suidical woman:

CASE

On October 29, 1995, twenty-year-old Dawn Renee Befano, a talented Maryland freelance journalist killed herself. She left behind twenty-two journals which are now in unpublished manuscript form. Excerpts from the journal written in the weeks leading up to her death show how unbearable her world had become, how her sense of her options had constricted them to nonexistence, and how an agonizing, suffusing hopelessness pervaded all reaches of her mind:

October 9th

I will not last another month feeling as I do now. I do not question that my eyes are brown, and I do not question my fate: I will die a suicide within the next month if relief does not come relatively quick. I am growing more and more tired, more and more desperate. I am dying. I know I am dying, and I know it will be by my own hand...

I am so bone-tired and everyone around me is tired of my illness.

October 10th

Outside the world is crisp and blue, refreshing fall weather, beautiful weather. I feel like hell, trapped in a black free-fall. The contrast between the two makes both seem more extreme.

In a strange way, however, I feel at peace, resigned to my fate. If I do not feel better by the end of November, I have decided to choose death over madness. I know, one way or another, that this will all be over with by the end of next month. This will all be over and done with...

I feel everything and all is pain. I do not want to live, but I must stick it out until my deadline.

October 23rd

I want to die. Today I feel even more vulnerable than usual. The pain is all-consuming, overwhelming. Last night I wanted to drown myself in the lake after everyone in the house had gone to sleep, but I managed to sleep through the impulse. When I awoke, the urgency had vanished. This morning, the urgency is back. I live in hell, day in and day out. I am not getting any better. "Better" is alien to me, I cannot get there. I am a hopeless case. I have lost my angel. I have lost my mind. The days are too long, too heavy; my bones are crushing under the weight of these days.

October 28th

I will not go back into the hospital. I will simply take a walk into the water.

The pain has become excruciating, constant and endless. It exists beyond time, beyond reality, beyond endurance. Tonight I would take an overdose, but I don't want to be sick, I just want to be dead.

The next morning Dawn woke early. She sat at the kitchen table, ate cold cereal, and worked on the crossword puzzle from the newspaper. After a short while, she left the kitchen and was not seen alive again.

The bed in her room was made neatly, according to her mother. There was "a stack of thirteen library books on the floor, and the contents of her backpack, including keys, cash, and her driver's license, stowed in a large envelope. Her great-grandmother's crystal rosary beads were spread out on the bed."

Her body was found months later, floating in a lake.

Adapted from Jamison, 1999b, pp. 94–97.

fering from other disorders such as schizophrenia (Chapter 12) and substance use disorders (Chapter 9).

In the effort to understand and hopefully prevent suicide, researchers use a variety of methods, including interviews with individuals who have survived suicide attempts and "psychological autopsies" on those who have not, to collect information on attempted and completed suicides. Some facts about *attempted* and *completed* suicide are described below (adapted from Kerkhof, 2000).

Facts about *attempted* suicide:

- Women are at least 1.5 times more likely to attempt suicide than men, with the highest rates of attempted suicide occurring among women between the ages of 15 and 24.

- People who are single or divorced are more likely to attempt suicide than people who are married.

- Low education, unemployment, poverty, and having a history of psychiatric treatment are all associated with increased rates of attempted suicide. Individuals with chronic illnesses, members of certain professions (including doctors, dentists, and law enforcement personnel), and gay and lesbian adolescents are also at higher risk for attempted suicide.

- People who are seriously depressed, abusing substances, suffering from a personality disorder, living in unstable conditions, have criminal records, and/or have a history of traumatic life events are at increased risk for making *repeated* suicide attempts.

- During the 1960s and 1970s there was a sharp rise in rates of attempted suicide, followed by a stabilization of these rates during the 1980s and another increase during the 1990s. Currently, there are several million suicide attempts per year in the United States, resulting in well over 30,000 deaths.

Facts about *completed* suicide:

- Worldwide, the highest rate of completed suicide is in people over 75 years of age (Harwood & Jacoby, 2000).

- In the United States, males are 4 to 5 times more likely to commit suicide than females. While women attempt suicide far more often than men, men are more likely to succeed in killing themselves because they typically use more lethal methods than women (Peters, Kochanek, & Murphy, 1998).

- In the United States, suicide rates among Caucasians are about twice as high as rates among African Americans (Peters et al., 1998). Native Americans, however, have an unusually high incidence of suicide that is well above the national average (NCIPC, 1999).

- Though the risk of suicide generally increases with age, suicide is the third leading cause of death among adolescents, following accidents and homicides (Diekstra, Kienhorst, & de Wilde, 1995). Rates of suicide among adolescents in the United States have risen dramatically in recent years.

Myths about suicide:

- *There are typically no warning signs of suicide attempts.* In fact, most individuals who attempt suicide have communicated their intentions to others. Accordingly, all suicidal remarks should be taken very seriously, even if they do not appear to indicate an imminent attempt.

- *Talking with a suicidal individual about their feelings will increase the likelihood of an attempt.* On the contrary, therapists know that talking with clients about suicidal feelings decreases clients' sense of isolation and hopelessness. Suicide can often be prevented, and suicide hotlines and prevention centers play an important role in this effort. However, working with suicidal clients requires special professional training, and friends and relatives of suicidal individuals should refer them to professionals for help.

- *"Manipulative" suicide attempts or gestures are not dangerous.* Many people have accidentally killed themselves in what were intended to be nonlethal suicide attempts.

- *Suicidal thoughts or attempts are a sign of severe mental illness.* Occasional thoughts about suicide are very common among the general population, and suicide attempts can occur for reasons unrelated to mental illness.

Virginia Woolf Woolf, the great English writer, committed suicide in 1941 at the age of 59. She probably suffered from what would today be diagnosed as schizoaffective disorder, a combination of a mood disorder and schizophrenia (Chapter 12). Woolf was portrayed by Nicole Kidman in the film *The Hours* (2002) based on the novel by Michael Cunningham.

The psychologist Kay Redfield Jamison, pictured here at the grave of Edgar Allan Poe, is an expert on mood disorders who has written about her own manic and depressive episodes.

Manic episode A one-week or longer period of manic symptoms causing impairment in functioning.

Manic Episode In many ways, mania is the opposite of depression. People experiencing a **manic episode** are sped up, bursting with energy, and tireless in their motivation (Table 6.3). They are often convinced of their own superiority, talk constantly, and switch rapidly from one topic to another. Much can be accomplished during a manic episode: artists, writers, and musicians with bipolar disorder often complete major pieces of work in marathon sessions fueled by mania. Kay Redfield Jamison described her experience of a manic episode in *An Unquiet Mind: A Memoir of Moods and Madness:*

> My memories of the garden party were that I had had a fabulous, bubbly, seductive, assured time. My psychiatrist [who happened to be at the party], however, in talking with me about it much later, recollected it very differently. I was, he said, dressed in a remarkably provocative way, totally unlike the conservative manner in which he had seen me dressed over the preceding year. I had on much more makeup than usual and seemed, to him, to be frenetic and far too talkative … I, on the other hand, had thought I was splendid…
>
> My mind was beginning to have to scramble a bit to keep up with itself, as ideas were coming so fast that they intersected one another at every conceivable angle… My enthusiasms were going into overdrive as well although there was often some underlying thread of logic in what I was doing… I found an exceedingly modern apartment in Santa Monica, although I hated modern architecture; I bought modern Finnish furniture, although I loved warm and old-fashioned things. Everything I acquired was cool, modern, angular, and, I suppose, strangely soothing and relatively uninvasive of my increasingly chaotic mind.

(Jamison, 1995, pp. 71–74)

Mania, like depression, involves emotional, cognitive, motivational, and physical symptoms. *Grandiosity,* an inflated sense of self-esteem, is a hallmark of mania and causes people to feel highly special, infallible, or in Jamison's words "fabulous." While experiencing a manic episode, one man jumped into his bright red sports car, put the radio at full-blast, rolled the windows down, and drove up and down the main street of his small town at 100 miles per hour. When he was pulled over by police, he argued that he could do as he pleased because he was "the greatest thing to happen to this town in

Table 6.3	Diagnostic Criteria for Manic Episode
Adapted from DSM-IV-TR (APA, 2000)	A distinct period of abnormally or persistently elevated, expansive, or irritable mood, lasting at least a week and including at least three of the following symptoms listed below. During a manic episode social or occupational functioning becomes impaired, and/or psychotic features are present. • Inflated self-esteem or grandiosity. • Decreased need for sleep. • Excessive talking and/or pressured speech. • Racing thoughts. • Extreme distractibility. • Increase in goal-directed activity (for example, highly productive at work or school, increased social and/or sexual activity). • Excessive pursuit of pleasurable but foolish activities (such as buying sprees, sexual promiscuity, worthless investments).

years!" During manic episodes some people sleep for only a couple of hours each night, if at all, and yet feel full of energy, hypersexual, and invincible. People who are manic often experience *racing thoughts,* and a rapid *flight of ideas* from topic to topic.

While energy is at a peak during a manic episode, judgment usually goes out the window. Manic episodes may cause people to spend recklessly, hatch crazy plans, have impulsive sexual relations, or abuse substances. Mood may progress from excited to short-tempered and irritable. At their most extreme, manic episodes can evolve into psychotic states in which people lose touch with reality and may develop *delusions* (fixed, false beliefs) or *hallucinations* (abnormal sensory experiences). Kay Redfield Jamison describes the following hallucination:

> One evening I stood in the middle of my living room and looked out at a blood-red sunset spreading out over the horizon of the Pacific. Suddenly I felt a strange sense of light at the back of my eyes and almost immediately saw a huge black centrifuge inside my head...
>
> Then, horrifyingly, the image that previously had been inside my head now was completely outside of it. I was paralyzed by fright. The spinning of the centrifuge and the clanking of the glass tube against the metal became louder and louder, and then the machine splintered into a thousand pieces. Blood was everywhere. It spattered against the windowpanes, against the walls and paintings, and soaked down into the carpets. I looked out toward the ocean and saw that the blood on the window had merged into the sunset. I couldn't tell where one ended and the other began. I screamed at the top of my lungs.

> (Jamison, 1995, pp. 79–80)

Manic episodes often come on quite quickly, building up over a few days or less. They may last for several weeks but are usually briefer than major depressive episodes. Manic episodes often end quite abruptly, and about half of the time they occur immediately after or immediately before a major depressive episode (APA, 2000).

Hypomanic Episode **Hypomania** is much like mania, only less severe (hence "hypo-," a prefix derived from the Greek word for "under"). People who are hypomanic engage in behaviors similar to those characterizing a manic state, but their elevated, expansive, or irritable mood never reaches a level that interferes with their functioning. Hypomanic episodes are often experienced as pleasurable periods in which self-confidence, sociability, and productivity are heightened. Why, then, is hypomania considered pathological? Keep in mind that hypomania is *not* a diagnostic category, just a mood episode. It is included in the DSM-IV-TR only for the purpose of diagnosing bipolar mood disorders in which hypomanic episodes alternate with different forms of depression (see Table 6.4).

Hypomania Robin Williams, shown here in a still from the movie *Patch Adams,* is well-known for his fast-moving, hyperactive, witty comedy that resembles a hypomanic state.

Hypomania A less extreme version of a manic episode that is not severe enough to significantly interfere with functioning.

Diagnostic Criteria for Hypomanic Episode	Table 6.4

Adapted from the DSM-IV-TR (APA, 2000)

A distinct period of persistently elevated, expansive, or irritable mood, lasting at least 4 days, that is clearly different from one's usual nondepressed mood.

- Presence of at least three of the symptoms of mania described in Table 6.3.
- The episode is not severe enough to cause marked impairment in social or occupational functioning.

Table 6.5	The DSM-IV-TR Mood Disorders
Adapted from APA, 2000	**Major depressive disorder** ▪ The occurrence of one or more major depressive episodes (lifetime prevalence: approximately 17% of the U.S. population). **Dysthymic disorder** ▪ Depression that is less severe but more chronic than a major depressive episode, lasting for at least 2 years in adults or 1 year in children and adolescents (lifetime prevalence: approximately 6%). **Bipolar I disorder** ▪ Combination of manic and major depressive episodes (lifetime prevalence: approximately 1%). **Bipolar II disorder** ▪ Combination of hypomanic and major depressive episodes (lifetime prevalence: approximately 0.5%). **Cyclothymic disorder** ▪ Combination of hypomanic and depressive mood swings that are less severe than in Bipolar I and II disorders but occur chronically for at least 2 years (lifetime prevalence: up to 1%).

The DSM-IV-TR Mood Disorders

Now that we have described the DSM-IV-TR mood episodes, we can turn to the DSM-IV-TR mood *disorders,* which are based on various combinations of the mood episodes.

The five DSM-IV-TR mood disorders, outlined in Table 6.5, have distinct patterns as you can see in Figure 6.2. For most people, mood centers around "normal" with minor fluctuations up and down. In contrast, the mood disorders are characterized by more extreme fluctuations in mood such as those shown below. As you examine the figure, keep in mind that no two cases of mood disorders follow the exact same course, and few follow the exact patterns shown. The figure simply shows prototypes of each mood disorder to assist in distinguishing among them.

Major Depressive Disorder People who have one or more major depressive episodes, and no history of a manic or hypomanic episode, meet the DSM-IV-TR criteria for **major depressive disorder.** (See Box 6.2 for a description of the DSM-IV-TR subtypes of major depressive disorder.) Not everyone who experiences one major depressive episode will go on to experience another, but the more major depressive episodes a person experiences, the more likely he or she is to continue to have episodes.

Major depressive disorder The occurrence of one or more major depressive episodes.

Figure 6.2 Different patterns of mood fluctuation in various mood disorders

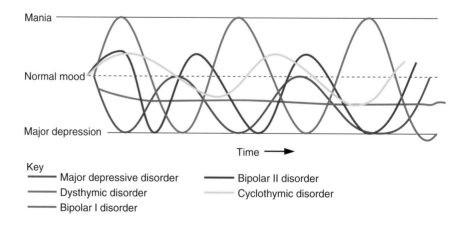

BOX 6.2   The Many Faces of Depression

Subtypes of Major Depressive Disorder

The DSM-IV-TR (APA, 2000) describes several subtypes of major depressive disorder. These so-called "specifiers" can be appended to a mood disorder diagnosis in order to further describe the symptoms of an individual who meets the basic diagnostic criteria for major depressive disorder. We include these specifiers here to highlight the many forms that depression can take.

Catatonic Features

In some cases, depression is characterized by profound changes in motoric activity. Catatonic mood states involve either physical immobility (sometimes referred to as *catatonic stupor*) or the opposite—extreme physical agitation. Catatonia that takes the form of physical immobility may be so severe that the person resists all efforts to be moved. People suffering from catatonic

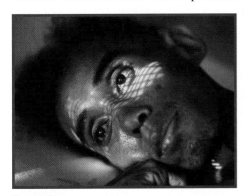
Catatonia

excitement may develop strange, stereotyped movements or mannerisms (such as hand-flapping), make repeated grimacing expressions with their faces, or mimic the words and physical actions of those around them.

Melancholic Features

Depressive episodes that are characterized by melancholic features involve a profound loss of the ability to experience pleasure. While some people who are depressed enjoy a temporary lift in their mood when something good happens, people suffering from depression with melancholic features seem to feel no pleasure at all. In addition, depression with melancholic features is characterized by a deepening of depression in the morning, early morning awakening (usually at least two hours earlier than normal), significant lethargy or physical agitation, loss of appetite and weight loss, and excessive and inappropriate guilt.

Atypical Features

Depression with atypical features is characterized by an improvement in mood in response to positive events and two or more of the following: increased appetite or weight gain, excessive sleeping, a heavy, leaden feeling in the arms or legs, and a hypersensitivity to believing that one has been or will be rejected by others (APA, 2000).

Postpartum Onset

Depression with postpartum onset is defined as major depression that occurs in women within four weeks of giving birth (remember the case of Charlotte Perkins Gilman in Chapter 1?). It is significantly more severe than the "baby blues" that many women feel from about 3 to 7 days after having a baby. Women suffering from postpartum depression may experience panic attacks, spontaneous crying, difficulty concentrating, physical agitation, and may even feel suicidal. In very severe cases of postpartum depression, women lose touch with reality and experience delusions or hallucinations that usually pertain to the baby, such as believing that the baby is possessed by the devil, or imagining that they are being given instructions to hurt or kill the baby. Though psychotic features sometimes

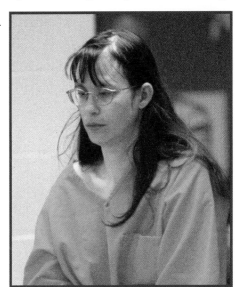
Andrea Yates In 2002, Yates was found guilty of murdering her children in the midst of a psychotic postpartum depression and sentenced to life in prison.

occur in depressions that do not involve the recent birth of a child, they are most common among postpartum women, occurring after as many as 1 in 500 deliveries.

Seasonal Pattern

In some cases, depressive symptoms regularly recur and remit at certain times of the year, with the most common pattern involving recurrences during the winter months. This pattern is called seasonal affective disorder. Winter onset of depressive symptoms may be related to the increased activity of the hormone *melatonin* which is secreted during darkness and decreases energy and activity levels. Interestingly, *phototherapy* (extra exposure to artificial bright white light) helps most clients who experience a seasonal pattern of depressive symptoms (Lam et al., 2000)

(Information from DSM-IV-TR, APA, 2000)

Case Illustration Sam, a pre-medical student, experienced his first bout of depression during his junior year of college. The school year started off well, but then Sam received two pieces of bad news in a short period of time. He received a "C" in organic chemistry, and a routine medical checkup yielded evidence that Sam might have skin cancer. While waiting for results of a tissue biopsy, Sam fell into a deep depression. He stopped attending class or going to the dining hall to eat. He spent all day in his dorm room sleeping and watching television reruns with the curtains drawn. Though Sam asked his friends to let him know what was due in class, he could not find the motivation to write papers or prepare for exams. After one week, Sam got the news that he did not have cancer but he remained depressed for another month. The following school year Sam became quite depressed again as he tried to prepare medical school applications. He spent nine days in his room before one of his friends insisted that he visit the campus infirmary to get help.

One year after being diagnosed with depression about 40% of people continue to meet the full diagnostic criteria for a major depressive episode, 20% continue to meet some of the criteria, and the remaining 40% are no longer depressed. The intensity of the first major depressive episode tends to predict how long the depression will last (APA, 2000). Like Sam, many people experience their first major depressive episode in the wake of a major stressor (such as the death of a family member or a serious medical illness). However, subsequent major depressive episodes are less likely to be precipitated by significant life stressors.

Dysthymic disorder Two years or more of consistently depressed mood and other symptoms that are not severe enough to meet criteria for a major depressive episode.

Dysthymic Disorder If major depression is like breaking an ankle, **dysthymic** (dis-THIGH-mick) **disorder** is like having a bad sprain that refuses to heal. While the symptoms are less severe than in major depression, dysthymia persists over long periods of time (Table 6.6).

Case Illustration When Mr. Wilson took a job with a company that offered excellent health insurance, his wife encouraged him to take advantage of their benefits by seeing a psychologist about his long-standing malaise. Agreeing that he had been feeling somewhat sad and listless for quite a while, Mr. Wilson took his wife's advice. In his first meeting with the therapist, Mr. Wilson explained that he had felt pessimistic for as long as he could remember—with the exception of a brief period of time during adolescence he did not recall ever feeling joyful and excited. He was almost always tired and could bring himself to do little but sit on the couch and watch television when he got home from work in the evening. Though he was very fond of his wife and two children, Mr. Wilson often felt like he was missing out on many of the simple pleasures that his life seemed like it should offer.

Table 6.6	Diagnostic Criteria for Dysthymic Disorder

Adapted from the DSM-IV-TR (APA, 2000)	• Depressed mood for most of the day, most days for at least two years.
	• Presence, while depressed, of at least two of the following:
	  • Poor appetite or over-eating
	  • Insomnia or hypersomnia
	  • Low energy or fatigue
	  • Low self-esteem
	  • Poor concentration or difficulty making decisions
	  • Feelings of hopelessness

Like many people who experience dysthymia, Mr. Wilson was able to function in his day-to-day life, but he generally felt sad, tired, and distracted. People who suffer from dysthymic disorder tend to feel inadequate, withdrawn, and ineffective. In some cases, dysthymia may periodically worsen and become a major depressive episode, a situation known as "double depression" in which both the diagnosis of dysthymic disorder and major depressive disorder simultaneously apply.

Bipolar I Disorder and Bipolar II Disorder In **bipolar I disorder** (formerly called *manic depression*), normal mood is interrupted by manic and major depressive episodes, or, occasionally, by what are referred to as *mixed episodes* in which manic and major depressive symptoms are both present. On average, people who develop bipolar I disorder go through about four mood cycles (mania and depression) during the first 10 years that they are affected. However, without treatment this pattern often intensifies and mood cycles occur more frequently (APA, 2000). There is considerable variation in the rate of mood cycling and the length of time between episodes. Some people, known as *rapid cyclers,* have as many as four or more mood episodes in the course of a year, while other individuals with bipolar I disorder may be free of symptoms for many years. The course of the disorder also varies within individuals; sometimes a rapid cluster of mood cycles can be followed by a long period in which no symptoms are present.

Bipolar I disorder Combination of major depressive episodes and manic episodes.

Bipolar II disorder Combination of major depressive episodes and hypomanic episodes.

Case Illustration **Rebecca's troubles with her mood became apparent during college when she would go through periods of having boundless energy and staying awake all night for several nights in a row. At first, she would spend the night in her room participating in Internet chat rooms or ordering expensive merchandise from online catalogs. Before long, she would spend several consecutive nights in bars drinking far more than normal, and going home with guys she had just met. She would tell her roommates all about her adventures, speaking so quickly and continuously that no one else could talk. Her roommates grew worried about the effect that her all-night carousing was having on her schoolwork and her reputation, but when they confronted her with their concerns she became enraged and accused them of being jealous of her "sky-rocketing popularity." Shortly after a period of staying up all night for three days in a row, Rebecca fell into a deep depression. Her roommates were shocked when they returned to the room one day to find Rebecca unconscious from having overdosed on Tylenol.**

Between manic and depressive states, most people with bipolar I disorder return to their typical level of functioning. However, as many as 20% to 30% of people with bipolar I continue to experience some level of mood disturbance when they are neither fully manic nor depressed (APA, 2000). For such individuals, what often appears to be the end of depression is really just the beginning of mania or vice versa. Robert Lowell (1917–1977), the American poet who suffered from bipolar I disorder, is famous for remarking "If we see light at the end of the tunnel, it's the light of the oncoming train" (1977). As noted, untreated bipolar I disorder usually gets worse over time. Mood starts to cycle more rapidly, both mania and depression can become more intense, and treatment using medications becomes less effective (Hopkins & Gelenberg, 1994) (see Table 6.7).

Bipolar II disorder is similar to bipolar I disorder except that hypomanic episodes occur instead of manic episodes. The distinction between these two disorders was clarified in the 1980s, and was included for the first time in the DSM-IV, published in 1994. Approximately 85% of people with bipolar II return to normal mood states between episodes of depression or hypomania (versus 70%–80% with bipolar I). As time goes on, between 5% and 15% of people with bipolar II develop full manic episodes, and thus their diagnosis is changed to bipolar I (APA, 2000).

Robert Lowell Lowell, a Pulitzer Prize-winning poet, suffered from bipolar I disorder, formerly called manic-depression.

Table 6.7	How Mood Episodes Form Mood Disorders

	MOOD EPISODE			
MOOD DISORDER	**MAJOR DEPRESSIVE EPISODE**	**MANIC EPISODE**	**HYPOMANIC EPISODE**	**DYSTHYMIA**[1]
Major depressive disorder	1 or more			
Dysthymic disorder				for at least 2 years
Bipolar I disorder	1 or more	1 or more		
Bipolar II disorder	1 or more		1 or more	
Cyclothymia			recurrent	recurrent

[1] Dysthymia is not considered a mood *episode* in the DSM-IV-TR.

Cyclothymic disorder Two years or more of consistent mood swings between hypomanic highs and dysthymic lows.

Cyclothymic Disorder **Cyclothymic** (SIGH-klo-thigh-mick) **disorder,** in contrast to bipolar I and II disorders, involves less severe, but more constant, mood swings that continue over a period of two years or more. In cyclothymia, mood alternates between hypomanic highs and dysthymic lows. Like bipolar I and II, cyclothymia has the potential to worsen over time; between 15% to 50% of people with cyclothymia go on to develop bipolar I or II (APA, 2000).

Case Illustration Phil had always been emotionally intense, but his parents became concerned about his moodiness when, even as an adolescent, he seemed to have more severe "ups and downs" than any of his friends. As an adult, Phil's friends noticed that he would go through phases when he was revved up, bursting with energy, and enormously fun to be with. These emotional highs were usually followed by periods when he would be sluggish, cranky, and full of self-recrimination about all of the "stupid" things he had done when full of energy. Phil was generally able to function adequately and meet his responsibilities, but his mood swings seemed to keep him from reaching his full potential in his career.

Brief Summary

- The DSM-IV-TR recognizes five main mood disorders: major depressive disorder, dysthymic disorder, bipolar disorder I, bipolar disorder II, and cyclothymic disorder.

- The DSM-IV-TR mood disorders are based on various combinations of the three types of mood episodes: major depressive episodes, manic episodes, and hypomanic episodes.

- Major depressive disorder involves one or more major depressive episodes.

- Dysthymic disorder involves less severe, but more chronic, depressive symptoms than major depressive disorder.

- Bipolar I disorder involves the recurrence of manic and major depressive episodes.

- Bipolar II disorder involves the recurrence of hypomanic and major depressive episodes.

- Cyclothymic disorder involves a chronic pattern of alternating hypomania and dysthymia.

Classification in Demographic Context

Depression is so prevalent that it is sometimes referred to as the "common cold" of mental illnesses (though clearly, this analogy should not be taken to imply that depression is not a serious condition). As many as one-quarter of all women and one-eighth of all men in the United States will meet the diagnostic criteria for major depressive disorder at some point during their lifetimes—truly alarming statistics (APA, 2000). Keep in mind that these figures do not even include people who suffer from dysthymic, bipolar I, bipolar II, and cyclothymic disorders. Given the high prevalence rates of mood disorders, it should come as no surprise that they affect all demographic groups, albeit in different ways. Let's take a look at these differences, which highlight again the core concept of the importance of *context* in understanding abnormality. Here, and throughout the rest of this chapter, the unipolar mood disorders (major depressive disorder and dysthmic disorder) will be referred to collectively as "depression" and the bipolar disorders (bipolar I, bipolar II, and cyclothymia) will be referred to collectively as "bipolar disorders," unless otherwise noted.

Age

The symptoms typically associated with depression differ dramatically based on age. Major depressive disorder, as defined by the DSM-IV-TR, emphasizes the symptoms usually seen in depressed people who are between the ages of approximately 20 and 60. Children, adolescents, and older adults can all become depressed, but they tend to exhibit depression in somewhat different ways. As a result, depression is often underdiagnosed or misdiagnosed in these groups.

While bipolar disorders typically do not develop until adolescence or later (Baron, Risch, & Mendlewicz, 1982), depression can occur at any age, even during infancy. In a classic study of infants between the ages of six and eight months who were separated from their mothers, Rene Spitz (1965) observed that the babies initially became despondent and withdrawn, and then, after two or three months, developed frozen facial expressions, lost weight, stopped sleeping, and developed myriad illnesses and infections. Amazingly, Spitz found that 30% of these institutionalized infants died by the end of their first year despite the fact that they received adequate nutritional and medical care. In less severe cases, infants who become depressed (usually due to maternal deprivation) withdraw, become listless, and may refuse to eat.

Between the ages of one and five, depression may take the form of the loss or delay of developmental achievements; children may stop feeding themselves, fail to become potty-trained, and so on. Young children who are depressed may lose their appetites, become excessively sleepy, develop nightmares, or be clingy or apathetic. Unlike normal preschoolers, depressed children aren't playful and often look sad. School-aged children who are depressed share many symptoms in common with depressed adults (such as sadness, self-criticism, and loss of motivation), but they may also complain of stomachaches and headaches, be more negative and aggressive with their peers, and be disruptive at school (Wenar & Kerig, 2000).

Depressed adolescents often have trouble at school—their grades typically drop and they may skip school or stop going altogether. Often the behavior of a depressed teenager is like that of a scared porcupine: he or she becomes very prickly and seems

Depression in adolescents Depressed teens may be obviously sad, or depression may be expressed in other forms such as apathy, irritability, or risk-taking behaviors.

to want to be left alone. To this end, depressed teenagers are often irritable, argumentative, and sometimes aggressive. They may withdraw from friends, pay little attention to their looks, and be overly sensitive. Unfortunately, adolescent depression often involves dangerous behaviors such as drug and alcohol abuse, sexual promiscuity, or extreme risk-taking (Wenar & Kerig, 2000).

Like depression among children and adolescents, depression in older adults can have a unique profile. In addition to the typical symptoms of depression, older individuals may be crabby, muddled and distracted, or have many physical complaints. Severe depression among older adults may include delusional concerns about becoming impoverished or severely ill and can involve confusion and stupor that may be mistaken for an organic delirium or dementia (Chapter 13).

Research indicates that depression is the most common psychiatric disorder among older adults (Reiger et al., 1988) although, on the whole, older people are generally less depressed than younger people (Chiu et al., 1999). The finding that depression occurs less often among the older individuals than the young seems counterintuitive given the various losses and indignities associated with aging, but some possible explanations have been proposed. This finding may reflect the fact that people who suffer from depression have a relatively high mortality rate and thus may not live to old age. Another possibility is that the particular group (or *cohort*) of older people in these studies endured significant hardships during their lifetimes (for example, the Great Depression and World War II) which may have "inoculated" them against depression in later life.

Gender

One of the most consistent and striking findings in the field of abnormal psychology is that females, beginning by about age 12, are twice as likely to be diagnosed with depression as males (McGrath et al., 1991; Nolen-Hoeksema & Girgus, 1995). Some arguments have been offered to suggest that these findings are illusory (for example, women might be more likely to admit to symptoms or seek help than men, or men might manifest depression differently than women), but none have held up under the microscope of empirical investigation (Nolen-Hoeksema, 1990). Rather, research suggests that the difference is real, and that sociocultural and psychological factors are largely responsible for it.

The sociocultural factors that contribute to the high rates of depression among females center on what is known as *role stress*. Women who pursue traditional female roles, such as full-time mother and homemaker, are at increased risk for depression because these roles are demanding, but traditionally undervalued, in American culture (Repetti & Crosby, 1984; Stoppard, 2000). Even women who have careers are usually responsible for the majority of housekeeping and child-care responsibilities, meaning that they are expected to fill several roles simultaneously. Research shows that this leads to increased rates of depression, especially when work and home demands come into conflict with each other (Napholz, 1995). However, working women tend to be less depressed when their husbands help with the housework and, interestingly, husbands who help around the home do not report more depression than other men (Ross, Mirowsky, & Huber, 1983). Discrimination against women may also contribute to high rates of depression among women. Women who work tend to be paid less and given harsher evaluations than men in the same positions who do work of equal quality (Nolen-Hoeksema, 1990).

A variety of psychological factors may also contribute to the high rates of depression among girls and women. From infancy on, boys still tend to be socialized to take risks and explore the outside world while girls are encouraged to stay closer to home and to their mothers. These early lessons in social behavior are thought to contribute

Depression and gender The prevalence of depressive disorders appears to be much higher for women than for men. One theory about this finding is that gender role stresses experienced by women contribute to depression.

to a pattern in which women tend to *internalize* psychological distress, especially in the form of rumination and self-criticism (Nolen-Hoeksema, 2003; Wolfe & Russianoff, 1997), while men are more likely to *externalize* psychological distress through behaviors such as substance abuse and aggression. (Indeed, while women are disproportionately represented among the ranks of the depressed, prison populations are overwhelmingly male.) Women are also far more likely to be subject to certain types of victimization than men. Sexual harassment, rape, spousal abuse, and childhood sexual abuse occur disproportionately among females, and all of these forms of victimization have been associated with heightened vulnerability to depression (Brems, 1995).

Unlike depression, bipolar I disorder seems to occur equally among men and women. However, bipolar II disorder may be more common among women, and women are at increased risk for developing all varieties of mood episodes (depressive episodes, mania, or hypomania) immediately after giving birth (APA, 2000).

Culture

Studies of the different racial groups in the United States have found that, over their lifetimes, African Americans are significantly less likely than whites to become depressed, while the rate of depression for Latinos falls about midway between these two groups (Weissman et al., 1991). International studies provide conflicting evidence about whether people of different nationalities are more or less likely to be depressed, but significant disparities may exist. For example, some studies have found lifetime prevalence rates for depression as low as 3.3% for people living in Seoul, South Korea; these are far lower than rates in the U.S. (Kessler et al., 1994; Lee et al., 1990). Though rates of bipolar illness appear to be quite consistent across cultures, there is some evidence that members of American minority populations with bipolar disorders are at heightened risk for being misdiagnosed with schizophrenia by clinicians (APA, 2000).

It is well established that the experience and expression of depression are ***culturally relative.*** Americans, for example, tend to communicate feelings of depression in terms of emotional symptoms—feeling sad, "down in the dumps," or irritable—while members of many Asian cultures may experience primarily physical symptoms, such as being weak or tired, when depressed. (These differences may partially account for the above-mentioned disparity in reported rates of depression between Koreans and Americans.) Latino and Mediterranean individuals often describe depression in terms of "nerves" or frequent headaches, while some Middle Eastern and Native American populations speak of being heartbroken or having a problem in the heart (APA, 2000).

Class

Rates of depression positively correlate with poverty, low levels of education, and unemployment or inadequate employment. Studies of people living in poor neighborhoods find that depression is associated with having limited economic resources and is further exacerbated by the stress of living in neighborhoods where social order has deteriorated (Ross, 2000). A major British study of depression found that being poor was a highly significant factor in determining who was depressed, and that poverty was also highly predictive of depression lasting six months or longer (Ostler et al., 2001). Researchers interested in the effects of unemployment on mood compared depression in a group of factory workers who were laid off to workers at a similar factory who kept their jobs. The unemployed factory workers were not only more depressed than the employed comparison group, but their depressions became increasingly severe the longer their unemployment lasted (Viinamaeki, Koskela, & Niskanen, 1996). While social class does not appear to be correlated

Depression and economic stress Research has shown that rates of depression are higher among those living in poverty and the unemployed, like these people waiting at an unemployment office in Boston.

with bipolar disorders, repeated manic and depressive episodes have consistently been found to interfere with work productivity and thereby to decrease the socioeconomic status of affected individuals.

Brief Summary

- Infants, children, adolescents, adults, and the elderly can all suffer from depression, but tend to experience and express their symptoms in different ways.

- After age 12, females are twice as likely to be depressed as males, partly due to sociocultural factors such as role stress, patterns of feminine socialization, and the fact that females are disproportionately subject to certain kinds of victimization.

- The prevalence of depression varies across cultures. In addition, the subjective experience of depression varies across cultures, highlighting the core concept of *cultural relativism.*

- Poverty, lack of education, and unemployment or inadequate employment are all positively correlated with depression. These sociocultural variables are related to single episodes of depression and to chronic and worsening mood disturbances.

EXPLAINING AND TREATING MOOD DISORDERS

All of the major theoretical perspectives in abnormal psychology have contributed to our understanding of mood disorders and their treatment. We'll review the explanatory concepts and treatment interventions associated with each perspective and then highlight areas in which they overlap or complement each other, in keeping with the principle of *multiple causality.* As before, the term "depression" will be used to refer to both major depressive disorder and dysthymic disorder, and the term "bipolar" will be used to refer to bipolar I, bipolar II, and cyclothymic disorders. We'll begin our exploration of the explanations and treatments of mood disorders by considering their biological components, since recent major breakthroughs in the understanding of the biology of mood disorders has brought the biological perspective on mood disorders into prominence.

Biological Components

Biological contributions to depression include genetic, neurochemical, and hormonal factors. Evidence from all three of the major genetic research strategies—family, adoption, and twin studies—demonstrates that a vulnerability to some forms of depression can be inherited. For example, family studies have found that both the first- and second-degree relatives of people who are depressed are significantly more likely to suffer from major depressive disorder than the relatives of nondepressed controls (Harrington et al., 1997). Adoption studies have found that the biological relatives of depressed adoptees may be 15 times as likely to commit suicide as the relatives of adoptees who are not depressed (Wender et al., 1986). Twin studies also support the hypothesis that depressive disorders have a genetic component; some research indicates that this is particularly true of severe, recurrent depressions (McGuffin et al., 1996). For example, in one study the concordance rate for identical (or *monozygotic*) twins with three or more episodes of major depression was 59%, while the concordance rate for identical twins with less than three major depressive episodes was 33% (Bertelsen, Harvald, & Hauge, 1977).

One specific genetic vulnerability to depression may involve the short form of the 5-HTT gene, sometimes referred to as the "mood gene." In one recent study of individuals with histories of exposure to severe stress, those with one or two short forms of this gene were much more likely to become depressed than those with two long forms of the gene (Caspi et al., 2003). These findings provide an excellent illustration of the diathesis-stress model and the principle of *multiple causality,* since they indicate that a combination of life stress and genetic vulnerability are necessary to produce depression.

Genetic factors may predispose a person to depression by affecting brain structures and functions involved in mood regulation. Recent research on brain functions in depression has focused on a certain class of neurotransmitters known as **monoamines:** especially *norepinephrine, dopamine,* and *serotonin.* Like all neurotransmitters, the monoamines act as chemical messengers that pass information among neurons in the brain. Electrophysiological impulses stimulate neurons to release neurotransmitters into the *synaptic cleft* (the space between neurons) where they can be absorbed by the membranes of adjacent neurons and stimulate further electrophysiological responses. Leftover neurotransmitters that are not absorbed by an adjacent neuron are either reabsorbed into the neuron that released them, or broken down by enzymes in the synaptic cleft (see Chapter 3 and Figure 3.7, p. 66).

The **monoamine hypothesis** argues that depression is related to insufficient transmission of monoamines between neurons. Evidence supporting this hypothesis comes from the fact that medications that increase the availability of monoamines can relieve depression, while medications that interfere with the functioning of monoamines or monoamine receptors can cause depression (Thase & Howland, 1995). While the monoamine hypothesis seems simple enough, the complete story is quite a bit more complicated. For example, medications that relieve depression usually must be taken for several weeks before they have a beneficial effect, despite the fact that they almost immediately increase the availability of monoamines at the synaptic cleft. As a result, researchers now speculate that it is not just the amount of neurotransmitter in the synaptic cleft that is important, but also the number of receptor sites available in the adjacent neurons. Higher concentrations of monoamines in the synaptic cleft (such as when stimulated by medication) may lead to the growth of more receptor sites in adjacent neurons through which monoamines can be absorbed—a process that may take several weeks. While the complex interactions between such brain functions (neurotransmission) and brain structure (neuron receptors) are not yet well understood, researchers increasingly appreciate that brain structures are highly *plastic,* meaning that they can change over time.

The *endocrine,* or hormonal, system in the body may also play an important role in some forms of depression. For a long time, clinicians have known that endocrine disorders such as hypothyroidism, hyperthyroidism, and Cushing's disease can cause depression. Research into the relationship between hormones and depression points to the role of the *HPA (hypothalamic-pituitary-adrenocortical) axis* (see Figure 5.6, p. 148), which responds to stress by releasing **cortisol** into the bloodstream. A significant percentage of people who are severely depressed have high blood levels of cortisol, indicating a possible failure of the HPA axis to properly suppress or inhibit cortisol release (Stokes & Sikes, 1988). Some researchers suggest that sustained stress during critical periods of development may damage the cells regulating feedback within the HPA axis. In other words, ongoing childhood stressors such as emotional neglect or an unstable home environment may lead to permanent dysregulation of the HPA axis and, possibly, predisposition to subsequent depression (Insel, 1991). This hypothesis provides a good example of the core concept of the *connection between mind and body* insofar as the emotional impact of early life events has the potential to

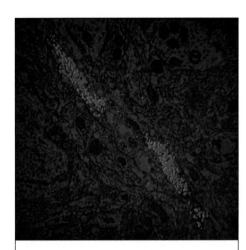

Depression and neurotransmitters This colorized electron micrograph shows a neurotransmitter being released from a neuron.

Monoamines A class of neurotransmitters involved in mood disorders, including norepinephrine, dopamine, and serotonin.

Monoamine hypothesis The hypothesis that depression is partially caused by insufficient neurotransmission of monoamines.

Cortisol A hormone released by the pituitary gland in response to stress.

shape the structures and functions of the developing brain. This is also one of the ways in which biological and psychological perspectives on mood disorders may be integrated in accordance with the principle of ***multiple causality***.

Bipolar disorders, especially bipolar I and II, have a significant genetic component: twin studies have found concordance rates as high as 87% for identical (or *monozygotic*) twins as compared to 39% for nonidentical (or *dizygotic*) twins (Bertelsen et al., 1977). Adoption and family studies of bipolar disorder have further confirmed the heritability of a predisposition to bipolar disorders (Harrington et al., 1997; Tsuang & Faraone, 1990). Researchers continue to search for the precise genes involved, and for indications of precisely how particular genes relate to the emotional and behavioral manifestations of the disorders (see Box 6.3).

Research on the biological mechanisms of bipolar disorders has also focused on neurotransmission. Studies have shown that the monoamines (norepinephrine, dopamine, and serotonin) seem to increase during mania and decrease during depression, but no conclusive evidence exists as to whether these changes in neurotransmitter levels are a *cause,* or an *effect,* of the mood swings (Anand & Charney, 2000). In addition, the *switch mechanism*—the process that triggers the switch from one mood state to another—is not well understood. In all likelihood, several neurotransmitter systems interact to bring about these abnormal alterations in mood.

Abnormal brain *structures* have also been investigated in relation to bipolar disorders. Brain imaging studies, which use computed tomography (CT) and magnetic resonance imaging (MRI) to study the living brain, have found some brain abnormalities that appear to be unique to bipolar disorders. While structural brain abnormalities in unipolar depression appear to be concentrated in the prefrontal cortex, basal ganglia, cerebellum, and hippocampus, bipolar disorders seem to be linked to anomalies in the amygdala, prefrontal cortex, and cerebellum (see Figure 3.6, p. 64, and Figure 5.4, p. 142) (Soares & Innis, 2000). In addition, some studies have found that people suffering from bipolar disorders have defects in the sodium ion channels of neural membranes which may cause neurons to be over- or under-sensitive to firing, resulting in mood swings (El Mallakh & Wyatt, 1995).

Biological Interventions

Biological interventions for unipolar depression have developed steadily over the last 50 years. At present, there are three major classes of medications used to treat depression: **tricyclics, monoamine oxidase inhibitors** (MAOIs), and **selective serotonin reuptake inhibitors** (SSRIs). Though each class of drugs is chemically unique, they all work by increasing levels of certain neurotransmitters (especially serotonin and norepinephrine) within the synaptic cleft. The tricyclics and MAOIs are often described as "first generation" antidepressants because they have been in use since the 1950s, while the SSRIs and their close relatives are considered "second generation" antidepressants because they were introduced in the 1980s. These second generation antidepressants such as fluoxetine—commonly known by its brand name, Prozac—have become the most common biological intervention for depression.

The tricyclic antidepressants take their name from their three-ring chemical structure. They exert their antidepressant effect by blocking the *reuptake* of monoamines back into the neuron from which they were released, thus increasing the likelihood that monoamines will be absorbed by adjacent neurons (see Figure 3.7, p. 66). While the tricyclic antidepressants have been found to be effective in relieving depression in the majority of clients who take them, they also have some unpleasant, common side effects including dry mouth, constipation, urinary retention, blurred vision, sedation, and weight gain. In addition, tricyclics must be taken for at least four to eight weeks in order to determine whether they are having a therapeutic effect (Carlson, 1986).

Tricyclics One of the "first generation" classes of antidepressant drugs; they block the reuptake of norepinephrine.

MAO (monoamine oxidase inhibitors) Antidepressant medications that inhibit an enzyme (monoamine oxidase), which degrades serotonin and norepinephrine, thus enhancing neurotransmission.

SSRIs (selective serotonin reuptake inhibitors) A "second generation" class of antidepressants; they inhibit the reuptake of serotonin.

Are Mood Disorders and Creativity Linked?

The apparent commonality of depression, mania, and sometimes suicide, among creatively talented people has lead to questions about whether there is such a thing as an "artistic temperament." Writers and poets such as Ernest Hemingway, Emily Dickinson, Sylvia Plath, Anne Sexton, and Lord Tennyson, and painters such as Vincent Van Gogh (Figure 6.3), Mark Rothko, and Jackson Pollock are nearly as well-known for their extreme moods as they are for their outstanding creative achievements. The question of whether there is, in fact, an association between mood disturbance and creativity has recently been held up to the light of scientific research and has yielded some interesting results.

In a large study of 1,005 individuals whose biographies were reviewed in the *New York Times Book Review,* Arnold Ludwig of the University of Kentucky (1992) compared the psychological histories of artists and writers with those of individuals in other professions such as business, science, and public service. He found significantly higher rates of mania, suicide, and involuntary hospitalizations among the artists and writers as compared to members of other professions. In a particularly clever study of the possibility that heightened creativity and mood disturbance might share a genetic basis, Ruth Richards and her colleagues at McLean Hospital (1988) compared levels of creativity among: (1) people suffering from bipolar disorders, (2) the first-degree relatives of the bipolar participants, and (3) a control group of participants who were neither bipolar nor closely related to someone who was. The members of the first two groups (those with bipolar disorder and their relatives) were significantly more creative than the control group. Further, the first-degree relatives of people suffering from bipolar disorders were *more* creative than their bipolar relatives! This second finding—that the relatives of the bipolar participants were the most creative of all—has an important implication. In addition to supporting the idea that some of the same genes which predispose a person to bipolar illness might also contribute to creativity, it indicates that these "creativity genes" may be more successfully expressed in individuals who do *not* also have mood disorders. Similarly, most artists and writers who experience extreme moods increase their productivity and vastly improve the quality of their lives when properly treated for their mood disorders (Hershman & Lieb, 1998).

Is there anything about mood disorders themselves, though, that might promote creativity? Kay Redfield Jamison (1999a), a well-known expert on the subject, notes that mania can be characterized by highly creative thinking as well as by increased productivity. Further, she notes that "when artists and writers who have mood disorders are asked what they think is the most important aspect of what happens to them, they will often say that it's the range and the intensity of their emotional experiences" (1999a, p. 73). However, many researchers point out that the extreme suffering and personal and professional disruptions caused by depression and mania hardly constitute a "blessing." As we noted, when mood disorders are treated, creativity usually remains and the artist is often better able to make use of his or her talent.

"Sorrow," drawing by Vincent Van Gogh
Van Gogh's drawing captures the anguish of depression.

Mood disorders and creativity
Emily Dickinson, Ernest Hemingway, and Jackson Pollack are three examples of the apparent link between mood disorders and creative talent.

The monoamine oxidase inhibitors (MAOIs) do what their name implies: they inhibit the enzymes that oxidize (or break down) monoamines which have been released into the synaptic cleft. This raises the monoamine level in the synaptic cleft and increases the chances that monoamines will be passed between neurons. The MAOIs have been found to be effective in alleviating depressive disorders, particularly those with atypical features (see Box 6.2), but they do have some significant drawbacks. First, like the tricyclics, the MAOIs must be taken for several weeks in order to determine whether they are effective for an individual client. Second, MAOIs generally have more side effects than tricyclics, including disrupting the body's ability to metabolize *tyramine,* an amino acid found in many common foods such as aged cheese, red wine, beer, and chocolate. People who ingest tyramine while taking MAOIs do so at the risk of having a severe, possibly life-threatening, hypertensive crisis (Carlson, 1986). In addition, both tricyclics and MAOIs can be fatal in overdose—a difficult problem when treating people who may be suicidal.

During the 1960s and 1970s, the tricyclics and MAOIs were the first-line biological interventions for depression. But, given the unpleasant physical side effects and potential dangers of these medications, many physicians only prescribed antidepressants to clients who were very seriously depressed. As we noted, a potentially lethal antidepressant presents a significant clinical dilemma: because the tricyclics and MAOIs take several weeks to work, writing a prescription for these medications can seem like handing a loaded gun to someone who might be feeling suicidal. This clinical dilemma accounts, in large part, for the enormous popularity of the newer "second-generation" SSRI antidepressants, which have roughly the same clinical effectiveness as the older medications but have fewer side effects and are less lethal in overdose, making them much safer to prescribe.

The SSRIs work by inhibiting the reuptake of serotonin after it has been released into the synaptic cleft, thereby leaving more serotonin available for absorption by nearby neurons. Compared to the tricyclics and MAOIs, the SSRIs tend to show effects more quickly (within 2–3 weeks), and they usually have less severe side effects, although they can cause restlessness, upset stomach, and sexual dysfunctions. Despite the advantages of the SSRIs and other related second-generation antidepressants, all three classes of antidepressants continue to be prescribed since different people respond differently to the same medications.

During the 1980s and 1990s, the SSRIs gained rapid popularity within the United States, due, in part, to aggressive marketing by their manufacturers in the $1 billion antidepressant market and glowing testimonials from some clients. Recent studies (Einarson et al., 1999) suggest that these drugs may have been over-hyped, and are at best only marginally more effective than tricyclics, MAOIs, or even placebos. Indeed, some researchers claim that the effectiveness of all antidepressants is mainly due to placebo effects (Kirsch & Saperstein, 1998), and studies are beginning to shed light on some of the neurological mechanisms involved in placebo responses (Leuchter et al., 2002; Mayberg, Silva, Brannan, Tekell et al., 2000). Given these factors, some experts question the wisdom of liberally prescribing SSRIs, especially since SSRIs are increasingly being prescribed by general practitioners and family physicians without a comprehensive psychological or psychiatric evaluation.

Electroconvulsive therapy (ECT) is another form of biological intervention for depression. First discovered in the 1930s, ECT involves sending an electrical current through the skull to trigger an electrical storm (or *seizure*) in the brain that lasts for a few minutes. For reasons that are not fully understood, several sessions of ECT spaced over a number of weeks are a highly effective treatment for severe depression (Rey & Walter, 1997).

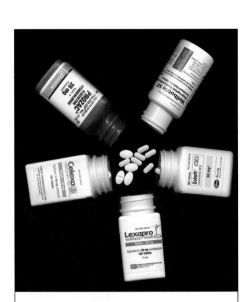

Antidepressant medication "Second-generation" antidepressants, like those shown here, have been hailed as a breakthrough in treating mood disorders. Studies show that these newer antidepressants are not significantly more effective than older medications but they usually have fewer side effects.

ECT (electroconvulsive therapy) A biological intervention for severe depression involving sending electric current through the skull to produce seizures.

As you might expect from this description of ECT, it has been a controversial treatment, and many people associate "shock therapy" with images such as the horrible punishment of the character Randall Patrick McMurphy in the film *One Flew Over the Cuckoo's Nest* (see Box 2.2, p. 17). Actually, the practice of ECT has changed considerably from the 1950s and 1960s when it was widely and somewhat dangerously prescribed. Today, patients are placed under general anesthesia and given muscle relaxants so that the motoric effects of the seizure are barely visible. In addition, the intensity of the electrical shock (approximately 100 volts) is carefully controlled and in some cases can be applied to just one hemisphere of the brain with equally good results. Nonetheless, ECT still has potentially troublesome side effects, the most common being amnesia for events and learning that occurred shortly before *(retrograde amnesia)* or after *(anterograde amnesia)* the ECT treatments. Over time, memory usually returns to normal, although some clients experience lasting memory problems (Calev et al., 1991).

Despite its relative safety and efficacy, ECT is not widely prescribed today, largely because many people are frightened by the idea of undergoing shock treatment and because of the availability of medications that are effective for most clients. ECT is now reserved mainly for people who are severely depressed (and often acutely suicidal) and either cannot take or have not been helped by antidepressant medications.

For bipolar I disorder, **lithium,** a naturally occurring mineral salt, has long been the "gold standard" of treatment. The discovery of lithium's potency as a *mood stabilizer* was made by an Australian physician in 1949, but it was not used widely outside of Australia until the 1960s. Given the absence of other effective treatments for bipolar disorders, lithium was hailed as a miracle drug once it became widely known. Though its mechanism of action is not well understood, lithium stabilizes mood in the majority individuals with bipolar illness who take it in adequate doses (Maj, 1999). For the approximately 30% to 40% of clients who do not respond well to lithium, some anticonvulsant (such as carbamazepine, valproate, lamotrigine, or gabapentin), calcium channel blocking (such as verapamil), or antipsychotic medications can have mood stabilizing effects.

Though lithium is an effective treatment for many people with bipolar mood disorders, it has several significant limitations and drawbacks. First, lithium must often be taken in combination with an antidepressant because lithium controls manic symptoms more effectively than depressive symptoms. Second, the difference between effective and toxic blood levels of lithium is rather small (see Table 6.8). People who take too little lithium may not improve, but too much lithium can cause severe nausea, kidney dysfunction, and other serious side effects. Even at a proper therapeutic dose, lithium can have several unpleasant side effects such as loss of appetite, mild diarrhea, increased urination, excessive thirst, and hand tremors.

Finally, lithium must be taken continually in order to be effective. Nearly half of all people who stop taking lithium when their mood stabilizes experience a manic or depressive episode within five months of discontinuing lithium use (Maj, 1999).

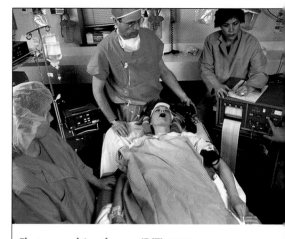

Electroconvulsive therapy (ECT) ECT is an effective, but controversial, treatment for severe depression. Recent improvements in ECT techniques have improved ECT's safety.

Lithium A naturally occurring salt that is the main mood stabilizing medication for bipolar disorders.

Lithium Toxicity	Table 6.8

- Effective dose (blood level of 0.5–0.7 mEq/L)
- Below 0.5—no therapeutic effect
- About 1.0—mild toxic effect
- Above 2.0—severe and potentially fatal toxic effects

Unfortunately, manic and depressive episodes seem to get worse the more often they occur. Thus, the best outcomes in bipolar I disorder involve an early diagnosis followed by consistent lithium use. In reality, many people with bipolar illnesses are not diagnosed until they have suffered for several years, and once diagnosed they are often ambivalent about taking an unpleasant medication, especially during periods when they are feeling well. Psychotherapy can be an especially important adjunct to lithium treatment in bipolar disorders partly because it can help support clients' compliance with their medication regimen.

Brief Summary

- Genetic factors play a predisposing role in depression, especially more severe depressions. Bipolar mood disorders also have a genetic component.

- Research on abnormal brain functions associated with depression has focused on the deficient availability of a class of neurotransmitters known as monoamines (norepinephrine, dopamine, and serotonin). In addition, hormonal changes can cause depressive symptoms.

- At present, there are three major classes of medications used to treat depression: tricyclics, monoamine oxidase inhibitors (MAOIs), and "second-generation" antidepressants such as the selective serotonin reuptake inhibitors (SSRIs). Each class of drugs is chemically different, but they all work by increasing available monoamine levels within the synaptic cleft.

- Electroconvulsive therapy (ECT) involves the use of an electrical current to induce seizures. Despite its relative efficacy and safety as practiced today, ECT remains controversial and is generally used only when other treatments have not been successful.

- Lithium is the most effective and widely prescribed treatment for bipolar mood disorders. Lithium stabilizes moods in the majority of clients who receive an adequate dose, but it does have potentially troubling side effects and typically must be taken consistently for long periods of time. Other mood stabilizing and/or antidepressant medications can also play a role in the treatment of bipolar disorders.

Cognitive Components

The cognitive perspective has become one of the most influential approaches to explaining and treating mood disorders, particularly depression. One of the founders of this perspective, Aaron Beck, noticed that many of his depressed patients shared certain cognitive patterns that seemed to contribute to their depression. Specifically, he noted that they seemed to hold irrationally negative views of *themselves,* their *worlds,* and their *futures* (which he called the **negative cognitive triad**) (Beck, 1967; 1987; 1997). Over the last 40 years, Beck and other cognitive theorists have developed numerous models of the cognitive patterns that contribute to the negative triad and, thus, to depression. Among the most important of these patterns are *negative automatic thoughts, cognitive distortions,* and *pessimistic explanations* of negative events.

Depression-prone individuals tend to have *negative self-schemas*—they view themselves as incompetent, unlucky, unlikable, and so on. These attitudes are expressed in an ongoing stream of **negative automatic thoughts.** For example, people may have negative automatic thoughts like "nothing ever works out for me" and "people will always be mean" that form the backdrop of their everyday lives. Negative automatic thoughts are often characterized by certain **cognitive distortions.** According to Beck (1967), several common distortions or logical errors contribute to depression; they are listed and described in Table 6.9.

Negative cognitive triad Irrationally negative thinking about the self, the world, and the future.

Negative automatic thoughts Negative thoughts generated by negative cognitive schemas.

Cognitive distortions Irrational beliefs and thinking processes.

Common Cognitive Distortions

Table 6.9

Based on Beck, 1967

COGNITIVE DISTORTIONS	DESCRIPTION	SAMPLE SITUATION	EXAMPLE
Arbitrary Inference	Drawing a conclusion based on absent or ambiguous evidence.	Greeting from neighbor, who has just received some bad news of her own, is less friendly than usual.	"Oh great, now my neighbor hates me and I don't even know why!"
Selective Abstraction	Tendency to focus on negative details to the exclusion of all else.	Student receives a "B+" on a paper with many encouraging comments and a few constructive criticisms.	"I can't believe I made those mistakes in my paper."
Over-generalization	Drawing a general conclusion on the basis of a single incident.	Babysitter cancels at last minute.	"Babysitters don't like my children… we'll never be able to get another babysitter…"
All-or-None Thinking	Thinking in black and white, or absolute terms.	Breakup of a relationship.	"If I'm not married by the time I'm 30, I'll never get married!"

Another influential cognitive approach to depression is based on the work of Martin Seligman and his colleagues, who have been exploring the relationship between cognition and depression since the 1960s. In a landmark series of studies, Seligman found that prolonged periods of helplessness in the face of misfortune can cause dogs to give up on trying to change unpleasant circumstances that are actually within their control (Seligman & Maier, 1967). Seligman's experiments involved subjecting dogs to unpleasant electric shocks. Using boxes that were separated into two compartments by a low barrier, one group of dogs was shocked after hearing a short tone. However, if they jumped over the barrier into the other side of the box after the tone sounded, they could avoid the shock. The dogs in this group quickly learned to move back and forth across the barrier when prompted by the tone. In a second group, the dogs also heard a tone, but they received a shock whether or not they jumped across the barrier. Before long, the dogs in this group laid down and gave up trying to avoid the shocks. Next, the researchers changed the conditions so that all of the dogs were able to avoid the shocks if they jumped over the barrier. The dogs in the first group continued to jump back and forth, while the dogs in the second group continued to passively accept the shocks even when the researchers pulled them back and forth across the barrier to show them that they need not be shocked. This phenomenon, which Seligman called **learned helplessness,** is the basis for a number of contemporary cognitive-behavioral approaches to explaining depression.

In its current form, learned helplessness theory focuses on certain cognitive factors that seem to be the key links between negative, uncontrollable events, which

Learned helplessness Martin Seligman pioneered the study of links between learned helplessness and depression. A woman who is repeatedly subjected to negative, uncontrollable events, like being battered by her partner, may exhibit learned helplessness.

Learned helplessness Cognitive-behavioral theory in which animals give up adaptive responding after prior experience with inescapable punishments.

Pessimistic explanatory (attributional) style
Cognitive theory concerning the tendency to make internal, global, and stable explanations of negative events as a risk factor for depression.

everyone experiences from time to time, and depression. Seligman and his colleagues have proposed that a **pessimistic explanatory (or attributional) style** in response to uncontrollable negative events—such as bad weather that interferes with a vacation—is a crucial risk factor for depression (Alloy, Abramson, & Francis, 1999; Peterson & Seligman, 1984). The characteristics of a pessimistic explanatory style are the consistent use of *internal, global,* and *stable* attributions (or explanations) concerning negative events. In other words, people who think this way tend to blame *themselves* when negative events occur (internal), feel that the negative event will *generalize* to other areas (global), and believe that the negative situation will be *lasting* (stable). Consider, for example, a minor negative uncontrollable event we have all experienced at one time or another: you're running late for an appointment because of an unforeseeable traffic jam. Table 6.10 illustrates the contrast between depressive and nondepressive attributions related this event.

Numerous studies have found a positive correlation between pessimistic explanatory style and depression (for example, Peterson & Seligman, 1984). Keep in mind that correlations do not prove causation; the positive correlation could mean that pessimism causes depression, depression causes pessimism, or that both are caused by a third, unidentified factor. However, *longitudinal* studies have suggested a causal relationship in which pessimistic explanatory style can precede and contribute to depression (this is sometimes referred to as a *cognitive vulnerability* theory) (Abramson, Metalsky, & Alloy, 1989; Beck, 1987). For example, researchers (Alloy, Abramson, & Francis, 1999) at Temple University and the University of Wisconsin studied nondepressed freshmen who were considered to be at high risk (HR) or low risk (LR) for depression based on their responses to measures of explanatory style. The researchers then conducted follow-up assessments every six weeks for two and a half years, and then every four months for three more years. During the first two and a half years of the study, HR freshmen were significantly more likely to develop major depressive disorders, minor depressive disorders (such as dysthymic disorder), and suicidal thoughts or actions than the LR freshmen (see Table 6.11).

Cognitive Interventions

Three assumptions underlie cognitive interventions for depression: (1) negative thinking contributes to depression; (2) negative thinking can be monitored and changed by directive, logical methods; and (3) such changes in thinking will improve mood and behavior. In general, cognitive therapies for depression are psychoeducational in their

Table 6.10	**Explanatory Styles in a Traffic Jam**	
	NONDEPRESSIVE ATTRIBUTIONS	**DEPRESSIVE ATTRIBUTIONS**
External vs. internal	"This is out of my control so I might as well relax."	"I am so stupid for not leaving earlier."
Specific vs. global	"Oh well, it's just one appointment."	"My whole day is going to be rotten!"
Unstable vs. stable	"It can't be backed up for too much longer."	"I'm sure this traffic jam will last for hours!"

SYMPTOMS AT FOLLOW-UP	HIGH-RISK FRESHMEN	LOW-RISK FRESHMEN
Major depressive disorder	17%	1%
Minor depressive disorder	39%	6%
Suicidality	28%	12.6%

Depression in High-Risk (Pessimistic Explanatory Style) and Low-Risk Freshmen

Table 6.11

Data from Alloy, Abramson, & Francis, 1999

approach, meaning that the therapist takes an active role in setting the agenda for each session and acts as a coach who helps the client to master new skills. Sacco and Beck (1995) describe the five steps of a typical cognitive intervention for depression (adapted from Sacco & Beck, 1995):

Step 1: Identify and Monitor Dysfunctional Automatic Thoughts Clients are taught to recognize their negative automatic thoughts. In-session exploration and homework assignments are used to identify and record prominent automatic thoughts.

Step 2: Recognize the Connections Among Thoughts, Emotions, and Behaviors Clients are helped to note their emotional and behavioral responses to their negative automatic thoughts, and reassured that anyone who had such negative thoughts would likely be depressed.

Step 3: Evaluate the Reasonableness of Negative Automatic Thoughts The negative automatic thoughts are evaluated to determine their accuracy. Clients are encouraged to look for evidence for and against their beliefs, to consider alternative explanations for events, and to evaluate the degree to which they make internal, global, and stable attributions about negative events. For example, the woman who attributed a babysitter's cancellation to the "fact" that "babysitters don't like my children" (Table 6.9) would be shown that she made *internal* (the problem is her children), *global* (*all* babysitters dislike her children), and *stable* (we'll *never* get another babysitter) attributions about the event. Finally, clients are reminded that even if their pessimism is accurate, things are probably not be as bad as they fear. For example, if babysitters do not, in fact, like this woman's children, is that necessarily a catastrophe? Babysitters don't have the last word on the merits of children; children who mistreat babysitters can be taught to behave differently, and so on.

Step 4: Substitute More Reasonable Interpretations for the Distorted Attributions This step flows directly from the one before it. Clients are usually encouraged to write down rational responses and to compare them with their dysfunctional thoughts. For example, the woman who concluded that babysitters don't like her children would be asked to evaluate whether other babysitters seemed to like her children, and what else could explain why the babysitter cancelled at the last minute.

Step 5: Identify and Alter Dysfunctional Assumptions In this step, the client and therapist explore the underlying assumptions that promote negative self-schemas and automatic thoughts. Dysfunctional assumptions are usually fundamental beliefs that the client may not even be aware of holding. Beck (1976) provides several examples of common problematic assumptions:

- To be happy, I must be accepted by all people at all times.
- My value as a person depends on what other people think of me.
- In order to be happy, I have to be successful in whatever I undertake.

Once such assumptions are brought to light, they may be evaluated and challenged in the same fashion as negative automatic thoughts. Cognitive interventions, either on their own or in combination with other approaches, have been shown in numerous studies to be effective in relieving depression.

Cognitive interventions for bipolar disorders use many of the same techniques described above for unipolar disorders, but also include some special features that apply specifically to the challenges of living with depression *and* mania or hypomania. Cory Newman, clinical director of the Center for Cognitive Therapy at the University of Pennsylvania, has developed a cognitive intervention for individuals with bipolar disorders that emphasizes empowering clients so that they do not see themselves as helpless victims of a disease (Newman et al., 2001). Basic cognitive techniques are extended and applied to several specific clinical topics including: the management of manic and hypomanic episodes, suicide prevention, how bipolar disorder affects family members, and clients' frequent reluctance to take needed medications. Clients provided with cognitive interventions in addition to medication have shown greater improvement in both symptoms and overall functioning than clients who were treated with medication alone (Scott, Garland, & Moorhead, 2001).

Brief Summary

- People who are depressed tend to take a negative view of themselves, their world, and their future (the negative cognitive triad).
- The negative cognitive triad is associated with negative automatic thoughts, cognitive distortions, and internal, global, and stable attributions about negative events.
- According to the cognitive-vulnerability theory of depression, pessimistic explanatory styles predispose individuals to depression when they encounter negative life events.
- Cognitive interventions for mood disorders focus on recording and evaluating negative automatic thoughts, challenging cognitive distortions, and modifying pessimistic attributions and assumptions. Such interventions are a helpful component of treatment for both unipolar and bipolar mood disorders.

> *Critical Thinking Question* | Imagine the following negative event—you've planned an outdoor graduation party and the weather is terrible. Can you construct hypothetical pessimistic (internal, global, stable) and nonpessimistic (external, specific, unstable) explanations of this event?

Behavioral Components

B. F. Skinner, one of the founders of behaviorism, proposed many years ago that depression results from the interruption of *reinforcements* (rewards) from the environment (Skinner, 1953). This view has been elaborated and modified over the past five decades. For example, the next generation of behavioral theorists added that increased frequency of *punishments* (negative consequences) or the decreased *effectiveness* of reinforcements contribute to depression, as expressed by a decrease in adaptive behaviors (Costello, 1972; Ferster, 1966). In other words, a student who has worked hard

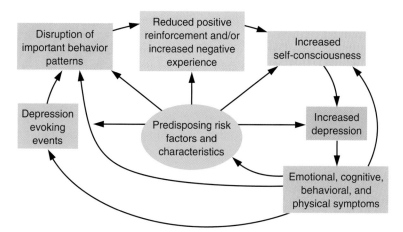

Figure 6.3 An Integrated Cognitive-Behavioral Model of Depression Lewinsohn and his colleagues have developed a model of depression that combines cognitive and behavioral causes that interact in a "vicious cycle."

(Adapted from Lewinsohn et al., 1985 and Lewinsohn, Gotlib, & Hautzinger, 1998)

with good results in the past may slack off if he starts to receive some negative feedback or becomes less encouraged by positive feedback.

Behavioral researchers have focused on understanding the conditions likely to cause reductions in reinforcement and, accordingly, depression. Lewinsohn identified three such conditions: (1) poor social skills; (2) an environment with low reinforcement potential and high punishment potential; and (3) a diminished capacity to enjoy positive events (reinforcements) or a heightened sensitivity to negative events (punishment) (Lewinsohn, Lobitz, & Wilson, 1973). Thus, a student who is awkward in so___ situations, has few supportive friends, hangs out with a critical roommate, an___ ___ praise but is hypersensitive to criticism is at high risk for depression.

Many contemporary behavioral approaches to explaining depre___ cognitive principles in a combined cognitive-behavioral perspectiv___ Lewinsohn and his colleagues view depression as the product of b___ cognitive processes (Lewinsohn, Gotlib, & Hautzinger, 1998). Be'___ tive factors contributing to depression can combine and intera___ vicious cycle, as shown in Figure 6.3.

Behavioral Interventions

Behavioral interventions for depression emphasize increasin___ ing punishments in the client's environment. To this end, reachable daily life goals with rewards for meeting them, ___ skill assistance to correct deficits in areas such as socia___ sohn et al., 1998). Such interventions can help clien___ with more active behaviors that are reinforced by th___ ple, a housebound depressed client might be encour___ such as having coffee or going to a movie with a f___ some research suggests that the effectiveness ___ largely to this *behavioral activation* aspect of ___

Lewinsohn and his colleagues (1980) d___ intervention to help clients understand ___ mood, learn techniques for relaxation, ___ aversive events, improve time manage___ ant activities. Interventions like these___ to minimize unpleasant events and ___ reduce levels of depression (Lew___ thought to be appropriate mainly ___ ple, a *meta-analysis* (combined___

studies of depressed outpatients found that behavioral therapy and cognitive therapy were both effective treatments, and both were more effective than no therapy, antidepressant medication, and a group of miscellaneous other therapies (Gloaguen et al., 1998). Numerous studies have also shown that *combined* cognitive-behavioral interventions can be very effective in alleviating depression (Evans et al., 1992; Sanderson & McGinn, 2001).

Cognitive-behavioral techniques have also been found to helpfully augment biological interventions for bipolar disorders. According to Bacso and Thase (1998, p. 531), cognitive-behavioral interventions for bipolar disorders have five major goals:

1. To educate patients and their families about the illness, its treatment, and its major complications.

2. To teach patients how to monitor the occurrence, severity, and course of manic and depressive symptoms in order to allow for early intervention should symptoms worsen.

3. To facilitate compliance with prescribed medication regimens by removing the obstacles that interfere with compliance.

4. To provide psychological strategies for coping with the cognitive and behavioral symptoms of mania and depression.

5. To teach skills for coping with common psychosocial problems that are the precipitants or results of depressive and manic episodes.

Cognitive-behavioral adjunctive interventions for clients with bipolar disorders have been shown to enhance the effectiveness of lithium treatment and to reduce the recurrence of manic and depressive symptoms in comparison to clients who are treated with lithium alone (Fava et al., 2001).

Brief Summary

- Behavioral theories of depression focus primarily on the relationship between depression and reductions in reinforcement and/or increases in punishments (negative consequences).

- Behavioral interventions for depression emphasize increasing reinforcements and reducing punishments through daily monitoring of activities and mood, setting reachable goals, and using skill specific training to correct behavioral deficits.

- Combined cognitive-behavioral interventions for depression integrate cognitive restructuring techniques with a focus on reinforcements and skills training.

- Cognitive-behavioral interventions have been found to effectively supplement medication treatment for bipolar disorders.

Psychodynamic Components

Sigmund Freud (1917/1957) and his associate Karl Abraham (1911/1960) proposed some of the earliest psychological theories of depression. Freud's essay on the relationship between childhood experiences, loss, and depression—*Mourning and Melancholia* (1917)—is a classic text that dominated thinking about depression for many

and Melancholia, Freud considers the differences between *mourn-* process after the death of a loved one) and *melancholia* (an old tes that have many common features. He noted that people reacting to a loss like people who are in mourning, always clear. But, unlike people in mourning, people who are depressed also tend to take harshly critical views of themselves. Based on these and other observations, Freud concluded that depression has its roots in experiences of loss or disappointment that generate anger at the lost or disappointing person. If, for some reason, this anger cannot be consciously acknowledged, it is turned on the self as self-criticism, resulting in depression. Freud's explanation for this was that the individual *internalizes* the lost or disappointing "object" (a psychodynamic term for the mental image of another person) by *identifying* (taking on their traits) with them, and therefore can indirectly express anger at the other person by criticizing him- or herself.

For example, when a child experiences the physical loss (through death or separation) or emotional loss (though neglect or depression) of a parent, the parent may become the focus of anger and sadness. If consciously feeling anger toward the absent parent is too upsetting, the child may direct anger inward at him- or herself instead, especially the part of the self that is most closely identified with the parent. In adulthood, actual or symbolic losses may then activate similar processes. A disappointment, such as a romantic breakup or the loss of a job, may be symbolically associated with earlier losses, reawakening depressive symptoms from the past. Depressive self-recriminations (such as, "I'm worthless") may be internalized versions of unconscious anger at others.

After developing the structural (id, ego, superego) theory (Chapter 3), Freud began emphasizing the role of the **superego** in the development of depression. As you know, Freud viewed the superego as the part of the mind that morally evaluates the self. It can sometimes be excessively harsh and critical, leading to depressive self-loathing. In the following passage from a book titled *Autobiography of a Face*, Lucy Grealy describes her experience of living with a severe facial deformity after being diagnosed with jaw cancer at age nine. It provides an excellent example of how depression can be caused by superego-induced guilt about "bad" thoughts and feelings.

Superego In Freud's structural theory, the part of the mind that acts as a censor and conscience.

> I hated Danny in my orchestra class because I had a crush on him and I knew that he would never have a crush on me. Anger scared me most of all, and I repressed every stirring. Every time I felt hatred, or any other "bad" thought I shooed it away with a broom of spiritual truisms. But the more I tried to negate my feelings, the more they crowded in. I not only harbored hatred for Danny even while I had a crush on him, I also hated Katherine, the girl in orchestra *he* had a crush on. Trying to repress that feeling, I found myself hating Katherine's cello, of all things, which she played exquisitely well. The cycle eventually ended with me: I hated myself for having even entertained the absurd notion that someone like Danny could like me.
>
> I didn't begrudge Danny his crush on Katherine. She was pretty and talented, so why shouldn't he want her? I was never going to have anyone want me in that way, so I mustn't desire such a thing; in this way I could be grateful to my face for "helping" me to see the error of earthly desire. This complicated gratitude usually lasted for about five minutes before giving way to depression, plain and simple.

(Grealy, 1994, p. 181)

Some psychodynamic theorists have also elaborated the links between depression and narcissistic personality traits (Bibring, 1953; Fenichel, 1945; Miller; 1979). As you will see in Chapter 11, people with narcissistic traits ward off feelings of inadequacy or unworthiness by trying to be seen as special, praiseworthy, and superior. But when a narcissistic man loses a competition for a promotion at work, or a narcissistic woman's beauty fades as she ages, they may be prone to depression as feelings of inadequacy resurface. The object relational and self-psychology schools of psychodynamic theory have further elaborated this perspective on depression by focusing on the many ways in which childhood losses, disappointments, excessive frustrations, and other interpersonal stresses can undermine self-esteem and feelings of security, putting individuals at risk for depression. As one psychodynamic theorist describes it:

> The combination of emotional or actual abandonment with parental criticism is particularly likely to create depressive dynamics. A patient of mine lost her mother to cancer when she was 11 and was left with a father who repeatedly complained that her unhappiness was aggravating his ulcer and hastening his death. Another client was called a sniveling baby by her mother when she cried because, at age 4, she was being shipped away to overnight camp for several weeks. A depressed man I worked with whose mother was severely depressed and unavailable emotionally during his early years was told he was selfish and insensitive for wanting her time, and that he should be grateful that she was not sending him to an orphanage. In such instances it is easy to see that angry reactions to emotional abuse by the parent would have felt too dangerous to the child who already feared rejection.
>
> …Finally, a powerful causative factor in depressive dynamics is significant depression in a parent, especially in a child's earliest years. Biologically inclined theorists have tended to attribute to genetic processes the fact that dysthymic illnesses run in families, but analytically oriented writers have been more cautious… Children are deeply bothered by a parent's depression; they feel guilty for making normal demands, and they come to believe that their needs drain and exhaust others. The earlier their dependence on someone who is deeply depressed, the greater is their emotional privation.
>
> (McWilliams, 1994, pp. 235–236)

Psychodynamic Interventions

Psychodynamic interventions for depression involve therapeutic techniques also used for other disorders; clients are encouraged to speak as freely as possible and to attend, with the therapist's help, to the repetitive patterns and emotional conflicts in the client's life. With depressed clients, clinicians pay special attention to psychodynamic issues such as loss (actual or symbolic), anger directed at the self, and the presence of an overly harsh superego. In addition, they assess the possibility that some of the client's personality traits (for example, narcissistic traits) and/or problematic early life experiences and relationships may have made him or her vulnerable to depression.

When clients discover earlier, unresolved losses in the course of a psychodynamic exploration of depression, therapists will try to facilitate normal grieving over these losses. For example, a man who sought therapy because he felt suicidal after the breakup of a brief relationship soon discovered that his sadness ultimately pertained to the death of his father when he was eight years old. The client's mother had been so devastated by her husband's death that the client had pushed aside his own feelings in order to support his mother. Over the course of the therapy, he began to belatedly grieve the death of his father and found that after doing so he was not so easily devastated by the ups and downs of his current relationships.

In addition to their effectiveness in addressing some depressive problems, psychodynamic interventions can also be helpful in the treatment of bipolar disorders (Deitz, 1995; Kahn, 1993; Teixeira, 1992). For bipolar disorders, psychodynamic interventions focus on identifying the emotional triggers of mood swings, supporting healthy coping mechanisms, and addressing issues that might interfere with compliance with necessary medication regimens.

Brief Summary

- Freud drew a parallel between mourning and depression and believed that depression was rooted in early childhood experiences of loss. Over time he amended his theory and emphasized the role of the overly harsh superego as the major agent in the development of depression.

- Recent psychodynamic theorists emphasize that problematic childhood relationships with caregivers are also risk factors for depression.

- Psychodynamic interventions for depression involve a focus on issues of loss, anger directed inward, the role of the superego, problematic childhood experiences and relationships, and, sometimes, predisposing personality traits.

> *Critical Thinking Question* | **William Faulkner once said: "The past isn't dead. It isn't even past." How could his words be said to characterize the psychodynamic perspective on depression?**

Sociocultural and Family Systems Components

As noted earlier in the chapter, a variety of demographic factors such as being female, unemployed, or poor are risk factors for depression. The link between these demographic factors and depression may be due to variables such as self-esteem and social support that have been shown to protect against depression (Scott, 1988). Specifically, self-esteem and social support may be compromised among members of groups faced with discrimination and socioeconomic disadvantage. Accordingly, sociocultural interventions to reduce depression focus on a number of areas that improve self-esteem and social support: problem-solving training, changing jobs or gaining employment, and developing social and coping skills (Scott, 1992). *Feminist therapy,* for example, focuses on the gender-related stresses and prejudices that may contribute to depression in women.

Family systems approaches to depression can be especially helpful when children or adolescents are depressed or when family relationships are taxed by recurrent or chronic depression in one family member. Children and adolescents who become depressed often do so in reaction to a problem within the broader family system, such as neglect, abuse, or divorce. Therapeutic interventions in such situations involve addressing the family situation that triggered the child's depression and then addressing the various psychological repercussions of family problems on all family members. In a review of the research on treatments for childhood depression, a team at the Menninger Clinic in Kansas found that family-focused treatments, especially treatments that address parent-child interactions and parental depression, are particularly effective in treating depressed children (Dujovne, Barnard, & Rapoff, 1995).

Mood disorders, both unipolar and bipolar, take a toll on the families of those afflicted. Following a model developed for the families of people with schizophrenia, a group of clinicians developed an inpatient family intervention (IFI) for the relatives of people suffering from depression or bipolar illness severe enough to require hospitalization (Haas et al., 1988). The IFI employs a brief, psychoeducational intervention to help families understand and accept their relative's illness, identify life stressors that might trigger relapses in the future, and strategize about how to manage unavoidable family conflicts. The IFI model has been especially useful for families of people with bipolar illness. Highly stressful life events and chronic stress in family relationships have both been found to predict the recurrence of mood episodes in people suffering from bipolar disorders (Miklowitz & Frank, 1999).

Interpersonal psychotherapy (IPT) An influential current treatment for depression that integrates psychodynamic, cognitive, and behavioral components.

Multiple Causality of Mood Disorders

An influential current treatment for depression that combines several theoretical components nicely illustrates the principle of ***multiple causality*** in explaining and treating mood disorders. **Interpersonal psychotherapy (IPT)**, developed by Klerman and Weissman (Klerman & Weissman 1992; Klerman et al., 1984), is designed for people suffering from mild to moderate depression. IPT incorporates aspects of object-relational (psychodynamic), behavioral, and cognitive perspectives on depression (Markowitz & Weissman, 1995). The interpersonal approach to depression assumes that there is a circular relationship between mood and relationships. For example, people who experience unfortunate events or high levels of stress may become depressed if they have not had or do not currently have supportive, empathic relationships. Once depressed, they likely become less capable of initiating gratifying interpersonal relationships, and thus are prone to deepening depression.

IPT is usually conducted as a time-limited, structured approach to treating depression. Clinician and client meet on a weekly basis for 12 to 20 weeks but may continue to meet on a monthly "maintenance" basis for several years (Klerman et al., 1984). During the initial sessions of therapy, the clinician and client work together to assess the client's current relationships and identify a specific area of interpersonal problems. The IPT model identifies four major categories of interpersonal problems: losses, role disputes, role transitions, and interpersonal deficits (see Table 6.12).

Regardless of the kinds of interpersonal problem identified in IPT, the clinician emphasizes helping the client to try out new interpersonal strategies and to understand the connection between his or her attributions concerning interpersonal events

Relationships and depression Interpersonal psychotherapy, which combines multiple theoretical components, focuses on the importance of close, supportive relationships in preventing depression and improving mood in those who are depressed.

Interpersonal Problems: Examples of the Four IPT Categories	Table 6.12

Information from Klerman et al., 1984

Interpersonal Loss ■ Client has been unable to appropriately grieve the death of a significant other and needs assistance with this in order to pursue new supportive relationships.

Interpersonal Role Dispute ■ Client is engaged in a struggle over job responsibilities with a boss and needs help understanding his or her role in the dispute and how to go about changing the relationship.

Interpersonal Role Transition ■ Client has experienced a recent divorce and needs help adjusting to a new interpersonal situation.

Interpersonal Deficit ■ Client has poor social skills and needs encouragement to try out new relationships and behavior patterns.

and his or her mood. Before treatment ends, the clinician and client assess what the client has accomplished and his or her role in improving mood and changing interpersonal relationships. Points of vulnerability that may trigger relapses are identified and plans may be made for monthly "booster" sessions to maintain therapeutic gains and provide a forum for ongoing work on interpersonal problems.

Finally, as we have noted, the combination of biological interventions with psychotherapeutic interventions is rapidly becoming the state of the art in treating mood disorders. Studies show that medication, interpersonal, cognitive, and behavioral interventions are all about equally effective in alleviating depression over about a four-month period (Jacobson & Hollon, 1996), but that a combination of medication and psychotherapy may be most effective of all, especially in preventing relapse (Frank et al., 1991). The decision about which treatment, or which combination of treatments, to pursue depends on a variety of factors. In some situations, clients prefer to see if they can overcome depression through psychotherapy before considering medications. In other cases, people who are very severely depressed may not be able to make use of psychotherapy until their depression has been partially alleviated with the help of medication. Such individuals may use medications to help manage an acute episode of depression, but pursue psychotherapy as a long-term approach to preventing future episodes. In some cases, as we have seen, psychotherapy is crucial for helping clients adhere to a medication regimen (see Table 6.13 for information on obstacles to medication compliance in bipolar disorder).

Brief Summary

- Sociocultural components of depression include low self-esteem and inadequate social support related to gender or socioeconomic factors. Sociocultural interventions aim to improve self-esteem and social support through assistance with problem solving, employment issues, and social and coping skills.

- Family therapy interventions for depression address family dynamics that may contribute to a client's depression, and the effects of a mood disorder on a client's family members.

- Interpersonal psychotherapy (IPT) is an integrated treatment that focuses on the circular relationship between mood and interpersonal events, combining object relational (psychodynamic), behavioral, and cognitive components in keeping with the principle of ***multiple causality.***

Table 6.13	Obstacles to Adherence with Medication Treatment for Bipolar Disorders

Adapted from Basco & Thase, 1998

Noncompliance with medication is a common problem for clients being treated for bipolar disorders. Among the common obstacles to medication adherence are the following factors:

Intrapersonal variables:

- Remission in symptoms causes client to see no need for further treatment
- Client runs out of medication/did not refill prescription
- Client denies he or she has a chronic illness/stigma associated with bipolar disorders
- Forgetfulness

Treatment variables:

- Side effects of medication
- Medication schedule does not conform to client's personal schedule
- Client assigned a new doctor who changes treatment plans

Social system variables:

- Psychosocial stressors
- Competing medical advice
- Discouragement from family and friends
- Publicized stories of others' bad experiences with medications

Interpersonal variables:

- Poor rapport with the therapist and/or psychiatrist
- Busy, uncomfortable, or otherwise unpleasant clinic environment

Cognitive variables:

- Client does not like the idea of having to depend on drugs
- Client thinks he or she should be able to handle mood swings on his or her own
- Client misattributes symptoms of bipolar disorder to another source
- Client is suspicious of the intentions of the doctor

Case Vignettes | **Treatment**
Tamara | Major Depressive Disorder

After meeting with Tamara for a few sessions, the psychologist offered her recommendations. She suggested that Tamara begin psychotherapy to address her feelings about the divorce and obtain additional emotional support. She also suggested that Tamara consider an evaluation for antidepressant medication, since Tamara's children were needing their mother to be more effective and available as soon as possible. Tamara was eager to begin therapy but felt reluctant to consider an antidepressant drug. She explained that she often reacted poorly to medications. Tamara and the psychologist agreed that they would monitor her progress and revisit the issue of medication if Tamara's mood did not improve within a few weeks.

As Tamara began therapy, she found herself becoming increasingly angry about her husband's behavior. She described how humiliated she felt by his abrupt departure, and spent several weeks vacillating between rage and despair as she wondered if he had fallen in love with someone else or if he had just fallen out of love with her. At times, Tamara was full of self-recrimination, making long mental lists of all of her failings as a wife that might have justified her husband's behavior. Tamara's psychologist pointed out how self-critical Tamara was being, and that there was no evidence that she was solely to blame for the divorce.

As time went on, Tamara's emotional expression became richer both inside and outside of therapy. She sobbed as she explained to her psychologist how pathetic she felt since she continued to love someone who had hurt her and her children so much. Tamara also began to talk about having had similar feelings of abandonment and betrayal twice before—when she was five years old and her mother gave birth to twins, and when her parents divorced when Tamara was 16. She remembered having had strong feelings of anger and desperation both times, but had tried very hard, even at five years old, to "calm down and be a good girl." Tamara began to see that these long suppressed feelings had been reawakened by her husband's behavior and were contributing to her depression. After a couple of months, Tamara started to feel more alive, and regained her appetite. She felt more connected to her work, and more present and effective in her role as a mother. Though Tamara felt much better, she was still not entirely back to her "old self." She became more open to the idea of trying an antidepressant and consulted with a psychiatrist who recommended an SSRI. Tamara found that the medication did, in fact, help her to feel even better. After nine months on the SSRI, Tamara was feeling well enough that she and her psychiatrist agreed to gradually reduce her dosage. She remained in therapy to complete the emotional work she had begun.

Case Discussion | Major Depressive Disorder

Tamara benefited from a psychotherapy that drew from a number of theoretical perspectives. Her psychologist used both psychodynamic and cognitive interventions, while also recommending biological treatment. As Tamara became aware of how angry she was about her husband's behavior, she felt less depressed, indicating that her depression arose, in part, from redirecting negative feelings about her husband back at herself. Tamara's psychologist also tried to correct cognitive distortions, such as Tamara's self-criticisms and tendency to take all the blame for the failure of her marriage. By doing so, the psychologist hoped to keep Tamara from ruminating over painful thoughts that might interfere with her ability to grieve the end of her marriage and move forward emotionally.

Mark | Bipolar I Disorder

Mark's psychiatrist quickly realized that Mark suffered from bipolar I disorder and that immediate treatment would be necessary to bring his manic and depressive mood swings under control. The psychiatrist prescribed lithium, and scheduled several follow-up appointments to monitor Mark's progress and to gradually increase the lithium dose until it reached a therapeutic blood level. Two months after beginning to take lithium, Mark was feeling more "even-keeled," but then suddenly became depressed after learning that his mother had been diagnosed with Alzheimer's disease. Mark was unable to get out of bed for several days in a row, lost 15 pounds in two weeks, and felt emotionally numb. His wife insisted that he meet with his psychiatrist who promptly prescribed an antidepressant to be taken in addition to the lithium.

Over the course of the next month Mark started to feel much better and reported to his psychiatrist that he did not feel like he was "riding on an emotional roller-coaster" as he had for most of his life. The psychiatrist suggested that the best thing that Mark could do for himself now would be to begin psychotherapy to help him adjust to the realities of managing his bipolar disorder. Mark met with a few different therapists until he found someone with whom he felt comfortable. He found that the therapy, in combination with medication, helped him feel that he was more in control of his mood swings, and as a result, of his life.

After about two years of medication and psychotherapy, Mark felt stable and decided that he wanted to stop taking his medications. Against the advice of his therapist and psychiatrist, Mark proceeded with his plan to wean himself off lithium. Within two months Mark experienced a dramatic manic episode in which he spent nearly $15,000 on plane tickets, hotel reservations, and video equipment for a spontaneous vacation that his family could not afford. Mark's wife insisted that if he did not return to taking lithium she would have to consider filing for divorce. Mark relented, became emotionally stabilized again, and spent several months in therapy assessing the damage his poor decision had done to his marriage and personal finances.

Case Discussion | Bipolar I Disorder

Not all cases of bipolar I disorder are as easily diagnosed as Mark's, but Mark's mood swings had become so severe that a clear pattern of manic and major depressive episodes was obvious to his psychiatrist. Like many people who are treated with medication for bipolar disorders, Mark needed both a mood-stabilizer (lithium) and an antidepressant in order to control both his manic and depressive episodes. Also, like many clients with bipolar disorders, Mark was tempted to discontinue his medication when he was feeling well, but he relapsed after doing so. Ultimately, Mark's therapist helped him to come to terms with the fact that he needed to take medication in order to have a "normal" life, and therapy gave him a forum where he could think about how to manage his mood swings which were so dangerous for him and his family.

Chapter Summary

- Moods have emotional, cognitive, motivational, and physical components.

- Variations in mood are normal aspects of living. It is partly the *context* in which moods occur that helps define whether they are abnormal.

- Variations in mood occur on the *continuum between normal and abnormal behavior*. Moods of unusual intensity and duration are more likely to be considered abnormal.

- Classfications of mood disorders are *historically relative*, having changed considerably over time. The DSM-IV-TR currently recognizes five main mood disorders: major depressive disorder, dysthymia, bipolar disorder I, bipolar disorder II, and cyclothymia. The DSM-IV-TR mood disorders consist of various combinations of three mood episodes: major depressive episodes, manic episodes, and hypomanic episodes.

- Demographic context factors such as age, gender, class, and culture influence the expression and prevalence of mood disorders. Depression may involve different symptoms in different age groups and it is seen disproportionately among females and the poor. Further, the experience and expression of depression is *culturally relative.*

- Biological components of mood disorders include predisposing genetic factors, deficits in the availability of monoamines (norepinephrine, dopamine, and serotonin), and dysregulation in the body's hormonal system. Bipolar mood disorders also have a genetic component. Neurotransmitters and neural anomalies in the amygdala, prefrontal cortex, and cerebellum are involved in bipolar illness, but their roles are not yet well understood.

- Cognitive theorists propose that people become depressed by holding negative views of themselves, their world, and their future, expressed in negative automatic thoughts, cognitive distortions, and pessimistic explanations of negative events.

- Behavioral theories of depression focus primarily on the relationship between depression and reductions in reinforcements and/or increase in aversive consequences (punishments).

- Psychodynamic theorists suggest that depression may be rooted in childhood experiences of loss, anger turned on the self, an overly harsh superego, and personality traits such as narcissism.

- Sociocultural interventions for depression focus on improving self-esteem and social support through assistance with problem solving, employment, and social skills. Family therapy interventions for depression address the family situation that may have contributed to a client's depression as well as addressing the effects of an individual's depression on family members.

- Interpersonal psychotherapy (IPT), an integrated treatment that focuses on the circular relationship between mood and interpersonal events, draws on object relational, behavioral, and cognitive theories of depression. The principle of *multiple causality* in mood disorders is well illustrated by IPT and other multi-modal treatments.

Joan Miró, *La Nuit,* 1953.
©Marlborough Graphics,
London, UK/Bridgeman Art
Library International Ltd.
©2004 Successio Miro/
Artists Rights Society
(ARS), New York

Joan Miró (1893–1983), a Spaniard considered to be one of the leading figures in the Surrealist art movement, emphasized simplified shapes and organic imagery in his abstract paintings. Miró often worked "automatically," using his brush without conscious intention, in the hopes that this would ......*continued on page 196*

joan miró

chapter seven

DISSOCIATION AND THE DISSOCIATIVE DISORDERS

Case Vignettes

John, a college sophomore, came for a walk-in appointment at his university counseling center because he was worried that his tendency to "space out" was getting in the way of his schoolwork. Though he had experienced what he called "spacey" episodes off and on since his senior year in high school, they had increased in intensity and duration around the time of his most recent midterm exams, sometimes happening while he was in the middle of taking a test. John had been able to continue working on the exams when this happened, but his academic performance was dropping and he was sure that "spacing out" during exams wasn't helping. When the counselor asked if anything important had occurred in John's life around the time the episodes began, John explained that his father had died shortly after being diagnosed with lung cancer in the summer before John's freshman year of college. However, John felt that his father's death was unrelated to the spacey episodes because he and his family were able to say their good-byes to their father and everyone handled the loss "very well." Further, John explained that when he felt spacey he didn't feel sad, or like he missed his father; he just felt nothing at all.

Margaret, a clerical worker at a manufacturing company, was contacted by the staff assistance program of her division due to her excessive absences. Though she did not feel comfortable giving the details of her many absences to the counselor, Margaret explained that she had been having "mental problems" and accepted a referral to a local psychologist. The psychologist was struck by Margaret's description of a typical week. On Mondays, she often awoke feeling miserable from the weekend's activities, though she could rarely remember what had occurred. Margaret was almost always terribly hungover and unable to go to work. Occasionally, she would find a strange man in her bed or would receive phone calls from men she had never met who seemed to know her, but who addressed her as "Janie." Margaret explained to the psychologist that she had been having similar experiences for the past nine years, since the time she was a sophomore in high school. Though genuine cases are rare, the psychologist began to suspect that Margaret might be suffering from multiple personality disorder.

As treatment progressed it became clear to Margaret and her therapist that over the weekends Margaret did indeed seem to exhibit an alternate personality who called herself "Janie" and would engage in impulsive and self-destructive behavior. During therapy sessions when Margaret was feeling especially upset she would suddenly begin to act and talk like a young child who did not know where she was. This little girl personality referred to herself as "Suzie," and in this way the therapist became aware of the existence of a third distinct personality within Margaret.

...*continued from page 194*

reveal the hidden contents of his unconscious mind. Like others in his circle, Miró was reputed to have sometimes fasted and deprived himself of sleep in order to generate hallucinatory experiences that could become fodder for future paintings. Miró's efforts to induce alterations in consciousness—dissociative states—may have helped secure his place as a key figure in the history of modern art.

Dissociation A significant disruption in one's conscious experience, memory, sense of identity, or any combination of the three.

DEFINING DISSOCIATION AND DISSOCIATIVE DISORDERS

The cases of John and Margaret—one relatively mild, one quite extreme—have a central feature in common. It is a process known as **dissociation,** which refers to a significant disruption in one's state of consciousness, memory, sense of identity, or any combination of the three. While the dissociative disorders are some of the most strange and fascinating of the mental disorders, mild forms of dissociation are common, everyday experiences. For example, if you have ever meditated, been lost in a daydream, or experienced déjà vu, you have had a mild dissociative experience. Such states are not necessarily unpleasant or pathological and are even sought out by some people through exercise or drug use. In other cases, people have dissociative symptoms during frightening experiences, such as being in a car crash or falling down stairs. They may feel as if the accident were happening in slow motion, or as if they were standing outside their bodies, watching it occur. Indeed, dissociation is particularly associated with trauma, and it represents one of the ways that the mind can protect itself against overwhelmingly frightening or painful experiences—in other words, it can be understood as one of the mind's defense mechanisms (Chapter 3). Like other defense mechanisms, dissociative experiences can be adaptive, such as when athletes are able to detach from pain and anxiety to perform at unusually high levels. Hypnosis, a form of induced dissociation, has been found to be effective in treating some anxiety disorders, and in helping people stop smoking (Green, 2000).

Because dissociative symptoms are common, and sometimes adaptive, it is a challenge to define *pathological* dissociation. As with the other disorders already

In the "zone" Dissociative experiences can be highly adaptive. Through meditation people can achieve deep states of relaxation; by ignoring pain, people can perform at remarkably high levels of athleticism. Donovan Bailey, a Canadian runner, appears to be truly transported as he sets the new world record in the Olympic 100 meter final.

discussed, two factors are critical: the severity of the dissociative symptoms on the continuum between normal and abnormal behavior and the context in which the dissociation occurs.

The Continuum Between Normal and Abnormal Dissociation

The *continuum between normal and abnormal behavior* must be considered in order to define *pathological* dissociation. On the normal side of the continuum are common dissociative experiences such as déjà vu or daydreaming. On the abnormal end of the continuum are extreme and chronic dissociative states in which people literally forget who they are or shift involuntarily between alternate identities. Between these two extremes are mildly disruptive dissociative symptoms, such as John's "spaciness." Whether or not dissociative symptoms constitute a dissociative *disorder* depends, in large part, on the severity of the dissociation and how much it interferes with overall functioning.

The Importance of Context in Defining Dissociative Disorders

As mentioned above, there are certain *contexts* in which dissociation is an adaptive response. For example, a person who is terrified of flying on airplanes may begin every flight by mentally transporting himself to a safe and familiar place while the plane takes off. Dissociation may also allow people to perform heroic feats in situations that would normally cause paralyzing fear and dread. We are all familiar with stories of people who rescue themselves and others from accidents with no apparent awareness of their own physical injuries. Once the danger has passed, the heroic individual may feel overwhelmed by the memory of the harrowing experience. However, at the time of the incident, he or she was able to create a profound detachment from normal consciousness.

Unfortunately, dissociation is not always helpful or adaptive. John, the college junior described at the beginning of the chapter, is having mild dissociative experiences during examinations. While his dissociation may be in part a reaction to anxiety about the exam, it is not helpful for him to be "spacing out" when he needs to be concentrating. So, when we are trying to determine whether a dissociative experience should be considered pathological or not, we need to ask ourselves if the dissociative symptoms are occurring in a context in which they assist or interfere with the individual's ability to function.

Brief Summary

- Dissociation refers to alterations in state of consciousness, memory, sense of identity, or any combination of the three.
- Dissociative disorders are defined by dissociative symptoms that occur in inappropriate *contexts* and are severe enough on the *continuum* of dissociative symptoms to interfere with functioning.

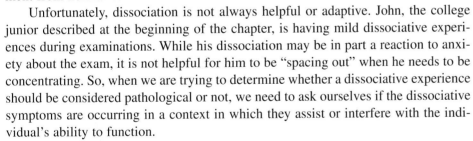

Critical Thinking Question | Everyone has had some form of a dissociative experience at one time or another, though, as we've seen, many common dissociative experiences are not pathological. Where would you draw the line between normal and abnormal dissociation?

CLASSIFYING DISSOCIATIVE DISORDERS

Dissociative symptoms sometimes occur as part of certain anxiety disorders (Chapter 5), or personality disorders (Chapter 11). However, the disorders that are classified as the dissociative disorders in the DSM-IV-TR are those in which dissociation is the *main symptom*.

The DSM-IV-TR Categories

The DSM-IV-TR recognizes four different dissociative disorders: *depersonalization disorder, dissociative amnesia, dissociative fugue,* and *dissociative identity disorder* (see Table 7.1).

Depersonalization Disorder

Depersonalization disorder Persistent and distressing feelings of being detached from one's mind or body.

People, like John (described at the beginning of the chapter), with **depersonalization disorder,** are distressed or impaired by persistent feelings of detachment and unreality. Individuals who suffer from depersonalization feel disconnected from their own mental processes, sometimes saying that they feel as if they were robots or living in a dream or a movie. At the time of a depersonalization experience, most people feel emotionally detached and numbed, though there may be some distress about the depersonalization experience itself (see Table 7.2).

> **Case Illustration** Mara, age 35, sought counseling for help with her long-standing sense of emotional detachment and repeated episodes during which she felt that "life doesn't seem real." During an intake interview Mara explained that as a child she could escape from the tension of her parents' loud arguments by immersing herself in imaginative play. As an adult, she found herself feeling strange, "non-human" and "unreal" during confrontational situations. She was scared and upset because the "unreal" episodes became more frequent.

Occasional symptoms of depersonalization are fairly common. Most people have experienced times when they feel disconnected from themselves and the world around

Table 7.1

Adapted from DSM-IV-TR (APA, 2000; prevalence data from Ross, 1996)

The DSM-IV-TR Dissociative Disorders

Depersonalization disorder ■ Persistent and distressing feelings of being detached from one's mind or body (lifetime prevalence estimate: up to 2.8% of the population).

Dissociative amnesia ■ Inability to recall important personal information, usually of a traumatic or stressful nature (lifetime prevalence estimate: up to 6% in some populations).

Dissociative fugue ■ Sudden and unexpected travel away from home accompanied by forgetting of one's past and personal identity (lifetime prevalence estimate: 0.2%).

Dissociative identity disorder (formerly *multiple personality disorder*) ■ Presence of two or more distinct personalities or identity states that recurrently control an individual's behavior (lifetime prevalence estimate: less than 1%).

Diagnostic Criteria for Depersonalization Disorder

Table 7.2

Adapted from DSM-IV-TR (APA, 2000)

- Persistent or recurrent experiences of feeling detached from one's body or mental processes, as if watching one's self from outside.
- During the period of depersonalization, the person is not psychotic; that is, he or she continues to know what is real and not real.
- The experience of depersonalization causes significant distress or difficulty in social, occupational, or other important areas of functioning.

them. Such experiences may be brought on by a stressful event, such as having to give a public talk, or may even result from feeling overly tired. Most of the time, temporary experiences of depersonalization are not particularly upsetting or problematic. The diagnosis of depersonalization disorder is reserved for situations in which depersonalization symptoms are frequent or persistent enough to become distressing or to interfere with normal functioning. Estimates of the prevalence of depersonalization disorder vary widely due, in part, to the fact that symptoms of depersonalization are often present in other psychological disorders (for example acute stress disorder and borderline personality disorder) and clients rarely seek treatment for depersonalization disorder itself (Moran, 1986).

Dissociative Amnesia

People with **dissociative amnesia** literally forget basic information about their identity or recent past, usually following a traumatic or emotionally upsetting event (see Table 7.3). Dissociative amnesia can take many forms (APA, 2000):

- **Localized amnesia** refers to forgetting that occurs within a circumscribed period of time, such as a person having amnesia for all of the events that happened on the same day that she witnessed a gruesome car accident.
- **Selective amnesia** refers to the ability to recall some but not all of the information from a specific period of time, such as someone who has forgotten many episodes from a recent combat experience.
- **Generalized amnesia** refers to the experience of forgetting everything about one's personal identity—having no knowledge of one's own name, background, family history, and so on. Nonpersonal aspects of memory remain intact, such as knowing about current events.

Portrait of Edward James René Magritte's painting communicates the feelings of detachment and disconnection often described by people suffering from depersonalization disorder.

Dissociative amnesia Psychogenic loss of ability to recall important personal information, usually of a traumatic or stressful nature.

Localized amnesia Loss of memory for all of the events that occurred within a circumscribed period of time.

Selective amnesia Loss of memory for some, but not all, of the events from a specific period of time.

Generalized amnesia Loss of memory for events and information, including information pertaining to personal identity.

Diagnostic Criteria for Dissociative Amnesia

Table 7.3

Adapted from DSM-IV-TR (APA, 2000)

- One or more episodes of being unable to recall important personal information, usually of a traumatic or stressful nature.
- The forgotten information is too extensive to be accounted for by ordinary forgetting.
- The forgetting causes clinically significant distress or impairment in social, occupational, or other important areas of functioning.

Dangerous information In the movie *Dead Again* (1991), Emma Thompson plays a woman whose dissociative amnesia seems to be triggered by her knowledge of a murder.

Continuous amnesia Loss of memory that begins at a specific time, continues through to the present, and prevents the retention in memory of new experiences.

Systematized amnesia The loss of memory for a certain category of information.

- **Continuous amnesia** refers to amnesia that begins at a specific time and continues through to the present, such as a man who cannot remember anything that has occurred since learning of the accidental death of his spouse a week ago.

- **Systematized amnesia** refers to the loss of memory for a certain category of information, such as memories related to a particular person.

Amnesias can also result from a head injury or medical illness, but these are classified as organic (that is, biologically caused) amnesias (see Box 7.1). Dissociative amnesia usually results from an emotionally traumatic experience and, by definition, does not have a biological cause.

Case Illustration Two police officers accompanied Mrs. Solon to her local emergency room after she flagged them down in the street and said that she could not remember her name or where she lived. As the emergency room physician asked her questions about her family, she recalled what had triggered her amnesia. On the previous day her husband of 15 years announced that he had been having an affair and wanted a divorce. Mrs. Solon was overwhelmed and devastated by the news. She left the house abruptly and apparently had been wandering for the past 24 hours, with no memory of these events. As the events came back to her, she began to shake and cry.

Case Illustration Sam, age 70, fought in the Korean War for nearly 2 years until he returned home with a shrapnel injury to his leg. Upon his return, he joined his father's printing company which he ran from the time of his father's death to his own retirement. Though Sam sometimes tells war stories to his friends and grandchildren, he is aware that there are large gaps in his memory of being in Korea. Sam knows better than to attribute this forgetting to old age. Even at the time of his return home, he was unable to recall anything at all about periods of several weeks when he had been stationed in areas of heavy fighting.

Mrs. Solon suffers from generalized amnesia while Sam suffers from selective amnesia. In both cases, upsetting or harrowing experiences appear to have triggered amnesia for these experiences or for aspects of personal identity. The symptoms of dissociative amnesia can take a variety of forms; Table 7.4 lists different experiences that can be characteristic of dissociative amnesia. In most cases of dissociative amnesia, the forgotten experiences or aspects of identity spontaneously return.

The major challenge in diagnosing patients with amnesia lies in determining whether their amnesia is dissociative or organic (biological). Both dissociative and

Table 7.4	Common Experiences in Dissociative Amnesia
Adapted from Loewenstein, 1996, p. 310	• Blackouts or "time loss" • Reports of disremembered behavior • Appearance of unexplained possessions • Perplexing changes in relationships • Fragmentary recall of life history • Brief, trancelike amnesia episodes ("microamnesias")

BOX 7.1 Organic Amnesias

The Forgetful Brain

Organic amnesias are caused by brain injury, disease, and/or neural deterioration. Organic amnesias are characterized by **anterograde amnesia,** or the inability to recall *new* information, though sometimes retrograde amnesia is also present. In contrast, people who suffer from dissociative amnesia usually experience only **retrograde amnesia,** meaning that they cannot remember what happened *before* the event that caused their amnesia. Some common causes of *organic* amnesia are presented here.

• *Brain injury* of the coconut-hits-someone-on-the-head variety can, indeed, cause amnesia. The severity of amnesia depends on the severity of the head injury. Amnesia caused by mild head injuries usually resolves quickly and spontaneously. More severe head injuries, such as those caused by serious automobile accidents, can cause irreversible damage to memory and to other brain functions such as speech and motor coordination. However, head injuries are not responsible for all forms of brain damage accompanied by amnesia. Blood clots and other vascular impairments that damage areas of the brain (such as "strokes"), severe nutri-tional deficiencies, and exposure to some toxins can also interfere with memory.

• *Korsakoff's syndrome* is a form of anterograde amnesia caused by chronic alcoholism. Alcohol interferes with the body's ability to metabolize vitamin B (thiamine), causing serious deficiencies to accrue after years of heavy drinking (Chapter 9). Not surprisingly, poor nutritional habits often go hand-in-hand with chronic alcoholism and only exacerbate the problem. Thiamine deficiencies damage the diencephalon, a part of the brain made up of the thalamus and hypothalamus, and lead to difficulty recalling newly acquired information. People suffering from Korsakoff's syndrome are highly forgetful, yet they may deny the extent of their amnesia to themselves and others by *confabulating*, creating stories or telling lies to hide their confusion. Interestingly, thiamine administered to recovering alcoholics improves the functioning of memory within a matter of days (Ambrose, Bowden, & Whelan, 2001). This phenomenon led one clinician from the Health Department of Western Australia to argue that thiamine should be added to the Australian beer supply (Finlay-Jones, 1986).

• *Delirium* and *dementia,* mental disorders frequently associated with aging, often involve amnesia as a result of brain disease or deterioration. These disorders are described in detail in Chapter 13.

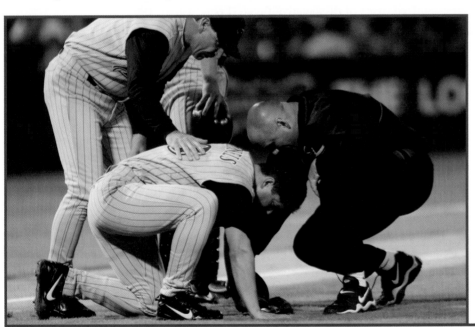

Occupational hazard Unlike dissociative amnesias, organic amnesias result from physical trauma to the brain. Here, third baseman Chris Donnels is attended to by the manager and trainer of the Arizona Diamondbacks after he experienced a concussion while fielding a bunt. Concussions and other head injuries often result in some degree of memory loss.

organic amnesias involve the inability to remember personal events from the past. However, organic amnesia is caused by biological factors—such as a head trauma, or illness—while dissociative amnesia is **psychogenic** (in fact, dissociative amnesia was called "psychogenic amnesia" in the DSM-III). One difference between the two is that people who suffer from organic amnesia usually forget both personal information (such as where they were born) and general information (such as the name of the current president), while people with dissociative amnesia typically only forget only personal information.

Anterograde amnesia The inability to recall events that occurred after a trauma.

Retrograde amnesia The inability to recall events that occurred before a trauma.

Psychogenic Originating from the mind or caused by psychological factors.

Table 7.5	Diagnostic Criteria for Dissociative Fugue

Adapted from DSM-IV-TR (APA, 2000)

- Sudden, unexpected travel away from one's home or place of work with inability to recall one's past.
- Confusion about personal identity or the assumption of a complete or partial new identity.
- The symptoms cause clinically significant distress or impairment in social, occupational, or other important areas of functioning.

Dissociative fugue Sudden and unexpected travel away from home accompanied by forgetting of one's past and personal identity.

Dissociative identity disorder Presence of two or more distinct personalities or identity states that recurrently control an individual's behavior.

Fugue on film Alfred Hitchcock's movie *Spellbound* (1945) tells the tale of a man (played by Gregory Peck) who cannot remember the details of his own life and assumes the identity of a psychiatrist named Dr. Anthony Edwardes. His love interest, a psychoanalyst named Dr. Constance Petersen (played by Ingrid Bergman), helps Edwardes unravel his dark and forgotten past.

Dissociative Fugue

The DSM-IV-TR criteria for **dissociative fugue** (listed in Table 7.5) involve the experience of dissociative amnesia plus two other features. After losing their memories, people with dissociative fugue leave their regular lives to travel to new areas, and typically assume new identities without any apparent recollection of the lives they've left behind. The dramatic nature of the disorder has inspired many fictional depictions, such as Alfred Hitchcock's famous movie *Spellbound*, and many soap opera plots. Dissociative fugue is considered to be rare, but some clinicians suspect that a significant number of missing persons and teenage runaways may involve unrecognized cases of dissociative fugue (Loewenstein, 1993).

Case Illustration Warren, age 25, had always dreamed of becoming a lawyer but had a great deal of trouble with the intellectual demands of law school. In his first semester Warren failed three of his four classes and was asked to leave school. After receiving the news, he walked out of the Dean's office and hailed a cab. Apparently, he found an apartment in a neighboring town, began introducing himself to others as "Bill", and did odd jobs for money for a period of several weeks. His parents filed a missing persons report with the local police department and circulated a recent photograph of their son. One of Warren's employers recognized the photograph and contacted the police. Only when he was reunited with his parents was Warren able to recall his previous identity, and the upsetting event that led to his sudden amnesia and travel.

Like dissociative amnesia, dissociative fugue usually occurs in the wake of an upsetting or traumatizing event. Fugue states appear to be more common in people who have had past incidents of amnesia and may also be more likely to occur in individuals who are highly suggestible (Kopelman, 1987). In most cases of dissociative amnesia or fugue, forgotten information about identity or recent events is recovered spontaneously, either in the course of a clinical intervention or simply with the passage of time (Kardiner, 1941). In other cases, the false identity may be discovered, or the individual may be located by family and friends. Upon recovering from a fugue state, the individual often has no recall for anything that occurred during the time of the fugue (APA, 2000).

Dissociative Identity Disorder

Dissociative identity disorder, better known by its former name, *multiple personality disorder,* is the most severe of the dissociative disorders, and one of the most fascinating and controversial of all mental disorders. A person with dissociative identity disorder (such as Margaret, described at the beginning of the chapter) typically maintains his or her own "original" identity, but also has other identities or personalities that intermittently replace the original personality. Dissociative identity disorder (DID) is often confused with schizophrenia (Chapter 12) because people sometimes mistakenly believe that schizophrenia involves "split personality." In fact, schizophrenia involves symptoms focusing on psychosis in the form of hallucinations and delusions. When an individual truly exhibits separate personalities, the appropriate diagnosis is DID (see Table 7.6).

The following case comes from a published account (Muller, 1998) of a woman with DID who sought help at a hospital emergency room.

> This was the third time I had been asked to see her [Nadine] in the ER. She was sitting on a royal blue mattress in the seclusion room, watched and comforted by a female technician who had a particularly gentle way with patients.
>
> Nadine seemed to be holding court, alternately speaking English and Russian, a language she later told me she had studied seriously. Her speech was rapid and pressured, loud and emphatic. Much of what she said was intelligible, some was not. She wrote in a notebook as she spoke, making bold strokes that produced lines and, occasionally, a few words. Nadine was childlike in appearance and manner—short, slightly built, with short brown hair and thick glasses that seemed too big for her sharp-featured, feral face.
>
> Nadine had come from the oncology unit upstairs. Proudly, she flashed a hospital badge with her picture and the word Volunteer printed in bold, black letters. She had two reasons for coming to the ER. She needed prescriptions for paroxetine (Paxil), trazodone (Desyrel) and levothyroxine (Synthroid); her psychiatrist was not due back from vacation for two weeks, and she had only enough medication for six days. The second reason was because, as she put it, "the children started coming out." These "children," as far as I could tell, were several of the more immature facets of her identity—the "alters"—who tended to cause trouble for the major identity, "Nadine" (a name she chose, not her legal first name).
>
> Whoever was speaking for the ensemble of labile identities constituting the consciousness of this patient, ostensibly Nadine, gave an agreeable and often cogent interview. Much of what she said made sense, but some of what she said did not and was clearly bizarre. Both the cogent and the bizarre were put forward with equal conviction, making me think she could not distinguish one from the other.
>
> Agitation quickly gave way to hysterics. The patient (whatever facet of her dissociated, fractured identity was paramount now, possibly not Nadine) was screaming, and drawing the attention of the ER staff, as well as other patients being evaluated or waiting to be seen. In a few seconds, she went from what appeared to

The real "Eve" Chris Sizemore, whose story was made famous by the movie *The Three Faces of Eve* (1957), struggled for years to reconcile and integrate three distinct personalities: a 1950s housewife, a racy seductress, and a high-functioning intellectual.

Diagnostic Criteria for Dissociative Identity Disorder	Table 7.6
<ul><li>Presence of two or more distinct identities or personality states within one person.</li><li>At least two of these identities or personality states recurrently take control of the person's behavior.</li><li>Forgetting of personal information that is too extensive to be explained by ordinary forgetfulness.</li></ul>	*Adapted from DSM-IV-TR (APA, 2000)*

Found guilty Kenneth Bianchi became known as the "Hillside Strangler" for his gruesome murders of several women in the Los Angeles area in the late 1970s. During his trial, he pretended to suffer from dissociative identity disorder in order to avoid being convicted for his crimes. He eventually confessed to five murders and was sentenced to life in prison.

be a composed young woman (Nadine?) to a hysterical child, (one of the "children" who "started coming out" just before she came to the ER? Or, alternatively, simply an hysterical adult), screaming that we were not giving her the attention she needed and was promised.

Excerpted from Muller, 1998.
(Available at: http://www.psychiatrictimes.com/p981107.html)

Although no two cases of DID are identical, the disorder has several common features (Coons, Bowman, & Milstein, 1988; Ross, 1997). Most people with DID have between two and four personalities at the time they are diagnosed. In the course of psychotherapy, an average of 13 to 15 personalities are discovered, but in a minority of complex cases more than 25 "alters," or alternate personalities, exist (Kluft, 1988; Kluft, 1996). Often, the various personalities are radically different from each other: young, old, gay, straight, male, female, and so on. One personality may be calm and thoughtful while another is cruel and aggressive; a pious and chaste personality might coexist with another personality that is wild and promiscuous. Usually, at least one of the alternate personalities is a child or teenager who has a joyful, happy-go-lucky demeanor, or who is terribly traumatized and frightened. Diametrically opposed pairs of personalities like these are typical in DID.

The *host* personality usually retains the individual's legal name and identity and may help the individual function by holding down a job, meeting responsibilities, and maintaining relationships, while other *persecutory* personalities act out aggressive and hostile impulses and may actively seek to undermine the more adaptive personalities. *Protector* personalities often work to avoid dangerous situations and they may be aggressive toward anyone who appears to pose a threat. Some individual personalities have their own names; others may use labels that describe their traits (such as "Fury," or "Tease") (see Box 7.2). In many cases, the host or protector personalities are aware of and can describe all of the other personalities, while other personalities may or may not be aware that they are one of many identities. Amnesia between certain personalities accounts for the common DID experience of *lost time* in which there is no memory for events during which another personality was dominant. Margaret's amnesia for the weekends in which Janie was dominant (described at the beginning of the chapter) is an example of this phenomenon.

DID provides one of the most fascinating and compelling examples of the ***connection between mind and body*** in abnormal behavior. For example, some research has shown that different subpersonalities may have distinct biological profiles. An early single-case study reported "consistent differences" in the skin conductance, heart rate, and respiratory activity of four different identities in one person with DID (Bahnson & Smith, 1975, cited in Zahn, Moraga, & Ray, 1996) (see also Figure 7.1). More recently, one group of researchers found that the individual subpersonalities of people with DID had different degrees of visual acuity (Miller et al., 1991) while another group found that different subpersonalities had unique profiles of autonomic nervous system activity (Putnam, Zahn, & Post, 1990). Some researchers interpret these physiological differences as proof of the validity of DID. However, studies have also found that hypnosis, or even the production of the facial expressions that accompany certain emotions, can also produce alterations in physiological indices (Braun, 1983; Levenson, Ekman, & Friesen, 1990).

Brief Summary

- The DSM-IV-TR lists four main dissociative disorders: depersonalization disorder, dissociative amnesia, dissociative fugue, and dissociative identity disorder (DID).

BOX 7.2   Life as a Multiple

"My Guys"

In a book titled *First Person Plural: My Life as a Multiple,* Cameron West, Ph.D., describes suffering from dissociative identity disorder, recovering lost memories of having been sexually abused as a child, being treated for his disorder, and, ultimately, becoming a psychologist. He begins his book with a description of his 24 alternate personalities. Here are a few of his descriptions:

Soul is an ageless alter who emerged early on and whose job it was to give me hope so I could survive. His presence is still felt but he rarely comes out, even in therapy.

Sharky is a private alter who at first couldn't form words at all. He would grunt and swing his head from side to side and bite things, like tables and clothes and plants. One of the other alters drew a picture of him as a limbless being with a huge toothy mouth. Sharky has learned to talk and eat with his hands or a fork. He doesn't come out too often, but he likes to share treats with the others.

Davy is four. He is sweet and sad. He was the first to emerge, but he doesn't come out much anymore.

Anna and *Trudi* are four-year-old twins. Anna is doe-eyed and happy, with a smile so big it makes my face hurt. She remembers her abuse, but feels no anger, no sadness. She loves a good cookie. Trudi is dark and brooding, a kid in the corner. She remembers, too, but only the pain and sadness and horror. Anna shares her cookies with her. Anna is a member of the core group of alters who come out most frequently...

Switch is eight years old. He held incredible rage for being abused, but he also felt a powerful allegiance to one of our abusers and turned that rage toward me and some of the others. Switch harmed my body many times. He is not so angry anymore and he has been accepted by everyone in the system. Switch has his own sheriff's badge now, which he likes to wear around. He is a member of the core group...

West, 1999 (pp. vii–viii)

Cameron West's alter "Davy" Davy made this drawing on his first day "out."
From West, 1999, p. 51

- Depersonalization disorder is characterized by persistent and distressing feelings of being detached from one's mind or body.

- People suffering from dissociative amnesia forget basic personal information usually related to traumatic or upsetting events.

- In dissociative fugue, the forgetting of one's personal identity is accompanied by travel away from home and sometimes by the assumption of a complete or partial new identity.

- DID involves the existence of two or more distinct personalities within one person that recurrently control the individual's behavior. Interestingly, some studies have reported that different personalities in DID have distinct biological profiles.

Critical Thinking Question | **S**ome experts see the four dissociative disorders as being on a continuum of severity, while other experts argue that depersonalization disorder is so much less disruptive than the other three dissociative disorders that it cannot be placed on a continuum with them. What do you think?

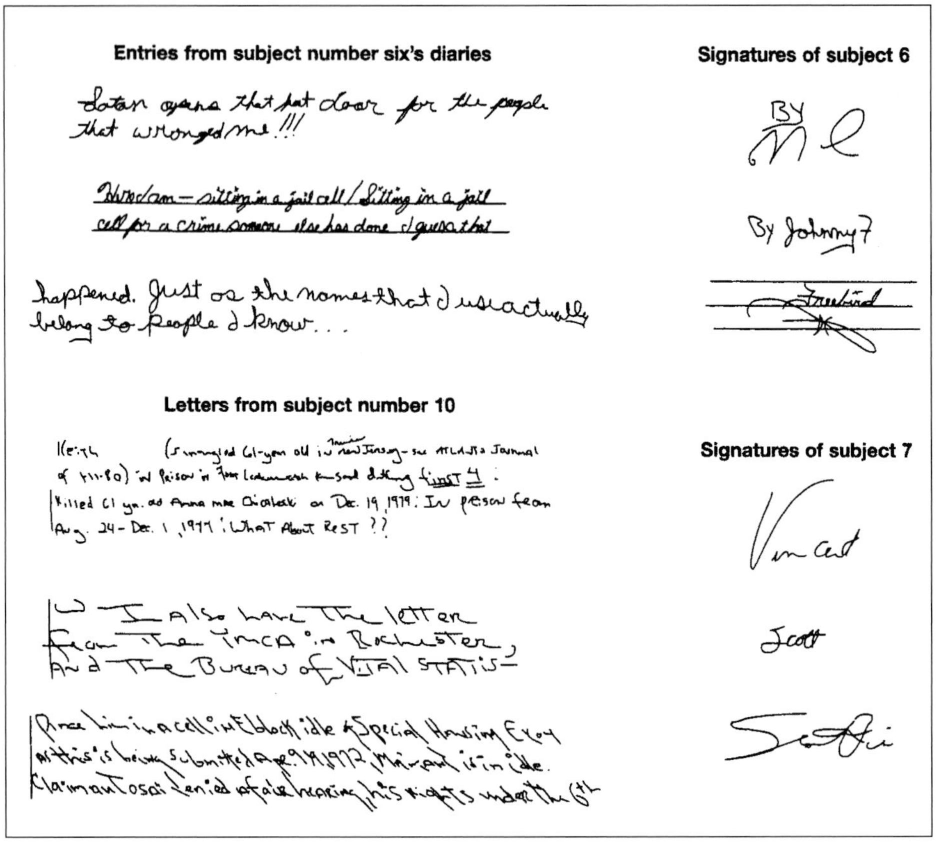

Figure 7.1 Handwriting samples of people suffering from DID A person's handwriting can be like a fingerprint—a unique reflection of individual identity. The wide variety of handwriting samples taken from those with DID appears to demonstrate the radical differences among various personalities within the same person.

From Lewis et al., 1997, p. 1706

Entries from subject number six's diaries

Signatures of subject 6

Letters from subject number 10

Signatures of subject 7

Classification in Demographic Context

We know less about the demographic factors associated with dissociative disorders than we do about many other disorders because, for many years, dissociative disorders were considered to be extremely uncommon and were rarely diagnosed. Despite recent evidence that dissociative disorders are more common than had been previously assumed, we are just beginning to learn about their demographic features (Ross, Joshi, & Currie, 1990). In particular, little is known about whether dissociative disorders occur at different rates or in different forms among members of various socioeconomic groups. In the following sections we describe what is known about age and gender factors in dissociative disorders; unique cultural aspects of dissociative phenomena are described later in the section on *cultural relativism.*

Age

Cases of dissociative disorders in children and adolescents have been reported for years (Fast & Chethik, 1976) but did not become the focus of systematic clinical studies until the mid-1980s (Kluft, 1984, 1985; Putnam, 1985). The dearth of information about childhood dissociation prior to the last two decades is due, in part, to the fact that descriptions of dissociative pathology in adults are not always applicable to children and adolescents. For example, many behaviors that might be considered examples of pathological dissociation in adults are normal aspects of child and adolescent development, such as the presence of an imaginary companion in childhood or fluctuations in sense of self or identity in adolescence.

More recent research and new diagnostic instruments designed especially for children (such as the Child Dissociative Checklist; Putnam, Helmers, & Trickett,

1993) have led to a more refined understanding of the nature of dissociative disorders in children and adolescents. In an extensive study of children with dissociative disorders, Nancy Hornstein and Frank Putnam (1992) found that dissociation in children and adolescents may take the form of extreme forgetfulness or strange variations in academic performance. In very young children with DID, alternate personalities may be seen as external imaginary companions, and they may be based on superheroes or other fictional characters. Unlike the imaginary companions that are often a part of normal child development, children with DID feel that the imaginary companion is in charge of their behavior and "making" them do dangerous or disturbing things. Severe and prolonged trancelike states in which children were unresponsive to and disengaged from their surroundings were also commonly found in children with dissociative disorders.

Lost in the "system" Men suffering from undiagnosed dissociative identity disorder may find themselves serving time for crimes committed by a criminal "alter." Women suffering from the disorder are more likely to be identified through their contact with mental health, as opposed to legal, systems.

Gender

Available evidence indicates that approximately 75% to 90% of the people diagnosed with DID are female (DSM-IV-TR, 2000). This may be due to the fact that girls are far more likely to be the victims of sexual abuse, a major predisposing factor for DID (Finkelhor, 1987). However, some experts believe that men with DID are more likely to become involved with the legal system, due to criminal behavior by one of their alters, than with the mental health system. Thus, prevalence data on DID may underestimate the number of men who might warrant the diagnosis. Indeed, some researchers (Bliss, 1986) have found high rates of DID among male sex offenders.

Less is known about the gender ratios of the other dissociative disorders, partly because studies of dissociative disorders have tended to focus on particular kinds of traumatic experiences that differentially affect men and women. For example, investigations into dissociative disorders in veterans of war have found high rates of dissociative disorders in men (Sargent & Slater, 1941), while studies of dissociative disorders in victims of physical and sexual abuse have found high rates of dissociative disorders in women (Leventhal & Midelfort, 1986).

Cultural and Historical Relativism in Defining and Classifying Dissociative Disorders

Studies indicate that the experience and description of dissociative phenomena are *culturally relative.* For example, the members of some South Asian cultures describe an experience called "spirit possession" which closely resembles the symptoms of dissociative amnesia or fugue (Castillo, 1994). Similarly, in some African and Asian cultures individuals (usually females) fall into what is known as a "possession trance" in which the body is believed to have been taken over by a spirit (Akhtar, 1988; Peltzer, 1989; Suryani, 1984). During a possession trance, the individual is unable to control his or her actions, takes on a new personality, and may demand gifts or favors from family and friends (Gonzales & Griffith, 1996). Clinical descriptions of such trances note that they often occur during times of stress, may last several days, and are not necessarily seen as pathological within their cultural context. Interestingly, most ancient religious texts also tell stories of individuals who become possessed or who enter trance or "altered" states (Castillo, 1991).

Some Eskimo and Central American cultures describe trancelike syndromes during which an individual runs or flees aimlessly until he or she becomes exhausted, and then has no memory of the incident. One dramatic version of this behavior is known as *amok,* a syndrome found in Malaysia (also described in Chapter 2). A person who "runs amok" experiences a period of brooding followed by a violent rampage which is later completely forgotten (APA, 2000). Finally, African Americans in the southern United States and inhabitants of the Bahamas use terms such as "falling out" or "blacking out" to describe a form of dissociation. An episode of falling or blacking out is usually triggered by an emotionally intense experience such as a religious ceremony or a family fight. People who fall or black out usually fall down and are temporarily unable to move, though they are still able to hear and comprehend what is going on around them (Gonzales & Griffith, 1996).

The definition and classification of dissociative disorders is also *historically relative*. As you may recall, dissociative symptoms were included as part of a syndrome classified as **hysteria** (described in detail in Chapter 2) from the days of the Greeks until the mid-twentieth century. When the DSM-I was published in 1952, dissociative disorders were placed together with what are now called the **somatoform disorders** in which physical symptoms are caused by psychological factors (Chapter 14) (APA, 1952). In the DSM-III (1980), dissociative and somatoform disorders were differentiated into separate diagnostic categories in keeping with the DSM-III's emphasis on descriptive diagnosis. The four major dissociative disorders included in the DSM-III are the same four dissociative disorders that are currently classified in the DSM-IV-TR.

The Advantages and Limitations of the DSM-IV-TR Dissociative Disorder Diagnoses

Perhaps one of the most heated debates in all of clinical psychology centers around the diagnosis of DID. Two major camps exist. On one side of the debate are the proponents of the **posttraumatic model** (PTM) who argue that DID is a real disorder which can result from overwhelming childhood experiences such as severe abuse. According to this model, a dissociative response served as a survival strategy that helped the child cope with the overwhelming trauma (Gleaves, 1996). In other words, people develop alternative identities as a way of escaping severe physical or sexual abuse. Colin Ross, a psychiatrist who is an expert in the field of dissociative disorders states that DID develops from "a little girl imagining that the abuse is happening to someone else" (Ross, 1997).

On the other side of the debate stand the proponents of the **sociocognitive model** (SCM) of DID. According to these theorists, the diagnosis of DID is an unfortunate contemporary fad which is fueled by naive or overzealous therapists and the media. For example, one expert describes DID as "a syndrome that consists of rule-governed and goal-directed experiences and displays of multiple role enactments that have been created, legitimized, and maintained by social reinforcement. Patients with DID synthesize these role enactments by drawing on a wide variety of sources of information, including the print and broadcast media, cues provided by therapists, personal experiences, and observations of individuals who have enacted multiple identities" (Lilienfeld et al., 1999, pp. 507–508). In other words, proponents of the sociocognitive model believe that DID is an **iatrogenic** (eye-at-row-GEN-ick) disorder, which translates from Greek to mean "doctor borne." They propose that the disorder is created in suggestible individuals by clinicians who encourage clients, sometimes under hypnosis, to see their complex and opposing traits as independently operating personalities, or who unwittingly communicate this view through various cues.

Consider the PTM and SCM positions on the following facts that are relevant to the debate about the validity of the DID diagnosis:

Hysteria A term used for centuries to describe a syndrome of symptoms that appear to be neurological but do not have a neurological cause; now classified as **conversion disorder.**

Somatoform disorders Disorders in which physical symptoms are caused by psychological factors.

Posttraumatic model A theory of dissociative identity disorder that argues that the disorder results from traumatic childhood experiences.

Sociocognitive model A theory of dissociative identity disorder that argues that the disorder is iatrogenic and/or that it results from socially reinforced multiple role enactments.

Iatrogenic A disorder unintentionally caused by a treatment.

The overwhelming majority of people diagnosed with DID report histories of extreme childhood abuse (Gleaves, 1996).

PTM The validity of the DID diagnosis is supported by its strong association with a history of extreme childhood abuse (see Table 7.7). Many empirical studies have found objective documentation of extreme abuse during the childhoods of individuals who later developed DID (Coons, 1994).

SCM Most reports of child abuse in DID are based exclusively on client recollections, which may or may not be accurate (see Box 7.3, p. 210, and Box 7.4, p. 211 on the recovered memories debate). Even if child abuse is highly correlated with the diagnosis of DID in adulthood, this does not prove either that abuse causes DID, or that DID is a valid diagnosis (Lilienfeld et al., 1999).

The diagnosis of DID has increased dramatically since 1980 (Goettman, Greaves, & Coons, 1992).

PTM DID was properly defined for the first time in the DSM-III, published in 1980 (although it was then called multiple personality disorder). With the growth in awareness and scientific knowledge about the disorder since then, fewer cases are being confused with other dissociative disorders, or with psychotic disorders, and more cases are accurately being diagnosed as DID (Gleaves, 1996).

SCM The increasing public fascination with the concept of multiple personalities has led clinicians to overdiagnose DID in their clients, and suggestible clients may begin to believe that they have multiple personalities (Spanos, 1994).

DID is diagnosed primarily within the United States and Canada.

PTM In the absence of large, systematic studies using standardized assessment measures, the higher rates of DID diagnosis in the U.S. and Canada cannot be assumed to indicate that cases are created iatrogenically in North America (Ross, 1997). DID is, in fact, diagnosed in many countries around the world (Coons et al.,

Percentage of Patients with DID and Reported Histories of Sexual or Physical Abuse				Table 7.7
RESEARCH STUDY	**NUMBER OF PARTICIPANTS IN STUDY**	**SEXUAL TRAUMA OR ABUSE**	**PHYSICAL TRAUMA OR ABUSE**	*From Gleaves, 1996, p. 53.*
Putnam et al. (1986)	100	83.0%	75.0%	
Coons et al. (1988)	50	68.0%	60.0%	
Ross, Norton, & Wozney (1989)	236	79.2%	74.9%	
Ellason et al. (1996)	135	92.3%	90.0%	
Ross et al. (1990)	102	90.2%	82.4%	
Sehultz et al. (1989)	355	86.0%	82.0%	
Boon & Draijer (1993a)	71	77.5%	80.3%	

The Limitations of Retrospective Research

While many clinicians believe that dissociative disorders in general, and DID in particular, are related to the experience of childhood trauma, the vast majority of research in this area has been **retrospective,** meaning that it is based on research participants' recollection of events that occurred in the past. By their very nature, retrospective studies are subject to recall and rumination bias and like many other kinds of studies, they also can suffer from selection, information, investigator, and other forms of bias, as described below.

- **Recall bias:** Human memory can be highly fallible (see Box 7.4, p. 211).

- **Rumination bias:** People who suffer from mental disorders may ruminate about the causes of their disorders and therefore may have more complete or detailed memories than members of a comparison group without mental disorders.

- **Selection bias:** Many retrospective studies only investigate people who already have the disorder in question, and do not survey a comparison group without the disorder.

- **Information bias:** Researchers often limit their investigation to variables they already believe contribute to the disorder in question.

- **Investigator bias:** When researchers ask about past events, they are typically expecting (and usually hoping) to find that the past events they ask about are related to the disorder in question.

An ideal study of the causes of dissociative disorders would involve several design features to minimize the types of bias described above. First, the study would be **prospective**, or forward-looking, in order to allow researchers to avoid the limitations of retrospective methodologies. Such a study would involve: collecting data on a large, random sample of children (minimizing selection bias); measuring a wide variety of variables such as family interactions, IQ, school performance, physical and sexual abuse, other forms of trauma, and so on (minimizing information and investigator bias); collecting objective measures in addition to personal reports (minimizing recall and rumination bias); and following the sample over time to see who develops dissociative disorders. Unfortunately, such studies are costly, time-consuming, and difficult to conduct with samples large enough to yield meaningful results. Further, even if a prospective study found that a variable such as childhood abuse was highly correlated with the later development of DID, we must remember the general principle that *correlation does not prove causation.* Correlational studies can demonstrate that two variables are related, and even that one systematically preceeds the other, but not that one *causes* the other. Only a true experimental design, in which one variable is manipulated while others are held constant, can prove causation.

For obvious moral and ethical reasons, true experimental studies cannot be employed to answer the question of whether trauma causes dissociative disorders. However, in the effort to find answers to this question, researchers can consider the role of trauma in other psychological disorders, look for evidence of nontraumatic causes of dissociation, and seek objective verification for reports of past traumas in people suffering from dissociative disorders.

Retrospective Research based on participants' recall of information about events that occurred in the past.

Recall bias Bias based on distortion of memories for past events.

Rumination bias Bias based on the fact that thinking about past events enhances the memory of such events.

Selection bias Bias based on researching nonrepresentative samples, such as when studies only investigate research subjects who already have the disorder in question and do not investigate a comparison group without the disorder.

Information bias Bias based on researchers only studying variables already believed to be related to the phenomena in question.

Investigator bias Bias based on the influence of the researchers' expectations or preferences on the study's results.

Prospective Research based on data that are collected as the events being studied are occurring, rather than recalling them retrospectively.

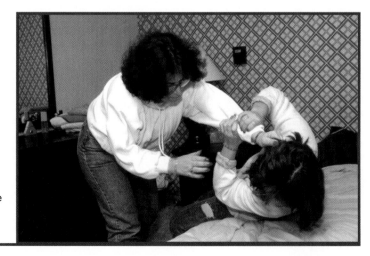

The origins of dissociative identity disorder Many experts on dissociative identity disorder believe that the disorder results from chronic and extreme childhood abuse.

BOX 7.4 From Freud to the American Psychological Association

One Hundred Years of the "Recovered Memories" Debate

How accurate are memories? Can highly significant events be forgotten? If so, can "lost" memories be found again? These questions arise in many areas of psychology but are perhaps most salient in the heated debate over memories of childhood sexual abuse that are "recovered" during adulthood, sometimes in the course of psychotherapy. The debate over the accuracy of such childhood memories is almost as old as the field of psychology itself.

Sigmund Freud, the first practitioner of psychotherapy as we now know it, struggled with this question, a struggle that continues for today's clinicians and researchers. Early in his psychotherapeutic career, Freud had many clients who recalled during therapy experiences of having been sexually exploited as children. Though Freud was initially surprised by these revelations, he believed the memories were real and, in fact, theorized that childhood sexual abuse caused his clients' symptoms of hysteria. In a summary report titled *The Aetiology of Hysteria* (1896), Freud proclaimed that "at the bottom of every case of hysteria there are one or more occurrences of premature sexual experiences, occurrences which belong to the earliest years of childhood, but which can be reproduced through the work of psycho-analysis in spite of the intervening decades." This became known as the "seduction theory" of hysteria.

Freud began to doubt his own theory within a year. As memories of childhood sexual abuse emerged in nearly every one of his clinical cases, he concluded that the sexual abuse of children could not be so rampant among the elite Viennese families whose members he treated. Furthermore, Freud began to see an alternative explanation for these memories; they could be distorted relics of conflicted childhood sexual feelings, in keeping with his emerging theory of childhood psychosexual development. Accordingly, Freud soon modified his original position, arguing that while sexual abuse occurred all too often, memories (which Freud called *psychic reality*) could not be assumed to correspond with *historical reality*, a perspective that became central to the psychodynamic focus on the subjectivity of recollections. Later, Freud explained the shift in his perspective: "I was at last obliged to recognize that these scenes of seduction had never taken place, and that they were only fantasies which my patients had made up" (Freud, 1925). Ultimately Freud took a nuanced position on the question of recovered memories of sexual abuse. According to one of his biographers, Peter Gay, "the col-

lapse of this [seduction] theory did not induce Freud to abandon his belief in the sexual etiology of neurosis or, for that matter, the conviction that some neurotics at least had been sexually victimized by their fathers" (Gay, 1988).

The two sides in the modern debate over recovered memories of sexual abuse echo Freud's struggle. On one side are expert clinicians who believe, based on numerous case examples, that memories of highly traumatic events are often repressed and may emerge years after an event took place. Supporting evidence that traumatic experiences can be exiled from memory comes from empirical studies that compare objective documentation of abuse with the victims' own recollection (or lack thereof) of traumatic experiences. For example, Williams (1994) sought out 129 adult women whose hospital records indicated that they had been treated for childhood sexual abuse. Thirty-eight percent of the women had no recollection of the documented incidents of childhood molestation. Further, the women who were quite young at the time of the abuse, or were molested by someone they knew, were the most likely to have forgotten the abuse.

On the other side of this debate are experts in the area of memory who argue that memories can be highly inaccurate and easily distorted. Elizabeth Loftus, a leader in such research, has shown that memories of childhood events can be retrospectively altered, or even implanted. For example, Loftus (1997) worked with the family members of college-aged research participants to "invent" incidents that never occurred (telling the participants that they had been lost in a mall for a long time or hospitalized overnight as a child) and then asked the family members to tell

(continues)

Recovered memories? In a highly controversial 1990 trial, George Franklin, Sr. was convicted of murdering the childhood friend of his daughter, Eileen Franklin-Lipsker (center). The trial was based on Franklin-Lipsker's sudden recollection of the crime 20 years after it occurred. Franklin's conviction was overturned six years later due, in part, to questions about the validity of Franklin-Lipsker's recovered memories.

BOX 7.4 (continued)

the research participant that such an event had occurred. Loftus found that within two or three interviews, roughly one-quarter of her research participants now "remembered" an event that had never actually happened. Evidence is mixed as to whether memory for events as traumatic as childhood sexual abuse are equally malleable (Pezdek & Hodge; 1999). However, work by Loftus and others (Clancy et al., 2000) shows that children who are asked specific, repeated questions about sexual abuse, or are told by a parent that such events occurred, could mistakenly remember such experiences.

In all likelihood, experts on both sides of the recovered memory debate are partly correct: sometimes memories for traumatic events that actually occurred are repressed and recovered, while in other situations memories of traumatic events have been distorted or created by the individual's imagination, or by parents, investigators, or clinicians. A panel of clinical and research experts convened by the American Psychological Association to study the controversy ended up taking this balanced position. It concluded that:

> Under certain circumstances, memories of abuse that have been forgotten for a long time can be remembered. The mechanism by which such delayed recall occurs is not currently well understood.

and that

> Under certain circumstances it is possible to construct pseudo-memories. These are potentially harmful and disruptive to the person in whom they are induced as well as to his or her social support network.

(APA, 1996)

Given the gravity of allegations of childhood sexual abuse—no one wants to disbelieve a victim or to accuse someone who is innocent—it is incumbent upon members of the clinical and legal professions to be sensitive yet cautious when dealing with recovered memories of abuse.

1991), and evidence suggests that it tends to be grossly underreported in countries where clinicians do not ask about dissociative symptoms (Boon & Draijer, 1993).

SCM Culture-bound examples of dissociative experiences demonstrate that DID-like symptoms are highly influenced by cultural factors. In the words of Nicholas Spanos, one of the leading critics of the posttraumatic model of DID: "When examined across cultures and historical eras, the rule-governed nature of multiple identity enactments and their embeddedness within a legitimizing social matrix becomes clear. Each culture develops its own indigenous theory of multiple identity enactments. These local theories reflect local social structures and institutions, and they translate into culturally specific expectations that guide both the performance of multiple identity enactments and the reactions of the audience to these enactments" (Spanos, 1994, p. 160). Such factors argue against the validity of DID as a unique, cross-cultural disorder.

The symptoms of DID can be convincingly faked or elicited in people who do not suffer from the disorder (Spanos et al., 1986).

PTM Whether or not the symptoms of a disorder can be created in a laboratory setting has nothing to do with the legitimacy of the diagnosis. Depression, psychotic symptoms, and eating disordered behaviors have all been created in "healthy" individuals through experimental methods (Gleaves, 1996).

SCM Studies demonstrating that college-aged subjects can convincingly enact multiple identities and other characteristics of DID support the idea that people may develop DID symptoms in response to external cues and prompts (Lilienfeld et al., 1999).

In all likelihood, the posttraumatic and sociocognitive models are both partly correct. In fact, one of the most prominent advocates of the posttraumatic model—a firm believer in the validity of the DID diagnosis—has reported that he has also seen cases of DID that were created iatrogenically by irresponsible therapists employing poor therapeutic technique (Ross, 1997).

Brief Summary

- Recent research suggests that dissociative disorders also occur in children and adolescents, but may have different clinical features than those usually seen in adults.

- Women are disproportionately represented among those diagnosed with dissociative identity disorder (DID), though the disorder is probably underdiagnosed in men.

- The diagnosis of dissociative disorders is **culturally relative** insofar as dissociative phenomena take different forms in various parts of the world.

- The definition and classification of dissociative symptoms has changed substantially over the last century, an example of **historical relativism**.

- Experts continue to debate the **advantages and limitations** of the DID diagnosis. The main controversy centers on whether DID is a valid disorder usually caused by childhood trauma, or a recent diagnostic fad supported by iatrogenically produced cases.

Critical Thinking Question	**D**o you think a therapist who was skeptical of the DID diagnosis could work effectively with a person who believed that he or she had the disorder?

EXPLAINING AND TREATING DISSOCIATION AND THE DISSOCIATIVE DISORDERS

Clinicians from most theoretical perspectives consider traumatic experiences to be the major cause of dissociative disorders (Kluft, 1996). As you may recall from the discussion of the anxiety disorders (Chapter 5) a *trauma* is an emotionally overwhelming event that falls outside the realm of expectable everyday occurrences. Traumatic experiences come in many forms: war combat, natural disasters, serious accidents, physical or sexual victimization, and so on.

DID, in particular, appears to be related to especially intense and prolonged physical and/or sexual abuse in childhood (Goodwin & Sachs, 1996). In a fascinating study of eleven men and one woman—all incarcerated for murder—who were diagnosed with DID, Dorothy Lewis and her colleagues (1997) used medical, psychiatric, social service, and school records to document histories of extreme abuse. The authors note that the individuals in their study were not just abused, but "tortured," by their caretakers: one man was purposely set on fire by his parents, another was dressed as up as a girl by his grandmother and then offered to his grandfather to be used for sexual gratification. Other accounts of DID, such as the book *Sybil* which tells the story of a woman with sixteen personalities, also detail childhoods filled with horrific physical and sexual abuse (Schreiber, 1973).

While clinicians from most theoretical perspectives agree that trauma is a major causal factor in the dissociative disorders, each theoretical approach offers its own perspective on how and why traumatic events contribute to dissociative phenomena. As is often the case, the various theoretical perspectives are complementary since each focuses on a different component of human functioning when explaining dissociative

Psychopathology and popular culture *Sybil,* a book which detailed the life story of a woman with sixteen personalities, quickly became a best-seller when it was published in 1973. Three years later, Sally Field played the title role in a movie of the same name. The public's fascination with accounts of dissociative identity disorder has fueled debate about the validity of the diagnosis.

experiences. Similarly, many contemporary treatments for dissociative disorders address psychodynamic, behavioral, cognitive, and biological components, another illustration of the core concept of ***multiple causality***. We will take a brief look at each theoretical component and then turn our attention to an integrated treatment model which draws on a variety of theoretical perspectives for treating DID.

Psychodynamic Components

Psychodynamic theorists suggest that dissociative disorders result from the extreme use of the defense mechanism of *dissociation*. Considered as a defense mechanism, dissociation can be understood as being an extreme form of **repression** (Shengold, 1989). As you know, in repression, painful thoughts and memories are split off from consciousness and "forgotten." The defense mechanism of repression is usually employed to forget specific painful memories, and doing so does not necessarily disrupt one's overall sense of identity. In contrast, the defense mechanism of dissociation involves forgetting large amounts of personal information and, accordingly, disrupts personal identity.

DID involves additional defense mechanisms that can contribute to the creation of multiple identities. For example, people with DID employ a form of the defense mechanism known as **splitting** (Kernberg, 1975). Typically, splitting refers to the tendency to see people as being "all good" or "all bad." In the case of DID, good and bad aspects of the self are split off from each other and treated as separate personalities. For the child who is being abused, a "bad" personality who is seen as deserving the abuse may be split off from a "good" personality who is innocent. Similarly, **identification**, the normal developmental experience of imitating and adopting admired qualities in others, may be used excessively as a defense mechanism in DID. For example, abused children who would like to forget what is happening to them may identify with, and adopt as *alters*, the personalities of various people in their surroundings.

The defense mechanisms operative in DID are believed to develop as a means of coping with chronic and severe childhood traumatization. Unfortunately, the same defense mechanisms which may have promoted emotional survival in a highly pathological childhood situation become maladaptive in later life. For obvious reasons, it is difficult to maintain relationships or hold a job if separate personalities take turns dominating one's consciousness.

Psychodynamic Interventions

Psychodynamic interventions for the dissociative disorders emphasize providing a safe and supportive environment for the exploration of past traumas and the defense mechanisms developed to protect against overwhelming emotions (Herman, 1997). The main goal of psychodynamic interventions is not necessarily to gain an accurate account of what occurred in childhood, which can be difficult to do (see Box 7.4), but to help the client improve his or her overall emotional functioning, though this usually involves processing the client's perceptions, thoughts, and feelings about what might have happened in the past (Ganaway, 1994). Some clinicians have suggested that psychodynamic interventions for dissociative disorders require an especially active and supportive approach (Horevitz & Loewenstein, 1994). Clients are encouraged to explore the meaning of painful experiences from the past and gently confronted when their defense mechanisms are employed to maladaptive ends. For example, a clinician using a psychodynamic technique might point out that a client emotionally detaches or switches to an aggressive personality when the therapist asks about traumatic childhood experiences. Therapists can help clients find better ways to cope—other than detaching or switching—with intense feelings of anxiety, anger, or despair.

Repression A defense mechanism consisting of the forgetting of painful or unacceptable mental context.

Splitting A defense mechanism in which one views the self or others as all-good or all-bad in order to ward off conflicted or ambivalent feelings.

Identification Taking on the traits of someone else; sometimes used as a defense mechanism.

Like mother, like daughter *Identification*, a normal developmental process whereby children adopt qualities of people they admire, may be employed to create alternate personalities in dissociative identity disorder.

Modern psychodynamic approaches to dissociative amnesia and fugue treat these conditions as defense mechanisms to protect against the emotional effects of a traumatic experience. Rather than seeking an immediate remission of amnesia, psychodynamic interventions focus on restoring the clients' sense of personal safety, developing a strong therapeutic alliance, and understanding the effects of trauma on the client's general functioning (Loewenstein, 1993). Case reports document that some clients are able to recover and process forgotten traumatic events in the context of safe and supportive long-term therapy (Briere, 1989).

Behavioral Components

Behavioral explanations of dissociative disorders focus mainly on the role of operant conditioning in the development of dissociative behaviors. As you recall, operant conditioning occurs when an individual's behaviors are reinforced or punished; behaviors that are reinforced are more likely to be repeated, while behaviors that are punished tend to disappear. In the midst of traumatic experiences, some people discover that they can remove themselves mentally, if not physically, from what is happening (Darlington, 1996). This splitting of consciousness is usually accompanied by feelings of relief, which, in behavioral terms, are negatively reinforcing (Farley & Barkan, 1997). Learning to dissociate is the psychological equivalent of learning to duck a punch; by dissociating, emotional pain is avoided and the behavior of dissociating is reinforced. When such a person subsequently remembers the traumatic event, or when another traumatic or highly upsetting circumstance occurs, dissociation may be repeated.

These behavioral principles apply to all four of the dissociative disorders. Depersonalization disorder could develop from episodes of depersonalization that provide relief from emotional pain. In dissociative amnesia and fugue, the amnesia for devastating personal events also provides negatively reinforcing relief. A similar principle applies to the dissociative shifts between personalities in DID. Unfortunately, while these behavioral "solutions" provide short-term emotional relief, they create other significant problems in people's lives.

Behavioral Interventions

Operant conditioning principles are involved in almost every approach to treating dissociative disorders and behavioral interventions are especially useful with clients who engage in behaviors that place their own health or the therapy in jeopardy (Linehan, 1993). For example, dissociative clients who threaten suicide, harm themselves in other ways (alcohol abuse, self-injury), or fail to attend sessions are taught how to manage overwhelming feelings in constructive ways, often through the suggestion of specific alternative behaviors (for example, phoning a friend, taking a walk, etc.) (Fine, 1991). Experts in the treatment of dissociative disorders generally agree that addressing self-harming and/or treatment-compromising behaviors should be the first priority in therapy with these clients (Horevitz & Loewenstein, 1994).

Brief Summary

- Clinicians from most theoretical perspectives agree that trauma is the major causal factor in dissociative disorders. Each theoretical approach offers a different perspective on how and why traumatic experiences contribute to dissociative phenomena.

- The psychodynamic approach explains dissociative disorders as resulting from the extreme use of several defense mechanisms, especially dissociation, repression, splitting, and identification. While these defense mechanisms may help people endure traumatic situations, they impair overall functioning. Psychodynamic interventions emphasize providing a supportive environment for helping clients develop adaptive responses to traumatic events.

- Behavioral explanations of dissociative disorders focus on operant-conditioning principles. During a traumatic experience, the splitting of consciousness can bring relief; this negatively reinforced behavior may then be repeated in response to new upsetting events. Behavioral interventions may be especially helpful in reducing self-harming behaviors.

Critical Thinking Question | **What do you think is the most persuasive point of view in the "recovered memory" debate?**

Cognitive Components

There are two predominant cognitive approaches to explaining dissociative disorders: the *self-hypnosis* theory and the *state-dependent learning* theory. The **self-hypnosis** theory suggests that people who dissociate are, in fact, putting themselves in a hypnotic trance state to remove themselves from painful experiences (Bliss, 1986; Frischholz, 1985; Hilgard, 1991). While self-hypnosis and dissociation may not be entirely the same, hypnotic and dissociative states both involve alterations and divisions in consciousness. Several other similarities between dissociation and hypnosis have also been observed. Both are marked by: periods of amnesia, the ability to disregard physically or psychologically painful experiences, the ability to recall previously forgotten memories, and the sense of a "hidden observer," or a part of the self who is not actively conscious, but is aware of what the conscious part of the self is doing.

Some research supports the relationship between hypnosis, dissociation, and trauma. A number of researchers have found that people who suffer from dissociative disorders also tend to score in the very high range on standard measures of hypnotizability (Carlson & Putnam, 1989). Further, some studies have found that children who are severely punished in childhood are more likely to be hypnotizable than children who are not mistreated (Nash & Lynn, 1986; Spiegel & Cardena, 1991). Despite these suggestive links among childhood maltreatment, hypnosis, and dissociative disorders, we are still a long way from understanding exactly how these three phenomena are related to each other.

The concept of **state-dependent learning** comes from research on memory which has shown that people are better able to remember information if they are in the same mood state when a memory is *retrieved* as they were when it was *encoded*. In other words, if you are in a particular mood when studying for a test, your test performance will likely be improved if you are in the same mood when you actually take the test (Bower, 1981). Psychologists believe that state similarity between encoding and retrieval improves memory by providing retrieval cues, such as similar thoughts or feelings, which facilitate the recollection of specific information. State-dependent learning theory has been used to explain the multiple identities and pervasive amnesia of DID. Specifically, some experts have proposed that the traits, abilities, and memories associated with specific personalities in DID are linked to particular states of emotional arousal and thus are forgotten during other emotional states (Putnam, 1992). However, a significant limitation of the state-dependent learning theory in dissociative disorders relates to the finding that state similarity between information encoding and retrieval promotes recall only if the emotional state is not too intense (Kenealy, 1997). As you know, intense emotional states are common in dissociative disorders.

Self-hypnosis The ability to put oneself in a trance state; may contribute to dissociative disorders according to some experts.

State-dependent learning Learning and memory that depend on emotional state similarity between encoding and retrieval.

The power of suggestion Here, a hypnotist puts a group of volunteers to sleep at a state fair. Some experts have raised questions about whether hypnotic interventions for dissociative identity disorder may, in fact, create the symptoms they are designed to treat.

Cognitive Interventions

We will describe two cognitively focused interventions for dissociative disorders: schema-focused cognitive therapy and hypnosis. Schema-focused cognitive therapy addresses maladaptive beliefs that contribute to dissociative disorders, while hypnosis is a widely used but controversial technique employed to help clients recover memories of traumatic events and to reintegrate dissociated mental states.

Schema-Focused Cognitive Therapy **Schema-focused cognitive therapy** (SFCT) assumes that **cognitive schemas**, or organized patterns of thought, are shaped by early life experiences. Emotionally charged schemas—those beliefs that were shaped by very strong feelings—are most likely to lead to cognitive distortions (Young, 1990). Given that dissociation is often triggered by overwhelming emotional experiences, the thinking processes of a person suffering from a dissociative disorder may be characterized by a variety of reality-distorting, maladaptive schemas about the self. Catherine Fine (1992, 1996), an expert in cognitive interventions for dissociative disorders, proposes that much of the disruptive behavior associated with DID can be attributed to processes called *schema maintenance, schema avoidance,* and *schema compensation.*

For example, a client suffering from DID might *maintain* an early maladaptive schema (EMS) that she is a bad person deserving of mistreatment by attending only to information that supports that schema. Cognitive techniques would focus on challenging the perceptions that maintain such a belief, while reframing the client's perception of her own and other people's behavior (for example, she acts "bad" only when she is feeling scared; people who mistreat others have their own problems; and so on). While some EMS are actively maintained, others are actively *avoided* due to their painful emotional content. An adult client who harbors the EMS that she is a helpless child may avoid thoughts and feelings associated with helplessness. For example, she might focus excessively on how she can be of help to others. Cognitive therapy would address how her thinking processes distort reality in order to avoid recognizing her upsetting EMS. Alternatively, the same client might *compensate* for the helpless child EMS by developing a tough and aggressive personality (Fine, 1996). A cognitive intervention would help the client make the connection between her EMS and her compensatory behaviors, and then attempt to correct the distortions of the EMS.

Hypnosis Many clinicians who specialize in the treatment of DID use hypnosis as one element of their work (Putnam, 1989). The aim of hypnotic interventions is to help

Schema-focused cognitive therapy A cognitive intervention for dissociative disorders that focuses on changing cognitive schemas that are based on traumatic childhood experiences.

Cognitive schema Mental models of the world that are used to organize information.

clients gain control over their dissociative reactions and to recover forgotten traumatic memories. By using hypnosis, clients can sometimes be helped to recall and address traumatic experiences at a pace that feels safe and tolerable. Hypnosis can also facilitate *cognitive restructuring* by providing access to memories that can then be considered from new perspectives. For example, a client who felt that she did not do enough to avoid her abusers may remember through hypnosis ways that she had tried, as a child, to protect herself from the abuse (Maldonado & Spiegel, 1998).

Though many clinicians consider hypnosis to be a helpful technique in treating clients with dissociative disorders, its use is controversial. As noted earlier, critics of the diagnosis of DID believe that hypnosis may have iatrogenic effects, meaning that symptoms could be unintentionally caused by hypnotic treatment. For example, memories of abuse, or the experience of separate identities, might be created, rather than discovered, under hypnosis (Spanos, 1994).

In some cases, people suffering from dissociative amnesia and fugue may not remember critical personal information even after a great deal of time has passed. Under these circumstances, hypnosis may be used to recover lost information (Kardiner, 1941). However, many clinicians are reluctant to use hypnosis to gain access to memories that clients may not be emotionally ready to recall. Instead, they may prefer to use traditional techniques or to wait for clients to recover their lost memories spontaneously (Briere, 1989).

Biological Components

Most of the research on the neurobiology of dissociative states has emerged within the last decade. One particularly interesting line of investigation explores how dissociative states can be medically induced in healthy research subjects. Three drugs have been studied in connection with dissociative states: NMDA receptor *antagonists* (which interfere with the functioning of neuronal receptor sites normally reserved for *N*-methyl-D-aspartate), cannabinoids, and serotonergic hallucinogens (Krystal et al., 1998). Research subjects who took ketamine or phencyclidine, both NMDA receptor antagonists, reported a wide variety of dissociative symptoms: the slowing of time, altered sensory experiences, impairment of identity awareness, and constricted attention in the form of "tunnel vision" or the feeling of being in a fog (Javitt & Zukin, 1991). Tetrahydrocannabinol (THC), the main psychoactive component in the cannabinoids (such as marijuana), can produce depersonalization, a sense that the external world is not real *(derealization),* perceptual changes, and disorientation to time (Krystal et al., 1998). Serotonergic hallucinogens, such as LSD (lysergic acid diethylamide) are also known to produce dissociative symptoms (Freedman, 1968). Indeed, many people recreationally use hallucinogens specifically to experience the dissociated states they induce (Chapter 9). While it remains unclear exactly how these drugs produce dissociative experiences, their effects suggest that glutamate receptors (which receive NMDA), G-protein-coupled receptors (which receive cannabinoids), and serotonin-2 receptors (which receive serotonergic hallucinogens) are involved in dissociation.

In addition to discovering some of the neurochemical pathways that may contribute to dissociative experiences, researchers are also learning more about the involvement of specific brain structures in dissociation. The thalamus, for example, which acts as a gateway between external sensory stimulation and higher mental functions (Chapter 3), may play a key role in dissociation. Among its functions, the thalamus aids in the regulation of sleep and dreaming (Steriade & McCarley, 1990). Given the similarities between dreaming and dissociative states, some researchers are investigating the possibility that dissociation involves alterations in the normal functioning of the thalamus (Llinas & Pare, 1991; Mahowald & Schenck, 1991).

Biological Interventions

Partly because neurobiological research on dissociation is relatively new, medications designed specifically to treat dissociation are not yet available (Krystal et al., 1998). However, the discovery that ketamine can generate dissociative experiences in healthy subjects has led some researchers to consider the possibility that drugs that enhance NMDA receptors could be used to alleviate dissociative symptoms (Domino, 1992).

Narcosynthesis, the use of barbiturates such as sodium amytal to gain access to forgotten experiences, was employed during World War II with soldiers suffering from dissociative amnesia or fugue. How these "amytal interviews" work is not well understood; some researchers suspect that the sedation and anxiety reduction caused by the medication simply lessens reluctance to recall anxiety-provoking experiences. Narcosynthesis is rarely used today as it is not always effective and people are often unable to recall what they remembered once the drug wears off (Krystal et al., 1998). Currently, antidepressants and anxiolytics (anti-anxiety drugs) are sometimes used to provide relief from depression and anxiety symptoms in individuals with dissociative disorders (Loewenstein, 1991).

The Multiple Causality of Dissociative Disorders

As we have noted, the dissociative disorders provide an excellent example of the core concept of *multiple causality* since the various theoretical explanations and interventions complement each other. For example, in all of the dissociative disorders, defense mechanisms (psychodynamic component) may be used to reduce overwhelming anxiety, and the subsequent reduction in anxiety negatively reinforces (behavioral component) the further use of these defense mechanisms. This cycle is supported by trauma-focused maladaptive schemas (cognitive component) that involve a preoccupation with traumatic experiences. Finally, each of these mental processes may be influenced by or contribute to changes in brain structures and functions that regulate dissociative experiences (biological component).

Accordingly, the general consensus among experts who treat dissociative disorders is that a **multi-modal,** integrated approach works best, especially when treating the most complex dissociative disorder: DID. Often, techniques associated with different theoretical approaches are employed at different stages of treatment (Braun, 1986; Horevitz & Loewenstein, 1994; Putnam, 1989). What follows is a summary of the stages of the treatment of DID as described by Richard Kluft (1993), who has integrated his own stage model of treatment with similar models proposed by other experts.

Stage One: Establishing the psychotherapy
The major goals of this stage are to introduce the client to the treatment plan, make an appropriate diagnosis, and establish feelings of hope and confidence that the therapy, though difficult at times, will be helpful. The clinician works hard to develop a relationship with the client and to establish the beginnings of a therapeutic alliance.

Stage Two: Preliminary interventions
In the second stage of therapy, the clinician seeks to establish a relationship with any subpersonalities that are readily accessible, and to convince them to accept the diagnosis of DID. This stage of treatment frequently involves interventions such as making agreements with self-destructive alters not to end the treatment prematurely and to reduce self-harming behaviors. When necessary, symptomatic relief may be sought by the adjunctive use of psychotropic drugs such as antidepressants or anti-anxiety medications.

"Truth serum" treatment World War II soldiers suffering from dissociative amnesia or fugue, often in the wake of highly traumatic war experiences, were sometimes given sodium amytal in order to help retrieve their lost memories.

Narcosynthesis The use of medication to promote therapeutic remembering; used during World War II to help soldiers remember forgotten traumatic incidents.

Multi-modal A treatment strategy that integrates a variety of theoretical perspectives.

Stage Three: *History gathering and mapping*

The clinician and client now work together to gather information about all of the subpersonalities. Each personality is assessed in terms of its age, traits, functions, problems, time of creation, and its knowledge of and relationships with the other personalities. With this information, the client and clinician can work together to understand how the subpersonalities interact with each other and encourage cooperation among the various alters.

Stage Four: *Metabolism of the trauma*

In this stage of treatment, the different subpersonalities discuss and explore traumatic memories from the past. If necessary, hypnosis may be used to help clients recall forgotten traumas. This stage is often extremely painful and taxing for the client, and may result in emotional crises or interruptions in the therapy if the earlier stages have not been managed adequately.

Stage Five: *Moving toward integration-resolution*

The client continues to work through each alters' traumatic memories and to promote further cooperation and communication among the subpersonalities. The various personalities are helped to recognize, understand, and empathize with each other; doing so may begin to dissolve some of the boundaries between particular alters. In this stage of therapy, the client begins to see what were previously separate personalities as potentially different sides of one, integrated personality.

Stage Six: *Integration-resolution*

The work from the previous stage continues as the therapist and client endeavor to blend the various traits of the different personalities into one complex, but unified, personality. If the client is unable to merge divergent personalities with each other, he or she may work toward what is known as a *resolution,* in which the various personalities agree to collaborate with each other rather than pursuing their own individual interests at each other's expense.

Stage Seven: *Learning new coping skills*

Once the client has consolidated multiple personalities, or achieved a resolution among various personalities, he or she will need to develop coping skills for managing stressful situations that were previously dealt with by dissociation. In this phase of therapy, the clinician may act as a "coach" who helps the client to consider, try, and evaluate new ways of handling old problems.

Stage Eight: *Solidification of gains and working-through*

Having achieved a more stable personality structure, the client may now be able to address problems that were obscured by the presence of multiple personalities. This stage of treatment may last at least as long as all of the stages that preceded it, especially as exploration is interwoven with interventions to improve functioning in current relationships and other aspects of daily life. When the client and therapist agree that they have accomplished as much as possible, a plan is made to complete the work, which allows plenty of time to address reactions to the ending of therapy and to review the achievements of treatment.

Stage Nine: *Follow-up*

After the psychotherapy has ended, clinicians arrange for periodic follow-up to assess the stability of therapeutic gains and to offer continued treatment, if needed.

Brief Summary

- Cognitive explanations of dissociative disorders focus on two areas: self-hypnosis and state-dependent learning. Cognitive interventions for dissociative disorders may involve the identification and evaluation of early maladaptive schemas (EMS) or the induction of hypnotic states in which clients suffering from dissociative identity disorder (DID) can gain control over their dissociative reactions and recall previously forgotten traumatic experiences. Hypnosis remains controversial because of its potential for iatrogenic effects.

- Biological research has focused on understanding how certain drugs produce dissociative states, and on the possibility that dissociation involves alterations in the normal functioning of the thalamus. Medications designed specifically to treat dissociative symptoms are not yet available but researchers are investigating the possibility that drugs that enhance NMDA receptors might be useful in treating dissociative disorders.

- In keeping with the principle of *multiple causality*, the various theoretical components provide complementary accounts of the processes underlying dissociative disorders. An integrated, multi-modal approach is particularly useful when attempting to conceptualize and treat a complex condition like dissociative identity disorder (DID).

Critical Thinking Question	You may have noticed substantial overlap in how the psychodynamic, cognitive, and behavioral approaches explain dissociative disorders. Where do the approaches overlap? Where do they diverge?

Case Vignettes | Treatment
John | Depersonalization Disorder

John sought help at his college counseling center because he was often feeling "spacey" in a way that interfered with his schoolwork. After an evaluation, the psychologist recommended therapy and noted that John's otherwise lively manner seemed to go flat when he talked about his father and the time around his father's death. The psychologist suggested that perhaps John was still struggling with feelings about his father's death. John asserted that he had already dealt with his father's death, especially since he had "two entire months of sadness" between the time of his father's cancer diagnosis and the time when he died.

However, in the next session, John reported the following dream: "I spent most of the evening at my own bachelor party, but it was never clear who I was marrying. Though I was at least 25, at the end of the evening I returned to my current dorm room where I found my father was sitting at my desk. When I told him that I missed him at the party he said that I should stop yelling at him, and he abruptly left the room." The dream helped John to recognize that he did continue to have a lot of thoughts and feelings about his father, such as feelings that his father was missing out on important events in his life (such as a future marriage) and that he felt abandoned and angered by his father's early death.

Over time, John was able to talk with his therapist in a heartfelt way about how he wished he could tell his father about his college life, and how sad he was that his father would not see him graduate from college. John began to cry during some sessions, especially when he talked about the enormous amount of physical pain his father had endured in the last months of his life and how difficult it had been to see his previously powerful father reduced to such a helpless state. Around the same time, John found that he was no longer experiencing depersonalization and he became convinced that his "spacing out" had been a way to avoid his grief.

Case Discussion | Depersonalization Disorder

John was able to benefit from psychodynamic interventions aimed at understanding the root causes of his depersonalization symptoms. As John became increasingly comfortable with and aware of the painful feelings he had about his father's death, he no longer needed to use dissociation as a defense mechanism to block out distressing emotions.

Margaret | Dissociative Identity Disorder

As noted earlier, Margaret and her therapist soon learned that mild-mannered Margaret had two additional personalities: the promiscuous Janie, and the terrified young girl, Suzie. Margaret spent a great deal of time in therapy trying to understand the roles that each personality played. It became clear that by becoming Janie, Margaret could act out impulses that she could not otherwise tolerate, and that Suzie served the function of containing all of the painful memories from the past that Margaret did not wish to recall. As the therapy progressed, Margaret would turn into Suzie frequently during the sessions. The therapist observed that this seemed to happen most often when Margaret spoke about her unstable father, who had raised her alone after her mother died when she was five. Margaret began to describe strange memories, starting just after her mother's death, of "games" with her father in which he would pretend she was "mommy" and he would teach her "how to make a baby." Then he would get mad, hit her, and leave, sometimes for days. Margaret began to understand that she had inexplicably "forgotten" so much of her childhood in an effort to forget how betrayed, debased, and damaged she felt by the sexual abuse and neglect she'd suffered.

As Margaret recalled more and more of what had happened to her when she was growing up, she became extremely depressed. She had difficulty sleeping, often missed work, was at risk of losing her job, and was frequently suicidal. Margaret's therapist suggested that perhaps Margaret would be better able to function if she were to begin a course of antidepressant medication. The antidepressants did help, and Margaret and her therapist returned to the task of working through the painful memories from Margaret's childhood. As Margaret remembered what had happened when she was young, Suzie made fewer appearances in the therapy. In time, Margaret was able to accept some of her own "darker" parts and many aspects of Janie were also integrated into Margaret's personality.

Occasionally, Margaret would "forget" to attend several sessions in a row. Together, Margaret and her therapist understood that Margaret would skip sessions when she was feeling afraid of what she might remember or discover about herself. At other times, Margaret would forget her appointments because she felt that her therapist was being "pushy" and making her feel bad in a way that felt uncomfortably familiar. They talked about how old feelings of being mistreated and manipulated had made their way into the therapy relationship. Margaret agreed that she would let the therapist know when she did not want to talk about certain things so that she wouldn't feel pushed or have to worry about being emotionally overwhelmed.

Margaret remained in therapy for many years. At times, she used the therapy to talk about newly remembered experiences with her father, and at other times, she sought the therapist's advice on how to approach new relationships in a less self-destructive manner. Though Margaret often became disconnected from her surroundings when painful feelings were triggered, she was much better able to tolerate and understand her emotions and no longer needed to use alters in order to feel safe.

Case Discussion | Dissociative Identity Disorder

Margaret's therapist employed the multi-modal, stage approach to treat dissociative identity disorder (DID), as described earlier in the chapter. Her therapist used psychodynamic methods to explore traumatic memories and to address transference feelings when they arose in the therapy relationship. Cognitive-behavioral techniques were used to "coach" Margaret on how to manage new relationships in her life. A biological intervention was included when Margaret's depressive symptoms interfered with her ability to function in her life, work, or in therapy. Like most people suffering from DID, Margaret required an open-ended therapy that lasted many years.

Chapter Summary

- *Dissociation* refers to alterations in consciousness, memory, sense of identity, or any combination of the three.

- Dissociation can be adaptive or maladaptive depending on how severe it is on the **continuum between normal and abnormal behavior** and on the **context** in which it occurs.

- The DSM-IV-TR describes four main dissociative disorders: depersonalization disorder, dissociative amnesia, dissociative fugue, and dissociative identity disorder (DID).

- The experience and classification of dissociative phenomena are **culturally and historically relative**. For example, dissociative phenomena take different forms in different parts of the world, and the classification of dissociative disorders has changed substantially over the past century.

- The major issue concerning the **advantages and limitations** of the DSM-IV-TR dissociative disorder diagnoses centers on whether DID is a valid diagnostic entity or whether it is a diagnostic fad in which symptoms are iatrogenically created in suggestible individuals.

- Clinicians from most theoretical perspectives agree that trauma is the major causal factor in most dissociative disorders, yet each theoretical approach offers its own way of understanding how and why traumatic experiences contribute to dissociative disorders.

- The various theoretical components provide complementary accounts of the processes underlying dissociative disorders, in keeping with the principle of **multiple causality.** An integrated multi-modal approach is particularly useful when attempting to conceptualize and treat a complex disorder like DID.

Van Gogh, *Interiuer d'un Restaurant*, 1887. ©Christie's Images.

Vincent van Gogh (1853–1890) drew upon the Impressionist movement's explorations of color and light to create paintings saturated with intense and often distorted hues. Many of Van Gogh's canvases have a tactile, sculptural quality as his thickly applied layers of paint and obvious brushstrokes *...continues on page 226*

vincent van gogh

chapter eight

EATING, WEIGHT, AND THE EATING DISORDERS

Case Vignettes

Megan, age 15, started to participate in competitive gymnastics when she was 8 years old. When puberty began at age 13 she was upset by the changes in her body. She felt that her widening hips and increasing breast size interfered with gymnastics and wished that she could keep her body in its prepubescent form. Megan decided to stop eating sweets and soon received some encouraging comments from her gymnastics coach about her weight loss. For the next four months, she began to monitor what and how much she ate and limited herself to a daily total of 1,000 calories. Megan lost weight quickly and before long she weighed only 85 pounds even though she was 5'4" tall. Her parents and coach became extremely concerned about her weight loss, especially when Megan began to faint after particularly intense practices. Megan, however, continued to feel that her hips were too big and that she had more weight to lose. Even though Megan looked like a walking skeleton, she persisted with her diet until she collapsed one day at school and was rushed to the hospital. She weighed 72 pounds.

Theresa, a 19-year-old sophomore, sought help at her college counseling center when she realized that she was unable to control her impulses to binge eat and then "purge" by making herself vomit. She told the therapist that she had never worried about her weight before coming to college, and that she had had a "normal, happy" childhood. Theresa explained that the first time she made herself throw up after eating occurred five months earlier after she had eaten some of a sorority sister's birthday cake shortly after deciding that she was going to give up sweets as part of a diet. Theresa felt guilty for breaking her diet and mentioned to her roommate that she wished that she had exercised more self-control. Theresa's roommate sympathized with her situation and showed Theresa how she could make herself vomit by putting a toothbrush down her throat. Theresa tried it and found that she no longer felt guilty and, in fact, felt thinner than she had before the birthday party.

Soon, Theresa began to eat much more food than she needed because she knew that she could "get rid of any extra." She began to worry about her new habit when she started to feel that she could not control her eating. Whenever she was stressed or upset, Theresa would eat a huge amount of food quickly. She hated the way that she shoved food into her mouth, but she could not make herself stop until she felt sick to her stomach. She felt "disgusting" and would relieve some of her discomfort by making herself vomit. This helped her to feel less physically ill but left her feeling ashamed for giving in to her urges to overeat and then throw up.

...continued from page 224

reveal the strength of his emotional response to his subjects. Van Gogh's famous act of cutting off his own ear provides only one example of his abnormal behaviors: he also experienced auditory and visual hallucinations, sometimes assaulted orderlies in the asylum to which he had himself committed, and even ate the paint with which he worked. This last symptom is technically known as *pica*, an eating disturbance in which an individual consumes nonnutritive substances.

DEFINING EATING DISORDERS

While Megan keeps extremely tight control of her diet and Theresa cannot control how much she eats, both are at the mercy of their feelings about food. Megan and Theresa suffer from what are known as *eating disorders*. Megan thinks about her weight constantly and is convinced that she weighs too much even though she is alarmingly thin. Megan is so preoccupied with being thin that she has put herself at risk for a variety of serious medical disorders. Theresa, in contrast, feels that her eating is out of control. She comforts herself by overeating when she is upset and cannot keep herself from eating much more food than her body needs. In order to manage her overeating she deliberately vomits. For Theresa, food is not simply a source of nourishment; it is an emotional comfort, but also an enemy.

Recent years have brought a growing awareness of the prevalence and severity of eating disorders, particularly among young women. In the last few decades eating disorders have become a part of mainstream culture as the fashion industry continues to feature increasingly thin models in popular advertisements. Indeed, one recent study found that half of *Playboy* centerfolds and a third of models meet criteria for being severely underweight (Oldenberg, 1998).

While there is a great deal of debate about what causes eating disorders (an issue we'll get to soon) there is no question that the rates of eating disorders in the United States are alarmingly high. Presently, between 0.5% and 3% of American women suffer from *anorexia nervosa,* which is technically defined as refusal to maintain a normal body weight, while 1% to 3% suffer from *bulimia nervosa,* which is characterized by repeated binge eating followed by compensatory measures, such as self-induced vomiting or excessive exercise, to avoid weight gain (APA, 2000a; Shisslak, Crago, & Estes, 1995). In addition, many individuals who are not technically anorexic or bulimic struggle in their relationships with food, exercise, and weight. How do we tell the difference between "normal" concerns about weight and

Starving for success Models, dancers, and members of other low-weight subcultures, are expected and encouraged to engage in many of the behaviors associated with eating disorders.

eating disorders? To answer that question, we return to two core concepts: the *continuum between normal and abnormal behavior* and the *importance of context* in defining and understanding abnormality.

The Continuum Between Normal and Abnormal Eating

While up to 6% of American women may suffer from anorexia or bulimia, many more suffer from "subclinical" eating disorders (meaning that they have some but not all of the symptoms of an eating disorder) and half of all American women are dieting at any given time (Brownell, 1995). On the *continuum between normal and abnormal* eating behavior, we could place people who are at a healthy weight and have no concerns about their weight at one end, and people who are severely anorexic or bulimic at the other. Between these two poles we would find a variety of conditions: people who are mildly overweight or underweight; people of normal weight who worry about their weight all the time; people who feel inordinately guilty when they eat unhealthy foods; people who radically restrict their food options for fear of gaining weight; people who engage in compulsive exercise to maintain normal weight, and so on. In other words, not everyone who has an eating-related problem fits the definitions of anorexia or bulimia, and not everyone with anorexic or bulimic tendencies has a full-blown eating disorder. As we'll see, the DSM-IV-TR criteria for anorexia and bulimia include guidelines for defining how much weight loss, and how much bingeing and purging is necessary for a diagnosis of anorexia or bulimia. Although these diagnoses reflect extreme versions of behaviors that are relatively common, the behaviors associated with anorexia and bulimia are still potentially problematic even in their milder forms.

The Importance of Context in Defining Abnormal Eating

In addition to considering the *continuum* of eating behaviors, we must also consider *context* when defining abnormal eating. In some subcultures, eating disordered behavior is the norm. For example, the fashion and entertainment industries are widely populated by women who weigh less than 85% of what is considered normal for their heights—one of the main diagnostic criteria for anorexia. Professional dancers and competitive gymnasts also commonly maintain very low body weights, and wrestlers, jockeys, and boxers engage in many of the behaviors associated with bulimia to drop weight when needed. Do most models, dancers, gymnasts, and jockeys therefore have eating disorders? The best answer is that some do and some do not. Members of these "low-weight" subcultures can point to those among them who are extreme even by the group's stringent weight standards, such as the actress Calista Flockhart of *Ally McBeal* fame. Yet there are also some models, gymnasts, and wrestlers who return to normal weights and eating patterns when they leave the *context* in which success depends on maintaining a very low weight. As with all disorders, eating disorders can only be defined and understood in the context of a particular individual's life circumstances. This complicates the task of defining abnormality among members of these groups, but clinicians can still make appropriate diagnoses by paying attention to each individual's circumstances when assessing whether an eating-related problem exists.

Brief Summary

- As many as 6% of American women suffer from the eating disorders anorexia nervosa and bulimia nervosa.
- Disordered eating occurs along a *continuum*. Eating disordered behavior (such as excessive worrying about food and weight) can be problematic even if it does not meet the diagnostic criteria for anorexia or bulimia.

Too thin? Calista Flockhart, star of the television show *Ally McBeal,* created quite a stir when she arrived at the 1998 Emmy awards looking gaunt and emaciated. Her extremely thin physique raised questions about whether she'd crossed the line to having an eating disorder.

Anorexia nervosa A disorder involving extreme thinness, often achieved through self-starvation.

- Eating disordered behavior must be considered within the **context** in which it occurs. In some subcultures (professional dance, boxing, etc.) eating disordered behavior is the norm, and this has to be taken into account in determining if an individual member of the subculture has an eating disorder.

Critical Thinking Question	**If Theresa (described at the beginning of the chapter) only binges and purges when she is at her sorority house and surrounded by other women who do the same, would you consider her to have an eating disorder? Why or why not?**

CLASSIFYING EATING DISORDERS

The DSM-IV-TR identifies three eating disorders: *anorexia nervosa, bulimia nervosa,* and *eating disorder not otherwise specified.*

Anorexia nervosa is primarily characterized by extreme thinness while bulimia nervosa involves episodes of consuming inordinately large amounts of food followed by compensatory behaviors, such as vomiting, to avoid weight gain. The diagnosis of eating disorder not otherwise specified applies to some eating disordered behaviors that do not meet the diagnostic criteria for anorexia or bulimia.

The DSM-IV-TR Categories

Having addressed some questions about how to define eating disorders, let's turn our attention to the DSM-IV-TR eating disorder diagnoses.

Anorexia Nervosa

Anorexia nervosa involves a refusal to maintain a body weight that is at least 85% of what would be considered normal for an individual's height and age. People who suffer from anorexia are usually very fearful of gaining weight and will persist in dieting even when they are bone-thin and experiencing many of the physical and psychological symptoms associated with severe malnutrition. Anorexia is often perpetuated by significant cognitive distortions in the perception of one's own weight and shape. Though emaciated, many people with anorexia believe that they are still overweight

Table 8.1	**The DSM-IV-TR Eating Disorders**
Adapted from DSM-IV-TR (APA, 2000); prevalence data from APA, 2000; Shisslak, Crago, & Estes, 1995	**Anorexia nervosa** ▪ Refusal to maintain a minimally normal body weight (prevalence estimate among women: 0.5%–1.0%; prevalence rates for men: 0.05%–0.1%.
	Bulimia nervosa ▪ Binge eating and inappropriate compensatory measures to avoid weight gain (prevalence estimate among women: 1%–3%; prevalence estimate among men: 0.1%–0.3%).
	Eating disorder not otherwise specified ▪ Disordered eating that does not meet the diagnostic criteria for anorexia or bulimia nervosa (prevalence rates unknown).

and continue to diet in order to lose what they consider to be excess weight. People with anorexia become obsessed with their efforts to stay thin; feelings of personal value or worth are often completely contingent upon success in losing weight. Women who suffer from anorexia also usually stop menstruating (see Table 8.2).

Case Illustration Janice, age 16, began to lose weight rapidly during her sophomore year in high school when she switched from the public school she had been attending to an elite private school. Though she was excited about the many opportunities available at her new school, Janice worried about her ability to keep up with her peers in the classroom. As her first year at the new school progressed, Janice developed an increasingly ascetic approach to life. She ran around the school track for an hour each day and would have joined the school's cross-country team if she hadn't worried that the meets would cut into her rigid study schedule. Before long, Janice started to skip all desserts and some entire meals because she felt that her body did not look quite the way she wanted. She took pride in limiting her caloric intake, sometimes eating only a few vegetables and a handful of crackers all day. By December of her sophomore year her weight had dropped from 115 to 90 pounds. Though Janice's parents expressed concern about her rapid weight loss, Janice interpreted their comments as praise for her self-discipline and strong academic showing at her new school and she returned for her second semester with a strengthened devotion to exercise, hard work, and dieting.

The severe weight loss associated with anorexia has a number of psychological and physical effects. Clients with anorexia are often irritable, have a diminished interest in sex, and may suffer from insomnia (APA, 2000a). Depression and anxiety occur in at least half of people with anorexia, though there is some question as to whether mood disturbances result from or contribute to eating disorders (Braun, Sunday, & Halmi, 1994). Individuals suffering from anorexia are also likely to have some dependent and perfectionistic personality traits, although again the direction of causality is not entirely clear (Herzog, Nussbaum, & Marmor, 1996).

The numerous physical symptoms associated with anorexia (see Table 8.4, page 231), such as the dramatic slowing of metabolism and hypotension (low blood pressure), represent the body's natural response to the effects of starvation. People suffering from anorexia or bulimia run the risk of inducing **electrolyte** imbalances in their bodies through chronic starvation and dehydration, or starvation followed by bingeing. Electrolytes are charged molecules that regulate nerve and muscle impulses throughout the body; accordingly, severe electrolyte imbalances may result in heart attacks and death. Anorexia is one of the most dangerous forms of psychopathology: up to 10% of people suffering from anorexia die of heart attacks or one of the other physi-

A deadly disorder Gymnast Christy Henrich competes at the 1988 Olympic Trials. Though she was 4 foot 10 inches and weighed only 90 pounds, an American judge remarked that Henrich would need to lose weight if she hoped to make the U.S. team. Six years later she was dead from the effects of severe anorexia.

Electrolytes Charged molecules that regulate nerve and muscle impulses throughout the body.

Diagnostic Criteria for Anorexia Nervosa	Table 8.2

Adapted from the DSM-IV-TR (APA, 2000)

- Refusal to maintain body weight at or above minimally normal weight for age and height (less than 85% of expectable weight).
- Intense fear of gaining weight or becoming fat, even though underweight.
- Disturbance in the way in which one's body or shape is experienced, undue influence of body weight or shape on self-evaluation, or denial of the seriousness of current low body weight.
- In women, the absence of at least three consecutive menstrual cycles.

Severe perceptual distortions Despite sometimes obvious emaciation, people suffering from anorexia have highly distorted perceptions of their own weight and shape and will continue to see themselves as being overweight.

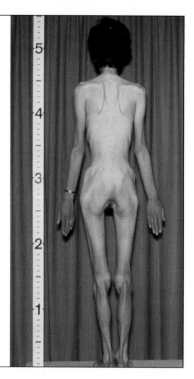

Restricting type anorexia Anorexia in which the individual loses weight by severely restricting food intake.

Binge-eating/purging type anorexia Anorexia in which the individual loses weight by bingeing and purging.

Bulimia nervosa A disorder involving repeated binge eating followed by compensatory measures to avoid weight gain.

cal effects of starvation (Nielsen, 2001). Even people who recover from anorexia face the possibility of having done permanent damage to their skeletal and reproductive systems.

The DSM-IV-TR distinguishes between two subtypes of anorexia nervosa based on the method of weight loss. People with anorexia who lose weight by restricting their food intake are classified as having **restricting type anorexia.** They do not binge eat and do not attempt to "purge" the food they eat through behaviors such as vomiting. In most cases, restricting type anorexics eat extremely small amounts of food (for example, only an apple and a piece of tofu each day). However, there are also restricting type anorexics who eat normal amounts of food but exercise so much that they remain significantly below normal body weight. People with anorexia who lose weight by bingeing and purging (usually by inducing vomiting or by abusing laxatives and water-reducing pills called diuretics) are classified as having **binge-eating/purging type anorexia.** Binge-eating/purging type anorexics differ from people with bulimia (see Table 8.3) because they lose weight to the point where they are 15% or more below normal body weight for their height.

Bulimia Nervosa

Bulimia nervosa is a repeated pattern of eating an excessive amount of food in a very short period of time (bingeing) and then engaging in behaviors to compensate for the extreme food intake and to avoid weight gain (purging). Most people with bulimia report that they feel out of control while bingeing and that they cannot stop eating until they are uncomfortably full or sick to their stomachs. The intense feeling of loss of control associated with bingeing is often described in terms similar to those used by alcoholics or drug addicts who cannot control their compulsive desire to use substances. Like people with anorexia, people with bulimia are preoccupied with their weight and may measure their self-worth mainly in terms of their weight and what they have (or haven't) eaten. However, in contrast to those suffering from anorexia, individuals with bulimia are typically at or above a normal weight.

Table 8.3	Diagnostic Criteria for Bulimia Nervosa
Adapted from DSM-IV-TR (APA, 2000)	• Recurrent episodes of binge eating characterized by eating an unusually large amount of food in a discrete period of time and feeling unable to stop eating or control what or how much one is eating. • Recurrent inappropriate compensatory behavior in order to prevent weight gain, such as self-induced vomiting, misuse of laxatives or diuretics, fasting, or excessive exercise. • The binge eating and inappropriate compensatory behaviors both occur, on average, at least twice a week for 3 months. • Self-evaluation is unduly influenced by body weight and shape.

Case Illustration Marsha, a buyer for a major department store, managed to maintain a façade of competence and control despite her difficult battle with bulimia. Soon after she turned 25, Marsha was given an exciting, but very stressful, promotion at her job. While celebrating the promotion with friends, Marsha ate much more food than usual and went home feeling upset with herself for eating so much. She resolved that she would join a gym the next day. Marsha followed through on her resolution and felt better about herself immediately after her first intense workout. In an effort to keep from gaining weight, Marsha decided to limit her food intake and to continue to work out. After several days of eating little and exercising a lot, Marsha "broke down" and ate an entire pizza and a gallon of ice cream in about 20 minutes. Feeling terrible about the binge, she marched off to the gym and exercised for five hours until the calorie count on her exercise machine indicated that she burned off all of the food she had just eaten. A pattern quickly developed: Marsha would undereat for several days, "break down" from hunger, binge, and then try to "exercise off" all of the calories she had consumed. Marsha sometimes spent hours exercising after a particularly large binge. Despite the exercise, Marsha slowly gained weight over the next several months and complained to her friends that she felt like "a horrible, fat pig."

Like anorexia, bulimia has powerful psychological and physical effects (see Box 8.1). People with bulimia also experience high levels of depression and anxiety, but they tend to suffer from even greater mood instability and have more difficulty controlling their impulses than people with anorexia (Braun, Sunday, & Halmi, 1994). For example, people suffering from bulimia are far more likely than people who are anorexic to abuse drugs and alcohol, even when factors such as age and eating disorder severity are taken into account (Weiderman & Pryor, 1996). Bulimia also commonly co-occurs with personality disorders, especially borderline personality disorder (Chapter 11), a disorder characterized by chronic mood instability and impulsive behavior (Diaz-Marsa, Carrasco, & Saiz, 2000). People with bulimia usually suffer from a variety of medical symptoms at the time of their eating disorder, and even after they have recovered. Many of the medical problems associated with bulimia are due to the damaging effects that chronic vomiting has on the throat, glands, and teeth (see Table 8.4).

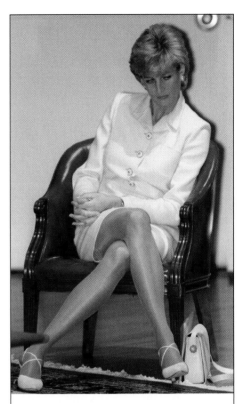

Tragic Princess Princess Diana, whose weight and appearance were constantly scrutinized by the media, was reputed to have suffered from bulimia.

Physical Symptoms Associated with Anorexia and Bulimia	Table 8.4

ANOREXIA	BULIMIA
• Lowered metabolism	• Corrosion of dental enamel by exposure to stomach acids during vomiting
• Dehydration and anemia	• Dehydration and anemia
• Reduced blood pressure and body temperature	• Irritation and enlargement of salivary glands due to frequent vomiting
• Development of lanugo (la-NEW-go), a pale, downy hair, on face and trunk	• Menstrual irregularities
• Electrolyte imbalances	• Electrolyte imbalances
• Cessation of menstrual cycle	
• Possible permanent damage to bones and reproductive system	

BOX 8.1	An 11-Year Struggle

Inside the Mind of Anorexia and Bulimia

In a book titled *Wasted: A Memoir of Anorexia and Bulimia,* Marya Hornbacher chronicles her 11-year struggle with anorexia and bulimia during which her weight ranged between 52 and 135 pounds. The following passage describes some of what went on in her mind.

Up to that point, the bulimia had had a life of its own. It was purely an emotional response to the world—under pressure, binge and purge; sad and lonely, binge and purge; feeling hungry, binge and purge—and actually had little to do, believe it or not, with a desire to lose weight. I'd always wanted to be thinner, sure, but I wanted to eat as well. The year I got to boarding school, I actually began to hate my body with such incredible force that my love of food was forced underground, my masochistic side surfaced, and anorexia became my goal.

Part of this had to do with the self-perpetuating nature of eating disorders: The worries about your weight do not decrease no matter how much weight you lose. Rather, they grow. And the more you worry about your weight, the more you are willing to act on that worry. You really do have to have an excessive level of body loathing to rationally convince yourself that starvation is a reasonable means to achieve thinness. Normally, there is a self-protective mechanism in the psyche that will dissuade the brain from truly dangerous activity, regardless of how desirable the effects of that activity may be. For example, a woman may wish to lose weight but have an essential respect for her physical self and therefore refrain from unhealthy eating. I had no such self-protective mechanism, no such essential self-respect. When you have no sense of physical integrity—a sense that your own health is important, that your body, regardless of shape, is something that requires care and feeding and a basic respect for the biological organism that it is—a very simple, all-too-common, truly frightening thing happens: you cross over from a vague wish to be thinner to a no-holds-barred attack on your flesh…

By winter, I was starving. Malnutrition is no joke. Whether you're skinny or not, your body is starving. As the temperature dropped, I began to grow fur, what is technically called lanugo. Your body grows it when you're not taking in enough calories to create internal heat … I liked my fur. I felt like a small bear. I grew fur on my belly, my ribs, the small of my back, my cheeks, fine downy fur, pale white. My skin grew whiter far north. I began to look a bit haunted. I stood in the shower, feeling the bones of my lower back, two small points at the top of my rear. I took hold of my pelvic bones, twin toy hatchets. I took Fiberall and Dexatrim. I drank gallons of water. I was perpetually cold.

Hornbacher, 1998
(pp. 108–109)

Marya Hornbacher

Purging type bulimia Bulimia in which individuals try to avoid weight gain from binges by physically removing ingested food from their bodies, usually through vomiting or the use of laxatives.

Nonpurging type bulimia Bulimia in which individuals try to avoid weight gain from binges by burning off calories, usually through fasting or engaging in excessive exercise.

The DSM-IV-TR distinguishes between two kinds of bulimia: purging and nonpurging types. Those with **purging type bulimia** try to avoid weight gain by making efforts to physically remove ingested food from their bodies. This can take the form of self-induced vomiting, or inappropriate use of laxatives, diuretics, or enemas. Those with **nonpurging type bulimia** try to avoid weight gain by burning off the calories they have eaten. Usually this takes the form of fasting for a period of days after a binge, or engaging in excessive exercise. All efforts to remove ingested food (through purging or nonpurging methods) usually result in extreme hunger and increase the chances of repeated bingeing.

For a long time, mental health professionals believed that people with eating disorders were *either* anorexic and always restricted food intake *or* were bulimic and engaged in chronic bingeing and purging. With this mistaken idea in mind, psychologists put a great deal of energy into delineating the differences between the "anorexic personality" and the "bulimic personality." More recent research shows that many people with anorexia have suffered from bulimia at some point, and vice versa (see Box 8.1) (Bulik et al., 1997; Raymond et al., 1995). The current eating

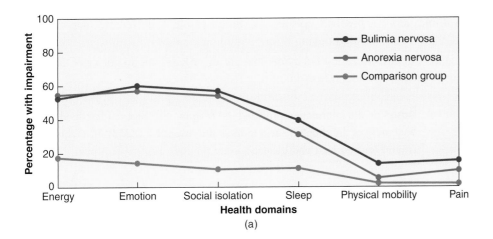

(a)

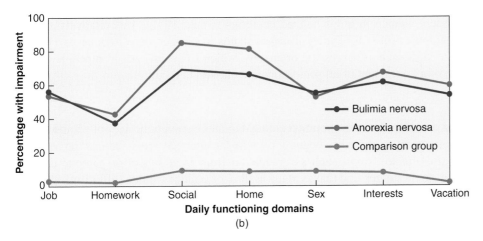

(b)

Figure 8.1 Impairments in health and daily functioning in people with anorexia or bulimia As these two graphs illustrate, anorexia and bulimia dramatically affect many aspects of health and daily functioning. In contrast to a comparison group of people without eating disorders, people suffering from anorexia or bulimia experience more difficulties related to energy level, emotional regulation, social isolation, sleeping, physical mobility, and pain management (a). Further, they are more likely to have difficulty functioning in a job, doing homework, engaging in social activities, enjoying life at home, pursuing sexual activity, maintaining other interests, or enjoying vacations (b).

Adapted from Treasure & Szmukler, 1995, pp. 198–199

disorder categories in the DSM-IV-TR demonstrate the growing awareness of the fluid boundaries between anorexia and bulimia. As you can see from Figure 8.1, both anorexia and bulimia exact a high toll on the lives of people who struggle with these disorders.

Eating Disorder Not Otherwise Specified

In addition to the diagnoses of anorexia and bulimia, the DSM-IV-TR includes the diagnostic category called **eating disorder not otherwise specified** (EDNOS) for eating behaviors that are disordered but do not meet diagnostic criteria for either anorexia or bulimia nervosa. EDNOS can be used as a diagnosis for behaviors such as:

- meeting all of the diagnostic criteria for anorexia while maintaining normal weight
- meeting all of the diagnostic criteria for bulimia, but bingeing less than twice a week, or for a duration of less than three months
- repeatedly chewing and spitting out (not swallowing) large amounts of food
- recurrent episodes of binge eating not followed by compensatory behaviors.

Brief Summary

- The DSM-IV-TR includes three diagnostic categories for eating disorders: anorexia nervosa, bulimia nervosa, and eating disorder not otherwise specified (EDNOS).
- Anorexia nervosa is characterized by significantly low body weight and distortions in how the body is perceived.

Eating disorder not otherwise specified The DSM-IV-TR diagnosis for eating behaviors that are disordered but do not meet diagnostic criteria for either anorexia or bulimia.

- Bulimia nervosa involves episodes of binge eating followed by inappropriate methods to avoid weight gain.

- EDNOS applies to eating behaviors that are disordered but do not meet the diagnostic criteria for anorexia or bulimia.

Critical Thinking Question | **B**ased on the information provided, do Megan and Theresa (described at the beginning of the chapter) seem to meet the respective DSM-IV-TR diagnostic criteria for anorexia and bulimia?

Classification in Demographic Context

The eating disorders are profoundly influenced by demographic factors such as age, gender, class, and culture. For example, the vast majority of eating disorders occur in adolescent women in industrialized countries (Hoek, 1995). This relatively specific demographic profile for eating disorders stands in stark contrast to other psychological disorders such as depression or anxiety, which frequently occur in people of both sexes, of all ages, and of all socioeconomic classes, and cultures.

Age

Eating disorders are most common among females between the ages of 15 and 25; the majority of eating disorders begin during the late teenage years and may be triggered by a stressful life event such as graduation from high school or parental divorce. Indeed, some studies find that as many as 20% of college women suffer from anorexia or bulimia, with many more having **subclinical** problems with eating, weight, or dieting (Attie & Brooks-Gunn, 1989). Some experts speak of an epidemic of eating disorders on college campuses, and the eating irregularities of college women have become a major public health concern. But eating disorders and excessive concern about weight are not limited to college students and young adult women. In her popular book, *Reviving Ophelia* (1994), Dr. Mary Pipher discusses the recent increase in eating disorders among preadolescent girls. The average age at which girls first report dieting appears to be dropping. One study found that children as young as eight years old expressed concerns about their weight and physique that reflected the current preoccupation many women have with thinness and dieting (Shapiro, Newcomb, & Loeb, 1997). Other researchers have found that many grade school girls diet, even if they are of normal weight or underweight (Maloney et al., 1989).

In recent years, clinicians have also begun to appreciate that anorexia has been underdiagnosed in older adult populations. While frailty and thinness are traditionally associated with growing older, accruing evidence suggests that some older people radically restrict food intake with the aim of losing weight. Anorexia among older adult women in particular appears to be related to depression, fear of aging, and a desire to conform to cultural ideals of beauty (Cosford & Arnold, 1992; Lewis & Cachelin, 2001).

Gender

Approximately 90% of eating disorders occur in women (APA, 2000a). Many experts argue that the dramatic difference in the rates of eating disorders for men and women results from social pressures on women to achieve an ideal of perfection and success partly measured by being thin. Some feminists, most notably Susan Faludi in her book *Backlash: The Undeclared War Against American Women,* propose that the current emaciated beauty ideal is intended to keep women physically frail in reaction to their increasing social and economic power.

Subclinical The presence of symptoms at levels below the full diagnostic criteria for a disorder.

Early worries Not only are eating disorders in teenage girls on the rise, girls as young as eight years old report concerns about their weights and diets.

BOX 8.2 Eating Disordered Behavior in Men

Ken Catches up with Barbie

Mental health professionals are learning that men *do* suffer from eating disorders, even if they don't have the same symptoms seen in women with anorexia or bulimia. There is a growing interest in what some researchers call *reverse anorexia,* the belief that one's body is small and weak, even in cases of male bodybuilders who have developed an unusual amount of muscle mass (Pope, Katz, & Hudson, 1993). Studies of competitive male bodybuilders find high levels of preoccupation with food (81%) and binge eating (10%) (Anderson et al., 1995). Researchers are also learning of bodybuilders who have not eaten in restaurants for years because they cannot control the exact carbohydrate and protein ratios of their food (Smith, 1997). Some reverse anorexics report avoiding social situations or wearing heavy clothes in order to hide their bodies.

Like females with eating disorders, male bodybuilders report high levels of body dissatisfaction and perfectionism, and low levels of self-esteem (Blouin & Gold-

field, 1995). One particularly concerning aspect of reverse anorexia in men is the use of anabolic steriods to promote muscle development. Steroid abuse can lead to increased aggression, as well as psychotic and manic symptoms. Major depression is also a common psychological side effect of steroid withdrawal (Pope & Katz, 1988).

It also seems that "Ken" may be catching up with "Barbie," the popular female doll whose physical proportions represent an impossible standard. A recent study of action figures for boys found that the waist, chest, and biceps of the most popular American action figures have been growing steadily over the last 30 years and are now much more muscular than even the largest human bodybuilders (Pope et al., 1999).

Man in the mirror In *reverse anorexia,* men see themselves as small and weak despite their obviously excessive muscle development. The focus on building muscle mass is often accompanied by preoccupations with what, and how much, they eat.

The standards for attractiveness in men are generally considered to be more flexible than they are for women. In particular, weight standards for men are closer to what most men naturally weigh. Despite significant gains in social equality for women, men tend to be valued for their talents and personal qualities while women are more likely to be hired and promoted, to have dates, and to be considered attractive if they are thin (Yuker & Allison, 1994). However, any discussion of beauty standards should also address the question of who is holding such standards. A number of studies have found that women believe that men prefer much thinner women than they actually do (Rozin & Fallon, 1988).

Some evidence indicates that eating disorders are increasing in men, but accurate prevalence data are hard to come by. Experts note that binge eating may be less noticeable in a man than in a woman because of different social expectations about how men and women should eat (Andersen, 1995). Further, men who suffer from anorexia or bulimia may be reluctant to seek help for what are traditionally "women's" problems. While men do not suffer from DSM-IV-TR eating disorders nearly as frequently as women, there are some experts who argue for the recognition of **reverse anorexia,** also known as *muscle dysmorphia,* as an eating and weight disorder (Pope, Katz, & Hudson, 1993). Men with *reverse anorexia* worry that their muscles are too small and underdeveloped (see Box 8.2). They are preoccupied with their perceived smallness and may spend an inordinate amount of time lifting weights and exercising, even if their muscles are obviously overdeveloped. Men

Reverse anorexia A condition, usually affecting men, that involves excessive worry that muscles are too small and underdeveloped.

From Johnson, Powers, & Dick, 1999, p. 182

Table 8.5	Rates of Vomiting, Laxative Use, Diet Pill Use, and Sauna/Steam Use Among Male and Female NCAA Athletes

	FREQUENCY	**FEMALES**	**MALES**
Vomiting	Lifetime	23.90%	5.93%
	Monthly	6.41%	2.04%
	Weekly	3.20%	1.13%
	Daily	1.42%	0.34%
Laxative use	Lifetime	11.72%	5.06%
	Monthly	1.78%	1.02%
	Weekly	0.36%	0.34%
	Daily	0.18%	0.23%
Diet pill use	Lifetime	14.30%	2.16%
	Monthly	1.42%	0.57%
	Weekly	1.25%	0.23%
	Daily	1.25%	0.23%
Sauna/Steam use	Lifetime	6.59%	24.26%
	In Last Year	2.50%	14.63%

with this syndrome may take potentially dangerous anabolic steroids in the effort to increase their muscle mass.

Female athletes in the "appearance" sports (ballet, figure skating, gymnastics) or "endurance" sports (track, cross-country) are at an extremely high risk for anorexia. Indeed, success in some activities, particularly ballet and other forms of dance, may depend on being unusually thin, and as many as 15% of "appearance" or "endurance" athletes may suffer from eating disorders (Sundgot-Borgen, 1994). However, not all athletes with eating disorders are female. In fact, as noted earlier, eating disordered behavior commonly occurs among males in competitive wrestling. Wrestlers often binge when training for competition in order to gain strength, then engage in dramatic weight loss measures including food restriction and fluid depletion through saunas, laxatives, and diuretics in order to cut weight before competition. Table 8.5 shows the rates of vomiting, laxative use, diet pill use, and sauna or steam use among male and female National Collegiate Athletic Association (NCAA) athletes. Such practices have resulted in the recent deaths of a number of college wrestlers and have led the NCAA to adopt rules prohibiting the use of "laxatives, emetics, excessive food and fluid restriction, self-induced vomiting, hot rooms, hot boxes, saunas and steam rooms [and] vapor-impermeable suits" (Renfro, 1998).

Class

Until recently, eating disorders occurred mostly in the higher socioeconomic classes, but new research shows that this is no longer the case. Recent studies have demonstrated that the prevalence of eating disorders does not vary significantly by socioeconomic class (Rogers et al., 1997). However, the same studies have shown that subclinical eating problems (such as unhealthy dieting behavior) are significantly more common among members of higher socioeconomic groups. It also continues to be the case that eating disorders are most prominent in affluent, developed countries where there is an abundance of food, and they are virtually nonexistent in cultures where food is scarce (Hoek, 1995).

Authors' Note: Eating disorders often develop during the college years. If you know someone who seems to be suffering from an eating disorder but does not feel that he or she has a problem, the following approaches are recommended by experts:

- Gently let your friend know that you are worried about his or her behavior by citing specific actions as examples (not eating meals, throwing up after meals).

- Encourage your friend to talk with someone who knows how to help solve eating problems (such as a mental health professional at your college or university counseling services).

- Don't be surprised if your friend denies that a problem exists.

- Let your friend know that you may need to alert his or her parents or a college official about the problem if the problem doesn't get better, or if your friend won't seek help.

Culture

Within the United States, eating disorders have been more common among white women than minority women, but this trend may be changing. Previously, minority women were believed to be less prone to eating disorders because they were exempted from the dominant cultural ideal for beauty (thin, blue-eyed, and blonde) and had more reasonable beauty standards. However, some studies indicate that that the rates of eating disorders among minority women are rising, especially among those who are heavier, well-educated, and more involved with middle-class white culture (Crago, Shisslak, & Estes, 1996). Indeed, some experts in the field of eating disorders believe that minority women may be prone to having poor body images *because* of cultural attitudes that denigrate the physical characteristics of minorities (Root, 1990).

Brief Summary

- Eating disorders are most common in women between the ages of 15 and 25, though there is evidence of increased dieting and weight-preoccupation among younger girls.

- Ninety percent of eating disorders occur in women. However there is growing awareness of a reverse anorexia syndrome among men.

- Eating disorders occur at approximately the same rate across different socioeconomic groups, but subclinical eating disorders are more common among members of the upper socioeconomic classes.

- While eating disorders have traditionally been most prevalent among white American women, the rates of eating disorders among minority women appear to be on the rise.

Critical Thinking Question | **H**ow do Megan and Theresa (described at the beginning of the chapter) reflect the demographic trends described above?

How the dominant culture dominates Once thought to be insulated from the beauty ideals of the dominant culture, it appears that African American women are increasingly affected by social attitudes that idealize a slim female form.

Cultural Relativism in Defining and Classifying Eating Disorders

The prevalence rates of eating disorders vary dramatically across cultures, highlighting the core concept of ***cultural relativism.*** As previously noted, anorexia and bulimia are virtually unheard of in underdeveloped and impoverished countries, while they are increasingly common in Western, industrialized societies (Garfinkel & Dorian, 2001). Interestingly, when non-Western cultures are exposed to Western media and its glorification of thinness, rates of eating disorders rise (see Box 8.3) (Lee & Lee, 1999). Most women, even very healthy ones, are not able to meet the female beauty standards presented to them in the media, but many may be willing to risk their health (and even their lives) in the effort to approximate the standard. The extremely thin standard for physical beauty is marketed to even the youngest members of our society; by one estimate the average Barbie doll would be 7′2″ and weigh 125 pounds if her height, weight, and proportions were converted to human form (Brownell & Napolitano, 1995).

The Advantages and Limitations of the DSM-IV-TR Eating Disorder Diagnoses

According to some researchers, between 25% and 60% of eating disorder cases are classified as eating disorder not otherwise specified (Andersen, Bowers, & Watson, 2001). The fact that so many people with eating disorders fit best in this residual

BOX 8.3 Exporting Eating Disorders

We Have to Have Those Thin, Slim Bodies

Sociocultural theorists are quick to say that women in Western, industrialized societies suffer from high rates of eating disorders because they are constantly exposed to media images of ultra-thin models and actresses. But do we really know that such images are to blame? Perhaps these media images don't *set* a trend but merely *reflect* a national obsession with physical beauty. Perhaps eating disorders would be just as common with or without slim-figured movie stars and svelte magazine models.

Remarkably, a group of researchers led by Dr. Anne Becker of Harvard Medical School was able to find a place where they could study this question (Becker et al., 2002). Prior to 1995, eating disorders were virtually non-existent on the island of Fiji, located in the South Pacific. Eating disorders were not only rare, but Fijians considered a hearty appetite and a robust figure to be signs of emotional well-being and physical health. In 1995, the island of Fiji began to receive Western television programs such as "Beverly Hills 90210" "Seinfeld" and "ER." Within three years, the number of teenage girls receiving high scores on a measure of eating disordered behaviors went from 12.7% to 29.2%. In 1995, not a single teenage girl included in the study had ever self-induced vomiting in an effort to control her weight; by 1998, 11.3% of the girls in the study reported having done so. In a culture where dieting had traditionally been frowned upon and discouraged, 69% of the girls surveyed in 1998 reported having dieted, and 74% said they sometimes felt that they were overweight.

Becker and her colleagues point out that the arrival of television is only one of many recent modernizations in Fijian culture. The gradual conversion from subsistence agriculture to a cash economy may also play a role in changing how girls feel about their bodies.

Yet when interviewed, the Fijian girls included in Becker's study made direct reference to the connection between what they saw on television and how they thought about themselves:

> When I look at the characters on TV, the way they act on TV and I just look at the body, the figure of that body, so I say, "look at them, they are thin and they all have this figure," so I myself want to become like that, to become thin.

> …it's good to watch [TV] because … it's encouraged me that what I'm doing is right; when I see the sexy ladies on the television, well, I want to be like them, too.

> …the actresses and all those girls … I just like, I just admire them and I want to be like them. I want their body, I want their size. I want to be [in] the same position as they are … Because Fijians are, most of us Fijians are, many of us, most, I can say most, we are brought up on these heavy foods, and our bodies are, we are getting fat. And now, we are feeling, we feel that it is bad to have this huge body. We have to have those thin, slim bodies.

> (Becker et al., 2002, p. 513)

Becker's findings raise questions about why some girls who watch American television go on crash diets and others don't. All the same, her study shows that Western television programming can have a powerful, noxious effect on the lives and bodies of those who watch it.

In traditional Fijian culture, a hearty appetite and a robust figure were viewed as signs of emotional well-being and physical health.

diagnostic category highlights the core concept of the ***advantages and limitations of diagnosis***. On the one hand, eating disorder experts are better able to communicate with each other about research findings and clinical phenomena when they have clearly defined diagnostic categories like anorexia and bulimia. On the other hand, these narrowly defined categories may represent only a minority of people suffering from disordered eating. Many people with significant eating problems do not fit into these categories as they are currently defined.

One of the most interesting controversies in the classification of eating disorders revolves around the problem of **obesity**, which is defined as being 20% or more over

Obesity The condition of being 20% or more over ideal weight.

the ideal weight as determined from life insurance statistics for a person's age, build, sex, and height. Obesity is extremely common in the United States; one in three American adults are significantly overweight or obese (Kuczmarski et al., 1994). Presently, obesity is *not* included in the DSM-IV-TR, despite strong evidence that obesity involves prominent behavioral and psychological factors.

Studies show that obesity involves a preference for fatty foods and the disinclination to engage in physical activity (Devlin, Yanovski, & Wilson, 2000). In addition, people experiencing emotional stress are more likely to eat unhealthy, fatty foods and to exercise less than people who report low levels of stress (Ng & Jeffery, 2003). Obesity also has a wide variety of negative psychological effects such as low self-esteem and depression (Miller & Downey, 1999). In his book *Food Fight: The Inside Story of the Food Industry, America's Obesity Crisis and What We Can Do About It,* psychologist Kelly Brownell points out that environmental factors, such as ballooning portion sizes and the savvy marketing techniques of the convenience-food industry, also contribute to epidemic rates of American obesity (Brownell & Horgen, 2003). Interestingly, binge eating that occurs without compensatory behavior may be diagnosed as an eating disorder not otherwise specified, but presently, no diagnosis describes the chronic overeating (not necessarily in the form of binges) that usually results in obesity. However, many mental health professionals *do* consider obesity to be a form of eating disorder.

Eating disorder? Obesity is not included in the DSM-IV-TR, but some experts contend that the condition involves prominent psychological and behavioral features, and should be classified as an eating disorder.

Brief Summary

- Eating disorders are most common among white women in Westernized industrialized countries. When non-Western countries are exposed to Western media, rates of eating disorder rise.

- Between 25% and 60% of eating disorder cases are diagnosed as eating disorder not otherwise specified, highlighting the core concept of the ***advantages and limitations of diagnosis.***

- Obesity is not currently listed in the DSM-IV-TR, even though there are significant psychological and behavioral factors associated with it.

> *Critical* | **Some people feel that the DSM-IV-TR should not include obesity as a**
> *Thinking* | **psychological/psychiatric disorder because people who are obese are**
> *Question* | **already stigmatized in our culture. Do you agree with this reasoning? Why or**
> | **why not?**

EXPLAINING AND TREATING EATING DISORDERS

Each of the major theoretical perspectives offers explanations of and interventions for eating disorders. As with the other disorders we have discussed, you will notice important areas of overlap and complementarity among the various approaches, as well as some critical differences.

Psychodynamic Components

Hilde Bruch's book, *The Golden Cage: The Enigma of Anorexia Nervosa* (1978), is considered one of the classic texts in the field of eating disorders. Bruch emphasizes that clients with anorexia are often so focussed on others' needs and desires that they lose awareness of what they want for themselves. In particular, young women who develop anorexia may be striving to live up to the high expectations they feel their parents have set for them. The constant struggle to meet parental expectations may take the form of over-compliance and high achievement in a number of areas. While the daughter suffering from anorexia may succeed in pleasing her parents, she is usually dogged by feelings of inferiority and believes that she must continue to be highly successful in order to ensure that she will be loved and supported by her parents. The daughter who develops anorexia may be striving for the "perfection" she feels her parents want from her, while simultaneously asserting her independence. Indeed, being able to achieve and maintain extreme levels of weight loss speaks to the daughter's ability to meet difficult goals while also proving her ability to chart a course separate from the one outlined for her by her parents.

Some empirical evidence supports Bruch's assertion that eating disorders are more likely to occur in families that are preoccupied with appearance and high achievement; families of women with eating disorders do tend to value perfectionism and control more than most families (Harding & Lachenmeyer, 1986; Woodside et al., 2002). Other studies have investigated the link between maternal attitudes toward weight and eating disorders in adolescent girls. For example, Pike and Rodin (1991) found that the mothers of daughters with eating disorders were more disordered in their own eating than mothers whose daughters ate normally. Further, compared to mothers of girls who ate normally, the mothers of eating disordered girls thought their daughters should lose more weight and rated their daughters as being less attractive than the girls rated themselves.

Recent psychodynamic explanations elaborate upon Bruch's view that eating disorders are fueled by complex, often unconscious feelings. For example, some psychodynamic theorists have suggested that anorexia may provide the sufferer with an opportunity to retain a childlike physical form and thereby avoid the sexual anxieties that accompany the physical and psychological move into adolescence (Swift & Stern, 1982). Others have noted the high incidence of sexual trauma, either during childhood or adulthood, in the lives of clients with bulimia or anorexia (Palmer, 1995). In the wake of a sexual trauma, a person with anorexia may aim to regain control over her body by ridding herself of sexual characteristics such as menses, shapely hips, or breasts. A client with bulimic symptoms may be unconsciously reenacting a sexual trauma: first by overwhelming herself, in this case with food, and then "undoing" the trauma by vomiting. In addition, young women who are highly emotionally conflicted about their own sexual desires may resist or restrict all forms of sensuality, including the pleasures of eating, in an ascetic anorexic life (Dare & Crowther, 1995). Needless to say, a high price is paid when people with anorexia or bulimia use their bodies as an arena for self-punishment, self-assertion, or self-control.

Psychodynamic Interventions

Psychodynamic interventions for eating disorders involve exploratory techniques such as free association, dream analysis, and the analysis of the relationship with the therapist (transference) to uncover the meaning and function of eating disorder symptoms. The following case description illustrates the use of transference interpretations in the treatment of an 18-year-old who had been anorexic since age 12. In this case, the client felt that she needed to surrender her own age-appropriate interests so that she could be a dutiful companion for her lonely and depressed mother.

> **Case Illustration** The patient's difficulties began when she had the opportunity to join school activities that took her away from her mother for hours over the weekend. The patient's mother was not overtly destructive, but the patient felt guilty about participating in age-appropriate activities because "[her] mother wanted [her] to stay home, watch TV with her, and go shopping."

In the therapy process, the patient would closely observe her therapist for any waning of interest when activities, school, and friendships were mentioned. The therapist pointed out that the patient seemed to stay on guard to "figure out what [the therapist] might want [the patient] to do." The therapist's sensitivity to the maternal transference issues enabled the clinician to gently wonder and later confront the patient for not permitting herself more participation in age-appropriate activities...

In this case, understanding how the patient was attempting to repeat in the transference an earlier, but ultimately unhealthy way of relating enabled the eating symptoms to subside. The patient did not have to "find [her] own space" by not eating, nor did she have to "stay a little girl" because this is what she assumed adults (e.g., her mother and her therapist) desired.

Zerbe, 2001 (pp. 310–311)

In another case:

Case Illustration A patient developed anorexia nervosa after her father had died of an emaciating illness. By her anorexic self-starvation she came to believe that, in relation to her father, her imitative emaciation made her a more faithfully loving daughter. ... It was as though the patient could believe herself to be under the approving gaze of her dead father.

Dare & Crowther, 1995 (p. 302)

While many case studies support the effectiveness of psychodynamic interventions for eating disorders, few studies have compared psychodynamic interventions to other therapeutic approaches. However, a recent a study of outpatient treatments for anorexic clients at the University of London found psychodynamic psychotherapy to be more effective than a control condition in which clients had regular nontherapeutic contact with a member of the hospital staff and also more effective than a cognitive intervention program (Dare et al., 2001).

Family Systems Components

As the work of Bruch suggests, family relationships and pathological family structures appear to play a role in the development or perpetuation of eating disorders (Eisler, 1995; Stern et al., 1989). Salvador Minuchin, an influential family systems theorist, was particularly interested in how disturbed family relationships might impede the normal tasks of separation and individuation during adolescence and contribute to the onset of eating disorders in teenaged girls (Minuchin, Rosman, & Baker, 1978). Like many family systems therapists, Minuchin focused on family boundaries, roles, and coalitions, and attributed psychopathology in any one family member to disruptions within the broader family system. Minuchin believed that eating disorders usually occur in families that are overly **enmeshed.** By this he meant that individual family members become too involved with the details of each other's lives: the parents might be directing every aspect of their children's school work while the children are overly involved in the details of their parents' finances. Enmeshed family members may provide a great deal of support to each other, but their over-involvement presents a problem for teenagers who, in the normal course of development, need to become increasingly private and independent.

Enmeshed Families in which boundaries between members are weak and relationships tend to be intrusive.

According to Minuchin, developing an eating disorder may be a particularly elegant, if dangerous, "solution" to the dilemma of being an adolescent in an overly enmeshed family. On the one hand, becoming anorexic is a profound statement of independence. In effect, the teenager is saying "You may be too involved in many areas of my life, but you can't make me eat!" On the other hand, having an eating disorder renders the young woman "sick" and causes her family to worry about what she eats, how much she exercises, and how much she weighs. Rather than gaining independence from her family, the eating disordered teenager may spend less time with her friends and find that her parents are more involved with the details of her daily life than ever before.

As you can see, family systems and psychodynamic approaches overlap; both view eating disorders as rooted in complex family problems. However, critics have noted the possibility that the enmeshed family style described by family systems and psychodynamic theorists could be a *result* of an eating disorder, not its *cause.* In other words, it may be expectable and desirable for parents to become heavily involved with children who are engaging in life-threatening behaviors, such as self-starvation; the family may not have been enmeshed prior to the onset of the eating disorder. Research efforts to verify the family systems belief that enmeshment preceeds and contributes to eating disorders have been largely unsuccessful (Eisler, 1995). Empirical investigations have failed to find specific family styles or patterns that are consistently associated with eating disorders, and community-based studies have found few differences between families in which a family member suffers from an eating disorder and matched controls (Rastam & Gilberg, 1991).

As a result, recent family theorists have shifted from thinking of enmeshment as simply a cause of eating disorders toward considering what kinds of family processes maintain eating disorders once they have begun. Consider the following description of Hannah, a 16-year-old who binges compulsively and who hurts herself when prevented from bingeing:

Case Illustration When Hannah gets distressed and feels the compulsive need to fill herself with food, the family responds: father tries to prevent her forcibly from doing so, Hannah fights back, he becomes enraged and breakages occur. If he does manage to prevent her from bingeing, she breaks the window, cuts herself, or hits her head against the wall until her agony subsides. Father is consumed with guilt at feeling he has harmed her, enraged that she has pushed him to such desperate measures and ends up feeling impotent and frustrated.

Meanwhile, Hannah calms down, phones her mother at work and tells her what her father has done. Mother returns from work, in a panic, furious with father, and berates him for being a useless violent brute … father in shame and despair goes to the pub; Hannah and mother console each other for having to put up with such a creature…

However, mother, whilst responding to Hannah's needs and joining her in unity against the father when he is out of favour, has adult needs of her own which require her to make choices in favour of her husband. Hannah's impossible desire for a symbiotic relationship with her mother is thus repeatedly frustrated, and the vicious cycle continues.

Colahan & Senior (1995, p. 250)

While a family systems approach may not be able to explain why Hannah developed bulimia in the first place, it does offer a framework for understanding the complex family processes that maintain her emotional and eating problems.

Family Systems Interventions

Despite the lack of consistent empirical support for family systems explanations of eating disorders, family systems interventions have been found to be effective in the treatment of anorexia and bulimia (Dare & Eisler, 1995). The major distinguishing characteristic of family systems interventions is that the therapist views the entire family as the "client." In family systems terms, the person suffering from anorexia or bulimia is simply the **identified patient**, meaning that her symptom is viewed as an index of difficulties within the whole family.

Identified patient The member of the family identified by the family as having problems; family systems theorists see this as a manifestation of a problem in the family system, not in an individual member.

Reasons for hope Family therapy interventions for eating disorders, especially in families that are otherwise functioning well, have been found to be highly effective.

When working with young clients, family therapists often encourage parents to take an active role in opposing the adolescent's eating-disordered symptoms. Once the eating-disordered symptoms begin to diminish, the therapist urges the family members to return to their individual interests and activities, many of which may have been ignored due to concerns about the adolescent's eating disorder (le Grange, 1999). Not surprisingly, family members often find that they have trouble operating independently, and family sessions can be used to address impediments to autonomous functioning. For Hannah and her family (described in the previous case), a family therapist would most likely address Hannah's wish to provoke and then exclude her father in order to have an exclusive relationship with her mother, and also confront the marital problems between Hannah's parents that allow for the maladaptive gratification of Hannah's wishes.

Family systems interventions seem to be especially helpful for families who are generally functioning well and do not feel overtly hostile toward the person with the eating disorder (Dare & Eisler, 1995). In contrast, families that feel highly critical toward their eating-disordered child seem to derive more benefit from meeting in separate parent and child psychotherapy sessions (Eisler et al., 2000). In either case, including parents in the treatment of adolescents with eating disorders appears to be an important component of therapeutic success.

Brief Summary

- Psychodynamic explanations of anorexia and bulimia have focused on anorexia as a complex reaction to perfection-oriented families, anorexia as a retreat from adult sexuality, and eating disorders as reactions to traumatic events such as sexual abuse or assault.

- Psychodynamic interventions aim to help clients understand how eating-disordered symptoms relate to their unconscious emotional conflicts.

- Salvador Minuchin believed that eating disorders occur in families that are overly enmeshed. Since empirical research has not supported the assertion that a specific kind of family dynamic causes eating disorders, recent family systems approaches emphasize family processes that perpetuate eating disorders once they have begun.

- Family systems interventions for eating disorders involve the whole family and assume that the eating disorder represents a problem within the broader family system.

Critical Thinking Question | While family systems explanations of eating disorders have received little research support, family systems interventions have proven to be quite useful. How might you explain this discrepancy?

Cognitive-Behavioral Components

From the cognitive-behavioral perspective, anorexia and bulimia result from a combination of dysfunctional thoughts and experiences that have reinforced eating disordered behaviors. For example, the belief that one's physical shape reflects one's value or worth as a person fuels a great deal of eating disordered behavior (APA, 2000a). Table 8.6 describes some of the common cognitive distortions in anorexia.

Both anorexia and bulimia are maintained by "black and white" thinking about food and weight. Many people with bulimia and anorexia have categories of "good" and "bad" foods that do not take into account nutritional values and normal dietary requirements. Foods containing fat may be considered to be "bad" even though they are required for healthy physical functioning. Similarly, people with eating disorders may create and follow arbitrary but rigid rules that perpetuate their problems. For

Table 8.6	Cognitive Distortions in Anorexia Nervosa

Adapted from De Silva, 1995, p. 145

	DYSFUNCTIONAL COGNITION	EXAMPLES
Selective abstraction	• One aspect of a complex situation is the focus of attention and other relevant aspects of the situation are ignored.	• "Yes I have friends, a great family, and good grades, but I gained two pounds this week—I'm such a loser."
Dichotomous reasoning	• Thinking in extreme and absolute terms.	• "If I am not in complete control, then I will lose all control."
Over-generalization	• Deriving a rule from one event and applying it to other situations or events.	• "I failed at controlling my eating last night. So I am going to fail today as well."
Magnification	• Exaggerating the significance of events.	• "I have gained a pound. I'll never be able to wear shorts again."

example, a client with anorexia may decide that it is "against the rules" to eat after 6 o'clock in the evening, or that it is imperative that she run 8 miles in the morning before eating anything. A client with bulimia may tell herself that she is not "allowed" to eat for a whole day to make up for bingeing, and then find herself bingeing all over again because she is so hungry from fasting. The weight loss in anorexia and the relief that comes from purging after a bulimic binge unfortunately reinforce anorexic and bulimic behaviors, creating a vicious cycle of disordered eating.

Terence Wilson's (1989) theoretical model of bulimia illustrates the cognitive and behavioral processes that perpetuate the disorder (Figure 8.2). As you can see, cognitive processes (dysfunctional thoughts about weight and fear of becoming fat) trigger behavioral responses (excessive dieting, binge eating, and purging) which lead to emotional reactions (reinforcing emotional relief, followed by guilt and depression) that renew the cycle of cognitive distortions and behavioral disruptions. While cognitive-behavioral approaches to eating disorders have received considerable empirical support (Wilson, 1989) they, like family systems descriptions, may explain more about how eating disorders are *maintained* than about how a person with weight concerns develops dysfunctional cognitions in the first place.

Cognitive-Behavioral Interventions

Cognitive-behavioral interventions for eating disorders usually involve a variety of techniques. In hospital settings, behavioral interventions are typically employed to help clients with severe anorexia gain weight when they are dangerously thin. For example, a client with anorexia may not be allowed to watch television or visit with friends until she eats regularly and begins to put on weight. Such behavioral interventions may help with initial weight gain, but they rarely work outside of a hospital setting and are not usually effective as a long-term solution for anorexia (Russell, 2001). Once basic health needs have been addressed, more complex cognitive-behavioral interventions have been found to be useful in the subsequent treatment of both anorexia and bulimia (APA, 2000b).

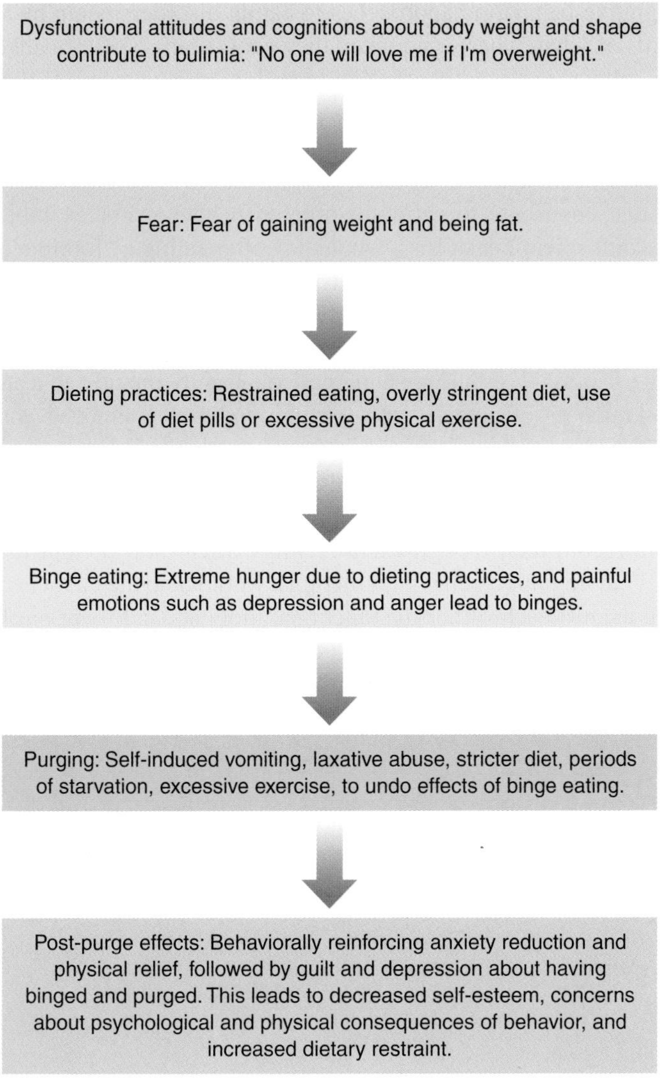

Dysfunctional attitudes and cognitions about body weight and shape contribute to bulimia: "No one will love me if I'm overweight."

Fear: Fear of gaining weight and being fat.

Dieting practices: Restrained eating, overly stringent diet, use of diet pills or excessive physical exercise.

Binge eating: Extreme hunger due to dieting practices, and painful emotions such as depression and anger lead to binges.

Purging: Self-induced vomiting, laxative abuse, stricter diet, periods of starvation, excessive exercise, to undo effects of binge eating.

Post-purge effects: Behaviorally reinforcing anxiety reduction and physical relief, followed by guilt and depression about having binged and purged. This leads to decreased self-esteem, concerns about psychological and physical consequences of behavior, and increased dietary restraint.

Figure 8.2 Cognitive-behavioral model of bulimia.
(Adapted from De Silva, 1995, pp. 148–149).

Self-monitoring Chart for Bulimia Nervosa			Table 8.7
TIME	**BEHAVIOR**	**CIRCUMSTANCES**	**FEELINGS**
3:00 P.M.	Binge: Two orders of pancakes, three milk-shakes, half of a pizza	Avoided food all day, felt like I was starving.	Furious with myself throughout binge, guilty afterwards.
5:00 P.M.	Exercised for an hour.	Trying to work off binge.	Feeling somewhat less guilty.
8:00 P.M.	Purged by vomiting.	Just finished normal-sized dinner.	Disgusted with myself.

Most cognitive-behavioral approaches to eating disorders begin by asking clients to keep records of what, where, and when they eat (Tobin, 2000). In addition to monitoring eating, clients are usually asked to record the thoughts and feelings they have about eating (see Table 8.7). Clients may also be asked to monitor and record their thoughts and feelings after they exercise, purge, or weigh themselves.

Therapists use the client's records to help the client understand the cognitive mechanisms that contribute to eating-disordered behavior. For example, a therapist might notice that a client fasted for a whole day after eating a "forbidden" food like a chocolate-chip cookie. The clinician would point out that such rigid and extreme rules increase the likelihood of bingeing and may result from a cognitive error, such as **catastrophizing** a minor event (such as "If I eat one cookie, I will get fat"). Cognitive-behavioral interventions for bulimia and anorexia usually include education about the physical consequences of binge-eating, fasting, and/or self-induced vomiting (Freeman, 1995). Clients are asked to consider the effects that maintaining an eating disorder may have, such as the serious physical consequences of anorexia and bulimia.

Cognitive-behavioral therapists may "prescribe" a pattern of regular eating and ask their clients to record their thoughts and feelings when they attempt to eat normally (Bowers, 2001). A cognitive-behavioral therapist would help the client evaluate the evidence for and against each of her dysfunctional thoughts and point out how errors in her thinking influence her eating behavior (see Table 8.8). For anorexic clients who are extremely reluctant to gain weight, a cognitive-behavioral therapist might need to focus

Catastrophizing A cognitive distortion involving the tendency to view minor problems as major catastrophes.

Table 8.8	A Cognitive Therapist's Questions: Helping Clients Look for Rational Answers

Adapted from Freeman, 1995, p. 321

- *What is the evidence?*
  What evidence do you have to support your thoughts?
  What evidence do you have against them?

- *What alternative views are there?*
  How would someone else view this situation?
  What evidence do you have to back alternative views of the situation?

- *What is the effect of thinking the way you do?*
  Does it help you, or hinder you from getting what you want? How?
  What would be the effect of looking at things a little differently?

- *What thinking error are you making?*
  Are you thinking in all-or-nothing terms?
  Are you condemning yourself totally as a person on the basis of a single event?
  Are you concentrating on your weaknesses and forgetting your strengths?
  Are you expecting yourself to be perfect?
  Are you using a double standard? How would you view someone else in your situation?
  Are you assuming that you can do nothing to change your situation?
  Are you overlooking solutions to problems on the assumption they won't work?

- *What action can you take?*
  What can you do to change your situation?
  What can you do to test out the validity of your rational answers?
  Can you use "I want," I need," and "I wish" instead of "I must," "I should," and "I ought"?

on other areas where the client with anorexia says that she is unhappy with her life and then help the client make the connection between her anorexia and her unhappiness.

Some cognitive-behavioral techniques are specific to the treatment of anorexia or bulimia. For example, a cognitive-behavioral intervention for a client with bulimia may focus primarily on the negative effects of dieting and other weight-loss measures (Tobin, 2000). Indeed, many people with bulimia find themselves in a cycle of purging in order to compensate for a binge and then bingeing again because they are extremely hungry after extended periods of fasting. When binge episodes are linked to feelings of emotional distress, cognitive-behavioral therapists may help clients to problem-solve around the source of their distress, or develop more adaptive means for managing their feelings. Cognitive-behavioral interventions for anorexia often include an effort to understand what triggered the anorexia, how it is maintained, and what "benefits" the client believes accrue from being anorexic. Distorted thoughts are challenged (for example, "If being very thin will make you perfect, why are you too tired to do many of the things you used to do?"), and the client and therapist work together to develop healthier ways of managing the problems that led to the anorexia in the first place (Bowers, 2001).

Cognitive-behavioral interventions are often highly effective in the treatment of bulimia nervosa (Wilson & Fairburn, 2002). For example, a large study comparing cognitive-behavioral therapy with an interpersonal therapy that emphasized the role of interpersonal problems in bulimic behavior found that only 8% of the people treated with interpersonal therapy had stopped bingeing and purging after 20 weeks of psychotherapy as compared to 45% of those treated with cognitive-behavioral therapy (Agras et al., 2000). Cognitive-behavioral interventions have not received the same strong support as a treatment for anorexia nervosa (Wilson & Fairburn, 2002); some studies have found cognitive approaches to be no more effective in promoting weight gain than nontherapeutic meetings with clinical staff (Dare et al., 2001).

Sociocultural Components

The sociocultural explanation of eating disorders emphasizes that in recent years, the prevalence of eating disorders has been increasing as images of women presented by the media have equated thinness and physical beauty with success, intelligence, popularity, power, and self-control (Szmukler & Patton, 1995). Further, the implicit message of these images is that being overweight (or even of normal weight) is a reflection of laziness, weakness, stupidity or, at best, lack of self-control. Adult women may have a hard enough time resisting such media messages, but teenagers are naturally preoccupied with how they are viewed by others and often find such messages almost impossible to ignore. Add to this scenario the natural tendency of the adolescent female body to begin to retain fat in late puberty and the stage is set for high rates of adolescent eating disorders.

Naomi Wolf, a feminist theorist, takes the sociocultural argument a step further. She asserts that cultural standards for beauty become more impossible for women to attain as women gain more equal economic status with men. Wolf argues that women are subjected to increasingly restrictive standards for beauty precisely *because* they are achieving economic independence:

> Dieting and thinness began to be female preoccupations when Western women received the vote around 1920; between 1918 and 1925, "the rapidity with which the new, linear form replaced the more curvaceous one is startling." In the regressive 1950s, women's natural fullness could be briefly enjoyed once more because their minds were occupied in domestic seclusion. But when women came en masse into male spheres, that pleasure had to be overriden by an urgent social expedient which would make women's bodies the prisons that their homes no longer were.

Wolf, 1990 (p. 150)

Changing beauty ideals The weight of historical "supermodels" has dropped fast—from Rubens' voluptuous nymphs, to Marilyn Monroe's abundant feminine form, to today's sleek ideal.

For Wolf, it is no accident that women feel compelled to starve themselves as they gain social power. She asserts that our culture requires women to keep themselves in a weakened state from which they will never be able to attain full equality with men. Despite the strengths of Wolf's argument, her work also highlights the major limitation of the sociocultural explanation of eating disorders: by asserting that eating disorders result from cultural forces, it fails to explain why only some women in our culture develop eating disorders while most do not.

Sociocultural Interventions

Recently, a number of studies have investigated the effectiveness of media literacy training to help young women question and resist the media's unrealistic standards for female beauty (Irving, DuPen, & Berel, 1998). Psychoeducational programs that describe the unnatural techniques required to create "perfect" images for magazines (plastic surgery, airbrushing, computer imaging) appear to have at least a short-term effect in helping to reduce body-image disturbances in many women (Posavac, Posavac, & Posavac, 1998). Sociocultural interventions for eating disorders have also taken the form of "media activism" including organized protests against unrealistic or harmful advertising images. Watchdog and advocacy groups, such as Eating Disorders Awareness and Prevention, Inc. (EDAP), which monitor and then criticize or praise media images of women have led several major corporations (including Nike and Kellogg) to discontinue ads that glorify unrealistic standards for female beauty (Levin, Piran, & Stoddard, 1999).

Sociocultural intervention An Eating Disorders Awareness and Prevention, Inc. (EDAP) poster promoting respect for all physical shapes and sizes.

Brief Summary

- Cognitive-behavioral explanations of eating disorders focus on faulty and distorted thoughts about food and weight, and experiences that have reinforced eating-disordered behaviors.

- Cognitive-behavioral interventions are particularly helpful in educating clients about the psychological effects of eating disorders and helping clients to identify the thoughts and feelings that support self-starvation or the cycle of bingeing and purging. In general, cognitive-behavioral interventions seem to be more effective for bulimia nervosa than for anorexia nervosa.

- The sociocultural explanation of eating disorders focuses on the unrealistic images of female beauty presented by the media and their negative effects on women.

- Sociocultural interventions focus on educating young women about distorted and unhealthy media images of women and use social activism to protest these harmful images.

| Critical Thinking Question | If you were to design an eating disorders prevention program for seventh grade girls, what information would you provide? |

Biological Components

Biological explanations of eating disorders focus on genetic factors, and on hormonal and neurotransmitter imbalances in anorexia and bulimia. On the genetic front, identical twins have a higher concordance rate for anorexia and bulimia than fraternal twins (Fichter & Noegel, 1990; Holland et al., 1984). Further, eating disorders often co-occur with two other disorders that are known to have a genetic component: depression and obsessive-compulsive anxiety disorder (Figure 8.3 shows self-portraits by women with anorexia that illustrate depressive features of the disorder) (Wonderlich & Mitchell, 2001). Some clinicians argue that eating disorders can be seen as a form of obsessive-compulsive anxiety disorder (Chapter 5), the disorder in which an individual is preoccupied by anxiety-provoking thoughts and feels compelled to perform ritual acts in order to relieve anxiety (Cooper, 1995). In the case of eating disorders the obsession might be the recurrent anxious thought "I am too fat" and the compulsions which reduce the anxiety can include vomiting, excessive exercising, or restricting food intake.

Some studies have shown that individuals with anorexia have lower levels of hormones produced by the hypothalamus than people without anorexia (Fairburn, 1995), while other studies have found that people with bulimia have unusually low levels of the neurotransmitters norepinephrine and serotonin (Pirke, 1995). However, researchers do not yet know whether these hormonal and neurotransmitter deficiencies are a cause or a result of eating disorders.

In addition, anorexia and bulimia may be perpetuated by stimulation of the body's **endorphins,** natural opiates that produce feelings of pleasure. Huebner (1993) proposes that the body secretes endorphins in response to the purging and/or self-starvation behaviors associated with anorexia and bulimia. The release of endorphins may then reinforce eating-disordered behavior.

Biological Interventions

Though biological interventions for eating disorders are relatively new, several studies have found **SSRI (selective serotonin reuptake inhibitor) antidepressants** (Chapter 6) to be effective in the treatment of bulimia whether or not the person suffering from bulimia is depressed (Mitchell et al., 2001). Research comparing cognitive-behavioral therapy (CBT), SSRI treatment, and a combination of CBT and SSRI treatment for bulimia has shown that CBT and SSRI treatment are most beneficial in combination, while CBT treatment alone is more effective than SSRI treatment alone (Walsh et al., 1997). However, SSRI treatment can be an alternative intervention for clients who do not respond to psychotherapy, or who relapse after a successful course of psychotherapy (Walsh et al., 2000). To date, there has been little experimental support for using SSRIs to treat anorexia nervosa, though some recent evidence indicates that the combination of SSRIs and psychotherapy may be effective in preventing relapses after weight recovery has occurred (Kaye et al., 2001).

Figure 8.3 Self-portraits by anorexic women
These self-portraits by women suffering from anorexia illustrate both the profound sense of suffering and isolation (top) and the harshly critical feelings (bottom) that are common among people with anorexia. In both drawings, the women hang their heads and depict the depression and lack of pleasure shared by many people who suffer from eating disorders.

From Claude-Pierre, 1999, p. 64

Endorphins Brain chemicals that reduce pain and produce pleasurable sensations; sometimes referred to as the body's "natural opioids."

SSRI (selective serotonin reuptake inhibitor) antidepressants A "second generation" class of antidepressant medications that block the reuptake of serotonin from the synapse; used in the treatment of depression and other disorders.

The Connection Between Mind and Body in Eating Disorders

Eating disorders profoundly illustrate the **connection between mind and body.** Think of how you feel after you have skipped a meal. Are you able to concentrate well? Is your abstract thinking as good as usual? Probably not. Now, multiply that condition by 10 and you may approximate the mental state of a person with anorexia. Indeed, many clinicians find that clients with anorexia are very difficult to treat precisely because they are famished. Their chronic hunger makes it difficult for them to think constructively about their problems. A classic study of healthy men who volunteered to severely restrict their diets for an extended period of time found that most changed from being pleasant, cooperative, and social to becoming cranky, self-centered, and cognitively impaired (Brozek, 1953). Hilde Bruch was among the first clinicians to emphasize the effects of starvation on an anorexic client's behavioral and cognitive style. The growing appreciation of the cognitive impairment caused by starvation has led clinicians to prioritize weight-gain interventions not only for health reasons, but also to restore the cognitive flexibility needed for psychotherapy.

The Multiple Causality of Eating Disorders

Eating disorders also illustrate the principle of **multiple causality**. For example, a young woman whose family emphasizes perfection and self-control may be at risk for anorexia, but might not develop the disorder unless she starts to gain weight in adolescence and happens to be highly attuned to media images of thin models. Or, a female athlete with mild concerns about weight and physical appearance may develop bulimia only after becoming upset about a disappointing period of athletic performance. Someone with a genetic predisposition to anorexia might cross the line from dieting to anorexia when faced with the stresses of leaving home to go to college.

Despite differences among the various theoretical perspectives on eating disorders, they also share some common ground. Both psychodynamic and family systems theorists focus on family dynamics and relationships in maintaining eating disorders. Several theoretical perspectives focus on the cognitive distortions that are central to eating disorders, such as overly rigid thinking about "good" and "bad" foods; while psychodynamic and family systems explanations emphasize the underlying causes of such cognitive distortions, cognitive-behavioral interventions focus directly on identifying the kinds of thinking and behavior that sustain eating disorders.

Treatment of a client with severe anorexia or bulimia often involves a team of specialists. A nutritionist, psychiatrist, and a psychologist or social worker may work together to tackle the multiple components of a client's eating disorder. In most cases, psychotherapy will draw on a variety of theoretical approaches. Cognitive-behavioral techniques might be used to help a client with anorexia gain weight, while psychodynamic interventions may be employed to address the roots of the eating disorder. Similarly, a cognitive-behavioral intervention for a client with bulimia may be supplemented by the prescription of an antidepressant. In cases where the eating disorder is less severe (intense dieting, but without significant weight loss, or occasional bingeing), a single treatment approach may be tried at first, with other treatments added if necessary.

Brief Summary

● Biological explanations of anorexia and bulimia focus on the role of genetic, hormonal, and neurotransmission factors. Studies of twins indicate that genetics play a role in the development of eating disorders, as they do with two other psychological disorders that often co-occur with anorexia and bulimia: depression and obsessive-compulsive disorder. It is not clear if the hormonal and neurotransmission differences between people with and without eating disorders are a cause or result of the eating disorders.

- SSRI antidepressants have been shown to be effective in the treatment of bulimia and may be useful in preventing relapse in people who have already recovered from anorexia.

- The cognitive impairment caused by starvation illustrates the **connection between mind and body** in eating disorders.

- Eating disorders usually arise from **multiple causes**. Most treatments, especially in cases where the eating-disordered behavior is severe, involve the combination of techniques from a variety of theoretical perspectives.

Critical	We have noted the connection between eating disorders and depression.
Thinking	What possibilities do you see for how and why these disorders might
Question	be related?

Case Vignettes | Treatment
Megan | Anorexia Nervosa

Megan's parents became terribly concerned when their daughter collapsed at school. The doctors at the ER determined that Megan needed to be hospitalized so that her electrolyte levels could be monitored. Megan insisted that she was not hungry and that she did not need or want to gain weight. A psychologist evaluated Megan and determined that it was impossible to assess her psychological make-up while she still suffered the effects of severe malnutrition. The psychologist worked with the hospital nutritionist and Megan's physician to develop a weight-gain plan that would be tolerable for Megan. They presented a plan in which she would be allowed to choose what she wanted to eat from a variety of foods as long as she made steady progress toward gaining weight. Megan and her physician determined that she could be released from the hospital to continue her weight recovery plan at home once she reached a weight of 85 pounds. Megan was very eager to leave the hospital, so she agreed to the plan without much protest.

At about the time she reached 82 pounds, Megan's attitude toward her anorexia began to change. No longer fighting the cognitive effects of starvation, she began to talk to her psychologist about how often she did feel hungry, but would deny this to herself and others because she did not want anyone to think she was "weak." Megan complained that giving up her anorexia meant giving up a feeling of being special and "tough," and different from the other teenage girls she knew.

Once Megan left the hospital and returned to living at home, she described to her therapist how her mother had been especially proud of her accomplishments in gymnastics. Megan's mother did not work outside the home and would spend hours driving Megan back and forth between gymnastic meets, or waiting in the back of the gym while Megan practiced. At times, Megan's mother credited her daughter's success in gymnastics to her own dedication and constant support. Megan appreciated her mother's interest in her sport and was happy that her successes pleased her mother, but she also felt angry and resentful that her mother seemed to be taking credit for her hard athletic work. Over time, Megan understood that she began to lose weight so that she could have a personal accomplishment that her mother could not take credit for.

As her therapy progressed, Megan discussed how she had enjoyed gymnastics tremendously when she first began, but that her interest waned over time. She did not tell her parents that she had thoughts of quitting gymnastics because she knew that it meant a lot to them that she was such an accomplished gymnast. Megan also worried that her mother would feel lonely and bored if she did not have Megan's gymnastics, and she felt that she owed it to her mother to keep competing since her mother had been so supportive. Eventually, Megan was convinced that she did want to continue to be a gymnast, but found that she became more worried than ever about what her parents thought of her performance at meets. In the final stages of therapy, Megan struggled to figure out what she wanted for herself and also worked to understand the origins of the strong sense of responsibility she had assumed for her mother's happiness.

Megan and her therapist decided that it would be helpful to begin a family therapy that included her parents. In the family therapy, Megan talked with her parents about how her anorexia stemmed from her desire both to please and to separate from them. The therapist also helped Megan's parents talk about their reactions to their daughter's anorexia and also confront some marital problems that Megan's anorexia had over-

shadowed. Throughout both therapies, Megan continued to meet on an outpatient basis with the hospital nutritionist who monitored her weight and made sure that Megan continued to gain weight until she reached 110 pounds.

Megan's weight stayed in the normal range until her sixteenth birthday. As soon as she began to drive, Megan spent more and more time away from home, missing meals and quickly losing weight. Despite her apparent recovery and therapeutic insights, Megan became severely anorexic again and needed to be re-hospitalized only a year after her first hospitalization.

Case Discussion | Anorexia Nervosa

A team approach was used to help Megan in the early stages of her recovery from anorexia. By including a nutritionist and a physician in Megan's treatment, the psychologist was able to share the responsibility for monitoring Megan's weight. Megan's psychologist decided not to begin therapy while Megan was still severely malnourished because he knew that she would not be cognitively equipped to consider her problems in a constructive way. A behavioral approach was used to help Megan regain weight; she was rewarded with being allowed to choose her own meals as long as she gained weight, and she was able to leave the hospital once her weight reached a satisfactory level.

Megan's individual therapist employed techniques from a variety of theoretical approaches. When therapy began, Megan and her therapist explored a number of psychodynamic themes, particularly ones related to Megan's feelings of wishing to be special and not knowing how to decide what she wanted for herself. They also considered some family systems themes which were addressed later on in family therapy. Yet despite Megan's apparent recovery, her anorexic symptoms returned. Like many suffering from anorexia, Megan faces a life-long struggle with the wish to starve herself when psychologically distressed.

Theresa | Bulimia Nervosa

In Theresa's first therapy session, the therapist discussed how dieting, over-concern about weight, and allowing oneself to purge all work to perpetuate the binge-purge cycle. Theresa began to understand how changing her thinking and behavior would be critical to controlling her bulimia. Before the end of the second session, Theresa's therapist showed her how to monitor everything she ate, to record when she binged and purged, and to keep track of the thoughts and feelings that influenced her eating behaviors.

Theresa felt embarrassed when she next returned to meet with her therapist because she had binged and purged three times in the week since they had met. Together they looked over Theresa's monitoring sheets. The therapist observed that Theresa always binged after a period of fasting for at least six hours. Theresa's therapist encouraged her to eat breakfast, lunch, and dinner every day for the next week. Theresa worried that this would cause her to gain weight, but her therapist reassured her that this would in all likelihood reduce her binges and help her to feel more in control of her eating and weight.

Theresa was surprised to find that she only binged and purged once in the next week, and by the time of her next appointment she thought that she might even be getting back a sense of what it felt like to be a little bit hungry and then to eat only until she was pleasantly full. Next, Theresa and her therapist began to focus on the thoughts and feelings that Theresa had been recording on her monitoring sheets. They talked about Theresa's sense that she could not control herself once she started eating. The therapist noted that there were bingeing episodes in which Theresa felt that she could not stop herself from eating, but the therapist also used the monitoring sheet to point out several other times during the week when Theresa had been able to eat a reasonable amount and then stop.

In the next session, Theresa talked about how she often felt pressured to eat at times when her sorority sisters were eating, even if she didn't feel hungry. Theresa worried that if she did not join her sisters in all their meals, or didn't eat the kinds of things they ate, they would feel that she was being aloof or "stuck-up." Theresa and her therapist talked about how Theresa was making extreme assumptions about what her sisters might be thinking about her. The therapist encouraged Theresa to join her sisters for meals only when she felt like eating, and then to eat only what she wanted. Theresa was instructed to watch carefully to see if her sisters treated her differently, and then report back in the next therapy session.

In the next session, Theresa reported that her sisters did not seem to mind, or even notice, the change in her eating patterns. The remainder of the therapy focused on helping Theresa maintain her improved eating habits and on identifying and challenging other cognitive distortions related to food and eating.

Case Discussion | Bulimia Nervosa

Theresa's therapist used cognitive-behavioral techniques to treat Theresa's bulimia. The therapist educated Theresa about healthy eating and the cognitive distortions that contributed to her unhealthy eating patterns. In addition, Theresa's therapist provided "homework" between sessions such as prescribing a regular pattern of eating, or encouraging Theresa to experiment with how her friends reacted when she did not eat what they ate. Ongoing psychotherapy sessions helped Theresa maintain her progress and provided a forum for addressing new, or as yet unexplored, cognitive distortions.

Chapter Summary

- Eating concerns and disorders occur along a **continuum** that ranges from mild worries about food and weight to severe anorexia or bulimia

- Problematic eating behavior must be considered within the **context** in which it occurs when assessing whether an eating disorder diagnosis is appropriate.

- The DSM-IV-TR includes three diagnostic categories for eating disorders: anorexia nervosa, bulimia nervosa, and eating disorder not otherwise specified.

- The majority of eating disorders occur in young adult women from Western, industrialized countries, highlighting the **cultural relativism** of eating disorders.

- While the categories of anorexia and bulimia characterize two prominent eating disorders, many people with significant eating problems do not meet the DSM-IV-TR diagnostic criteria for either disorder highlighting the **advantages and limitations** of the DSM-IV-TR eating disorder diagnoses.

- The cognitive effects of physical starvation, which can interfere with psychotherapy, illustrate the **connection between mind and body** in eating disorders.

- Eating disorders arise from **multiple causes**, making it important to include a variety of interventions in most treatments.

Jean-Michel Basquiat,
Furious Man, 1982
© Christie's Images.
© 2004 Artists Rights
Society (ARS), New
York/ADAGP, Paris.

Brooklyn-born Jean-Michel Basquiat
(1960–1988) was a major figure in the New
York art scene of the 1980s. He skyrocketed to
fame when his graffiti-inspired creations were
hailed by Rene Ricard of *Artforum* magazine.
Soon after, he began to engage in artistic collab-
orations with ....*continues on page 256*

jean-michel basquiat

chapter nine

DRUG USE AND THE SUBSTANCE USE DISORDERS

Case Vignettes

Rob is a 21-year-old philosophy major at a large Eastern university. He enjoys school and his friends, but feels that he is not functioning at his best, possibly because of his marijuana use. Rob and his friends began drinking on weekends in ninth grade, but after getting very sick at a party Rob decided that alcohol was not for him. In tenth grade, Rob tried marijuana for the first time and found that he enjoyed it a great deal. The high relaxed him and made him feel more creative and intelligent. Also, it seemed to help him forget about the painful turmoil of his parents' recent divorce. Since tenth grade, Rob has gotten high on a regular basis, usually about three times each week. At times, Rob smoked pot every day, but he was always able to cut back after doing so. He even stopped smoking entirely for two months during his senior year in high school when his girlfriend complained that his marijuana use was interfering with their relationship.

During college, Rob has tried a few other drugs, including LSD, ecstasy, and cocaine, but he rarely uses them, as he much prefers the marijuana high. Rob wonders at times if his pot use is a problem. He knows that he could do better in school if he was not smoking marijuana. However, he reassures himself by noting that he has decent grades and that he is so accustomed to being high that people usually can't tell when he is stoned.

Dr. Bryce consulted a psychologist after being denied tenure at the business school where she had been teaching. Dr. Bryce was furious about the decision and told the psychologist that she was considering suing the university. She wanted the psychologist's help in preparing her case and testifying to her emotional turmoil, as she had been agitated, anxious, and unable to sleep since receiving the news two weeks ago. When the psychologist asked Dr. Bryce about the grounds on which tenure had been denied, she reported that the committee had claimed that her teaching and research records were extremely poor, and they attributed this to her alcoholism. Dr. Bryce insisted that she was not an alcoholic and that her weak academic record was due to unfairly burdensome administrative responsibilities. When the psychologist gently questioned Dr. Bryce about her use of alcohol, she admitted to drinking daily to the point of intoxication for the past seven years. She also acknowledged having failed at several important projects and relationships during this time, but argued that these stresses were the cause of her drinking not the result of it. Dr. Bryce claimed that alcohol helped her cope with her difficult situation, and since she could hold her liquor well, she saw no harm in it.

...*continued from page 254*

Andy Warhol and to show his work with Keith Haring and other famed contemporary artists of the time. Basquiat's promising career was tragically cut short when he died of a heroin overdose in 1988 after several years of struggling with drug addiction.

Binge drinking A dangerous practice of rapid alcohol consumption, defined as four or more drinks in a row for a woman or five or more drinks in a row for a man.

Denial A defense mechanism in which an individual fails to acknowledge an obvious reality.

Consequences of substance misuse Experts estimate the annual cost of substance-related disorders in the U.S. at up to $300 billion, but the human cost of substance misuse is incaluable.

DEFINING SUBSTANCE USE DISORDERS

Drug abuse (classified as the "Substance Related Disorders" in the DSM-IV-TR) is considered a major public health problem in the United States. At least one-quarter of the U. S. population will meet the criteria for a substance use disorder over the course of their lifetimes, making substance misuse the most common of all mental disorders (Kessler et al., 1994). In addition, alcohol, nicotine, and other drugs contribute to 25% of all deaths in the United States each year (McGinnis & Feage, 1993; Neumark, Van Etten, & Anthony, 2000). Practically everyone in this country, therefore, will at some point be personally affected by substance misuse—if not their own, then that of friends or family members (see Table 9.1). The social and economic price of substance misuse is staggering. By some estimates, the total annual cost of substance-related disorders in the United States reaches $300 billion; this figure includes the cost of drug-related crime and mental health problems (Shuckit, 2000; Rouse, 1995). The human cost—in deadly car accidents, dysfunctional families, lost achievement potential (such as in the case of Dr. Bryce), violence, and so on—is incalculable.

Among college students, substance misuse is a particularly serious problem. While college has always been a time of experimentation with new and sometimes risky behaviors, American college campuses are currently experiencing an epidemic of a particularly dangerous form of substance abuse known as **binge drinking** (Miller, 2001; Mooney, 2001; Nelson & Wechsler, 2001; Schulenberg et al., 2001). Every year, several students die as a result of binge drinking, which is technically defined as drinking five or more drinks in a row for a man, or four or more drinks in a row for a woman. Drinking-related fatalities aside, the lives of thousands of college students are disrupted by their own or others' alcohol misuse. As a result, the topic of drug use is particularly relevant to a college-age population.

But how do we know when drug or alcohol use is a problem, rather than a harmless recreational activity? In severe cases like Dr. Bryce's, we can easily label her alcohol use as problematic, despite her **denial** of the problem. (Denial is a defense mechanism commonly found among drug users who minimize or deny the seriousness of their problem in order to keep using their drug.) Heavy substance users often become physically and emotionally dependent on a drug, and their daily functioning becomes seriously impaired. But what about Rob, or less extreme examples, in which substance use seems to cause few, if any, obvious problems? Drug and alcohol use is not always abnormal or problematic. We will return to the issue of how to define problematic substance use shortly. First, however, we must start with even more fundamental issues: what are drugs, and why, in general, are they used?

Experts in the field of substance misuse insist that in order to understand drug problems we have to understand two basic facts. First, we must get past the misconception that the term "drugs" refers only to illegal substances such as marijuana, cocaine, or heroin. In fact, any *psychoactive* (that is, brain-affecting) substance is a drug and can potentially be abused. Accordingly, caffeine, alcohol, and nicotine are all drugs. Some drugs are legal, some illegal, and some legal only by prescription. In order to address the misconception that only illegal drugs are abused, most experts have come to prefer the term "substance" to "drug." This is why the relevant DSM-IV-TR category is called Substance-Related Disorders (APA, 2000).

The second point follows from the first. Drug, or substance, use is universal (Garrick et al., 2000; Gerostamoulos, Staikos, & Drummer, 2001; Laranjeira et al., 2001; Shewan et al., 2000). We all use psychoactive chemicals at times, most of us on a daily basis. While legal and consumed in relatively small doses, our daily cup of coffee, cigarette, or glass of wine are forms of substance use (see Box 9.1). Every known soci-

Prevalence Estimates for Substance Use in the United States

Table 9.1

Adapted from Anthony & Arria, 1999

SUBSTANCES	EVER USED (%)	PAST YEAR USE (%)	DEPENDENCE RATE AMONG USERS (%)
Alcohol	83.6	66.9	15.4
Tobacco	73.3	31.7	31.9
Marijuana	33.7	8.5	9.1
Cocaine	11.3	1.7	16.7
Stimulants	6.0	0.7	11.2
Sedatives (anxiolytics and hypnotics)	3.4	0.4	9.2
Analgesics	6.8	2.0	7.5
Inhalants	5.3	1.1	3.7
Hallucinogens	8.7	1.3	4.9
Heroin	1.1	0.1	23.1

Note: "Ever Used" and "Past Year" data based on individuals age 12 and up from the National Household Survey on Drug Abuse, Office of Applied Studies, Substance Abuse and Mental Health Services Administration. Dependence data is from the National Comorbidity Study (Kessler, et al., 1994).

ety—across cultures and across historical epochs—has engaged in substance use of some kind (Rassool, 1998).

Since substance use is so ubiquitous, we must also look at the question of *why* people use drugs. In a general sense, the answer is simple. People use substances in order to obtain feelings of pleasure, or to decrease feelings of distress or tension. In this way, substance use follows the fundamental laws of pleasure seeking and pain aversion that shape all behavior according to behavioral and psychodynamic theories (da Silva et al., 2000; Nesse & Berridge, 1997; Ng, George, & O' Dowd, 1997). As one heroin addict put it, "I use drugs to feel good and to stop feeling bad." This basic explanation applies to all substance use, from the heroin addict to the college student who has one cup of coffee in the morning to feel more alert and one beer in the evening to "take the edge off" a stressful day. While pleasure seeking and pain aversion explain substance use in general, they do not explain why some people can use substances in moderation while others become pathological users. To answer *this* question, we will turn to the various explanatory theories which offer much more detail about the biological, psychological, and sociocultural factors involved in substance misuse (in the Explaining and Treating Substance Use Disorders section later in this chapter).

Binge drinking Binge drinking, a popular activity among college students, is shown here during spring break in Cancun, Mexico. It is serious public health problem on college campuses.

The Importance of Context in Defining Substance Use Disorders

For many years, clinicians viewed substance misuse as a symptom of personality pathology rather than as a distinct syndrome of its own. In the DSM-I and DSM-II, for example, the diagnoses called "addiction" and "drug dependence" were classified under the personality disorders (Fleming, Potter, & Kettyle, 1996). When clinicians tried to evaluate whether someone had a drug problem, they usually relied on relatively crude *quantitative* (numerical) criteria. For example, clinicians focused on *how*

BOX 9.1   College Guerrilla Theatre: Are Coffee Drinkers Drug Addicts?

"At Amherst, the Day the Urns Went Dry" *By Julie Flaherty*

The following article describes a "guerrilla theatre" project by a group of students at Amherst College that aimed to highlight hypocritical attitudes about substance use.

On any given day, the coffee house in the Amherst College campus center offers a dozen brews, plus espresso. But today the pots were covered with white shrouds, and the dispensers in the dining hall were empty.

This was the day that coffee was banned forever from the campus.

Or so it seemed. Actually, it was an elaborate class project staged by an art student, Andrew Epstein, and pulled off with the help of friends and the administration.

While not exactly the War of the Worlds, students and staff did panic when they showed up for their morning cup and found signs that read: "In order to curb the use of caffeine at Amherst College, the sale and distribution of coffee are no longer permitted on campus. Effective Immediately." Questions were to be directed to the Caffeine Control Coordinator.

And indeed, the dining services, which were in on the joke, brewed not a drop today.

Mr. Epstein, who is 22, conceived the Day of No Joe as a final project for his art class on social sculpture, to draw attention to what he regards as the hypocrisy of drug laws. A painting is easily ignored, he said, but remove part of a person's daily routine, and notice is taken.

"I came upon this idea of trying to re-create Prohibition by taking away a substance that's been culturally domesticated to make people aware of their own substance abuse," Mr. Epstein said.

He recruited friends to act as black-market coffee dealers, who sat outside the dining hall and offered bootleg java at inflated prices. "Hey, you need coffee?" Dan Frabman, 22, a senior, hissed from behind his dark glasses. To entice hard-core addicts looking for a quick hit, he added: "Espresso beans, 10 cents a bean." Some bought: many averted their eyes or just said no.

Several confused students—"Is this for real?" one asked—attended a news conference at which Mr. Epstein enumerated the dangers of caffeine. Mr. Epstein later said he studied the speeches of Barry R. McCaffrey and William J. Bennett, two former federal drug-policy czars, to get in character.

The true art of Mr. Epstein's work was in convincing the college to go along with his scheme. The student government approved his plan in a closed-door session late one night. He also met with Charles Thompson, the director of dining services, and Tom Gerety, president of the college, who gave their tacit blessing.

Mr. Gerety said through a spokesman that the project was "a wonderful piece of guerrilla theater."

A college administration supporting the legalization of drugs, however indirectly? DeWitt Godfrey, the assistant professor who oversaw the art projects, said Mr. Epstein, who is known around campus for his involvement in Students for a Sensible Drug Policy, was wise to couch his proposal as art, not policy.

"I suspect if he had come to the administration as an activist, there would have been much stronger resistance," Mr. Godfrey said. "It shows us how art has this kind of peculiar permission."

Mr. Thompson, the head of dining services, said he had trouble sleeping the last several nights, knowing that he and his staff would be on the front lines when people discovered that coffee was no more.

Denying his customers a product "went against everything I believe in my job," he said. He planned to post signs on Wednesday apologizing for the inconvenience, and offering hazelnut and other specialty coffees in the dining hall as penance.

"It wasn't as bad as I thought it would be," Mr. Thompson admitted.

Mr. Epstein had originally proposed to stage his coffee ban next week—finals week. But Mr. Thompson objected, feeling that that would constitute cruel and unusual punishment.

The New York Times, May 9, 2001

Students at Amherst College confronting the absence of coffee in the dining hall.

much of the substance was used, *how often* it was used, and *when* it was typically used during the day. This approach was communicated to the general public, so that as recently as the 1970s high school students were sometimes taught that "an alcoholic is someone who has a drink every day at the same time."

By the time the DSM-III was published (APA, 1980), most clinicians and researchers had come to believe that substance misuse was a distinct syndrome, not a type of personality disorder, and the DSM-III reflected this by placing substance use disorders in their own category. Concurrently, the quantitative approach to defining drug problems fell into disfavor as clinicians realized that numerical criteria did not usefully distinguish problematic from nonproblematic substance use. The major inadequacy of the quantitative approach is that it disregards the importance of **context** in assessing drug use. For example, one drink every day with dinner may not be problematic for a 250-pound man who is only mildly affected by the alcohol because of his body size. The same drink may cause significant impairment in a 95-pound woman and could be quite problematic if consumed on a daily basis. Similarly, assessing alcohol misuse among college students requires careful consideration of the context of their subculture, which differs considerably from other subcultures of our society in terms of its norms for alcohol use (Miller, Stout, & Sheppard, 2000; Weitzman & Wechsler, 2000).

In order to improve upon the quantitative approach to determining pathological drug use, some clinicians began to emphasize the nature of the *relationship* between the user and the drug (Adalbjarnardottir & Rafnsson, 2001; Camlibel, 2000). The relationship approach proposes that users have a complex relationship with the substances they use, and that this relationship can be healthy or pathological, just like interpersonal relationships. Assessing a drug relationship, then, is much like assessing any human relationship. The clinician obtains a history of the relationship, looking for indications as to whether the relationship is adaptive or maladaptive (O'Farrell, 2001). Does the substance use harm the user? How much does it interfere with everyday life? These questions cannot be answered by simply looking at quantitative criteria; they can only be answered by assessing the unique role of substance use in each user's life.

The relationship model for defining pathological drug use has been incorporated into the DSM criteria for diagnosing substance misuse since the DSM-III (APA, 1980). While there have been some modifications in the specific DSM criteria since DSM-III, the basic definition of Substance Use Disorders is "a maladaptive pattern of substance use, leading to clinically significant impairment or distress" (APA, 2000, p. 197; Landry, 1988; Netherton & Walker, 1999). Notice that the emphasis is on *a pattern of use that causes distress or impairment,* rather than on quantitative criteria. Again, it is the particular relationship between the user and the drug that determines whether or not the drug use is pathological.

Legal drugs Millions of people use caffeine to regulate their moods and levels of alertness; Starbucks alone expects to have 10,000 stores in 60 countries by 2005.

The Continuum Between Normal and Abnormal Substance Use

If we return to the cases of Rob and Dr. Bryce, we see that the relationship model can help us define whether or not their drug use is pathological. The relationship model takes into consideration the **continuum between normal and abnormal behavior,** since all relationships can be placed on a continuum from healthy to pathological. On this continuum, the case of Dr. Bryce is an easy call. Her relationship with alcohol is clearly extreme, maladaptive, and a cause of significant impairment. Rob's marijuana use, and the degree of impairment it causes, are less extreme, but still sufficient to suggest that the relationship is maladaptive since it is interfering with his academic performance. Nonetheless, Rob's case, being closer to the middle of the continuum between normality and abnormality, highlights another core concept: the ***advantages and limitations of diagnosis***. Even though the relationship approach helps define pathological substance use, it cannot provide an *absolute* definition of pathology because there will always be some approximation in drawing the line between normality and pathology for any type of mental disorder.

Brief Summary

● Substance misuse is a serious public health problem in our society.

● Psychoactive chemicals, legal and illegal, are universally used, generally in order to increase pleasure and decrease distress or tension.

● The core concepts of the ***importance of context*** and the ***continuum between normality and abnormality*** help define pathological substance use. These core concepts inform the relationship model which has replaced quantitative criteria for defining substance misuse.

Critical Thinking Question	In Rob's case, how might the frequency of his marijuana use (a quantitative factor) play a role in defining whether his use is pathological?

CLASSIFYING SUBSTANCE USE DISORDERS

As we described, the DSM-IV-TR substance use disorders are defined in a manner consistent with a relationship model. The DSM-IV-TR identifies two distinct patterns of substance misuse: *substance abuse* and *substance dependence*. Each of these diagnoses identifies a *pathological relationship between a user and a drug* (or drugs) being used.

The DSM-IV-TR Substance Use Disorders

Substance abuse is the less severe of the two DSM-IV-TR diagnoses, although substance abuse may develop into substance dependence, a diagnosis roughly equivalent to the popular term "addiction." To understand the distinction between substance abuse and substance dependence, let's consider three criteria known informally among clinicians as the "three C's" of substance misuse (see Table 9.2) (Committee on Problems of Drug Dependence, 1984). These criteria describe three features of a pathological drug relationship: a pattern of ongoing use of a substance despite experiencing negative **c**onsequences, a pattern of **c**ompulsive use (that is, significant time and resources are devoted to the substance) and a loss of **c**ontrol over use of the substance, such as using the substance in greater amounts or with greater frequency than intended.

Substance abuse and substance dependence can be distinguished on the basis of the three C's. **Substance abuse** consists of only the first C—continued use of a substance despite negative consequences, such as the case of Rob's slipping grades due to

Substance abuse The DSM-IV-TR diagnosis for substance use that has negative consequences.

Table 9.2	The "Three C's" of Substance Misuse
	1. Continued use despite negative **c**onsequences
	2. **C**ompulsive use
	3. Loss of **c**ontrol of use

Diagnostic Criteria for Substance Abuse

Substance abuse is a maladaptive pattern of substance use leading to clinically significant impairment or distress, as manifested by one (or more) of the following occurring within a 12-month period:

- Recurrent substance use resulting in a failure to fulfill major role obligations at work, school, or home.
- Recurrent substance use in physically hazardous situations.
- Recurrent substance-related legal problems.
- Continued substance use despite having persistent or recurrent social or interpersonal problems caused by or exacerbated by the effects of the substance.

Table 9.3

Adapted from the DSM-IV-TR (APA, 2000)

his marijuana use. Negative consequences may include failure to fulfill one's family, work, or school obligations, the development of substance-related legal or medical problems, or even the presence of dangerous behaviors such as driving while intoxicated (APA, 2000, see Table 9.3). **Substance dependence,** on the other hand, usually involves all three C's (see Table 9.4), as in the case of Dr. Bryce. In addition, substance dependence often (though not always) involves symptoms of physical dependence. Physiological dependence is defined by the presence of one or both of two physical symptoms: **tolerance** and **withdrawal.** Tolerance refers to the body's adaptation to the

Substance dependence The DSM-IV-TR diagnosis for substance use that is compulsive, out of control, and has negative consequences including physical dependence on the substance.

Tolerance The body's adaptation to a substance as indicated by the need for increased amounts of the substance to achieve the desired effect or obtaining less effect in response to using the same amount over time.

Withdrawal Physical or psychological symptoms that occur when substance use is decreased or stopped.

Diagnostic Criteria for Substance Dependence

Substance dependence is a maladaptive pattern of substance use leading to clinically significant impairment or distress, as manifested by three (or more) of the following occurring at any time in the same 12-month period:

- Tolerance, as defined by either of the following:
  - The need for markedly increased amounts of the substance to achieve intoxication.
  - Markedly diminished effect with continued use of the same amount of the substance.
- Withdrawal, as manifested by either of the following:
  - The characteristic withdrawal syndrome for the substance.
  - The same or a related substance is taken to relieve or avoid withdrawal symptoms.
- The substance is taken in larger amounts or over a longer time than was intended.
- There is a persistent desire or unsuccessful effort to reduce or control use.
- A great deal of time is spent in activities necessary to obtain the substance or recover from its use.
- Important social, occupational, or recreational activities are reduced due to use.
- Substance use is continued despite knowledge of having a recurrent physical or psychological problem that is likely to have been caused by or exacerbated by the substance.

Table 9.4

Adapted from DSM-IV-TR (APA, 2000)

Withdrawal Withdrawal, one of the common symptoms of substance dependence, can be excruciatingly unpleasant, frightening, and sometimes medically dangerous.

substance as indicated by the need for increased amounts of the substance to achieve the desired effect or obtaining less effect in response to using the same amount over time (APA, 2000). Frequent drinkers, for example, often find that they must consume ever-increasing amounts of alcohol in order to feel intoxicated. Withdrawal refers to the occurrence of physical or psychological symptoms if substance use is decreased or stopped. For example, regular heroin users typically go through an excruciatingly unpleasant period of withdrawal if they abruptly stop using heroin. It is important to

Table 9.5 | **Addictiveness and Effects of Some Commonly Abused Substances**

From Ray & Ksir, 2002, inside cover

	DRUGS	TRADE/STREET NAMES	MEDICAL USES	PHYSICAL DEPENDENCE
Stimulants	Cocaine	Coke, crack, snow	Local anesthetic	Possible
	Amphetamines	Biphetamine, Desoxyn, Dexedrine, Obetrol	Weight control, hyperactivity, narcolepsy	
	Methylphenidate	Ritalin		
	Phenmetrazine	Preludin		
	Other stimulants	Adipex, Bacarate, Cylert, Didrex, Sanorex, Tenuate, Tepanil		
Depressants	Chloral hydrate	Noctec	Hypnotic	Moderate
	Barbiturates	Amytal, Alurate, Butisol, Mebaral, Numbutol, Seconal	Anesthetic, anticonvulsant, sedative, hypnotic	Moderate to High
	Methaqualone	Quaalude	None	High
	Benzodiazepines	Ativan, Dalmane, Halcion, Librium, Valium, Xanax	Anesthetic, anticonvulsant, sedative, hypnotic	Low to Moderate
	Alcohol	Many types	None	Moderate
Opiates	Opium	Pantofen, Paregoric, Parepectolin	Analgesic, antidiarrheal	High
	Morphine	Morphine	Analgesic	High
	Codeine	Many brands	Analgesic, antitussive	Moderate
	Heroin	Many street names	None in U.S.	High
	Methadone	Dolophine	Analgesic, addict maintenance	High
	Other opiates	Demerol, Dilaudid, Fentanyl, Percodan, Talwin	Analgesic	Varies
Hallucinogens	LSD	Acid, many others	None	None
	Psilocybin	Mushrooms, shrooms		
	Mescaline, peyote	Mesc, cactus, others		
Other Drugs	Amphetamine variants	DOM, STP, MDA, MDMA, ecstasy, MMDA, TMA		Unknown
	Phencyclidine	PCP, angel dust	Veterinary anesthetic	Very low
	Marijuana	Pot, grass, weed, many others	Under investigation	Very low
	Tetrahydrocannibinol	THC, Marinol	Nausea	
	Hashish	Hash	None	

keep in mind that withdrawal can occur even with less potent, legal drugs. The slight headache you may experience if you skip your morning cup of coffee is very likely a mild symptom of caffeine withdrawal!

Substance abuse and substance dependence can be diagnosed with regard to any psychoactive substance. (Table 9.5 lists the addictiveness and effects of various substances.) The DSM-IV-TR lists 11 commonly misused substances but also allows for diagnoses related to other unlisted substances such as anabolic steroids and nitrous

PSYCHOLOGICAL DEPENDENCE	TOLERANCE	USUAL METHODS OF ADMINISTRATION	POSSIBLE EFFECTS	EFFECTS OF OVERDOSE	WITHDRAWAL SYNDROME
Moderate (oral); Very high (injected IV or smoked)	Possible	Sniffed, smoked, injected	Increased alertness, excitation, euphoria, increased pulse rate and blood pressure, insomnia, loss of appetite	Agitation, increased body temperature, hallucinations, convulsions, possible death	Severely depressed mood, prolonged sleep, apathy, irritability, disorientation
	Yes	Oral, injected			
Moderate	Possible	Oral	Slurred speech, disorientation, staggering, drunken behavior	Shallow respiration, cold and clammy skin, weak and rapid pulse, coma, possible death	Anxiety, insomnia, tremors, convulsions, possible death
Moderate to High	Yes	Oral, injected			
High					
Moderate to High					
Moderate		Oral			
Moderate (oral) High (smoked)	Yes	Oral, smoked	Euphoria, drowsiness, slowed respiration, nausea	Slow and shallow breathing, clammy skin, constricted pupils, coma, possible death	Watery eyes, runny nose, yawning, loss of appetite, tremors, panic, chills and sweating, cramps, nausea
Moderate		Oral, injected			
Moderate		Oral			
Very high (IV)		Injected, smoked			
Moderate		Oral, injected			
Varies					
Low	Yes	Oral	Visual illusions, hallucinations, altered perception of one's own body, increased emotionality	More prolonged episodes that many resemble psychotic states	Not reported
Unknown					
High		Oral, smoked			
Moderate	Yes	Smoked	Euphoria, relaxed inhibitions, increased appetite, impaired memory and attention	Fatigue, paranoia, at very high doses a hallucinogen-like psychotic state	Insomnia hyperactivity (syndrome is rare)
		Oral			
		Smoke			

Polysubstance abuse The misuse of three or more substances.

Dual diagnosis The coexistence of a substance use diagnosis and another Axis I or II diagnosis for a client.

oxide (laughing gas). In addition the DSM-IV-TR provides a diagnosis for situations of **polysubstance dependence,** in which three or more substances are misused (see Box 9.2). Because substance use disorders have significant *comorbidity* (co-occurrence) with other Axis I or II disorders, clients can receive a **dual diagnosis** when appropriate, and certain treatment approaches are specifically geared toward dual-diagnosis clients (Den Bleyker, 2000; Drake & Mueser, 2001; Evans & Sullivan, 2001; Hwang & Bermanzohn, 2001; Steele, 2000). For example, an individual with an anxiety disorder may misuse alcohol, or someone with schizophrenia may also have a heroin addiction. We will return to the topic of dual diagnosis in the Explaining and Treating Substance Use Disorders section, because the question of whether substance misuse is the *cause* or the *result* of a client's other psychological problems is a complex and important one.

The Advantages and Limitations of the DSM-IV-TR Diagnoses

One current controversy related to the classification of substance use disorders involves other kinds of compulsive, maladaptive behaviors that are sometimes referred to as "addictions." For example, you may have heard about "food addiction," "sexual addiction," "work addiction," or "gambling addiction" and treatment groups for each of them. Since the "relationship model" implies that any kind of addiction can be viewed as a pathological relationship with a substance or activity, it seems plausible that the DSM-IV-TR might group these other "addictive" behaviors together with substance use disorders. However, this is not the case. As we noted earlier, the tendency over the past few editions of the DSM has been to increasingly separate substance use disorders from other disorders. In addition, many experts are skeptical about whether these other problems are truly addictions in a technical, physical sense (Fisher & Harrison, 1997). As a result, food, sex, work, and gambling "addictions" are not found in the DSM-IV-TR, although they share features with other mental disorders. For example, food addiction resembles some of the eating disorders (Chapter 8), sexual addiction resembles some of the sexual disorders (Chapter 10), and work addiction resembles obsessive-compulsive personality disorder (Chapter 11). Gambling addiction is described in the DSM-IV-TR as "pathological gambling," a disorder listed under the heading "Impulse Control Disorders Not Otherwise Specified" (APA, 2000). The issue of how closely these other "addictions" resemble substance addiction, and how they can best be classified remains controversial and unresolved (Fisher & Harrison, 1997).

Brief Summary

- The current DSM-IV-TR categories for substance use disorders are based on maladaptive relationships between a user and a drug (or drugs) as shown by a pattern of compulsive use, a loss of control over use, and continued use despite negative consequences (the "Three C's")

- Substance abuse is diagnosed when the main symptom is continued use despite negative consequences, while substance dependence involves all three of the "Three C's" including, in some cases, physical dependence as indicated by tolerance and withdrawal symptoms.

Commonly Abused Substances

Let's turn now to a description of some of the most commonly misused substances (Table 9.6). Understanding the characteristics, properties, and effects of different kinds of drugs will help us to address the two major topics to be covered later in the chapter: how substance misuse can be *explained* and *treated.*

BOX 9.2   An Addict's Firsthand Account

"Dope, A Love Story"   *by Patti Davis*

This article by Patti Davis, daughter of Nancy and Ronald Reagan, chronicles her struggle with polysubstance addiction.

I once knew a girl who fell deeply in love at the vulnerable age of 15; her paramour was drugs. The girl would look at you with wide, dark eyes that seemed simultaneously to plead for understanding while pushing you away. There wasn't much room for anyone else in her life. Every time I see another mug shot of Robert Downey Jr., I think of that girl. Those eyes…

I overheard a comment by a stranger last Tuesday, when the news of Downey's latest arrest was released. "Did you see his mug shot?" the man was saying to his companion. "More like a smug shot. He was practically smirking."

No, I wanted to say. You don't understand. He was wishing that he could hide.

I knew a girl whose lover came in several disguises—white cross Methedrine, orange triangles of Dexedrine, "black beauties," long white lines of coke. She followed her lover everywhere—into parking lots with strangers. Into dark cars, into the shadows along steep mountain roads, into apartments that smelled like stale smoke and had three or four locks on every door. When her lover wasn't with her, she was left with her own terror of how to move through the world alone. She didn't know how to deal with people alone; she needed her partner, her other half. You need to know this about drugs: unlike people, drugs don't judge you or look at you too closely, too intimately. They don't ask you to reveal yourself or confide your secrets. They just take you away—far away; they let you hide, which is what frightened people want to do.

One night this girl's terror became too much. She sat alone in a bathroom, dark except for the blue-white light of the streetlamp outside spilling across her hands, her wrists, the small square of the razor blade as it moved closer to her soft web of veins. She imagined blood spilling over white porcelain; she imagined the end. But someone had told her something long ago when she was a child—that God put each of us here for a reason. A thought took shape in her mind, even through the jangle of nerves and the blur of the emotions, ragged by then from years of drug use. She felt God's heart breaking at the touch of cold steel on her soft young wrist; a little more pressure was all it would take. She felt like she was betraying him. She put the blade back in the medicine cabinet.

That girl was me. I never got arrested like Robert Downey Jr.—more because of dumb luck or chance than anything else. But if I had been arrested, my eyes would have looked the same as his—a hard, puzzling, faraway stare into the camera. It isn't smugness. It's actually honesty, as strange as that sounds. It's a look that says, There, now you know who I really am. I'm not lying and pretending I know how to live in this world. I don't. Not alone, not without my lover.

Remember how Robert Downey Jr. described his relationship with drugs at one of his hearings? He said it's like he has a gun in his mouth, and he loves the taste of the gunmetal. You will never understand drug addiction unless you understand that it's a love story.

My story would be neatly tied up if I said that, after that night, after I put away the razor blade, I never did drugs again. But stories are rarely that neat. It was years before I stopped. I lost work, I risked my life, I even stole prescription drugs from people's medicine cabinets. I would reach past the razor blades and grab the pills. Dying can be accomplished in many ways.

I finally stopped because I kept feeling I was letting God down. Because I didn't want to die like that. Because even though I was in love, my lover was cold and cruel, and hardly faithful.

But I never fell out of love. Every time I see a movie in which people are doing coke, I want it. I can almost taste it in the back of my throat, and I still love the taste. You don't get over drugs; you don't ever fall out of love. You just—somehow—tell yourself every morning that you can go through that day, that

night, without the one lover who took away your fear. If Robert Downey Jr., ever leaves his lover, you will see a different look in his eyes—more frightened, I suspect, but with a bravery that will move you to tears. I don't know why the world is so hard for some people, why some of us run for the refuge of drugs. I do know why some of us quit though. I followed the white lines of coke laid out on mirror after mirror. In the end there was only the mirror left. I had to look at myself.

Time Magazine, May 7, 2001

Patti Davis

Table 9.6	Categories of Commonly Abused Substances

DEPRESSANTS	STIMULANTS	HALLUCINOGENS	OTHER DRUGS
Alcohol	Cocaine	LSD	Marijuana
Sedative-Hypnotics	Amphetamines	Psilocybin	Ecstasy
Opioids	Nicotine	Mescaline	PCP/Ketamine
	Caffeine		GHB
			Inhalants
			Steroids

Depressants Substances that slow CNS functions.

Alcoholism Another term for alcohol dependence.

Depressants

Substances classified as central nervous system (CNS) **depressants** slow down the processes of the CNS by reducing the activity of some nerve cells (Ledig et al., 1998; McCann et al., 1998; Schuckit, 2000). Heart rate, breathing, alertness, and other CNS functions decrease. In small doses, depressants produce a mild tranquilizing, sedative, or numbing effect and impair psychomotor performance (Blin et al., 2001; Seligman, Walker, & Rosenhan, 2001). At higher doses, CNS effects become increasingly dangerous. Anesthesia (loss of sensation), coma, and even death can occur (Dodgen & Shea, 2000; Lazorthes et al., 2000; Oestroem & Eriksson, 2001). The most commonly used and abused depressant substances are alcohol, sedative-hypnotics (mostly anti-anxiety and sleeping pills), and opioids (derivates of opium).

Alcohol Ninety percent of Americans use alcohol at some point in their lives, and 60% to 70% are current drinkers (McDowell & Spitz, 1999). Alcohol is also the most commonly abused substance in the United States (Dodgen & Shea, 2000; National Clearinghouse for Alcohol and Drug Information Services, 2000), but whites consume more and binge drink more frequently than blacks or Hispanics (Wallace, 1999). By some estimates, 40% of Americans will experience alcohol-related problems in their lifetimes. Around 25% will meet DSM-IV-TR criteria for alcohol *abuse* at some point in their lives; up to 10% will meet criteria for alcohol *dependence,* commonly known as **alcoholism** (McDowell & Spitz, 1999).

Alcohol is typically ingested by drinking beverages containing ethyl alcohol, or ethanol, a simple two-carbon molecule. Alcoholic beverages vary widely in the amount of ethanol they contain, ranging from approximately 4% in beer to up to 50% in liquors and distilled spirits (Dodgen & Shea, 2000). Ethanol is easily absorbed into the bloodstream through the lining of the entire digestive tract. The rate of absorption varies according to several factors such as the amount of food in the stomach, body weight, and the speed at which the alcohol is consumed. As alcohol travels to the CNS it affects a number of neurotransmission systems in the brain. For example, alcohol appears to increase the activity of the neurotransmitters serotonin, dopamine, and gamma-aminobutyric acid (GABA) (Lappalainen et al., 1998; Schuckit, 2000), contributing to the sense of well-being and decreased anxiety associated with alcohol use (Larkin, 1998). It also decreases the activity of glutamate, a major excitatory neurotransmitter in the brain.

Simultaneously, alcohol decreases the activity of neurological systems responsible for emotional and physical self-control, causing the well-known disinhibiting

Depressants Depressant substances commonly cause loss of coordination and decreased inhibition, in addition to other effects.

effects of the drug. With a moderate dose of alcohol, a person may become louder and more impulsive. (An old psychiatric joke has it that the superego is the only part of the mind that dissolves in alcohol!) With increasing intoxication, brain centers controlling memory, balance, speech, and coordination are also affected (see Table 9.7). The intoxicated person may slur his or her speech, stagger clumsily, and generally become physically incompetent. Shakespeare famously described a common sexual version of emotional disinhibition combined with physical incapacity when the Porter tells Macduff (Macbeth, Act II, Scene iii) that alcohol "provokes the desire but takes away the performance."

The degree of intoxication from alcohol is primarily determined by the amount consumed. One drink is usually defined as 12 grams of ethanol, an amount found in one 12-ounce can of beer, a 5-ounce glass of wine, or 1.5 ounces of an 80-proof liquor ("proof" is double the percentage of alcohol in the beverage). On average, one drink usually raises the blood alcohol level by 0.02% to 0.04% (McDowell & Spitz, 1999). However, there is a great deal of variability among people in the rate at which alcohol is metabolized in the liver (see Table 9.8). For example, women tend to manifest higher blood levels of alcohol than men after ingesting equivalent doses. This may occur in part because they have lower activity levels of the enzyme *alcohol dehydrogenase,* which breaks down alcohol and contributes to its elimination from the body. As a result, women are typically twice as affected as men by the same amount of alcohol. Thus, for a man, it may take four or six drinks to produce a blood alcohol level in the range of legal intoxication (0.08–0.10 g/100 mL, depending on the state), but only two or three drinks for a woman.

The physical and psychological effects of long-term alcohol misuse can be devastating. Chronic alcohol use damages almost every important system in the body (APA, 2000; Salaspuro, 1995). For example, the CNS can be profoundly affected in a

Relationship Between Blood Alcohol Concentration (BAC) and Behavior	Table 9.7

From Ray & Ksir, 2002, pp. 254 & 255

PERCENT BAC	BEHAVIORAL EFFECTS
0.05	Lowered alertness, usually good feeling, release of inhibitions, impaired judgment
0.10	Slower reaction times and impaired motor function, less caution
0.15	Large, consistent increases in reaction time
0.20	Marked depression in sensory and motor capability, intoxication
0.25	Severe motor disturbance, staggering, sensory perceptions, great impairment
0.30	Stuporous but conscious—no comprehension of what's going on
0.35	Surgical anesthesia; about LD, minimal level causing death
0.40	About LD

LD = Lethal dose

Table 9.8 — Relationships Among Gender, Weight, Alcohol Consumption, and Blood Alcohol Concentration

From Ray & Ksir, 2002, p. 256

Blood alcohol concentrations (g/100 mL)

ABSOLUTE ALCOHOL (OUNCES)	BEVERAGE INTAKE[1]	FEMALE (100 LB)	MALE (100 LB)	FEMALE (150 LB)	MALE (150 LB)	FEMALE (200 LB)	MALE (200 LB)
$1/2$	1 oz spirits[2] 1 glass wine 1 can beer	0.045	0.037	0.03	0.025	0.022	0.019
1	2 oz spirits[2] 2 glasses wine 2 cans beer	0.090	0.075	0.06	0.050	0.045	0.037
2	4 oz spirits[2] 4 glasses wine 4 cans beer	0.180	0.150	0.12	0.100	0.090	0.070
3	6 oz spirits[2] 6 glasses wine 6 cans beer	0.270	0.220	0.18	0.150	0.130	0.110
4	8 oz spirits[2] 8 glasses wine 8 cans beer	0.360	0.300	0.24	0.200	0.180	0.150
5	10 oz spirits[2] 10 glasses wine 10 cans beer	0.450	0.370	0.30	0.250	0.220	0.180

[1] In one hour [2] 100-proof

number of ways. Chronic drinkers often become vitamin B (especially thiamine) deficient as alcohol replaces food in their diets, the capacity to absorb vitamin B decreases, and additional vitamin B is needed to metabolize alcohol (Brun & Andersson, 2001; Hope, Cook, & Thomson, 1999). Vitamin B deficiency can lead to severe neurological impairments such as *Wernicke's encephalopathy,* a syndrome of cognitive, visual, and motor deterioration, and *Korsakoff's syndrome,* which involves amnesia and other cognitive symptoms (Chapter 7). Gastrointestinal problems associated

Cirrhosis of the liver These pictures contrast a healthy liver (left) with one damaged by cirrhosis. Long-term alcohol use can lead to cirrhosis of the liver, a chronic disease in which scarring of the liver tissue blocks the flow of blood through the liver from the intestines.

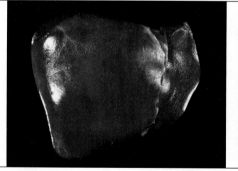

with prolonged alcohol use include cancers, ulcers, gastritis, cirrhosis of the liver, and pancreatitis. Hypertension (high blood pressure) and cardiomyopathy (heart muscle damage) are among the cardiovascular effects of chronic alcohol use.

Among the many other medical problems associated with alcohol use, one deserves special mention because it directly affects someone other than the user: *fetal alcohol effects* (FAE), the most serious form of which is called **fetal alcohol syndrome (FAS)** (Raut, Stephen, & Kosofsky, 1996). FAS consists of mental retardation, growth impairment, and facial distortions as a result of intrauterine alcohol exposure related to a mother's drinking during pregnancy. FAS also results in increased mortality in affected children, the need for long-term special education and medical services, and high levels of family stress (Greenfield & Sugarman, 2001). Women who consume 5 ounces of alcohol per day during pregnancy have a 33% chance that their child will develop FAS, a 33% chance that their child will experience more moderate fetal alcohol effects, and only a 33% of having a normal child (Raut, Stephen, & Kosofsky, 1996). As a result, it is strongly advised that pregnant women refrain from alcohol consumption.

In addition to the serious physical risks of alcohol-related disorders, heavy alcohol users run the risk of causing serious psychological damage to themselves and those around them. Alcoholism can lead directly or indirectly—because of the havoc it causes in a person's life—to anxiety, depression, and a variety of other psychological symptoms including changes in personality (Brun & Andersson, 2001; Roberts & Linney, 2000; Zernig et al., 2000). It is often noted by clinicians that when serious substance problems begin, an individual's emotional development stops (Krystal & Raskin, 1994; Leonard & Blane, 1999). For example, Dr. Bryce (described in one of the chapter-opening case vignettes) was in her 30s when she sought help, but her psychologist noted that she seemed to have the emotional maturity of an adolescent, the point at which she began drinking.

Finally, as our awareness of the effects of alcohol misuse has increased, clinicians have become increasingly sensitive to the effects of alcoholism on the family members of the alcoholic. Having an alcoholic parent or spouse can be a profoundly damaging experience that is associated with increased risk for a variety of emotional problems (Barber & Gilbertson, 1999; Malpique et al., 1998; Roberts & Linney, 2000). The current popularity of therapy groups such as Adult Children of Alcoholics (ACOA) testifies to the wide-ranging effects of alcoholism on family members (Haaken, 1993; Sussman & Smith, 1992), although some experts question the usefulness of the ACOA label (Fisher & Harrison, 1997).

Sedative-Hypnotics

For centuries, human beings have searched for substances that might promote relaxation and sleep. Such substances, of course, fall under the general heading of depressants, and alcohol is one substance that has been widely (though not necessarily effectively) used for these purposes. In the 1800s, bromide salts were a popular form of sleeping medication, so much so that the word *bromide* entered our vocabulary as a term for a tiresome idea or person (Ray & Ksir, 2002). Unfortunately, most of the substances used to promote relaxation (**sedatives**) and sleep (**hypnotics**) have turned out to be problematic. Many are habit forming or have troublesome side effects. In addition, while these drugs produce anxiety relief (known as an **anxiolytic** effect) at low doses, and sleep at higher doses, overdoses can be lethal because depressants slow respiration and heartbeat.

As our understanding of neurochemistry has accelerated over the past 50 years, many new sedative-hypnotic drugs have been discovered and marketed. They have important medical uses in the treatment of anxiety and anxiety disorders, sleep disorders, seizure disorders, and for anesthesia during medical procedures. But they are

Fetal Alcohol Syndrome This Sioux Indian child living on the Pine Ridge Reservation suffers from FAS.

Fetal alcohol syndrome (FAS) A syndrome consisting of mental retardation, growth impairment, and facial distortions in a child caused by intrauterine alcohol exposure related to a mother's drinking during pregnancy.

Sedatives Substances used to promote relaxation.

Hypnotics Substances used to promote sleep.

Anxiolytic An anxiety-reducing effect.

also widely misused. As we describe the history and nature of sedative-hypnotics, you will see that researchers have been able to develop increasingly safe and effective sedative-hypnotics, although misuse of these drugs remains a major problem.

Barbiturates, a major class of sedative-hypnotic drugs, were first discovered and marketed in the early 1900s. In 1903, barbitol—"named after a charming lady named Barbara"—was the first barbiturate to be marketed (Robson, 1999). Barbiturates became so popular as anxiolytics and hypnotics that before long 2,000 different barbiturates were on the market. However, it soon became clear that barbiturates were dangerously addictive. By the 1960s, there were 2,000 deaths per year from barbiturate overdose in Great Britain alone; among the notable casualties of barbiturate overdose in the 1960s and 1970s were the musicians Brian Jones, Jimi Hendrix, Janis Joplin, and Elvis Presley (Robson, 1999). As a result, the market for newer, safer, nonaddictive sedative-hypnotics was enormous.

Fortunately, in the meantime, another class of sedative-hypnotic drugs was being developed—the *benzodiazepines.* The benzodiazepines showed promise as nonaddictive, nonsedating anxiety medications. Like barbiturates, benzodiazepines enhance the activity of GABA, an inhibitory neurotransmitter. Benzodiazapines calm nerve cells by increasing GABA's inhibitory role in neural transmission (Friedman et al., 1996; Nishino, Mignot, & Dement, 2001). In early experiments, mice given chlordiazepoxide (a benzodiazepine later marketed as Librium) loosened their grip on wire screen cages and fell to the floor, and then walked around sniffing normally. In contrast, mice given barbiturates immediately fell asleep (Ray & Ksir, 2002). Librium was introduced as a medication in 1961, followed two years later by diazepam (trade name Valium), another benzodiazepine. These medications were aggressively and successfully marketed by their manufacturers; between 1972 and 1978, Valium was the most frequently prescribed drug in the United States (Friedman et al., 1996).

Benzodiazepines are still widely used for anxiety problems, sleep problems, and other medical conditions and procedures (see Table 9.9). Because they share CNS depressant properties with other depressant substances such as alcohol, benzodiazepines can exhibit **cross-tolerance**, meaning that when tolerance develops for one drug in the class it may automatically be present for others. (As a result, benzodiazepines can relieve symptoms of alcohol withdrawal and are often used in treating alcohol dependence.) The combined depressant properties of different drugs in the

Cross-tolerance Tolerance extending across drugs within a class.

Table 9.9	**Some Popular Benzodiazepines**	
From Ray & Ksir, 2002, p. 208	**TYPE**	**HALF-LIFE (HOURS)**[1]
Anxiolytics	Alprazolam (Xanax)	6–20
	Chlordiazepoxide (Librium)	5–30
	Clonazepam (Klonopin)	30–40
	Clorazepate (Tranxene)	30–200
	Diazepam (Valium)	20–100
	Lorazepam (Ativan)	10–20
	Oxazepam (Serax)	5–15
Hypnotics	Flurazepam (Dalmane)	40–250
	Temazepam (Restoril)	5–25
	Triazolam (Halcion)	1.7–3

[1] Amount of time for half the drug to be eliminated from the body.

depressant class can also result in dangerous **synergistic** effects—that is, a multiplication of effects when two or more drugs of the same class are taken together. This is why combinations of alcohol and benzodiazepines (such as Valium) or other sedative-hypnotics are so dangerous. The multiplied effects of these depressants can readily lead to coma and even death.

It is estimated that 12.5% of the U. S. population uses benzodiazepines each year, mostly to treat anxiety (Fingerhood, 2000; Kendler et al., 2000; Kendler, Karkowski, & Prescott, 1999). This rate is especially high compared to rates of usage in other countries; for example, in China the current use rate is 0.1% (Teesson, Hodder & Buhrich, 2000; Zhimin et al., 2001). Currently, alprazolam (trade name Xanax) is the most commonly prescribed benzodiazepine.

Benzodiazepines are typically taken orally, although they can be administered intramuscularly or intravenously. Despite their main advantage of causing less respiratory depression than barbiturates, benzodiazepines are not without problems. They can be addictive when used for four weeks or more and can produce tolerance and withdrawal symptoms (Brady, Myrick, & Malcom, 1999; McCrady & Epstein, 1999). In addition, they are widely abused as street drugs (Levinthal, 1999).

A particularly disturbing form of benzodiazepine misuse has come to public attention recently as flunitrazepan (Rohypnol, sometimes referred to on the street as "roofies") has gained notoriety as a "date rape" drug (Calhoun et al., 1996; Galvan et al., 2000). Added to alcohol, this benzodiazepine—which has not been approved for use in the United States but is widely available on the black market—causes disinhibition and loss of memory (Daderman & Lidberg, 1999). In 1997, the manufacturer altered the composition of Rohypnol so that it would change the color of alcoholic beverages and thereby warn potential victims of its misuse (Ray & Ksir, 2002).

Opioids The term **opioids** refers to all of the derivatives—natural and synthetic—of the opium poppy, and chemically similar drugs. The opium poppy produces opium for only a few days of its annual life cycle, right after the petals drop and before the seed pod matures (Ray & Ksir, 2002). The thick substance that oozes out of the unripe seedpod at this time contains morphine and codeine, natural products of the opium plant. Heroin, methadone, and analgesics (painkillers) such as Vicodin, Dilaudid, Darvon, and Demerol are synthetic opioids that mimic morphine's action on the CNS

Synergistic The multiplication of effects when two or more drugs of the same class are taken together.

Opioids All of the derivatives—natural and synthetic—of the opium poppy.

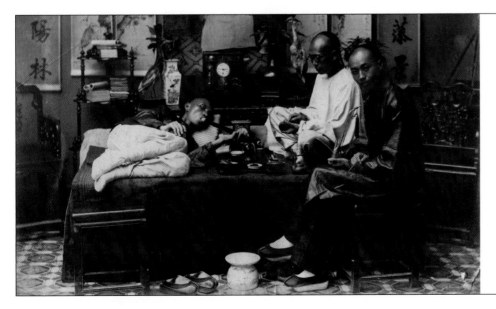

Opioids Opium has been used around much of the world for centuries; experts estimate that opiate use dates back at least 3500 years. By the early nineteenth century, opium use had spread across Europe, the Middle East, and the Far East. Opium was often consumed in smoking dens like the one pictured here.

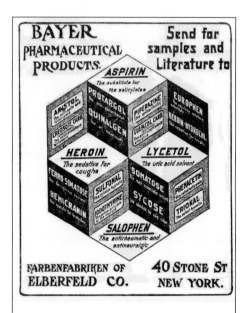

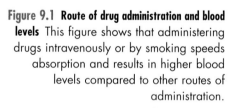

Historical relativism Heroin was a legal cough remedy at one time, as seen here in a advertisement for Bayer Heroin.

Narcotics Another term for opioids

Analgesia The effect of pain relief.

Endogenous Internal or natural.

Enkephalins The first endogenous opioids to be discovered.

Endorphins A class of endogenous opioids known as the cause of "runner's high."

Stimulants Substances that increase CNS functions.

(Sloan & Wala, 1998). Heroin was once marketed by Bayer as an over-the-counter cough suppressant before its dangers were understood.

The opioids are sometimes also referred to as the **narcotics**, a term derived from the Greek word for "stupor." The term is appropriate, since opioids are powerful CNS depressants whose main effects include **analgesia** (pain relief), a feeling of euphoria, and sedation. In addition, opioids decrease respiration and smooth muscle motility, resulting in, among other things, constipation and cough suppression (Galanter & Kleber, 1999). Opioids cause these changes, and differ from other depressant drugs, by binding with specific opioid receptor sites throughout the body, rather than affecting the CNS generally (Carvey, 1998; McDowell & Spitz, 1999). These inborn opiate receptors exist in order to be available for the body's **endogenous** (natural, internal) opioids, which help regulate feelings of pleasure and pain. The first endogenous opioids, the **enkephalins,** were discovered in 1975; since then the **endorphins,** known to runners as the cause of the "runner's high," and at least 18 other endogenous opioids have been identified (Lichtman & Martin, 1999).

Opiates can be taken orally, intravenously, snorted, or smoked; the resulting blood levels of opiates, and the time it takes to achieve them, depend upon the route of administration (see Figure 9.1). Physical and psychological tolerance (including cross-tolerance to all other opioids) develops quickly; an opioid addict uses doses that would kill a first-time user. Dependence can develop in as little as one week for regular intravenous (IV) users (Fisher & Harrison, 1997). Withdrawal from opioids can be excruciatingly uncomfortable. During withdrawal, the ex-user experiences severe flulike symptoms including vomiting, sweating, aching, and diarrhea along with cravings for the drug (Senay, 1998). An old adage states that "no one ever dies of heroin withdrawal—they just wish they did" (McDowell & Spitz, 1999).

Stimulants

Stimulant is the general name given to psychoactive substances that increase CNS activity; stimulants have essentially the opposite effect of depressants (Fisher & Harrison, 1997). Stimulants enhance arousal, alertness, and energy. Mild stimulants, such as nicotine and caffeine, have relatively subtle effects, such as relief from fatigue and improved concentration (Leon, 2000; Liguori, Grass, & Hughes, 1999). Stronger stimulants, such as amphetamines and cocaine, can produce powerful feelings of euphoria and dramatically increase energy level. Stimulants have safe and appropriate medical uses, but when misused recreationally they can cause psychosis and even death.

Figure 9.1 Route of drug administration and blood levels This figure shows that administering drugs intravenously or by smoking speeds absorption and results in higher blood levels compared to other routes of administration.
From McDowell & Spitz, 1999

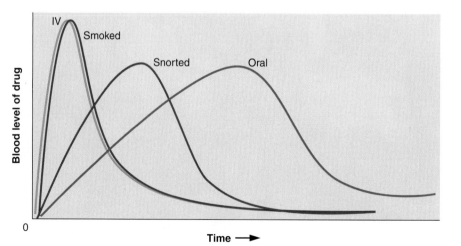

As with other psychoactive substances already discussed, stimulants have a long history of use. Humans have always been interested in substances that could relieve fatigue, enhance performance, and produce ecstatic feelings. For example, ancient Chinese cultures used a medicinal herbal tea known as Mahuang over 5,000 years ago (Jacobs & Hirsch, 2000; McDowell & Spitz, 1999). The active ingredient in Mahuang is ephedrine, a stimulant still used medically for bronchodilation in asthma and as a treatment for urinary incontinence (Vernon et al., 2000). Cocaine was cultivated by the Incas in South America 4,000 years ago, and spread rapidly through Europe in the 1800s (McDowell & Spitz, 1999). Nicotine, present in tobacco, was cultivated by Native Americans for many centuries before being exported to Europe. Finally, caffeine, found in coffees and teas, has long been the world's most popular stimulant (Ray & Ksir, 2002: Wilson, 2000). Let's take a closer look at each of these stimulants.

Cocaine (Coke, Rock, Snow) **Cocaine,** perhaps the most powerful known stimulant, has had a long and interesting history (see Table 9.10). It is derived from the leaves of the coca plant, which grows mostly in South America. The effects of cocaine are rapid and intense. Cocaine appears to block the reuptake of the neurotransmitters dopamine, norepinephrine, and serotonin, causing increased transmission of these chemicals in the brain (Sizemore, Co, & Smith, 2000), resulting in powerful feelings of euphoria, confidence, energy, and excitement that last a relatively brief time (Ray & Ksir, 2002; Regan, 2001). Unfortunately, cocaine use can lead to addiction and withdrawal syndromes, causing numerous physical, psychological, and social problems (Lex, 2000).

Recreational cocaine use involves the ingestion of the drug through chewing, snorting, smoking (after conversion of cocaine into crack), or IV administration. Inhaling the heated vapors of pure cocaine, a technique known as freebasing, was also briefly popular in the 1970s until the dangers of heating the volatile chemicals involved became widely known. The comedian Richard Pryor, for example, was severely burned while freebasing cocaine. Windle and Welch (1995) noted a threefold increase in freebasing and injecting cocaine among recent users, suggesting that this trend is on the rise again.

The effects of cocaine begin within minutes, especially after IV use, snorting, or smoking, all of which lead to rapid absorption. Some experts believe that cocaine is

Cocaine A powerful stimulant derived from the leaves of the coca plant.

Early History of Cocaine	Table 9.10

From Kerfoot, Sakoulas, & Hyman, 1996, p. 158

6th century C.E. ■ Peruvians bury coca leaves as a "necessity" for the afterlife, likely indicating use at that time.

16th century C.E. ■ Spaniards pay gold/silver mine slaves with coca leaves to improve performance.

1859 ■ Alkaloid cocaine isolated from coca leaves.

1884 ■ Freud publishes "Uber Coca" describing cocaine as a central nervous system stimulant useful in treatment of numerous ailments.

1886 ■ Coca-Cola, containing cocaine, produced by Georgia pharmacist Pemberton as "brain tonic" drink (caffeine substituted for cocaine in 1906).

1906/1914 ■ Federal Acts require cocaine listed as an ingredient in patent medicines and registration of those involved in trade of coca products.

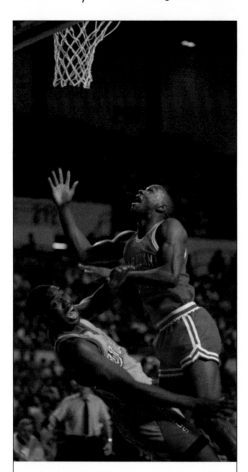

Dangers of cocaine use Len Bias, shown in the red uniform during an NCAA tournament game, died of a heart attack after using cocaine. Bias, who played at the University of Maryland, was a first round NBA draft pick, but he never played professionally because of his untimely death.

Amphetamines Synthetic stimulants with a chemical structure similar to the neurotransmitters dopamine and norepinephrine.

the most reinforcing of all drugs (McDowell & Spitz, 1999; Wilcox et al., 2000). Laboratory animals offered cocaine will prefer it to food, sex, or warmth (Robson, 1999; McDowell & Spitz, 1999). While not all users become addicted, the powerful physical and psychological reinforcement of the drug can lead relatively quickly to dependence. Cocaine "binges"—a compulsive pattern of frequent re-dosing—can sometimes last for days (Robson, 1999). Tolerance also develops rapidly. Withdrawal from cocaine is not as dramatic as withdrawal from alcohol or opioids, but it can be very unpleasant. The infamous "crash" of cocaine withdrawal involves cravings, depression, and irritability. Users sometimes combine cocaine with heroin (known as a "speedball") in order to lessen the effects of the crash (David et al., 2001). The less dramatic withdrawal syndrome associated with cocaine as compared to some other drugs has misled users and even health care professionals, at times, into believing that cocaine is not addictive (Fleming et al., 1996).

One of the greatest dangers of cocaine use is overdose, even from relatively small amounts of the drug. Overdoses of cocaine, like amphetamines, can cause psychosis, seizures, and fatal heart attacks. This danger of cocaine use received heavy press coverage in 1986 when Len Bias, a University of Maryland basketball star, died of a heart attack caused by an apparently modest dose of cocaine, shortly after he was chosen by the Boston Celtics in the first round of the NBA draft (Smith, 1992).

Amphetamines (Speed, Uppers, Bennies, Crank, Ice, Crystal Meth) **Amphetamines** are drugs with a chemical structure quite similar to those of the neurotransmitters norepinephrine and dopamine, and they produce their stimulant effects by increasing the availability of these neurotransmitters (Palfai & Jankiewicz, 1997). Amphetamines were first synthesized in the 1880s, but they were not introduced medically until almost 50 years later (McDowell & Spitz, 1996). The first medical stimulants were made available in 1932 as appetite suppressants for weight loss, and this has continued to be one of their common uses and abuses (Kanayama et al., 2001).

When they first became available in the 1930s, amphetamines were hailed as wonder drugs. As with so many other drugs, this period of wild enthusiasm was only later tempered by a more balanced understanding of the risks associated with their use. Methamphetamine, the most popular early form of amphetamine, was widely used as a "pep pill" throughout the 1940s and 1950s (McDowell & Spitz, 1996). Truck drivers, students, and others who needed to stay awake for long periods were eager users. Some of the popularity of amphetamines during this era can be attributed to their widespread use during World War II. The American, British, Japanese, and German militaries all experimented with giving amphetamines to soldiers in order to enhance performance. Large stockpiles of amphetamines remaining after the war were made easily available, without a prescription, to the general population through aggressive marketing by drug companies (Ray & Ksir, 2002). In fact, the first recorded instance of widespread amphetamine abuse occurred among the Japanese population following World War II, when a significant percentage of the Japanese population became amphetamine-dependent (Robson, 1999).

As a result of increasing abuse, the United States government established tighter controls over amphetamines in the late 1940s and 1950s. But by the 1960s, amphetamine use was soaring. Amphetamines were being widely prescribed to facilitate weight loss and to treat depression (King & Ellinwood, 1997)—two uses that are now considered medically questionable. The term "speed freak" became commonplace as recreational IV methamphetamine use increased (Ray & Ksir, 2002). Between 1969 and 1971, the U.S. government embarked on a campaign to reduce amphetamine production and to educate doctors and the public about the dangers of amphetamine abuse (using the "speed kills" slogan) (King & Ellinwood, 1997; McDowell & Spitz, 1996).

Production of amphetamines dropped by 80% during this period, and many abusers shifted to cocaine, which was became increasingly available in the 1970s (Erickson et al., 1994). Other abusers began manufacturing their own amphetamines in homemade labs, a practice that continues today and is a primary source of "crank" (methamphetamine) and "ice" (a smokable form of methamphetamine) (Lit et al., 1996; Wilson, 2000).

Currently, amphetamines do have some appropriate medical uses. They are considered a standard treatment for narcolepsy (a sleep disorder characterized by sudden and frequent onset of sleep) and for attention-deficit/hyperactivity disorder (ADHD; see Chapter 13) (Littner et al., 2001). Methylphenidate (Ritalin), a milder stimulant than amphetamine, has been shown, paradoxically, to have a calming effect in treating ADHD, probably because it stimulates attentional and behavioral inhibition centers in the brain (King & Ellinwood, 1997; Solanto, Arnsten, & Castellanos, 2001). However, there is controversy surrounding the use of stimulants in treating ADHD, as critics charge that ADHD is over-diagnosed and stimulant treatments are over-prescribed (Chapter 13).

While the use of stimulants as a primary treatment for depression has been discredited and replaced by far more effective treatments, amphetamines are still prescribed for weight loss. However, this practice has been particularly controversial because research indicates that the weight-reducing effects of amphetamines are only temporary, and the drugs usually have side effects (Bessesen, 2002). Furthermore, some stimulants marketed as weight loss agents have been later shown to pose health risks. For example, the combination of fenfluramine and phentermine (known as "fenphen") was first thought to be a breakthrough in longer-term weight reduction, but was later withdrawn from the market in 1997 after reports of serious heart and lung disease associated with their use (Stahl, 1997).

Currently, amphetamines and related drugs continue to be widely abused, twice as often by men as women (Lit et al., 1996). They can be ingested, taken intravenously, or smoked. Amphetamines are as potent as cocaine, and the high lasts longer (de la Torre et al., 2000). However, street amphetamines are often diluted; were this not the case, most stimulant users would not be able to distinguish between a cocaine and an amphetamine high (Robson, 1999). Tolerance and dependence on these drugs can develop relatively quickly, sometimes within weeks (Jansen & Darracot-Cankovic, 2001). Amphetamine withdrawal is similar to cocaine withdrawal; it is not usually medically dangerous, but it does involve a very unpleasant "crash" consisting of depressed mood, decreased energy, increased appetite, and irritability in addition to powerful cravings for the drug, which can last for days (Fisher & Harrison, 1997; Rothman et al., 2000). Even within the drug culture, amphetamines have a mixed reputation. Frank Zappa, the rock musician, once said: "I would like to suggest that you don't use speed, and here is why: it will mess up your liver, your kidneys, rot out your mind. In general, these drugs will make you just like your parents" (quoted by Robson in Shapiro, 1989).

Nicotine **Nicotine** is a mild stimulant found in the leaves of the tobacco plant, which can be chewed or smoked after drying. Nicotine is highly addictive and very toxic in large doses. Sixty milligrams of nicotine—half the amount in a typical cigar—is enough to kill a person within minutes (Ray & Ksir, 2002). However, nicotine is absorbed gradually while smoking, and it is typically taken in smaller doses (an average cigarette contains 1 mg) that are not very toxic.

Nicotine is rapidly absorbed and reaches the brain within 20 seconds (McDowell & Spitz, 1999). Its stimulant effects include increased heart rate, elevated blood pressure, and improved mood. Nicotine is highly reinforcing; experiments demon-

Nicotine A mild stimulant found in the leaves of the tobacco plant.

Nicotine dependence Although it is legal for adults, nicotine can cause dependency, and it is the world's deadliest drug because of the harmful effects of smoking.

strate that monkeys will engage in strenuous work if rewarded with nicotine injections. In humans, the reinforcing effects include pleasant mood, anxiety reduction, and relief from withdrawal symptoms that occur when nicotine is withheld. These withdrawal symptoms can include depression, irritability, insomnia, restlessness, increased appetite, and weight gain (McDowell & Spitz, 1999; Slade, 1999). All of these factors contribute to the addictive power of smoking and the difficulties associated with quitting.

The major health problem associated with nicotine use is due to its delivery system—smoking. The chemicals ingested into the lungs in the process of smoking make nicotine the world's deadliest, albeit legal, drug (Kozlowski, Henningfield, & Brigham, 2001). Smoking causes over 400,000 deaths each year in the United States, one-fifth of all deaths (Fisher & Harrison, 1997). The former Surgeon General of the United States, Antonia Novello, put it simply: "Smoking represents the most extensively documented cause of disease ever investigated in the history of biomedical research" (McDowell & Spitz, 1999). Accordingly, there is currently a fierce debate among health professionals about whether greater restrictions should be placed on the sale and use of tobacco (Arjonilla, Pelcastre, & Orozco, 2000; MacFadyen, Hastings, & MacKintosh, 2001; O'Grady, Asbridge, & Abernathy, 2000). While smoking rates in the United States have steadily declined since 1964, rates continue to increase overseas as tobacco companies look to replace the shrinking U.S. market with other markets (Dunphy, 2000; McDowell & Spitz, 1999) (see Figure 9.2). In Vietnam, for example, it is estimated that 77% of the population smokes, mostly using American brands.

Figure 9.2 Trends in cigarette sales in the United States since 1945 This figure highlights the dramatic decrease in per capita sales of cigarettes since government efforts to reduce smoking began in the 1960s and 1970s. However, total sales of cigarettes continued to increase until around 1980 because of the overall growth of the adult population.
From Ray & Ksir, 2002, p. 308

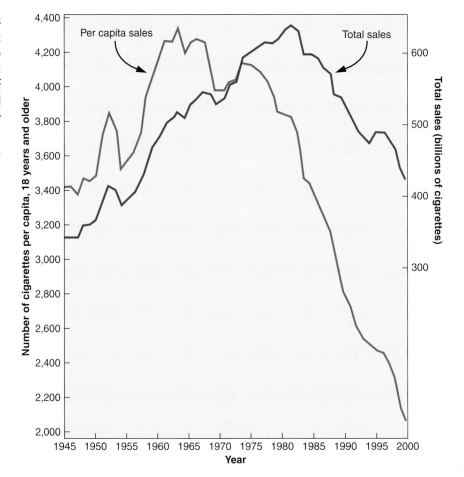

Caffeine **Caffeine** is a mild stimulant found in many foods and beverages, including coffee, tea, soft drinks, and chocolate, and in various over-the-counter (OTC) drugs (see Table 9.11). Caffeine has been used for centuries, primarily in coffees and teas, for its pleasant stimulant effects. At times throughout history, people have argued that caffeine has either magically medicinal, or devilishly immoral, properties (Ray & Ksir, 2002). In reality, caffeine has relatively mild effects when taken in moderate doses (Hughes et al., 1993). Its effects include relief from fatigue, enhanced alertness, and relief from headaches. While caffeine can offset fatigue-induced performance deficits, it may also decrease mental performance at high doses (Williams & Knight, 1995).

Caffeine is a highly reinforcing drug, and regular caffeine intake can lead to physical and psychological dependence, with tolerance and withdrawal symptoms. Withdrawal usually consists of a headache, and regular coffee drinkers often notice this symptom if they decrease their intake. However, caffeine is not particularly toxic; the lethal dose for humans is around 10 grams, the equivalent of 100 cups of coffee (Ray & Ksir, 2002).

Moderate caffeine use is probably not a health risk for most people, although questions remain about the medical consequences of high consumption. Researchers have examined possible links between caffeine intake and cancer, fibrocystic breast disease, heart disease, and other illnesses, with mixed results. At this point, most medical experts suggest that it is not harmful to use moderate amounts of caffeine, except possibly during pregnancy (Hutchings, 1989; Pressman & Orr, 1997).

Caffeine A mild stimulant found in many foods and beverages.

Caffeine Doses in Common Foods, Beverages, and Medicines			Table 9.11

From Ray & Ksir, 2002,
pp. 337 & 340

Caffeine in Beverages and Foods	CAFFEINE (mg)	
ITEM	**AVERAGE**	**RANGE**
Coffee (5 oz cup)		
Brewed, drip method	115	60–180
Brewed, percolater	80	40–170
Instant	65	30–120
Decaffeinated, brewed	3	2–5
Decaffeinated, instant	2	1–5
Tea (5 oz cup)		
Brewed, major U.S. brands	40	20–90
Brewed, imported brands	60	25–110
Instant	30	25–50
Iced (12 oz glass)	70	67–76
Cocoa beverage (5 oz cup)	4	2–20
Chocolate milk beverage (8 oz glass)	5	2–7
Milk chocolate (1 oz)	6	1–15
Dark chocolate, semisweet (1 oz)	20	5–35
Baker's chocolate (1 oz)	26	26
Chocolate-flavored syrup (1 oz)	4	4

(Table continues)

Table 9.11	(Continued)

Caffeine in Popular Soft Drinks

BRAND	CAFFEINE* (mg)
Sugar-Free Mr. Pibb	58.8
Mountain Dew	54.0
Mello Yello	52.8
Tab	46.8
Coca-Cola	45.6
Diet Coke	45.6
Shasta Cola	44.4
Mr. Pibb	40.8
Dr Pepper	39.6
Big Red	38.4
Pepsi-Cola	38.4
Diet Pepsi	36.0
Pepsi Light	36.0
RC Cola	36.0
Diet Rite	36.0
Canada Dry Jamaica Cola	30.0
Canada Dry Diet Cola	1.2

Caffeine Content of Nonprescription Drugs

DRUG	CAFFEINE (mg)
Stimulants	
No Doz	100.0
Vivarin	200.0
Analgesics	
Anacin	32.0
Excedrin	65.0
Goody's Headache Powders	32.5
Midol	32.4
Vanquish	33.0
Diuretics	
Aqua-Ban	100.0
Maximum-Strength Aqua-Ban Plus	200.0

* Per 12-oz serving

Caffeine is not specifically listed as a substance associated with either abuse or dependence in the DSM-IV-TR (APA, 2000), but many researchers do believe that a caffeine dependence syndrome exists (Pressman & Orr, 1997; Widiger et al., 1994). *Caffeinism,* a related condition, can include symptoms of irritability, insomnia, nervousness, twitching, heart arrhythmias and palpitations, and gastrointestinal disturbances due to high caffeine intake (Baer & Pinkston, 1997; Tarter, Ammerman, & Ott, 1998).

Hallucinogens

Hallucinogens are so named because of their tendency to produce *hallucinations,* internally generated sensory perceptions. The term *hallucinogen* applies to all natural or synthetic substances that have this effect. This class of substances is also sometimes referred to as *psychedelic* (literally, "mind-viewing") or *psychotomimetic* (psychosis mimicking) drugs. Some enthusiasts describe them as *entheogens,* substances that produce spiritual or religious experiences (Strassman, 1995).

Plants and fungi with hallucinogenic properties are found throughout the world. Hallucinogens have been used for centuries, in many cases as part of religious practices. Scholars have speculated that hallucinogenic drugs may be responsible for phenomena ranging from the wild imagery of the Book of Ezekiel in the Bible to the behavior of the women who were burned as witches during the Salem witch trials (Ray & Ksir, 2002). At various times, hallucinogens have been used by spiritual seekers, artists, and those in the counterculture wishing to open the "Doors of Perception" (the title of Aldous Huxley's famous book about his experiments with hallucinogens). However, hallucinogens have been illegal in the United States since 1965.

LSD (Acid)

Lysergic acid diethylamide (**LSD**) was originally synthesized in 1938 from alkaloids extracted from a fungus. A related compound was later found to exist naturally in the seeds of the morning glory plant (Littell, 1996; Robson, 1999). LSD has a chemical structure similar to the neurotransmitter *serotonin,* and binds at a type of serotonin receptor (Stain-Malmgren et al., 2001). LSD, which is usually taken orally, is one of the most potent known psychotropic substances. Physically, it causes sympathetic nervous system effects such as dilated pupils and increased temperature and blood pressure (Ghuran & Nolan, 2000). LSD's psychological effects include profound perceptual changes, depersonalization (Chapter 7), and enhanced emotionality, typically either along grandiose/spiritual or anxious/paranoid lines. Effects usually last six to nine hours (Ghuran & Nolan, 2000; Littell, 1996).

Albert Hofmann discovered LSD while working as a chemist working for Sandoz Labs in Basel, Switzerland. In 1943, Dr. Hofmann was attempting to develop new stimulant medications when he had a pleasant hallucinatory experience that resulted from the accidental absorption of LSD. Subsequently, he deliberately ingested LSD to study its effects. In the company of an assistant, Dr. Hofmann tried to dutifully record his experience. Unfortunately for him, he took what is now recognized as a huge dose of this powerful drug—0.25 milligrams, 10 times more than the minimal effective dose of around 20 to 25 micrograms (Brendel, West, & Hyman, 1996). Dr. Hofmann had the first recorded "bad trip" (McDowell & Spitz, 1999)! He had an intense, unpleasant hallucinatory experience, which included *synthesesia* (the mixing of sensory experiences, such as "seeing" sounds).

Between 1953 and 1966, Sandoz Labs distributed LSD to many researchers for further study. Various uses for LSD were investigated, such as to enhance psychotherapy, as a treatment for alcoholism, and as a model for studying psychosis, but none panned out (Hofmann, 1994; Mangini, 1998; Novak, 1997). When LSD gained popularity as a street drug during the 1960s, Sandoz Labs stopped sponsoring LSD research and distributing the substance.

Also during the 1950s and 1960s, the U.S. military and the Central Intelligence Agency (CIA) engaged in some disturbing research with LSD despite evidence that the dangers of the drug were already well understood (Neill, 1987; Novak, 1998). LSD was given to at least 585 soldiers and 900 civilians, often without their knowledge or consent (Strassman, 1995). One subject, a biochemist named Frank Olson, suffered an extended psychotic reaction and committed suicide two weeks after he

---

Hallucinogens Substances that produce hallucinatory changes in sensory perception.

LSD Lysergic acid diethylamide, a potent synthetic hallucinogen.

Psychedelic art The popularity of psychedelic drugs in the 1960s led to psychedelic art such as this 1967 work by Minnie Evans (1892–1987), now housed at the Smithsonian Institution in Washington, DC.

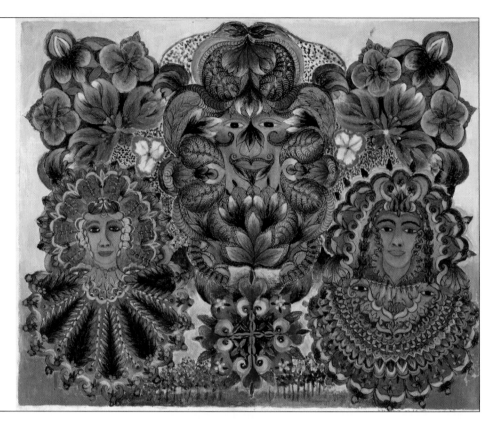

had LSD secretly slipped into his drink during an experiment. His family was told at the time only that he had fallen or jumped out of a window. The full extent of these government LSD experiments was revealed later in part due to the investigation of Dr. Olson's death over 20 years after the experiments occurred (Robson, 1999).

LSD was popularized as a street drug in the 1960s largely as a result of the efforts of Timothy Leary, who was, at the time, a Harvard professor. When Dr. Leary began violating research guidelines while conducting LSD experiments, he was dismissed from Harvard, but continued to advocate LSD use through his League for Spiritual Discovery (also known as "LSD"). Street use of LSD reached a peak around 1968, and then declined, due in part to fears concerning the possibility of "bad trips," psychotic reactions, flashbacks, and rumors about possible chromosome damage from LSD use (Batzer, Ditzler, & Brown, 1999; Littell, 1996; Ulrich & Patten, 1991). Recently, however, LSD usage appears to have increased again among young people (Abraham & Aldridge, 1993; Novak, 1998; Taylor, 1996).

LSD use does not seem to cause physical dependence or withdrawal, but tolerance does occur; a person taking the same daily dose of LSD will find that the drug becomes completely ineffective within days (Ray & Ksir, 2002). In addition, cross-tolerance occurs with other hallucinogens. LSD can apparently precipitate an ongoing psychotic condition in a vulnerable individual, and treatment is sometimes required for users having temporary panic or distressing psychotic symptoms (Batzer et al., 1999). These individuals are kept safe, reassured ("talked down"), and occasionally given benzodiazepines to help reduce anxiety (Littell, 1996).

Psilocybin The active ingredient found in mushrooms with hallucinogenic properties.

Psilocybin (Mushrooms) **Psilocybin** is the active ingredient found in scores of mushrooms with hallucinogenic properties that grow worldwide (Ghuran & Nolan, 2000; Robson, 1999). Psilocybin, like LSD, is chemically quite similar to the neurotransmitter serotonin, and its effects are nearly identical to those of LSD, though it is far less potent (Ghuran & Nolan, 2000). The Aztec Indians have used psilocybin in religious ceremonies for hundreds of years, and early Western explorers learned from the Aztecs about its hallucinatory properties. However, Western knowledge of psilocybin was suppressed for centuries because Spanish priests were offended by the religious practices of the Aztecs and destroyed their writings and teachings (Ray & Ksir, 2002). Western knowledge of psilocybin did not resurface until the mid-1900s (Smith, 1995). In 1955, an American ethnobotanist and former banker named Gordon Wasson gained access to ceremonies of an indigenous group using "magic mushrooms." He described his experience as follows: "It permits you to travel backwards and forwards in time, to enter other planes of existence, even (as the Indians say), to know God" (Ray & Ksir, 2002, p. 380). Psychedelic mushrooms became popular during the counterculture movement of the 1960s.

Peyote/Mescaline **Peyote** is a small, carrot-shaped cactus found mostly in Mexico and Central America. **Mescaline**, the primary active ingredient in peyote, was first isolated in the 1890s and first synthesized in 1918 (Robson, 1999). Mescaline causes euphoric and hallucinatory experiences very similar to those associated with LSD and psilocybin, but its chemical structure is different—less like serotonin and more like the neurotransmitters norepinephrine and dopamine (Ray & Ksir, 2002). Peyote is usually eaten, in the form of sun-dried "buttons" taken from the cactus (Brendel et al., 1996). As with other hallucinogens, tolerance does occur, but dependence and withdrawal are rare (Ellison et al., 1980; Stephens, 1999).

Many Native American tribes have used peyote for centuries in religious rituals, and as recently as 1960 "peyotism" was the major religion of Native Americans in the Western United States (Garrity, 2000; Hopgood, 2000; Swan & Perez, 2000; Weaver, 2001). Peyote is legal in some states when used by Native Americans for religious purposes—an interesting example of *cultural relativism* concerning substance use. This legal protection has been challenged in some states, but peyote currently remains the only legally sanctioned hallucinogen in the Western world (Brooke, 1997; Epps, 2001; Robson, 1999).

Other Drugs

The following drugs do not easily fit into the categories of depressants, stimulants, and hallucinogens. They have properties similar to some of the substances already discussed, but have unique properties as well.

Marijuana (Pot, Weed, Reefer, Grass) **Marijuana** is the most widely used illegal drug in the world (Fisher & Harrison, 1997; Wallace, 1999). In a recent survey, 23% of Americans between the ages of 19 to 32 admitted having used marijuana. Pot is America's number one cash crop, to the tune of $30 billion per year (Vinluan, 1996). Worldwide, it is estimated that hundreds of millions of people use marijuana daily (Dawsey, 1996; Strassman, 1988).

Marijuana comes from the dried and crushed flowers, leaves, seeds, and stems of some strains of the *cannabis* plant. The primary psychoactive ingredient in these plants is tetrahydrocannabinol, abbreviated as *THC*, which is concentrated in the resin of the plant (Monroe, 1998). The different parts of the cannabis plant have different concentrations of THC-containing resin, which are reflected in the different potencies of several related substances. Marijuana, made primarily from the leaves and seeds, typically contains between 1% and 8% THC. More potent substances such as hashish (hash) and sinsemilla are made specifically from the resin-rich flowering tops of the plant which contain up to 14% THC.

Peyote A small, carrot-shaped cactus containing mescaline found mostly in Mexico and Central America.

Mescaline A hallucinogenic substance found in peyote.

Marijuana The world's most widely used illegal substance; derived from the cannabis plant.

Legal marijuana This man is smoking marijuana in the "Cannabis Castle" outside Nijmegen, Holland. Marijuana was decriminalized in Holland in the 1970s.

Half-life The amount of time it takes for half of a substance to be eliminated from the body.

Ecstasy (MDMA) A synthetic amphetamine/stimulant with some hallucinogenic properties.

Marijuana and its related substances are typically smoked, but they can also be eaten (usually baked into food), or used as teas. Marijuana is rapidly absorbed when smoked, and its effects begin within minutes, reaching a peak within about two hours. However, marijuana is metabolized slowly, with a high that can last several hours and a **half-life** of about two days (Losken, Maviglia, & Friedman, 1996). The half-life of a drug is the amount of time it takes for half of the substance to be eliminated from the body. In general, the shorter the half-life of a substance, the sooner its effects dissipate (Dodgen & Shea, 2000.) Because of its long half-life, regular marijuana users, like Rob (described in one of the chapter opening case vignettes), can easily become chronically "stoned" (McDowell & Spitz, 1999).

The effects of marijuana are varied, and include some depressant, hallucinogenic, and stimulant properties which have made the classification of marijuana controversial (Losken, Maviglia, & Friedman, 1996). The most common effects are enhanced sensory experience, relaxation, euphoria, altered time sense, increased appetite, and, for some users, anxiety and paranoia. Physical changes include increased pulse and blood pressure, dilation of blood vessels (causing bloodshot eyes), dry mouth, and decreased reaction time (Fisher & Harrison, 1997). The brain mechanisms of marijuana are not fully understood, but THC seems to bind at endogenous cannabinoid receptors which may have a role in mood, memory, and sensory regulation (Robson, 1999). These receptors appear to be designed for an endogenous substance called *anandamide* that shares marijuana-like properties (Ray & Ksir, 2002). Marijuana also has some medically beneficial effects, which have ignited controversy about its illegal status. For example, there is evidence that marijuana can help treat loss of appetite, severe nausea (as from chemotherapies for cancer), glaucoma, and pain (Nichols, 2000).

Regular marijuana use can cause tolerance, withdrawal, and both physical and psychological dependence (Losken, Maviglia, & Friedman, 1996). Withdrawal symptoms can include irritability, restlessness, insomnia, craving, tremors, and chills (Monroe, 1998). While overdoses of marijuana are very unusual, the drug can cause both acute and chronic health problems. Some marijuana users experience flashbacks and panic reactions, which can be treated with supportive reassurance and anti-anxiety medications if necessary (Losken, Maviglia, & Friedman, 1996).

Long-term problems associated with marijuana use are more varied and complex. Marijuana use has been known to precipitate psychosis and may also contribute to problems with learning and short-term memory, impaired judgment and problem solving, loss of balance and coordination, anxiety and panic attacks, and an increased risk of engaging in unsafe behaviors (Harrigan, 1999). In addition, some researchers claim that long-term marijuana use is associated with a controversial condition known as *amotivational syndrome* in which individuals lose their drive and purpose (Losken, Maviglia, & Friedman, 1996). However, it remains unclear whether this syndrome is actually caused by marijuana use or only correlated with it. Physical problems related to long-term marijuana use include decreased reaction time, immune suppression, lung damage (marijuana contains carcinogens, and one marijuana joint is as toxic as five cigarettes), decreased hormone production, and possible memory loss (Fisher & Harrison, 1997; Robson, 1999).

Ecstasy (MDMA, XTC, X, Adam, E) **Ecstasy** is a synthetic amphetamine/stimulant with some hallucinogenic properties. MDMA (methylenedioxymethamphetamine), the chemical compound in ecstasy, was originally patented by the German pharmaceutical company Merck in 1914. MDMA was used in the 1950s and 1960s by the U. S. Army (as a stimulant), by some psychotherapists (to enhance client insight), and recreationally by members of the drug culture of the era (McDowell & Spitz, 1999). Ecstasy has been illegal since 1985, largely through the efforts of Senator Lloyd Bentsen of Texas who became concerned about the easy availability of ecstasy in Texas, where it was sold over the counter, at bars, and through 800 numbers (McDowell & Spitz, 1999).

Ecstasy has recently become popular as a "club" drug and on college campuses (Doyon, 2001; Graeme, 2000). Its popularity is in large part due to its reputation for inducing a pleasurable feeling of empathy, closeness, and connection with other people. Ecstasy is usually taken as a 100 to 150 mg pill. Effects begin approximately 20 minutes after ingestion and last from three to six hours, although larger doses can result in reactions for up to two days. The drug affects many neurotransmitters, particularly the serotonin system (Ghuran & Nolan, 2000). Tolerance does develop, with regular usage resulting in a decrease in the desired effects and increasingly prominent side effects.

Despite its seemingly benign nature, ecstasy is a potentially dangerous drug. It causes permanent damage to serotonin neurons in monkeys and may do so in humans (Kish et al., 2000; McDowell & Spitz, 1999). In addition, many ecstasy-related deaths have been reported. These appear to be due to dehydration and hyperthermia caused by using the drug in hot, crowded dance clubs (Cloud, 2001; Doyon, 2001; Ling et al., 2001).

Ecstasy "raves" The popularity of ecstasy raves among young people has been a cause for concern due to the potential dangers of ecstasy use.

PCP (Phencyclidine, Angel Dust) and Ketamine (Special K)

PCP was developed by the Parke-Davis pharmaceutical company in the 1950s for possible use as an anesthetic. Because of side effects associated with it, PCP was designated for use only as an animal anesthetic, and then withdrawn from the market altogether in 1965 when it began to appear on the streets (Giannini, 1998; Senay, 1998). **Ketamine,** a shorter-acting and safer derivative of PCP, is still used as an anesthetic (Robson, 1999).

PCP and ketamine are sometimes classified as hallucinogens because they do have some hallucinatory effects. However, their mechanism of action in the brain is very different from the hallucinogens, and many experts disagree with this classification (Brendel et al., 1996). PCP is usually smoked (it is often "laced," or mixed with, other substances such as marijuana), but it can also be snorted, injected, or ingested. It produces several hours of a euphoric state, often with hallucinations. Ketamine is more often sniffed as a powder, and it has a highly reinforcing, dissociative effect (McDowell & Spitz, 1999). Police officers are well aware that PCP can also cause bizarre and violent behavior. Because of PCP's anesthetic properties, users can be impervious to pain yet retain full use of their muscles. As a result, they can be very hard to subdue (Brendel et al., 1996).

Overdoses of PCP can cause a psychosis resembling schizophrenia, or even coma (Fisher & Harrison, 1997). Treatment of acute PCP intoxication and prolonged psychotic reactions can require medications, restraints, and a quiet, low-stimulation environment (Giannini, 1998; Senay, 1998).

GHB (Gamma-hydroxybutyrate)

GHB was also developed for possible use as an anesthetic but was withdrawn from use as a medical drug in 1990. However, it has been widely used as a so-called "natural" bodybuilding and sleep aid (since it is probably a naturally occurring neurotransmitter), and has recently become popular as a "club" drug (Graeme, 2000; McDowell & Spitz, 1999). GHB acts mostly like a depressant and thus has dangerous synergistic effects with alcohol (Nicholson & Balster, 2001). Deaths due to this combination have been reported (McDowell & Spitz, 1999). Dependence can develop with GHB, and the withdrawal syndrome is similar to that observed with alcohol and the benzodiazepines. GHB is usually taken in liquid form (and is sometimes called "liquid ecstasy") in doses of about 5 mg, and it causes a highly reinforcing, pleasant dissociative state, most likely mediated by the

PCP Phencyclidine, a substance of abuse originally developed as an animal anesthetic.

Ketamine A shorter-acting derivative of PCP still used as an anesthetic.

GHB Gamma-hydroxybutyrate, a so-called natural bodybuilding and sleep aid that has become a popular club drug.

dopamine system (McDowell & Spitz, 1999; Nicholson & Balster, 2001). Because GHB, like flunitrazepam (Rohypnol) and ketamine, is colorless, odorless, and tasteless, all three have been implicated as potential "date rape" drugs when slipped into beverages.

Inhalants The term **inhalants** refers to a wide range of chemicals that produce a "high" when inhaled. Many inhalants are common household products, including solvents such as gasoline, kerosene, glue, nail polish remover, lighter fluid, and paint. Medical drugs, including gaseous anesthetics like nitrous oxide (laughing gas) and chloroform, or nitrates, such as amyl nitrite ("poppers"), can also be abused as inhalants. Solvents are typically used by spraying or soaking a rag, from which the individual then inhales, sometimes under a plastic bag (Fisher & Harrison, 1997). Because they are cheap, readily available, and easy to administer, inhalants are often abused by young adolescents or impoverished individuals (Brooks, Leung, & Shannon, 1996; Robson, 1999).

Inhalants cause a variety of relatively short-lived effects. Most create temporary dizziness, drowsiness, euphoric feelings, giddiness, slurred speech, and decreased inhibitions (Fisher & Harrison, 1997; Robson, 1999). Nitrates cause a faintness (by reducing blood pressure to the brain) which is reputed to enhance sexual pleasure; hence their notorious popularity in sex clubs. Most inhalants do not produce significant tolerance or withdrawal effects, although there are some exceptions to this rule (Robson, 1999). Unfortunately, most inhalants are quite toxic. Acute effects can include hallucinations, headaches, loss of consciousness, cardiac arrhythmias, coma, and death. Permanent liver, kidney, lung, and brain damage can also result from the repeated use of inhalants.

Anabolic Steroids Gonadal steroids are hormones that regulate the functioning of the reproductive system and include the male sex hormone *testosterone*. **Anabolic steroids**—a synthetic subtype of steroids resembling testosterone that tends to increase muscle mass—are often abused with the aim of enhancing athletic performance or physique. The use of substances to improve physical performance has a long history; ancient Greek and Aztec athletes are known to have used various substances to increase endurance and strength (Ray & Ksir, 2002). Many athletes around the world began to use steroids avidly once it was discovered, during the 1930s, that male hormones could increase muscle mass. Soviet athletic teams experimented with the use of testosterone in the 1950s, while Americans began using anabolic steroids. In the 1970s, some Eastern European Olympic teams were using steroids routinely. In one infamous incident, an East German Olympic coach was asked why all his female swimmers had deep voices; he replied "We have come here to swim, not to sing" (Ray & Ksir, 2002). Steroid abuse was so widespread that a 1972 survey of Olympic athletes indicated that 68% had used steroids. As a result of these abuses, bans on steroid use and testing for the banned substances began during the 1970s in many amateur and professional sports. However, steroids remain popular among many athletes and bodybuilders.

Steroid use spread to more casual athletes and younger people, male and female, during the 1980s (Kaufman & Friedman, 1996; Peters & Phelps, 2001). In a 1988 survey, 6.6% of high school seniors reported having used steroids. Concern over this phenomenon led to the passage of the Anabolic Steroids Act of 1990 in the United States, which placed tight control over the distribution and sale of the drugs (Fisher & Harrison, 1997). Since then, illicit steroid users have typically obtained black market steroids which often contain impurities and may be derived from veterinary substances (Kaufman & Friedman, 1996).

Inhalants Chemicals that produce a "high" when inhaled.

Anabolic steroids A synthetic subtype of steroids resembling testosterone that tend to increase muscle mass and are often abused with the aim of enhancing athletic performance or physique.

Steroid abuse These bodybuilders at the Mr. Universe competition in 2002 highlight the growing obsession with muscularity that has contributed to steroid abuse.

Anabolic steroids do have some legitimate medical uses, such as the treatment of muscle loss, blood anemia, HIV, and testosterone replacement (Newshan & Leon, 2001; Rabkin et al., 2000). Illicit steroid users tend to use much higher doses (10–100 times higher) of the substance than medically approved amounts. Ironically, it is not clear that anabolic steroid use actually improves athletic performance, although it can increase muscle mass. If it does enhance performance, the effect is probably minor, and may be due to the *placebo effect* which relies on the power of suggestion (Wichstrom & Pedersen, 2001).

There is no doubt, however, about many of the psychological and physical side effects of these drugs. Anabolic steroids increase aggressiveness, and have been anecdotally connected with a syndrome of belligerent behavior known as "roid rage" (Thiblin, Kristiansson, & Rajs, 1997). While overdose is not a common danger with these drugs, they do pose serious long-term health risks. Among the side effects of ongoing use are testicular atrophy, impotence, acne, baldness, hepatitis, high blood pressure, liver damage, and masculinization in women (Fisher & Harrison, 1997; Midgley et al., 2000). Tolerance does not seem to occur, but there is a withdrawal syndrome with anabolic steroids involving depression, insomnia, fatigue, and decreased sex drive (Brower, 2000a; Gruber & Pope, 2000; Riem & Hursey, 1995). Treatment for steroid abuse focuses on establishing discontinuation and maintaining abstinence through therapy and educational interventions (Brower, 2000b; Kaufman & Friedman, 1996).

Classification in Demographic Context

As we've already noted, substance use and misuse pervades all cultures and has occurred during all historical periods. There are, however, some noteworthy demographic trends with regard to substance misuse in the United States over the last several decades.

Age

With the exception of young children, people of all ages abuse drugs. However, certain developmental periods are a significant risk factor for substance misuse. Peer pressure can make adolescence a high-risk time for drug abuse, and adolescents' feelings of invincibility and immortality often exacerbate their risk-taking behaviors. Some drugs, including marijuana and the current "club drugs" (such as ecstasy and GHB), are used primarily by adolescents and young adults. Marijuana became increasingly popular among young people during the 1950s and 1960s when their sense of the relatively benign effects of the drug, in contrast to official government statements about its lurid dangers, fed the distrust of authority in the counter culture of the time (Sloman, 1998). Marijuana remains a popular drug among today's teenagers and young adults.

Most experts agree that substance misuse problems are under-diagnosed and under-treated among the elderly (Weintraub et al., 2002). Evidence suggests that substance misuse among geriatric populations centers on the unintentional misuse of prescription medications, but researchers warn that the number of elderly people abusing illicit drugs and alcohol will likely spike as the baby boom generation ages (Patterson & Jeste, 1999). Substance use problems among the elderly are of special concern given that treatment outcomes are poorer among people with cognitive impairment, and that special treatment strategies are required for elderly persons with dementia (Patterson & Jeste, 1999).

Gender

In general, men are significantly more likely than women to abuse drugs and alcohol (Warner et al., 1995). A genetic predisposition to alcoholism appears to be more common in men than it is in women (an issue we'll return to shortly), and men are twice as likely to abuse amphetamines and related drugs (Lit et al., 1996).

Interestingly, a shift in gender trends has occurred with regard to nicotine consumption. When tobacco use peaked in the 1950s, cigarette smoking was advertised as a highly masculine activity. Marlboro brand cigarettes became famous, and extremely profitable, thanks to ads featuring the "Marlboro Man," a ruggedly handsome cowboy riding the range, cigarette in mouth. When the feminist movement gained popularity in the 1960s and 1970s, cigarette manufacturers responded by advertising smoking as a "liberated" activity for women. Virginia Slims created a brand of cigarettes especially for the women and advertised using the slogan "You've come a long way, baby." Such aggressive marketing campaigns are believed to account for the dramatic recent increases in lung cancer rates among women (McDowell & Spitz, 1999).

Class

Large epidemiological studies have found that drug use in the United States is, in general, positively correlated with being Caucasian, well-educated, and living in an urban environment in the northeastern and western regions of the country (Warner et al., 1995). However, young, underemployed men have been specifically found to have much higher rates of alcoholism than the population at large (Dodgen & Shea, 2000).

An interesting, but tragic, demographic shift in cocaine use occurred during the 1980s. Throughout the 1970s and 1980s, cocaine was a glamorous society drug, snorted through rolled up hundred dollar bills. At its height, cocaine became so popular as a recreational drug that public health officials spoke of a "cocaine epidemic." Toward the end of the 1980s, rates of cocaine use dropped in high-income groups due, in part, to the cocaine-related deaths of stars like John Belushi and Len Bias. However, cocaine use soared in low-income, inner-city communities when it was discovered that cocaine could be mixed with common household chemicals and dried into a smokable form. This new product, called crack because of the crackling sound make by the impurities as it burned, could be bought for as little as $10 on the streets.

Brief Summary

- Most commonly abused substances fall into one of three categories: stimulants, depressants, or hallucinogens.
- Depressants, which slow central nervous system (CNS) activity, include alcohol, sedative-hypnotics, and opioids.
- Stimulants, which increase CNS activity, include cocaine, amphetamines, nicotine, and caffeine.
- Hallucinogens, which cause altered sensory perception, include LSD, psilocybin, and mescaline.
- Other commonly abused substances include marijuana, ecstasy, PCP/ketamine, GHB, inhalants, and steroids.
- Demographic trends regarding substance misuse in the United States highlight the importance of *context* in understanding substance-related disorders.

Critical Thinking Question | **Do** the current U.S. policies concerning which substances are legal and illegal seem appropriate to you? Why or why not?

EXPLAINING AND TREATING SUBSTANCE USE DISORDERS

Current ideas about how to explain and treat substance use problems have been shaped by historical and ideological factors in a way that is somewhat unique in the field of abnormal psychology. Today's dominant approach to explaining and treating substance use disorders is often referred to as the *disease model,* which argues that substance dependence is a disease akin to other medical diseases. The disease model's dominance does not necessarily result from its clear scientific superiority to other approaches—it has both strengths and limitations—but from complex historical, social, psychological, and economic forces (Epstein, 2001; Schaler, 2000).

Theories of the causes and treatment of substance use problems provide an excellent example of **historical relativism** because they have dramatically changed over time. In particular, explanations of substance misuse have tended to swing between the poles of moral/legal approaches and disease/medical approaches. As a society, we are still struggling to find a balanced approach to substance misuse. During colonial times, for example, alcohol was widely abused in America, but it was not considered addictive, and alcoholism was not considered a disease (Thombs, 1999). Rather, it was viewed as a moral problem, and many well-known figures such as Cotton Mather, John Adams, and Ben Franklin spoke out against drunks and taverns as "pests to society" (Rorabaugh, 1979). Dr. Benjamin Rush, the "father of American psychiatry" and a signer of the Declaration of Independence, first popularized an alternative view. Rush argued that alcohol was addictive, alcoholism a disease, and abstinence the only cure—very much in line with the contemporary disease model (Widiger et al., 1998). Rush's work led to the founding of an influential anti-alcohol organization, the American Temperance Society. This group started off promoting moderation in alcohol use but later advocated abstinence and the prohibition of alcohol. They viewed alcoholism as both a sin *and* a disease, reflecting the unresolved tension between moral and disease models which still exists today (Levin & Weiss, 1994).

As psychological perspectives within the field of abnormal psychology flourished during the middle of the twentieth century, a third way of explaining and treating substance misuse, neither moral nor medical, emerged. Psychological models tended to conceptualize substance misuse as a *symptom* caused by underlying motivational, emotional, cognitive, or learning problems. However, the symptom model, as a general approach to explaining and treating substance misuse, has fallen out of favor for a variety of reasons. First, people seem to have difficulty distinguishing between the symptom approach and the moral approach, causing many clients and their families to feel blamed and shamed. Second, the symptom model has been unable to demonstrate that severe substance misuse (such as substance dependence) can be effectively treated by focusing exclusively on underlying psychological problems (Maunder & Hunter, 2001).

The net result is that the disease model currently dominates the field of substance use disorders. Many forces support the disease model. The alcohol industry prefers the disease model because it implies that the biologically vulnerable individual, not the addictive substance, lies at the root of the problem. The medical system benefits because drug problems and their treatment fall within its purview. And many clients and their families feel that the disease model eases the shame and stigma of their problems, making it possible for more people to seek help, more research to be done, and better treatments to be developed. In fact, the entire *recovery movement*—a loose term for the plethora of self-help groups, such as Alcoholics Anonymous, that focus on helping people with substance problems—is based upon the disease model. The proliferation of self-help and group treatments testifies to the importance of reducing the shame and stigma surrounding substance misuse (Bennett & Lehman, 2001; Buchanan & Young, 2000; Gribble et al., 2000).

BOX 9.3 Is There Room for Free Will in the Disease Model?

"Don't Forget the Addict's Role in Addiction" *by* Sally L. Satel

Dr. Sally Satel is one of the foremost critics of the disease model of substance dependence. In this Op-Ed piece from *The New York Times* she outlines her views.

From the first installment of Bill Moyers's widely publicized television special, "Addiction: Close to Home," on Sunday night, viewers learned that addiction is a chronic and relapsing brain disease.

The addict's brain "is hijacked by drugs," Mr. Moyers said that morning on "Meet the Press," adding that "relapse is normal."

These are the words of a loving father who was once at his wits' end over his son's drug and alcohol habit. But as a public health message, they miss the mark. First, addiction is not a brain disease. And second, relapse is not inevitable.

The National Institute on Drug Abuse, part of the National Institutes of Health, is waging an all-out campaign to label addiction a chronic and relapsing brain disease. It seems a logical scientific leap.

Obviously, heavy drug use affects the brain, often to a point where self-control is utterly lost—for example, when a person is in the throes of alcohol or heroin withdrawal or in the midst of a cocaine binge. Scientists have even identified parts of the brain that "light up," presumably reflecting damage, after long-term exposure to drugs. Yet as dramatic as the images of this phenomenon are, there is wide disagreement on what they mean.

"Saying these changes predict that someone will relapse amounts to modern phrenology," John P. Seibyl, a nuclear radiologist and psychiatrist at the Yale School of Medicine, told me. "We don't have any data linking these images to behavior, so how can we call addiction a disease of the brain?"

One of my colleagues puts it this way: You can examine brains all day, but you'd never call anyone an addict unless he acted like one. That's what is really misleading about the Moyers assertion that "addiction is primarily a brain disease"—it omits the voluntary aspects of an addict's behavior.

Addicts' brains are not always in a state of siege. Many addicts have episodes of clean time that last for weeks, months or years. During these periods it is the individual's responsibility to make himself less vulnerable to drug craving and relapse.

Treatment can help the addict learn how to fight urges and find alternative ways to meet emotional and spiritual needs. But will he take the advice? Maybe. More likely, he will begin a revolving-door dance with the treatment system. A recent study showed that only 1 in every 21 patients complete a year in a treatment clinic. To drop out generally means to relapse.

"Addicts make decision about use all the time," Dr. Robert L. DuPont, a former director of the national institute, points out. Researchers have found that the amount of alcohol consumed by alcoholics is related to its cost and the effort required to obtain it. Two decades ago Lee Robins, a professor of psychiatry at Washington University in St. Louis, in a classic study of returning Vietnam veterans, found that only 14 percent of men who were addicted to heroin in Vietnam resumed regular use back home. The culture surrounding heroin use, the price and fear of arrest helped keep the rest off the needle.

Thus drug addicts and alcoholics respond to rewards and consequences, not just to physiology. Relapse should not be regarded as an inevitable, involuntary product of a diseased brain.

Turning addiction into a medical problem serves a purpose, of course. The idea is to reduce stigma and get better financing and more insurance coverage for treatment.

As a psychiatrist, I'm all for treatment, but when the national institute says that addiction is just like diabetes or asthma, it has the equation backward. A diabetic or asthmatic who relapses because he ignores his doctor's advice is more like an addict, as his relapses result from forsaking the behavioral regimens that he knows can keep him clean.

True, former addicts are vulnerable to resuming use—hence the "one day at a time" slogan of Alcoholics Anonymous. But they are by no means destined to do so. The message that addiction is chronic and relapse inevitable is demoralizing to patients and gives the treatment system an excuse if it doesn't serve them well.

Calling addiction a behavioral condition, as I prefer, emphasizes that the person, not his autonomous brain, is the instigator of his relapse and the agent of his recovery. The experts on Bill Moyers's program say that making addiction more like heart disease or cancer will reduce stigma. They're wrong. The best way to combat stigma is to expect drug users to take advantage of treatment, harness their will to prevent relapse and become visible symbols of hard work and responsibility.

This prescription does not deny the existence of vulnerabilities, biological or otherwise. Instead it makes the struggle to relinquish drugs all the more ennobling.

The New York Times, April 4, 1998

While the disease model has many advantages, critics argue that it is more ideological than scientific (Robson, 1999; Skolnik, 2000) (see Box 9.3). For example, the disease model's tenet that total abstinence is the only appropriate goal for most clients misusing substances has been highly controversial. Researchers who have suggested that controlled substance use might be a reasonable goal for some clients have come under fierce attack (for example, Sobell & Sobell, 1984). Given the intense controversies about how to explain and treat substance misuse, it is especially important to keep in mind the core concept of ***multiple causality***. With substance misuse, as with other disorders, the use of multiple components in explanations and treatments is the most helpful complete approach (Brower et al., 1989).

Biological Components

We begin with biological components for several reasons. The first is the current dominance of the disease model and its close relation to the biological perspective. Second, as psychoactive substances, all drugs have biological properties and effects that must be considered when trying to understand substance misuse. Third, many of the prominent symptoms of drug addiction, such as drug tolerance and withdrawal, have powerful biological features. Finally, the recent "decade of the brain" (a phrase used to describe the emphasis on brain research in the mental health field during the 1990s) brought about many new insights into the biochemistry of addiction.

The biological approach to explaining and treating substance misuse includes any explanation or treatment focused on the body and biological processes. The biological approach overlaps substantially, then, with the "disease model," but the biological perspective and the disease model are not synonymous since the biological perspective can be integrated with other theoretical perspectives.

Despite its earlier roots, the origin of the disease model as a scientific perspective on substance misuse is usually credited to Jellineck (1946), who proposed that alcoholism could be characterized as a chronic, progressive, and incurable disease (Popham, 1976; Tarter et al., 1971). The emergence of the disease model spawned important research into the biology of addiction. For example, the discovery of *endorphins* (naturally occurring, or *endogenous,* opiates) in the 1970s led to speculation that some people might use drugs in order to compensate for inborn or acquired deficiencies in their neurochemistry (Berti, 1994; Erickson, 1996; Kosten, 1990). This hypothesis is sometimes referred to as a **self-medication** theory of substance use (we will see slightly different, *psychological* versions of this self-medication theory later in the chapter). More recently, evidence has emerged that virtually all drugs affect the dopamine neurotransmitter system, which can provide surges of pleasure when stimulated and therefore can account for the powerful reinforcing effects of many abused substances (Wise, 1988).

Biological researchers have also focused on genetic factors that may contribute to substance misuse. Our review of the role of inheritance in substance misuse will focus on the study of genetic factors in alcoholism, which have been thoroughly investigated. As you know, the role of genetic factors in mental illnesses (and other behavioral traits) is generally explored through family, adoption, and twin studies. Family studies show that alcoholism runs strongly in families. For example, about one-quarter of the sons of alcoholics become alcoholic themselves (Dodgen & Shea, 2000). However, this is the weakest form of genetic evidence, as families share environments as well as genes, and the shared environment could explain why alcoholism runs in families.

Much stronger evidence of a genetic role in alcoholism comes from adoption studies, which separate out, to a large extent, the influence of genes from the influence of the environment. Studies have shown that the adopted-out sons of alcoholics are three to four times more likely to become alcoholic than the adopted-out sons of nonalcoholics (Dodgen & Shea, 2000). Interestingly, the correlations between alcoholic mothers and alcoholic daughters are much lower, suggesting that the heritability of at least some forms of alcoholism may be greater in males. While we must keep in mind that adoption studies never totally eliminate the potential confound of

Self-medication The abuse of substances to compensate for deficiencies in neurochemistry or to soothe unpleasant emotional states.

environmental factors—because there is still a shared environment up until the adoption, and possible environmental influences from selective adoption placement and later contact with the biological family—these studies provide powerful evidence of a genetic role in alcoholism.

Further genetic evidence, along with an estimate of the relative strength of genetic and environmental influences, comes from twin studies. Recall that most twin studies are based on the comparison of concordance rates of identical (monozygotic) twins and fraternal (dizygotic) twins. In one large Swedish study, identical twins had a concordance rate for alcoholism of 58% compared to a rate of 28% for fraternal twins (Scandinavian countries are often the best source of genetic data since many of them have extensive medical databases on their entire populations) (McDowell & Spitz, 1999). Remember that the most likely explanation of this 30% difference is that identical twins, originating from a single, fertilized ovum that divides in two, share 100% of their genes. Fraternal twins, on the other hand, originating from two separate fertilized ova, share, on average, about 50% of their genes, just like regular siblings. Other twin studies have shown similar results, supporting the hypothesis of a substantial genetic role in alcoholism (Cloninger, Sigvardsson, & Bohman, 1996; Cook & Gurling, 2001; Thombs, 1999). However, the evidence to date suggests that the role of genetic factors in alcoholism is partial; otherwise the concordance rate for identical twins would be 100%. Genetic factors may predispose an individual to alcoholism (and other drug addictions), but environmental factors also play a significant role (Cadoret et al., 1995; Heath et al., 2001; Rose et al., 2001).

How, precisely, do genetic factors lead to alcoholism? While no one knows yet for sure—researchers keep hunting, so far unsuccessfully, for the specific genes involved—several possibilities have been explored. One scenario suggests that genes determine a person's susceptibility to the reinforcing effects of alcohol—in other words, how much pleasure or tension reduction alcohol causes. For instance, some people may be biologically predisposed to find alcohol consumption especially pleasurable and/or to not experience aversive effects such as "hangovers." Additionally, genes may affect general sensitivity to alcohol, including how quickly tolerance develops and how unpleasant withdrawal feels. These genetically determined biological factors may be rooted in individual differences within the limbic system and/or in the liver enzymes, which metabolize alcohol (Dodgen & Shea, 2000; Thombs, 1999). According to the **flipped switch theory** of addiction, genetic differences may explain observed differences in how quickly addiction develops. This theory suggests that after using a drug for a prolonged period, it is as though a biological switch is flipped and a person crosses the threshold from controlled use to addiction (McDowell & Spitz, 1999). However, the amount of use that causes the switch to flip varies a great deal from person to person, possibly as a result of predisposing genetic factors.

Flipped switch theory The hypothesis that continued use of a substance can precipitate a biologically based switch from controlled use to addiction.

Biological Interventions

Biological interventions are currently used for many substance misuse problems, and we have already mentioned some treatments as we reviewed the list of commonly abused substances. Here we describe the most common and successful biological interventions.

Alcohol Treatment of alcoholism usually begins with a medically supervised withdrawal period, which is carefully managed in order to prevent the development of seizures or other medically dangerous symptoms. Benzodiazepines, which are *cross-tolerant* with alcohol, are often used to ease withdrawal. After withdrawal, medications can continue to play a role in the long-term treatment of alcoholism. One commonly used medication is *disulfiram (Antabuse),* which causes very unpleasant reactions such as nausea, headache, and flushing when combined with alcohol. Disulfiram inhibits the liver enzyme *alcohol dehydrogenese,* which normally breaks down alcohol (McDowell & Spitz, 1999; Moss, 1999). Clients can choose to take disulfiram regularly to prevent impulse drinking. However, many clients who are initially willing to take disulfiram fail to stay on the medication; psychotherapy can have a crucial role in helping maintain medication compliance. Selective serotonin reuptake inhibitor (SSRI) antidepressants (Chapter 6) and opiate *antagonists,* such as naltrexone, can also be helpful in maintaining abstinence from alcohol in some circumstances (Gitlow, 2001; Sadock & Sadock, 2001).

Opioids The first step for treating active addiction (for example, to heroin) is detoxification and medically supervised withdrawal, often using opiate *antagonists* such as naloxone and naltrexone. These antagonists block opiate receptors and thereby displace opiates, precipitating withdrawal (Boyarsky & McCance-Katz, 2000; McDowell & Spitz, 1999; Sadock & Sadock, 2001). The next step is to prevent relapse. The primary biological intervention for this "maintenance" phase is a controversial practice known as **substitution** or **maintenance therapy** in which addicts are provided with a safer opioid in a medically monitored setting. For many years, *methadone* was the standard substitute, but recently two longer-acting substitutes, *levo-alpha-acetyl methadol* and *buprenorphine* (byoo-pre-NOR-feen), have become available. Substitution therapy works by reducing the craving for heroin without causing the intense high and "doped" effect of heroin.

The controversy surrounding substitution therapy involves the ethics of substituting one addiction for another. However, most clinicians believe that the advantages of substitution therapy—such as the ability of the substitute opioids to ward off withdrawal without causing a debilitating "high," the use of oral rather than IV administration, thus eliminating needle sharing, and the longer action of the substitute opioids resulting in a less frequent dosing need—outweigh the disadvantages. Weaning from opiate substitutes remains the long-term goal, and many clients are eventually able to do so. Until opioid use stops, psychotherapies aimed at improving medication compliance and improving psychosocial adjustment are an important adjunct to biological interventions (Dodgen & Shea, 2000).

The long-term process of dealing with the underlying physical and psychological causes of the addiction poses an additional challenge. Self-help groups, therapeutic communities, and psychotherapy for recovering addicts are all used to prevent relapse, though with mixed success (Klingemann & Hunt, 1998). (See Table 9.12 for some data on long-term outcomes of heroin addiction.)

Substitution (or maintainance) therapy The practice of a providing opioid addicts with a substitute opioid in a safe, medically monitored setting.

Substitution therapy This man is taking methadone, a synthetic opiate, at a clinic; substitution therapy remains a controversial treatment for opiate dependence.

Twenty-Year Follow-up of Male Heroin Addicts

Table 9.12

From Robson, 1999, based on Vaillant, 1988

	TIME AFTER FIRST HOSPITALIZATION (YEARS)		
	5	10	18
Stable abstinence	10%	23%	35%
Dead	6%	11%	23%
Active narcotic addiction	53%	41%	25%
Uncertain status	31%	25%	17%

Cocaine Many medications have been tested as possible treatments for cocaine addiction in the hopes that they might reduce cocaine cravings and restore neurotransmitter balances (Sadock & Sadock, 2001). Among these medications are tricyclic and SSRI antidepressants, dopamine agonists, opiate agonists and antagonists, and antiseizure medications (Anton, Brady, & Moak, 1999). Unfortunately, the results of these efforts have been mixed, and the search for effective biological treatments for cocaine addiction continues (Elman et al., 2001).

Treatment of cocaine dependence is difficult and usually involves multiple interventions including individual therapy and group therapy (Barber et al., 2001; Petry, Tedford, & Martin, 2001). Treatment typically begins with initiating abstinence from the drug, and then proceeds to preventing relapse (Kerfoot, Sakoulas, & Hyman, 1996). Some treatment programs have been able to increase abstinence by paying patients to go to work at a job that tests for drugs on a daily basis (Silverman et al., 2001). Treatment may take place in an inpatient, outpatient, or partial hospital setting.

Nicotine Quitting smoking can be extremely difficult. Mark Twain said it best: "It's easy to quit smoking; I've done it hundreds of times!" Fortunately, several relatively effective biological treatments for nicotine addiction have been developed in recent years. One strategy involves having the client ingest aversive agents, such as silver acetate lozenges, which create a bitter taste when combined with smoke (this is analogous to the use of disulfiram in alcoholism). Alternatively, nicotine can be delivered through chewing gum, nasal spray, inhaler, or a transdermal (skin) patch, allowing the client to avoid the health risks of smoking (West et al., 2001). These approaches are referred to as *nicotine replacement* strategies, and the user is then weaned off of nicotine altogether. Finally, the antidepressant bupropion (brand named Wellbutrin but renamed for this use as Zyban by the manufacturer) has shown promise as a treatment for smoking cessation, although its use over the long-term has not been proven (Anton et al., 1999; Hughes et al., 1993).

Sociocultural and Family Systems Components

Sociocultural and family systems perspectives focus on the role of larger social institutions in causing and treating substance misuse problems. We begin with an overview of the sociocultural model, which takes the broadest perspective on substance use disorders, and then look more closely at issues involving the specific role of the family.

Sociocultural Components and Interventions

The sociocultural perspective emphasizes that substance misuse problems are strongly correlated with social variables. For example, we have already noted that young, underemployed, urban men have much higher rates of alcoholism than the population at large. Interestingly, high stress professions such as the medical and dental fields also appear to have higher rates of substance abuse (Dodgen & Shea, 2000). U.S. soldiers fighting in the Vietnam War had high rates of opiate addiction while in Vietnam, but relatively few of them continued as opiate users after they returned home (Robson, 1999). All of these examples illustrate the profound effects of specific social circumstances on drug use and abuse. Obviously, these sociocultural forces cannot entirely explain substance misuse, since not all individuals in these high-risk groups develop drug problems. However, evidence suggests that social stresses and cultural pressures in these high-risk groups play a partial role in the etiology of substance misuse. Accordingly, sociocultural theorists encourage the engagement of the client's social network of friends and family in treatment, an approach known as **network therapy** (Galanter & Brook, 2001).

Network therapy A treatment for substance misuse that emphasizes engagement of the client's social network of friends and family in treatment.

Family Systems Components and Interventions

Family systems theorists have focused on certain family patterns that seem to be associated with substance misuse (Kaufman, 1986). As we have seen, the family systems approach analyzes the boundaries, subsystems, and homeostatic forces within families. Families of substance abusers appear to have certain characteristic patterns of interaction, including family-wide *denial, co-dependent* relationships, and *enabling* of the substance abuser (Dodgen & Shea, 2000). **Co-dependency,** a concept that has become widely used, refers to a relationship in which family members unconsciously collude with, or *enable,* a family member's substance misuse even though they may consciously oppose it (Fisher & Harrison, 1997). For example, the wife of an alcoholic might complain about her husband's drinking, yet call in sick for him at work and assume his responsibilities at home.

Denial and other family-wide defense mechanisms often keep substance abuse a highly protected secret within families. As a result, families may seek treatment with a focus on some other problem in another family member. Family therapists are therefore careful not to focus on the **identified patient** (the family's perception of who in the family is troubled), and, instead, attend to the possibility that the family is really organized around protecting the secret addiction of a substance abuser (McDowell & Spitz, 1999). Family therapy in these situations focuses on confronting family defenses such as denial and co-dependency, and establishing more appropriate family roles and boundaries (Dodgen & Shea, 2000).

Behavioral Components

Behavioral perspectives make an important contribution to the explanation and treatment of substance misuse. The three pillars of behavioral theory—operant conditioning, classical conditioning, and social learning/modeling—all play an important part in explaining and treating substance misuse (Rutgers, 1996).

Behavioral Explanations

In operant conditioning terms, drugs can be highly *reinforcing* because they both induce powerfully pleasurable emotional states (positive reinforcement) or alleviate unpleasant ones (negative reinforcement). The ability of drugs to relieve distress (negative reinforcement) is sometimes referred to as the **tension reduction** motive for substance misuse.

Classical conditioning—learning resulting from automatic mental associations—also contributes to substance misuse. For drug addicts, cues associated with their drug use, such as neighborhoods, friends, and drug paraphernalia, can become conditioned stimuli capable of producing strong cravings (Collins, Blane, & Leonard, 1999). Alcoholics Anonymous cautions recovering alcoholics to "stay away from people, places, and things" associated with drinking for precisely this reason. Even drug tolerance, usually thought of as a strictly biological phenomenon, is partly explained by conditioning (Thombs, 1999). This effect, known as *behavioral tolerance,* involves subtle forms of operant and classical conditioning that cause the drug user to experience decreased effects from the same dosage over time, leading to increased usage.

Finally, social learning—also referred to as vicarious learning or modeling (Bandura, 1977)—can be a powerful influence in drug abuse. Family learning contributes to the familial transmission of drug addiction above and beyond genetic factors (Zucker et al., 1995). Other social causes of addiction include learning about drug use from peers and the media. Advertisers know the power of social learning well; alcohol and cigarette ads that feature attractive and famous people are based on the effectiveness of modeling (Robson, 1999).

Codependency A relationship in which family member(s) unconsciously collude with the substance misuse of another member even though they may consciously oppose it.

Identified patient In family therapy, the family's perception of who in the family is troubled.

Tension reduction A behavioral explanation of substance misuse based on the ability of drugs to relieve distress (negative reinforcement).

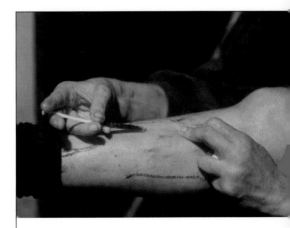

Classical conditioning and substance use
Drug paraphernalia, such as syringes, can become associated with drug effects through classical conditioning.

Covert sensitization Behavioral intervention involving pairing unpleasant emotional images with unwanted behaviors, such as drug use.

Aversion therapy Behavioral technique involving pairing an unwanted behavior with an aversive stimulus in order to classically condition a connection between them.

Contingency management The use of reinforcements and punishments to shape behavior in adaptive directions.

Behavioral Interventions

Behavioral interventions for substance misuse are also based on classical conditioning, operant conditioning, and social learning/modeling (Brooks, Karamanlian, & Foster, 2001; Kim & Siegel, 2001; Taylor & Jentsche, 2001). For example, when drug cravings have become classically conditioned responses to various cues (such as a drug dealer's neighborhood, or a hypodermic syringe), exposure to these cues in the absence of reinforcing drug use can be helpful in extinguishing cravings (Monti, Colby, & O'Leary, 2001). Relaxation training can also assist addicts in extinguishing conditioned craving responses. In another classical conditioning treatment technique known as **covert sensitization**, clients are taught to associate unpleasant emotional images with thoughts about drug use in order to pair drugs with aversive rather than rewarding consequences (Dodgen & Shea, 2000). For example, clients might be instructed to imagine what it would be like to have lung cancer whenever they start thinking about having a cigarette. Covert sensitization techniques are closely related to **aversion therapies**, in which drug use is connected to an unpleasant state such as nausea; the use of disulfiram (Antabuse) to prevent alcohol misuse is an example of aversion therapy.

A comprehensive form of treatment based on operant conditioning known as **contingency management** systematically rewards healthy behavior by the client (for example, with approval, increased privileges, or material rewards) and punishes or withholds rewards for drug-oriented behavior. With cocaine abusers, contingency management has been shown to be helpful as part of a comprehensive community intervention including counseling, recreation, and social support (Thombs, 1999).

Social learning interventions include everything from social skills and drug refusal training to anger management and support for appropriate life planning. Two specific treatment models based on social learning principles provide useful illustrations. Marlott and Gordon's (1985) *relapse prevention model,* for example, focuses on helping clients to identify and avoid high-risk situations in order to prevent relapse, while simultaneously promoting healthier modes of coping with stress. Another treatment model, known as *behavioral self-control training* (BSCT), emphasizes careful recording of drug use patterns, the development of social skills, and planning of healthy activities (Hester & Miller, 1995). BSCT seems to help a small but significant percentage (15%–25%) of problem drinkers to achieve controlled drinking (Thombs, 1999).

Because substance misuse poses a major public health problem around the world, public health officials have encouraged campaigns aimed at the *prevention* of substance misuse in addition to promoting the development of effective treatments. Prevention efforts aimed at instilling anti-drug attitudes and peer pressure resistance skills in children, based mostly on behavioral and cognitive principles, have become commonplace in elementary, middle, and high schools in the United States. The most widely known of these, the *DARE* (Drug Abuse Resistance Education) program, was developed by Daryl Gates, the former police chief of Los Angeles. The DARE program has been heavily supported by law enforcement organizations, and it claims to reach 5 million children each year (DARE America, 1991). However, as recent research on its effectiveness is mixed, the program has become controversial (Clayton et al., 1996; Fisher & Harrison, 1997).

Cognitive Components

Cognitive approaches to explaining and treating substance misuse began proliferating as the "cognitive revolution" swept through psychology in the 1970s. In one line of research, cognitive psychologists demonstrated that cognitions are heavily involved in the subjective experience of drug effects. For example, subjects' *expectancies* about how they will feel when drinking powerfully influence how they

DARE These fifth graders are receiving drug prevention instruction through the DARE program; research on its effectiveness has shown mixed results.

actually feel (Thombs, 1999). Thus the expectation of feeling good, relaxed, or less distressed can be an important motive for drug use and a self-fulfilling prophecy. In addition, researchers have found that, among problem drinkers, thoughts involving a fear of negative social evaluation may precipitate drinking episodes and relapses (Collins et al., 1999). In general, poor self-esteem and low *self-efficacy* (self-effectiveness) expectations seem to be risk factors for drug problems (Robson, 1999). For example, Ellis and his colleagues in the *Rational Emotive Therapy* (RET) school of cognitive clinical psychology have established that stress and negative thinking patterns can contribute to relapses (Ellis & MacLaven, 1999). Cognitive theorists also use their general emphasis on negative cognitive **schemas**, and resulting **negative automatic thoughts**, in explaining substance misuse. For instance, the schema "Drugs are the only reliable friend" may produce negative automatic thoughts such as "I'm lonely, so why not get high?"

Finally, social learning approaches, which we also discussed in the Behavioral Components section, have a significant cognitive element. Social learning, or modeling, involves cognitive processes that influence self-efficacy expectations and self-esteem (Bandura, 1977). For example, children of alcoholics are at risk for alcoholism not just because of behavioral learning involved in imitating their parents' behavior but also because of the dysfunctional cognitions (such as, "If dad drinks, it can't be so bad") they may develop from observing their parents' drinking.

Cognitive Interventions

Some of the relapse prevention treatments described in the Behavioral Components section include a cognitive component, and the two perspectives are often combined (McDowell & Spitz, 1999). The cognitive component emphasizes **cognitive restructuring** in the form of challenging and changing distorted cognitive schemas, teaching clients improved social skills, helping them to identify relapse dangers, and improving their poor self-efficacy expectations. In cognitive therapy for drug abuse, the therapist assists the client in examining drug-related cognitive schemas (such as, "drugs aren't that dangerous"), challenging automatic negative thought patterns (such as, "I'm boring when I'm sober"), and building positive coping self-statements (for example, "I can recover") (Dodgen & Shea, 2000).

Psychodynamic Components

The psychodynamic perspective on substance misuse was the first comprehensive psychological approach to addiction, and it is a foundation for many other contemporary psychological approaches. Currently, however, the psychodynamic perspective has a negative reputation in some parts of the "recovery movement." This is partly because the psychodynamic model is somewhat at odds with the disease model, and also because some clinicians have inappropriately used older psychodynamic theories and techniques to treat addiction, with poor results. However, the psychodynamic perspective does have a great deal to offer to the understanding and treatment of substance misuse, particularly as psychodynamic theory has been updated and revised (McDowell & Spitz, 1999). Although it is true that traditional psychodynamic interventions alone are not considered effective for substance dependence, psychodynamic principles have an important role in explaining and treating substance misuse (Allen, 2001; Felix & Wine, 2001; Herman, 2000).

Like the other psychological approaches, psychodynamic theory views substance misuse as a symptom, or result, of other forces and problems within the client. As psychodynamic theory has changed over the past century, ideas about the specific emotional factors causing substance misuse have shifted. During the early

Cognitive schemas Mental models of the world used to organize information.

Negative automatic thoughts Negative thoughts generated by negative cognitive schemas.

Cognitive restructuring Therapy techniques that focus on changing irrational and problematic thoughts.

psychodynamic period, clinicians emphasized the addict's strong oral phase needs for comfort and dependency, and devotion to pleasure seeking. The addict was seen as someone who was emotionally fixated at an early stage of childhood, seeking nurturance and pleasure at all costs. As psychodynamic theory developed, more complex ideas about addiction arose in connection with the newer emphasis on ego and superego development, object (interpersonal) relations, attachment issues, and self-esteem. Current psychodynamic explanations, for example, tend to view substance misuse as a maladaptive coping (or defense) strategy. In other words, drug abuse is viewed as a way of numbing or avoiding painful emotions that the ego cannot tolerate. For example, clients with severe substance use problems may have been overwhelmed by traumatic experiences, and may not have developed adequate ego skills to cope effectively with them. Such clients often have profound difficulty identifying and verbalizing their feelings, a condition sometimes referred to as **alexithymia,** and frequently numb intense emotions through substance misuse (Koocher, Norcross, & Hill, 1998; Krystal, 1979). In this sense, current psychodynamic theorists use a *self-medication* model to explain substance misuse, but they emphasize the psychological, rather than the biological, deficits and experiences being "medicated" with drugs (McDougall, 1980).

Along with their emphasis on emotion-regulation problems as the underlying cause of the symptom of substance misuse, psychodynamic clinicians focus on the role of defense mechanisms in the development and maintenance of addictions. For example, the addict protects himself from painful awareness of the problems and feelings surrounding his addiction through the defense mechanism of *denial*—a refusal to acknowledge an obvious reality. Denial is so central to the process of addiction that it has become a cornerstone of most theoretical explanations and interventions (Herman, 2000; Shaffer & Simoneau, 2001; Miller & Flaherty, 2000). Another prominent defense mechanism in addictions is *omnipotent thinking*—the wishful belief that one has control over uncontrollable situations. Addicts often seem to believe that they can control and master a drug which actually has taken control of them (McDowell & Spitz, 1999). As the ancient Japanese proverb puts it: "First the man takes a drink, then the drink takes a drink, then the drink takes the man."

As we have seen, the symptom model to which psychodynamic theory subscribes is not currently in favor for a variety of complex reasons. However, there is research support for the symptom model as an *explanation* for some cases of substance misuse. Shedler and Block (1990), in a landmark study, were able to test the symptom model by using a longitudinal study design. **Longitudinal** studies are those that follow their research subjects over an extended period of time. This is the only way to be certain about sequences of cause and effect that cannot be sorted out in correlational studies. Shedler and Block analyzed data on approximately 100 children growing up in Berkeley, California. The children were studied extensively at ages 7, 11, and 18. Among other things, Shedler and Block examined the subjects' patterns of drug use at age 18. They found that research participants who had drug problems at age 18 had consistently experienced emotional, family, and school problems since age 7. Furthermore, they found that most of the emotionally well-adjusted research participants experimented with drugs during high school without developing drug problems.

Shedler and Block's findings support the symptom model of substance misuse because they indicate that substance misuse develops from underlying emotional problems, not from drug use per se. But it is important here to distinguish again between explanations and treatments. Just because drug problems may develop as a symptom of underlying emotional problems does not mean that the most effective way to treat drug problems is to focus exclusively on the underlying concerns.

Alexithymia Profound difficulty in identifying and verbalizing emotions.

Longitudinal Research that studies subjects over time.

Psychodynamic Interventions

Because substance addictions usually require structured, directive therapies, often with a biological component, traditional psychodynamic interventions are rarely a primary intervention for substance dependence (Khantzian, Halliday, & McAuliffe, 1990). However, psychodynamic interventions can have an important adjunctive role in the treatment of substance dependence, and psychodynamic interventions are often useful in the treatment of less severe cases, such as those diagnosed with substance abuse (Herman, 2000). In these cases, focusing on the underlying emotional problems contributing to the substance misuse can be effective (Khantzian et al., 1990; Reder, McClure, & Jolley, 2000). Psychodynamic interventions for substance misuse have several goals. In keeping with the self-medication hypothesis, interventions aim at helping the individual discover and cope with painful emotions that are being avoided through drug use. The therapist attempts, through the use of interpretations and a supportive emotional relationship, to help the client develop better skills for dealing with troublesome emotions. Psychodynamic interventions also aim to improve self-esteem, self-acceptance, ego skills, and relationships in order to reduce the need for drug use (Allen, 2001; Felix & Wine, 2001; Leeds & Morgenstern, 1996).

The Twelve-Step Approach

The most prevalent current approach to treating substance misuse does not fit neatly into any of the theoretical perspectives we have discussed, though it relies on principles from many of them. Today's dominant approach is a collection of self-help treatments based on the Alcoholics Anonymous **twelve-step method**, which is at the core of the "recovery movement." Alcoholics Anonymous was born in 1935 when two men, Bill Wilson, a stockbroker, and Bob Smith, a surgeon, sat down one afternoon and talked together about their struggles with alcoholism. Wilson had been trying valiantly to stay sober after years of problem drinking, and he had a religious awakening after reading William James' classic book, *The Varieties of Religious Experience*. The combination of this experience with the recognition by the two men of the helpful power of their mutual support, empathy, and advice led them to co-found Alcoholics Anonymous (Fisher & Harrison, 1997; McDowell & Spitz, 1999). Since then, the organization has grown exponentially, based on the simple principles of Wilson and Smith's initial conversations which are embodied in the "Twelve Steps" (see Table 9.13). The twelve step principles now form the foundation of the many support groups that deal with a wide variety of addictive problems.

The actual process of Alcoholics Anonymous (AA) and other twelve-step meetings consists of a first-name only sharing of experiences and encouragement to follow the twelve steps. In addition to meetings, each participant works with a sponsor (an experienced AA member) who is available to offer advice and support on the challenging path to sobriety. Throughout the process, AA embodies the disease model of addiction, and participants are confronted when they are "in denial" about the severity of their problems or believe that they are in control of their substance use.

The AA model draws on some of the theoretical perspectives described above, even though it was developed independently by laypeople. For example, the AA model includes cognitive-behavioral (for example, contingency management and identification of relapse dangers), psychodynamic (empathy, ego support), and sociocultural (social support) principles, along with its core focus on spirituality (Brower et al., 1989; McDowell & Spitz, 1999; Miller & Kurtz, 1994).

Currently, there are also alternative self-help groups which make use of some aspects of the twelve-step method but reject parts they find objectionable, such as its religious elements or its endorsement of the disease model with its goal of total

Twelve-step method A popular self-help approach to substance misuse problems based on the twelve-step recovery process of Alcoholics Anonymous.

Alcoholics Anonymous These individuals are participating in an AA meeting as part of an alcohol treatment program. AA appears to be one of the most effective treatments for alcoholism.

Table 9.13	The Twelve Steps of Alcoholics Anonymous

1. We admitted we were powerless over alcohol and that our lives had become unmanageable.
2. Came to believe that a Power greater than ourselves could restore us to sanity.
3. Made a decision to turn our will and our lives over to the care of God as we understood Him.
4. Made a searching and fearless moral inventory of ourselves.
5. Admitted to God, to ourselves, and to another human being the exact nature of our wrongs.
6. Were entirely ready to have God remove all these defects of character.
7. Humbly asked Him to remove our shortcomings.
8. Made a list of all persons we had harmed, and became willing to make amends to them all.
9. Made direct amends to such people wherever possible, except when to do so would injure them or others.
10. Continued to take personal inventory and when we were wrong promptly admitted it.
11. Sought through prayer and meditation to improve our conscious contact with God as we understood Him, praying only for knowledge of His will for us and the power to carry that out.
12. Having had a spiritual awakening as the result of these steps, we tried to carry this message to alcoholics, and to practice these principles in all our affairs.

abstinence from alcohol and drugs. Rational Recovery, one such group, uses the principles of Ellis's Rational Emotive Therapy as an alternative to the twelve-step approach (Fisher & Harrison, 1997).

As the popularity of the twelve-step approach has grown, researchers have been eager to evaluate its effectiveness and to compare it to other treatments. Overall, studies of AA's effectiveness have shown mixed results, but it is difficult to study the program rigorously because of the anonymity of the group members (McCrady & Miller, 1993). However, one recent influential government study attempted to compare the twelve-step approach with two other popular treatments. Project MATCH (an abbreviation for Matching Alcoholism Treatment to Client Heterogeneity), sponsored by the National Institute for Alcohol Abuse and Alcoholism (NIAAA), was so named because one of its research questions was whether certain clients did better when matched with certain treatment approaches. Clients were randomly assigned either to a program facilitating and encouraging attendance at AA meetings, to a cognitive-behavioral treatment, or to *motivational enhancement* therapy, a treatment that addresses ambivalence about drinking in a nonconfrontational way (Carroll et al., 1998; Zywiak, Longabough & Wirtz, 2002). The treatments were equally effective. After 12 weeks of treatment, most clients had improved, and they had maintained improvement at a 15-month follow-up (Thombs, 1999). The effectiveness of all three treatments is good news on many levels. Not only does it provide hope for alcoholics and their families, but it also provides hope for our society, given the enormous human and economic costs of alcoholism. More generally, the Rand Corporation (Ebener, McCaffrey & Sane, 1994) estimated that for every dollar spent on treating addiction, seven dollars is ultimately saved as a result of reduced crime and increased productivity.

Multiple Causality and the Connection Between Mind and Body in Substance Use Disorders

In keeping with the core concept of *multiple causality,* many experts now agree that the most effective explanations and treatments for addiction draw on multiple theoretical perspectives (Brower et al., 1989). For example, explaining and treating alcohol dependence in a college student requires consideration of genetic vulnerability (biological), peer influences (sociocultural), the reinforcement provided by alcohol (behavioral), cognitive expectancies about drinking (cognitive), and the possibility of self-medicating painful emotions (psychodynamic). Similarly, as we have noted, the success of AA seems to be due, in part, to its use of principles associated with several different theoretical approaches. Increasingly, *multimodal* explanations and treatments for substance misuse integrate these different perspectives and view them as congruent (or overlapping) rather than competing.

In addition, substance use disorders highlight the **connection between mind and body** and we have seen that understanding this connection is crucial to explaining and treating substance use problems. For example, neurochemical deficits can create subjective states of drug craving, and behavioral responses to these cravings, such as drug use, in turn, can cause further changes in neurochemistry that can sustain the vicious cycle of addiction. We return now to the case vignettes of substance misuse from the beginning of the chapter to further illustrate these core concepts.

Brief Summary

- For a variety of reasons, the disease model is currently the dominant paradigm for explaining and treating substance use disorders, even though the symptom model has some merit.

- Biological explanations of substance use disorders include the hypothesis that drug use is a form of self-medication for biochemical deficiencies, and an emphasis on the role of genetic factors in substance use disorders. Biological interventions include the use of aversive agents that make drug use noxious, substitution therapies, and the provision of medications that can help reduce drug cravings.

- Sociocultural and family systems approaches emphasize social and family dynamics that can contribute to substance misuse. Social support and family treatment can also contribute to recovery from substance use disorders.

- Behavioral and cognitive perspectives highlight the role of tension reduction, classical conditioning, and negative beliefs and expectancies in substance use disorders. Classical conditioning interventions such as covert sensitization, operant conditioning techniques such as aversion therapies and contingency management, and cognitive restructuring methods are among the important behavioral and cognitive treatment components.

- Early psychodynamic explanations for substance misuse focused on the hypothesis of emotional fixation at an oral, pleasure-addicted developmental stage. Current psychodynamic theorists view substance misuse as a maladaptive defense mechanism for coping with painful emotions. While psychodynamic interventions by themselves are not considered effective for treating serious substance misuse, psychodynamic concepts are an important component of many treatments.

- Twelve-step models, such as the Alcoholics Anonymous approach, combine principles of many theoretical perspectives with a spiritual emphasis. Multimodal approaches to substance misuse are increasingly embraced by experts on substance misuse, highlighting the core concepts of *multiple causality* and the *connection between mind and body.*

> Critical Thinking Question | The AA approach to treating substance dependence, developed and conducted by laypeople, seems to be at least as effective as treatments designed by mental health professionals. What components seem to you to account for its effectiveness?

Case Vignettes | Treatment
Rob | Substance Abuse

Rob decided to seek therapy after the fall semester of his senior year. His GPA for the fall was a 2.5, far below the 3.3 average of his first three years. Rob was upset about this, as he was intent on attending law school. Still, Rob was ambivalent about seeking help. He was worried that a therapist would focus on his pot use and tell him that he had to quit. Rob wasn't sure that quitting would solve his academic problems, and he was reluctant to give up something he enjoyed so much. Nevertheless, he agreed to meet one time with a therapist when his father encouraged him to do so.

The therapist suggested that Rob complete a standard three-session evaluation, so that they could thoroughly review his situation and decide what might be helpful. The subject of Rob's marijuana use did come up in the first session. Rob told the therapist that he was smoking only on weekends, although he actually was getting high occasionally during the week as well. Rob's therapist noticed that Rob seemed to have trouble describing his emotions, and stayed away from any troubling subjects, such as his parents' divorce. The therapist mentioned to Rob that sometimes drug use is a way to "numb out" difficult feelings, and that he might find himself tempted to smoke even more as painful feelings came up in therapy. She encouraged Rob to begin keeping a journal of his feelings and his urges to get high, and to try to substitute writing for pot smoking.

Rob felt very uncomfortable after the first session. He decided that he could handle his problems on his own and that he didn't need professional help. When he told his father about his decision, however, Rob's father urged him to at least finish the evaluation. Rob agreed to do so, and felt more comfortable after seeing the therapist again and feeling that she was genuinely interested in helping him. After three sessions, they agreed that it would make sense to meet once weekly for the winter term to try to help Rob get back on track. Rob found that the sessions and the journal writing were more interesting and worthwhile than he'd expected, and he decided that he wanted to meet twice each week to further his progress. Rob was surprised to find that his thoughts kept returning to his parents' divorce, even though he believed he had "put that behind" him. Rob's therapist helped him to realize that he still had intensely sad, angry, and guilty feelings about the divorce that he had been avoiding by getting high. As they examined these feelings, it became clear that many of Rob's feelings were based on misperceptions of the situation, such as Rob's idea that he should have been able to keep his parents happy. As Rob became better able to notice, identify, and tolerate his feelings, his urges to smoke pot decreased, and he felt more in control of his moods. By the middle of the semester, Rob decided to stop smoking for the rest of the term, and his grades returned to his usual A's and B's.

Case Discussion | Substance Abuse

Rob was clearly experiencing negative consequences from his marijuana use, but the therapist believed that he had not crossed the threshold from abuse to dependence. Accordingly, she felt that it would be possible and appropriate to treat the marijuana use as a symptom of Rob's underlying emotional conflicts, especially the avoidance of his feelings about his parents' divorce. She used a variety of psychodynamic (exploring feelings) and cognitive-behavioral techniques (journal writing; challenging beliefs) to help him learn to understand and tolerate his feelings without having to rely on pot smoking to "numb out."

Dr. Bryce | Substance Dependence

Dr. Bryce was furious when the psychologist continued to question her about her alcohol use. Finally, she stormed out of the session, yelling "I came here for help with my case against the University, not for unwanted advice about my so-called alcoholism!" Like many addicts, Dr. Bryce might never have admitted her problem or sought treatment for it on her own. However, a group of her friends and colleagues had been very worried about her drinking for years. Several of them tried to approach her about it and were rudely rebuffed. Now, after hearing from her about her session with the psychologist, and seeing her preparing to further destroy her career by suing the University, Dr. Bryce's friends decided to act. They contacted a local therapist who agreed to act as a facilitator for an "intervention." After some careful planning, eight friends arrived at Dr. Bryce's house with the facilitator. They told her that they cared about her, were concerned about her, and were determined that she get immediate help. Dr. Bryce was enraged and humiliated. She said that she would only promise to think about it and insisted that they leave. As they had planned with the therapist, the friends refused to leave, insisting that they were going to take her directly to an inpatient treatment center. After two hours, Dr. Bryce capitulated.

At the hospital, a team of substance abuse specialists evaluated Dr. Bryce. They noted that she met all the criteria for alcohol dependence of several years' duration and began developing a treatment plan. The first step was detoxification, which, given the severity and duration of Dr Bryce's alcoholism, would require careful medical supervision. To ease the withdrawal process, Dr. Bryce was put on benzodiazepines. She was also required to attend AA meetings. After two weeks in the hospital, Dr. Bryce had completed the detox program. She was transferred to a day treatment program which included therapy, AA meetings, and disulfiram (Antabuse) for those clients who agreed to it. Dr. Bryce refused to try disulfiram. She remained bitter about having been forced into treatment, even though she admitted that she felt healthier without alcohol. Over the next several months, Dr. Bryce wavered between sobriety and relapse. She attended AA meetings sporadically, and began drinking again in between meetings. Eventually, she found an AA sponsor who she liked and trusted. With her sponsor's help, Dr. Bryce began attending meetings more regularly and admitting that she still had a problem. She acknowledged that controlled drinking was not a realistic option for her. By the first anniversary of the "intervention," Dr. Bryce had been completely sober for six months.

Case Discussion | Substance Dependence

Dr. Bryce's alcohol use had reached the point of severe dependence, but her extreme denial prevented her from seeking treatment; she required the intervention of friends before treatment could begin. Given the intensity and long duration of her drinking, careful management of the withdrawal process was critical. A medical, hospital-based program of supervised withdrawal was necessary, after which it was possible for Dr. Bryce to be treated on an outpatient basis. Her motivation for treatment often wavered, and her compliance was inconsistent, as is often the case with people who are substance dependent. Eventually, Dr. Bryce had a positive response to the AA process, especially after bonding with a sponsor. Like so many others who have struggled with alcoholism, Dr. Bryce was finally able to acknowledge her problem and reach sobriety primarily through the help of AA.

Chapter Summary

- In defining pathological drug use, experts prefer the term "substance" instead of "drug" because it conveys that drug use is universal and misuse can involve legal or illegal substances. Definitions and classifications of substance misuse are ***culturally and historically relative***.

- The current method for defining pathological substance use assesses the relationship between the user and the substances they use; a relationship causing distress or impairment is viewed as pathological regardless of whether the substance is legal or illegal. This method, which highlights ***the importance of context*** in defining substance misuse and the ***continuum*** between normal and abnormal substance use, is preferable to earlier quantitative approaches to defining pathological substance use.

- The DSM-IV-TR includes two main diagnoses of pathological substance use. Substance abuse refers to situations in which a person's use of a substance is causing negative consequences for him or her. Substance dependence, the more severe diagnosis often referred to as addiction, involves not just negative consequences but also compulsive use of the substance, loss of control over its use, and, in some cases, physical or psychological dependence. One ***limitation*** of these diagnoses is that it is not entirely clear how addiction to substance use differs from "addictions" to other activities such as work, sex, or gambling.

- Multimodal approaches, which endorse the principle of ***multiple causality*** of substance misuse and attend to the ***connection between mind and body***, are increasingly the norm in explaining and treating substance use disorders.

APPENDIX: HISTORIES OF SOME COMMONLY ABUSED SUBSTANCES

Opioids

Because of their powerful effects, opioids have been used and misused for centuries, for both medicinal and recreational purposes. The history of opioid use and abuse is a fascinating story in its own right. As you will see, there have been enormous changes over time and across cultures in the way that the opioids have been viewed, used, and regulated—another illustration of the core concept of ***cultural and historical relativism***.

The use of *opiates* (the term for substances derived directly from the opium poppy) dates back at least 3,500 years. Evidence of opium use has been found in ancient Sumerian, Greek, Egyptian, Persian, Roman, and Arabic cultures. During the last two millennia, the use of opiates and the cultivation of poppies spread around the globe as a result of conquest and trade. By the beginning of the nineteenth century, opium use was widespread across Europe, the Middle East, and the Far East.

During the 1800s, several important scientific advances occurred regarding the opioids, leading to increasing medical and recreational uses of these drugs. In 1806, a 20-year-old German pharmacist's assistant named Frederich Sertuerner published a paper demonstrating that he had isolated the primary active ingredient in opium. He named this ingredient morphine, after Morpheus, the Greek god of dreams. Pure morphine was 10 times more potent than opium. It became one of the most important medications in the history of medicine, providing powerful pain relief, and Sertuerner received the French equivalent of the Nobel Prize for his work (Ray & Ksir, 2002). Twenty-six years later, the second most important ingredient in

opium, *codeine,* was isolated. It, too, has played an enormous role in medical history because of its analgesic and cough suppressive properties. Finally, in 1874, chemists at the Bayer Pharmaceutical Company slightly altered the chemical structure of morphine and created a new compound, which was three times more potent than morphine and acted more quickly. In 1898, Bayer gave this new chemical the brand name Heroin (from the German word "heroisch," meaning powerful) and marketed it as a nonaddicting substitute for codeine (Hirsch, Paley, & Renner, 1996; McDowell & Spitz, 1999; Robson, 1999). The highly addictive nature of heroin was not understood until several years later.

In the meantime, Alexander Wood, a Scottish surgeon, had invented the hypodermic syringe (needle). This transformed both medical practice and substance misuse because it created a more potent intravenous method for the delivery of substances that previously could only be ingested, smoked, or absorbed through the skin. Concurrent with these scientific discoveries, opiate use was becoming increasingly widespread. In 1805, a 20-year-old Englishman bought some opium for a toothache in the form of laudanum, a common, legal, over-the-counter preparation typically containing opium, spices, and some alcohol. Laudanum translates from the Latin, meaning "worthy of praise." The young man described his experience as follows:

> I took it: and in an hour, O heavens! ... Here was a
> panacea ... for all human woes; here was the secret of
> happiness, about which philosophers had disputed for so
> many ages, at once discovered; happiness might now be

bought for a penny, and carried in the waistcoat pocket; portable ecstasies might be had corked up in a pint-bottle; and peace of mind could be sent down by the mail.

Quoted in Ray & Ksir, 2002 (p. 337)

This young man, Thomas De Quincey, later became famous as the author of a widely read article, "The Confessions of an English Opium Eater" (laudanum was actually a liquid, but consumption of it was referred to as "opium eating"), in which he described his life as an opium addict. He was by no means unusual in nineteenth century England. Opium was used then like aspirin is now. Many famous English writers were regular users, including Samuel Taylor Coleridge, Charles Dickens, and Elizabeth Barrett Browning (Robson, 1999). As late as World War I, the famous London department store Harrods sold morphine (and cocaine) kits complete with syringes labeled "A Useful Gift for Friends at the Front" (Robson, 1999). England was also heavily involved in the proliferation of opiate use around the world (Anderson & Berridge, 2000). In the infamous "Opium Wars" (1839–1842) the British forced the Chinese to give them continued control of the opium market in China. As a result, it is estimated that at one point 15 to 20 million Chinese were addicted to opiates (Robson, 1999).

Meanwhile, in the United States, opiate use was also commonplace. During the Civil War, opium addiction by soldiers who had used it for pain relief was so common that it was referred to as the "soldier's disease" (Robson, 1999). Yet, addiction was not considered a significant social or legal problem at this time. Addicts who sought treatment were usually given another opiate as a "treatment" for their addiction. By the turn of the twentieth century, approximately 1% of the U.S. population was addicted to an opiate (Ray & Ksir, 2002). The typical addict was a middle-aged housewife, who could buy laudanum (for 9 cents an ounce) by mail from Sears & Roebuck (Ray & Ksir, 2002).

This picture of widespread opiate use and addiction changed dramatically in the United States following the passage of the Harrison Act in 1914. This legislation was prompted by growing concern about opiate addiction, and it outlawed all nonmedical uses of opiates. Suddenly, a legal group of drugs became illegal, and has remained so to this day. Opiate use became a criminal issue (Wilson, 2000). Even the medical use of opiates was restricted by a 1919 Supreme Court ruling that prescribing maintenance opiates to addicts was not acceptable medical practice (Robson, 1999). Opiate use plummeted, but it was also pushed increasingly into the criminal underworld, much as was the case with alcohol during the Prohibition period.

The United States and many Western countries experienced sharp increases in opioid use again during the 1960s and 1970s. Some of this was a result of the experiences of soldiers serving in Vietnam, where heroin was easily available and 95% pure (compared to 5%–20% in the U.S.) (Robson, 1999). The counterculture movement of the 1960s also contributed to more widespread drug use, including use of opioids. Opioid addiction once again became a major legal and medical problem and has continued to be so. The AIDS epidemic, since the beginning of the 1980s, has intensified concern about heroin addiction since the virus is frequently spread through needle sharing (Alcabes, Beniowski, & Grund, 1999; Metzger, Navaline, & Woody, 2000; Somaini et al., 2000). More recently, the "heroin chic" fashion style of the 1990s, which featured waiflike models with sunken eye sockets, caused concern about a glorification and resurgence of heroin use among young people. It is currently estimated that there are about 500,000 heroin addicts in the United States (Ray & Ksir, 2002), and addiction is a major problem in many other countries as well, such as China (McCoy et al., 2001), Afganistan (Macdonald & Mansfield, 2001), Thailand (Cheurprakobkit, 2000) and Great Britain (Anderson & Berridge, 2000).

Cocaine

At several points in human history, a cycle of enthusiasm about the wonderful effects of cocaine has been followed by awareness of its dangers and increased regulation of the drug. Each time, the lessons from the past have been forgotten by later generations. Cocaine, then, provides another vivid example of the enduring issue of *historical relativism*. Let's explore some of the historical and cultural changes which are part of the story of this fascinating substance.

Although the active ingredient in coca leaves, known as cocaine, was not isolated until 1859, the substance has been used for centuries. The native people of the Andes Mountains have probably chewed coca leaves since 5,000 B.C.E. (see Table 9.10 on the early history of cocaine). This helped give them the energy for carrying large bundles across the high mountains and accounts for one of cocaine's many nicknames: "Bolivian marching powder." Cocaine was also used in religious rituals and as a form of currency by these native peoples.

During the 1800s, cocaine was brought to Europe and became immensely popular as a supposedly safe, mild stimulant. Its virtues were promoted by many respectable medical people, among them Angelo Mariani, a French chemist, W.S. Halsted, an American surgeon, and Sigmund Freud, the founder of psychoanalysis. Mariani imported huge amounts of cocaine to make a coca wine which became so popular that the Pope awarded him a medal of appreciation. Halsted, considered the "father of modern surgery," pioneered the use of cocaine as an anesthetic for surgery.

Freud's role in the history of cocaine is a particularly interesting one, especially given his later importance in the field of psychopathology. Early in his medical career, while he was still yearning for fame and the financial security that would enable him to marry his fiancée, Freud began to study the effects of cocaine. It was believed at the time that cocaine might be beneficial in the treatment of morphine addiction—a major problem then—as well as for treating certain heart conditions, depression, and as an anesthetic. Freud wrapped up his research on cocaine quickly, because he had an opportunity to visit his fiancée whom he had not seen in two years. The paper he published, "Uber Coca" ("On Cocaine"), was enthusiastic about the usefulness of cocaine, and it earned Freud some mild acclaim. However, upon returning from his visit to his fiancée, Freud discovered that a colleague, Carl Koller, had finished the crucial experiments demonstrating that cocaine was a breakthrough in anesthesia for eye surgery. Freud was frustrated that he had barely missed this opportunity for great fame, and later, of course, turned his ambitions in a different direction—the founding of psychoanalysis. In the meantime, Freud was an avid user of cocaine and provided samples to his friends. He wrote to his fiancée that a little cocaine helped him feel confident enough to speak to his esteemed professors, and he teased her that when he visited her she would behold "a big, wild man with cocaine in his body" (Gay, 1988). Only after one of his good friends became addicted—Freud was giving him cocaine to treat his morphine addiction—did Freud's enthusiasm for the drug wane.

In the United States, a similar cycle of enthusiasm for cocaine, followed by increased awareness of its dangers, occurred. In 1885, the Parke-Davis pharmaceutical firm described cocaine as a "wonder drug," and claimed that it "can supply the place of food, make the coward brave, and the silent eloquent" (Ray & Ksir, 2002). In 1886, the Coca-Cola Company began marketing a soft drink containing cocaine (thus the name Coca-Cola) based on the patented formula of an Atlanta druggist named John Pemberton. Coca-Cola, containing 60 milligrams of cocaine in every 8-ounce bottle, was promoted as a substitute for alcoholic beverages (Kerfoot, Sakoulas, & Hyman, 1996). But the tide soon began to turn against cocaine as concerns grew about its increasing use among the poor and its association with crime (Wilson, 2000). Cocaine was removed from Coca-Cola in 1906 and replaced with caffeine, a milder stimulant still found in many soft drinks. The government began to regulate the use of cocaine in the early 1900s along with the increasing regulation of opioids and other substances. Cocaine use also diminished because of the advent of amphetamines, developed in the 1930s. It was not until the 1970s, when increased regulation of amphetamines made them harder to obtain, that the popularity of cocaine resurfaced.

During the 1970s and 1980s, cocaine became so popular as a recreational drug that public health officials spoke of a "cocaine epidemic" (Rassool, 1998). The lessons of the previous century seemed to be forgotten as some physicians claimed that cocaine was a nonaddictive, relatively safe drug (Kerfoot et al., 1996; McDowell & Spitz, 1999). By 1990, it is estimated that 30 million Americans had tried cocaine, and 50% of Americans between the ages of 25 and 30 were thought to have used it. Finally, the new cocaine epidemic came full circle; as the public health community warned of the dangers of cocaine addiction, public sentiment turned more negative, and law enforcement against cocaine trafficking and use became a high national priority (Bowling, 1999; Furst et al., 1999; Nappo, Galduroz, & Carlini, 2000). Currently, rates of cocaine use are well below their peak about 20 years ago, although it remains a widely used drug (Blanken, Barendregt, & Zuidmulder, 1999).

Cocaine still has a small role in medical practice. It is used as an anesthetic for medical procedures involving the nasal, laryngeal, and esophageal regions as well as the eyes—just as Freud and his colleagues suggested over 100 years ago. Derivatives of cocaine, such as novocaine, are also used by dentists for numbing and anesthesia. However, other medications have proven superior to cocaine for most anesthetic purposes and have replaced it as a medical tool.

Nicotine

Native Americans had been using tobacco for centuries when it was "discovered" by European explorers in the New World. Christopher Columbus reported that the native people of San Salvador gave him tobacco on his birthday in 1492. Tobacco quickly became very popular among the growing European population in the American colonies. In fact, the economic growth of the colonies was largely financed through the sale of tobacco, their most important cash crop. Tobacco smoking spread quickly through Europe as well. Sir Walter Raleigh is thought to have introduced tobacco to the court of Queen Elizabeth. It was widely believed to have significant medical benefits and was used to treat everything from headaches to flatulence in sixteenth century Europe. The active ingredient in tobacco, nicotine, was isolated in 1828. Nicotine was named after Jean Nicot, a sixteenth century Frenchman who had supposedly used tobacco to "cure" the headaches of Catherine de Medicis, the wife of King Henry II. By the nineteenth century, the medicinal value of tobacco and nicotine had been disproved, and nicotine addiction had been identified as a problem. However, tobacco remained very popular, primarily in the form of snuff and chew products. Cigarettes did not become a popular form of tobacco use until the twentieth century. Tobacco use, primarily in the form of cigarettes, peaked in the 1950s.

In 1964, the Surgeon General of the United States officially reported that smoking was medically dangerous. In 1971, cigarette commercials were banned from television. In recent decades, the profoundly toxic effects of direct and secondhand smoke have been documented over and over again. In response to this, tobacco companies have gradually decreased the amounts of nicotine and tars (which contain most of the carcinogens in smoke) in cigarettes. However, these companies have often been accused of misleading the public about the dangers of smoking and the addictiveness of nicotine. Some tobacco companies had evidence of the addictiveness of nicotine to rats in the early 1980s, but did not publish the results (Ray & Ksir, 2002). It was not until the 1990s that tobacco companies began to admit their awareness of nicotine's addictive properties.

Marijuana

Like most other popular drugs, marijuana has been used for centuries; experts believe that it has been cultivated for at least 8,000 years (Losken, Maviglia, & Friedman, 1996). There are references to marijuana in ancient Chinese medical texts and on ancient Egyptian papyrus tracts. Over the centuries, the cannabis plant has been used to make rope fiber as well as for its mind-altering/medicinal properties. George Washington grew cannabis plants at Mt. Vernon in the 1700s, and marijuana was a popular drug in certain artistic and high society circles in Europe in the 1800s (Iversen, 2000). However, concern about marijuana use grew during the 1920s and 1930s, leading many states, and eventually the United States government, to outlaw the drug. This concern was based on the widespread belief that marijuana was linked to criminal behavior (Fisher & Harrison, 1997). For example, a 1936 article in *Scientific American* claimed that:

> Marijuana produces a wide variety of symptoms in the user, including hilarity, swooning, and sexual excitement. Com-
> bined with intoxicants, it often makes the smoker vicious, with a desire to fight and kill.
>
> Quoted in Ray & Ksir, 2002 (p. 407)

During the 1950s and 1960s, marijuana became increasingly popular, especially with young people. Marijuana use peaked around 1978, then declined until 1992, and has recently increased again (McDowell & Spitz, 1999; Sloman, 1998). During the 1970s, several states decriminalized (lessened legal penalties against) marijuana in keeping with the popular view at the time that it was a relatively mild drug (Iversen, 2000). However, the conservative trend during the 1980s and 1990s caused a return to harsher legal treatment of marijuana possession, and, by 1996, 600,000 arrests on marijuana charges were made in the United States alone (Ray & Ksir, 2002). The position of recent U.S. administrations concerning marijuana has also caused controversy concerning the medical use of the drug. During the 1990s, some states attempted to make marijuana available for medical uses, such as treating glaucoma or severe nausea, over the objections of the Drug Enforcement Administration (DEA). The Supreme Court upheld the ban on medical uses of marijuana in May 2001, but the issue remains a controversial one (Nichols, 2000; Sloman, 1998).

Duchamp, *Nude Descending a Staircase No. 2,* 1912. © Philadelphia Museum of Art, Philadelphia, PA/Bridgeman Art Library International, Ltd. © 2003 Artists Rights Society (ARS), New York/ADAGP, Paris/Succession Marcel Duchamp

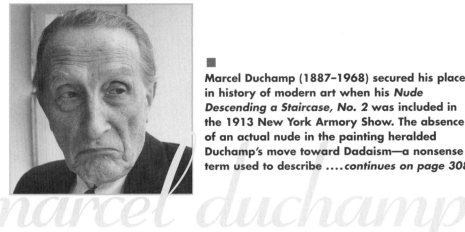

Marcel Duchamp (1887–1968) secured his place in history of modern art when his *Nude Descending a Staircase, No. 2* was included in the 1913 New York Armory Show. The absence of an actual nude in the painting heralded Duchamp's move toward Dadaism—a nonsense term used to describe ....*continues on page 308*

marcel duchamp

chapter ten

SEX, GENDER, AND THE SEXUAL DISORDERS

Case Vignettes

Laurie is a 29-year-old, married attorney; she and her husband are planning to start having children in a couple of years. Laurie is mostly satisfied with her life except for one thing: she has never enjoyed sex as much as she thinks she should, and rarely has orgasms. This has particularly bothered Laurie recently because she believes that once she becomes pregnant and starts having children her chances of having a satisfying sex life will be over. Laurie feels that she is missing out on something important, and this upsets her. She has always felt that she could get whatever she wanted in life by being focused and determined.

Until she met the man who became her husband, Laurie's sexual problem didn't bother her much. Laurie had only two serious boyfriends before she married, and she'd always focused more on school and career than on her personal life. When Laurie was growing up, her family life was very chaotic, largely due to her mother's emotional instability. Laurie decided at an early age that her life would be different: orderly and organized. When sex wasn't satisfying with her boyfriends, Laurie assumed that it would get better when she met the right man. But with Sam, her husband, things aren't much different. Laurie finds that while she likes the idea of sex, she has difficulty becoming aroused. She feels self-conscious about her body, and ashamed about her "animal-like" feelings. Laurie rarely masturbates because she finds it too embarrassing. After confiding to a friend for the first time about her problem, Laurie decided to accept her friend's suggestion and consult a sex therapist.

Rick, a 28-year-old computer programmer, was arrested late one summer night for exposing his genitals to a woman who was walking in a park near his office. To his dismay, she calmly pulled out a cell phone and called the police, rather than giving him the look of shock and the scream of terror that he had expected and wanted. While this was the first time Rick had been arrested, he had been exposing himself to women in situations like this for years. After exposing himself to an attractive woman, Rick would go to his car and masturbate.

Rick was concerned about his behavior, but mainly because he feared what his parents would think if they ever found out. Rick's parents were very religious and extremely puritanical about sex; all sexual topics were off-limits in his family. Rick felt that it might literally kill his parents if they ever discovered what he had been doing. He told himself that if he was careful they would never know, and that he wasn't really hurting anybody. However, Rick felt very ashamed whenever people made comments about "perverts," and he told no one about his secret. His few friends and occasional girlfriends had no idea about his behavior. Rick did have sex with the women he dated, but he never enjoyed it as much as his "secret" behavior. Now that he had been caught, Rick

...continued from page 306

art about life's absurdity and absence of meaning. Duchamp explored humor and absurdity in other ways as well. He enjoyed cross-dressing as a female alter-ego whose name, Rose Sélavy, was a play on the words *"Eros, c'est la vie"* (Desire, that is life).

was thinking for the first time about getting help for his problem. He knew that doing so might make a judge more sympathetic, and he hoped that "curing" his problem would prevent his parents from ever finding out about it.

Phil, a 35-year-old anthropologist, has never felt comfortable being male. As a toddler, he was more interested in playing with girls and dolls than with boys and trucks. When Phil was four, his father, an abusive alcoholic, beat his mother so badly that she was hospitalized for a week. Thereafter, Phil, an only child, was terrified whenever he was left with his father, and he formed an especially close bond with his mother. They would whisper to each other about the father's whereabouts and moods to protect each other. Around his fifth birthday, Phil insisted to his parents that he was really a girl, and that his penis would fall off soon. His parents were alarmed, and had Phil see a child therapist at the time. Things seemed to get better as Phil began school. He made friends with girls, not boys, but he stopped saying that he was, or wanted to be, a girl. In junior high school, Phil began to realize that he was sexually attracted to boys. His father had left the family by then, and Phil confided to his mother about these attractions. She told him that he was probably gay and was very accepting. In high school, Phil came "out" and began having homosexual relationships. However, he never felt comfortable with his male body, and found himself still drawn to emotionally intimate relationships with women, whom he admired and envied.

Phil became fascinated with anthropology in college, and devoted himself to becoming an anthropologist. He loved the idea of immersing himself in a foreign culture so much that he could almost transform himself into a member of the other group. Phil was aware of the connection between this and his lifelong feelings of alienation as a man and his fascination with women. He also explored his fascination with woman by occasionally cross-dressing and by taking a feminine role with his lovers. But Phil could never shake his unhappiness and a feeling that something was wrong in his life. After establishing himself as a successful professor of anthropology, Phil began to think seriously about pursuing a sex change. As he learned more about his situation and options, Phil became convinced that he was psychologically female, and would only be happy in a woman's body.

Sexuality is an area of intense interest to most people. It has been said that sex is an amalgam of "friction and fantasy" (Kaplan, 1974). The former (friction) involves a powerful hormonal and biological reflex system, and the latter (fantasy) involves a powerful psychological drive. In our current culture, there are many available outlets for people's sexual interests. For example, when the Internet company Yahoo! began restricting access to sex-oriented chat rooms during the spring of 2001, there was an enormous outcry from thousands of disappointed users. But sexuality is also an area of emotional and moral conflict for many people—in fact, Yahoo! began blocking the sex-oriented chat rooms as a result of protests from religious organizations opposed to the chat room content (Schwartz, 2001). In brief, sex is an arena of excitement, passion, guilt, anxiety, shame, and many other intense feelings. It is no wonder, then, that people are especially interested in, and sometimes worried about, their own sexuality and whether it is "normal."

The three cases described above, each very different from the others, give some idea of the wide range of problems that fall under the heading of "sexual disorders." Laurie's problem is a limitation in her enjoyment of "normal" sexual activity, Rick has an "abnormal" sexual desire, and Phil's problem is not in the area of sex per se, but in the arena of gender identity which is closely related to sex. We have put the words normal and abnormal above in quotes in order to make the familiar point that it is not easy to precisely define normality and abnormality. We have seen that this is true for many disorders, but defining abnormality is especially problematic when it comes to sexuality.

DEFINING SEXUAL DISORDERS

Defining abnormality in the area of sexuality is challenging, mainly because of three core concepts in abnormal psychology: the *continuum between normal and abnormal behavior,* the *importance of context,* and *cultural and historical relativism* (Kernberg, 2001; Laws & O'Donohue, 1997; Munroe & Gauvain, 1997; Romano, DeLuca, & Rayleen, 2001).

The Continuum Between Normal and Abnormal Sexuality and the Importance of Context in Defining Abnormality

To illustrate the *continuum* between normal and abnormal sexuality, let's return to the cases at the beginning of the chapter. In each case, it is clear that something is wrong, although one might hesitate to use terms such as "abnormal" or "disordered." In particular, Laurie seems to be happy and to function well aside from her sexual frustration. Yet from a DSM-IV-TR standpoint, her condition can be considered a disorder because it causes significant distress and impairment. (In fact, as we will see, there are at least two DSM-IV-TR diagnoses that might apply to Laurie, female sexual arousal disorder and female orgasmic disorder, both described later in the chapter.) But what if Laurie were not distressed by her situation? Or, what if she were able to have orgasms regularly by masturbating, even though sex with her husband wasn't fully satisfying? What if she lived in a culture in which women were not expected to enjoy sex? With this last example, we are foreshadowing the discussion of *cultural relativism*, but all three examples illustrate once again how difficult it can be to draw the line between normal and abnormal behavior.

The cases of Rick and Phil probably seem like more clear-cut examples of abnormal sexuality. However, some members of the "transgender" movement (a movement supporting people who want to change their gender) would argue that the only problem with Phil's situation is society's intolerance of it, and that there is no mental disorder involved. And in Rick's case, what if he only had *fantasies* of exhibiting himself, or acted his fantasies out with a consenting partner? For that matter, how different is Rick's behavior from the behavior of someone who goes out in public dressed to shock people, or from someone who strips for money? These questions highlight the importance of *context* in defining abnormal sexuality; sexual behaviors that would be considered inappropriate and abnormal in one context might seem normal in another context. The DSM-IV-TR provides diagnostic criteria (which we will review later in the chapter) that attempt to draw a line between normal and abnormal sexuality, but they contain many vague and even contradictory elements (Laws & O'Donohue, 1997; Parsons, 2000; Szuchman & Muscarella, 2000).

Cultural and Historical Relativism in Defining and Classifying Sexual Disorders

The concepts of *cultural and historical relativism* are especially relevant to the area of sexual disorders, and contribute to the challenges of defining abnormal sexuality.

Dr. Jocelyn Elders Dr. Elders sparked controversy as the U.S. Surgeon General for her strong support of sex education in schools.

Ego-dystonic homosexuality A DSM-III diagnosis, since eliminated, that referred to homosexuality that was distressing and unwanted by the client.

Kellogg's cereals and sexuality It is a little known fact that J. H. Kellogg invented his breakfast cereals as part of his mission to discourage sexuality in young people; he hoped that feeding them bland food in the morning would decrease their excitability.

Let's consider two sexual practices that have been viewed very differently during different historical periods and in different cultures: masturbation and homosexuality.

In 1994, the Surgeon General of the United States, Dr. Jocelyn Elders, was fired by President Clinton after she made remarks suggesting that masturbation should be discussed in school as part of sex education (Frisby, 1994; Kolata, 1994). Her dismissal demonstrates how much tension and anxiety still surrounds the topic of masturbation, and sexuality in general, even though Dr. Elders' views were well within the scientific mainstream. Masturbation is generally considered a harmless, normal, and nearly universal activity (Baumeister, Kathleen, & Vohs, 2001; Halpern et al., 2000; Szuchman & Muscarella, 2000). It is nearly unthinkable that someone would be considered mentally ill because he or she masturbates. In fact, it is far more common today to consider the *absence* of masturbation, at least during adolescence, to be a sign of pathology (Laufer, 1981; McCarthy & McCarthy, 1998; Money, 1986).

However, in the nineteenth century people sometimes *were* considered mentally ill, and even hospitalized, because they masturbated (Hare, 1962). A medical anti-masturbation movement began in the 1700s, launched by a Swiss psychiatrist named S. D. D. Tissot, whose book, *Onanism, or a Treatise on the Disorders of Masturbation,* warned of the dangers of the practice (Bullough, 1987; Kolata, 1994; Tissot, 1817). Benjamin Rush, the father of American psychiatry, also argued against masturbation and considered it physically and psychologically damaging (Switzer, 1967). In the nineteenth century, two American industrialists took the anti-masturbation campaign to the cupboards of America's kitchens. Both Sylvester Graham, the inventor of the graham cracker, and J. H. Kellogg, the founder of the Kellogg cereal company, wrote books on the evils of masturbation (Kellogg suggested "curing" girls by putting carbolic acid on the clitoris). Graham's and Kellogg's food products were designed to keep children from masturbating by feeding them bland foods in an effort to decrease their excitability (Graham, 1854; Kellogg, 1881; Sokolow, 1983). Anti-masturbation views were so widespread that inventors developed genital cages that would sound an alarm when an erection occurred while a boy was sleeping (Kolata, 1994; Money, 1985). Even Freud, who popularized a more permissive and accepting view of childhood and adult sexuality, believed for some time that masturbation could cause a form of neurosis (Bonaparte, 1954/2000; Gay, 1988).

Homosexuality has been subject to similarly bizarre and shifting social judgments, which further illustrate the principle of ***historical relativism***. Until 1973, homosexuality was listed in the DSM-II as a mental disorder. Thereafter, the diagnosis of homosexuality was replaced by the diagnosis of **ego-dystonic homosexuality** (that is, homosexuality that is distressing and unwanted by the client). The reasons for this change were complex and involved a variety of scientific, cultural, and political developments reflected in the increasingly widespread view that homosexuality per se was not a disorder, but a normal variation of sexuality (Bayer, 1981; Bullough, 1976; Laws & O'Donohue, 1997). Later, even ego-dystonic homosexuality was removed from the diagnostic manual on the grounds that it usually reflected internalized homophobia and prejudice and did not constitute a mental disorder (Cohler & Galatzer-Levy, 2000). In the most current DSM, the DSM-IV-TR, homosexuality is not mentioned (APA, 2000).

The fact that only 30 years ago, many clients were in treatment with a diagnosis of "homosexuality" shows how much and how quickly norms regarding sexuality can change, causing our definitions of abnormality to change along with them. Definitions of sexual abnormality also vary greatly across cultures (Bullough, 1976, 1987; Nye, 1999)—reflecting the core concept of ***cultural relativism***. For example, China only removed homosexuality as a psychiatric diagnosis in 2001 (Heng, 2001). In another culture, that of the Sambia people of Papua New Guinea, ritualized male homosexu-

Sexuality and historical relativism This painting from the Classical period of ancient Greece showing a man kissing a young boy illustrates the historical relativism of attitudes about homosexuality.

ality is the norm before the birth of a man's first child (Herdt & Stoller, 1990). More generally, the liberal and liberated sexual mores of the contemporary Western world are considered bizarre and abnormal in conservative, traditional cultures around the world (Davidson & Moore, 2001; Nye, 1999; Tseng, 2001). Also, disorders such as Rick's *exhibitionism* (one of the disorders within a category called *paraphilias,* described later in the chapter) are found primarily in Western societies (Bhugra, 2000). Other sexual disorders are found only in non-Western cultures. For example, a syndrome known as *dhat,* which consists of severe anxiety associated with the loss of semen in ejaculation, is found primarily in India, Sri Lanka, and China (APA, 2000; Shukla & Singh, 2000).

The bottom line is that the core concepts involving the importance of ***context***, the ***continuum between normal and abnormal behavior*** and ***cultural and historical relativism*** make it so difficult to define the concept of a sexual disorder that many experts eschew the phrase "sexual disorder" altogether and use the term "sexual deviation" instead (Willerman & Cohen, 1990). This latter term is meant to convey that it may be more appropriate, scientifically speaking, to describe certain unusual sexual practices as "deviant" (that is, statistically rare) rather than "disordered" (implying a mental disease). Some theorists take the concepts of the ***continuum*** and ***relativism*** to extremes, arguing that all sexual taboos are based upon cultural biases and prejudices (an argument presented in Box 10.1). However, it remains important to try to define, classify, and understand abnormal sexual behaviors so that we can offer treatments to those who may be suffering because of them. Experts have attempted to classify sexual disorders for hundreds of years. We now turn to a review of these classification schemes and their frequently changing categories, and then examine the current DSM-IV-TR sexual disorder diagnoses.

Brief Summary

- Sexuality is a ubiquitous, intense, and emotionally conflicted aspect of human life.
- The core concepts of the ***continuum between normal and abnormal behavior***, the importance of ***context***, and ***historical and cultural relativism*** make it especially difficult to define abnormal sexuality.

"Yes, But Did Anyone Ask the Animals' Opinion?" *by Sarah Boxer*

The following article from *The New York Times* describes a controversy over the question of whether taboos against bestiality (a sexual disorder listed in the DSM-IV-TR as zoophilia) are a form of historically and culturally based prejudice against animals, an issue that has divided the animal rights movement.

The controversy came with the first daffodils in March, shortly after Peter Singer, the father of the animal rights movement, reviewed a reissue of the book *Dearest Pet: On Bestiality* (Verso), by the Dutch biologist Midas Dekkers, for *Nerve,* an online sex magazine. Three months have passed and still the sun has not set on the latest tempest surrounding Mr. Singer, the provocative author of *Animal Liberation* and a professor of bioethics at Princeton University's Center for Human Values.

Mr. Singer has received his share of human venom before this. Protesters have called him a Nazi for his view that in some cases infanticide and euthanasia are morally justifiable.

The furor this time concerns sex with animals.

In his review, titled "Heavy Petting," Mr. Singer noted that almost all of the taboos on nonprocreative sex (taboos against homosexuality, oral sex, contraception and masturbation) have vanished. But one notable exception still stands: the taboo on sex with animals. "Heard anyone chatting at parties lately about how good it is having sex with their dog?" he asked. The persistence of the bestiality taboo, he wrote, reflects humans' ambivalence about animals. We know we are like them, but we think we are better, and so we want "to differentiate ourselves, erotically and in every other way, from animals."

Of course, the taboo does not prevent fantasies. Mr. Singer described the illustrations in Mr. Dekkers' book, including "a 17th-century Indian miniature of a deer mounting a woman" and a 19th-century Japanese drawing of a very busy giant octopus groping a woman. Nor is the taboo always effective in real life. Mr. Singer noted that some men have sex with hens, and certain people don't stop the family dog from making free with them, which occasionally leads to "mutually satisfying activities."

The moral problem with human beings' consorting with animals, Mr. Singer suggested, is not human indignity and depravity but rather cruelty to animals. But as he put it, "Sex with animals does not always involve cruelty." And if cruelty is the problem, isn't raising them to kill them generally worse than coupling with them? *The San Francisco Chronicle* summed up Mr. Singer's position on animals thus: "You can have sex with them, but don't eat them."

The reaction was swift and prolonged. Some critics were appalled on behalf of humans, others on behalf of animals. And the headlines flowed—"Lock the Barn Door," "Puppy Love," and "The Love That Dare Not Bark Its Name."

As word of Mr. Singer's review spread, the debate began to shift from cruelty to consent. *Slate,* an online magazine, said Mr. Singer hadn't explained "how an animal can go about giving consent because, well, you know, animals can't talk." And *The New Republic* went further: "If animals are entitled to the protection of what we today call human rights, Isn't sex with them, absent consent, rape?"

Pretty soon animal rights groups began weighing in, from the president of the Animal Sexual Abuse Information and Resource Site, a group that fights bestiality, to the president of United Poultry Concerns Inc., a group based in Machipongo, Va., that stands up for the rights of domestic fowl.

Priscilla Feral, the president of Friends of Animals, wrote that "bestiality is wrong for the same reason pedophilia is wrong." Gary Francione who, like Mr. Singer, is one of the signers of the Declaration on the Rights of Great Apes, said Mr. Singer could no longer be trusted with the rights of apes.

There was one important exception. Ingrid Newkirk, the president of People for the Ethical Treatment of Animals, not only stood by Mr. Singer but also imagined a few perfectly innocent human-animal sex acts: "If a girl gets sexual pleasure from riding a horse, does the horse suffer? If not, who cares? If you French kiss your dog and he or she thinks it's great, is it wrong? We believe all exploitation and abuse is wrong." But she added, "If it isn't exploitation and abuse, it may not be wrong."

Mr. Singer said the fuss over his review was largely "hysterical" and a big waste of time. "This country is in the grip of a Puritan worldview," he added. When it comes to bestiality, the stakes are relatively small: while factory farming kills billions of animals a year, he said, human-animal sexual interactions involve only hundreds or thousands.

To some degree, the subject of bestiality represents the extreme edge of a larger discussion about whether animals have rights and what they are. But a legal issue is also at stake. In an essay reproduced at www.asairs.com, Piers Beirne, chairman of the department of criminology at the University of Southern Maine, in Portland, where he teaches a course on animal abuse, wrote that 24 states now have laws against bestiality, and seven more are considering them.

In Maine, he said, bestiality was once considered a crime against God and brought a sentence of 10 years of hard labor. The law loosened up after World War II. But now a bill before the Maine State Legislature proposes to recriminalize bestiality on the ground that it is cruel to animals and linked with domestic violence. The Bangor Daily News quoted Philip Buble, a man who came to testify, as saying that he often has sex with his dog-spouse, Lady Buble. "In the eyes of God," he said, "we are truly married."

The main effect of Mr. Singer's review Mr. Beirne said, will be the one that he intended: "A subject which for centuries was taboo will now be out in the open." But something else has changed. Now when it comes to bestiality, the debate is not so much about what God wants as what animals want.

The New York Times, June 9, 2001, p. A19

Critical Thinking Question | **A**re there any forms of sexual behavior that can be absolutely defined as abnormal regardless of the issues of the *continuum, context,* and *relativism?*

CLASSIFYING SEXUAL DISORDERS

Contemporary classifications of sexual abnormality in Western cultures have their roots in the mid-1800s. At that time, medical scientists began to view sexuality as a legitimate area of scientific investigation, beginning a process of the "medicalization of sexuality" which continues to this day (King, in Krafft-Ebing, 1999). Prior to the 1800s, aberrant sexuality had been considered an issue of sin or vice, within the purview of the Church rather than science or the state. During the 1800s, several scientific books dealing with sexual abnormality were written, the most important of which was Dr. Richard von Krafft-Ebing's *Psychopathia Sexualis,* first published in Germany in 1886. Krafft-Ebing's book (which was so successful both as a scientific work and as pornography to a titillated public that it went through 12 editions) organized sexual pathology into some still familiar categories such as *sexual sadism, sexual masochism,* and *fetishism,* illustrated with hundreds of case studies he had collected (see Figure 10.1). To give a flavor of the book and of the times, here is Krafft-Ebing's case number 43, an example of sexual sadism.

> P., aged fifteen, of high social position, came from a hysterical mother whose brother and father died in an asylum. Two children in the family died early in childhood of convulsions. Although the patient was talented, virtuous, and quiet, at times he was very disobedient, stubborn, and of violent temper. He had epilepsy, and practiced masturbation. One day it was learned that P., with money, induced a comrade of fourteen, B., to allow himself to be pinched on the arms, genitals, and thighs. When B. cried, P. became excited and struck at B. with his right hand, while with his left he made manipulations in the left pocket of his trousers. P. confessed that to maltreat his friend, of whom he was very fond, gave him peculiar delight, and that ejaculation while hurting his friend gave him much more pleasure than when he masturbated alone.

> Quoted in Krafft-Ebing, 1999 (p. 113)

Krafft-Ebing's work greatly influenced the next major figure to study sexuality, Sigmund Freud. Freud's early work in psychoanalysis, as you know, focused on sexuality, which was still a relatively taboo subject in Victorian Europe. Freud was especially interested in the role of emotional conflicts about sexuality as a causal factor in all sorts of mental disorders ranging from anxiety to schizophrenia. Like others at the time, Freud used the term *perversion* as a diagnostic label to refer to "sexual behavior that accompanies…atypical means of obtaining sexual pleasure" (Laplanche & Pontalis, 1973). Freud's unique contribution was to relate "perverse" behaviors to a theory of the development of the sexual instinct during childhood. Freud believed that human beings are born with a bisexual disposition that sought oral, anal, and phallic forms of pleasure in infancy and childhood before developing into the familiar form of genitally focused heterosexuality at adolescence (Freud, 1905). He argued that "perversions" were formed when sexual development got stuck, or "fixated," at one of the stages along the way, such as an oral, anal, or homosexual stage. If the person resisted his or her perverse wishes with defense mechanisms, a neurosis would develop, while if the person allowed his or her desires to be expressed they would con-

Case 93. A gentleman of very bad heredity consulted me concerning impotence that was driving him almost to despair. While he was young, his fetich (sic) was women of plump form. He married such a lady, and was happy and potent with her. After a few months the lady fell very ill, and lost much of her flesh. When, one day, he tried to resume his marital duty, he was absolutely impotent, and remained so. If, however, he attempted coitus with plump women, he was perfectly potent.

Case 99. X., aged twenty, inverted sexually (authors' note: "inverted" was the then-current term for homosexual). Only loved men with a large bushy mustache. One day he met a man who answered his ideal. He invited him to his home, but was unspeakably disappointed when this man removed an artificial mustache. Only when the visitor put the ornament on the upper lip again, he exercised his charm over X. once more and restored him to the full possesion of virility....

Figure 10.1 Cases from Krafft-Ebing's Psychopathia Sexualis (1886) Brief case descriptions from Krafft-Ebing's influential book are presented here.

Michelangelo The painter Michelangelo was one of many great individuals cited by Freud as evidence that homosexuality was not a defect.

stitute a perversion; thus Freud's famous dictum that "neuroses are the negative of perversions" (Freud, 1905). It is also notable that Freud was rather unique in his day for his sympathetic attitude toward homosexuality, which he viewed as a developmental fixation but not as a disorder. For example, when the worried mother of a young gay man in the United States wrote Freud for advice, he replied that the man need not, and probably could not, change his sexual orientation. Freud encouraged the mother and son to accept the son's homosexuality as nothing to be ashamed of, noting that several of the greatest men in history (he cited Plato, Michelangelo, and Leonardo da Vinci) had been gay. Freud concluded: "It is a great injustice to persecute homosexuality as a crime—and a cruelty, too" (Gay, 1988).

It is important to note that in Freud's time, the terms "perverse" and "perversion" were used as scientific, diagnostic terms, and did not have the negative, derogatory connotations they have since assumed. Early editions of the DSM continued to use the term *perversion* in connection with sexual disorders, and also continued to use many of the other categories developed by Krafft-Ebing and Freud. In more recent editions, however, the DSM has substituted the term *paraphilia* (from the Greek for "abnormal love") to describe the conditions formerly labeled "perversions" because the latter term had developed negative connotations (Charlton & Quatman, 1997; Moser, 2001; Suppe, 1984).

The DSM-IV-TR Categories

We have seen in previous chapters that sexuality and sexual conflicts can play a large role in many emotional disorders. Freud, for example, originally thought that most forms of psychopathology were caused by sexual conflict, such as Little Hans' phobia (Chapter 5) resulting from his Oedipal conflicts (Freud, 1954/1909; Gay, 1988). Even though current psychodynamic theorists take a broader view of the etiology of mental disorders, sexuality remains a focus in many of their theories, and most theoretical perspectives include sexuality as an important causal factor in some disorders. However, it is important to keep in mind that when we talk about the DSM-IV-TR category called sexual disorders we are referring to disorders in which the *symptoms* are sexual. Thus, we would not consider a phobia—like Little Hans' fear of horses—a sexual disorder even though the root cause may have been sexual conflict. Classifying disorders on the basis of symptoms rather than causes, of course, is at the heart of the DSM-IV-TR approach, and it has advantages and limitations as we have seen. Symptom-based diagnosis can be a useful way of grouping disorders as long as one keeps in mind that the symptoms of a disorder are not necessarily indicative of its causes. In fact, you will see that one of the leading theoretical explanations of sexual disorders like Rick's *exhibitionism* focuses on underlying causes that have little to do with sex and much more to do with aggression that is acted out in the sexual domain. Thus, as we cover the DSM-IV-TR sexual disorder diagnoses, keep in mind the core concept of the ***advantages and limitations*** of symptom-based diagnosis.

The DSM-IV-TR includes three very different groups of conditions under the general heading of "sexual disorders." The first group, the **sexual dysfunctions**, refers to persistent problems with sexual interest, sexual arousal, or orgasm—the major components of the human "sexual response cycle"—in the context of "normal" sexual relationships. Sexual dysfunctions are quite common in both men and women (as in the chapter opening case of Laurie), can have psychological and/or biological causes, and are usually quite treatable. The second group is the **paraphilias**—the same group Freud classified as "perversions"—in which a person's sexual desires and preferences are considered abnormal (as in the case of Rick). The causes of paraphilias—disorders such as *sexual sadism* and *exhibitionism*—are more complex, and treatment is more difficult. Interestingly, for reasons we will discuss later in the chapter, paraphilias are almost exclusively found in men. Finally, the DSM-IV-TR includes under the rubric of sexual disorders a relatively rare condition called *gender identity disorder* (as in the case of Phil). This is a disorder in which individuals—men about twice as often as women—feel that they have the body of the wrong sex and want to change sexes. We now turn to a more detailed consideration of each of these disorders.

Sexual dysfunctions DSM-IV-TR disorders involving persistent problems with sexual interest, sexual arousal, or orgasm.

Paraphilias DSM-IV-TR disorders involving persistent sexual desires or preferences that are considered abnormal.

The Sexual Dysfunctions

The sexual dysfunctions are best defined in terms of the sexual response process (Kaplan, 1974, 1995; Sadock & Sadock, 2000). Normal sexual response is currently understood as a process involving four stages: (1) *sexual interest or desire;* (2) *sexual excitement or arousal;* (3) *orgasm;* and (4) *resolution* (see Figure 10.2). This four-stage model of sexual response was developed by Kaplan (1974, 1995) who slightly modified the pioneering work on sexual response by Masters and Johnson (1970). Sexual dysfunctions consist of *persistent* problems at any stage of the sexual response process (*occasional* problems with sexual response are extremely common and not considered dysfunctions). Since there are no dysfunctions associated with the resolution phase of the cycle, the sexual dysfunctions involve persistent problems with sexual desire, sexual excitement, orgasm, or with pain related to sexual activity (APA, 2000). Clients can be diagnosed with one or more sexual dysfunctions according to the criteria listed in the DSM-IV-TR (see Table 10.1). Overall, the sexual dysfunctions are relatively common (prevalence data are included in the description of each dysfunction listed in the following paragraphs), much more so than the other, more severe sexual disorders (paraphilias and gender identity disorder).

Figure 10.2 The sexual response process The graph illustrates the four stages of normal sexual response; dysfunctions can occur during the first three stages of the process.

Adapted from Masters, Johnson, & Kolodny, 1986

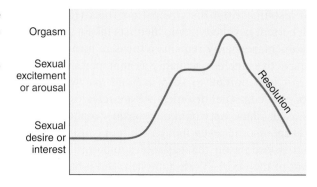

In general, the sexual dysfunctions are considered quite treatable (Rosen & Leiblum, 1995; Segraves & Althof, 1998; Wylie, 1997). In many cases, especially in younger people, sexual dysfunctions are a result of sexual inexperience or lack of adequate sexual information (Charlton & Quatman, 1997). In other cases, a wide range of psychological and biological factors can be involved. On the psychological side, Masters and Johnson (1966, 1970) emphasized the role of sexual *performance anxiety* (worries about sexual competence) and *spectatoring* (anxious, detached self-observation) in causing sexual dysfunctions. Masters and Johnson developed couple-based treatment techniques such as *sensate focus,* which involves exercises to enhance sensual awareness, and *nondemand pleasuring,* a graduated series of "petting" exercises that initially deemphasize intercourse and orgasm so as to create a nonpressured atmosphere for sensual exploration (Masters, Johnson, & Kolodny, 1986). In addition to these widely used behavioral methods, the treatment of sexual dysfunctions often involves discussion of emotions such as guilt, shame, and anxiety that may be interfering with normal sexual response. Emotional conflicts relating to the present, the recent past, and childhood (such as sexual abuse or other sexual traumas, or problematic sexual learning experiences) can all play an important role in the sexual dysfunctions (Levine & Althof, 1997; Rosen & Leiblum, 1995). In keeping with the core concept of the **connection between mind and body**, all of the psychological factors noted above can influence the physical aspects of sexual functioning, and psychological interventions can restore the physical capacities necessary for pleasurable sexual activity.

On the biological side, medical illnesses (such as diabetes and heart conditions), numerous medications, poor diet, aging, and substance use (including cigarette smoking) can all contribute to sexual dysfunctions. For example, medications that inhibit the parasympathetic division of the autonomic nervous system can adversely affect sexual arousal, while medications that inhibit the sympathetic branch of the system can affect orgasm (Charlton & Quatman, 1997) (see Table 10.2).

Because of the range of causes associated with the sexual dysfunctions, the DSM-IV-TR provides subtypes for each diagnosis according to etiology (if known). Sexual dysfunctions can be subtyped as "due to psychological factors," "due to combined factors," "due to a general medical condition," or "substance-induced." In addition, subtypes are listed according to whether the dysfunction is lifelong or acquired (beginning after a period of normal functioning), and generalized or situational (APA, 2000). With these general comments on the sexual dysfunctions in mind, we now turn to a more detailed discussion of each of the dysfunctions.

Hypoactive sexual desire Persistently deficient sexual fantasies and desire for sexual activity causing distress or interpersonal difficulty.

Sexual Desire Disorders **Hypoactive sexual desire** consists of a lack of interest in sex. While most people take interest in sex for granted, this first stage of the sexual response cycle is problematic for some. Prevalence estimates for this disorder vary

Diagnostic Criteria for the Sexual Dysfunctions	Table 10.1

Adapted from DSM-IV-TR (APA, 2000)

Sexual desire disorders

Hypoactive sexual desire ▪ Persistently deficient sexual fantasies and deficient desire for sexual activity causing distress or interpersonal difficulty.

Sexual aversion ▪ Persistent extreme aversion to, and avoidance of, genital sexual contact with a sexual partner causing distress or interpersonal difficulty.

Sexual arousal disorders

Female sexual arousal disorder ▪ Persistent inability to attain, or maintain, an adequate lubrication-swelling response of sexual excitement, causing distress or interpersonal difficulty.

Male erectile disorder ▪ Persistent inability to attain, or maintain, an adequate erection, causing distress or interpersonal difficulty.

Orgasmic disorders

Female orgasmic disorder ▪ Persistent delay in, or absence of, orgasm following a normal sexual excitement phase, causing distress or interpersonal difficulty.

Male orgasmic disorder ▪ Persistent delay in, or absence of, orgasm following a normal sexual excitement phase, causing distress or interpersonal difficulty.

Premature ejaculation ▪ Persistent ejaculation with minimal sexual stimulation before, on, or shortly after penetration and before the person wishes it, causing distress or interpersonal difficulty.

Sexual pain disorders

Vaginismus ▪ Persistent involuntary spasm of the musculature of the outer third of the vagina that interferes with sexual intercourse, causing distress or interpersonal difficulty.

Dyspareunia ▪ Persistent genital pain associated with sexual intercourse, causing distress or interpersonal difficulty.

widely; a conservative estimate would be that in a given year 10% of women and probably less than 3% of men experience persistent lack of desire (Hall et al., 2000; Simons & Carey, 2001). However, rates appear to be increasing, especially among men (Beck, 1995; Hall et al., 2000). Part of the difficulty in accurately estimating the prevalence of this dysfunction is the lack of uniform criteria in studies; there is a pressing need for more research using standard criteria (Beck, 1995).

Loss of interest in sex is a common symptom of many medical conditions, and of many mental disorders such as depression (Hall et al., 2000). Ironically, decreased sexual desire can also be a side effect of numerous medications, including some antidepressants (Beck, 1995; Wise, 1999). Aging processes and hormonal changes, such as menopause in women, are often a factor; in such cases hormone treatments may be helpful in restoring sexual interest (Renshaw, 1996; Warnock, Bundren, & Morris,

| Table 10.2 | **Medications That Can Influence Sexual Function (partial list)** |

Adapted from Charlton & Quatman, 1997

DRUG NAME	POTENTIAL EFFECT
Paroxietine (Paxil)	Decreased desire; delayed or no orgasm
Perphenazine (Trilafon)	Decreased or no ejaculation
Phenelzine (Nardil)	Impotence; retarded or no ejaculation; delayed or no orgasm
Phenytoin (Dilantin)	Decreased desire; impotence; priapism (prolonged, painful erection)
Prazosin (Minipress)	Impotence
Propantheline (Pro-Banthine)	Impotence
Propranolol (Inderal)	Loss of desire; impotence
Protriptyline (Vivactil)	Loss of desire; impotence; painful ejaculation
Ranitidine (Zantac)	Impotence; loss of desire
Reserpine	Decreased desire; impotence; decreased or no ejaculation
Sertraline (Zoloft)	Decreased desire; retarded or no orgasm
Spironolactone (Aldactone)	Decrease desire; impotence
Sulfasalazine (Azulfidine)	Impotence
Tamoxifen (Nolvadex)	Priapism
Testosterone	Priapism
Thiazide diuretics	Impotence
Thioridazine (Mellaril)	Impotence; retrograde, painful, or no ejaculation
Thiothixene (Navane)	Spontaneous ejaculations; impotence; priapism
Tranylcypromine (Parnate)	Impotence; painful ejaculation; retarded ejaculation

Sexual aversion Persistent extreme aversion to, and avoidance of, genital sexual contact with a sexual partner causing distress or interpersonal difficulty.

Female sexual arousal disorder Persistent inability to attain or maintain an adequate lubrication-swelling response of sexual excitement, causing distress or interpersonal difficulty.

1999). And, of course, emotional conflicts about sex, bodily functions, and pregnancy can contribute to a lack of sexual interest (Katz & David, 1999; Klein, 1997).

Sexual aversion is a more extreme form of disinterest in sex—an actual aversion to and avoidance of sexual activity (APA, 2000). The same range of psychological and biological factors that can contribute to decreased desire can also contribute to sexual aversion, but the active feelings of disgust about sex in sexual aversion usually signal the significant influence of emotional conflicts in this disorder (Carnes, 1998; Rosen & Leiblum, 1995).

Sexual Arousal Disorders The second phase of the sexual response cycle, the arousal/excitement phase, involves distinct physical changes that accompany the subjective feelings of arousal. In women, the primary physical process involves lubrication and swelling of the vaginal tissue in anticipation of sexual intercourse. For men, erection of the penis occurs during this phase.

Female sexual arousal disorder involves persistently insufficient lubrication responses to sexual stimuli—a condition sometimes referred to, somewhat disparagingly, as "frigidity" (Masters, Johnson, & Kolodny, 1986). Prevalence research on this disorder is inadequate, but most estimates suggest that between 10% and 20% of women experience this condition over the course of a lifetime (Simons & Carey, 2001). Female sexual arousal disorder is often associated with hypoactive sexual desire (and female orgasmic disorder, discussed later), and has a similar range of psychological and biological causes (Spector et al., 1993). Consequences of the disorder include painful intercourse, sexual aversion, and relationship difficulties (APA, 2000).

Male erectile disorder (also known as *erectile dysfunction, ED,* and *impotence*) involves the persistent inability to attain, or maintain, an erection. Most estimates of its annual incidence among adult men are in the 5% to 15% range (Charlton & Quatman, 1997; Masters, Johnson, & Kolodny, 1986; Simons & Carey, 2001), although these estimates are considered somewhat unreliable because of the lack of definitive research and the reluctance of many men to report accurately. Certainly the huge popularity and success of Viagra and similar medications (which normalize blood flow to the penis facilitating erection) indicates the enormous number of men with this dysfunction.

Prior to the development of Viagra, the major treatments for erectile disorder were penile tension rings, vacuum pumps, penile prostheses, and penile injections (Ramage, 1998). These methods can all be problematic psychologically (Levine & Althof, 1997); as one researcher put it "putting a needle in your penis is not everybody's idea of foreplay" (Dr. John Seely, quoted in Kolata, 2000). Some experts have argued that the success of Viagra is actually in part a result of the relatively new diagnostic term "erectile dysfunction" or ED. This medical sounding term is apparently much more palatable to most men than the old term "impotence," which seemed to imply that the client's masculinity was inadequate. Some critics have complained that the current emphasis on developing medications to treat erectile disorder reflects a sexist overemphasis on men's potency problems at the expense of emphasizing help for the millions of women with sexual dysfunctions (Kolata, 2000; Leiblum & Sharon, 2001; Segraves & Althof, 1998). However, as it became clear that the market for treating female dysfunctions was potentially lucrative, drug companies began testing Viagra and other medications as possible treatments for women as well (Stahl, 2001; Warnock et al., 1997).

The causes of erectile disorder include a wide range of psychological and biological factors. Medical conditions (such as diabetes), certain medications, smoking, poor diet, and psychological conflicts can all interfere with the blood flow necessary to produce and maintain an erection (Ramage, 1998). The absence of erections during sleep, when they normally occur, suggests a biological etiology. *Nocturnal penile tumescence* (erection) can be assessed with a *snap gauge* that is fastened around the penis at bedtime and will break if an erection occurs. Medications like Viagra can be helpful by enhancing blood flow regardless of whether the underlying cause of the problem is psychological or medical (Byne, 1993; McCarthy & McCarthy, 1998; Weisberg et al., 2001). Psychotherapy can also be helpful in treating psychogenic cases of erectile dysfunction (Althof, 2000; Masters, Johnson, & Kolodny, 1986).

Orgasmic Disorders **Female orgasmic disorder** (formerly known as *inhibited female orgasm,* and sometimes referred to as *anorgasmia*) involves persistent and distressing difficulties in reaching orgasm despite sexual excitement and appropriate sexual stimulation (APA, 2000). This is believed to be a fairly common dysfunction, affecting perhaps 7% to 10% of women (Simons & Carey, 2001). It is important to note that difficulty in achieving orgasm is only considered a dysfunction when it occurs persistently despite adequate sexual stimulation (Charlton & Quatman, 1997). Sexual

Male erectile disorder Persistent inability to attain, or maintain, an adequate erection, causing distress or interpersonal difficulty.

Female orgasmic disorder Persistent delay in, or absence of, orgasm following a normal sexual excitement phase, causing distress or interpersonal difficulty.

Viagra salesman Former U.S. Senator Bob Dole has helped reduce the stigma surrounding erectile problems by discussing his own use of Viagra in an advertising campaign.

Male orgasmic disorder Persistent delay in, or absence of, orgasm following a normal sexual excitement phase, causing distress or interpersonal difficulty.

Premature ejaculation Persistent ejaculation with minimal sexual stimulation before, on, or shortly after penetration and before the person wishes it, causing distress or interpersonal difficulty.

intercourse, by itself, is *not* assumed to provide adequate stimulation; in fact, it is estimated that only about half of women regularly have orgasms during intercourse (Baumeister, 2000; Baumeister et al., 2001; Laumann, Paik, & Rosen, 1999). Largely through the work of Masters and Johnson, it has become more widely known and accepted that most women require direct clitoral stimulation to reach orgasm (Masters & Johnson, 1970). Prior to this, women who did not regularly reach a climax during sexual intercourse were often assumed, unfairly, to be dysfunctional, and the diagnosis became controversial as a result. As currently defined, women with female orgasmic disorder have difficulty coming to climax even with direct clitoral stimulation through manual or oral sex, or masturbation (APA, 2000; Carnes, 1998; Leiblum, 2000).

Male orgasmic disorder involves the same scenario in men—persistent difficulty reaching orgasm despite adequate stimulation (APA, 2000; Brindley & Gillian, 1982). It appears to be somewhat less common than the female variant, affecting about 3% of men (Simons & Carey, 2000). For both men and women, the orgasmic dysfunctions often seem to be caused by emotional conflicts over sexuality, and about orgasm in particular, which can be associated with a frightening loss of control. However, physical conditions and medications may also play a role. For example, many of the widely prescribed selective serotonin reuptake inhibitor (SSRI) antidepressant medications can cause delay in or absence of orgasm (Coleman et al., 2001; Wise, 1999).

Premature ejaculation is probably the most common male sexual dysfunction, affecting as many as 29% of all men (Athanasiadis, 1998; Metz & Pryor, 2000). It is defined as a persistent tendency to ejaculate with minimal sexual stimulation, before the man wishes it, and often before sexual intercourse has begun (APA, 2000; Kaplan, 1995). In making this diagnosis, clinicians have to take into account that occasional premature ejaculation is very common, especially in younger and sexually inexperienced men, in novel sexual situations, and after long periods without ejaculation (Kaplan, 1995; Leiblum, 2000). When premature ejaculation occurs regularly, however, it can be quite distressing and can lead to avoidance of sexual relationships (APA, 2000; Athanasiades, 1998).

Many experts argue that there has not been enough sound research using standard criteria for assessing premature ejaculation, resulting in a limited understanding of its causes (Athanasiadis, 1998; Rowland, Cooper, & Schneider, 2001). However, most agree that a variety of psychological and biological factors can contribute to premature ejaculation, including emotional problems, relationship problems, poor sexual skills, neurological factors, illnesses, physical injuries, and medication side effects (Malatesta & Henry, 2001; Metz & Pryor, 2000). Accordingly, many different interventions can be appropriate, and treatment must be geared to the particular situation of the client (Metz & Pryor, 2000). Psychological interventions can include everything from traditional psychotherapies for resolving contributing emotional problems to more focal sex therapies. These focal treatments include individual relaxation, sexual self-pacing and pubococcygeal muscle training, and direct work with couples (Metz & Pryor, 2000; Pridal & Joseph, 2000). Two widely used techniques with couples are the *stop-start* method, in which the couple repeatedly decreases stimulation just before ejaculation would occur, and the *penile squeeze* technique, in which the client or partner gently squeezes the head of the penis to prevent ejaculation (Kaplan, 1995; Masters, Johnson, & Kolodny, 1986). While many researchers report very high success rates with these techniques, their long-term effectiveness has been questioned (Athanasiadis, 1998). Medications can be helpful in delaying orgasm in cases in which psychological methods are not effective (Metz & Pryor, 2000).

Sexual Pain Disorders The sexual pain disorders are somewhat distinct from the other sexual dysfunctions in that they are not defined by the phases of the sexual response cycle. Rather, they involve recurrent experiences of physical pain during sex that interfere with sexual activity and cause distress.

Vaginismus refers to recurrent muscle spasms in the outer third of the vagina, which interfere with sexual intercourse by making penetration difficult or painful (APA, 2000). Research on vaginismus has been limited, and no reliable prevalence data are available (Reissing, Yitzchak, & Khalife, 1999); however, Masters, Johnson, and Kolodny (1986) estimated that 2% to 3% of postadolescent women experience vaginismus. Some experts suggest that vaginismus can be best understood as a phobia of vaginal penetration, in which the fear of physical and/or emotional pain from intercourse leads to the muscle contractions, but the relationships among these factors remain somewhat unclear (Leiblum, 2000). Reports that vaginismus is easily resolved with vaginal dilation techniques and psychosexual education appear to be exaggerated (Reissing et al., 1999). When treatment does succeed, it seems that the crucial ingredients are attention to both the physical (such as genital pain) and psychological (for example, a history of sexual abuse) aspects of the problem.

Dyspareunia (dis-par-OON-ya) involves recurrent genital pain associated with sexual intercourse in a man or woman. Most cases of painful intercourse (which is a far more common problem for women than men) are caused by physical factors such as genital infections or scarring, lack of lubrication, medication side effects, or in some parts of the world, culturally sanctioned "female circumcision" in which parts of the female genitals are cut and damaged as a childhood or adolescent rite of passage (El-Defrawi et al., 2001; Graziottin, 2001). However, the DSM-IV-TR specifically excludes medical causes in the diagnosis of dyspareunia proper (APA, 2000), which is meant to be reserved for cases in which the pain is partially or entirely caused by psychological factors. Nonetheless, the term *dyspareunia* is frequently used—even by health professionals—to refer more broadly to any condition of recurrent sexual pain. Common physical causes of sexual pain are usually investigated first, with further exploration of emotional factors or more unusual physical causes if necessary (Graziottin, 2001).

Brief Summary

- The work of Krafft-Ebing, Freud, and others paved the way for the current DSM-IV-TR classification of sexual disorders.
- The DSM-IV-TR identifies three types of sexual disorders: sexual dysfunctions, paraphilias, and gender identity disorder.
- The sexual dysfunctions are recurrent, distressing, and/or impairing problems in the desire, arousal, and orgasm phases of the normal human sexual response cycle.
- The sexual desire dysfunctions include hypoactive sexual desire and sexual aversion.
- The sexual arousal dysfunctions include female arousal disorder and male erectile disorder.
- The orgasmic disorders include female orgasmic disorder, male orgasmic disorder, and premature ejaculation.
- Sexual pain disorders include vaginismus and dyspareunia.
- Sexual dysfunctions can be caused by a wide variety of psychological and biological factors. Most can be effectively treated with psychotherapy and/or medications.

Vaginismus Persistent involuntary spasm of the musculature of the outer third of the vagina that interferes with sexual intercourse, causing distress or interpersonal difficulty.

Dyspareunia Persistent genital pain associated with sexual intercourse, causing distress or interpersonal difficulty.

Female circumcision This 16-year-old girl in northern Kenya has just undergone a ritual circumcision. Such practices can be traumatizing and frequently lead to sexual dysfunctions.

Critical Thinking Question	**G**iven that they are so common, do you think the sexual dysfunctions should be considered mental disorders and listed in the DSM-IV-TR?

The Paraphilias

The **paraphilias,** formerly known as the *perversions,* are less common than the sexual dysfunctions, but they are considered more pathological—true disorders rather than dysfunctions. While the sexual dysfunctions involve persistent sexual difficulties in the context of normal sexual relationships, the paraphilias involve disordered sexual relationships and aberrant sexual preferences. A paraphilia consists of sexual arousal by, and sexual preference for, atypical sexual "objects" (or "stimuli") (see Table 10.3). In the most common paraphilias, the atypical stimuli involve either nonhuman objects (such as inanimate objects, or animals), hostile rather than affectionate human relationships (such as sexual sadism), or nonconsenting human relationships (for example, with children). Because many paraphilias involve nonconsensual sexual activity, several of them, such as exhibitionism, voyeurism, and pedophilia, are illegal. As a result, people with paraphilias often seek treatment after they have been caught, prosecuted, and either ordered or encouraged to do so by legal authorities (Brockman & Bluglass, 1996). Others have been pressured to get

Table 10.3	**Diagnostic Criteria for the Paraphilias**
Adapted from DSM-IV-TR (APA, 2000)	**Exhibitionism** ▪ Recurrent, intense sexually arousing fantasies, sexual urges, or behaviors involving the exposure of one's genitals to an unsuspecting person. **Voyeurism** ▪ Recurrent, intense sexually arousing fantasies, sexual urges, or behaviors involving the act of observing an unsuspecting person who is naked, in the process of disrobing, or engaging in sexual activity. **Fetishism** ▪ Recurrent, intense sexually arousing fantasies, sexual urges, or behaviors involving the use of nonliving objects. **Transvestic fetishism** ▪ Recurrent, intense sexually arousing fantasies, sexual urges, or behaviors involving cross-dressing in a heterosexual male. **Sexual sadism** ▪ Recurrent, intense sexually arousing fantasies, sexual urges, or behaviors involving acts in which a victim's psychological or physical suffering is sexually exciting. **Sexual masochism** ▪ Recurrent, intense sexually arousing fantasies, sexual urges, or behaviors involving the act of being humiliated, beaten, bound, or otherwise made to suffer. **Pedophilia** ▪ Recurrent, intense sexually arousing fantasies, sexual urges, or behaviors involving sexual activity with a prepubescent child or children. **Frotteurism** ▪ Recurrent, intense sexually arousing fantasies, sexual urges, or behaviors involving touching and rubbing against a nonconsenting person. **Paraphilias not otherwise specified (NOS)** ▪ Includes necrophilia (sexual interest in dead bodies), zoophilia (animals), coprophilia (feces), urophilia (urine), and telephone scatologia (obscene telephone calls).

help by spouses or other family members. In fact, it is relatively unusual for individuals with paraphilias to seek help on their own (Doerman, 1999). These individuals are often distressed by their paraphilias, but their motivation to seek treatment is often diminished by feelings of shame and/or reluctance to give up their primary form of sexual pleasure.

One of the most difficult problems involved in defining and classifying the paraphilias relates to the core concept of the ***continuum between normal and abnormal behavior***. Many of the sexual practices that are central to the paraphilias are considered normal when practiced consensually and in moderation (Brownell, Steven, & Barlow, 1977; Furnham & Haraldsen, 1998; Stoller, 1985b, 1989). For example, it is relatively common for people to include mildly exhibitionistic, voyeuristic, and sadomasochistic practices in their sex lives (Kinsey et al., 1948, 1953; Strauss & Donnelly, 1994). But several things distinguish these normal activities from a paraphilia. First of all, in a paraphilia, the sexual behavior in question is *persistent* (the DSM-IV-TR requires at least six months' duration), often nonconsensual, and may be necessary for sexual arousal (APA, 2000). Second, to meet the criteria for a paraphilia in the DSM-IV-TR, a sexual urge or fantasy pattern must either be distressing to the individual or cause impairment in his or her life (APA, 2000; Brockman & Bluglass, 1996). Thus, it is the compulsive, maladaptive, and extreme quality of paraphilias that distinguish them from variations of normal sexuality.

The prevalence of paraphilias appears to have increased over the last decade (Rosler & Witzum, 2000; Weiner & Rosen, 1999). While epidemiological data suggest that the paraphilias are much less common than sexual dysfunctions, the popularity of paraphilic pornography indicates that actual rates of paraphilia are much higher than official estimates (APA, 2000). Interestingly, paraphilias are found almost exclusively in men, about half of whom are married (Brockman & Bluglass, 1996; Money, 1986; Rosler & Witztum, 2000). While the reasons for this striking gender disparity are not fully understood, we will review some theories about it below. In addition, while there have been references to paraphilic sexual practices in cultures around the world for millennia, the paraphilias appear to be primarily found in Western cultures (de Silva, 1999). Paraphilias typically begin in adolescence, and rates of youthful paraphilia-related criminal offenses are on the rise (Brockman & Bluglass, 1996).

Over the years, researchers have offered various lists of common paraphilias; Money (1986), for example, described 30 different types. In the DSM-IV-TR, eight specific paraphilias are listed (see Table 10.3), along with a residual category (paraphilia not otherwise specified) that allows for the diagnosis of unusual forms of paraphilia (APA, 2000). Frequently, individuals with one paraphilia also have others (de Silva, 1999). Accordingly, some researchers view these disorders as a related set of "courtship disorders," in which evolutionarily designed, normal human courtship practices have become disordered (Freund, Seto, & Kuban, 1997; Horley, 2001).

You may be surprised to note that rape is not included as a DSM-IV-TR paraphilia even though it would seem to fit the definition of aberrant, nonconsensual sexual behavior. The exclusion of rape as a separate diagnosis in the DSM-IV-TR has been controversial and puzzling even to some experts on sexual disorders, although others argue that it is sufficient that rape is included as a subtype of the paraphilia known as sexual sadism (Horley, 2001; Hudson & Ward, 1997; Laws & O'Donahue, 1997). Part of the reason that rape has not been included separately relates to a concern that the diagnosis could be used by rapists as a legal defense (Boehnert, 1989; Hudson & Ward, 1997; Noffsinger & Resnick, 2000), although this concern could also apply to other illegal paraphilias, such as pedophilia, which *are* listed in the DSM-IV-TR (Eads, Shuman, & DeLipsey, 2000; Marshall, 1997). Another argument against including rape as a separate diagnosis is that some scientific evidence supports the view that rape is motivated more by hostility toward women than by aberrant sexual arousal. For example, Lalumiere and Quinsey (1996) found that antisocial tendencies were more consistently characteristic of sexually coercive males than deviant sexual arousal patterns. On the other hand, similar antisocial tendencies and hostile motivations may also be involved in paraphilias that *are* included in the DSM-IV-TR. This controversy offers another illustration of the ***advantages and limitations*** of the sexual disorder diagnoses. We now turn to a description of the paraphilias listed in the DSM-IV-TR.

Exhibitionism Recurrent, intense sexually arousing fantasies, sexual urges, or behaviors involving the exposure of one's genitals to an unsuspecting person.

Voyeurism Recurrent, intense sexually arousing fantasies, sexual urges, or behaviors involving the act of observing an unsuspecting person who is naked, in the process of disrobing, or engaging in sexual activity.

Fetishism Recurrent, intense sexually arousing fantasies, sexual urges, or behaviors involving the use of nonliving objects.

Exhibitionism **Exhibitionism** involves exposing one's genitals to an unsuspecting stranger. In the DSM-IV-TR, the criteria for exhibitionism consist of six months or more of recurrent, intense, sexually arousing behaviors (or distressing/impairing fantasies and urges) involving genital exposure (APA, 2000). Exhibitionism is generally considered the most common paraphilia (Brockman & Bluglass, 1996; Murphy, 1997). To the lay public, exhibitionists are known as "flashers." The stereotype of an exhibitionist is of a "dirty old man" who opens his raincoat to expose himself to little girls. In fact, most men diagnosed with exhibitionism are young to middle aged, and sexual exposure to children is more characteristic of pedophilia than exhibitionism (Hall et al., 2000; Weiner & Rosen, 1999). When an elderly person exposes himself or herself, it is most likely a result of disinhibition due to a dementia (Chapter 13) and not a paraphilia (Brockman & Bluglass, 1996; Jordan & Stein, 2000).

Typically, exhibitionists become aroused and masturbate during or after exposing themselves. Exhibitionists rarely seek out actual contact with the women to whom they expose themselves. Rather, they typically describe a wish to shock, humiliate, or sexually arouse women they encounter as strangers (APA, 2000; Black et al., 1997; Nye, 1999). While individuals with exhibitionism are often thought to be fearful, shy, passive, and avoidant of real contact with women, researchers have not been able to identify a clear personality profile for people with the disorder (Laws & O'Donohue, 1997; Murphy, 1997). The general advice to victims of exhibitionism is to remain calm, walk away, and report the incident (Marshall, 1997).

Voyeurism **Voyeurism** can be thought of as the opposite of exhibitionism, as voyeurism involves the practice of watching unsuspecting others who are disrobing or engaging in sex. Voyeurism, sometimes also referred to as *scoptophilia* (literally, the "love of seeing"), is commonly understood in the figure of the "Peeping Tom" who peers into strangers' bedrooms at night (Brockman & Bluglass, 1996).

Obviously, experiencing sexual arousal from seeing others naked or having sex, in and of itself, is common and not abnormal—as the television and film industries know well. But voyeurism differs, in several respects, from this normal reaction. The DSM-IV-TR specifies that in order to be diagnosed with voyeurism, an individual must have experienced a period of six months or more of recurrent, intense sexual pleasure from watching nonconsenting others (or distressing/impairing fantasies and urges to do so). Usually the individual masturbates during the voyeuristic episodes, often with a fantasy involving the person or people observed. Voyeurism usually begins before age 15 and tends to become chronic (APA, 2000).

Fetishism **Fetishism** consists of intense, recurrent sexual arousal involving inanimate objects. The DSM-IV-TR criteria for fetishism describe six months or more of distressing and/or impairing sexual urges or behaviors related to nonliving objects (APA, 2000). Common fetish objects include female undergarments, other articles of clothing such as shoes, and rubber or leather objects. The individual will typically mastur-

Voyeurism This painting, "Susanna Bathing," by Tintoretto (1518–1594) depicts a famous biblical scene of voyeurism, the practice of watching unsuspecting people for sexual purposes.

bate alone with the object or ask a sexual partner to wear it (Charlton & Quatman, 1997; de Silva, 1999). Any object can be the focus of fetishism, and there are published reports of clients with fetishes involving objects ranging from pacifiers to radio static (Junginger, 1997; Stoller, 1987). (Table 10.4 lists some Internet forums with primarily fetish themes.) Some researchers also include compulsive sexual arousal to specific body parts within the definition of fetishism (such as a foot, or hair, fetish). An unusual variant of this type of fetish involves sexual arousal related to amputees. Wise and Kalyaanam (2000) describe the case of a 49-year-old accountant with a life-long amputee fetish who was easily able to find pornographic materials to satisfy his fetish over the Internet. Eventually, this individual cut off his own penis, a practice that has also been reported in other cases of amputee fetishism (Wise & Kalyanam, 2000).

Like exhibitionism and voyeurism, fetishism is an extreme form of a normal sexual arousal pattern (Mason, 1997). Sexual arousal in response to seeing undergarments

Sex Forums on the Internet with Primarily Fetish Themes			Table 10.4
The following is a partial list of alternative sex forums with fetish themes found on the Internet			*Adapted from Junginger, 1997*
Pantyhose	Amputee	Hair	
Underwear	Diapers	Fur	
Jock strap	Feet	Fat	
Uniforms	Latex	Bottles	
Wax	Leather	Vegetables	
Smoking	Trees	Tools	

Transvestism Individuals with transvestism are motivated to cross-dress because it provides sexual satisfaction.

Transvestic fetishism (or **transvestism**)
Recurrent, intense sexually arousing fantasies, sexual urges, or behaviors involving cross-dressing in a heterosexual male.

Sexual masochism Recurrent, intense sexually arousing fantasies, sexual urges, or behaviors involving the act of being humiliated, beaten, bound, or otherwise made to suffer.

Sexual sadism Recurrent, intense sexually arousing fantasies, sexual urges, or behaviors involving acts in which the psychological or physical suffering of the victim is sexually exciting to the person inflicting the suffering.

or body areas is a part of normal sexual response, and the lingerie, perfume, and hair care industries capitalize on this natural tendency. In fact, the word "fetish" in common usage refers not just to the sexual disorder but to any object imbued with special power. As a result, drawing the line between normal sexual response and fetishism can be difficult (Brockman & Bluglass, 1996; Junginger, 1988, 1997). However, one key difference between normal arousal to female undergarments, for example, and an underwear fetish is that in the latter case the undergarments actually become necessary, or at least strongly preferred, for sexual arousal and performance to occur (APA, 2000).

Transvestic Fetishism **Transvestic fetishism,** or **transvestism,** is a particular form of fetishism in which men become sexually aroused by *wearing* women's clothing. This form of cross-dressing for sexual arousal is distinct from cross-dressing due to *gender dysphoria* (the wish *to be* the opposite sex, as in *gender identity disorder* which is discussed later in the chapter.), although the former sometimes evolves into the latter (APA, 2000; Zucker & Blanchard, 1997). Transvestism should also be distinguished from cross-dressing for other purposes that do not involve sexual arousal. In transvestism, the individual, typically a heterosexual man, becomes aroused by cross-dressing. He may simply wear female underwear under his normal attire, or dress completely as a woman, commonly referred to as being "in drag" (APA, 2000). Some individuals experience maximum arousal by going out in public cross-dressed, while others prefer to cross-dress in private. Frequently, the sexual arousal seems to be associated with fantasies of being female (*autogynephilia,* or love of oneself as a woman), or as having characteristics of both sexes (Person & Ovesey, 1978; Stoller, 1971; Zucker & Blanchard, 1997), although transvestites do not wish to literally become women.

Sexual Sadism **Sexual sadism** refers to the recurrent need to imagine, or act out, the infliction of pain on a suffering victim in order become sexually aroused. Once again, it is important, though not always easy, to distinguish normal variations of sexual "play" from a paraphilia. Many people are aroused by aggressiveness as part of sex. For example, Kinsey and colleagues (1948, 1953) found in their groundbreaking surveys of sexual habits that half of Americans enjoyed mildly sadomasochistic activities such as biting and spanking during sex (see the report in Box 10.2 on S&M). In a more recent survey of college students, Straus & Donnelly (1994), found that 61% of the students reported sexual arousal while imagining or participating in similar activities. However, in sexual sadism the infliction of physical or psychological pain (for example, humiliation) is a recurrent, and often necessary, condition of sexual arousal, and it causes distress and/or impairment for the sexual sadist (APA, 2000). In some cases, the individual has not acted on these fantasies and urges but is troubled by them. In other cases, fantasies are acted out with either consenting or nonconsenting others. Sadistic sexual behaviors can include a wide range of physical practices such as restraining, slapping, whipping, burning, and beating, and/or psychological activities such as dominating, humiliating, and degrading the other person (APA, 2000; Alison, Santtila, & Sandnabba, 2001). In severe cases, especially in conjunction with antisocial personality disorder, sexual sadism may involve rape and other acts which can seriously injure or even kill the victim.

Sexual Masochism In contrast to sexual sadism, **sexual masochism** involves the need or strong preference for physical or psychological suffering in order to produce sexual arousal. Typical behaviors and fantasies include being bound, forced, beaten, cut, urinated or defected upon, berated, or humiliated (Brockman & Bluglass, 1996). In some cases, the individual only fantasizes about masochistic situations during

BOX 10.2   The Mainstreaming of S&M: Just Another Lifestyle Choice?

"Lick Me, Flog Me, Buy Me!"   *by* Rick Marin with Nadine Joseph

This article suggests that sadomasochism, or S&M, has become commonplace in contemporary American culture, raising questions about when such behavior should be considered "abnormal."

Surely you've seen the ad by now. Young man in a business suit. On all fours. Depraved leer in his eye. His tongue licking a spiky, thigh-high boot of shiny blue vinyl. You can't see the boot's owner, just a long fishnet leg disappearing out of the frame. Presumably a woman's, but who knows? The caption: "In a world of strange tastes, there's always Bass Ale." S&M has become so common place, so banal, that it can safely be used to sell beer.

And just about anything else. Look at Gucci's voyeuristic, lust-in-an-elevator ad bilitz. How can you not? On [the TV show] *Friends,* Chandler dated a woman with a predilection for handcuffs and dominance. ("She's the boss of me," he swooned.) Janet Jackson's album *Velvet Rope* features a bondage fantasy called "Rope Burn." (Michael's little sister!) And the Internet? As they say in Brooklyn—fuggedaboutit!

S&M—or B&D, for bondage and discipline—has been mainstreamed from deviant perversion to just another wacky lifestyle choice. Everybody's into it, from Marv Albert to Marilyn Manson. So whether you're a disgraced sports-caster, a freaky crossdressing rock star or the rest of us gawking in disgust/amusement/whatever, it was a very kinky year.

If the Marquis de Sade were alive to see his subversive sexual directives submitted to such mercenary use, he'd be fit to be tied. La Nouvelle Justine, Manhattan's latest theme restaurant, takes its name from a Sade novel. The theme is S&M. It's Planet Kinkywood, outfitted with all the requisite tools of this potentially very rough trade. Patrons can opt to dine in a confining little jail called the Prisoner's Cell. A scaffold with manacles is available for those whose idea of a tasty appetizer is flagellation with a cat-o'-nine-tails. The menu also includes Verbal Abuse and Spanking, at just $20 a pop. (Warning: the chicken receives similarly nasty treatment in the kitchen.) "It's a lot like dinner theater," says Hane Jason, one of the owners, adding, "People bring their clients here to impress them." So much for the three-martini lunch.

New York is the Sodom of the new S&M craze. You can guess Gomorrah. Every Wednesday night a San Francisco club called Trocadero Transfer is themed Bondage à Go-Go. Stockbrokers, lawyers, secretaries, shipping clerks and the occasional off-duty cop turn up regularly for a flogging, maybe some elective shock therapy. "Most people come here for S&M 101, the introduction course," says Hawk, a burly 28-year-old ex-roadie with a black goatee and satanic grin. Many of the students bear the marks of their major: tattoos, pierced everything, second-skin latex. Tiffany, a 24-year-old former teacher, flips her long jet-black hair and explains, "When the electric shock runs through your hair and scalp, it's thrilling." Couldn't she just stick her finger in a light socket like when we were kids? And lest you think fetish indulgence is a strictly bicoastal phenomenon, club employee Jennifer, 28, notes that when she visited relatives in Wisconsin, they took her to a garage sale where all manner of smutty lingerie and bondage hardware were for sale. Apparently, she says, "people don't think of it as perverse."

Are we that jaded? Is there no shame anymore? Is nothing beyond the pale? In Woody Allen's new movie, "Deconstructing Harry," he casually instructs a hooker, "Tie me up, beat me, then give me a—" Hello! He never talked like that to Annie Hall. But the audience barely bats an eye. It's seen worse. New York Gov. George Pataki registered a rare note of complaint against creeping kink when a women's studies conference at one of his state universities conducted a seminar on "Safe, Sane and Consensual S&M: An Alternate Way of Loving." He decried the event as an inappropriate "expenditure of tax dollars." But boredom will likely snuff S&M before outrage. "Last year's trend," sniffs Kate Betts, a top editor at *Vogue,* of fetish fashion. "You can buy leather pants at the Gap." True, but those perky salesclerks really need to work on their verbal abuse.

Newsweek Magazine, January 5, 1998

Sexual sadism Sexual sadism and masochism sometimes involves a woman in the role of a "dominatrix" who humiliates, and sometimes physically hurts, her sexual partner. The dominatrix may engage in such behavior for her own sexual pleasure or when asked or paid to do so by a sexual masochist.

Pedophilia Recurrent, intense sexually arousing fantasies, sexual urges, or behaviors involving sexual activity with a prepubescent child or children.

Frotteurism Recurrent, intense sexually arousing fantasies, sexual urges, or behaviors involving touching or rubbing against a nonconsenting person.

masturbation or sex; in other cases masochism is acted out. One particularly dangerous form of masochistic sexual behavior is the deprivation of oxygen (hypoxia) by strangulation, noose, plastic bag, or other means (APA, 2000). This sexual practice causes up to 200 deaths per year in England (Brockman & Bluglass, 1996), and similar fatality rates have been reported in the United States, Australia, and Canada (APA, 2000).

Sexual masochism is one of the only paraphilias commonly diagnosed in women, although it is still 20 times more common in men (APA, 2000). As with other paraphilias, it can be difficult to distinguish the disorder of sexual masochism from "normal" masochistic sexual interests pursued in the context of a safe, consenting relationship. We include in Box 10.3 an excerpt from an essay by the writer Daphne Merkin about her own sexual masochism in which she raises questions about the boundary between normal and abnormal sexual masochism.

Pedophilia Pedophilia (literally, "love of children") involves sexual attraction to, or sexual activity with, prepubescent children. The DSM-IV-TR defines pedophilia in terms of recurrent sexual behavior with, or distressing/impairing fantasies and urges toward, prepubescent children on the part of someone at least 16 years old and 5 years older than the child (APA, 2000). While some experts have questioned various aspects of the DSM-IV-TR criteria (such as whether the "recurrent" criterion is too restrictive; see Marshall, 1997), the DSM-IV-TR provides the most widely used formal definition of pedophilia. Individuals who meet DSM-IV-TR criteria for pedophilia may target boys, girls, or both, but they more commonly seek boys (Blanchard et al., 1999). Some experts believe that young boys are the more common targets because men with pedophilia are trying to find sexual "partners" who are as different as possible from adult women in terms of age and gender (Blanchard et al., 1999). Victims may be family members, or strangers to whom the pedophile gains access by "befriending" the child or winning the trust of adults in the child's life. The sexual contact can include anything from watching the child undress, to fondling, to actual penetration. Pedophiles typically rationalize their behavior as harmless, good for the child, or as something the victim wanted (APA, 2000; Brockman & Bluglass, 1996). Often, the victims are threatened in some way so as to prevent them from telling others about the molestation.

While no reliable data exist on the prevalence of pedophilia, it is clear that child sexual abuse is pandemic and a national crisis in the United States (Laws & O'Donohue, 1997). Current estimates are that between 100,000 and 500,000 children in the United States are sexually molested by adults every year, resulting in 10% to 20% of all children having experienced sexual abuse by the time they reach age 18 (Rosler & Witztum, 1998). Pedophiles appear to be a diverse group, with no clear personality profile (Bickley & Beech, 2001). The vast majority are men, but pedophilia is one of the few paraphilias in which a significant percentage of cases involve women.

Frotteurism Frotteurism (sometimes also referred to as *toucheurism*) is less well known than the other DSM-IV-TR paraphilias. A frotteur (almost invariably male) rubs up against or touches a stranger (usually a female) for sexual gratification. Typically, frotteurism occurs in a crowded place such as subway trains or busy sidewalks where quick escape is possible (APA, 2000). Frotteurists often fantasize about having a meaningful relationship with the victim, and often engage in other kinds of paraphilic behaviors (Freund et al., 1997). Frotteurism is often treated lightly by the criminal justice system, a fact that is deplored by some researchers who see it as having some similarities to rape (Laws & O'Donohue, 1997).

BOX 10.3 Sexual Masochism in a Woman: A First Person Account

"Unlikely Obsession" *by Daphne Merkin*

Daphne Merkin, a well-known writer, describes her own struggle with masochistic sexual tendencies in an excerpt from her article "Unlikely Obsession" which was published in *The New Yorker* Magazine.

All the while, I continued to read and dream, feeding my appetite. In my mid-twenties, I met a man who had fairly advanced sadistic skills, albeit of a psychological rather than a physical variety. His wish to control me—to offer and then withdraw affection on an erratic and hurtful schedule of his own devising—coincided with my secret wish to be mastered, but it never occurred to him to spank me, and I never asked. (I was undoubtedly afraid of what I might unleash: I had visions of being splattered against the wall.) Our relationship may not have taken on an explicitly S&M aspect, but it was riddled with those impulses: once, after a fight, he ordered me to get down on my knees before his standing, undressed self; another time, he lay on the bed and languidly suggested that I crawl across the floor in order to win back his favor. Although these were not things I wanted to be told to do on a regular basis, my mind read both of these demands as a signal for arousal. I experienced degradation (or, at least, a degree of degradation) as a thrill; there was no mistaking it. I wondered with growing anxiety how I would ever make do with less dubious forms of sexual engagement.

Finally, in my late twenties, I admitted my wish to be spanked to a man who seemed distant from my world, and thus not in a position to assess how fitting or incongruous this wish might be with the rest of me. He was from the West Coast; to my intractably Manhattanite sensibilities, he might as well have hailed from Sri Lanka. Whereas I was accustomed to the edgy New York style, this man's way of looking at things seemed slower and less driven by the need to evaluate. He also had a receptive quality that made me think I could trust him with my fantasy, and, after we'd been going out for several months, I did. He appeared delighted at the prospect of implementing my wishes, and so it was that I found myself in the position I had been dreaming of for years: thrust over a man's knee, being soundly spanked for some concocted misdeed. (How much I liked those adverbs—"soundly," "firmly," "roundly," "thoroughly"—leading up to the most resonant verb I knew of in the English language.) The sheer tactile stimulation of it—the chastening sting—would have been enough to arouse me, but there was also, at last, the heady sense of emotional release: I was and was not a child; was and was not a sensual being; was and was not being reduced; was and was not being forced into letting go; was and was not the one in control. I had fantasized about this event for so long that in the back of my mind there had always lurked the fear that its gratification would prove disappointing. I needn't have worried: the reality of spanking, at least initially, was as good as the dream.

I eventually married this man, after dillydallying for six years. By then, sex between us had lost some of its sheen, and somewhere along the way I had begun to tire of the spankings; I found them too hard, and then again not hard enough, to excite me. If, as I have come to think, mine was an addictive personality, kept in line by the tight parameters of my upbringing and by some exertion of will, then spankings were my drug of choice: they were meant to blunt the edges of my existence. But the edges kept springing back into sight again, resilient as weeds. I had veered in and out of depression since adolescence, and began to think that my depression was intimately linked to the whole spanking thing. (What I actually suspected was that I wanted to be spanked to death—transported out of my sorrow into a state of numbness, of permanent *un*feeling.) Then, too, I found that domesticity, with its dirty dishes and regular hours, didn't mesh particularly well with the role-playing agenda of erotic discipline, which required the sort of imaginative space that was compromised by the rut of daily life. A year after we married, I gave birth to a daughter; I was now a parent myself, attending to the needs of an imperious infant while fighting off freshly ignited feelings about the lack of mothering in my own childhood. The fantasy receded, its urgent claim on my imagination muted by the realization that I had to look toward the future, for my child's sake if not for my own.

I have no doubt that there are people who are into S&M—or believe that they are into it, which comes to the same thing—for the sophisticated experimentation, the "gourmet sex" of it. I suppose, too, that sadomasochism can be dispassionately viewed as a heightened paradigm for the discrepancies in power and control which run in a more diffuse fashion through all human relations. One can class such behavior as pathological or, with greater poetic license and less clinical judgment, as part of the infinite human variety, but I have come to believe that for me it was about nothing less gripping than stating and restating, in an adult arena, the emotional conditions of my childhood, where accepting pain was the price of affection. I believed in a magic trick, an impossible reversal: if you chose of your own free will to let someone hurt you, then all past hurt would be wondrously undone.

"The desires of the heart," Auden observed, "are as crooked as corkscrews." I don't expect my own desires to ever straighten out completely, but I am beginning to see an opening in the maze—to see that I can rise to the occasion of erotic affection without first wrapping my arms around a punitive fantasy.

Excerpted from *The New Yorker Magazine,* February 26 and March 4, 1996 (pp. 98–100, 102–108).

Frotteurism Froutteurism usually occurs in crowded places such as subways.

Other Paraphilias The DSM-IV-TR also lists a category called *paraphilias not otherwise specified (NOS)* which includes relatively rare behaviors that meet the definition of a paraphilia (APA, 2000) (see Table 10.5). *Necrophilia,* for example, involves sexual urges and activities with dead bodies. *Zoophilia* (or *bestiality*) pertains to sexual interest in animals (see Box 10.1). *Coprophilia* and *urophilia* involve sexual arousal to feces and urine, respectively. *Telephone scatologia* refers to compulsive sexual interest in making obscene telephone calls.

Related Disorders The phrase "sexual addiction" has been a focus of a great deal of recent attention and debate. While not found in the DSM-IV-TR, some experts argue that sexual addiction is a real and important syndrome of disordered sexuality (Carnes, 1990, 2000). The term sexual addiction overlaps with several other quasi-diagnostic labels such as "nonparaphilic hypersexuality" (Kafka & Hennen, 1999), "sexual dependence," "compulsive sexual behavior" (for example, compulsive promiscuity or masturbation), "pornography dependence," "on-line sexual dependence," "erotomania," or "erotic obsession" (Kaplan, 1996). The common denominator in these problems is seen as a loss of control over sexual behavior, much as the substance-use disorders are understood as a loss of control over substance use. Carnes estimates that 3% to 6% of the U.S. population suffers from some form of sexual addiction (Carnes, 1990, 2000). But other experts have questioned whether a syndrome of sexual addiction actually exists. While there is little empirical evidence to date on the subject (Gold & Heffner, 1998), studies suggest that clients identified as "sex addicts" are a heterogeneous group, tending to suffer from other significant psychopathology, often including paraphilias (Black et al., 1997; Kafka, 1997; Kafka & Hennen, 1999).

Brief Summary

- The paraphilias are more severe disorders than the sexual dysfunctions, involving aberrant sexual relationships and preferences.

- The most common paraphilias are exhibitionism, voyeurism, fetishism, sexual sadism, sexual masochism, pedophilia, and frotteurism.

Critical Thinking Question | **S**ome experts classify the paraphilias as addictive behaviors similar to substance misuse. The DSM-IV-TR does not. What do you think about this classification issue?

EXPLAINING AND TREATING SEXUAL DISORDERS: THE PARAPHILIAS

We have already touched on the issues of explanation and treatment for the sexual dysfunctions. In this section, we go into greater detail about how sexual abnormality is explained and treated, focusing on the paraphilias. While there are many theories about what causes paraphilias, experts generally agree that no fully satisfactory explanation has yet been developed. Studies have found that many individuals with paraphilias experienced childhood sexual traumas, such as sexual abuse, or other childhood stressors, such as attachment difficulties (Brockman & Bluglass, 1996; Sawle & Kear-Colwell, 2001). However, the various theoretical perspectives explain the connection between these childhood experiences and later paraphilias differently, as we will see. The most influential theoretical perspectives

Table 10.5

Adapted from
Milner & Dopke,
1997

PARAPHILIA NOS CATEGORIES	EROTIC FOCUS	POSSIBLE OVERLAPPING PARAPHILIA CATEGORIES
Nonhuman objects		
Zoophilia (zooerasty, zooerastia, bestiality, bestiosexuality)	Animals	
Formicophilia	Small creatures	Zoophilia
Klismaphilia	Enemas	
Olfactophilia	Odors	
Mysophilia	Filth	
Urophilia (urolagnia, urophagia, ondinisme, renifleurism, undinism)	Urine	Fetishism, sexual masochism, sexual sadism
Coprophilia	Feces	
Vampirism	Blood	Sexual sadism
Suffering or humiliation of oneself or one's partner		
Telephone scatophilia	Obscenities over phone	Exhibitionism
Narratophillia	Obscene language with partner	
Chrematistophilia	Being charged or forced to pay for sex	
Saliromania	Soiling/damaging clothing or body	Sexual sadism
Vomerophilia	Vomiting	
Children or other nonconsenting persons		
Necrophilia	Corpses	
Somnophilia	Sleeping partner	
Atypical focus involving human objects (self and others)		
Hypoxyphilia	Reduced oxygen intake	Sexual masochism
Urethral manipulation	Insertion of objects	Fetishism, sexual masochism
Morphophilia	One or more body characteristics of partner	
Partialism	Focus on a body part	
Stigmatophilia	Partner tattooed, scarified, or pierced for wearing jewelry	
Abasiophilia	Lamed or crippled partner	
Acrotomophilia	Amputation in partner	
Apotemnophilia	Own amputation	Sexual masochism
Infantilism	Impersonating or being treated as an infant	Sexual masochism
Adolescentilism	Impersonating or being treated as an adolescent	Sexual masochism
Gerontophilia	Elderly partner	
Andromimetophilia	Andromimetic (a woman posing as a man) partner	
Gynemimetophilia	Gynemimetic (a man posing as a woman) partner	
Autogynephilia	Image of self as woman	Transvestic fetishism
Gynandromorphophilia	Cross-dressed feminized male	
Scoptophilia	Viewing sexual activity	Voyeurism
Mixoscopia	Viewing couple having intercourse	Voyeurism
Triolism	Observing partner having sex	Voyeurism
Pictophilia	Pornographic pictures, movies, or videos	Voyeurism
Autagonistophilia	Being observed/being on stage	
Hybristophilia	Partner must have committed an outrageous act or crime	
Kleptophilia	Stealing	

for explaining the paraphilias are the psychodynamic, cognitive-behavioral, and biological approaches.

Treatment of the paraphilias is generally considered very difficult, and most experts are not very optimistic about its effectiveness (Laws & O'Donohue, 1997). Not only do we have an incomplete understanding of these disorders, but in addition most individuals with paraphilias deny the seriousness of the problem and lack motivation to change (Charlton & Quatman, 1997). Violent sexual offenders tend to be especially unresponsive to treatment (Gacano, Meloy, & Bridges, 2000). Even those with nonviolent paraphilias usually do not seek treatment unless they have been confronted or arrested. As a result, group treatments, many of which use confrontive techniques to address clients' denial, are often used for paraphilias.

Clients with paraphilias can evoke difficult feelings in their therapists (technically known as **countertransference,** the therapist's feelings about the client), posing another barrier to successful treatment. Therapists have to be able to appropriately manage their own possible feelings of disgust, excitement, or moral disapproval that can easily arise when working with individuals with paraphilias.

Countertransference The therapist's feelings about the client.

The primary treatments for paraphilias are psychological, although biological treatments can play a significant role. Once again, it is important to keep in mind the core concept of *the connection between mind and body.* A biological treatment can sometimes be useful even if the cause of a paraphilia is clearly psychological, and vice versa. The goals of treatment are usually to eliminate or significantly reduce the paraphilic behaviors (Wood, Grossman, & Fichtner, 2000). In order for this to occur, it is usually necessary to help the client develop substitute satisfactions through more "normal" sexual outlets (de Silva, 1999).

We now turn to a description of each approach, viewing them as complementary components in accord with the *principle of multiple causality*.

Psychodynamic Components

Psychodynamic explanations of paraphilias have significantly changed over time. As we have noted, Freud's first explanations of "perversions" emphasized the idea that perversions represented the direct expression in adulthood of "fixated" sexual interests from the developmental phases of childhood (for example, exhibitionism as a holdover from the phallic phase when children enjoy showing off their bodies) (Freud, 1905). Later, Freud and other psychodynamic theorists shifted their emphasis to the idea that "perverse" sexual behavior is a particular kind of defense mechanism in response to an underlying emotional conflict. For example, Freud argued that every boy (remember Little Hans?) goes through a phase of *castration anxiety* during childhood in which he fears that his penis (or, symbolically, his emerging sense of masculinity) could be at risk at the hands of the big, powerful adults in his life. A mild version of this anxiety continues throughout life for most men, but some men remain, consciously or unconsciously, haunted by it, and they need constant reassurance that their genitals and their masculinity are intact. Freud believed that perverse sexual behaviors were designed, in a complex way, to provide this reassurance, and therefore could be seen as defense mechanisms against the fear of castration (or emasculation) (Fenichel, 1945; Freud, 1940a, 1940b). For instance, the exhibitionist reassures himself by revealing that his penis is still there for all to see; the fetishist symbolically equates his fetish object with a penis and therefore requires that it be present during sex; the pedophile seeks out children which reassures him that he is bigger and more masculine than they are.

Contemporary psychodynamic explanations continue to emphasize the defensive function of paraphilias, but in a somewhat different way. The most influential contemporary psychodynamic theorist, Robert Stoller, modified Freud's theories based on his study of hundreds of individuals with paraphilias. He argued that men with paraphilias all seemed to have one thing in common—childhood experiences in which they felt utterly humiliated to such a degree that it profoundly threatened their sense of masculinity (Stoller, 1975, 1980, 1987). Some of the men Stoller studied experienced sexual abuse; others experienced less dramatic yet nonetheless emotionally traumatic events. In any case, these individuals developed a common defense mechanism for protecting themselves from these feelings of humiliation and inadequacy: **turning passive into active** (also known as **identification with the aggressor**). In lay terms, these individuals "do unto others before others can do unto them" and attempt to humiliate others sexually. Thus, for Stoller, paraphilic behaviors are a form of hostility expressed sexually—specifically, a need to humiliate someone else in order to get revenge for past childhood humiliations. In most cases, the individual is not consciously aware of these motives, but can become aware of them in therapy. For example, Charlton and Quatman (1997) describe a case involving a man whose symptoms met the criteria for sexual sadism; his greatest sexual excitement came from the idea of spanking a woman while having sex. The man's father had punished him in childhood by forcing him to wait in the bathroom naked while his father retrieved a belt with which to whip him. In therapy, this man discovered that his paraphilia was related to three remnants of his childhood experiences: (1) his own hostility, now sexualized and directed toward doing to a woman what was done to him; (2) his own sense that he was less than adequate as a man; and (3) the rage that lay deep in his heart toward his father for beating him and toward his mother for allowing it to happen (quoted in Charlton & Quatman, 1997). Stoller viewed all of the different forms of paraphilias as different "scripts" for unconsciously enacting an identification with the aggressor (Stoller, 1975, 1987). The exhibitionist, the voyeur, the pedophile, the frotteurist, the sadist, the masochist (by believing he or she secretly controls the sadist), and the fetishist (by imagining that the object has symbolic power) all wish to undo past humiliating experiences by humiliating someone else in the present.

Turning passive into active (identification with the aggressor) A defense mechanism involving doing unto others what was done to oneself.

Psychodynamic Interventions

Psychodynamic interventions for paraphilias focus on addressing the roots of the paraphilia in early sexual traumas, problematic emotions such as humiliation, shame, and rage, defense mechanisms against these painful feelings, and ineffective emotional (ego) and moral (superego) self-regulation (Laws & O'Donohue, 1997; Stoller, 1975). The psychodynamic approach has the advantage of dealing with the problem in depth, but the typically nondirective nature of psychodynamic interventions can also be problematic with clients who are unmotivated or behaving in aggressive or self-destructive ways that might require a more structured approach. In order to motivate clients to collaborate in therapy, psychodynamic treatments for paraphilias emphasize the importance of establishing a strong *therapeutic alliance*, the collaborative bond between client and therapist (Charlton & Quatman, 1997; Kear-Colwell & Boer, 2000). This can be especially challenging given the ambivalence many paraphilic clients have about treatment, and the fact that many legal jurisdictions require that therapists break the normal guarantee of therapeutic confidentiality and report certain sexual behaviors, such as child abuse, to government authorities (Charlton & Quatman, 1997).

Cognitive-Behavioral Components

Cognitive-behavioral perspectives on paraphilias focus on two familiar principles: *classical (or Pavlovian) conditioning,* and *social learning* (Brockman & Bluglass,

1996; Laws & O'Donohue, 1997). In many ways, the cognitive-behavioral explanation of paraphilias is similar to the cognitive-behavioral explanation of phobias: both can be conceptualized as a physical reaction (sexual arousal, or fear) occurring in response to an inappropriate stimulus (something that would not normally arouse sexual excitement or fear). The theory of classical conditioning can explain these abnormal "pairings" as the product of accidental, automatic learning. Remember that when a "neutral" stimulus is coincidentally present and associated with an emotional reflex, the two can become powerfully and lastingly connected in the mind. Just as hearing a loud noise (the *unconditioned stimulus*) in the presence of a rat (the *neutral stimulus*) made Little Albert afraid of rats (that is, the rats became a *conditioned stimulus*), sexual arousal in the presence of an inanimate object could theoretically produce a fetish. Behavioral theorists have described numerous cases in which accidental learning of this kind seemed to lead to the development of various paraphilias (Laws & Marshall, 1990; Marshall & Eccles, 1993).

Another cognitive-behavioral process relevant to the development of paraphilias involves social learning (Bandura, 1999). Children's behaviors are shaped not only by classical and operant conditioning but also through their observations of others. Children who observe other people behaving in sexually deviant ways (for example, overly aggressive), children who lack the social and cognitive skills for relating in a sexually appropriate manner, and children who are rewarded for inappropriate sexual behavior all can develop a tendency toward paraphilic behaviors (Nichols, 1998; Pithers et al., 1998).

Behavioral and Cognitive Interventions

Behavioral treatments involve a directive, interventionist approach. Using the principles of classical and operant conditioning, behavioral interventions attempt to alter learned, maladaptive patterns of deviant sexual arousal, and to replace them with new, more appropriate patterns (Brockman & Bluglass, 1996). Paraphilic arousal tendencies are first assessed using a *penile plethysmograph,* which measures penile responses to various paraphilic stimuli (a process known as **phallometric assessment**). While the reliability and validity of phallometric assessment are not well established (APA, 2000), many experts find that it can be a useful tool in designing behavioral treatments (Laws & O'Donohue, 1997). Once a client's deviant sexual arousal patterns have been established, classical and operant conditioning principles can be employed to attempt to change them. Behavioral treatment techniques include *aversion therapies,* in which electric shocks or noxious odors are paired with deviant sexual thoughts (Laws & O'Donohue, 1997; Wood et al., 2000). *Covert sensitization,* another conditioning technique, involves having the client imagine unpleasant consequences, such as public humiliation, or a prison sentence, in connection with their paraphilic urges (Wood et al., 2000). Two additional conditioning methods are *systematic desensitization* and **masturbatory satiation** (or **orgasmic reconditioning**). In the former, the client learns to relax, rather than respond erotically, to problematic sexual stimuli, just as a phobic client can learn to relax in the presence of a phobic stimulus through systematic desensitization (as discussed in Chapter 5) (Wood et al., 2000). The latter technique relies on the powerful reinforcing properties of a sexual orgasm. Clients are asked to masturbate to "normal," rather than paraphilic, fantasies to reinforce "normal" fantasies with the pleasure of sexual climax (Laws & Marshall, 1991; Laws & O'Donohue, 1997). All of these techniques rely on a combination of classical and operant conditioning principles. While some ethical concerns have been raised about the potential coerciveness of behavioral treatment techniques (Fog, 1992), they have been shown to reduce paraphilic behaviors (Wood et al., 2000).

Phallometric assessment Measurement of penile responses to various stimuli.

Masturbatory satiation (or **orgasmic reconditioning**) A behavioral treatment for paraphilias in which the client masturbates to "normal" sexual stimuli in order to reinforce this behavior.

Cognitive techniques are often paired with behavioral methods, and the combination of the two is currently a common approach to treating paraphilias (Laws & O'Donohue, 1997). Cognitive treatments include *cognitive restructuring,* in which paraphilic fantasies and related interpersonal schemas are challenged and revised (Laws & O'Donohue, 1997). In addition, cognitive therapists focus on clients' cognitive deficits in areas such as empathy *(empathy training),* social skills *(social skills training),* impulse control, and healthy coping strategies (Brockman & Bluglass, 1996; Laws & O'Donohue, 1997).

Biological Components

Most explanations of paraphilias emphasize psychological factors (Laws & O'Donohue, 1997). However, biological factors can contribute to paraphilias, particularly in the form of injuries or illnesses that have a *disinhibiting* effect on behavior. For example, temporal lobe epilepsy, brain tumors or injuries, and degenerative diseases have all been occasionally implicated in cases of paraphilias (Brockman & Bluglass, 1996). In addition, Lewis and Stanley (2000) found that among women accused of sexual offenses, mental retardation, and a history of current physical abuse and childhood physical and sexual abuse, were common.

Biological Interventions

While psychological interventions are currently the primary approach to treating paraphilias, biological treatments also play a role in some cases. In the recent past, surgical castration was sometimes employed to "treat" sexual criminals and treatment-resistant paraphilics (Rosler & Witztum. 1998; 2000). This practice dramatically decreased sexually deviant behavior (see Table 10.6), but legal and ethical concerns have almost eliminated its use (Rosler & Witztum, 2000). However, medical interventions designed to suppress testosterone levels (sometimes referred to as **chemical castration**) are still in use. Some experts consider anti-androgenic treatments (testosterone is the main androgen, or male hormone), and other hormonal treatments to be promising interventions for severe paraphilias (Rosler & Witztum, 1998, 2000). However, ethical concerns remain, especially when dealing with criminals where the issue of obtaining valid consent for treatment is quite problematic (Brockman & Bluglass, 1996). Antidepressant medications have also recently been tested as a partial treatment for paraphilias, but current evidence suggests that they are only helpful in some cases (Rosler & Witztum, 2000).

Chemical castration A biological intervention for some paraphilias designed to suppress testosterone levels.

Brief Summary

- Psychodynamic explanations of paraphilias originally focused on fixations in sexual development, and currently focus on defense mechanisms related to humiliating sexual traumas from childhood.

- Cognitive-behavioral explanations of paraphilias emphasize classically conditioned sexual arousal to deviant stimuli, reinforcement of aberrant sexual behavior, and social learning of abnormal sexuality.

- Biological factors are generally not a central focus in explaining paraphilias, but some disinhibiting diseases or injuries, and mental retardation, can contribute to paraphilic behavior.

- Treatment of the paraphilias is difficult, partly because clients often come for treatment because of external (for example, legal) pressures rather than internal desire to change. Psychodynamic, cognitive-behavioral, and biological interventions can all be employed as treatment strategies.

Table 10.6	Recidivism Rates Following Castration of Sex Offenders

From Bradford, 1997. Data from Heim & Hursch (1977); Bradford & Pawlak (1987).

	RECIDIVISM RATES FOLLOWING CASTRATION			
STUDIES	**FOLLOW-UP PERIOD (YEARS)**	*N*	**PRE-RATE (%)**	**POST-RATE (%)**
Langeluddeke (1963)	20	1,036	84	2.3
Cornu (1973)	5	127	76.8	4.1
Bremer (1959)	5–10	216	58	2.9
Sturup[1]	30	900		2.2

Pre-rate, the recidivism rate prior to castration; Post-rate, the recidivism rate after castration.
[1] Mostly rapists.

GENDER IDENTITY DISORDERS

Gender identity disorder (transsexualism) A DSM-IV-TR disorder involving intense discomfort with one's biological sex and the desire to change it.

Gender A person's psychological sense of being male or female.

Gender identity disorder (sometimes referred to in adults as **transsexualism**) is listed as a sexual disorder in the DSM-IV-TR, although GID does not focus on sexual symptoms per se. Rather, GID involves a disruption in *gender identity,* which is, of course, closely related to sexuality. Gender identity disorder is most clearly defined in terms of two variables: *sex,* which refers to a person's *biological* body (either male or female), and **gender,** which refers to a person's *psychological* sense of being male or female (Zucker & Bradley, 1995). GID consists of three symptoms. First, a person's psychological gender identity is the opposite of his or her biological sex. Second, the person is extremely uncomfortable with his or her biological sex (APA, 2000). Third, the person experiences significant distress or impairment in functioning. Thus, GID involves either men (or boys) who dislike being male and want to be female, or women (or girls) who dislike being female and wish to be male (see Table 10.7).

It is important to emphasize that simple gender nonconformity, such as a girl behaving as a "tomboy" or effeminacy in a boy, does not constitute GID. Nor is GID diagnosed when a person may have cross-gender identifications that are related to some of the *intersex* physical conditions in which children are born with ambiguous genitalia (APA, 2000). Rather, GID is diagnosed only when a person's gender and sex are fundamentally at odds, and the person experiences distress and impairment as a result. In typical cases, people with GID are tormented by feelings of having been born into the wrong body (such as "I feel like a woman trapped in a man's body").

Gender identity disorder is very rare, but over the past decade it has become much more widely publicized. Not long ago, only a few celebrated cases of GID were well known, such as the case of Renee Richards, a biologically male eye doctor and tennis player who wanted to join the women's professional tennis tour in 1976 after undergoing a sex change (Masters, Johnson, & Kolodny, 1986). More recently, as a result of the efforts of the transgender community to raise awareness of the condition combined with the propensity of the media to sensationalize cases of GID, the disorder has been more broadly recognized. While GID may be more visible and socially accepted, there is no indication that the disorder is becoming more prevalent. GID remains quite unusual, probably affecting less than 1 in 10,000 people, although no sound data on the prevalence of GID yet exist (Zucker & Bradley, 1995).

Gender Identity Disorders | **337**

| Diagnostic Criteria for Gender Identity Disorder | Table 10.7 |

- A strong and persistent cross-gender identification.
- A persistent discomfort with one's sex or sense of inappropriateness in the gender role of that sex.
- Significant distress or impairment of functioning related to the condition.

*Adapted from DSM-IV-TR
(APA, 2000)*

Adults with GID usually try to live as members of the opposite sex. Because they cross-dress, individuals with GID are often confused with transvestites (see Box 10.4 for an example of this confusion). However, there is an important difference between the two conditions: transvestites (a form of fetishism) cross-dress because it is sexually arousing; people with GID cross-dress to feel in harmony with their gender identity.

Many clients with GID seek hormonal, surgical, and other forms of treatment to transform their bodies to conform to their gender identity. Often they are able to "pass" effectively as members of the opposite sex and can interact with others who never suspect the condition. Nonetheless, GID does seem to take a psychological toll. Many individuals with GID are reported to have significant relationship problems and generally impaired functioning. These difficulties are not surprising, given that individuals with GID face discrimination and ostracism in addition to struggling with emotional problems related to their condition (the struggles of one transsexual are described in Box 10.4).

Adult GID seems to be two to three times more common in biological men than in women (APA, 2000). This skewed ratio may be due to the fact that in our society men are more stigmatized for having effeminate traits than women are for having masculine traits; for example, the label "sissy" is much more negative than "tomboy." As a result, males with cross-gender identifications may have a harder time than cross-gender identified females. Interestingly, while virtually all women with GID are sexually attracted to women, sexual orientation varies much more in GID men. Males who experienced a childhood onset of GID are most likely to be sexually attracted to

Gender nonconformity Gender nonconformity, such as a "tomboy"-ish girl, is very common and not the same as a gender identity disorder.

Transsexualism Dr. Richard Raskin is shown in 1974 before his sex-change operation. By 1977, Dr. Raskin, known postsurgically as Renee Richards, caused a brief controversey when she tried to join the women's professional tennis tour.

BOX 10.4 The Struggles of a Transsexual in an Unusual Profession

"Auto Racing: Driver with Sex Change Finds Her Career Stalled" *by Tarik El-Bashir*

The following article from *The New York Times* describes some of the special difficulties encountered by the transsexual race car driver Terri O'Connell.

For more than a year, Terri O'Connell has been tireless in her pursuit of a sponsor. She spends hours on the phone daily. She spends even longer preparing and mailing proposals, trying to come up with the money she needs to resume her career as a race car driver.

O'Connell is hardly alone, for there are scores of other drivers—some young and looking for a break, some old and aching for a comeback—out hustling their talents and tales. Every sell is a hard one. No one's pitch, though, is more difficult to make than O'Connell's. The 35-year-old driver, after all, used to be a man.

"It's tough to find sponsors if you're normal," O'Connell said. It has been near hopeless, she said, given her life story—the saga of a promising young driver who prospered in the hard-living, macho world of race car driving, only to abandon the sport in order to end the torment of an identity crisis that ultimately resulted in a sex change.

While her story has elicited curiosity among the sponsors whose finances determine what cars run on the professional circuits, no one has agreed to back O'Connell with the $250,000 or so she needs to put together an Indy Racing League team. They all have declined politely, but repeatedly. No one has said O'Connell's sex change was the deciding factor, but she has her suspicions.

"I'm controversial because of a biological problem," said O'Connell, who, after having won dozens of sprint car races as well as having run in a Winston Cup race as a young driver, has not turned a lap in a race car since her sex change operation in 1992. "It's been incredibly difficult because of the stereotypes. People don't understand my situation. They think that I'm a freak."

And so, day after day, O'Connell works the phones and knocks on doors. Last week, one door opened slightly. Volkswagen and Candies, a women's shoe company, agreed to let O'Connell drive a Beetle from coast to coast next month in the Cannonball Run, a race for charity. It is a start, but it is not mainstream racing.

"It's going to be tough for her," said Brittan Schnell, a Winston Cup team owner who knows O'Connell. "Terri's got a long road ahead to earn the respect of people in the sport."

High-stakes professional car racing can often be a closed, conservative world, one dominated by men. Nearly two decades ago, Janet Guthrie, the first woman to race in the Indianapolis 500, endured years of hardship in the world of stock car and Indy car racing, forced to drive inferior cars when she could get the financing to drive at all. Only two women are now competing in North America's three major racing leagues, the Indy Racing League, Championship Auto Racing Teams and Nascar.

Still, many of the principals in the world of racing deny that there is any bar to women—or women who used to be men. Some team owners, including Junie Donlavey, for whom O'Connell once raced years ago, think that her trouble in finding a sponsor comes more from her long layoff than from her sex change.

It has been eight years since she drove Donlavey's car in her only Winston Cup race, in Rockingham, N.C. Then known as J. T. Hayes, she was the teammate of Ernie Irvan.

"I don't see sex as a factor," said Donlavey, who is now the owner of Dick Trickle's Winston Cup car. "We had Janet Guthrie down here years ago, and everybody treated her with respect. Lyn St. James, who drives in Indy, has really been an asset to her sport. I think it's just tough to get a sponsor, period."

But Shand Tillman, the promoter for the Riverside Speedway in West Memphis, Ark., believes there is more to it than that. Tillman said that when O'Connell was regularly competing at tracks like Riverside, "she was as good a sprint car driver as they come." Now, Tillman said, "People are scared to put their name on a car she is driving because of what effects it might have on their product."

(continues)

Terri O'Connell, formerly J.T. Hayes, at the wheel.

BOX 10.4 (continued)

"I don't agree with what she has done at all," Tillman added. "I don't know where in the Bible it says it, but if you are made a man, you should stay a man."

Growing up in Corinth, Miss., J. T. Hayes appeared to be a prototypical race car driver, a Southern boy with a lead foot. With his father, he spent weekends competing at Southern tracks like Riverside and Devil's Bowl in Dallas. He developed into an accomplished driver, reaching the podium more than 300 times in Go-Kart, midget, and sprint car races.

But O'Connell felt trapped, her very identity wrong. She tried hard to pretend otherwise. Fearing rejection from the father she loved, O'Connell kept up a very male persona. She dated girls in high school and even married briefly. It was always a struggle.

"Being feminine was like eating for me," O'Connell said. "Imagine what it's like for you not to eat, and you'll understand the nightmare I was living."

That nightmare reached its unsettling nadir when O'Connell smashed into a wall during a race at Houston's Astrodome. Her first thoughts, she said, were not about her broken bones, but about what the medics would say when they discovered she was wearing women's underwear and pink toenail polish.

Depressed and confused, O'Connell, good enough to have raced in Nascar's top circuit, walked away from racing in 1990. Two years later, she underwent the sex change.

"I had to do it," O'Connell said. "I was at the point where I could let racing go. I had to get my life straight."

But once a woman, the desire to drive endured, and it has brought her back to the fringes of the sport. Nothing has come easy since she has been back. But against the resistance, O'Connell, who has been working as a fashion model, keeps pushing. She lives in Charlotte, not far from Charlotte Motor Speedway.

"As it turned out," O'Connell said, "motorsports were my blessing and my curse."

The New York Times, May 17, 1998.

---

men, while those with later onset may be attracted to women or consider themselves bisexual. Sexual orientation in transsexuals is defined in terms of the person's original biological sex, so that a female-to-male transsexual who is attracted to women is classified as homosexual, even though her sexual fantasies are most likely heterosexual (herself as a man having sex with a woman). A small percentage of transsexuals report little sexual interest in either sex.

GID occurs much more often in children than in adults, because most children with GID "outgrow" the problem by adolescence. For example, 75% of boys diagnosed with GID as children no longer have the disorder by late adolescence (APA, 2000). However, most of these boys have developed a homosexual or bisexual orientation by this time. In general, GID in childhood is strongly associated with later homosexuality, which has led to some controversy about treating GID in childhood. Critics have called such treatment "anti-homosexual" and unnecessary (Pleak, 1999). Other experts contend that it is legitimate and important to treat childhood GID since the symptoms of the disorder cause considerable suffering (Zucker & Bradley, 1995). (See Explaining Gender Identity Disorders and Treating Gender Identity Disorders sections for more details.)

Boys with GID typically show stereotypically feminine interests, avoid "rough and tumble" play, and express the wish to be a girl. Girls with GID usually resist feminine activities and dress, prefer to play with boys, and often insist that they are or will become male (for example, "I'm going to grow a penis" or "my testicles are hidden"). (Table 10.8 presents an interview protocol that can be helpful in assessing childhood GID; Figure 10.3 shows drawings by children with GID.) Both boys and girls with the condition may experience serious peer relationship problems including isolation and teasing, and are considered at risk for depression and suicide. Adolescence is often particularly traumatic for these children, as their bodies develop into the adult form of the sex that feels foreign to them.

In order to provide a descriptive picture of GID in children, we include the following case report of GID in a 6 year-old girl.

Table 10.8	Gender Identity Interview for Children (Version for Boys)

Zucker et al., 1993

The following interview format can be helpful in assessing childhood GID.

1. Are you a boy or a girl? BOY ___ GIRL___
2. Are you a (opposite of first response)?___
3. When you grow up, will you be a Mommy or a Daddy? MOMMY ___ DADDY___
4. Could you ever grow up to be a (opposite of first response)? YES ___ NO___
5. Are there any good things about being a boy? YES ___ NO___
   If YES, say: Tell me some of the good things about being a boy.
   (Probe for a maximum of three responses.)
   If YES or NO, ask: Are there any things that you don't like about being a boy? YES ___ NO___
   If child answers YES, say: Tell me some of the things thar you don't like about being a boy. (Probe for a maximum of three responses.)
6. Do you think it is better to be a boy or a girl? YES ___ NO ___ Why?
   (Probe for a maximum of three responses.)
7. In your mind, do you ever think that you would like to be a girl? YES ___ NO ___
   If YES, ask: Can you tell me why? (Probe for a maximum of three responses.)
8. In your mind, do you ever get mixed up and you're not really sure if you are a boy or a girl?
   YES ___ NO___
   If YES, say: Tell me more about that. (Probe until satisfied.)
9. Do you ever feel more like a girl than like a boy? YES ___ NO___
   If YES, say: Tell me more about that. (Probe until satisfied.)
10. You know what dreams are, right? Well, when you dream at night, are you ever in the dream?
    YES ___ NO___
    If YES, ask: In your dreams, are you a boy, a girl, or sometimes a boy and sometimes a girl?
    BOY ___ GIRL ___ BOTH ___ NOT IN DREAMS___
    (Probe regarding content of dreams.)
11. Do you ever think that you really are a girl? YES ___ NO___
    If YES, say: Tell me more about that. (Probe until satisfied.)

Case Illustration Toni, a 6-year-old girl with an IQ of 123…was referred because of increasing parental concern over her gender identity development… At times she displayed exaggerated masculine motoric movements and would lower her voice. She was adamantly opposed to wearing stereotypically feminine clothes and dressed almost exclusively in pants. Her only concession was wearing a dress to church. She stated that she dressed "like a gentleman" during the week but for church she dressed "like a lady."

Toni was quite outspoken in her desire to be a boy. At school, she began to call herself a boy, and to spell her name as "Tony," which greatly alarmed her teacher. Toni had heard from neighborhood boys about "sex change" and subsequently asked her parents more about this. Toni's mother, perhaps because of her "liberal" or "permissive" child-rearing style, explained the mechanics of sex-reassignment surgery to her; after that, she became, in her parents' words, "obsessed" with the idea.

Toni was persistent in claiming that she had male genitalia "hidden inside"… If hit in the stomach with a hockey puck, she would clutch herself and exclaim, "Oh, my balls!" Information from psychological testing indicated that Toni knew that she was a girl but was struggling with intense desires that this not be so. For example, she stated that she knew she didn't really have a penis and testes hidden inside her, but

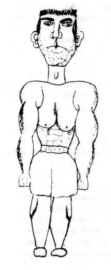

Drawing by a 10-year-old boy with gender identity disorder during an individual therapy session. At the time, the boy was talking about the unpredictability of his mother's moods.

Drawing of a man by an 11-year-old girl with gender identity disorder who wanted to be a weightlifter so that she could be strong enough to protect her mother from potential rapists.

Drawing of a girl (left) and a boy (right) by an 8-year-old boy with gender identity disorder. Note the marked difference in height. The youngster remarked that the boy was drawn with a "dress on" because he "didn't know how" to wear pants.

Drawing of a boy by a girl with gender identity disorder. Note the presence of the third leg.

Figure 10.3 Drawings by children with gender identity disorder Zucker and Bradley (1995) compiled these annotated drawings of children with gender identity disorder.

From Zucker & Bradley 1995, pp. 19, 63, 65, and 230

that she said so "just to be like a boy." At a later point, she tried to explain her feelings thus: "I am a girl but I'm not."

Quoted in Minter, 1999, from Zucker, 1990

Explaining Gender Identity Disorders

The development of gender identity in general, and GID in particular, are complex processes that are not fully understood. We do know that for most children a relatively stable and unchangeable gender identity as either male or female is well established by the age of three or four (Bradley & Zucker, 1997). While the factors responsible for producing gender identity are hotly debated, most experts agree that a combination of biological, psychological, and social factors are involved. We turn now to a summary of some of the current explanations of GID. At the end of this summary, we describe an integrated explanatory model, in keeping with the core concept of *multiple causality*.

Biological Components

Temperament Inborn behavioral tendencies.

There is a small but growing literature on the possible role of biological factors in the development of GID (Zucker & Bradley, 1995). One area of research involves connections between **temperament**—inborn behavioral tendencies—and GID. For example, boys with GID seem to have generally lower activity levels, and less interest in rough-and-tumble play, than other boys. These temperamental differences probably have some genetic basis (Zucker & Bradley, 1995).

The mechanism of these genetic temperamental differences probably involves the hormonal system, which influences many sexual- and gender-linked behaviors. For example, chromosomal females with a rare genetic condition known as *congenital virilizing adrenal hyperplasia* (CVAH or CAH) receive excess androgen, the male sex hormone, in utero. As a result, these girls not only develop some masculine physical characteristics, but they have more masculine personality traits as well (Money, 1994) (Figure 10.4 shows the masculine play preferences of CVAH girls). Similarly, chromosomal males with the rare genetic condition called *androgen insensitivity syndrome* are unable to process androgen in utero. They are born looking female, raised as girls, and generally found to be psychologically hyper-feminine in later life (Money, 1994). While these conditions are not the same as GID, they do demonstrate the influence of hormones on gender identity as well as on sexual anatomy. Accordingly, some experts suspect that prenatal, postnatal, or even postpubertal hormonal abnormalities could contribute to the gender anomalies seen in GID, although no consistent evidence for this has yet been reported (Bradley & Zucker, 1997). There is, however, some preliminary evidence of differences in brain structure in transsexual men as compared to control subjects. Zhou and colleagues (1997) found that an area of the hypothalamus in six transsexual males was half the normal size of that in nontranssexual men, making it close to its typical size in women.

Psychodynamic Components

Psychodynamic theories of GID have emphasized the role of disturbed mother-son relationships in the development of GID in boys. However, there has been some disagreement among psychodynamic theorists as to the nature of the mother-son problem (Zucker & Bradley, 1995). Stoller (1979) and Greenson (1968) believed that an overly close and gratifying mother-son relationship (what they described as a "blissful sym-

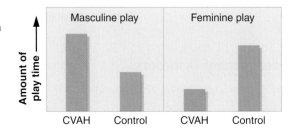

Figure 10.4 Differences in Masculine versus Feminine Play in Girls with Congenital Virilizing Adrenal Hyperplasia (CVAH) versus Controls The graph shows that the girls with CVAH spent more time in "masculine" play and less time time in "feminine" play with gender-typed toys, compared to control girls.

Adapted from Zucker & Bradley, 1995, based on Berenbaum & Hines, 1992, p. 205

biosis"), combined with a too-distant father, were the key factors in producing a female identification in a boy. However, Coates and her colleagues (Coates, 1992; Coates, Freidman, & Wolfe, 1991; Coates & Wolf, 1995) found in their empirical studies of GID that the GID boy's feminine behaviors and interests were often an attempt to connect with a depressed, withdrawn mother rather than a symbiosis with an overly gratifying mother.

Behavioral Components

From a behavioral standpoint, gender behavior, like all behavior, is shaped by the environment. Accordingly, behavioral theorists see the primary cause of GID as a set of reinforcements in the child's environment which lead the child to learn that cross-gender behavior will be rewarded and gender consistent behavior will be punished (Rekers & Varni, 1977). Cross-gender behavior and identity, in other words, could be formed through operant conditioning. This perspective overlaps with some psychodynamic theories about the influence of parents' conscious and unconscious wishes in shaping their child's gender identity and behavior. Evidence for these hypotheses is mixed. Parental preference for an opposite-sex child does not seem to be associated with GID, but some evidence suggests that social reinforcement of cross-gender behavior can contribute to the disorder (Zucker & Bradley, 1995).

Sociocultural and Family Systems Components

In addition to the evidence that social reinforcement of cross-gender behavior outside the family can contribute to GID, several family variables have been associated with the disorder. Demographically, GID boys tend to have a large number of brothers and to be among the younger siblings in their families (Bradley & Zucker, 1997). In addition, the families of children with GID tend to have significant family-wide psychopathology, a great deal of family stress and frustration, and difficulty with effective limit setting (Zucker & Bradley, 1995).

The Principle of Multiple Causality in Gender Identity Disorders

Coates and her colleagues offer an integrated *biopsychodevelopmental* explanation of the multiple factors that contribute to GID—an approach that reflects the core concept of ***multiple causality*** (Coates, 1990, 1992; Coates et al., 1991; Coates & Wolfe, 1995). For GID in boys, such factors include: a relatively passive temperament; high levels of anxiety and insecurity among immediate family members; the boy's acute sensitivity to parents' emotions; mothers who are uncomfortable with male aggressiveness; fathers who feel inadequate and defer to their wives; a depressive withdrawal of the mother leading to separation anxiety for the boy; parental emotional problems leading to insecure attachments with their children; inadequate family limit setting; and parental tolerance or reinforcement of cross-gender behavior when it begins to emerge during the critical early childhood period of gender identity development. In this context, the GID boy may begin to identify as female, either because he wants to regain his connection with his mother by becoming like her (Coates et al., 1991; Hansell, 1998) or because it feels emotionally safer to be female than male. For girls with GID, different family factors are involved. In these families, fathers are often abusive and appear to devalue femininity. Mothers tend to feel inadequate and to adopt a victim role within the family. This combination of factors may lead a girl to feel that it is far preferable to be male than female.

Treating Gender Identity Disorders

The treatment of GID has been an area of great controversy. Part of the controversy has to do with the fact that the basic treatment approach for GID fundamentally differs depending on whether the client is a child or an adult, mainly because gender identity appears to be somewhat changeable during childhood but unchangeable in adults (Masters, Johnson, & Kolodny, 1986). Accordingly, treatment for children involves trying to readjust their gender identity to fit their biological sex, while treatment of adults involves **sex change,** or **sex reassignment**, to make biological sex conform to gender identity. However, both approaches have been challenged in terms of effectiveness and ethics (Minter, 1999; Zucker & Bradley, 1995). We now turn to a description of some of the treatments for GID, including some discussion of the efficacy and ethical issues.

Sex change (or **sex reassignment**) A treatment for gender identity disorder in which the client's body is altered through various means to conform with his or her gender identity.

Treatment of Childhood Gender Identity Disorder

Because gender identity is still somewhat fluid during childhood, most experts on GID believe that children with the disorder can and should be helped to become more comfortable with their biological sex through psychotherapy. A number of treatment approaches have been developed; all have had mixed results (Zucker & Bradley, 1995). Beginning in the 1970s, George Rekers and his colleagues reported success in extinguishing feminine behaviors and developing masculine behaviors in GID boys using rewards and punishments in a behavioral conditioning paradigm (Rekers et al., 1977; Rekers & Lovaas, 1974). However, the long-term success and generalizability of these results have since been questioned. In addition, some critics have argued that these behavioral treatment methods are coercive and cruel (Minter, 1999; Pleak, 1999).

Psychodynamic interventions for children with GID were pioneered by Robert Stoller. With colleagues (Green, Newman, & Stoller, 1972), he developed an integrated therapy for GID in boys based on four principles: (1) developing a trusting relationship with the child; (2) increasing the parents' concern about cross-gender behavior; (3) increasing the father's involvement with his son; and (4) improving the marital relationship.

While reliable statistics on treatment efficacy with GID are lacking, there is reason to be optimistic that most children can be helped. Most therapists believe that it is optimal for the therapist to be of the same sex as the child in order to provide a role model, but there is no systematic evidence that opposite gender therapists are less effective (Zucker & Bradley, 1995). Finally, some clinicians have experimented with group therapy for GID children and provided anecdotal reports of success, but there are as yet no quantitative data on this form of therapy with GID.

As mentioned earlier, some critics believe that treatment of children with GID is unethical. They argue that since most GID children grow up to be homosexual, but not transsexual, treatment of childhood GID has simply become a new locus for the old psychiatric tendency to pathologize and "treat" homosexuality (Minter, 1999; Pleak, 1999). The counter-argument is that children with GID experience distress and impairment in the form of depression, isolation, stigmatization, and a range of other problems. Furthermore, many experts believe that GID is usually part of a broader set of psychological problems requiring treatment (Coates, 1992; Coates & Wolfe, 1995), although evidence for this is mixed. In any case, the current mainstream opinion seems to be that the respectful treatment of childhood GID is appropriate and helpful in most cases (Zucker & Bradley, 1995).

Treatment of Adult Gender Identity Disorders

As clinicians began to realize the futility of attempting to change the gender identity of adult transsexuals through psychotherapy, *sex change* or *sex-reassignment* developed as an alternative treatment approach. Essentially, the goal of sex-reassignment is to facilitate the client's wish to live as a member of the opposite sex, thereby eliminating the symptoms of GID. The complete sex change process is long, complex, expensive, and stressful, and not possible or appropriate for all transsexuals (Masters, Johnson, & Kolodny, 1986). It usually begins with a trial period during which the client undergoes a psychological evaluation while experimenting with living as a member of the opposite sex. During this period, the individual may begin hormone treatments, which shift secondary sex characteristics toward those of the opposite sex. Concurrently, clients can receive physical therapy, voice training, psychotherapy, and other adjunctive services to assist them in their complex transition (Cohen-Kettenis & Gooren, 1999). If the client still wishes to proceed to the final and irreversible stage of sex-change surgery, and if he or she has "passed" the psychological and physical screening criteria, specialized medical centers offer sex change procedures (for discussion of the issue of medical insurance coverage for sex change surgery, see Box 10.5).

During the 1960s and 1970s, sex-change surgery was enthusiastically embraced by many experts in the field, and it was widely available. Since then, professional enthusiasm has been more tempered. On the one hand, sex-change surgical techniques have improved for both male-to-female and female-to-male procedures. While the latter is more complex—for example, *phalloplasty* techniques (creating an artificial penis) are not yet perfected—there are many reports of satisfactory sexual functioning, including orgasmic capacity, in postsurgical transsexuals (Lief & Hubschman, 1993; Masters, Johnson, & Kolodny; 1986). On the other hand, reports on the long-term psychological effects of sex-change surgery have been mixed (Wolfradt & Neumann, 2001). The ethics of sex-change surgery have also been hotly debated. Some experts see sex-change surgery as a humane solution to a vexing psychological problem that cannot be effectively treated in any other way. Others view it as a barbaric practice similar to discredited psychiatric "treatments" of the past such as the prefrontal lobotomy. While the technical success of the surgery continues to improve, it may be many years before the efficacy and ethical issues concerning sex-change procedures are resolved (Masters, Johnson, & Kolodny, 1986). Who knows how our current understanding and treatment of GID will sound to the experts in the next century?

Brief Summary

- Gender identity disorder (GID) is a rare condition involving the wish to be the opposite sex and a dislike of one's own sex. It usually begins in childhood, but most children with GID become homosexual adults rather than adults with GID.

- Various psychological, social, and biological theories have been proposed to explain GID, but the causes are still not fully understood.

- Treatment of GID is controversial for practical and ethical reasons. Children with GID usually receive psychotherapy to stabilize a gender identity consistent with their biological sex. Adults, whose gender identities are less malleable, may pursue a sex change, a complex process of altering the body to conform to one's gender identity. The long-term effectiveness and the ethics of these forms of treatment remain open questions.

FOCUS ON PSYCHOLOGY IN SOCIETY

BOX 10.5 | **Insurance Coverage for Sex-Change Surgery?**

San Francisco Says Yes

This report from *The New York Times* describes the decision by the city of San Francisco to include coverage for sex-change treatment under its health insurance policies.

The city of San Francisco is planning to extend its health insurance to cover sex-change operations for municipal employees.

The Board of Supervisors and Mayor Willie Brown are expected to sign the measure within the next couple of weeks. It will extend up to $50,000 in benefits to city workers who want to switch their gender.

San Francisco may become the only governmental body in the nation to make sex-change benefits available. The state of Minnesota offered such benefits, but the program was phased out in 1998. The issue was discussed in Oregon, but a commission decided against it in 1999.

"I'm very pleased that we're doing it," Tom Ammiano, president of the Board of Supervisors, said today. "We have a noticeable transgender, population in San Francisco, and many are city employees."

The benefits would be available starting July 1.

The benefit would cover male-to-female surgery, which costs about $37,000, as well as female-to-male surgery, which runs about $77,000. It also would cover hormone therapy and other procedures.

Cecilia Chung, a city employee who has had medical problems since sex-change surgery in Thailand two years ago, said she wanted to be first in line to take advantage of the new insurance.

"I've been trying to get the problem corrected, but it's not covered by my regular health insurance," said Ms. Chung, 35, who works for the Department of Public Health.

Transgender advocates said the measure's, symbolism was more valuable than the benefits.

"I think it's really politically important to do that," said Susan Stryker, the executive director of the Gay, Lesbian, Bisexual, Transgender Historical Society of Northern California. "Transgender rights are often considered as a joke: 'What are those wacky San Franciscans going to do next?'"

Ms. Stryker, who had male-to-female surgery 10 years ago, said there were about 15,000 transgendered people in San Francisco.

The term transgender covers a of categories including cross-dressers, transvestites, transsexuals and those born with characteristics of both sexes. Employees would have to work for the city at least one-year before they would be eligible.

"Sex-change coverage to San Francisco workers."
The New York Times, February 28, 2001.

Case Vignettes | Treatment
Laurie | Sexual Dysfunction

Laurie (the 29-year-old, married attorney described at the beginning of the chapter) consulted a sex therapist recommended by her gynecologist after deciding, with her husband, that she wanted to try to do something about her limited enjoyment of sex. The therapist met with Laurie and her husband for two evaluation sessions. She suggested that Laurie's sexual problems could best be addressed by a combination of a focal behavioral sex therapy to address her sexual dysfunction and a more exploratory psychodynamic intervention to

deal with related emotional conflicts about sex. In six sessions with the sex therapist, Laurie was taught sensate focus, relaxation, directed masturbation, and sexual communication techniques. After practicing these techniques, Laurie was more easily able to have orgasms while masturbating, but she still felt inhibited about masturbating and about having sex with her husband. In her concurrent exploratory sessions with a colleague of the sex therapist, Laurie discovered that her inhibitions were related to her need to feel constantly "in control."

She equated sexual arousal and orgasm with "losing control," which felt frightening to her. As Laurie explored this with the therapist, she discovered that her preoccupation with control stemmed from her unresolved anger toward and her childhood fear of her "out-of-control" mother. As Laurie worked out her feelings about her mother, she was able to become a more relaxed, less "driven" person. She began to recognize that she didn't have to feel embarrassed, weak, or scared about feeling emotional or sexually excited. Laurie was able to combine these insights from her exploratory work with the greater sexual responsiveness she had developed from her sessions with the sex therapist. Her husband was very encouraged by these changes, and their sex life improved significantly.

Case Discussion | Sexual Dysfunction

As it turned out, Laurie's sexual difficulties had a psychological basis. Focal sex therapy was helpful, but did not address the emotional conflicts underlying Laurie's sexual inhibitions. Psychodynamic sessions helped Laurie to recognize these conflicts, which in turn allowed her to make better use of the new skills learned in the sex therapy.

Rick | Exhibitionism

Rick (the 28-year-old computer programmer with exhibitionism) was prosecuted following his arrest for indecent exposure. In return for a guilty plea, he was placed on probation and ordered to participate in a state-sponsored group treatment program for sex offenders. Rick was able to keep his family from finding out about his arrest. Once he realized that his "secret" was still safe, Rick's interest in treatment diminished. He had tearfully assured the judge that he desperately wanted to get help for his problem, but after his sentencing he told himself that as soon as he could get his probation officer off of his back by completing the 20-week group therapy he would return, more carefully, to his exhibitionism.

Rick's attitude changed during his first group therapy session. To his surprise, the "experienced" members of the group, all of whom had committed a variety of sex offenses, immediately picked up on Rick's denial of his problem and confronted him. They told him of their own stories of sexual misconduct, denial, repeated arrests, and public humiliation. Rick was horrified to think that he might end up like some of the men in the group—disowned by their families, fired from their jobs, and living marginal lives. In addition, as the men in the group talked about the connections between their personal histories and their sexual misconduct, Rick began to realize that he, too, had some "skeletons in the closet." Rick had been sexually molested by two 14-year-old neighborhood boys when he was

9. Rick had never told anyone about it, and had rarely thought of the experience since. However, when Rick was 14, he had tried to force his younger brother to suck his penis. The brother told their parents; Rick was beaten with a belt by his father, told not to tell anyone else about it, and the incident was never again mentioned in the family. Now, as he heard others tell their stories, Rick realized that he was still affected by these experiences. He knew they were somehow related to his exhibitionism, but he did not understand exactly how.

When the 20-session group treatment came to an end, Rick decided to pursue individual therapy to continue to gain insight into his problems. Rick ended up working with his therapist for several years. During the early part of the therapy, Rick still struggled repeatedly with an irresistible urge to expose himself to women. With his therapist's help, he discovered that the impulse to "act out" was always stimulated by an experience in which he felt humiliated or emasculated. Exposing himself had become a way to reassure himself that he "had the guts" to be successful as a man. Rick discovered that his vulnerability to feeling very easily humiliated did indeed stem from his childhood experience of abuse, and his family's shame and silence about it. By gradually learning to understand these urges, Rick was eventually able to keep himself from acting on them though he still felt a strong desire to do so.

Case Discussion | Exhibitionism

Rick was not highly motivated to change initially. Like many individuals with paraphilias, he wanted to avoid the negative consequences of his behavior while continuing to pursue it. However, the group treatment was effective in confronting Rick's denial of the seriousness of his problem and increasing his motivation to change. Further individual therapy allowed Rick to address the earlier sexual traumas that contributed to his exhibitionism, leading to a more favorable outcome than is the case for most men with exhibitionism.

Phil | Gender Identity Disorder

Phil (the 35-year-old anthropology professor) consulted with a psychologist who was experienced in working with GID and affiliated with a sexual disorders clinic. The psychologist explained to Phil what the sex-change process would entail, and encouraged him to read more about it and to talk to others who had undergone a sex change. As he did so, Phil became even more convinced that he wanted to proceed with a sex change. He felt that he could only be happy living as the woman he felt he was, sharing "girl talk" with close female friends, and having a male sexual partner. Phil applied to the sex-change treatment program. The program began with a psychological evaluation, counseling, and support for the first stage of the process—successfully living as a woman for a year. The psychological evaluation indicated that Phil was emotionally stable and realistically motivated to pursue a sex change.

Phil found this first year "liberating." It began with telling his friends, family, and colleagues about his decision, and most were quite accepting. Phil began female hormone treatment; with daily estrogen doses, he developed breasts, his muscles and skin softened, and he reported that he "felt womanly." Phil met with a team of speech and physical therapists who helped him to learn to talk and move like the woman he was becoming. Electrolysis allowed him to remove his unwanted facial and body hair. By now, Phil easily passed as a woman, yet he felt his change was not complete as long as he had a penis instead of a vagina. He wanted to feel like "a complete, genuine woman able to have a full relationship with a man." Since everything had proceeded well up to this point, Phil was scheduled for sex-change surgery. The surgeon removed Phil's penis and testicles, and fashioned a vaginal pouch using tissue from the male genitals in order to preserve some sexual sensitivity. The surgery was a physical and emotional success. Phil (now Phyllis) finally felt that she had become the woman she was meant to be. Five years later, she was living happily as a woman in a committed relationship with a man, and coping reasonably well with the occasional hostility and discrimination faced by most transsexuals.

Case Discussion | Gender Identity Disorder

Phil was convinced that he could only be happy by transforming himself completely into a woman. Fortunately, he had the emotional and financial resources to successfully pursue and achieve this goal. Phil's GID was treated with a complete sex change process. His positive result was one of the best outcomes achieved for GID by this particular sexual disorders clinic.

Chapter Summary

- *Cultural and historical relativism* regarding sexual norms, the *continuum between normal and abnormal* sexual behavior, and the *importance of context* in sexual behavior all complicate the tasks of defining and classifying abnormal sexuality.

- Currently, the DSM-IV-TR identifies three types of sexual disorders based on symptoms related to disturbances in sexual behavior or gender identity: sexual dysfunctions, paraphilias, and gender identity disorder (GID).

- Sexual dysfunctions are recurrent, distressing, and/or impairing problems in the desire, arousal, or orgasm phases of sexual response. Desire phase dysfunctions include hypoactive sexual desire and sexual aversion. Arousal phase dysfunctions include female arousal disorder and male erectile disorder. Orgasm phase dysfunctions include female and male orgasmic disorders and premature ejaculation. Two sexual pain disorders, vaginismus and dyspareunia, are also listed as sexual dysfuntions. The sexual dysfunctions have a wide variety of psychological and biological causes, and are usually responsive to treatment.

- Paraphilias are recurrent, intense, abnormal sexual preferences that cause distress or impairment. They include: exhibitionism, voyeurism, fetishism, sexual sadism, sexual masochism, pedophilia, and frotteurism. Paraphilias illustrate the principle of *multiple causality* and the *connection between mind and body* in that psychodynamic, behavioral, cognitive, and biological components are involved in their etiology and treatment. Paraphilias are considered difficult to change.

- GID is a severe disturbance in gender identity involving the wish to be the opposite sex and extreme discomfort with one's own sex. The causes of GID are not well understood, although several biological and psychological models have been offered to explain it. Children with GID are generally treated with psychotherapy in an effort to help them better adapt to their biological sex. However, adults with GID may seek sex reasssignment (or sex change) as a treatment for the condition.

Salvador Dali, *The Triangular House,* 1933. ©Private Collection/Art Resource, NY. ©2003 Salvador Dali, Gala-Salvador Dali Foundation/ Artists Rights Society (ARS), New York

■ Spanish born, Salvador Dali (1904–1989) created strikingly bizarre Surrealist paintings rich with symbolic meanings and strangely juxtaposed objects. Despite Dali's reputation as one of the most influential painters in the modern art move-ment, he was almost as famous for his flam-boyant personality ....*continues on page 352*

salvador dali

chapter eleven

PERSONALITY AND THE PERSONALITY DISORDERS

Case Vignettes

Tyler, a 33-year-old medical student, contacted a psychologist at his girlfriend Sarah's urging. She was concerned about his irrational suspiciousness, jealousy, and hostility. Tyler and Sarah had started dating two years earlier. Even at the beginning of the relationship, Sarah knew that Tyler tended to be very suspicious, often distrusting his friends and feeling that for most of his life other people "had it in for me." Over time, Tyler began to doubt Sarah's fidelity. Despite Sarah's commitment to the relationship, Tyler insisted that she was dating other men. Just last month, Tyler angrily confronted one of Sarah's male friends and accused him of having an affair with Sarah. When Sarah attempted to reason with Tyler and reassure him of her loyalty, he said that she was just trying to "trick me again."

Beth, age 28, sought therapy at her university counseling center when she became distressed at the prospect of the upcoming completion of her Ph.D. Beth told her therapist that she felt extremely worried about how she would spend her time after graduation. Despite her high level of academic achievement, Beth had not been able to decide on what kind of career interested her and thus had not applied for a single job. Beth was tempted by her parent's suggestion that she come home to live with them for as long as she wanted. She spoke fondly of how much her mother and father cared for her, and how they had continued to come by campus to do her laundry, clean her apartment, and pay her bills throughout college and graduate school. Beth had been living with college friends throughout graduate school. She was hoping that another friend might invite her to move in with her after graduation but Beth knew that her friends felt a little overburdened by her constant need for support. In fact, she looked to them for advice on everything from deciding what classes to take, what clothes to wear to class, what she should eat for lunch, and which guys she should like.

DEFINING PERSONALITY AND THE PERSONALITY DISORDERS

Tyler and Beth both exhibit extreme *personality traits*—Tyler is overly suspicious and Beth is overly dependent. **Personality traits** are patterns of inner experience and behavior that are relatively stable across time. Unlike *symptoms,* traits do not come and go. For example, you may have a friend who is highly intelligent (trait) and who sometimes gets depressed (symptom). Another friend who is very assertive (trait), may experience occasional episodes of intense anxiety (symptom). The dis-

Personality traits Behavioral tendencies that are relatively stable across time and place.

...continued from page 350

and skill at self-publicity as he was for his art. Dali's histrionic behavior included arriving at an event in a limousine filled with cauliflower and wearing a deep-sea diving suit to the opening of the London Surrealist exhibit in 1936.

Ego-dystonic Behaviors, thoughts, or feelings that are experienced by an individual as distressing and unwelcome.

Ego-syntonic Behavior, thoughts, or feelings that are experienced by an individual as consistent with his or her sense of self.

Personality disorders Disorders characterized by extreme and rigid personality traits that cause distress or impairment.

Personality An individual's unique and stable way of experiencing the world that is reflected in a predictable set of reactions to a variety of situations.

tinction between traits and symptoms goes back to early psychodynamic theorists who noted that emotional conflicts could be expressed either in symptoms, which the individual experiences as unwanted, uncomfortable, and inconsistent with their sense of self (**ego-dystonic**), or in personality traits, which are consistent with the individual's sense of self, (**ego-syntonic**). While the difference between symptoms and traits is not entirely clear-cut (for example, is a "depressive person" manifesting a symptom or a trait?), it is a helpful and widely used distinction. As you recall, the difference between traits and symptoms is the basis of the distinction between Axis I and Axis II in the modern DSM system: symptom disorders are classified on Axis I, and trait-based disorders are classified on Axis II. The primary trait-based disorders are known as the **personality disorders,** and the DSM-IV-TR currently includes 10 different personality disorders. (The only other disorders classified on Axis II of the DSM-IV-TR are various forms of mental retardation.) All other psychological disorders categorized by the DSM-IV-TR are classified on Axis I (see Chapter 4 for more information on multiaxial classification in the DSM).

Before we begin to explore the nature of abnormal personality, it is important to consider some questions about personality in general. Does such a thing as stable personality exist, or are people's thoughts, feelings, and behaviors simply reactions to the shifting characteristics of their environments? If there is such a thing as personality, can it be measured? Can personality traits be reliably described and categorized? Most personality researchers agree that individuals *do* have relatively stable personality traits that can be measured and categorized. Experts define **personality** as an individual's unique and stable way of experiencing the world that is reflected in a predictable set of reactions to a variety of situations (Costa & McCrae, 1989).

In general, the personality disorders are characterized by rigid, extreme, and maladaptive personality traits. In other words, people with personality disorders behave in ways that do not fit with accepted social standards and they are unable to adapt their behaviors to better suit their environments. The DSM-IV-TR provides the following definition of a personality disorder: "an enduring pattern of inner experience and behavior that deviates markedly from the expectations of the individual's culture, is pervasive and inflexible, has an onset in adolescence or early adulthood, is stable over time, and leads to distress or impairment" (APA, 2000).

The Continuum Between Normal and Abnormal Personality

Many of the traits associated with personality disorders are exaggerated versions of normal traits. For example, we all feel preoccupied with ourselves and our own self-interest at times, but in the extreme such behavior characterizes one of the personality disorders: *narcissistic personality disorder*. Similarly, most people need emotional support and reassurance from time to time, but people with *dependent personality disorder* have a chronic and excessive need for reassurance and caretaking. Thus, like most other disorders, the personality disorders represent an extreme end of the ***continuum between normal and abnormal behavior***. When trying to determine where to draw the line between normal and abnormal personality, it is crucial to consider how extreme, rigid, and maladaptive an individual's personality traits are. For example, Beth (described in one of the chapter-opening case vignettes) is so dependent upon other people that she seems to be unable to care for herself, and she is extremely upset about what she will do when graduate school ends; her dependence upon others impairs her functioning. The case of Beth also illustrates the ego-syntonic quality of personality disorders. Beth is not distressed by her dependency—she is only distressed that others will not meet her dependency needs! In some cases, people with personality disorders are aware of and concerned about their extreme traits, but in general they are unlikely to seek treatment and can be difficult to help when they do, as we will discuss later in the chapter (see Box 11.2, page 381, Focus on Research: Psychotherapy Outcome Studies).

Brief Summary

- Unlike symptoms, personality traits are patterns of inner experience and behavior that are relatively stable across time.

- Personality is considered to be disordered when personality traits are maladaptive, rigid, and extreme.

- Most of the traits associated with personality disorders occur on a **continuum between normal and abnormal behavior.** Personality disorders usually involve extreme versions of common personality traits.

Critical Thinking Question | Tyler's suspicious behavior (described in one of the chapter-opening case vignettes) makes sense to him (it's ego-syntonic) but does not make sense to his girlfriend. Why might Tyler be unable to see his behavior as irrational?

Going to extremes Personality disorders are diagnosed when personality traits are rigid, extreme, and maladaptive. Feeling occasionally clingy with a loved one is very different from chronic and extreme clinginess, a trait associated with dependent personality disorder.

CLASSIFYING, EXPLAINING, AND TREATING PERSONALITY DISORDERS

As noted previously, the DSM-IV-TR currently includes 10 personality disorders (see Table 11.1). The 10 DSM-IV-TR personality disorders are grouped into three *clusters* based on some common features:

- *Cluster A* (odd or eccentric) includes *paranoid, schizoid,* and *schizotypal* personality disorders.

- *Cluster B* (dramatic, emotional, or erratic) includes *antisocial, borderline, histrionic,* and *narcissistic* personality disorders.

- *Cluster C* (anxious or fearful) includes *avoidant, dependent,* and *obsessive-compulsive* personality disorders.

Cluster A: Odd or Eccentric Personality Disorders

Paranoid Personality Disorder

People with **paranoid personality disorder** believe, in almost all situations, that other people are "out to get" them. They frequently assume that they are being talked about maliciously, that other people are attempting to take advantage of them, or that they are being betrayed by their friends or lovers. In some cases, there may be a grain of truth in their suspicions, as suggested by the aphorism that "even paranoids sometimes have real enemies." But in paranoid personality disorder the suspicions are enormously exaggerated, or, if they are warranted, they are usually provoked by the paranoid individual's hostile behavior. Paranoid personality disorder differs from paranoid schizophrenia (Chapter 12) in that people with paranoid personality disorder are sufficiently in touch with reality to be able to function in daily life, sometimes at a very high level (see Table 11.2).

Paranoid personality disorder Personality traits involving extreme distrust and suspiciousness.

Table 11.1 | **The DSM-IV-TR Personality Disorders**

Adapted from DSM-IV-TR (APA, 2000; prevalence data from APA, 2000; Torgersen, Kringlen, & Cramer, 2001)

Paranoid personality disorder ▪ A pattern of extreme distrust and suspiciousness (lifetime prevalence estimate: 0.5%–2.5% of the population).

Schizoid personality disorder ▪ A pattern of detachment from social relationships and a restricted range of emotional expression (lifetime prevalence estimate: 0.8%).

Schizotypal personality disorder ▪ A pattern of eccentricities of behavior, cognitive or perceptual distortions, and acute discomfort in close relationships (lifetime prevalence estimate: 3%).

Antisocial personality disorder ▪ A pattern of disregard for, and violation of, the rights of others (lifetime prevalence estimate: 2%).

Borderline personality disorder ▪ A pattern of instability in interpersonal relationships, self-image, and emotions, impulsivity, and self-destructive behavior (lifetime prevalence estimate: 2%).

Histrionic personality disorder ▪ A pattern of excessive, superficial emotionality and attention seeking (lifetime prevalence estimate: 2%–3%).

Narcissistic personality disorder ▪ A pattern of grandiosity, need for admiration, and lack of empathy (lifetime prevalence estimate: less than 1%).

Avoidant personality disorder ▪ A pattern of social inhibition, feelings of inadequacy, and hypersensitivity to negative evaluation (lifetime prevalence estimate: 0.5%–1.0%).

Dependent personality disorder ▪ A pattern of submissive and clinging behavior related to an excessive need to be cared for by others (lifetime prevalence estimate: 2%).

Obsessive-compulsive personality disorder ▪ A pattern of preoccupation with orderliness, perfectionism, and control at the expense of spontaneity, flexibility, and enjoyment (lifetime prevalence estimate: 1%).

Presidential paranoia Those close to Richard Nixon were familiar with his paranoid view of the world. He trusted few people, even in his inner circle, and surrounded himself with "yes-men" who refused to challenge him.

Case Illustration Jennifer, age 29, is convinced that her coworkers gossip about her when she is not around. Despite the fact that her colleagues are quite friendly, Jennifer is sure that their kindness is just a "front" and that they are secretly plotting ways to make her look bad in front of her boss. Recently, Jennifer discovered that she was missing some pages from an important presentation she'd been preparing for months. Though her coworkers offered to help her look for the missing pages, Jennifer was convinced that one of them had stolen the pages in order to undermine her presentation. Jennifer had left her last job abruptly when she decided that she could no longer stand the "horrible backstabbing" that went on around the company. At that job, Jennifer was passed over for a promotion that ultimately went to a pleasant but slightly less competent colleague. Jennifer confronted her boss, accused him of sabotaging her chances of promotion, and then quit. Ever since childhood, Jennifer was given to angry outbursts, and she was acutely sensitive to her parents' and teachers' moods. For example, when she sensed that one of her teachers was in a bad mood, Jennifer would decide that the teacher no longer liked her; Jennifer would then become cold and hostile toward the teacher. She has always had trouble maintaining relationships because she invariably becomes jealous, suspicious, and vengeful.

Diagnostic Criteria for Paranoid Personality Disorder	Table 11.2

Adapted from DSM-IV-TR (APA, 2000)

A *pervasive distrust and suspiciousness* of others such that their motives are interpreted as malevolent, beginning by early adulthood and present in a variety of contexts, as indicated by four (or more) of the following:

- Suspects, without sufficient basis, that others are exploiting, harming, or deceiving him or her.
- Is preoccupied with unjustified doubts about the loyalty or trustworthiness of friends or associates.
- Is reluctant to confide in others because of unwarranted fear that the information will be used maliciously against him or her.
- Reads hidden demeaning or threatening meanings into benign remarks or events.
- Persistently bears grudges; that is, is unforgiving of insults, injuries, or slights.
- Perceives attacks on his or her character or reputation that are not apparent to others and is quick to react angrily or to counterattack.
- Has recurrent suspicions, without justification, regarding fidelity of spouse or sexual partner.

Like Jennifer, people with paranoid personality disorder tend to assume that others have hostile motives and cannot be trusted, even in the absence of objective evidence to confirm such suspicions. It is common for people with paranoid personality disorder to have difficulty in relationships because they are often antagonistic, full of complaints, or highly guarded and emotionally withdrawn (APA, 2000). A hallmark of paranoid personality disorder is the tendency to "take things the wrong way." People with this disorder often hear criticism or condescension where it does not exist and then go on to hold extended grudges in reaction to imagined or unintentional insults or slights. At times, the reaction to perceived slights may go beyond a mere grudge and may take the form of an angry, defensive outburst. Most people with paranoid personality disorder are acutely attentive to cues in their environments, but tend to distort information to support their own paranoid ideas (Shapiro, 1965). For example, as a child Jennifer may have been accurate in her perception that her teacher was sometimes in a bad mood. However, she was probably quite wrong in her assumption that her teacher had developed a sudden dislike of her.

Explaining and Treating Paranoid Personality Disorder

Personality disorders, like personality in general, are currently believed to result from the interaction of the psychosocial experiences during childhood and inherited temperamental traits. Psychodynamic perspectives, which emphasize the lasting effects of early experiences, have dominated the explanation of personality disorders for many years. More recently, cognitive-behavioral and biological approaches have offered important perspectives on explaining and treating personality disorders. We'll begin by describing the cognitive-behavioral and psychodynamic approaches to personality disorders in general and then proceed to specific explanations of particular personality disorders. Summary tables of the psychodynamic, cognitive-behavioral, and biological perspectives on personality disorders are provided at the end of this section (Tables 11.12, 11.13, & 11.14).

Cognitive-Behavioral Components
In general, cognitive-behavioral approaches to personality disorders view people's beliefs and expectancies as the basis for the stable aspects

of behavior we call personality. In "normal" individuals, these beliefs and expectancies are relatively flexible and adaptive, while in personality disorders they have become rigid and maladaptive. In other words, people with personality disorders impose rigid preexisting beliefs on almost every situation, have difficulty questioning their beliefs, and will continue to act on their beliefs even when such behavior is self-defeating (Beck & Freeman, 1990).

Cognitive schemas Mental models of the world that are used to organize information

The cognitive-behavioral perspective on personality disorders holds that personality disorders often develop out of early life experiences. According to Aaron Beck, childhood experiences establish fixed thought patterns (**cognitive schemas**) that shape interpersonal behavioral strategies and influence how people perceive and interpret all subsequent experiences (Pretzer & Beck, 1996). When maladaptive cognitive schemas are formed early in life, they often persist because "individuals tend to selectively attend to experiences that are consistent with their preconceptions and to be biased toward interpreting their experiences as confirming these preconceptions" (Pretzer & Beck, 1996, p. 64). For example, a person who was taught by his or her parents that other people can't be trusted might recall every example of having been taken advantage of and forget times when he or she was treated fairly. In this way, a person might develop traits associated with paranoid personality disorder.

Cognitive-behavioral approaches to the personality disorders also focus on how maladaptive beliefs and behavioral strategies become self-perpetuating through "self-fulfilling prophecies." In other words, people with personality disorders hold certain interpersonal beliefs, act in accordance with those beliefs in such a way as to influence others to respond accordingly, and then perceive others' responses as evidence in support of their beliefs (see Figure 11.1 for a graphic representation of this cycle in paranoid personality disorder). For example, an overly suspicious, paranoid man might anger his friends with his constant doubts about their loyalty. Unfortunately, the paranoid man will likely see their anger as proof that his friends cannot be trusted.

Cognitive-behavioral interventions for personality disorders aim to identify and challenge distorted cognitive schemas, and to help alter maladaptive behavioral patterns. Not surprisingly, people with paranoid personality disorder are often reluctant to have their perceptions challenged by a therapist, and they may see such challenges as evidence that the therapist is also "against" them. As a result, cognitive interventions for people with paranoid traits do not aim to alter the client's fundamental

Figure 11.1 Cognitive Conceptualization of Paranoid Personality Disorder. As you can see in this model, paranoid assumptions lead to interpersonal behavior that elicits confirmatory responses from others.

Adapted from Freeman et al., 1990, p. 161

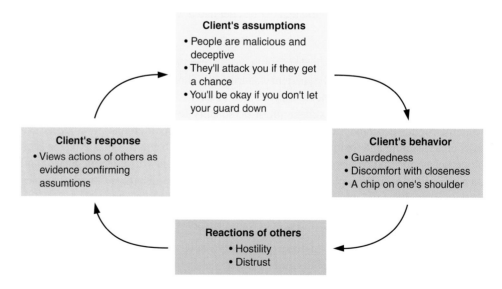

assumptions (that people are malicious and cannot be trusted) but instead encourage the client to evaluate the threat posed by particular situations and his or her capacity for coping with these situations (Freeman et al., 1990). For example, a paranoid person might be helped to recognize that a neighbor who is "out to get him" probably won't resort to violence or do anything else to seriously undermine the client. When clients feel that external threats are less pernicious than originally thought, they may be open to reevaluating their assumption that people are generally malevolent. In the following description Gary, a paranoid man, reconsiders his dichotomous view that people are either fully trustworthy or untrustworthy:

> Once he delineated the behaviors that he saw as being characteristic of truly trustworthy and completely untrustworthy individuals and considered whether his acquaintances completely fit into one category or the other, it became clear that few people actually fell at either extreme... When this was followed by raising the question of whether his (consistently malevolent) family was typical of people in general, he was able to gradually risk trusting colleagues and acquaintances in small things and was pleasantly surprised to discover that the world at large was much less malevolent than he had believed.
>
> Freeman et al., 1990 (p. 168)

Psychodynamic Components The psychodynamic perspective on personality disorders in general focuses primarily on two areas—problematic childhood relationships and maladaptive defense mechanisms. For example, from a psychodynamic perspective, paranoid personality disorder often begins with repeated childhood experiences of humiliation, criticism, and ridicule (McWilliams, 1994). Such family histories are believed to foster the "attacking" style of the paranoid adult who is often hostile toward others because he or she anticipates being criticized or hurt by them (Nydes, 1963). At the same time, people with paranoid personality disorder often have a distorted view of others due to their frequent and extreme use of the defense mechanism of **projection.** They unconsciously attribute their own hostile feelings to others and then feel threatened and react accordingly. Psychodynamic clinicians also emphasize that paranoid personality disorder involves the paradoxical combination of feelings of inferiority and self-centeredness. A paranoid person focuses on his or her own weaknesses and how they might be exploited. Concurrently, paranoid individuals assume that other people are intently focused on them and their weaknesses.

Projection A defense mechanism in which an individual attributes his or her own unacceptable emotions to someone or something else.

The psychodynamic concept of *transference,* the phenomenon by which patterns from other relationships are repeated in the therapy relationship, is especially relevant in the treatment of the personality disorders. For example, a paranoid person who goes to psychotherapy may quickly become suspicious of what his or her therapist is "really" thinking. When these feelings, thoughts, and interaction patterns occur (or are "transferred") into the relationship with the therapist, the client and therapist can try to understand and change the client's inappropriate expectations and distortions. The therapist will also address these problematic patterns as they appear in other relationships described by the client.

The psychodynamic emphasis on the importance of the *therapeutic alliance*—a positive, collaborative bond between client and therapist—can pose special challenges for psychotherapy with clients suffering from personality disorders, since people with personality disorders tend to have significant interpersonal difficulties. For example, people with paranoid personality disorder are often extremely uncomfortable in the role of a client and may be reluctant to trust their therapists with information that feels personal or sensitive. Indeed, it is a major therapeutic achievement when a paranoid client begins to believe that a therapist's expressions of interest and concern are benign and genuine (McWilliams, 1994).

Brief Summary

- The cognitive-behavioral perspective on personality and personality disorders emphasizes that childhood experiences shape thought patterns (cognitive schemas), establish interpersonal strategies, and influence the patterns of perception and behavior that become personality traits. Parents influence personality development through direct instruction and by modeling behavior. Cognitive-behavioral interventions for paranoid personality disorder focus on the maladaptive beliefs and behaviors that perpetuate a cycle of paranoia.

- The psychodynamic perspective on personality disorders in general emphasizes disruptive early childhood experiences with caretakers and a reliance on maladaptive defense mechanisms. In paranoid personality disorder, parental criticism and ridicule, and the extreme use of projection, are thought to be central factors.

Schizoid Personality Disorder

Schizoid personality disorder Personality traits involving detachment from social relationships and a restricted range of emotional expression.

Schizoid personality disorder is characterized by emotional detachment and a lack of interest in personal relationships—extending even to indifference toward relationships with family members or potential sexual partners. People who suffer from this disorder are usually considered to be "loners," although unlike people with *autism* and *Asperger's disorder* (which are also characterized, in part, by social and emotional detachment; see Chapter 13) they can function adequately in social situations when they need to. However, people with schizoid personality disorder tend to keep to themselves, enjoy a very limited range of interests, and are detached to the point of seeming emotionless (see Table 11.3).

> **Case Illustration** Jenine has spent most of her life doing things alone. Even though she grew up in a neighborhood where children played games at the local park after school, she preferred to spend afternoons watching television by herself or working on her computer. She expressed little interest in making friends in high school and, to her parent's surprise, did not seem to mind the fact that she never went to a school dance or out on a date. Currently employed at a factory, she has one friend who will sometimes call and ask her to go to video gaming, but otherwise Jenine spends her spare time reading or

Table 11.3	Diagnostic Criteria for Schizoid Personality Disorder
Adapted from DSM-IV-TR (APA, 2000)	A pervasive pattern of *detachment from social relationships and a restricted range of expression of emotions* in interpersonal settings, beginning by early adulthood and present in a variety of contexts, as indicated by four (or more) of the following: • Neither desires nor enjoys close relationships, including being part of a family. • Almost always chooses solitary activities. • Has little, if any, interest in having sexual experiences with another person. • Takes pleasure in few, if any, activities. • Lacks close friends or confidants other than first-degree relatives. • Appears indifferent to the praise or criticism of others. • Shows emotional coldness, detachment, or flattened affect.

watching television. Jenine's parents are quite upset about her limited social life but they are aware that she does not seem to be particularly sad or joyful about anything, including the fact that she spends most of her time by herself.

Like Jenine, most people with schizoid personality disorder appear to be indifferent to interpersonal relationships. They appear to be unemotional and often try to spend as much time alone as possible. In most cases, people with schizoid personality disorder have few, if any, friendships and do not seem to derive any pleasure from spending time with people (APA, 2000). Occasionally, they may be drawn into a relationship by an extremely gregarious person, but they will likely remain passive and indifferent with regard to the relationship as they seem to have a fundamental inability to sense what other people feel and want (Millon & Davis, 1996). They tend to seek out vocations that do not involve interpersonal contact, such as programming computers or working as a nighttime security guard. Indeed, people with schizoid personality disorder may flourish in careers that reward long hours of solitary work.

Explaining and Treating Schizoid Personality Disorder

Recent evidence suggests that some of the personality disorders, including schizoid personality disorder, may involve a significant biological component. Accordingly we'll begin our explanation of the causes and treatments for schizoid personality disorder with a look at the biological perspective and then turn our attention to the disorder's psychodynamic and cognitive-behavioral components.

Biological Components While personality disorders are usually explained in terms of psychosocial influences (for example, family relationships) on personality development, many normal personality traits have a substantial genetic basis, and the same may be true of abnormal personality traits. Research on **temperament**—innate behavioral tendencies that are present at birth—indicates that some personality disorders may result from an interaction between genetically determined temperament and specific environmental influences. For example, some evidence suggests that babies who are born with highly sensitive and easily over-stimulated temperaments might "pull back" emotionally from caregivers who are too active or intrusive (Thomas, Chess, & Birch, 1970; Winnicott, 1965). This kind of temperament, sometimes referred to as "difficult" temperament, has been linked with schizoid and schizotypal (described subsequently) personality disorders (Coid, 1999).

Temperament Innate behavioral tendencies.

Withdrawal A defense mechanism in which an individual retreats from emotional engagement with others.

Intellectualization A defense mechanism in which a detached rational approach is used to protect against upsetting emotions.

Psychodynamic Components Psychodynamic theorists view schizoid personality disorder as a defensive **withdrawal** from full human connectedness and feeling, in response to the expectation of overwhelming pain in relationships (Joseph, 1989; Klein, 1946). Difficult early attachments to parental figures are assumed to have carried forward to adulthood, where relationships are seen as distressing, not pleasurable, and are consequently avoided. Some psychodynamic clinicians have also suggested that ambiguous or perplexing parental communications which leave children unsure about how to appropriately attach to and engage important emotional figures may contribute to the development of schizoid personality disorder (Searles, 1959). In keeping with the *principle of multiple causality*, schizoid traits might emerge from an unfortunate combination of a child's biological predisposition to a "difficult" temperament in combination with a painful relationship with his or her parents.

In addition to *withdrawal*, the defense mechanism of **intellectualization** is also associated with schizoid traits (McWilliams, 1994). In intellectualization, emotions and emotional experiences are thought about, not felt, thus accounting for the "cold fish" style in people with schizoid personality disorder. People with schizoid personality disorder rarely seek therapy of their own accord, but when they do, psychodynamic interventions emphasize patience and careful attention to clear interpersonal boundaries as a way to help a person with schizoid traits feel safe in a psychotherapy relationship (Hammer, 1990; Robbins, 1988).

Cognitive-Behavioral Components As described earlier, the cognitive-behavioral perspective on personality disorders in general emphasizes rigid and maladaptive beliefs and expectancies, fixed thought patterns, and self-defeating and self-perpetuating behavioral strategies. People with schizoid personality disorder tend to think of themselves as "loners" and to value their seclusion from others. While they may notice that other people derive pleasure from interpersonal relationships, people with schizoid personality are unresponsive to, or have difficulty interpreting, emotional cues from others. As a result, they are inclined to believe that human involvement is unnecessarily complicated and painful (Beck & Freeman, 1990). Thus, they isolate themselves and withdraw into their own private mental lives to avoid pain; the comfort they experience when alone negatively reinforces their withdrawal behavior.

Schizotypal Personality Disorder

Schizotypal personality disorder Personality traits involving eccentricities of behavior, cognitive or perceptual distortions, and acute discomfort in close relationships.

Psychotic Out of contact with reality, such as experiencing hallucinations or delusions.

Schizotypal personality disorder is characterized by a pervasive, chronic, and dysfunctional eccentricity in behavior, appearance, and thinking. People with this disorder tend to be anxious, suspicious, socially awkward, and somewhat isolated. They also have some of the thought and perceptual disturbances associated with schizophrenia, a **psychotic** disorder (Chapter 12), and genetic and biological evidence suggests that schizotypal personality disorder may, in fact, be closely related to schizophrenia (Kendler & Gardner, 1997). However, while people with schizotypal personality disorder have distinctly odd thoughts, perceptions, and behaviors, they are not out of touch with reality, as a psychotic person would be (see Table 11.4).

Table 11.4	Diagnostic Criteria for Schizotypal Personality Disorder
Adapted from DSM-IV-TR (APA, 2000)	A pervasive pattern of *social and interpersonal deficits* marked by acute discomfort with, and reduced capacity for, close relationships as well as by *cognitive or perceptual distortions and eccentricities of behavior,* beginning by early adulthood and present in a variety of contexts, as indicated by five (or more) of the following: • The feeling that casual incidents and external events have a particular and unusual self-referential meaning (ideas of reference). • Odd beliefs or magical thinking that influence behavior and are inconsistent with subcultural norms (for example, suspiciousness, belief in clairvoyance, etc.). • Unusual perceptual experiences, including bodily illusions. • Suspiciousness or paranoid ideas. • Inappropriate or constricted affect. • Behavior or appearance that is odd, eccentric, or peculiar. • Lack of close friends or confidants other than first-degree relatives. • Excessive social anxiety that does not diminish with familiarity and tends to be associated with paranoid fears rather than feeling negatively about oneself.

Case Illustration Martin has always been considered somewhat eccentric. As a teenager he developed a habit of dressing in colors that he felt characterized his mood for the day. When in a good mood he would wear clothes that were all yellow or all red; when feeling down he wore all blue or all black. Martin also believed that the color of his clothing could influence the moods of others—if a sad person saw Martin wearing red, Martin imagined that the person would cheer up. After finishing high school, Martin went to work at a convenience store near his home, and he lost contact with his few friends from school. Though he liked the job he often felt quite uncomfortable around customers because he suspected that they said mean things about him when they left the store. For a while, Martin developed a crush on a woman named Shelia, one of his coworkers at the convenience store, but his strange behavior and ideas put her off. He wrote her long and rambling love letters that never seemed to come to a point and told her that he was sure that they were meant for each other because they both chose the same kind of employment. After a while, Shelia complained to her manager about Martin's odd attempts at courtship. When confronted by the manager, Martin agreed to "back off" but continued, for several years, to hope that he could make Shelia develop an interest in him by thinking nice thoughts about her every day.

Strange habits People suffering from schizotypal personality disorder dress and conduct themselves in ways that are odd, eccentric, or peculiar.

Schizotypal personality disorder shares several features with both paranoid and schizoid personality disorder. Like people with paranoid personality disorder, people with schizotypal personality disorder tend to be suspicious of others and distrusting of their motives, and fail to develop close relationships, even with people they know well. Like people with schizoid personality disorder, those with schizotypal personality disorder frequently lack interest in or understanding of close relationships and have a constricted range of emotions. However, the disorder differs from the paranoid and schizoid personality disorders in that it is characterized by strange or eccentric thinking, appearance, and behavior. **Ideas of reference**—beliefs that normal events contain special, personal meanings—and **magical thinking**—the idea that one can control events with thoughts—are common in schizotypal personality disorder. For example, a person with this disorder might believe that he had caused a rain shower by making a plan to rent the movie *Singing in the Rain.* People with this disorder often have strange patterns of speech, such as being excessively vague or circumstantial, or they may use words in unusual ways (for example, saying that one is "underready" to take on a new task) (APA, 2000).

Ideas of reference Idiosyncratic beliefs that normal events contain "special" meanings.

Magical thinking Believing that one's thoughts influence external events.

Explaining and Treating Schizotypal Personality Disorder

Like schizoid personality disorder, schizotypal personality disorder appears to have a significant genetic component. As noted earlier, research evidence suggests that schizotypal personality disorder and schizophrenia share a common genetic basis, even though the specific genes involved in each of these disorders have not yet been identified.

Biological Components People who suffer from schizotypal personality disorder have some of the structural and functional brain abnormalities typically seen in schizophrenia. For example, a study comparing the *ventricles* (fluid-filled spaces within the brain) of people with schizophrenia, people with schizotypal personality disorder, and normal individuals found that the left frontal lobe ventricles were significantly enlarged in schizophrenics, somewhat less enlarged among people with schizotypal personality disorder, and of normal size in the unaffected research participants (Buschsbaum et al., 1997). Further, people suffering from schizotypal personality disorder share many of the same neurotransmitter abnormalities seen among people suffering from schizophrenia (Siever, 1995; Walker, Logan, & Walder, 1999) and are at an increased risk for developing schizophrenia (Miller et al., 2002). Antipsychotic drugs which are typically used to treat schizophrenia have been found, in low doses, to help clients with schizotypal personality disorder control their unusual thoughts and perceptions (Coccaro, 1998).

Cognitive-Behavioral Components While schizotypal personality disorder may have a substantially genetic basis, the disorder is characterized by a particular cognitive style. People with schizotypal personality disorder make strange connections among disparate phenomena and have highly idiosyncratic views of causal relationships (such as Martin's belief that the color of one's clothes can alter another person's mood) (Millon & Davis, 2000). People with schizotypal personality disorder have poor interpersonal relationships, largely because they have unusual thought patterns and difficulty reading interpersonal cues. Not surprisingly, schizotypal personality disorder presents a challenge for cognitive interventions which use reason, logic, and objective evaluation to examine maladaptive thought patterns. Cognitive-behavioral interventions for schizotypal personality disorder tend to focus on improving social skills and social problem solving (Freeman et al., 1990).

Cluster B: Dramatic, Emotional, or Erratic Personality Disorders

Antisocial Personality Disorder

Antisocial personality disorder Personality traits involving profound disregard for, and violation of, the rights of others.

People with **antisocial personality disorder** are not "antisocial" in the everyday vernacular sense of avoiding social contact. Rather, the term "antisocial" indicates a profound disregard for other people's rights. People with antisocial personality disorder focus solely on their own interests and do so at the expense of others. A critical feature of this disorder is lack of remorse: individuals with the disorder feel little, if any, guilt about their misbehavior. When confronted about their misdeeds they typically feel angry about being accused, not apologetic for their actions. It is important to note that while antisocial behavior often involves criminal acts, not all criminals suffer from antisocial personality disorder; criminal acts can be committed by people who do not have the pervasive, long-standing personality patterns that characterize antisocial personality disorder (see Table 11.5).

Table 11.5	**Diagnostic Criteria for Antisocial Personality Disorder**
Adapted from DSM-IV-TR (APA, 2000)	A pervasive pattern of *disregard for and violation of the rights of others,* beginning in childhood or adolescence and continuing into adulthood, as indicated by three or more of the following: • Failure to conform to social norms with respect to lawful behaviors as indicated by repeatedly performing acts that are grounds for arrest. • Deceitfulness, as indicated by repeated lying, use of aliases, or conning others for personal profit or pleasure. • Impulsivity or failure to plan ahead. • Irritability or aggressiveness, as indicated by repeated physical fights or assaults. • Reckless disregard for safety of self or others. • Consistent irresponsibility, as indicated by repeated failure to sustain consistent work behavior or to honor financial obligations. • Lack of remorse, as indicated by being indifferent to or rationalizing having hurt, mistreated, or stolen from another person.

Case Illustration When the police arrested Nick, a 24-year-old unemployed man, for mugging a 65-year-old woman as she walked home from church, he denied that he had been anywhere near her neighborhood and seemed appalled at the implication that he might have committed a crime. As the investigation continued the police discovered that Nick had a long history of similar crimes, and they also found two eyewitnesses to the mugging. When confronted with this evidence, Nick admitted that he had mugged the woman, explaining that he needed the money to visit a friend. When the police asked why he had hit a defenseless 65-year-old woman, Nick stated matter-of-factly that she had hesitated too long before handing over her purse. Nick was convicted and jailed, and in prison he quickly developed a reputation for having an uncanny ability to get his way. For example, Nick charmed one of the guards into buying him a carton of cigarettes each week in exchange for Nick's promise that he would exert his influence to keep order among the other prisoners. When one of the supervisory staff became aware of the contraband cigarettes, Nick did not hesitate to turn in the guard who purchased the cigarettes in order to avoid being punished himself.

Grinning criminals Gary Gilmore arrives at court on December 1, 1976 for a hearing to set the date of his execution. Gilmore was convicted of killing two men. The smirk on his face exemplifies the lack of remorse that is one of the features of antisocial personality disorder.

While the DSM-IV-TR criteria highlight the criminal aspects of antisocial behavior, personality disorder experts point out that people with antisocial traits do not necessarily break laws. In fact, they can flourish in careers that require a "take no prisoners" and "look out for number one" approach (Millon & Davis, 1996, p. 429). Experts do emphasize, however, that people with antisocial personality disorder are emotionally callous and indifferent to accepted social morality. Such individuals have no compunction about lying, manipulating, and taking advantage of others. They may be aggressive, impulsive, and quick-tempered, sometimes leading to assaultive behavior. But a central feature of the disorder is the lack of regard or empathic concern for others' rights or feelings. In his book, *Shot in the Heart,* Mikal Gilmore includes the following description of the childhood activities of his brother, Gary Gilmore, who became infamous as an adult for committing two senseless murders and being put to death in 1977.

> One day Gary and a couple of other toughs pantsed some guy in the school yard. They held him down and pulled his pants and shorts off him and ran them up the flagpole… Gary didn't do it for any reason except to be funny. But I could see right then, there was a cruel streak developing in him. Ripping some poor guy's shorts off and running them up the flagpole, leaving the guy standing there in his buff, trying to find something to cover himself with. That wouldn't have been much fun. The guy was a nice guy. He was someone I got along with.
>
> Gilmore, 1994 (p. 132)

Explaining and Treating Antisocial Personality Disorder

The high social costs of antisocial personality traits have fostered a great deal of research on the causes of and treatments for the disorder. Explanations of antisocial personality disorder provide an especially good illustration of the ***principle of multiple causality***, since current evidence suggests that biological, cognitive, psychodynamic, and sociocultural factors interact to cause the disturbing behavior associated with this disorder.

Biological Components Research has demonstrated that antisocial personality disorder may involve a deficiency in normal anxiety reactions (see Box 5.1, "Too Little Anxiety?"). Actions that would make most people uncomfortably anxious, such as committing a violent crime, are not anxiety provoking to a person with antisocial traits. In other words, people with antisocial personality disorder fall at the other end of the anxiety continuum from people who are over-anxious and vulnerable to anxiety disorders (Patrick, Bradley,

Interacting risk factors Biological causes of antisocial personality disorder may interact with broader sociocultural factors. For example, in utero drug exposure appears to be linked with childhood aggression, and mothers who abuse drugs while pregnant are more likely to live in poor, crime-ridden neighborhoods where children are just as likely to play with guns as they are to play with bikes.

& Lang, 1993). While the cause of this "anxiety deficiency" is not fully understood at present, researchers generally assume that it has a genetic basis.

Another biological perspective on antisocial personality disorder draws on research findings that prenatal drug exposure leads to negative social, psychological, and academic outcomes. In utero exposure to cocaine, nicotine, marijuana, and a variety of other drugs has been linked to attention-deficit problems, impulsivity, and delinquency in childhood (Goldschmidt, Day, & Richardson, 2000; Mayes, 1999; Wakschlag et al., 2002). Unfortunately, mothers who abuse substances while pregnant are also more likely to mistreat their children, have large families, have closely spaced pregnancies, and be poor. In keeping with the ***principle of multiple causality*** these factors, especially in combination, further increase the risk of antisocial behavior in their children (Olds et al., 1998).

One study evaluated anxiety impairment and structural brain abnormalities in antisocial personality disorder by comparing men with the disorder with men in three comparison groups: men who had no diagnosis, men who were substance dependent, and men with other psychiatric diagnoses. The prefrontal white and gray brain matter of the antisocial research participants was significantly smaller than that of members of all three comparison groups. In turn, small prefrontal gray matter volumes were associated with lower rates of skin conductance (a measure of anxiety) during a stressful social interaction (Raine et al., 2000).

Some researchers have speculated that people with antisocial personality disorder feel chronically under-stimulated and engage in dangerous or risky behaviors partly in order to raise their level of physiological arousal. Paradoxically, anxiety-reducing and mood-stabilizing drugs have been found to decrease antisocial behaviors in some people with antisocial personality disorder (Moleman, van Dam, & Dings, 1999).

Modeling Learning based on observing and imitating the behavior of others; see also: **social/observational learning.**

Neurotic mobster Despite his deeply antisocial behavior, Tony Soprano (played by James Gandolfini) of HBO's *Sopranos* engages in an on-again, off-again psychotherapy with Dr. Melfi (played by Lorraine Bracco). Clinicians and nonclinicians alike have been fascinated by the fictional gangster's efforts to come to terms with his anxiety, depression, and feelings about his mother.

Cognitive-Behavioral Components A number of research studies have found that many antisocial adults are the children of antisocial parents (Eron, 1997). While this link is partly genetic, parents who **model** behaviors associated with antisocial personality disorder (such as violence, deceitfulness, or impulsivity) may teach their children that such behaviors are acceptable and rewarded. Other behavior theorists emphasize that antisocial traits are *reinforced* when parents reward manipulative or abusive behavior. For example, a parent who congratulates a child for getting away with misdeeds may teach the child that he can get what he wants by being hostile and coercive (Capaldi & Patterson, 1994).

In addition, antisocial personality disorder is characterized by a variety of cognitive deficits. The impulsive and aggressive behavior commonly associated with antisocial personality disorder reflects impairment in the ability to connect actions and their consequences (Millon & Davis, 2000). Similarly, people with antisocial traits attend largely to their own self-interests and appear to lack the ability or interest to consider how their actions might be damaging or hurtful to others. While cognitive interventions can be used to try to address these deficits, most therapists are pessimistic about outcomes when working with clients with antisocial personality disorder. Of the small percentage of individuals with antisocial personality disorder who receive treatment, most are required to pursue treatment by a legal mandate, and most drop out of therapy (Gabbard & Coyne, 1987). Behavioral interventions which aim to teach responsible behavior through the use of consistent punishments for inappropriate behavior and rewards for positive behavior may be more effective than cognitive techniques for individuals with this disorder.

Psychodynamic Components Research evidence suggests that people who develop antisocial personality disorder tend to come from families that are emotionally turbulent, cruel, and prone to physical abuse (Akhtar, 1992). Children in these families often experience feelings of helplessness in the face of their parents' anger and violence. Psychodynamic clinicians emphasize that such individuals may begin to use the defense mechanism of **identification with the aggressor** in which they cause *others* to experience the victimization, powerlessness, and helplessness that they felt overwhelmed by as children. In other words, the antisocial person who spent his childhood feeling like a scared and helpless victim may spend his adulthood scaring and victimizing others. People with antisocial personality disorder are rarely able to talk about their own emotional experiences; the antisocial person *acts* instead of feels. Psychodynamic clinicians have also focused on other problematic aspects of early childhood attachments among people who develop antisocial personality disorder. Normal parent-child attachment paves the way for the internalization of a morally guiding *superego* and the ability to empathize with others. People with antisocial personality disorder show abnormal superego functioning and a lack of empathic ability to imagine how others feel, presumably due to disrupted parent-child relationships (Grotstein, 1982).

Borderline Personality Disorder

Borderline personality disorder is one of the most dramatic mental disorders (see Box 11.1 for more on the term "borderline"). People with this disorder struggle with chronic instability and disruption in their relationships, their sense of themselves, and their behavior (APA, 2000). They exhibit emotional volatility, impulsivity, and self-destructive or suicidal behavior. Borderline personality disorder may also include episodes of *depersonalization* (feeling extremely detached from oneself, a *dissociative* symptom; see Chapter 7) and self-injury, often in the form of cutting or burning one's own skin. The self-injurious and suicidal behaviors associated with borderline personality disorder are often used to manipulate others, such as threatening to commit suicide if a romantic partner decides to leave. The extreme quality of these behaviors speaks to the intense fear of abandonment that is one of the hallmarks of borderline personality disorder (see Table 11.6).

Identification with the aggressor A defense mechanism in which an individual causes others to experience the victimization, powerlessness, or helplessness that he or she has experienced in the past.

Borderline personality disorder Personality traits involving instability in interpersonal relationships, self-image, and emotions, as well as impulsivity and self-destructive behavior.

Diagnostic Criteria for Borderline Personality Disorder	Table 11.6

Adapted from DSM-IV-TR (APA, 2000)

A pervasive pattern of *instability of interpersonal relationships, self-image, emotions, and impulsivity,* beginning by early adulthood and present in a variety of contexts, as indicated by five (or more) of the following:

- Frantic efforts to avoid real or imagined abandonment.
- A pattern of unstable and intense interpersonal relationships characterized by alternating between extremes of idealization and devaluation.
- Identity disturbance: markedly and persistently unstable self-image or sense of self.
- Impulsivity in at least two areas that are potentially self-damaging (for example, spending, sex, substance abuse).
- Recurrent suicidal behavior, gestures, or threats, or self-mutilating behavior.
- Affective instability due to marked reactivity of mood (for example, intense episodic sadness, irritability, or anxiety usually lasting a few hours and rarely more than a few days).
- Chronic feelings of emptiness.
- Inappropriate, intense anger or difficulty controlling anger (for example, frequent displays of temper, constant anger, recurrent physical fights).
- Transient, stress-related paranoid thinking or severe dissociative symptoms.

BOX 11.1 Naming a Disorder

Why "Borderline?"

Personality disorder experts have pointed out that "borderline" is not really a very good name for a psychological disorder (Aronson, 1985; Fromm, 1995). The term "borderline" does not refer to behaviors or emotional experiences as do most other diagnostic labels (such as "substance dependence" or "depression"). The word is really better suited to descriptions of physical locations, such as the edge or border of an area, or a space between two identifiable points on a continuum. Yet, despite the term's lack of descriptive specificity, "borderline" does capture several salient features of this syndrome of maladaptive personality traits.

The "Border" Between Neurotic and Psychotic Functioning

People with borderline personality disorder seem to function at a level in between (or on the "borderline" between) neurotic and psychotic functioning. Much of the time they seem neurotic, meaning that they—like many people—experience some impairments in functioning as a result of trying to manage emotional conflicts, but they do not lose touch with reality. However, there are times when people with borderline personality disorder may lose contact with reality and become psychotic. Even though these episodes are usually brief, their presence marks an important distinction between borderline personality disorder and most other personality disorders.

The "Border" Between Emotional Extremes

People with borderline traits are known for moving quickly from one emotional extreme to another. A man with borderline personality disorder who deeply admires one of his colleagues might soon find the same colleague utterly detestable if the colleague disappoints or lets him down. Similarly, people with borderline personality disorder often struggle with wild and unstable moods. They may appear to be quite happy one minute and then enraged the next, without any obvious reasons for the radical changes in their feelings. Such emotional flip-flopping can give the impression that they exist on the border of a number of feeling states and can move very rapidly from one to another.

Poor Interpersonal "Borders"

Normal interpersonal boundaries or "borders" are frequently disregarded by people with borderline personality disorder. For example, people with borderline traits may be overly hostile, or flirtatious and familiar, with new acquaintances. They throw themselves into relationships; after one date, a woman with borderline personality disorder declared that she had found "the love of her life" and "the most interesting and loyal person I have ever known." While these feelings are often short-lived (and are likely to switch quickly to the polar opposite), in the moment they are very real and intense.

Case Illustration Lou, a 27-year-old salesman, has long-term friendships with several male friends, but he has what he calls "trouble with women." Lou's good looks and charm make it easy for him to get dates, but he has difficulty sustaining a relationship over a long period of time. In his most recent relationship he fell "madly in love" in just a few days, and he and his girlfriend enjoyed a whirlwind beginning to their romance. But, when his new girlfriend needed to leave town for a short business trip, Lou was devastated. After a long night of drinking he called his girlfriend at her hotel to say that he felt unwanted and alone and that if she did not cut her trip short he might hurt himself. Lou's friends have watched him go through several similar experiences with other women. His friends have even noticed that Lou becomes surprisingly angry with them when they have to change or cancel plans they have made with him. Recently, Lou received a somewhat critical evaluation from one of his supervisors at work. The negative tone of the evaluation came as a complete surprise to Lou despite the fact that he had missed work repeatedly over the prior six months. He impulsively confronted his supervisor, who he had previously liked, and bad-mouthed him as an "evil idiot" to his coworkers. Lou then left work early, went home, and drank from his liquor cabinet until he passed out.

Many of the problem behaviors associated with borderline personality disorder stem from maladaptive attempts to cope with extreme emotional distress. People with borderline personality disorder often report that they feel "empty" and that they long for close relationships to help them feel secure. However, such heavy dependence on others for emotional security results in anxiety or anger about the possibility of losing a meaningful relationship. Not surprisingly, the friends and lovers of people with borderline personality disorder often feel "burned out" by the excessive demands and expectations placed on their relationships; a vicious cycle ensues as the borderline person's neediness only increases the likelihood that he or she *will* be abandoned.

People with borderline personality disorder often become quickly and deeply involved in new relationships, and any perception that a relationship might end sets off feelings of terror, desolation, and fury. What might feel like a painful but tolerable breakup to most people creates an emotional firestorm for people with borderline personality disorder. Much of the "acting out" and manipulative behavior associated with the disorder (binge drinking and eating, sexual promiscuity, self-mutilation, suicidal gestures) can be understood as maladaptive efforts to control or numb painful feelings or to regain a threatened relationship. Similarly, people with this disorder sometimes describe feeling so overwhelmed by confusing emotions that relief comes only from making emotional pain "concrete" in the form of an injury such as cutting oneself with a knife or burning oneself with cigarettes. At other times, intense emotions can cause people with borderline personality disorder to become extremely detached from themselves and their surroundings. Many people with this disorder report that they can only feel "real" again if they see themselves bleed or feel the physical pain of a self-induced injury (APA, 2000).

Avoiding abandonment at all costs In the 1987 film *Fatal Attraction*, Glenn Close plays a woman with many features of borderline personality disorder. When her married lover (played by Michael Douglas) attempts to cut ties with her after a weekend-long whirlwind affair, she threatens suicide to keep him from leaving.

Explaining and Treating Borderline Personality Disorder

We'll begin by considering how the psychodynamic, biological, and cognitive-behavioral perspectives explain and treat borderline personality disorder and then turn our attention to an innovative treatment approach that effectively combines all three perspectives.

Psychodynamic Components Some psychodynamic theorists have focused on difficulties in the mother-child relationship as a contributing cause of borderline personality disorder. For example, Mahler (1971) concluded that adults who manifest borderline traits were raised by unreliable and inconsistent primary caretakers who interfered with the normal process by which children learn to manage difficult feelings and to function independently. Recent research suggests that the parents of people who develop borderline traits are not merely unreliable, they are often abusive. Several studies have shown that a high percentage of borderline adults were physically and/or sexually abused as children (Westen et al., 1990). For example, one study found that 75% of clients with borderline personality disorder had histories of some type of abuse, compared with 33% of clients with other diagnoses (Oldham et al., 1996). Thus, it appears that many people who develop borderline personality disorder grow up with a particularly unfortunate combination of circumstances: exposure to trauma (such as emotional, physical, or sexual abuse) and inadequate parental help with managing the painful emotions that inevitably result from trauma. Even in the absence of trauma, studies have found that many people with borderline personality disorder have parents they experienced as unempathic, and they report being raised in stressful and chaotic environmental circumstances (Golomb et al., 1994).

People with borderline personality disorder tend to see others (and themselves) as all-good *(idealized)* or all-bad *(devalued)*. This is often referred to as **splitting**, a defense mechanism that protects against painful mixed, or ambivalent, feelings by resorting to "black and white" thinking. By idealizing others ("Bill is the kindest, warmest, most gentle person ever!") a person with borderline traits attempts to reassure herself that she will not be hurt or disappointed and that all bad feelings have been

Splitting A defense mechanism in which one views the self or others as all-good or all-bad in order to ward off conflicted or ambivalent feelings.

banished. But any disappointment, even a minor one such as a failure to return a phone call promptly, may lead to devaluation, the other side of the idealization coin ("I hate Bill, he is a selfish, unreliable jerk!"). Devaluation works as a defense mechanism by decreasing the importance of the person who has just inflicted a painful emotional injury and by externalizing all feelings of "badness" outside the self.

Biological Components Researchers have found that some of the impulsive behaviors associated with borderline personality disorder may be related to low levels of the neurotransmitter serotonin (Silk, 1994). Serotonin also happens to be one of the major neurotransmitters implicated in depression (Chapter 6), and some genetic evidence indicates that the first-degree relatives of people with borderline personality disorder may be likely to suffer from depression (Schulz et al., 1989). A wide range of medications—especially antidepressants—can be used to manage some of the emotional symptoms associated with borderline personality disorder (Grossman, 2002; Koenigsberg, Woo-Ming, & Siever, 2002).

Cognitive-Behavioral Components Cognitive-behavioral explanations of borderline personality disorder focus on the predominance of dichotomous thinking (seeing things as all good or all bad), which results in extreme interpretations of events, and dramatic, impulsive behavioral responses. In order to establish a productive working relationship with clients with borderline personality disorder, cognitive therapists often begin with a focus on concrete behavioral goals, such as reducing impulsive behavior, while remaining flexible when it comes to allotting therapy time to address inevitable emotional crises (Freeman et al., 1990). Over time, cognitive interventions can be employed to address borderline clients' propensity for dichotomous thinking and problematic interpersonal behaviors that are repeated within the therapy relationship (Sperry, 1999) (see Figure 11.2).

Dialectical Behavior Therapy One of the most promising treatments for borderline personality disorder, dialectical behavioral training (DBT), was developed by Marsha Line-

Figure 11.2 The Impulse Control Process in the Cognitive-Behavioral Treatment of Borderline Personality Disorder Impulse control training in cognitive-behavioral interventions helps people with borderline personality disorder use a step-by-step process to choose thoughtful, effective, and adaptive responses to difficult situations, rather than engaging in damaging, impulsive behaviors.
Adapted from Freeman et al., 1990, p. 199

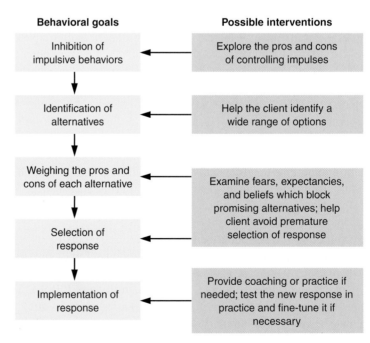

han, a psychologist at the University of Washington, Seattle. Consistent with the ***principle of multiple causality***, DBT recognizes that borderline personality disorder involves disturbances of thought, action, emotion, and neurotransmission. Consequently, DBT interventions draw upon cognitive-behavioral, psychodynamic, biological, and even Zen Buddhist principles. DBT focuses on the role of emotional dysregulation (resulting from childhood traumatization and emotional invalidation) in borderline personality disorder. As a result, DBT therapists are warmly validating of their clients' intense emotional experiences while using cognitive-behavioral techniques to help clients solve day-to-day problems effectively and better manage intense emotional experiences. Individual DBT sessions are complemented by group meetings in which clients focus on developing skills in four specific areas: improving attentional focus ("mindfulness" in Zen terms), increasing emotional control, improving interpersonal effectiveness, and tolerating distress. The skill-training component of DBT uses cognitive-behavioral principles as it aims to change how clients think about their experiences (accepting reality, challenging distorted cognitions about interpersonal interactions), while teaching new behaviors for dealing with emotional crises (self-soothing techniques, assertiveness training, increasing opportunities for positive emotions).

DBT proceeds in a hierarchical fashion by addressing a series of "behavioral targets" (Kim & Goff, 2000). The therapist and client address the following behaviors in order: life-threatening behaviors, therapy-interfering behaviors, quality-of-life-interfering behaviors, behaviors related to posttraumatic stress reactions, and finally, behaviors that interfere with self-respect and general quality of life. Sessions can also include psychodynamic exploration of long-standing emotional conflicts, but only after the client has become adept at using new emotional skills (often practiced in a group setting) to manage intense feelings. Medications are prescribed, as needed, to help clients who have persistent difficulties tolerating intense emotions. DBT appears to be highly effective with borderline personality disorder clients who have not improved in other forms of psychotherapy (Crits-Christoph & Barber, 2002; Linehan, 1993).

Histrionic Personality Disorder

Histrionic personality disorder is characterized by a strong and constant need to be noticed and by superficial emotions. People with this disorder tend to engage others through flirtatiousness, self-dramatization, or an attention-grabbing appearance. While they may strive to be the "life of the party" they are often felt by others to be long on style but short on substance. Their engagement with their own emotions, other people, and with the world has a superficial, impressionistic quality (Shapiro, 1965) (see Table 11.7).

Histrionic personality disorder Personality traits involving excessive, superficial emotionality and attention-seeking.

Case Illustration Kathy sought psychotherapy because she was very upset about the recent breakup of a romantic relationship. She explained to the therapist that her boyfriend seemed to lose interest in the relationship over time, and that this had happened repeatedly in other relationships. Despite the fact that Kathy was initially quite charming and engaging, her therapist soon noticed that her emotions had a superficial quality. Even when Kathy would weep throughout the entire session, he had the feeling that she cried merely to get sympathy. When pressed to explore the cause of her distress, Kathy's responses were usually vague and imprecise. She would say things like "it's so tragic—you know how men can be!" in a dramatic, even theatrical way, but she would then change the subject. Though Kathy had a number of acquaintances, she didn't really have any close friends. Her coworkers liked her but described her as "flashy and shallow" and found it difficult to develop a relationship with her that went beyond a surface friendship.

Table 11.7	Diagnostic Criteria for Histrionic Personality Disorder
Adapted from DSM-IV-TR (APA, 2000)	A pervasive pattern of *excessive emotionality and attention-seeking,* beginning by early adulthood and present in a variety of contexts, as indicated by five (or more) of the following: • Is uncomfortable in situations in which he or she is not the center of attention. • Interaction with others is often characterized by inappropriate sexually seductive or provocative behavior. • Displays rapidly shifting and shallow expression of emotion. • Consistently uses physical appearance to draw attention to self. • Has a style of speech that is excessively impressionistic and lacking in detail. • Shows self-dramatization, theatricality, and exaggerated expression of emotion. • Is suggestible, or easily influenced by others or circumstances. • Considers relationships to be more intimate than they actually are.

Too feminine? The character of Scarlet O'Hara, from *Gone with the Wind* (1939) displays the dramatic, yet emotionally superficial, qualities typically associated with histrionic personality disorder. Some critics have argued that the diagnosis of histrionic personality disorder pathologizes traits that have been considered, in certain times and places, to be the essence of appealing, feminine behavior.

Repression A defense mechanism consisting of the forgetting of painful or unacceptable mental content.

People with histrionic personality disorder will dramatize themselves (such as picking a loud fight or bursting into tears) in order to draw attention that may be focused elsewhere. When they do receive attention, they often interpret it as more intimate than it really is. Someone with histrionic personality disorder may claim to have numerous "best friends," all of whom see themselves as only casual friends. Histrionic emotions shift rapidly—from crying one moment to laughing hysterically the next—in a way that appears to be trite and artificial. Even feelings that seem to be intensely experienced often lack depth. For example, when asked for details about why his mother is the "most wonderful woman in the world" a histrionic man might explain "well, she is just superb!" People with this disorder are also easily influenced by others, as they can be quickly carried away by emotion and surface impressions.

Explaining and Treating Histrionic Personality Disorder

The psychodynamic and cognitive-behavioral perspectives on histrionic personality disorder provide different, but complementary, views on what causes histrionic behavior.

Psychodynamic Components As you may recall, Freud's initial work focused on *hysteria* (Chapter 3)—a disorder involving strange physical symptoms (such as the paralysis, pain, or loss of feeling) in the absence of any physical cause (Breuer & Freud, 1955). Freud concluded that these "hysterical" symptoms resulted from **repressed** emotional conflicts and the conversion of emotional tension into physical symptoms. Freud believed that the repressed emotions usually had to do with memories of premature sexual experiences or childhood sexual conflicts. Later psychodynamic theorists extended this explanation to account for hysterical personality traits such as those seen in histrionic personality disorder. They also noted that the emotional insecurity of these individuals, which leads to a craving for attention, is often rooted in insecure childhood attachments to their parents. Thus, from a modern psychodynamic perspective, conflicts about sexuality and insecurity in relationships with others are seen as central causes of histrionic personality disorder (Herman, 1981).

While the flirtatious and seductive behavior of people with histrionic personality disorder expresses their sexual impulses and their desire for attention and security, the defense mechanism of repression keeps the individual from having to be aware of these "unacceptable" needs. Unfortunately, this extreme use of repression interferes with genuine feelings and contributes to the naive, shallow, and emotionally superficial traits associated with histrionic behavior. Psychodynamic interventions for histrionic personality disorder focus on the role of *transference* in the psychotherapeutic relationship. By paying close attention to the way in which a histrionic client engages with his or her therapist (such as being overly flirtatious, dramatic, or vague), the clinician can help the client to identify and understand the unconscious roots and function of the client's histrionic interpersonal style.

Cognitive-Behavioral Components Cognitive theorists suggest that people with histrionic personality disorder believe that they cannot care for themselves and must seek out attention and approval from others (Beck & Freeman, 1990). As a result, they engage in self-dramatizing behaviors in order to obtain the attention and concern they long for. People with histrionic personality disorder have a cognitive style that relies on vague impressions instead of precision, reason, and concrete facts. Accordingly, cognitive-behavioral therapists must often be patient yet firm when trying to hold histrionic clients to a therapeutic agenda or specific and concrete treatment goals. When they succeed in doing so, therapists can help histrionic clients to identify and revise distorted thoughts at the root of their dramatic and overly emotional behavior. Therapeutic goals usually focus on helping histrionic clients learn to identify what they want and ask for it directly rather than resorting to indirect and usually ineffective attention-seeking behaviors (Freeman et al., 1990).

Narcissistic Personality Disorder

Narcissistic personality disorder is characterized by a profound sense of entitlement and superiority with regard to others which usually masks underlying problems with self-esteem (APA, 2000). People who are severely narcissistic feel jealous of other people's accomplishments, work to convince others that they are special or important, and are often quite offended when their "specialness" seems to go unnoticed. They expect to be treated favorably, even if such treatment comes at other people's expense. For example, a person with narcissistic personality disorder is likely to feel offended when given a "bad" table at a restaurant and may demand that the waiter make another party give up a preferred table. Because they are so focused on their own needs, people with narcissistic personality disorder usually disregard other people's feelings. They may cruelly "put down" other people or thoughtlessly boast about accomplishments. For example, one man with narcissistic personality disorder bragged about being admitted to a choice medical school every time he encountered someone he knew who had been rejected (see Table 11.8).

Narcissistic personality disorder Personality traits involving extreme grandiosity, need for admiration, and lack of empathy.

Narcissus at the Fountain The term "narcissism" comes from the myth of Narcissus, a young man who became so enchanted by the beauty of his own reflection that the gods punished him with transformation into a flower that grows at the water's edge.

Case Illustration Monica, who works as a sales representative for a pharmaceutical company, is quite unhappy at work. Though she is very good at her job, she is painfully aware that she is not the top salesperson in her region. Monica makes frequent appointments with her boss to complain about her assignments, arguing that she is entitled to the best territory so that she can "blow everyone else away." When Monica boss refused to assign her to a hospital where a colleague was achieving record sales, Monica stormed out of his office complaining enviously about the colleague and bad-mouthing her boss to anyone who would listen. Monica has some friends, but she has always had difficulty holding on to any one friend for very long. Most people find

Table 11.8	Diagnostic Criteria for Narcissistic Personality Disorder
Adapted from DSM-IV-TR (APA, 2000)	A pervasive pattern of *grandiosity (in fantasy or behavior), need for admiration, and lack of empathy for others,* beginning by early adulthood and present in a variety of contexts, as indicated by five (or more) of the following: • Has a grandiose sense of self-importance (for example, exaggerates achievements and talents, expects to be recognized as superior without commensurate achievements). • Is preoccupied with fantasies of unlimited success, power, brilliance, beauty, or ideal love. • Believes that he or she is "special" and unique and can only be understood by, or should associate with, other special or high-status people (or institutions). • Requires excessive admiration. • Has a sense of entitlement: has unreasonable expectations of especially favorable treatment or automatic compliance with his or her expectations. • Is interpersonally exploitative: takes advantage of others to achieve his or her own ends. • Lacks empathy: is unwilling to recognize or identify with the feelings and needs of others. • Is often envious of others or believes that others are envious of him or her. • Shows arrogant, haughty behaviors or attitudes.

Monica to be impressive when they first meet her, but after a while they tire of her constant preoccupation with herself and her own achievements and her minimal interest in other people. When friends do share news of their accomplishments with Monica, she often responds by pointing out how she has had a similar, but superior, personal success.

Explaining and Treating Narcissistic Personality Disorder

On the surface, narcissistic personality disorder may seem to be caused by too much self-esteem. However, both the psychodynamic and cognitive-explanations of narcissistic personality disorder focus on how narcissistic traits typically result when people are unable to feel good about themselves in realistic and constructive ways.

Psychodynamic Components From a psychodynamic perspective, the vanity, arrogance, and self-centeredness associated with narcissistic personality disorder represents an effort to counteract underlying feelings of inadequacy. For example, people with this disorder may have been emotionally neglected by their parents or valued mainly for their external qualities—what they accomplished, how they looked, or how their behavior reflected upon the family—rather than loved unconditionally. Under these conditions they grow to feel that they are only appreciated for what they do, not for who they are (Kohut, 1977; Miller, 1981). Lorna Benjamin, a modern interpersonal theorist, argues that narcissism can also result from excessive indulgence by parents. Benjamin points out that indulgent parents may subtly convey the message "we need to see you as fabulous and perfect because acknowledging your imperfections would make you impossible to love." In addition, parents who accommodate too readily to

Only skin deep For people with narcissistic personality disorder, external sources of self-esteem, such as physical beauty, praise from others, or owning a fancy car, may be required to counteract feelings of inadequacy.

their children's wishes may raise children who don't think about other people's needs and feelings, leading to the kind of entitlement that characterizes narcissistic personality disorder (Benjamin, 1996). In other words, over-indulged children may have a precarious sense of self-esteem and rely heavily on praise from others in order to feel good about themselves. Similarly, they may use relationships to enhance their self-esteem by constantly reminding others of their accomplishments or pointing out how they are superior to the people who surround them.

People with narcissistic personality disorder rely heavily on the defense mechanisms of **idealization** and **devaluation** (McWilliams, 1994). They tend to idealize themselves—to tell themselves and others that they are flawless and worthy of admiration—in order to ward off their own feelings of inferiority. People who are narcissistic also aim to bolster their self-esteem by associating with people and objects that can be idealized (Kohut, 1977). A narcissistic attorney might focus most of his energy on a celebrity client or insist that his car is the finest one available. In addition to idealizing themselves, narcissists must often defensively devalue others; people who fail to support their need to feel superior may be dismissed as "stupid" or "useless."

There are two major psychodynamic approaches to treating narcissistic personality disorder. Heinz Kohut (1977) believed that therapists should provide consistent empathy and be tolerant of clients' grandiosity in order to allow them to move forward developmentally. In contrast, Otto Kernberg (1989) stresses the importance of kind but consistent confrontation of the grandiose beliefs held by narcissistic clients. Psychodynamic therapists report that some narcissistic clients are best helped with "Kohutian" empathy while others are served better served by "Kernbergian" confrontation (McWilliams, 1994).

Cognitive-Behavioral Components When individuals with narcissistic personality disorder seek therapy it is typically because they are experiencing painful symptoms (such as depression after the loss of a relationship), not because of concern about their personality traits, which are ego-syntonic. However, using cognitive and behavioral techniques to address the painful symptoms the client is experiencing often leads to a focus on the problematic personality traits. For example, a therapist might observe that the client's depression is linked to a distorted view of himself as either completely superior or totally worthless. Such extreme forms of self-evaluation are not only inherently inaccurate, but they pave the way for feelings of inferiority and inadequacy (Beck & Freeman, 1990). The distorted *cognitive schema* behind the depression, in other words, is likely to be closely related to the schema behind the narcissistic problems. Cognitive-behavioral interventions focus on helping the client to take a more realistic view of himself and others.

The culture of narcissism In his 1978 book *The Culture of Narcissism*, Christopher Lasch argued that modern Western culture promotes narcissistic traits by valuing the individual above the group, and style over substance. The excesses of Beverly Hill's Rodeo Drive seem to support Lasch's view.

Idealization A defense mechanism in which someone or something is seen as being perfect or wonderful in order to protect against negative feelings.

Devaluation A defense mechanism in which someone or something external is disparaged in order to protect against negative feelings about oneself.

Avoidant personality disorder Personality traits involving social inhibition, feelings of inadequacy, and hypersensitivity to negative evaluation.

Cluster C: Anxious or Fearful Personality Disorders

Avoidant Personality Disorder

Avoidant personality disorder can be thought of as shyness taken to a pathological extreme. People with avoidant personality disorder are usually extremely tense in social situations and convinced that they will be seen as inadequate. As a result, they avoid new or unpredictable social situations and may only socialize when they can be ensured that they will be liked. Considering that it is quite difficult to *guarantee* anyone that he or she will be liked by others, it is easy to imagine how such a prerequisite for social interaction could significantly interfere with one's functioning (see Table 11.9).

Table 11.9	Diagnostic Criteria for Avoidant Personality Disorder

Adapted from DSM-IV-TR (APA, 2000)

A pervasive pattern of *social inhibition, feelings of inadequacy, and hypersensitivity to negative evaluation,* beginning by early adulthood and present in a variety of contexts, as indicated by four (or more) of the following:

- Avoids occupational activities that involve significant interpersonal contact due to fears of criticism, disapproval, or rejection.
- Is unwilling to get involved with people unless certain of being liked.
- Shows restraint within intimate relationships because of the fear of being shamed or ridiculed.
- Is preoccupied with being criticized or rejected in social situations.
- Is inhibited in new interpersonal situations because of feelings of inadequacy.
- Views self as socially inept, personally unappealing, or inferior to others.
- Is unusually reluctant to take personal risks or to engage in any new activities because they may prove embarrassing.

Case Illustration From early childhood, Claire has been described by her family as "painfully shy." In elementary school she would watch her classmates play while she stood at the edge of the playground. While it was clear that she longed to join in the daily games, Claire felt sure that her classmates did not like her and thought she was a "dork." Encouragement from her teachers and invitations to birthday parties did not help Claire to feel more confident about making friends. Claire found some relief from her social difficulties by throwing herself into her schoolwork when she reached high school. She achieved extremely high grades and scored well on her college entrance exams. Claire and her parents were pleased with her academic achievement, but Claire also felt that her academic ability simply affirmed her reputation as a "geeky girl with no friends." When it came time to apply to college, Claire decided that she would prefer to attend a trade school where she could learn secretarial skills while living at home with her parents. When asked about her reluctance to attend college, Claire explained that she was worried that her professors would think that she had nothing of substance to offer in class, and her classmates and potential friends would find her boring. Though Claire tended to focus on her academic concerns, her parents also knew that she was worried about what it would be like to move away from home and live in a dorm. Even though Claire had managed to develop a few superficial friendships in high school, she continued to feel that she could not make friends and would perceive even the most minor interactions (such as a friend saying that she already had plans for a coming weekend) as proof that others disliked her.

People with avoidant personality disorder are often "loners," but unlike people with schizoid personality disorder they strongly desire relationships with others yet are convinced that they will be rejected or disliked. They are frightened of taking the risks necessary to develop new friendships and are preoccupied with how they might potentially embarrass or humiliate themselves. The withdrawal from social relationships in avoidant personality disorder means that people with this disorder do not have many opportunities to develop the social skills necessary to facilitate friendships. For the person with avoidant personality disorder, the failure to make a new friend on the first try is usually perceived as proof of social inadequacy and can lead to further social withdrawal.

Avoidant personality disorder differs from social phobia (Chapter 5) because it is pervasive and chronic. People who suffer from social phobia feel anxious in circumscribed social situations such as eating in public or giving a speech. In contrast, people with avoidant personality disorder feel anxious and inadequate in almost all social situations over many years and can engage in interpersonal intimacy only when they feel assured of uncritical acceptance (APA, 2000).

Explaining and Treating Avoidant Personality Disorder

The psychodynamic perspective on avoidant personality disorder focuses on how childhood experiences can lead to lasting interpersonal anxiety, while the cognitive-behavioral approach focuses on the thought processes that perpetuate and reinforce social avoidance. The biological perspective adds an understanding that some people can be born with a predisposition to pathological shyness.

Psychodynamic Components The psychodynamic perspective focuses on the developmental roots of avoidant personality disorder—specifically, painful childhood experiences involving extreme shame. For example, individuals with avoidant personality disorder may have been excessively shamed by their parents during childhood or adolescence (Gabbard, 1990). As a result, they tend to assume that their vulnerabilities will be pointed out by others, and they shun contact with unfamiliar people or situations in order to minimize the chances of being rejected (Millon & Davis, 2000). People with avoidant personality traits may rely heavily on the defense mechanisms of *withdrawal* and **escape into fantasy**—imagining that they will be completely accepted or revered by others, or that they might be able to self-assuredly defend themselves against any criticism (Millon & Davis, 2000).

People with avoidant personality disorder often have difficulty engaging in psychotherapy because of their intense concerns about how they are seen by others. As a result, clinicians working with them must be carefully attuned to the clients' anxieties about the psychotherapy situation itself. Clinicians must also pay special attention to gradually developing a trusting therapeutic relationship in which the roots of the client's social anxieties can be understood (Gabbard, 1990).

Cognitive-Behavioral Components As described previously, people with avoidant personality disorder assume that they will be criticized and rejected by others. Like people with paranoid traits, people who are avoidant scan their environment and attend to minute details, selectively attending to those details that fit their negative assumptions (Millon & Davis, 2000). Cognitive-behavioral interventions help people with avoidant personality disorder pay attention to the disconfirming (that is, positive) feedback that they tend to ignore. In addition, therapists attempt to increase their clients' tolerance for the painful emotions (such as fear of rejection) that perpetuate avoidant behavior. For example, a cognitive-behavioral therapist might challenge her client's assumption that rejection is intolerably painful and should be avoided at all costs (Beck & Freeman, 1990). Group therapy can also been an effective way for people with avoidant personality to gather more accurate "data" about how they are perceived in social situations and to boost their confidence about seeking out new social situations (Azima, 1993).

Biological Components Biological investigations of avoidant personality disorder have focused on the role of a particular *temperament* in the development of the disorder. Babies who tend to withdraw from new experiences and adapt slowly to change are categorized as having "slow-to-warm-up" temperaments. Interestingly, the "slow-to-warm-up" temperament has been associated with intense shyness in childhood and avoidant personality disorder in adulthood (Kernberg, Weiner, & Bardenstien, 2000).

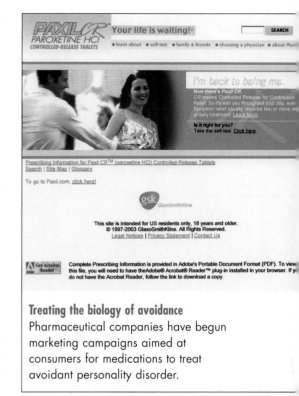

Treating the biology of avoidance
Pharmaceutical companies have begun marketing campaigns aimed at consumers for medications to treat avoidant personality disorder.

Escape into fantasy A defense mechanism in which an individual avoids unpleasant feelings by focusing on pleasant daydreams.

Antidepressant medications can be used to minimize some of the depressive and anxiety symptoms often associated avoidant personality disorder and may make it possible for people with the disorder to make better use of psychotherapy (Koenigsberg, Woo-Ming, & Siever, 2002).

Dependent Personality Disorder

Dependent personality disorder Personality traits involving submissive and clinging behavior related to an excessive need to be cared for by others.

People with **dependent personality disorder** feel that they cannot care for themselves, make decisions, or take responsibility for everyday aspects of their own lives. They depend on others for help with everything, from the most minor decisions such as where to go to lunch, to major life choices such as the type of career to pursue. Like Beth (described at the beginning of the chapter) people with dependent personality disorder rely almost entirely on others even though they are, in fact, capable adults (see Table 11.10).

Case Illustration **William, 32, sought therapy because he was extremely distraught after being left by his wife of 10 years. Though William makes a comfortable living as a systems analyst at a large company, he is extremely worried that he won't be able to care for himself now that his wife is gone, and he pleaded with her not to divorce him. Indeed, he had relied on her to make or approve of most of the major decisions in his life, from what tie to wear each to day to whether he should ask for a promotion at work. William's wife tired of his lack of independence and encouraged him, to no avail, to do things on his own. Interestingly, William's boss has told William many of the same things that William heard from his wife. In the annual evaluations of William's work performance, his boss has noted that William is overly hesitant and**

Table 11.10	Diagnostic Criteria for Dependent Personality Disorder
Adapted from DSM-IV-TR (APA, 2000)	A *pervasive and excessive need to be taken care of that leads to submissive and clinging behavior and fears of separation,* beginning by early adulthood and present in a variety of contexts, as indicated by five (or more) of the following: • Has difficulty making everyday decisions without an excessive amount of advice and reassurance from others. • Needs others to assume responsibility for most major areas of his or her life. • Has difficulty expressing disagreement with others because of unrealistic fears of retribution, or loss of support or approval. • Has difficulty initiating projects or doing things on his or her own (because of a lack of self-confidence in judgment or abilities rather than a lack of motivation or energy). • Goes to excessive lengths to obtain nurturance and support from others, to the point of volunteering to do things that are unpleasant. • Feels uncomfortable or helpless when alone because of exaggerated fears of being unable to care for himself or herself. • Urgently seeks another relationship as a source of care and support when a close relationship ends. • Is unrealistically preoccupied with fears of being left to take care of himself or herself.

cautious when making routine decisions, and that he tends to go from colleague to colleague asking advice, even in familiar situations where he has been successful in the past.

Clearly, William possesses the intelligence, education, and physical ability to take charge of his own life, yet he is dogged by the feeling that he cannot care for himself or make decisions on his own. Like William, people with dependent personality disorder are clingy and needy in their relationships with others and worry excessively about what will happen if they are left to care for themselves. They often feel devastated and terrified when a close relationship ends and actively seek another care-taking relationship to take its place. In some cases, people with this disorder allow others to take advantage of them, or even volunteer to do unpleasant tasks (such as cleaning a friend's home) in order to maintain what feels like a desperately needed care-taking relationship (APA, 2000).

Explaining and Treating Dependent Personality Disorder

Both cognitive-behavioral and psychodynamic explanations of dependent personality disorder focus on the role of childhood experiences. The cognitive-behavioral perspective suggests that lifelong patterns of extreme neediness might emerge from the early reinforcement of dependent behavior, while the psychodynamic approach focuses on various ways in which parent-child relationships can lead to excessive dependence. Research also suggests that the "slow-to-warm-up" temperament (described earlier) which contributes to avoidant personality disorder is also a risk factor for dependent personality disorder.

Cognitive-Behavioral Components People with dependent personality disorder feel that they are helpless and inadequate in spite of ample evidence to the contrary. Research indicates that some highly dependent adults have been raised by parents who punished their children for independent and assertive behaviors and instead rewarded needy, clinging behavior (Bornstein, 1997). Cognitive-behavioral interventions challenge dependent clients' deeply entrenched, but distorted, beliefs that they are unable to care for themselves and create opportunities for clients to function independently (Beck & Freeman, 1990). Even small steps in the direction of autonomy (such as a client's successful execution of a therapeutic homework assignment to buy groceries without soliciting advice) provide concrete proof that clients are not nearly as helpless and ineffectual as they believe themselves to be (Freeman et al., 1990).

Cognitive-behavioral interventions for dependent personality disorder also focus on assertiveness training. Assertive behaviors are modeled and practiced, with the aim of helping people to develop a broader array of behaviors for meeting their own needs (Sperry, 1999). Often, the results of the newly assertive behaviors are inherently rewarding (such as getting more of what one wants), but clients may also be encouraged to find additional ways to reward themselves for taking risks and striving to be more independent.

Psychodynamic Components Early psychodynamic theorists hypothesized that dependent personality traits resulted from fixation at the oral stage of psychosexual development (Fenichel, 1945). Children who were either overindulged or who were not sufficiently gratified during the oral stage were thought likely to become adults who were preoccupied with being nurtured and cared for by others. Contemporary psychodynamic ideas about dependency are more complex. For example, the **regression** (reversion to earlier, childlike behavior) seen in people with dependent personality disorder can be a defense mechanism protecting the individual from anxieties associated with

Comic relief In the 1991 movie *What About Bob?* Bill Murray provides a humorous portrait of a man with such intense dependency needs that he exhausts, annoys, and ultimately maddens his psychiatrist (played by Richard Dreyfuss) by following him on a family vacation.

Regression A defense mechanism that involves a return to childlike behavior in order to avoid anxieties associated with progressive development.

independent, adult roles. In other cases, individuals may have developed fears of being unable to care for themselves because of *identifications* with parents who seemed dependent or helpless. A dependent person may also believe that a relationship is a loving one only if his or her partner agrees to take over most of the decisions and responsibilities. Finally, the defense mechanism of *idealization* is common among people with dependent personality disorder (Millon & Davis, 2000). The people who are depended upon may be seen as all-knowing and all-powerful, similar to the way that many young children view their parents.

The psychodynamic concept of transference is especially important in the treatment of dependent personality disorder. For example, a client with dependent personality disorder may look to the therapist to give him or her all the answers about how to save the client's marriage. When these typical feelings, thoughts, and interaction patterns are brought into the relationship with the therapist, the client and therapist can work together to try to understand and change the client's inappropriate expectations. The therapist will also address these problematic patterns as they appear in other relationships described by the client.

Obsessive-Compulsive Personality Disorder

Obsessive-compulsive personality disorder
Personality traits involving preoccupation with orderliness, perfectionism, and control at the expense of spontaneity, flexibility, and enjoyment.

People with **obsessive-compulsive personality disorder** have an extreme need for order and control. Typically, they rigidly adhere to what they believe to be the "right" way to conduct themselves—even to the degree of missing the point of an activity or taking the pleasure out of leisure. For example, an obsessive-compulsive boss might insist that all of her employees arrive at the company picnic on time so that they do not disrupt her schedule of "fun" activities (tug-of-war from 10:00–10:20, touch football from 10:20–11:00, etc.). Another person with this disorder may make a habit of turning projects in late because he cannot let go of the work until it seems to be "perfect." Perfectionism and procrastination are common problems in such individuals (see Table 11.11).

Case Illustration Natalie is a supervisor at a company that distributes cleaning supplies. The person who works directly below her just quit her job after only four months, and the person who held the spot before that quit after only three weeks. Neither employee could stand Natalie's exacting and seemingly meaningless guidelines for how work had to be done. For example, Natalie was preoccupied with the company's regulations and would insist that those who worked for her provide proof of illness if they called in sick. She made detailed lists that specified how every task had to be done, down to the correct procedure for making coffee in the company lounge. Natalie is at her office for long hours each day, making sure that her work is "perfect" and keeping a close eye on the quality of the work done by her subordinates. Little time is left over for a social life, which has contributed to Natalie's difficulties in finding and maintaining a romantic relationship. Several months ago Natalie started to date a man whom she liked very much. Though their relationship got off to a good start, he soon started to feel that Natalie was "bossy" and "rigid." For example, she refused to stay out late on weekend evenings because it would disrupt her strict sleep schedule. Similarly, her friends and family had complained for years that Natalie's inflexibility made it difficult to enjoy time with her.

People with obsessive-compulsive personality disorder can be highly productive, but they are unable to relax. They are often difficult colleagues, friends, or family members as they typically insist on doing everything their way and have a hard time acting as a member of a group or team. In addition to their rigid approach to work and play, obsessive-compulsive people also tend to be "pack rats." They hoard possessions, even those that have no sentimental value (such as old magazines or broken appliances), with

Diagnostic Criteria for Obsessive-Compulsive Personality Disorder	Table 11.11

Adapted from DSM-IV-TR (APA, 2000)

A pervasive pattern of *preoccupation with orderliness, perfectionism, and mental and interpersonal control,* at the expense of flexibility, openness, and efficiency, beginning by early adulthood and present in a variety of contexts, as indicated by four (or more) of the following:

- Is preoccupied with details, rules, lists, order, organization, or schedules to the extent that the major point of the activity is lost.
- Shows perfectionism that interferes with task completion (for example, is unable to complete a project because his or her own overly strict standards are not met).
- Is excessively devoted to work and productivity to the exclusion of leisure activities and friendships (not accounted for by obvious economic necessity).
- Is over-conscientious, scrupulous, and inflexible about matters of morality, ethics, or values (not accounted for by cultural or religious identification).
- Is unable to discard worn-out or worthless objects even when they have no sentimental value.
- Is reluctant to delegate tasks or to work with others unless they submit to exactly his or her way of doing things.
- Adopts a miserly spending style toward both self and others; money is viewed as something to be hoarded for future catastrophes.
- Shows rigidity and stubbornness.

the idea that the object might somehow be useful in the future (APA, 2000). Similarly, they are often reluctant to spend money and are frequently perceived as "stingy."

Obsessive-compulsive personality disorder differs from obsessive-compulsive *anxiety* disorder (Chapter 5) in several ways. First, the personality disorder is pervasive and chronic, reflecting traits rather than specific symptoms of compulsive rituals and/or obsessional thoughts. Second, while some people with obsessive-compulsive personality disorder may see their need for control as excessive, usually the obsessive-compulsive traits are not distressing to the person who has them, and may, in fact, be highly valued (ego-syntonic) personal qualities. Typically, people with obsessive-compulsive personality disorder pride themselves on being highly organized perfectionists without being aware of how their rigid and controlling behavior affects others. It is possible for a person to have both obsessive-compulsive personality disorder *and* obsessive-compulsive anxiety disorder.

Explaining and Treating Obsessive-Compulsive Personality Disorder

People often refer to their own or their friends' obsessive-compulsive traits as "anal." We'll explore the meaning behind this strange, if familiar, psychodynamic term and then consider the cognitive and behavioral mechanisms that perpetuate obsessive-compulsive traits.

Psychodynamic Components Early psychodynamic explanations for obsessive-compulsive personality disorder focused on fixation at a particular childhood psychosexual stage—in this case the anal stage of development (Freud, 1913). Taken to an extreme, many of the developmental tasks of the toilet-training period, such as staying clean and learning

Reaction formation A defense mechanism in which an unwanted impulse or emotion is turned into its opposite.

Undoing A defense mechanism in which one action or thought is used to "cancel out" another action or thought.

Isolation of affect A defense mechanism in which thoughts occur without associated feelings.

self-control, resemble obsessive-compulsive traits. Fixation at or regression to the anal stage, possibly related to parenting that was overly controlling, anxious, or punitive concerning childhood messes, is still considered relevant to the development of obsessive-compulsive personality disorder (McWilliams, 1994). However, contemporary psychodynamic thinking about this disorder emphasizes the maladaptive use of three defense mechanisms: *reaction formation, undoing,* and *isolation of affect.*

In **reaction formation,** a person turns an unacceptable impulse into its opposite to make it more acceptable. In obsessive-compulsive traits, the wish to make a mess causes anxiety, leading to its opposite: excessive organization and tight control. The defense mechanism of **undoing** refers to the use of symbolic rituals to magically counteract unacceptable feelings. For instance, a physician struggling with extreme guilt about his sexual desires ritually straightened up every desk that he came across in the hospital. Undoing is related to the compulsive traits of obsessive-compulsive personality disorder. **Isolation of affect** refers to the separation of thought and emotions in order to distance oneself from painful feelings. The use of this defense mechanism is responsible for the hyper-rational, emotionless tendencies in obsessive-compulsive personality disorder. All of these defense mechanisms and traits have in common an effort to achieve emotional and interpersonal control, which is the hallmark of this personality disorder. Psychodynamic interventions for obsessive-compulsive personality disorder focus on developing more adaptive means of managing the emotions that are warded off by reaction formation, undoing, and isolation of affect.

Cognitive-Behavioral Components The cognitive style of people with obsessive-compulsive traits can be summed up by the familiar expression "missing the forest for the trees." In other words, a person with obsessive-compulsive personality disorder is likely to focus on details or rules to the extent that the relevance of an activity is lost. Cognitive-behavioral interventions address the irrationality of this cognitive style. For example, an obsessive-compulsive client may start to question his desire to meticulously review every minor decision once it is pointed out to him how his constant ruminations actually get in the way of goals he has set for himself (Beck & Freeman, 1990). Because they are so oriented toward rational analysis, clients with obsessive-compulsive personality disorder easily embrace the cognitive technique of examining and evaluating the evidence for their assumptions. Obsessive-compulsive clients may also be asked to engage in behavioral experiments that address maladaptive assumptions, such as the idea that productivity is more important than pleasure. Beck and Freeman (1990) provide the following example:

> [I]f an obsessive businessman thinks that he does not have time to relax during the day the therapist can have him try relaxation for a few days and then measure how much he accomplishes on the days he uses a relaxation tape and how much he accomplishes on the days he does not. It would also be beneficial to assess to what degree the patient enjoys the days he uses the relaxation technique in contrast to the days he does not. Obsessives tend to value pleasure much less than productivity. It is often therapeutic to help them become aware of this and to evaluate with them the assumptions behind their value system concerning the place of pleasure in their lives.

Beck & Freeman, 1990 (p. 324)

Brief Summary

- The 10 DSM-IV-TR personality disorders are organized into three groups: Cluster A includes three personality disorders characterized by odd or eccentric behavior; Cluster B includes four personality disorders characterized by dramatic,

BOX 11.2 Psychotherapy Outcome Studies

Evaluating the Treatment of Personality Disorders

Regardless of the type of intervention employed, the personality disorders do not tend to have very good treatment outcomes. Since the personality disorders are ego-syntonic and usually life-long patterns of behavior, lasting change is hard to achieve. Though medications (such as anxiolytics or antidepressants) are sometimes helpful in the treatment of personality disorders, they are mainly prescribed to manage emotional symptoms associated with personality disorders, not to modify personality traits.

Most psychotherapy outcome studies fall into one of three categories: *uncontrolled clinical reports, single-case design* studies, and *controlled outcome* studies. **Uncontrolled clinical reports** are descriptive case studies of individual treatments. **Single-case design** studies also evaluate individual treatments but use standardized research measures. **Controlled outcome** studies systematically examine groups of clients being treated for the same disorder, ideally in comparison to a control group not receiving treatment.

Single-case design and controlled outcome studies have found that psychodynamic psychotherapy can be an effective form of treatment for avoidant, obsessive-compulsive, and borderline personality disorders (Barber et al., 1997; Stevenson & Meares, 1999). While uncontrolled clinical reports suggest that psychodynamic interventions can also be helpful for people suffering from other personality disorders (Jorstad, 2001), controlled outcome studies have not yet confirmed this (Crits-Christoph & Barber, 2002). Few controlled outcome studies of cognitive-behavioral treatment of personality disorders exist (Crits-Christoph & Barber, 2002), but, as you can see in the table below, studies have found cognitive-behavioral treatment to be effective for avoidant personality disorder, and of mixed effectiveness for borderline personality disorder. Uncontrolled reports and single-case design studies of cognitive-behavioral interventions have reported more promising results (Beck & Freeman, 1990).

Effectiveness of Cognitive-Behavioral Interventions for Personality Disorders

PERSONALITY DISORDER	UNCONTROLLED CLINICAL REPORTS	SINGLE-CASE DESIGN STUDIES	CONTROLLED OUTCOME STUDIES
Antisocial	+	−	
Avoidant	+	+	+
Borderline	±	−	±
Dependent	+	+	
Histrionic	+		
Narcissistic	+	+	
Obsessive-compulsive	+	−	
Paranoid	+	+	
Schizoid	+		
Schizotypal	+		

Adapted from Beck & Freeman, 1990, p. 12

Note: + indicates cognitive-behavioral interventions found to be effective; − indicates cognitive-behavioral interventions found not to be effective; ± indicates mixed findings.

Uncontrolled clinical reports Descriptive case studies of individual treatments.

Single-case design Studies that evaluate individual treatments but utilize standardized research measures.

Controlled outcome research Studies that systematically examine groups of clients being treated for the same disorder.

Table 11.12 | **Psychodynamic Components of Personality Disorders**

PERSONALITY DISORDER	CHILDHOOD EXPERIENCES	PROMINENT DEFENSE MECHANISMS
Paranoid	• Humiliation, criticism, and ridicule.	• Projection
Schizoid	• Difficult early attachments.	• Withdrawal
	• Ambiguous or perplexing parental communications.	• Intellectualization
Antisocial	• Emotionally turbulent families, cruel and abusive parenting.	• Identification with the aggressor
Borderline	• Inconsistent, unempathic parenting; chaotic or abusive environments.	• Splitting
Histrionic	• Premature sexual experiences.	• Repression
	• Inattentive parenting.	
Narcissistic	• Valued for external qualities.	• Idealization
	• Neglected or highly indulged.	• Devaluation
Avoidant	• Painful interactions involving shame and anxiety.	• Withdrawal • Escape into fantasy
Dependent	• Fixation at the oral phase.	• Regression
	• Belief that relationship is a loving one only if partner takes over decisions and responsibilities.	• Idealization
Obsessive-compulsive	• Fixation at the anal phase related to overly controlling, anxious, or punitive parenting concerning childhood messes.	• Reaction formation • Undoing • Isolation of affect

emotional, or highly erratic behavior; and Cluster C includes three personality disorders characterized by anxious or fearful behavior.

- Cluster A
  - Paranoid personality disorder involves a pattern of distrust and suspiciousness such that others' motives are interpreted as malevolent.
  - Schizoid personality disorder is characterized by detachment from social relationships and a restricted range of emotional expression.
  - Schizotypal personality disorder involves a pattern of acute discomfort in close relationships, cognitive or perceptual distortions, and eccentricities of behavior.
- Cluster B
  - Antisocial personality disorder is characterized by disregard for, and violation of, the rights of others.

Cognitive-Behavioral Components of Personality Disorders

Table 11.13

Condensed from Millon & Davis, 2000; Beck & Freeman, 1990, pp. 54–55

PERSONALITY DISORDER	VIEW OF SELF	VIEW OF OTHERS	BASIC BELIEFS	OVER-DEVELOPED BEHAVIORAL STRATEGIES	UNDER-DEVELOPED BEHAVIORAL STRATEGIES
Paranoid	Righteous Innocent Vulnerable	Interfering Malicious Discriminatory	People are potential enemies.	Vigilance Mistrust Suspiciousness	Serenity Trust Acceptance
Schizoid	Self-sufficient Loner	Intrusive	I need plenty of space.	Autonomy Isolation	Intimacy Reciprocity
Schizotypal	Estranged	Dangerous Confusing	People are perplexing and strange.	Isolation	Reciprocity Social sensitivity
Antisocial	Loner Autonomous Strong	Vulnerable Exploitative	People are there to be taken advantage of.	Combativeness Exploitativeness Predation	Empathy Reciprocity Social sensitivity
Borderline	Unstable Empty	Ideal Worthless	I must feel close to someone.	Manipulation Acting out (drinking, spending, etc.)	Self-soothing Patience Modulated reactions
Histrionic	Glamorous Impressive	Seducible Receptive Admirers	I need to impress.	Exhibitionism Expressiveness Impressionism	Reflectiveness Control
Narcissistic	Special Unique Superior	Inferior Admirers	I am special.	Self-aggrandizement Competitiveness	Sharing Group identification
Avoidant	Vulnerable Socially inept Incompetent	Critical Demeaning Superior	I may get hurt.	Social vulnerability Avoidance Inhibition	Self-assertion Gregariousness
Dependent	Needy Weak Helpless Incompetent	Nurturant Supportive Competent	I am helpless.	Help seeking Clinging	Self-sufficiency Mobility
Obsessive-compulsive	Responsible Fastidious Competent	Irresponsible Casual Incompetent	Errors are bad. I must not err.	Control Responsibility Systematization	Spontaneity Playfulness

Table 11.14 | **Biological Components of Personality Disorders**

PERSONALITY DISORDER	BIOLOGICAL COMPONENT
Schizoid	• "Difficult" temperament
Schizotypal	• Enlarged left frontal lobe ventricles
	• Neurotransmitter abnormalities
Antisocial	• Diminished anxiety reactions
	• Prenatal drug exposure
	• Reduced prefrontal gray and white matter volume
Borderline	• Low serotonin levels
Avoidant	• "Slow-to-warm-up" temperament
Dependent	• "Slow-to-warm-up" temperament

- Borderline personality disorder involves a pattern of instability in interpersonal relationships, self-image, emotions, and marked impulsivity.
- Histrionic personality disorder is marked by excessive emotionality and attention-seeking.
- Narcissistic personality disorder involves chronic and extreme grandiosity, need for admiration, and lack of empathy.
- Cluster C
  - Avoidant personality disorder involves a pattern of social inhibition, feelings of inadequacy, and hypersensitivity to negative evaluation.
  - Dependent personality disorder is characterized by submissive and clinging behavior related to an excessive need to be taken care of.
  - Obsessive-compulsive personality disorder is characterized by preoccupation with orderliness, perfectionism, and control.

Classification in Demographic Context

Demographic factors such as age, gender, and social class are highly relevant in the epidemiology of personality disorders. As you will see, there is also a significant risk of class and gender bias in diagnosing personality disorders.

Age

Personality disorders are rarely diagnosed in children or teenagers, even in cases where such a diagnosis might appear to be warranted. While experts differ about when personality becomes fully developed, most agree that personalities grow and change during childhood and adolescence. Since the personality disorder diagnoses assume that personality has become fixed and rigid, the DSM-IV-TR criteria include the stipulation that an individual must be over 18 to be diagnosed with a personality disorder. To illustrate, the trait of narcissism (need for admiration, preoccupation with the self, fixation on status) is quite common among adolescents, but this is a normal developmental phenomenon, and by adulthood less than 1% of the population meet the criteria for narcissistic personality disorder (APA, 2000). Similarly, many adolescents experience identity crises and experiment with behaviors associated with borderline personality disorder (for example, self-injury, binge drinking, and sexual promiscuity), but these behaviors in adolescence are not necessarily precursors of borderline personality disorder in adulthood (Block et al., 1991).

However, many adults with personality disorders have exhibited traits associated with their disorder throughout their lifetime. Among the Cluster A disorders (paranoid, schizoid, and schizotypal personality disorders) social anxiety, hypersensitivity to others, and poor peer relations are common childhood traits (APA, 2000). As already noted, extreme shyness in childhood is common among people who later develop avoidant personality disorder (Kernberg, Weiner, & Bardenstein, 2000), though not all shy children go on to become avoident. Antisocial personality disorder is frequently heralded by *oppositional defiant disorder* and/or *conduct disorder* during childhood (Lahey & Loeber, 1997), diagnoses involving hostile and delinquent behaviors in children and adolescents (Chapter 13).

Just a phase? Extreme traits and behaviors are common in adolescence, so that clinicians usually defer the diagnosis of a personality disorder until after age 18.

Gender

One of the major controversies in the field of psychopathology centers on the issue of gender bias in the diagnosis of personality disorders. Since personality disorders describe extreme and maladaptive versions of everyday traits, it is not surprising that the personality disorders diagnosed more commonly in women (histrionic, borderline, and dependent personality disorders) involve extremes of stereotypically feminine traits (for example, emotionality and dependence), just as the disorders more commonly diagnosed in men (paranoid, schizoid, schizotypal, antisocial, narcissistic, and obsessive-compulsive) involve extremes of stereotypically masculine traits (such as emotional withdrawal, aggression, and control) (Widiger & Costa, 1994). However, some researchers have suggested that a significant gender bias influences the diagnosis of personality disorders (Caplan, 1987, 1991; Kaplan, 1983). For example, several studies have found that clinicians are more likely to give a "typically female" diagnosis, such as histrionic personality disorder, to a female client than to a male client, even if both clients meet diagnostic criteria for the disorder (Adler, Drake, & Teague, 1990; Slavney & Chase, 1985). Some personality disorder experts have argued that the DSM-IV-TR diagnostic criteria themselves are gender-biased (Bornstein, 1996, 1997). For example, the criteria for dependent personality disorder describe ways that women tend to be dependent (asking or pleading for assistance) but do not describe more typically male forms of dependence (relying on others to maintain their homes and care for their children) (Brown, 1992).

To the extent that gender bias influences the diagnosis of personality disorders, it is not clear that this bias mainly stigmatizes women. For example, when male and female clients both show traits indicative of antisocial personality disorder (a "typically male" diagnosis), clinicians are more likely to assign this disorder to men than to women (Ford & Widiger, 1989). While it is true that women are more frequently diagnosed with histrionic, dependent, and borderline personality disorders, six of the seven other personality disorders (all except avoidant personality disorder) are diagnosed more frequently in men.

Gender bias Women with histrionic traits are more likely to be diagnosed with histrionic personality disorder than men who display the same behaviors. However, men are more likely to receive a "typically male" diagnosis, such as antisocial personality disorder, than women with the same personality features.

Full of promise Claude Brown, author of *Manchild in the Promised Land,* a thinly disguised autobiography in which he details his efforts to escape a life of hustling, drug-dealing, and violence as a young man growing up in Harlem in the 1950s. Here he revisits his old neighborhood.

Class

Most of the personality disorders seem to occur evenly across different socioeconomic groups, although there are a few exceptions. For example, there is some evidence that borderline and dependent personality disorder may occur more frequently among people of lower socioeconomic status (Reich, 1996; Swartz et al., 1990) and strong evidence that the criminal behaviors associated with the diagnosis of antisocial personality disorder occur disproportionately among members of lower socioeconomic classes (Alarcon & Foulks, 1995). Given the realities of living in poverty, it is not surprising that some researchers have questioned whether it is appropriate to apply the antisocial personality disorder diagnosis to people who live in communities where engaging in violence and theft can be seen as survival strategies and where prison life may be preferable to living in poverty (Alarcon & Foulks, 1995). Indeed, in his book *Manchild in the Promised Land,* Claude Brown speaks of the security and care provided by the juvenile detention system and how it compared favorably with his life in his neighborhood.

> I was only about fifteen, and I couldn't get a job. I couldn't do anything. I didn't like the idea of not being able to get a place and having to stay out on the street. So I just got fed up one day and went back to Warwick [a juvenile detention facility]. I went down to the Youth House where the bus used to pick up all the boys going to Warwick every other Friday. I just told the bus driver and the other cat that was on the bus that my name was Claude Brown, that I had stayed down from Warwick, and that they were looking for me. They said, "Hop on." So I just hopped on and went up to Warwick.
>
> Brown, 1965 (p. 152)

Brief Summary

- According to the DSM-IV-TR, personality disorders should not be diagnosed in clients under the age of 18 because personality has not yet stabilized.

- Some experts contend that there is considerable gender bias in the diagnosis of personality disorders.

- Most of the personality disorders appear to occur at the same rates regardless of social class, with the exception of antisocial personality disorder and possibly borderline and dependent personality disorders, which occur disproportionately among members of lower socioeconomic groups.

Critical Thinking Question | In your view, would diagnosing Beth (described in one of the case vignettes at the beginning of the chapter) with dependent personality disorder be a gender-biased diagnosis? Why or why not?

Cultural and Historical Relativism in Defining and Classifying Personality Disorders

When we say that someone has a personality disorder, we are saying that he or she consistently exhibits extreme and maladaptive personality traits that do not fit with accepted social standards for behavior. Of course, different cultures have different ideas about what are considered acceptable behaviors (see Table 11.16) so that the definition of specific personality disorders is **culturally relative**. For example, Buddhist priests might meet DSM-IV-TR diagnostic criteria for schizoid personality disorder (engaging

| Culturally Normative Examples of Traits Associated with DSM-IV-TR Personality Disorders | Table 11.16 |

Based on Buffenstein, 1997 and Foulks, 1996

Paranoid ■ Immigrant and minority populations may express extreme mistrust of institutions and authorities.

Schizotypal ■ Shaman or mystics in some societies engage in magical thinking and have unusual perceptual experiences.

Histrionics ■ An intensely expressive emotional style that appears excessive or flamboyant by American standards is not unusual in some Mediterranean cultures. Margaret Mead documented similar traits among the males of the Tchambuli tribe of New Guinea (1963).

Narcissistic ■ The culturally valued trait of "machismo", as sometimes expressed by young Latino males, can be mistaken for narcissism.

Avoidant ■ Immigrant and minority cultures may have avoidant traits while in the process of becoming acculturated to a new culture or community.

Dependent ■ Passivity, extreme politeness, and deference to others and their opinions is a normal, culturally valued behavior in some Asian and Arctic societies.

Obsessive-compulsive ■ Devout religious believers may appear to be overly scrupulous with regard to morality and preoccupied with rules and rituals.

Cultural relativism Though some of the diagnostic criteria of schizoid personality disorder might describe the life of a Buddhist monk, such a diagnosis is obviously inappropriate when applied outside of the cultural context for which it was designed.

in solitary activity, lack of emotion, appearing to lack sexual desire, etc.) (Roland, 1988), but this diagnosis would obviously be inappropriate in light of the fact that such behavior is not only appropriate and accepted, but revered within its cultural context.

The core concept of *historical relativism* is also important in regard to the personality disorders. Needless to say, norms for social behavior change over time. A twenty-first century middle-class American woman who expects her husband to make all of the significant family decisions, who does not disagree with her husband for fear of losing his support, and who worries that she will be unable to care for herself if left alone might receive a diagnosis of dependent personality disorder. But in the 1950s the same woman might have been considered a typical housewife.

Not surprisingly, the criteria for diagnosing personality disorder diagnoses have changed considerably over time. The original *Diagnostic and Statistical Manual*, published in 1952, contained the first broad, systematic attempt to provide a classification system for personality disorders (APA, 1952). Eleven personality types were described; some (paranoid, schizoid, and antisocial personality disorders) have been retained in every subsequent edition of the DSM, others ("dissocial," "inadequate," and "emotionally unstable" personality disorders) have been altered or dropped altogether, and still others ("addictions" and "sexual deviations") have been reclassified and renamed as symptom disorders on Axis I.

In addition, the DSM-IV-TR includes an appendix titled "Criteria Sets and Axes Provided for Further Study" which lists new diagnostic categories being considered for inclusion in future editions of the DSM. The disorders in this appendix are usually controversial or not yet well-validated; they may later be removed from the DSM altogether or "upgraded" to the status of a new disorder. For example, self-defeating personality disorder was included in the appendix of the DSM-III-R (1987) but removed

Historical relativism June Cleaver, of the TV show *Leave it to Beaver*, was considered to represent the ideal 1950s mother. A woman, in today's world, who similarly defers to her husband on all major decisions might be viewed as overly dependent.

from the DSM-IV (1994) due to protests that it could be unfairly applied to women who are coerced into remaining in abusive relationships (Walker, 1987). At present, two proposed personality disorder diagnoses (depressive personality disorder and passive-aggressive personality disorder) are being studied for possible inclusion on Axis II in the next edition of the DSM.

The Advantages and Limitations of the DSM-IV-TR Personality Disorder Diagnoses

For a variety of reasons, the DSM personality disorder diagnoses have historically shown relatively weak **reliability** and **validity** (Zimmerman & Coryell, 1989); the reliability of most Axis I disorders is considerably higher (Chapter 4). This poor reliability and validity stems, in part, from the fact that many personality disorders, especially those within the same cluster, have overlapping diagnostic criteria. For example, attention-seeking behavior is common in both histrionic and narcissistic personality disorders, while social withdrawal is an important component of schizoid, schizotypal, and avoidant personality disorders.

In fact, a high percentage of people who meet criteria for one personality disorder diagnosis also meet criteria for another. In a study of 627 people with personality disorders, researchers found that more than half of the participants met the diagnostic criteria for two or more personality disorder diagnoses (Stuart et al., 1998). Several personality disorders frequently co-occur: schizotypal and paranoid, schizotypal and schizoid, narcissistic and histrionic, and avoidant and schizotypal. Indeed, real-life examples of people who have traits associated with many different personality disorders are commonplace (see Box 11.3). The common co-occurrence of some personality disorder diagnoses has caused researchers to wonder whether personality disorders that tend to be diagnosed together (such as schizoid and schizotypal) are really two distinct conditions, or simply variations on a single underlying theme.

Another limitation of the personality disorder diagnoses stems from the fact that the DSM-IV-TR relies on **polythetic**, or multiple, criteria sets (Segal & Falk, 1998). While polythetic criteria sets can enhance the reliability of diagnoses—since a person is required to meet a minimum number of criteria in order to be diagnosed with a disorder—no one criterion is critical to the overall diagnosis. For example, there are seven symptoms listed in the DSM-IV-TR for the diagnosis of antisocial personality disorder but only three of the seven symptoms need to be present to warrant the diagnosis (see Table 11.5). Thus, two people who do not share a single trait could be assigned the same personality disorder diagnosis. To address these problems, some experts have proposed that personality disorders should be reclassified in **dimensional** terms (in which clinicians would rate *how much* of a given trait a client exhibits) rather than using the current **categorical** method (in which clinicians have to arrive at a "yes" or "no" answer as to whether a client meets criteria for various personality disorders). This proposal is under consideration for future editions of the DSM.

Brief Summary

- The classification of personality disorders is **culturally and historically relative** because different cultures and historical periods have different norms for behavior.

- The DSM personality disorder diagnoses have undergone considerable changes over time.

- Some personality disorders have overlapping diagnostic criteria and often co-occur, posing challenges to the reliability and validity of the diagnoses.

Reliability The consistency of a test, measurement, or category system.

Validity The accuracy of a test, measurement, or category system.

Polythetic Diagnostic criteria sets in which a person is required to meet a minimum number of predetermined diagnostic criteria in order to warrant a diagnosis—no one criterion is critical to the overall diagnosis.

Dimensional system A diagnostic system in which individuals are rated for the degree to which they exhibit certain traits.

Categorical system A diagnostic system, like the DSM system, in which individuals are diagnosed according to whether or not they fit certain defined categories.

BOX 11.3 One Man, Three (or More) Diagnoses

Theodore Kaczynski

Theodore Kaczynski—also known as the Unabomber—seems to suffer from profound personality pathology, but he is very difficult to categorize. Kaczynski's mail bombs killed 3 and injured 23 people, but throughout his trial he maintained that his actions were justified. His remorseless disregard for the rights (and lives!) of others clearly suggests the diagnosis of antisocial personality disorder. Yet prior to his arrest in 1996, his behavior was also consistent with schizoid and schizotypal personality disorders and schizophrenia (Chapter 12). Kaczynski lived alone in a remote cabin, expressed little interest in relationships with others, even members of his own family, and was extremely eccentric in appearance, thinking, and behavior. Extensive investigations into Kaczynski's background found that from earliest childhood on he had never had a real friend other than his brother (McFadden, 1996). Kaczynski also has traits that are consistent with paranoid personality disorder, such as his extreme distrust of others and tendency to hold grudges for extended periods of time.

Kaczynski confounded authorities for over 18 years. He was finally caught after *The Washington Post* agreed to publish his manifesto against technology in exchange for his promise to end his violent behavior. Kaczynski's brother recognized his sibling's words and notified the FBI that the man they were looking for was a mathematical genius living in a Montana cabin. The following excerpts from a biographical account document Ted Kaczynski's complex and lifelong emotional troubles.

Teddy once showed a school wrestler how to make a more powerful mini-bomb. It went off one day in chemistry class, blowing out two windows and inflicting temporary hearing damage on a girl. Everyone was reprimanded, but Teddy was unfazed. He later set off blasts that echoed across the neighborhood and sent garbage cans flying...

Teddy skipped another grade and after only three years graduated from high school in 1958, and won a scholarship to Harvard. He was only 16. "The thought was, if he went to a university, such as Harvard, he might not have the pressure to conform in a working-type class community like Evergreen Park, and that the experience might be liberating for him socially" David [his brother] explained...

In the next three years, Mr. Kaczynski lived in a seven-man suite at Eliot House, one of a dozen residential dormitories overlooking the Charles River, but he had almost no contact with his suitemates. ... One suitemate, Patrick McIntosh, now a Colorado astronomer, said that in three years, "I don't recall more than 10 words being spoken by him." ... "He was intensely introverted ... he wouldn't allow us to know him. I never met anybody like him who was as extreme in avoiding socialization. He would almost run to his room to avoid conversation if one of us tried to approach him"...

David Kaczynski said his brother wrote some letters home, and one mentioned "a girl he kind of admired from afar." He added, "He eventually asked her for a date and was rebuffed." If Ted was miserable, he never mentioned it, David said. He was "a person who nursed a sense of injury."

After graduating from Harvard, Ted Kaczynski received a Ph.D. in mathematics at the University of Michigan and then secured a prestigious position as a professor at the University of California at Berkeley. He abruptly quit the position after only two years.

David [his brother] saw the decision to quit mathematics as part of a pattern in his brother's life. "He was a person who seemed capable of closing doors on things, on people, on stages of his life," he said. "That cutting himself off was part of what he was about. At some point, it happened with me. At some point, it happened with our parents. ... It was also true with a friend of his who would call in high school. 'Hi, it's Mosny. Is Ted around?' 'I don't want to talk to him.' You can expand that whole theme of cutting oneself off."

McFadden, 1996, (pp. 12–13)

Brotherly love After 18 years of searching, the FBI ultimately located Ted Kaczynski based on information they received from his brother, David. Kaczynski's brother asked the FBI to rule out the death penalty in exchange for information about Ted's whereabouts.

- Polythetic criteria sets have improved the reliability of the personality disorder diagnoses, but some experts argue in favor of dimensional, rather than categorical, diagnoses for personality disorders.

Critical Thinking Question | **C**an you think of other personality traits that might be valued in one cultural context, but considered abnormal in another?

Case Vignettes | **Treatment**

Tyler | Paranoid Personality Disorder

Tyler began his first therapy session by explaining to his therapist that he was worried that his girlfriend Sarah was having an affair. When the therapist asked what made Tyler think that she was unfaithful, he could offer little in the way of objective evidence, but said that he could just "tell" that things between them had changed. As the evaluation continued, the therapist asked about Tyler's experience of medical school. Tyler seemed guarded in his response and complained about many of his classmates, saying that they were excessively competitive and that he had found it better not to associate too closely with anyone. He was sure that, given the opportunity, they would make every effort to ruin his reputation. To this end, he had told few classmates about his long-standing relationship with Sarah for fear they would try to sabotage it.

Tyler agreed to begin therapy, hoping to get some relief from his suspicions about Sarah. Before too long, Tyler told his therapist about his attraction to one of his medical school classmates and his worry that Sarah would think him unfaithful for looking at other women. The therapist suggested that perhaps Tyler's concern about Sarah's fidelity was partly a concern about his own.

In a subsequent session, Tyler's therapist pointed out that he seemed to be somewhat angry with her (the therapist) that day. Tyler told her that he had seen her when she was out enjoying herself with friends at a restaurant, and he had begun to feel that she found him boring and repetitive, not nearly as interesting as her other clients. The therapist was able to use this transference reaction to help Tyler see that his anger toward others was related to worries about whether he was interesting and worthwhile. Over time, Tyler's doubts about Sarah's fidelity diminished somewhat, and he was able to appreciate that he often had such doubts when he was feeling insecure or disappointed in the relationship. The therapy continued to focus on the ways that these emotional conflicts contributed to his general suspiciousness and hostility.

Case Discussion | Paranoid Personality Disorder

Tyler's therapist focused on psychodynamic exploration of Tyler's paranoid beliefs that most people are malicious and untrustworthy. Using traditional psychodynamic techniques (attention to defense mechanisms and transference phenomena) Tyler and his therapist were able to learn how his feelings of inadequacy, his fear of being disappointed in relationships, and his projection of his own unacceptable impulses fueled Tyler's paranoia, such as his fear that Sarah was cheating on him. This understanding led to a decrease in Tyler's paranoia, though he remained somewhat guarded and aloof.

Beth | Dependent Personality Disorder

Beth was very glad to begin therapy and hoped that her therapist would help her to make the important decisions she now faced. The therapist avoided offering advice to Beth (feeling certain that Beth would accept any suggestion uncritically and become dependent on her) and instead began the therapy by trying to help Beth improve her mood. After several weeks of talking about the stresses of the upcoming graduation, and with the help of antidepressant medication, Beth's mood did begin to improve.

Once Beth was feeling less depressed, her therapist began to challenge Beth about her difficulty deciding on a career or motivating herself to find a job. Beth said that she worried that she would be unable to do the work expected of her in a job. Using cognitive techniques, the therapist helped Beth to evaluate the evidence for and against this belief. Given Beth's excellent academic record, it was not hard to highlight the distortions in her thinking. Over time, Beth became increasingly aware that her beliefs about her own incompetence did not really reflect reality. She began to use her therapy to talk about how she had been "coddled" by her parents. She was torn between feeling that their extreme devotion was the "essence of love" and being envious of her friends whose parents seemed to encourage and expect their children to become independent adults. As Beth began to apply for jobs and look for a place to live, she was met with surprising resistance from her family. In therapy, Beth began to explore the reasons behind her parents' growing insistence that she come home after graduation. During a weekend visit with her family she observed that her parents seemed to have difficulty talking with each other and wondered why they focused so much on her instead of dealing with problems in their marriage.

Case Discussion | Dependent Personality Disorder

Beth's therapist combined a number of interventions to address Beth's excessive dependence. An initial focus on her depressive symptoms and a trial of antidepressant medication lifted Beth's mood enough that she could begin to work on other issues. Beth and her therapist began to evaluate the evidence for and against her dysfunctional beliefs, and as Beth came to appreciate the distortions inherent in these beliefs she recognized that her parents fostered and rewarded her excessive dependence and that they might have done so in order to distract themselves from their own troubles.

Chapter Summary

- Personality is considered to be disordered when personality traits are maladaptive, rigid, and extreme.

- Most of the traits associated with personality disorders occur on a ***continuum between normal and abnormal behavior***. Personality disorders usually involve extreme versions of common personality traits.

- The DSM-IV-TR personality disorders are organized into three groups:

  - *Cluster A* (characterized by odd or eccentric behavior): paranoid, schizoid, and schizotypal personality disorders

  - *Cluster B* (characterized by dramatic, emotional or highly erratic behavior): antisocial, borderline, histrionic, and narcissistic personality disorders

  - *Cluster C* (characterized by anxious or fearful behavior): avoidant, dependant, obsessive-compulsive personality disorders

- In keeping with the ***principle of multiple causality***, the psychodynamic, cognitive-behavioral, sociocultural, and biological perspectives have different, but often overlapping or complementary, ideas about the causes and treatments of personality disorders.

- Demographic ***context*** factors, such as age, gender, and social class are highly relevant to the personality disorder diagnoses.

- The classification of personality disorders is ***culturally and historically relative*** because different cultures and historical periods have different norms for behavior.

- Some personality disorders have overlapping diagnostic criteria and personality disorders often co-occur, posing challenges to the reliability and validity of the diagnoses and highlighting the ***advantages and limitations of diagnosis***.

Henry Darger, *After M. Whurther Run Glandelinians Attack and Blow up Train Carrying Children to Refuge.* **Collection of the American Folk Art Museum, New York. Gift of Sam and Betsey Farber. ©Kiyoko Lerner. Photo by Gavin Ashworth, New York. P10.2000.1b**

Henry Darger (1892–1972), who probably suffered from schizophrenia, lived in almost complete seclusion in a Chicago apartment for most of his life. Upon his death, Darger's landlord found that he had written a 15,145-page epic story titled *The Story of the Vivian Girls, in What Is Known as the* ....continues on page 394

henry darger

PSYCHOSIS AND SCHIZOPHRENIA

Case Vignette

Peter had a relatively happy and uneventful childhood. As the only child of older parents, Peter enjoyed their exclusive attention. He was a highly intelligent boy, with a tendency to be somewhat shy and quiet. Peter's parents were also introverted, and the family was oriented toward intellectual rather than social pursuits. Peter got along well with peers in grade school, but he never had close friends and preferred playing by himself with his toys. In middle school, Peter became fascinated with music, and by high school he was an accomplished cellist. He was accepted at a nearby college where he decided to major in music.

Peter's freshman year went well. He liked the music program and did outstanding work. Peter was not very social, but this didn't bother him or concern his parents since that was typical for him. However, when Peter returned for his sophomore year, everything seemed different to him. He told his parents that he felt strange, alienated, and unreal. He was having trouble concentrating, and his music suffered. At first, his parents suspected that he was experiencing a "sophomore slump" or that he might be physically sick. Then, during the winter term, Peter began to behave bizarrely and clearly was not himself. He would not wash or change clothes for days and sometimes only left his room to eat. Peter began to babble and talk strangely over the phone to his parents. Classmates and faculty noticed that he seemed to be talking to himself. After a few weeks of this behavior, Peter's parents came to visit and see what was wrong. When they saw Peter they were immediately alarmed. He looked disheveled, and had a blank, hollow expression in his eyes. Their concerns only increased when they spoke to him. Peter seemed scared and accused them of being terrorists and "devils." He ran around his room in circles mumbling that he was the Messiah, and he appeared to be responding to imaginary voices. Peter's parents immediately called campus security, who escorted the family to a nearby hospital.

DEFINING PSYCHOSIS AND SCHIZOPHRENIA

Peter is exhibiting a symptom known as **psychosis**—a state of being profoundly out of touch with reality. Psychosis can take many forms. People who are psychotic may experience **hallucinations**—abnormal sensory experiences such as hearing or seeing nonexistent things—and/or **delusions**, which are fixed, false, and often bizarre beliefs, such as Peter's idea that he is the Messiah. Psychosis can also take other forms, as we'll see, and it can occur as a symptom in several different mental disorders as well as in some medical conditions. For example, we saw in Chapter 6 that some severe mood disorders can include psychosis among their symptoms. But one mental disorder is most closely associated with psychosis: *schizophrenia.* When people equate schizophrenia with true madness or insanity, as they often do, it is usually because of schizophrenia's prominent psychotic symptoms.

Psychosis A state of being profoundly out of touch with reality.

Hallucinations Abnormal sensory experiences such as hearing or seeing nonexistent things.

Delusions Fixed, false, and often bizarre beliefs.

...continued from page 392

Realms of the Unreal, of the Glandeco-Angelinnion War Storm, Caused by the Child Slave Rebellion. **The text—a tale of seven young girls under attack from a group of men known as the Glandelinians—was accompanied by over 150 watercolor and pencil illustrations depicting the strange and gory battles between the Vivian girls and their enemies. Darger's work is considered one of the twentieth century's most significant collections of "outsider art," or artwork by a person with no formal training.**

As you can see in the case of Peter, schizophrenia is a terribly incapacitating disorder. In addition to psychosis, schizophrenia causes impairment in many mental functions and a general disruption and decline in one's ability to function normally. While there are now treatments available that can significantly help most clients with schizophrenia, the disorder still takes an enormous toll on clients, their families, and society. Though it is not a common disorder, schizophrenia is hardly rare: it is found across almost all known cultures in approximately 1 out of every 100 people (Harrap & Trower, 2001). In 1990, it was estimated that the total socioeconomic impact of schizophrenia in the United States alone was $32.5 billion (Coleman & Gillburg, 1996; Taber, Lewis, & Hurley, 2001). The human cost of schizophrenia, in diminished human potential, disrupted families, and suicide, is, of course, incalculable. Suicide, in fact, is a tragically common occurrence in people with schizophrenia (Loas, Yon, & Bralet, 2001; Raymont, 2001; Torrey, 2001). According to two Swedish studies, up to 12% of individuals diagnosed with schizophrenia committed suicide within 17 years of their first hospitalization (Allebeck & Wistedt, 1986; Coleman & Gillberg, 1996). Twenty to forty percent of people diagnosed with schizophrenia attempt suicide at some point in their lives (APA, 2000).

Because schizophrenia is such a profound and often frightening disorder, it is frequently misunderstood, and many popular myths about it are widespread. As a result, we'll begin by discussing what schizophrenia is *not* before discussing what it *is*. Perhaps the two most common myths about schizophrenia are that it consists of a "split personality," and that individuals with schizophrenia are dangerously violent. As to the former, schizophrenia actually involves disruptions of mental functions rather than a division into multiple identities. Having multiple, alternating identities constitutes a totally separate disorder—the dissociative disorder known as *dissociative identity disorder* (Chapter 7). As for the second myth, it is true that a subset of individuals with schizophrenia are often violent, and that impulsive, disorganized behavior can be among the symptoms of the disorder. However, the majority of individuals with schizophrenia, especially those receiving treatment, are no more dangerous than anyone else, and they are just as likely to be withdrawn and inhibited as they are to be impulsive (Gut-Fayand et al., 2001; Hausmann & Fleischhacker, 2000).

Unfortunately, it is easier to describe what schizophrenia is *not* than to describe what it is. Schizophrenia is a complex disorder that has always eluded clear definition (Coleman & Gillberg, 1996; Jablensky, 1997). Despite our rapidly increasing knowledge of the disorder and increasingly refined criteria for diagnosing it, there remains much debate over the essential nature and symptoms of schizophrenia and what distinguishes it from related disorders (Torrey, 1999; Tsuang, Stone, & Faraone, 2000). These debates involve some of the core concepts in abnormal psychology, which, as we have seen, affect the definitions, classifications, explanations, and treatments of all mental disorders. With respect to schizophrenia, the core concepts of **cultural and historical relativism** and the **principle of multiple causality** are especially relevant.

CLASSIFYING PSYCHOSIS AND SCHIZOPHRENIA

We begin our study of schizophrenia with a discussion of some of the cultural and historical factors that have affected the ways in which schizophrenia has been defined and classified (Thomas, 1997).

Cultural and Historical Relativism in Defining and Classifying Schizophrenia

Psychotic madness has been observed and documented since ancient times (Libbrecht, 1995; Palha & Esteves, 1997). Descriptions of psychosis can be found in the Hindu Ayur Veda texts, the Old and New Testaments, and many other ancient sources (Johnstone, 1994; Sutker & Adams, 2001). People suffering from psychosis have not always been regarded as sick. At some times and in certain cultures, psychotic individuals have been viewed as especially creative, spiritual, wise, or enlightened (Schuldberg, 2001). In fact, this attitude resurfaced in the Western world during the 1960s, when certain theorists romanticized schizophrenic psychosis as a heightened appreciation of reality or an effort to be sane in an insane world (see Box 12.1).

Within the Western scientific and medical traditions, however, psychosis has been generally regarded as a symptom of illness. Interest in classifying different forms and causes of psychosis began to flourish in the 1800s as part of the overall progress in medical science. At that time, most descriptions of psychosis involved people who seemed to become psychotic in the context of severe, episodic *mood* states—such as what we would now call major depression with psychosis (Johnstone, 1994). However, written descriptions of another pattern of psychotic disorder—more chronic, and not associated with extreme mood fluctuations—began to appear in the early nineteenth century in publications by Phillipe Pinel, the psychiatric reformer, and others (Gottesman, 1991; Johnstone, 1994). Throughout the nineteenth century, medical authorities attempted to come up with classification systems for different forms of psychosis. Near the end of the century, a useful distinction was proposed by Emil Kraepelin (1856–1926), a professor of psychiatry in Heidelberg and Munich who is often referred to as the "father of modern psychiatry." In the sixth edition of his textbook, Kraepelin (1923) suggested that psychoses could be divided into two broad classes: manic-depressive psychosis (now called bipolar disorder) and **dementia praecox**, which comes from the Greek for "premature dementia." This name, which Kraepelin borrowed from Benedict Morel's 1852 case description of a psychotic adolescent, reflected the fact that this second pattern of psychosis seemed to be characterized by an early adult onset, a progressive deteriorating course, and a global disruption of perceptual and cognitive functions (Gottesman, 1991; Johnstone, 1994; Tsuang et al., 2000). This was in contrast to manic-depressive psychosis, which typically had a later onset, periods of normal functioning in between episodes, and relatively normal cognitive functioning. Here is Kraepelin's description of a typical case of dementia praecox.

Dementia praecox An early term for schizophrenia, from the Greek for "premature dementia."

> The patient was a 21-year-old man who had become more and more solitary over the past few years. A year previously he had failed university examinations and then became preoccupied with the belief that he was ugly, that he had a rupture and that he was suffering from wasting of the spinal cord, which he believed was the result of masturbation. He had stopped seeing friends because he believed they knew about this and were making fun of him about it. Prior to admission he began crying a great deal, masturbated, ran about aimlessly, was occasionally excited and disturbed at night, played senseless tunes on the piano, and began to write obscure observations on life.
>
> In hospital he was in a state of excitement for several days, during which he chattered in a confused way, made faces, ran about, wrote in disconnected scraps, which were crossed and recrossed with flourishes and meaningless combinations of letters. After this a tranquil state ensued. The patient would lie in bed for weeks or months, or sit around without feeling the slightest need to occupy himself, or at best turning over the pages of a book. He would stare ahead with expressionless features,

BOX 12.1 The Politics of Psychosis

Mark Vonnegut and *The Eden Express*

Mark Vonnegut's memoir of his schizophrenic breakdown, *The Eden Express* (1975), chronicles the contrast between his terrifying ordeal and the romanticized view of psychosis held by his friends in the 1960s counterculture and supported by the anti-psychiatry writings of R. D. Laing and Thomas Szasz. Vonnegut, the son of the novelist Kurt Vonnegut, Jr., had been sympathetic to these radical views of psychosis as a creative or healthy process before his breakdown, but his "not-so-cheery" experience changed his mind. Here are some excepts from his book.

If I had had a well defined role in a stable culture, it might have been far simpler to sort things out. For a hippie, son of a counterculture hero, B.A. in religion, genetic biochemical disposition to schizophrenia, setting up a commune in the wilds of British Columbia, things tended to run together...

(p. ix)

At first my friends and I were doubtful that there was any medical problem. It was all politics and philosophy. The hospital bit was just grasping at straws when all else failed. It took quite a bit to convince us that anything as pedestrian as biochemistry was relevant to something as profound and poetic as what I was going through. For me to admit the possibility that I might not have gone nuts had they given me pills when I left was a tremendous concession...

(p. 248)

I myself was a Laing-Szasz fan and didn't believe there was really any such thing as schizophrenia. I thought it was just a convenient label for patients whom doctors were confused about. I even worked in a mental hospital for several months without being convinced otherwise...

(p. 265)

I cracked in very hip surroundings. While it has advantages in terms of people being willing to go the extra mile, having more respect and sympathy for the terrors you're going through, it can also add some new problems. I was often afraid to tell my friends what was going on, not so much because they'd think I was nuts, but more because it might sound like bragging. Many of the things that were happening to me were things I was supposed to like: ego death, communicating the supernatural, hypersensitivity of all sorts. If there's anything worse than bragging about such things, it's not liking them...

(p. 268)

over which a vacant smile would play. When he had visitors he would sit without showing any interest, would not ask what was happening at home, hardly ever greeted his parents, and would go back indifferently to the ward.

McKenna, 2001 (p. 169)

The term "schizophrenia" was coined about 15 years later by Eugen Bleuler, a Swiss psychiatrist. Bleuler (1911/1950) intended to further Kraepelin's work, although Bleuler felt that Kraepelin's diagnostic category was too narrow because in some cases, he felt, there were no prominent psychotic symptoms or evidence of early onset and gradual deteriorating course. As a result, Bleuler was more optimistic than Kraepelin about the prognosis of the disorder (Bleuler, 1911/1950; Coleman & Gillberg, 1996; Wyatt, 2001). Bleuler's focus was on symptoms that have become known as the "4 A's" of schizophrenia: (1) extreme *Ambivalence* (referring to a kind of paralysis of the will); (2) abnormal *Associations* in thinking; (3) disturbed *Affect* (emotion); and (4) *Autism* (a withdrawal into fantasy instead of focus on reality). (Incidentally, the term "autism," which Bleuler coined, is now used to describe a separate disorder of childhood involving profound social, communicative, and behavioral disturbances—see Chapter 13.) Bleuler renamed this syndrome of symptoms **schizophre-nia**, from the Greek for "split mind" (*schizo* = schism or split; *phrenia* = mind). This term has contributed to the common misunderstanding that schizophrenia involves multiple personalities, but Bleuler's intention was to highlight the profound disruptions in thought, emotion, and behavior in schizophrenia, not a condition of multiple identities. "I call dementia praecox 'schizophrenia,'" Bleuler (1911/1950) wrote, "because the 'splitting' of different psychic functions is one of its most important characteristics."

Bleuler also believed that schizophrenia was probably not a single disorder, but a group of related "schizophrenias," which foreshadowed current thinking about the disorder (Bleuler, 1911/1950). His approach—including his expansion of the diagnostic category—became widely accepted, particularly in the United States. However, this led to problems in the *reliability* of the diagnosis of schizophrenia (Bentall, 1990), since European psychiatrists tended to stay closer to Kraepelin's narrower definition even though they used Bleuler's new diagnostic term. This problem persisted for decades, and it resulted in many more diagnoses of schizophrenia in the United States than in Europe, where the same types of patients were often classified as manic-depressive, as shown in Figure 12.1 (Cooper et al., 1972; Wing, Cooper, & Sartorius, 1974). Reliability did not improve until the 1970s, when more uniform criteria were agreed upon (Wing et al., 1974). For example, the first two editions of the DSM generally followed Bleuler's model in defining schizophrenia, although they did include psychosis as a central symptom (Tsuang et al., 2000). The DSM-I (1952) and DSM-II (1968) criteria for diagnosing schizophrenia were also somewhat vague and imprecise. Because of the reliability and validity problems associated with these vague criteria, and in keeping with the reform mission of the DSM-III (1980) emphasizing reliability and empirical observation, the criteria for schizophrenia were clari-

Schizophrenia A disorder marked by psychosis and a decline in adaptive functioning.

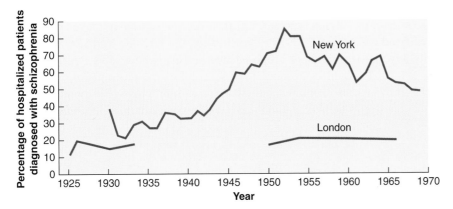

Figure 12.1 Differences in Diagnosing Schizophrenia Between the United States and United Kingdom This graph shows the enormous difference in the percentage of hospitalized psychiatric patients diagnosed with schizophrenia in the United States as compared to the United Kingdom, especially during the 1950s and 1960s. This difference highlights the core concept of *cultural relativism* in classifying schizophrenia since the difference cannot be accounted for by actual differences in the prevalence of schizophrenia between the two countries. In addition, the large increase in the percentage of patients diagnosed with schizophrenia within the United States between the 1930s and the 1950s illustrates *historical relativism* in classifying schizophrenia since the profound increase was largely due to changes in diagnostic practice over that time period.

Gottesman, 1991, p. 32

fied and narrowed in the third edition. Psychosis was maintained as central to the diagnosis of schizophrenia in the DSM-III. This brings us to the current DSM-IV-TR criteria for schizophrenia, which we turn to next.

Brief Summary

- Psychosis is a symptom involving a profound loss of contact with normal reality. Hallucinations—abnormal sensory perceptions—and delusions—false, fixed, and often bizarre beliefs—are the most common forms of psychosis.

- Psychosis can occur in many mental disorders, but it is most frequently associated with schizophrenia.

- Although it has been described for hundreds of years, schizophrenia still eludes clear definition. Kraepelin pioneered modern attempts to define the disorder with his category called dementia praecox, or premature dementia. Bleuler coined a different term for the disorder—schizophrenia—in 1911 because he was not convinced that the disorder really involved premature, progressive dementia.

- Despite considerable overlap in Kraepelin's and Bleuler's views of schizophrenia, the differences between them led to problems with the reliability of the diagnosis. The diagnostic criteria for schizophrenia have been refined and standardized in the recent editions of the DSM.

| *Critical* *Thinking* *Question* | **D**oes the case of Peter help you understand why schizophrenia has been subject to so much misunderstanding and confusion? How so? |

The DSM-IV-TR Categories

For many years, researchers have tried to identify and clarify the core symptoms of schizophrenia. Empirical studies attempting to do so have yielded conflicting results, perhaps because schizophrenia is not a single disorder, but a group of related disorders or subtypes (Andreason et al., 1995; Roy, Merette, & Maziade, 2001; Stuart et al., 1999). This hypothesis, originally proposed by Bleuler, is now supported by many researchers, and up to 70 different subtypes of schizophrenia have been proposed. The DSM-IV-TR provides an operational, or working, definition of schizophrenia, but many experts question whether it captures the "true" essence of the syndrome (Tsuang et al., 2000).

Schizophrenia

The DSM-IV-TR currently defines schizophrenia in terms of a constellation of severe cognitive and behavioral symptoms that last for a certain length of time (six months or more) and result in significant life impairment. The symptoms are divided into five types; in most cases, two or more symptom types must be present in order to make the diagnosis (see Table 12.1). The first two types of symptoms—delusions and hallucinations—are familiar as the most common forms of psychosis. The next two symptom types—**disorganized speech** and **grossly disorganized behavior** (discussed in detail later in the chapter), are also considered psychotic under the broadest definition of the term. As a result, they are grouped together with delusions and hallucinations as what are called the **positive** or **type I** symptoms of schizophrenia (Crow, 1985; Ho & Andreason, 2001). The term "positive" is not meant to imply that these symptoms are good. Rather, it conveys that all of these symptoms represent *excesses,* exaggerations, or distortions from normal functioning—the presence of something that is normally

Disorganized speech Severe disruptions in the process of speech.

Grossly disorganized behavior Bizarre or disrupted behavioral patterns, such as dishevelment, extreme agitation, uncontrollable childlike silliness, or an inability to perform simple activities of daily living.

Positive or **type I symptoms of schizophrenia** Symptoms that represent pathological excesses, exaggerations, or distortions from normal functioning, such as delusions, hallucinations, and disorganized speech, thought, or behavior.

Diagnostic Criteria for Schizophrenia	Table 12.1

Adapted from DSM-IV-TR (APA, 2000)

- Two or more of the following five symptoms:
  - Delusions
  - Hallucinations
  - Disorganized speech
  - Grossly disorganized or catatonic behavior
  - Negative symptoms (such as lack of emotion, speech, or motivation)
- Social/occupational dysfunction and decline
- Continuous signs of the disorder for at least 6 months

absent. Positive symptoms contrast with the **negative**, or **type II** symptoms of schizophrenia, which constitute the fifth symptom listed in the DSM-IV-TR. The negative symptoms refer to the *deficit* aspects of schizophrenia—the absence of functions that are normally present—such as apathy, withdrawal, poor concentration, and lack of emotion (Limpert & Amador, 2001) (see Table 12.2). Let's look at each symptom type in more detail.

Negative or **type II symptoms of schizophrenia** Symptoms that represent pathological deficits, such as flat affect, loss of motivation, and poverty of speech.

Positive Symptoms of Schizophrenia: Delusions As we have seen, delusions are defined as fixed, false beliefs, such as Peter's belief that he is the Messiah. Obviously, it can be difficult under some circumstances—particularly across cultural contexts—to distinguish a true delusion from a strongly held but sane belief that may seem bizarre to an outsider. For example, many Americans viewed the September 11, 2001 hijackers' belief that they would be rewarded in paradise for their acts as delusional, but experts caution that this belief was not necessarily delusional within the hijackers' religious/cultural subculture.

Delusional beliefs are impervious to reason or refutation by evidence; as a result, it is futile to argue with someone holding a delusional belief. An old psychiatric joke humorously illustrates the fixed nature of delusions.

Delusional Patient: Doctor, you have to help me! I'm dead—literally dead!

Doctor (thinking he can reason with the delusional patient): Of course you're not dead—you're walking and talking! Tell me this: do dead men bleed?

Patient: No—everyone knows that!

Doctor (feeling smug): Then why is your face bleeding where you cut yourself shaving?

Patient: I'll be darned—dead men *do* bleed!

Positive (Type I) and Negative (Type II) Symptoms of Schizophrenia	Table 12.2

Positive/Type I symptoms ■ Pathological *excesses,* such as delusions, hallucinations, and disorganized speech, thought, or behavior.

Negative/Type II symptoms ■ Pathological *deficits,* such as flat affect, loss of motivation, and poverty of speech.

BOX 12.2   A Study in Delusions

The Three Christs of Ypsilanti

In 1959, a Michigan State University Professor named Milton Rokeach conducted an unprecedented study on delusional thinking. He discovered that each of three patients at the nearby Ypsilanti State Mental Hospital held the delusional belief that he was Jesus Christ. Rokeach wondered whether the men might alter their delusional thinking if confronted with each other. He arranged to have the three men live and work together for two years. At the end of that time, all three still held fast to their delusions; they simply managed to convince themselves that the others were imposters! Of course, this study occurred before the wide availability of effective antipsychotic medications. Today, the three men would undoubtedly have had their delusions treated more successfully. Here some excerpts from Rokeach's book *The Three Christs of Ypsilanti* (Rokeach, 1964):

> The Three Christs met for the first time in a small room off the large ward where they live. The date was July 1, 1959. All three had been transferred to Ward D-23 of Ypsilanti State Hospital a few days before and had been assigned to adjacent beds, a shared table in the dining hall, and similar jobs in the laundry room.
>
> It is difficult to convey my exact feelings at that moment. I approached the task with mixed emotions:

curiosity and apprehension, high hopes for what the research project might reveal and concern for the welfare of the men. Initially, my main purpose in bringing them together was to explore the processes by which their delusional systems of belief and behavior might change if they were confronted with the ultimate contradiction conceivable for human beings: more than one person claiming the same identity…

> (p. 3).

Rokeach describes one early encounter among the men ("Leon," "Joseph," and "Clyde"):

> "As I was stating before I was interrupted," Leon went on, "it so happens that I was the first human spirit to be created with a glorified body before time existed."
>
> "Ah, well, he is just simply a creature, that's all," Joseph put it. "Man created by me when I created the world, nothing else."
>
> "Did you create Clyde, too?" Rokeach asked.
>
> "Uh-huh. Him and a good many others."
>
> At this, Clyde laughed.

> (p. 10–11)

This hypothetical patient's ability to incorporate any contradictory evidence into his delusion is typical of delusional thinking. (For another example, see Box 12.2.)

The DSM-IV-TR distinguishes between *bizarre* and *nonbizarre* delusions, although it can be difficult to make this distinction in practice. Bizarre delusions are those that do not relate to ordinary life experience. For example, the idea that a secret race of aliens is controlling one's actions through invisible rays from their home planet would be considered a bizarre delusion. In contrast, the belief that one is being followed by the CIA would be considered a nonbizarre delusion (assuming that it is not true!).

In terms of content, *delusions of persecution*—the idea that one is being attacked, followed, controlled, and so on—are the most common. *Delusions of grandeur,* such as Peter's belief that he is the Messiah, and *delusions of reference,* which involve the false assumption that external events are connected to oneself (such as the idea that a TV announcer is specifically talking to you) also occur frequently. Other common themes in delusions include guilt (*delusions of sin*), illness (*hypochondriacal delusions*), and the impending end of the world (*nihilistic delusions*). The following description of a man suffering from schizophrenic delusions illustrates bizarre delusions of persecution and grandeur.

> [He believes that] transmitters control his thoughts, tape recorders control his actions. The skin behind his eyes was broken away and there is nothing behind them. When he urinates, his nipples move up his chest and lodge in his forehead.

His nipples control the traffic. His brain is upside down; there is a plastic bag in his brain; there is a man cycling in his brain. He built the hospital. When he first came to the hospital it was because he had been found at the bottom of a river, together with pieces of other bodies in plastic bags. He has 500 bodies some or all of which are dead.

McKenna, 2001 (p. 171)

Hallucinations Hallucinations are abnormal sensory perceptions in which an internally generated perception is perceived as if it were external and real. Hallucinations can occur in any sensory modality: hearing (auditory hallucinations), seeing (visual), smelling (olfactory), tasting (gustatory), or touching (tactile). Auditory and visual hallucinations, in that order, are the most common forms of hallucinations in schizophrenia (Benson et al., 2000). Auditory hallucinations, which are experienced by most people with schizophrenia, usually consist of hearing voices; hallucinations of two or more voices conversing, or of voices giving a running commentary on one's behavior, are especially characteristic of schizophrenia (Morrison & Baker, 2000). Here is one client's description of his auditory hallucinations:

For about almost seven years—except during sleep—I have never had a single moment in which I did not hear the voices. They accompany me to every place and at all times; they continue to sound even when I am in conversation with other people, they persist undeterred even when I concentrate on other things, for instance read a book or a newspaper, play the piano, etc.

Quoted in Torrey, 2001

"A Geometry of Hallucinations" This painting by Adolph Gottlieb conveys a sense of the perceptual distortions in some visual hallucinations. Gottlieb (1903–1974) was an important figure among American Abstract Impressionist painters.

Delusions and hallucinations can be thought of as severely distorted mental *content,* and, interestingly, the subject matter of psychotic content tends to focus on relatively few themes. As with delusions, the most common themes in hallucinations involve persecution, destruction, sin and punishment, hypochondria (imagined bodily ailments), and grandiosity. In most cases, as this list implies, the content of delusions and hallucinations is emotionally negative, even terrifying, to the individual, but in some cases hallucinations are experienced as comforting and reassuring (Bowins & Shugar, 1998; Houran & Lange, 1997). There is also considerable variation in the extent to which psychotic individuals are aware that they are psychotic (Torrey, 2001). Some know that their hallucinations are not real, while others are unable to make this distinction (Daprati et al., 1997).

Disorganized Speech or Thought As we have seen, delusions and hallucinations are severe aberrations in the *content* of thoughts (delusions) or perceptions (hallucinations). But it is also possible to have severe aberrations in the *process* of thinking or behaving which are also considered psychotic. For example, severely **disorganized speech or thought** (sometimes referred to as *formal thought disorder*) is considered by many experts to be the central symptom of schizophrenia (APA, 2000) (see Table 12.3 for examples). Schizophrenic speech often sounds like a sequence of logically disconnected thoughts (a symptom known as **loose associations**). In some cases, schizophrenic speech includes other oddities such as **neologisms** (made-up words, like "headvise" for headache), **clang associations** (nonsense sequences of rhyming or like-sounding words, such as "I'm out sprout, shout! Shout me shoot me shoe me shoe! shoe! shoe!"), **echolalia** (repeating verbatim what others say), and **echopraxia** (repeating the gestures of others). At its most extreme, schizophrenic speech can deteriorate into *incoherence* and even **word salad**—a seemingly random collection of disorganized words. It is not the case, however, that these disorganized thoughts and expressions are meaningless (see Box 12.3 for a dis-

Disorganized speech or thought Severe disruptions in the process of speaking or thinking.

Loose associations A sequence of logically disconnected thoughts.

Neologisms Made-up words, like "headvise" for headache.

Clang associations Nonsense sequences of rhyming or like-sounding words.

Echolalia A speech abnormality in which a person mimics what they have just heard.

Echopraxia Repeating the gestures of others.

Word salad A seemingly random collection of disorganized words.

Table 12.3	**Examples of Disorganized Schizophrenic Speech**

- I am not artificial. I am life. The theatre is not life. I know the customs of the theatre. The theatre becomes a habit. Life does not. I do not like the theatre with a square stage. I like a round stage. I will build a theatre which will have round shape, like an eye. I like to look closely in the mirror and I see only one eye in my forehead.

  Spoken by the Russian dancer Vaslav Nijinsky, who suffered from schizophrenia, as quoted in Torrey, 2001.

- I have schizophrenia—cancer of the nerves. My body is overcrowded with nerves. This is going to win me the Nobel Prize for medicine. I don't consider myself schizophrenic anymore. There's no such thing as schizophrenia, there's only mental telepathy.

  Quoted in Sheehan, 1982

- [Medication] can kill the space area off if I died, space areas are normally after I died. Cubic space area and nature. That syrup does kill us off if we have it three or four times a day. It does kill us off, it does. Some of it is quite kind but some of it is duff bottles some of it. It deads me off I can't awake all the time, day and night, to take medication all at once.

  Quoted in McKenna, 2001 (p. 171)

BOX 12.3   Madness and Modernism

Are Psychosis and Modernism Related?

In his influential book *Madness and Modernism* (1992), Rutgers psychology professor Louis Sass compares *modernism,* the late nineteenth and twentieth century movement in art, literature, and philosophy, to schizophrenic psychosis. His thesis is that some essential features of modern art and literature—such as hyper self-consciousness and the fragmentation of the self—are also characteristic of schizophrenia. Sass does not argue that modernist culture *causes* schizophrenia (although some experts do argue that schizophrenia was not found before the early nineteenth century), but he does suggest that understanding modernism might help in the understanding of schizophrenic symptoms. Here are excerpts from his book, along with reproductions of some classic modernist art works which convey a fragmented experience of the world.

> The notion that too much consciousness might be a thorough-going illness (as Dostoevsky's narrator puts it in *Notes From the Underground*) has been, then, a common enough idea in the last two centuries, yet it has had little impact on the understanding of the psychoses; the truly insane, it is nearly always argued, are those who have failed to attain, or else have lapsed or retreated from, the higher levels of mental life. Nearly always insanity involves a shift from the human to the animal, from culture to nature, from thought to emotion, from maturity to the infantile and the archaic. If we harbor insanity, it is always in the depths of our souls, in those primitive strata where the human being becomes beast and the human essence dissolves in the universal well of desire.
>
> Another possibility does suggest itself, however: What if madness were to involve not an escape, but an exacerbation of that thoroughgoing illness Dostoevsky imagined? What if madness, in at least some of its forms, were to derive from a heightening rather than a dimming of conscious awareness, and an alienation not from reason but from the emotions, instincts and the body. This, in essence, is the basic thesis of this book.
>
> (p. 4).

T. S. Eliot diagnosed the modern condition as a "dissociation of sensibility:" a widening rift between thought and emotion, intellect and sensation, and a general failure to achieve "unification of sensibility." This is remarkably close to Emil Kraepelin's and Erwin Stransky's classic definition of dementia praecox—as "a loss of inner unity of intellect, emotions and volition, in themselves and among one another," or as "disturbances of the smooth interplay" between ideational and emotional layers of the psyche.

(p. 357)

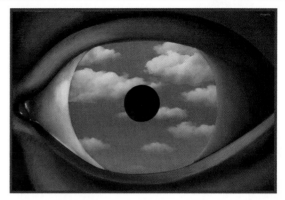

René Magritte, *The False Mirror* (1928). This painting is evocative of the schizophrenic experience of a solipsistic universe.

Oil on canvas, 21¼″ × 31⅞″. Collection, The Museum of Modern Art, New York; Purchase.

Fruit bowl drawn by a schizophrenic patient. Evocative of the fragmentation vision: objects seen in isolation, separated from one another and from their overall context.

From Arieti, S. (1974). Interpretation of schizophrenia, 2nd ed. (New York: Basic Books, 1974).

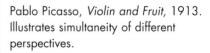

Pablo Picasso, *Violin and Fruit,* 1913. Illustrates simultaneity of different perspectives.

The Philadelphia Museum of Art, The A. E. Gallatin Collection. ©2003 Estate of Pablo Picasso/Artists Rights Society (ARS), New York

cussion of the relationship between psychosis and modern art). After getting to know a person with schizophrenia, it is often possible to decipher the meanings of their garbled communications. Here one client describes her loose associations:

> My thoughts get all jumbled up. I start thinking about something but I never get there. Instead I wander off in the wrong direction and get caught up with all sorts of things that might be connected with the things I want to say but in a way I can't explain. People listening to me get more lost than I do.
>
> Quoted in Torrey, 2001 (p. 47)

Grossly disorganized behavior The DSM-IV-TR identifies grossly *disorganized behavior* as another example of a positive symptom of schizophrenia. This refers to a wide variety of bizarre or disrupted behavioral patterns which can include dishevelment, extreme agitation, uncontrollable childlike silliness, inability to perform simple activities of daily living, and other similar symptoms (APA, 2000). Bizarre *motoric* behaviors are known as **catatonic** symptoms. These can range from extreme immobility and unresponsiveness (known as *catatonic rigidity* and *catatonic stupor,* respectively) to extreme agitation, such as a purposeless flailing, pacing, or spinning (*catatonic excitement).* Catatonic rigidity sometimes includes an unusual symptom known as **waxy flexibility** in which patients' limbs, often held in rigid posture for hours, can be bent and reshaped as though made of wax (Fink & Taylor, 2001; Peralta & Cuesta, 2001) Interestingly, catatonic symptoms are more common in non-Western cultures than in the United States and other Western countries (Mimica, Folnegovic-Smalc, & Folnegovic, 2001).

Negative Symptoms of Schizophrenia The negative symptoms of schizophrenia (also referred to as *type II symptoms*) are those in which a deficit—a loss or absence of a normal function—exists. These symptoms are less dramatic than the bizarre and excessive positive symptoms, but they are often more incapacitating in the long run, as they rob people of some basic human attributes—the ability to feel, communicate, and maintain goal-directed behavior (see Table 12.4) (Goldberg & Schmidt, 2001; Jogems-Kosterman et al., 2001; Limpert & Amador, 2001; Trumbetta & Mueser, 2001). The DSM-IV-TR identifies three specific negative symptoms that are particularly characteristic of schizophrenia: *affective (emotional) flattening, alogia,* and *avolition* (APA, 2000; Fleischhacker, 2000).

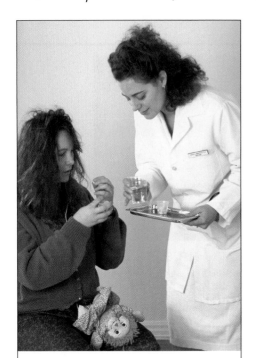

Disorganized behavior This client's disheveled state is an example of disorganized behavior in schizophrenia.

Catatonia Psychomotoric symptoms ranging from extreme immobility and unresponsiveness to extreme agitation.

Waxy flexibility Catatonic symptom in which clients' limbs, often held in rigid posture for hours, can be bent and reshaped as though made of wax.

Table 12.4	Symptoms of Schizophrenia and the Systems They Involve	
(Adapted from Ho & Andreason, in Breier, 2001, p. 411)	**SYMPTOM**	**SYSTEM INVOLVED**
Positive Symptoms	Hallucinations	Perceptual
	Delusions	Cognitive
	Disorganized speech	Linguistic
	Disorganized behavior	Behavioral self-regulation
Negative Symptoms	Alogia (decrease in speech)	Speech fluency
	Emotional flattening	Affective
	Avolition (lack of motivation)	Motivational
	Anhedonia (lack of pleasure)	Hedonic (pleasure/pain)

Affective flattening, a very common symptom of schizophrenia, refers to a reduction or absence of normal emotion. Schizophrenic clients may appear unresponsive and emotionally blunted, and emotions, if present, are typically restricted in range and often inappropriate to the situation (Alpert et al., 2000; Limpert & Amador, 2001). **Alogia** (from the Greek for "absence of words"), or **poverty of speech**, refers to the paucity of verbal communication in many people with schizophrenia. They may be entirely mute, or prone to giving only short and empty responses to direct questions. Some clients appear to be trying to talk but seem unable to do so, a symptom known as **thought blocking**. **Avolition** refers to a lack of motivation. Many people with schizophrenia find it impossible to initiate or persist in even simple activities like making a bed or going for a walk. They may sit inactive all day long, and show little interest in planful activity or goal-directed behavior.

Another relatively common and devastating negative symptom of schizophrenia is **anhedonia**, the loss of a sense of pleasure. However, anhedonia is not listed as a diagnostic example of negative symptoms of schizophrenia in the DSM-IV-TR, partly because it is a common symptom of depression as well. In fact, the major difficulty in assessing negative symptoms in general is to determine whether they are indeed symptoms of schizophrenia or related to other factors such as medication side effects, depression, and the demoralizing living conditions often endured by people with schizophrenia (Galynker, Cohen, & Cai, 2000; Malla, Norman, & Scholten, 2000; Tsuang, Stone, & Faraone, 2000).

Other Diagnostic Criteria In addition to the positive and negative symptoms of schizophrenia, the DSM-IV-TR also lists two additional criteria that relate to the course of the disorder over time and are therefore sometimes referred to as the *temporal criteria*. First, signs of the disorder must be present for at least six months, with at least one month's existence of two or more clear examples of positive or negative symptoms from the five types listed previously (see Table 12.1). When the symptoms last for a briefer time, a different diagnosis applies: these are described in the Other Related Disorders section of this chapter. Schizophrenia, then, tends to have a chronic, rather than an acute, course.

Second, there must be evidence of significant impairment and deterioration over time in an individual's ability to function in his or her social and occupational world (APA, 2000). People with schizophrenia have significant difficulties with work, school, and relationships. For example, 60% to 70% of individuals with schizophrenia never marry, and those who do often report poor quality marriages (Li et al., 2001) and high rates of separation and divorce, especially if one or both of the individuals developed schizophrenia between the ages of 19 and 25 (Stromwall, 1997). Typically, the socioeconomic status of individuals with schizophrenia is below that of their family of origin and of their unaffected parents and siblings—a phenomenon known as the **downward drift** of schizophrenia. This downward drift probably partially accounts for the fact that rates of schizophrenia are significantly higher among lower socioeconomic classes (Dohrenwend et al., 1992; Goldberg & Morrison, 1963; see the Classification in Demographic Context section, and Table 12.7 later in this chapter for more on this topic).

Taken together, these temporal criteria highlight the long-term and downward course typical of schizophrenia and say a good deal about why schizophrenia is such a devastating disorder. But as if this were not enough, it is also common for individuals with schizophrenia to experience symptoms of anxiety and dissociation. In addition, *comorbidity* with substance abuse may be as high as 50% (Clark, 2001; Hwang & Bermanzohn, 2001; Kamali et al., 2001). Further, the profound cognitive disturbances associated with schizophrenia interfere with clients' awareness that they are

Catatonic behavior This client exhibits the odd, frozen posture seen in some individuals with catatonic symptoms of schizophrenia.

Affective flattening A reduction or absence of normal emotion.

Alogia or **poverty of speech** Minimal or absent verbal communication.

Thought blocking Inability to talk despite trying to do so.

Avolition Reduced or absent motivation.

Anhedonia Loss of a sense of pleasure.

Downward drift The decline in socioeconomic status of individuals with schizophrenia relative to their families of origin.

not well; individuals with schizophrenia often lack insight into the fact that they have a disorder. This frequently results in noncompliance with treatment, which contributes to relapses and a generally poor course for the disorder (Kamali et al., 2001; Kingsbury & Yi, 2001; Tattan & Creed, 2001).

Subtypes of Schizophrenia How to best categorize subtypes of schizophrenia continues to be a subject of debate, with many alternate typologies being suggested (Fossati et al., 2001; Gutkind et al., 2001; Lucas et al., 2001; Roy et al. 2001). The DSM-IV-TR currently lists five subtypes of schizophrenia (Table 12.5), based on the most prominent symptoms at the time of evaluation. However, there is some debate over the stability and application of these subtypes (Torrey, 2001).

The **paranoid** subtype, the most common and usually the least severe, refers to cases in which the predominant symptoms are delusions and auditory hallucinations, with relatively intact cognitive and emotional functioning. The **disorganized** subtype, typically the most severe, is characterized by the prominence of disorganized speech, disorganized behavior, and flat or inappropriate affect. The **catatonic** subtype is marked by strange psychomotoric symptoms, such as rigid physical immobility and unresponsiveness *(catatonic stupor)* or extreme behavioral agitation *(catatonic excitement),* muteness, and, occasionally, *echolalia* and *echopraxia.* Finally, the DSM-IV-TR includes two additional categories for cases in which none of the first three subtypes apply. If the client clearly meets the general criteria for schizophrenia yet does not fit into any of the three subtypes above, then the subtype **undifferentiated** applies. If the client has clearly met the criteria for schizophrenia in the past, and there is ongoing evidence of the disorder in the absence of current psychotic symptoms, the subtype **residual schizophrenia** applies. (It is worth noting that residual schizophrenia is the diagnosis that was given to David Rosenhan and most of his confederate "pseudopatients" upon discharge from the hospitals to which they were admitted in his study; see Chapter 2.) Residual schizophrenia can occur as a transitional phase when a client improves after an episode of schizophrenia, but it can also persist as a chronic condition.

Paranoid schizophrenia The most common subtype, characterized by predominant symptoms of delusions and auditory hallucinations, with relatively intact cognitive and emotional functioning.

Disorganized schizophrenia Typically the most severe subtype, characterized by the prominence of disorganized speech, disorganized behavior, and flat or inappropriate affect.

Catatonic schizophrenia Subtype marked by psychomotoric symptoms, such as rigid physical immobility and unresponsiveness (catatonic stupor) or extreme behavioral agitation (catatonic excitement), muteness, and, occasionally, echolalia and echopraxia.

Undifferentiated schizophrenia Subtype in which clients clearly meet the general criteria for schizophrenia, yet do not fit into any of the other three subtypes.

Residual schizophrenia Subtype in which clients have clearly met the criteria for schizophrenia in the past, and there is ongoing evidence of the disorder but without current psychotic symptoms.

Table 12.5	Subtypes of Schizophrenia	
Adapted from APA, 2000	**SUBTYPE**	**DEFINING FEATURES**
	Paranoid	• Prominent delusions or auditory hallucinations.
	Disorganized	• Prominent disorganized speech, disorganized behavior, and flat or inappropriate affect.
	Catatonic	• Prominent psychomotoric symptoms, such as rigid physical immobility, and unresponsiveness or extreme behavioral agitation, muteness, echolalia, and echopraxia.
	Undifferentiated	• Active schizophrenic symptoms that do not fit the paranoid, disorganized, or catatonic subtypes.
	Residual	• Following at least one episode of schizophrenia, a state in which there are no prominent positive symptoms of schizophrenia but some negative symptoms and milder positive symptoms remain.

Other Related Disorders

As we have mentioned, many experts believe that schizophrenia is actually a cluster of related disorders rather than a single entity—a viewpoint that touches on the ***advantages and limitations*** of the DSM-IV-TR diagnosis of schizophrenia. Accordingly, some experts refer to what is known as the **schizophrenic spectrum** of disorders—a group of related and overlapping disorders that may have a common etiological basis (Cassano et al., 1998; Meyer, 1998) (see Table 12.6). Disorders considered to be on the schizophrenic spectrum include the schizotypal and paranoid personality disorders (described in Chapter 11). In addition, you may recall that the diagnosis of schizophrenia developed out of the observation that the disorder seemed to follow a different course than mood disorders with psychotic features. However, there are cases in which symptoms of both a mood disorder *and* schizophrenia are present (Atre-Vaidyn & Taylor, 1997). As noted earlier, the DSM-IV-TR provides a diagnosis of **schizoaffective disorder** for these situations (APA, 2000). The diagnosis of schizoaffective disorder is further specified as either *bipolar type* or *depressive type* depending on the nature of the mood symptoms (see Chapter 6).

There are two additional disorders on the schizophrenic spectrum listed in the DSM-IV-TR that differ from schizophrenia only in terms of the temporal criteria. **Schizophreniform disorder** involves a psychotic episode that has all the features of schizophrenia but *has not lasted the required six months.* Ultimately, about two-thirds of cases of schizophreniform disorder continue beyond six months at which point the diagnosis of schizophrenia would apply (Wyatt, 2001). As a result, if the diagnosis of schizophreniform disorder is made before six months have elapsed (that is, not in regard to a prior episode from which the individual has recovered) the diagnosis is listed as "provisional." In cases in which positive symptoms of schizophrenia (delusions, hallucinations, disorganized speech, or grossly disorganized behavior) are present but last *less than one month,* the DSM-IV-TR diagnosis **brief psychotic disorder** applies. The symptoms of brief psychotic disorder may last anywhere from 1 to 30 days, usually with a return to normal, baseline functioning after recovery. Schizophreniform disorder and brief psychotic disorder both appear to be less prevalent than schizophrenia in the United States and other developed countries, although they appear to be significantly more common in developing countries (Jablensky, 2000; Mojtabai et al., 2001; Selten et al., 2001).

In some cases, an individual may become delusional over an extended period of time without any other symptoms of schizophrenia. When symptoms are limited to

Schizophrenic spectrum A group of related and overlapping disorders that may have a common etiological basis.

Schizoaffective disorder DSM-IV-TR diagnosis involving symptoms of both a mood disorder and schizophrenia.

Schizophreniform disorder DSM-IV-TR diagnosis involving a psychotic episode that has all the features of schizophrenia but has not lasted six months.

Brief psychotic disorder DSM-IV-TR diagnosis involving a psychotic episode that has all the features of schizophrenia but lasts less than one month.

Differences Among Some Disorders on the "Schizophrenic Spectrum"	Table 12.6

Schizophrenia ■ Symptoms last at least 6 months.

Schizophreniform disorder ■ Symptoms last between 1 and 6 months.

Brief psychotic disorder ■ Symptoms last less than 1 month.

Delusional disorder ■ Nonbizarre delusions, without other symptoms, lasting at least 1 month.

Shared delusional disorder ■ Delusions that develop in the context of a close relationship with a psychotic person.

Schizoaffective disorder ■ Symptoms of both schizophrenia and a mood disorder.

Delusional disorder DSM-IV-TR diagnosis involving nonbizarre delusions lasting at least one month.

Shared delusional disorder or **folie à deux** DSM-IV-TR diagnosis involving delusions that develop in the context of a close relationship with a psychotic person.

nonbizarre delusions (such as jealous delusions) lasting longer than one month, the DSM-IV-TR classification is **delusional disorder**. In rare cases, an individual will develop delusions, without other psychotic symptoms, in the context of a close relationship with someone else who has a psychotic disorder. This is known as **shared delusional disorder** or **folie à deux** (fo-lee-ah-DU). In these cases, the client is typically in a submissive, long-term relationship with a person with schizophrenia or another psychotic disorder. For example, the child of a father with paranoid schizophrenia may begin to share his father's paranoid delusions.

Brief Summary

- The DSM-IV-TR defines schizophrenia as a constellation of severe cognitive and behavioral symptoms lasting six months or more and causing significant impairment.

- The main symptoms of schizophrenia fall into two categories: positive or type I and negative or type II. The positive symptoms are pathological excesses—delusions, hallucinations, disorganized speech, thought, and behavior. The negative symptoms are pathological deficits—emotional flatness, loss of motivation, diminished cognitive skills, and withdrawal.

- The DSM-IV-TR lists five subtypes of schizophrenia. Paranoid schizophrenia is diagnosed in cases in which the main symptoms are delusions and hallucinations. Disorganized schizophrenia is diagnosed in cases in which the main symptoms are disorganized speech, behavior, and affect. Catatonic schizophrenia is diagnosed when the main symptoms are in the psychomotor area. If none of these three subtypes clearly applies, the diagnosis is undifferentiated schizophrenia. If an individual is no longer psychotic but still has other ongoing expressions of schizophrenia, the diagnosis is residual schizophrenia.

- Schizophrenia is one of several disorders on the schizophrenic spectrum—a group of related and overlapping disorders that may have a common etiological base. They include: schizophreniform disorder (symptoms of schizophrenia for one to six months), brief psychotic disorder (symptoms of schizophrenia for less than one month), delusional disorder (nonbizarre delusions lasting more than one month, without other symptoms of schizophrenia), shared delusional disorder (the development of delusions in the context of a close relationship with a psychotic individual), schizoaffective disorder (a combination of symptoms of schizophrenia and mood disorders), and the schizotypal and paranoid personality disorders (Chapter 11).

Classification in Demographic Context

The epidemiology and course of schizophrenia vary considerably depending on several demographic variables (Fabrega, Ahn, & Mezzich, 1992; Peralta & Cuesta, 2000; Vocisano et al., 1996).

Class and Culture

As we have seen, the lifetime prevalence of schizophrenia hovers around 1% of the population worldwide (Jablensky, 1997). However, the prevalence of schizophrenia is notably higher in certain demographic groups, such as second generation African Caribbeans in Great Britain, and people of African heritage in London and in the United States (Baker & Bell, 1999; Bhugra et al., 1997). The last difference is probably an artifact of the overall higher rates of schizophrenia in lower socioeconomic groups (with lifetime risk as high as 2%) in which African Americans are disproportionately represented (Dohrenwend et al., 1992, 1998; Keith, Regier, & Rae, 1991).

Indeed, severe socioeconomic stress may be a contributing cause of schizophrenia (see the Family Systems and Sociocultural Components section later in the chapter), explaining, along with the *downward drift* in socioeconomic status of many schizophrenic individuals, the positive correlation between low socioeconomic status and higher rates of the disorder (see Table 12.7) (Cohen, 1993; Freeman, 1994; Levav et al., 1998). Interestingly, the long-term outcome of schizophrenia is significantly better in "developing" as opposed to industrialized countries, although the cause of this difference is unknown (Jablensky, 2000).

Other risk factors for schizophrenia include slightly higher rates of the disorder among persons born in urban areas (Mueser et al., 2001; Svedberg, Mesterton, & Cullberg, 2001) and slightly lower rates for later-born siblings (APA, 2000). Overall, however, the greatest risk factors involve having biological relatives with schizophrenia or other disorders on the schizophrenic spectrum.

Age and Gender

In general, the course of schizophrenia has three phases, although not all cases follow this pattern exactly: (1) **prodromal** (developing); (2) **active** (psychotic symptoms); and (3) **residual** (no longer psychotic, but still showing signs of schizophrenia) (APA, 2000). Onset can occur as early as five years of age, although the disorder is rare before adolescence (Howard et al., 2000). Late onset, even among those over 60, is possible, and occurs more often among women (Coleman & Gillburg, 1996; Howard et al., 2000). The onset of schizophrenia can be sudden—over a matter of days—or there may be a gradual prodromal phase as in the case of Peter. Over time, three characteristic long-term patterns of schizophrenia have been observed: (1) occasional episodes with good recovery (if the episodes do not last six months, then diagnoses of schizophreniform disorder or brief psychotic disorder would apply); (2) occasional episodes with some gradual deterioration; and (3) chronic symptoms with steady "downward drift" (an der Heiden & Haefner, 2000; DeSisto et al., 1999; Gaebel et al., 2000; Harrison et al., 2001; Mojtabai et al., 2001). Unfortunately, about 60% of people with schizophrenia follow the last, chronic course, and relatively few experience the first of the three patterns with full recovery (an der Heiden & Hafner, 2000).

The course of schizophrenia differs by age and gender. Despite the fact that schizophrenia occurs roughly equally across genders (with only slightly higher rates for young men) it follows a somewhat different pattern in men and women (Goldstein,

Schizophrenia and Social Class
Schizophrenia is more common among the urban poor, such as this homeless man.

Prodromal phase The first stage of schizophrenia in which symptoms are developing.

Active phase The second phase of schizophrenia, involving psychotic symptoms.

Residual phase The third stage of schizophrenia, in which the individual is no longer psychotic but still shows signs of the disorder.

Downward Drift in Schizophrenia	Table 12.7

Gottesman, 1991, p. 78, after Goldberg & Morrison, 1963

The downward socioeconomic drift of schizophrenic patients between the ages of 25 and 34 in England and Wales in the 1950s is shown below. As you can see, these patients were almost all categorized as in the middle and lower classes when they were admitted to hospitals, and, on average, they had "drifted down" below the ratings of their fathers and brothers.

SOCIAL CLASS	PATIENTS (%)	THEIR FATHERS (%)	THEIR BROTHERS (%)	CENSUS NORMS (%)
Higher (classes 1 and 2)	4	29	21	16
Middle (class 3)	48	48	56	58
Lower (classes 4 and 5)	48	23	23	27

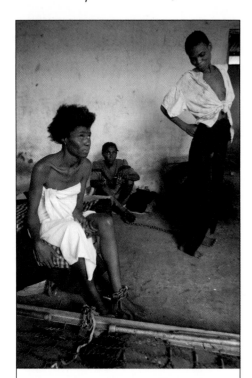

Schizophrenia and Culture Schizophrenia is found worldwide, but for unknown reasons the long-term outcome of schizophrenia appears to be better in "developing" countries than in industrialized societies.

1995; Raesaenen et al., 1999). For instance, the median age of onset of schizophrenia is later for women than men. Men tend to have first episodes in their early 20s, while for women onset more often occurs in their late 20s (APA, 2000). Also, women tend to have somewhat better pre-morbid (pre-illness) levels of functioning and fewer negative symptoms (Roy et al., 2001).

Interestingly, all of the variables associated with schizophrenia in women (later onset, better pre-morbid functioning, and fewer negative symptoms) are also associated with better prognosis (an der Heiden & Hafner, 2000; Goldstein, 1995; McGurk et al., 2000; Siris, 2001). Other variables associated with a better prognosis include: relatively acute onset in the context of stressful events; early detection and treatment; prominent mood symptoms; normal neuropsychological findings; compliance with treatment; family history of mood disorders rather than schizophrenia; and lack of substance abuse (Blanchard et al., 2000; Gross, 1997).

Brief Summary

- Schizophrenia develops in about 1% of the population worldwide, but the prevalence and course of the disorder differ across different demographic groups. For example, the rate of schizophrenia is almost twice as high among the urban poor, either because the stress of urban poverty can be a contributing cause of the disorder, because people with schizophrenia experience a socioeconomic "downward drift," or both.

- The course of schizophrenia is usually divided into three phases: prodromal (developing), active (psychotic), and residual (no longer psychotic but still affected). The onset of schizophrenia is usually in early adulthood, although it can be earlier or much later.

- Schizophrenia manifests differently in men and women. Men tend to have slightly higher rates of the disorder, earlier onset, more negative symptoms, and a poorer course and outcome.

EXPLAINING AND TREATING SCHIZOPHRENIA

The understanding and treatment of schizophrenia have come a long way in a relatively short time. As recently as the 1950s, explanations of schizophrenia were rudimentary and most individuals with schizophrenia endured the disorder without hope of effective treatment (Cooper, 1999; Fink, 1999). Now, dozens of promising explanatory theories are being actively researched, and there are many useful treatments available that help most clients. However, experts in the field agree that there is still a long way to go. We do not yet have a comprehensive understanding of the etiology of schizophrenia, or even whether schizophrenia is a single disorder. The treatments for schizophrenia, while better than ever, are far from cures. And among other formidable obstacles to research on schizophrenia, most research subjects with the disorder have been medicated and/or hospitalized, adding confounding variables to the search for the essence and causes of schizophrenia (Hardy et al., 2001; Keefe & McEvoy, 2001; O'Doherty, 1998; Pakaslahti, 1994). As a result, while reviewing the various models of explanation and treatment, we will highlight both the answers that have been found and the many questions that still remain.

As we have seen, the pioneers who developed and refined the diagnosis of schizophrenia around the turn of the twentieth century were mostly medical scientists, like Kraepelin, who firmly believed that the disorder was essentially biological—caused by a diseased brain—and probably of genetic origin (Athanasiadis, 1997; DeLisi,

1997; Marshall, 1996). Biological research on schizophrenia during the first half of the twentieth century seemed to support this view, as abnormalities in the brain structure of people suffering from schizophrenia were discovered (Johnstone, 1994). However, much of this research was conducted by German scientists working during the Nazi era, and was tainted by the ethical outrage about Nazi medical experiments. Partly in reaction to this, the biological approach to explaining and treating schizophrenia took a back seat to psychological approaches in the post-World War II period (Johnstone, 1994). In the 1970s, biological research regained momentum, and in the decades since then the biological perspective has dominated explanations and treatments for schizophrenia. (The biological perspective on schizophrenia also has its critics: see Box 12.4.) Accordingly, we begin our review by describing the biological components of and interventions for schizophrenia. However, we will see that the state-of-the-art in explaining and treating schizophrenia involves combining components from multiple theoretical perspectives. Because of its importance in understanding schizophrenia, we will return to the core concept of *multiple causality* at the end of the chapter.

Progress and hope Until recently, clients with schizophrenia were often "warehoused" in substandard hospitals, such as the one above, with little hope of improvement. The past fifty years have brought enormous progress in the treatment of schizophrenia.

Biological Components

In order to organize the enormous amount of information now available about biological aspects of schizophrenia, it is helpful to distinguish between the immediate (or *proximal*) causes of the symptoms of schizophrenia and the **predisposing** (or *distal*) causes of the disorder. The proximal causes of the symptoms involve various abnormalities in brain function, brain structure, and neuropsychological/neurophysiological status that may cause schizophrenic symptoms (though it is also possible that some of them are *effects*, not causes, of schizophrenia). The predisposing factors involve possible answers to the question: what are the *underlying* causes—for example, genetic or viral—of schizophrenia?

Immediate Causes

Brain Function Abnormalities Biological researchers have long been interested in links between the symptoms of schizophrenia and neurochemical abnormalities. In recent years, brain imaging techniques such as positron emission tomography (PET scans), single-photon emission computed tomography (SPECT), and magnetic resonance spectroscopy (MRS) have provided powerful new tools for studying the functioning of the schizophrenic brain.

Several abnormalities in brain function appear to be associated with schizophrenia. For example, studies have shown a general decrease in activity in the prefrontal cortex (anterior region of the frontal lobe)—a syndrome known as **hypofrontality**—that seems to be particularly associated with the negative symptoms of schizophrenia (Keshavan, Stanley, & Pettegrew, 2000). MRS studies have also suggested altered cell membrane metabolism in the prefrontal region of the brain (Stanley, Pettegrew, & Keshavan, 2000; Vance et al., 2000). While these findings represent important leads, current technical limitations of the imaging methods have limited their reliability thus far (Keshavan et al., 2000; Stanley et al., 2000; Zakzanis et al., 2002).

Perhaps the most prominent findings regarding brain function and schizophrenia focus on abnormal neurotransmission. Neuroimaging and postmortem studies have shown abnormalities in several neurotransmitter systems of people with schizophrenia, including the **dopamine, serotonin, glutamine,** and **gamma-aminobutyric acid (GABA)** systems (Dean, 2000; Taber et al., 2001). In fact, the dopamine system has been at the heart of biological research on schizophrenia for many years. Interest in the dopamine system began in the 1950s when French researchers discovered that the drug

Predisposing cause The underlying processes that create the conditions which make it possible for a precipitating cause to trigger an event.

Hypofrontality A general decrease in activity in the prefrontal cortex.

Glutamine A neurotransmitter involved in schizophrenia symptoms.

Dopamine A neurotransmitter thought to be specifically related to positive symptoms of schizophrenia and to pleasure regulation.

Serotonin A neurotransmitter associated with depression and anxiety

Gamma-aminobutyric acid (GABA) A neurotransmitter that suppresses nervous system activity

"We've Been Misled by the Drug Industry" *by Daniel B. Fisher*

Fueled by discoveries during the 1990s "decade of the brain," the biological perspective on schizophrenia has become dominant, but it is not without critics. In this article, Dr. Daniel Fisher, a biochemist and psychiatrist who himself suffered from schizophrenia, challenges reductionistic biological approaches to the disorder and the drug companies that seem to support them.

I have recovered from schizophrenia. If that statement surprises you—if you think schizophrenia is a lifelong brain disease that cannot be escaped—you have been misled by a cultural misapprehension that needlessly imprisons millions under the label of mental illness.

In the last 20 years, the pharmaceutical industry has become the major force behind the belief that mental illness is a brain disorder and that its victims need to take medications for the rest of their lives. It's a clever sales strategy: If people believe mental illness is purely biological, they will only treat it with a pill.

Drug companies have virtually bought the psychiatric profession. Their profits fund the research, the journals and the departments of psychiatry. Not surprisingly, many researchers have concluded that medication alone is best for the treatment for mental illness. Despite recent convincing research showing the usefulness of psychotherapy in treating schizophrenia, psychiatric trainees are still told "you can't talk to a disease." This is why psychiatrists today spend more time prescribing drugs than getting to know the people taking them.

I, too, used to believe in the biological model of mental illness. Thirty-one years ago, as a Ph.D biochemist with the National Institute of Mental Health, I researched and wrote papers on neurotransmitters such as serotonin and dopamine. Then I was diagnosed with schizophrenia—and my experience taught me that our feelings and dreams cannot be analyzed under a microscope.

Despite what many people assume when they hear about my recovery, that original diagnosis was no mistake: It was confirmed by a board of six Navy psychiatrists after my four-month inpatient stay at Bethesda Naval Hospital. I was devastated by being branded a schizophrenic. My life seemed over. Six years later, however, I had defied everyone's expectations and recovered. The most important elements in my recovery were a therapist who believed in me, the support of my family, steadfast friends and meaningful work. And I had a new goal: I wanted to become a psychiatrist. My therapist validated that dream, saying, "I will go to your graduation." (When I received my degree from George Washington University Medical School in 1976, he was there.) Drugs were a tool I used during crises, but I have been completely off medication for 25 years.

I am not an anomaly. Thousands of others have recovered, but are afraid to disclose their past due to the stigma of mental illness. The definitive Vermont Longitudinal Study, led by Courtenay Harding, followed 269 patients diagnosed in the late 1950s with severe schizophrenia. Three decades later, Harding found that two-thirds of them were living and functioning independ-

ently; and of those, half were completely recovered and medication-free.

The Swiss psychiatrist Manfred Bleuler—whose father, Eugen, coined the term schizophrenia in 1908—obtained similar results. His father had mistakenly concluded that people did not recover from schizophrenia—because he rarely saw his patients after discharge. Our own research at the National Empowerment Center (NEC), funded by the federal Center for Mental Health Services, shows that the most important factor in recovery from mental illness is people who believe in patients and give them hope: medications are a less important factor.

But that is not how psychiatrists are being taught; recently I was reminded of how tightly training is controlled. I contacted a colleague at a major West Coast medical school to see if he could get me an invitation to conduct one of their teaching rounds. He apologetically told me that he couldn't: since he had published a critique of the biological model of mental illness, demonstrating that people could recover from schizophrenia without medication, he himself was no longer allowed to speak to the residents in training—even though he was on the faculty.

The pharmaceutical industry also controls the public's education. Who can avoid the TV image of the phobic man who needs Paxil to socialize? Industry-funded research and experts have a huge impact on media coverage. Finally, the drug companies have taken advantage of well-intentioned advocacy groups who support the biological model of mental illness—and they give those groups much-needed financial support.

Schizophrenia is more often due to a loss of dreams than a loss of dopamine. At the NEC, we try to reach out across the chasm of chaos. I know there are many people who feel they have done all they can, have struggled against mental illness to no avail, and we understand their pain. Yet we believe that recovery is eventually possible for everyone—although it can take a long time to undo the negative messages of past treatments. We can offer hope from first-hand experience.

Addressing the needs of people with mental illness will require a large-scale retraining of mental health workers, decision-makers, families and the public. There will need to be more research into the ways that people recover. There will need to be more jobs, housing, peer support and self-help, for these are the pathways to self-determination and independence. And there needs to be a cultural shift toward people rather than pills to alleviate this form of human suffering.

The Washington Post, August 19, 2001; p. B03

chlorpromazine, an antihistamine being tested as a sedative, appeared to eliminate delusions and hallucinations in psychotic patients (Delay & Deniker, 1952; Sandler, 1999). When these drugs were introduced to treat schizophrenia, it became evident that they often caused side effects known as **parkinsonism**, the stiffness and tremors associated with Parkinson's disease. Since it had been discovered that parkinsonism was caused by a reduction in dopamine in the basal ganglia, it was logical to assume that chlorpromazine and other similar antipsychotic (or **neuroleptic**) drugs might also be creating their antipsychotic effects by reducing the availability of dopamine in the brain.

Several lines of evidence support this **dopamine hypothesis**. Carlsson and Lindqvist (1963) demonstrated that neuroleptic drugs did indeed affect the dopamine system, and hypothesized that their antipsychotic action was due to their ability to block dopamine receptor sites. Furthermore, L-DOPA, a dopamine precursor used to alleviate parkinsonian symptoms, can cause psychosis with overuse (Faustman, 1995; Friedhoff & Silva, 1997; Sandler, 1999). Similarly, stimulant drugs such as amphetamines and cocaine will produce psychosis in overdose, partly by blocking dopamine reuptake and thereby causing excess dopamine transmission (Dalmau, Bergman, & Brismar, 1999; Poole & Brabbins, 1996; Sandler, 1999; Schlemmer, Young, & Davis, 1996). (See Table 12.8 for a selected list of drugs that can induce schizophrenia-like psychosis.) Finally, it was discovered that many individuals with schizophrenia, particularly those with a preponderance of positive, psychotic symptoms, had an excess of dopamine receptors in the brain, particularly a variety known as D_2 receptors (Faustman, 1995; Murugaiah et al., 1982).

For many years, the dopamine hypothesis held sway as the leading explanation of the positive symptoms of schizophrenia. Currently, however, researchers regard the

Parkinsonian symptoms The stiffness and tremors associated with Parkinson's disease.

Neuroleptic Another name for antipsychotic medications.

Dopamine hypothesis The hypothesis that excess dopamine transmission causes the psychotic symptoms of schizophrenia.

D_2 receptors Receptors involved in dopamine transmission that are thought to play a role in symptoms of schizophrenia.

Selected Drugs That Can Induce Schizophrenia-like Psychosis		Table 12.8
Alcohol (withdrawal hallucinosis)	Disulfiram (Antabuse)	*Gottesman, 1991, p. 29*
Amantadine	Ephedrine	
Amphetamine (speed, crank, crystal, ice)	Ibuprofen (Motrin)	
Atropine	Indomethacin	
Bromide	Isoniazid	
Bromocriptine	Levodopa	
Cannabis (marijuana)	Lidocain	
Carbon monoxide	LSD	
Chloroquine	Methamphetamine	
Cimetidine	Monoamine oxidase (MAO) inhibitors	
Clonidine	Pentazocine (Talwin)	
Cocaine (and crack)	Phencyclidine (PCP, angel dust)	
Corticosteroids (adrenocorticotropic hormone, cortisone, etc.)	Phenelzine (Nardil)	
Dexatrim	Propanolol (Inderal)	
Diazepam (Valium)	Propoxyphene (Darvon)	
Digitalis	Tricyclic antidepressants	

dopamine hypothesis as only a partial explanation of the positive symptoms of schizophrenia for several reasons (Sandler, 1999; Valenstein, 1998; Weinberger, 1997). First, not all individuals with schizophrenic psychosis respond to dopamine-reducing antipsychotic medications, and even when antipsychotics are effective there is some delay in the effects even though the dopamine blockade begins immediately. Second, antipsychotic medications can be used to treat psychosis of any origin, not just schizophrenic psychosis (Chou et al., 2001; Currier & Simpson, 2001; Salzman, 2001). Third, the development of new antipsychotic medications that affect different neurotransmitter systems made it clear that multiple neurotransmitters are involved in schizophrenic psychosis (Abi-Dargham et al., 1998; Benes, 1998; Lewis et al., 1999; Vollenweier, 1998). Nonetheless, the dopamine hypothesis remains an important element of the current understanding of schizophrenia.

Brain Structure Abnormalities In addition to looking for abnormalities in brain function and metabolism, researchers have also investigated whether the brains of people with schizophrenia are anatomically or structurally different than the brains of normal individuals. Brain imaging techniques such as computed tomography (CT) and magnetic resonance imaging (MRI) provide a way of looking at the structure of the living brain and thereby augment postmortem research on the brains of deceased people who had schizophrenia. One of the earliest and most robust findings in this area is an association between enlarged lateral **ventricles** (fluid-filled cavities in the brain) and schizophrenia, particularly in cases with prominent negative symptoms (Cannon & Marco, 1994; Chua & McKenna, 2000; Corey-Bloom et al., 1995) (see

Ventricles Fluid-filled cavities in the brain.

Figure 12.2 Increased Ventricle Size in Schizophrenia as seen in Magnetic Resonance Imaging (MRI) Brain Section (a) These magnetic resonance imaging (MRI) scans show the increased ventricle size in a patient with schizophrenia (*right,* see arrows: *top arrow,* lateral ventricles; *bottom arrow,* third ventricle) compared to a healthy control (*left*). (b) A view of the brain showing the location of the ventricles.

From Schultz & Andreason, 2000

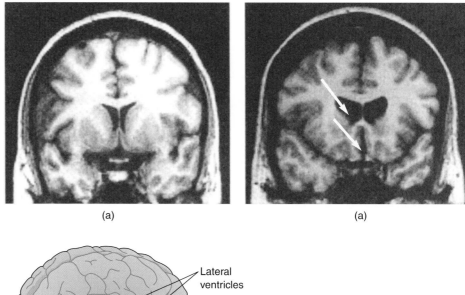

(a)   (a)

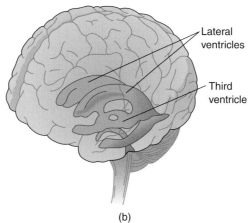

Lateral ventricles

Third ventricle

(b)

Figure 12.2). While the differences in ventricle size between clients with schizophrenia versus control groups are relatively small and subtle (Shenton et al., 2001), they may indicate a loss of brain tissue in schizophrenia (Barto et al., 1997; Sullivan et al., 1996), possibly due to reduced blood flow to the brain (Sagawa et al., 1990). These findings contributed to Crow's (1980; 1985) proposal to distinguish between the Type I and Type II aspects of schizophrenia, the former consisting of increased D_2 dopamine receptors associated with the positive symptoms of schizophrenia, and the latter consisting of enlarged ventricles and a loss of cortical tissue associated with the negative symptoms (Wyatt, 2001). Most individuals with schizophrenia have a combination of both Type I, positive and Type II, negative symptoms, but the relative preponderance of each varies across cases (Crow, 1995; Fenton & McGlashan, 1991, 1994).

Other neuroanatomical findings in schizophrenia include a decrease in the size of the temporal lobe (especially in the medial temporal structures such as the hippocampus and the amygdala), and abnormalities in the frontal and parietal lobes (Andreason et al., 1997; Shenton et al., 2001). In particular, cell membrane degradation has been seen in the prefrontal cortex, and decreases in the mass of neuronal cells have been found in the hippocampus (Stanley et al., 2000; Taber et al., 2001; Vance et al., 2000). Finally, some studies have indicated abnormalities in subcortical structures such as the corpus callosum and the thalamus (Ettinger et al., 2001; Shenton et al., 2001) (see Figure 12.3). Some researchers suggest that the neuroanatomic changes seen in MRIs of schizophrenic brains suggest an abnormality in large brain "networks" that connect the cortex, thalamus, and cerebellum (Andreason, 1999). However, many of these findings regarding brain structure abnormalities in schizophrenia have not been consistently replicated (Taber, 2001). To date, the only certain differences are those involving ventricle size and, possibly, decreased neuron mass in the hippocampus (Chua & McKenna, 2000; Zakzanis & Hansen, 1998).

Neuropsychological and Neurophysiological Abnormalities Clients with schizophrenia show a variety of neuropsychological deficits, which contribute to impairments in functioning (Addington & Addington, 2000; Heinrichs & Zakzanis, 1998). Cognitive abilities such as verbal fluency, learning, memory, attention, and psychomotor skills are all reduced compared to control subjects (Censits et al., 1997; Young et al., 1998; Zakzanis et al., 2000b), consistent with neuroanatomical research suggesting abnormalities in the frontal and temporal lobes of the brain (Centis et al., 1997). Interestingly, similar frontal and temporal lobe deficits are also found in healthy close relatives of individ-

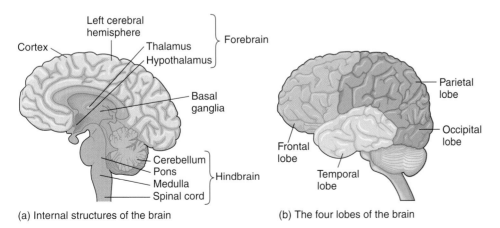

(a) Internal structures of the brain

(b) The four lobes of the brain

Figure 12.3 The Brain Brain structures that play important roles schizophrenia. (a) Internal structures of the brain. (b) The four lobes of the brain.

Impaired sensory gating Many individuals with schizophrenia describe feeling constantly "flooded" by overwhelming stimuli, much as normal individuals might feel in an overstimulating environment like the trading floor of a stock exchange or Times Square in New York.

Impaired sensory gating Difficulty processing sensory input.

uals with schizophrenia, suggesting that such deficits may constitute a necessary but not sufficient risk factor for the disorder (APA, 2000).

People with schizophrenia have difficulty processing sensory input, and often describe feeling "flooded" with stimulation (Hetrick & Smith, 2000). This deficit is known as **impaired sensory gating**. One client described such "flooding" as follows:

> Sometimes when people speak to me my head is overloaded. It's too much to hold at once. It goes out as quick as it goes in.
>
> Quoted in Torrey, 2001 (p. 37)

In addition, researchers have found neurophysiological differences between individuals with schizophrenia and control subjects. Individuals with schizophrenia often show abnormal visual tracking (visually following moving objects), slow reaction times, and abnormal brain wave patterns (as measured by electroencephalograms) (Bahramali et al., 1998; Iwanami et al., 1998; Laurent et al., 2000; Pigache, 1999; Sweeney et al., 1998). However, many of the neurophysiological signs found in schizophrenia are also found in people with mood disorders, so they are not uniquely associated with schizophrenia (Boks et al., 2000).

Predisposing Causes

Researchers are especially interested in discovering the underlying causes of the brain function, brain structure, and neuropsychological abnormalities in schizophrenia. There are several theories at this level, focusing on everything from genetic, viral, nutritional, and chemical variables to physical injuries and traumatic experiences (Johnstone, 1994; Torrey et al., 1997). We will focus on the major biological theories. One overarching concept is the growing consensus that schizophrenia is a *neurodevelopmental* disorder rather than a *neurodegenerative* disorder as was suggested by Kraepelin and others (Censits et al., 1997). In other words, it appears that the brain abnormalities present in schizophrenia begin early in life—even though they may not be evident until later when the disorder appears—rather than stemming from a degenerative process. Studies suggest that the cognitive abilities of people with schizophrenia, for example, are already deficient at the onset of their illness, and do not decline further (Censits et al., 1997). Some researchers refer to a *potential* for the disorder that may or may not progress into full-blown schizophrenia. The renowned psychologist Paul Meehl (1990) refers to such potential as **schizotaxia**, a sort of halfway point on the *continuum* between normality and schizophrenia. Schizotaxia is characterized by mild negative symptoms, deviant eye tracking, and abnormalities in brain structure and neuropsychological function, but not necessarily by psychosis (Tsuang et al., 2000; Tsuang, Stone, & Faraone, 2001).

A second area of consensus concerning the predisposing biological causes of schizophrenia is that they include both genetic and environmental biological factors. Possible environmental causes include some surprising candidates. For example, over 250 studies across 39 countries demonstrate that children born during the winter or spring have a slightly higher chance of developing schizophrenia (Procopio & Marriott, 1998; Torrey et al., 1997). This is true of only a few other mental disorders, including bipolar disorder, schizoaffective disorders, major depression, and autism (Torrey et al., 1997). While the meaning of this pattern is not yet understood, possibilities include exposure to viruses more common in the winter months that could affect brain development during gestation, seasonal nutritional changes, seasonal toxins, effects of temperature changes, and even changes in daylight (Torrey et al., 1997). Other biological environmental risk factors for schizophrenia include pregnancy and birth complications, perinatal (after birth) viruses, and maternal drug use (Van Os & Marcelis, 1998). The fact that similar risk factors also apply to bipolar disorder and a few other mental disorders supports the idea that schizophrenia may best be conceptualized as on a continuum with other disorders (especially those on the schizophrenic spectrum) rather than as an entirely distinct disorder (Jones & Tarrant, 2000; Torrey, 1999; Tsuang et al., 2000).

Genetic Factors Genetic factors clearly play a substantial, although partial, role in the etiology of schizophrenia. However, many questions remain about the how genes contribute to the disorder, and whether the contribution is unique to schizophrenia or more generally to a range of related disorders (Bradshaw & Sheppard, 2000; Breier et al., 2001; Citrome & Volavka, 2001; Goodman et al., 2000; Martens, 2000; Siris, 2001). The evidence for the genetic contribution to schizophrenia comes from a combination of familiar research strategies: family studies, twin studies, and adoption studies.

As we have seen in discussing other disorders, the first step in establishing whether a disorder has a genetic basis is to see whether the disorder runs in families. Schizophrenia clearly does run in families. Figure 12.4 shows that when one member of a family has schizophrenia, other family members are far more likely than the general population (where the rate is around 1%) to also have the disorder. In fact, the closer a person's biological relationship to a schizophrenic family member, the greater the chances the person also has schizophrenia. Thus, a first cousin (known as a third-degree relative) of someone with schizophrenia has a 2% chance of having the disorder; a nephew or niece (second-degree relative) a 4% chance; a sibling (first-degree relative) has a 9% chance; and an identical (monozygotic) twin, the closest possible biological relative, has a 48% chance of having schizophrenia. (This is according to Gottesman's 1991 summary of European studies between 1920–1987; other studies have shown different concordance rates but with similar overall patterns.) While such findings may seem to provide convincing evidence of a genetic role in schizophrenia, recall that family studies can only suggest, not prove, a genetic contribution because families share environments as well as genes, and the shared environment could also

Schizotaxia A potential for developing schizophrenia that may or may not progress into full-blown schizophrenia.

Figure 12.4 Risk for Developing Schizophrenia This graph shows the lifetime risk of developing schizophrenia for various hypothetical relatives of someone with schizophrenia.
Gottesman, 1991, p. 96

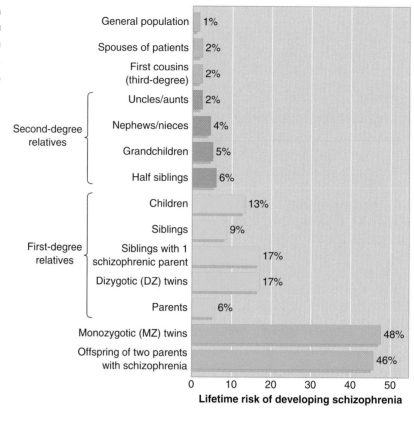

Relative	Risk
General population	1%
Spouses of patients	2%
First cousins (third-degree)	2%
Second-degree relatives	
Uncles/aunts	2%
Nephews/nieces	4%
Grandchildren	5%
Half siblings	6%
First-degree relatives	
Children	13%
Siblings	9%
Siblings with 1 schizophrenic parent	17%
Dizygotic (DZ) twins	17%
Parents	6%
Monozygotic (MZ) twins	48%
Offspring of two parents with schizophrenia	46%

Lifetime risk of developing schizophrenia

Concordance rates In a group of twins, the percentage who both have the same disorder.

explain why schizophrenia runs in families. For example, attending certain colleges and universities also strongly runs in families—but no one suspects that this has a genetic basis!

Twin studies are intended to substantially reduce the confounding of genes and environment that limit family studies. Recall that most twin studies are based on the comparison of **concordance rates** (the percentage of cases in which *both* twins have the same disorder) of identical (monozygotic, or MZ) twins with the concordance rates of fraternal (dizygotic, or DZ) twins. If schizophrenia (or any trait) has a genetic contribution, the concordance rates for MZ twins should be significantly higher than for DZ twins, since the MZ twins are genetic carbon copies derived from the splitting of a single fertilized egg and have 100% genetic similarity, while the DZ twins, originating from two separate fertilized eggs share, like ordinary siblings, 50% of their genes on average (see Figure 12.5). As you can see from Figure 12.4, MZ twins do indeed

The Genain quadruplets These famous quadruplets, pictured as young girls and as adults, all developed schizophrenia.

Degrees of relationship

	Identical	First	Second	Third
−3				Great-grandparent
−2			Grandparent	Great-uncle
−1		Parent	Uncle	Half uncle
Current	Identical twin	Full sibling / Fraternal twin	Half sibling	First cousin
+1		Child	Nephew	Half nephew
+2			Grandchild	Grandnephew
+3				Great-grandchild
Genetic correlation	1.0	0.5	0.25	0.125
Percentage of genes in common with client with schizophrenia	100%	50%	25%	12.5%

(Left axis label: Generation)

Figure 12.5 Degrees of Genetic Relatedness The chart illustrates the percentage of genes in common between identical twins, and first-, second-, and third-degree relatives. Research strategies for determining the genetic contribution to various disorders depend upon comparisons among these groups.

Gottesman, 1991, p. 85

have substantially higher concordance rates for schizophrenia than DZ twins, by 48% to 17% based on Gottesman's (1991) data.

Twin studies provide powerful evidence for a genetic contribution to schizophrenia, but with two important caveats. First, subtle environmental confounds can affect twin studies, since identical twins are more likely to imitate each other and to be treated similarly than fraternal twins (Lewontin, Rose, & Kamin, 1984). Also, MZ twins sometimes uniquely share another environment—the placenta—which may be implicated in schizophrenia through prenatal illnesses or injuries (Brown et al., 2001; MacDonald et al., 2001; Tekell, 2001; Urakubo et al., 2001). Indeed, Davis and Phelps (1995) found that the concordance rate for schizophrenic MZ twins was twice as high when the twins shared the same placenta as opposed to having separate placentas. Second, twin studies clearly indicate that the genetic contribution to schizophrenia is a partial one and that environment plays an equally large role, since if genes were the complete cause of schizophrenia the concordance rate for MZ twins would be 100%, not 48%. In fact, some of the data from twin studies specifically demonstrate the importance of environmental factors in the etiology of schizophrenia. Note that the concordance rate in Gottesman's samples for regular (nontwin) siblings is 9%, substantially lower than the 17% rate for DZ twins. Genetically speaking, regular siblings and DZ twins are no different; each shares, on average, 50% of their genetic material with their sibling. But DZ twins share more in the way of environment—prenatal and postnatal—since they are conceived, born, and raised together. This environmental similarity, therefore, must be responsible for their higher concordance rates (Joseph, 2000; Lewontin et al., 1984; MacDonald et al., 2001).

Adoption studies make up the third side of the genetic research triangle; they attempt to further isolate genetic factors from environmental factors. There are two main strategies in adoption studies. One is to find parents with schizophrenia who have given up children for adoption (and therefore not raised them) and to look at concordance rates among these biologically but not environmentally related parent-child pairs. The other strategy is to find adoptees who developed schizophrenia and to look at concordance rates with their biological relatives, if they can be located. Clearly, some environmental confounds can remain in these studies, since the postnatal environment is shared with the biological parent(s) up until the adoption, and there could be additional environmental confounds from selective adoption placement with families similar to the biological family, and from later contact with the biological family. With these caveats in mind, we will describe the results of two classic adoption studies. The first, Heston's (1966) study of adoptions from schizophrenic mothers in Oregon, shows that, of 47 adopted children born to mothers with schizophrenia, 5 developed schizophrenia, and over half developed other significant types of psychopathology (see Table 12.9). By contrast, of the 50 adoptees from normal mothers, none developed schizophrenia, and less than 20% developed other disorders. Even these compelling results, however, are consistent with a significant environmental role in schizophrenia. For example, recent studies suggest that whether adoptees from schizophrenic mothers develop schizophrenia depends, in part, upon the psychological health of their adoptive families (Tienari et al., 1994; Wahlberg et al., 1997).

Building upon the pioneering work of Seymour Kety and his associates (Kety, 1988) with a Danish sample (Denmark keeps a remarkable register of demographic and health data on all its citizens), Kendler, Gruenberg, and Kinney (1994) examined the concordance rates for schizophrenia among the biological relatives of schizophrenic adoptees. The results showed significant rates of schizophrenia and schizophrenic spectrum disorders among the first- and second-degree biological relatives of schizophrenic adoptees—much higher rates than among control subjects (Gottesman, 1991). Thus, evidence from all three sides of the genetic research triangle—family, twin, and adoption studies—point to a significant, though partial, role of genetic fac-

---

Table 12.9

Adapted from Gottesman, 1991, p. 138

Heston's Study of Adopted Children of Schizophrenic Mothers

The table shows that adopted children with birth mothers who suffered from schizophrenia had higher rates of schizophrenia and other disorders, and lower IQs and educational attainment, than adopted children whose birth mothers did not have schizophrenia.

	BIRTH MOTHER WITH SCHIZOPHRENIA	BIRTH MOTHER WITHOUT SCHIZOPHRENIA
Number of adoptees	47	50
Adoptees with:		
Schizophrenia	5	0
Antisocial personality	9	2
Other mental disorders	13	7
Mental retardation	2	0
Adoptees average psychological adjustment rating (100 = best)	65.2	80.1
Adoptees average IQ	94.0	103.7
Adoptees average education (in years)	11.6	13.4

tors in the development of schizophrenia and related disorders. The questions are: what genes are involved, and what do they do?

Genetic Linkage Thus far, at least seven different chromosomal regions have been identified in genetic linkage studies as possible sites for schizophrenia susceptibility genes (Lichterman, Karbe, & Maier, 2000). The fact that different, rather than consistent, sites have emerged in these studies underscores that the mechanism for the genetic transmission of schizophrenia remains unknown (DeLisi et al., 2000; Wade, 2002). It is now considered probable that schizophrenia is genetically complex, with a **polygenic** (multiple genes) transmission of a vulnerability to the disorder that depends heavily on environmental triggers for expression (Jablensky, 2000; Lichterman et al., 2000). This view is supported by the cultural differences in the course of schizophrenia; similar patterns are found in complex, polygenic, environmentally influenced diseases such as diabetes, hypertension, and cancer (Jablensky, 2000). The polygenic hypothesis is also consistent with the general *diathesis-stress* model of psychopathology, which holds that most disorders are caused by a combination of a predisposing vulnerability *(diathesis)* and some form of precipitating circumstances *(stress)*.

Some researchers hypothesize that as yet unidentified genetic defects affect brain development, growth, and plasticity so as to produce sensitivity to environmental risk factors such as childhood emotional trauma, severe life stress, brain infections, and drug use (DeLisi, 1997; Van Os & Marcelis, 1998). This neurologically based vulnerability or sensitivity might take the form of Meehl's *schizotaxia,* or similar traits which only progress to schizophrenia when combined with certain stressful life events (Lichterman et al., 2000; Van Os & Marcelis, 1998).

Polygenic Involving multiple genes.

Brief Summary

- Information on the biology of schizophrenia has increased dramatically in recent decades. Researchers have discovered brain function, brain structure, neuropsychological, and neurophysiological abnormalities associated with schizophrenia.

- The dopamine hypothesis—that excessive dopamine transmission causes psychosis—was the leading biological explanation of schizophrenic symptoms for many years. More recently, it has become clear that schizophrenia has a complex neurodevelopmental basis that includes abnormalities in several neurotransmitter and structural systems.

- At the predisposing level, several biological theories have been offered to explain the underlying causes of schizophrenia. Genetic evidence suggests that a predisposition to schizophrenia is inherited, but that genetic factors must interact with environmental factors for the disorder to develop. Possible biological environmental factors include viruses, toxins, drug use, and prenatal or postnatal injuries.

Critical Thinking Question | Can you think of other mental or physical disorders that also result from a complex mix of genetic and environmental causes?

Biological Interventions

The introduction of **antipsychotic medications** during the 1950s created a revolution in the treatment of schizophrenia (Gelman, 1999; Shen, 1999). These drugs, also known by their chemical name **phenothiazines** (also referred to as the **major tranquilizers** and the *neuroleptics*), created significant improvement in thousands of patients, many of whom had long been relegated to the back wards of overcrowded

Antipsychotic medication Medications that reduce psychotic symptoms.

Phenothiazines Chemical name for the first generation antipsychotic medications.

Major tranquilizers Another name for antipsychotic medications.

mental institutions under scandalous conditions (Bane, 1951; Gelman, 1999). Until the 1950s, the main biological treatments for clients with schizophrenia had been electroconvulsive therapy (ECT), insulin-induced coma, and prefrontal lobotomy, which were not particularly effective and frequently harmful (Lokshin, Prolov, & Belmaker, 1994; Sakel, 1994). Psychotherapy was helpful in some cases, but most patients were too psychotic to benefit from the "talking cure." Suddenly, with the availability of antipsychotic medications, hospitals could provide treatment rather than merely custodial care (Gelman, 1999).

Deinstitutionalization The social policy, beginning in the 1960s, of discharging large numbers of hospitalized psychiatric clients into the community.

The public's growing awareness of the deplorable conditions in many psychiatric hospitals increased the call to take advantage of the improvements made possible by the new antipsychotic medications. Individuals with schizophrenia were rapidly discharged from hospitals into community life (Rosenstein, Milazzo-Sayre, & Manderscheid, 1990; Torrey, 2001). The United States government officially endorsed and funded this **deinstitutionalization** movement during the Kennedy administration of the early 1960s (Olshansky, 1980; Robbins et al., 1979). However, the era of hope and enthusiasm created by these medications had all but disappeared by 1980 (Gelman, 1999); it had become clear that the antipsychotic medications were not a "magic bullet" after all. A significant number of people with schizophrenia (up to 40%) did not improve on these medications, and those who did saw little improvement in their negative symptoms (such as apathy, social withdrawal, and flat affect). In addition, the phenothiazines commonly caused troubling side effects such as sedation, apathy, constipation, dry mouth, stuttering, menstrual and sexual dysfunctions, blurred vision, and other less obvious physiological changes, including cardiac irregularities and increased photosensitivity (Fayek et al., 2001; Hsiao, 2001; Nayudu & Scheftner, 2000; Pollmaecher et al., 2000; Unis & Rose, 1996). More serious potential side effects of these medications include *tardive dyskinesia,* a late developing but sometimes irreversible condition consisting of involuntary movements of the tongue, jaw, trunk, or extremities; *neuroleptic-induced parkinsonian* symptoms, and *neuroleptic malignant syndrome,* a rare but potentially life-threatening condition characterized by extreme muscle rigidity and elevated body temperature (Pollmaecher et al., 2000).

Furthermore, many of the discharged patients deteriorated in community settings, partly because of the lack of adequate social services for them and the loss of the structured environment that the hospitals had provided (Rachlin, 1978). It became clear that the antipsychotic medications were only a first step; clients with schizophrenia also needed help with their negative symptoms and greater community support (Meltzer, 1999a; Zahniser, Coursey, & Hershberger, 1991). Without these resources, many individuals with schizophrenia quickly relapsed, and often became stuck in "revolving door" hospitalizations in which they would be frequently readmitted after being discharged into the community.

In this context, a new class of medications for schizophrenia created a fresh wave of enthusiasm in the late 1980s. A medication called clozapine (marketed as Clozaril) had been shown in Europe during the 1970s, and in trials in the United States during the 1980s, to treat both the positive and negative symptoms of schizophrenia without the side effects of the phenothiazines (Hsiao, 2001). The phenothiazines (the "first generation" antipsychotics) reduced psychotic symptoms primarily by blocking D_2 and other dopamine receptors. Clozapine, by contrast, produced much less dopamine blockade and actually seemed to increase dopamine transmission in the prefrontal cortex, leading to improvements in cognitive deficits and other negative symptoms (Meltzer, 1999b). However, there was one significant downside to this new medication. In a small percentage of patients (1%–2%) clozapine caused a potentially fatal side effect known as *agranulocytosis,* a lowering of white blood cell counts (Horacek et al., 2001; Kodesh et al., 2001). As a result, when the Food and Drug Administration approved Clozaril in 1990, it mandated that patients taking the drug had to receive weekly blood tests to screen for agranulocytosis (Honigfield et al., 1996). The combined price for the medication and blood tests reached $9,000 per year—a cost that was hardly realistic for most people, let alone individuals debilitated by schizophrenia. After years of litigation, Clozaril was made available in a more affordable package; fortunately, in the meantime, similar new medications became available as well (Breier, 2001). The effectiveness of these medications, known collectively as the **atypical** or **second-generation antipsychotics** (see Table 12.10), seems to be related to their *antagonistic* targeting of certain serotonin receptors in addition to their effects on various dopamine receptors (Hsiao, 2001; Sadock & Sadock, 2001; Svensson, 2000). For some clients, the effects of the atypical antipsychotics have been nearly miraculous (Keefe, 2001; Meltzer, 1999a). In most cases, however, the major advantage of the atypical antipsychotics has been a modest improvement in negative symptoms and less severe side effects than the earlier medications. Some critics argue that the advantages of the atypical antipsychotics over first generation antipsychotics have been oversold by the pharmaceutical companies that manufacture them (Czekalla, Kollack-Walker, & Beasley, 2001; Keefe, 2001; Torrey, 2001). Most clients on the new medications show significant improvement in their positive and negative symptoms but remain moderately to severely affected by schizophrenia (Kapur & Remington, 2001; Sadock & Sadock, 2001; Schatzberg & Nemeroff, 2001). The diminished side effects of the second generation medicines reduces one barrier to compliance with treatment, but noncompliance remains a serious problem in the treatment of schizophrenia because the disorder involves such major impairments in judgment, insight, and self-care (Kemp & David, 2001; see Table 12.11).

Currently, the cutting edge in the biological treatment of schizophrenia is the effort to treat, or even prevent, the disorder before it fully develops in high-risk individuals (Goode, 1999; Hsiao, 2001; Meltzer, 1999a). Treatment with atypical antipsychotics appears to help mildly affected first-degree relatives of clients with schizophrenia even if they have only minor impairments and no psychosis (Metzer, 1999). Hopefully, treatment with these medications during the *prodromal* (developing) phase of schizophrenia could head off full-blown active episodes, reducing considerable suffering and saving on later treatment expenses (Hsiao, 2001). However, treating *developing* schizophrenia also raises a host of complex practical and ethical problems. Identifying people who may be at risk, and treating them with powerful antipsychotic medications in the absence of actual schizophrenia, could expose them to unnecessary side effects and stigmatization (Goode, 1999).

Atypical or **second generation antipsychotics** Newer antipsychotic medications that seem to more effectively reduce both positive and negative symptoms of schizophrenia.

The Atypical Antipsychotics	Table 12.10

CHEMICAL NAME	BRAND NAME
Clozapine	Clozaril
Risperidone	Risperdal
Olanzapine	Zyprexa
Quetiapine	Seroquel
Ziprasidone	Zeldox, Geodon

Table 12.11	**Rates of Treatment Noncompliance in Schizophrenia**

Adapted from Kemp & David, 2001, p. 270

STUDY	SETTING	MEASURE	NONCOMPLIANCE RATE
Forrest et al. (1961)	Inpatient	Urine assay	15%
Irwin et al. (1971)	Open ward	Urine assay	32%
Scottish Schizophrenia Research Group (1987)	Inpatient	Serum assay	46%
Serban & Thomas (1974)	Outpatient	Self-report	42%
Weiden et al. (1991)	Outpatient	Observer and self-report	48% 1st year 70% 2nd year
Carney & Sheffield (1976)	Clinics	Missed injection	40%

A similarly complex legal and ethical issue involves the right of psychotic clients to refuse treatment. In most jurisdictions, people cannot be treated involuntarily unless they pose an imminent danger to themselves or others (Dignam, 2000; Griswold, 2000; Heath, 2000). But it is often not possible to accurately assess and predict dangerousness. On August 17, 2000, a man who had begun to hallucinate after he stopped taking his medication for schizophrenia murdered 24-year-old Kevin Heisinger, a social work student, in a bus station bathroom in Kalamazoo, Michigan. Subsequently, legislation was introduced in Michigan to make it easier to compel psychotic clients to take medication. Given the apparent recent increase in violent acts by individuals with untreated schizophrenia, and the fact that at least 40% of people with schizophrenia are not receiving treatment at any given time, this is likely to become a prominent national issue (Torrey, 2001). We discuss this, and other issues at the interface of abnormal psychology and the legal system, in more detail in Box 12.5.

Brief Summary

- The development in the 1950s of antipsychotic medications, which seemed to operate by reducing dopamine transmission, was a major breakthrough in the treatment of schizophrenia. These drugs provided the first generally effective treatment for schizophrenia and led to the deinstitutionalization movement in which the long-term treatment of schizophrenia shifted from hospitals to community settings.

- By 1980, it was clear that these first generation antipsychotic medications, though helpful, did little to treat the negative symptoms of schizophrenia, and that most clients needed additional help. Subsequently, atypical, or second generation, antipsychotics showed promise in treating both the positive and negative symptoms of schizophrenia with fewer side effects than their predecessors. However, it is not yet clear how effective these new medications will prove to be over time.

- One current focus in the biological treatment of schizophrenia is on preventing the disorder, through early treatment, among those who may be at high risk.

Critical Thinking Question | **Which of Peter's symptoms do you think would improve on a first generation antipsychotic medication, and why?**

FOCUS ON PSYCHOLOGY IN SOCIETY

BOX 12.5   Abnormal Psychology and the Law

Patients' Rights and the Insanity Defense

The field of abnormal psychology intersects with the legal system in several areas. For example, the civil rights of people with mental illnesses and the confidentiality of mental health treatments have specific legal protection. But society also has a compelling interest in seeing that mentally ill individuals who are at risk for harming themselves or others are not free to do so; this issue is particularly relevant to the most severe disorders, such as schizophrenia. Sometimes individual civil rights are in conflict with the need to protect people from harm, and state and federal courts are continually called upon to balance these competing interests. For example, courts may order a *civil commitment*—forcing an individual to be hospitalized for treatment against his or her will—when they are presented with compelling evidence that the individual poses a significant danger (the exact procedures vary from state to state). Obviously, the government's power to hospitalize people against their will poses risks to civil liberties, and there has been vigorous debate over the proper balance between the protection of individual liberty and the need for society to protect individuals from harm. In recent decades, the balance has tilted increasingly in the direction of emphasizing patients' rights, although in some states the trend has moved in the opposite direction. While specific protections vary by state, many jurisdictions have established patients' rights to receive treatment while hospitalized (not to simply be "warehoused"), to refuse treatments they do not want, to be treated in a humane and minimally restrictive environment, to be paid for work they perform while institutionalized, and to be treated in the community after discharge.

A similar balancing act exists with regard to the confidentiality of mental health treatment records. In 1996, the U.S. Supreme Court affirmed (in *Jaffe v. Redmond*) the principle that the confidentiality of mental health information must be maintained in federal courts on the grounds that confidentiality is essential to psychotherapy and that viable psychotherapy is essential to society. Most states have similar protections, but exceptions are mandated in certain circumstances. For example, in 1976 the California Supreme Court (in *Tarasoff v. Regents of the University of California*) ruled that therapists must break confidentiality and warn potential victims if a client specifically threatens to harm someone. The case involved a man, Prosenjit Poddar, who told his therapist at the University of California that he wanted to hurt his ex-girlfriend, Tatania Tarasoff. The therapist warned the campus police but did not notify Ms. Tarasoff, and she was subsequently murdered by Mr. Poddar. Similarly, many states require that therapists break confidentiality and report to authorities any client disclosures of information indicating that a child or elderly person is being abused.

Courts must also, in a just society, be able to determine whether people accused of crimes might not be (a) responsible

(continues)

John Hinckley, Jr., and the insanity defense Hinkley, shown here in custody, acted on his delusional belief that attempting to assassinate President Reagan would win the love of actress Jodie Foster (right). He was later found not guilty by reason of insanity.

BOX 12.5 (continued)

for their criminal act or (b) able to assist in their defense in court, due to mental illness. In such cases, a court may institute a *criminal commitment*—commitment to a mental institution until the disorder that led to the criminal acts, or the incompetence to stand trial, has been treated or found to be untreatable. *Mental incompetence* to stand trial is a actually a much more common reason for criminal commitment than a verdict of *not guilty by reason of insanity*; only about 1% of all criminal defendants plead not guilty by reason of insanity, and only one-quarter of those are acquitted (Callahan et al., 1991; Melton et al., 1997). Nonetheless, the insanity defense has been quite controversial as it focuses on the question of whether or not individuals should always be held responsible for criminal actions. Over the past 200 years, various courts have established, defined, and redefined the criteria for determining *insanity* (a legal, not a diagnostic, term). The first legal test of insanity was the M'Naghten rule, which states that an individual is not responsible for criminal behavior if he did *not know what he was doing* or was *unable to distinguish right from wrong* at the time of committing the crime. This rule was established by an English court in 1843 which held that Daniel M'Naghten was not criminally responsible for murder (he had killed the Prime Minister Sir Robert Peel's secretary while aiming for Peel, claiming that the voice of God had ordered him to do it). The M'Naghten rule was widely adopted in the United States, but in the late nineteenth century some jurisdictions adopted another standard–the *irresistible impulse test*.

By this test, someone who commits a crime in an uncontrollable fit of passion could not be held responsible for the crime. Another test, the *Durham test,* was briefly popular after it was offered in a 1954 U.S. Supreme Court decision *(Durham v. United States)*. The Durham test suggested that a person should not be found guilty if their crime was a result of a "mental disease or defect," a more liberal, but also more technical, standard.

Concerns about the limitations of all of these tests contributed to the formulation in 1955 of the *American Law Institute (ALI) test,* which combines elements of all of the aforementioned tests. The ALI test states that individuals are not responsible for criminal conduct if they have a mental disorder (specifically excluding antisocial personality disorder) that prevents them from understanding right from wrong or from controlling their behavior to comply with the law. The ALI test was widely praised and adopted until John Hinckley, Jr. successfully used the insanity defense in his 1982 trial for shooting President Ronald Reagan, one of his aides, and two police officers. In response to a strong public outcry, the federal government and many states returned to the stricter M'Naghten test. In addition, many jurisdictions shifted the burden of proof of insanity from the prosecution—which previously had to prove that the defendant was sane—to the defense, which now had to prove that the defendant was insane at the time of the crime. Many other states continue to use the ALI standard, while three states—Idaho, Utah, and Montana—do not currently recognize insanity pleas at all.

Psychodynamic Components

Although most of Freud's work was devoted to neurotic rather than psychotic disorders, he was interested in schizophrenia. Freud believed, as do most contemporary experts, that schizophrenia had a substantially biological basis, and he was pessimistic about the value of psychotherapy in treating the disorder (Freud, 1924). Freud's pessimism about treating schizophrenia with psychotherapy was also related to his theory that schizophrenia involved a profound withdrawal of emotional investment in the external world so that individuals with the disorder could not form deep relationships with others, including relationships with psychotherapists (LaPlanche & Pontalis, 1973). He presumed that this withdrawal occurred partly in reaction to emotional traumas very early in life and represented a fixation at an infantile stage (Freud, 1914). Freud suggested that hallucinations and other psychotic symptoms were secondary symptoms of schizophrenia related to the individual's attempt to reconnect with the outside world, an idea that overlaps with some contemporary cognitive and sociocultural theories.

A number of later psychodynamic theorists differed from Freud in their beliefs that schizophrenia could be of entirely psychological origin and effectively treated by psychodynamic psychotherapy. Therapists such as Frieda Fromm-Reichmann (1943, 1948, 1950) and Harry Stack Sullivan (1962) were gifted at understanding clients with schizophrenia and making them feel safe. Fromm-Reichmann's successful therapy with a young woman with schizophrenia has been immortalized in the client's fictionalized, best-selling memoir, *I Never Promised You A Rose Garden* (Greenberg,

1964), which was later made into a movie. Fromm-Reichmann also became infamous for coining the phrase *schizophrenogenic mother,* or schizophrenia-causing mother. This expressed her belief that schizophrenia could be caused by mothers who were alternately or simultaneously cold, overprotective, and demanding. Fromm-Reichmann's theory pre-dated the contemporary biological discoveries about schizophrenia, and is now considered misguided and obsolete.

Psychodynamic Interventions

Today, most psychodynamic theorists take a balanced approach, believing that biological factors play a central role in the development of schizophrenia but that psychotherapy can be a helpful part of the treatment process. Psychotherapy can be a crucial adjunct to medication since the effects of medication are typically limited in scope, and the combination of the two has been shown to improve personal adjustment, prevent relapse, and increase ongoing treatment compliance (Grady, 1998; Hogarty et al., 1997; Steele, 2001). Individuals with schizophrenia have wishes, fears, hopes and conflicts that can be helpfully addressed in a caring therapeutic relationship (Davidson, Stayner, & Haglund, 1998; Karon, 1992; Robbins, 1993). As one client with schizophrenia put it:

> My relationship with my therapist … was the first real relationship I ever had; that
> is, the first I felt safe enough to invest myself in …. I had drawn so far inside
> myself and so far away from the world, I had to be shown not only that the world
> was safe but also that I belonged to it, that I was in fact a person. This grew from
> years of our working together to develop mutual respect and acceptance and a
> forum of understanding, in which I believed that he had the capacity to comprehend
> what I said and that I had the potential to be understood.

> Anonymous, 1986, "Can We Talk?:" The Schizophrenic Patient in
> Psychotherapy. *American Journal of Psychiatry, 143,* pp. 68–70.

Cognitive Components

Cognitive theorists have developed several influential ideas about the role of cognitive processes in schizophrenia. Some researchers focus on the role of abnormal *attentional* processes. For example, the positive symptoms of schizophrenia may be related to a problem of *overattention* in which individuals with schizophrenia are unable to screen out irrelevant stimuli (*impaired sensory gating*), possibly because of dopaminergic (dopamine-related) abnormalities (Swerdlow et al., 1994). This overattention leads to difficulties coping with stress, and possibly further to psychotic symptoms such as delusions when clients attempt to explain their odd subjective experiences to themselves (Blaney, 1999; Kennedy, 1995; Perry & Braff, 1994; Schwartz, 1998). One client described his overattention as follows:

> Everything seems to grip my attention although I am not particularly interested in
> anything. I am speaking to you just now, but I can hear noises going on next door
> and in the corridor. I find it difficult to concentrate on what I am saying to you.
> Often the silliest little things that are going on seem to interest me. That's not even
> true; they don't interest me, but I find myself attending to them and wasting a lot of
> time this way.

> Quoted in Torrey, 2001 (p. 36)

Conversely, the negative symptoms of schizophrenia may be related to an equally problematic *underattention* to important stimuli, leading to withdrawal and apathy

(Cadenhead & Braff, 1999; Dawson et al., 2000; Moser et al., 2000). For example, studies have shown that individuals with prominent negative symptoms do not have a normal *orienting* response—physical changes associated with sharpened attention—to novel stimuli (Braunstein-Bercovitz, Dimentman-Ashkenazi, & Lubow, 2001; Lee et al., 2001; Lubow et al., 2000). Interestingly, attentional problems remain present in residual schizophrenia, and are found in the nonschizophrenic relatives of individuals with schizophrenia, suggesting that they may be fundamental to schizophrenia (Faraone et al., 1999; Kalayciougly et al., 2000).

Cognitive Inverventions

Cognitive therapists have developed a number of interventions for schizophrenia in recent years. In addition to using *cognitive rehabilitation* techniques to address over- and under-attention, cognitive therapists also use standard cognitive techniques such as *cognitive restructuring* to challenge delusional beliefs (Buchanan & Wessely, 1998; Chadwick, Birchwood, & Trower, 1996; Nelson, 1997). They emphasize that normal, but exaggerated, cognitive processes and emotional problems can underlie the bizarre symptoms of schizophrenia. For example, cognitive theorists understand persecutory delusions and hallucinations to be exaggerations of expectable reactions to the fear and mistreatment that individuals with schizophrenia often experience in their daily lives (Beck & Rector, 2000). Cognitive interventions have been shown to be effective in both the treatment and prevention of some schizophrenic symptoms (Beck & Rector, 2000; Gottdiener, 2001; Gould et al., 2001; Spaulding, Johnson, & Coursey, 2001). When combined with behavioral treatments in the form of cognitive-behavioral therapy, they have been especially beneficial in reducing the severity of delusions (Bustillo et al., 2001, Dickerson, 2000; Torrey, 2001).

Behavioral Components

Behavioral theorists focus on the importance of *learning* in the development and treatment of schizophrenia. In particular, behaviorists have argued that reinforcement of abnormal responses, such as positive attention for disorganized speech, can contribute to the abnormal behaviors of schizophrenia through the principles of operant conditioning (Willis & Walker, 1989). For the most part, behaviorists do not argue that schizophrenia is entirely caused by conditioning, and they emphasize the role of biological factors that may predispose someone to learn abnormal responses. For example, biological abnormalities may lead individuals with schizophrenia to respond to atypical, rather than normal, social cues, with resulting social difficulties (Lawrie et al., 2001; Willis & Walker, 1989).

Behavioral Interventions

The main focus of behavioral perspectives on schizophrenia has been around intervention, not explanation. Reinforcement-based techniques using operant conditioning principles can be used to increase appropriate behaviors and decrease inappropriate ones in clients with schizophrenia (Black & Bruce, 1989; Durand & Carr, 1989; Silverstein, Menditto, & Stuve, 2001). The **token economy** is one widely used intervention based on such principles (Foxx, 1998; Silverstein, Hitzel, & Schenkel, 1998). In token economies (which are often used in hospital or other institutional settings) clients who engage in desired behaviors earn coinlike tokens that can be exchanged for privileges such as watching television or having extra snacks. Such systems can effectively promote behavior change in schizophrenia (Foxx, 1998; Silverstein et al., 1998).

Social skills training, another widely used behavioral treatment for clients with schizophrenia, educates clients about appropriate interpersonal behavior (Smith, Bel-

Token economy The systematic use of coinlike tokens as rewards in an operant conditioning treatment program.

lack, & Liberman, 1996). Social skills training has been shown to improve clients' social and interpersonal functioning (Heinssen, Liberman, & Kopelowicz, 2000; Liberman, Eckman, & Marder, 2001; McQuaid et al., 2000), although there is some debate about the extent of these improvements (Bustillo et al., 2001).

Family Systems Components

Family theorists have long been interested in schizophrenia, and have proposed a variety of theories about its causes and treatment. Family theorists have focused on the possibility that overly hostile, confusing, or otherwise pathological family environments could contribute to, or even cause, schizophrenia (Gromska et al., 1972; Lidz et al., 1965, 1985; Mirsky & Duncan-Johnson, 1984; Upton & Hoogkamer, 1994). For example, Bateson and colleagues developed an influential early theory that ongoing **double-bind communications** from parents to children—contradictory messages such as "Be independent!" but "Never leave me!" that put the child in a "damned if you do, damned if you don't" position—could lead to the cognitive confusion and emotional paralysis characteristic of schizophrenia (Bateson et al., 1956).

Contemporary researchers have focused on specific, measurable variables related to pathological family communication. For example, researchers have explored different aspects of **communication deviance**—odd or idiosyncratic communications— within families (Goldstein, 1998; Hooley & Hiller, 2001). Many studies have also examined how individuals are affected by **expressed emotion (EE)**—high levels of criticism and over-involvement among family members. Linszen and colleagues (1997) showed that higher levels of EE, which correlate with communication deviance (Miklowitz et al., 1986), are present in the families of individuals with schizophrenia and predict relapse in the affected family members. Furthermore, when EE levels in the family decrease, the functioning of the family member with schizophrenia improves (see Figure 12.6). Whether EE is a risk factor for developing schizophrenia, or just for relapsing, continues to be debated. In addition, questions remain as to whether abnormal family communication patterns are indeed *causes* of schizophrenia, or, alternatively, *effects* of having a member of the family with schizophrenia (Goldstein, 1984; Gromska et al., 1972; Lidz et al., 1965, 1985; Mirsky & Duncan-Johnson, 1984; Upton & Hoogkamer, 1994). If family patterns are causal, they must be viewed as partial causes interacting with other biological and psychological components, in keeping with the core concept of *multiple causality*.

Double-bind communication Contradictory messages such as 'Be independent!' but "Never leave me!" that put the child in a "damned if you do, damned if you don't" position.

Communication deviance Odd or idiosyncratic communications in families

Expressed emotion High levels of criticism and overinvolvement in families.

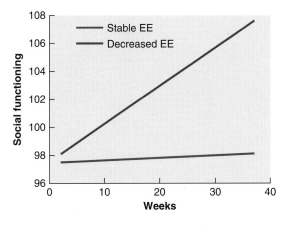

Figure 12.6 Effects of Expressed Emotion (EE) on Schizophrenic Clients' Social Functioning The graph shows that as relatives' expressed emotion (EE) decreased, schizophrenic clients' social functioning improved. When EE was stable, there was no significant improvement in clients' functioning.

Barrowclough & Tarrier, 1998

Shine This 1996 movie, which won a best actor award for Geoffrey Rush and was nominated for Best Picture, portrays the life of pianist David Helfgott, who suffers from schizophrenia. The film was somewhat controversial for its implication that Helfgott's schizophrenia was caused by his father's overbearing behavior and by pathological family dynamics.

Milieu treatment An institutional treatment philosphy in which clients take active responsibility for decisions about the management of their environment and their therapies.

Family Systems Interventions

Regardless of the role of the family in the *etiology* of schizophrenia, there is no doubt that family therapy can be a helpful component of treatment. Family interventions have been shown to reduce communication deviance and expressed emotion, and to lower the risk of relapse of schizophrenic symptoms in previously diagnosed clients (Bustillo et al., 2001). These, in turn, reduce the number of rehospitalizations for clients with schizophrenia.

Sociocultural Components

The sociocultural perspective on schizophrenia focuses on larger social and institutional forces that may have a role in the development and treatment of the disorder. For example, we have already discussed the epidemiological evidence that rates of schizophrenia are higher in lower socioeconomic classes and among those born in urban areas. These data suggest that stresses associated with urban poverty could be one contributing factor in the onset of schizophrenia. Another emphasis in sociocultural work on schizophrenia concerns the effects of social institutions, such as the medical establishment, on the symptoms and identity of those with severe mental illnesses (Wing & Brown, 1961). You may recall that David Rosenhan's famous "pseudopatient" study (Chapter 2) argued that the dehumanizing conditions of the psychiatric hospitals contributed to the actual patients' symptomatic behaviors (Rosenhan, 1973). Thus, social and institutional forces may play a role in the stabilization and maintenance of schizophrenic behaviors and identity.

A more extreme view associated with both the sociocultural and existential models is represented in the work of the Scottish psychiatrist R. D. Laing (1927–1989). Laing, a founder of the radical *antipsychiatry* movement and a kindred spirit with psychiatry critic Thomas Szasz (Chapter 2), argued that schizophrenia is a healthy, constructive reaction to pathological social and family pressures. As such, he advocated that it should not be "treated," or seen as an illness, but rather allowed to run its course as individuals try to find a solution to their problems (Laing, 1959). Laing's critics, however, have labeled his views irresponsible and insensitive to the suffering of people with the disorder (Torrey, 2001). This issue is discussed more fully in Box 12.1; Mark Vonnegut, who suffered from psychotic symptoms, challenges Laing's views.

Sociocultural Interventions

The sociocultural perspective is important in the treatment of schizophrenia, both in terms of hospital and outpatient care. In inpatient settings, the **milieu treatment** movement developed in response to concerns about the potentially dehumanizing effects of institutional treatment, especially in settings in which clients were "warehoused" rather than treated. In milieu treatment, clients take active responsibility for decisions about the management of their environment and therapy programs (Raesaenen, Nieminen, & Isohanni, 1999; Schermer & Pines, 1999).

On the outpatient side, the failure of the deinstitutionalization movement of the 1960s heightened awareness of the need for better community support and services for clients released from hospitals. The federally supported Community Mental Health movement began in this context, and it has continued to emphasize the need for outpatient treatment options, including *partial or day hospitalization* programs (which clients attend from 9:00 A.M. to 5:00 P.M. each day) and *halfway houses* (group homes where clients can live and readjust to life in the community), for the seriously mentally ill. However, most experts and advocates for the mentally ill have been extremely disappointed with the quantity and quality of available services, and they cite the high frequency of mental illness among the homeless population as one indicator of the problem. In recent years, as hospital stays have been drastically shortened by economic pressures, the need for quality outpatient services is especially great. People with schizophrenia are often hospitalized for only a few days, during which they are simply stabilized, medically evaluated, and started or re-started on medication. The most important factor in effective community care appears to be the coordination of services to protect against relapse. A program called **assertive community treatment (ACT)**, which offers frequent and coordinated contact with a wide variety of professionals, has been shown to decrease relapses and rehospitalizations (Bustillo et al., 2001; Scott & Dixon, 1995).

Assertive community treatment (ACT) A treatment program for schizophrenia which offers frequent and coordinated contact with a wide variety of professionals in an effort to decrease relapses and rehospitalizations.

The Multiple Causality of Schizophrenia

Our review of the multiple components that contribute to the understanding of schizophrenia highlights the *principle of multiple causality.* For example, while we have learned a great deal about the genetic aspects of schizophrenia, we also know that genetic factors are only partly responsible for the disorder. The possible environmental contributions to schizophrenia include some biological factors, such as viruses, but they also include pathological interpersonal, social, and learning experiences. Most experts agree that the development of schizophrenia typically requires a combination of vulnerabilities and stressors, as described by the *diathesis-stress* model. Accordingly, reductionistic theories of schizophrenia that focus on only a single theoretical approach to the disorder are increasingly being viewed as unhelpful and over-simplistic. The state-of-the-art in understanding and treating schizophrenia involves the integration of multiple theoretical components. For example, Hogarty and colleagues (1997a, 1997b) have developed an adjunctive therapy for schizophrenia called **personal therapy** which combines cognitive, behavioral, psychodynamic, and humanistic principles. Personal therapy, which focuses on helping clients with schizophrenia to solve the practical problems of daily life, has been shown to produce general improvement and prevent relapse (Hogarty et al., 1997a, 1997b).

Personal therapy An adjunctive therapy for schizophrenia that combines cognitive, behavioral, psychodynamic, and humanistic principles and helps clients solve the practical problems of daily life.

Brief Summary

- While Freud believed that biological factors played an important role in schizophrenia and was pessimistic about the value of psychotherapy, some of his followers developed psychodynamic explanations and treatments for the disorder. Most current psychodynamic theorists emphasize the role of biological and psychological factors in schizophrenia and see psychotherapy as a helpful adjunctive treatment.

- Cognitive theorists have focused on the role of attention and reasoning deficits in schizophrenia. Cognitive interventions address these deficits and are increasingly used in the treatment of schizophrenia often in combined cognitive-behavioral interventions.

- Behavioral theorists focus on the role of operant conditioning, along with other factors, in the development and maintenance of schizophrenic behaviors. Treatments based on behavioral principles, including token economies and social skills training, are widely used as adjunctive treatments for schizophrenia.

- Family theorists have explored the hypothesis that pathological family environments can contribute to schizophrenia. They focus on the role of pathological communication patterns, such as "double-bind" communications and "expressed emotion," which they address in family therapy.

- Sociocultural theorists focus on the role of larger social and institutional forces, such as urban poverty and labeling, in contributing to and maintaining schizophrenia. Sociocultural theorists have called attention to the failures of the deinstitutionalization movement, and they have developed milieu therapies and integrated community treatments to deal with sociocultural problems in schizophrenia.

- The *principle of multiple causality* is crucial to explanations of schizophrenia. The state-of-the-art in understanding and treating schizophrenia increasingly incorporates multiple theoretical perspectives.

Critical Thinking Question | **D**o you see much overlap among the psychological perspectives on schizophrenia. If so, where?

Case Vignette | Treatment
Peter | Schizophrenia, Paranoid Type

Peter was admitted to the hospital through the emergency room and placed on a psychiatric unit for observation and treatment. He was immediately given antipsychotic medication in an effort to reduce his psychotic symptoms and agitation. Within two days, Peter was calm and coherent, although he was very subdued and seemed sedated by the medication. Meanwhile, a team consisting of a psychiatrist, psychologist, social worker, nurse, and occupational therapist were working together to arrive at a diagnosis and treatment plan. In talking to Peter's parents, it became clear that he had grown increasingly withdrawn, with occasional oddities of speech and behavior, for well over a year. In addition, his parents revealed that relatives on both sides of the family had experienced psychotic disorders. Since the content of Peter's delusions and hallucinations was paranoid, and his cognition and psychomotor functioning seemed otherwise intact, he was diagnosed with schizophrenia, paranoid subtype.

Peter's parents were devastated by the diagnosis. The team worked with them to provide education about the breakthroughs in biological and psychosocial treatments, and the increased chance for a favorable outcome when premorbid functioning is good, as it had been in Peter's case. Peter was discharged from the hospital after only five days. Peter was fortunate to have responded well to an atypical antipsychotic

that reduced both his positive and negative symptoms (although his symptoms were primarily positive) without serious side effects. Peter had to withdraw from school for the semester, but he was able to continue his music studies while living at home. The hospital staff referred Peter to a local psychiatrist who monitored his medication and provided weekly psychotherapy. In this respect, Peter was more fortunate than most individuals with schizophrenia because his parents were able to pay for this care. He was also referred to a group for clients newly diagnosed with schizophrenia at a local community mental health center. However, Peter found these meetings uncomfortable and soon stopped going. He was compliant with his medication and therapy, but despite this he started becoming psychotic again when he was about to return to school for the next semester. In his therapy sessions, Peter realized that his fears about leaving home, and the pressures to excel in music, had contributed to his relapse. With support from his therapist and parents, and a temporary increase in his medication dosage, the relapse was short-lived, and Peter was able to return to school. He completed his degree in six years. Peter never completely returned to his premorbid level of functioning, and he had occasional relapses under stress, but six years after his initial episode he was living and working independently and his parents described him as "75% well."

Case Discussion | Schizophrenia

The onset and symptoms of Peter's schizophrenia were fairly typical of the disorder, but a number of factors contributed to an unusually positive outcome in his case. First, Peter had good premorbid functioning, and his schizophrenia was properly diagnosed and treated relatively early. In addition, Peter's family support and resources allowed him to obtain high-quality, ongoing treatment. Even with these advantages, however, Peter has never fully recovered, and it appears that he will be affected by the disorder for his entire life. Nonetheless, his condition is far better than those of the majority of clients with schizophrenia who have poorer premorbid functioning, fewer resources, and less access to appropriate treatment.

Chapter Summary

- *Cultural and historical relativism* have influenced the classification of disorders involving psychosis (a profound loss of contact with normal reality) resulting in different classification practices in different regions and historical periods. Currently, the term *schizophrenia* is used to describe the most common psychotic syndrome.

- The DSM-IV-TR defines schizophrenia as a constellation of severe cognitive and behavioral symptoms lasting six months or more and causing significant distress.

- Demographic *context* variables including culture, class, age, and gender affect the epidemiology and course of schizophrenia.

- Experts are unsure whether schizophrenia is a single disorder or a group of related disorders on a schizophrenic spectrum, highlighting the *advantages and limitations of the DSM-IV-TR diagnosis* of schizophrenia.

- *The principle of multiple causality* is crucial to the explanation and treatment of schizophrenia since the disorder is so complex. Biological, psychological, and sociocultural components interact to cause schizophrenia, and current treatments are also multi-modal.

Willem de Kooning, *Untitled,* 1950. ©Bridge-
man Art Library International Ltd. ©2004 The
Willem de Kooning Foundation/Artists Rights
Society (ARS), New York

Dutch-born Willem de Kooning (1904–1997)
was a central figure in New York City Action
Painting movement during the 1940s and
1950s. His paintings are known for their
ambiguous nature, seeming simultaneously
to be carefully designed yet impulsively ren-
dered. Though ....*continues on page 436*

chapter thirteen

LIFESPAN

DEVELOPMENT

DISORDERS OF CHILDHOOD

AND OLD AGE

Many of the mental disorders described in this textbook can occur in the very young and in the very old. Psychopathology among children and older adults often shares the same features as psychopathology at other times of life; exceptions to this rule are discussed in the Classification in Demographic Context section of relevant chapters. In this chapter, we turn our attention to disorders that occur, or are first diagnosed, almost exclusively during specific developmental periods. In Part One, we'll consider the mental disorders most often seen during childhood; in Part Two, we'll consider disorders of old age.

PART ONE: DISORDERS OF CHILDHOOD

Case Vignettes

Molly, age two, has yet to speak. As a baby, she expressed little interest in people. She did not watch her parents, but was transfixed by the rhythmic movements of an oscillating fan or by her own rocking motions. Now a toddler, she is preoccupied with the wheels on toy cars and will sit for hours in the living room holding toy cars near her face while spinning their wheels in front of her eyes. Her parents are greatly pained by her seeming disinterest in them (or anyone else) and are very worried about their daughter.

Shane, age eight, is a human tornado. From the moment he wakes in the morning until late at night, he goes at full speed. His mother says that she knew that she was in for trouble while she was pregnant with him: throughout the pregnancy he kicked and moved so much that she was often unable to sleep through the night. When he was three, his mother went to get him out of bed one morning and found him missing. Panicked, she searched the house for him until a phone call came from a friend who lived two blocks away. The friend had seen Shane playing on her neighbor's lawn and brought him inside. Apparently he had let himself out of his own house early in the morning and decided to explore the neighborhood. Now in the third grade, Shane struggles mightily at school. Though he wants to be "a good boy," he finds it nearly impossible to sit quietly in his seat or to wait his turn in line. His parents have started to receive almost daily calls from the teacher about his behavior: Shane yells out answers without waiting his turn and gets up out of his seat during quiet time. Last week he punched one of his friends during a playground dispute and then called the teacher a "butt head" when she tried to intervene.

...continued from page 434

he suffered from dementia which began sometime in his late 70s, de Kooning continued to create new art until the end of his life.

DEFINING DISORDERS OF CHILDHOOD

The effort to describe the psychopathologies of childhood has a remarkably short history. Despite the fact that some children have always struggled with emotional problems, the first attempts to systematically describe and classify the distinct disorders of childhood did not occur until the beginning of the twentieth century (Terman, 1916). In part, childhood psychopathology has received less attention than adult psychopathology because "abnormality" in childhood behavior is harder to define than abnormality in adult behavior. Consider some of the common criteria for defining adult psychopathology, as described in Chapter 2:

- Help seeking
- Irrational or dangerous behavior
- Deviant behavior
- Emotional distress
- Significant impairment in functioning

How might these criteria apply to children? The first, *help seeking,* is a poor criterion for psychopathology in adults (as you know, most people who suffer from mental disorders never seek help) and it is even less helpful in children. Children rarely understand the concept of seeking treatment for psychological distress and, by virtue of being children, are far more likely to *act out* their distress than to seek help for it. The second criterion, *irrational or dangerous behavior,* can sometimes be useful in defining and identifying adult psychopathology; if a grown man decides that he will jump from a high building because he believes he can fly, chances are he has fairly significant psychological troubles. But what should we make of a four-year-old girl who arrives at the breakfast table insisting that she *is* Ariel, the star of the movie *The Little Mermaid?* She may refuse to answer to her given name, responding only to "Ariel" and even insist that she is going to jump in the neighbor's swimming pool. This anecdote (a true one) is amusing, not alarming, and it reminds us that normal children go through periods of

Miniature adults? Adult definitions of psychopathology, like adult clothes and fashions, don't always suit children very well.

Acting out Though some children with emotional disorders experience intense psychological distress, most children express emotional difficulties through disruptive behavior that upsets the people around them.

blending fantasy and reality, such as when they have imaginary friends. Only later in life is irrational or dangerous behavior seen as a possible sign of psychopathology.

What about the third criterion, the presence of *deviant behavior?* Deviant behavior in adults may be a sign of psychopathology, despite the limitations of this criterion as discussed in Chapter 2. Consider, for example, a grown man who refuses to bathe or dress normally even though he is competent to do so, or an adult woman who flies into rages at the first sign that she might not get her way. But these kinds of behaviors are normative and expectable in children of certain ages. The criterion of "deviant behavior" can sometimes be useful for defining abnormality in children, but it has even more limitations with children than with adults.

Does *emotional distress,* our fourth criterion for adult psychopathology, apply to children? Some disorders of childhood, such as separation anxiety disorder, do involve significant distress. However, many childhood disorders seem to cause little, if any, conscious distress for the child. Disorders such as autism, mental retardation, attention deficit/hyperactivity disorder, and conduct disorder are far more upsetting to the adults in the child's environment than to the affected child. Consider, for example, parents who consulted a psychologist because their five-year-old daughter was not yet toilet trained—a task usually mastered by age three. The young girl did not appear to be the least bit bothered by the problem and stated simply that she found it a bother to have to stop what she was doing to go to the bathroom. Her parents, on the other hand, were extremely worried that she wouldn't be allowed to begin kindergarten (where diapers are usually forbidden) if she did not start to use the toilet soon. Children do sometimes complain about emotional distress, but they are usually brought to mental health professionals when their behaviors distress the people around them, such as their parents and teachers.

What about the fifth criterion, *significant impairment in functioning?* Again, standards that indicate a possible emotional problem in an adult—such as the inability to care for one's own basic needs or to establish lasting romantic relationships—are problematic when applied to children. Nobody expects young children to care for themselves or to have romantic partners. Yet certain age appropriate functioning is expected of children, and delays or disruptions in functioning can be indicative of psychopathology. Given the limitations of adult definitions of psychopathology, how do we define childhood psychopathology? To begin, we must consider the core concepts of the importance of *context* and the *continuum between normal and abnormal* childhood behavior.

The Importance of Context in Defining and Understanding Childhood Disorders

Trying to come up with a simple definition of childhood psychopathology is like trying to hit a moving target. Because of normal developmental processes, children are always growing and changing. What is perfectly normal at one age might be a marker of significant trouble at another; we wouldn't think twice about a toddler who sucks her thumb, but we would be concerned about the same "symptom" in a thirteen-year-old. Arnold Gesell, a developmental psychologist, observed that "If a group of nursery school parents should cast a secret ballot to determine the most exasperating age in the preschool period, it is quite likely that the honors would fall to the two-and-a-half-year-old" (Gesell & Ilg, 1943, p. 177). But he observes that the two-and-a-half-year-old "acts that way because he is built that way" (p. 178). Gesell's research on normal developmental processes highlights the core concept of the importance of *context* in defining and understanding abnormality. Childhood behavior must be considered within the context of what is developmentally appropriate for a child of a given age. Bedwetting is normal at age two and abnormal at twelve; preferring to be with peers instead of parents is normal at age twelve and abnormal at two.

One of the most useful definitions of childhood psychopathology comes from Anna Freud, the youngest of Sigmund and Martha Freud's six children, who followed in her father's footsteps by elaborating his theories. According to Anna Freud, identifying psychopathology in children "implies asking whether the child under examination has reached developmental levels which are adequate for his age, whether and in what respects he has either gone beyond or remained behind them; whether maturation and development are ongoing processes or to what degree they are affected as a result of the child's disturbance..." (Freud, 1965, p. 124). In other words, child psychopathology can be defined as behavior that interferes with normal, progressive development. The effort to define what constitutes psychological normality and abnormality in developing children has given rise to a field within abnormal psychology known as **developmental psychopathology** (Cicchetti & Cohen, 1995) which aims to "understand troublesome behavior in light of the developmental tasks, sequences, and processes that characterize human growth" (Achenbach, 1982, p. 1).

In her father's footsteps Anna Freud elaborated on her father's psychoanalytic theories and pioneered techniques for psychoanalytic treatment of children.

Developmental psychopathology A subfield within abnormal psychology that considers abnormal behavior in light of developmental processes.

The Continuum Between Normal and Abnormal Childhood Behavior

As implied above, the core concept of the *continuum between normal and abnormal* behavior is especially relevant to childhood psychopathology. For example, all children are inattentive, clingy, or aggressive at times. But these behaviors are on the normal side of the normality-abnormality continuum so long as they *do not interfere with progressive development*. A twelve-year old girl who is developing normally may cling to her parents for a few days before leaving for her first sleep-away camp, but a girl of her same age who clings to her parents so much that she consistently refuses to play with age-mates is certainly having trouble with social development. Anna Freud also pointed out that each child develops along several different developmental lines simultaneously: from play to work, toward independent body management, toward mature peer relationships, and so on (Freud, 1981). Thus, a six-year-old boy who refuses to leave his mother may have a serious developmental delay in his social and emotional skills, but have age-appropriate or even advanced intellectual abilities.

Terms like "delay," "age appropriate," and "advanced" accurately suggest that standards exist for what is considered to be normal social, emotional, cognitive, and physical development in children of different ages. In this context, *deviance* can be a useful criterion for identifying disorders in children, since developmental norms provide a yardstick for measuring deviance against age-appropriate behaviors and expected developmental gains; these norms can help locate childhood behavior on the **continuum between normal and abnormal** behavior.

Brief Summary

● Many of the criteria used to define adult psychopathology are problematic when used to define child psychopathology.

● The core concepts of the importance of **context** and the **continuum between normal and abnormal** behavior are crucial to defining childhood psychopathology. Definitions of child psychopathology must take into account what behaviors are developmentally appropriate for a child of a given age. Behavior that is normal at one age may be highly abnormal at another, and standards exist that help define "normal" behavior at each age.

● The study of normal and pathological development is sometimes referred to as developmental psychopathology.

Critical Thinking Question **Can you think of childhood behaviors that are abnormal, regardless of age?**

CLASSIFYING, EXPLAINING, AND TREATING DISORDERS OF CHILDHOOD

Childhood behavior has always been explained in terms of the dominant *paradigms* for thinking about development. One early and still influential view of the nature of childhood came from the philosopher John Locke (1632–1704), who believed that children's minds were blank slates (or *tabula rasa*) at birth, which were then shaped entirely by external experiences (Locke, 1950). The philosopher, Jean Jacques Rousseau (1712–1788) proposed a somewhat different view: he believed that children were by their very nature good, but often corrupted by harmful environmental influences.

In the first half of the twentieth century, the psychologists G. Stanley Hall and Arnold Gesell proposed a **maturationist** approach in which childhood development was seen as analogous to embryologic growth, with specific developmental and behavioral stages naturally unfolding in a predictable fashion (Gesell, 1940; Hall, 1921). Simultaneously, John Watson's **behaviorism** (see Chapter 5) held that childhood fears, interests, talents, and even personality characteristics could be shaped by early environmental experiences, as is clear in his famous quotation:

> Give me a dozen healthy infants, well-formed, and my own specified world to bring them up in and I'll guarantee to take any one at random and train him to become any type of specialist I might select—doctor, lawyer, artist, merchant-chief, and yes, even beggarman and thief, regardless of his talents, penchants, tendencies, abilities, vocations, and race of his ancestors.

1925/1970 (p. 82)

Maturationist A theory of child development in which specific developmental stages are believed to unfold in a natural and predictable fashion.

Behaviorism The theoretical perspective that emphasizes the influence of learning, via classical conditioning, operant conditioning, and modeling, on behavior.

Staunch behaviorist John Watson, widely known for his experiments with Little Albert (see Chapter 5), saw no limits to the power of the environment when it came to shaping human behavior.

Table 13.1	Complete List of DSM-IV-TR Disorders Usually First Diagnosed in Infancy, Childhood, or Adolescence
Adapted from the DSM-IV-TR (APA, 2000).	• **Mental retardation:** Mild, moderate, severe, or profound • **Learning disorders:** Reading disorder; mathematics disorder; disorder of written expression • **Motor skills disorders:** Developmental coordination disorder • **Communication disorders:** Expressive language disorder; mixed receptive-expressive language disorder; phonological disorder; stuttering • **Pervasive developmental disorders:** Autistic disorder; Rett's disorder; childhood disintegrative disorder; Asperger's disorder • **Attention deficit and disruptive behavior disorders:** Attention deficit/hyperactivity disorder; conduct disorder; oppositional defiant disorder • **Feeding and eating disorders of infancy or early childhood:** Pica (eating nonfood substances); rumination disorder (regurgitation and rechewing of food) • **Tic disorders:** Tourette's disorder; chronic motor or vocal tic disorder; transient tic disorder • **Elimination disorders:** Encopresis (defecating in inappropriate places); enuresis (urinating in inappropriate places) • **Other disorders of infancy, childhood, or adolescence:** Separation anxiety disorder; selective mutism; reactive attachment disorder of infancy or early childhood; stereotypic movement disorder

Watch and learn Children are, indeed, highly responsive to their environments. Their behavior can reflect both the best and the worst of what they see in the adults who surround them.

Freudian theories of child development and behavior sit somewhere between Hall and Gesell's focus on internal processes and Watson's focus on external factors. As you know, Freud and his followers maintained that children proceed through a predictable sequence of maturational stages: oral, anal, phallic, latency, and genital. But Freud also believed that environmental factors, such as the relationship with members of one's immediate family, interact with internal processes to shape personality development and, in some situations, to produce mental disorders.

Given that efforts to describe and classify psychopathology in children have lagged behind similar efforts with regard to adults, you may not be surprised to learn that the first edition of the DSM (APA, 1952) contained only two diagnostic categories for childhood disorders: adjustment reaction and childhood schizophrenia (APA, 1952). A third category—behavior disorders of childhood—was added to the DSM-II (APA, 1968), but it was not until the publication of the DSM-III and DSM-IV that the classification of childhood disorders blossomed (APA, 1980, 1987, 1994). The DSM-IV-TR contains ten general categories of disorders specific to childhood or adolescence, each with several subcategories of its own (see Table 13.1).

In this chapter, we will focus on five of the most prominent DSM-IV-TR childhood disorders: *mental retardation, learning disorders, pervasive developmental disorders, attention deficit and disruptive behavior disorders,* and *separation anxiety disorder* (see Table 13.2).

Five Prominent DSM-IV-TR Childhood Disorders	Table 13.2

Adapted from the DSM-IV-TR (APA, 2000)

- **Mental retardation:** Significantly impaired intellectual functioning and adaptive behavior (lifetime prevalence estimate: 1% of the population).

- **Learning disorders:** Deficits in specific academic skills (lifetime prevalence estimate: 2%–10%).

- **Pervasive developmental disorders:** Severe impairment in several areas of development (lifetime prevalence estimate: approximately 5 cases per 10,000 individuals).

- **Attention deficit and disruptive behavior disorders:** Inattentive, hyperactive, impulsive, dangerous, and/or disobedient behaviors (prevalence estimates: attention deficit/hyperactivity disorder: 3%–7% of school-age children; conduct disorder: 1%–10% of school-age population; oppositional defiant disorder: 2%–16% of school-age population).

- **Separation anxiety disorder:** Excessive anxiety concerning separation from home or attachment figures, usually parents (prevalence estimate: 4% of children and young adolescents).

Mental Retardation

Mental retardation is one of the few mental disorders that is usually present at birth and persists throughout life. Due to its chronicity, mental retardation is the only disorder besides the personality disorders to be listed on Axis II of the DSM-IV-TR. In order to be diagnosed as mentally retarded, an individual must have an IQ score below 70 and also have significant trouble functioning independently (see Table 13.3).

Case Illustration Howard was a happy and responsive infant, though by the time he was six months old, his parents noticed that he was not as responsive and engaged as the other babies in his play group. They became concerned when he failed to reach several developmental milestones within normal ranges—he sat, stood, and walked much later than his peers or siblings did. As a toddler he seemed to be "slow" but he was also friendly and affectionate with his parents and with other children. When Howard was five years old he scored a 55 on an IQ test, indicating that he was mildly mentally retarded. He was placed in special education classes at school. As a teenager, Howard was able to work as a stock boy at a convenience store near his home. Though Howard could dress and feed himself, he was unable to take the bus to work or to figure out the proper amounts of money when shopping.

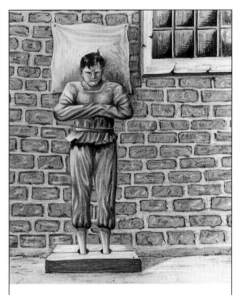

Treating the "feeble-minded" Depiction of nineteenth century conditions for "feeble-minded" children.

Mental retardation Severely impaired intellectual functioning and adaptive behavior.

Diagnostic Criteria for Mental Retardation	Table 13.3

Adapted from the DSM-IV-TR (APA, 2000)

- Significantly subaverage general intellectual functioning (IQ below 70).

- Significant limitations in at least two of the following areas of adaptive functioning: communication, self-care, home living, social/interpersonal skills, use of community resources, self-direction, functional academic skills, work, leisure, health, and safety.

- Onset before age 18.

The DSM-IV-TR distinguishes among four different levels of severity of mental retardation: mild, moderate, severe, and profound. The distinction is made largely on the basis of IQ score, which is strongly correlated with social competence and adaptive behavior (Reynolds, 1981). The following descriptions are adapted from the DSM-IV-TR (APA, 2000).

Mild mental retardation: IQ = 50–70   Approximately 85% of people who are mentally retarded are classified in the mild range. Historically referred to as "educable" retardation, this category includes individuals who typically have adequate social and communication skills and who may acquire school skills as high as the sixth-grade level. As adults, the mildly mentally retarded are often able to work in simple jobs and to live independently or with intermittent support and supervision from others.

Moderate mental retardation: IQ = 35–50   The classification of moderate mental retardation is appropriate for about 10% of all mentally retarded individuals. As teenagers, moderately retarded individuals may have significant difficulty with even simple social interactions and need extra help in attending to their own personal care. In adulthood, they often live in supervised settings and are able to engage in simple vocational tasks though they rarely achieve academic skills above the second-grade level.

Severe mental retardation: IQ = 20–35   Comprising approximately 3% of all mentally retarded individuals, those with severe retardation usually cannot read or use complex sentences in speech. While they may be able to learn some simple tasks and basic self-care skills they rarely learn more than the most elementary of school skills. As adults, the severely mentally retarded cannot care for themselves or travel alone but may be able to partially support themselves in jobs that require unskilled labor.

Profound mental retardation: IQ = <20   Individuals suffering from profound mental retardation make up roughly 2% of the mentally retarded population and usually require full-time custodial care throughout their lifetimes. Under optimal conditions, the profoundly retarded may develop some communication and self-care skills. In most cases, individuals with severe mental retardation have an identifiable neurological disorder that causes their mental retardation and is also often responsible for significantly shortened life expectancies.

Explaining and Treating Mental Retardation

Mental retardation is one of the best understood childhood psychopathologies. It is a clearly defined and identifiable syndrome that usually results from one of two causes: biological abnormalities or sociocultural and family systems factors.

Biological Components   Moderate, severe, and profound mental retardation usually have a biological basis (Scott, 1994). While several hundred organic causes of mental retardation have been identified, the major biological factors associated with mental retardation are genetic abnormalities, metabolic deficiencies, and prenatal and postnatal complications.

Genetic Abnormalities   Most cases of mental retardation result from genetic abnormalities. **Down syndrome**, which occurs in 1 out of every 1,000 births, is the leading cause of mental retardation (Simonoff et al., 1996). Individuals with Down syndrome have what is known as **trisomy 21**; they have three, not two, twenty-first chromosomes. Trisomy 21 results when chromosomes fail to divide properly during cell division (meiosis)—an anomaly that is more likely to occur in the pregnancies of older

Down syndrome   A form of mental retardation caused by having three twenty-first chromosomes; characterized by mild mental retardation and distinctive physical features.

Trisomy 21   The phenomenon of having three, not two, twenty-first chromosomes, causing Down syndrome.

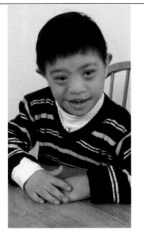

Physical features of Down syndrome   This boy displays the physical abnormalities typically associated with Down syndrome: almond-shaped eyes, flat face, small mouth, and broad hands.

women. John Langdon Down, a physician, originally described the physical abnormalities associated with the syndrome in 1866: almond-shaped and upwardly slanting eyes (resulting in the now outdated term "mongolism"), flat face, large tongue and small mouth, broad hands, and shortened life expectancy.

The second most common genetic cause of mental retardation is known as the **Fragile X syndrome** because it involves any one of a number of genetic abnormalities of the X chromosome. Males with Fragile X syndrome are almost always mentally retarded, have long faces and large ears, and often are hyperactive (State, King, & Dykens, 1997). Girls with Fragile X syndrome are less likely to display mental retardation than boys, but do have high levels of learning disabilities and behavior problems.

Metabolic Deficiencies Metabolic disorders that affect intelligence usually result when both parents contribute a pathogenic recessive gene to a child's genetic material. The most common metabolic disorder associated with mental retardation, known as **phenylketonuria** (PKU), results when the liver fails to produce an enzyme that breaks down a common amino acid called phenylalanine. Unmetabolized phenylalanine is toxic to humans and causes retardation, hyperactivity, and seizures. When detected before three months of age, PKU can be effectively treated (and mental retardation can be avoided) by restricting the intake of phenylalanine. (You may have seen the warning found on diet cans of soda—Phenylketonuriacs: Contains phenylalanine.) Similar to PKU, **Tay-Sachs disease** occurs when a child receives a recessive gene from both parents. Tay-Sachs causes the progressive deterioration of the nervous system and usually results in childhood death. The gene for Tay-Sachs is particularly prominent among Jewish populations and, presently, the disease is untreatable.

Prenatal and Postnatal Complications Mental retardation can result when fetuses or children are exposed to poisons, diseases, or physical traumas that damage the brain. Cocaine, marijuana, and nicotine are among the many drugs known to cause fetal brain damage when used by pregnant women. Women who drink alcohol during pregnancy may cause **fetal alcohol syndrome** in which babies are born with mental retardation and a host of physical abnormalities (see Chapter 9). Maternal rubella, herpes, or syphilis infections during pregnancy can also cause prenatal brain damage. Premature birth and postnatal exposure to toxins such as lead or mercury are another known cause of mental retardation. **Shaken baby syndrome** is the most common childhood physical trauma associated with permanent brain damage. It results when a caretaker who is angered and overwhelmed by the demands of caring for an infant violently shakes a baby back and forth. Given that babies lack the strength to control the movement of their heads, such shaking can result in severe bruising of the brain and heavy bleeding within the skull, leading to cognitive impairments.

Sociocultural and Family Systems Components Some mentally retarded children have what is known as *cultural-familial retardation*. On the sociocultural side, retardation may be related to extreme poverty and its attendant difficulties: inadequate prenatal care, meager nutrition, substandard schools, and overwhelmed families. While it is impossible to completely untangle biological and sociocultural causes of mental retardation because poverty inevitably affects overall health, poverty can undoubtedly contribute to intellectual impairment (McLoyd, 1998). On the familial side, retardation can result from extreme sensory deprivation. A physically healthy child may fail to develop intellectually if his or her parents do not provide an adequately stimulating home environment (Singh, Oswald, & Ellis, 1998).

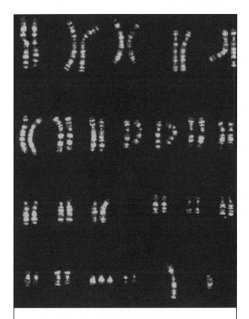

Down syndrome karyotype In karyotyping, chromosomes are arranged in pairs. As you can see in this karyotype of a boy with Down syndrome, there are three, not two, chromosomes in the twenty-first set.

Fragile X syndrome A chromosomal disorder resulting in learning disabilities or mental retardation, distinctive physical features such as long faces and large ears, and behavioral difficulties.

Phenylketonuria A genetic disorder in which the liver fails to produce an enzyme that metabolizes phenylalanine; it can cause retardation, hyperactivity, and seizures.

Tay-Sachs disease A genetic disorder that leads to the progressive deterioration of the nervous system and usually results in childhood death.

Fetal alcohol syndrome (FAS) Mental retardation and a variety of physical abnormalities that result from prenatal exposure to alcohol.

Shaken baby syndrome Severe bruising of the brain resulting in heavy bleeding within the skull that can result when an infant is shaken violently.

Intervention programs designed to address the effects of chronic poverty and/or sensory deprivation have been found to prevent or remediate the effects of cultural-familial retardation. Head Start, a national early intervention program, has successfully promoted the intellectual development of poor children who otherwise may lag behind their middle-class peers even by the time they start kindergarten (Zigler, Styfco, & Gilman, 1993). Programs that work directly with families have also been found to foster intellectual growth in children. One study of low-birthweight premature infants investigated the effects of three kinds of familial intervention: home visits to provide support and information, drop-in child care centers, and meetings for parents. The researchers found that involvement in any one of the available interventions was associated with increases in the children's IQs (Blair, Ramey, & Hardin, 1995).

Most of the available interventions for children and adults with mental retardation focus on providing appropriate educational and personal support for the mentally impaired. Educational interventions have been the predominant form of treatment for the mentally impaired, but the nature of educational interventions has changed radically over the last several decades. The "warehousing" of retarded individuals in state institutions prior to the 1960s gave way to the current focus on **normalization**, which aims to promote the most normal functioning possible (Handen, 1998). To this end, mentally retarded children are taught academic skills as well as language, social, and daily living skills. Behavioral modification techniques based on operant-conditioning principles are central to normalization (Handen, 1998). Tasks are broken down into discrete components and rewards are provided for the competent execution of each component, and ultimately of the entire task. A major controversy in the education of the mentally retarded has centered on whether they should be taught in **special education** classes with other mentally retarded individuals, or placed in **inclusion classrooms** with children of normal intelligence. Despite years of controversy, neither special education nor full inclusion has been shown to be clearly superior for all mentally retarded individuals.

Most mentally retarded individuals live in group homes, supervised apartments, or in their own family home (Burchard et al., 1992). The residential placement of each mentally retarded person must take into account the availability of family support and the degree of intervention and supervision required. Individuals living in group homes share a communal living arrangement that is supervised by a full-time staff of paraprofessionals. Mildly mentally retarded adults are often able to live independently in supervised apartments, and to work in **sheltered workshops** that provide work appropriate to each individual's skills.

The "mainstreaming" debate Proponents of the inclusion approach argue that mentally retarded individuals benefit most when integrated into academic and social settings with normally developing age-mates, like the young people shown here. To date, research studies indicate that mainstreaming suits some mentally retarded individuals well, while others benefit from special education settings.

Normalization An intervention approach for people suffering from mental retardation which aims to promote the most normal functioning possible by teaching academic, language, social, and daily living skills.

Special education Classes tailored to individuals with learning impairments or mental retardation.

Inclusion classrooms Classrooms where children with special academic needs (learning impairments, mental retardation) are taught in the same classrooms as normally functioning children rather than in special education classrooms.

Sheltered workshops Supervised work settings for people suffering from mental retardation or other impairments.

Brief Summary

- Mental retardation is characterized by intellectual functioning and adaptive behavior that are significantly impaired.

- Mental retardation results primarily from genetic abnormalities such as Down syndrome, metabolic deficiencies such as phenylketonuria (PKU), and prenatal and postnatal complications such as maternal rubella during pregnancy or shaken baby syndrome after birth.

- Mental retardation can also be caused by sociocultural and familial factors such as inadequate nutrition or lack of environmental stimulation.

- Mentally retarded children are usually schooled in special education classes and live either with their families or in group-home settings as adults.

Critical Thinking Question **D**o you think that low IQ related to poverty (cultural-familial retardation) should be considered a "mental disorder?"

Learning Disorders

While the intellectual deficits associated with mental retardation tend to impair all areas of cognitive functioning, individuals suffering from **learning disorders** usually have trouble with a specific kind of academic skill (Table 13.4). For example, some children do well in math and music classes but have extreme difficulty learning to read. In contrast other children read and write fluently, but are unable to master even the most basic mathematical concepts. Many people assume that individuals with learning disorders are not intelligent. On the contrary, learning disorders are usually identified by a notable lack of achievement in one area in the context of average or superior ability in other academic domains (APA, 2000).

Learning disorders Deficits in specific academic skills compared to what would be expected given a child's age, schooling, and intelligence.

Dyslexia A learning disorder in which academic achievement in reading is substantially below what would be expected given the child's age, intelligence, or education.

Case Illustration When Jessica, who is in the third grade, failed the first two math tests of the school year, her teacher contacted her parents. Though Jessica struggled with mathematical concepts in first and second grade, her parents and teachers assumed that she was simply making the adjustment to elementary school and that her math abilities would improve gradually over the course of the next school year. On the school's recommendation, Jessica was tested for a learning disorder. She received a full scale IQ score of 112, which included a verbal IQ of 118 (a measure of language-related skills) and performance IQ of 105 (a measure of nonverbal skills such as working with puzzles and symbols). All of Jessica's IQ scores fell in the average to high-average range. However, Jessica's scores on the achievement tests (which measure grade and percentile equivalents for a variety of school skills) placed her in the fifth percentile for math achievement, though she performed close to grade level in nearly every other academic subject. Based on the large discrepancy between Jessica's IQ scores and her low achievement test scores for math, the evaluating psychologist concluded that Jessica suffered from dyscalculia, a learning disorder that pertains specifically to math skills.

Learning disorders are diagnosed when there is a significant discrepancy between a child's general intellectual ability and what the child *actually achieves* in specific academic subjects. Jessica's testing revealed that her overall intelligence is good, yet she has specific difficulties with age-appropriate math skills. The DSM-IV-TR distinguishes among three types of learning disorders—one for each of the traditional "three R's" of academics: reading disorder, disorder of written expression, and mathematics disorder (APA, 2000). These diagnostic categories are known respectively as **dyslexia,**

Diagnostic Criteria for Learning Disorders	Table 13.4

Adapted from the DSM-IV-TR (APA, 2000)

- Academic achievement in reading, mathematics, or written expression is substantially below what would be expected given the child's age, overall intelligence, or general education.

- The disturbance significantly interferes with academic achievement or activities of daily living.

Dysgraphia A learning disorder in which academic achievement in written expression is substantially below what would be expected given the child's age, intelligence, or education.

Dyscalculia A learning disorder in which academic achievement in mathematics is substantially below what would be expected given the child's age, intelligence, or education.

Comorbidity The presence of two or more disorders in one person, or a general association between two or more different disorders.

dysgraphia, and **dyscalculia**. (Some people who specialize in evaluating learning disorders measure a wider variety of skill deficits, such as problems with speech or physical coordination, that are not as closely associated with school performance.) Since reading, writing, and arithmetic each involve several interdependent mental skills, the DSM-IV-TR diagnostic categories for learning disorders are deceptively simple. For example, performing calculations requires understanding that numbers (2, 3, 4) are symbolic of values (a conceptual skill), that values can be placed into relationships with each other (added, subtracted, multiplied, and so on—an abstract reasoning skill), and that the value of the product of such abstract relationships can, again, be expressed in the form of a symbol (6, 9, 12) (abstract reasoning, verbal, and memory skills). A deficit in one or more of the necessary mental skills may produce a learning disorder, or as is often the case, multiple learning difficulties across a variety of subjects. Children who fall within the same learning disorder diagnostic category may have little in common with each other, and children who are not classified within the same category of learning disorder may nonetheless share similar cognitive deficits. The DSM-IV-TR is a blunt instrument when it comes to diagnosing learning disorders and, as such, it reminds us of the core concept of the ***advantages and limitations of diagnosis***.

Explaining and Treating Learning Disorders

Like mental retardation, learning disorders result primarily from biological factors but can be complicated by psychological components. Indeed, learning disorders highlight the core concept of the ***multiple causality*** because they often result from a complex cycle of factors including cognitive deficits, diminished self-esteem, and reduced motivation and effort (see Figure 13.1).

Biological Components There are two predominant biological factors in learning disorders: genetic influences and brain abnormalities. Family, sibling, and twin studies indicate that learning disorders often have a genetic component (Rack & Olson, 1993; Silver, 1994). One study found that the concordance rates for reading disorders was 68% for identical twins compared to 40% for fraternal twins (DeFries & Light, 1996). The exact genes and chromosomes involved in various learning disorders have not yet been identified, but available evidence indicates that many different genes are likely involved.

Technological advances, such as magnetic resonance imaging (MRI), allow researchers to study the workings of the living brain and to identify previously undetectable brain anomalies. Recent neuroimaging research on reading disorders has found a relationship between dyslexia and abnormal functioning in two systems in the posterior (back) section of the brain's left hemisphere. Individuals with a reading disorder seem to compensate for difficulties in their posterior left hemisphere (a center of language processing) by relying instead on the brain's frontal left hemisphere and right hemisphere—areas ill-equipped for fluent word recognition (Pugh et al., 2000). Other researchers have found measurable differences in the brain functioning of children with other language-related learning impairments as compared to intellectually unimpaired children (Cohen, Riccio, & Hynd, 1999).

To date, there are no biological interventions specifically for learning disorders. However, learning disorders and attention deficit/hyperactivity disorder (ADHD) (described in detail below) are highly **comorbid**, meaning that many children diagnosed with one disorder are also diagnosed with the other. Indeed, some studies have shown that as many as 70% of children with ADHD are also diagnosed with a learning disorder (Mayes, Calhoun, & Crowell, 2000). As a result, a high percentage of children with learning disorders are taking medications for ADHD which may help improve academic performance by increasing attention and focus.

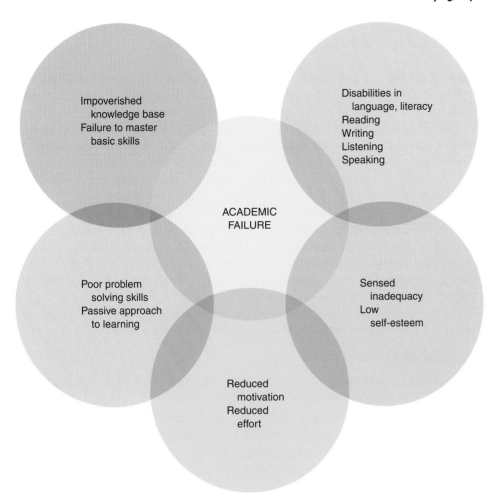

Figure 13.1 The Multiple Causality of Academic Failure Due to Language-related Learning Disorders Children who suffer from learning disorders often develop psychosocial and motivational problems as they become increasingly frustrated by their academic difficulties. Not surprisingly, psychosocial and motivational difficulties interfere with the ability to manage a learning disorder. Here we see how cognitive deficits, linguistic deficits, and psychosocial problems can combine to produce academic failure.

Adapted from Gerber, 1993, p. 269.

Family Systems Components Gerald Coles (1989) proposes an "interactivity theory" of learning difficulties. According to interactivity theory, families and schools can interact with each other in ways that contribute to the development of learning deficits. For example, not all families support early learning experiences by reading stories to their children or actively engaging their children in conversation. When children from educationally impoverished environments begin school, they are already behind their peers from more educationally oriented families. School systems may mistakenly assume that children from educationally impoverished environments are less intelligent or capable than their well-prepared peers; the school system may then treat these children accordingly by placing them in remedial classrooms which may ask and expect less of them academically. Insofar as the growing brain is shaped by environmental experiences, Coles argues that neurological differences between "learning disordered" and "normal" children could be the *result* of environmental factors that caused the learning disorder, not the *cause* of the disorder itself. In a similar vein, some clinicians have described cases in which a learning disorder appeared to have a psychosocial origin (Day & Moore, 1976; Garber, 1993). For example, a child who feels anxiety about "knowing" something at home, such as a situation that the family treats as a secret (a father's affair, a mother's alcoholism) may have difficulty letting herself know and learn at school.

Having a learning disorder is an emotionally painful experience for most children, considering that school is the major focus of a child's life. Many children with learning disorders feel anxious and depressed and assume that they are "dumb" and incompetent in general. Family and individual psychotherapy to address the negative emotional effects of having a learning disorder can be a crucial component of a multifaceted intervention (Pickar, 1986; Zigler & Holden, 1988).

Behavioral and Cognitive Components The most common interventions for learning disorders involve remedial education using behavioral and cognitive principles. Academic skills are broken down into specific components that are modeled by teachers, and then rewarded when properly executed (Nelson, 1987). As noted, many children with learning disorders feel anxious and depressed about their academic troubles and often manifest their distress and frustration by misbehaving in school. Behavioral interventions for children with learning disorders can address both academic and behavioral difficulties simultaneously. For example, a child with a learning disorder might be rewarded for completing a set of math exercises and for staying on-task all morning.

Cognitive interventions for learning disorders help children to identify their problem areas and to develop techniques for tackling specific academic problems. Children are helped to devise new strategies for problem solving, to assess the effectiveness of whatever strategy they have chosen, and to try another strategy when needed. This approach to helping children with learning disorders has been found to be highly effective, especially when combined with the direct training and rewards typical of a behavioral intervention (Swanson, 2000; Swanson & Hoskyn, 1998).

Brief Summary

- Learning disorders are specific deficits in academic skills such as reading, mathematics, or written expression.

- Learning disorders are usually caused by genetic and/or neurological abnormalities that interfere with the performance of specific academic tasks.

- Some theorists suggest that learning disorders may also arise from environmental causes such as an interaction between home and school problems.

- Learning disorders are most often addressed with remedial education that involves behavioral and cognitive components.

> *Critical Thinking Question* **How might you design a research study that could distinguish between biologically based learning disorders and environmentally based learning disorders?**

Pervasive Developmental Disorders

Pervasive developmental disorders Severe impairment in several areas of development.

Autism A pervasive developmental disorder characterized by impaired social and communication skills, and rigid and repetitive patterns of behavior.

As a group, the **pervasive developmental disorders** are characterized by profound and persistent impairment in several areas of functioning. In contrast to mild mental retardation and the learning disorders, in which mainly intellectual functions are affected, children suffering from pervasive developmental disorders fail to develop normal social and communication skills and fail to engage in typical childhood behaviors, interests, and activities (APA, 2000). Like mental retardation, the pervasive developmental disorders are lifelong conditions that are usually diagnosed in childhood. **Autism** is the most common diagnosis within the category of pervasive developmental disorders (see Table 13.5). The other DSM-IV-TR disorders within this category (Rett's disorder, childhood disintegrative disorder, and Asperger's disorder) will be discussed briefly as they are defined largely by how they differ from autism.

Like Molly (described at the beginning of the chapter), children suffering from autism are impaired in three major areas: (1) social interaction, (2) communication, and (3) behaviors, interests, or activities. In terms of social interaction, fluency in

Diagnostic Criteria for Autism	Table 13.5

Adapted from the DSM-IV-TR (APA, 2000)

Diagnosis of autism is based on meeting specific criteria for at least six items across the three categories below (with at least two criteria from the first category, and at least one criterion from the second and third categories).

- Impaired social interaction, as demonstrated by: absence of nonverbal behaviors; disinterest in developing age-appropriate friendships with peers; general lack of interest in relationships; lack of social or emotional exchange with others.

- Impaired communication as demonstrated by: delayed or absent spoken language; when speech is present, inability to maintain a conversation; odd language, or repetitive use of words; absence of age-appropriate pretend play.

- Rigid and repetitive patterns of behavior, interests, and activities: abnormally intense and narrow patterns of interest; inflexible adherence to meaningless routines; odd and repetitive physical movements; preoccupation with parts of objects.

nonverbal social cues is a subtle but critical component of human relationships. Most interpersonal interactions rely heavily on eye contact, nodding, facial expressions, and body posture. Children and adults with autism seem to be unable to send or receive the nonverbal messages that act as the "glue" that holds social interactions together. Many people with autism can be taught some of the basic rules that guide social behavior (such as greeting people with "Hello, how are you?" and a handshake), but their interpersonal styles often seem stiff, scripted, and lacking in spontaneity. Individuals with autism do not seem to be bothered by their failure to make social contact with others. Indeed, they often prefer the inanimate world to the animate and treat human beings as if they were inanimate objects. For example, while playing at blocks with his mother, an autistic child might pick up his mother's hand by the wrist and use her hand to lift a block without ever looking at his mother's face or acknowledging her presence.

Difficulties with communication are pervasive in autism: nearly half of all people with autism fail to develop useful speech. Those who do speak are generally considered to be in the "high functioning" range of autism (Tager-Flüsberg, 1993). People with autism often sound mechanical or robotic when they talk because their speech usually lacks normal cadence and intonation. Autistic speech is often limited and repetitive and people with autism have a tendency to reverse pronouns (such as saying "you" where "I" would be appropriate), or to mimic what they hear—a behavior known as **echolalia**.

Individuals with autism often have unusual and narrow areas of interest. For example, an autistic child may spend hours rearranging bottle caps into a series of patterns, or stare intently at her fingers as she wiggles them in front of her eyes. Rather than using a whole object for pretend play, such as dressing up a baby doll and pretending to be a mother, an autistic child might become preoccupied by the snap closure on the baby doll's diaper, or like Molly, play only with the wheels of her toy cars. Many people who suffer from autism rely heavily on sameness and routine, and may become quite distressed when changes, however insignificant, occur. This aspect of autism was highlighted in the 1988 movie *Rain Man* in which Dustin Hoffman plays

Echolalia A speech abnormality in which a person mimics what they have just heard; seen in autism.

an autistic man who becomes hysterical when prevented from watching *The People's Court,* his favorite daily television show.

Savant Someone possessing an exceptional or unusual intellectual skill in one area.

A common misconception is that all people with autism are **savants**, meaning that they each possess some outstanding and unusual intellectual skill. For example, in *Rain Man,* Dustin Hoffman's character was able to execute complex calculations in his head and to memorize vast amounts of information—thus inspiring his sleazy long-lost brother, played by Tom Cruise, to take him to Las Vegas to count cards. While not typical of autism, examples of isolated but highly developed intellectual skills among people with autism have been documented by authors such as the neurologist Oliver Sacks (1985, 1995) (see also Box 13.1). For example, when writing about a young autistic man with uncanny artistic skills, Sacks comments:

> Steven, only thirteen, was now famous throughout England—but as autistic, as disabled, as ever. He could draw, with the greatest ease, any street he had seen; but he could not, unaided, cross one by himself. He could see all London in his mind's eye, but its human aspects were unintelligible to him. He could not maintain a real conversation with anyone, though, increasingly, he now showed a sort of pseudosocial conduct, talking to strangers in an indiscriminate and bizarre way.

Sacks, 1995 (p. 203)

Though savant skills are fascinating, they occur in less than 2 out of every 1,000 people with pervasive developmental disorders (Saloviita, Ruusila, & Ruusila, 2000), and even autistic savants tend to score in the mentally retarded range of tests of general intelligence. Recent research on savant artistic skill has noted that the careful attention to visual detail, compulsive repetition, and narrow interests often associated with autism may promote the development of special, but limited, artistic abilities (Hou et al., 2000).

The DSM-IV-TR also classifies Rett's disorder, childhood disintegrative disorder, and Asperger's disorder as pervasive developmental disorders. Rett's disorder shares many of its major features with autism (stereotyped behaviors, social isolation, language difficulties) but differs from autism in that it occurs only in girls and begins after a period of apparently normal development. Girls with Rett's disorder develop normally for the first six months of life. After that time, a genetic anomaly causes a slowing of head growth, and the loss of previously acquired social skills, motor skills, and physical coordination (APA, 2000).

Childhood disintegrative disorder is much like Rett's disorder, but it afflicts both boys and girls, and occurs after at least two years of normal development (APA, 2000). Children with childhood disintegrative disorder develop age-appropriate verbal, social, physical, and play skills until they are at least two years old. When the disorder begins, they abruptly lose language abilities, social skills, and motor skills and develop many of the characteristics usually associated with autism (social difficulties, impaired communication, rigid and repetitive behavioral patterns). The cause of childhood disintegrative disorder is unknown, but several lines of research suggest that it results from central nervous system pathology (Volkmar et al., 1997).

Asperger's disorder differs from autism in that people with Asperger's disorder have unimpaired and often superior language and cognitive skills. Individuals with Asperger's have many of the social impairments typical of autism but may function well in academic settings due to their verbal skills and intense and narrow focus on specific topics. Many people with Asperger's develop an encyclopedic knowledge of specialized subjects, such as knowing everything there is to know about snakes, or memorizing complex train schedules. There is an ongoing debate about whether Asperger's is a unique clinical syndrome, or a high-functioning form of autism.

BOX 13.1   Thinking in Pictures

The Tale of Temple Grandin

Temple Grandin holds a Ph.D. in animal science, sits on the faculty at Colorado State University, and also happens to be autistic. Temple Grandin is both like and unlike other people with autism. Like many people with autism, she feels confused by and disconnected from interpersonal interactions. Oliver Sacks took the title of his book, *An Anthropologist on Mars,* from Dr. Grandin's comment that she feels as if she were an observer from another planet who witnesses social interactions between people, but lacks an intuitive understanding of such behavior. Dr. Grandin differs from most people with autism in that she has enjoyed enormous professional success as a leading expert on the design of livestock management systems. In fact, Dr. Grandin's intellectual abilities have caused several experts to question whether she truly suffers from autism; her correct diagnosis may be Asperger's disorder, a closely related syndrome that shares the same social impairments as autism, yet in which language and cognitive skills are normal, and sometimes exceptionally well-developed.

Caring for animals Temple Grandin, a high-functioning autistic woman, credits her success as a designer of livestock handling systems to her empathy with animals and her concern about their humane treatment.

Dr. Grandin attributes the success of her designs to two things: her deep empathy for animals, and her extraordinary ability to develop complex architectural designs in her head (see Figure 13.2). Here, Dr. Grandin describes her acute visualization skills as well as her interpersonal limitations:

> I think in pictures. Words are like a second language to me. I translate both spoken and written words into full-color movies, complete with sound, which run like a VCR tape in my head. When somebody speaks to me, his words are instantly translated into pictures. Language-based thinkers often find this phenomenon difficult to understand, but in my job as an equipment designer for the livestock industry, visual thinking is a tremendous advantage.
>
> Visual thinking has enabled me to build entire systems in my imagination. During my career I have designed all kinds of equipment, ranging from corrals for handling cattle on ranches to systems for handling cattle and hogs during veterinary procedures and slaughter. I have worked for many major livestock companies. In fact, one third of the cattle and hogs in the United States are handled in equipment I have designed. Some of the people I've worked for don't even know that their systems were designed by someone with autism. I value my ability to think visually, and I would never want to lose it…
>
> At [the beginning of graduate school] I still struggled in the social arena, largely because I didn't have a concrete visual corollary for the abstraction known as "getting along with people." An image finally presented itself to me while I was washing the bay windows in the cafeteria. … The bay windows consisted of three glass sliding doors enclosed by storm windows. To wash the inside of the bay window, I had to crawl through the sliding door. The door jammed while I was washing the inside panes, and I was imprisoned between the two windows. … While I was trapped between the windows, it was almost impossible to communicate through the glass. Being autistic is like being trapped like this. The windows symbolized my feelings of disconnection from other people and helped me cope with the isolation.

Grandin, 1995 (pp. 20–36)

Figure 13.2 Drawing of Cattle Barns by Temple Grandin Temple Grandin, who has no formal training in drafting, uses her unusual visualization skills to create highly technical drawings of her architectural and engineering designs. This blueprint of cattle barns was generated, by hand, in only one try.

From, Grandin, T. 1995

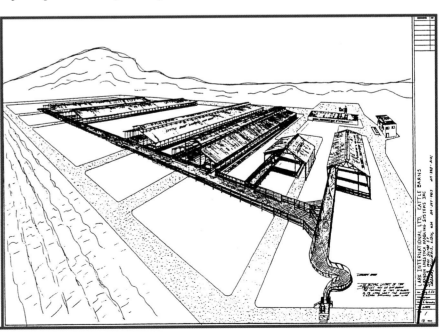

Explaining and Treating Pervasive Developmental Disorders

We will focus our discussion of the explanations and interventions for pervasive developmental disorders on autism, the most common and most thoroughly studied of these disorders.

Biological Components Despite a consensus among experts that autism is caused by biological factors, the precise causes of autism have yet to be identified. Various biological markers have been observed in some cases of autism, but not in others.

Genetic Factors Studies of monozygotic (MZ) and dizygotic (DZ) twin pairs show that autism has an extremely strong genetic component: several researchers report concordance rates at or above 90% for MZ twins compared with 0% for DZ twins (Rutter et al., 1997). Interestingly, in the rare identical twin pairs in which only one twin is autistic, researchers have found that the nonautistic twin frequently displays autistic qualities, such as delayed language or marked social difficulties (Bailey, Phillips, & Rutter, 1996). Further evidence that autism has a genetic basis comes from studies showing that individuals with autism have unusually high rates of other genetically based disorders such as seizures, Fragile X syndrome, and tuberous sclerosis (frequent benign brain and organ tumors) (Dykens & Volkmar, 1997). The linkage between autism and other genetic disorders is unclear: autism may cause or be caused by other disorders, or an abnormal *genotype* (genetic makeup) may express itself in a variety of *phenotypes* (observable characteristics) such as autism, seizure disorder, and so on.

Prenatal, Birth, and Neurological Factors A wide variety of prenatal and birth complications have been associated with autism, but none of them have been found to be a definitive cause of the disorder. Maternal bleeding or rubella during pregnancy, prematurity, breech birth, and forceps deliveries have all been found to be stastically associated with autism. Various studies of people with autism have also identified neuroanatomical anomalies in the cerebellum, in overall brain weight, and in the functioning of the limbic system, a part of the brain involved in regulating social behavior (Minshew, Sweeney, & Bauman, 1997), but studies of brain abnormalities must be interpreted cautiously since we know little about how often the same anomalies occur in nonautistic individuals. Neurochemical studies have found that a significant percentage of autistic individuals have unusually high blood levels of the neurotransmitter **serotonin** (Anderson & Hoshino, 1997). This finding, too, is as yet inconclusive and poorly understood, but it lends support to the argument that a variety of biological factors interact to cause the various clinical features of autism.

Serotonin A neurotransmitter associated with depression and anxiety.

Biological Interventions Given that the biological causes of autism are still unclear, it should come as no surprise that an effective biological treatment for the disorder has yet to be discovered. The current state of the art in the biological treatment of autism employs various psychotropic medications to treat some of the behavioral symptoms associated with the disorder. Antipsychotic medications are frequently used to help calm agitated and aggressive autistic individuals, though this intervention has not proven to be consistently effective (McDougle, 1997). Antidepressants, anxiolytics (anti-anxiety medications), stimulants, opiate antagonists, and lithium have also been used to address the irritability and emotional reactivity sometimes associated with autism (Buitelaar, 1995). While some medications help some people with autism, no one medication works for everyone or treats the primary symptoms of the disorder.

Behavioral Components Behavioral programs are the most effective and widely used interventions for autism. Using the principles of operant conditioning, behavioral interventions can be used to teach autistic children language and communication skills, self-care, and community adaptation. For example, an autistic child being taught to ask for juice would first be rewarded (with candy, hugs, etc.) for making eye contact with the person responsible for giving out juice. Next the child would be prompted to say "juice," with successive approximations of the word being rewarded (thus **shaping** the behavior in the appropriate direction). Next, the child would be taught to say "I want juice" using the same techniques.

Ivar Lovaas and his colleagues at the University of California, Los Angeles have used behavioral techniques to develop a comprehensive and intensive intervention program for autistic children (Lovaas & Smith, 1988). By employing undergraduate and graduate students, Lovaas developed what he calls the Early Intervention Project in which young autistic children receive 40 hours of behavioral intervention each week. They are taught both expressive and receptive language, play behaviors, affectionate behaviors, emotional expression, and school skills. The UCLA program has been hailed by some as a "cure" for autism, and by others for its ability to help many autistic children function much more normally than expected. But, Lovaas's intervention program has also been harshly criticized (Gresham & MacMillan, 1998). Some critics wonder whether it is appropriate to subject very young children to 40 or more hours of behavioral training each week, others suggest that it is a waste of time to teach "affection" skills to a child who may be destined to remain emotionally detached, and still others criticize Lovaas for having employed harsh punishments at times. Other educational programs for autistic children, such as TEACCH (Treatment and Education of Autistic and related Communication handicapped CHildren) are less intensive than the UCLA model but focus more on promoting home adjustment and community adaptation (Schopler, 1997). TEACCH is based at the University of North Carolina, but uses regional centers to work closely with families and vocational training programs throughout the entire state of North Carolina.

As adults, individuals with autism have many of the same living and treatment options as those available to the mentally retarded. Placement in a group home, supervised apartment, family home, or independent living depends largely upon the skills of the autistic individual. People with autism who speak, care for themselves, and perform skilled or unskilled labor are often able to live independently. However, like Temple Grandin, even the most high-functioning people with autism continue to be socially impaired throughout their lives.

Psychodynamic Components The psychodynamic perspective has a particularly unfortunate history related to autism. For many years, some psychodynamic theorists considered the parents of autistic children to be the cause of the disorder. Psychodynamic theorists believed that autistic children were born normal, and only became autistic after withdrawing from painful interactions with their hostile and cold parents (sometimes referred to as "refrigerator mothers"). This view was articulated in a widely read tract on autism by Bruno Bettleheim titled *The Empty Fortress* (1967). Bettleheim argued that autistic children responded to their disturbed and hostile parents by retreating to a protected inner world, and that the most hopeful interventions involved separating autistic children from their parents. This view is widely rejected by contemporary psychodynamic theorists and clinicians who now, in combination with other interventions, tend to focus on helping children and families cope optimally with the disorder.

Brief Summary

- Pervasive developmental disorders such as autism, Rett's disorder, childhood disintegrative disorder, or Asperger's disorder are characterized by severe impairments in several areas of development.

Shaping Behavioral term for an operant-conditioning procedure in which successive approximations of a desired behavior are rewarded until the target behavior is achieved.

- A variety of biological anomalies have been associated with autism, though no single factor has been identified as the main cause of the disorder.

- Autism is usually treated with behavioral interventions that aim to increase functional skills and promote the use of speech by rewarding appropriate behaviors.

Critical Thinking Question | **If your child were autistic, would you prefer that he or she be treated using the UCLA or TEACCH model? Why?**

Attention Deficit and Disruptive Behavior Disorders

The attention deficit and disruptive behavior disorder category of the DSM-IV-TR includes three diagnoses: attention deficit/hyperactivity disorder (ADHD), oppositional defiant disorder (ODD), and conduct disorder (CD). All three of these disorders are characterized by *externalizing* behaviors in which children "act out" and fail to conform to the behavioral standards of their homes, schools, and/or communities.

Attention Deficit/Hyperactivity Disorder

Case Illustration Eleven-year-old Mary's middle school teachers told her parents that Mary's academic performance did not seem to reflect her high intelligence, causing them to wonder if she had an undiagnosed learning disability. The results of diagnostic testing indicated that Mary's academic skills were strong, but that she had a great deal of difficulty attending to what was happening around her. When Mary's parents were asked about her ability to pay attention at home, they reported that she always had to be asked to do a task several times before she would remember to complete it. Mary would gladly agree to do things, such as loading the dishwasher, but would then be found playing with the family cat, having completely forgotten about the dishes. Mary's parents also explained that Mary lost things so frequently that the family joked that "if you want to get rid of something, give it to Mary."

Attention deficit/hyperactivity disorder A disruptive behavior disorder involving symptoms of inattention, hyperactivity, and impulsivity.

Attention deficit/hyperactivity disorder (ADHD) is one of the most frequently diagnosed childhood disorders (see Table 13.6). Though the DSM-IV-TR estimates that one out of every 20 to 30 children suffers from ADHD (APA, 2000), prevalence rates in several countries exceed these estimates (Searight & McLaren, 1998). The number of American children diagnosed with ADHD and treated with medications has sky-rocketed since the early 1980s when Ritalin, a psychostimulant drug treatment for ADHD, was found to have a calming effect on hyperactive and inattentive children. Prescriptions for Ritalin increased almost three-fold during the 1990s, and roughly 2.5 million American children are now treated with psychostimulant medications (Safer & Zito, 1999). The sharp rise in the diagnosis and medical treatment of ADHD is not well understood. Some experts contend that ADHD was vastly underdiagnosed prior to the 1980s, others say that the pharmaceutical industry has used massively-funded advertising campaigns to pathologize behaviors that can be "treated" with their products, while still others argue that some physicians and parents prefer to use drugs as "chemical restraints" for difficult children instead of seeking environmental or psychological explanations for a child's troubles. As the number of children diagnosed with ADHD and treated with psychostimulant medication continues to grow, the diagnosis has become increasingly controversial.

Children like Mary may be diagnosed with ADHD, predominately inattentive type when they have a great deal of difficulty attending to and remembering what is going on around them. Other children, like Shane (described at the beginning of the chap-

Diagnostic Criteria for Attention Deficit/Hyperactivity Disorder (ADHD)	Table 13.6

Adapted from the DSM-IV-TR (APA, 2000)

ADHD involves symptoms of inattention, hyperactivity, and impulsivity. The DSM-IV-TR identifies three subtypes based on which symptoms predominate. The diagnosis of *ADHD, combined type* is made when children exhibit at least six symptoms of inattention *and* six symptoms of hyperactivity and/or impulsivity. *ADHD, predominately inattentive type* is diagnosed when children have at least six symptoms of inattention, but fewer than six symptoms of hyperactivity-impulsivity; *ADHD, predominately hyperactive-impulsive type* is diagnosed when children have at least six symptoms of hyperactivity-impulsivity, but fewer than six symptoms of inattention.

- **Symptoms of inattention:** Missing important details when working; having trouble paying attention to one thing for a sustained period of time; not listening to others; forgetting instructions; being disorganized, easily distracted, and/or forgetful; frequently losing things.

- **Symptoms of hyperactivity:** Frequent fidgeting or squirming; inability to remain seated when expected to do so; excessive motor activity; difficulty relaxing quietly; excessive talking.

- **Symptoms of impulsivity:** Blurts out answers to questions; can't wait for his or her turn; interrupts or bothers others.

Some inattentive or hyperactive-impulsive symptoms must be present and cause impairment before seven years of age; impairment from the symptoms must occur in two or more settings (for example, at school and at home).

ter), may be diagnosed with ADHD, predominantly hyperactive-impulsive type when they are unable to control their behavior and excessive energy, especially in comparison to other children of the same age. The diagnosis of ADHD, combined type is the most widely used; it describes children who have problems with attention, hyperactivity, and impulsivity.

ADHD is often first diagnosed when children enter school and are required to pay attention to teachers and to sit quietly for extended periods of time (Campbell, 1995). The school setting may also be the first in which a child can easily be compared with his or her age-mates; unusually distracted or hyperactive children start to stand out when surrounded by their peers. In school, hyperactive and impulsive children tend to fidget in their seats, get up and roam around the classroom when they should be at their desks, and shout out answers to questions when they are supposed to be raising their hands. Inattentive children often seem to be daydreaming when they should be listening to the teacher, fail to follow simple directions, turn in work that is incomplete or filled with mistakes, and frequently misplace needed items like pencils and books. Many children with ADHD also have difficulty getting along with their peers (Pfiffner, Calzada, & McBurnett, 2000). The impulsivity associated with ADHD may cause children to act before thinking—often in ways that annoy their classmates. They may push or cut ahead in line or take things from peers without first asking to share. Inattentive children may also miss out on the subtle social cues that increasingly guide social interactions between children as they grow up.

In order to warrant a diagnosis of ADHD, a child must exhibit symptoms in at least two different settings (home, school, during play, etc.). If a child is inattentive or

Attention grabbers Not only do children suffering from attention deficit/hyperactivity disorders (ADHD) have difficulty paying attention to their own work, their hyperactive and impulsive behaviors often disrupt the studies of other children in their classrooms.

hyperactive in only one setting, clinicians are inclined to think that the child is having an emotional problem that is exacerbated by being in that particular setting.

About 30% of children diagnosed with ADHD "grow out" of their symptoms by the time they have completed adolescence while the remaining 70% continue to have difficulty with restlessness, inattention, and impulsivity or go on to develop other kinds of behavioral difficulties (Cantwell, 1996). Longitudinal studies have found that children diagnosed with ADHD are more likely than their peers to have social, academic, and emotional difficulties as adults and to engage in antisocial behavior and substance abuse (Greenfield, Hechtman, & Weiss, 1988; Mannuzza & Klein, 2000).

Explaining and Treating Attention Deficit/Hyperactivity Disorder

ADHD is a controversial disorder not only because of the frequency with which it is diagnosed but also because treatment often involves using a controlled substance to medicate children. The pervasive use of medication to treat ADHD is often interpreted to mean that the disorder results largely from biological causes. While this may be true in many cases of ADHD, the symptoms of ADHD can also be caused by psychological factors. Accordingly, ADHD highlights the core concept of the **connection between mind and body** because it is one of many disorders in which psychologically based cases may respond to biological treatment, and, conversely, biologically based cases can sometimes be treated with psychotherapy.

Biological Components At present, evidence suggests that many cases of ADHD result, at least in part, from genetic and neurological factors (Barkley, 1998).

Genetic Factors Research from family, adoption, and twin studies indicates that ADHD is partly inherited. Recent studies have found that ADHD is usually present in 10% to 35% of the immediate family members of a child with ADHD, and that ADHD occurs in 57% of the children born to adults with the disorder (Biederman et al., 1992, 1995). Evidence from adoption studies demonstrates that hyperactive children who are adopted take after their biological, not adoptive, parents in terms of levels of hyperactivity (van den Oord et al., 1994). Twin studies have found concordance rates of 67% to 81% for MZ twins compared with 0 to 29% concordance for DZ twins (Gilger, Pennington, & DeFries, 1992; Sherman, McGue, & Iacono, 1997).

Neurological Factors The search for brain anomalies has been at the center of research on ADHD since the disorder was originally conceptualized as resulting from "minimal brain dysfunction" in the 1930s and 1940s. While some children with ADHD are known to have experienced brain damage as a result of head trauma or illness, the current consensus is that brain damage is not a major cause of the disorder. Instead, recent research suggests that ADHD is associated with congenital abnormalities in the development of the frontal and striatal regions of the brain which seem to regulate vigilance and sustained attention (Barkley, 1998). Several studies have found a smaller right prefrontal cortical region and a smaller caudate nucleus in people with ADHD when compared to control subjects (Filipek et al., 1997) (see Figure 13.3). Other studies have found diminished blood flow to the same prefrontal and striate regions of the brain in people with ADHD (Sieg et al., 1995). Studies of brain waves during attentional tasks indicate that the prefrontal and striate regions of the brain among people with ADHD may be under-responsive or "asleep on the job" (Kuperman et al., 1996). Interestingly, adults and children who suffer injuries to the prefrontal region of the brain have long been known to develop difficulties with attention, impulse control, and organization—many of the same symptoms seen in ADHD (Benton, 1991).

Prenatal Factors The prenatal factors that may be related to ADHD are not as well documented as the genetic and neurological factors previously described. However,

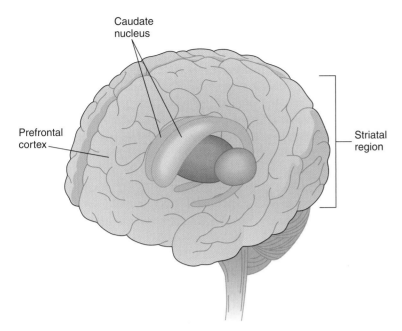

Caudate nucleus

Prefrontal cortex

Striatal region

Figure 13.3 Brain Anomalies in Attention Deficit/Hyperactivity Disorder (ADHD) Some studies suggest that children suffering from ADHD have abnormalities in the frontal and striatal regions of the brain; specifically, they may have a smaller right prefrontal cortical region, a smaller caudate nucleus, and diminished blood flow to the prefrontal and striate areas of the brain.

some preliminary studies indicate that prenatal exposure to alcohol and tobacco smoke may be causally related to the development of ADHD in children (Milberger et al., 1996; Streissguth et al., 1995).

Biological Interventions Medications that stimulate the central nervous system (CNS) are the most common form of biological intervention for ADHD. Methylphenidate (Ritalin, Concerta), dextroamphetamine (Dexedrine), and a combination of amphetamine and dextroamphetamine (Adderall) are among the most frequently prescribed medications (Barkley, 1998). Though it might seem strange to give a stimulant medication to children who are frequently hyperactive, stimulants seem to promote activity in the prefrontal and striate regions of the brain that help children to focus their attention. Thus, Ritalin and its analogs effectively calm children down and help them to focus on one thing at a time. Many children who take Ritalin experience side effects such as insomnia or reduced appetite. Interestingly, Ritalin and other psychostimulant drugs improve attention and concentration in anyone who takes them; this being the case, a positive reaction to Ritalin should not be taken as "proof" that an ADHD diagnosis is accurate or appropriate. There is considerable interest in a recently approved nonstimulant medication known as Strattera which appears to treat the symptoms of ADHD by selectively inhibiting the reuptake of norepinephrine. Though there are side effects associated with Strattera (upset stomach and fatigue being among the most common), parents and physicians are encouraged by the prospect of being able to treat ADHD with a drug that, unlike the psychostimulants, is not a controlled substance.

Family Systems Components Some researchers have suggested that ADHD symptoms can develop when parents are unable to help a child develop skills for emotional and behavioral self-regulation, and/or they regularly allow their young child to become overstimulated or overwhelmed (Silverman & Ragusa, 1992). Of course, it is difficult to separate environmental causes (such as parenting style) from genetic or other biological factors. For instance, the parents of children with ADHD may have ADHD traits

Controversial treatment By some estimates, two and a half million school-age children (roughly 8% of the school-age population) are currently taking Ritalin.

themselves that affect the quality of their parenting. Further, a child with biologically based ADHD symptoms might be particularly difficult to parent, and thus elicit less-than-optimal parenting from an otherwise competent parent. Biological influences on families aside, studies indicate that the severity of family dysfunction appears to correlate with the severity of ADHD symptoms. For example, a large community-based study found that children with symptoms of ADHD were more likely to have mothers with a history of psychiatric treatment, fathers with a history of excessive alcohol use, to live in low-income families, and to experience higher levels of family dysfunction than children without ADHD symptoms (Scahill et al., 1999).

Psychodynamic Components The cardinal symptoms of ADHD (inattention, hyperactivity, and impulsivity) are also behaviors frequently seen in children who are experiencing emotional distress. Accordingly, careful clinicians do not jump to the conclusion that an inattentive or hyperactive child has biologically based ADHD, but first try to rule out other possible causes of the symptoms (Gilmore, 2000; Yeschin, 2000). Often this can be done by establishing when the symptoms began and where they tend to occur. In many cases, a child with biologically based ADHD symptoms will have displayed inattention, impulsivity, and possibly hyperactivity in most settings since early childhood, while an emotionally distressed child might misbehave in some settings and not in others, or the problem behaviors might occur around the time of stressful life events. For example, psychodynamic authors note that ADHD symptoms may occur in response to overwhelming or overstimulating events (Rosenblitt, 1996).

When ADHD-like symptoms seem to result from emotional distress, psychodynamic interventions seek to understand the source of the child's distress and to help the child to better cope with his or her conflicts. Single case studies report positive outcomes from psychodynamic interventions for children with emotionally based ADHD symptoms (Gilmore, 2000; Gilmore, 2002).

Behavioral and Cognitive Components Russell Barkley, an expert on the diagnosis of ADHD, has developed a parent training program for the parents of children with ADHD (Barkley, 1998). A good example of theoretical integration, Barkley's program focuses on parents, using a family systems perspective, but it also incorporates behavioral and cognitive components. The behavioral component of the parent training program works on establishing appropriate reinforcement and punishments in the home environment. For example, when making a request, parents are instructed to establish eye contact with the child, give a simple command, have the child repeat the command back to the parent, and then praise the child for completing the request. When praise is not sufficient to reinforce the desired behavior, parents are instructed to use a point and reward system to promote desired behaviors, and a "time out" system to reduce undesirable behaviors. Cognitive interventions are used throughout the training program to help parents correct their own problematic assumptions about parenting a child with ADHD. For example, parents are helped to see that maintaining parental control is a constructive responsibility that is in the best interest of their child.

There are many ways in which schools can also use behavioral programs to help children with ADHD (Robin, 1998) (see Table 13.7). Ideally, behavioral interventions target specific behaviors such as staying in one's seat, increasing homework accuracy, improving transitions between classrooms, and so on. A sample program might give a child with ADHD a sticker chart to keep on her desk. The classroom teacher would then give the child a sticker for every 15-minute period that she stays on-task. Once the child earns a certain number of stickers, she would receive a suitable reward. Such a program would usually start small (requiring only a couple of stickers for a whole morning) and then increase in difficulty as the child became increasingly able to focus

Classroom Behavioral Management Worksheet for Children with ADHD	Table 13.7

Adapted from Pfiffner, 1996 (p. 103)

On-Task Behavior

Staying Seated: Receive one sticker for every 15 minutes that you remain seated. Getting out of seat with teacher's permission is O.K.

8:15	8:30	8:45	9:00	9:15	9:30	Snack
10:15	10:30	10:45	11:00	11:30	11:45	

Working Quietly: Receive one sticker for every 15 minutes you do not visit with your neighbor or make distracting noises or gestures. Visiting neighbor with teacher's permission is O.K.

8:15	8:30	8:45	9:00	9:15	9:30	Snack
10:15	10:30	10:45	11:00	11:30	11:45	

Academic Performance

Amount of Work Completed: Receive one sticker for every 15 minutes if you complete assigned work during that period. During class discussions, stickers will be awarded if you are paying attention to the activity.

8:15	8:30	8:45	9:00	9:15	9:30	Snack
10:15	10:30	10:45	11:00	11:30	11:45	

Accuracy of Work: If 90% or more of work is completed accurately and your work is neat you will receive one sticker every 15 minutes. During class discussions, stickers will be awarded if contributions are accurate or task-related.

8:15	8:30	8:45	9:00	9:15	9:30	Snack
10:15	10:30	10:45	11:00	11:30	11:45	

Reward

Total stickers possible = 52   Total stickers earned = _____

47 or more stickers = 90%; reward is computer games

42–46 stickers = 80%; reward is free reading time

36–41 stickers = 70%; reward is study hall

---

her attention (Barkley, 1998). In general, behavioral management programs have been found to work well in the short term, but the reduction in ADHD symptoms does not appear to last beyond the period of the intervention or to generalize to other settings (Hinshaw, Klein, & Abikoff, 2002).

Evaluating and Comparing Interventions for ADHD In recent years, the National Institute of Mental Health (NIMH) has undertaken a large-scale clinical trial to compare the effectiveness of various ADHD interventions. The *Multimodal Treatment Study of Children with Attention Deficit Hyperactivity Disorder* (known as the "MTA study") randomly assigned nearly 600 children between the ages of 7 and 9 to one of the following treatments: (a) medication management alone, with medications being monitored by an MTA physician; (b) behavioral interventions alone; (c) a combination of both medical and behavioral interventions; or (d) routine community care (usually meaning medication management by the child's pediatrician).

In the first 14 months of the study, almost all of the children demonstrated some level of improvement (MTA Cooperative Group, 1999). However, children in the various treatment groups differed in the nature and degree of symptomatic change. Children in groups "a" and "c" whose medications were carefully monitored by an MTA physician (who stayed in close contact with the child and his or her parents and teachers) demonstrated greater reductions in inattentiveness, hyperactivity, and impulsivity than children in the behavioral treatment (group "b") or routine community care (group "d") groups. However, when it came to also reducing anxiety and oppositional symptoms and improving academic performance, social skills, and parent-child relations, children who had both medical and behavioral interventions (group "c") improved more than children in the other three groups. Interestingly, both parents and teachers expressed greater satisfaction with interventions that included behavioral (as opposed to strictly medical) components. Longer-term outcome results from the MTA study are still being compiled, but the early results suggest that multimodal treatments that combine both medical and behavioral interventions are highly effective, and also well-received by many families.

Brief Summary

- Attention deficit disorders involve symptoms of inattention, impulsivity, and hyperactivity.

- Attention deficit/hyperactivity disorder (ADHD) appears to have a significant genetic component; ADHD symptoms appear to be associated with impairments in the frontal-striatal region of the brain.

- Stimulant medications are the main biological intervention for ADHD. They increase attention and decrease hyperactivity by stimulating the part of the brain that helps individuals to focus attention.

- The family systems perspective focuses on the connections between parent-child interactions and ADHD symptoms.

- The psychodynamic perspective emphasizes that many of the behaviors associated with ADHD can also be caused by emotional distress.

- Parent training and school-based interventions that incorporate behavioral and cognitive components are sometimes used in the treatment of ADHD.

- Results from large-scale studies suggest that multimodal treatments are most effective when it comes to treating the wide variety of symptoms associated with ADHD.

Critical Thinking Question	**S**ome clinicians take a "try it and see if it helps" attitude toward using Ritalin for children with ADHD symptoms. What are the potential disadvantages of this approach?

Oppositional Defiant Disorder

Case Illustration **Alana's mother consulted a psychologist in the hope that she could get some advice about how to bring her 12-year-old daughter under control. In the first meeting, Alana's mother explained that her daughter had been a hot-tempered but manageable child until a year ago when she suddenly stopped caring about school, listening to adults, or being civil toward her little sister. Alana refuses to join her mother and sister for dinner and insists on spending the evening in her room talking on the phone with friends. When asked to do chores, she scowls and asks why she should be expected to help out around the house. Alana especially seems to enjoy tormenting her little sister: more days than not she hides one of her sister's favorite toys or books and then claims that her (usually tearful) sister must have misplaced it. Though Alana is often quite humorous with her friends, she becomes instantly hostile when her mother tries to talk to her. She is also so rude with teachers that her mother has received several phone calls from the school about Alana's behavior.**

Diagnostic Criteria for Oppositional Defiant Disorder (ODD)	Table 13.8

Adapted from the DSM-IV-TR (APA, 2000)

ODD involves consistently negativistic, hostile, and defiant behavior for at least six months as demonstrated by the presence of at least four of the following symptoms:

- Losing temper
- Arguing with adults
- Defying rules and/or refusing to comply with requests from adults
- Deliberately annoying people
- Blaming others for personal mistakes and misbehavior
- Being touchy or reactive
- Being angry and resentful
- Being spiteful and vindictive

The behavioral symptoms significantly interfere with social, academic, or occupational functioning.

Children who meet the diagnostic criteria for **oppositional defiant disorder** (ODD) are usually irritable and irritating. The antagonistic behavior associated with ODD reminds us of the core concept of the ***continuum between normal and abnormal behavior***, because ODD involves an exaggeration of many normal childhood behaviors. Negative mood, tantrums, and deliberate defiance are expectable behaviors during toddlerhood, and are often revived when older children are emotionally upset (Campbell, 1995). Only when children or adolescents become chronically oppositional in ways that impede development does their behavior cross the threshold from normal to abnormal (see Table 13.8).

Interestingly, the *comorbidity* between ODD and ADHD ranges from 20% to 57% (Rey, 1993). Several possible (and not necessarily contradictory) explanations for the frequent co-occurrence of ODD and ADHD exist: the same environmental or biological conditions may foster both disorders; children with ADHD may have personal difficulties at home and school which might contribute to the development of ODD; or the behaviors associated with both ODD and ADHD may be surface manifestations of an underlying emotional problem.

The behaviors associated with ODD usually begin in the preschool years and persist at least through adolescence in about 50% of all children diagnosed with the disorder. Another 25% of the children diagnosed with ODD appear to "outgrow" their symptoms, while the remaining 25% go on to develop the next disorder to be discussed: conduct disorder (Rey, 1993).

Oppositional defiant disorder A disruptive behavior disorder involving consistently negativistic, hostile, and defiant behavior.

Conduct Disorder

 **Case Illustration** Phil, age 14, was sentenced to placement in a juvenile detention home after being convicted of arson. He had been experimenting with fire-setting since age 12 when a couple of older boys in his neighborhood asked him to keep lookout while they set fire to an abandoned car. Phil's mother works two jobs, leaving Phil with long hours of unsupervised time in which he can make trouble at home and in the neighborhood. Phil and his mother were kicked out of their apartment after he twice set fire to the apartment kitchen. By the time he was 13, Phil was roaming the streets and

dealing drugs with older boys in his neighborhood. On several occasions he has engaged in fights, once seriously injuring another boy with a broken beer bottle. Phil was convicted of arson for setting fire to a storage building at his school after the school counseling office reported his frequent absences to his mother.

Conduct disorder A disruptive behavior disorder involving the consistent violation of the rights of others and significant age-appropriate norms.

The diagnosis of **conduct disorder** (CD) essentially describes criminal behavior when it occurs in children and adolescents (see Table 13.9). Children who meet the diagnostic criteria for ODD are often extremely unpleasant, but unlike children and adolescents with CD, they typically do not engage in illegal acts. However, as previously noted, about 25% of children who are diagnosed with ODD eventually engage in the behaviors associated with CD. In turn, as many as 61% of children and adolescents diagnosed with CD later warrant the diagnosis of antisocial personality disorder, which involves similar behaviors in adults (Myers et al., 1998) (see Chapter 11).

Several controversies exist with regard to the diagnosis of CD. One critique of the DSM-IV-TR diagnosis of CD highlights the core concept of the ***advantages and limitations of diagnosis:*** the diagnostic criteria for CD describe an extremely wide range of behaviors—from shoplifting to rape—and may therefore lump together in one diagnostic category individuals who have little in common. Further, leading researchers, John Richters and Dante Cicchetti, have observed that two of Mark Twain's most lovable characters, Tom Sawyer and Huckleberry Finn, would have qualified for the diagnosis of CD based on their behavior, yet neither boy appeared to suffer from an underlying mental disturbance (Richters & Cicchetti, 1993). A related complaint about the diagnosis of CD is that it may inappropriately place a mental health label on what is essentially a legal and social problem. This criticism is particularly salient when one considers that the diagnostic criteria for CD apply to the behaviors of many urban youths living in poor neighborhoods and participating in gang cultures. While many gang members are extremely troubled, some urban youths join gangs or carry weapons

Table 13.9	Diagnostic Criteria for Conduct Disorder (CD)
Adapted from the DSM-IV-TR (APA, 2000)	CD applies to children or adolescents who consistently violate the rights of others and significant age-appropriate norms. In order to warrant the diagnosis, three or more of the following behaviors must have been present within the last year, and at least one must have been present within the last six months. • **Aggression toward people and animals:** Bullying, threatening, or intimidating others; starting physical fights; using dangerous weapons; physical cruelty to people or animals; stealing while confronting a victim (mugging, extortion, etc.); forcing someone into sexual activity. • **Destruction of property:** Deliberate fire setting or other forms of major property destruction. • **Deceitfulness or theft:** Breaking and entering into someone else's house, building, or car; "conning" others to gain goods or favors or avoid obligations; stealing without confronting a victim (shoplifting, forgery, etc.). • **Serious violation of rules:** Staying out at night before age 13 and despite parental prohibitions; running away from home overnight at least twice; frequent truancy from school before age 13. The behavioral symptoms significantly interfere with social, academic, and/or occupational functioning.

in order to gain a sense of safety in otherwise dangerous inner-city communities (Kazdin, 1995).

Explaining and Treating Oppositional Defiant Disorder and Conduct Disorder

ODD and CD differ both in terms of severity and age of onset. ODD usually occurs in younger children; CD usually occurs in older children and adolescents.

Sociocultural and Family Systems Components Sociocultural and family systems factors can significantly contribute to both ODD and CD. Children living in poverty, dangerous neighborhoods, and overcrowded and substandard housing are at increased risk for developing disruptive behavior disorders (Hawkins, Catalano, & Miller, 1992). Not all children living in poor and dangerous neighborhoods develop ODD or CD, but children living in highly dysfunctional families in poor and dangerous neighborhoods are especially vulnerable to this type of psychopathology highlighting

Family Factors Consistently Associated with Conduct Disorders — Table 13.10

Adapted from Frick, 1998 (p. 224)

GENERAL TYPE OF DYSFUNCTION	SPECIFIC ASPECTS OF DYSFUNCTION	SUMMARY OF KEY FINDINGS
Parental psychopathology	Parental depression Parental substance abuse Parental antisocial/criminal behavior	Parental depression and substance use have nonspecific associations with child psychopathology. That is, they are associated with many types of child problems including conduct disorders (Downey & Coyne, 1990; West & Prinz, 1987). Parental antisocial behavior shows a more specific relationship with conduct disorders (Frick et al., 1992), one that may have a genetic component (Jarey & Stewart, 1985).
Parental marital relationship	Divorce Marital dissatisfaction Marital conflict	The key predictor of child adjustment seems to be the degree of overt conflict witnessed by the child (Amato & Keith, 1991).

Parental socialization practices	Lack of parental involvement
	Poor parental supervision and monitoring
	Ineffective discipline practices
	  Inconsistency
	  Failure to use positive change strategies
	  Harsh discipline
		In a meta-analysis of several hundred studies, Loeber and Stouthamer-Loeber (1986) found that lack of parental involvement in their child's activities and inadequate parental supervision and monitoring of their child showed the strongest and most consistent association with conduct disorders across all areas of family dysfunction studied. Inadequate parental discipline exhibited a less consistent relationship with CD across studies, but discipline seems to be a critical focus of some of the most successful interventions for conduct disorders (Kazdin, 1987, 1993).

the principle of ***multiple causality*** (Deater-Deckard et al., 1998) (see Table 13.10). However, as noted earlier, engaging in disruptive behavior can be seen as adaptive for some children and adolescents living in particularly dangerous neighborhoods.

A variety of family systems factors can also contribute to the development of disruptive behavior. Parental alcoholism, antisocial personality disorder, and/or criminal behaviors place children at high risk for developing ODD or CD symptoms (Kuperman et al., 1999). Studies of parent-child interactions have also yielded several important findings. The parents of children with ODD and CD tend to be harsh and inconsistent in their discipline, to abuse their children and otherwise model aggressive behavior, and to be less supportive, warm, and accepting of their children than other parents. They are also more likely to reward disruptive behavior with attention and compliance, to ignore positive social behaviors, and to leave their children unsupervised (Kazdin, 1995).

Sociocultural interventions for disruptive behavior disorders take a preventative approach by teaching positive social behaviors and problem-solving skills at neighborhood centers (see Box 13.2). The effectiveness of such programs has been mixed, but they appear to be most useful for children who have already started to have some trouble with the law (O'Donnell, 1992). Functional family therapy (FFT) and parent management training (PMT) are the most widely studied interventions for disruptive behavior disorders (Kazdin, 1995). FFT incorporates family systems, behavioral, and cognitive principles by focusing on the role the disruptive behavior serves in the family, how disruptive behaviors are reinforced, and what attributions and assumptions the family makes about the behaviors. PMT programs focus specifically on reversing problematic parenting practices. Parents are taught to be consistent and predictable, and to discipline their children using rewards and appropriate punishments, not coercion. PMT has been found to have broad, positive effects; in one study improvements were maintained for at least a decade after the original intervention (Long et al., 1994).

Cognitive Components Children and adolescents with disruptive behavior disorders tend to have specific distortions and deficiencies in their thinking (Coy et al., 2001). In general, they make hostile attributions about the behavior of others, come up with primarily aggressive solutions to interpersonal problems, and fail to consider the consequences of their own actions. For example, imagine that Chris, a boy with conduct disorder, is bumped in a busy school hallway by another boy named Scott. Though several possible explanations of the bump are possible (Scott was just in a hurry; the hallway is simply too crowded) Chris is likely to assume the worst ("Scott's trying to push me around") and to respond with an aggressive solution, such as giving Scott a strong shove back. Needless to say, what may have been a meaningless bump could now turn into a fight. Interestingly, researchers have shown that children who wrongly attribute hostile intent to others have often been mistreated in their own families (Dodge et al., 1995). As a result of having harsh or abusive parents, these children may expect hostility in other relationships and use aggression to protect themselves.

Cognitive interventions for disruptive behavior disorders focus on helping children and adolescents: (1) make more accurate attributions about other people's behaviors; (2) generate several possible options for how to respond to threatening situations; and (3) evaluate the likely outcome of each option *before* acting. Therapists may model problem-solving behaviors, engage in role-play exercises, and offer constructive criticism and praise to shape skills. Such problem-solving skills training programs have been found to be effective in modifying the behavior of impulsive and aggressive children (Kazdin, Siegel, & Bass, 1992).

BOX 13.2 | Primary, Secondary, and Tertiary Prevention

Savings to Society

Mental health experts not only classify and treat various forms of psychopathology, they also aim to *prevent* emotional problems from occurring in the first place or worsening once they've begun. Prevention takes one of three forms: primary, secondary, or tertiary. **Primary prevention** aims to stop problems before they begin, **secondary prevention** aims to identify problems when they are minor and to keep them from getting worse, and **tertiary prevention** aims to prevent significant problems from continuing and worsening. Here are some examples of successful prevention efforts.

Primary Prevention

"Teen Outreach," a program that focuses on enhancing normative social development in adolescence, was designed to reduce rates of teen pregnancy and academic failure among high school students (Allen et al., 1997). A total of 695 students in 25 different high schools nationwide were randomly assigned to the Teen Outreach program or to a control group. Students in the Teen Outreach group participated in highly structured volunteer programs within their communities that were coordinated with classroom-based discussions of career and relationship choices. Further, emphasis was placed on helping students in the Teen Outreach

Primary prevention Interventions that aim to prevent problems before they begin.

Secondary prevention Interventions that aim to identify problems when they are minor and to keep them from getting worse.

Tertiary prevention Interventions that aim to prevent significant problems from continuing and worsening.

program to develop positive relationships with their peers in the program, the program facilitators, and the adults at their volunteer sites. Students who were assigned to the control group simply participated in the standard curricular offerings in Health or Social Studies available at their high school.

After participating in the study for nine months, students in the Teen Outreach program had significantly lower rates of teen pregnancy, course failure, and school suspension as compared to their peers in the control group. As you can see in Figure 13.4, even when controlling for differences in parental education, racial/ethnic minority status, and prior behavioral problems, students in the control group were more than twice as likely as their Teen Outreach peers to become pregnant, fail a course, or be suspended from school. Given the enormous social and financial costs of teen parenthood and school failure, programs like Teen Outreach provide an excellent example of how a primary prevention program can have a dramatic impact.

Secondary Prevention

The Child Development-Community Policing program in New Haven, Connecticut is a model secondary prevention program for children who have been exposed to violence (Marans, Berkowitz, & Cohen, 1998). Historically, when police officers arrived at crime scenes where children are present they have ignored the children, or interviewed them as witnesses, victims, or perpetrators of violent acts. Since 1991, the New Haven police department has collaborated with child mental health experts at the Yale Child Study Center to train its officers in the principles of child development and to help officers respond sensitively to children who have been traumatized. Since the program's incep-

(continues)

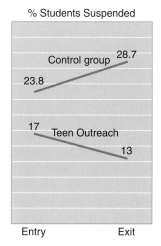

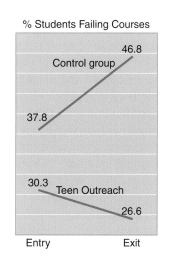

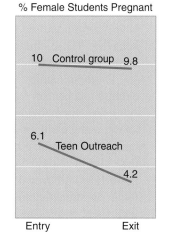

Figure 13.4 Preventing Teen Pregnancy and Academic Failure Participants in the Teen Outreach program had significantly lower rates of suspension, failed courses, and pregnancies from the time they began the program (entry) until its completion (exit). As you can see, participants in the control group worsened, or failed to improve over the same period of time.

Allen et al., 1997 (p. 734)

BOX 13.2 **(continued)**

tion, hundreds of children who have witnessed, experienced, or committed a violent offense have been referred to a mental health professional by the police. In addition, the Yale Child Study Center maintains a 24-hour on-call system so that police can call a clinician to the scene of a violent crime to address the immediate emotional needs of affected children and families. Due to the program's enormous popularity and success, the United States Department of Justice has funded similar programs in communities around the country.

Tertiary Prevention

A team of clinicians at the University of Florida in Gainesville have developed a program called "Project Back-on-Track" to improve the futures of young juvenile offenders (Myers et al.,

2000). Children and adolescents who had already committed violent offenses, or who met the diagnostic criteria for conduct disorder were enrolled in a four-week intensive after-school program. Participants in the program attended group and family therapies, joined community service projects, and engaged in empathy-building exercises for a total of two hours each day, four days each week. Their parents also participated in parenting groups and educational sessions. When compared to a matched control sample one year after completing the program, participants in Project Back-on-Track were significantly less likely to have committed a criminal offense. By reducing criminal recidivism in young juvenile offenders, the program's organizers estimated that Project Back-on-Track resulted in a "savings to society" of approximately $1,800 per participant.

Superego In Freud's structural theory, the part of the mind that contains moral judgments and evaluates the self.

Identification with the aggressor A defense mechanism in which an individual causes others to experience the victimization, powerlessness, or helplessness that he or she has experienced in the past.

Biological Components Evidence indicates that genetic factors may play a role in the development of disruptive behavior disorders. Several studies have found higher concordance rates for delinquency and criminal behavior among monozygotic (MZ) twins as compared to dizygotic (DZ) twins, and studies of conduct disorder specifically have found concordance rates of 44% for MZ twins compared to 24% for DZ twins (Silberg et al., 1996). Interestingly, evidence suggests that some individuals with conduct problems have impairments in a neural circuit system known as the behavior inhibition system (BIS) which inhibits behaviors that are expected to lead to negative outcomes. Aggressive and impulsive actions may be tied to deficiencies in the neurotransmitters that influence the functioning of the BIS, such as serotonin and norepinephrine (Dodge, 2000). Neuroleptic medications (Chapter 12), stimulants, and antidepressants, many of which increase levels of serotonin and norepinephrine, are sometimes used to treat children with ODD and CD (Lavin & Rifkin, 1993).

Psychodynamic Components In psychodynamic terms, children who suffer from disruptive behavior disorders have some deficiency in the functioning of their conscience or **superego.** Kessler (1988) outlines three levels of superego impairment. Children with the most extreme superego impairments are aggressive, dangerous, and remorseless when they hurt others. Children with less extreme superego impairments do have a conscience, but it is somewhat weak and inconsistent. Children in the third category have strong impulses and poor impulse control, but feel very guilty about their misbehavior. These children suffer less from superego impairments than from impairments in the ego functions of self-control and frustration tolerance.

Psychodynamic explanations of disruptive behavior disorders also center on the defense mechanism called **identification with the aggressor.** When exposed to terrifying and traumatizing situations, such as witnessing a shooting or being a victim of abuse, many children and adolescents try to ward off feelings of helplessness by imitating the aggressive behavior they have seen. When identifying with the aggressor, the child or adolescent exchanges the role of helpless victim for that of seemingly powerful victimizer. Psychodynamic interventions for disruptive behavior disorders focus on strengthening superego functioning and helping children to work through feelings of helplessness without resorting to aggressive behavior as a defense mechanism (Marans, 2000).

Brief Summary

- The disruptive behavior disorders—oppositional defiant disorder (ODD) and conduct disorder (CD)—are characterized by disobedient and/or dangerous behaviors.

- Poverty, living in a dangerous neighborhood, and disturbed parent-child relations can contribute to disruptive behavior disorders.

- Family therapy and parent management training have been found to help parents improve their parenting skills and thereby address their children's disruptive behaviors.

- Cognitive interventions help children reduce the distortions and deficiencies in their thinking that promote disruptive behavior. Role-play exercises are often used to help children practice problem-evaluation and problem-solving skills.

- The aggressive and impulsive behaviors associated with disruptive behavior disorders may be related to impairments of the brain's behavioral inhibition system (BIS).

- Psychodynamic interventions focus on strengthening superego functioning and reducing reliance on aggressive behavior as a defense mechanism.

Critical *Thinking* *Question*	**If you were to design an intervention program for disruptive behavior disorders, would you aim your efforts at the level of the individual child, the family, or the community? Why?**

Separation Anxiety Disorder

Case Illustration **Janel's parents went through an amicable divorce two years ago when she was seven years old. Though she was saddened by the divorce, Janel initially adapted well to the change and to her new living arrangement in which she spent alternate weeks with each of her parents. Three months ago, Janel stayed with her father while her mother was away for two weeks on an extended business trip. She had a good time with her father, but when her mother returned Janel became extremely clingy and anxious around her mother in a way she had never been before. As time went on, Janel's behavior only seemed to get worse. She started to sob every morning before school, saying that she wanted to go to work with her mother instead of getting on the school bus. She also started crawling into her mother's bed at night, complaining that she was having nightmares in which her mother died. Janel even became reluctant to go on her regular visits to her father's house and when she was there would insist on calling her mother several times each night to check to see if she was okay.**

As noted in Chapter 5, symptoms of anxiety occur in individuals of all ages. While children develop some of the same anxiety disorders seen in adults (such as phobias and obsessive-compulsive disorders) **separation anxiety disorder** (SAD) is a diagnosis reserved for children and adolescents (see Table 13.11).

Separation anxiety disorder highlights the core concept of the ***continuum between normal and abnormal behavior***. Many children go through periods of being clingy and anxious about being alone. However, children and adolescents with SAD exhibit an extreme version of these behaviors. They cannot be reassured that they and their parents will be safe during a brief separation. Instead of being able to let their parents go, children with SAD cling, cry, and beg their parents to stay nearby. Like Janel, many children with SAD have nightmares or daydreams about what horrible fate

Separation anxiety disorder Excessive anxiety concerning separation from home or attachment figures, usually parents.

Table 13.11	Diagnostic Criteria for Separation Anxiety Disorder (SAD)
Adapted from the DSM-IV-TR (APA, 2000)	Separation anxiety disorder involves excessive and unwarranted anxiety for at least four weeks when separated from home or from major attachment figures as demonstrated by the presence of at least three of the following symptoms: • Chronic and extreme emotional distress when separations occur or are anticipated. • Recurrent fears that major attachment figures will be lost or badly hurt. • Recurrent fears of unusual separation from attachment figures, such as being kidnapped. • Chronic reluctance or refusal to leave attachment figures, even to go to school. • Extreme fearfulness about being alone, even in familiar places. • Chronic reluctance or refusal to fall asleep if attachment figure is not nearby. • Nightmares involving the theme of separation. • Recurrent complaints of physical symptoms (headaches, stomachaches, etc.) around separations. The behavioral and emotional symptoms significantly interfere with social, academic (occupational), or other important areas of functioning.

Developmental interference While many children become upset when their parents or caretakers leave, children suffering from separation anxiety disorder (SAD) become so upset that they experience significant delays in their social, emotional, or academic development.

Projection A defense mechanism in which an individual attributes his or her own unacceptable emotions to someone or something else.

might befall themselves or their parents, resulting in a permanent separation. Some children become so fearful of leaving their parents that they refuse to go to school, spend time with other children, or sleep in their own beds.

Explaining and Treating Separation Anxiety Disorder

SAD is one of the most common anxiety disorders in children. By most estimates, SAD affects roughly 1 out of every 25 (4%) children and adolescents (Silverman & Ginsburg, 1998). The high prevalence rate of this disorder probably results from the fact that a wide variety of emotional concerns are expressed in fearful and clinging behaviors in children.

Sociocultural and Family Systems Components SAD is often linked to psychosocial stressors. Many children who develop symptoms of the disorder do so in the wake of traumatic events such as war or natural disasters. In other cases, nervous and over-protective parents may unwittingly contribute to SAD by indicating to their children that separations are potentially dangerous (Kearney & Silverman, 1995). Parents can help their children feel comfortable with separations by providing reasonable reassurance to a child who has been traumatized, and by modeling appropriate separation behaviors such as saying goodbye in a way that expresses a confidence that they will return as planned.

Psychodynamic Components Psychodynamic explanations of SAD emphasize the possibility that children who excessively cling to their parents or worry about them are using the defense mechanism of **projection** to cope with rejecting or angry feelings toward their parents. Unconscious anger by a child toward a parent may be experienced consciously as a fear that the parent is in danger from someone or something else. By clinging to his or her parent, a child feels reassured that the parent is unharmed by the child's projected aggressive impulses (Kessler, 1988).

A psychodynamic intervention for SAD would aim to explore all of a child's feelings toward his or her parents (loving, rejecting, caring, aggressive, and so on) and try to determine why rejecting or angry feelings are warded off through fearful and clinging behavior. The source of a child's anger may be related to family events such as the birth of a sibling, parental divorce, or overly harsh punishment.

Cognitive-Behavioral Components Philip Kendall and his colleagues at Temple University in Philadelphia have developed a comprehensive cognitive-behavioral training program for treating separation anxiety disorders in children (1994). Anxious children are taught to attend to the physical and emotional signs of anxiety and to use relaxation techniques involving deep breathing and progressive muscle relaxation to keep their anxiety at low to moderate levels. Next, children are taught "coping self-talk" to reduce anxiety and increase tolerance for separations. Children are helped to attend to the thoughts that increase their anxiety such as "Mommy might never return" or "something bad might happen to me while my parents are gone." Then, children are coached to develop "self-talk statements" to counteract their anxiety-provoking thoughts. For SAD, coping self-talk might include statements like "Mom and Dad have always come back in the past" and "If something goes wrong, I can call my parents and they'll come right home." Finally, children are helped to evaluate how they managed an anxiety-provoking situation and to reward themselves when appropriate. Preliminary research on cognitive-behavioral interventions for children suggests that these programs are effective, and that reductions in anxiety are sustained over time (Kendall & Treadwell, 1996).

Biological Components Considerable evidence suggests that many adult anxiety disorders have a genetic component. Since some cases of SAD lead to adult anxiety disorders such as agorophobia and social anxiety disorder, SAD may share the genetic basis as these adult anxiety disorders (Silove & Manicavasagar, 2001). One study of the mothers of children with SAD and other anxiety disorders found that the mothers had an 83% lifetime incidence of anxiety disorders compared to a 40% rate in the mothers of children with other psychiatric disorders (Last et al., 1987). Benzodiazepines and antidepressants can reduce severe anxiety symptoms in children, just as they can for adults. However, benzodiazepines are addictive and may have undesirable side effects.

Stories with meaning Psychodynamic interventions for children are based on the assumption that children communicate their emotional conflicts through imaginative play. Clinicians carefully observe and comment on their young clients' games and stories, and sometimes make direct connections between a child's pretend play, and the troubles the child is having in his or her own life.

Brief Summary

- Children suffering from separation anxiety disorder (SAD) become excessively anxious when required to separate from home or attachment figures, such as their parents.

- Many children who develop SAD do so after a traumatic event has occurred and can be helped to feel less anxious when reassured appropriately by their parents.

- Psychodynamic explanations of SAD emphasize that clingy children may be reacting to projected rejecting or angry feelings about their parents.

- Cognitive-behavioral interventions involving relaxation training, "self-talk", self-evaluation, and rewards can help children to manage anxiety symptoms and tolerate separations.

- Anxiety disorders often run in families and have a genetic component. Children with SAD sometimes benefit from medications designed to reduce anxiety symptoms.

Critical Thinking Question | **W**ell-meaning parents sometimes unwittingly reinforce abnormal behaviors in their children. How might parents unwittingly reinforce SAD?

Reliability The consistency of a test, measurement, or category system.

Validity The accuracy of a test, measurement, or category system.

The Advantages and Limitations of the DSM-IV-TR Childhood Diagnoses

The proliferation of DSM diagnostic categories for children has raised a number of questions about the **reliability** and **validity** of childhood diagnoses. First, the reliability of some childhood diagnoses depends on the age and sex of the child being assessed and, interestingly, the source of diagnostic information (parent, teacher, child); a teacher may see a "problem" child when parents do not, or vice versa (Rapee et al., 1994). Second, the childhood DSM-IV-TR disorders have high rates of *comorbidity* (Nottleman & Jensen, 1995). Several experts have pointed out that high comorbidity rates call into question the DSM-IV-TR's categorical diagnostic system that treats psychological disorders as distinct syndromes that are either present or absent (Scotti et al., 1996). Alternative diagnostic systems, such as those that rate the severity of symptom clusters on a continuum (a *dimensional* approach) or those that focus on age-appropriate development (a *developmental profile* approach) are described below. Third, some experts have suggested that there are simply too many diagnoses in the DSM-IV-TR for children and that some typical childhood behaviors (such as oppositionality) or academic problems (such as learning disorders) should not be classified as mental disorders at all (Cantwell, 1996; Wicks-Nelson & Israel, 2000).

Alternative Diagnostic Systems

The DSM-IV-TR is only one of several diagnostic systems available for classifying child psychopathology. For example, Anna Freud and her successors constructed a developmental profile that can be used to organize information about a child's development in a number of psychodynamically relevant areas such as the focus of the child's instinctual energies, the maturity of the ego and superego, the nature of interpersonal relationships, progress in toilet training and self-care, and so on (Freud, 1962; Furman, 1992). Children are diagnosed in terms of specific areas of developmental regression or fixation as measured against expectable achievements for children in different developmental phases.

Empirically derived systems based on extensive checklists of behavioral symptoms may also be used to classify child psychopathology. The classification systems most often referred to as "empirically derived" are those that use statistical techniques to identify clusters of behaviors usually associated with child psychopathology. Typically, parents, teachers, and in some cases the children themselves, are given a long list of possible symptoms and asked to indicate which symptoms are present and the severity of the identified symptomatology. Two "broadband" clusters of behaviors have emerged from years of research using behavioral checklists: *externalizing* behaviors, in which children are usually under controlled, impulsive, or violent, and *internalizing* behaviors in which children are usually over controlled, withdrawn, or depressed (Achenbach, 1985). As noted subsequently in our discussion on gender, externalizing behaviors occur more frequently in boys while internalizing behaviors are more likely to occur in girls.

The most popular empirically derived classification system, the Child Behavior Checklist (CBCL) (see Figure 13.5), comes in three different forms: a parent report form, a teacher report form, and a youth self-report form that can be given to children and adolescents between ages 11 and 18. In addition to identifying children with predominantly internalizing or externalizing problems, the CBCL can also be used to identify eight "narrowband" clusters of behavioral symptoms: withdrawal, somatic (bodily) complaints, anxiety/depression, social problems, thought problems, attention problems, delinquent behavior, and aggressive behavior (Achenbach, 1993). Areas of clinical concern can be identified by comparing individual broadband and narrowband scores on the CBCL against established norms for specific behavioral problems. The CBCL is a pop-

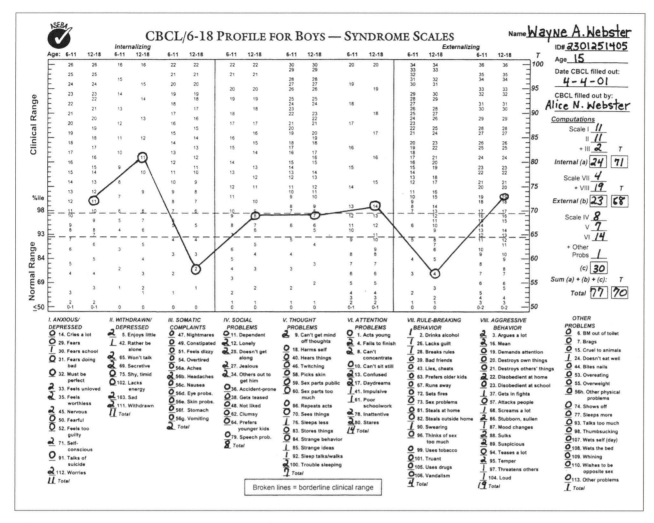

Figure 13.5 Child Behavior Checklist (CBCL)—Parent Report Form, with Profile of Narrowband Scores The CBCL generates a child behavior profile by asking parents, teachers, and children to rate 118 behavior problems as 0 if the item is *not true*, 1 if the item is *somewhat or sometimes true*, and 2 if the item is *very true or often true*. The scores for each item are organized under eight different behavioral clusters where each child's total score can be compared with scores from other children of the same sex and similar age.

From Achenbach & Rescorla, 2001 (p. 23).

ular classification tool because it measures several problem areas simultaneously and indicates the relative severity of specific difficulties. Some clinicians treat CBCL results as alternative, independent diagnoses, but the CBCL is often used as one component of an overall assessment in combination with one or more DSM-IV-TR diagnoses.

Brief Summary

- Diagnostic categories for childhood psychopathology have proliferated in recent editions of the DSM. However, this has raised a number of questions about the reliability and validity of the DSM-IV-TR childhood diagnoses.

- Psychodynamic developmental profiles and empirically derived behavioral checklists such as the Child Behavior Checklist (CBCL) can be used as alternatives to or in conjunction with the DSM-IV-TR to describe and categorize child psychopathology.

Critical | **W**hat seem to be the advantages and limitations of each of the classification
Thinking | systems for childhood psychopathology described in this section: DSM-IV-TR,
Question | psychodynamic, and empirically derived?

Classification in Demographic Context

Like all mental disorders, the psychopathologies of childhood are best understood
when demographic factors are taken into account. Even within the age range of birth
through adolescence, factors such as age, gender, and class shape both the prevalence
and characteristics of each disorder.

Age

Many learning disorders and even mild mental retardation may go unnoticed until
children begin school, and subtle learning disorders may not become obvious until a
child has been in school for several years. Mental retardation, learning disorders, and
pervasive developmental disorders persist throughout the lifetime though they may
remediate to a degree with the help of educational and psychotherapeutic interventions. As noted earlier, ADHD seems to become less severe as children grow older, but
effects of the disorder, such as delayed academic achievement or social skills, sometimes last well into adulthood. Symptoms of ODD are usually present before children
are eight years old (APA, 1994), and though many children "outgrow" the diagnosis,
aggressive children with ODD are likely to go on to develop CD symptoms (Loeber,
Lahey, & Thomas, 1991). Finally, it is important to note that the same psychological
problem can be marked by a different set of symptoms depending on the child's age.
For example, depression may take the form of listlessness in an infant, distractability
in a young child, and irritability in a teenager.

Gender

Four out of the five childhood disorders described in this chapter occur predominantly
in boys, with SAD as the only exception. There are approximately three mentally
retarded boys, four or five autistic boys, and four to *nine* boys with ADHD for every
girl with the same disorder (APA, 2000). The learning disorders are also diagnosed
more frequently in boys than in girls, perhaps because boys with learning disorders are
likely to have accompanying behavior problems that call attention to a learning disorder diagnosis (APA, 2000). Oppositional and conduct disordered behavior occurs more
frequently in boys than in girls, though girls are as likely as boys to warrant a diagnosis of ODD after the onset of puberty (APA, 2000). Interestingly, the boys and girls who
are diagnosed with ODD and CD tend to display very different kinds of behaviors: boys
usually engage in behaviors that involve aggression against others (fighting, vandal-
ism), while girls typically show nonviolent forms of delinquency (lying, truancy). The
different prevalence rates between boys and girls for disorders that are usually present
from birth (such as mental retardation and autism) may also derive from the fact that
many inherited disorders are linked to the Y chromosome (Jensen et al., 1990).

Why do most child psychopathologies appear to be so disproportionately male?
One possibility is that the disparity is an artifact of the tendency for boys to *externalize*
distress, while girls often *internalize* distress (Kazdin, 1995). Externalizing behaviors
(aggression, restlessness, impulsivity) are more likely to upset adults and thus be
brought to clinical attention. In contrast, many of the internalizing behaviors frequently
seen in distressed girls can seem acceptable, even pleasing, to adults. Parents are less
likely to contact a psychologist for help if their previously high-spirited daughter has
suddenly become quieter and extremely compliant than if their son is suddenly getting
into trouble at school, though both are possible signs of emotional trouble.

Class

One major class-related issue in child psychopathology involves cultural-familial retardation. As described earlier, this label reflects the fact that some children and adults meet the diagnostic criteria for mental retardation (IQ below 70, impairment in at least two areas of adaptive functioning) without any apparent biological cause for mental retardation. Cultural-familial retardation tends to be mild and to predominate in poor families and communities where children may receive meager stimulation or educational support from their (usually overwhelmed) parents and thus may fail to flourish intellectually or to learn age-appropriate adaptive functioning skills (Camp et al., 1998; Stromme & Magnus, 2000).

Perhaps the most dramatic demonstration of the effects of the environment on intelligence came from the work of Harold Skeels, an Iowa psychologist who studied the development of institutionalized children in the 1930s and followed the progress of many of his subjects through adulthood (Skeels, 1966). Skeels noticed that two 1-year-old girls who appeared to be mentally retarded seemed to blossom intellectually and emotionally when moved from an orphanage to a home for the mentally impaired. Skeels suspected that the girls were improving because they were doted on by the mildly mentally retarded women housed at the same institution. To test his hypothesis, he moved 10 more children from the orphanage to the institution for the retarded. He followed the development of the transferred children and of a comparison group of children who remained at the orphanage where busy nurses provided little stimulation or individualized care. By age six, the children in the home for the retarded achieved an average IQ of 96 while the typical IQ of the orphanage comparison group was in the low 60s. As adults, the average child raised in the institution for the retarded had completed the twelfth grade and had an income above the Iowa state average. In stark contrast, the orphanage group had, on average, reached only fourth grade and many were unskilled laborers.

Brief Summary

- Childhood psychopathology can only be properly diagnosed and treated when the behaviors of concern are considered within the context of the child's age.

- Childhood psychopathology occurs disproportionately among males. Aside from those disorders linked to the Y chromosome, this may be because boys tend to externalize distress while girls tend to internalize distress.

- Cultural-familial mental retardation is most likely to occur in poverty-stricken families that are unable to provide adequate intellectual and emotional stimulation for their children.

Critical Thinking Question | **W**hy might a clinician say that Shane's behavior (described at the beginning of this chapter) is "typically male" when it comes to childhood psychopathology?

Cultural and Historical Relativism in Defining and Classifying Childhood Disorders

The definition and classification of child psychopathology is highly ***culturally relative***. When asked to describe their children, American parents often talk in terms of intelligence and school achievement, Dutch parents tend to address their child's social behavior and personal qualities, and Asian Indian parents may describe the degree to which their children are obedient and respectful (Harkness & Super, 2000). Insofar as psychopathology partially involves deviations from what is culturally valued, varying cultural expectations shape culturally unique definitions of child psychopathology. For example, an Asian child who is viewed by his parents as overtly disrespectful might be seen, by American standards, as impressively assertive.

The sweeping changes we have described in the diagnostic classification of childhood psychopathology underscore the core concept of *historical relativism:* not a single one of the childhood diagnoses recognized today existed in its same form 50 years ago. For example, ADHD symptoms were previously associated with mental retardation or labeled as MBD for "minimal brain dysfunction." In the DSM-II (APA, 1968), the diagnosis for these symptoms changed to "hyperkinetic reaction of childhood," which focused primarily on hyperactivity. This was followed by the DSM-III which highlighted the symptom of inattention in the new diagnosis of "attention deficit disorder" (APA, 1980); finally, this evolved into the current DSM-IV-TR category of "attention deficit/hyperactivity disorder" with its three subcategories (see Table 13.6).

Brief Summary

● The definition and diagnosis of child psychopathology is culturally relative insofar as different cultures value different qualities in children and therefore have different standards for defining "deviant" behavior.

● The classification of childhood psychopathology is also historically relative as evidenced by major changes in the DSM diagnostic categories for children over the last five decades.

Critical *Thinking* *Question*	**C**an you imagine an historical era or cultural setting in which Shane or Molly's behavior would not seem to be pathological?

Case Vignettes | **Treatment**
Molly | **Autism**

Molly's parents, Sue and Tom, hoped that she would become more outgoing and start talking if they signed her up for a playgroup with other two-year-olds. Rather than helping Molly's social skills, the gregarious and chatty children in the playgroup highlighted the fact that Molly was starkly unlike other children her age. Tom made an appointment with Molly's pediatrician; he and Sue were upset, but not surprised, when the pediatrician referred Molly to the local children's hospital for a complete neurologic and psychiatric evaluation.

The pediatric psychiatrist who conducted the evaluation concluded that Molly probably had autism and that the diagnosis would become more certain if she continued to be disinterested in social interactions. Molly's parents were devastated by the news that their daughter had a serious psychiatric illness. They contacted the local chapter for parents with autistic children to begin to educate themselves about what they could do to help Molly. Upon learning that "high-functioning" people with autism can almost always speak,

they committed themselves to doing everything they could to help Molly learn spoken language. Sue quit her job and began to spend five hours a day doing "language time" with Molly. They sat at the kitchen table for an hour at a time with a bowl of grapes (Molly's favorite fruit) between them. Sue started by teaching Molly the word "spoon." First, she gave Molly a grape every time she looked toward her mother and at the spoon. Next, Sue said the word "spoon" and then used her hand to move Molly's mouth into the position needed to say the word. Sue heartily rewarded Molly when she made an "ooh," sound, and continued to offer grapes, cheers, and smiles as Molly gradually made sounds similar to the word "spoon." After two weeks of practice, Molly said "spoon" when prompted by her mother.

Molly and Sue continued to work together for several months, with each word coming a little quicker than the one before it. When Sue felt that she wanted to go back to work, she and Tom hired and trained college students to take over as

Molly's language teachers. By the time Molly was six, she had a vocabulary of about 400 words and was able to form simple sentences like "want soda." Molly started to spend her days in a special education program where she continued to learn words and basic self-care skills; in the afternoons she kept up her language training at home or watched television. Though Molly continued to learn words and simple grammatical structures she also developed several odd behaviors such as staring at the palms of her hands or rocking back and forth from her heels to her toes when not otherwise occupied.

Molly stayed in special education classes for the duration of her school years. In some ways, she appeared to become more social as she grew older. As a teenager, Molly declared that she would like to have a boyfriend and was fascinated by television programs about other teenagers and their romantic lives. In reality, Molly never approached other people her age or initiated conversations. When in a group situation, such as a field trip with her classmates, Molly wandered along by herself seeming indifferent to the people around her.

Case Discussion | Autism

Molly's parents created their own intensive behavioral training program for their daughter. Using operant-conditioning principles, Molly's mother and trained college students taught Molly how to speak. Like many autistic children, Molly was able to use the intensive training to make steady progress in acquiring language, but she remained autistic. She was unable to maintain a conversation or to send or receive social cues. When left to her own devices, she reverted to self-stimulating behaviors, such as staring at her hands, without any awareness that her behavior was socially inappropriate. With continued support and training, Molly should be able to live in a group setting with other autistic adults and to work in a supervised, unskilled job.

Shane | Attention Deficit/Hyperactivity Disorder

Toward the end of the school year, a standardized assessment confirmed that Shane was reading and doing math at only a first-grade level, though he was in the third grade. Interviews and testing by the school psychologist indicated that Shane had an above average IQ, did not have a learning disability, and was not emotionally troubled; rather, his distractibility and energy level seemed to be a temperamental trait. The school psychologist recommended that Shane should not be promoted to the fourth grade with the rest of his class unless he were prescribed Ritalin to help contain his behavior and focus his attention.

Shane's parents agreed that Shane should try Ritalin but decided that he would use the medication only for the first half of fourth grade with the hope that he could learn to control his own behavior and stop taking the medication by Christmas. In conjunction with the school psychologist, Shane's parents and teachers also developed a behavioral intervention to help Shane learn to control his own behavior. At the start of the day, Shane's teacher put an empty cup on the corner of his desk. For every half-hour in which he remained in his seat and did not bother other children, the teacher put a peg in his cup. Every time Shane got out of his seat without permission or disrupted a classmate, a peg was removed. The pegs were counted before morning and afternoon recess and if Shane had enough pegs, he was allowed to join his classmates outdoors; if not, he stayed in the classroom and continued his schoolwork.

The program was successful at the start of the school year, but Shane's parents suspected that it was the Ritalin that was really keeping Shane under control. In mid-October, Shane's teacher agreed to try a "Ritalin-free" week to see how he performed. The week was an unmitigated disaster: Shane flew around the classroom for most of the mornings and then spent the afternoons grousing about his punishment of having to miss recess for the next two days. Shane's teacher and parents agreed that he could not function adequately in school without medication. He stayed on Ritalin for the remainder of the fourth-grade school year, and to his parents' delight, caught up to his classmates in both math and reading.

Case Discussion | Attention Deficit/Hyperactivity Disorder

Shane's symptoms are typical of ADHD: the lifelong nature of the symptoms and the absence of any evidence of anxiety or emotional conflict suggests that they are primarily biological in origin. Stimulant medication was highly effective in reducing Shane's symptoms, much more so than other interventions. Treatment allowed Shane to overcome his academic problems and learn in accordance with his intellectual ability.

PART TWO: DISORDERS OF OLD AGE

Case Vignette

One morning Joseph, age 80, poured his coffee into his cereal while eating breakfast with his wife. Though they both thought his behavior was strange, they wrote it off as "one of those crazy things that happen when you get old!" A few days later, he surprised his wife again by asking if their grandson Mark had left for boarding school yet. Only a week before Joseph had driven with his son to drop Mark off at boarding school. Over the next several months, Joseph's memory problems seemed to worsen. He often asked the same question several times in a row, forgot where he put his shoes and glasses, and regularly asked his wife what day it was. Joseph also seemed to be forgetting familiar words like "car" and "couch"—saying instead that he would be cleaning "that thing we drive around in" or watching television on that "big soft seat."

DEFINING AND CLASSIFYING DISORDERS OF OLD AGE

Anxiety disorders, mood disorders, dissociative disorders, eating disorders, substance abuse problems, sexual disorders and personality disorders can continue into or begin toward the end of life, and we have discussed the nature of these disorders when they occur in older adults in the relevant chapters. There are, however, two mental disorders, both cognitively focused, that occur primarily among older adults and thus are considered separately here: delirium and dementia.

The DSM-IV-TR Categories

In the past, the cognitive disorders of aging were often described with the blanket term "senility." Today, the DSM-IV-TR describes two distinct, but sometimes co-occurring, mental disorders: delirium and dementia (Tables 13.12 and 13.13).

Delirium

Case Illustration Martha, age 74, became delirious while vacationing with her family at the beach. After a long day in the sun, she went back to her hotel room to take a shower and get ready for dinner. When Martha's daughter went to her room, she found the door unlocked and Martha sitting in a chair, still in her bathing suit. She

Table 13.12	Diagnostic Criteria for Delirium
Adapted from the DSM-IV-TR (APA, 2000)	• Disturbed consciousness with difficulty focusing, sustaining, or shifting attention.
	• Marked changes in cognitive capacity such as memory loss, disorientation, or language problems.
	• Difficulties develop rapidly over the course of a few hours or days and tend to be more or less severe at different times during the day.

Diagnostic Criteria for Dementia	Table 13.13

Adapted from the DSM-IV-TR (APA, 2000)

- Development of multiple cognitive deficits including both memory impairment and one or more of the following cognitive disturbances: aphasia (difficulty with language), apraxia (impaired motor abilities), agnosia (difficulty recognizing things), and disturbance in executive functioning (the ability to plan, initiate, monitor, and stop complex behaviors).
- The cognitive deficits interfere with social or occupational functioning and represent a significant decline from previous levels of functioning.

yelled at her daughter saying that she "refused to go to the reception because she did not want to dance with that strange neighbor-boy." Martha did not seem to recognize her daughter and was puzzled about why she was wearing a bathing suit. Martha's daughter contacted the hotel's doctor, who diagnosed Martha as having become delirious as a result of fatigue and dehydration. After several hours of rest and intravenous hydration, Martha was back to behaving normally again. A follow-up visit to her physician found that Martha had not fully recovered from a bout of pneumonia, leaving her vulnerable to delirium when she became dehydrated.

The mental state of **delirium** can occur in people of any age as a result of exposure to toxins, use of or withdrawal from drugs or alcohol, electrolyte imbalances, high body temperatures, or medical illness. People who are delirious lose track of time, place, and person. They usually don't know what day it is or where they are and they often fail to recognize familiar people. In addition, people who are delirious often forget recent events and find that they cannot focus their attention *or* they fix their attention on a single topic and cannot be induced to think about anything else. If untreated, delirium can progress to a sustained state of confusion in which recent and distant memories become permanently impaired. Delirium can appear very suddenly and is usually short-lived when the underlying cause is treated (APA, 2000).

Delirium An acute cognitive disorder involving disruptions in attention, and changes to cognitive capacity such as memory loss, disorientation, or language problems.

Dementia A progressive cognitive disorder usually seen among older adults involving the development of multiple cognitive deficits including memory impairment, aphasia, apraxia, agnosia, or disturbance in executive functioning.

Aphasia Deterioration of receptive or expressive language skills.

Apraxia Difficulty executing common physical actions due to impairments in the brain's ability to signal specific physical movements.

Dementia

Unlike delirium, which can come and go quickly, **dementia** usually involves a gradual and permanent decline in cognitive functioning. Delirium can be likened to a "brain flu" because its effects, though serious, are usually temporary. In contrast, dementia is more like "brain decay" because the effects are permanent and progressive. Joseph, described at the beginning of this section, suffers from dementia.

People who develop dementia *always* have difficulties with memory. They may have trouble remembering new information, recalling information that they knew before, or both. Memory impairment usually increases as dementia worsens over time: in the early stages of dementia, a person might not remember events from the last year, but in the later stages he or she might not recall what happened during the last 10 years.

A variety of other cognitive deficits are also common in dementia. **Aphasia** is a term used to describe the deterioration of language skills. People who become aphasic forget common words—like Joseph forgetting the words "car" and "couch"—and may have difficulty expressing themselves to others, or understanding what other people are saying to them. In **apraxia**, the brain has difficulty sending the necessary signals to execute common physical actions. A woman with apraxia may find that she can no longer button or unbutton her clothes even though there may be nothing wrong with her hands or arms—her brain has simply forgotten how to tell her hands how to make

Loss of function Due to impairments in executive functioning, people with severe dementia often need a great deal of help executing seemingly simple tasks.

Agnosia Loss of the ability to recognize familiar objects or people.

Executive functioning Ability to develop and execute complex plans.

"buttoning" and "unbuttoning" movements. **Agnosia** (from the Greek word meaning "not knowing") involves losing the ability to recognize familiar objects or people. People in the early stages of dementia might not recognize distant relatives, but as the disease progresses they might not recognize their own spouse, children, or even common household object such as tables and chairs.

Another major impairment associated with dementia is the loss of **executive functioning**—the ability to create and execute plans. For example, before going to the grocery store we have to decide what we want to eat, then determine what foods we already have and what we need to buy, then take our list and money to the store, locate the correct items, pay for them, and then bring them home. This sounds simple enough, but people who lose their executive functioning skills lose track of where they are in a sequence of tasks. They may get themselves to the store, forget why they came in the first place, and leave empty-handed.

Brief Summary

- Delirium and dementia are the two mental disorders that occur primarily among older adults.

- Delirium is usually a temporary condition in which people experience disturbed consciousness with difficulty focusing, sustaining, or shifting attention.

- Dementia is usually a progressive and permanent condition that impairs memory and other forms of cognition.

Critical Thinking Question | **The adult children of older people suffering from dementia are often reluctant to take their parents to be evaluated by a physician, even when symptoms are quite severe. Why might this be?**

EXPLAINING AND TREATING DISORDERS OF OLD AGE

As mentioned earlier, delirium and dementia usually result from medical conditions, but psychological interventions are often an important component of a multimodal treatment.

Delirium

Older adults are particularly susceptible to delirium because their physical health is often quite fragile. As many as 10% of people over the age of 65 are delirious when admitted to the hospital for a general medical condition and another 10% to 15% have been found to develop delirium while hospitalized (APA, 2000).

Biological Components and Interventions

The list of medical conditions associated with delirium in older adults is long and varied (see Table 13.14).

The first line of intervention for delirium is to address the underlying problem, which is usually a medical condition. However, the medical situation responsible for inducing delirium cannot always be identified, or, if it is known, cannot be completely treated. Low doses of antipsychotic medications are sometimes prescribed for delirious patients who are extremely agitated, but in most cases physicians are reluctant to add medications to the regimen of a physically compromised older patient (Raskind & Peskind, 1992).

Some Known Causes of Delirium in Older Adults	Table 13.14

Based on Caine & Grossman, 1992 (p. 628)

- **Brain:** Brain tumors, head traumas, strokes, meningitis, encephalitis
- **Cardiovascular system:** Heart attacks, congestive heart failure, hypertension, and arrhythmia
- **Endocrine system:** Hyper- and hypothyroidism, hyper- and hypoglycemia, Addison's disease
- **Anoxia (insufficient oxygen):** Pneumonia, chronic obstructive pulmonary disease, acute carbon monoxide poisoning
- **Drugs:** Psychotropics, anticonvulsants, antihistamines, analgesics, anticholinergics, postanesthesia

Other Interventions

Patients with mild symptoms of delirium may be calmed and reassured by the presence of a comforting family member or trusted physician. Some delirious patients appear to be more lucid in the mornings and then become more agitated and cognitively impaired as the day goes on—a phenomenon known as "sundowning"—which can result when the normal sleep-wake cycle becomes disrupted. Light treatments—in which "sundowning" patients are exposed to pulses of bright light during the evening—have been found to improve circadian rhythms and reduce afternoon and evening agitation (Satlin et al., 1992).

Dementia

The symptoms of dementia are usually confusing, exasperating, and devastating to those with the disorder. Not surprisingly, people with dementia also suffer from high rates of depression and anxiety, yet the relationships among depression, anxiety, and dementia are very complex (Burn, 2002; Porter et al., 2003). Some experts suggest that symptoms of depression and anxiety can be early signs of dementia (Kennedy & Scalmati, 2001); others suggest that neuroanatomical problems related to dementia may also cause depression and anxiety (McDonald, Richard, & DeLong, 2003); still others suggest that depression and anxiety are expectable and understandable reactions to the psychosocial stress associated with dementia (Orrel & Bebbington, 1996). In any event, experts in the treatment of older individuals have begun to recognize the importance of identifying and treating the symptoms of depression and anxiety when they co-occur with dementia (Burn, 2002; Mintzer et al., 2000).

Dementia can also confuse, exasperate, and devastate the friends and family members of the person with the disorder. Thus, psychosocial support for the friends and relatives of the patient with dementia is a critical part of a complete intervention.

Biological Components and Interventions

Dementia arises from the progressive deterioration of the brain. A variety of specific illnesses are known to produce dementia, though in many cases the cause of an individual's dementia remains unknown.

Alzheimer's Dementia Alzheimer's dementia accounts for more than half of all cases of dementia (Brookmeyer, Gray, & Kawas, 1998). The brains of people with

Living with Alzheimer's Former President Ronald Reagan and his wife Nancy became increasingly private as President Reagan lived out his final days while suffering from Alzheimer's disease.

Neuritic plaques Abnormal protein deposits surrounded by clusters of degenerated nerve endings; they are typically found at the end of neuronal axons in people suffering from Alzheimer's dementia.

Neurofibrillary tangles Tangled strands of the fibers that normally make up a cortical cell's internal skeleton; they are typically found in people suffering from Alzheimer's dementia.

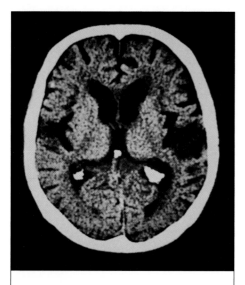

Visible deterioration The large, dark, fluid-filled spaces in this computerized axial tomography (CAT) scan of the brain of a 60-year-old woman illustrates the cell death and resulting cerebral atrophy often seen in people with Alzheimer's disease.

Alzheimer's shrink in size due to extensive cell death and reduction in the number of dendrites connecting neurons to each other. Upon autopsy, the presence in the brain of **neuritic plaques** and **neurofibrillary tangles** confirms the diagnosis of Alzheimer's disease. Neuritic plaques are found at axon terminals where abnormal protein deposits are surrounded by clusters of degenerated nerve endings; neurofibrillary tangles occur when the fibers that normally make up a cortical cell's internal skeleton develop tangled strands. Put simply, neuritic plaques and neurofibrillary tangles "gum up the works" of previously healthy cortical cells and synapses. As these physical changes in the brain progress, patients with Alzheimer's often become confused depressed, paranoid, delusional, agitated, or psychotic (see Box 13.3). They experience significant alterations in personality and are at times aggressive, sexually disinhibited, or prone to wandering away from familiar places. Eventually, patients with Alzheimer's lose the ability to speak, walk, or care for themselves and usually die from medical complications such as pneumonia or infections that arise from being bed-ridden. Alzheimer's disease is sometimes confused with *Pick's disease,* a rare degenerative brain disorder that damages the frontal and temporal lobes. Like Alzheimer's, Pick's disease cannot be conclusively diagnosed until autopsy (APA, 2000).

Research into the causes of Alzheimer's disease focuses on genetic factors, such as the predisposition toward unusually high levels of the amyloid proteins involved in the formation of neuritic plaques. Evidence for the genetic basis of Alzheimer's disease comes from a variety of sources. Family studies of Alzheimer's indicate that first-degree relatives of people with the disease have a 50% lifetime chance of developing Alzheimer's, but these findings need to be considered in the context of indications that at least 20% of all people over the age of 85 may have Alzheimer's disease (APA, 2000, Raskind & Peskind, 1992). Genetic studies of Alzheimer's have been further complicated by two facts. First, the disorder can only be confirmed by autopsy and therefore cannot be definitively detected among living relatives. Second, Alzheimer's may not manifest itself until people are of advanced age and may therefore seem to be absent in the autopsy of a person who dies at a relatively young age from another cause, even if he or she would have ultimately developed Alzheimer's. The protein found in neuritic plaques and the peptide (beta-amyloid) responsible for its formation have been carefully studied in recent years, and their function in the development of Alzheimer's disease continues to be the focus of research (Xu et al., 1999).

There is no known cure for Alzheimer's disease, but medical interventions that enhance neurotransmission systems and interfere with neurodegenerative processes have been found to slow or delay cognitive deterioration and, in some cases, improve memory. Medications, like tacrine (trade name Cognex) and donepezil (trade name Aricept), that prevent the breakdown of the neurotransmitter acetylcholine appear to benefit a significant subset of those with Alzheimer's. Antiinflammatory agents and estrogen replacement also appear to slow the progress of neurological degeneration (Marin, 1999). Antipsychotics, antidepressants, and benzodiazepines are sometimes used to treat the agitation, depression, and/or sleeplessness associated with Alzheimer's (Corey-Bloom, 2000).

Vascular Dementia Vascular dementia results when cerebrovascular diseases block blood flow to areas of the brain, resulting in the death of brain tissue. Symptoms of dementia can result when a large section or several small areas of brain tissue die. In contrast to the gradual progression of cognitive problems in Alzheimer's, vascular dementia often comes on suddenly and proceeds in a step-wise deteriorating course. High blood pressure and coronary artery disease are among several vascular diseases that increase

BOX 13.3 Personal Reflections

Life with Alzheimer's Disease

Jean, age 71, describes how frustrating and unsettling it can be to live with Alzheimer's disease. She addresses her own experience of the disease as well as how it affects those with whom she comes into contact.

I know there are areas that are slipping, but I don't quite know offhand what they are. The other day I was going to put some laundry in the laundry room and I had to get the keys to open the door and get the soap and all that stuff you have to schlep with you. I found it very difficult to get it all together. But it was of no significance that day. No one was waiting for me, and I didn't really care if it took me another 20 minutes to get it together. I wasn't functioning well that particular day, and I couldn't even do the little stuff. I recognized that and accepted it and thought, "Well, just keep going till you get it all together and then you'll go and do the laundry." It wasn't a shame because nobody else was involved.

There are some scary things, like not remembering my name. I remember the first time it happened: I was in a bank and I had to tell my name. I always thought I had enough trouble telling what my mother's name was! But I couldn't think of my own name and I said, "Oh, never mind. I'll come back." That was really difficult. It's like something hit me hard. I'd already indicated that I was going to give this important material and then all of the sudden I wasn't going to. So it's not being able to meet their expectations, or even my own. I certainly don't feel like I have full control. And some days I don't feel like I have any!

Quoted in Snyder, 2000 (pp. 63–64)

Social support Here, a staff member at a residential facility reassures a woman suffering from dementia.

the risk of developing vascular dementia. Controlling high blood pressure and cessation of smoking have both been associated with improved cognitive functioning in patients with vascular dementia (Raskind & Peskind, 1992).

Parkinson's Disease Parkinson's disease involves the gradual deterioration of the *substantia nigra,* an area of dark cells within the brain that produces the neurotransmitter dopamine. Muscle tremors, rigidity, and difficulty initiating movements are among the physical symptoms of Parkinson's disease caused by the decrease in dopamine. Twin studies indicate that Parkinson's disease results from genetic factors in some cases and environmental factors in others. One large-scale study found a 100% concordance rate in monozygotic (MZ) twins diagnosed with Parkinson's disease before age 50, compared to a 16.7% concordance rate in dizygotic (DZ) twins. After age 50, concordance rates for MZ and DZ twins were 15.5% and 11.1% respectively (Tanner et al., 1999). These findings indicate that genetics play the major role in early-onset Parkinson's, as diagnosed in former heavyweight boxing champion Muhammed Ali and actor Michael J. Fox, while as-yet-undetermined environmental causes are crucial when Parkinson's begins after age 50. As treatment with synthetic dopamine has helped people with

A personal choice Nancy Wexler, Ph.D., a leading expert in Huntington's disease, played a critical role in developing a test to detect the gene that causes Huntington's. Though Dr. Wexler's mother died of the disease in 1978, Dr. Wexler has chosen not to take the genetic test for Huntington's that she helped to develop.

Parkinson's to live longer, we have learned that symptoms of dementia frequently occur in the later stages of the disease. Patients with Parkinson's who develop dementia become forgetful and slow in their thinking, but usually retain their language skills (Murray, 2000).

Huntington's Disease Huntington's disease results from the gradual degeneration of specific areas of the brain, including the caudate nucleus (see Figure 13.3) which helps to inhibit physical movements. Irritability and depression are early signs of the disease. As Huntington's progresses, symptoms of dementia increase while speech, emotional control, and balance also become increasingly impaired. Most people with the disorder develop jerky, involuntary movements known as Huntington's chorea (or *dance*). The disorder is caused by a single dominant gene located on the fourth chromosome, meaning that every child born to someone with Huntington's has a 50% chance of developing the disease (APA, 2000).

HIV HIV, which causes AIDS, enters the brain shortly after the virus is contracted while the immune system of a person in the early stages of the disease can still ward off brain infection. However, as the disease progresses, and the immune system becomes compromised, the virus replicates rapidly within the central nervous system and can cause a wide range of dementia symptoms by killing areas of the central white matter, the basal ganglia, the thalamus, and the brain stem.

Family Systems Interventions

Many people who develop dementia live with severe cognitive impairment for years, if not decades. Professionally staffed residential care facilities can provide safe housing for those needing constant care and supervision. However, as the older adult population grows and the average life span increases, more attention is being paid to the stresses placed upon the "sandwich generation"—middle-aged adults who are sandwiched between the needs of their own children and their aging parents. Supportive group therapies have proved to be useful for the children of people suffering from dementia who often feel that the parent they knew and loved has been replaced by a demanding, confused, and emotionally volatile stranger (Schmidt & Keyes, 1985).

Brief Summary

- Delirium is caused by a wide variety of medical conditions or other factors that temporarily compromise cognitive functions. Treatment involves addressing the underlying cause and providing social support until the delirium has passed.

- Dementia usually results from the death of brain cells and is most commonly caused by Alzheimer's disease, vascular problems, or Parkinson's, Huntington's, or HIV disease. Some medications seem to slow brain cell death or reduce the negative effects of neurological degeneration. Residential treatment centers for people with dementia and support groups for their family members are important components of the treatment of dementia.

Classification in Demographic Context

Demographic factors such as age, gender, class, and culture significantly affect the frequency and intensity of delirium and dementia among older individuals.

Age

Normal physical processes associated with aging predispose older adults to age-related mental disorders such as delirium and dementia. Neural cells die, and the brain shrinks in size and decreases in weight as a function of aging. At the neurochemical level, studies have found that healthy humans lose about 50% of D_2 dopamine and acetylcholine receptors and about 20% to 40% of serotonin receptors over the course of their lifetimes (Morgan, 1992). However, the core concept of the ***continuum between normal and abnormal behavior*** is relevant here: the degree of cognitive impairment in dementia and delirium is much more severe than the mild forgetfulness normally associated with aging.

Alzheimer's disease, a prominent cause of dementia, rarely develops before age 50, occurs in 2% to 4% of people over 65, becomes increasingly prevalent among people over age 75, and, as noted, may occur in as many as 20% of all people over age 85 (APA, 2000). In contrast, the early symptoms of Huntington's disease may appear in people who are in their 40s and 50s. Delirium occurs primarily in older adults suffering from medical illnesses, though, as mentioned, it can occur in younger people with high fevers, certain medical illnesses, or other brain-altering conditions.

Gender

The mental disorders of old age are more likely to occur among women because women consistently outlive men. Women outnumber men by 127 to 100 between the ages of 65 and 69 and by 220 to 100 after age 85. Interestingly, three-quarters of all men over the age of 65 are married as compared to one-third of women over the age of 65 (Strain & DuBois, 1992). Marriage has consistently been found to reduce rates of psychopathology among older individuals. However, when compared to women who have lost their husbands (widows), men who have lost their wives (widowers) have more health problems, fewer social ties, and are less likely to have a close companion. The differences between widows and widowers, however, become less prominent as men and women age (Strain & DuBois, 1992).

Class and Culture

Increasing evidence suggests that assessment measures often used to assess cognitive impairments may be biased against people who have little formal education. For example, the Mini-Mental Status Examination and the Short Portable Mental Status Questionnaire—both widely used to assess cognitive impairment—have items that require basic literacy skills and calculation abilities and thus may falsely indicate a cognitive impairment in a healthy, but poorly educated, person (Teresi et al., 2001).

Interestingly, educational activity may have a *preventative* effect when it comes to dementias that reduce the number of interneuronal connections in the brain (Gatz et al., 2001). In an example of the ***connection between mind and body,*** research indicates that people who are engaged in lifelong learning (academic or otherwise) continuously create new interneuronal connections. Through constant learning they add more branches—which are technically known as **dendrite arbors**—to their neural dendrites and thus suffer less cognitive impairment when affected by diseases, like Alzheimer's, that "cut" dendrite arbors.

Good mental health is generally associated with life satisfaction among older adults (Michalos et al., 2001). Cross-cultural comparisons of life satisfaction among African Americans and whites in the United States have found that African Americans report significantly higher levels of life satisfaction after age 65, possibly because they are more likely to be members of religious communities than older whites (Ortega, Crutchfield, & Rushing, 1983). However, African Americans tend to have higher rates of hypertension and diabetes than whites and thus may be at higher risk for developing vascular dementia (Heyman et al., 1991).

Dendrite arbors Neuronal branches that allow neurons to communicate with each other by sending chemical messengers (neurotransmitters).

Brief Summary

● Normal physical processes associated with aging, such as the death of brain cells, predispose older adults to delirium and dementia.

● Mental disorders among older adults occur disproportionately among women because they tend to outlive men.

● Assessment measures of cognitive ability may be unfairly biased against those with little formal education. Lifelong learning appears to reduce the effects of late-life neurological deterioration.

Critical Thinking Question | **A** genetic test can ascertain whether someone carries the gene for Huntington's disease and thus will develop the disease as they age. People with the gene in their families have different feelings about whether or not to take the test. If Huntington's ran in your family, do you think you would want to have the test? Why or why not?

Case Vignette | Treatment
Joseph | Alzheimer's Dementia

Joseph, who had forgotten the entire trip in which he helped take his grandson to boarding school, continued to have trouble with his memory. He often forgot the names of his children and grandchildren, and his wife was particularly distressed one afternoon when Joseph asked her how they happened to know each other. Early one morning Joseph's wife woke up and found herself alone in bed. She searched the house, and then the neighborhood for her husband, finding him several blocks from home, still wearing his pajamas. At that point, she knew that it was time to take her husband to the doctor, though she felt scared of what they might learn. The physician said that Joseph was suffering from dementia, most likely due to Alzheimer's disease. She prescribed medications to improve Joseph's memory and asked if they had considered moving Joseph into a supervised living arrangement.

Joseph's children were strongly supportive of placing their father in residential care because they had become increasingly worried about what their father might do or forget next, and they did not want their mother to be solely responsible for his care. After Joseph had two more incidents of wandering and also threw a temper tantrum, his wife reluctantly agreed to move him out of their house but was insistent that she be able to move with him. After a great deal of searching the family found a facility that had apartments and a full-time staff that was available to provide whatever supervision and care Joseph required. Joseph did not seem to understand the move but accepted his new living arrangement. His wife hated giving up their house and found it extremely painful to watch her husband of 60 years continue to deteriorate both cognitively and physically.

Case Discussion | Alzheimer's Dementia

Like many people suffering from Alzheimer's disease, Joseph's difficulties came on slowly. The initial stages of his disease were easy to ignore, but over time his cognitive symptoms worsened significantly. His memory failed him frequently and he developed agnosia (failure to recognize familiar things or people) and aphasia (language difficulties). Joseph's cognitive impairment was also evident in his strange behavior, such as wandering away from home in his pajamas and in the lack of inhibition that likely contributed to his temper tantrums. Joseph's wife and children faced many dilemmas when making decisions about his care. They were initially reluctant to move him out of his house and into residential care despite evidence that he was not safe at home.

Chapter Summary

- The study of childhood psychopathology highlights the core concept of the importance of *context* in defining and understanding abnormality. Definitions of child psychopathology must take into account what behaviors are developmentally appropriate for a child of a given age.

- When assessing psychopathology in children it is important to consider the *continuum between normal and abnormal behavior*. Childhood behaviors are considered abnormal mainly when they begin to interfere with progressive development.

- This chapter describes five of the most prominent DSM-IV-TR categories that relate specifically to children and adolescents: mental retardation, learning disorders, pervasive development disorders, attention deficit and disruptive behavior disorders, and separation anxiety disorder.

- Demographic factors such as age, gender, class, and culture significantly affect the prevalence and the manifestations of psychopathology in both children and older adults.

- There are several *advantages and limitations of the DSM-IV-TR childhood diagnoses*. While the recent proliferation of child-related diagnostic categories has increased diagnostic specificity, it has raised questions about the usefulness of the DSM-IV-TR childhood diagnoses as compared to those of alternative diagnostic systems.

- Definitions of childhood psychopathology are *culturally and historically relative* insofar as different cultures value different qualities in their children and the classification of childhood disorders changes substantially over time.

- Several disorders of early and late life point to the *connection between mind and body* insofar as psychologically based symptoms may sometimes respond to biological treatments, and some biologically based symptoms may be helped with psychological interventions.

- Biological, psychological, family, and community factors contribute to the development of many childhood disorders, providing an excellent example of the principle of *multiple causality*.

- Delirium and dementia, the mental disorders that occur almost exclusively among older people, are generally caused by medical conditions. Delirium is usually a temporary condition in which people experience disturbed consciousness with difficulty focusing, sustaining, or shifting attention. Dementia is a progressive and permanent condition which impairs memory and other forms of cognition.

Pablo Picasso, *Melancholy Woman,* 1902. Bridgeman Art Library/London. ©2004 Estate of Pablo Picasso/ Artist Rights Society (ARS), New York

■ Pablo Picasso (1881–1973), a towering figure in the history of art, mastered the techniques of Realism and Impressionism, and was also one of the major figures in the creation of Cubism, an art form that explored simplified, geometrical shapes and shifting points of view. In addition to his reputation for a ....*continues on page 488*

pablo picasso

chapter fourteen

PSYCHOLOGICAL STRESS AND PHYSICAL DISORDERS

Case Vignettes

Robert, age 45, was admired by his colleagues for his ability to close large and complicated real estate deals quickly and efficiently and for his capacity to work with several developers and contractors simultaneously on a variety of different projects. Yet, despite the fact that he was one of the most productive members of his company, he was generally disliked for being short-tempered and impatient. Much of the gossip around Robert's office focused on his latest antics: throwing his cellular phone at an assistant who interrupted him in the middle of a call, loudly berating a waitress for bringing him a medium-rare, not well-done, hamburger, openly referring to his own secretary as "the idiot," and insisting on smoking in areas of the office where smoking was forbidden. When he suffered a heart attack while caught in a traffic jam the consensus at the office water-cooler was that he "had it coming" despite his young age.

David, a 24-year-old construction worker who lives at home with his parents, suffers from a wide variety of physical symptoms for which doctors can find no explanation: chronic pain in his neck, arms, lower back, and lower legs, frequent nausea and constipation, and occasional dizziness. Though David occasionally dated in high school, his physical symptoms have caused him to lose interest in romantic or sexual relationships with women. David finds that, due to his chronic pain, he cannot stand the physical demands of construction work and he has been unemployed for most of the past three years. While David's mother has been glad to support him while he convalesces, David's father doubts the legitimacy of his son's symptoms and has begun to resent his son's ongoing unemployment and dependence.

This chapter explores the various ways that psychological stress interacts with physical health. We'll begin with an exploration of the field of **psychophysiology**—the study of actual physical illnesses caused or exacerbated by psychological stress. Then we'll turn our attention to the **somatoform disorders**, in which psychological stress causes physical symptoms or distress about physical features but no actual medical disorder is present. Our discussions of psychophysiology and the somatoform disorders will provide a detailed look at the core concept of the ***connection between mind and body***.

Psychophysiology The study of physical disorders caused or exacerbated by stress or emotional factors.

Somatoform disorders Disorders in which physical symptoms are caused by psychological factors.

- **Explaining and Treating Somatoform Disorders**
  - Psychodynamic Components
  - Cognitive-Behavioral Components
  - Sociocultural Components
  - Biological Components
  - The Connection Between Mind and Body in Somatoform Disorders

Case Vignettes - **Treatment**

...continued from page 486

passionate, sometimes consuming, approach to his work and his relationships, Picasso was also considered to be something of a hypochondriac.

Cognitive appraisal An individual's subjective perception of a potentially stressful event that weighs the event's potential threat against resources available for managing the event.

Tough day at the office Some jobs are more stressful than others: here, Indian bomb squad officers investigate an abandoned bag found near a passenger bus.

PSYCHOPHYSIOLOGY: DEFINING PSYCHOLOGICAL STRESS

The concept of stress is familiar to most people. In all likelihood you have felt "stressed" during final exams, encouraged a good friend not to be "too stressed out," and can list several experiences or events that are "stressful." While stress is a familiar concept, the term has many uses and means different things to different people. Not surprisingly, psychologists have attempted to define stress in order to facilitate communication about the topic and to advance empirical research on stress and related phenomena.

Stress is sometimes conceptualized as a *reaction* to physically and psychologically taxing events (Selye, 1993) but a more sophisticated definition views stress as a complex *interaction* between people and their environments (Lazarus, 1999). In other words, what feels stressful to one person might feel boring, pleasant, or even exciting to someone else; some people are thrilled by the excitement of jumping off the high dive, others *greatly* prefer to watch the divers from the pool deck. Further, an individual's perception of stressful events might change over time and will likely depend on other events occurring at or around the same time. Discovering, as you head out for a leisurely jog, that your parked car has a flat tire won't be nearly as stressful as making the same discovery when you are about to drive your car to an important meeting.

Cognitive Appraisal of Stress

Stress researchers have found that the degree to which an event is experienced as stressful depends upon an individual's subjective perception, or **cognitive appraisal**, of the event (Lazarus, 1999). Cognitive appraisals (which can occur rapidly and unconsciously) of potentially stressful events generally focus on two factors: (1) whether the event poses a threat to immediate or long-term well-being and (2) whether adequate resources (personal, emotional, social, financial, etc.) are available for managing the threat (Lazarus & Folkman, 1984). Getting a costly speeding ticket (a potential threat to one's financial well-being) is not nearly as stressful if you have lots of money in the bank (resources to address the threat), just as breaking your leg (a potential threat to one's physical and occupational well-being) is not nearly so stressful if you have good medical care and an accommodating boss (resources to address the threat).

Stress experts have identified several specific conditions that influence whether or not an event will be appraised as stressful. The most stressful events are those that are felt to be negative, uncontrollable, ambiguous, unpredictable, and/or require significant adaptation (DiMatteo & Martin, 2002; Dougall & Baum, 2001). Consider, for example, a common, potentially stressful situation: going to an interview for a strongly desired job.

- *Felt to be negative*—If you've had very unpleasant job interviews in the past or have been told by friends that interviews with the company you're interested in are often "brutal," the interview process will likely be perceived as a negative experience and therefore be more stressful.

- *Uncontrollability*—Perhaps you've heard from friends or colleagues that people who felt they had great interviews with the company you're interested in were rarely offered jobs. The experience of being interviewed will likely be more stressful if you want the job but know that having a good interview may have little to do with being hired.

- *Ambiguity*—If the interviewer asks clear questions and provides lots of positive feedback about how your skills fit with the company's needs, the interview will probably feel less stressful than if the interviewer asks vague questions and provides little feedback.

- *Unpredictability*—Imagine that the company you are interested in tells applicants in advance which questions they will be asked during the interview. Having time to prepare answers in advance is usually less stressful than walking into an interview not knowing what to expect.

- *Requiring significant adaptation*—If the interview process is lengthy and demanding, the amount of adaptation required will likely increase your sense that the process is stressful.

Brief Summary

- Stress is sometimes conceptualized as a reaction to physically and psychologically taxing events, but a more sophisticated definition views stress as an interaction between people and their environments.

- Cognitive appraisals of potentially stressful events generally focus on two factors: (1) whether the event poses a threat to immediate or long-term well-being and (2) whether adequate resources (personal, emotional, social, financial, etc.) are available for managing the threat.

- Stress experts have identified several specific conditions that influence whether an event will be appraised as stressful or not; the most stressful events are those that are felt to be negative, uncontrollable, ambiguous, unpredictable, and/or requiring significant adaptation.

Critical Thinking Question **C**an you think of an event (such as taking a final exam or speaking in front of an audience) that would be highly stressful for you under one circumstance, but not under another?

CATEGORIZING STRESSORS

Stressful events, or **stressors**, range from the annoyance of misplacing one's house keys to the trauma of being raped. Stress experts have grouped stressors into the following general categories: *life events, chronic stressors, daily hassles,* and *catastrophic events.*

Life Events

In the late 1960s, researchers began to conceptualize stress as a function of the impact of significant life changes and hypothesized that the more life change an event required (whether positive or negative) the more stressful the event would be. To test this hypothesis, researchers developed a list of 43 positive and negative **life events** and asked 394 individuals to rate how much adjustment, or life change, each event would require (Holmes & Rahe, 1967). Based on the participants' responses, the researchers developed a mean "stress score" on a scale from zero to 100 for each type of life event. These stress scores were then used to develop the **Social Readjustment Rating Scale** (SRRS), a commonly used stress measure (Table 14.1). An individual's total stress score on the SRRS is the sum of the assigned values for stressful life events experienced within the past year. While SRRS scores have been correlated with various health problems including sudden hair loss (York et al., 1998) and pregnancy complications (Kalil

Stressors Stressful events, ranging from minor annoyances to traumatic experiences.

Life events Life changes, both positive and negative, that require adaptation.

Social Readjustment Rating Scale A scale used to rate stress by quantifying the amount of adaptation required by a variety of life events.

Table 14.1 | **The Holmes-Rahe Social Readjustment Rating Scale**

Adapted from Holmes & Rahe, 1967

LIFE EVENT	STRESS VALUE
1. Death of a spouse	100
2. Divorce	73
3. Marital separation	65
4. Jail term	63
5. Death of a close family member	63
6. Personal injury or illness	53
7. Marriage	50
8. Fired at work	47
9. Marital reconciliation	45
10. Retirement	45
11. Change in health of family member	44
12. Pregnancy	40
13. Sexual difficulties	39
14. Gained a new family member	39
15. Business readjustment	39
16. Change in financial status	38
17. Death of a close friend	37
18. Change to a different line of work	36
19. Change in number of arguments with spouse	35
20. Mortgage or loan of more than $100,000	31
21. Foreclosure of mortgage or loan	30
22. Change in responsibilities at work	29
23. Son or daughter left home	29
24. Trouble with in-laws	29
25. Outstanding personal achievement	28
26. Spouse began or stopped work	26
27. Began or ended school	26
28. Change in living conditions	25
29. Revision of personal habits	24
30. Trouble with boss	23
31. Change in work hours or conditions	20
32. Change in residence	20
33. Change in schools	20
34. Change in recreation	19
35. Change in church activities	19
36. Change in social activities	18
37. Mortgage or loan of less than $100,000	17
38. Change in sleeping habits	16
39. Change in number of family get-togethers	15
40. Change in eating habits	15
41. Vacation	13
42. Christmas	12
43. Minor law violations	11

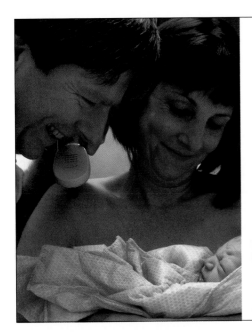 

Defining stress Happy events, such as the birth of a child, or the move to a new home, can be stressful because they require significant adaptation and life changes.

et al., 1995), the SRRS does not account for the fact everyone experiences stressful events differently; a highly stressful event for one person might be a minor distraction to someone else. However, the SRRS made a major contribution to the study of stress by pointing out that even *positive* life events, like marriage (#7), outstanding personal achievement (#25), and vacations (#41) can be quite stressful because they usually demand significant life changes.

Chronic stress Ongoing stress related to difficult everyday life circumstances such as poverty or long-term family strife.

Chronic Stress

In addition to experiencing acute stress from major life events, many people experience **chronic stress** due to the basic circumstances of their everyday lives. For example, being fired from one's job is a significantly stressful life event that ranks just below getting married on the SRRS. But consider the situation of a person employed by a large company that has been drastically reducing its workforce through layoffs. While the employee may continue to keep her job, she will spend a lot of time worrying that she is *about* to be laid off, and she will be surrounded by other employees who share her same concerns—certainly a chronically stressful experience even if she keeps her job.

Research into chronic stress has connected ongoing stress with psychological and physical symptoms. For example, a study of community-wide stressors found that people living in low-quality neighborhoods reported worse physical health and greater psychological distress than a control sample living in better neighborhoods (Steptoe & Feldman, 2001). This was true even when factors like socioeconomic status and social support were controlled for statistically. Another study found that the chronic stress of caring for a spouse suffering from dementia (such as that brought on by Alzheimer's disease or Parkinson's disease) was associated with elevated cortisol levels (a physical sign of stress) and compromised immune functioning (Bauer et al., 2000). In a clever study of the effects of chronic stress on children, researchers examined the relationships among the environmental stressor of household density (the number of people living in a single household), cardiovascular reactivity as measured by elevated heart rate and blood pressure, and school absences due to illness in 81 nine- to twelve-year-old boys (Johnston-Brooks et al., 1998). Interestingly, greater household density correlated with higher levels of cardiovascular reactivity (a physical sign of stress

The daily grind Living in a crowded urban environment can, all by itself, contribute to chronic stress and its damaging effects.

Spread thin "Daily hassles," like those involved with caring for small children while working, play a role in the negative emotional and health outcomes related to stress.

Daily hassles Minor stresses of everyday life.

Prospective study Research based on data that are collected as the events being studied are occurring, rather than recalling them retrospectively.

Catastrophes Extreme and unusual negative events that invariably cause significant stress.

Trauma An emotionally overwhelming experience in which there is a possibility of death or serious injury to oneself or a loved one.

Enduring disaster Catastrophic events, such as the floods in Mozambique in 2000, are associated with extreme stress reactions.

described in detail later in the chapter) which, in turn, was associated with a greater number of school days missed due to illness.

Daily Hassles

Since the early 1980s, researchers have investigated how minor life events or **daily hassles**, such as being caught in a traffic jam or worrying about one's appearance, contribute to stress and its emotional and physical effects (Hansell, 1989; Kanner et al., 1981). For example, a study of the effects of daily hassles, or "microstressors," such as having a fight with a friend, found that hassles predicted headache frequency and intensity in people who were headache-prone more accurately than measures of major life events (Fernanadez & Sheffield, 1996). There is also some evidence that daily hassles mediate the relationship between major life events and physical or emotional symptoms. For example, a **prospective study** of 144 undergraduates found that major life events measured at the beginning of the study were more likely to result in emotional difficulty at follow-up when daily hassles were also present (Johnson & Sherman, 1997). Not surprisingly, major life events, such as the death of a spouse, inevitably trigger a cascade of daily hassles: increased responsibility for household chores, changes in financial resources and their management, increased obligations to family and friends, and so on (Fernandez & Sheffield, 1996). Further, researchers have learned that daily hassles, like most stressors, are largely subjective; what feels like a hassle to one person may fall below the stress threshold of someone else. To this end, investigators have turned their attention from counting "objective" daily hassles to measuring the degree to which daily hassles are *felt* to be psychologically stressful (Crowther et al., 2001; Lazarus, 1999).

Catastrophic Events

Catastrophes are extreme and unusual events that invariably cause significant stress. These events come in many forms and may be experienced by an entire community or by an isolated individual. Natural disasters such as hurricanes, earthquakes and floods, or human-made disasters such as war, genocide, torture, or rape are all considered to be events of catastrophic proportions. Much of what we know about the effects of catastrophic events comes from psychological research on **trauma**, a term referring to threatening experiences that are psychologically overwhelming. Several factors influence the degree to which a catastrophe is experienced as traumatic (Shalev et al., 1996; Ullman & Filipas, 2001):

- The *duration* of the catastrophic event: one experience of torture versus repeated torture over a period of several months.

- The *severity* of the catastrophe: losing one's home in a hurricane versus losing one's home *and* experiencing major physical injuries.

- The *proximity* of the catastrophic event: having relatives who are Holocaust survivors versus being a Holocaust survivor.

- The degree of *psychological difficulty* experienced by an individual *prior to* the catastrophic event: an assault experienced by a man who is emotionally stable and healthy versus an assault on a man who has a long history of anxiety and depression.

- The availability of *social support* following a catastrophe: the celebration and veneration of World War II veterans versus open hostility directed toward veterans of the war in Vietnam.

Often, the psychological stress associated with a catastrophe is not limited to the duration of the event itself, but persists for years or even decades in the form of **post-traumatic stress disorder** (PTSD), an anxiety disorder described in detail in Chapter 5. In addition to suffering from a number of anxiety symptoms, people with PTSD also continue to relive the catastrophic event in the form of nightmares, flashbacks, and intrusive memories of the experience.

Studies of the effects of the September 11, 2001 terrorist attacks in the United States are currently under way. We can get a sense of the severe and long-term stress associated with this kind of catastrophe by considering what is known about the long-term effects of the 1995 terrorist bombing of the of Alfred P. Murrah Federal Building in Oklahoma City. A study of 182 adults who were direct survivors of the Oklahoma City bombing found that nearly every survivor continued to experience emotional hyperarousal and intrusive recollections of the event when interviewed six months after the attack. Further, 34% of the survivors suffered from full-blown PTSD, while 45% suffered from some other kind of psychological disorder (North et al., 1999). Not surprisingly, children who lost a parent in the Oklahoma City bombing experienced high levels of ongoing arousal and fear, and persistent post-traumatic stress symptoms, when compared to their nonbereaved peers (Pfefferbaum et al., 1999). Studies of Oklahoma sixth graders who had not been physically exposed to the bombing and who did not know anyone killed or injured in the attack found that even watching media coverage of the bombing, or knowing someone who knew someone killed or injured in the attack, was associated with posttraumatic stress symptoms and functional impairment two years after the catastrophe (Pfefferbaum et al., 2000).

Initial reports about the psychological aftermath of the September 11th attacks confirm the expectation of massive posttraumatic effects. Using random-digit dialing to contact a sample of 1,008 adults living in Manhattan, investigators found that 5 to 8 weeks after the attacks 7.5% of the people they contacted reported several symptoms consistent with a diagnosis of current PTSD related to the events of September 11th. The prevalence of PTSD was 20% for research participants living in close proximity to the World Trade Center (Galea et al., 2002). A nation-wide phone survey of 560 adults conducted in the week immediately after the attacks found that 44% of adults and 35% of children reported one or more symptoms of PTSD (Schuster et al., 2001). Mental health experts have every reason to expect that ongoing stress reactions to the destruction of the World Trade Center will be severe, pervasive, and lasting for thousands of directly affected individuals.

Brief Summary

- Stress experts have grouped stressors into the following categories: major life events, chronic stressors, daily hassles, and catastrophic events.

- Studies of major life events hypothesize that the more life change an event requires (whether positive or negative), the more stressful it is.

- Chronic stress can result from everyday life situations such as living in a low-quality neighborhood or a crowded household, or caring for a sick relative.

- Daily hassles, such as being caught in a traffic jam or worrying about one's appearance, can be perceived as stressful and contribute to physical or emotional symptoms.

- Catastrophes are extreme and unusual events that invariably cause significant psychological stress; they are sometimes experienced as traumatic or psychologically overwhelming.

Posttraumatic stress disorder Significant posttraumatic anxiety symptoms occurring more than one month after a traumatic experience.

Critical Thinking Question   **A**lmost every American experienced some form of psychological stress as a result of the events of September 11, 2001. What do you think was specifically most stressful for you about the September 11 attacks?

EXPLAINING STRESS AND HEALTH: PSYCHOPHYSIOLOGICAL DISORDERS

Now that we have described how psychologists define and categorize stress we can turn our attention to understanding how psychological stress influences physical health. We will begin by considering three pathways by which stress contributes to **psychophysiological disorders**, illnesses significantly influenced by emotional factors. These are: (1) the effects of psychological stress on health-related behaviors; (2) the effects of psychological stress on physiological reactions; and (3) the effects of certain personality traits on the management of psychological stress and, consequently, on health-related behaviors (see Figure 14.1).

Psychophysiological disorders Physical disorders caused or exacerbated by stress or emotional factors.

Psychological Stress and Unhealthy Behaviors

Stress can contribute to the development of physical illness by influencing health-related behaviors. Common sense and everyday experience tell us that even the most health-conscious college students are less likely to exercise and more likely to eat junk food during final exams than they are at the start of the semester. Research evidence shows that psychological stress decreases health-promoting behaviors, such as exercising and getting enough sleep, and increases unhealthy behaviors such as consumption of caffeine, nicotine, alcohol, and foods high in fat, salt, and sugar (Steptoe et al., 1998; Wardle et al., 2000). In a fascinating study of the relationship between work stress and car accidents, Bruce Kirkcaldy and his colleagues measured the working conditions of a German medical staff and the number of car accidents they had during a 12-month period (Kirkcaldy, Trimpop, & Cooper, 1997). They found that the age of the driver and the number of hours spent at work predicted the overall frequency of car accidents during the year but that the number of accidents that occurred on the way *to and from* work depended on factors such as working climate, hours spent at work, and length of lunchtime break.

Figure 14.1 Three Pathways by Which Stress Can Contribute to Physical Illness Psychological stress can influence health in more ways than one.

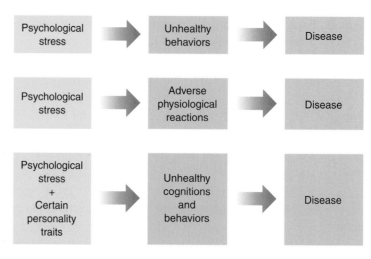

Psychological Stress and Adverse Physiological Reactions

In 1932 Walter Cannon, an American physiologist, described what has become known as the **fight-or-flight response** (Cannon, 1932). This primitive physiological response is rooted in an evolutionarily based instinct to go on the attack or run away when faced with danger or extreme stress (Chapter 5). The fight-or-flight response involves a cascade of physical reactions within the sympathetic branch of the *autonomic nervous system:* increased blood pressure and heart rate, dilation of the pupils, muscle tension, deepened and quickened breathing, and secretion of stress hormones. This physiological response to an environmental stressor is adaptive if it helps a person to meet or avoid a serious threat, but it places a great deal of strain on the body and can cause permanent harm if it occurs repeatedly (DiMatteo & Martin, 2002).

General Adaptation Syndrome

Following a tradition begun by Cannon, Hans Selye devoted his career to investigating the physiological effects of chronic stress in animals (Selye, 1956, 1976). Selye observed that when laboratory rats were put through a variety of highly stressful medical experiments they tended to develop a set of physical symptoms: enlarged adrenal glands, atrophied lymph nodes, and an increased number of stomach ulcers. Based on these observations, Selye developed a theory of a three-stage **General Adaptation Syndrome** (GAS) that occurs when animals (including humans) are faced with chronically stressful circumstances. The first phase of the GAS, known as the *alarm phase,* involves the mobilization of the body's defenses, especially those associated with the pituitary-adrenocortical systems. This is followed by the *resistance stage* in which the pituitary-adrenocortical system attempts to adapt to the external stressor, and then the *exhaustion* stage in which the body loses its ability to adapt to chronic stress and suffers significant physical damage (Marks et al., 2000). While Selye's work fostered interest in the relationship between chronic stress and physical illness, subsequent research found that environmental stressors and specific emotions interact to produce various physiological effects, not just one general physiological syndrome (Mason, 1975). Let's turn our attention to what we now know about how psychological stress alters and damages *specific* biological systems.

Stress and the Immune System

As we mentioned, many college students have noticed that they survive final exams (often on a steady diet of chips, cookies, and caffeine) only to go on vacation and come down with a bad cold. The field of **psychoneuroimmunology** aims to provide a scientific explanation for what college students frequently experience: that periods of high stress interfere with immune functioning and increase susceptibility to infectious diseases. Ample anecdotal evidence supports the relationship between heightened stress and vulnerability to viral or bacterial infections, but well-controlled studies of this phenomenon have only emerged in the last decade. State-of-the-art research in this field involves **viral challenge studies** in which healthy research participants are first evaluated for the degree of stress in their lives, then *deliberately* exposed to cold or flu viruses, then quarantined and monitored to see who gets sick and who doesn't (Marsland et al., 2001). For example, Sheldon Cohen and his colleagues in the Department of Psychology at Carnegie Mellon University measured the psychological stress of 55 research participants before infecting them with an influenza virus and placing them in quarantine (Cohen, Doyle, & Skoner, 1999). While in quarantine, the research participants were assessed on a number of objective measures of infection, such as upper respiratory symptoms and weight of mucus production. Consistent with findings from other studies and in keeping with the ***connection between mind and body***, Cohen's group learned that higher levels of preinfection psychological stress predicted increased severity of

Fight-or-flight response Extreme sympathetic nervous system arousal that prepares animals to flee or attack when faced with danger.

General Adaptation Syndrome According to some theories, a three-stage response—alarm, resistance, and exhaustion—that occurs when animals (including humans) are faced with chronically stressful circumstances.

Psychoneuroimmunology A field that investigates the interaction between emotional phenomena and immune system functioning.

Viral challenge studies Studies in which research participants are deliberately exposed to an infectious agent in order to assess immune system response.

influenza infection. Using similar methods, Cohen and colleagues learned that people are more likely to contract a common cold when they are faced with chronically stressful experiences (lack of employment, underemployment, ongoing relationship problems with family or friends) than when faced with an acute, but brief (less than one month) stressor (Cohen et al., 1998).

Findings from the field of psychoneuroimmunology also highlight the core concept of ***multiple causality.*** Illness typically results when individuals are faced with the combination of psychological stress and exposure to an infectious agent, not just one or the other. Stomach ulcers provide an excellent example of the principle of ***multiple causality***. For many years, the medical community believed that ulcers (small holes in the gastrointestinal tract) were caused by psychological stress alone. However, in the mid-1980s, researchers discovered that ulcers involve infection with the bacterium *Helicobacter pylori* (Marshall & Warren, 1984). While exposure to *H. pylori* is common, the bacterium is far more likely to contribute to the development of an ulcer when the stomach's protective mucosal lining has been weakened by the effects of psychological stress.

But what, exactly, does stress do to inhibit the functioning of the immune system? This simple question has a complicated answer because the immune system is made up of many types of immune cells which work together to prevent disease. *B cells, T cells,* and *natural killer cells* are some of the major players in the complex yet elegant design of the human immune system. B and T cells and natural killer cells help the body to recognize and attack external (viral or bacterial illnesses) or internal (cancer cells) causes of disease. A subclass of T cells known as *T-helper cells* mobilizes other immune cells into action. The HIV virus is particularly dangerous because it attacks the T-helper cells and prevents them from alerting the rest of the immune system to dangerous foreign substances known as **antigens**, giving even the most minor virus or bacterium lethal potential.

Research evidence suggests that acute stress leads to a brief *increase* in the production and activity of immune cells, but that sustained or chronic stress leads to **immunosuppression,** or sustained *decreases* in immune functioning (Herbert & Cohen, 1993). While the latest research indicates that the activation of the sympathetic branch of the nervous system (as in the fight-or-flight response) accounts, in part, for these effects on the immune system, researchers do not yet understand the exact mechanisms by which sympathetic stress hormones such as epinephrine, norepinephrine, and cortisone influence immune-cell activity (Marsland et al., 1997).

Stress and Cardiovascular Disorders (CVDs)

Physiologists have discovered that there is a great deal of individual variation in *cardiovascular reactivity*—the degree to which people react to environmental stressors with an increase in heart rate and blood pressure. Cardiovascular reactivity can be assessed under controlled conditions by measuring heart rate and blood pressure in volunteers while they participate in stressful activities such as the *Stroop task* (1935) or the *cold pressor task.* In the Stroop task (Table 14.2) volunteers are asked to identify, as quickly as possible, the *color* of the ink in which a word is spelled. Research participants are then presented with a highly frustrating list like the following:

The immune system at work T-cells attacking a cancer cell.

Antigens Foreign substances, such as viruses or bacteria, that typically trigger an immune system response.

Immunosuppression Subnormal functioning of the immune system.

Table 14.2	Sample Stroop Task
	RED GREEN
	BLUE PURPLE
	BLACK ORANGE

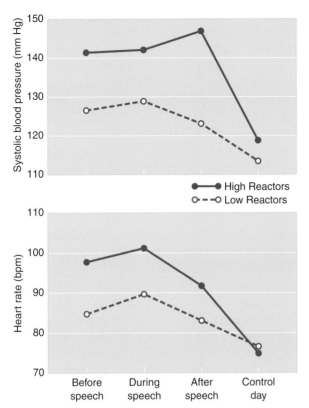

Figure 14.2 Heart Rate and Blood Pressure in High- and Low-Reactive Individuals Before, During, and After Giving a Speech As you can see, "high reactors" and "low reactors" had similar blood pressure and heart rate readings on a control day when no speeches were scheduled. However, when scheduled to give a speech, the "high reactors" had higher blood pressure and heart rate readings before, during, and even *after* delivering their speeches than the "low reactors" did.

Hugdahl, 1995 (p. 202), adapted from Manuck, Kasprowicz, & Muldoon, 1990

The cold pressor task requires research participants to hold their hands and arms under ice water for as long as possible; though the ice water does no physical damage, it quickly becomes quite painful. Measures of heart rate and blood pressure taken during these tasks provide an index of an individual's cardiovascular reactivity that appears to be stable across time and in a variety of situations (Hugdahl, 1995). "High reactors" experience dramatic increases in their heart rate and blood pressure when faced with a stressful situation, while "low reactors" do not. As you can see from Figure 14.2, even a common stressful situation, such as giving a classroom speech, will cause heart rate and blood pressure to be much higher in "high reactors" than in "low reactors." By understanding the relationship between external stressors and individual differences in cardiovascular reactivity, researchers have gained important insights into how stress plays a role in two common cardiovascular disorders: hypertension and coronary heart disease.

Stress and Hypertension While a temporary increase in blood pressure is an adaptive component of the fight-or-flight response, *chronically* elevated blood pressure, known as **hypertension**, increases the risk for stroke, coronary heart disease, and kidney failure by placing unnecessary and damaging strain on the walls of coronary arteries. A variety of factors contribute to the development of hypertension: being severely overweight, eating a diet high in sodium, failing to exercise, and having a genetic predisposition toward hypertension. Stress experts are especially interested in what is known as **essential hypertension**—hypertension not caused by biological factors. A variety of environmental stressors such as having a stressful job, living in a city, or living in a war-torn area have been found to contribute to essential hypertension (Nyklicek, Vingerhoets, & Van Heck, 2000; Shapiro, 2001).

Stress and Coronary Heart Disease Coronary heart disease (CHD) is the leading cause of death in the United States and many other industrialized countries. Nearly half a mil-

Hypertension Chronically elevated blood pressure.

Essential hypertension Hypertension for which no physiological cause can be found.

lion Americans die from the effects of CHD each year, and the Centers for Disease Control estimates that 12.4 million Americans currently suffer from CHD (CDC, 2001). While CHD is responsible for one out of every five deaths nationally, deaths from heart disease occur disproportionately among African Americans and people living in southern states such as Mississippi, West Virginia, and Kentucky (CDC, 2001) (see Box 14.1).

CHD is a blanket term used to describe several different kinds of heart problems including *arteriosclerosis, atherosclerosis,* and *myocardial infarction.* Arteriosclerosis, the thickening and stiffening of coronary arteries, often results from the excessive pressure that chronic hypertension places upon the arteries. Atherosclerosis occurs when cholesterol deposits collect within the coronary arteries causing the artery walls to become narrow and stiff and impeding the flow of blood to the heart. Arteriosclerosis and atherosclerosis both lead to myocardial infarctions, or "heart attacks," when artery damage prevents sufficient amounts of oxygenated blood from reaching the heart. Like all muscles, the heart requires a constant supply of oxygen and areas of heart tissue die when oxygen becomes unavailable.

A variety of factors contribute to the risk of developing CHD: smoking, being significantly overweight, failing to exercise, having uncontrolled hypertension or diabetes, having high levels of blood cholesterol, and having a genetic predisposition to heart problems (DiMatteo & Martin, 2002). In addition to these biological factors, researchers have learned that how a person reacts to stressful situations constitutes a significant *psychological* risk factor for CHD. The first observations that personality factors might play a significant role in CHD came in the 1950s when two cardiologists, Meyer Friedman and Ray Rosenman, observed that many of their patients were intense and impatient, even to the degree that they were wearing out the upholstery on the front of the waiting room chairs by constantly sitting on the edge of their seats (Friedman & Rosenman, 1974). Upon further investigation, Friedman and Rosenman found that a disproportionate number of their cardiology patients suffered from what they called "type A" personality: their patients were hard-driving, felt an urgent need to do as many things as quickly as possible, and had little patience for others (Friedman & Rosenman, 1974).

In recent years, the conceptualization of what constitutes type A behavior has shifted away from competitive and time-conscious behavior toward hostile, irritable, and antagonistic behavior (Siegman et al., 2000). As the definition of what constitutes a "heart-damaging" personality becomes increasingly refined, researchers are finding more robust connections between personality factors and CHD. Even when other coronary risk factors such as smoking, obesity, exercise, family history, and socioeconomic status are taken into account, hostile behavior constitutes a significant risk factor for developing CHD (Miller et al., 1996).

Stress and Other Medical Disorders

In addition to compromising the functioning of the immune system and being a major causal factor in disorders such as essential hypertension and coronary heart disease, psychosocial stress has been found to contribute to a number of other medical disorders such as **asthma, migraine headaches,** and **cancer**. Asthma, a medical condition in which the airways to and from the lungs become periodically constricted, tends to begin during childhood and adolescence. Research on the relationship between stress and asthma has found that healthy children and adolescents experience increases in respiration rate and airway resistance when faced with a highly stressful situation such as being required to play a frustrating computer game (Rietveld, Beest, & Everaerd, 1999; Ritz et al., 2000). However, these effects are especially problematic for children who also happen to suffer from asthma, which may cause mild airway constriction to turn into a full-blown asthma attack (McQuaid et al., 2000).

Asthma A medical condition in which the airways to and from the lungs become periodically constricted.

Migraine headaches Painful headaches that result from the constriction of blood vessels in the cranium and are often heralded by extreme sensitivity to light and sound, dizziness, nausea, or vomiting.

Cancer A disease characterized by the uncontrolled growth of malignant cells in some part of the body.

FOCUS ON PSYCHOLOGY IN SOCIETY

BOX 14.1   Hypertension Among African American Men

John Henryism

John Henry was an African American man born in the mid-1800s who, according to legend, was one of the most industrious and powerful men working on the U.S. railroad system during the Reconstruction period following the Civil War. While hand-drilling through a mountain with his team, John Henry was challenged by a salesman who claimed that his steam-powered machine could drill faster than any human. John Henry raced against the machine and won, only to die from exhaustion immediately thereafter. The term **John Henryism** was coined by Dr. Sherman James, a social psychologist, and his colleagues to describe a style of active coping fueled by the belief that *any* environmental obstacle can be overcome with enough hard work and persistence (1983).

Though John Henryism may seem on its surface to be an adaptive response to the social and economic pressures placed upon ethnic minorities, this active coping style has been linked repeatedly with high rates of hypertension, particularly among poor, African American men (Dressler, Bindon, & Neggers, 1998; Wright et al., 1996). Unfortunately, some economically disadvantaged minority men who are doing their best to succeed against enormous odds may be risking their own health in the process.

If you were asked to develop an intervention program to address the negative effects of John Henryism, how might you proceed? In designing your program, be sure to consider psychological, medical, and economic options.

He Laid Down His Hammer and Cried   A depiction of John Henry, shortly after he has beaten the steam-powered machine, and shortly before his death from exhaustion.

Palmer Hayden, *He Laid Down His Hammer and Cried*, 1944–1947. ©Museum of African American Art.

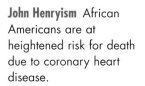

John Henryism African Americans are at heightened risk for death due to coronary heart disease.

Migraine headaches result from the constriction of blood vessels in the cranium and are often heralded by extreme sensitivity to light and sound, dizziness, nausea, or vomiting. Though migraine headaches are different for everyone who experiences them, many people suffer completely debilitating aching or throbbing pain. Stress seems to trigger migraine headaches which then cause additional stress as a result of physical pain, lost sleep and productivity, and so on; increased levels of stress then appear to contribute to future migraines (Holm, Lokken, & Myers, 1997; Sorbi, Maassen, & Spierings, 1996).

John Henryism An active coping style fueled by the belief that *any* environmental obstacle can be overcome with enough hard work and persistence.

Given the strength of the association between type A personality and coronary heart disease, researchers were eager to explore whether a particular personality profile might be linked to another major disease: cancer. Early research indicated that certain personality traits might predispose people to cancer. By studying people who had just received a cancer diagnosis, two psychologists (LeShan & Worthington, 1956) developed a "cancer personality" profile which "included the tendency to deny and suppress emotions, to avoid conflict, and to be overly agreeable" (DiMatteo & Martin, 2002, p. 350). However, subsequent work in this area revealed that this original formulation of a "cancer personality" involved the major methodological flaw of assessing people who had recently been diagnosed with life-threatening cancers. Under these circumstances, research participants may have been understandably reluctant to share intense feelings with a virtual stranger during the personality assessment rather than displaying pathological personality traits.

Well-designed prospective studies (which conduct personality evaluations of a large number of individuals and then see who goes on to develop cancer) have failed to find a direct connection between any particular personality profile and cancer (Levenson & Bemis, 1995). However, stress may promote the development of cancer through indirect routes. Physically harmful stress-related behaviors, such as smoking or eating an unhealthy diet, are known to increase cancer risk. Stress-related immunosuppression, particularly among the natural killer cells, also interferes with the body's natural ability to identify and destroy cancer cells (Anderson, Golden-Kreutz, & DiLillo, 2001).

Psychological Stress, Personality Traits, and Health

In addition to the type A personality style which has been linked with coronary heart disease, psychologists have found that cognitive and behavioral tendencies such as *pessimism, optimism,* and *repressive coping* influence health. Pessimism, optimism, and repressive coping shape how individuals manage psychologically stressful circumstances and have a general impact on health-related behaviors and physiological reactions to stress.

Pessimism and Optimism

Substantial research evidence indicates that **pessimism** increases the likelihood that one will become ill while **optimism** has salutary effects. For research purposes, psychologists have defined *pessimistic explanatory style* as the tendency to attribute negative events to stable, global, and internal factors; optimism is the opposite tendency. When a pessimist loses his car keys he may think "I always lose things (stable), I can't keep track of anything (global), I'm totally irresponsible (internal)" while the optimist may think "It's not really like me to lose my keys (unstable), I keep track of everything else (specific), I must have been distracted by all of the work I have this week (external)."

In one of the most interesting investigations into the relationship between optimism, pessimism, and health, psychologists analyzed surveys filled out by 99 Harvard University graduates from the classes of 1942 to 1944 when they were about 25 years old (Peterson, Seligman, & Vaillant, 1988). In follow-up health evaluations of the men when they were between 45 and 60, those men with pessimistic explanatory styles were far more likely to have died or to be in poor physical health than their optimistic peers, even when mental and physical health at age 25 were taken into account. But, does an optimistic attitude by itself keep people in good health? Not necessarily. Researchers have found that people with optimistic explanatory styles are more likely to be and stay healthy if their optimism influences them to engage in behaviors, such

Pessimism In cognitive terms, the tendency to make internal, global, and stable explanations of negative events; associated with depression and poor health.

Optimism In cognitive terms, the tendency to make external, specific, and unstable explanations of negative events; associated with good health.

Attitude counts Pessimism, written all over this man's face, appears to contribute to long-term negative health outcomes.

as exercising, that are known to promote good health (Peterson & Bossio, 2001). Put another way, optimism promotes good health because people feel optimistic that healthy choices in the present (exercising, eating a healthy diet) will contribute to future physical well-being. Pessimism, apparently, has the opposite effect; people with a pessimistic explanatory style are likely to think "Why should I worry about my health now, it won't make a difference anyway!"

Repressive Coping

While the open hostility of type A behavior has been linked to CHD, consistently *repressing* hostile emotions also seems to have negative health effects. Psychologists have identified a pattern of emotional behavior called **repressive coping** in which people actively suppress negative emotions to the degree that they may not even know that they are experiencing these feelings (see Chapter 3 on the defense mechanism of repression for more on this topic). To identify people with repressive coping styles, researchers typically compare self-report measures of anxiety with self-report measures of social desirability (social desirability is defined as the tendency to distort the truth in order to "look good"). People who report little or no anxiety, but who also score very high on measures of social desirability (endorsing statements like "I like everyone I know") are considered to be repressive copers: they under-report feelings of subjective distress and exaggerate cheerful, happy, and content feelings. The constant effort required to keep negative feelings at bay seems to have a damaging effect on health. People who use a repressive coping style have been found to have fewer circulating T-helper cells and higher blood cholesterol levels than non-repressors. When faced with a laboratory stressor designed to trigger an immune system response (the Stroop task), repressors also exhibited a smaller increase in the availability of natural killer immune cells than non-repressors (Barger et al., 2000; Niaura et al., 1992).

Repressive coping A coping style characterized by general suppression of negative emotions.

Brief Summary

- There are three distinct pathways by which stress contributes to physical illness:
  - The effects of psychological stress on health-related behaviors.
  - The effects of psychological stress on physiological reactions.
  - The effects of certain personality traits on the management of psychological stress and consequently on health-related behaviors.
- Stress contributes to the development of physical illness by influencing health-related behaviors such as getting enough exercise and sleep and limiting consumption of caffeine, nicotine, alcohol, and foods high in fat and sugar.
- Adverse physiological reactions to stress can take the form of a persistent fight-or-flight response, suppressed immune functioning, and/or heightened cardiovascular reactivity.
- Cardiovascular reactivity contributes to two serious heart conditions: hypertension (chronically elevated blood pressure) and coronary heart disease (CHD).
- "Type A" behavior (hostile, irritable, and antagonistic) also appears to be a significant risk factor for developing CHD.
- Stress has been found to contribute to medical disorders such as asthma, migraine headaches, and cancer.
- In addition to "type A" personality features, psychologists have found that cognitive and behavioral tendencies, such as pessimism, optimism, and repressive coping, influence health.

Critical Thinking Question | **N**ow that you know about three different pathways by which stress can influence health, can you think of a situation in which all three of these pathways could combine to produce a negative health outcome?

REDUCING STRESS AND TREATING PSYCHOPHYSIOLOGICAL DISORDERS

As experts in the mental health and medical fields began to learn about the relationship between psychological stress and physical health they became interested in developing preventative interventions to reduce stress. A wide variety of psychophysiological interventions have been developed over the past three decades. Some psychophysiological interventions fall squarely within established Western medical and psychological traditions while others, such as meditation and yoga, have been borrowed from Eastern spiritual practices. The interventions described below serve two important purposes: reducing stress to prevent disease, and managing the stressful effects of physical illness to improve prognosis.

Relaxation Techniques

Relaxation training Training people how to calm themselves by regulating their breathing and attending to bodily sensations.

As you will recall from Chapter 5, **relaxation training** can be used to reduce and prevent episodes of intense anxiety. Even people who don't suffer from panic disorder (for which relaxation training is frequently employed) can benefit from learning how to calm their body by systematically tightening and relaxing their muscles and focusing on their breathing. *Progressive muscle relaxation* has been found to reduce sympathetic nervous system activity, lower heart rate, and enhance immune response (Gatchel, 2001; van Dixhoorn, 1998). Eastern meditation and exercise practices, such as yoga, that focus on controlled breathing and reducing mental distractions, have also been found to have a significant salutary effect on a variety of physiological measures of stress (Gatchel, 2001). Recent research has found that people who write about stressful experiences in a way that enhances the meaning of stressful events may boost their immune systems (see Box 14.2)

In order to study the effects of relaxation training on the immune system, Janice Kiecolt-Glaser and her colleagues studied T-helper cells and natural killer cells in the blood samples of first-year medical students taken one month before a scheduled exam, and again on the day of the examination. After the first blood sample was collected, half of the students were assigned to a relaxation training group, and the other half were left to their own devices. At exam time, students in the relaxation group not only reported feeling less distressed than their peers, but more frequent relaxation practice among individuals in the relaxation group was associated with heightened T-helper cell and natural killer cell activity (Kiecolt-Glaser et al., 1986).

Relaxation techniques, meditation, and breathing exercises not only reduce stress and thereby prevent certain psychophysiological diseases but they can also be used to alleviate a variety of physical symptoms. Relaxation techniques have been found to be effective in the treatment of insomnia, muscle contraction headaches, and premenstrual syndrome and also work to reduce some of the side effects (such as nausea) associated with cancer chemotherapy (Gatchel, 2001).

Improving health through relaxation Yoga and other Eastern meditation and exercise practices have been found to reduce stress and, thereby, contribute to improved health.

Biofeedback

In the 1960s, behavioral scientists discovered that humans could be taught to control a variety of autonomic nervous system responses that were previously thought to be

BOX 14.2	Strengthening the Immune System

Writing to Heal *by* Bridget Murray

Emerging research indicates that writing can help strengthen immune functioning and prevent deterioration due to disease when it is used to help people understand, learn, and derive meaning from negative experiences.

Writing is no stranger to therapy. For years, practitioners have used logs, questionnaires, journals and other writing forms to help people heal from stresses and traumas.

Now, new research suggests that expressive writing may also offer physical benefits to people battling terminal or life-threatening diseases. Studies by those in the forefront of this research—psychologists James Pennebaker, Ph.D., of the University of Texas at Austin, and Joshua Smyth, Ph.D., of Syracuse University—suggest that writing about emotions can boost immune functioning in patients with such illness as HIV/AIDS, asthma and arthritis.

Researchers are only beginning to get at how and why writing might benefit the immune system, and why some people appear to benefit more than others. There is emerging agreement, however, that the key to writing's effectiveness is in the way people use it to interpret their experiences, right down to the words they choose. Venting emotions alone—whether through writing or talking—is not enough to relieve stress, and thereby improve health, Smyth emphasizes. To tap writing's healing power, people must use it to better understand and learn from their emotions, he says.

A ground-breaking study of writing's physical effects appeared in the *Journal of the American Medical Association* (Vol. 281, No. 14) three years ago. In the study, led by Smyth, 107 asthma and rheumatoid arthritis patients wrote for 20 minutes on each of three consecutive days—71 of them about the most stressful event of their lives and the rest about the emotionally

neutral subject of their daily plans. Four months after the writing exercise, 70 patients in the stressful-writing group showed improvement on objective, clinical evaluations compared with 37 of the control patients. In addition, those who wrote about stress improved more, and deteriorated less, than controls for both diseases. "So writing helped patients get better, and also kept them from getting worse," says Smyth.

Not everyone agrees, though, that the mere act of writing is necessarily beneficial. In fact, initial writing about trauma triggers distress and physical and emotional arousal, researchers have found.

But there is evidence that the nature of a person's writing is key to its health effects, notes health psychology researcher Susan Lutgendorf, Ph.D., of the University of Iowa. An intensive journaling study (Ullrich & Lutgendorf, 2002) she conducted recently with her doctoral student Phil Ullrich suggests that people who relive upsetting events without focusing on meaning report poorer health than those who derive meaning from the writing. They even fare worse than people who write about neutral events.

"You need focused thought as well as emotions," says Lutgendorf. "An individual needs to find meaning in a traumatic memory as well as to feel the related emotions to reap the positive benefits from the writing exercise."

Monitor on Psychology, June 2002 (pp. 54–55)

James Pennebaker *(left)*
Joshua Smyth

involuntary, such as heart rate and blood pressure. When connected to monitors that provide visual feedback about heart rate, blood pressure, and even skin temperature most people can learn to modify these physiological responses. **Biofeedback training** teaches people to attend to and partially control certain problematic physiological processes with the help of such feedback.

One study of biofeedback efficacy evaluated the effects of 12 sessions of biofeedback training for pain management in patients suffering from chronic temporomandibular disorders—discomfort or pain in the muscles and joints that control jaw function. When compared to patients who had received no training, patients in the biofeedback group reported less pain, decreased pain-related disability, and improved jaw functioning one year after treatment was completed (Gardea, Gatchel, & Mishra, 2001). Biofeedback training has also been found to be an effective aid in the treatment of asthma, essential hypertension, gastrointestinal disorders, insomnia, migraine

Biofeedback training Training people to attend to and partially control autonomic physiological functions with the help of visual feedback.

Monitoring the autonomic nervous system
Here, a person engages in biofeedback training. With practice and the availability of visual feedback, people can learn to modify and control certain physiological responses.

Cognitive-behavioral stress management An intervention designed to enhance or maintain adaptive coping strategies and decrease maladaptive coping strategies.

headaches, Raynaud's disease (a painful vascular disorder), and possibly even epileptic seizures (Gatchel, 2001).

Cognitive Retraining

As you recall from the study of the Harvard graduates described earlier, men who exhibited pessimistic explanatory styles at age 25 were more likely than their optimistic classmates to be ill or to have died when they were evaluated again at ages 45 to 60 (Peterson et al., 1988). Based on these and other findings, psychologists have sought out ways to change how people think about negative events in the hope that this will lead to better health outcomes. Cognitive interventions can be employed to improve physical health in two important ways: by reducing the kinds of thoughts that cause stress and increase susceptibility to disease, and by helping patients who are already ill to adopt adaptive attitudes and behaviors.

Cognitive retraining interventions to reduce stress focus on changing pessimistic explanatory styles which may leave people feeling helpless and overwhelmed in the face of negative life events. Standard cognitive interventions help clients to replace cognitive distortions ("I'm hopelessly irresponsible!") with rational thinking ("I've lost something today, but if I pay attention in the future, I'll keep better track of my things."). It is important to recall that stress is best defined as an *interaction* between an event and a person's subjective perception or cognitive appraisal of the event. While it is not possible to prevent bad things from happening, it is possible to reduce stress by changing how people interpret negative events (see Figure 14.3).

Cognitive-behavioral stress management (CBSM) techniques have been found to improve the health status of people who have already been diagnosed with an illness. For example, a group of men diagnosed with HIV participated in a CBSM training program that enhanced or maintained adaptive coping strategies such as exercising and taking advantage of social support and reduced maladaptive coping strategies such as denial or repression. The training program prevented some of the immune changes typically associated with HIV and also decreased social isolation. Research participants who maintained maladaptive cognitive styles were more depressed, more immunosuppressed, and more symptomatic one year after the intervention when compared to men who developed or maintained adaptive coping styles (Ironson et al., 2000).

Cognitive-behavioral interventions can be especially useful in the treatment of disease when they help people to reduce *catastrophizing* cognitions. Not surprisingly,

Figure 14.3 How Cognitive Retraining Reduces Stress Cognitive retraining programs that help decrease pessimism and increase sense of control have been found to reduce stress and improve prognosis in people suffering from some medical disorders.
Adapted from Helgeson et al., 2001, p. 274.

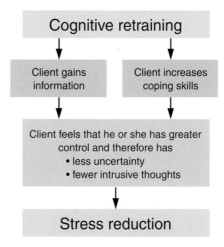

many people who are diagnosed with serious illnesses such as cancer and heart disease are quick to think "I'm going to die from this," "The doctors won't be able to help me," and "All hope is lost." When such beliefs are maintained, patients are often reluctant to engage in a wide variety of activities (exercise, support groups, improved diet) that are known to improve the outcome of many health problems.

Social Support

Social support is closely associated with health. Studies of social networks and mortality rates have consistently found that the more social connections a person has, the less likely he or she is to die prematurely (Welin et al., 1992). Social support comes in many forms. *Emotional support* can help reduce stress by providing an outlet for worries, a confidante in difficult times, and feelings of connection and acceptance; *instrumental support* reduces stress by providing practical, tangible support such as financial loans or extra help around the house, and *informational support* reduces stress through the provision of useful advice or helpful feedback (Wills & Filer Fegan, 2001).

Ample evidence suggests that people who have solid social connections are less likely to become ill. A prospective study of 736 healthy Swedish men found that research participants with the highest levels of emotional support and social integration were the least likely to have developed heart disease when evaluated six years later (Orth-Gomer, Rosengren, & Wilhelmsen, 1993). Several models have been offered to explain *how* social support prevents disease; Table 14.3 illustrates a variety ways in which social support might reduce stress and improve health outcomes.

Social support not only protects against the onset of disease, but it also improves physical and mental health outcomes in people who are already sick. Researchers have found that social support in the form of being married, participating in social activities, and/or maintaining relationships with friends increases survival time in cancer patients even when factors such as socioeconomic status and severity of cancer at time of diagnosis are taken into account (Waxler-Morrison et al., 1991). In addition to prolonging the lives of people suffering from life-threatening disorders like cancer, social support also seems to ward off anxiety and depression in people with chronic illnesses. Strong interpersonal relationships have also been found to improve mental health outcomes in patients suffering from chronic diseases such as arthritis, diabetes, kidney failure, and HIV infection (Wills & Filer Fegan, 2001). While some experts have

A little help from one's friends Social support, as depicted in the close friendships between the characters of the television show *Dawson's Creek,* helps to reduce stress and, as a result, improve physical health.

Possible Ways that Social Support Reduces Stress and Improves Health Outcomes	Table 14.3

Adapted from Wills & Filer Fegan, 2001 (p. 214)

- Promotes physical calming
- Reduces anxiety and depression
- Improves immune functioning
- Alters appraisals of threats
- Lowers physiological reactivity
- Reduces harmful behaviors
- Promotes healthful behaviors
- Results in better coping with stressors.

observed that having numerous social ties and their attendant obligations can also *increase* stress, most research indicates that the health and stress-reduction benefits of social support far outweigh the costs.

Brief Summary

- Interventions to reduce stress serve two major purposes: the prevention of disease and the management of the physical effects of illness in order to improve prognosis.

- Relaxation training involves systematically tightening and relaxing muscles while focusing on breathing. It has been found to reduce sympathetic nervous system activity, lower heart rate, and enhance immune response.

- Biofeedback training teaches people to attend to and partially control physiological processes with the help of visual feedback provided by monitors that measure physical indices such as heart rate, blood pressure, or skin temperature.

- Cognitive retraining that alters pessimistic explanatory styles, or enhances adaptive coping strategies, can reduce stress and susceptibility to disease and also help patients who are already ill to improve their medical prognosis.

- Social support comes in several forms: emotional (having a confidante, feeling connected and accepted), instrumental (financial support, help with chores), and informational (advice and feedback). Social support not only protects against the onset of disease, but it also improves physical and mental health outcomes in people who are already sick.

Critical Thinking Question | **Consider Robert, the heart attack patient described in the chapter-opening vignette. Do you think that he would benefit from participating in relaxation training, biofeedback, and/or cognitive retraining to reduce the chances of having another heart attack? Why or why not?**

DEFINING THE SOMATOFORM DISORDERS

Somatoform disorders Disorders in which physical symptoms are caused by psychological factors

Factitious disorders Physical disorders that are intentionally produced, or faked, because the person wants to be perceived as sick.

Hysteria A term used for centuries to describe a syndrome of symptoms that appear to be neurological but do not have a neurological cause; now classified as **conversion disorder**.

The **somatoform disorders** are characterized by the presence of physical symptoms or concerns that are not due to a medical disorder. The term "somatoform" comes from the ancient Greek word *soma,* which means body. People suffering from somatoform disorders experience symptoms of physical disease or defect even though there is nothing medically wrong with their bodies. **Factitious disorders** are similar to somatoform disorders in that bodily symptoms are the focus of concern. However, unlike the somatoform disorders, factitious disorders are intentionally produced, or faked, because the person wants to be perceived as sick (see Box 14.3).

CLASSIFYING THE SOMATOFORM DISORDERS

Accounts of fascinating but medically impossible physical complaints date back to the *Papyrus Ebers,* an ancient Egyptian medical document from 1600 B.C.E. (Phillips, 2001). Somatoform symptoms were for a long time included as part of an old diagnostic category known as **hysteria**. You may recall that Freud described hysteria as a disorder involving physical symptoms resulting from the repression of

BOX 14.3   *Deliberately Feigning Illness*

Factitious Disorders and Malingering

The factitious, or faked, disorders have been recognized by savvy physicians for many centuries; a medical essay written in 1838 and titled "On Feigned and Factitious Diseases" tells us faking illness is nothing new (Gavin, 1838). In the 1950s a physician named Richard Asher identified a particularly severe form of factitious disorder which he named Munchausen's syndrome after a German cavalry officer, Baron von Munchausen (1720–1797) who was reputed to have made up fantastic, but untrue, tales about his military exploits and heroism. Individuals suffering from Munchausen's syndrome create real, self-induced disease symptoms by ingesting toxic substances, misusing medications, or employing other, similar means. They usually have extensive medical histories marked by multiple hospitalizations, surgeries, and medical tests, tell elaborate tales about their own medical problems, and often travel from one area to the next to keep hospital staff members from becoming familiar with their ruse (Eisendrath, 1996; Feldman, Hamilton, & Deemer, 2001). People with Munchausen's syndrome are usually motivated by a desire for the care and attention provided by medical staff members.

In one particularly disturbing form of factitious disorder, known as *Munchausen syndrome by proxy,* parents exaggerate or induce physical symptoms in their children in order to draw medical attention and to provide an arena for acting as self-sacrificing, devoted caretakers. Here is a case of a 6-year-old boy whose mother was ultimately discovered to have been injecting her son with infectious microbes:

> A 6-year-old white male was transferred to the University of Chicago Children's Hospital for evaluation of headaches, fever, and vomiting. The patient was well until 6 weeks before admission when he began having recurrent headaches. Phenobarbital was prescribed for presumptive migraine headaches. Despite this treatment, the symptoms persisted and the patient presented to a local hospital with severe headache and vomiting… To evaluate the headaches, magnetic resonance imaging (MRI), magnetic resonance angiography (MRA), and [electroencephalography] EEG were performed; results were normal. To evaluate the abdominal pain, an ultrasound was performed, which appeared normal… Fevers persisted and subsequent blood cultures grew *E[scherichia] coli, Enterococcus faecium,* and *Candida albicans*…
>
> Because no anatomic source for the polymicrobial sepsis could be identified despite extensive investigation, the possibility of external contamination of the intravenous lines was considered… A review of the chart revealed that the mother was the patient's most frequent visitor, having stayed in the child's room overnight and most of each day. She helped with nursing chores including monitoring intravenous infusions… The parents were interviewed separately regarding the possibility that microorganisms were being introduced externally into the intravenous lines. The mother denied any wrongdoing, but the father was willing to consider the diagnosis and offered additional family history. It was learned that the mother had a history of laxative abuse and anorexia nervosa/bulimia… A sibling had had a prolonged hospitalization at another institution for chronic diarrhea. The etiology was never determined despite an extensive evaluation.
>
> The patient was transferred to the Intensive Care Unit for continuous monitoring and observation. All intravenous lines were removed. The patient remained afebrile [without a fever] with marked clinical improvement in all symptoms. After a meeting among the primary medical team, the multiple consult services, child psychiatry, and social work, Munchausen syndrome by proxy was diagnosed. The state's attorney was contacted and the child was placed in protective custody…The [woman's] children were placed in foster care for 15 months and subsequently have been returned to the father's custody. The patient has had no further infections or hospitalizations. The mother eventually confessed to contaminating the child's intravenous lines.
>
> Seferian, 1997 (pp. 419–422)

Like many victims of Munchausen by proxy, this boy endured painful physical symptoms, multiple hospitalizations, and intrusive diagnostic procedures. Parents who engage in Munchausen by proxy are often quite adept at hiding their behaviors and may even be well-liked by the hospital staff for their patience with extensive medical procedures and eagerness to help with their child's care. Many of these parents have also been found to have their own histories of factitious or somatoform disorders, self-harming behaviors, and histrionic or borderline personality disorders (Bools, Neale, & Meadow, 1994).

Factitious disorders differ slightly from **malingering** in which individuals also feign or deliberately induce illness. While people with factitious disorder fake illness in order to garner medical concern and attention, malingerers have a clear and specific external incentive to be sick. For example, they fake illness to avoid having to work, to get out of unpleasant duties, or to evade military service.

Malingering The act of purposely feigning illness in order to get out of an obligation.

Telling tall tales An artist's rendition of Baron von Munchausen on one of his fantastic adventures.

anxiety-provoking impulses. Beginning with the DSM-III in 1980, there was a deliberate move away from theoretically laden terms like hysteria—a word closely associated with psychoanalysis—to more symptom-based descriptions of psychological disorders. In the DSM-III, and subsequent editions of the DSM, the symptoms associated with hysteria have been categorized as specific somatoform disorders.

The DSM-IV-TR Categories

The DSM-IV-TR includes five different somatoform disorders: *conversion disorder, somatization disorder, pain disorder, hypochondriasis, and body dysmorphic disorder* (APA, 2000). These disorders are encountered primarily in medical settings and have two important features in common: a focus on bodily complaints that have no physical basis, and symptoms that are not being intentionally produced or faked. Of course, before a diagnosis of a somatoform disorder can be made, all plausible medical explanations have to be evaluated and ruled out. Thus, these disorders are generally diagnosed after extensive medical testing, and clinicians must be careful not to jump to a conclusion that a physical symptom is somatoform just because no immediate medical explanation can be found.

We'll begin our explanation of the DSM-IV-TR somatoform disorders with the description of conversion disorder.

Conversion Disorder

Conversion disorder Specific symptoms or deficits in voluntary motor or sensory functions with no physiological cause.

The modern history of abnormal psychology began with the study of **conversion disorder** (see Table 14.5), then called *hysteria*. As described in Chapter 3, in the 1890s Sigmund Freud and Josef Breuer were struggling to understand clients who would today be diagnosed with conversion disorder. Breuer's famous patient, Anna O., had a variety of bizarre and unexplainable physical symptoms:

Table 14.4	The DSM-IV-TR Somatoform Disorders
Adapted from the DSM-IV-TR (APA, 2000)	**Conversion disorder:** Specific symptoms or deficits in voluntary motor or sensory functions with no physiological cause (prevalence rate among referrals to outpatient mental health clinics: 1.0% to 3.0%; prevalence rate in general population: 1 to 3 cases per 10,000 people). **Somatization disorder:** Recurrent gastrointestinal, sexual, or pseudoneurological symptoms without a physiological cause (prevalence rate among women: 0.2% to 2.0%; among men: less than 0.2%). **Pain disorder:** Physical pain without a physiological cause (prevalence rate: unknown, but physical pains that are difficult to diagnose occur frequently in the general population). **Hypochondriasis:** Preoccupation with the fear of contracting, or the mistaken idea that one has a serious disease (prevalence rate in a general medical practice: 4.0% to 9.0%). **Body dysmorphic disorder:** Preoccupation with an imagined or exaggerated defect in physical appearance (prevalence rate unknown).

Diagnostic Criteria for Conversion Disorder

Table 14.5

Adapted from the DSM-IV-TR (APA, 2000)

- One or more symptoms or deficits affecting voluntary motor or sensory function that suggest a neurological or other general medical condition.
- Psychological factors are judged to be associated with the symptom or deficit because the initiation or exacerbation of the symptom or deficit is preceded by conflicts or stressors.
- The symptom or deficit is not intentionally produced or feigned.
- The symptom or deficit cannot be fully explained by a general medical condition, or by the direct effects of a substance, or as a culturally sanctioned behavior or experience.
- The symptom or deficit causes clinically significant distress or impairment in social, occupational, or other important areas of functioning or warrants medical evaluation.

There developed in rapid succession a series of severe disturbances which were apparently quite new: left-sided occipital headache...disturbances of vision which were hard to analyse; paresis of the muscles of the front of the neck, so that finally the patient could only move her head by pressing it backwards between her raised shoulders and moving her whole back; contracture and anesthesia of the right upper, and, after a time, of the right lower extremity. The latter was fully extended, adducted [drawn close to the body] and rotated inwards. Later the same symptom appeared in the left lower extremity and finally in the left arm, of which, however, the fingers to some extent retained the power of movement. So, too, there was complete rigidity in the shoulder-joints...

Studies in Hysteria, 1893/1955 (p. 23)

Anna O.'s symptoms fit the current definition of conversion disorder insofar as she precipitously developed a variety of physical impairments: disturbances of vision, paralyzed neck muscles, loss of feeling in her arms and legs, and so on, without any medical basis. Anna O.'s symptoms mimicked a neurological condition, even though nothing was actually wrong with her brain. Physicians are often able to detect conversion symptoms because they "typically do not conform to known anatomical pathways and physiological mechanisms" (APA, 1994, p. 453). For example, a person who claims to have a paralyzed leg may still have the normal reflex when hit below the knee with a rubber mallet, or complain that she has lost all feeling in her hand from her wrist down, even though this contradicts what is known about nerve pathways in the body (Figure 14.4). People suffering from conversion symptoms frequently display an attitude known as *la belle indifference,* (literally "the beautiful indifference"), meaning that they do not seem to be particularly bothered by their strange symptoms.

Trailblazer Joseph Breuer's famous patient, Anna O., was actually named Bertha Pappenheim. In later years, Ms. Pappenheim became a staunch advocate for women's rights.

Somatization Disorder

Somatization disorder differs from conversion disorder in that it involves a collection of physical complaints occurring over an extended period of time (see Table 14.6), while conversion disorder tends to focus on a specific functional deficit (for example, loss of feeling in one's arm) that occurs in the wake of a psychological conflict or stressor. Sufferers of somatization disorder often make repeated visits to

Somatization disorder Recurrent pain, gastrointestinal, sexual, and pseudoneurological symptoms without a physiological cause.

Figure 14.4 Glove Anesthesia Conversion anesthesias (loss of feeling) can often be detected when an area of numbness does not correspond to known neural pathways. Normal neural innervation pathways are shown in the hand on the left; the shaded area, indicating loss of feeling in the hand on the right, shows a medically impossible conversion symptom known as "glove anesthesia."

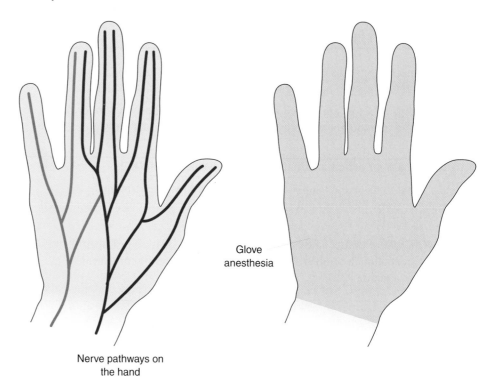

Glove anesthesia

Nerve pathways on the hand

Table 14.6	Diagnostic Criteria for Somatization Disorder

Adapted from the DSM-IV-TR (APA, 2000)	• A history of physical complaints beginning before age 30 that occur over the course of several years and result in treatment being sought or significant impairment in social, occupational, or other important areas of functioning.
	
	 • Each of the following criteria must be met, with individual symptoms occurring at any time in the history of physical complaints:
	    • Four pain symptoms: pain related to at least four different sites or functions (head, abdomen, back, etc.).
	    • Two gastrointestinal symptoms other than pain: such as nausea, bloating, vomiting, etc.
	    • One sexual symptom other than pain: such as sexual indifference, erectile dysfunction, etc.
	    • One pseudoneurological symptom other than pain: impaired coordination or balance, paralysis or localized weakness, etc.
	
	 • Either of the following:
	    • Physical symptoms cannot be explained by a general medical condition or the direct effects of a substance.
	    • If there is a general medical condition, the physical complaints or resulting functional impairment cannot be fully explained by the medical condition.
	
	 • The symptoms are not intentionally produced or faked.

physicians to complain of physical symptoms which turn out to have no physiological basis. Health care utilization studies find that people with somatization disorder are three times more likely to use walk-in services and spend *nine times* more money on health care services than people without the disorder (Hollifield et al., 1999). People with somatization disorder often describe their medical complaints in an exaggerated, dramatic manner that lacks concrete details, and may seek treatment from several different doctors simultaneously, thus making the diagnosis of somatization difficult (APA, 2000).

> **Case Illustration** **Donna, a 25-year-old department store clerk, was asked to report to her company's human resources office to discuss her unusually high number of absences due to illness. In her meeting with the personnel director Donna explained that she had been experiencing headaches, nausea, an aching sensation in her arms, and dizziness for the last several years. She missed work often because her visits to several primary care physicians had failed to find a medical explanation for her problems. As a result, she had been sent from one subspecialist to the next and undergone multiple medical tests to see if a diagnosis could be determined. While Donna seemed to be quite distressed about her physical discomfort (she cried when describing her symptoms), she seemed to be quite indifferent to the personnel director's hopefulness that she would find a diagnosis and proper treatment soon. After the meeting, the personnel director placed a call to Donna's boss at the last place she was employed before coming to the department store. He was disheartened, but not surprised, to learn that she had been fired from that job for excessive absenteeism due to vague medical complaints, related to her menstrual cycle, that could not be diagnosed or treated.**

Like most people suffering from somatization disorder Donna complains of diffuse medical symptoms that are not related to each other, or to an actual medical condition. Her symptoms have been present for several years, and include pain (headaches, arms), gastrointestinal (nausea), pseudoneurological (dizziness), and sexual (menstrual) complaints. This pattern of multiple and chronic medical complaints that defy explanation was called *Briquet's syndrome* in the first two editions of the DSM (APA 1952, 1968) in honor of the French physician Pierre Briquet who published a description of a young woman with diffuse somatization complaints in 1859 (Holder-Perkins & Wise, 2001).

Pain Disorder

Somatization and **pain disorder** have much in common, but pain disorder is characterized specifically by complaints of *physical pain* that cannot be accounted for, or accounted for fully, by a medical condition (see Table 14.7).

Pain disorder Physical pain without a physiological cause.

> **Case Illustration** **Steven, age 44, has complained of neck pain for years. Despite extensive medical evaluations, no doctor has been able to come up with an explanation or treatment for Steven's discomfort. At times, Steven's pain is so severe that he cannot drive, go to work, or even get out of bed. His family members have noticed that Steven's neck pain came on shortly after he was divorced by his wife, and that it seems to be worse when he sees her at family events involving their children.**

People suffering from pain disorders may experience physical pain that is severe enough to interfere with their ability to work or maintain relationships. They may spend a great deal of time seeking medical care, may rely heavily on analgesic (pain-killing) medications, and may become preoccupied with their pain to the exclusion of most other things (APA, 2000).

Table 14.7	Diagnostic Criteria for Pain Disorder

Adapted from the DSM-IV-TR (APA, 2000)	• Pain in one or more anatomical sites is the major focus of complaint and is sufficiently severe to warrant clinical attention.
	
	• The pain causes clinically significant distress or impairment in social, occupational, or other important areas of functioning.
	
	• Psychological factors are judged to have an important role in the onset, severity, exacerbation, or maintenance of the pain.
	
	• The symptoms are not intentionally produced or faked.
	
	• Subtypes of pain disorder:
	  • Pain disorder associated with psychological factors.
	  • Pain disorder associated with both psychological factors and a general medical condition.

Hypochondriasis

Hypochondriasis Preoccupation with the fear of contracting, or the mistaken idea that one has, a serious disease.

Hypochondriasis could be characterized as the tendency to make medical mountains out of benign molehills. People with hypochondriasis constantly worry that there is something terribly wrong with their bodies and often interpret the most minor symptom to be a sign of serious disease. They worry that an occasional cough is actually tuberculosis, that a stomachache heralds a severe bout of severe food poisoning, and that a garden-variety pimple is actually a tumor. Hypochondriacal concerns may also focus on normal bodily processes and cause sufferers to seek medical care for having a quick heartbeat after exercising, for the appearance of freckles, and so on (see Table 14.8).

> **Case Illustration** Leslie, age 18, has missed most of her classes this semester. Though she is quite healthy, she is constantly worried that she might have some horrible disease. As a result, she often stays in bed in her dormitory room or goes to the doctor's office rather than going to class. On a recent morning, she woke up feeling a bit dizzy. She was afraid that the dizziness was due to viral meningitis and took herself to the emergency room. The physicians at the hospital agreed to test her for meningitis, but the

Table 14.8	Diagnostic Criteria for Hypochondriasis
Adapted from the DSM-IV-TR (APA, 2000)	• Preoccupation with fears of having, or the idea that one has, a serious disease based on the person's misinterpretation of bodily symptoms. • The preoccupation persists despite appropriate medical evaluation and reassurance. • The belief in having a serious disease is not of delusional intensity and is not limited to a circumscribed concern about appearance (a body dysmorphic disorder, described on page 513). • The preoccupation causes clinically significant distress or impairment in social, occupational, or other important areas of functioning. • The duration of the disturbance is at least 6 months.

tests came back negative. At that point she insisted that she be given a computerized axial tomography (CAT) scan to rule out a brain tumor. Rather than give her an unwarranted CAT scan, the physician referred her to the school's counseling services for a psychological evaluation.

Despite frequent medical visits, hypochondriacs are rarely reassured that their bodies and their health are normal. They are known for going from doctor to doctor for medical advice, or for wearing out and frustrating their regular physicians with a constant stream of medical worries (APA, 2000). Personal and family relationships may be focused almost exclusively on the hypochondriac's medical concerns and conditions, and work or school may suffer due to excessive absences for unnecessary medical appointments or "sick days" for minor physical ailments.

Body Dysmorphic Disorder

A person suffering from **body dysmorphic disorder** is convinced that there is something horribly wrong with his or her physical appearance even though a defect is rarely present, or, if one does exist, it is not nearly as severe or unusual as believed to be. Concerns are often focused on anomalies of the head and face, such as "hair thinning, acne, wrinkles, scars, vascular markings, paleness or redness of the complexion, swelling, facial symmetry or disproportion, or excessive facial hair" (APA, 2000, p. 507). The symptoms of body dysmorphic disorder highlight the *continuum between normal and abnormal behavior*. Though most of us can point to something about our physical appearance that we wish were different, people suffering from body dysmorphic disorder become utterly preoccupied with their imagined defect and may come to organize their lives around altering or hiding a part, or several parts of their bodies (see Table 14.9).

Body dysmorphic disorder Preoccupation with an imagined or exaggerated defect in physical appearance.

Case Illustration Marjorie, age 30, is convinced that she has (in her words) "hideously shaped, ugly breasts," despite the reassurance of her husband and doctor that her breasts are normal. For many years she insisted on wearing bulky sweaters all year round in order to hide her breasts. She also tried out a wide variety of bras and prosthetic breasts, but was never satisfied with the outcome. Eventually, she decided to get plastic surgery to change the shape of her breasts, but she was not pleased with the results and continued to feel terribly self-conscious.

Some people with body dysmorphic disorder become profoundly socially isolated because they do not want others to observe what they believe to be wrong with their bodies. Others, like Marjorie (described above) or the singer Michael Jackson, may undergo multiple surgeries in an effort to "fix" something that was never broken in the first place. The constant preoccupation with having an abnormal (or "hideous" or "disgusting") body part may become so severe as to interfere with an individual's ability to work or attend school, and may result in depression and/or suicidal behavior (APA, 2000).

Diagnostic Criteria for Body Dysmorphic Disorder	Table 14.9

Adapted from the DSM-IV-TR (APA, 2000)

- Preoccupation with an imagined defect in appearance. If a slight physical anomaly is present, the person's concern is markedly excessive.
- The preoccupation causes clinically significant distress or impairment in social, occupational, or other important areas of functioning.

Dramatic change Michael Jackson in 1972, and 30 years later in 2002, after numerous plastic surgeries to alter his appearance.

Brief Summary

- The somatoform disorders are characterized by the presence of physical symptoms that are not explained by a medical disorder.

- Factitious disorders are similar to somatoform disorders in that bodily symptoms are the focus of concern. However, unlike the somatoform disorders, factitious disorders are intentionally produced, or faked, because the person wants to be perceived as sick.

- The DSM-IV-TR includes five different somatoform disorders: conversion disorder, somatization disorder, pain disorder, hypochondriasis, and body dysmorphic disorder. These disorders have two important features in common: a focus on bodily complaints that have no physical basis, and symptoms that are not being intentionally produced or faked.

- Conversion disorder is characterized by specific symptoms or deficits in voluntary motor or sensory functions with no physiological cause.

- Somatization disorder involves recurrent gastrointestinal, sexual, or pseudoneurological symptoms without a physiological cause.

- Pain disorder involves the experience of physical pain without a physiological cause.

- Hypochondriasis is defined as a preoccupation with the fear of contracting, or the mistaken idea that one has, a serious disease.

- Body dysmorphic disorder involves a preoccupation with an imagined or exaggerated defect in physical appearance.

Critical Thinking Question | **Do you think that plastic surgeons should encourage patients like Marjorie (described in this section) to seek psychotherapy instead of plastic surgery?**

The Advantages and Limitations of the DSM-IV-TR Somatoform Diagnoses

The DSM-IV-TR classification of somatoform disorders has both ***advantages and limitations***. The somatoform disorders category has the advantage of separating out, on the basis of the primary symptom of physical complaints, disorders that were previously lumped together with other categories, such as the dissociative disorders (Chapter 7). Yet, despite the fact that, as a group, the somatoform disorders are characterized by a focus on bodily concerns, they do not necessarily have similar causes or psychological mechanisms. In fact, some of the somatoform disorders may share more descriptive and causal features with disorders in other DSM-IV-TR diagnostic categories than they do with each other.

For example, conversion disorder can have a great deal in common with some of the dissociative disorders when conversion disorder involves symptoms of alterations in consciousness and sensory disruptions (as in the case of Anna O.) (Oakley, 1999). Further, some cases of hypochondriasis and most cases of body dysmorphic disorder share common features with obsessive-compulsive disorder (OCD), the anxiety disorder described in Chapter 5. Like OCD, body dysmorphic disorder and hypochondriasis are often characterized by intense preoccupations ("my nose is disgusting" or "this spot on my hand is cancerous") and repetitive behaviors designed to reduce the anxiety brought on by the thoughts. In body dysmorphic disorder and hypochondriasis, the behaviors may take the form of repeatedly checking one's face in the mirror or constantly seeking medical evaluation and advice (Phillips, 2001). Body dysmorphic disorder may also share a common boundary with anorexia, an eating disorder described in Chapter 8. Like body dysmorphic disorder, anorexia involves significant perceptual distortions with regard to one's body—believing one's body to be fat when it is in fact emaciated—and intense concerns about monitoring and regulating one's weight and shape.

Cultural and Historical Relativism in Defining and Classifying Somatoform Disorders

While somatization symptoms are observed around the world, the different forms of somatization symptoms highlight the role of ***cultural and historical relativism*** in abnormality. For example, many experts agree that the disorder previously known as hysteria hasn't disappeared, but merely changed forms as Western culture has evolved over time (see Box 3.2 Modern Hysteria: New Forms for an Old Disorder?). In the words of one expert:

> It is safe to conclude that while classic conversion symptoms of motor paralysis and sensory loss are seen more commonly in clinics in many developing countries, they have diminished in westernized health care settings. However, if disorders of pain, fatigue, dizziness, or vague malaise are understood as equivalent, then conversion disorders have not so much disappeared as changed shape to fit common health beliefs and expectations in the health care system.

Kirmayer & Santhanam, 2001 (p. 256)

Further, different cultures seem to promote different physical pathways for expressing psychological distress. For example, in regions of India, Sri Lanka, and China, men sometimes complain of *dhat* (DOT), a syndrome characterized by intense anxiety, hypochondriacal concerns about loss of semen, and feelings of physical exhaustion. In Korea, pent-up rage is believed to cause *hwa-byung* (WA-bung), which results in a wide variety of physical symptoms including fatigue, indigestion, and palpitations,

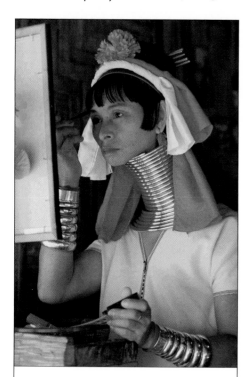

Cultural relativism Women in the Padaung tribes of Thailand use metal rings to gradually elongate their necks to startling lengths. This practice reflects the degree to which physical concerns and preoccupations can be highly culturally relative. While an elongated neck is not considered to be a sign of beauty in our culture, other physical features such as shapely breasts or flawless skin are valued in Western society. Not surprisingly, these features are often the focus of body dysmorphic concerns among Americans.

aches and pains. *Koro* (CORE-oh), a syndrome reported in south and east Asia, involves an intense fear that one's penis (or, in women, vulva and nipples) will withdraw into the body, possibly causing death. And Portugese Cape Verde Islanders sometimes complain of *sangue dormido* or "sleeping blood" (SAHN-greh dor-ME-doh) a syndrome that causes numbness, tremor, paralysis, blindness, and other physical symptoms (APA, 2000).

In contrast, body dysmorphic disorder seems to have virtually identical features regardless of the culture in which it occurs. Karen Phillips, a psychiatrist who specializes in body dysmorphic disorder, observes that case studies from Eastern and Western Europe, Russia, Japan—and even reports from 100 years ago—have the same characteristics of recently diagnosed cases in the United States (Phillips, 1996).

Critical Thinking Question	**W**hy might body dysmorphic disorder appear in a similar form across cultures while somatization disorder appears to be significantly shaped by its cultural context?

Classification in Demographic Context

Like all mental disorders, the somatoform disorders are best understood when demographic factors are taken into account. Factors such as gender, age, and class influence both the prevalence and characteristics of the various somatoform disorders.

Gender

Conversion symptoms occur disproportionately in women, with studies finding that American women are between two and ten times more likely to be diagnosed with conversion disorders as men (APA, 2000). Explanations for the different rates of conversion symptoms in men and women have ranged from the ancient Greek idea that hysteria was caused by a wandering uterus (Chapter 3) to the contemporary finding that women are more likely than men to *internalize* emotional distress, possibly leading to conversion symptoms, while men tend to *externalize* (or act out) emotional distress. (Women also experience higher rates of depression and anxiety than men, while men are far more likely to engage in antisocial behavior or abuse substances.) Men who are diagnosed with conversion disorder often have many of the personality characteristics associated with antisocial personality disorder (Chapter 11) such as being irresponsible, deceitful, and having little remorse when it comes to violating the rights of others. Conversion disorders in antisocial men often take the form of physical disabilities that prevent them from working or engaging in military service.

Both hypochodriasis and body dysmorphic disorder occur with roughly equal frequency in men and women. However, women suffering from body dysmorphic disorder are likely to focus their concerns on their hips and weight, use makeup to hide their "flaws," and to also suffer from bulimia nervosa (Chapter 8). Men with this disorder tend to be preoccupied with concerns about their body build, genitalia, or thinning hair, to be unmarried, and to have problems with alcohol abuse or dependence (Phillips & Diaz, 1997). Rates of somatization disorder are more equal between men and women in Greece and Puerto Rico than in the United States (where the disorder is somewhat more likely to occur in women), indicating that cultural factors may influence the degree to which men express emotional distress through physical symptoms (APA, 2000).

Age

Occasional somatization symptoms, such as the common nervous stomach before the first day of school, are often seen in children. However, full-fledged somatoform disorders usually begin during adolescence or early adulthood. First episodes of conversion disorder are rarely diagnosed before age 10 or after age 35, while hypochondriasis typically begins in early adulthood and often persists as a chronic condition throughout an individual's lifetime. Body dysmorphic disorder usually begins in adolescence, but proper diagnosis may be delayed because many parents and doctors are prone to consider even extreme bodily concerns to be examples of "typical teenage behavior" (APA, 2000).

Class

Epidemiological studies have found that somatization disorder and hypochondriasis are more likely to occur among members of lower socioeconomic classes, especially those who have little formal education and are unemployed (Wool & Barsky, 1994; Kirmayer & Looper, 2001). Conversion disorder has also been found to occur more frequently among members of rural populations, people of lower socioeconomic status, and those less fluent in medical and psychological concepts (APA, 2000). Interestingly, a 15-year follow-up study of prevalence rates for conversion disorder and depression in two rural Indian villages found that improvement in housing, educational facilities, health care deliver and the social status of women led to a dramatic drop in the rate of conversion disorder from 16.9 to 4.6 per 1,000 (Nandi et al., 1992). However, rates of depression rose significantly over the same time period—from 37.7 to 53.3 per 1,000.

Brief Summary

- Some somatoform disorders share features with disorders in other DSM-IV-TR diagnostic categories (such as dissociative, anxiety, or eating disorders) highlighting the *advantages and limitations* of the DSM-IV-TR somatoform disorder diagnoses.

- While somatization symptoms are observed around the world, the form taken by somatization symptoms often appears to be dictated by cultural or historical factors highlighting the role of *cultural and historical relativism* in abnormality.

- Conversion symptoms occur disproportionately in women in the United States, with studies finding that they are between two and ten times more likely than men to be diagnosed with conversion disorders. Both hypochodriasis and body dysmorphic disorder occur with roughly equal frequency among men and women.

- Though occasional somatization symptoms are often seen in children, diagnosable somatoform disorders usually begin during late adolescence or early adulthood.

- Somatization disorder and hypochondriasis are more likely to occur among members of lower socioeconomic classes, especially those who are not well educated and unemployed.

- Conversion disorder has also been found to occur more frequently among members of rural populations, people of lower socioeconomic status, and those less fluent in medical and psychological concepts.

Critical Thinking Question | **W**hy might complaints of depression take the place of conversion symptoms when groups gain in economic and social status?

EXPLAINING AND TREATING THE SOMATOFORM DISORDERS

Several theoretical perspectives have developed explanations and interventions for the somatoform disorders. For historical purposes we'll begin with the psychodynamic perspective which has its roots in treatments for conversion symptoms. As you read about interventions for somatoform disorders, keep in mind the delicate task of encouraging a person to seek psychological help for physical complaints. Consider the advice of one expert in the treatment of somatoform disorders:

> The first step in treating conversion disorder involves reassuring the patient that the symptoms are not the result of a medical or neurological condition, but are secondary to an underlying psychological conflict. However, it is wise to present this information to patients and their families in a manner that does not imply that the patients have been faking their symptoms, or that their symptoms do not have a physical component. Rather, an approach that conveys that there are physical and psychological aspects of the illness that can best be addressed by a rehabilitation approach invites the patient to engage in treatment without feeling humiliated.
>
> Maldonado & Spiegel, 2001 (pp. 117–118)

Psychodynamic Components

As you know, the modern history of abnormal psychology began with Sigmund Freud and Josef Breuer's work with conversion disorder, then known as *hysteria* (Breuer & Freud, 1893/1955). In his treatment of Anna O., Breuer discovered that each of her physical complaints, such as her coughing spells, was rooted in an emotional conflict. Breuer noted that "she began coughing for the first time when once, as she was sitting at her [dying] father's bedside, she heard the sound of dance music coming from a neighbouring house, felt a sudden wish to be there, and was overcome with self-reproaches" (Breuer & Freud, 1893/1955, p. 40). Freud and Breuer coined the term "hysterical conversion" to describe the conversion of uncomfortable emotions into physical symptoms. Later, Freud postulated that conversion symptoms typically arose from emotional conflicts over sexual feelings, wishes, or impulses. Modern psychodynamic theorists emphasize that conversion symptoms can result from the repression of any feeling that a person considers "forbidden" or intolerable, whether it is anger, jealousy, sadness, or sexual excitement.

The psychodynamic approach assumes that conversion symptoms often symbolically represent some aspect of a repressed wish or feeling. For example, a boy repressing "forbidden" wishes to scream in rage at his sickly younger brother might lose his voice; a person who has witnessed something horrible or shocking might temporarily lose her eyesight. Psychodynamic clinicians have also noted that conversion symptoms can be particularly tenacious because they confer some advantages on their sufferers (McWilliams, 1994). The symptoms effect a **primary gain** by temporarily resolving the emotional conflict (you can't yell at your brother if you can't speak at all) and a **secondary gain** because they often bring desired attention and concern from others.

Psychodynamic explanations of somatization disorder, pain disorder, hypochondriasis, and body dysmorphic disorder are similar to psychodynamic explanations of conversion symptoms. In all of these disorders, physical distress is seen as an indirect expression of and metaphor for unconscious emotional distress. Clients who complain of imagined or exaggerated physical symptoms (as in somatization and pain disorder),

Primary gain In psychodynamic terms, the relief of anxiety that occurs when an emotional conflict is converted into a physical symptom.

Secondary gain In psychodynamic terms, the desired attention and concern from others that results from the "sick" role.

or who worry excessively about health (as in hypochondriasis) are indirectly saying "I am in (psychological) pain and I need help." Similarly, clients with body dysmorphic disorder may be expressing the idea "something (psychological) is not right with me, I need to be altered or repaired" (Phillips, 2001). Accordingly, when working with clients with somatoform symptoms, psychodynamic clinicians ask themselves two questions: what is the nature of this client's *emotional* distress and why is this psychological distress being expressed as a bodily symptom?

Psychodynamic Interventions

As noted, engaging a person in a psychotherapy for a somatoform disorder can be difficult. Initially, what the client sees as the problem (physical pain) and what the clinician sees as the problem (underlying emotional distress) may be quite different. Given this possible discrepancy in goals, psychodynamic clinicians emphasize the importance of "meeting the client where he/she is" in order to develop a therapeutic alliance. For example, a therapist might begin with a focus on the client's physical concerns and only address deeper issues over time. By developing a therapeutic alliance, the clinician lays the groundwork for investigating—through free associations, reflections, memories, dreams, and transferences—the unconscious thoughts and feelings that might be responsible for the presenting somatic symptoms. When working with clients suffering from somatoform disorders, clinicians employing psychodynamic techniques are especially watchful for the workings of defense mechanisms such as **repression**, the motivated forgetting of upsetting events or experiences that might contribute to the conversion of emotional distress into physical distress, and **regression**, the tendency to return to more dependent, childlike functioning (McWilliams, 1994). The clinician would aim to help his or her client understand the connection between conflicted emotions, the use of repression, regression and other defense mechanisms, and the development or exaggeration of somatic symptoms. Psychodynamic interventions have been found to be effective treatments for some somatic symptoms (Moran et al., 1991); these techniques appear to be most helpful for people who are also experiencing psychological distress, such as anxiety or depression (Guthrie, 1995).

Cognitive-Behavioral Components

Cognitive-behavioral theorists generally agree with the psychodynamic view that conversion, somatization, and pain disorder result when emotional distress finds expression in physical symptoms, but they emphasize specific behavioral and cognitive processes by which somatic symptoms are developed and maintained. For example, behavioral principles such as **modeling** or *social learning* and **reinforcement** play a role in the development of somatic symptoms. Children whose parents express their emotional pain in a physical form may follow in their parents' footsteps, and parents may reinforce their children's somatic expressions of distress by being warm and caring about physical symptoms and making fewer demands on children who are not feeling well (Bonner & Finney, 1996). Empirical evidence strongly supports the modeling hypothesis, but it is less robust for reinforcement theories of somatization (Garralda, 2000; Lipowski, 1987).

Cognitive explanations of hypochondriasis emphasize two cognitive processes: the **amplification** and **catastrophizing** of physical symptoms (Botella & Narvaez, 1998). In symptom amplification, hypochondriacs pay extremely close attention to their bodies and bodily sensations and experience even minor physical sensations as intense. Once physical sensations are perceived, hypochondriacs interpret the symptoms in catastrophic terms. Consider the following example: two college students, John and Harry, stand up quickly after sitting through a long lecture. Each experiences

Repression A defense mechanism consisting of the forgetting of painful or unacceptable mental content.

Regression A defense mechanism that involves a return to childlike behavior in order to avoid anxieties associated with progressive development.

Modeling Learning based on observing and imitating the behavior of others; see also: **social/observational learning.**

Reinforcement In operant conditioning theory, an environmental response to a behavior that increases the probability that the behavior will be repeated.

Amplification The anxious magnification of minor physical sensations, such as in people with hypochondriasis.

Catastrophizing Cognitive distortion involving the tendency to view minor problems as major catastrophes.

Pass the aspirin Children whose parents express emotional distress through physical symptoms may quickly learn to do the same.

a brief "head rush" as his blood pressure adjusts to the change in bodily position. John notices the head rush but knows that it comes from standing quickly after sitting so long and gives it little thought. Harry also notices the head rush, but he focuses on it to the point of becoming a little dizzy (symptom amplification) and then begins to worry "What's wrong with me!? Why am I feeling dizzy!? Maybe I have a brain tumor!" (catastrophic interpretation). Symptom amplification and catastrophic interpretations usually cause intense anxiety that may lead to withdrawal from regular activities and/or seeking medical care. If suspending normal activities or seeing a physician helps someone with hypochondriasis feel better, the accompanying anxiety reduction may also reinforce the withdrawal and help-seeking behaviors (Warwick & Salkovskis, 1990).

Body dysmorphic disorder involves a chain of similar cognitive distortions that begins with the belief that one has a significant physical defect. From there, people with body dysmorphic disorder go on to amplify and catastrophize: "I look defective, other people notice and are interested in my defect, they view me as unattractive (ugly, deformed, deviant, etc.) and evaluate me negatively as a person, and consequently my appearance proves something negative about my character and worth to other people" (Rosen, 1998, p. 366). Not surprisingly, these cognitive distortions leave people with body dysmorphic disorder feeling depressed and anxious and lead to behaviors such as mirror checking, seeking reassurance from others, and undergoing cosmetic surgery.

Cognitive-Behavioral Interventions

Cognitive interventions often focus on providing rational reasons for clients to consider addressing their physical symptoms differently than they have in the past. For example, a therapist working with a client whose conversion symptom involves difficulty using his legs might explain the following:

> So, even though it is understandable that you rest when you feel weak and that it probably feels impossible to move your legs, immobility in the long term can only result in one thing...more weakness and loss of muscle bulk and fitness. In fact, did you know that bed rest results in a 3 per cent reduction in muscle bulk per day? So, in the long term, inactivity and lack of exercise will contribute to you remaining disabled.
>
> Chalder, 2001 (p. 306)

Cognitive-behavioral interventions often involve a variety of specific behavioral prescriptions to reduce the reinforcement of somatization or conversion symptoms and to provide alternative coping mechanisms. Clients may be encouraged to engage in a variety of physical activities that had been avoided in the past and discouraged from seeking reassurance from others about their physical complaints. They may also be urged to seek assertiveness training or anger management instruction so that the emotional distress communicated by their physical symptoms can find a more adaptive route for expression (Chalder, 2001). **Exposure and response prevention** treatments have been found to be particularly effective for people suffering from body dysmorphic disorder (McKay, 1999). For example, a client who believes that her facial freckles make her look "diseased" could be exposed to an anxiety-provoking situation, such as sitting in a crowded place without wearing heavy cover-up makeup, and prevented from executing her typical responses, such as applying makeup, checking herself in the mirror, or hiding her face. The goal of this technique would be to break the connection between her anxiety and her maladaptive behavioral response, while teaching a more adaptive way of dealing with her irrational anxiety.

Exposure and response prevention A behavioral intervention in which clients are encouraged to confront a frightening thought or situation and then prevented from engaging in anxiety-reducing behaviors.

Cognitive restructuring, which identifies, evaluates, and changes harmful negative thoughts, is widely used in treating all of the somatoform disorders. Clients are encouraged to write down concerns about their bodies as they occur ("If I use my arm today, it will be unbearably painful again tomorrow," or "My sore throat may be a sign of cancer") and to evaluate them objectively (see Figure 14.5). Special consideration is given to alternative (and nonpathological) explanations for their physical symptoms and sensations.

Cognitive restructuring techniques can be especially helpful for clients suffering from body dysmorphic disorder (Rosen, 1998). Clinicians focus on the distorted negative thoughts and assumptions that cause physical idiosyncrasies to feel like major defects. For example, a clinician might acknowledge a client's perception that his nose is large ("Yes, I can see that your nose has a different shape than most people's") but challenge the client's belief that strangers are disgusted by his "hideous" nose and consequently judge him to be a worthless person. This technique not only encourages the client to evaluate the evidence for his beliefs about how people react to his appearance but also enables the clinician to model an attitude of acceptance and tolerance of physical differences. Cognitive therapists may also encourage clients with body dys-

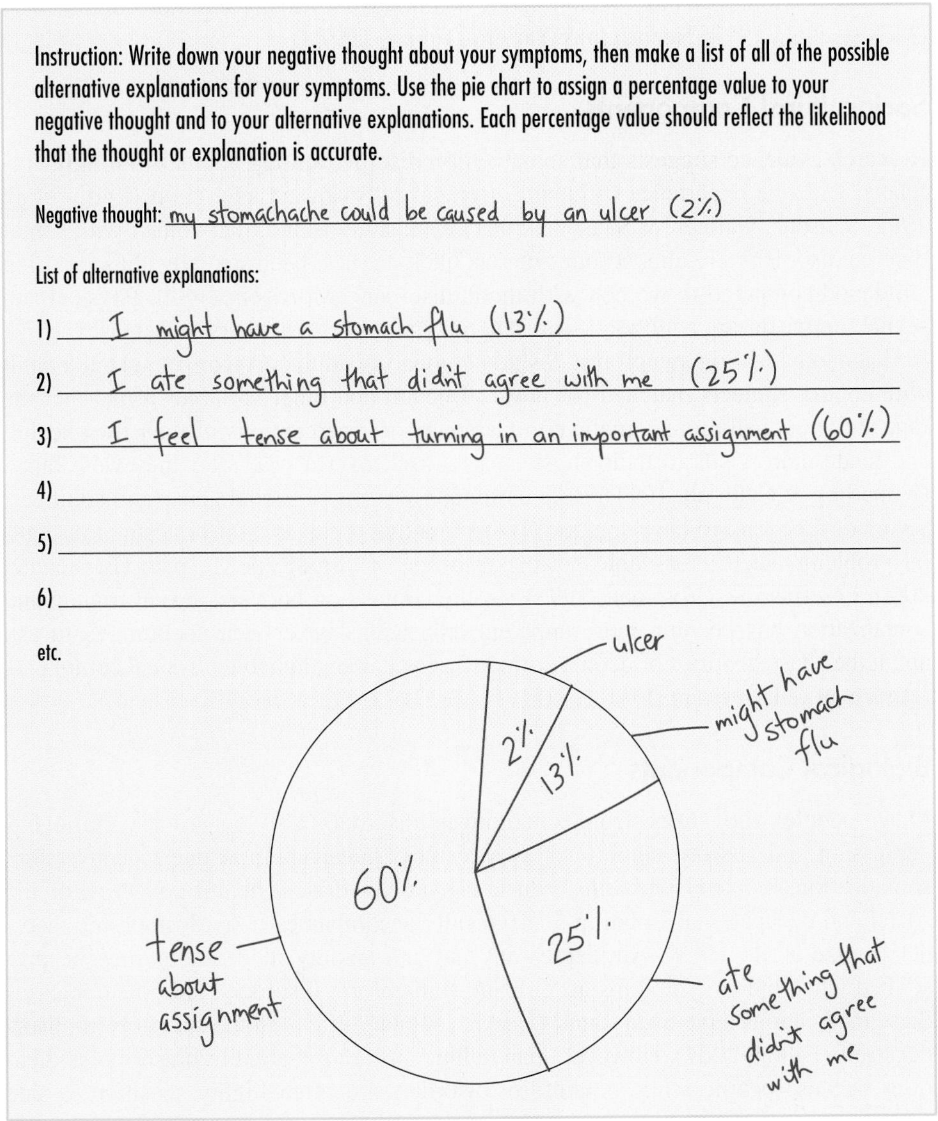

Cognitive restructuring Therapy techniques that focus on changing irrational and problematic thoughts.

Instruction: Write down your negative thought about your symptoms, then make a list of all of the possible alternative explanations for your symptoms. Use the pie chart to assign a percentage value to your negative thought and to your alternative explanations. Each percentage value should reflect the likelihood that the thought or explanation is accurate.

Negative thought: my stomachache could be caused by an ulcer (2%)

List of alternative explanations:

1) I might have a stomach flu (13%)

2) I ate something that didn't agree with me (25%)

3) I feel tense about turning in an important assignment (60%)

4) _____

5) _____

6) _____

etc.

Figure 14.5 Cognitive Behavioral Intervention for Somatoform Disorders Worksheets like this one can be used to help people suffering from somatoform disorders to take a more rational, objective, and adaptive view of their physical symptoms.

Adapted from Botella & Narvaes, 1998, p. 359.

morphic disorder to use a self-monitoring diary in which they record their experiences in an A-B-C-D-E format (after Rosen, 1998):

Activating events—the situation or event that activated body concerns:
> "The waitress at the coffee shop looked at me in a strange way."

Beliefs—your thoughts about yourself, your situation, or your body:
> "I'm deformed—she sees it."

Consequences—how you feel or what you do as a result of your beliefs:
> "I feel mortified and leave the coffee shop without getting my drink."

Disputing thoughts—alternative beliefs that could explain activating event:
> "The waitress was tired or was having a bad day."

Effects of corrective thinking—describe benefits of alternative beliefs:
> "Tomorrow I'll go back to the coffee shop and see if she is friendly to me when I am friendly to her."

In general, cognitive-behavioral interventions, especially those that focus on developing a therapeutic alliance as a basis for helping clients evaluate their reactions to physical symptoms, have been found to be effective for many somatoform disorders (McKay et al., 1997; Neziroglu & Yaryura-Tobias, 1997).

Sociocultural Components

Research evidence suggests that somatization disorder among adults is strongly correlated with the experience of having been sexually abused as a child (Reilly et al, 1999; Sansone, Gaither, & Sansone, 2001). One study found that women with somatization disorder were almost four times as likely to have been sexually abused during childhood compared to women with mood disorders (Morrison, 1989). Physical and sexual trauma during adulthood—most notably rape—also appears to increase the risk for later somatization symptoms. A study comparing adult survivors of sexual assault with control subjects matched for physical health and other variables found that the rape survivors had more somatic complaints, poorer perceptions of their own health, and made more visits to their physicians for well over a year after they were raped (Kimerling & Calhoun, 1994). Both childhood victims of sexual abuse and adult survivors of rape tend to have somatic complaints that focus on gastrointestinal or genital problems, such as irritable bowel syndrome or chronic pelvic pain (Berkowitz, 2000; Leserman & Drossman, 1995). As the connection between sexual trauma and somatization has become more apparent, physicians have been encouraged to ask about the abuse histories of people with diffuse and unexplainable physical complaints (Leserman & Drossman, 1995).

Biological Components

Comorbidity The presence of two or more disorders in one person, or a general association between two or more different disorders.

Many people who suffer from somatoform disorders also experience **comorbid** depression and anxiety, sometimes as a result of incapacitation due to conversion, somatization, or pain symptoms, constant hypochondriacal health concerns, or the social and occupational isolation that typically accompanies body dysmorphic disorder (Lenze et al., 1999). Antidepressant and anti-anxiety medications may be prescribed when mood symptoms accompany somatoform disorders, and in some cases these medications have been found to have a salutary effect on the somatoform disorder itself (Fallon, 2001). However, many clinicians are reluctant to prescribe medications because people with somatoform disorders are often highly sensitive to side effects, are at risk for abusing medications, and may already be taking several medications simultaneously (Holder-Perkins & Wise, 2001). Medications are more commonly used to treat body dysmorphic disorder and some extreme cases of hypochondriasis that, as noted previously, share a common diagnostic boundary with obsessive-compulsive disorder. For example, elective serotonin reuptake inhibitors (SSRIs) can be an effective treatment for the preoccupations found in body dysmorphic disorder and hypochondriasis (Phillips, 2000).

The Connection Between Mind and Body in Somatoform Disorders

By their very nature, the somatoform disorders profoundly illustrate the *conection between mind and body.* The relationship between somatoform disorders and hypnosis further amplifies this connection. Some experts in the area of conversion disorders have noted that a person suffering from leg paralysis due to conversion disorder has a great deal in common with a person who has been hypnotized and told that her legs are paralyzed (Oakley, 1999). Each feels that her legs are genuinely paralyzed, each seems to have lost voluntary control over her legs, and yet neither person actually has anything physically wrong with her legs. Indeed, research suggests that there may be some similarities in the neurological bases of hypnosis and conversion disorder. Both hypnosis and conversion symptoms appear to involve the activation of the anterior frontal cortex, a part of the brain that regulates attention and can coordinate or inhibit the functioning of other cortical systems, such as the motor cortex which regulates physical movement (Crawford, Knebel, & Vendemia, 1998; Tiihonen et al., 1995). With these similarities in mind, some clinicians have suggested viewing conversion disorder as an **autosuggestive disorder**, meaning that people with conversion symptoms have essentially hypnotized themselves into believing that they have lost some form of physical functioning (Oakley, 1999). While the autosuggestive theory may explain part of the mechanism for conversion disorders, it still leaves room for psychodynamic, cognitive, and behavioral perspectives on what might *motivate* a person to inhibit a physical function in the first place.

Autosuggestive disorder Disorder in which individuals convince themselves, through a process akin to self-hypnosis, that they have lost some form of physical functioning.

Interestingly, Sigmund Freud and Josef Breuer's first treatments for patients with hysteria involved using hypnosis to treat conversion symptoms. Breuer triumphantly describes how he used hypnotic suggestion to cure Anna O.:

> …the hysterical phenomena disappeared as soon as the event which had given rise to them was reproduced in her hypnosis…Each individual symptom in this complicated case was taken separately in hand; all the occasions on which it had appeared were described in reverse order, starting before the time when the patient became bed-ridden and going back to the event which had led to its first appearance. When this had been described the symptom was permanently removed.
>
> From *Studies in Hysteria,* 1893/1955 (p. 35)

Freud ultimately abandoned hypnosis as a therapeutic technique because he felt he was not skilled at it and because he came to doubt its long-term effectiveness. However, hypnosis is still used by some contemporary clinicians to treat conversion symptoms (Davies & Wagstaff, 1991; Moene, Hoogduin, & van Dyck, 1998).

Brief Summary

- Psychodynamic theorists emphasize that conversion symptoms can result from the repression of feelings that a person considers "forbidden" or intolerable. Psychodynamic interventions emphasize addressing defense mechanisms such as *repression,* the motivated forgetting of upsetting events or experiences and *regression,* the tendency to return to more dependent, childlike functioning.

- Behavioral principles such as modeling (or social learning) and reinforcement explain how children may develop behaviors associated with somatoform disorders. Cognitive approaches to somatoform disorders such as hypochondriasis emphasize two cognitive processes: the amplification of symptoms (experiencing even minor physical symptoms as intense), and the catastrophic interpretation of physical symptoms (minor physical symptoms are believed to herald dire consequences).

- Exposure and response prevention techniques have been found to be particularly effective for people suffering from body dysmorphic disorder. Cognitive restructuring is also a widely used intervention in the treatment of the somatoform disorders.

- Somatization disorder among adults appears to be strongly correlated with the experience of having been sexually abused as a child or having experienced physical and sexual trauma during adulthood.

- Many people who suffer from somatoform disorders also experience depression and anxiety. Antidepressant and anti-anxiety medications may be prescribed when mood symptoms accompany somatoform disorders, and in some cases medication has been found to have a salutary effect on the somatoform disorder itself.

- In keeping the with core concept of the *connection between mind and body* some experts view conversion disorder as an autosuggestive disorder, meaning that people with conversion symptoms have essentially hypnotized themselves into believing that they have lost some form of physical functioning.

Case Vignettes | Treatment
Robert | Coronary Heart Disease

After his heart attack, Robert spent several days in the hospital undergoing a variety of medical tests and working with his doctors to evaluate the risk factors which contributed to his recent heart attack. Despite their experience with many "intense" patients, Robert's doctors and nurses felt that he was one of the most aggressive and unpleasant patients they had ever treated. After his second day in the hospital he began to pester the staff about when he would be released and he insisted on spending most of his time making business calls regardless of his doctor's orders to the contrary.

Upon release, he was referred to a cardiac rehabilitation unit where he was encouraged to adopt a routine of regular exercise and to give up smoking. He was also referred to the rehabilitation unit's psychiatric staff for help with smoking cessation, but also in the hope that the rehab psychiatrist could direct Robert toward stress and anger management training and psychotherapy. The rehab psychiatrist strongly encouraged Robert to consider psychotherapy so that he could "blow off steam" about events at work, but Robert was offended by the implication that his difficulties had a psychological component. Robert also rejected the recommendation for stress and anger management classes, insisting that stress was just part of his job and that he could "handle it." Though Robert did agree to start walking for exercise three days a week and to cut back on smoking, his cardiologist was not surprised when Robert suffered another, more severe, heart attack only eight months after the first.

Case Discussion | Coronary Heart Disease

Robert fits the profile of a type A personality—right down to his refusal to accept psychological help. His hostile and aggressive behavior likely contributes to chronic hypertension (high blood pressure) which has the effect of stiffening and narrowing his coronary arteries. Though engaging in a regular program of exercise and cutting back on smoking should improve the health of his heart, research suggests that Robert's lifestyle and personality will continue to place him at risk for heart attacks.

David | Somatization Disorder

David's father became increasingly frustrated by the debilitating effects of his son's physical symptoms, and the failure of any doctor to render a diagnosis or suggest a treatment that could get David back on his feet. Eventually, David's father insisted that David attend a chronic pain support group run by a social worker at a nearby YMCA. During meetings, David and the other participants were encouraged to articulate their negative thoughts about their pain symptoms, and then to evaluate their thoughts objectively. When David stated that he believed that he might never be able to work again because of his neck, arm, and back pain, the social worker (and other group members) observed how quickly David gave up on considering interventions for his physical problems, or other lines of employment where his pain symptoms might not be exacerbated. Over time, David was able to use support and encouragement from the group to find work as a janitor at a local school, but he continued to live with his parents.

Case Discussion | Somatization Disorder

Cognitive restructuring techniques helped David to notice and evaluate the extreme assumptions he made about his own pain symptoms and his willingness to be debilitated by them. Drawing on the encouragement of the support group, David was able to find and maintain employment despite his ongoing physical discomfort. However, David did not use the support group setting to address the likely psychological causes of physical symptoms, or to question his reasons for continuing to live with his parents, especially after he became employed. Like many people with somatization symptoms, David was able to make some gains through a psychotherapeutic intervention, but remained somewhat resistant to considering the deeper psychological roots of his troubles.

Chapter Summary

- Psychophysiology (the study of actual physical illnesses caused or exacerbated by psychological stress) and the somatoform disorders (physical symptoms caused by psychological stress), provide a detailed look at the core concept of the *connection between mind and body.*

- Findings from the field of psychoneuroimmunology highlight the core concept of *multiple causality* in that illness often results when individuals are faced with the combination of psychological stress and exposure to an infectious agent, not just one or the other.

- The DSM-IV-TR includes five different somatoform disorders: conversion disorder, somatization disorder, pain disorder, hypochondriasis, and body dysmorphic disorder.

- The DSM-IV-TR classification of somatoform disorders has both *advantages and limitations.* While the somatoform disorders are characterized by a common focus on bodily concerns, they do not necessarily have similar causes or psychological mechanisms.

- Like all mental disorders, the somatoform disorders are best understood when demographic *context* factors such as gender, age, and social class are taken into account.

- The form taken by somatization symptoms is often influenced by cultural and historical factors, highlighting the role of ***cultural and historical relativism*** in abnormality.

- Psychodynamic, cognitive, behavioral, neuropsychological, sociocultural, and biological perspectives all contribute to the understanding and treatment of somatoform disorders.

A

Abnormal psychology/psychopathology The subfield of psychology devoted to the study of mental disorders.

Active phase The second phase of schizophrenia involving psychotic symptoms.

Acute stress disorder Significant posttraumatic anxiety symptoms that occur within one month of a traumatic experience.

Adoption studies Studies designed to compare the concordance rates for a given disorder of biological versus nonbiological parent-child pairs.

Affective flattening A reduction or absence of normal emotion.

Agnosia Loss of the ability to recognize familiar objects or people.

Agonists Drugs that increase neurotransmission.

Agoraphobia A phobia of wide open spaces or crowded places.

Alcoholism Another term for alcohol dependence.

Alexithymia Profound difficulty in identifying and verbalizing emotions.

Alogia or **poverty of speech** Minimal or absent verbal communication.

Amphetamines Synthetic stimulants with a chemical structure similar to the neurotransmitters dopamine and norepinephrine.

Amplification The anxious magnification of minor physical sensations, such as in people with hypochondriasis.

Amygdala A brain structure that registers the emotional significance of the sensory signals and contributes to the expression of emotion.

Anabolic steroids A synthetic subtype of steroids resembling testosterone that tend to increase muscle mass and are often abused with the aim of enhancing athletic performance or physique.

Analgesia The effect of pain relief.

Anhedonia Loss of a sense of pleasure.

Animism Belief in the existence and power of a spirit world.

Anorexia nervosa A disorder involving extreme thinness, often achieved through self-starvation.

Antagonists Drugs that reduce or block neurotransmission.

Anterograde amnesia The inability to recall events that occurred after a trauma.

Antigens Foreign substances, such as viruses or bacteria, that typically trigger an immune system response.

Antipsychotic medication Medications that reduce psychotic symptoms.

Antisocial personality disorder Personality traits involving profound disregard for, and violation of, the rights of others.

Anxiety An unpleasant emotion characterized by a general sense of danger, dread, and physiological arousal.

Anxiolytic An anxiety-reducing effect.

Aphasia Deterioration of receptive or expressive language skills.

Apraxia Difficulty executing common physical actions due to impairments in the brain's ability to signal specific physical movements.

Assertive community treatment (ACT) A treatment program for schizophrenia that offers frequent and coordinated contact with a wide variety of professionals in an effort to decrease relapses and rehospitalizations.

Assessment The process of gathering information in order to make a diagnosis.

Asthma A medical condition in which the airways to and from the lungs become periodically constricted.

Ataque de nervios A term used in some Latino cultures to describe an episode of intense anxiety.

Attention deficit/hyperactivity disorder A disruptive behavior disorder involving symptoms of inattention, hyperactivity, and impulsivity.

Attributions People's beliefs about the causes of events.

Atypical or **second-generation antipsychotics** Antipsychotic medications that seem to effectively reduce both positive and negative symptoms of schizophrenia.

Autism A pervasive developmental disorder characterized by impaired social and communication skills, and rigid and repetitive patterns of behavior.

Autonomic nervous system (ANS) The part of the peripheral nervous system that regulates involuntary bodily systems, such as breathing and heart rate; it is made up of the sympathetic and parasympathetic nervous system.

Autosuggestive disorder Disorder in which individuals convince themselves, through a process akin to self-hypnosis, that they have lost some form of physical functioning.

Aversion therapy Behavioral technique involving pairing an unwanted behavior with an aversive stimulus in order to classically condition a connection between them.

Avoidant personality disorder Personality traits involving social inhibition, feelings of inadequacy, and hypersensitivity to negative evaluation.

Avolition Reduced or absent motivation.

Azaspirones Drugs that treat anxiety by regulating serotonin.

B

Barbiturates Sedative drugs sometimes used to treat anxiety.

Basal ganglia A subcortical brain structure involved in the regulation of movement.

Beck Depression Inventory-II (BDI-II) A widely used depression symptom questionnaire.

Behaviorism The theoretical perspective that emphasizes the influence of learning, via classical conditioning, operant conditioning, and modeling, on behavior.

Benzodiazepines Sedative drugs that treat anxiety by increasing the activity of gamma-aminobutyric acid (GABA).

Beta-blockers Drugs that treat anxiety by decreasing the activity of norepinephrine.

Binge drinking A dangerous practice of rapid alcohol consumption, defined as four or more drinks in a row for a woman or five in a row for a man.

Binge-eating/purging type anorexia Anorexia in which the individual loses weight by bingeing and purging.

Biofeedback training Training people to attend to and partially control autonomic physiological functions with the help of visual feedback.

Biopsychosocial model A perspective in abnormal psychology that integrates biological, psychological, and social components.

Bipolar disorders Mood disorders in which an individual experiences both abnormally low and high moods.

Bipolar I disorder Combination of major depressive episodes and manic episodes.

Bipolar II disorder Combination of major depressive episodes and hypomanic episodes.

Body dysmorphic disorder Preoccupation with an imagined or exaggerated defect in physical appearance.

Borderline personality disorder Personality traits involving instability in interpersonal relationships, self-image, and emotions, as well as impulsivity and self-destructive behavior.

Brief psychotic disorder Diagnosis involving a psychotic episode that has all the features of schizophrenia but lasts less than one month.

Bulimia nervosa A disorder involving repeated binge eating followed by compensatory measures to avoid weight gain.

C

Caffeine A mild stimulant found in many foods and beverages.

Cancer A disease characterized by the uncontrolled growth of malignant cells in some part of the body.

Catastrophes Extreme and unusual negative events that invariably cause significant stress.

Catastrophizing A cognitive distortion involving the tendency to view minor problems as major catastrophes.

Catatonia Psychomotoric symptoms ranging from extreme immobility and unresponsiveness to extreme agitation.

Catatonic schizophrenia Subtype of schizophrenia marked by psychomotoric symptoms, such as rigid physical immobility and unresponsiveness (catatonic stupor) or extreme behavioral agitation (catatonic excitement), muteness, and, occasionally, echolalia and echopraxia.

Categorical system A diagnostic system, like the DSM system, in which individuals are diagnosed according to whether or not they fit certain defined categories.

Central nervous system (CNS) The control center for transmitting information and impulses throughout the body, consisting of the brain and the spinal cord.

Chemical castration A biological intervention for some paraphilias designed to suppress testosterone levels.

Chronic stress Ongoing stress related to difficult everyday life circumstances such as poverty or long-term family strife.

Clang associations Nonsense sequences of rhyming or like-sounding words.

Classical conditioning Learning that takes place via automatic associations between neutral stimuli and unconditioned stimuli.

Client-centered therapy A humanistic treatment approach developed by Carl Rogers.

Cocaine A powerful stimulant derived from the leaves of the coca plant.

Co-dependency A relationship in which family members unconsciously collude with the substance misuse of another member even though they may consciously oppose it.

Cognitive The theoretical perspective that focuses on the influence of thoughts on behavior.

Cognitive appraisal An individual's subjective perception of a potentially stressful event that weighs the event's potential threat against resources available for managing the event.

Cognitive-behavioral Approaches that combine cognitive and behavioral principles.

Cognitive-behavioral stress management An intervention designed to enhance or maintain adaptive coping strategies and decrease maladaptive coping strategies.

Cognitive distortions Irrational beliefs and thinking processes.

Cognitive restructuring Therapy techniques that focus on changing irrational and problematic thoughts.

Cognitive schemas Mental models of the world that are used to organize information.

Cognitive triad In cognitive theory, the triad consisting of one's self, one's future, and one's world.

Communication deviance Odd or idiosyncratic communications in families.

Comorbidity The presence of two or more disorders in one person, or a general association between two or more different disorders.

Compulsions Irrational rituals that are repeated in an effort to control or neutralize the anxiety brought on by obsessional thoughts.

Concordance Situation in which two twins both have the same disorder.

Concordance rate In a group of twins, the percentage that both have the same disorder.

Conditioned response The response elicited by a conditioned stimulus.

Conditioned stimulus A previously neutral stimulus that acquires the ability to elicit a response through classical conditioning.

Conduct disorder A disruptive behavior disorder involving the consistent violation of the rights of others and significant age-appropriate norms.

Confabulating The act of making up stories or fabricating events to hide gaps in memory; typically seen in people suffering from Korsakoff's syndrome.

Conscious Descriptively, mental contents that are within awareness; also, the rational part of the mind in Freud's topographic theory.

Contingency management The use of reinforcements and punishments to shape behavior in adaptive directions.

Continuous amnesia Loss of memory that begins at a specific time, continues through to the present, and prevents the retention in memory of new experiences.

Controlled outcome research Studies that systematically examine groups of clients being treated for the same disorder.

Conversion disorder Specific symptoms or deficits in voluntary motor or sensory functions with no physiological cause.

Correlation A statistical term for a systematic association between variables.

Cortisol A hormone released by the pituitary gland in response to stress.

Counterconditioning The process of de-linking a conditioned stimulus with an unconditioned stimulus, leading to **extinction** of the conditioned response.

Countertransference The therapist's feelings about the client.

Covert desensitization Behavioral desensitization intervention for phobias in which the client practices relaxation techniques while imagining being confronted with the feared stimulus.

Covert sensitization Behavioral intervention involving pairing unpleasant emotional images with unwanted behaviors, such as drug use.

Covert response prevention Exposure and response prevention in obsessive-compulsive disorder for clients whose compulsions are mental processes (not behaviors).

Cyclothymic disorder Two years or more of consistent mood swings between hypomanic highs and dysthymic lows.

D

D$_2$ receptors Receptors involved in dopamine transmission that are thought to play a role in symptoms of schizophrenia.

Daily hassles Minor stresses of everyday life.

Defense mechanisms Unconscious, automatic mental processes that reduce anxiety by warding off unacceptable thoughts and feelings.

Deinstitutionalization The social policy, beginning in the 1960s, of discharging large numbers hospitalized psychiatric patients into the community.

Delirium   An acute cognitive disorder involving disruptions in attention, and changes to cognitive capacity such as memory loss, disorientation, or language problems.

Delusional disorder   Diagnosis involving nonbizarre delusions lasting at least one month.

Delusions   Fixed, false, and often bizarre beliefs.

Dementia   A progressive cognitive disorder usually seen among older adults involving the development of multiple cognitive deficits including memory impairment, aphasia, apraxia, agnosia, or disturbance in executive functioning.

Dementia praecox   An early term for schizophrenia, from the Greek for "premature dementia."

Dendrite arbors   Neuronal branches that allow neurons to communicate with each other by sending chemical messengers (neurotransmitters).

Denial   A defense mechanism in which an individual fails to acknowledge an obvious reality.

Dependent personality disorder   Personality traits involving submissive and clinging behavior related to an excessive need to be cared for by others.

Depersonalization disorder   Persistent and distressing feelings of being detached from one's mind or body.

Depressants   Substances that slow CNS functions.

Depression   State of abnormally low mood, with emotional, cognitive, motivational, and/or physical features.

Developmental psychopathology   A subfield within abnormal psychology that considers abnormal behavior in light of developmental processes.

Devaluation   A defense mechanism in which someone or something external is disparaged in order to protect against negative feelings about oneself.

Diagnoses   Categories of disorders or diseases according to a classification system.

Diathesis-stress model   The view that the development of a disorder requires the interaction of a diathesis (predisposing cause) and a stress (precipitating cause).

Dichotomous reasoning   A cognitive distortion involving thinking in terms of extremes and absolutes

Dimensional system   A diagnostic system in which individuals are rated for the degree to which they exhibit certain traits.

Disengaged families   Families in which relationships tend to be distant and unemotional.

Disorganized schizophrenia   Typically the most severe subtype of schizophrenia, characterized by the prominence of disorganized speech, disorganized behavior, and flat or inappropriate affect.

Disorganized speech/thought   Severe disruptions in the process of speaking or thinking.

Displacement   A defense mechanism in which feelings about someone or something are unconsciously shifted to someone or something else.

Dissociation   A significant disruption in one's conscious experience, memory, sense of identity, or any combination of the three.

Dissociative amnesia   Psychogenic loss of ability to recall important personal information, usually of a traumatic or stressful nature.

Dissociative fugue   Sudden and unexpected travel away from home accompanied by forgetting of one's past and personal identity.

Dissociative identity disorder   Presence of two or more distinct personalities or identity states that recurrently control an individual's behavior.

Dopamine hypothesis   The hypothesis that excess dopamine transmission causes the psychotic symptoms of schizophrenia.

Double-bind communication   Contradictory messages such as "Be independent!" but "Never leave me!" that put the child in a "damned if you do, damned if you don't" position.

Down syndrome   A form of mental retardation caused by having three twenty-first chromosomes; characterized by mild mental retardation and distinctive physical features.

Downward drift   The decline in socioeconomic status of individuals with schizophrenia relative to their families of origin.

Draw-A-Person Test (DAP)   A projective test in which clients are asked to draw pictures of themselves and other people.

DSM   The Diagnostic and Statistical Manual of Mental Disorders published by the American Psychiatric Association, currently in its 4th revised edition (DSM-IV-TR).

Dual diagnosis   The coexistence of a substance use diagnosis and another Axis I or II diagnosis for a client.

Dyscalculia   A learning disorder in which academic achievement in mathematics is substantially below what would be expected given the child's age, intelligence, or education.

Dysgraphia   A learning disorder in which academic achievement in written expression is substantially below what would be expected given the child's age, intelligence, or education.

Dyslexia   A learning disorder in which academic achievement in reading is substantially below what would be expected given the child's age, intelligence, or education.

Dyspareunia   Persistent genital pain associated with sexual intercourse, causing distress or interpersonal difficulty.

Dysthymic disorder Two years or more of consistently depressed mood and other symptoms that are not severe enough to meet criteria for a major depressive episode.

E

Eating disorder not otherwise specified The DSM-IV-TR diagnosis for eating behaviors that are disordered but do not meet diagnostic criteria for either anorexia or bulimia.

Echolalia A speech abnormality in which a person mimics what they have just heard; seen in autism.

Echopraxia Repeating the gestures of others.

ECT (electroconvulsive therapy) A biological intervention for severe depression involving sending electric current through the skull to produce seizures.

Ecstasy (MDMA) A synthetic amphetamine/stimulant with some hallucinogenic properties.

Ego In Freud's structural theory, the part of the mind that is oriented to the external world and mediates the demands of the id and superego.

Ego-dystonic Behaviors, thought, or feelings that are experienced by an individual as distressing and unwelcome.

Ego-dystonic homosexuality A DSM-III diagnosis, since eliminated, that referred to homosexuality that was distressing and unwanted by the client.

Ego-syntonic Behavior, thoughts, or feelings that are experienced by an individual as consistent with his or her sense of self.

Electrolytes Charged molecules that regulate nerve and muscle impulses throughout the body.

Empirically supported treatments (ESTs) Specific forms of therapy that have been shown, by certain standards, to be helpful for specific disorders.

Endocrine system The system of glands that controls the production and release of hormones.

Endogenous Internal or natural.

Endorphins Brain chemicals that reduce pain and produce pleasurable sensations; sometimes referred to as the body's "natural opioids."

Enkephalins The first endogenous opioids to be discovered.

Enmeshed Families in which boundaries between members are weak and relationships tend to be intrusive.

Escape into fantasy A defense mechanism in which an individual avoids unpleasant feelings by focusing on pleasant daydreams.

Essential hypertension Hypertension for which no physiological cause can be found.

Executive functioning The ability to develop and execute complex plans.

Exhibitionism Recurrent, intense sexually arousing fantasies, sexual urges, or behaviors involving the exposure of one's genitals to an unsuspecting person.

Existential The theoretical perspective that emphasizes individual responsibility for creating meaning in life in the face of universal anxiety about death.

Explanatory styles The patterned ways (such as pessimism) in which people perceive and explain the causes of life events.

Exposure and response prevention A behavioral intervention in which clients are encouraged to confront a frightening thought or situation and then prevented from engaging in anxiety-reducing behaviors.

Exposure Technique of deliberately confronting a conditioned stimulus (such as a feared object) in order to promote **extinction**.

Expressed emotion (EE) High levels of criticism and over-involvement in families.

Extinction The weakening of a connection between a conditioned stimulus and a conditioned response.

F

Factitious disorders Physical disorders that are intentionally produced, or faked, because the person wants to be perceived as sick.

Family pedigree studies Studies designed to investigate whether a disorder runs in families.

Family systems The theoretical perspective that focuses on the importance of family dynamics in understanding and treating mental disorders.

Fear hierarchy In systematic desensitization, a list of feared situations ranging from least to most terrifying.

Female orgasmic disorder Persistent delay in, or absence of, orgasm following a normal sexual excitement phase, causing distress or interpersonal difficulty.

Female sexual arousal disorder Persistent inability to attain or maintain an adequate lubrication-swelling response of sexual excitement, causing distress or interpersonal difficulty.

Fetal alcohol syndrome (FAS) Mental retardation and a variety of physical abnormalities that result from prenatal exposure to alcohol.

Fetishism Recurrent, intense sexually arousing fantasies, sexual urges, or behaviors involving the use of nonliving objects.

Fight-or-flight response Extreme sympathetic nervous system arousal that prepares animals to flee or attack when faced with danger.

Flashback A vivid and often overwhelming recollection of a past traumatic experience

Flipped switch theory The hypothesis that continued use of a substance can precipitate a biologically based switch from controlled use to addiction.

Flooding Intensive exposure to a feared stimulus.

Fragile X syndrome A chromosomal disorder resulting in learning disabilities or mental retardation, distinctive physical features such as long faces and large ears, and behavioral difficulties.

Frotteurism Recurrent, intense sexually arousing fantasies, sexual urges, or behaviors involving touching or rubbing against a nonconsenting person.

G

Gamma-aminobutyric acid (GABA) A neurotransmitter that inhibits nervous system activity.

Gender A person's psychological sense of being male or female.

Gender identity disorder (transsexualism) A *DSM-IV-TR* disorder involving intense discomfort with one's biological sex and the desire to change it.

General adaptation syndrome According to some theories, a three-stage response—alarm, resistance, and exhaustion—that occurs when animals (including humans) are faced with chronically stressful circumstances.

General paresis A disease, due to a syphilis infection, that can cause psychosis, paralysis, and death.

Generalized amnesia Loss of memory for events and information, including information pertaining to personal identity.

Generalized anxiety disorder Chronic, pervasive, and debilitating nervousness.

Genetic linkage Studies looking for the specific genetic material that may be responsible for the genetic influence on particular disorders.

Genogram Diagram of the structure of a family.

GHB Gamma-hydroxybutyrate, a so-called natural body-building and sleep aid that has become a popular club drug.

Global Assessment of Functioning (GAF) A scale rating an individual's level of functioning used for Axis V of the DSM-IV-TR.

Glutamine A neurotransmitter involved in schizophrenia symptoms.

Grossly disorganized behavior Bizarre or disrupted behavioral patterns, such as dishevelment, extreme agitation, uncontrollable childlike silliness, or an inability to perform simple activities of daily living, often seen in schizophrenia.

H

Half-life The amount of time it takes for half of a substance to be eliminated from the body.

Hallucinations Abnormal sensory experiences such as hearing or seeing nonexistent things.

Hallucinogens Substances that produce hallucinatory changes in sensory perception.

Hippocampus A brain structure involved in the formation of memories.

Histrionic personality disorder Personality traits involving excessive, superficial emotionality and attention seeking.

Homeostasis The tendency of systems, such as family systems, to maintain a stable pattern.

Hormones Chemicals released by the endocrine system that regulate sexual behavior, metabolism, and physical growth.

HPA axis A brain system involving the hypothalamus, pituitary gland, and adrenal cortex that regulates the release of stress hormones into the bloodstream.

Humanistic The theoretical perspective that emphasizes the importance of self-actualization in human life and unconditional positive regard in relationships.

Humours Four bodily fluids believed, by Hippocrates and Greek doctors, to control health and disease.

Hypertension Chronically elevated blood pressure.

Hypnotics Substances used to promote sleep.

Hypochondriasis Preoccupation with the fear of contracting, or the mistaken idea that one has, a serious disease.

Hypofrontality A general decrease in activity in the prefrontal cortex.

Hypomanic episode A less extreme version of a manic episode that is not severe enough to significantly interfere with functioning.

Hypothalamus A subcortical brain structure that controls the endocrine, or hormonal, system.

Hysteria A term used for centuries to describe a syndrome of symptoms that appear neurological, but do not have a neurological cause; now classified as **conversion disorder**.

I

Iatrogenic A disorder unintentionally caused by a treatment.

Id In Freud's structural theory, the part of the mind containing instinctual urges.

Idealization A defense mechanism in which someone or something is seen as being perfect or wonderful in order to protect against negative feelings.

Ideas of reference Idiosyncratic beliefs that normal events contain "special" meanings.

Identification   Taking on the traits of someone else; sometimes used as a defense mechanism.

Identification with the aggressor   A defense mechanism in which an individual causes others to experience the victimization, powerlessness, or helplessness that he or she has experienced in the past.

Identified patient   The member of a family identified by the family as having problems; family systems theorists see this as a manifestation of a problem in the family system, not in an individual member.

Immunosuppression   Subnormal functioning of the immune system.

Impaired sensory gating   Difficulty processing sensory input.

In vivo desensitization   Behavioral desensitization training in which the client is actually confronted with the feared stimulus.

Inclusion classrooms   Teaching children with special academic needs (learning impairments, mental retardation) in the same classrooms as normally functioning children rather than in special education classrooms.

Information bias   Bias based on researchers only studying variables already believed to be related to the phenomena in question.

Inhalants   Chemicals that produce a "high" when inhaled.

Insulin coma   The deliberate induction of a seizure and coma using insulin; formerly used to treat certain mental disorders.

Intellectualization   A defense mechanism in which a detached rational approach is used to protect against upsetting emotions.

Intelligence quotient (IQ)   A measurement, obtained by intelligence tests, of overall intellectual ability.

Interjudge reliability   Consistency or agreement between multiple judges.

Interoceptive exposure   Deliberate induction of the physiological sensations typically associated with a panic attack.

Interpersonal psychotherapy (IPT)   An influential current treatment for depression that integrates psychodynamic, cognitive, and behavioral components.

Investigator bias   Bias based on the influence of the researchers' expectations or preferences on the study's results.

Isolation of affect   A defense mechanism in which thoughts occur without associated feelings.

J

John Henryism   An active coping style fueled by the belief that *any* environmental obstacle can be overcome with enough hard work and persistence.

K

Ketamine   A short-acting derivative of PCP still used as an anesthetic.

L

Labeling   A cognitive distortion in which people or situations are characterized on the basis of global, not specific, features.

Law of effect   Thorndike's principle that behaviors followed by pleasurable consequences are likely to be repeated while behaviors followed by aversive consequences are not.

Learned helplessness   Cognitive-behavioral theory in which animals give up adaptive responding after prior experience with inescapable punishments.

Learning disorders   Deficits in specific academic skills relative to what would be expected given a child's age, schooling, and intelligence.

Life events   Life changes, both positive and negative, that require adaptation.

Limbic system   A group of subcortical structures involved in the experience and expression of emotions and the formation of memories.

Lithium   A naturally occurring salt that is the main mood stabilizing medication for bipolar disorders.

Lobotomy   The surgical destruction of brain tissue as a treatment for a mental disorder.

Localized amnesia   Loss of memory for all of the events that occurred within a circumscribed period of time.

Locus coeruleus   A part of the brain stem associated with activation of the sympathetic nervous system.

Longitudinal   Research that studies subjects over time.

Loose associations   A sequence of logically disconnected thoughts.

LSD   Lysergic acid diethylamide, a potent synthetic hallucinogen.

M

Magical thinking   Believing that one's thoughts influence external events.

Major depressive disorder   The occurrence of one or more major depressive episodes.

Major depressive episode   A two-week or longer period of depressed mood along with several other significant depressive symptoms.

Major tranquilizers   Another name for antipsychotic medications.

Male erectile disorder Persistent inability to attain, or maintain, an adequate erection, causing distress or interpersonal difficulty.

Male orgasmic disorder Persistent delay in, or absence of, orgasm following a normal sexual excitement phase, causing distress or interpersonal difficulty.

Malingering The act of purposely feigning illness in order to get out of an obligation.

Mania State of abnormally high mood, with emotional, cognitive, motivational, and/or physical features.

Manic episode A one-week or longer period of manic symptoms causing impairment in functioning.

Marijuana The world's most widely used illegal substance; derived from the cannabis plant.

MAO inhibitors (monoamine oxidase inhibitors) A "first-generation" antidepressant; they inhibit the enzymes that oxidize monoamines thus enhancing neurotransmission.

Masturbatory satiation (or *orgasmic reconditioning*) A behavioral treatment for paraphilias in which the client masturbates to "normal" sexual stimuli in order to reinforce "normal" sexual interests.

Maturationist A theory of child development in which specific developmental stages are believed to unfold in a natural and predictable fashion.

Melancholia An early historical term for depression.

Mental health parity A political movement advocating that mental disorders should be covered by health insurance on par with physical disorders.

Mental retardation Severely impaired intellectual functioning and adaptive behavior.

Mental Status Exam A series of questions designed to assess whether a client has major problems with cognitive functions and orientation to reality.

Mescaline A hallucinogenic substance found in peyote.

Migraine headaches Painful headaches that result from the constriction of blood vessels in the cranium and are often heralded by extreme sensitivity to light and sound, dizziness, nausea, or vomiting.

Milieu treatment An institutional treatment philosophy in which clients take active responsibility for decisions about the management of their environment and their therapies.

Minnesota Multiphasic Personality Inventory-2 (MMPI-2) A widely used personality questionnaire.

Modeling Learning based on observing and imitating the behavior of others; see also: **social/observational learning**.

Monoamine hypothesis The hypothesis that depression is partially caused by insufficient neurotransmission of monoamines.

Monoamines A class of neurotransmitters involved in mood disorders, including norepinephrine, dopamine, and serotonin.

Mood episodes Periods of abnormal mood that are the building blocks of the DSM-IV-TR mood disorders.

Multimodal A treatment strategy that integrates a variety of theoretical perspectives.

N

Narcissistic personality disorder Personality traits involving extreme grandiosity, need for admiration, and lack of empathy.

Narcosynthesis The use of medication to promote therapeutic remembering; used during World War II to help soldiers remember forgotten traumatic incidents.

Narcotics Another term for opioids

Natural categories Categories that usually work reasonably well in everyday use, despite their lack of precision.

Natural selection The evolutionary theory and process by which organisms, over generations, tend to change and develop traits and behaviors that enhance survival and reproduction.

Negative automatic thoughts Negative thoughts generated by negative cognitive schemas.

Negative cognitive triad Irrationally negative thinking about the self, the world, and the future.

Negative reinforcement Increasing the probability of a behavior by removing an unpleasant stimulus when the behavior occurs.

Negative or type II symptoms of schizophrenia Symptoms that represent pathological deficits, such as flat affect, loss of motivation, and poverty of speech.

Neologisms Made-up words, like "headvise" for headache.

Nervios A term used by Latino populations in Latin America and in the United States to describe a range of symptoms of nervous distress.

Network therapy A treatment for substance misuse that emphasizes engagement of the client's social network of friends and family in treatment.

Neuritic plaques Abnormal protein deposits surrounded by clusters of degenerated nerve endings; they are typically found at the end of neuronal axons in people suffering from Alzheimer's dementia.

Neurofibrillary tangles Tangled strands of the fibers that normally make up a cortical cell's internal skeleton; they are typically found in people suffering from Alzheimer's dementia.

Neuroleptic Another name for antipsychotic medications.

Neuron An individual nerve cell.

Neurotransmitters Chemicals that allow neurons in the brain to communicate by traveling between them.

Nicotine A mild stimulant found in the leaves of the tobacco plant.

Nonpurging type bulimia Bulimia in which individuals try to avoid weight gain from binges by burning off calories, usually through fasting or engaging in excessive exercise.

Norepinephrine A neurotransmitter associated with the activation of the sympathetic nervous system; involved in depression and panic attacks.

Normalization An intervention approach for people suffering from mental retardation that aims to promote the most normal functioning possible by teaching academic, language, social, and daily living skills.

O

Obesity The condition of being 20% or more over ideal weight.

Obsession Unwanted and upsetting thoughts or impulses.

Obsessive-compulsive disorder An anxiety disorder in which distressing and unwanted thoughts lead to compulsive rituals that significantly interfere with daily functioning.

Obsessive-compulsive personality disorder Personality traits involving preoccupation with orderliness, perfectionism, and control at the expense of spontaneity, flexibility, and enjoyment.

Oedipus complex A phase during normal development when children desire an exclusive loving relationship with the parent of the opposite sex.

Operant conditioning A form of learning in which behaviors are shaped through rewards and punishments.

Opioids All of the derivatives—natural and synthetic—of the opium poppy.

Oppositional defiant disorder A disruptive behavior disorder involving consistently negativistic, hostile, and defiant behavior.

Optimism In cognitive terms, the tendency to make external, specific, and unstable explanations of negative events; associated with good health.

P

Pain disorder Physical pain without a physiological cause.

Panic attack Discrete episodes of acute terror in the absence of real danger.

Panic disorder Panic attacks that cause ongoing distress or impairment.

Paradigms Overall scientific worldviews, which according to philosopher of science Thomas Kuhn, radically shift at various points in history.

Paranoid personality disorder Personality traits involving extreme distrust and suspiciousness.

Paranoid schizophrenia The most common subtype of schizophrenia, characterized by predominant symptoms of delusions and auditory hallucinations, with relatively intact cognitive and emotional functioning.

Paraphilias DSM-IV-TR disorders involving persistent sexual desires or preferences that are considered abnormal.

Parasympathetic nervous system The part of the autonomic nervous system that regulates the body's calming and energy-conserving functions.

Parkinsonian symptoms The stiffness and tremors associated with Parkinson's disease.

PCP Phencyclidine, a substance of abuse originally developed as an animal anesthetic.

Pedophilia Recurrent, intense sexually arousing fantasies, sexual urges, or sexual activity involving a prepubescent child or children.

Peripheral nervous system (PNS) Network of nerves throughout the body that carries information and impulses to and from the CNS.

Personal therapy An adjunctive therapy for schizophrenia that combines cognitive, behavioral, psychodynamic, and humanistic principles and helps clients solve the practical problems of daily life.

Personality An individual's unique and stable way of experiencing the world that is reflected in a predictable set of reactions to a variety of situations.

Personality disorders Disorders characterized by extreme and rigid personality traits that cause distress or impairment.

Personality traits Behavioral tendencies that are relatively stable across time and place.

Personalization A cognitive distortion in which one wrongly assumes that he or she is the cause of a particular event.

Pervasive developmental disorders Severe impairment in several areas of development.

Pessimism In cognitive terms, the tendency to make internal, global, and stable explanations of negative events; associated with depression and poor health.

Pessimistic explanatory (attributional) style The tendency to make internal, global, and stable explanations of negative events.

Peyote A small, carrot-shaped cactus containing mescaline found mostly in Mexico and Central America.

Phallometric assessment Measurement of penile responses to various stimuli.

Phenothiazines Chemical name for the first-generation antipsychotic medications.

Phenylketonuria A genetic disorder in which the liver fails to produce an enzyme that metabolizes phenylalanine; it can cause retardation, hyperactivity, and seizures in humans.

Phobia An intense, persistent, and irrational fear of a specific object or situation.

Polygenic Involving multiple genes.

Polysubstance abuse The misuse of three or more substances.

Polythetic Diagnostic criteria sets in which a person is required to meet a minimum number of predetermined diagnostic criteria in order to warrant a diagnosis—no one criterion is critical to the overall diagnosis.

Positive or **Type I symptoms of schizophrenia** Symptoms that represent pathological excesses, exaggerations, or distortions from normal functioning, such as delusions, hallucinations, and disorganized speech, thought, or behavior.

Posttraumatic model A theory of dissociative identity disorder that argues that the disorder results from traumatic childhood experiences.

Post-traumatic stress disorder Significant posttraumatic anxiety symptoms occurring more than one month after a traumatic experience.

Precipitating cause The immediate trigger or precipitant of an event.

Preconscious In Freud's topographic model, mental contents that are not the focus of conscious attention but are accessible because they are not repressed.

Predisposing cause The underlying processes that create the conditions making it possible for a precipitating cause to trigger an event.

Premature ejaculation Persistent ejaculation with minimal sexual stimulation before, on, or shortly after penetration and before the person wishes it, causing distress or interpersonal difficulty.

Prepared conditioning Classical conditioning based on an evolutionarily derived sensitivity to certain stimuli that were dangerous in an ancestral environment.

Primary gain In psychodynamic terms, the relief of anxiety that occurs when an emotional conflict is converted into a physical symptom.

Primary prevention Interventions that aim to prevent problems before they begin.

Prodromal phase The first stage of schizophrenia in which the symptoms are developing.

Projection A defense mechanism in which an individual attributes his or her own unacceptable emotions to someone or something else.

Projective tests Tests designed to measure client characteristics based on clients' responses to and interpretations of ambiguous stimuli.

Prolonged imaginal exposure A behavioral intervention in which clients suffering from posttraumatic stress disorder are encouraged to describe the traumatizing experience(s) in detail.

Prospective study Research based on data that are collected as the events being studied are occurring, rather than recalling them retrospectively.

Psilocybin The active ingredient found in mushrooms with hallucinogenic properties.

Psychodynamic The theoretical perspective that began with Freud's work and is associated with emphasis on unconscious mental processes, emotional conflict, and the influence of childhood on adult life.

Psychogenic Originating from the mind or caused by psychological factors.

Psychoneuroimmunology A field that investigates the interaction between emotional phenomena and immune system functioning.

Psychopathology The subfield of psychology devoted to the study of mental disorders.

Psychophysiological disorders Physical disorders caused or exacerbated by stress or emotional factors.

Psychophysiology The study of physical disorders caused or exacerbated by stress or emotional factors.

Psychosocial dwarfism A rare disorder in which the physical growth of children deprived of emotional care is stunted.

Psychosis A state of being profoundly out of touch with reality.

Psychotic Out of contact with reality, such as experiencing hallucinations or delusions.

Psychotropic Medications designed to affect mental functioning.

Punishment In operant conditioning theory, any environmental response to a behavior that decreases the probability that the behavior will be repeated.

Purging type bulimia Bulimia in which individuals try to avoid weight gain from binges by physically removing ingested food from their bodies, usually through vomiting or the use of laxatives.

R

Reaction formation A defense mechanism in which an unwanted impulse or emotion is turned into its opposite.

Recall bias Bias based on distortion of memories for past events.

Receptors The areas of a neuron that receive neurotransmitters from adjacent neurons.

Reductionism Explaining a disorder or other complex phenomenon using only a single idea or perspective.

Regression A defense mechanism that involves a return to childlike behavior in order to avoid anxieties associated with progressive development.

Reinforcement In operant conditioning theory, any environmental response to a behavior that increases the probability that the behavior will be repeated.

Relaxation training Technique for teaching people to calm themselves by regulating their breathing and attending to bodily sensations.

Reliability The consistency of a test, measurement, or category system.

Repression A defense mechanism consisting of the forgetting of painful or unacceptable mental content.

Repressive coping A coping style characterized by general suppression of negative emotions.

Residual phase The third stage of schizophrenia in which the individual is no longer psychotic but still shows signs of the disorder.

Residual schizophrenia Subtype of schizophrenia in which clients have clearly met the criteria for schizophrenia in the past, and there is ongoing evidence of the disorder in the absence of current psychotic symptoms.

Restricting type anorexia Anorexia in which the individual loses weight by severely restricting food intake.

Retrograde amnesia The inability to recall events that occurred before a trauma.

Retrospective Research based on participants' recall of information about events that occurred in the past.

Reverse anorexia A condition, usually affecting men, that involves excessive worry that muscles are too small and underdeveloped.

Rorschach test A projective test in which clients' responses to inkblots are interpreted and scored.

Rumination bias Bias based on the fact that thinking about past events enhances the memory of such events.

S

Savant Someone possessing an exceptional or unusual intellectual skill in one area.

Schema-focused cognitive therapy A cognitive intervention for dissociative disorders that focuses on changing cognitive schemas that are based on traumatic childhood experiences.

Schemas See **cognitive schemas.**

Schizoaffective disorder Diagnosis involving symptoms of both a mood disorder and schizophrenia.

Schizoid personality disorder Personality traits involving detachment from social relationships and a restricted range of emotional expression.

Schizophrenia A disorder marked by psychosis and a decline in adaptive functioning.

Schizophrenic spectrum A group of related and overlapping disorders that may have a common etiological basis.

Schizophreniform disorder Diagnosis, involving a psychotic episode, that has all the features of schizophrenia but has not lasted six months.

Schizotaxia A potential for developing schizophrenia that may or may not progress into full-blown schizophrenia.

Schizotypal personality disorder Personality traits involving eccentricities of behavior, cognitive or perceptual distortions, and acute discomfort in close relationships.

Secondary gain In psychodynamic terms, the desired attention and concern from others that results from the "sick" role.

Secondary prevention Interventions that aim to identify problems when they are minor and to keep them from getting worse.

Sedatives Substances used to promote relaxation.

Selection bias Bias based on researching nonrepresentative samples, such as when studies only investigate research subjects who already have the disorder in question and do not investigate a comparison group without the disorder.

Selective amnesia Loss of memory for some, but not all, of the events from a specific period of time.

SSRIs (Selective serotonin reuptake inhibitors) A "second generation" class of antidepressant medications that block the reuptake of serotonin from the synapse; used in the treatment of depression and other disorders.

Self-actualization In humanistic theory, the pursuit of one's true self and needs.

Self-hypnosis The ability to put oneself in a trance state; may contribute to dissociative disorders according to some experts.

Self-medication The abuse of substances to compensate for deficiencies in neurochemistry or to soothe unpleasant emotional states.

Separation anxiety disorder Excessive anxiety concerning separation from home or attachment figures, usually parents.

Serotonin A neurotransmitter associated with depression and anxiety.

Sexual aversion Persistent extreme aversion to, and avoidance of, genital sexual contact with a sexual partner causing distress or interpersonal difficulty.

Sex change (or *sex reassignment*) A treatment for gender identity disorder in which the client's body is altered through various means to conform with his or her gender identity.

Sexual dysfunctions DSM-IV-TR disorders involving persistent problems with sexual interest, sexual arousal, or orgasm.

Sexual masochism Recurrent, intense sexually arousing fantasies, sexual urges, or behaviors involving the act of being humiliated, beaten, bound, or otherwise made to suffer.

Sexual sadism Recurrent, intense sexually arousing fantasies, sexual urges, or behaviors involving acts in which the psychological or physical suffering of a victim is sexually exciting to a person inflicting or witnessing the acts.

Shaken baby syndrome Severe bruising of the brain and heavy bleeding within the skull that can result when an infant is shaken violently.

Shared delusional disorder Diagnosis involving delusions that develop in the context of a close relationship with a psychotic person.

Shaping Behavioral term for an operant conditioning procedure in which successive approximations of a desired behavior are rewarded until the target behavior is achieved.

Sheltered workshops Supervised work settings for people suffering from mental retardation or other impairments.

Shenjing shuairuo An anxiety syndrome, recognized in China, including symptoms of physical or mental exhaustion, difficulty sleeping and concentrating, physical pains, dizziness, headaches, and memory loss.

Simple phobia The former name for specific phobias.

Single-case design Studies that evaluate individual treatments but utilize standardized research measures.

Social phobia A phobia in which fears are focused on social situations or other activities where there is a possibility of being observed and judged.

Social Readjustment Rating Scale A scale used to rate stress by quantifying the amount of adaptation required by a variety of life events.

Social skills training The use of operant conditioning techniques and modeling in order to improve social skills.

Social/observational learning Learning based on observing and imitating the behavior of others; see also: **modeling**.

Sociocognitive model A theory of dissociative identity disorder that argues that the disorder is iatrogenic and/or that it results from socially reinforced multiple role enactments.

Sociocultural The theoretical perspective that focuses on the influence of large social and cultural forces on individual functioning.

Somatic nervous system Connects the central nervous system with the sensory organs and skeletal muscles.

Somatization disorder Recurrent pain, gastrointestinal, sexual, and pseudoneurological symptoms without a physiological cause.

Somatoform disorders Disorders in which physical symptoms are caused by psychological factors.

Special education Classes tailored to individuals with learning impairments or mental retardation.

Special phobia Any phobia that is not a social phobia or agoraphobia.

Splitting A defense mechanism in which one views the self or others as all-good or all-bad in order to ward off conflicted or ambivalent feelings.

Stanford-Binet The first widely used intelligence test.

State anxiety An individual's level of anxiety at a specific time.

State-dependent learning Learning and memory that depend on emotional state similarity between encoding and retrieval.

Stimulants Substances that increase CNS functions.

Stressors Stressful events, ranging from minor annoyances to traumatic experiences.

Structural theory Freud's final model of the mind, divided into the id, the ego, and the superego.

Subclinical The presence of symptoms at levels below the full diagnostic criteria for a disorder.

Substance abuse The DSM-IV-TR diagnosis for substance use that has negative consequences.

Substance dependence The DSM-IV-TR diagnosis for substance use that is compulsive, out of control, and has negative consequences including physical dependence on the substance.

Substitution (or maintenance) therapy The practice of providing opioid addicts with a substitute opioid in a safe, medically monitored setting.

Suggestion The physical and psychological effects of mental states such as belief, confidence, submission to authority, and hope.

Superego In Freud's structural theory, the part of the mind that contains moral judgments and evaluates the self.

Sympathetic nervous system The part of the autonomic nervous system that activates the body's response to emergency and arousal situations.

Symptom and personality questionnaires Tests designed to measure symptoms or personality traits based on clients' responses to structured questions.

Symptom disorders Disorders characterized by the unpleasant and unwanted forms of distress and/or impairment.

Synapse Point of connection between neurons.

Synaptic cleft The tiny gap between one neuron and the next at a synapse.

Synergistic The multiplication of effects when two or more drugs of the same class are taken together.

Systematic desensitization Intervention involving gradually increased exposure to a conditioned stimulus (such as a feared object) while practicing relaxation techniques.

Systematized amnesia The loss of memory for a certain category of information.

T

Taijin kyofusho An anxiety disorder, recognized in Japan, characterized by worry that one's body or aspects of one's body will be displeasing or offensive to others.

Tay-Sachs disease A genetic disorder that leads to the progressive deterioration of the nervous system and usually results in childhood death.

Temperament Innate behavioral tendencies.

Temporal contiguity Two events occurring closely together in time.

Tension reduction A behavioral explanation of substance misuse based on the ability of drugs to relieve distress (negative reinforcement).

Tertiary prevention Interventions that aim to prevent significant problems from continuing and worsening.

Test-retest reliability Consistency or agreement between multiple administrations of the same test.

Thalamus A subcortical brain structure involved in routing and filtering sensory input.

Thematic Apperception Test (TAT) A projective test in which clients are asked to make up stories about pictures of people in ambiguous situations.

Therapeutic alliance The positive, collaborative partnership between client and therapist.

Thought blocking Inability to talk despite trying to do so.

Token economies The systematic use of coinlike tokens as rewards in an operant-conditioning treatment program.

Tolerance The body's adaptation to a substance as indicated by the need for increased amounts of the substance to achieve the desired effect or obtaining less effect in response to using the same amount over time.

Topographic theory Freud's first model of the mind, divided into the unconscious, conscious, and preconscious parts.

Trait anxiety An individual's tendency to respond to a variety of situations with more or less anxiety.

Transvestic fetishism (or **transvestism**) Recurrent, intense sexually arousing fantasies, sexual urges, or behaviors involving cross-dressing in a heterosexual male.

Trauma An emotionally overwhelming experience in which there is a possibility of death or serious injury to oneself or a loved one.

Tricyclics A "first-generation" class of antidepressant medications which increases the availability of both serotonin and norepinephrine.

Trisomy 21 The phenomenon of having three, not two, twenty-first chromosomes, causing Down syndrome.

Turning passive into active (or identification with the aggressor) A defense mechanism involving doing unto others what was done to oneself.

Twelve-step method A popular self-help approach to substance misuse problems based on the twelve-step recovery process of Alcoholics Anonymous.

Twin studies Studies which compare concordance rates for identical and nonidentical twins for a given disorder.

U

Unconditional positive regard In humanistic theory, the provision of unconditional love, empathy, and acceptance in relationships.

Unconditioned response The natural reflex response elicited by an unconditioned stimulus.

Unconditioned stimulus A stimulus that automatically elicits a response through a natural reflex.

Unconscious Descriptively, mental contents that are outside of awareness; also, the irrational, instinctual part of the mind in Freud's topographic theory.

Uncontrolled clinical reports Descriptive case studies of individual treatments.

Undifferentiated schizophrenia Subtype of schizophrenia in which clients clearly meet the general criteria for schizophrenia yet do not fit into any of the other three subtypes.

Undoing A defense mechanism in which one action or thought is used to "cancel out" another action or thought.

Unipolar disorders Mood disorders in which an individual experiences only abnormally low moods.

V

Vaginismus Persistent involuntary spasm of the musculature of the outer third of the vagina that interferes with sexual intercourse, causing distress or interpersonal difficulty.

Validity The accuracy of a test, measurement, or category system.

Ventricles Fluid-filled cavities in the brain.

Vicarious conditioning When the consequences of behavior are learned through modeling.

Viral challenge studies Studies in which research participants are deliberately exposed to an infectious agent in order to assess immune system response.

Voyeurism Recurrent, intense sexually arousing fantasies, sexual urges, or behaviors involving the act of observing an unsuspecting person who is naked, in the process of disrobing, or engaging in sexual activity.

W

Waxy flexibility Catatonic symptom in which clients' limbs, often held in rigid posture for hours, can be bent and reshaped as though made of wax.

Wechsler Adult Intelligence Test (WAIS) Currently, the most widely used intelligence test.

Withdrawal A defense mechanism in which an individual retreats from emotional engagement with others.

Word salad A seemingly random collection of disorganized words.

A

Abend, S. M. (1996). Psychoanalytic psychotherapy. In C. Lindemann (Ed.), *Handbook of the treatment of anxiety disorders* (pp. 401–410). Northvale, NJ: Jason Aronson, Inc.

Abi-Dargham, A., Gil, R., Krystal, J., Balwin, R. M., et al. (1998). Increased striatal dopamine transmission in schizophrenia: Confirmation in a second cohort. *American Journal of Psychiatry, 155,* 761–767.

Abraham, K. (1960). Notes on the psychoanalytic treatment of manic depressive insanity and allied conditions. In K. Abraham, *Selected papers on psychoanalysis.* New York: Basic Books. (Original work published 1911)

Abrams, R. D., & Finesinger, J. E. (1953). Guilt reactions in patients with cancer. *Cancer, 6,* 474–482.

Abramson, L. Y., Metalsky, G. I., & Alloy, L. B. (1989). Hopelessness depression: A theory-based subtype of depression. *Psychological Review, 96,* 358–372.

Achenbach, T. M. (1982). *Developmental psychopathology.* New York: John Wiley & Sons.

Achenbach, T. M. (1985). *Assessment and taxonomy of child and adolescent psychopathology.* Beverly Hills, CA: Sage Publications.

Achenbach, T. M. (1993). *Empirically based taxonomy: How to use syndromes and profile types derived from the CBCL/4–18, TRF, and YSR.* Burlington: University of Vermont, Department of Psychiatry.

Achenbach, T. M., & Edelbrock, C. (1986). *Manual for the Teacher's Report Form and Teacher Version of the Child Behavior Profile.* Burlington: University of Vermont, Department of Psychiatry.

Ackerman, B. P., Izard, C. E., Schoff, K., Youngstrom, E. A., et al. (1999). Contextual risk, caregiver emotionality, and the problem behaviors of six- and seven-year-old children from economically disadvantaged families. *Source Child Development, 70*(6), 1415–1427.

Adalbjarnardottir, S., & Rafnsson, F. D. (2001). Perceived control in adolescent substance use: Concurrent and longitudinal analyses. *Psychology of Addictive Behaviors, 15*(1), 25–32.

Addington, D., & Addington, O. (2000). Neurocognitive and social functioning in schizophrenia. *Schizophrenia Research, 44,* 47–56.

Adler, D., Drake, R., & Teague, G. (1990). Clinicians' practices in personality assessment: Does gender influence the use of DSM-III Axis II? *Comprehensive Psychiatry, 31,* 125–133.

Agras, W. S., Walsh, T., Fairburn, C. G., Wilson, G. T., et al. (2000). A multicenter comparison of cognitive-behavioral therapy and interpersonal psychotherapy for bulimia nervosa. *Archives of General Psychiatry, 57,* 459–466.

Aguayo, J. (2000). Patronage in the dispute over child analysis between Melanie Klein and Anna Freud—1927–1932. *International Journal of Psychoanalysis, 81*(4), 733–752.

Aiken, L. R. (1987). *Assessment of intellectual functioning.* Boston: Allyn & Bacon.

Aiken, L. R. (1999). *Personality assessment methods and practice* (3rd rev. ed.). Seattle, WA: Hogrefe & Huber Publishers.

Akhtar, S. (1988). Four culture-bound psychiatric syndromes in India. *International Journal of Social Psychiatry, 34,* 70–74.

Akhtar, S. (1992). *Broken structures: Severe personality disorders and their treatment.* Northvale, NJ: Jason Aronson.

Akhtar, S., Wig, N. N., Varma, V. K., Pershad, D., et al. (1975). A phenomenological analysis of symptoms in obsessive-compulsive neurosis. *British Journal of Psychiatry, 127,* 342–348.

Alarcon, R. D., & Foulks, E. F. (1995). Personality disorders and culture: Contemporary clinical views (Part A). *Cultural Diversity & Mental Health, 1*(1) 3–17.

Alarcon, R., Foulks, E., & Vakkur, M. (1998). *Personality disorders and culture: Clinical and conceptual interactions.* New York: John Wiley & Sons.

Albano, A. M., Chorpita, B. F., & Barlow, D. H. (1996). Childhood anxiety disorders. In E. J. Mash & R. A. Barkley (Eds.) *Child psychopathology.* New York: Guilford Press.

Alcabes, P., Beniowski, M., & Grund, J-P. C. (1999). Needle and syringe exchange in Poland and the former Soviet Union: A new approach to community-impact studies. *Journal of Drug Issues, 29*(4), 861–660.

Alden, L. E., & Wallace, S. T. (1995). Social phobia and social appraisal in successful and unsuccessful social interactions. *Behavior Research Therapy, 33*(5), 497–505.

Alexander, M., & Waxman, D. (2000). Cinemedication: Teaching family systems through the movies. *Family Systems & Health, 18*(4), 455–466.

Alison, L., Santtila, P., & Sandnabba, N. (2001). Sadomasochistically oriented behavior: Diversity in practice and meaning. *Archives of Sexual Behavior: Special Issue, 30*(1), 1–12.

Allebeck, P., & Wistedt, B. (1986). Mortality in schizophrenia. *Archives of General Psychiatry, 43*(7), 650–653.

Allen, D., Seaton, B., Goldstein, G., Sanders, R., et al. (2000). Neuroanatomic differences among cognitive and symptom subtypes of schizophrenia. *Journal of Nervous & Mental Diseases, 188*(6), 381–384.

Allen, J. G. (2001). *Traumatic relationships and serious mental disorders.* New York: John Wiley & Sons.

Allen, J. P., Philliber, S., Herrling, S., & Kupermin, G. P. (1997). Preventing teen pregnancy and academic failure: Experimental evaluation of a developmentally based approach. *Child Development, 64,* 729–742.

Allison, J., Blatt, S., & Zimet, C. N. (1968). *The interpretation of psychological tests.* Washington, DC: Hemisphere Publishing/Harper Row.

Alloy, L. B., Abramson, L. Y., & Francis, E. L. (1999). Do negative cognitive styles confer vulnerability to depression? *Current Directions in Psychological Science, 8,* 128–132.

Alpert, M., Rosenberg, S. D., Pouget, E. R., & Shaw, R. J. (2000). Prosody and lexical accuracy in flat affect schizophrenia. *Psychiatry Research (Special Issue), 97*(2–3), 107–118.

Althof, S. E. (2000). Erectile dysfunction: Psychotherapy with men and couples. In S. Leiblum & C. Raymond (Eds.), *Principles and practice of sex therapy* (pp. 242–275). New York: Guilford Press.

Ambrose, M. L., Bowden, S. C., & Whelan, G. (2001). Thiamin treatment and working memory function of alcohol-dependent people: Preliminary findings. *Alcoholism: Clinical & Experimental Research, 25,* 112–116.

American Medical Association. (1992). *Diagnostic treatment guidelines on domestic violence.* Washingtono, DC: Author.

American Psychiatric Association. (1952). *Diagnostic and statistical manual of mental disorders.* Washington, DC: Author.

American Psychiatric Association. (1968). *Diagnostic and statistical manual of mental disorders* (2nd ed.). Washington, DC: Author.

American Psychiatric Association. (1980). *Diagnostic and statistical manual of mental disorders, third edition.* Washington, DC: Author.

American Psychiatric Association. (1987). *Diagnostic and statistical manual of mental disorders* (3rd ed., rev.). Washington, DC: Author.

American Psychiatric Association. (1994). *Diagnostic and statistical manual of mental disorders, fourth edition.* Washington DC: Author.

American Psychiatric Association. (1996). *APA panel addresses controversy over adult memories of childhood sexual abuse.* Washington, DC: Author.

American Psychiatric Association (1999). *Journal of Abnormal Psychology, 108*(3). Washington, DC: American Psychological Association.

American Psychiatric Association. (2000). *Diagnostic and statistical manual of mental disorders* (DSM-IV-TR) (4th ed.–text revision). Washington, DC: Author.

American Psychiatric Association. (2000). Practice guidelines for the treatment of patients with eating disorders [revised]. *American Journal of Psychiatry, 157* (suppl.), 1–39.

an der Heiden, W., & Hafner, H. (2000). The epidemiology of onset and course of schizophrenia. *European Archives of Psychiatry & Clinical Neuroscience, 250*(6), 292–303.

Anand, A., & Charney, D. S. (2000). Abnormalities in catecholamines and pathophysiology of biopolar disorder. In J. C. Soares & S. Gershon (Eds.), *Bipolar disorders: Basic mechanisms and therapeutic implications* (pp. 59–94). New York: Marcel Dekker.

Andersen, A. (1995). Eating disorders in males. In K. D. Brownell & C. G. Fairburn (Eds.), *Eating disorders and obesity.* New York: Guilford Press.

Andersen, A. E., Bowers, W. A., & Watson, T. (2001). A slimming program for eating disorders not otherwise specified: Reconceptualizing a confusing, residual diagnostic category. *Psychiatric Clinics of North America, 24,* 271–291.

Andersen, R. E., Barlett, S. J., Morgan, G. D., & Brownell, K. D. (1995). Weight loss, pscyhological, and nutritional patterns in competitive male body builders. *International Journal of Eating Disorders, 18,* 49–57.

Anderson, B. L., Golden-Kreutz, D. M., & DiLillo, V. (2001). Cancer. In A. Baum, T. A. Revenson, & J. E. Singer (Eds.), *Handbook of health psychology* (pp. 709–725). Mahwah, NJ: Lawrence Erlbaum.

Anderson, G. K., & Hoshino, Y. (1997). Neurochemical studies of autism. In D. J. Cohen & F. R. Volkmar (Eds.), *Handbook of autism and pervasive developmental disorders.* New York: John Wiley & Sons.

Anderson, S., & Berridge, V. (2000). Opium in 20th-century Britain: Pharmacists, regulation and the people. *Addiction, 95*(1), 23–36. England: Carfax Publishing Limited.

Andreasen, N. C. (1999). A unitary model of schizophrenia: Bleuler's "fragmented phrene" as schizencephaly. *Archives of General Psychiatry, 56*(9), 781–787.

Andreasen, N. C., O'Leary, D. S., Flaum, M., Nopoulos, P., et al. (1997). "Hypofrontality" in schizophrenia: Distributed dysfunctional circuits in neuroleptic naïve patients. *Lancet 349,* p. 173.

Andreasen, N. C., Rezai, K., Alliger, R., Swayze, V. W., et al. (1992). Hypofrontality in neuroleptic-naïve patients and in patients with chronic schizophrenia: Assessment with xenon 133 single-photon emission computed tomography and the Tower of London. *Archives of General Psychiatry, 49*(12), 943–958.

Andreason, N. (1984). *The broken brain.* New York: Harper & Row.

Andreason, N. C., Swazye, V., O'Leary, D. S., Nopoulos, P., et al. (1995). Abnormalities in midline attentional circuitry in schizophrenia: Evidence from magnetic resonance and positron emission tomography. *European Neuropsychopharmacology, 5,* S37–S41.

Andrews, G., Stewart, G., Allen, R., & Henderson, A. S. (1990). The genetics of six neurotic disorders: A twin study. *Journal of Affective Disorders, 19,* 23–29.

Aneshensel, C. S., & Sucoff, C. A. (1996). The neighborhood context of adolescent mental health. *Journal of Health & Social Behavior, 37*(4), 293–310.

Anonymous (1986). "Can we talk?": The schizophrenic patient in psychotherapy. *American Journal of Psychiatry, 143,* 68–70.

Anthony, J., & Arria, A. (1999). Epidemiology of substance abuse in adulthood. In P. Ott, R. Tarter, & R. Ammerman (Eds.), *Sourcebook on substance abuse* (pp. 32–49). Boston: Allyn & Bacon.

Anton, R., Brady, K., & Moak, D. (1999). Pharmacotherapy in P. Ott, R. Tarter, & R. Ammerman (Eds.), *Sourcebook on substance abuse: Etiology; epidemiology, assessment, and treatment* (pp. 303–314). Boston: Allyn & Bacon.

Antoni, M. H., Cruess, D. G., Cruess, S., Lutgendorf, S., et al. (2000). Cognitive-behavioral stress management intervention effects of anxiety, 24-hr urinary norepinephrine output, and T-cytotoxic/suppressor cells over time among symptomatic HIV-infected gay men. *Journal of Counsulting and Clinical Psychology, 68*(1).

Arjonilla, S., Pelcastre, B., & Orozco, E. (2000). [Social representation of tobacco consumption in a health institution]. *Salud Mental, 23*(3), 2–12.

Aron, L. (1996). *A meeting of minds.* Hillsdale, NJ: Analytic Press.

Aronow, E., Reznikoff, M., & Rauchway, A. (1979). Some old and new directions in Rorschach testing. *Journal of Personality Assessment, 43,* 227–234.

Aronson, T. A. (1985). Historical perspectives on the borderline concept: A review and critique. *Psychiatry, 48,* 209–222.

Arrington, R. (1979). Practical reason, responsibility and the psychopath. *Journal for the Theory of Social Behavior, 9*(1), 71–89.

Asher, R. (1951). Munchausen's syndrome. *Lancet, 1,* 339–341.

Athanasiadis, L. (1997). Greek mythology and medical and psychiatric terminology. *Psychiatric Bulletin, 21*(12), 781–782.

Athanasiadis, L. (1998). Premature ejaculation: Is it a biogenic or a psychogenic disorder? *Sexual and Marital Therapy (Special Issue: Integrated Interventions: Physical and Psychological Treatments), 13*(3), 241–255.

Atre-Vaidya, N., & Taylor, M. A. (1997). Differences in the prevalence of psychosensory features among schizophrenic, schizoaffective, and manic patients. *Comprehensive Psychiatry, 8*(2), 88–92.

Attie, I., & Brooks-Gunn, J. (1989). The development of eating problems in adolescent girls: A longitudinal study. *Developmental Psychology, 25,* 70–79.

Attkinson, C. C., Waidler, V. J., Jeffrey, P. M., & Lambert, E. W. (1974). Interrater reliability of the Handler Draw-a-Person scoring. *Perceptual & Motor Skills, 38*(2), 567–573.

Axelrod, S., & Apsche, J. (Eds.). (1983). *The effects of punishment on human behavior.* New York: Academic Press.

Azima, F. J. C. (1993). Group psychotherapy with personality disorders. In H. I. Kaplan & B. J. Sadock (Eds.), *Comprehensive group psychotherapy* (3rd ed.). Baltimore: Williams & Wilkins.

B

Baer, D. M., & Pinkston, E. M. (Eds.). (1997). *Environment and behavior.* Boulder, CO: Westview Press.

Bahramali, H., Gordon, E., Li, W. M., Rennie, C., et al. (1998). Fast and slow reaction times and associated ERPs in patients with schizophrenia and controls. *International Journal of Neuroscience, 95*(3–4), 155–165.

Bailey, A., Phillips, W., & Rutter, M. (1996). Autism: Toward an integration of clinical, genetic, neuropsychological, and neurobiological perspectives. *Journal of Child Psychology and Psychiatry, 37,* 89–126.

Baker, F. M., & Bell, C. C. (1999). Issues in the psychiatric treatment of African Americans. *Psychiatric Services, 50*(3), 362–368.

Ban, T. A., & Guy, W. (1985). Conditioning and learning in relation to disease. *Activitas Nervosa Superior, 27*(4), 236–245.

Bandura, A. (1977). Self-efficacy: Toward a unifying theory of behavioral change. *Psychology Review, 84*(2), 191–215.

Bandura, A. (1986). *Social foundations of thought and action.* Engelwood Cliffs, NJ: Prentice Hall.

Bandura, A. (1999). Social cognitive theory of personality. In *Handbook of personality: Theory and research* (2nd ed., pp. 154–196). New York: Guilford Press.

Bandura, A., Ross, D., & Ross, S. A. (1963). Vicarious reinforcement and imitative learning. *Journal of Abnormal & Social Psychology, 67*(6), 601–607.

Bane, F. (1951). The governors' study on mental hospitals. *Mental Hygiene, 35,* 10–13.

Banhson, C. B., & Smith, K. (1975). Autonomic changes in a multiple personality patient. *Psychosomatic Medicine, 37,* 85–86.

Barber, J. G., & Gilbertson, R. (1999). The drinker's children. *Substance Use & Misuse, 34*(3), 383–402.

Barber, J. P., Morse, J. Q., Krakauer, I., Chittams, J., et al. (1997). Change in obsessive-compulsive and avoidant personality disorders following time-limited supportive-expressive therapy. *Psychotherapy, 34,* 133–143.

Barber, J., Luborsky, L., Gallop, R., Crits-Christoph, P., et al. (2001). Therapeutic alliance as a predictor of outcome and retention in the National Institute on Drug Abuse Collaborative Cocaine Treatment Study. *Journal of Consulting & Clinical Psychology (Special Issue), 69*(1), 119–124.

Bard, R. A. (1996, June). Charlotte Perkins Gilman: A psychobiography. *Dissertation Abstracts International: Section B: The Sciences & Engineering, 56*(12-B), University Microfilms International; 1996. 7038. AAM9612582.

Barger, S. D., Marsland, A. L., Bachen, E. A., & Manuck, S. B. (2000). Repressive coping and blood measures of disease risk: Lipids and endocrine and immunological responses to a laboratory stressor. *Journal of Applied Social Psychology, 30,* 1619–1638.

Bark, N. M. (1988). On the history of schizophrenia: Evidence of its existence before 1800. *New York State Journal of Medicine, 88*(7), 374–383.

Barker, C., Pistrang, N., & Elliott, R. (1994). *Research methods in clinical and counseling psychology.* Chichester, England: John Wiley & Sons.

Barkley, R. A. (1997). *Manual to accompany the workshop on Attention-Deficit/Hyperactivity Disorder.* Worcester, MA: Author.

Barkley, R. A. (1998). *Attention-deficit hyperactivity disorder: A handbook for diagnosis and treatment.* New York: Guilford Press.

Barlow, D. H., & Cerny, J. A. (1988). *Psychological treatment of panic.* New York: Guilford Press.

Barlow, D. H., Raffa, S. D., & Cohen, E. M. (2002). Psychosocial treatments for panic disorders, phobias, and generalized anxiety disorder. In P. E. Nathan & J. M. Gorman, (Eds.), *A guide to treatments that work* (2nd ed., pp. 301–335). New York: Oxford University Press.

Barnes, R. C. (2000). Viktor Frankl's logotherapy: Spirituality and meaning in the new millennium. *Texas Counseling Association Journal: Special Issue: Counseling theory, 28*(1), 24–31.

Baron, M., Risch, N., & Mendlewicz, J. (1982). Age at onset in bipolar-related major affective illness: Clinical and genetic implications. *Journal of Psychiatric Research, 17,* 5–18.

Barron, J. W. (1998). *Making diagnosis meaningful: Enhancing evaluation and treatment of psychological disorders.* Washington, DC: American Psychological Association.

Barrowclough, C., & Tarrier, N. (1998). Social functioning and family interventions. In *Handbook of social functioning in schizophrenia* (pp. 327–341). Needham Heights, MA: Allyn & Bacon.

Barto, P. E., Pearlson, G. D., Brill, L. B., II, Royall, R., et al. (1997). Planum temporale asymmetry reversal in schizophrenia: Replication and relationship to gray matter abnormalities. *American Journal of Psychiatry, 154*(5), 661–667.

Basco, M. R., & Rush, A. J. (1996). *Cognitive-behavioral therapy for bipolar disorder.* New York: Guilford Press.

Basco, M. R., & Thase, M. E. (1998). Cognitive-behavioral treatment of bipolar disorder. In V. E. Caballo (Ed.), *International handbook of cognitive and behavioural treatments for psychological disorders* (pp. 521–550). Oxford, England: Elsevier Science.

Bateson, G., Jackson, O., Haley, J., & Weakland, J. (1956). Towards a theory of schizophrenia. *Behavioral Science, 1,* 251.

Batzer, W., Ditzler, T., & Brown, C. (1999). LSD use and flashbacks in alcoholic patients. *Journal of Addictive Diseases, 18*(2), 57–63.

Bauer, K. (2000). The therapeutic role of regression: Comparing the perspectives of Michael Balint and Melanie Klein. *Dissertation Abstracts International: Section B: The Sciences & Engineering, 61*(3-B). University Microfilms International. Ann Arbor, MI 1624. AAI9965294.

Bauer, M. E., Vedhara, K., Perks, P., Wilcock, G. K., et al. (2000). Chronic stress in caregivers of dementia patients is associated with reduced lymphocyte sensitivity to glucocorticoids. *Journal of Neuroimmunology, 103,* 84–92.

Baumeister, R. (2000). Gender differences in erotic plasticity: The female sex drive as socially flexible and responsive. *Psychological Bulletin, 126*(3), 347–374.

Baumeister, R., Kathleen, R., & Vohs, K. (2001). Is there a gender difference in strength of sex drive? Theoretical views, conceptual distinctions, and a review of relevant evidence. *Personality & Social Psychology Review (Special Issue), 5*(3), 242–273.

Baxter, L., Schwartz, J., Bergman, K., Szuba, M., et al. (1992). Caudate glucose metabolic rate changes with both drug and behavior therapy for obsessive-compulsive disorder. *Archives of General Psychiatry, 49,* 681–689.

Bayer, R. (1981). *Homosexuality and American psychiatry: The politics of diagnosis.* New York: Basic Books.

Beck, A. T. (1967). *Depression: causes and treatment.* Philadelphia: University of Pennsylvania Press.

Beck, A. T. (1967). *Depression: Clinical, experimental, and theoretical aspects.* New York: International Universities Press.

Beck, A. T. (1976). *Cognitive theory and emotional disorders.* New York: Harper & Row.

Beck, A. T. (1976). *Cognitive therapy and the emotional disorders.* New York: International University Press.

Beck, A. T. (1987). Cognitive models of depression. *Journal of Cognitive Psychotherapy: An International Quarterly, 1,* 5–37.

Beck, A. T. (1991). Cognitive therapy: A 30-year retrospective. *American Psychologist, 46*(4), 368–375.

Beck, A. T. (1996). *The Beck Depression Inventory.* New York: Harcourt.

Beck, A. T. (1997). *BDI-II, Beck Depression Inventory manual* (2nd ed.). New York: Harcourt.

Beck, A. T. (1997). Cognitive therapy: Reflections. In J. K. Zeig (Ed.), *The evolution of psychotherapy: The third conference.* New York: Brunner/Mazel.

Beck, A. T. (1999). *Prisoners of hate: The cognitive basis of anger, hostility, and violence.* New York: HarperCollins.

Beck, A. T., & Clark, D. A. (1997). An information processing model of anxiety: Automatic and strategic processes. *Behaviour Research & Therapy, 35,* 49–58.

Beck, A. T., & Freeman, N. (1990). *Cognitive therapy of personality disorders.* New York: Guilford.

Beck, A. T., & Rector, N. A. (2000). Cognitive therapy of schizophrenia: A new therapy for the new millennium. *American Journal of Psychotherapy, 54*(3), 291–300.

Beck, A. T., Emery, G., & Greenberg, R. L. (1985). *Anxiety disorders and phobias: A cognitive perspective.* New York: Basic Books.

Beck, A. T., Rush, A. J., Shaw, B. F., & Emery, G. (1979). *Cognitive therapy of depression.* New York: Guilford Press.

Beck, A. T., Sokol, L., Clark, D. A., Berchick, R., et al. (1992). A crossover study of focused cognitive therapy for panic disorder. *American Journal of Psychiatry, 149,* 778–783.

Beck, A. T., Steer, R. A., & Epstein, N. (1992). Self-concept dimensions of clinically depressed and anxious outpatients. *Journal of Clinical Psychology, 48,* 423–432.

Beck, A. T., Ward, C. H., Mendelson, M., Mock, J. E., et al. (1961). An inventory for measuring depression. *Archives of General Psychiatry, 4,* 561–571.

Beck, A. T., Ward, C. H., Mendelson, M., Mock, J. E., et al. (1962). Reliability of psychiatric diagnosis. 2: A study of consistency of clinical judgments and ratings. *American Journal of Psychiatry, 119,* 351–357.

Beck, J. (1995). Hypoactive sexual desire disorder: An overview. *Journal of Consulting and Clinical Psychology, 63*(6), 919–927.

Becker, A. E., Burwell, R. A., Gilman, S. E., Herzog, D. B., et al. (2002). Eating behaviours and attitudes following prolonged exposure to television among ethnic Fijian adolescent girls. *British Journal of Psychiatry, 180,* 509–514.

Begley, S. (1995). Promises, promises. *Newsweek,* 60–62.

Bell-Dolan, D. J., Last, C. G., & Strauss, C. C. (1990). Symptoms of anxiety disorders in normal children. *Journal of the American Academy of Child & Adolescent Psychiatry, 29,* 759–765.

Benes, F. M. (1998). Model generation and testing to probe neural circuitry in the cingulate cortex of postmortem schizophrenic brain. *Schizophrenia Bulletin, 24,* 219–230.

Benjamin, L. S, (1996). *Interpersonal diagnosis and treatment of personality disorders.* New York: Guilford Press.

Bennett, J. B., & Lehman, W. E. K. (2001). Workplace substance abuse prevention and help seeking. Comparing team-oriented and informational training. *Journal of Occupational Health Psychology: Special Issue, 6*(3), 243–254.

Bennett, M. B. (1987). Afro-American women, poverty and mental health: A social essay. *Women and Health, 12*(3–4), 213–228.

Benson, D., Gorman, D., Jeste, D., Galasko, D., et al. (2000). Psychosis. In B. Fogel, R. Schiffer, & S. Rao (Eds.), *Synopsis of neuropsychiatry.* Philadelphia: Lippincott Williams & Wilkins.

Bentall, R. P. (1990). *Reconstructing schizophrenia.* Florence, KY: Taylor & Francis/Routledge.

Benton, A. (1991). Prefrontal injury and behavior in children. *Developmental Neuropsychology, 7,* 275–282.

Ben-Zion, I. Z., Meiri, G., Greenberg, B. D., Murphy, D. L., et al. (1999). Enhancement of CO-sub-2-induced anxiety in healthy volunteers with the serotonin antagonist metergoline. *American Journal of Psychiatry, 156,* 1635–1637.

Berenbaum, S., & Hines, M. (1992). Early androgens are related to childhood sex-typed toy preferences. *Psychological Science, 3*(3), 203–206.

Bergner, S. (2000). Resolution: The metabolization of early loss in the life of the self. (Sigmund Freud, Melanie Klein). *Dissertation Abstracts International: Section B: The Sciences & Engineering, 60*(9-B). University Microfilms International. Ann Arbor, MI 4876. AAI9946140.

Berkowitz, C. D. (2000). The long-term medical consequences of sexual abuse. In R. M. Reece (Ed.), *Treatment of child abuse: Common ground for mental health, medical, and legal practitioners* (pp. 54–64). Baltimore: Johns Hopkins University Press.

Bermann, E. (1973). The uses of scapegoating. In *Scapegoat: The impact of death fear on an American family.* Ann Arbor, MI: University of Michigan Press.

Berridge, K. C., & Robinson, T. E. (1995). The mind of an addicted brain: Neural sensitization of wanting versus liking. *Current Directions in Psychological Science, 4*(3), 71–76. United States: Blackwell Publishers.

Berrios, G. E., & Hauser, R. (1988). The early development of Kraepelin's ideas on classification: A conceptual history. *Psychological Medicine, 18*(4), 813–821.

Bertelsen, A., Harvald, B., & Hauge, M. (1977). A Danish twin study of manic-depressive disorders. *British Journal of Psychiatry, 130,* 330–351.

Berti, A. (1994). Schizophrenia and substance abuse: The interface. *Progress in Neuro-Psychopharmacology & Biological Psychiatry, 18*(2), 279–284. Oxford, England: Elsevier.

Bessesen, D. E. (2002). *Evaluation and management of obesity.* Philadelphia: Hanley & Belfus.

Bettleheim, B. (1967). *The empty fortress.* New York: Free Press.

Bhugra, D., Leff, J., Mallett, R., Der, G., et al. (1997). Incidence and outcome of schizophrenia in Whites, African-Caribbeans and Asians in London. *Psychological Medicine, 27*(4), 791–798.

Bhurga, D. (2000). Disturbances in objects of desire: Cross cultural issues. *Sexual and Relationship Therapy, 15*(1), 67–77.

Bibring, E. (1953). The mechanism of depression. In P. Greenacre (Ed.), *Affective disorders.* New York: International Universities Press.

Bickley, J., & Beech, A. (2001). Classifying child abusers: Its relevance to theory and clinical practice. *International Journal of Offender Therapy & Comparative Criminology (Special Issue: Sex Offenders), 45*(1), 51–69.

Biederman, J., Faraone, S. V., Keenan, K., Benjamin, J., et al. (1992). Further evidence for family-genetic risk factors in attention deficit hyperactivity disorder: Patterns of comorbidity in probands and relatives in psychiatrically and pediatrically referred samples. *Archives of General Psychiatry, 49,* 728–738.

Black, D., Kehrberg, L., Flumerfelt, D., & Schlosser, S. (1997). Characteristics of 36 subjects reporting compulsive sexual behavior. *American Journal of Psychiatry, 154*(2), 243–249.

Black, D. W., Wesner, R., & Bowers, W. (1993). A comparison of fluvoxamine, cognitive therapy and placebo in the treatment of panic disorder. *Archives of General Psychiatry, 50,* 44–50.

Black, J. L., & Bruce, B. K. (1989). Behavior therapy: A clinical update. *Hospital & Community Psychiatry, 40*(11), 1152–1158.

Blackburn, R. (1995). Psychopaths: Are they bad or mad? *Issues in Criminological and Legal Psychology, 22,* 97–103.

Blair, C., Ramey, C. T., & Hardin, J. M. (1995). Early intervention for low birthweight, premature infants: Participation and intellectual development. *American Journal on Mental Retardation, 99,* 542–554.

Blanchard, E. B. (1994). Behavioral medicine and health psychology. In A. E. Bergin & S. L. Garfield (Eds.), *Handbook of psychotherapy and behavior change.* New York: John Wiley & Sons.

Blanchard, E. B. (2001). Irritable bowel syndrome: Psychosocial assessment and treatment (pp. xi, 1–373). Washington, DC: American Psychological Association.

Blanchard, J., Brown, S., Haran, W., & Sherwood, A. (2000). Substance use disorders in schizophrenia: Review, integration and a proposed model. *Clinical Psychology Review, 20*(2), 207–234.

Blanchard, R., Steiner, B., & Clemmensen, L. (1985). Gender dysphoria, gender reorientation, and the clinical management of transsexualism. *Journal of Consulting & Clinical Psychology, 53*(3), 295–304.

Blaney, P. H. (1999). Paranoid conditions. In *Oxford textbook of psychopathology* (pp. 339–361). New York: Oxford University Press.

Blanken, P., Barendregt, C., & Zuidmulder, L. (1999). The evolution of crack and basing cocaine in the Rotterdam heroin scene. *Journal of Drug Issues, 29*(3), 609–626.

Blatt, S. J. (1990). The Rorschach: A test of perception or an evaluation of representation. *Journal of Personality Assessment, 55,* 394–416.

Blazer, D. G. (1997). Generalized anxiety disorder and panic disorder in the elderly: A review. *Harvard Review of Psychiatry, 5*(1), 18–27.

Blazer, D. G., George, L. K., Swartz, M., & Boyer, D. (1991). Generalized anxiety disorder. In L. N. Robins & D. A. Regier (Eds.), *Psychiatric disorders in America: The epidemiological catchment area study.* New York: Maxwell Macmillan International.

Blechner, M. (2001). Clinical wisdom and theoretical advances: Albert Szalita's contributions to psychoanalysis. *Contemporary Psychoanalysis: Special Issue, 37*(1), 63–76.

Bleuler, E. (1950). *Dementia praecox or the group of schizophrenias.* New York: International Universities Press. (Original work published 1911)

Blin, O., Simon, N., Jouve, E., Habib, M., et al. (2001). Pharmacokinetic and pharmacodynamic analysis of sedative and amnesic effects of lorazepam in healthy volunteers. *Clinical Neuropharmacology (Special Issue), 24*(2), 71–81.

Bliss, E. L. (1986). *Multiple personality, allied disorders and hypnosis.* New York: Oxford University Press.

Blouin, A. G., & Goldfield, G. S. (1995). Body image and steroid use in male bodybuilders. *International Journal of Eating Disorders, 18*, 159–165.

Boehnert, C. (1989). Characteristics of successful and unsuccessful insanity pleas. *Law & Human Behavior, 13*(1), 31–39.

Boks, M., Russo, S., Knegtering, R., & van den Bosch, R. (2000). The specificity of neurological signs in schizophrenia: A review. *Schizophrenia Research, 43*(2–3), 109–116.

Bonaparte, M. (Ed.). (2000). *The origins of psychoanalysis: Letters to William Fliess.* New York: Basic Books. (Original work published 1954.)

Bonner, M. J., & Finney, J. W. (1996). A psychosocial model of children's health. In T. H. Ollendick & R. J. Prinz (Eds.), *Advances in clinical child psychology* (Vol. 18, pp. 231–282). New York: Plenum Press.

Bonnie, R. J. (1990). Soviet psychiatry and human rights: Reflections on the report of the U. S. delegation. *Law, Medicine, and Health Care, 18*(1–2), 123–131.

Bools, C., Neale, B., & Meadow, R. (1994). Munchausen syndrome by proxy: A study of psychopathology. *Child Abuse & Neglect, 18*, 773–788.

Boon, S., & Draijer, N. (1993). *Multiple personality disorder in the Netherlands: A study on reliability and validity of the diagnosis.* Bristol, PA: Swets & Zeitlinger Publishers.

Borkovec, T. D., & Costello, E. (1993). Efficacy of applied relaxation and cognitive-behavioral therapy in the treatment of generalized anxiety disorder. *Journal of Consulting and Clinical Psychology, 61*, 611–619.

Bornstein, R. F. (1996). Sex difference in dependent personality disorder prevalence rates. *Clinical Psychology: Science and Practice, 3*, 1–12.

Bornstein, R. F. (1997). Dependent personality disorder in the DSM-IV and beyond. *Clinical Psychology: Science and Practice, 4*, 175–187.

Botella, C., & Narvaes, P. M. (1998). Cognitive behavioral treatment for hypochondriasis. In V. E. Caballo (Ed.), *International handbook of cognitive and behavioural treatments for psychological disorders* (pp. 313–361). Oxford, England: Elsevier Science.

Bower, G. H. (1981). Mood and memory. *American Psychologist, 36*, 129–148.

Bowers, W. A. (2001). Basic principles for applying cognitive-behavioral therapy to anorexia nervosa. *Psychiatric Clinics of North America, 24*, 293–303.

Bowins, B., & Shugar, G. (1998). Delusions and self-esteem. *Canadian Journal of Psychiatry, 43*(2), 154–158.

Bowlby, J. (1982). *Attachment and loss.* New York: Basic Books.

Bowling, B. (1999). The rise and fall of New York murder: Zero tolerance or crack's decline? *British Journal of Criminology: Special Issue: Drugs at the end of the century (Special Issue), 39*(4), 531–554. England: Oxford University Press.

Boxer, S. (2001, June 9). Yes, but did anyone ask the animals' opinion. *The New York Times.*

Boyarsky, B. K., & McCance-Katz, E. F. (2000). Improving the quality of substance dependency treatment with pharmacotherapy. *Substance Use & Misuse, 35*(12–14), 2095–2125.

Bradford, J. (1997). Medical interventions in sexual deviance. In D. Laws & W. O'Donohue (Eds.), *Sexual deviance: Theory, assessment, and treatment.* New York: Guilford Press.

Bradford, J. M. W., & Pawlak, A. (1987). Sadistic homosexual pedophilia: Treatment with eyperterone acetate. A single case study. *Canadian Journal of Psychiatry, 32*, 22–31.

Bradley, S., & Zucker, K. (1997). Gender identity disorder: A review of the past 10 years. *Journal of the American Academy of Child & Adolescent Psychiatry, 36*(7), 872–880.

Brady, K. T., Myrick, H., & Malcolm, R. (1999). Sedative-hypnotic and anxiolytic agents. In B. S. McCrady (Ed.), *Addictions: A comprehensive guidebook* (pp. 95–104). New York: Oxford University Press.

Braun, B. G. (1983). Psychophysiologic phenomena in multiple personality and hyponosis. *American Journal of Clinical Hypnosis, 26*, 124–137.

Braun, B. G. (1986). Issues in the psychotherapy of multiple personality. In B. G. Braun (Ed.), *Treatment of multiple personality disorder.* Washington, DC: American Psychiatric Press.

Braun, D. L., Sunday, S. R., & Halmi, K. A. (1994). Psychiatric comorbidity in patients with eating disorders. *Psychological Medicine, 24*, 859–867.

Braunstein-Bercovitz, H., Dimentman-Ashkenazi, I., & Lubow, R. E. (2001). Stress affects the selection of relevant from irrelevant stimuli. *Emotion (Special Issue), 1*(2), 182–192.

Breier, A. (2001). A new era in the pharmacotherapy of psychotic disorders. *Journal of Clinical Psychiatry, 62* (2), S3–S5.

Breier, A., Tran, P. V., Herrera, J. M., Tollefson, G. D., et al. (2001). *Current issues in the psychopharmacology of schizophrenia.* Philadelphia: Lippincott Williams & Wilkins.

Breivik, G. (1996). Personality, sensation seeking and risk taking among Everest climbers. *International Journal of Sport Psychology, 27*(3), 308–320.

Bremer, J. (1959). *Asexualization: A follow-up study of 244 cases.* New York: Macmillan.

Bremner, J. D. (1999). Does stress damage the brain? *Biological Psychiatry, 45*, 797–805.

Bremner, J. D., & Vermetten, E. (2001). Stress and development: Behavioral and biological consequences. *Development & Psychopathology, 13*, 473–489.

Brems, C. (1995). Women and depression: A comprehensive analysis. In E. E. Beckham & W. R. Leber (Eds.), *Handbook of depression* (2nd ed., pp. 539–366). New York: Guilford Press.

Brendel, West, & Hyman, S. (1996). In L. Friedman, N. Fleming, D. Roberts, & S. Hyman (Eds.), *Sourcebook of substance abuse and addiction.* Baltimore: Williams & Wilkins.

Brenner, C. (2000). Observations on some aspects of psychoanalytic theories. *Psychoanalysis Quarterly 66*, 597–632.

Breslau, N., Chilcoat, H. D., Kessler, R. C., Peterson, E. L., et al. (1999). Vulnerability to assaultive violence: Further specification of the sex difference in post-traumatic stress disorder. *Psychological Medicine, 29*, 813–821.

Breslau, N., Davis, G. C., & Andreski, P. (1995). Risk factors for PTSD-related traumatic events: A prospective analysis. *American Journal of Psychiatry, 152*, 529–535.

Breslau, N., Davis, G. C.; Andreski, P., Peterson, E. L., et al. (1997). Sex differences in posttraumatic stress disorder. *Archives of General Psychiatry, 54,* 1044–1048.

Brett, E. A. (1996). The classification of Posttraumatic Stress Disorder. In B. A. van der Kolk, A. C. McFarlane, & L. Weisaeth (Eds.), *Traumatic stress: The effects of overwhelming experience on mind, body and society.* New York: Guilford Press.

Breuer, J., & Freud, S. (1955). Studies on hysteria. In J. Strachey (Ed. and Trans.), *The standard edition of the complete psychological works of Sigmund Freud* (Vol. 2). London: Hogarth Press. (Original work published 1893)

Briere, J. (1989). *Therapy for adults molested as children: Beyond survival.* New York: Springer.

Brindley, G., & Gillian, P. (1982). Men and women who do not have orgasms. *British Journal of Psychiatry, 140*(1982), 351–356.

Brink, A. (2000). The creative matrix: Anxiety and the origin of creativity. New York: Peter Lang Publishing, Inc. (pp. vii, 221). Book Series: *The reshaping of psychoanalysis.* (Vol. 10).

Brockman, B., & Bluglass, R. (1996). A general psychiatric approach to sexual deviation. In I. Rosen (Ed.), *Sexual deviation* (pp. 1–42). New York: Oxford University Press.

Brooke, J. (1997, May 7). Military ends conflict of career and religion: American Indians win ritual peyote use. *The New York Times* (late New York edition), p. A16.

Brookmeyer, R., Gray, S., & Kawas, C. (1998). Projections of Alzheimer's disease in the United States and the public health impact of delaying disease onset. *American Journal of Public Health, 88,* 1337–1342.

Brooks, J. (1985). Polygraph testing: Thoughts of a skeptical legislator. *American Psychologist, 40*(3), 348–354.

Brooks, J., Leung, G., & Shannon, M. (in press). In L. Friedman, N. Fleming, D. Roberts, & S. Hyman, (Eds.), *Sourcebook of substance abuse and addiction.* Baltimore: Williams & Wilkins.

Brooks, O., Karamanlian, B., & Foster, V. (2001). Extinction and spontaneous recovery of ataxic tolerance to rats. *Psychopharmacology (Special Issue), 153*(4), 491–496.

Brower, K. J. (2000a). Anabolic steroids: Potential for physical and psychological addiction. In C. E. Yesalis (Ed.), *Anabolic steroids in sport and exercise* (2nd ed., pp. 279–304). Champaign, IL: Human Kinetics.

Brower, K. J. (2000b). Assessment and treatment of anabolic steroid abuse, dependence, and withdrawal. In C. E. Yesalis (Ed.), *Anabolic steroids in sport and exercise* (2nd ed., pp. 305–332). Champaign, IL: Human Kinetics.

Brower, K. J., Blow, F. C., & Beresford, T. P. (1989). Treatment implications of chemical dependency models, an integrative approach. *Journal of Substance Abuse Treatment, 6*(3), 147–157.

Brown, A. S., Cohen, P., Harkavy-Friedman, J., Babulas, V., et al. (2001). Prenatal rubella, premorbid abnormalities, and adult schizophrenia. *Biological Psychiatry (Special Issue), 49*(6), 473–486.

Brown, C. (1965). *Manchild in the promised land.* New York: Macmillan.

Brown, G. P., & Beck, A. T. (2002). Dysfunctional attitudes, perfectionism, and models of vulnerability to depression. In G. L. Flett & P. L. Hewitt (Eds.), *Perfectionism: Theory, research, and treatment* (pp. 231–251). Washington, DC: American Psychological Association.

Brown, L. (1992). A feminist critique of personality disorders. In L. Brown & M. Ballou (Eds.), *Personality and psychopathology* (pp. 206–228). New York: Guilford Press.

Brown, T. A. (1996). Validity of the DSM-III-R and DSM-IV classification systems for anxiety disorders. In R. M. Rapee (Ed.), *Current controversies in the anxiety disorders* (pp. 21–45). New York: Guilford Press.

Brownell, K., & Horgen, K. B. (2003). Food fight: The inside story of the food industry, America's obesity crisis, and what we can do about it. Boston: McGraw-Hill.

Brownell, K., Steven, C., & Barlow, D. (1977). Patterns of appropriate and deviant sexual arousal: The behavioral treatment of multiple sexual deviations. *Journal of Consulting and Clinical Psychology, 45*(6), 1144–1155.

Brownell, K. D. (1995). Effects of weight cycling on metabolism, health, and psychological factors. In K. D. Brownell & C. G. Fairburn (Eds.), *Eating disorders and obesity.* New York: Guilford Press.

Brownell, K. D., & Napolitano, M. A. (1995). Distorting reality for children: Body size proportions of Barbie and Ken dolls. *International Journal of Eating Disorders, 18,* 295–298.

Brozek, J. (1953). Semi-starvation and nutritional rehabilitation: A qualitative case study, with emphasis on behavior. *Journal of Clinical Nutrition. 1,* 107–118.

Bruch, H. (1978). *The golden cage: The enigma of anorexia nervosa.* Cambridge, MA: Harvard University Press.

Brun, A., & Andersson, J. (2001). Frontal dysfunction and frontal cortical synapse loss in alcoholism: The main cause of alcohol dementia? *Dementia & Geriatric Cognitive Disorders (Special Issue), 12*(4), 289–294.

Buchanan, A., & Wessely, S. (1998). Delusions, action, and insight. In *Insight and psychosis* (pp. 241–268). New York: Oxford University Press.

Buchanan, J., & Young, L. (2000). The war on drugs—A war on drug users? *Drugs: Education, Prevention & Policy, 7*(4), 409–422.

Buchsbaum, M. S., Haier, R. J., Potkin, S. G., & Nuechterlein, K. (1992). Fronostriatal disorder of cerebral metabolism in never-medicated schizophrenics. *Archives of General Psychiatry, 49,* 935–942.

Buffenstein, A. (1997). Personality disorders. In W. Teng, & J. Streltzer (Eds.), *Culture and psychopathology: A guide to clinical assessment* (pp. 190–205). New York: Brunner/Mazel.

Buikhuisen, W., Bontekoe, E. H., van der Plas-Korenhoff, C., & Van Buren, S. (1984). Characteristics of criminals: The privileged offender. *International Journal of Law & Psychiatry, 7*(3–4), 301–313.

Buitelaar, J. K. (1995), Psychopharmacologic approaches to childhood psychotic disorders. In J. A. Den Boer, H. G. M. Westenberg, et al., (Eds), *Advances in the neurobiology of schizophrenia* (pp. 429–457). New York: John Wiley & Sons.

Buka, S. L., Stichick, T. L., Birdthistle, I., & Earls, F. J. (2001). Youth exposure to violence: Prevalence, risks and consequences. *American Journal of Orthopsychiatry, 71,* 298–310.

Bulik, C. M., Sullivan, P. F., Fear, J., & Pickering, A. (1997). Predictors of the development of bulimia nervosa in women with anorexia nervosa. *Journal of Nervous and Mental Disease, 185,* 704–707.

Bullough, V. (1976). *Sexual variance in society and history.* New York: John Wiley & Sons.

Bullough, V. (1987). Male and female homosexuality: Psychological approaches. In L. Diamant (Ed.), *The first clinicians* (pp. 21–30). Washington, DC: Hemisphere.

Bullough, V. L., & Bullough, B. (1997). The history of the science of sexual orientation 1880–1980: An overview. *Journal of Psychology & Human Sexuality, 9*(2), 1–16.

Burchard, S. N., Rosen, J. W., Gordon, L. R., Hasazi, J. E., et al. (1992). A comparison of social support and satisfaction among adults with mental retardation living in three types of community residential alternatives. In J. W. Jacobson & S. N. Burchard (Eds.), *Community living for people with developmental and psychiatric disabilities* (pp. 137–154). Baltimore, MD: Johns Hopkins University Press.

Burn, D. J. (2002). Depression in Parkinson's disease. *European Journal of Neurology, 9*(3), 44–54.

Burston, D. (2000). *The crucible of experience: R.D. Laing and the crisis of psychotherapy* (pp. vii, 168). Cambridge, MA: Harvard University Press.

Busch, F. (1998). *Rethinking clinical technique.* New York: Jason Aronson.

Bustillo, J., Lauriello, J., Horan, W., & Keith, S. (2001). The psychosocial treatment of schizophrenia: An update. *American Journal of Psychiatry, 158,* 163–175.

Butcher, J. (1999). *A beginner's guide to the MMPI-2.* Washington, DC: American Psychological Association.

Butcher, J., Dahlstrom, W., Graham, J., Tellegen, A., & Kaemmer, B. (1989). *MMPI-2 manual for administration and scoring.* Minneapolis: University of Minnesota Press.

C

Caballo, V. E. (1998). *International handbook of cognitive and behavioural treatments for psychological disorders.* Oxford, UK: Pergamon Press.

Cadenhead, K. S., & Braff, D. L. (1999). Schizophrenia spectrum disorders. In *Startle modification: Implications for neuroscience, cognitive science, and clinical science* (pp. 231–244). New York: Cambridge University Press.

Cadoret, R. J., Yates, W. R., Troughton, E., Woodworth, G., et al. (1995). Adoption study demonstrating two genetic pathways to drug abuse. *Archives of General Psychiatry, 52,* 42–52.

Caine, E. D., & Grossman, H. (1992). Neuropsychiatric assessment. In J. E. Birren, R. B. Sloane, & G. D. Cohen (Eds.), *Handbook of mental health and aging* (2nd ed.). San Diego, CA: Academic Press.

Calev, A., Nigal, D., Shapira, B., Tubi, N., et al. (1991). Early and long-term effects of electroconvulsive therapy: Effects of treatment, time since treatment, and severity of depression. *Convulsive Therapy, 7*(3), 184–189.

Calhoun, S. R., Wesson, D. R., Galloway, G. P., & Smith, D. E. (1996). Abuse of flunitrazepam (Rohypnol) and other benzodiazepines in Austin and South Texas. *Journal of Psychoactive Drugs, 28*(2), 183–189.

Callahan, L., Steadman, H., McGreevy, M., & Robbins, P. (1991). The volume and characteristics of insanity defense pleas: An eight-state study. *Bulletin of the American Academy of Psychiatry Law, 19*(4), 331–338.

Cameron, O. G., Kuttesch, D., McPhee, K., & Curtis, G. C. (1988). Menstrual fluctuation in the symptoms of panic anxiety. *Journal of Affective Disorders, 15*(2), 169–174.

Camlibel, A. R. (2000). Affectivity and attachment: A comparison of binge drinking and non-binge drinking first-year college students. *Dissertation Abstracts International: Section B: The Sciences & Engineering, 60*(11-B). Ann Arbor, MI: University Microfilms International.

Camp, B. W., Broman, S. H., Nichols, P. L., & Leff, M. (1998). Maternal and neonatal risk factors for mental retardation: Defining the "at-risk" child. *Early Human Development, 50,* 159–173.

Campbell, S. B. (1995). Behavior problems in preschool children: A review of recent research. *Journal of Child Psychiatry and Psychology, 36,* 113–149.

Cannon, T. D., & Marco, E. (1994). Structural brain abnormalities as indicators of vulnerability to schizophrenia. *Schizophrenia Bulletin, 20*(1), 89–102.

Cannon, W. B. (1932). *The wisdom of the body.* New York: Norton.

Cantwell, D. P. (1996). Classification of child and adolescent psychopathology. *Journal of Child Psychology and Psychiatry and Allied Disciplines, 37,* 3–12.

Capaldi, D. M., & Patterson, G. R. (1994). Interrelated influences of contextual factors on antisocial behavior in childhood and adolescence for males. In D. C. Fowler, P. Sutker, & S. H. Goodman (Eds.), *Progress in experimental personality and psychopathology research.* New York: Springer.

Caper, R. (2000). *Immaterial facts: Freud's discovery of psychic reality and Klein's development of his work* (pp. xiv, 161). London: Routledge.

Caplan, P. J. (1987). The Psychiatric Association's failure to meet its own standards: The dangers of self-defeating personality disorder as a category. *Journal of Personality Disorders, 1,* 178–182.

Caplan, P. J. (1991). How do they decide what is normal? The bizarre, but true, tale of the DSM process. *Canadian Psychologist, 32*(2), 162–170.

Carlson, E. B., & Putnam, F. W. (1989). Integrating research on dissociation and hypnotizability: Are there two pathways to hypnotizability? *Dissociation, 2,* 32–38.

Carlson, N. R. (1986). *Physiology of behavior* (3rd ed.). Boston: Allyn & Bacon.

Carlsson, A., & Lindqvist, P. (1963). Effect of chlorpromazine. *Actua Pharmacologica et Toxicologica, 20,* 140–144.

Carnes, P. (1990). Sexual addiction. *The incest perpetrator: A family member no one wants to treat* (pp. 126–143). Thousand Oaks, CA: Sage.

Carnes, P. (1998). The case for sexual anorexia: An interim report on 144 patients with sexual disorders. *Sexual Addiction & Compulsivity, 5*(4), 293–309.

Carnes, P. (2000). *Out of the shadows: Understanding sexual addiction.* Center City, MN: Hazelden Information Education.

Carpenter, W. T. (1992). The negative symptom challenge [Comment]. *Archives of General Psychiatry, 49*(3), 236–237.

Carroll, B. J., et al. (1980). Diagnosis of endogenous depression: Comparison of clinical, research and neuroendocrine criteria. *Journal of Affective Disorders, 2*(3), 177–194.

Carroll, K., Connors, G., Cooney, N., DiClemente, C., et al. (1998). Internal validity of project MATCH treatments: Discriminability and integrity. *Journal of Consulting & Clinical Psychology, 66*(2), 290–303.

Carroll, R. (2000). Assessment and treatment of gender dysphoria. In S. Leiblum & C. Raymond (Eds.), *Principles and practice of sex therapy* (3rd ed., pp. 368–397). New York: Guilford Press.

Carvey, P. M. (1998). *Drug action in the central nervous system.* New York: Oxford University Press.

Caspi, A., Sugden, K., Moffitt, T., Taylor, A., et al. (2003, July 18). Influence of life stress on depression: Moderation by a polymorphism in the 5-HTT gene. *Science, 301,* 386–389.

Cassano, G. B., Pini, S., Saettoni, M., Rucci, P., et al. (1998). Correlates of 8 comorbidity in patients with psychotic disorders. *Journal of Clinical Psychiatry, 59*(2), 60–68.

Castillo, R. J. (1991). Divided consciousness and enlightenment in Hindu yogis. *Anthropology of Consciousness, 2,* 1–6.

Castillo, R. J. (1994). Spirit possession in South Asia, dissociation or hysteria? Part 2: Case histories. *Culture, Medicine, and Psychiatry, 18,* 141–162.

Censits, D. M., Ragland, J. D., Gur, R. C., & Gur, R. E. (1997). Neuropsychological evidence supporting a neurodevelopmental model of schizophrenia: A longitudinal study. *Schizophrenia Research, 24*(3), 289–298.

Centers for Disease Control. (2001). *Morbidity and Mortality Weekly Report, 50,* 90–93.

Chadwick, P. D., Birchwood, M. J., & Trower, P. (1996). *Cognitive therapy for delusions, voices and paranoia.* New York: John Wiley & Sons.

Chalder, T. (2001). Cognitive behavioural therapy as a treatment for conversion disorders. In P. W. Halligan, C. Bass, & J. C. Marshall (Eds.), *Contemporary approaches to the study of hysteria* (pp. 298–311). Oxford, England: Oxford University Press.

Chambless, D. (1996). In defense of empirically supported psychological interventions. *Clinical Psychology: Science & Practice, 3*(3), 230–235.

Chambless, D. L., & Mason, J. (1986). Sex, sex-role stereotyping and agoraphobia. *Behaviour Research & Therapy, 24*(2), 231–235.

Chang, E. C. (Ed.). (2001). *Optimism & pessimism: Implications for theory, research, and practice* (pp. xxi, 395). Washington, DC: American Psychological Association.

Charlton, R., & Quatman, A. (1997). A therapist's guide to the physiology of sexual response. In R. Charlton & I. Yalom. (Eds.), *Treating sexual dysfunction.* San Francisco: Jossey-Bass.

Charney, D. S., Heninger, G. R., & Breier, A. (1984). Noradrenergic function in panic anxiety. *Archives of General Psychiatry, 41,* 751–763.

Chen, Y. R., Swann, A. C., & Burt, D. B. (1996). Stability of diagnosis in schizophrenia. *American Journal of Psychiatry, 153*(5), 682–686.

Cheurprakobkit, S. (2000). The drug situation in Thailand: The role of government and the police. *Drug & Alcohol Review, 19*(1), 17–26.

Chiu, E., Ames, A., Draper, B., & Snowdon, J. (1999). Depressive disorders in the elderly: A review. In M. Maj & N. Sartorius (Eds.), *Depressive disorders* (pp. 313–363).

Chou, J. C.-Y., Czobor, P., Dacpano, G., Richardson, N., et al. (2001). Haloperidol blood levels in acute mania with psychosis. *Journal of Clinical Psychopharmacology (Special Issue), 21*(4), 445–447.

Chua, S., & McKenna, P. (2000). A skeptical view of the neuropathology of schizophrenia. In P. Harrison & G. Roberts (Eds.), *The neuropathology of schizophrenia: Progress and interpretation.* New York: Oxford University Press.

Cicchetti, D., & Cohen, D. J. (1995). Perspectives on developmental psychopathology. In D. Cicchetti & D. J. Cohen (Eds.), *Developmental psychopathology* (Vol. 1. Theory and methods, pp. 3–20). New York: John Wiley & Sons.

Clancy, S. A., Schacter, D. L., McNally, R. J., & Pitman, R. K. (2000). False recognition in women reporting recovered memories of sexual abuse. *Psychological Science, 11,* 26–31.

Clark, D. M. (1989). Anxiety states. In K. Hawton, P. M. Salkovskis, J. Kirk, & D. M. Clark (Eds.), *Cognitive behavior therapy for psychiatric problems* (pp. 52–96). New York: Oxford Medical Publications.

Clark, R. E. (2001). Family support and substance use outcomes for persons with mental illness and substance use disorders. *Schizophrenia Bulletin, 27*(1), 93–101.

Claude-Pierre, P. (1999). *The secret language of eating disorders: The revolutionary approach to understanding and curing anorexia and bulimia.* New York: Vintage Books.

Clayton, R. R., Leukefeld, C. G., Harrington, N. G., & Cattarello, A. (1996). DARE (Drug Abuse Resistance Education): Very popular but not very effective. In *Intervening with drug-involved youth* (pp. 101–109). Thousand Oaks, CA: Sage.

Cloitre, M., & Liebowitz, M. R. (1991). Memory bias in panic disorder: An investigation of the cognitive avoidance hypothesis. *Cognitive Therapy & Research, 15,* 371–386.

Cloninger, C. R., Sigvardsson, S., & Bohman, M. (1996). Type I and type II alcoholism: An update. *Alcohol Health & Research World, 20*(1), 18–23.

Cloud, J. (2001, Jan. 15). Recreational pharmaceuticals. *Time Magazine,* p. 100.

Coates, S. (1990). Ontogenesis of boyhood gender identity disorder. *Journal of the American Academy of Psychoanalysis, 18*(3), 414–438.

Coates, S. (1992). The etiology of boyhood gender identity disorder: An integrative model. In *Interface of psychoanalysis and psychology* (pp. 245–265). Washington, DC: American Psychological Association.

Coates, S., Friedman, R., & Wolfe, S. (1991). The etiology of boyhood gender identity disorder: A model for integrating temperament, development, and psychodynamics. *Psychoanalytic Dialogues, 1*(4), 481–523.

Coates, S., & Wolfe, S. (1995). Gender identity disorder in boys: The interface of constitution and early experience. *Psychoanalytic Inquiry, 15*(1), 6–38.

Coccaro, E. F. (1998). Clinical outcome of psychopharmacologic treatment of borderline and schizotypal personality disordered subjects. *Journal of Clinical Psychiatry, 59,* 30–35.

Cohen, C. I. (1993). Poverty and the course of schizophrenia: Implications for research and policy. *Hospital and Community Psychiatry, 44,* 951.

Cohen, M. (1998). *Culture of intolerance: Chauvinism, class, and racism in the United States.* New Haven, CT: Yale University Press.

Cohen, M. J., Riccio, C. A., & Hynd, G. W. (1999). Children with specific language impairment: Quantitative and qualitative analysis of dichotic listening performance. *Developmental Neuropsychology, 16,* 243–252.

Cohen, S., Doyle, W. J., & Skoner, D. P. (1999). Psychological stress, cytokine production, and severity of upper respiratory illness. *Psychosomatic Medicine. 61,* 175–180.

Cohen, S., Frank, E., Doyle, W. J., Skoner, D. P., et al. (1998). Types of stressors that increase susceptibility to the common cold in healthy adults. *Health Psychology, 17,* 214–223.

Cohen-Kettenis, P. (2001). Gender identity disorder in DSM? *Journal of the American Academy of Child & Adolescent Psychiatry (Special Issue), 40*(4), 391.

Cohen-Kettenis, P., & Gooren, L. (1999). Transsexualism: A review of etiology, diagnosis, and treatment. *Journal of Psychosomatic Research, 46*(4), 315–333.

Cohler, B., & Galatzer-Levy, R. (2000). *The course of gay and lesbian lives: Social and psychoanalytic perspectives.* Chicago: University of Chicago Press.

Coid, J. W. (1999). Aetiological risk factors for personality disorders. *British Journal of Psychiatry, 174,* 530–588.

Colahan, M., & Senior, R. (1995). Family patterns in eating disorders: Going round in circles, getting nowhere fast. In G. Szmukler, C. Dare, & J. Treasure (Eds.), *Handbook of eating disorders: Theory, treatment and research* (pp. 243–257). New York: John Wiley & Sons.

Coleman, C., Benjamin, R., Bolden-Watson, C., Book, M., et al. (2001). A placebo-controlled comparison of the effects on sexual functioning of bupropion sustained release and fluoxetine. *Clinical Therapeutics: The International Peer-Reviewed Journal of Drug Therapy (Special Issue), 23*(7), 1040–1058.

Coleman, M., & Gillburg, C. (1996). *The schizophrenias: A biological approach to the schizophrenia spectrum disorders.* New York: Springer.

Coles, G. (1989). *The learning mystique: A critical look at "learning disabilities."* New York: Fawcett Columbine.

Collins, R., Blane, H., & Leonard, K. (1999). Psychological theories of etiology. In P. Ott, R. Tarter, & R. Ammerman (Eds.), *Sourcebook on substance abuse: Etiology, epidemiology, assessment, and treatment.* Boston: Allyn & Bacon.

Committee on Problems of Drug Dependence. (1984). Testing drugs for physical dependence potential and abuse liability. *National Institute on Drug Abuse: Research Monograph Series, No. 52.* Washington, DC: U.S. Department of Health & Human Services.

Comunian, A., & Gielen, U. (Eds.). *International perspectives on human development.* Lengerich, Germany: Pabst Science Publishers.

Conners, C. K. (1997). *Conners' Rating Scales–revised: Technical manual.* North Tonawanda, NY: Multi-Health Systems, Inc.

Consumer Reports. (1995). Mental health: Does therapy help? pp. 734–739.

Cook, C. H., & Gurling, H. D. (2001). Genetic predisposition to alcohol dependence and problems. In N. Heather (Ed.), *International handbook of alcohol dependence and problems* (pp. 257–279). New York: John Wiley & Sons.

Coons, P. M. (1994). Confirmation of child abuse in child and adolescent cases of multiple personality disorder not otherwise specified. *Journal of Nervous and Mental Disease, 182,* 461–464.

Coons, P. M., Bowman, E. S., & Milstein, V. (1988). Multiple personality disorder: A clinical investigation of 50 cases. *Journal of Nervous and Mental Disease, 176,* 519–527.

Coons, P. M., Bowman, E. S., Kluft, R. P., & Milstein, V. (1991). The cross-cultural occurrence of multiple personality disorder: Additional cases from a recent survey. *Dissociation, 4,* 124–128.

Cooper, J., Kendell, R., Gurland, B., Sharpe, L., Copeland, J., & Simon, R. (1972). *Psychiatric diagnosis in New York and London.* New York: Oxford University Press.

Cooper, P. J. (1995). Eating disorders and their relationship to mood and anxiety disorders. In K. D. Brownell & C. G. Fairburn (Eds.), *Eating disorders and obesity.* New York: Guilford Press.

Cooper, R. S. (1999). Treatments for schizophrenia: Implications for cognitive rehabilitation therapy. *Journal of Cognitive Rehabilitation, 17*(3), 8–11.

Corey-Bloom, J. (2000). Dementia. In S. K. Whitbourne (Ed.), *Psychopathology in later adulthood.* New York: John Wiley & Sons.

Corey-Bloom, J., Jernigan, T., Archibald, S., Harris, M. J., et al. (1995). Quantitative magnetic resonance imaging of the brain in late-life schizophrenia. *American Journal of Psychiatry, 152*(3), 447–449.

Cornoldi, C., Rigoni, F., Tressoldi, P. E., & Vio, C. (1999). Imagery deficits in nonverbal learning disabilities. *Journal of Learning Disabilities, 32*(1), 48–57.

Cornu, F. (1973). *Katamnesen bein kastrierten sttlichkeits—dekinquenten aus forensisch—psychiatrischer sicht.* Basel, Switzerland: Karger.

Cosford, P. A., & Arnold, E. (1992). Eating disorders in later life: A review. *International Journal of Geriatric Psychiatry, 7* (7), 491–498.

Costa, P. T., Jr., & McCrae, R. R. (1989). Personality continuity and the changes of adult life. In M. Storandt & G. R. VandenBos (Eds.), *The adult years: Continuity and change.* Washington, DC: American Psychological Association.

Costello, C. G. (1972). Depression: Loss of reinforcers or loss of reinforcer effectiveness? *Behavior Therapy, 3,* 240–247.

Coy, K., Speltz, M. L., DeKlyen, M., & Jones, K. (2001). Social-cognitive practices in preschool boys with and without oppositional defiant disorder. *Journal of Abnormal Child Psychology, 29,* 107–119.

Crago, M., Shisslak, C. M., & Estes, L. S. (1996). Eating disturbances among American minority groups: A review. *International Journal of Eating Disorders, 19,* 239–248.

Craske, M. G. (1999). *Anxiety disorders: Psychological approaches to theory and treatment.* Boulder, CO: Westview Press.

Crawford, H. H., Knebel, T., & Vendemia, J. M. C. (1998). The nature of hypnotic analgesia: Neuropsychological foundation and evidence. *Contemporary Hypnosis, 15*, 22–33.

Crits-Cristoph, P. (1996). The dissemination of efficacious psychological treatments. *Clinical Psychology: Science and Practice, 3*, 260–263.

Crits-Christoph, P., & Barber, J. P. (2002). Psychological treatments of personality disorders. In P. E. Nathan & J. M. German (Eds.), *A guide to treatments that work* (2nd ed., pp. 611–623). New York: Oxford University Press.

Crits-Cristoph, P., Connolly, M., Azarian, K., Crits-Cristoph, K., et al. (1996). An open trial of brief supportive-expressive psychotherapy in the treatment of generalized anxiety disorder. *Psychotherapy, 33*(3), 418–430.

Crow, T. J. (1980). Positive and negative schizophrenic symptoms and the role of dopamine: II. *British Journal of Psychiatry, 137*, 383–386.

Crow, T. J. (1985). The two-syndrome concept: Origins and current status. *Schizophrenia Bulletin, 11*(3), 471–486.

Crow, T. J. (1995). Brain changes and negative symptoms in schizophrenia. 9th World Congress of psychiatry (1993, Rio de Janeiro, Brazil). *Psychopathology, 28*(1), 18–21.

Crowe, R. R., Noyes, R., Pauls, D. L., & Slymen, D. J. (1983). A family study of panic disorder. *Archives of General Psychiatry, 40*, 1065–1069.

Crowther, J. H., Snaftner, J., Bonifazi, D. Z., & Shepherd, K. L. (2001). The role of daily hassles in binge eating. *International Journal of Eating Disorders, 29*, 449–454.

Currier, G. W., & Simpson, G. M. (2001). Risperidone liquid concentrate and oral lorazepam versus intramuscular haloperidol and intramuscular lorazepam for treatment of psychotic agitation. *Journal of Clinical Psychiatry (Special Issue), 62*(3), 153–157.

Czekalla, J., Kollack-Walker, S., & Beasley, C. M. (2001). Cardiac safety parameters of olanzapine: Comparison with other atypical and typical antipsychotics. *Journal of Clinical Psychiatry, 62* (2), S35–S40.

D

Daderman, A. M., & Lidberg, L. (1999). Flunitrazepam (Rohypnol) abuse in combination with alcohol causes premeditated grievous violence in male juvenile offenders. *Journal of the American Academy of Psychiatry & the Law, 27*(1), 83–99.

Dalmau, A., Bergman, B., & Brismar, B. (1999). Psychotic disorders among inpatients with abuse of cannabis, amphetamaine and opiates. Do dopaminergic stimulants facilitate psychiatric illness? *European Psychiatry, 14*(7), 366–371.

Danforth, M. (2000). Listen to my words, give meaning to my sorrow: A study in perspective transformation in middle aged women who experience loss of spouse. *Dissertation Abstracts International, Section A: Humanities and Social Sciences, 60*(9-A), Ann Arbor, MI: Univ. of Microfilms International.

Daprati, E., Franck, N., Georgieff, N., Proust, J., et al. (1997). Looking for the agent: An investigation into consciousness of action and self-consciousness in schizophrenic patients. *Cognition, 65*(1), 71–86.

DARE America. (1991). *The DARE Regional Training Center Policy Board's manual for training law enforcement officers in the DARE program.* Washington, DC: Bureau of Justice Assistance.

Dare, C., & Crowther, C. (1995). Psychodynamic models of eating disorders. In G. Szmukler, C. Dare, & J. Treasure (Eds.), *Handbook of eating disorders: Theory, treatment and research* (pp. 125–139). New York: John Wiley & Sons.

Dare, C., & Eisler, E. (1995). Family therapy. In G. Szmukler, C. Dare, & J. Treasure (Eds.), *Handbook of eating disorders: Theory, treatment and research* (pp. 334–349). New York: John Wiley & Sons.

Dare, C., Eisler, I., Russell, G., Treasure, J., et al. (2001). Psychological therapies for adults with anorexia nervosa: Randomised controlled trial of out-patient treatments. *British Journal of Psychiatry, 178*, 216–221.

Darlington, Y. (1996). Escape as a response to childhood sexual abuse. *Journal of Child Sexual Abuse, 5*, 77–94.

David, V., Polis, I., McDonald, J., & Gold, L. (2001). Intravenous self-administration of heroin/cocaine combinations (speedball) using nose-poke or lever-press operant responding in mice. *Behavioural Pharmacology, 12*(1), 25–34.

Davidson, J., & Moore, N. (2001). *Speaking of sexuality: Interdisciplinary readings.* London: Pergamon/Elsevier Science.

Davidson, J. R., Hughes, D., Blazer, D. G., & George, L. K. (1991). Post-traumatic stress disorder in the community: An epidemiological study. *Psychological Medicine, 21*(3), 713–721.

Davidson, J. R., Swartz, M., Storck. M., Krishnan, R. R., et al. (1985). A diagnostic and family study of post-traumatic stress disorder. *American Journal of Psychiatry, 142*, 90–93.

Davidson, J. R. T., & Foa, E. B. (1991). Diagnostic issues in posttraumatic stress disorder: Considerations for the DSM-IV. *Journal of Abnormal Psychology,100*(3), 346–355.

Davidson, L., Stayner, D., & Haglund, K. (1998). Phenomenological perspectives on the social functioning of people with schizophrenia. In K. Muser & N. Tarrier (Eds.), *Handbook of social functioning in schizophrenia* (pp. 307–326). Needham Heights, MA: Allyn & Bacon.

Davies, A. D. M., & Wagstaff, G. F. (1991). The use of creative imagery in the behavioural treatment of an elderly woman diagnosed as an hysterical ataxic. *Contemporary Hypnosis, 8*, 147–152.

Davis, J., & Phelps, J. (1995). Twins with schizophrenia: Genes or germs? *Schizophrenia Bulletin, 21*, 13–18.

Davis, M. (1999). Functional neuroanatomy of anxiety and fear: a focus on the amygdala. In D. S. Charney, E. J. Nestler, & B. S. Bunney (Eds.), *Neurobiology of mental illness* (pp. 463–474). New York: Oxford University Press.

Davis, M., Rainnie, D., & Cassell, M. (1994). Neurotransmission in the rat amygdala related to fear and anxiety. *Trends in Neuroscience, 17*, 208–224.

Davis, P. (2001, May 7). Dope: A love story. *Time Magazine*, p. 62.

Dawsey, K. M. (1996, Aug.). Blunted. *Essence, 27*, 73–74.

Day, J. R., & Moore, M. E. (1976). Individual and family psychodynamic contributions to learning disability. *Journal of the National Association of Private Psychiatric Hospitals, 8*, 27–30.

de Haan, L., van Raaij, B., van den Berg, R., & Jager, M., et al. (2001). Preferences for treatment during a first pscyhotic episode. *European Psychiatry, 16*(2), 83–89.

de la Torre, R., Farre, M., Roset, P. N., Hernandez Lopez, C., et al. (2000). Pharmacology of MDMA in humans. In S. F. Ali (Ed.), *Neurobiological mechanisms of drugs of abuse: Cocaine, ibogaine, and substituted amphetamines* (pp. 225–237). New York: New York Academy of Sciences.

De Silva, P. (1995). Cognitive-behavioural models of eating disorders. In G. Szmukler, C. Dare, & J. Treasure (Eds.), *Handbook of eating disorders: Theory, treatment and research* (pp. 141–153). New York: John Wiley & Sons.

de Silva, W. (1999). ABC of sexual health: Sexual perversions [Review]. *British Medical Journal, 318*(7184), 654–656.

Deakin, J. W., & Graeff, F. G. (1991). 5-HT and mechanisms of defense. *Journal of Psychopharmacology, 54*(4), 305–315.

Dean, B. (2000). Signal transmission. *Australian & New Zealand Journal of Psychiatry, 34,* 560–569.

Deater-Deckard, K., Dodge, K. A., Bates, J. E., & Pettie, G. S. (1998). Multiple risk factors in the development of externalizing behavior problems: Group and individual differences. *Development and Psychopathology, 10,* 469–493.

DeFries, J. C., & Light, J. G. (1996). Twin studies of reading disability. In J. H. Beitchman & N. J. Cohen (Eds.), *Language, learning, and behavior disorders: Developmental, biological, and clinical perspectives* (pp. 272–292). New York: Cambridge University Press.

Deitz, I. J. (1995). The self-psychological approach to the bipolar spectrum disorders. *Journal of the American Academy of Psychoanalysis, 23,* 475–492.

Delay, J., & Deniker, P. (1952). Le traitment des psychoses par une methode neurolyptique derivee d'hibernotherapie: Le 4560 RP utilize seul en cure prolngee et continuee. *Congres des Medicins Alienistes et Neuologistes de France des Pays du Langue Francaise, 50,* 503–513.

Delgado, P., & Moreno, F. (2000). The role of norepinephrine in depression. *Journal of Clinical Psychiatry, 61*(suppl), 5–12.

DeLisi, L. E. (1997). The genetics of schizophrenia. *Schizophrenia Research, 28,* 163–175.

DeLisi, L. E., Razi, K., Stewart, J., Relja, M., et al. (2000). No evidence for a parent-of-origin effect detected in the pattern of inheritance of schizophrenia. *Biological Psychiatry, 48*(7), 706–709.

Den Bleyker, K. (2000). The dual diagnosis of posttraumatic stress disorder and substance abuse: A literature review and treatment protocol. *Dissertation Abstracts International: Section B: The Sciences & Engineering, 60*(8-B). Ann Arbor, MI: University Microfilms International.

Den Boer, J. A., van Vliet, I. M., & Westenberg, H. G. M. (1996). Advances in the psychopharmocology of social phobia. In H. G. M. Westenberg, J. A. Den Boer, & D. L. Murphy (Eds.), *Advances in the neurobiology of anxiety disorders* (pp. 401–418). New York: John Wiley & Sons.

Devlin, M. J., Yanovski, S. Z., & Wilson, G. T. (2000). Obesity: What mental health professionals need to know. *American Journal of Psychiatry, 157,* 854–866.

Diaz-Marsa, M., Carrasco, J. L., & Saiz, J. (2000). A study of temperament and personality in anorexia and bulimia nervosa. *Journal of Personality Disorders, 14,* 352–359.

Dickerson, F. B. (2000). Cognitive behavioral psychotherapy for schizophrenia: A review of recent empirical studies. *Schizophrenia Research, 43*(2–3), 71–90.

Diekstra, R. F., Kienhorst, C. W. M., & de Wilde, E. J. (1995). Suicide and suicidal behavior among adolescents. In M. Rutter & D. J. Smith (Eds.), *Psychosocial disorders in young people.* Chichester, England: John Wiley & Sons.

Dignam, P. T. (2000). Criteria for involuntary hospitalisation [Comment]. *Australian & New Zealand Journal of Psychiatry, 34*(2), 337.

Dilts, S. L., Jr. (2001). *Models of the mind: A framework for biopsychosocial psychiatry* (pp. xix, 327). Philadelphia: Brunner-Routledge.

DiMatteo, M. R., & Martin, L. R. (2002). *Health psychology.* Boston: Allyn & Bacon.

Dodge, K. A. (2000). Conduct disorders. In A. J. Sameroff, M. Lewis, & S. M. Miller (Eds.), *Handbook of developmental psychopathology* (2nd ed.). New York: Plenum Press.

Dodge, K. A., Pettit, G. S., Bates, J. E., & Valente, E. (1995). Social information-processing patterns partialy mediate the effect of early physical abuse on later conduct problems. *Journal of Abnormal Psychology, 104,* 632–643.

Dodgen, C., & Shea, W. (2000). *Substance use disorders: Assessment and treatment.* San Diego, CA: Academic Press.

Doerman, D. (1999). Sexual perversion. In D. Olendorf, C. Jeryan, & K. Boyden (Eds.), *Gale encyclopedia of medicine.* Detroit: Gale Research.

Dohrenwend, B. P., Levav, I., Shrout, P. E., Schwartz, S., et al. (1992). Socioeconomic status and psychiatric disorders: The causation-selection issue. *Science, 255*(5047), 946–952.

Dohrenwend, B., Levav, I., Shrout, P., Schwartz, S., et al. (1998). Ethnicity, socioeconomic status, and psychiatric disorders: A test of the social causation-social selection issue. In *Adversity, stress & psychopathology* (pp. 285–318). New York: Oxford University Press.

Domino, E. F. (1992). Chemical dissociation of human awareness: Focus on non-competitive NMDA receptor antagonists. *Journal of Psychopharmacology, 6*(3), 418–424.

Dostoevsky, F. (1993). *Notes from the underground.* New York: Knopf.

Dougall, A. L., & Baum, A. (2001). Stress, health, and illness. In A. Baum, T. A. Revenson, & J. E. Singer (Eds.), *Handbook of health psychology* (pp. 321–337). Mahwah, NJ: Lawrence Erlbaum.

Douglass, H. M., Moffitt, T. E., Dar, R., McGee, R., et al. (1995). Obsessive-compulsive disorder in a birth cohort of 18-year-olds: Prevalence and predictors. *Journal of the American Academy of Child and Adolescent Psychiatry, 34*(11), 1424–1431.

Doyle, A. D., Biederman, J., Seidman, L. J., Weber, W., et al. (2000). Diagnostic efficiency of neuropsychological test scores for discriminating boys with and without attention deficit-hyperactivity disorder. *Journal of Consulting and Clinical Psychology, 68*(3), 477–488.

Doyon, S. (2001). The many faces of ecstasy. *Current Opinion in Pediatrics, 13*(2), 170–176.

Drake, R. E., & Mueser, K. T. (2000). Psychosocial approaches to dual diagnosis. *Schizophrenia Bulletin (Special Issue: Psychosocial Treatment for Schizophrenia), 26*(1), 105–118.

Dressler, W. W., Bindon, J. R., & Neggers, Y. H. (1998). John Henryism, gender, and arterial blood pressure in an African American community. *Psychosomatic Medicine, 60,* 620–624.

Dujovne, V. F., Barnard, M. U., & Rapoff, M. A. (1995). Pharmacological and cognitive behavioral approaches in the treatment of childhood depression: A review and critique. *Clinical Psychology Review, 15,* 589–611.

Dunphy, P. M. (2000). Using an empowerment and education intervention to prevent smoking relapse in the early postpartum period. *Dissertation Abstracts International: Section B: The Sciences & Engineering, 61*(6-B), 2986. Ann Arbor, MI: University Microfilms International.

Durand, V. M., & Carr, E. G. (1989). Operant learning methods with chronic schizophrenia and autism: Aberrant behavior. In *Chronic schizophrenia and adult autism: Issues in diagnosis, assessment, and psychological treatment* (pp. 231–273). New York: Springer.

Dykens, E. M., & Volkmar, F. R. (1997). Medical conditions associated with autism. In D. J. Cohen & F. R. Volkmar (Eds.), *Handbook of autism and pervasive developmental disorders.* New York: John Wiley & Sons.

E

Eads, L., Shuman, D., & DeLipsey, J. (2000). Getting it right: The trial of sexual assault and child molestation cases under Federal Rules of Evidence 413–415. *Behavioral Sciences & the Law (Special Issue: Sex Offenders: Part two/three), 18*(2–3), 169–216.

Eaton, W. W., Kramer, M., Anthony, J. C., Chee, E. M. L., et al. (1989). Conceptual and methodological problems in estimation of the incidence of mental disorders. In B. Cooper & T. Helgason (Eds.), *Epidemiology and the prevention of mental disorders.* London: Routledge.

Ebener, P., McCaffrey, D., & Saner, H. (1994). *Prevalence of alcohol and drug use in California's household population, 1988–1991; Analysis of the California subsample, from the National Household Survey on Drug Abuse.* Santa Monica, CA: RAND Corporation.

Edelstein, B., Kalish, K., Drzdick, L., & McKee, D. (1999). Assessment of depression and bereavement in older adults. In P. Lichtenberg (Ed.), *Handbook of assessment in clinical gerontology.* New York: John Wiley & Sons.

Einarson, T. R., Arikian, S. R., Casciano, J., & Doyle, J. J. (1999). Comparison of extended release venlafaxine, selective serotonin reuptake inhibitors, and tricyclic antidepressants in the treatment of depression: A meta-analysis of randomized controlled trials. *Clinical Therapeutics: International Journal of Drug Therapy, 21*(2), 296–308.

Eisendrath, S. J. (1996). Current overview of factitious physical disorders. In M D. Feldman & S. J. Eisendrath (Eds.), *The spectrum of factitious disorders* (pp. 21–36). Washington, DC: American Psychiatric Press.

Eisler, I. (1995). Family models of eating disorders. In G. Szmukler, C. Dare, & J. Treasure (Eds.), *Handbook of eating disorders: Theory, treatment and research* (pp. 155–176). New York: John Wiley & Sons.

Eisler, I., Dare, C., Hodes, M., Russell, G., et al. (2000). Family therapy for adolescent anorexia nervosa: The results of a controlled comparison of two family interventions. *Journal of Child Psychology & Psychiatry & Allied Disciplines, 41,* 727–736.

El Mallakh, R. S., & Wyatt, R. J. (1995). The Na,K-ATPase hypothesis for bipolar illness. *Biological Psychiatry, 37,* 235–244.

El-Bashir, T. (1998, May 17). Auto Racing: Driver with sex change finds her career stalled. *The New York Times,* p. B1.

El-Defrawi, M., Lotfy, G., Dandash, K., Refaat, A., et al. (2001). Female genital mutilation and its psychosexual impact. *Journal of Sex & Marital Therapy, 27*(5), 465–473.

Ellason, J. W., Ross, C. A., & Fuchs, D. L. (1996). Lifetime Axis I and II comorbidity and childhood trauma history in dissociative identity disorder. *Psychiatry: Interpersonal & Biological Processes, 59*(3), 255–266.

Ellis, A. (1962). *Reason and emotion in psychotherapy.* Secaucus, NJ: Lyle Stuart.

Ellis, A. (1979). The theory of rational-emotive therapy. In A. Ellis & J. M. Whitely (Eds.), *Theoretical and empirical foundations of rational-emotive therapy.* Monterey, CA: Brooks/Cole.

Ellis, A. (1996). *Better, deeper, and more enduring brief therapy: The rational-emotive behavior therapy approach.* New York: Bruner/Mazel.

Ellis, A. (1997). The evolution of Albert Ellis and rational emotive behavior therapy. In J. K. Zeig (Ed.), *The evolution of psychotherapy: The third conference.* New York: Brunner/Mazel.

Ellis, A. (2000). Rational emotive behavior therapy. In R. Corsini & D. Wedding (Eds.). *Current Psychotherapies* (6th ed., pp. 168–204). Itasca, IL: FE. Peacock Publishing Inc.

Ellis, A., & MacLaren, C. (1998). *Regional emotive behavior therapy: A therapist's guide.* Atascadero, CA: Impact Publishers.

Ellison, G., & Switzer, R. C. (1993). Dissimilar patterns of degeneration in brain following four different addictive stimulants. *Neuroreport: An International Journal for the Rapid Communication of Research in Neuroscience, 5*(1), 17–20.

Ellison, G., Ring, M., Ross, D., & Axelrood, B. (1980). Cumulative alterations in rat behavior during continuous administration of LSD or mescaline: Absence of tolerance? *Biological Psychiatry, 15*(1), 95–102.

Elman, I., Krause, S., Karlsgodt, K., Schoenfeld, D. A., et al. (2001). Clinical outcomes following cocaine infusion in non-treatment seeking individuals with cocaine dependence. *Biological Psychiatry (Special Issue), 49*(6), 553–555.

Endler, N. S., & Kocovski, N. L. (2001). State and trait anxietyrevisited. *Journal of Anxiety Disorders, 15*(3), 231–245.

Engel, G. L. (1977). The need for a new medical model: A challenge to biomedicine. *Science, 196*(4286), 129–136.

Epps, G. (2001). *To an unknown God: religious freedom on trial.* New York: St. Martin's Press.

Epstein, E. E. (2001). Classification of alcohol-related problems and dependence. In N. Heather (Ed.), *International handbook of alco-*

hol dependence and problems (pp. 47–70). New York: John Wiley & Sons.

Erdelyi, M. (1985). *Psychoanalysis: Freud's cognitive therapy.* New York: W. H. Freeman.

Erickson, C. K. (1996). Review of neurotransmitters and their role in alcoholism treatment. *Alcohol & Alcoholism, 31*(1), S5–S11.

Erickson, P. G., Adlaf, E. M., Smart, R. G., & Murray, G. F. (1994). *The steel drug: Cocaine and crack in perspective* (2nd ed.). New York: Lexington Books/Macmillan.

Eron, L. D. (1997). The development of antisocial behavior from a learning perspective. In D. M. Stoff, J. Breiling, & J. D. Maser (Eds.), *Handbook of antisocial behavior* (pp. 140–147). New York: John Wiley & Sons, Inc.

Esper, E. A. (1964). *A history of psychology.* Philadelphia: Saunders.

Ettinger, U., Chitnis, X., Kumari, V., Fannon, D., et al. (2001). Magnetic resonance imaging of the thalamus in first-episode psychosis. *American Journal of Psychiatry, 158*(1), 116–118.

Evans, K., & Sullivan, J. M. (2001). *Dual diagnosis: Counseling the mentally ill substance abuser* (2nd ed.). New York: Guilford Press.

Evans, M. D., Hallon, S. S., DeRubies, R. J., Piasecki, J. M., et al. (1992). Differential relapse following cognitive therapy and pharmacotherapy for depression. *Archives of General Psychiatry, 49,* 802–808.

Exner, J. E. (1976). Projective techniques. In I. B. Weiner (Ed.), *Clinical methods in psychology.* New York: John Wiley & Sons.

Exner, J. E. (1995). *The Rorschach: A comprehensive system, volume 1: Basic foundations* (3rd ed.). New York: John Wiley & Sons.

F

Fabrega, H. (1982/1984). Culture and psychiatric illness: Biomedical and ethnomedical aspects. In A. J. Marsella & G. M. White (Eds.), *Cultural conceptions of mental health and therapy.* Dordecht, Holland: D. Reidel Publishing Co.

Fabrega, H. (1995). Cultural challenges to the psychiatric enterprise. *Comprehensive Psychiatry, 36*(5), 377–383.

Fabrega, H., Ahn, C., & Mezzich, J. E. (1992). On the descriptive validity of DSM III schizophrenia. *Psychopathology, 25*(2), 79–89.

Fairburn, C. G. (1995). Physiology of anorexia nervosa. In K. D. Brownell & C. G. Fairburn (Eds.), *Eating disorders and obesity.* New York: Guilford Press.

Fallon, B. A. (2001). Pharmacologic strategies for hypochondriasis. In V. Starcevic & D. R. Lipsitt (Eds.), *Hypochondriasis: Modern perspectives on an ancient malady* (pp. 329–351). New York: Oxford University Press.

Faludi, S. (1991). *Backlash: The undeclared war against American women.* New York: Crown Publishers.

Faraone, S. V., Seidman, L. J., Kremen, W. S., Toomey, R., et al. (1999). Neuropsychological functioning among the nonpsychotic relatives of schizophrenic patients: A 4-year follow-up study. *Journal of Abnormal Psychology, 108*(1), 176–181.

Farley, M., & Barkan, H. (1997). Somatization, dissociation, and tension-reducing behaviors in psychiatric outpatients. *Psychotherapy and Psychosomatics, 66,* 133–140.

Fast, I., & Chethik, M. (1976). Aspects of depersonalization-derealization in the experience of children. *International Review of Psychoanalysis, 3,* 483–490.

Faustman, W. O. (1995). What causes schizophrenia? In *Treating schizophrenia* (pp. 57–80). San Francisco: Jossey-Bass.

Fava, G. A., Bartolucci, G., Rafanelli, C., & Mangelli, L. (2001). Cognitive-behavioral management of patients with bipolar disorder who relapsed while on lithium prophylaxis. *Journal of Clinical Psychiatry, 62,* 556–559.

Fayek, M., Kingsbury, S. J., Zada, J., & Simpson, G. M. (2001). Cardiac effects of antipsychotic medications. *Psychiatric Services (Special Issue), 52*(5), 607–609.

Feldman, M. D., Hamilton, J. C., & Deemer, H. N. (2001). Factitious disorder. In K. A.. Phillips (Ed.), *Somatoform and factitious disorders* (pp. 129–166). Washington, DC: American Psychiatric Publishing.

Felix, A. D., & Wine, P. R. (2001). From the couch to the street: Applications of psychoanalysis to work with individuals who are homeless and mentally ill. *Journal of Applied Psychoanalytic Studies (Special Issue), 3*(1), 17–32.

Fenichel, O. (1945). *The psychoanalytic theory of neurosis.* New York: Norton.

Fenton, W. S., & McGlashan, T. H. (1991). Natural history of schizophrenia sybtypes. I. Longituinal study of paranoid, hebephrenic, an undifferentiate schizophrenia. *Archives of General Psychiatry, 48*(11), 969–977.

Fenton, W. S., & McGlashan, T. H. (1994). Antecedents, symptom progression, and long-term outcome of the deficit syndrome in schizophrenia. *American Journal of Psychiatry, 151*(3), 351–356.

Fergusson, D., Horwood, L., & Beautrais, A. (1999). Is sexual orientation related to mental health problems and suicidality in young people? *Archives of General Psychiatry, 56*(10), 876–880.

Fernandez, E., & Sheffield, J. (1996). Relative contributions of life events versus daily hassles to the frequency and intensity of headaches. *Headache, 36,* 595–602.

Ferster, C. B. (1966). Animal behavior and mental illness. *Psychological Record, 16,* 345–356.

Fichter, M. M., & Noegel, R. (1990). Concordance for bulimia nervosa in twins. *International Journal of Eating Disorders, 9,* 425–436.

Fichter, M. M., Narrow, W. E., Roper, M. T., Rehm, J., et al. (1996). Prevalence of mental illness in Germany and the United States: Comparison of the Upper Bavarian Study and the Epidemiologic Catchment Area Program. *The Journal of Nervous and Mental Disease, 184*(10), 598–606.

Fields, L. (1996). "Sanity and irresponsibility": Comment. *Philosophy, Psychiatry & Psychology, 3*(4), 303–304.

Filipek, P. A. (1999). Neuroimaging in the developmental disorders: The state of the science. *Journal of Child Psychology and Psychiatry and Allied Disciplines, 40*(1), 113–128.

Fine, C. G. (1991). Treatment stabilization and crisis prevention: Pacing the therapy of the multiple personality disorders patient. *Psychiatric Clinics of North America, 14,* 661–675.

Fine, C. G. (1992). Multiple personality disorder. In A. Freeman & F. M. Dittilio (Eds.), *Comprehensive casebook of cognitive therapy* (pp. 347–360). New York: Plenum Press.

Fine, C. G. (1996). A cognitively based treatment model for DSM-IV dissociative identity disorder. In L. K. Michelson & W. J. Ray (Eds.), *Handbook of dissociation: Theoretical, empirical, and clinical perspectives* (pp. 401–411). New York: Plenum Press.

Fingerhood, M. (2000). Substance abuse in older people. *Journal of the American Geriatrics Society, 48*(8), 985–995.

Fink, M. (1999). *Electroshock: Restoring the mind.* New York: Oxford University Press.

Fink, M., & Taylor, M. A. (2001). The many varieties of catatonia. *European Archives of Psychiatry & Clinical Neuroscience (Special Issue: Catatonia: A New Focus of Research, 251* (1), S8–S13.

Finkelhor, D. (1987). The sexual abuse of children: Current research reviewed. *Psychiatric Annals, 17,* 233–241.

Finlay-Jones, R. (1986). Should thiamine be added to beer? *Australian & New Zealand Journal of Psychiatry, 20,* 3–6.

First, M. B., Spitzer, R. L., Gibbon, M., & Williams, J. B. W. (1997). *SCID I/P (for DSM-IV) patient edition structured clinical interview for DSM-IV Axis I disorders.* New York: Biometrics Research, New York State Psychiatric Institute.

Fisher, D. (2001, Aug 19). We've been misled by the drug industry. *The Washington Post,* p. B03.

Fisher, G. L., & Harrison, T. C. (1997). *Substance abuse.* Boston: Allyn & Bacon.

Fiske, S., & Taylor, S. (1991). *Social cognition* (2nd ed). New York: McGraw-Hill.

Flaherty, J. (2001, May 9). At Amherst , the day the urns went dry. *The New York Times,* p. A26.

Flament, M. F., Rapoport, J. L., Berg, W., Sceery, C., et al. (1985). Cominpramine treatment of childhood obsessive-compulsive disorder: A double-blind controlled study. *Archives of General Psychiatry, 429*(10), 977–983.

Fleet, R. P., Dupuis, G., Marchand, A., Burelle, D., et al. (1996). Panic disorder in emergency department chest pain patients: prevalence, comorbidity, suicidal ideation, and physician recognition. *American Journal of Medicine, 101,* 371–380.

Fleischhacker, W. (2000). Negative symptoms in patients with schizophrenia with special reference to the primary versus secondary distinction. *Encephale (Special Issue), 26*(1), 12–14.

Fleming, N., Potter, & Kettyle. (1996). In L. Friedman, N. Fleming, D. Roberts, & S. Hyman (Eds.), *Sourcebook of substance abuse and addiction.* Baltimore: Williams & Wilkins.

Flint, A. J., & Rifat, S. L. (2002). Relationship between clinical variables and symptomatic anxiety in late-life depression. *American Journal of Geriatric Psychiatry, 10*(3), 292–296.

Foa, E. P., & Kozak, M. J. (1996). Obsessive-compulsive disorder. In C. Lindemann (Ed.), *Handbook of the treatment of anxiety disorders* (pp. 139–171). Northvale, NJ: Jason Aronson, Inc.

Fodor, I. E. (1974). Sex role conflict and symptom formation in women: Can behavior therapy help? *Psychotherapy: Theory, Research & Practice, 11*(1), 22–29.

Fog, A. (1992). Paraphilias and therapy. *Nordisk Sexologi, 10*(4), 236–242.

Follette, W. C., & Houts, A. C. (1996). Models of scientific progress and the role of theory in taxonomy development: A case study of the DSM. *Journal of Consulting and Clinical Psychology, 64*(6), 1120–1132.

Ford, M., & Widiger, T. A. (1989). Sex bias in the diagnosis of histrionic and antisocial personality disorders. *Journal of Consulting and Clinical Psychology, 57,* 301–305.

Fossati, A., Maffei, C., Battaglia, M., Bagnato, M., et al. (2001). Latent class analysis of DSM-IV schizotypal personality disorder criteria in psychiatric patients. *Schizophrenia Bulletin, 27*(1), 59–71.

Foulks, E. F. (1996). Culture and personality disorders. In J. E. Mezzich, A. Kleinman, H. Fabrega, & D. Parron (Eds.), *Culture and psychiatric diagnosis* (pp. 243–252). Washington, DC: American Psychiatric Press, Inc.

Foxx, R. M. (1998). A comprehensive treatment program for inpatient adolescents. *Behavioral Interventions, 13*(1), 67–77.

France, R., & Robson, M. (1997). *Cognitive behaivoural therapy in primary care: A practical guide.* London: Jessica Kingsley Publishers.

Frank, E., Kupfer, D., Wagner, E., & McEachran, A. (1991). Efficacy of interpersonal psychotherapy as a maintenance treatment of recurrent depression: Contributing factors. *Archives of General Psychiatry, 48,* 1053–1059.

Frank, L. K. (1939). Projective methods for the study of personality. *Journal of Psychology, 8,* 343–389.

Frankl, I. D. (1980). *Existential psychotherapy.* New York: Basic Books.

Franklin, M. E., Abramowitz, J. S., Kozak, M. J., Levitt, J. T., et al. (2000). Effectiveness of exposure and ritual prevention for obsessive-compulsive disorder: Randomized compared with nonrandomized samples. *Journal of Consulting & Clinical Psychology, 68,* 594–602.

Franzen, M. D., & Smith-Seemiller, L. (1998). Behavioral neuropsychology. In A. S. Bellack & M. E. Hersen (Eds.), *Behavioral assessment: A practical handbook* (4th ed.). Boston: Allyn & Bacon.

Fredrikson, M., Annas, P., Fischer, H., & Wik, G. (1996). Gender and age differences in the prevalence of specific fears and phobias. *Behaviour Research & Therapy, 34,* 33–39.

Freedman, D. X. (1968). On the use and abuse of LSD. *Archives of General Psychiatry, 18,* 330–347.

Freeman, A., Pretzer, B., Fleming, B., & Simon, K. M. (1990). *Clinical applications of cognitive therapy.* New York: Plenum Press.

Freeman, C. (1995). Cognitive therapy. In G. Szmukler, C. Dare, & J. Treasure (Eds.), *Handbook of eating disorders: Theory, treatment and research* (pp. 309–331). New York: John Wiley & Sons.

Freeman, H. (1994). Schizophrenia and city residence. *British Journal of Psychiatry, 164* (23), S39–S50.

Freud, A. (1937). *The ego and the mechanisms of defense.* London: Hogarth Press.

Freud, A. (1939). *The ego and mechanisms of defense.* New York: International Universities Press.

Freud, A. (1962). Assessment of childhood disturbances. *Psychoanalytic Study of the Child, 17,* 149–158.

Freud, A. (1965). *Normality and pathology in childhood: Assessments of development.* Madison, WI: International Universities Press.

Freud, A. (1981). *Psychoanalytic psychology of normal development.* New York: International Universities Press.

Freud, S. (1894). The neuro-psychoses of defense. In J. Strachey (Ed. & Trans.), *The standard edition of the complete psychological works of Sigmund Freud* (Vol. 3). London: Hogarth Press.

Freud, S. (1895). A reply to criticisms on the anxiety neurosis. In *Collected Works* (Vol. 1). London: Hogarth Press.

Freud, S. (with J. Breuer) (1895). *Studies in hysteria.* Standard Edition of the *Complete psychological works of Sigmund Freud,* (Vol. II). London: Hogarth Press.

Freud, S. (1905). Three essays on the theory of sexuality. In *Standard Edition of the Complete Psychological Works of Sigmund Freud* (Vol. 7, pp. 125–245). London: Hogarth Press.

Freud, S. (1909). Analysis of a phobia in a five-year-old boy (The case of "Little Hans"). In *Standard Edition of the Complete Psychological Works of Sigmund Freud* (Vol. 10, pp 1–149). London: Hogarth Press.

Freud, S. (1913). The disposition to obsessional neurosis. *Standard edition of the complete psychological works of Sigmund Freud* (Vol. 12). London: Hogarth Press, pp. 311–326.

Freud, S. (1914). On narcissism. In *The standard edition of the complete psychological works of Sigmund Freud* (Vol. 14). London: Hogarth Press.

Freud, S. (1923). *The ego and the id.* London: Hogarth Press.

Freud, S. (1924). The loss of reality in neurosis and psychosis. In *The standard edition of the complete psychological works of Sigmund Freud* (Vol). London: Hogarth Press.

Freud, S. (1925). *Collected papers, volume 4.* London: Hogarth Press.

Freud, S. (1926). Inhibitions, symptoms and anxiety. In J. Strachey (Ed. & Trans.), *The standard edition of the complete psychological works of Sigmund Freud* (Vol. 3). London: Hogarth Press.

Freud, S. (1940a). Splitting of the ego in the defensive process (1938). In *Standard Edition of the Complete Psychological Works of Sigmund Freud* (Vol. 23; pp. 271–278). London: Hogarth Press.

Freud, S. (1940b). An outline of psychoanalysis. In *Standard Edition of the Complete Psychological Works of Sigmund Freud* (Vol. 23, pp. 141–207). London: Hogarth Press.

Freud, S. (1952). *An autobiographical study.* J. Strachey (Ed. & Trans.), *The standard edition of the complete psychological works of Sigmund Freud,* Vol. 20 (p. 34). London: Hogarth Press. (Original work published 1925)

Freud, S. (1953–1966). In J. Strachey (Ed. & Trans.) *The standard edition of the complete psychological works of Sigmund Freud* (Vols. 1–23). London: Hogarth Press.

Freud, S. (1957). Mourning and melancholia. In J. Strachey (Ed. & Trans.) *The standard edition of the complete psychological works of Sigmund Freud* (Vol. 14). London: Hogarth Press. (Original work published 1917)

Freud, S. (1962). *The aetiology of hysteria.* In J. Strachey (Ed. & Trans.), *The standard edition of the complete psychological works of Sigmund Freud,* Vol. 3 (p. 203). London: Hogarth Press. (Original work published 1896)

Freud, S. (1964). New introductory lectures on psychoanalysis. In J. Strachey (Ed. & Trans.) *The standard edition of the complete psychological works of Sigmund Freud* (Vol. 22). London: Hogarth Press. (Original work published 1933)

Freund, K., Seto, M., & Kuban, M. (1997). Frotteurism: The theory of courtship disorder. In *Sexual deviance: Theory, assessment, and treatment* (pp. 111–130). New York: Guilford Press.

Frick, P. J. (1998). Conduct disorders. In T. H. Ollendick & M. Hersen (Eds.), *Handbook of child psychopathology* (pp. 213–237). New York: Plenum Press.

Friedhoff, A. J., & Silva, R. R. (1997). Stabilizing systems in the brain. In *Plasma homovanillic acid in schizophrenia: Implications for presynaptic dopamine dysfunction* (pp. 79–87). Washington, DC: American Psychiatric Press.

Friedman, M., & Rosenman, R. H. (1974). *Type A behavior and your heart.* New York: Alfred A. Knopf.

Friedman, M. J., Schnurr, P. P., & McDonagh-Coyle, A. (1994). Posttraumatic stress disorder in military veterans. *Psychiatric Clinics of North American, 17,* 265–277.

Frisby, M. K. (1994, Dec. 10). Clinton fires surgeon general Elders citing differences in opinion, policy. *Wall Street Journal,* p. 16.

Frischholz, E. J. (1985). The relationship among dissociation, hypnosis, and child abuse in the development of multiple personality disorder. In R. P. Kluft (Ed.) *Childhood antecedents of multiple personality* (pp. 99–126). Washington, DC: American Psychiatric Press.

Fromm, M. G. (1995). What does borderline mean? *Psychoanalytic Psychology, 12,* 233–245.

Fromm-Reichmann, F. (1943). Psychotherapy of schizophrenia. *American Journal of Psychiatry, 111,* 410–419.

Fromm-Reichmann, F. (1948). Notes on the development of treatment of schizophrenia by psychoanalytic psychotherapy. *Psychiatry, 11,* 263–273.

Fromm-Reichmann, F. (1950). *Principles of intensive psychotherapy.* Chicago: University of Chicago.

Fullerton, C. S., Ursano, R. J., Epstein, R. S., Crowley, B., et al. (2001). Gender differences in posttraumatic stress disorder after motor vehicle accidents. *American Journal of Psychiatry, 158,* 1486–1491.

Furman, E. (1992). Constructing and using the toddler profile. In *Toddlers and their mothers: A study in early personality development.* Madison, WI: International Universities Press.

Furnham, A., & Haraldsen, E. (1998). Lay theories of etiology and "cure" for four types of paraphilia: Fetishism, pedophilia, sexual sadism, and voyeurism. *Journal of Clinical Psychology, 54*(4), 689–700.

Furst, R. T., Johnson, B. D., Dunlap, E., & Curtis, R. (1999). The stigmatized image of the "crack head": A sociocultural exploration of a barrier to cocaine smoking among a cohort of youth in New York City. *Deviant Behavior, 20*(2), 153–181.

Fyer, A. J., Mannuzza, S., Chapman, T. F., Liebowitz, M. P., et al. (1993). A direct interview family study of social phobia. *Archives of General Psychiatry, 50,* 286–293.

G

Gabbard, G. (1990). *Psychodynamic psychiatry in clinical practice.* Washington, DC: American Psychiatric Press.

Gabbard, G., & Coyne, L. (1987). Predictors of response of antisocial patients to hospital treatment. *Hospital & Community Psychiatry, 38*(11), 1181–1185.

Gacono, C., Meloy, J., & Bridges, M. (2000). A Rorschach comparison of psychopaths, sexual homicide perpetrators, and nonviolent pedophiles: Where angels fear to tread. *Journal of Clinical Psychology, 56*(6), 757–777.

Gaither, G. A., & Plaud, J. J. (1997). The effects of secondary stimulus characteristics on men's sexual arousal. *Journal of Sex Research, 34*(3), 231–236.

Galanter, M., & Brook, D. (2001). Network therapy for addiction: bringing family and peer support into office practice. *International Journal of Group Psychotherapy, 51*(1), 101–122.

Galanter, M., & Kleber, H. D. (1999). *Textbook of substance abuse treatment* (2nd ed.). Washington, DC: American Psychiatric Press.

Galea, S., Ahern, J., Resnick, H., Kilpatrick, D., et al. (2002). Psychological sequelae of the September 11 terrorist attacks in New York City. *New England Journal of Medicine, 346,* 982–987.

Galynker, I. I., Cohen, L. J., & Cai, J. (2000). Negative symptoms in patients with major depressive disorder: A preliminary report. *Neuropsychiatry, Neuropsychology, & Behavioral Neurology, 13*(3), 171–176.

Ganaway, G. K. (1994). Transference and countertransference shaping influences on dissociative syndromes. In S. J. Lynn & J. Rhue (Eds.), *Dissociation: Clinical and theoretical perspectives* (pp. 317–337). New York: Guilford Press.

Garber, B. (1993). A contribution to the etiology of learning disabilities. In T. B. Cohen, M. H. Etezady, et al., (Eds.) *The vulnerable child* (Vol. 1, p. 139–154). Madison, CT: International Universities Press.

Gardea, M. A., Gatchel, R. J., & Mishra, K. D. (2001). Long-term efficacy of biobehavioral treatment of temporomandibular disorders. *Journal of Behavioral Medicine, 24,* 341–359.

Gardner, J. M., Grantham-McGregor, S. M., Himes, J., Chang, S. (1999). Behaviour and development of stunted and nonstunted Jamaican children. *Journal of Child Psychology & Psychiatry & Allied Disciplines, 40*(5), 819–827.

Garfield, S. L. (1996). Some problems associated with "validated" forms of psychotherapy. *Clinical Psychology, Science and Practice, 3,* 218–229.

Garfinkle, P. E., & Dorian, B. J. (2001). Improving understanding and care for the eating disorders. In R. H. Striegel-Moore & L. Smolak (Eds.), *Eating disorders: Innovative directions in research and practice* (pp. 9–26). Washington, DC: American Psychological Association.

Garralda, M. E. (2000). The links between somatisation in children and in adults. In P. Reder & M. McClure (Eds.), *Family matters: Interfaces between child and adult mental health* (pp. 122–134). London: Routledge.

Garrick, T. M., Sheedy, D., Abernethy, J., Hodda, A. E., et al. (2000). Heroin-related deaths in Sydney, Australia. How common are they? *American Journal on Addictions, 9*(2), 172–178.

Garrity, J. F. (2000). Jesus, peyote, and the holy people: Alcohol abuse and the ethos of power in Navajo healing. *Medical Anthropology Quarterly, 14*(4), 521–542.

Gatchel, R. J. (2001). Biofeedback and self-regulation of physiological activity: A major adjunctive treatment modality in health psychology. In A. Baum, T. A. Revenson, & J. E. Singer (Eds.),

Handbook of health psychology (pp. 95–115). Mahwah, NJ: Lawrence Erlbaum.

Gatz, M., Svedberg, P., Pedersen, N. L., Mortimer, J. A., et al. (2001). Education and the risk of Alzheimer's disease: Findings from the study of dementia in Swedish twins. *Journals of Gerontology: Series B: Psychological Sciences & Social Sciences, 56B,* 292–300.

Gavin, H. (1838). *On feigned and factitious diseases* (pp. 51–83). Edinburgh, Scotland: Edinburgh University Press.

Gay, P. (1988). *Freud: A life for our time.* New York: Norton.

Gay, P. (1988). Psycholanalysis in history. In W. M. Runyan (Ed.), *Psychology and historical interpretation* (pp. 107–120). New York: Oxford University Press.

Geller, D., Biederman, J., Jones, J., Park, K., et al. (1998). Is juvenile obsessive compulsive disorder a developmental subtype of the disorder? A review of the pediatric literature. *Journal of the American Academy of Child & Adolescent Psychiatry, 37,* 420–427.

Gelman, S. (1999). *Medicating schizophrenia: A history.* New Brunswick, NJ: Rutgers University Press.

Gerber, A. (1993). *Language-related learning disabilities: Their nature and treatment.* Baltimore: Paul H. Brookes.

Gerostamoulos, J., Staikos, V., & Drummer, O. H. (2001). Heroin-related deaths in Victoria: A review of cases for 1997 and 1998. *Drug & Alcohol Dependence, 61*(2), 123–127.

Gershon, E. S., & Nurnberger, J. I. (1995). Bipolar illness. In J. M Oldham & M. B. Riba (Eds.), *American Psychiatric Press review of psychiatry.* Washington, DC: American Psychiatric Press.

Gersons, B. P., & Carlier, I. V. (1993). Plane crash crisis intervention: A preliminary report from the Bijlmermeer, Amsterdam. *Crisis, 14*(3), 109–116.

Gesell, A. (1940). *The first five years of life: A guide to the study of the preschool child.* New York: Harper & Row.

Gesell, A., & Ilg, F. L. (1943). *Infant and child in the culture of today.* New York: Harper.

Ghuran, A., & Nolan, J. (2000, June 1). Recreational drug misuse: issues for the cardiologist. *Heart, 83*(6), 627–633.

Giannini, A. J. (1998). Phencyclidine. In *Handbook of substance abuse: Neurobehavioral pharmacology* (pp. 579–587). New York: Plenum Press.

Gilger, J. W., Pennington, B. F., & DeFries, J. C. (1992). A twin study of the etiology of comorbidity: Attention-deficit hyperactivity disorder and dyslexia. *Journal of the American Academy of Child and Adolescent Psychiatry, 31,* 343–348.

Gilman, C. (1913). Why I Wrote "The Yellow Wallpaper". *The Forerunner, 4,* 271.

Gilman, C. (1935). *The living of Charlotte Perkins Gilman: An autobiography.* New York: D. Appleton-Century Company. Reprint. Madison: University of Wisconsin Press 1991.

Gilmore, K. (2000). A psychoanalytic perspective on attention-deficit/hyperactivity disorder. *Journal of the American Psychoanalytic Association, 48,* 1259-1293.

Gilmore, K. (2002). Diagnosis, dynamics, and development: Considerations in the psychoanalytic assessment of children with AD/HD. *Psychoanalytic Inquiry, 22,* 372–390.

Gilmore, M. (1994). *Shot in the heart.* New York: Anchor Books.

Gitlow, S. (2001). *Substance use disorders: Practical guides in psychiatry*. Philadelphia: Lippincott Williams & Wilkins.

Gleaves, D. H. (1996). The sociocognitive model of dissociative identity disorder: A reexamination of the evidence. *Psychological Bulletin, 120*, 42–59.

Gloaguen, V., Cottraux, J., Cucherat, M., & Blackburn, I. (1998). A meta-analysis of the effects of cognitive therapy in depressed patients. *Journal of Affective Disorders, 49*, 59–72.

Goenjian, A. K., Najarian, L. M., Pynoos, R. S., & Steinberg, A. M. (1994). Posttraumatic stress disorder in elderly and younger adults after the 1988 earthquake in Armenia. *American Journal of Psychiatry, 151*(6), 895–901.

Goettman, C., Greaves, G. B., & Coons, P. M. (1992). *Multiple personality and dissociation, 1791–1991. A complete bibliography*. Lutherville, MD: Sidran Press.

Golberg, E. M., & Morrison, S. K. (1963). Schizophrenia and social class. *British Journal of Psychiatry, 109*, 785–802.

Gold, S., & Heffner, C. (1998). Sexual addiction: Many conceptions, minimal data. *Clinical Psychology Review, 18*(3), 367–381.

Goldberg, J. O., & Schmidt, L. A. (2001). Shyness, sociability, and social dysfunction in schizophrenia. *Schizophrenia Research (Special Issue), 48*(2–3), 343–349.

Golden, C. J. (1989). The Luria-Nebraska Neuropsychological Battery. In C. S. Newark (Ed.), *Major psychological assessment instruments*. (Vol. 2). Needham Heights, MA: Allyn & Bacon.

Golden, C., ed. (1992). *The captive imagination*. New York: The Feminist Press.

Goldstein, E. (1975). Compulsory treatment in Soviet psychiatric hospitals: A view from the inside. *International Journal of Offender Therapy & Comparative Criminology, 19*(2), 121–128.

Goldstein, G., & Hersen, M. (1990). *Handbook of psychological assessment* (2nd ed.). New York: Pergamon Press.

Goldstein, M. J. (1984). Family affect and communication related to schizophrenia. *New Directions for Child Development, 24*, 47–62.

Goldstein, M. J. (1995). The impact of gender on understanding the epidemiology of schizophrenia. In M. V. Seeman (Ed.), *Gender and psychopathology* (pp. 159–200). Washington, DC: American Psychiatric Press.

Goldstein, M. J. (1998). Adolescent behavioral and intrafamilial precursors of schizophrenia spectrum disorders. *International Clinical Psychopharmacology, 13* (1), S101.

Golomb, A., Ludolph, P., Westen, D., Block, M. J., et al., (1994). Maternal empathy, family chaos, and the etiology of borderline personality disorder. *Journal of the American Psychoanalytic Association, 42(2)*, 525–548.

Gonzalez, C. A., & Griffith, E. E. H. (1996). Culture and the diagnosis of somatoform and dissociaitive disorders. In J. E. Mezzich, A. Kleinman, H. Fabrega Jr., & D. L. Parron (Eds.), *Culture and psychiatric diagnosis: A DSM-IV perspective* (pp. 137–167). Washington, DC: American Psychiatric Press.

Goode, E. (1999, Dec. 7). Doctors try a bold new move against schizophrenia. *The New York Times*, D1.

Goode, E. (2001, November 20). Treatment can ease the lingering trauma of Sept. 11. *New York Times*, pp. D1, D6.

Goode, E. (2002, March 28). Thousands in Manhattan needed therapy after attack, study finds. *New York Times*, p. A15.

Goodman, E. (1999, May 28). Teaching young girls to harm themselves. *The Boston Globe*.

Goodwin, C. J. (1995). *Research in psychology: Methods and design*. New York: John Wiley & Sons.

Goodwin, J. M., & Sachs, R. G. (1996). Child abuse in the etiology of dissociative disorders. In L. K. Michelson & W. J. Ray (Eds.), *Handbook of dissociation: Theoretical, empirical, and clinical perspectives* (pp. 91–105). New York: Plenum Press.

Gorey K. M., & Leslie, D. R. (1997). The prevalence of child sexual abuse: Integrative review adjustment for potential response and measurement biases. *Child Abuse & Neglect, 21* (4), 391–398.

Gottdiener, W. H. (2001). The benefits of individual psychotherapy for schizophrenic patients: A meta-analytic review of the psychotherapy outcome literature. *Dissertation Abstracts International: Section B: The Sciences & Engineering, 61*, 7-B. Ann Arbor, MI: University Microfilms International.

Gottesman, I. (1991). *Schizophrenia genesis: The origins of madness*. New York: Freeman.

Gould, R. A., Mueser, K. T., Bolton, E., Mays, V., et al. (2001). Cognitive therapy for psychosis in schizophrenia: An effect size analysis. *Schizophrenia Research (Special Issue), 48*(2–3), 335–342.

Gould, S. J. (1993). *The mismeasure of man*. New York, London: W. W. Norton. (Original work published 1981)

Grady, D. (1998, Jan. 20). Studies of schizophrenia vindicate psychotherapy. The New York Times, B17.

Graeme, K. A. (2000). New drugs of abuse. *Emergency Medicine Clinics of North America, 18*(4), 625–636.

Graham, J. R. (1987). *The MMPI: A practical guide* (2nd ed.). New York: Oxford University Press.

Graham, S. (1854). *Lectures on the science of human life*. London: W. Horsell.

Grandin, T. (1995). *Thinking in pictures and other reports from my life with autism*. New York: Doubleday.

Graziottin, A. (2001). Clinical approach to dyspareunia. *Journal of Sex & Marital Therapy, 27*(5), 489–501.

Grealy, L. (1994). *Autobiography of a face*. Boston: Houghton Mifflin.

Green, J. P. (2000). Treating women who smoke: The benefits of using hypnosis. In L. M. Hornyak & J. P. Green (Eds.), *Healing from within: The use of hypnosis in women's health care* (pp. 91–117). Washington, DC: American Psychological Association.

Green, R., Newman, E., & Stoller, R. (1972). Treatment of boyhood "transsexualism". *Archives of General Psychiatry, 26*(3), 213–217.

Greenberg, J. (1964). *I never promised you a rose garden*. New York: Holt, Rinehart & Winston.

Greenberg, J., & Mitchell, S. (1983). *Object relations in psychoanalytic theory*. Cambridge, MA: Harvard University Press.

Greenberg. J. R., & Mitchell, S. (1983). *Object relations in psychoanalytic theory*. Cambridge, MA: Harvard University Press.

Greenfield, B., Hechtman, L., & Weiss, G. (1988). Two subgroups of hyperactives as adults: Correlations of outcome. *Canadian Journal of Psychiatry, 33,* 505–508.

Greenfield, S. F., & Sugarman, D. E. (2001). The treatment and consequences of alcohol abuse and dependence during pregnancy. *Management of psychiatric disorders in pregnancy.* New York: Oxford University Press.

Greenson, R. (1968). Dis-identifying from mother: Its special importance for the boy. *International Journal of Psycho-Analysis, 49*(2–3), 370–374.

Gregory, R. J. (1999). *Foundations of intellectual assessment: The WAIS-III and other tests in clinical practice.* Boston: Allyn & Bacon.

Gresham, F. M., & MacMillan, D. L. (1998). Early Intervention Project: Can its claims be substantiated and its effects replicated? *Journal of Autism and Developmental Disorders, 28,* 5–13.

Gribble, J. N., Miller, H. G., Cooley, P. C., Catania, J. A., et al. (2000). The impact of T-ACASI interviewing on reported drug use among men who have sex with men. *Substance Use & Misuse (Special Issue: Methodological Issues in the Measurement of Drug Use), 35*(6–8), 869–890.

Grisaru, N., Budowsky, D., & Witztum, E. (1997). Possession by the "Zar" among Ethiopian immigrants to Israel: Psychopathology or culture-bound syndrome? *Psychopathology, 30*(4), 223–233.

Griswold, T. (2000). Psychotherapy in emergency situations. In *The real world guide to psychotherapy practice* (pp. 121–148). Cambridge, MA: Harvard University Press.

Gromska, J., Labon, T., Tyszkiewica, M., & de Walden K. J. (1972). Familial and environmental factors in the occurrence of mental illness and neurosis. *Psychiatria Polska, 6*(2), 175–182.

Gross, G. (1997). The onset of schizophrenia. *Schizophrenia Research, 28,* 187–198.

Grossman, R. (2002). Psychopharmacologic treatment of patients with borderline personality disorder. *Psychiatric Annals, 32*(6), 357–370.

Grotstein, J. (1982). Newer perspectives in object relations theory. *Contemporary Psychoanalysis, 18,* 43–91.

Gruenbaum, A. (1996). Is psychoanalysis viable? In W. O'Donohue (Ed.), *The philosophy of psychology* (pp. 281–290). Thousand Oaks, CA: Sage Publications.

Guarnaccia, P. J. (1997). A cross-cultural perspective on anxiety disorders. In S. Friedman (Ed.), *Cultural issues in the treatment of anxiety* (pp. 3–20). New York: Guilford Press.

Gurman, A., & Messer, S. (Eds.). (1995). *Essential psychotherapies.* New York: Guilford Press.

Gut-Fayand, A. Dervaux, A., Olie, J-P., Loo, H., et al. (2001). Substance abuse and suicidality in schizophrenia: A common risk factor linked to impulsivity. *Psychiatry Research (Special Issue), 102*(1), 65–72.

Guthrie, E. (1995). Treatment of functional somatic symptoms: Psychodynamic treatment. In R. Mayou, C. Bass, & M. Sharpe (Eds.), *Treatment of functional somatic symptoms* (pp. 144–160). Oxford, England: Oxford University Press.

Gutkind, D., Ventur, J., Barr, C., Shaner, A., et al. (2001). Factors affecting reliability and confidence of DSM-III-R psychosis-related diagnosis. *Psychiatry Research (Special Issue), 101*(3), 269–275.

H

Haaken, J. (1993). From Al-Anon to ACOA: Codependence and the reconstruction of caregiving. *Signs 18,* 321–345.

Haaken, J. (1995). A critical analysis of the codependency construct. In M. Babcock (Ed.), *Challenging codependency: Feminist critiques* (pp. xix, 240, 53–69). Buffalo, NY: University of Toronto Press.

Haas, G. J., Glick, I. D., Clarkin, J. F., Spencer, J. H., et al. (1988). Inpatient family intervention: A randomized clinical trial. II. Results at hospital discharge. *Archives of General Psychiatry, 45,* 217–224.

Hadley N. (1985). *Foundations of aversion therapy.* New York: SP Medical and Scientific Books.

Haley, J. (1987). *Problem solving therapy* (2nd ed.). San Francisco: Jossey Bass.

Hall, G., Andersen, B., Aarestad, S., & Barongan, C. (2000). Sexual dysfunction and deviation. In M. Hersen, & A. Bellack (Eds.), *Psychopathology in adulthood* (2nd ed., pp. 390–418). Needham Heights, MA: Allyn & Bacon.

Hall, G. S. (1921). *Aspects of child life and education.* New York: D. Appleton and Company.

Halpern, C., Udry, J., Suchindran, C., & Campbell, B. (2000). Adolescent males' willingness to report masturbation. *Journal of Sex Research (Special Issue), 37*(4), 327–332.

Hammer, E. (1990). *Reaching the affect: Style in the psychodynamic therapies.* New York: Jason Aronson.

Handen, B. L. (1998). Mental retardation. In E. J. Mash & L. G. Terdal (Eds.), *Treatment of childhood disorders.* New York: Guilford Press.

Hansell, J. (1997). Take third parties out of mental health plans [Op-Ed]. *Detroit Free Press.*

Hansell, J. (1998). Gender anxiety, gender melancholia, gender perversion. *Psychoanalytic Dialogues, 8*(3), 337–351.

Hansell, J. (2002). Rigor and Reductionism: Commentory on Brenner. *Journal of Clinical Psychoanalysis, 11*(1), 83–89.

Hansell, J. H. (1989). Cognitive and affective determinants of coping: A study of divorced women. *Dissertation Abstracts International, 50,* (3B). University Microfilms International.

Harding, T. P., & Lachenmeyer, J. R. (1986). Family interaction patterns and locus of control as predictors of the presence and severity of anorexia nervosa. *Journal of Clinical Psychology, 42,* 440–448.

Hardy, M. S., & Calhoun, L. G. (1997). Psychological distress and the "medical student syndrome" in abnormal psychology students. *Teaching of Psychology, 24*(3), 192–193.

Hardy, P., Payan, C., Bisserbe, J. C., & Lepine, J. P. (1999). Anxiolytic and hypnotic use in 376 psychiatric inpatients. *European Psychiatry, 14*(1), 25–32.

Hare, E. (1962). Masturbatory insanity: The history of an idea. *Journal of Mental Science, 108,* 1–25.

Hare, R. (1999). *Without conscience: The disturbing world of the psychopaths among us.* New York: Guilford Press.

Harkness, S., & Super, C. M. (2000). Culture and psychopathology. In A. J. Sameroff, M. Lewis, & S. M. Miller (Eds.), *Handbook of developmental psychopathology* (2nd ed.). New York: Kluwer Academic/Plenum Press.

Harrap, C., & Trower, P. (2001). Why does schizophrenia develop at late adolescence? *Clinical Psychology Review, 21*(2), 241–266.

Harrigan, P. (1999). Are cannabis and psychosis linked? *Lancet (North American ed.), 353*(9154), 730.

Harrington, R., Rutter, M., Weissman, M., Fudge, H., et al. (1997). Psychiatric disorders in the relatives of depressed probands. I. Comparison of prepubertal, adolescent, and early adult onset cases. *Journal of Affective Disorders, 42*, 9–22.

Harris, B. (1979). Whatever happened to Little Albert? *American Psychologist, 34*, 151–160.

Harris, M. M. (1989). Reconsidering the employment interview: A review of recent literature and suggestions for future research. *Personnel Psychology, 42*, 691–726.

Harrison, G., Hopper, K., Craig, T., Laska, E., et al. (2001). Recovery from psychotic illness: A 15- and 25-year international follow-up study. *British Journal of Psychiatry: (Special Issue), 178*, 506–517.

Hart, B. (1988). Biological basis of the behavior of sick animals. *Neuroscience and Biobehavioral Reviews, 12*(2), 123–137.

Harwood, D., & Jacoby, R. (2000). Suicidal behavior among the elderly. In K. Hawton & K. van Heeringen (Eds.), *The international handbook of suicide and attempted suicide* (pp. 275–292). New York: John Wiley & Sons.

Hatcher, R., Barends, A., Hansell, J., & Gutfreund, J. (1995). Patients' and therapists' shared and unique views of the therapeutic alliance: An investigation using confirmatory factor analysis in a nested design. *Journal of Consulting and Clinical Psychology, 63*(4), 636–643.

Hathaway, S., & McKinley, J. (1989). *Manual for administration and scoring of the MMPI-2.* Minneapolis: University of Minnesota Press.

Hausmann, A., & Fleischhacker, W. W. (2000). Depression in patients with schizophrenia: Prevalence and diagnostic and treatment considerations. *CNS Drugs, 14*(4), 289–299.

Hawkins, J. D., Catalano, R. F., & Miller, J. Y. (1992). Risk and protective factors for alcohol and other drug problems in adolescence and early adulthood: Implications for substance abuse prevention. *Psychological Bulletin, 112*, 64–105.

Hayes, S., Follette, W., & Follette, V. (1995). Behavior therapy: A contextual approach. In A. Gurman & S. Messer (Eds.), *Essential psychotherapies.* New York: Guilford.

Hayes, S., Jacobson, N., Follette, V., & Dougher, M. (1994). *Acceptance and change in psychotherapy.* Reno, NV: Context Press.

Haynes, S. N., & O'Brien, W. H. (1990). Functional analysis in behavior therapy. *Clinical Psychology Review, 10*(6) 649–668.

Heath, A. C., Whitfield, J. B., Madden, P. A. F., Bucholz, K. K., et al. (2001). Towards a molecular epidemiology of alcohol dependence: Analyzing the interplay of genetic and environmental risk factors. *British Journal of Psychiatry (Special Issue), 78*(40), S33–S40.

Heath, I. (2000). May state treat, over his objection, a capital murder inmate who, as a result of mental illness, is found to be a danger to self and others, when a concurrent effect of the treatment is the restoration of competency to be executed. *Journal of the American Academy of Psychiatry & the Law, 28*(2), 247–248.

Heider, F. (1958). *Interpersonal relations.* New York: John Wiley & Sons.

Heim, C., Newport, D. J., Heit, S., Graham, Y. P., et al. (2000). Pituitary-adrenal and autonomic responses to stress in women after sexual and physical abuse in childhood. *Journal of the American Medical Association, 284*, 592–597.

Heim, N., & Hursch, C. J. (1977). Castration and sexual offenders: Treatment or punishment? A review and critique of recent European literature. *Archives of Sexual Behavior, 8*, 281–304.

Heinrichs, R. W., & Zakzanis, K. K. (1998). Neurocognitive deficit in schizophrenia: A quantitative review of the evidence. *Neuropsychology, 12*(3), 426–445.

Heinssen, R. K., Liberman, R. P., & Kopelowicz, A. (2000). Psychosocial skills training for schizophrenia: Lessons from the laboratory. *Schizophrenia Bulletin (Special Issue: Psychosocial Treatment for Schizophrenia), 26*(1), 21–46.

Helgeson, V. S., Cohen, S., Schulz, R., & Yasko, J. (2001). Group support interventions for people with cancer: Benefits and hazards. In A. Baum & B. L. Andersen (Eds.), *Psychosocial interventions for cancer* (pp. 269–286). Washington, DC: American Psychological Association.

Heng, L. (2001, March 12, 2001). *Mental disorder redefined, Homosexuality excluded.* Retrieved January 16, 2004 from (*People's Daily,* electronic English edition).

Herbert, T. B., & Cohen, S. (1993). Stress and immunity in humans: A metaanalytic review. *Psychosomatic Medicine, 55*, 364–379.

Herman, J. L. (1997). *Trauma and recovery.* New York: Basic Books.

Herman, J. L. (1981). *Father-daughter incest.* Cambridge, MA: Harvard University Press.

Herman, M. (2000). Psychotherapy with substance abusers: Integration of psychodynamic and cognitive-behavioral approaches. *American Journal of Psychotherapy, 54*(4), 574–579.

Hershman, D. J., & Lieb, J. (1998). *Manic depression and creativity.* Amherst, NY: Prometheus Books.

Herzog, D. B., Keller, M. B., Sacks, N. R., Yeh, C. J., et al. (1992). Psychiatric comorbidity in treatment-seeking anorexics and bulimics. *Journal of the American Academy of Child & Adolescent Psychiatry, 31*, 810–818.

Herzog, D. B., Nussbaum, K. M., & Marmor, A. K. (1996). Comorbidity and outcome in eating disorders. *Psychiatric Clinics of North America, 19*, 843–859.

Hester, R., & Miller, W. (1995). *Handbook of alcoholism treatment approaches: Effective alternatives* (2nd ed.). Needham Heights, MA: Allyn & Bacon.

Heston, L. (1996). Psychiatric disorders in foster home reared children of schizophrenic mothers. *British Journal of Psychiatry, 112*, 819–825.

Hetrick, W., & Smith, D. (2000). Sensory gating: Construct definition, development of a self-report rating instrument, and comparison with a psychophysiological measure. *Dissertation Abstracts International, Section B: The sciences and engineering, 60*(11-B). University Microfilms International.

Heyman, A., Fillenbaum, G., Prosnitz, B., & Raiford, K. (1991). Estimated prevalence of dementia among elderly Black and White community residents. *Archives of Neurology, 48,* 594–598.

Hien, D., & Bukszpan, C. (1999). Interpersonal violence in a "normal" low-income control group. *Women & Health, 29,* 1–16.

Hilgard, J. R. (1991). A neodissociation theory of hypnosis. In S. J. Lynn & J. Rhue (Eds.), *Theories of hypnosis: Current models and perspectives* (pp. 83–104). New York: Guilford Press.

Hiller, J. B., Rosenthal, R., Bornstein, R. F., Berry, D. T., et al. (1999). A comparative meta-analysis of Rorschach and MMPI validity. *Psychological Assessment, 11*(3), 278–296.

Hinshaw, S. P., Klein, R. G., & Abikoff, H. B. (2002). Childhood attention-deficit hyperactivity disorder: Nonpharmacological treatments and their combination with medication. In P. E. Nathan, P. E., & J. M. Gorman, (Eds.), *A guide to treatments that work* (2nd ed., pp. 3–23). New York: Oxford University Press.

Hirsch, D., Paley, J. E., & Renner, J. A. (1996). In L. Friedman, N. Fleming, D. Roberts, & S. Hyman (Eds.), *Sourcebook of substance abuse and addiction.* Baltimore: Williams & Wilkins.

Ho, B.-C., & Andreason, N. (2001). Positive symptoms, negative symptoms and beyond. In A. Brier, P. Tran, J. Herrera, G. Tollefson, et al. (Eds.), *Current issues in the psychopharmacology of schizophrenia* (pp. 407–416). Philadelphia: Lippincott Williams & Wilkins.

Hoek, H. W. (1995). The distribution of eating disorders. In K. D. Brownell & C. G. Fairburn (Eds.), *Eating disorders and obesity.* New York: Guilford Press.

Hofmann, A. (1994). Notes and documents concerning the discovery of LSD. 1970. *Agents & Actions, 43*(3–4), 79–81.

Hogarty, G. E., Greenwald, D., Ulrich, R. F., Kornblith, S. J., et al. (1997b). Three-year trials of personal therapy among schizophrenic patients living with or independent of family: II. Effects of adjustment of patients. *American Journal of Psychiatry, 154*(11), 1514–1524.

Hogarty, G. E., Kornblith, S. J., Greenwald, D., DiBarry, A. L., et al. (1997a). Three-year trials of personal therapy among schizophrenic patients living with or independent of family: I. Description of study and effects of relapse rates. *American Journal of Psychiatry, 154*(11), 1504–1513.

Holder-Perkins, V., & Wise, T. N. (2001). Somatization disorder. In K. A. Phillips (Ed.), *Somatoform and factitious disorders* (pp. 1–26). Washington, DC: American Psychiatric Publishing.

Holland, A. J., Hall, A., Murray, R., Russell. G. F. M., et al. (1984). Anorexia nervosa: A study of 34 twin pairs and one set of triplets. *British Journal of Psychiatry, 145,* 414–419.

Hollifield, M., Paine, S., Tuttle, L., & Kellner, R. (1999). Hypochondriasis, somatization, and perceived health and utilization of health care services. *Psychosomatics, 40,* 380–386.

Hollon, S. (1996). The efficacy and effectiveness of psychotherapy relative to medications. *American Psychologist, 51,* 1025–1030.

Holm, J. E., Lokken, C., & Myers, T. C. (1997). Migraine and stress: A daily examination of temporal relationships in women migraineurs. *Headache, 37,* 553–558.

Holmes, T. H., & Rahe, R. H. (1967). The social readjustment rating scale. *Journal of Psychosomatic Research, 11,* 213–218.

Honigfield, G. (1996). Effects of the clozapine national registry system on incidence of deaths related to agranulocytosis. *Psychiatric Services, 47*(1), 52–56.

Hooley, J. M., & Hiller, J. B. (2001). Family relationships and major mental disorder: Risk factors and preventive strategies. In *Personal relationships: Implications for clinical and community psychology* (pp. 61–87). Chichester, England: Wiley.

Hope, L. C., Cook, C. C. H., & Thomson, A. D. (1999). A survey of the current clinical practice of psychiatrists and accident and emergency specialists in the United Kingdom concerning vitamin supplementation for chronic alcohol misusers. *Alcohol & Alcoholism, 34*(6), 862–867.

Hopgood, J. F. (2000). People of the peyote [Book review] Huichol Indian history, religion & survival. *Latin American Research Review, 35*(2), 204–215.

Hopkins, H. S., & Gelenberg, A. J. (1994). Treatment of bipolar disorder: How far have we come? *Psychopharmacology Bulletin, 30,* 27–38.

Horacek, J., Libiger, J., Hoeschl, C., Borzova, K., et al. (2001). Clozapine-induced concordant agranulocytosis in monozygotic twins. *International Journal of Psychiatry in Clinical Practice (Special Issue), 5*(1), 71–73.

Horevitz, R., & Loewenstein, R. J. (1994). The rational treatment of multiple personality disorder. In S. J. Lynn & J. Rhue (Eds.), *Dissociation: Clinical and theoretical perspectives* (pp. 298–316). New York: Guilford Press.

Horley, J. (2001). Frotteurism: A term in search of an underlying disorder? *Journal of Sexual Aggression (Special Issue), 7*(1), 51–55.

Hornbacher, M. (1998). *Wasted: A memoir of anorexia and bulimia.* New York: HarperCollins.

Hornstein, N., & Putnam, F. W. (1992). Clinical phenomenology of child and adolescent dissociative disorders. *Journal of the American Academy of Child and Adolescent Psychiatry, 31,* 1077–1085.

Horvath, A. (1994). *The working alliance: Theory, research, and practice.* New York: John Wiley & Sons.

Horwath, E., & Weissman, M. M. (1997). Epidemiology of anxiety disorders across cultural groups. In S. Friedman (Ed.), *Cultural issues in the treatment of anxiety* (pp. 21–39). New York: Guilford Press.

Hou, C., Miller, B. L., Cummings, J. L., Goldberg, M., et al. (2000). Autistic savants. *Neuropsychiatry, Neuropsychology, and Behavioral Neurology, 13,* 29–38.

Houlihan, D., Schwartz, C., Miltenberger, R., & Heuton, D. (1993). The rapid treatment of a young man's balloon (noise) phobia using in vivo flooding. *Journal of Behavior Therapy & Experimental Psychiatry, 24,* 233–240.

Houran, J., & Lange, R. (1997). Hallucinations that comfort: Contextual mediation of deathbed visions. *Perceptual & Motor Skills, 84*(3, Pt. 2), 1491–1504.

Howard, R., Rabins, P. V., Seeman, M. V., & Jeste, D. V. (2000). Late-onset schizophrenia and very-late-onset schizophrenia-like psychosis: An international consensus. *American Journal of Psychiatry, 157*(2), 172–178.

Hsiao, J. (2001). Curing schizophrenia, treating schizophrenia: Translating research into practice. In J. Lieberman & R. Murray (Eds.), *Comprehensive care of schizophrenia.* London: Martin Dunitz.

Hudson, S., & Ward, T. (1997). Rape: Psychopathology and theory. In *Sexual deviance: Theory, assessment, and treatment* (pp. 332–355). New York: Guilford Press.

Huebner, H. F. (1993). *Endorphins, eating disorders and other addictive behaviors.* New York: W. W. Norton.

Hugdahl, K. (1995). *Psychophysiology: The mind-body perspective.* Cambridge, MA: Harvard University Press.

Hughes, J. R., Oliveto, A. H., Bickel, W. K., Higgins, S. T., et al. (1993). Caffeine self-administration and withdrawal: Incidence, individual differences and interrelationships. *Drug & Alcohol Dependence, 32*(3), 239–246.

Hutchings, D. E. (1989). *Prenatal abuse of licit and illicit drugs.* New York: New York Academy of Sciences.

Huyse, F. J., Lyons, J. S., Stiefel, F., Slaets, J., et al. (2001). Operationalizing the biopsychosocial model: The *Psychosomatics; Vol 42(1),* 5–13.

Hwang, M. Y., & Bermanzohn, P. C. (2001). *Schizophrenia and comorbid conditions: Diagnosis and treatment.* Washington, DC: American Psychiatric Press, Inc.

Hwang, M. Y., & Bermanzohn, P. C. (Eds.). (2001). *Schizophrenia and comorbid conditions: Diagnosis and treatment.* Washington, DC: American Psychiatric Press.

Hyman, S. & Moldin, S. (2001). Genetic Science and depression: Implications for research and treatment. In *Treatment of depression: Bridging the 21st century.* M. Weissman (Ed.), Washington DC: American Psychiatric Press, 83–103.

I

Iacono, W. G., & Patrick, C. J. (1997). Polygraphy and integrity testing. In R. Richards (Ed.), *Clinical assessment of malingering and deception* (2nd ed.). New York: Guilford Press.

Illness, H. (1999). Homosexuality and mental illness. *Archives of General Psychiatry, 56*(10), 883–884.

Insel, T. R. (1991). Long-term neural consequences of stress during development: Is early experience a form of chemical imprinting? In B. J. Carroll & J. E. Barrett (Eds.), *Psychopathology and the brain* (pp. 133–152). New York: Raven Press.

Insel, T. R., Zahn, T., & Murphy, D. L. (1985). Obsessive compulsive disorder: An anxiety disorder? In A. H. Turner & J. Maser (Eds.), *Anxiety and the anxiety disorders.* Hillsdale, NJ: Lawrence Earlbaum Associates.

Irving, L. M., DuPen, J., & Berel, S. (1998). A media literacy program for high school females. *Eating Disorders: The Journal of Treatment and Prevention, 6,* 119–131.

Isay, R. (1996). *Becoming gay: The journey to self-acceptance.* New York: Pantheon Books.

Iversen, L. L. (2000). *The science of marijuana.* New York: Oxford University Press.

Iverson, G. L., Turner, R. A., & Green, P. (1999). Predictive validity of WAIS-R VIQ-PIQ splits in persons with major depression. *Journal of Clinical Psychology, 55*(4), 519–524.

Iwanami, A., Isono, H., Okajima, Y., Noda, Y., et al. (1998). Event-related potentials during a selective attention task with short interstimulus intervals in patients with schizophrenia. *Journal of Psychiatry & Neuroscience, 23*(1), 45–50.

J

Jablensky, A. (1995). Kraepelin's legacy. Paradigm or pitfall of modern psychiatry? *European Archives of Psychiatry, 245*(4–5), 186–188.

Jablensky, A. (1997). The 100 year epidemiology of schizophrenia. *Schizophrenia Research, 28,* 111–125.

Jablensky, A. (2000). Epidemiology of schizophrenia: The global burden of disease and disability. *European Archives of Psychiatry & Clinical Neuroscience 250*(6), 274–285.

Jacobs, K. M., & Hirsch, K. A. (2000). Psychiatric complications of Ma-huang. *Psychosomatics, 41*(1), 58–62.

Jacobson, E. (1964). *The self and the object world.* New York: International Universities Press.

Jacobson, N., Dobson, K., Truax, P. A., Addis, M. E., et al. (2000). A component analysis of cognitive-behavioral treatment for depression. *Journal of Consulting and Clinical Psychology, 64,*(2), 295–304.

Jacobson, N. S., & Hollon, S. D. (1996). Cognitive-behavior therapy versus pharmacotherapy: Now that the jury's returned its verdict, it's time to present the rest of the evidence. *Journal of Consulting and Clinical Psychology, 64,* 74–80.

Jacobson, W., & Cooper, A. M. (1993). Psychodynamic diagnosis in the era of the current DSM's. In N. Miller, L. Luborsky, J. P. Barker, & J. P. Docherty (Eds.), *Psychodynamic treatment research: A handbook for clinical practice.* New York: Basic Books.

James, S. A., Hartnett, S. A., & Kalsbeek, W. (1983). John Henryism and blood pressure differences among Black men. *Journal of Behavioral Medicine, 6,* 259–278.

James, W. (1936). *The varieties of religious experience.* New York: Modern Library.

Jamieson, E., Butwell, M., Taylor, P., & Leese, M. (2000). Trends in special (high security) hospitals: Referrals and admissions. *British Journal of Psychiatry, 176,* 253–259.

Jamison, K. R. (1995). *An unquiet mind: A memoir of moods and madness.* New York: Vintage Books.

Jamison, K. R. (1999a). A magical orange grove in a nightmare. In R. Conlan (Ed.), *States of mind: New discoveries about how our brains make us who we are.* New York: John Wiley & Sons.

Jamison, K. R. (1999b). *Night falls fast: Understanding suicide.* New York: Knopf.

Jansen, K. L. R., & Darracot-Cankovic, R. (2001). The nonmedical use of ketamine, part two: A review of problem use and dependence. *Journal of Psychoactive Drugs (Special Issue), 33*(2), 151–158.

Javitt, D. C., & Zukin, S. R. (1991). Recent advances in the phencyclidine model of schizophrenia. *American Journal of Psychiatry, 148,* 1301–1308.

Jellineck, E. (1946). *Phases in the drinking history of alcoholics.* New Haven, CT: Hillhouse Press.

Jensen, P. S., Bloedau, L., Degroot, J., Ussery, T., et al. (1990). Children at risk I: Risk factors and child symptomatology. *Journal of the American Academy of Child and Adolescent Psychiatry, 29,* 51–59.

Jensen, P. S., & Hoagwood, K. (1997). The book of names: DSM-IV in context. *Development & Psychopathology, 9*(2), 231–249.

Jex, S. M., Bliese, P. D., Buzzell, S., & Primeau, J. (2001). The impact of self-efficacy on stressor-strain relations: Coping style as an explanatory mechanism. *Journal of Applied Psychology: Special Issue, 86*(3), 401–409.

Jogems-Kosterman, B. J. M., Zitman, F. G., VanHoof, J. J. M., & Hulstijn, W. (2001). Psychomotor slowing and planning deficits in schizophrenia. *Schizophrenia Research (Special Issue), 48*(2–3), 317–333.

Johnson, C., Powers, P. S., & Dick, R. (1999). Athletes and eating disorders: The National Collegiate Athletic Association Study. *International Journal of Eating Disorders, 25*, 179–188.

Johnson, J. G., & Sherman, M. F. (1997). Daily hassles mediate the relationship between major life events and psychiatric symptomatology: Longitudinal findings from an adolescent sample. *Journal of Social & Clinical Psychology, 16*, 389–404.

Johnson, M. E., Jones, G., & Brems, C. (1996). Concurrent validity of the MMPI-2 feminine gender role (GF) and masculine gender role (GM) scales. *Journal of Personality Assessment, 66*(1), 153–168.

Johnson, S. P. (2001). Short-term play therapy. In *Innovations in play therapy: Issues, process, and special populations* (pp. 217–235). Philadelphia: Brunner-Routledge.

Johnston-Brooks, C. H., Lewis, M. A., Evans, G. W., & Whalen, C. K. (1998). Chronic stress and illness in children: The role of allostatic load. *Psychosomatic Medicine, 60*, 597–603.

Johnstone, E. (1994). *Searching for the causes of schizophrenia.* New York: Oxford University Press.

Johnstone, E. C., Humphreys, M. S., Lang, F. H., Lawrie, S. M., et al. (1999). *Schizophrenia: Concepts and clinical management.* New York: Cambridge University Press.

Jones, E. & Pulos S. M. (1993). Comparing the process in psychodynamic and cognitive-behavioral therapies. *Jounal of Consulting and Clinical Psychology, 61*(2), 306–316.

Jones, P. B., & Tarrant, C. J. (2000). Developmental precursors and biological markers for schizophrenia and affective disorders: Specificity and public health implications. *European Archives of Psychiatry & Clinical Neuroscience, 25*(6), 286–291.

Jordan, G., & Stein, D. (2000). Mental disorders due to a general medical condition. *Psychosomatics, 41*(4), 370.

Jorstad, J. (2001). Avoiding unbearable pain: Resistance and defence in the psychoanalysis of a man with a narcissistic personality disorder. *Scandinavian Psychoanalytic Review, 24*, 34–45.

Joseph, B. (1989). *Psychic equilibrium and psychic change.* London: Routledge.

Joseph, J. J. (2000). A critical analysis of the genetic theory of schizophrenia. *Dissertation Abstracts International: Section B: The Sciences & Engineering, 60*(11-B). Ann Arbor, MI: University Microfilms International.

Junginger, J. (1988). Summation of arousal in partial fetishism. *Journal of Behavior Therapy & Experimental Psychiatry, 19*(4), 297–300.

Junginger, J. (1997). Fetishism: Assessment and treatment. In D. Laws & W. O'Donohue (Eds.), *Sexual deviance: Theory, assessment, and treatment* (pp. 92–110). New York: Guilford Press.

K

Kafka, M. (1997). Hypersexual desire in males: An operational definition and clinical implications for males with paraphilias and paraphilia-related disorders. *Archives of Sexual Behavior, 26*(5), 505–526.

Kafka, M., & Hennen, J. (1999). The paraphilia-related disorders: An empirical investigation of nonparaphilic hypersexuality disorders in outpatient males. *Journal of Sex & Marital Therapy, 25*(4), 305–319.

Kafka, M., & Prentky, R. (1997). Compulsive sexual behavior characteristics. *American Journal of Psychiatry, 154*(11), 1632.

Kagitcibasi, C. (2000). Cultural contextualism without complete relativism in the study of human development. In A. Comunian (Ed.), *International perspectives on human development.* Lengerich, Germany: Pabst Science Publishers.

Kahn, D. A. (1993). The use of psychodynamic psychotherapy in manic-depressive illness. *Journal of the American Academy of Psychoanalysis. 21*, 441–455.

Kahn, J. H., with Solomon, H. (1975). *Job's illness: Loss, grief and integration: a psychological interpretation.* New York: Pergamon Press.

Kahn, S. (2001). A matter of life and death: The case of Jan. In S. Kahn (Ed.), *Changes in the therapist.* Mahwah, NJ: Lawrence Erlbaum Associates, Inc.

Kalil, K. M., Gruber, J. E., Conley, J. G., & LaGrandeur, R. M. (1995). Relationships among stress, anxiety, Type A, and pregnancy-related complications. *Pre- & Peri-Natal Psychology Journal, 9*, 221–232.

Kamali, M., Kelly, L., Gervin, M., Browne, S., et al. (2001). Insight and comorbid substance misuse and medication compliance among patients with schizophrenia. *Psychiatric Services (Special Issue), 52*(2), 161–163.

Kanayama, G., Gruber, A. J., Pope, H. G., Jr., Borowiecki, J. J., et al. (2001). Over-the-counter drug use in gymnasiums: An underrecognized substance abuse problem? *Psychotherapy & Psychosomatics (Special Issue), 70*(3), 137–140.

Kanner, A., Coyne, J. C., Scaefer, C., & Lazarus, R. S. (1981). Comparison of two modes of stress measurement: Daily hassles and uplifts versus major life events. *Journal of Behavioral Medicine, 4*, 1–39.

Kaplan, H. (1974). *The new sex therapy; active treatment of sexual dysfunctions.* New York: Brunner/Mazel.

Kaplan, H. (1995). *New directions in sex therapy: Innovations and alternatives.* New York: Brunner/Mazel.

Kaplan, H. (1996). Erotic obsession: Relationship to hypoactive sexual desire disorder and paraphilia. *American Journal of Psychiatry, 153*(Suppl), 30–41.

Kaplan, M. (1983). A woman's view of the DSM-III. *American Psychologist, 28*, 786–792.

Kaplan, R. M., & Saccuzzo, D. P. (1993). *Psychological testing: Principles, applications and issues* (3rd ed.). Pacific Grove, CA: Brooks/Cole.

Kapur, S., & Remington, G. (2001). Atypical antipsychotics: New directions and new challenges in the treatment of schizophrenia. *Annual Review of Medicine (Special Issue), 52*, 503–517.

Kardiner, A. (1941). *The traumatic neuroses of war.* New York: Paul B. Hoeber.

Karon, B. P. (1992). The fear of understanding schizophrenia. *Psychoanalytic Psychology, 9*(2), 191–211.

Kaslow, N., & Celano, M. (1995). The family therapies. In A. Gurman & S. Messner (Eds.) Essential psychotherapies. New York: Guilford Press, pp. 343–402.

Kathol, R. G., Carter, J., & Yates, W. R. (1990). *Clinical psychiatry for medical students.* Philadelphia: J. P. Lippincott.

Katz, R., & David, J. (1999). The relationship between worry, sexual aversion, and low sexual desire. *Journal of Sex & Marital Therapy, 25*(4), 293–296.

Kaufman, D., & Friedman, L. (1996). In L. Friedman, N. Fleming, D. Roberts, & S. Hyman (Eds.), *Sourcebook of substance abuse and addiction.* Baltimore: Williams & Wilkins.

Kaufman, E. (1986). A contemporary approach to the family treatment of substance abuse disorders. *American Journal of Drug & Alcohol Abuse, 12*(3), 199–211.

Kaye, W. H., Nagata, T., Weltzin, T. E., Hsu, L. K. G., et al. (2001). Double-blind placebo-controlled administration of fluoxetine in restricting- and restricting-purging-type anorexia nervosa. *Biological Psychiatry, 49,* 644–652.

Kazdin, A. E. (1995). *Conduct disorders in childhood and adolescence* (2nd ed.). Thousand Oaks, CA: Sage Publications.

Kazdin, A. E., Siegel, T. C., & Bass, D. (1992). Cognitive problem-solving skills training and parent management training in the treatment of antisocial behavior in children. *Journal of Consulting and Clinical Psychology, 60,* 733–747.

Keane, T. M., Zimering, R. T., & Caddell, J. M. (1985). A behavioral formulation of posttraumatic stress disorder in Vietnam veterans. *Behavior Therapist, 8,* 9–12.

Kear-Colwell, J., & Boer, D. (2000). The treatment of pedophiles: Clinical experience and the implications of recent research. *International Journal of Offender Therapy & Comparative Criminology (Special Issue), 44*(5), 593–605.

Kearney, C. A., & Silverman, W. K. (1995). Family environment in youngsters with school refusal behavior: A synopsis with implications for assessment and treatment. *American Journal of Family Therapy, 23,* 59–72.

Keefe, R. S. E. (2001). Negative symptoms and the assessment of neurocognitive treatment response. In *Negative symptom and cognitive deficit treatment response in schizophrenia* (pp. 85–110). Washington, DC: American Psychiatric Press.

Keefe, R. S. E., & McEvoy, J. P. (2001). *Negative symptom and cognitive deficit treatment response in schizophrenia.* Washington, DC: American Psychiatric Press.

Keijers, G., Schoop, C., & Hoogdvin, C. (2000). The impact of interpersonal patient and therapist behaviors on outcome in cognitive-behavioral therapy: A review of empirical studies. *Behavior Modification, 24*(2), 264–297.

Keith, S. J., Regier, D. S., & Rae, D. A. (1991). Schizophrenic disorders. In L. N. Robins & D. S. Regier (Eds.), *Psychiatric disorders in America: The epidemiological catchment area study.* New York: Free Press.

Kellogg, J. (1881). *Plain facts for young and old embracing the natural history and hygiene of organic life.* Burlington, IA: I. F. Segner & Condit Co.

Kemp, R., & David, A. (2001). Patient compliance. In J. Lieberman & R. Murray (Eds.), *Comprehensive care of schizophrenia.* London: Martin Dunitz.

Kendall, P. C., & Gosch, E. A. (1994). Cognitive-behavioral interventions. In T. H. Ollendick, N. J. King, & W. Yule (Eds.), *International handbook of phobic and anxiety disorders in children and adolescents.* New York: Plenum Press.

Kendall, P. C., Haaga, D. A., Ellis, A., & Bernard, M. (1995). Rational-emotive therapy in the 1990s and beyond: Current status, recent revisions, and research questions. *Clinical Psychology Review, 15*(3), 269–85.

Kendall, P. C., & Treadwell, K. R. H. (1996). Cognitive-behavioral treatment for childhood anxiety disorders. In E. D. Hibbs & P. S. Jensen (Eds.), *Psychosocial treatments for child and adolescent disorders: Empirically based strategies for clinical practice* (pp. 23–41). Washington, DC: American Psychological Association.

Kendler, K., Bulik, C, Silberg, J., Hettema, J., et al. (2000). Childhood sexual abuse and adult psychiatric and substance use disorders in women: An epidemiological and cotwin control analysis. *Archives of General Psychiatry, 57*(10), 953–959.

Kendler, K., Gruenberg, A., & Kinney, D. (1994). Independent diagnoses of adoptees and relatives as defined by DSM-III in the provincial and national samples of the Danish Adoption Study of Schizophrenia. *Archives of General Psychiatry, 51*(6), 456–468.

Kendler, K. S., & Diehle, S. R. (1993). The genetics of schizophrenia: A current, genetic-epidemiologic perspective. *Schizophrenia Bulletin, 19,* 261–285.

Kendler, K. S., & Gardner, C. O. (1997). The risk for psychiatric disorder in relatives of schizophrenic and control probands: A comparison of three independent studies. *Psychological Medicine, 27,* 411–419.

Kendler, K. S., Karkowski, L. M., Neale, M. C., & Prescott, C. A. (2000). Illicit psychoactive substance use, heavy use, abuse, and dependence in a U.S. population-based sample of male twins. *Archives of General Psychiatry, 57*(3), 261–269.

Kendler, K. S., Karkowski, L., & Prescott, C. A. (1999). Hallucinogen, opiate, sedative and stimulant use and abuse in a population-based sample of female twins. *Acta Psychiatrica Scandinavica, 99*(5), 268–276.

Kendler, K. S., Neale, M. C., Kessler, R. C., Heath, A. C., et al. (1992). Generalized anxiety disorder in women: A population-based twin study. *Archives of General Psychiatry, 49*(4), 267–272.

Kenealy, P. M. (1997). Mood-state-dependent retrieval: The effects of induced mood on memory reconsidered. *Quarterly Journal of Experimental Psychology: Human Experimental Psychology, 50,* 290–317.

Kennedy, G. J., & Scalmati, A. (2001). The interface of depression and dementia. *Current Opinion in Psychiatry, 14*(4), 367–369.

Kennedy, M. G. (1995). Relapse in schizophrenia: The relationships among insight, symptom recognition, symptom self-management, and perceived effectiveness of symptom self-management at the time of hospitalization. *Dissertation Abstracts International: Sec-*

tion B: The Sciences 55(10-B), 4321. Ann Arbor, MI: University Microfilms International.

Kensit, D. A. (2000). Rogerian theory: A critique of the effectiveness of pure client-centred therapy. *Counselling Psychology Quarterly: Special Issue, 13*(4), 345–351.

Kerfoot, Sakoulas, & Hyman, S. (1996). In L. Friedman, N. Fleming, D. Roberts, & S. Hyman (Eds.), *Sourcebook of substance abuse and addiction.* Baltimore: Williams & Wilkins.

Kerkhof, A. J. F. M. (2000). Attempted suicide: Patterns and trends. In K. Hawton & K. van Heeringen (Eds.), *The international handbook of suicide and attempted suicide* (pp. 49–64). New York: John Wiley & Sons.

Kernberg, O. (1975). *Borderline conditions and pathological narcissism.* Northvale, NJ: Jason Aronson.

Kernberg, O. (2001). The concept of libido in the light of contemporary psychoanalytic theorizing. In *Mankind's oedipal destiny: Libidinal and aggressive aspects of sexuality* (pp. 95–111). Madison, CT: International Universities Press.

Kernberg, O. F. (1989). An ego psychology object relations theory of the structure and treatment of pathological narcissism: An overview. *Psychiatric Clinics of North America, 12,* 723–729.

Kernberg, O. F. (1995). *Love relations: Normality and pathology.* New Haven, CT: Yale University Press.

Kernberg, P. F., Weiner, A. S., & Bardenstein, K. K. (2000). *Personality disorders in children and adolescents.* New York: Basic Books.

Kesey, K. (1973). *One flew over the cuckoo's nest.* New York: Viking.

Keshavan, M., Stanley, J., & Pettegrew, J. (2000). Magnetic resonance spetroscopy in schizophrenia: Methodological issues and findings—Part II. *Biological Psychiatry, 48,* 369–380.

Kessler, J. W. (1988). *Psychopathology of childhood* (2nd ed.). Englewood Cliffs, NJ: Prentice Hall.

Kessler, R. C., McGonagle, K. A., Zhao, S., Nelson, C. B., et al. (1994). Lifetime and 12-month prevalence of DSM-III–R psychiatric disorders in the United States: Results from the National Comorbidity Study. *Archives of General Psychiatry, 51,* 8–19.

Kety, S. S. (1988). Schizophrenic illness in the families of schizophrenic adoptees: Findings from the Danish national sample. *Schizophrenia Bulletin, 114*(2), 217–222.

Kety, S. S., Woodford, R. B., Harmel, M. H., Freyman, F. A., et al. (1994). Cerebral blood flow and metabolism in schizophrenia: The effects of barbiturate semi-narcosis, insulin coma and electroshock. *American Journal of Psychiatry, 151*(6), S203–S207.

Khantzian, E. J., Halliday, K. S., & McAuliffe, W. E. (1990). *Addiction and the vulnerable self: Modified dynamic group therapy for substance abusers.* New York: Guilford Press.

Kiecolt-Glaser, J. K., Glaser, R., Strain, E. C., Stout, J. C., et al. (1986). Modulation of cellular immunity in medical students. *Journal of Behavioral Medicine, 9,* 5–21.

Kim, J., & Siegel, S. (2001). The role of cholecystokinin in conditional compensatory responding and morphine tolerance in rats. *Behavioral Neuroscience (Special Issue), 115*(3), 704–709.

Kim, S. A., & Goff, B. C. (2000). Borderline personality disorder. In M. Hersen & M. Biaggio (Eds.), *Effective brief therapies* (pp. 335–354). San Diego, CA: Academic Press.

Kim, U. (2000). Indigenous, cultural, and cross-cultural psychology: A theoretical, conceptual, and epistemological analysis. *Asian Journal of Social Psychology:* Special Issue: Indigenous, cultural and cross-cultural psychologies, *3*(3), 265–287.

Kimerling, R., & Calhoun, K. S. (1994). Somatic symptoms, social support, and treatment seeking among sexual assault victims. *Journal of Consulting & Clinical Psychology, 62,* 333–340.

King, G., & Ellinwood, E. (1997). In J. Lowinson, P. Rulz, R. Millman, & J. Langrad (Eds.), *Substance abuse: A comprehensive textbook* (3rd ed). Baltimore: Williams & Wilkins.

King, M., & Bartlett, A. (1999). British psychiatry and homosexuality. *British Journal of Psychiatry, 175,* 106–113.

Kingsbury, S. J., & Yi, D. (2001). Insight and moderating variables. *Psychiatric Services (Special Issue), 52*(3), 387–388.

Kinsey, A., Pomeroy, W., & Martin, C. (1948). *Sexual behavior in the human male.* Philadelphia: W. B. Saunders.

Kinsey, A., Pomeroy, W., Martin, C., & Gebhard, P. (1953). *Sexual behavior in the human female.* Philadelphia: W. B. Saunders.

Kirk, S. A., & Kutchins, H. (1992). The selling of DSM: *The rhetoric of science in psychiatry.* New York: Aldine de Gruyter.

Kirk, S. A., & Kutchins, H. (1994). The myth of the reliability of DSM. *The Journal of Mind and Behavior, 15*(1–2), 71–86.

Kirkcaldy, B. D., Trimpop, R., & Cooper, C. L. (1997). Working hours, job stress, work satisfaction, and accident rates among medical practitioners and allied personnel. *International Journal of Stress Management, 4*(2), 79–87.

Kirmayer, L. J., & Looper, K. J. (2001). Hypochondriasis in primary care. In V. Starcevic & D. R. Lipsitt (Eds.), *Hypochondriasis: Modern perspectives on an ancient malady* (pp. 155–180). New York: Oxford University Press.

Kirmayer, L. J., & Santhanam, R. (2001). The anthropology of hysteria. In P. W. Halligan, C. Bass, & J. C. Marshall (Eds.), *Contemporary approaches to the study of hysteria* (pp. 251–270). Oxford, England: Oxford University Press.

Kirmayer, L. J., & Young, A. (1999). Culture and context in the evolutionary concept of mental disorder. *Journal of Abnormal Psychology, 108*(3), 446–452.

Kirsch, I., & Saperstein, G. (1998). Listening to Prozac but hearing placebo: A meta-analysis of antidepressant medication. *Prevention & Treatment, 1,* Article 0002a. Available on the World Wide Web: http://journals.apa.org/prevention/volume1/pre0010002a.html.

Kish, S. J., Furukawa, Y., Ang, L., Vorce, S. P., et al. (2000). Striatal serotonin is depleted in brain of a human MDMA (ecstasy) user. *Neurology, 55*(2), 294–296.

Klamen, D., Grossman, L., & Kopacz, D. (1999). Medical student homophobia. *Journal of Homosexuality, 37*(1), 53–63.

Klein, D. (1964). Delineation of two drug responsive anxiety syndromes. *Psychopharmacologia, 5,* 397–408.

Klein, M. (1946). Notes on some schizoid mechanism. In *Envy and gratitude and other works* (Vol. 3 of *The writings of Melanie Klein,* pp. 1–24). London: Hogarth Press.

Klein, M. (1997). Disorders of desire. In R. Charlton (Ed.), *Treating sexual disorders* (pp. 201–236). San Francisco: Jossey-Bass.

Klein, M., & Riviere, J. (1967/1937). *Love, hate and reparation.* London: Hogarth Press and the Institute of Psycho-analysis.

Kleinknecht, R. A. (1994). Aquisition of blood, injury, and needle fears and phobias. *Behaviour Research & Therapy, 32,* 817–823.

Kleinman, A. (1987). Culture and clinical reality: Commentary on "culture-bound syndromes and international disease classifications." *Culture, Medicine & Psychiatry, 11*(1), 49–52.

Kleinman, A. (1996). How is culture important for DSM-IV? In J. E. Mezzich, A. Kleinman, H. Fabrega, & D. L. Parron (Eds.), *Culture and psychiatric diagnosis: A DSM-IV perspective.* Washington, DC: American Psychiatric Press.

Klerman, G. L., & Weissman, M. M. (1992). Interpersonal psychotherapy. In E. S. Paykel (Ed.), *Handbook of affective disorders.* New York: Guilford Press.

Klerman, G. L., Weissman, M. M., Rounsaville, B. J., & Chevron, E. (1984). *Interpersonal psychotherapy of depression.* New York: Basic Books.

Klingemann, H., & Hunt, G. (Eds.). (1998). *Drug treatment systems in an international perspective: Drugs, demons, and delinquents.* Thousand Oaks, CA: Sage.

Kluft, R. P. (1984). Multiple personality in childhood. *Psychiatric Clinics of North America, 14,* 631–648.

Kluft, R. P. (1985). Hypnotherapy of childhood multiple personality disorder. *American Journal of Clinical Hypnosis, 27*(4), 201–210.

Kluft, R. P. (1988). The phenomenology and treatment of extremely complex multiple personality disorder. *Dissociation, 1,* 47–58.

Kluft, R. P. (1993). Multiple personality disorder. In D. Spiegel (Ed.), *Dissociative disorders: A clinical review* (pp. 17–44). Lutherville, MD: Sidran Press.

Kluft, R. P. (1996). Dissociative identity disorder. In L. K. Michelson & W. J. Ray (Eds.), *Handbook of dissociation: Theoretical, empirical, and clinical perspectives* (pp. 337–366). New York: Plenum Press.

Kodesh, A., Finkel, B., Lerner, A. G., Kretzmer, G., et al. (2001). Dose-dependent olanxapine-associated leukopenia: Three case reports. *International Clinical Psychopharmacology (Special Issue), 16*(2), 117–119.

Koenigsberg, H. W., Woo-Ming, A. M., & Siever, L. J. (2002). Pharmacological treatments for personality disorders. In P. E. Nathan & J. M. Gorman (Eds.), *A guide to treatments that work* (2nd ed., pp. 625–641). New York: Oxford University Press.

Kohlenberg, R. & Tsai, M. (1992). *Functional analytic psychotherapy: Creating intense and curative therapeutic relationships.* New York: Plenum Press.

Kohut, H. (1977). *The restoration of the self.* Madison, CT: International Universities Press.

Kolata, G. (1994, Dec. 18). The rule Dr. Elders forgot; America keeps Onan in the closet. *The New York Times,* p. 5.

Kolata, G. (2000, April 18). Impotence is given another name, and a drug market grows. *The New York Times,* p. 6.

Koocher, G., Norcross, J., Hill, S. (Eds.). (1998). *Psychologists' desk reference.* New York: Oxford University Press.

Kopelman, M. D. (1987). Crime and amnesia: A review. *Behavioral Sciences and the Law, 5,* 323–342.

Koss, M. P. (1998). Hidden rape: Sexual aggression and victimization in a national sample of students in higher education. In M. E. Odem & J. Clay-Warner (Eds.); *Confronting rape and sexual assault* (pp. 51–69). Wilmington, DE: SR Books/Scholarly Resources Inc.

Kosten, T. R. (1990). Neurobiology of abused drugs: Opioids and stimulants. *Journal of Nervous & Mental Disease, 178*(4), 217–227.

Kozlowski, L., Henningfield, J., & Brigham, J. (2001). *Cigarettes, nicotine, & health: A biobehavioral approach.* Thousand Oaks, CA: Sage.

Kraepelin, E. (1899/1904). *Clinical psychiatry: a text-book for students and physicians.* Abstracted and adapted from the 6th German edition of Kraepelin (Author) *Psychiatrie; ein lehrbuch für studierend ünd ärzte,* by A. R. Defendorf (Trans.). New York: Macmillan.

Kraepelin, E. (1923). *Textbook of psychiatry.* New York: Macmillan. (Original work published 1883)

Krafft-Ebing, von R. (1999). *Psychopathia sexualis: With especial reference to contrary sexual instinct: a clinical-forensic study.* [Translated by B. King] (12th ed., unabridged). Burbank, CA: Bloat Publishing. (Original work published in 1886.)

Kramer, A., & Buck, L. A. (1997). Encountering people labeled "schizophrenic." *Journal of Humanistic Psychology, 37*(4), 12–29.

Kramer, P. (1993). *Listening to Prozac.* New York: Viking.

Krystal, H. (1979). Alexithymia and psychotherapy. *American Journal of Psychotherapy, 33*(1).

Krystal, J. H., Bremner, J. D., Southwick, S. M., & Charney, D. S. (1998). The emerging neurobiology of dissociation: Implications for treatment of posttraumatic stress disorder. In J. D. Bremner & C. R. Marmar (Eds.), *Trauma, memory, and dissociation* (pp. 321–363). Washington, DC: American Psychiatric Press, Inc.

Krystal, H., & Raskin, H. (1994). Affect tolerance. In J. D. Levin (Ed.), *The dynamics and treatment of alcoholism: Essential papers* (pp. 158–175). Northvale, NJ: Jason Aronson.

Kuczmarski, R. J., Flegel, K. M., Campbell, S. M., & Johnson, C. L. (1994). Increasing prevalence of overweight among US adults. *Journal of the American Medical Association, 272,* 205–211.

Kuhn, J. L. (2001). Toward an ecological humanistic psychology. *Journal of Humanistic Psychology: Special Issue, 41*(2), 9–24.

Kuhn, T. (1962). *The structure of scientific revolutions.* Chicago: University of Chicago Press.

Kulish, N. (1991). The mental representation of the clitoris: The fear of female sexuality. *Psychoanalytic Inquiry, 11*(4), 511–536.

Kuperman, S., Johnson, B., Arndt, S., Lindgren, S., et al. (1996). Quantitative EEG differences in a nonclinical sample of children with ADHD and undifferentiated ADD. *Journal of the American Academy of Child and Adolescent Psychiatry, 27,* 330–335.

Kuperman, S., Schloser, S. S., Lidral, J., & Reich, W. (1999). Relationship of child psychopathology to parental alcoholism and antisocial personality disorder. *Journal of the American Academy of Child and Adolescent Psychiatry, 38,* 686–692.

L

Lahey, B. B., & Loeber, R. (1997). Attention-deficit/hyperactivity disorder, oppositional defiant disorder, conduct disorder, and adult antisocial behavior: A life span perspective. In D. M. Stoff, J. Breiling, & J. D. Maser (Eds.), *Handbook of antisocial behavior* (pp. 51–59). New York: John Wiley & Sons.

Laing, R. D. (1959). *The divided self: An existential study in sanity and madness.* London: Tavistock.

Lalumiere, M., & Quinsey, V. (1996). Sexual deviance, antisociality, mating effort, and the use of sexually coercive behaviors. *Personality & Individual Differences, 21*(1), 33–48.

Lam, R., Tam, E., Shiah, I.-S., Yatham, L., & Zis, A. (2000). Effects of light therapy on suicidal ideation in patients with winter depression. *Journal of Clinical Psychiatry, 61*(1), 30–32.

Lambert, M., & Bergin, A. (1994). The effectiveness of psychotherapy. In S. L. Garfield & A. E. Bergin (Eds.), *Handbook of psychotherapy and behavior change* (4th ed., pp. 143–189). New York: John Wiley & Sons.

Lambert, M., Weber, F., & Sykes, J. (1993). *Psychotherapy versus placebo.* Poster presented at the annual meeting of the Western Psychological Association, Phoenix, Arizona.

Langeluddeke, A. (1963). *Die entmannung von sittlich—keitsverbrecher.* Berlin: de Gruyter.

Lanyon, R. I. (1984). Personality assessment. *Annual Review of Psychology, 35,* 667–701.

LaPlanche, J., & Pontalis J.-B. (1973). *The language of psychoanalysis.* New York: Norton.

Laranjeira, R., Rassi, R., Dunn, J., Fernandes, M., et al. (2001). Crack cocaine: A two-year follow-up of treated patients. *Journal of Addictive Diseases (Special Issue), 20*(1), 43–48.

Larkin, M. (1998). Festive drinking's slippery slope beckons. *Lancet, 352,* 19–26.

Lasch, C. (1978). *The culture of narcissism: American life in an age of diminishing expectations.* New York: Guilford Press.

Laufer, M. (1981). The psychoanalyst and the adolescent's sexual development. *Psychoanalytic Study of the Child, 36,* 181–191.

Laumann, E., Paik, A., & Rosen, R. (1999). Sexual dysfunction in the United States: Prevalence and predictors. *Journal of the American Medical Association, 281*(6), 537–544.

Laurent, A., Rochet, T., d'Amato, T., Anchisi, A.-M., et al. (2000). Vulnerability to schizophrenia: III. Interests and limits of the Continuous Performance Test-Identical Pairs (CPT-IP). *Encephale, 26*(2), 48–55.

Lavin, M. R., & Rifkin, A. (1993). Diagnosis and pharmacotherapy of conduct disorder. *Progress in Neuro-Psychopharmacology & Biological Psychiatry, 17,* 875–885.

Lawrie, S. M., Whalley, H. C., Abukmeil, S. S., Kestelman, J. N., et al. (2001). Brain structure, genetic liability, and psychotic symptoms in subjects at high risk of developing schizophrenia. *Biological Psychiatry (Special Issue), 49*(10), 811–823.

Laws, D., & Marshall, W. (1990). A conditioning theory of the etiology and maintainance of deviant sexual preference and behavior. In *Handbook of sexual assualt: Issues, theories, and treatment of the offender* (pp. 209–229). New York: Plenum Press.

Laws, D., & Marshall, W. (1991). Masturbatory reconditioning with sexual deviates: An evaluative review. *Advances in Behaviour Research and Therapy, 13*(1), 13–25.

Laws, D., & O'Donohue, W. (1997). *Sexual deviance: Theory, assessment, and treatment.* New York: Guilford Press.

Lazarus, R. S. (1999). *Fifty years of the research and theory of R. S. Lazarus: An analysis of historical and perennial issues.* Mahwah, NJ: Lawrence Erlbaum.

Lazarus, R. S., & Folkman, S. (1984). *Stress, appraisal, and coping.* New York: Springer.

Lazorthes, Y., Sagen, J., Sallerin, B., Tkaczuk, J., et al. (2000). Human chromaffin cell graft into the CSF for cancer pain management: A prospective phase II clinical study. *Pain, 87*(1), 19–32.

le Grange, D. (1999). Family therapy for adolescent anorexia nervosa. *Journal of Clinical Psychology, 55,* 727–739.

Leahy, R. L. (1997). *Practicing cognitive therapy: A guide to interventions.* Northvale, NJ: Jason Aronson, Inc.

Leary, K. (2000). Racial enactments in dynamic treatment. *Psychoanalytic Dialogues, 10*(4), 639–653.

Ledig, M., Misslin, R., Vogel, E., Holownia, A., et al. (1998). Paternal alcohol exposure: Developmental and behavioral effects on the offspring of rats. *Neuropharmacology, 37*(1), 57–66.

Lee, C. K., Kwak, Y. S., Yamamoto, J., Rhee, H., et al. (1990). Psychiatric epidemiology in Korea: Part II. Urban and rural differences. *Journal of Nervous and Mental Disease, 178,* 247–252.

Lee, K.-H., Williams, L. M., Haig, A., Goldberg, E., et al. (2001). An integration of 40Hz gamma and phasic arousal: Novelty and routinization processing in schizophrenia. *Clinical Neurophysiology, 112*(8), 1499–1507.

Lee, S. (1999). Psychiatry and homosexuality. *British Journal of Psychiatry, 175,* 492–493.

Lee, S., & Lee, A. M. (1999). Disordered eating in three communities of China: A comparative study of female high school students in Hong Kong, Shenzen, and rural Hunan. *International Journal of Eating Disorders, 27,* 317–327.

Leeds, J., & Morgenstern, J. (1996). Psychoanalytic theories of substance abuse. *Treating substance abuse: Theory and technique.* New York: Guilford Press.

Leff, J. (1988). *Psychiatry around the globe: A transcultural view.* London: Gaskell/Royal College of Psychiatrists.

Leiblum, S. (2000). Vaginismus: A most perplexing problem. In S. Leiblum & C. Raymond (Eds.), *Principles and practice of sex therapy* (3rd ed. pp. 181–202). New York: Guilford Press.

Leiblum, S., & Sharon, G. (2001). Persistent sexual arousal syndrome: A newly discovered pattern of female sexuality. *Journal of Sex & Marital Therapy (Special Issue: Historical and International Context of Nosology of Female Sexual Disorders), 27*(4), 365–380.

Leifer, R. (1966). Involuntary psychiatric hospitalization and social control. *International Journal of Social Psychiatry, 13*(1), 53–58.

Lenze, E. J., Miller, A. R., Munir, Z. B., Pornnoppadol, C., et al. (1999). Psychiatric symptoms endorsed by somatization disorder in a psychiatric clinic. *Annals of Clinical Psychiatry, 11,* 73–79.

Leon, M. R. (2000). Effects of caffeine on cognitive, psychomotor, and affective performance of children with attention-deficit/hyperactivity disorder. *Journal of Attention Disorders, 4*(1), 27–47.

Leonard, K. E., & Blane, H. T. (Eds.). (1999). *Psychological theories of drinking and alcoholism* (2nd ed.). New York: Guilford Press.

Leonhard, K. (1957). *Aufteilung der Endogenen Psychosen* [Partitioning the endogenous psychoses]. Berlin: Akademieverlag.

Leserman, J., & Drossman, D. A. (1995). Sexual and physical abuse history and medical practice. *General Hospital Psychiatry, 17,* 71–74.

LeShan, L. L., & Worthington, R. E. (1956). Personality as a factor in the pathogenesis of cancer: Review of the literature. *British Journal of Medical Psychology, 29,* 49–55.

Leuchter, A. F., Cook, I. A., Witte, E. A., Morgan, M., et al. (2002). Changes in brain function of depressed subjects during treatment with placebo. *American Journal of Psychiatry, 159*(1), 122–129.

Levav, M., Mirsky, A. F., French, L. M., & Bartko, J. J. (1998). Multinational neuropsychological testing: Performance of children and adults. *Journal of Clinical & Experimental Neuropsychology, 20*(5), 658–672.

Levenson, J. L., & Bemis, C. (1995). Cancer onset and progression. In A. Stoudemire (Ed.), *Psychological factors affecting medical conditions* (pp. 81–97). Washington, DC: American Psychiatric Press.

Levenson, R. W., Ekman, P., & Friesen, W. V. (1990). Voluntary facial action generates emotion-specific autonomicnervous system activity. *Psychophysiology, 27,* 363–384.

Leventhal, B. L., & Midelfort, H. B. (1986). The physical abuse of children: a hurt greater than pain. *Advances in Psychosomatic Medicine, 16,* 48–83.

Levin, J. D., & Weiss, R. H. (Eds.). (1994). *The dynamics and treatment of alcoholism: Essential papers.* Northvale, NJ: Jason Aronson.

Levin, M. P., Piran, N., & Stoddard, C. (1999). Mission more probable: Media literacy, activism, and advocacy as primary prevention. In N. Piran, M. P. Levin, & C. Steiner-Adair (Eds.), *Preventing eating disorders: A handbook of interventions and special challenges.* Philadelphia: Brunner/Mazel.

Levine, S., & Althof, S. (1997). Psychological evaluation and sex therapy. In J. Mulcahy (Ed.), *Diagnosis and management of male sexual dysfunction* (pp. 262). New York: Igaku-Shoin.

Levinthal, C. F. (1999). *Drugs, behavior, and modern society* (2nd ed.). Needham Heights, MA: Allyn & Bacon.

Levy, D. (1997). *Tools of critical thinking.* Boston: Allyn & Bacon.

Lewinsohn, P., Joiner, T., & Rohde, P. (2001). Evaluation of cognitive diathesis-stress models in predicting major depressive disorder in adolescents. *Journal of Abnormal Psychology, Special Issue, 11*(2), 203–215.

Lewinsohn, P. M., Gotlib, I. H., & Hautzinger, M. (1998). Behavioral treatment of unipolar depression. In V. E. Caballo (Ed.), *International handbook of cognitive and behavioural treatments for psychological disorders* (pp. 441–488). Oxford, England: Elsevier Science.

Lewinsohn, P. M., Hoberman, H., Teri, L., & Hautzinger, M. (1985). An integrative theory of depression. In S. Reiss & R. Bootzin (Eds.), *Theoretical issues in behavior therapy.* New York: Academic Press.

Lewinsohn, P. M., Lobitz, W. C., & Wilson, S. (1973). "Sensitivity" of depressed individuals to aversive stimuli. *Journal of Abnormal Psychology, 81,* 259–263.

Lewis, C., & Stanley, C. (2000). Women accused of sexual offenses. *Behavioral Sciences and the Law, 18,* 73–81.

Lewis, D. M., & Cachelin, F. M. (2001). Body image, body dissatisfaction, and eating attitudes in midlife and elderly women. *Eating Disorders: The Journal of Treatment & Prevention, 9*(1), 29–39.

Lewis, D. O., Yeager, C. A., Swica, Y., Pincus, J. H., et al. (1997). Objective documentation of child abuse and dissociation in 12 murderers with dissociative identity disorder. *American Journal of Psychiatry, 154,* 1703–1710.

Lewis, R., Kapur, S., Jones, C., DaSilva, J., et al. (1999). Serotonin 5-HT$_2$ receptors in schizophrenia: A PET study using (-sup-1-sup-8F) setoperone in neuroleptic-naïve patients and normal subjects. *American Journal of Psychiatry, 156,* 72–78.

Lewontin, R., Rose, S., & Kamin, L. (1984). *Not in our genes: Biology, ideology and human nature.* New York: Pantheon.

Lezak, M. D. (1976). *Neuropsychological assessment.* New York: Oxford University Press.

Li, C., Gu, G., Xu, J., & Lei, S. (2001). Quality of marriage and child bearing of married female schizophrenics. *Chinese Mental Health Journal (Special Issue), 15*(3), 193.

Libbrecht, K. (1995). *Hysterical psychosis: A historical survey.* New Brunswick, NJ: Transaction Publishers.

Liberman, R. P., Eckman, T. A., & Marder, S. R. (2001). Training in social problem solving among persons with schizophrenia. *Psychiatric Services, 52*(1), 31–33.

Lichterman, D., Karbe, E., & Maier, W. (2000). The genetic epidemiology of schizophrenia and of some schizophrenia spectrum disorders. *European Archives of Psychiatric Clinical Neuroscience, 250,* 304–310.

Lichtman, A. H., & Martin, B. R. (1999). Analgesic properties of THC and its synthetic derivatives. In G. G. Nahas (Ed.), *Marihuana and medicine* (pp. 511–526). Clifton, NJ: Humana Press, Inc.

Lidz, T., Fleck, S., & Cornelison, A. R. (1965). *Schizophrenia and the family.* New York: International Universities Press.

Lidz, T., Fleck, S., Cornelison, A. R., Alanen, Y. A., et al. (1985). *Schizophrenia and the family* (2nd ed.). Madison, CT: International Universities Press.

Lief, H., & Hubschman, L. (1993). Orgasm in the postoperative transsexual. *Archives of Sexual Behavior, 22*(2), 145–155.

Liester, M. B. (1998). Toward a new definition of hallucinations. *American Journal of Orthopsychiatry, 68*(2), 305–312.

Liguori, A., Grass, J. A., & Hughes, J. R. (1999). Subjective effects of caffeine among introverts and extraverts in the morning and evening. *Experimental & Clinical Psychopharmacology, 7*(3), 244–249.

Liiceanu, A. (2000). Parallel selves as the end of grief work. In J. Harvey (Ed.), *Loss and trauma: General and close relationship perspectives.* Philadelphia: Brunner-Routledge.

Likierman, M. (2001). *Melanie Klein: Her work in context* (p. 202). New York: Continuum.

Lilienfeld, S. O., Kirsch, I., Sarbin, T. R., Lynn, S. J., et al. (1999). Dissociative identity disorder and the sociocognitive model: Recalling the lessons of the past. *Psychological Bulletin, 125,* 507–523.

Limpert, C., & Amador, X. F. (2001). Negative symptoms and the experience of emotion. In *Negative symptom and cognitive deficit treatment response in schizophrenia* (pp. 111–137). Washington, DC: American Psychiatric Press.

Lindemann, C. (1996). *Handbook of the treatment of anxiety disorders.* Northvale, NJ: Jason Aronson, Inc.

Linehan, M. (1993). *Cognitive behavioral treatment of borderline personality disorder: The dialectics of effective treatment.* New York: Guilford Press.

Ling, L. H., Marchant, C., Buckley, N. A., Prior, M., et al. (2001). Poisoning with the recreational drug paramethoxyamphetamine ("death"). *Medical Journal of Australia, 174*(9), 453–455.

Linszen, D. H., Dingemans, P. M., Nugter, M. A., Van der Does, A. J. W., et al. (1997). Patient attributes and expressed emotion as risk factors for psychotic relapse. *Schizophrenia Bulletin, 23*(1), 119–130.

Lipowski, Z. J. (1987). Somatization: Medicine's unsolved problem. *Psychodmatics, 28,* 294–297.

Lit, Wiviott-Tishlor, Wong, & Hyman (1996). In L. Friedman, N. Fleming, D. Roberts, & S. Hyman (Eds.), *Sourcebook of substance abuse and addiction.* Baltimore: Williams & Wilkins.

Litman, R., & Farberow, N. (1994). Pop-rock music as precipitating cause in youth suicide. *Journal of Forensic Sciences, 39*(2), 494–499.

Little, K. B., & Schneidman, E. S. (1959). Congruences among interpretations of psychological tests and amamnestic data. *Psychological Monographs, 73*(6, Whole No. 476).

Llinas, R. R., & Pare, D. (1991). Of dreaming and wakefulness. *Neuroscience, 44,* 521–535.

Loas, G., Yon, V., & Bralet, M. C. (Eds.). (2001). Anhedonia and suicide in chronic schizophrenia: A follow-up study. *Schizophrenia Research, 47*(1), 105–106.

Locke, J. (1950). *An essay concerning human understanding.* New York: Dover.

Loeber, R., Lahey, B. B., & Thomas, C. (1991). Diagnostic conundrum of oppositional defiant disorder and conduct disorder. *Journal of Abnormal Psychology, 100,* 379–390.

Loewenstein, R. J. (1991). Rational psychopharmacotherapy in the treatment of multiple personality disorder. *Psychiatric Clinics of North America, 14,* 721–740.

Loewenstein, R. J. (1993). Psychogenic amnesia and psychogenic fugue: A comprehensive review. In D. Spiegel (Ed.), *Dissociative disorders: A clinical review* (pp. 45–78). Lutherville, MD: Sidran Press.

Loewenstein, R. J. (1996). Dissociative amnesia and dissociative fugue. In L. K. Michelson & W. J. Ray (Eds.), *Handbook of dissociation: Theoretical, empirical, and clinical perspectives* (pp. 307–336.). New York: Plenum Press.

Loftus, E. F. (1997). Creating childhood memories. *Applied Cognitive Psychology, 11,* S75–S86.

Lokshin, P., Prolov, K., & Belmaker, R. H. (1994). A survey of insulin coma experience among former Soviet psychiatrists in Israel. *Human Psychopharmacology Clinical & Experimental, 9*(4), 307.

Long, P., Forehand, R., Wierson, M., & Morgan, A. (1994). Does parent training with young noncompliant children have long-term effects? *Behaviour Research and Therapy, 32,* 101–107.

Lopez, S. R., & Guarnaccia, P. J. J. (2000). Cultural psychopathology: Uncovering the social world of mental illness. *Annual Review of Psychology, 52,* 571–598.

Lorr, M., & Strack, S. (1994). Personality profiles of police candidates. *Journal of Clinical Psychology, 50*(2), 200–207.

Losken, A., Maviglia, S., & Friedman, L. (in press). In L. Friedman, N. Fleming, D. Roberts, S. Hyman (Eds.), *Sourcebook of substance abuse and addiction.* Baltimore: Williams & Wilkins.

Lowell, R. (1977). *Day by day.* New York: Farrar, Straus and Giroux.

Luborsky, L., Diguer, L., Luborsky, E., & Schmidt, K. (1999). The efficacy of dynamic versus other psychotherapies: Is it true that "everyone has won and all must have prizes"?—An update. In D. S. Janowsky, et al. (Eds.), *Psychotherapy indications and outcomes.* Washington DC: American Psychiatric Press.

Lubow, R. E., Kaplan, O., Abramovich, P., Rudnick, A., et al. (2000). Visual search in schizophrenia: Latent inhibition and novel pop-out effects. *Schizophrenia Research, 45*(1–2), 145–156.

Lucas, C. P., Zhang, H., Fisher, P. W., Shaffer, D., et al. (2001). The DISC Predictive Scales (DPS): Efficiently screening for diagnoses. *Journal of the American Academy of Child & Adolescent Psychiatry (Special Issue), 40*(4), 443–449.

Ludwig, A. M. (1992). Creative achievement and psychopathology: Comparison among professions. *American Journal of Psychotherapy, 46,* 330–356.

Lykken, D. T. (1957). A study of anxiety in the sociopathic personality. *Journal of Abnormal and Social Psychology, 55,* 6–10.

Lykken, D. T. (1995). *The antisocial personalities.* Hillsdale, NJ: Erlbaum.

M

MacDonald, A. W. III., Pogue-Geile, M. F., Debski, T. T., & Manuck, S. (2001). Genetic and environmental influences on schizotypy: A community-based twin study. *Schizophrenia Bulletin, 27*(1), 47–58.

Macdonald, D., & Mansfield, D. (2001). Drugs and Afghanistan. *Drugs: Education, Prevention & Policy, 8*(1), 1–6.

MacFadyen, L., Hastings, G., & MacKintosh, A. M. (2001). Cross sectional study of young people's awareness of and involvement with tobacco marketing. *British Medical Journal (Special Issue), 322*(7285), 513–517.

Machlin, G. (1996). Some causes of genotypic and phenotypic discordance in monozygotic twin pairs. *American Journal of Psychiatry, 137,* 216–228.

Machover, K. (1949). *Personality projection in the drawing of the human figure.* Springfield, IL: Charles C Thomas.

MacKinnon, A., & Foley, D. (1996). The genetics of anxiety disorders. In H. G. M. Westenberg, J. A. Den Boer, & D. L. Murphy (Eds.), *Advances in the neurobiology of anxiety disorders* (pp. 39–59). New York: John Wiley & Sons.

Macleod, A. K., & Cropley, M. L. (1995). Depressive future thinking: The role of valence and specificity. *Cognitive Therapy and Reserch, 19*(1), 35–50.

Madianos, M., Zacharakis, C., & Tsitsa, C. (2000). Utilization of psychiatric inpatient care in Greece: A nationwide study. *International Journal of Psychology, 46*(2), 89–100.

Maes, M., De Vos, N., Van Hunsel, F., Van West, D., et al. (2001). Pedophilia is accompanied by increased plasma concentrations of catecholamines, in particular epinephrine. *Psychiatry Research (Special Issue), 103*(1), 43–49.

Mahler, M. (1971). A study of the separation-individuation process and its possible application to the borderline phenomena in the psychoanalytic situation. *Psychoanalytic Study of the Child, 26,* 403–424.

Mahler, M. S. (1975). On the current status of infantile neurosis. *Journal of the American Psychoanalytic Association, 23*(2), 327–333.

Mahoney, M. J. (1993). Introduction to special section: Theoretical developments in the cognitive psychotherapies. *Journal of Consulting and Clinical Psychology, 61*(2), 187–193.

Mahowald, M. W., & Schenck, C. H. (1991). Status dissociatus: A perspective on states of being. *Sleep, 4,* 69–79.

Maj, M. (1999). Lithium prophylaxis of bipolar disorder in ordinary clinical conditions: Patterns of long-term outcome. In J. F. Goldberg & M. Harrow (Eds.), *Bipolar disorders: Clinical course and outcome.* Washington, DC: American Psychiatric Press.

Major, B., Mueller, P., & Hildenbrandt, K. (1985). Attributions, expectations, and coping with abortion. *Journal of Personality and Social Psychology, 48,* 585–599.

Maldonado, J. R., & Spiegel, D. (1998). Trauma, dissociation, and hypnotizability. In J. D. Bremner & C. R. Marmar (Eds.), *Trauma, memory, and dissociation* (pp. 57–106). Washington, DC: American Psychiatric Press.

Maldonado, J. R., & Spiegel, D. (2001). Conversion disorder. In K. A. Phillips (Ed.), *Somatoform and factitious disorders* (pp. 95–128). Washington, DC: American Psychiatric Publishing.

Malla, A. K., Norman, R. M. G., & Scholten, D. (2000). Predictors of service use and social conditions in patients with psychotic disorders. *Canadian Journal of Psychiatry 45*(3), 269–273.

Mallery, S. (1999). Zar possession as psychiatric diagnosis: Problems and possibilities. *Dissertation Abstracts International: Section B: The Sciences & Engineering, 59*(7-B).

Maloney, M. J., McGuire, J., Daniels, S. R., & Specker, B. (1989). Dieting behavior and eating attitudes in children. *Pediatrics, 84,* 482–489.

Malt, U. F. (1986). Five years of experience with the DSM-III system in clinical work and research: Some concluding remarks. *Acta Psychiatrica Scandinavica, 73*(328 suppl), 76–84.

Mangini, M. (1998). Treatment of alcoholism using psychedelic drugs: A review of the program of research. *Journal of Psychoactive Drugs, 30*(4), 381–418.

Mannuzza, S., & Klein, R. G. (2000). Long-term prognosis in attention-deficit/hyperactivity disorder. *Child and Adolescent Psychiatric Clinics of North America, 9,* 711–726.

Manson, S., Beals, J., O'Nell, T., Piasecki, J., et al. (1996). Wounded spirits, ailing hearts: PTSD and related disorders among American Indians. In A. J. Marsella, M. G. Friedman, E. T. Gerrity, & R. M. Scurfield (Eds.), *Ethnocultural aspects of posttraumatic stress disorder* (pp. 255–283). Washington, DC: American Psychiatric Press.

Manuck, S. B., Kasprowicz, A. L., & Muldoon, M. (1990). Behaviorally-evoked cardiovascular reactivity and hypertension: Conceptual issues and potential associations. *Annals of Behavioral Medicine, 12,* 17–29.

Marans, S. (2000). "That's what my imagination says:" A study of antisocial behavior in two boys. *Psychoanalytic Study of the Child, 55,* 61–86.

Marans, S., Berkowitz, S. J., & Cohen, D. J. (1998). Police and mental health professionals: Collaborative response to the impact of violence on children and families. *Child and Adolescent Psychiatric Clinics of North America, 7,* 635–651.

Marantz, S., & Coates, S. (1991). Mothers of boys with gender identity disorder: A comparison of matched controls. *Journal of the American Academy of Child & Adolescent Psychiatry, 30*(2), 310–315.

Marin, D. B. (1999). Principles of the pharmacotherapy of dementia. In D. S. Charney, E. J. Nestler, & B. S. Bunney (Eds.), *Neurobiology of mental illness* (pp. 735–744). New York: Oxford University Press.

Marin, R., with Joseph, N. (1998, January 5). Lick me, flog me, buy me. *Newsweek Magazine,* p. 85.

Markowitz, J. C., & Weissman, M. M. (1995). Interpersonal psychotherapy. In E. E. Beckham & W. R. Leber (Eds.), *Handbook of depression* (2nd ed., pp. 376–390). New York: Guilford Press.

Marks, D. F., Murray, M., Evans, B., & Willig, C. (2000). *Health psychology: Theory, research and practice.* London: Sage.

Marks, I. M. (1990). Behavioral therapy of anxiety states. In N. Sartorius, V. Andreoli, G. Cassano, L. Eisenberg, et al. (Eds.), *Anxiety: Psychobiological and clinical perspectives.* New York: Hemisphere Publishing.

Markus, H. (1977). Self-schemata and processing information about the self. *Journal of Personality & Social Psychology, 35,* 63–78.

Marlatt, G. A., & Gordon, J. R. (Eds.). (1985). *Relapse prevention: maintenance strategies in the treatment of addictive behaviors.* New York: Guilford Press.

Marshall, B. J., & Warren, J. R. (1984). Unidentified curved bacilli in the stomach of patients with gastritis and peptic ulceration. *Lancet, 1,* 1311–1315.

Marshall, J. R. (1996). Science, "schizophrenia," and genetics: The creation of myths. *Journal of Primary Prevention, 17*(1), 99–115.

Marshall, W. (1997). Pedophilia: Psychopathology and theory, *Sexual deviance: Theory, assessment, and treatment* (pp. 152–174). New York: Guilford Press.

Marshall, W., & Eccles, A. (1993). Pavlovian conditioning processes in adolescent sex offenders. In H. Barbaree, W. Marshall, & S. Hudson (Eds.), *The juvenile sex offender* (118–142). New York: Guilford Press.

Marsland, A. L., Bachen, E. A., Cohen, S., & Maunck, S. B. (2001). Stress, immunity, and susceptibility to infections disease. In A. Baum, T. A. Revenson, & J. E. Singer (Eds.), *Handbook of health psychology* (pp. 683–695). Mahwah, NJ: Lawrence Erlbaum.

Marsland, A. L., Herbert, T. B., Muldoon, M. F., Bachen, E. A., et al. (1997). Lymphocyet subset redistribution during acute laboratory stress in young adults: Mediating effects of hemoconcentration. *Health Psychology, 16,* 1–8.

Marteau, T., & Lerman, C. (2001). Genetic risk and behavioral change. *BMJ: British Medical Journal Special Issue, 322*(7293), 1056–1059.

Martens, W. H. J. (2000). Antisocial and psychopathic personality disorders: Causes, course, and remission—a review article. *International Journal of Offender Therapy & Comparative Criminology (Special Issue), 44*(4), 406–430.

Maruish, M. E. (1999). *The use of psychological testing for treatment planning and outcomes assessment* (2nd ed.). Mahwah, NJ: Lawrence Elbaum.

Marx, B., Calhoun, K., Wilson, A., & Meyerson, L. (2001). Sexual revictimization prevention: An outcome evaluation. *Journal of Consulting and Clinical Psychology, 69*(1), 25–32.

Maslow, A. H., & Mittelmann, B. (1951). *Principles of abnormal psychology: The dynamics of psychic illness.* New York: Harper.

Mason, F. (1997). Fetishism: Psychopathology and theory. In *Sexual deviance: Theory, assessment, and treatment* (pp. 75–91). New York: Guilford Press.

Mason, J. W. (1975). A historical view of the stress field: Parts 1 & 2. *Journal of Human Stress, 1,* 6–12, 22–36.

Massaro, D. W. (1987). Categorical partition: A fuzzy-logical model of categorization behavior. In S. Harnad (Ed.), *Categorical perception: The groundwork of cognition.* New York: Cambridge University Press.

Masters, W., & Johnson, V. (1970). *Human sexual inadequacy.* Boston: Little, Brown.

Masters, W., Johnson, V., & Kolodny, R. (1986). *Masters and Johnson on sex and human loving.* Boston: Little, Brown.

Maunder, R. G., & Hunter, J. J. (2001). Attachment and psychosomatic medicine: Developmental contributions to stress and disease. *Psychosomatic Medicine (Special Issue), 63*(4), 556–567.

Maxwell, H. (2000). Developments within psychoanalytic theory and practice. In H. Maxwell (Ed.), *Clinical psychotherapy for health professionals* (pp. xiii, 207, 32–41) London: Whurr Publishers, Ltd.

May, R. (1961). *Existential psychology.* New York: Random House.

May, R. (1967). *Psychology and the human dilemma.* New York: Van Nostrand-Reinhold.

Mayberg, H. S., Silva, J., Brannan, S., Tekell, J., et al. (2002). The functional neuroanatomy of the placebo effect. *American Journal of Psychiatry, 159*(May), 728–735.

Mayes, L. C. (1999). Developing brain and in utero cocaine exposure: Effects on neural ontogeny. *Development & Psychopathology, 11*(4), 685–714.

Mayes, S. D. (1992). Eating disorders of infancy and early childhood. In S. R. Cooper, G. W. Hynd, & R. E. Mattison (Eds.), *Child psychopathology: Diagnostic criteria and clinical assessment.* New York: Lawrence Erlbaum Associates.

Mayes, S. D., Calhoun, S. L., & Crowell, E. W. (2000). Learning disabilities and ADHD: Overlapping spectrum disorders. *Journal of Learning Disabilities, 33,* 417–424.

McCann, S. M., Lipton, J. M., Sternberg, E. M., Chrousos, G. P., et al. (Eds.). (1998). Neuroimmunomodulation: Molecular aspects, integrative systems, and clinical advances. *Annals of the New York Academy of Sciences, 840.*

McCarthy, B., & McCarthy, E. (1998). *Male sexual awareness: Increasing sexual satisfaction* (rev. ed.). New York: Carroll & Graf.

McCloskey, M. E., & Glucksberg, S. (1978). Natural categories: Well defined or fuzzy sets? *Memory & Cognition, 6*(4), 462–472.

McCoy, C. B., McCoy, H., Lai, S., Yu, Z., et al. (2001). Reawakening the dragon: Changing patterns of opiate use in Asia, with particular emphasis on China's Yunnan Province. *Substance Use & Misuse (Special Issue: Emergent Drug Issues for the 21st Century), 36*(1–2), 49–69.

McCrady, B. S., & Epstein, E. E. (Eds.). (1999). *Addictions: A comprehensive guidebook.* New York: Oxford University Press.

McCrady, B. S., & Miller, W. R. (Eds.). (1993). *Research on Alcoholics Anonymous: Opportunities and alternatives.* New Brunswick, NJ: Rutgers Center of Alcohol Studies.

McDonald, W. M., Richard, I. H., & DeLong, M. R. (2003). Prevalence, etiology, and treatment of depression in Parkinson's disease. *Biological Psychiatry, 54*(3), 363–375.

McDougal, J. (1980). *Plea for a measure of abnormality.* New York: International Universities Press.

McDougle, C. J. (1997). Psychopharmacology. In D. J. Cohen & F. R. Volkmar (Eds.), *Handbook of autism and pervasive developmental disorders.* New York: John Wiley & Sons.

McDowell, D., & Spitz, H. (1999). *Substance abuse: From principles to practice.* Philadelphia: Brunner/Mazel.

McEwen, B. S. (1999). The effect of stress on the functional plasticity in the hippocampus. In D. S. Charney, E. J. Nestler, & B. S. Bunney (Eds.), *Neurobiology of mental illness* (pp. 475–495). New York: Oxford University Press.

McFadden, R. D. (1996, May 26). From a child of promise to a Unabom suspect. *The New York Times,* pp. 1, 12–15.

McFall, R. (1990). The enhancement of social skills: An information processing analysis. In W. L. Marshall, D. L., Laws, & H. E. Barboree (Eds.), *Handbook of sexual assualt: Issues, theories and treatment of the offender.* New York: Plenum.

McGrath, E., Keita, G. P., Strickland, B. R., & Russo, N. F. (1991). *Women and depression.* Washington, DC: American Psychological Association.

McGuffin, P., Katz, R., Watkins, S., & Rutherford, J. (1996). A hospital-based twin register of the heritability of DSM-IV unipolar depression. *Archives of General Psychiatry, 53,* 129–136.

McHugh, P. R. (1999). How psychiatry lost its way. *Commentary, 108*(5), 32–38.

McKay, D. (1999). Two-year follow-up of behavioral treatment and maintenance for body dysmorphic disorer. *Behavioral Modification, 23,* 620–629.

McKay, D., Todaro, J., Neziroglu, F., & Campisi, T. (1997). Body dysmorphic disorder: A preliminary evaluation of treatment and maintenance using exposure with response prevention. *Behaviour Research & Therapy, 35,* 67–70.

McKenna, P. (2001). *Chronic schizophrenia.* In J. Lieberman & R. Murray (Eds.), *Comprehensive care of schizophrenia.* London: Martin Dunitz.

McLoyd, V. C. (1998). Socioeconomic disadvantage and child development. *American Psychologist, 53,* 185–204.

McQuaid, J. R., Granholm, E., McClure, F. S., Roepke, S., et al. (2000). Development of an integrated cognitive-behavioral and social skills training intervention for older patients with schizophrenia. *Journal of Psychotherapy Practice & Research, 9*(3), 149–156.

McWilliams, N. (1994). *Psychoanalytic diagnosis: Understanding personality structure in the clinical process.* New York: Guilford Press.

Mead, M. (1963). *Sex and temperament in three primitive societies.* New York: Dell.

Meehl, P. (1962). Schizotaxia, schizotype, and schizophrenia. *American Psychologist, 17,* 827–838.

Meehl, P. E. (1990). Toward an integrated theory of schizotaxia, schizotypy, and schizophrenia. *Journal of Personality Disorders, 4*(1), 1–99.

Meichenbaum, D. (Ed.) (1997). *Cognitive behavior modification: An integrative approach.* New York: Plenum.

Melnick, J., & Nevis, S. M. (1998). Diagnosing in the here and now: A Gestalt therapy approach. In L. S. Greenberg, J. C. Watson, et al. (Eds.), *Handbook of experiential psychotherapy* (pp. 428–447). New York: Guilford Press.

Meloy, J., & Gothard, S. (1995). Demographic and clinical comparison of obsessional followers and offenders with mental disorders. *American Journal of Psychiatry, 152*(2), 258–263.

Melton, G., Pertila, J., Poythress, N., & Slobogin, P. (1997). *Psychological evaluation for the courts* (2nd ed.). New York: Guilford Press.

Meltzer, H. Y. (1999a). Treatment of schizophrenia and spectrum disorders: Pharmacotherapy, psychosocial treatments, and neurotransmitter interactions. *Biological Psychiatry, 46*(10), 1321–1327.

Meltzer, H. Y. (1999b). Dopamine$_2$ receptor occupancy and the action of clozapine: Does it make a difference to add a neuroleptic? *Biological Psychiatry, 46*(1), 114–147.

Menzies, R. G., & Clarke, J. C. (1993). The etiology of childhood water phobia. *Behaviour Research & Therapy, 31*, 499–501.

Merkin, D. (1996, Feb. 26 & March 4). Unlikely obsession. *The New Yorker Magazine*, pp. 98–100, 102–108.

Metz, M., & Pryor, J. (2000). Premature ejaculation: A psychophysiological approach for assessment and management. *Journal of Sex & Marital Therapy (Special Issue: Historical and International Context of Nosology of Female Sexual Disorders), 26*(4), 293–320.

Metzger, D. S., Navaline, H., & Woody, G. E. (2000). The role of drug abuse treatment in the prevention of HIV infection. In J. L. Peterson (Ed.), *Handbook of HIV prevention* (pp. 147–157). New York: Kluwer Academic/Plenum Publishers.

Meyer, R. G. (1998). *Case studies in abnormal behavior* (4th ed.). Needham Heights, MA: Allyn & Bacon.

Miach, P., Berah, E., Butcher, J., & Rouse, S. (2000). Utility of the MMPI-2 in assessing gender dysphoric patients. *Journal of Personality Assessment, 75*(2), 268–279.

Micallef, J., & Blin, O. (2001). Neurobiology and clinical pharmacology of obsessive-compulsive disorder. *Clinical Neuropharmacology, 24*, 191–207.

Michalos, A. C., Hubley, A. M., Zumbo, B. D., & Hemingway, D. (2001). Health and other aspects of the quality of life of older people. *Social Indicators Research, 54*, 239–274.

Miklowitz, D., Strachan, A., Goldstein, M., Doane, J., et al. (1986). Expressed emotion and communication deviance in the families of schizophrenics. *Journal of Abnormal Psychology, 95*, 60–66.

Miklowitz, D. J., & Frank, E. (1999). New psychotherapies for bipolar disorder. In J. F. Goldberg & M. Harrow (Eds.), *Bipolar disorders: Clinical course and outcome* (pp. 57–84). Washington, DC: American Psychiatric Press.

Milberger, S., Biederman, J., Faraone, S. V., Chen, L., et al. (1996). Is maternal smoking during pregnancy a risk factor for attention deficit hyperactivity disorder in children? *American Journal of Psychiatry, 153*, 1138–1142.

Miller, A. (1979). Depression and grandiosity as related narcissistic disturbances. *International Review of Psychoanalysis, 6*, 61–76.

Miller, A. (1981). *Prisoners of childhood: The drama of the gifted child and the search for the true self.* New York: Basic Books.

Miller, C. T., & Downey, K. T. (1999). A meta-analysis of heavyweight and self-esteem. *Personality and Social Psychology, 3*, 68–84.

Miller, I. (1997). Beware of a Trojan horse for managed care: Dangerous provisions in parity legislation. *The Independent Practitioner, 17*(3), 138–143.

Miller, J. L. (2001). Alcohol use and abuse among college women: A one-year follow-up study. *Dissertation Abstracts International: Section B: The Sciences & Engineering, 61*(8-B), 4384. Ann Arbor, MI: University Microfilms International.

Miller, N. S., & Flaherty, J. A. (2000). Effectiveness of coerced addiction treatment (alternative consequences): A review of the clinical research. *Journal of Substance Abuse Treatment, 18*(1), 9–16.

Miller, N. S., Stout, A. W., & Sheppard, L. M. (2000). Underage drinking among college students. *Psychiatric Annals, 30*(9), 597–601.

Miller, P., Byrne, M., Hodges, A., Lawrie, S. M., et al. (2002). Schizotypal components in people at high risk of developing schizophrenia: Early findings from the Edinburgh high-risk study. *British Journal of Psychiatry, 180*, 179–184.

Miller, S. D., Blackburn, T., Scholes, G., White, G. L., et al. (1991). Optical differences in multiple personality disorder: A second look. *Journal of Nervous & Mental Disease, 179*, 132–135.

Miller, T. Q., Smith, T. W., Turner, C. W., Guijarro, M. L., et al. (1996). Meta-analytic review of research on hostility and physical health. *Psychological Bulletin, 119*, 322–348.

Miller, W. R., & Kurtz, E. (1994). Models of alcoholism used in treatment: Contrasting AA and other perspectives with which it is often confused. *Journal of Studies on Alcohol, 55*, 159–166.

Millon, T., & Davis, R. (1996). *Disorders of personality: DSM-IV and beyond.* New York: John Wiley & Sons.

Millon, T., & Davis, R. (2000). *Personality disorders in modern life.* New York: John Wiley & Sons.

Milner, J., & Dopke, C. (1997). Paraphilia not otherwise specified: Psychopathology and theory. In D. Laws & W. O'Donohue (Eds.), *Sexual deviance: Theory, assessment and treatment.* New York: Guilford Press.

Mimica, N., Folnegovic-Smalc, V., & Folnegovic, Z. (2001). Catatonic schizophrenia in Croatia. *European Archives of Psychiatry & Clinical Neuroscience (Special Issue: Catatonia: A New Focus of Research), 251*(1), S17–S20.

Minshew, N. J., Sweeney, J. A., & Bauman, M. L. (1997). Neurological aspects of autism. In D. J. Cohen & F. R. Volkmar (Eds.), *Handbook of autism and pervasive developmental disorders.* New York: John Wiley & Sons.

Minter, S. (1999). Diagnosis and treatment of gender identity disorder in children. In M. Rotnek (Ed.), *Sissies and tomboys: Gender nonconformity and homosexual childhood* (pp. 9–33). New York: New York University Press.

Mintzer, J. E., Brawman-Mintzer, O., Mirski, D. F., & Barkin, K. (2000). Anxiety in the behavioral and psychological symptoms of dementia. *International Psychogeriatrics, 12*(1), 139–142.

Minuchin, S. (1974). *Families and family therapy.* Cambridge, MA: Harvard University Press.

Minuchin, S., Rosman, B. L., & Baker, L. (1978). *Psychosomatic families: Anorexia nervosa in context.* Cambridge, MA: Harvard University Press.

Mirsky, A. F., & Duncan-Johnson, C. C. (1984). Nature versus nurture in schizophrenia: The struggle continues. *Integrative Psychiatry, 2*(4), 137–141.

Mitchell, J. E., Peterson, C. B., Myers, T., & Wonderlich, S. (2001). Combining pharmacotherapy and psychotherapy in the treatment of patients with eating disorders. *Psychiatric Clinics of North America, 24,* 315–323.

Mitchell, S. (2000). *Relationality: From attachment to intersubjectivity.* Hillsdale, NJ: Analytic Press.

Mitchell, S., & Aron, L. (1999). *Relational psychoanalysis: The emergence of a tradition.* Hillsdale, NJ: Analytic Press.

Moehle, K. A., & Levitt, E. E. (1991). The history of the concepts of fear and anxiety. In C. E. Walker (Ed.), *Clinical psychology: Historical and research foundations.* New York: Plenum Press.

Moene, F. C., Hoogduin, K. A. L., & van Dyck. R. (1998). The inpatient treatment of patients suffering from (motor) conversion symptoms: A description of eight cases. *International Journal of Clinical and Experimental Hypnosis, 46,* 171–190.

Mogg, K., Millar, N., & Bradley, B. P. (2000). Biases in eye movements to threatening facial expressions in generalized anxiety disorder and depressive disorder. *Journal of Abnormal Psychology, 109,* 695–704.

Mojtabai, R., Varma, V. K., Malhotra, S., Mattoo, S. K., et al. (2001). Mortality and long-term course in schizophrenia with a poor 2-year course: A study in a developing country. *British Journal of Psychiatry, 178,* 71–75.

Moleman, P., van Dam, K., & Dings, V. (1999). Psychopharmacological treatment of personality disorders: A review. In J. Derksen, C. Maffei, & H. Groen (Eds.), *Treatment of personality disorders* (pp. 207–227). New York: Kluwer Academic/Plenum Publishers.

Monahan, J. (1992). Mental disorder and violent behavior: Perceptions and evidence. *American Psychologist, 47*(4), 511–521.

Monahan, J. (1993). Mental disorder and violence: Another look. In S. Hodgins (Ed.), *Mental disorder and crime.* Newbury Park, CA: Sage Publications Co.

Money, J. (1985). *The destroying angel: Sex, fitness & food in the legacy of degeneracy theory, graham crackers, Kellogg's corn flakes & American health history.* Buffalo, NY: Prometheus Books.

Money, J. (1986). *Lovemaps: Clinical concepts of sexual/erotic health and pathology, paraphilia, and gender transposition of childhood, adolescence, and maturity.* New York: Irvington.

Money, J. (1992). *The Kaspar Hauser syndrome of "psychological dwarfism": Deficient statural, intellectual and social growth induced by child abuse.* Buffalo, NY: Prometheus Books.

Money, J. (1994). The concept of gender identity disorder in childhood and adolescence after 39 years. *Journal of Sex & Marital Therapy, 20*(3), 163–177.

Monroe, J. (1998). Marijuana—A mind-altering drug. *Current Health 2*(24), 16–19.

Monti, P. M., Colby, S. M., & O'Leary, T. A. (Eds.). (2001). *Adolescents, alcohol, and substance abuse: Reaching teens through brief interventions.* New York: Guilford Press

Mooney, D. K. (2001). Assessing binge drinking: What you get is what you … ask! *Journal of American College Health (Special Issue), 49*(5), 243.

Moran, C. (1986). Depersonalization and agoraphobia associated with marijuana use. *British Journal of Medical Psychology, 59,* 187–196.

Moran, G., Fonagy, P., Kurtz, A., Bolton, A., et al. (1991). A controlled study of the psychoanalytic treatment of brittle diabetes. *Journal of the American Academy of Child and Adolescent Psychiatry, 30,* 926–935.

Morgan, C. D., & Murray, H. A. (1935). A method for investigating fantasies. The Thematic Apperception Test. *American Medical Association Archives of Neurology and Psychiatry, 34,* 289–306.

Morgan, D. G. (1992). Neurochemical changes with aging: Predisposition toward age-related mental disorders. In J. E. Birren, R. B. Sloane, & G. D. Cohen (Eds.), *Handbook of mental health and aging* (2nd ed.). San Diego, CA: Academic Press.

Morrison, A., & Baker, C. A. (2000). Intrusive thoughts and auditory hallucinations: A comparative study of intrusions in psychosis. *Behavior Research & Therapy, 38*(11), 1097–1106.

Morrison, J. (1989). Childhood molestation reported by women with somatization disorder. *Annals of Clinical Psychiatry, 1,* 25–32.

Moser, C. (2001). Paraphilia: A critique of a confused concept. In P. Kleinplatz (Ed.), *New directions in sex therapy: Innovations and alternatives* (pp. 91–108). Philadelphia: Brunner-Rutledge.

Moser, P. C., Hitchcock, J. M., Lister, S., & Moran, P. M. (2000). The pharmacology of latent inhibition as an animal model of schizophrenia. *Brain Research Reviews, 33*(2–3), 275–307.

Moss, H. B. (1999). Pharmacotherapy. In M. Hersen (Ed.), *Handbook of comparative interventions for adult disorders* (2nd ed., pp. 652–676). New York: John Wiley & Sons.

MTA Cooperative Group. (1999). A 14-month randomised clinical trial of treatment strategies for attention-deficit/hyperactivity disorder. *Archives of General Psychiatry, 56,* 1073–1086.

Muller, R. J. (1998). A patient with dissociative identity disorder "switches" in the emergency room. *Psychiatric Times, 15*(11). Retrieved December 19, 2003, from www.psychiatrictimes.com/p981107.html.

Munroe, R., & Gauvain, M. (2001). Why the paraphilias? Domesticating strange sex. *Cross-Cultural Research: The Journal of Comparative Social Science (Special Issue in Honor of Ruth H. Munroe: Part 2), 35*(1), 44–64.

Murphy, W. (1997). Exhibitionism: Psychopathology and theory. In D. Laws & W. O'Donohue (Eds.), *Sexual deviance: Theory, assessment, and treatment* (pp. 22–39). New York: Guilford Press.

Murray, B. (2002). Writing to heal. *Monitor on Psychology, 33,* 54–55.

Murray, H. A. (1938). *Explorations in personality.* New York: Oxford University Press.

Murray, H. A. (1943). *Thematic Apperception Test manual.* Cambridge, MA: Harvard University Press.

Murray, L. L. (2000). Spoken language production in Huntington's and Parkinson's diseases. *Journal of Speech, Language, & Hearing Research, 43,* 1350–1366.

Murugaiah, K., et al. (1982). Chronic continuous administration of neuroleptic drugs alters cerebral dopamine receptors and increases spontaneous dopaminergic action in the striatum. *Nature, 296*(5857), 570–572.

Myers, M. G., Stewart, D. G., & Brown, S. A. (1998). Progression from conduct disorder to antisocial personality disorder following treatment for adolescent substance abuse. *American Journal of Psychiatry, 155,* 479–485.

Myers, W. C., Burton, P. R. S., Sanders, P. D., Donat, K. M., et al. (2000). Project Back-on-Track at 1 year: A delinquency treatment program for early-career juvenile offenders. *Journal of the American Academy of Child and Adolescent Psychiatry, 39,* 127–1134.

N

Nakamagoe, K., Iwamoto, Y., & Yoshida, K. (2000). Evidence for brainstem structures participating in oculomotor integration. *Science, 288*(5467), 857–859.

Nandi, D. N., Banerjee, G., Nandi, S., & Nandi, P. (1992). Is hysteria on the wane? A community survey in West Bengal, India. *British Journal of Psychiatry, 160,* 87–91.

Napholz, L. (1995). Indexes of psychological well-being and role commitment among working women. *Journal of Employment Counseling, 32,* 22–31.

Nappo, S. A., Galduroz, J. C. F., & Carlini, E. A. (2000). Cocaine use: Key informant (KY) report from Sao Paulo, Brazil. *Journal Brasileiro de Psiquiatria, 49*(5), 149–166.

Nardi, A. E., Valenca, A. M., Nascimento, I., Mezzasalma, M. A., et al. (2001). Hyperventilation in panic disorder and social phobia. *Psychopathology, 34,* 123–127.

Nash, M. R., & Lynn, S. J. (1986). Child abuse and hypnotic ability. *Imagination, Cognition, and Personality, 5,* 211–218.

Nathan, P. E. (1995). DSM-IV process and outcomes. In F. Kessell (Ed.), *Psychology, science, and human affairs: Essays in honor of William Bevan.* Boulder, CO: Westview Press.

Nathan, P. E., & Gorman, J. M. (2002). *A guide to treatments that work* (2nd ed.). New York: Oxford University Press.

Nathan, P. E., & Lagenbucher, J. W. (1999). Psychopathology: Description and classification. *Annual Review of Psychology, 50,* 79–107.

National Institute of Mental Health. (1998). *New study on financing mental health parity in managed behavioral health care.* Press Release. Rockville, MD.

Nayudu, S. K., & Scheftner, W. A. (2000). Case report of withdrawal syndrome after olanzapine discontinuation. *Journal of Clinical Psychopharmacology, 20*(4), 489–490.

NCIPC (National Center for Injury Prevention and Control). (1999, February 20). *Suicide in the United States.* Atlanta, GA: Author.

Neill, J. R. (1987). More than medical significance: LSD and American psychiatry: 1953 to 1966. *Journal of Psychoactive Drugs, 19*(1), 39–45.

Nelissen, I., Muris, P., & Merckelbach, H. (1995). Computerized exposure and in vivo exposure treatments of spider fear in children: Two case reports. *Journal of Behavior Therapy and Experimental Psychiatry, 26*(2), 153–156.

Nelson, C. M. (1987). Behavioral interventions: What works and what doesn't. *Pointer, 31,* 45–50.

Nelson, H. E. (1997). *Cognitive behavioral therapy with schizophrenia: A practice manual.* Cheltenham, England: Stanley Thornes (Publishers).

Nelson, T. F., & Wechsler, H. (2001). Alcohol and college athletes. *Medicine & Science in Sports & Exercise, 33*(1), 43–47.

Nesse, R. (1998). Emotional disorders in evolutionary perspective. *British Journal of Medical Psychology, 71,* 397–415.

Nesse, R. M., & Berridge, K. C. (1997). Psychoactive drug use in evolutionary perspective. *Science, 278*(5335), 63–66.

Netherton, S. D., & Walker, C. E. (1999). Brief history of DSM-IV and ICD-10. In *Child & adolescent psychological disorders: A comprehensive textbook.* New York: Oxford University Press.

Neumark, Y. D., Van Etten, M. L., & Anthony, J. C. (2000). "Drug dependence" and death: Survival analysis of the Baltimore ECA sample from 1981 to 1995. *Substance Use & Misuse, 35*(3), 313–327.

Newman, C. F., Leahy, R. L., Beck, A. T., Reilly-Harrington, N. A., et al. (2001). *Bipolar disorder: A cognitive therapy approach.* Washington, DC: American Psychological Association.

Newshan, G., & Leon, W. (2001). The use of anabolic agents in HIV disease. *International Journal of STD & AIDS (Special Issue), 12*(3), 141–144.

Neziroglu, F., & Yaryura-Tobias, J. A. (1997). A review of cognitive behavioral and pharmacological treatment of body dysmorphic disorder. *Behavior Modification, 21,* 324–340.

Ng, D. M., & Jeffery, R. W. (2003). Relationships between perceived stress and health behaviors in a sample of working adults. *Health Psychology, 22*(6), 638–642.

Ngcobo, H., & Edwards, S. (1998). Violence and psychoanalysis: Zululand perspectives. *Psycho-analytic Psychotherapy in South Africa, 6*(1), 63–66.

Niaura, R., Herbert, P. N., McMahon, N., & Sommerville, L. (1992). Repressive coping and blood lipids in men and women. *Psychosomatic Medicine, 54,* 698–706.

Nichols, B. (1998). Predictors of sexual offending: Fantasy proneness, deviant sexual modeling in childhood, and paraphilic fantasy. *Dissertation Abstracts International: Section B: The Sciences and Engineering, 59*(6-B). Ann Arbor, MI: University Microfilms International.

Nichols, M. (2000). Roll-your-own medicine. *Maclean's, 113*(33), 22.

Nicholson, K. L., & Balster, R. L. (2001). GHB: A new and novel drug of abuse. *Drug & Alcohol Dependence (Special Issue), 63*(1), 1–22.

Nielsen, S. (2001). Epidemiology and mortality of eating disorders. *Psychiatric Clinics of North America: Eating Disorders, 24,* 201–214.

Nietzel, M. T., Bernstein, D. A., & Milich, R. (1994). *Introduction to clinical psychology* (4th ed.). Englewood Cliffs, NJ: Prentice Hall.

Nieves-Rivera, F., Gonzalez de Pijem, L., & Mirabal, B. (1998). Reversible growth failure among Hispanic children: Instances of psychosocial short stature. *Puerto Rico Health Sciences Journal, 17*(2), 107–112.

Ninan, P. T. (1999). The functional anatomy, neurochemistry, and pharmacology of anxiety. *Journal of Clinical Psychiarty, 60*(22 suppl), 12–17.

Nishino, S., Mignot, E., & Dement, W. C. (2001). Sedative-hypnotics. In A. F. Schatzberg (Ed.), *Essentials of clinical psychopharmacology* (pp. 283–301). Washington, DC: American Psychiatric Association.

Noffsinger, S., & Resnick, P. (2000). Sexual predator laws and offenders with addictions. *Psychiatric Annals, 30*(9), 602–608.

Nohr, R. W. (2000). Outcome effects of receiving a spiritually informed vs. a standard cognitive-behavioral stress management workshop. In *Dissertation Abstracts International: Section B: The Sciences & Engineering, 61*(7-B). University Microfilm International. 3855. AAI9977718. Ann Arbor, MI.

Nolen-Hoeksema, S. (1990). *Sex differences in depression.* Stanford, CA: Stanford University Press.

Nolen-Hoeksema, S. (1998). The other end of the continuum: The costs of rumination. *Psychological Inquiry, 9*(3), 216–219.

Nolen-Hoeksema, S. (2003). *Women who think too much.* New York: Henry Holt & Co.

Nolen-Hoeksema, S., & Girgus, J. (1995). Explanatory style and achievement, depression, and gender differences in childhood and early adolescence. In G. Buchanan & M. Seligman (Eds.), *Explanatory style.* Hillsdale, NJ: Lawrence Erlbaum.

Nolen-Hoeksema, S., Girgus, J. S., & Seligman, M. E. P. (1986). Learned helplessness in children: A longitudinal study of depression, achievement, and explanatory style. *Journal of Personality and Social Psychology, 51,* 435–442.

North, C. S., Nixon, S. J., Shariat, S., Mallonee, S., et al. (1999). Psychiatric disorders among survivors of the Oklahoma City bombing. *Journal of the American Medical Association, 282,* 755–762.

Noshirvani, H. F., Kasvikis, Y., Marks, I. M., Tsakiris, F., et al. (1991). Gender-divergent aetiological factors in obsessive-compulsive disorder. *British Journal of Psychiatry, 158,* 260–267.

Nottleman, E. D., & Jensen, P. S. (1995). Comorbidity of disorders in children and adolescents: Developmental perspectives. In T. H. Ollendick & R. J. Prinz (Eds.), *Advances in clinical child psychology* (Vol. 17). New York: Plenum Press.

Novak, S. J. (1997). LSD before Leary. Sidney Cohen's critique of 1950s psychedelic drug research. *Isis, 88*(1), 87–110.

Novak, S. J. (1998). Second thoughts on psychedelic drugs. *Endeavour, 22*(1), 21–23.

Noyes, R., & Hoehn-Saric, R. (1998). *The anxiety disorders.* Cambridge, UK: Cambridge University Press.

Noyes, R., Clarkson, C., Crowe, R. R., Yates, W. R., et al. (1987). A family study of generalized anxiety disorder. *American Journal of Psychiatry, 144,* 1019–1024.

Nydes, J. (1963). The paranoid-masochistic character. *Psychoanalytic Review, 50,* 215–251.

Nye, R. (1999). *Sexuality.* New York: Oxford University Press.

Nyklicek, I., Vingerhoets, A. J. J. M., & Van Heck, G. L. (2000). Blood pressure, appraisal, and coping with stressors. In P. M. McCabe, N. Schneiderman, T. Field, & A. R. Wellens (Eds.), *Stress, coping, and cardiovascular disease* (pp. 123–144). Mahwah, NJ: Lawrence Erlbaum.

O

O'Brien, M., & Houston, G. (2000). *Integrative therapy: A practitioner's guide.* Thousand Oaks, CA: Sage Publications.

O'Doherty, M. (1998). Acute psychiatric services: An appraisal of a major change in service delivery within one catchment area. *Irish Journal of Psychological Medicine, 15*(3), 84–87.

O'Farrell, T. J. (2001). Substance abuse disorders. In M. Hersen (Ed.), *Advanced abnormal psychology* (2nd ed., pp. 355–377). New York: Kluwer Academic/Plenum Publishers.

O'Grady, W., Asbridge, M., & Abernathy, T. (2000). Illegal tobacco sales to youth: A view from rational choice theory. *Canadian Journal of Criminology, 42*(1), 1–20.

Oakley, D. (1999). Hypnosis and conversion hysteria: A unifying model. *Cognitive Neuropsychiatry, 4,* 243–265.

Oehman, A., & Mineka, S. (2001). Fears, phobias, and preparedness: Toward an evolved module of fear and fear learning. *Psychological Review, 108,* 483–522.

Oestroem, M., & Eriksson, A. (2001). Pedestrian fatalities and alcohol. *Accident Analysis & Prevention, 33*(2), 173–180.

Oldenberg, D. (1998, June 23). On thin ground. *The Washington Post,* p. B4.

Oldham, J. M. (1994). Personality disorders: Current perspectives. *Journal of the American Medical Association, 272*(22), 1770–1776.

Oldham, J. M., & Skodol, A. E. (2000). Charting the future of Axis II. *Journal of Personality Disorders, 14*(1), 17–29.

Oldham, J. M., Skodol, A. E., Gallaher, P. E., & Kroll, M. E. (1996). Relationship of borderline symptoms to histories of abuse and neglect: A pilot study. *Psychiatric Quarterly, 67*(4), 287–295.

Olds, D., Pettitt, L. M., Robinson, J., Henderson, C. Jr., et al. (1998). Reducing risks for antisocial behavior with a program of prenatal and early childhood home visitation. *Journal of Community Psychology, 26*(1), 65–83.

Ollendick, T. H., Mattis, S. G., & King, N. J. (1994). Panic in children and adolescents: A review. *Journal of Child Psychology & Psychiatry & Allied Disciplines, 35*(1), 113–134.

Olshansky, S. (1980). The deinstitutionalization of schizophrenics: A challenge to rehabilitation. *Rehabilitation Literature, 41*(5–6), S127–S129.

Orrell, M., & Bebbington, P. (1996). Psychosocial stress and anxiety in senile dementia. *Journal of Affective Disorders, 39*(3), 165–173.

Ortega, S. T., Crutchfield, R. D., & Rushing, W. A. (1983). Race differences in elderly personal well-being. *Research on Aging, 5,* 101–118.

Orth-Gomer, K., Rosengren, A., & Wilhelmsen, L. (1993). Lack of social support and incidence of coronary heart disease in middle-aged Swedish men. *Psychosomatic Medicine, 55,* 37–43.

Oscar-Berman, M., Shagrin, B., Evert, D. L., & Epstein, C. (1997). Impairments of brain and behavior: The neurological effects of alcohol. *Alcohol Health & Research World, 21*(1), 65–75.

Ost, L. G., Alm, T., Brandberg, M., & Breitholtz, E. (2001). One vs five sessions of exposure and five sessions of cognitive therapy in the treatment of claustrophobia. *Behaviour Research & Therapy, 39,* 167–183.

Ostler, K., Thompson, C., Kinmonth, A. L. K., Peveler, R. C., et al. (2001). Influence of socio-economic deprivation on the prevalence and outcome of depression in primary care: The Hampshire Depression Project. *British Journal of Psychiatry, 178,* 12–17.

Otto, M. W., & Deckersbach, T. (1998). Cognitive-behavioral therapy for panic disorder. In J. F. Rosenbaum & M. H. Pollack (Eds.), *Panic disorder and its treatment* (pp. 181–203). New York: Marcel Dekker, Inc.

Owen, F., Crow, T. J., & Poulter, M. (1987). Central dopaminergic mechanisms in schizophrenia. *Acta Psychiatrica Belgica, 87*(5), 552–565.

P

Palfai, T., & Jankiewicz, H. (1997). *Drugs and human behavior* (2nd ed.). Madison, WI: Brown & Benchmark Publishers.

Palha, A. P., & Esteves, M. F. (1997). The origin of dementia praecox. *Schizophrenia Research: (Special Issue: 100 Years of Dementia Praecox), 28*(2–3), 99–103.

Palmer, R. L. (1995). Sexual abuse and eating disorders. In K. D. Brownell & C. G. Fairburn (Eds.), *Eating disorders and obesity.* New York: Guilford Press.

Parsons, M. (2000). Sexuality and perversion a hundred years on: Discovering what Freud discovered. *International Journal of Psycho-Analysis, 81*(1), 37–51.

Pato, M. T., Pato, C. N., & Gunn, S. A. (1998). Biological treatments for obsessive-compulsive disorder. In R. P. Swinson, M. M. Antony, S. Rachman, & M. A. Richter (Eds.), *Obsessive-compulsive disorder: Theory, research, and treatment* (pp. 327–348). London: Guilford Press.

Patrick, C. J., Bradley, M. M., & Lang, P. J. (1993). Emotion in the criminal psychopath: Startle reflex modulation. *Journal of Abnormal Psychology, 102,* 82–92.

Patterson, T. L. & Joste, D. V. (1999). The potential impact of baby-boom generation substance abuse among elderly persons. *Psychiatric Services 50,* 1184–1188.

Peltzer, K. (1989). Nosology and etiology of a spirit disorder (Vimbuza) in Malawi. *Psychopathology, 22,* 145–151.

Peralta, V., & Cuesta, M. J. (2000). Clinical models of schizophrenia: A critical approach to competing conceptions. *Psychopathology, 33*(5), 252–258.

Peralta, V., & Cuesta, M. J. (2001). Motor features in psychotic disorders. II: Development of diagnostic criteria for catatonia. *Schizophrenia Research: (Special Issue), 47*(2–3), 117–126.

Perna, G., Brambilla, F., Arancio, C., & Bellodi, L. (1995). Menstrual cycle-related sensitivity to 35% CO_2 in panic patients. *Biological Psychiatry, 37*(8), 528–532.

Perry, W., & Braff, D. L. (1994). Information-processing deficits and thought disorder in schizophrenia. *American Journal of Psychiatry, 151*(3), 363–367.

Person, E., & Ovesey, L. (1978). Transvestism: New perspectives. *Journal of the American Academy of Psychoanalysis, 6*(3), 301–323.

Peszke, M. A. (1975). Is dangerousness an issue for physicians in emergency commitment? *American Journal of Psychiatry 132*(8), 825–828.

Peters, K. D., Kochanek, K. D., & Murphy, S. L. (1998). Deaths: Final data for 1996. *National Vital Statistics Reports, 47*(9). Hyattsville, MD: National Center for Health Statistics.

Peters, M. A., & Phelps, L. (2001). Body image dissatisfaction and distortion, steroid use, and sex differences in college age body-builders. *Psychology in the Schools (Special Issue), 38*(3), 283–289. New York: John Wiley & Sons.

Peterson, C., & Bossio, L. M. (1991). *Health and optimism.* New York: Free Press.

Peterson, C., & Bossio, L. M. (2001). Optimism and physical well-being. In E. C. Chang (Ed.), *Optimism & pessimism: Implications for theory, research, and practice* (pp. 127–145). Washington, DC: American Psychological Association.

Peterson, C., Maier, S. F., & Seligman, M. E. (1993). *Learned helplessness: A theory for the age of personal control.* New York/Oxford: Oxford University Press.

Peterson, C., & Seligman, M. E. (1984). Causal explanations as a risk factor for depression: Theory and evidence. *Psychological Review, 91,* 347–374.

Peterson, C., Seligman, M. E., & Vaillant, G. E. (1988). Pessimistic explanatory style is a risk factor for physical illness: A thirty-five-year longitudinal study. *Journal of Personality & Social Psychology, 55,* 23–27.

Petry, N. M., Tedford, J., & Martin, B. (2001). Reinforcing compliance with non-drug-related activities. *Journal of Substance Abuse Treatment (Special Issue), 20*(1), 33–44.

Pezdek, K., & Hodge, D. (1999). Planting false childhood memories in children: The role of event plausibility. *Child Development, 70,* 887–895.

Pfefferbaum, B., Seale, T. W., McDonald, N. B., Brandt, E. N. Jr., et al. (2000). Posttraumatic stress two years after the Oklahoma City bombing in youths geographically distant from the explosion. *Psychiatry: Interpersonal & Biological Processes, 63,* 358–370.

Pfiffner, L. (1996). *All about ADHD: The complete practical guide for classroom teachers.* New York: Scholastic Professional Books.

Pfiffner, L. J., Calzada, E., & McBurnett, K. (2000). Interventions to enhance social competence. *Child and Adolescent Psychiatric Clinics of North America, 9,* 689–709.

Phelps, R., Eisman, E., & Kohut, J. (1998). Psychological practice and managed care: Results of the CAPP practitioner survey. *Professional Psychology: Research and Practice, 29,* 31–36.

Phillips, K. A. (1996). *The broken mirror: Understanding and treating body dysmorphic disorder.* New York: Oxford University Press.

Phillips, K. A. (2000). Pharamacological treatment of body dysmorphic disorder: A review of empirical data and a proposed treatment algorithm. *Psychiatric Clinics of North America, 7,* 59–82.

Phillips, K. A. (2001). *Somatoform and factitious disorders.* Washington, DC: American Psychiatric Publishing.

Phillips, K. A., & Diaz, S. F. (1997). Gender differences in body dysmorphic disorder. *Journal of Nervous Mental Diseases, 188,* 170–175.

Pichot, P. (1997). DSM-III and its reception. *American Journal of Psychiatry:* Special Issue, *154*(6 suppl), 47–54.

Pickar, D. B. (1986). Psychosocial aspects of learning disabilities: A review of research. *Bulletin of the Menninger Clinic, 50,* 22–32.

Pigache, R. M. (1999). Vigilance in schizophrenia and its disruption by impaired preattentive selection: A dysintegration hypothesis. *Cognitive Neuropsychiatry, 4*(2), 119–144.

Pike, K. M., & Rodin, J. (1991). Mothers, daughters, and disordered eating. *Journal of Abnormal Psychology, 100,* 198–204.

Pine, F. (1990). *Drive, ego, self and object.* New York: Basic Books.

Pinel, P. (1802/1803). *Nosographie philosophique, ou La méthode de l'analyse appliquée à la médecine.* [Philosophical classification or the analytic method applied to medicine.] Paris: J. A. Brosson.

Pipher, M. B. (1994). *Reviving Ophelia: Saving the selves of adolescent girls.* New York: Putnam.

Pirke, K. M. (1995). Physiology of bulimia nervosa. In K. D. Brownell & C. G. Fairburn (Eds.), *Eating disorders and obesity.* New York: Guilford Press.

Pithers, W., Gray, A., Busconi, A., & Houchens, P. (1998). Five empirically-derived subtypes of children with sexual behaviour problems: Characteristics potentially related to juvenile delinquency and adult criminality. *Irish Journal of Psychology (Special Issue: Understanding, Assessing and Treating Juvenile and Adult Sex Offenders), 19*(1), 49–67.

Plante, T. (1999). *Contemporary clinical psychology.* Hoboken, NJ: John Wiley & Sons.

Plath, S. (1966). *The bell jar.* London: Faber.

Pleak, R. (1999). Ethical issues in diagnosing and treating gender-dysphoric children and adolescents. In *Sissies and tomboys: Gender nonconformity and homosexual childhood* (pp. 34–51). New York: New York University Press.

Pollard, C. M., & Henderson, J. G. (1988). Four types of social phobia in a community sample. *Journal of Nervous and Mental Disorders, 176,* 440–449.

Pollmaecher, T., Haack, M., Schuld, A., Kraus, T., et al. (2000). Effects of antipsychotic drugs on cytokine networks. *Journal of Psychiatric Research: (Special Issue), 34*(6), 369–382.

Poole, R., & Brabbins, C. (1996). Drug induced psychosis. *British Journal of Psychiatry, 168*(2), 135–138.

Pope, H. G., & Katz, D. L. (1988). Affective and psychotic symptoms associated with anabolic steroid use. *American Journal of Psychiatry, 145,* 487–490.

Pope, H. G., Katz, D. L., & Hudson, J. I. (1993). Anorexia nervosa and "reverse anorexia" among 108 male bodybuilders. *Comprehensive Psychiatry, 34,* 406–409.

Pope, H. G., Olivardia, R., Gruber, A., & Borowiecki, J. (1999). Evolving ideals of male body image as seen through action toys. *International Journal of Eating Disorders, 26,* 65–72.

Popper, K. (1959). *The logic of scientific discovery.* London: Hutchinson & Co.

Popper, K. (1986). Predicting overt behavior versus predicting hidden states. *Behavioral & Brain Sciences, 9*(2), 254.

Porter, V. R., Buxton, W. G., Fairbanks, L. A., Strickland, T., et al. (2003). Frequency and characteristics of anxiety among patients with Alzheimer's disease and related dementias. *Journal of Neuropsychiatry & Clinical Neurosciences, 15*(2), 180–186.

Posavac, H. D., Posavac, S. S., & Posavac, E. J. (1998). Exposure to media images of female attractiveness and concern with body weight among young women. *Sex Roles, 38,* 187–201.

Power, K. G., Simpson, R. J., Swanson, V., & Wallace, L. A. (1990). A controlled comparison of cognitive-behavior therapy, diazepam, and placebo, alone and in combination, for the treatment of generalized anxiety disorder. *Journal of Anxiety Disorders, 4,* 267–292.

Pretzer, J. L., & Beck, A. T. (1996). A cognitive theory of personality disorders. In J. F. Clarkin & M. F. Lenzenweger (Eds.), *Major theories of personality disorder* (pp. 36–105). New York: Guilford Press.

Prince-Embury, S., & Rooney, J. F. (1988). Psychological symptoms of residents in the aftermath of the Three Mile Island nuclear accident and restart. *Journal of Social Psychology, 128*(6), 779–790.

Procopio, M., & Marriott, P. K. (1998). Is the decline in diagnoses of schizophrenia caused by the disappearance of a seasonal aetiological agent? An epidemiological study in England and Wales. *Psychological Medicine, 28*(2), 367–373.

Protter, B. (2001). Knowing the self in psychotherapy: Toward a postmodern integrative approach. In J. C. Muran (Ed.), *Self-relations in the psychotherapy process* (pp. xv, 391, 313–345). Washington, DC: American Psychological Association.

Putnam, F. (1985). Dissociation as a response to extreme trauma. In R. P. Kluft (Ed.), *Childhood antecedents of multiple personality* (pp. 66–97). Washington, DC: American Psychiatric Press.

Putnam, F. (1989). *Diagnosis and treatment of multiple personality disorder.* New York: Guilford Press.

Putnam, F. W. (1992). Are alter personalities fragments or figments? *Psychoanalytic Inquiry, 12,* 95–111.

Putnam, F. W., Guroff, J. J., Silberman, E. K., Barban, L., et al. (1986). The clinical phenomenology of multiple personality disorder: Review of 100 recent cases. *Journal of Clinical Psychiatry, 47,* 285–293.

Putnam, F. W., Helmers, K., & Trickett, P. K. (1993). Development, reliability and validity of a child dissociation scale. *Child Abuse and Neglect, 17,* 731–741.

Putnam, F. W., Zahn, T. P., & Post, R. M. (1990). Differential autonomic nervous system activity in multiple personality disorder. *Psychiatry Research, 31,* 251–260.

R

Rachlin, S. (1978). When schizophrenia comes marching home. *Psychiatric Quarterly, 50*(3), 202–210.

Rack, J. P., & Olson, R. K. (1993). Phonological deficits, IQ, and individual differences in reading disability: Genetic and environmental influences. *Developmental Review, 13,* 269–278.

Raesaenen, S., Nieminen, P., & Isohanni, M. (1999). Gender differences in treatment and outcome in a therapeutic community ward, with special reference to schizophrenic patients. *Psychiatry: Interpersonal & Biological Processes, 62*(3), 235–249.

Raesaenen, S., Veijola, J., Hakko, H., Joukamaa, M., et al. (1999). Gender differences in incidence and age of onset of DSM-III-R schizophrenia: Preliminary results of the Northern Finland 1966 birth cohort study. *Schizophrenia Research, 37*(2), 197–198.

Raine, A., Lencz, T., Bihrle, S., LaCasse, L., et al. (2000). Reduced prefrontal gray matter volume and reduced autonomic activity in antisocial personality disorder. *Archives of General Psychiatry, 57*(2), 119–127.

Ramage, M. (1998). ABC of sexual problems: Management of sexual problems. *British Medical Journal, 317*(7171), 1470.

Rao, S. M. (2000). Neuropsychological evaluation. In B. S. Fogel, R. B. Schiffer, & S. M. Rao (Eds.), *Synopsis of neuropsychiatry.* Philadelphia: Lippincott-Raven.

Rapee, R. M. (1994). Failure to replicate a memory bias in panic disorder. *Journal of Anxiety Disorders, 8,* 291–300.

Rapee, R. M., Barrett, P. M., Dadds, M. R., & Evans, L. (1994). Reliability of the DSM-III-R childhood anxiety disorders using structured interviews: Interrater and parent-child agreement. *Journal of the American Academy of Child and Adolescent Psychiatry, 33,* 984–992.

Rapoport, J. L. (1991). Recent advances in obsessive-compulsive disorder. *Neuropsychopharmacology, 5*(1), 1–10.

Raschka, L. B. (2000). Paternal age and schizophrenia in dizygotic twins. *British Journal of Psychiatry, 176,* 400–401.

Raskin, N., & Rogers, C. (2000). Person centered therapy. In R. Corsini & D. Wedding (Eds.), *Current psychotherapies* (6th ed.). Itasca, IL: Peacock Publishers.

Raskind, M. A., & Peskind, E. P. (1992). Alzheimer's disease and other dementing disorders. In J. E. Birren, R. B. Sloane, & G. D. Cohen (Eds.), *Handbook of mental health and aging* (2nd ed.). San Diego, CA: Academic Press.

Rasmussen, S. A., & Eisen, J. L. (1990). Epidemiology of obsessive compuslive disorder. *Journal of Clinical Psychiatry, 45,* 450–457.

Rassool, G. H. (Ed.). (1998). *Substance use and misuse: Nature, context and clinical interventions.* London: Blackwell Science.

Rastam, M., & Gilberg, C. (1991). The family background in anorexia nervosa: a population-based study. *Journal of the American Academy of Child & Adolescent Psychiatry, 30,* 283–289.

Ratey, J. J., & Johnson, C. (1997). *Shadow syndromes.* New York: Pantheon Books.

Raut, C., Stephen, A., & Kosofsky, B. (in press). In L. Friedman, N. Fleming, D. Roberts, & S. Hyman (Eds.), *Sourcebook of substance abuse and addiction.* Baltimore: Williams & Wilkins.

Ray, O., & Ksir, C. (2002). *Drugs, society and human behavior* (9th ed.). Boston: McGraw-Hill.

Raymond, N. C., Mussell, M. P., Mitchell, J. E., deZwann, M., et al. (1995). An age-matched comparison of subjects with binge eating disorder and bulimia nervosa. *International Journal of Eating Disorders, 18,* 135–143.

Raymont, V. (2001). Suicide in schizophrenia—how can research influence training and clinical practice? *Psychiatric Bulletin 25*(2), 46–50.

Reder, P., McClure, M., & Jolley, A. (Eds.). (2000). *Family matters: Interfaces between child and adult mental health.* London: Routledge.

Regan, C. (2001). *Intoxicating minds: How drugs work.* New York: Columbia University Press.

Regier, D. A., Narrow, W. E., Rae, D. S., Manderscheid, R. W., et al. (1993). The de facto U. S. mental health and addictive disorders service system: Epidemiologic Catchment Area prospective 1-year prevalence rates of disorders and services. *Archives of General Psychiatry, 50,* 85–94.

Reich, J. (1996). The morbidity of DSM-III-R dependent personality disorder. *Journal of Nervous and Mental Disease, 184,* 22–26.

Reichlin, S. (1998). Treatment of men with paraphilia with a long-acting analogue of gonadotropin-relaeasing hormone [Comment]. *New England Journal of Medicine, 338*(26), 1923.

Reiger, D. A., Boyd, J. H., Burke, J. D., Rae, D. S., et al. (1988). One month prevalence of mental disorders in the United States. *Archives of General Psychiatry, 45,* 977–986.

Reilly, J., Baker, G. A., Rhodes, J., & Salmon, P. (1999). The association of sexual and physical abuse with somatization: Characteristics of patients presenting with irritable bowel syndrome and non-epileptic attack disorder. *Psychological Medicine, 29,* 399–406.

Reissing, E., Yitzchak, M., & Khalife, S. (1999). Does vaginismus exist? A critical review of the literature. *Journal of Nervous & Mental Disease, 187*(5), 261–274.

Reitan, R. M., & Wolfson, D. (1986). The Halstead-Reitan Neuropsychological Test Battery. In D. Wedding, A. M. Horton, & J. Webster (Eds.), *The neuropsychology handbook: Behavioral and clinical perspectives.* New York: Springer Publishing.

Rekers, G., Bentler, P., Rosen, A., & Lovaas, O. (1977). Child gender disturbances: A clinical rationale for intervention. *Psychotherapy: Theory, Research & Practice, 14*(1), 2–11.

Rekers, G., & Kilgus, M. (1998). Diagnosis and treatment of gender identity disorders in children and adolescents. In *Innovations in clinical practice: A source book* (Vol. 16, pp. 127–141). Sarasota, FL: Professional Resource Press/Professional Resource Exchange, Inc.

Rekers, G., & Lovaas, O. (1974). Behavioral treatment of deviant sex-role behaviors in a male child. *Journal of Applied Behavior Analysis,* 173–190.

Rekers, G., & Varni, W. (1977). Self-monitoring and self-reinforcement in a pre-transsexual boy. *Behavioral Research and Therapy, 15*(2), 177–180.

Renfro, W. I. (1998). Wrestling rules changes address dehydration. *NCAA News Release.*

Renshaw, D. (1996). Sexuality and aging. In J. Sadavoy (Ed.), *Comprehensive review of geriatric psychiatry—II* (2nd ed., pp. 713–729). Washington, DC: American Psychiatric Press.

Repetti, R. L., & Crosby, F. (1984). Women and depression: Exploring the adult role explanation. *Journal of Social and Clinical Psychology, 2,* 5–70.

Resnick, P. A. (1993). The psychological impact of rape. *Journal of Interpersonal Violence, 8,* 223–255.

Rey, J. M. (1993). Oppositional defiant disorder. *American Journal of Psychiatry, 150,* 1769–1777.

Rey, J. M., & Walter, G. (1997). Half a century of ECT use in young people. *American Journal of Psychiatry, 154,* 595–602.

Reynolds, W. M. (1981). Measurement of personal competence of mentally retarded individuals. *American Journal of Mental Deficiency, 85,* 368–376.

Richards, R., Kinney, D. K., Lunde, I., & Benet, M. (1988). Creativity in manicdepressives, cyclothymes, their normal relatives, and control subjects. *Journal of Abnormal Psychology, 97,* 281–288.

Richardson, W. (2000). Criminal behavior fueled by attention deficit hyperactivity disorder and addiction. In D. Fishbein (Ed.), *The science, treatment, and prevention of antisocial behaviors: Application to the criminal justice system.* Kingston, NJ: Civic Reseach Institute.

Richters, J. E., & Cicchetti, D. (1993). Mark Twain meets DSM-III-R: Conduct disorder, development, and the concept of harmful dysfunction. *Development and Psychopathology, 5,* 5–29.

Riem, K. E., & Hursey, K. G. (1995). Using anabolic-androgenic steroids to enhance physique and performance: Effects on moods and behavior. *Clinical Psychology Review, 15*(3), 235–256.

Riese, W. (1969). *The legacy of Phillippe Pinel: An inquiry into thought on mental alienation.* New York: Springer Publishing.

Rietveld, S., Beest, I. V., & Everaerd, W. (1999). Stress-induced breathlessness in asthma. *Psychological Medicine, 29,* 1359–1366.

Rilling, M. (2000). John Watson's paradoxical struggle to explain Freud. *American Psychologist, 55*(3), 301–312.

Ritchie, W. F. (2000). An exploration of college student explanatory style and its relationship to academic performance. *Dissertation Abstracts International Section A: Humanities & Social Sciences, 60*(7-A). University Microfilms International. 2375. AEH9939922. Ann Arbor, MI.

Ritz, T., Steptoe, A., DeWilde, S., & Costa, M. (2000). Emotions and stress increase respiratory resistance in asthma. *Psychosomatic Medicine, 62,* 401–412.

Robbins, A. (1988). The interface of the real and transference relationships in the treatment of schizoid phenomena. *Psychoanalytic Review, 75,* 393–417.

Robbins, E. S., Robbins, L., Katz, S. E., & Stern, M. (1979). Psychiatry in New York City: Five systems, all overwhelmed. *Psychiatric Annals, 9*(5), 14–27.

Robbins, M. (1993). *Experiences of schizophrenia.* Boston: Guilford Press.

Robin, A. L. (1998). *ADHD in adolescents.* New York: Guilford Press.

Robson, P. (1999). *Forbidden drugs* (2nd ed.). New York: Oxford University Press.

Rogers, C. (1987). Rogers, Kohut, and Erikson: A personal perspective on some similarities and differences. In J. K. Zeig (Ed.), *The evolution of psychotherapy.* New York: Brunner/Mazel.

Rogers, C. R. (1961). *On becoming a person.* Boston: Houghton Mifflin.

Rogers, L., Resnick, M. D., Mitchell, J. E., & Blum, R. W. (1997). The relationship between socioeconomic status and eating-disordered behavior in a sample of adolescent girls. *International Journal of Eating Disorders, 22,* 15–23.

Rogler, R. H. (1993). Culture in psychiatric diagnosis: An issue of scientific accuracy. *Psychiatry: Interpersonal & Biological Processes, 56*(4), 324–327.

Rokeach, M. (1964). *The three Christs of Ypsilanti.* New York: Knopf.

Roland, A. (1988). *In search of self in India and Japan.* Princeton, NJ: Princeton University Press.

Romano, E., & De Luca, R. (2001). Male sexual abuse: A review of effects, abuse characteristics, and links with later psychological functioning. *Aggression & Violent Behavior, 6*(1), 55–78.

Root, M. P. (1990). Disordered eating in women of color. *Sex Roles, 22,* 525–536

Rorabaugh, W. (1979). *The alcoholic republic, An American Tradition.* New York: Oxford University Press.

Rosch, E., & Mervis, C. B. (1975). Family resemblances: Studies in the internal structure of categories. *Cognitive Psychology, 7*(4), 573–605.

Rose, R. J., Dick, D. M., Viken, R. J., & Kaprio, J. (2001). Gene-environment interaction in patterns of adolescent drinking: Regional residency moderates longitudinal influences on alcohol use. *Alcoholism: Clinical & Experimental Research (Special Issue), 25*(5), 637–643.

Rosen, J. C. (1998). Cognitive behavior therapy for body dysmorphic disorder. In V. E. Caballo (Ed.), *International handbook of cognitive and behavioural treatments for psychological disorders* (pp. 363–391). Oxford, England: Elsevier Science.

Rosen, R., Lane, R., & Menza, M. (1999). Effects of SSRIs on sexual function: A critical review. *Journal of Clinical Psychopharmacology, 19*(1), 67–85.

Rosen, R., & Leiblum, S. (1995). Treatment of sexual disorders in the 1990's: An integrated approach. *Journal of Consulting and Clinical Psychology, 63*(6), 877–890.

Rosen, W. G. (1990). Neuropsychological evaluation of children. In A. Weizman & R. Weizman (Eds.), *Application of basic neuroscience to child psychiatry.* New York: Plenum Medical Books/Plenum Press.

Rosenblitt, D. L. (1996). States of overstimulation in early childhood. *Psychoanalytic Study of the Child, 51,* 542–561.

Rosenhan, D. (1973). On being sane in insane places. *Science,* 179, 250–258.

Rosenhan, D. L. (1973). On being sane in insane places. *Science, 179,* 250–258.

Rosenstein, M. J., Milazzo-Sayre, L. J., & Manderscheid, R. W. (1990). Characteristics of persons using specialty inpatient, outpatient, and partial care programs in 1986. In R. W. Manderscheid & M. A. Sonnenschein (Eds.), *Mental health in the United States* (pp. 139–172). Washington, DC: U.S. Government Printing Office.

Rosler, A., & Witztum, E. (1998). Treatment of men with paraphilia with a long-acting analogue of gonadotropin-releasing hormone. *New England Journal of Medicine, 338*(7), 416–422.

Rosler, A., & Witztum, E. (2000). Pharmacotherapy of paraphilias in the next millennium. *Behavioral Sciences & the Law, 18*(1), 43–56.

Ross, C. A. (1996). History, phenomenology, and epidemiology of dissociation. In L. K. Michelson & W. J. Ray (Eds.), *Handbook of dissociation: Theoretical, empirical, and clinical perspectives* (pp. 3–24). New York: Plenum Press.

Ross, C. A. (1997). *Dissociative identity disorder: Diagnosis, clinical features, and treatment of multiple personality* (2nd ed.). New York: John Wiley & Sons.

Ross, C. A., Joshi, S., & Currie, R. (1990). Dissociative experiences in the general population. *American Journal of Psychiatry, 147,* 1547–1552.

Ross, C. A., Miller, S. D., Reagor, P., Bjornson, L., et al. (1990). Structured interview data on 102 cases of multiple personality disorder from four centers. *American Journal of Psychiatry, 147,* 596–601.

Ross, C. A., Norton, G. R., & Wozney, K. (1989). Multiple personality disorder: An analysis of 236 cases. *Canadian Journal of Psychiatry, 34,* 413–418.

Ross, C. E. (2000). Neighborhood disadvantage and adult depression. *Journla of Health and Social Behavior, 41,* 177–187.

Ross, C. E., Mirowsky, J., & Huber, J. (1983). Dividing work, sharing work, and in-between: Marriage patterns and depression. *American Sociological Review, 48,* 809–823.

Rotgers, F. (1996). Behavioral theory of substance abuse treatment: Bringing science to bear on practice. In F. Rotgers, D. Keller, and J. Morgenstern (Eds.), *Treating substance abuse: Theory and technique.* New York: Guilford Press.

Rothbaum, B. O., Foa, E. D., Riggs, D. S., & Murdock, T. (1992). A prospective examination of post-traumatic stress disorder in rape victims. *Journal of Traumatic Stress, 5,* 455-475.

Rothblum, E. D., Solomon, L. J., & Albee, G. W. (1986). A sociopolitical perspective on DSM-III. In T. Millon & G. L. Klerman (Eds.), *Contemporary directions in psychopathology: Toward the DSM-IV.* New York: Guilford Press.

Rothstein, A., & Glenn, J. (1999). *Learning disabilities and psychic conflict: A psychoanalytic casebook* (pp. viii, 504, 37–85). Madison, CT: International Universities Press, Inc.

Rottnek, M. (Ed.) (1999). *Sissies and tomboys: Gender nonconformity and homosexual childhood.* New York: New York University Press.

Rourke, B. P. (1989). *Nonverbal learning disabilities: The syndrome and the model.* New York: Guilford Press.

Rouse, B. A. (1995). *Substance abuse and mental health statistic sourcebook.* Washington, DC: U.S. Department of Health and Human Services.

Rowland, D., Cooper, S., & Schneider, M. (2001). Defining premature ejaculation for experimental and clinical investigations. *Archives of Sexual Behavior, 30*(3), 235–253.

Roy, M. A., Merette, C., & Maziade, M. (2001). Subtyping schizophrenia according to outcome or severity: A search for homogeneous subgroups. *Schizophrenia Bulletin, 27*(1), 115–138.

Rozin, P., & Fallon, A. (1988). Body image, attitudes to weight, and misperceptions of figure preferences of the opposite sex: A comparison of men and women in two generations. *Journal of Abnormal Psychology, 97,* 342–345.

Ruchkin, V. (2000) The forensic psychiatric system of Russia. *International Journal of Law & Psychiatry, Special Issue, 23*(5–6), 555–565.

Russell, G. F. M. (2001). Involuntary treatment in anorexia nervosa. *Psychiatric Clinics of North America, 24,* 337–349.

Rutter, M., Bailey, A., Simonoff, E., & Pickles, A. (1997). Genetic influences in autism. In D. J. Cohen & F. R. Volkmar (Eds.), *Handbook of autism and pervasive developmental disorders.* New York: John Wiley & Sons.

Ryan, C. (1995). Mental health law and dangerousness. *Australian & New Zealand Journal of Psychiatry 29*(1), 154–155.

S

Sacco, W. P., & Beck, A. T. (1995). Cognitive theory and therapy. In E. E. Beckham & W. R. Leber (Eds.), *Handbook of depression* (2nd ed., pp. 329–351). New York: Guilford Press.

Sacks, M. (1999). Mothers' and fathers' responses to SIDS. *Dissertation Abstracts International Section A: Humanities and Social Sciences, 59*(7-A), 2366, Ann Arbor, MI: Univ. Microfilms International.

Sacks, O. W. (1985). *The man who mistook his wife for a hat and other clinical tales.* New York: Summit Books.

Sacks, O. W. (1995). *An anthropologist on Mars: Seven paradoxical tales.* New York: Vintage Books.

Sadock, B. J., & Sadock, V. A. (2001). *Kaplan & Sadock's pocket handbook of psychiatric drug treatment* (3rd ed.). Philadelphia: Lippincott Williams & Wilkins.

Sadock, B., & Sadock, V. (2000). *Kaplan & Sadock's comprehensive textbook of psychiatry* (7th ed., Vols. 1 & 2). Philadelphia: Lippincott, Williams & Wilkins.

Safer, D. J. & Zito, J. M. (1999). Psychotropic medication for ADHD. *Mental Retardation & Developmental Disabilities Research Reviews, 53,* 237–242.

Sagawa, K., Kawakatsy, S., Shibuya, I., Oija, A., et al. (1990). Correlation of regional cerebral blood flow with performance on neuropsychological tests in schizophrenic patients. *Schizophrenia Research, 3*(4), 241–246.

Sakel, M. (1994). The methodical use of hypoglycemia in the treatment of psychoses. *American Journal of Psychiatry 151*(6), S241–S247.

Salaspuro, M. (1995). Biological markers of alcohol consumption. In B. Tabakoff (Ed.), *Biological aspects of alcoholism* (pp. 123–162). Kirkland, WA: Hogrefe & Huber Publishers.

Salloway, S., & Cummings, J. (1996). Subcortical structures and neuropsychiatric illnesses. *Neuroscientist, 2,* 66–75.

Saloviita, T., Ruusila, L., & Ruusila, U. (2000). Incidence of savant syndrome in Finland. *Perceptual & Motor Skills, 91,* 120–122.

Salzman, C. (2001). *Psychiatric medications for older adults: The concise guide.* New York: Guilford Press.

Sanderson, W. C., & McGinn, L. K. (2001). Cognitive-behavioral therapy of depression. In M. M. Weissman (Ed.), *Treatment of depression: Bridging the 21st century* (pp. 249–279). Washington, DC: American Psychiatric Press.

Sandler, R. (1999). The pharmacological basis for schizophrenia. In E. Johnstone, M. Humphreys, F. Lang, S. Lawrie, et al. (Eds.), *Schizophrenia: Concepts and clinical management.* New York: Cambridge University Press.

Sansone, R. A., Gaither, G. A., & Sansone, L. A. (2001). Childhood trauma and adult somatic preoccupation by body area among women in an internal medicine setting: A pilot study. *International Journal of Psychiatry in Medicine, 31,* 147–154.

Sargent, W., & Slater, E. (1941). Amnesic syndromes in war. *Proceedings of the Royal Society of Medicine, 34,* 757–764.

Sarte, J. P. (1953). *Existential psychoanalysis.* New York: Philosophical Library.

Sartre, J. P. (1956). *Being and nothingness.* New York: Philosophical Library.

Sass, L. (1992). *Madness and modernism.* New York: Basic Books.

Satel, S. L. (1998, April 4) Don't forget the addict's role in addiction. *The New York Times.*

Satlin, A., Volicer, L., Ross, V., Herz, L. R., et al. (1992). Bright light treatment of behavioral and sleep disturbances in patients with Alzheimer's disease. *American Journal of Psychiatry, 149,* 1028–1032.

Sattler, J. M. (1988). *Assessment of children* (3rd ed.). San Diego, CA: Author.

Saunders, D. G. (1994). Posttraumatic stress symptom profiles of battered women: A comparison of survivors in two settings. *Violence & Victims, 9* (1), 31–44.

Sawle, G., & Kear-Colwell, J. (2001). Adult attachment style and pedophilia: A developmental perspective. *International Journal of Offender Therapy & Comparative Criminology (Special Issue: Sex Offenders), 45*(1), 32–50.

Saxe, L., & Ben-Shakhar, G. (1999). Admissibility of polygraph tests: The application of scientific standards post-Daubert. *Psychology, Public Policy, & Law, 5*(1), 203–223.

Scahill, L., Schwab-Stone, M., Merikangas, K. R., Leckman, J. F., Zhang, H., & Kasl, S. (1999). Psychosocial and clinical correlates of ADHD in a community sample of school-age children. *Journal of the American Academy of Child & Adolescent Psychiatry, 38*, 976–984.

Schafer, R. (1997). *The contemporary Kleinians of London.* Madison, CT: International University Press.

Schaler, J. A. (2000). *Addiction is a choice.* Chicago: Open Court Publishing.

Schatzberg, A. F., & Nemeroff, C. B. (Eds.). (2001). *Essentials of clinical psychopharmacology.* Washington, DC: American Psychiatric Association.

Schermer, V. L., & Pines, M. (1999). Group psychotherapy of the psychoses: Concepts, interventions and contexts. Bristol, PA: Jessica Kingsley Publishers, Ltd.

Schlemmer, R. F., Jr., Young, J. E., & Davis, J. M. (1996). Stimulant-induced disruption of non-human primate social behavior and the psychopharmacology of schizophrenia. *Journal of Psychopharmacology, 10*(1), 64–76.

Schmidt, G. L., & Keyes, B. (1985). Group psychotherapy with family caregivers of demented patients. *Gerontologist, 25*, 347–350.

Schmidt, K., Nolte-Zenker, R., Patzer, J., Bouer, M., et al. (2001). Psychopathological correlates of reduced dopamine receptor sensitivity in depression, schizophrenia, and alcohol dependence. *Pharmacopsychiatry Special Issue, 34*(2), 66–72.

Schopler, E. (1997). Implementation of TEACCH philosophy. In D. J. Cohen & F. R. Volkmar (Eds.), *Handbook of autism and pervasive developmental disorders.* New York: John Wiley & Sons.

Schreiber, F. R. (1973). *Sybil.* Chicago: Regnery

Schuckit, M. (2000). *Drug and alcohol abuse: A clinical guide to diagnosis and treatment* (5th ed). New York: Kluwer Academic/ Plenum Publishers.

Schuldberg, D. (2001). Six subclinical spectrum traits in normal creativity. *Creativity Research Journal (Special Issue: Creativity and the Schizophrenia Spectrum), 13*(1), 5–16.

Schulenberg, J., Maggs, J. L., Long, S. W., Sher, K. J., et al. (2001). The problem of college drinking: Insights from a developmental perspective. *Alcoholism: Clinical & Experimental Research (Special Issue), 25*(3), 473–477.

Schulz, P. M., Soloff, P. H., Kelly, T. Morgenstern, M., et al. (1989). A family history study of borderline subtypes. *Journal of Personality Disorders, 3*, 217–229.

Schultz, R., Braun, B. G., & Kluft, R. P. (1989). Multiple personality disorder: Phenomenology of selected variables in comparison to major depression. *Dissociation, 2*, 45–51.

Schultz, S., & Andreason, N. (2000). Functional imaging and neural circuitry in schizophrenia. In P. Harrison & G. Roberts (Eds.), *The neuropathology of schizophrenia: Progress and Interpretation.* New York: Oxford University Press.

Schwartz, J. (2001, May 16, 2001). Yahoo goes beyond initial plan against adult sites. *The New York Times,* p. C6.

Schwartz, R. C. (1998). The relationship among insight, illness, and psychosocial impairments in psychotic clients. *Dissertation Abstracts International: Section B: The Sciences & Engineering, 59*(2-B). Ann Arbor, MI: University Microfilms International.

Scott, J. (1988). Chronic depression. *British Journal of Psychiatry, 153*, 287–297.

Scott, J. (1992). Social and community approaches. In E. S. Paykel (Ed.), *Handbook of affective disorders* (2nd ed., pp. 525–535). New York: Guilford Press.

Scott, J. E., & Dixon, L. B. (1995). Psychological interventions for schizophrenia. Assertive community treatment and case management for schizophrenia. *Schizophrenia Bulletin, 21*(4), 621–630 & 657–668, respectively.

Scott, J., Garland, A., & Moorhead, S. (2001). A pilot study of cognitive therapy in bipolar disorders. *Psychological Medicine, 31*, 459–467.

Scott, S. (1994). Mental retardation. In M. Rutter, E. Taylor, & L. Hersov (Eds.), *Child and adolescent psychiatry: Modern approaches.* Cambridge, MA: Blackwell.

Scotti, J. R., Morris, T. L., McNeil, C. B., & Hawkins, R. P. (1996). DSM-IV and disorders of childhood and adolescence: Can structural criteria be functional? *Journal of Consulting and Clinical Psychology, 64*(6), 1177–1191.

Scotti, J. R., Morris, T. L., McNeil, C. B., & Hawkins, R. P. (1996). DSM-IV and disorders of childhood and adolescence: Can structural criteria be functional? *Journal of Consulting and Clinical Psychology, 64*, 1177–1191.

Searight, H. R., & McLaren, A. L. (1998). Attention-deficit hyperactivity disorder: The medicalization of misbehavior. *Journal of Clinical Psychology in Medical Settings, 5*(4), 467–495.

Searles, H. F. (1959). The effort to drive the other person crazy. An element in the aetiology and psychotherapy of schizophrenia. *British Journal of Medical Psychology, 32*, 1–18.

Seferian, E. G. (1997). Polymicrobial bacteremia: A presentation of Munchausen syndrome by proxy. *Clinical Pediatrics, 36*, 419–422.

Segal, D. L., & Falk, S. B. (1998). Structured interviews and rating scales. In A. S. Bellack & M. Hersen (Eds.), *Behavioral assessment: A practical handbook* (4th ed., pp. 158–178). Boston: Allyn & Bacon.

Segraves, R., & Althof, S. (1998). Paraphilias: research and treatment. In P. Nathan & J. Gorman (Eds.), *A guide to treatments that work* (pp. 594). New York: Oxford University Press.

Seligman, M. E., & Maier, S. F. (1967). Failure to escape traumatic shock. *Journal of Experimental Psychology, 74*, 1–9.

Seligman, M. E. P. (1971). Phobias and preparedness. *Behavior Therapy, 2*, 307–320.

Seligman, M. E. P. (1995). The effectiveness of psychotherapy: The *Consumer Reports* Study. *American Psychologist, 51*, 1072–1079.

Seligman, M. E. P., Abramson, L. Y., Semmel, A., & Von Baeyer, C. (1979). Depressive attributional style. *Journal of Abnormal Psychology, 88,* 242–247.

Seligman, M. E. P., Walker, E. F., & Rosenhan, D. L. (2001). *Abnormal psychology* (4th ed.). New York: W. W. Norton.

Selling, L. S. (1940). *Men against madness.* New York: Greenberg.

Selten, J.-P., Veen, N., Feller, W., Blom, J. D., et al. (2001). Incidence of psychotic disorders in immigrant groups to The Netherlands. *British Journal of Psychiatry (Special Issue) 178,* 367–372.

Selye, H. (1956). *The stress of life.* New York: McGraw-Hill.

Selye, H. (1976). *The stress of life* (rev. ed.). New York: McGraw-Hill.

Selye, H. (1993). History of the stress concept. In L. Goldberger & S. Breznitz (Eds.), *Handbook of stress: Theoretical and clinical aspects* (2nd ed.). New York: Free Press.

Semple, S., Patterson, T., & Grant, I. (2000). The sexual negotiation behavior of HIV-positive gay and bisexual men. *Journal of Consulting and Clinical Psychology, 68*(5), 934–937.

Senay, E. C. (1998). *Substance abuse disorders in clinical practice* (2nd ed.). New York: W. W. Norton.

Senf, M. L. (1995). The revaluation of the feminine in psychoanalytic theory and practice. *Dissertation Abstracts International: Section B: The Sciences & Engineering, 56*(3-B). University Microfilms International. 1686. AAM9522463. Ann Arbor, MI.

Sex-change coverage to San Francisco workers. (2001, Feb. 28). *The New York Times*

Shaffer, H. J., & Simoneau, G. (2001). Reducing resistance and denial by exercising ambivalence during the treatment of addiction. *Journal of Substance Abuse Treatment (Special Issue), 20*(1), 99–105.

Shakespeare, W. *Macbeth.* (Act II, Scene iii). *The complete Pelican Shakespeare.* London: Penguin.

Shalev, A. Y., Peri, T., Canetti, L., & Schreiber, S. (1996). Predictors of PTSD in injured trauma survivors: A prospective study. *American Journal of Psychiatry, 153,* 219–225.

Shapiro, A. P. (2001). Nonpharmacological treatment of hypertension. In A. Baum, T. A. Revenson, & J. E. Singer (Eds.), *Handbook of health psychology* (pp. 697–708). Mahwah, NJ: Lawrence Erlbaum.

Shapiro, D. (1965). *Neurotic styles.* New York: Basic Books.

Shapiro, H. (1989). Crack: A briefing from the Institute for the Study of Drug Dependence, *Drug Link,* (Sept./Oct.), 8–11.

Shapiro, S., Newcomb, M., & Loeb, T. B. (1997). Fear of fat, disregulated-restrained eating, and body-esteem: Prevalence and gender differences among eight- to ten-year-old children. *Journal of Clinical Child Psychology, 26*(4), 358–365.

Shedler, J., & Block, J. (1990). Adolescent drug use and psychological health: A longitudinal inquiry. *American Psychologist, 45*(5), 612–630.

Sheehan, S. (1982). *Is there no place on earth for me?* New York: Vintage.

Shekhar, A., Katner, J. S., Sajdyk, T. J., & Kohl, R. R. (2002). Role of norepinephrine in the dorsomedial hypothalamic panic response: An in vivo microdialysis study. *Pharmacology, Biochemistry & Behavior, 71,* 493–500.

Shen, W. W. (1999). A history of antipsychotic drug development. *Comprehensive Psychiatry, 40*(6), 407–414.

Shengold, L. (1989). *Soul murder: The effects of childhood abuse and deprivation.* New Haven, CT: Yale University Press.

Shenton, M., Dickey, C., Frumin, M., & McCarley, R. (2001). A review of MRI findings in schizophrenia. *Schizophrenia Research, 49,* 1–52.

Sherman, D. K., McGue, M. K., & Iacono, W. G. (1997). Twin concordance for attention deficit hyperactivity disorder: A comparison of teachers' and mothers' reports. *American Journal of Psychiatry, 154,* 532–535.

Shewan, D., Hammersley, R., Oliver, J., & MacPherson, S. (2000). Fatal drug overdose after liberation from prison: A retrospective study of female ex-prisoners from Strathclyde region (Scotland). *Addiction Research, 8*(3), 267–278.

Shisslak, C. M., Crago, M., & Estes, L. S. (1995). The spectrum of eating disorders. *International Journal of Eating Disorders, 18,* 209–219.

Showalter, E. (1997). *Hystories.* New York: Columbia University Press.

Sibille, E., Pavlides, C., Benke, D., & Toth, M. (2000). Genetic inactivation of the serotonin$_{1A}$ receptor in mice results in downregulation of major GABA$_A$ receptor alphasubunits, reduction of GABA$_A$ receptor binding, and benzodiazepine-resistant anxiety. *Journal of Neuroscience, 20,* 2758–2765.

Sieg, K. G., Gaffney, G. R., Preston, D. F., & Hellings, J. A. (1995). SPECT brain inaging abnormalities in attention deficit hyperactivity disorder. *Clinical Nuclear Medicine, 20,* 55–60.

Siegman, A. W., Townsend, S. T., Civelek, A. C., & Blumenthal, R. S. (2000). Antagonistic behavior, dominance, hostility, and coronary heart disease. *Psychosomatic Medicine, 62,* 248–257.

Siever, L. J. (1995). Brain structure/function and the dopamine system in schizotypal personality disorder. In A. Raine, T. Lencz, & S. A. Mednick (Eds.), *Schizotypal personality* (pp. 272–286). New York: Cambridge University Press.

Siever, M. (1994). Sexual orientation and gender as factors in socioculturally acquired vulnerability to body dissatisfaction and eating disorders. *Journal of Consulting and Clinical Psychology, 62*(2), 252–260.

Sigmon, S. T., Dorhofer, D. M., Rohan, K. J., Hotovy, L. A., et al. (2000). Psychophysiological, somatic, and affective changes across the menstrual cycle in women with panic disorder. *Journal of Consulting and Clinical Psychology, 68*(3), 425–431.

Silberg, J., Rutter, M., Meyer, J., Maes, H., et al. (1996). Genetic and environmental influences on the covariation between hyperctivity and conduct disturbance in juvenile twins. *Journal of Child Psychology and Psychiatry, 37,* 803–816.

Silk, K. R. (1994). *Biological and neurobehavioral studies of borderline personality disorder.* Washington, DC: American Psychiatric Press.

Silove, D., & Manicavasagar, V. (2001). Early separation anxiety and its relationship to adult anxiety disorders. In M. W. Vasey & M. R. Dadds (Eds.), *The developmental psychopathology of anxiety* (pp. 459–480). New York: Oxford University Press.

Silver, A. A. (1994). Biology of specific (developmental) learning disabilities. In N. J. Ellsworth & C. Hedley, et al., (Eds), Literacy: A redefinition (pp. 187–210). Hillsdale, NJ: Lawrence Erlbaum.

Silverman, I. W., & Ragusa, D. M. (1992). A short-term longitudinal study of the early development of self-regulation. *Journal of Abnormal Child Psychology, 20,* 415–435.

Silverman, K., Svikis, D., Robles, E., Stitzer, M., & Bigelow, G. (2001). A reinforcement based therapeutic workplace for the treatment of drug abuse: Six-month abtinence outcomes. *Experimental & Clinical Psychopharmacology, 9*(1), 14–23.

Silverman, W. K., & Ginsburg, G. S. (1998). Anxiety disorders. In T. H. Ollendick & M. Hersen (Eds.), *Handbook of child psychopathology* (pp. 239–268). New York: Plenum Press.

Silverman, W. K., & Nelles, W. B. (1990). Simple phobia in childhood. In M. Hersen & C. G. Last (Eds.), *Handbook of child and adult psychopathology: A longitudinal perspective* pp. 183–195. New York: Pergamon Press.

Silverstein, S. M., Hitzel, H., & Schenkel, L. (1998). Identifying and addressing cognitive barriers to rehabilitation readiness. *Psychiatric Services, 49*(1), 34–36.

Silverstein, S. M., Menditto, A. A., & Stuve, P. (2001). Shaping attention span: An operant conditioning procedure to improve neurocognition and functioning in schizophrenia. *Schizophrenia Bulletin (Special Issue), 27*(2), 247–257.

Simons, J., & Carey, M. (2001). Prevalence of sexual dysfunctions: Results from a decade of research. *Archives of Sexual Behavior, 30*(2), 177–219.

Singh, N. N., Oswald, D. P., & Ellis, C. R. (1998). Mental retardation. In T. H. Ollendick & M. Hersen (Eds.), *Handbook of child psychopathology* (pp. 91–116). New York: Plenum Press.

Sintchak, G., & Geer, J. H. (1975). A vaginal plethysmograph system. *Psychophysiology, 12*(1), 113–115.

Siris, S. G. (2001). Depression in the course of schizophrenia. *Schizophrenia and comorbid conditions: Diagnosis and treatment.* Washington, DC: American Psychiatric Press.

Siris, S. G. (2001). Suicide and schizophrenia. *Journal of Psychopharmacology (Special Issue) 15*(2), 127–135.

Sizemore, G. M., Co, C., & Smith, J. E. (2000). Ventral pallidal extracellular fluid levels of dopamine, serotonin, gamma amino butyric acid, and glutamate during cocaine self-administration in rats. *Psychopharmacology, 150*(4), 391–398.

Skeels, H. M. (1966). Adult status of children with contrasting early life experiences. *Monographs of the Society for Research in Child Development, 31,* Serial No. 105.

Skinner, B. F. (1953). *Science and human behavior.* New York: Free Press.

Skolnik, M. E. (2000). Postmodernism in practice: Implications of the disease model of alcoholism. *Dissertation Abstracts International: Section B: The Sciences & Engineering, 61*(5-B), 2782. Ann Arbor, MI: University Microfilms International.

Slade, J. (1999). Nicotine. In B. S. McCrady (Ed.). *Addictions: A comprehensive guidebook* (pp. 162–170). New York: Oxford University Press.

Slavney, P. R., & Chase, G. A. (1985) Clinical judgments of self-dramatisation. A test of the sexist hypothesis. *British Journal of Psychiatry, 146,* 129–141.

Sloan, J. W., & Wala, E. P. (1998). Pharmacology of sedatives, hypnotics, and anxiolytics. In R. E. Tarter (Ed.), *Handbook of substance abuse: Neurobehavioral pharmacology* (pp. 395–433). New York: Plenum Press.

Sloman, L. (1998). *Reefer madness: The history of marijuana in America.* New York: St. Martin's Press/Griffin.

Smith, C. (1992). *Lenny, Lefty and the chancellor: The Len Bias tragedy and the search for reform.* Baltimore: Bancroft Press.

Smith, E. (1997, Nov. 24). Bodybuilders face "flip side" of anorexia. *USA Today,* A1–A2.

Smith, M., Glass, G., & Miller, T. (1980). *The benefits of psychotherapy.* Baltimore: Johns Hopkins University Press.

Smith, S. L. (1995). *Peyote and magic mushrooms.* New York: Rosen Publishing Group.

Smith, T. E., Bellack, A. S., & Liberman, R. P. (1996). Social skills training for schizophrenia: Review and future directions. *Clinical Psychology Review, 16*(7), 599–617.

Smock, T. (1999). *Physiological Psychology: A neuroscience approach.* Upper Saddle River, NJ: Prentice Hall.

Snyder, L. (1999). *Speaking our minds: Personal reflections from individual's with Alzheimer's.* New York: W. H. Freeman.

Soares, J. C., & Innes, R. B. (2000). Brain imaging findings in bipolar disorder. In J. C. Soares & S. Gershon (Eds.), *Bipolar disorders: Basic mechanisms and therapeutic implications* (pp. 227–252). New York: Marcel Dekker.

Sobell, M. B., & Sobell, L. C. (1984). The aftermath of heresay: A response to Penderay et al.'s (1982) critique of "Individualized Behavior Therapy for Alcoholics." *Behavior Research and Therapy, 22*(4), 413–440.

Sokolow, J. (1983). *Eros and modernization: Sylvester Graham, health reform, and the origins of Victorian sexuality in America.* Rutherford, NJ: Fairleigh Dickinson University Press.

Solanto, M. V., Arnsten, A. F. T., & Castellanos, F. X. (Eds.). (2001). *Stimulant drugs and ADHD: Basic and clinical neuroscience.* New York: Oxford University Press.

Soloman, A. (1998, January 12). Anatomy of melancholy. *The New Yorker,* 46–61.

Somaini, B., Wang, J., Perozo, M., Kuhn, F., et al. (2000). A continuing concern: HIV and hepatitis testing and prevalence among drug users in substitution programmes in Zurich, Switzerland. *AIDS Care, 12*(4), 449–460.

Sorbi, M. J., Maassen, G. H., & Spierings, E. L. H. (1996). A time series analysis of daily hassles and mood changes in the 3 days before the migraine attack. *Behavioral Medicine, 22,* 102–113.

Southwick, S. M., Bremner, J. D., Rasmussen, A., Morgan, C. A., et al. (1999). Role of norepinephrine in the pathophysiology and treatment of posttraumatic stress disorder. *Biological Psychiatry, 46*(9), 1192–1204.

Southwick, S. M., Krystal, J. H., Morgan, C. A., Johnson, D., et al. (1993). Abnormal noradrenergic function in posttraumatic stress disorder. *Archives of General Psychiatry, 50,* 266–274.

Spanos, N. P. (1994). Multiple identity enactments and multiple personality disorder: A sociocognitive perspective. *Psychological Bulletin, 116,* 143–165.

Spanos, N. P., Weekes, J. R., Menary, E., & Bertrand, L. D. (1986). Hypnotic interview and age regression procedures in the elicitation of multiple personality symptoms. *Psychiatry, 49,* 298–311.

Spaulding, W. D., Johnson, D. L., & Coursey, R. D. (2001). Combined treatments and rehabilitation of schizophrenia. In *Combined treatment for mental disorders: A guide to psychological and pharmacological interventions* (pp. 161–190). Washington, DC: American Psychological Association.

Spector, I., Sandra, R., Carey, M., & Rosen, R. (1993). Diabetes and female sexual function: A critical review. *Annals of Behavioral Medicine, 15*(4), 257–264.

Sperry, L. (1999). *Cognitive-behavior therapy of DSM-IV personality disorders.* Philadelphia: Brunner/Mazel.

Sperry, L. (Ed.). (2001). *Integrative and biopsychosocial therapy: Maximizing treatment outcomes with individuals and couples* (pp. xiv, 110). Alexandria, VA: American Counseling Association.

Spiegel, D., & Cardena, E. (1991). Disintegrated experience: The dissociative disorders revisited. *Journal of Abnormal Psychology, 100,* 366–378.

Spitz, R. A. (1965). *The first year of life.* New York: International Universities Press.

Spitzberg, B. H. (1999). An analysis of empirical estimates of sexual aggression victimization and perpetration. *Violence & Victims, 14* (3), 241–260.

Spitzer, R. L. (1975). On pseudoscience in science, logic in remission and psychiatric diagnosis. *Journal of Abnormal Psychology, 8*(5), 442–452.

Spitzer, R. L. (1999). Harmful dysfunction and the DSM definition of mental disorder. *Journal of Abnormal Psychology, 108*(3), 430–432.

Spitzer, R. L., Forman, J. B., & Nee, J. (1979). DSM-III field trials. I: Initial interrater reliability. *American Journal of Psychiatry, 136*(6), 815–817.

Spitzer, R. L., Williams, J. B., & Skodol, A. E. (1980). DSM-III: The major achievements and an overview. *American Journal of Psychiatry, 137*(2), 151–164.

Stahl, S. (2001). Sex and psychopharmacology: Is natural estrogen a psychotropic drug in women? *Archives of General Psychiatry, 58*(6), 537–538.

Stahl, S. M. (1997). Serotonin: It's possible to have too much of a good thing. *Journal of Clinical Psychiatry, 58*(12), 520–521.

Stain-Malmgren, R., El Khoury, A., Aberg-Wistedt, A., & Tham, A. (2001). Serotonergic function in major depression and effect of sertraline and paroxetine treatment. *International Clinical Psychopharmacology (Special Issue), 16*(2), 93–101.

Stanley, J., Pettegrew, J., & Keshavan, M. (2000). Magnetic resonance spectroscopy in schizophrenia: Methodological issues and findings—Part I. *Biological Psychiatry, 48,* 357–368.

State, M. W., King, B. H., & Dykens, E. (1997). Mental retardation: A review of the past 10 years. Part II. *Journal of the American Academy of Child and Adolescent Psychology, 15,* 91–113.

Steele, C. T. (2000). Providing clinical treatment to substance abusing trauma survivors. *Alcoholism Treatment Quarterly, 18*(3), 71–81.

Steele, K. (2001). *The day the voices stopped: A schizophrenic's journey from madness to hope.* New York: Basic Books.

Stefanis, C. N., & Stefanis, N. C. (1999). Diagnosis of depressive disorders: A review. In M. Maj & N. Sartoris (Eds.), *Depressive disorders* (pp. 1–51). New York: John Wiley & Sons.

Steinglass, P. (1987). A systems view of family interaction and psychopathology. In T. Jacob (Ed.), *Family interaction and psychopathology.* New York: Plenum Press.

Stephens, R. S. (1999). Cannabis and hallucinogens. *Addictions: A comprehensive guidebook* (pp. 121–140). New York: Oxford University Press.

Steptoe, A., & Feldman, P. J. (2001). Neighborhood problems as sources of chronic stress: Development of a measure of neighborhood problems, and associations with socioeconomic status and health. *Annals of Behavioral Medicine, 23,* 177–185.

Steptoe, A., Wardle, J., Lipsey, Z., Mills, R., et al. (1998). A longitudinal study of work load and variations in psychological well-being, cortisol, smoking, and alcohol consumption. *Annals of Behavioral Medicine, 20,* 84–91.

Steriade, M., & McCarley, R. W. (1990). *Brainstem control of wakefulness and sleep.* New York: Plenum Press.

Stern, S. L., Dixon, K. N., Jones, D., Lake, M., et al. (1989). Family environment in anorexia nervosa and bulimia. *International Journal of Eating Disorders, 8,* 25–31.

Stevenson, J., & Meares, R., (1999). Psychotherapy with borderline patients: 2. A preliminary cost benefit study. *Australian and New Zealand Journal of Psychiatry, 33,* 473–477.

Stiles, W. (2003, Spring). When is a case study scientific research? *The Psychotherapy Bulletin,* 6–11.

Stiles, W., Shapiro, D., & Elliott, R. (1986). Are all psychotherapies equivalent? *American Psychologist, 41,* 165–180.

Stokes, P. E., & Sikes, C. R. (1988). The hypothalamic-pituitary-adrenocortical axis in major depression. *Endorcrinology and Metabolism Clinics of North America, 17,* 1–19.

Stoller, R. (1971). The term "transvestism". *Archives of General Psychiatry, 24*(3), 230–237.

Stoller, R. (1975). *Perversion: The erotic form of hatred.* New York: Pantheon Books.

Stoller, R. (1979). A contribution to the study of gender identity: Follow-up. *International Journal of Psycho-Analysis, 60*(4), 433–441.

Stoller, R. (1980). Problems with the term "homosexuality". *Hillside Journal of Clinical Psychiatry, 2*(1), 3–25.

Stoller, R. (1985). *Observing the erotic imagination.* New Haven, CT: Yale University Press.

Stoller, R. (1987). Perversion and the desire to harm, *Theories of the unconscious and theories of the self* (pp. 221–234). Hillsdale, NJ: Analytic Press.

Stoller, R. (1989). Consensual sadomasochistic perversions. In *The psychoanalytic core: Essays in honor of Leo Rangell, M. D.* (pp. 265–282). Madison, CT: International Universities Press.

Stoppard, J. M. (2000). *Understanding depression: Feminist social constructionist approaches.* New York: Routledge.

Stoyva, J. M., & Budzynski, T. H. (1993). Biofeedback methods in the treatment of anxiety and stress disorder. In P. M. Lehrer & R. L. Woolfolk (Eds.), *Principles and practices of stress management* (2nd ed.). New York: Guilford Press.

Strassman, R. J. (1988). Living high: Daily marijuana use among adults. *American Journal of Psychiatry, 145,* 1467–1468.

Strassman, R. J. (1995). Hallucinogenic drugs in psychiatric research and treatment. Perspectives and prospects. *Journal of Nervous & Mental Disease, 183*(3), 127–138.

Straus, M., & Donnelly, D. (1994). *Beating the devil out of them: Corporal punishment in American families.* New York: Lexington Books/Macmillan.

Streissguth, A. P., Bookstein, F. L., Sampson, P. D., & Barr, H. M. (1995). Attention: Prenatal alcohol and continuities of vigilance and attentional problems from 4 through 14 years. *Development & Psychopathology, 7,* 419–446.

Stricker, G., & Trierweiler, S. J. (1995). The local clinical scientist: A bridge between science and practice. *American Psychologist, 50*(12), 995–1002.

Stromme, P., & Magnus, P. (2000). Correlations between socioeconomic status, IQ and aetiology in mental retardation: A population-based study of Norwegian children. *Social Psychiatry & Psychiatric Epidemiology, 35,* 12–18.

Stromwall, L. K. (1997). Gender differences in the social roles of parent and partner: The case of women and men with schizophrenic disorders. *Dissertation Abstracts International Section A: Humanities & Social Sciences, 58*(1-A). Ann Arbor, MI: University Microfilms International.

Stroop, J. R. (1935). Studies of interference in serial verbal reactions. *Journal of Experimental Psychology, 18,* 643–662.

Strupp, H. (1995). The psychotherapist's skill revisited. *Clinical Psychology: Science and Practice, 2,* 70–74.

Stuart, S., Pfohl, B., Battaglia, M., Bellodi, L., et al. (1998). The cooccurrence of DSM-III-R personality disorders. *Journal of Personality Disorders, 12,* 302–315.

Sturup, G. K. (1972). Castration: The total treatment. In H. L. P. Resnik, & M. E. Wofgang (Eds.), *Sexual behavior: Social, clinical, and legal aspects* (pp. 361–382). Boston: Little, Brown.

Sullivan, E. V., Shear, P. K., Lim, K. O., Zipursky, R. B., et al. (1996). Cognitive and motor impairments are relate to gray matter volume deficits in schizophrenia. *Biological Psychiatry, 39,* 234–240.

Sullivan, H. S. (1953). *The interpersonal theory of psychiatry.* New York: W. W. Norton.

Sullivan, H. S. (1962). *Schizophrenia as a human process.* New York: Norton.

Sundgot-Borgen, J. (1994). Risk and trigger factors for the development of eating disorders in female elite athletes. *Medicine and Science in Sports and Exercise, 26,* 414–419.

Suppe, F. (1984). Classifying sexual disorders: The Diagnostic and Statistical Manual of the American Psychiatric Association. *Journal of Homosexuality (Special Issue: Bisexual and Homosexual Identities: Critical Clinical Issues), 9*(4), 9–28.

Suryani, L. K. (1984). Culture and mental disorder: The case of the bebainan in Bali. *Cultural Medical Psychiatry, 8,* 95–113.

Sussman, L., & Smith, M. (1992). Working with adult children of alcoholics. *HR Magazine 37,* 68–70.

Sutker, P., & Adams, H. (Eds.). (2001). *Comprehensive handbook of psychopathology* (3rd ed.). New York: Kluwer Academic/Plenum Publishers.

Suzuki, L. A., & Valencia, R. R. (1997). Race-ethnicity and measured intelligence: Educational implications. *American Psychologist, 52*(10), 1103–1114.

Svedberg, B., Mesterton, A., & Cullberg, J. (2001). First-episode non-affective psychosis in a total urban population: A 5-year follow-up. *Social Psychiatry & Psychiatric Epidemiology, 36*(7), 332–337.

Svensson, T. J. (2000). Dysfunctional brain dopamine systems induced by psychotomimetic NMDA-receptor antagonists and the effects of antipsychotic drugs. *Brain Research Reviews (Special Issue Nobel Symposium 111: Schizophrenia: Pathophysiological Mechanisms), 31*(2–3), 320–329.

Swan, D. C., & Perez, B. (2000). Peyote religious art [Book review]. Symbols of faith and belief. *American Indian Culture and Research Journal, 24*(1), 248–250.

Swanson, H. L. (2000). Searching for the best cognitive model for instructing students with learning disabilities: A component and composite analysis. *Educational and Child Psychology, 17,* 101–121.

Swanson, H. L., & Hoskyn, M. (1998). Experimental intervention research on students with learning disabilities: A meta-analysis of treatment outcomes. *Review of Educational Research, 68,* 277–321.

Swartz, M., Blazer, D., George, L., & Winfield, I. (1990). Estimating the prevalence of borderline personality disorder in the community. *Journal of Personality Disorders, 4,* 257–272.

Sweeney, J. A., Luna, B., Srinivasagam, N. M., Keshavan, M. S., et al. (1998). Eye tracking abnormalities in schizophrenia: Evidence for dysfunction in the frontal eye fields. *Biological Psychiatry, 44*(8), 698–708.

Swerdlow, N. R., Braff, D. L., Taaid, N., & Geyer, M. A. (1994). Assessing the validity of an animal model of deficient sensorimotor gating in schizophrenic patients. *Archives of General Psychiatry, 51*(2), 139–154.

Swift, W. J., & Stern, S. (1982). The psychodynamic diversity of anorexia nervosa. *International Journal of Eating Disorders, 2,* 17–35.

Switzer, C. (1967). *The political, philosophical, and religious thought of Dr. Benjamin Rush.* [Unpublished dissertation]. East Lansing, MI: Michigan State University.

Szasz, T. (1960). The myth of mental illness. *American Psychologist, 15,* 113–118.

Szasz, T. S. (1960). The myth of mental illness. *American Psychologist, 15,* 113–118.

Szasz, T. S. (1973). *The age of madness: The history of involuntary mental hospitalization presented in selected texts.* Garden City, NY: Anchor.

Szasz, T. S. (1975). Medical metaphorology. *American Psychologist, 30*(8), 859–861.

Szasz, T. S. (1975). Medicine and madness. *Journal of Psychiatry and the Law, 3*(2), 215–222.

Szasz, T. S. (1994). *Cruel compassion: Psychiatric control of society's unwanted.* New York: John Wiley & Sons.

Szasz, T. S., Reiman, J., & Chambliss, W. J. (1995). Constructing difference: Social deviance. In J. S. Fleisher (Ed.), *Sociology:*

Exploring the architecture of everyday life: Readings. Thousand Oaks, CA: Pine Forge Press/Sage Publications Co.

Szmukler, G. I., & Patton, G. (1995). Sociocultural models of eating disorders. In G. Szmukler, C. Dare, & J. Treasure (Eds.), *Handbook of eating disorders: Theory, treatment and research* (pp. 197–220). New York: John Wiley & Sons.

Szuchman, L., & Muscarella, F. (2000). *Psychological perspectives on human sexuality.* New York: John Wiley & Sons.

T

Taber, K., Lewis, D., & Hurley, R. (2001). Schizophrenia: What's under the microscope? *Journal of Neuropsychiatry and Clinical Neuroscience, 13*(1), 1–4.

Taber, K. H., Lewis, D. A., & Hurley, R. A. (2001). Schizophrenia: What's under the microscope? *Journal of Neuropsychiatry & Clinical Neurosciences, 13*(1), 1–4.

Tanner, C. M., Ottman, R., Goldman, S. M., Ellenberg, J., et al. (1999). Parkinson disease in twins: an etiologic study. *Journal of the American Medical Association, 281*(4), 341–346.

Tarter, R. E., Ammerman, R. T., & Ott, P. J. (Eds.). (1998). *Handbook of substance abuse: Neurobehavioral pharmacology.* New York: Plenum Press.

Tarter, R. E., Jones, B. M., Simpson, C. D., & Vega, A. (1971). Effects of task complexity and practice on performance during acute alcohol intoxication. *Perceptual & Motor Skills, 33*(1), 307–318.

Tarter, R. E., Templer, D. I., & Hardy, C. (1975). *Reliability of the psychiatric diagnosis. Diseases of the Nervous System, 36*(1), 30–31.

Tattan, T. M. G., & Creed, F. H. (2001). Negative symptoms of schizophrenia and compliance with medication. *Schizophrenia Bulletin, 27*(1), 149–155.

Taylor, D., & Warner, R. (1994). Does substance use precipitate the onset of functional psychosis? *Social Work & Social Sciences Review, 5*(1), 64–75.

Taylor, E. (1996). Psychedelics: the second coming. *Psychology Today, 29,* 56–59.

Taylor, J. R., & Jentsch, J. D. (2001). Repeated intermittent administration of psychomotor stimulant drugs alters the acquisition of Pavlovian approach behavior in rats: Differential effects of cocaine, d-amphetamine and 3, 4-methylenedioxymethamphetamine ("ecstasy"). *Biological Psychiatry (Special Issue), 50*(2), 137–143.

Taylor, S. (1995). *Health psychology* (3rd ed.). New York: McGraw-Hill.

Teesson, M., Hodder, T., & Buhrich, N. (2000). Substance use disorders among homeless people in inner Sydney. *Social Psychiatry & Psychiatric Epidemiology, 35*(10), 451–456.

Teixeria, M. A. (1992). Psychoanalytic theory and therapy in the treatment of manic-depressive disorders. *Psychoanalysis & Psychotherapy, 10,* 162–177.

Tekell, J. L. (2001). Management of pregnancy in the schizophrenic woman. In *Management of psychiatric disorders in pregnancy* (pp. 188–212). New York: Oxford University Press.

Teresi, J. A., Holmes, D., Ramirez, M., Gurland, B. J., et al. (2001). Performance of cognitive tests among different racial/ethnic and education groups: Findings of differential item functioning and possible item bias. *Journal of Mental Health & Aging, 7,* 79–89.

Terman, L. M. (1916). *The measurement of intelligence.* Boston: Houghton-Mifflin.

Terr, L. C. (1983). Chowchilla revisited: The effects of psychic trauma four years after a school-bus kidnapping. *American Journal of Psychiatry, 140*(12), 1543–1550.

Terr, L. C. (1990). *Too scared to cry: Psychic trauma in childhood.* Grand Rapids, MI: Harper & Row Publishers, Inc.

Terr, L. C. (1991). Childhood traumas: An outline and overview. *American Journal of Psychiatry, 148*(1), 10–20.

Thase, M. E., & Howland, R. H. (1995). Biochemical processes in depression: An updated review and integration. In E. E. Beckham & W. R. Leber (Eds.), *Handbook of depression* (2nd ed., pp. 213–279). New York: Guilford Press.

Thiblin, I., Kristiansson, M., & Rajs, J. (1997). Anabolic androgenic steroids and behavioural patterns among violent offenders. *Journal of Forensic Psychiatry, 8*(2), 299–310.

Thomas, A., Chess, S., & Birch, H. (1970). *Temperament and behavior disorders in children.* New York: New York University Press.

Thomas, P. (1997). *The dialectics of schizophrenia.* London: Free Association Books.

Thombs, D. L. (1999). *Introduction to addictive behaviors* (2nd ed.). New York: Guilford Press.

Thompson, D., Hylan, T., McMullen, W., Romeis, M., et al. (1998). Predictors and effects of a medical offset effect among patients receiving antidepressant therapy. *American Journal of Psychiatry, 155,* 824–827.

Thompson, J. K., Heinberg, L. J., Altable, M., & Tantleff-Dunn, S. (1999). Feminist perspectives. In *Exacting beauty: Theory, assessment, and treatment of body image disturbances.* Washington, DC: American Psychological Association.

Thorndike, R. L., Hagen, E. P., & Sattler, J. M. (1986). *Guide for administering and scoring the fourth edition Stanford-Binet Intelligence Scale.* Chicago: Riverside.

Tienari, P., Wynne, L. C., Moring, J., Lahti, I., et al. (1994). The Finnish adoptive family study of schizophrenia: Implications for family research. *British Journal of Psychiatry, 164* (23), S20–S26.

Tiihonen, J., Kuikka, J., Vinamaki, H., Lehtonen, J., et al. (1995). Altered cerebral blood flow during hysterical paraesthesia. *Biological Psychiatry, 37,* 134–135.

Tissot, S. (1817). *L'onanisme. Dissertation sur les maladies produites par la masturbation.* Paris: Avignon.

Tobin, D. L. (2000). *Coping strategies therapy for bulimia nervosa.* Washington, DC: American Psychological Press.

Torgersen, S., Kringlen, E., & Cramer, V. (2001). The prevalence of personality disorders in a community sample. *Archives of General Psychiatry, 58,* 590–596.

Torrey, E. (1999). Epidemiological comparison of schizophrenia and bipolar disorder. *Scizophrenia Research, 39,* 101–106.

Torrey, E. F. (2001). *Surviving schizophrenia.* New York: Harper Collins.

Torrey, E. F., Miller, J., Rawlings, R., & Yolken, R. H. (1997). Seasonality of births in schizophrenia and bipolar disorder: A review of the literature. *Schizophrenia Research, 28*(1), 1–38.

Treasure, J., & Szmukler, G. (1995). Medical complications of anorexia nervosa. In G. Szmukler, C. Dare, & J. Treasure (Eds.), *Handbook of eating disorders: Theory, treatment and research* (pp. 197–220). New York: John Wiley & Sons.

Trevisan, M. S. (1996). Review of the Draw a Person: Screening procedure for emotional disturbance. *Measurement & Evaluation in Counseling & Development, 28*(4), 225–228.

Trierweiler, S. J., Neighbors, H. W., Munday, C., Thompson, E. E., et al. (2000). Clinician attributions associated with the diagnosis of schizophrenia in African American and non-African American patients. *Journal of Consulting & Clinical Psychology, 68*(1), 171–175.

Trumbetta, S. L., & Mueser, K. T. (2001). Social functioning and its relationship to cognitive deficits over the course of schizophrenia. In *Negative symptom and cognitive deficit treatment response in schizophrenia* (pp. 33–67). Washington, DC: American Psychiatric Press.

Trzepacz, P. T., & Baker, R. W. (1993). *The psychiatric mental status examination.* New York: Oxford University Press.

Tseng, W., Di, X., Ebata, K., Hsu, J., et al. (1986). Diagnostic pattern for neuroses in China, Japan and the United States. *American Journal of Psychiatry, 143*(8), 1010–1014.

Tseng, W.-S. (2001). *Handbook of cultural psychiatry.* San Diego, CA: Academic Press.

Tsuang, M. T., & Faraone, S. S. V. (1990). *The genetics of mood disorders.* Baltimore: Johns Hopkins University Press.

Tsuang, M. T., Stone, W. S., & Faraone, S. V. (2000). Toward reformulating the diagnosis of schizophrenia. *American Journal of Psychiatry, 157*(7), 1041–1050.

Tsuang, M. T., Stone, W. S., & Faraone, S. V. (2001). Genes, environment, and schizophrenia. *British Journal of Psychiatry, 178*(40), S18–S24.

Tuiten, A., Van Honk, J., Koppeschaar, H., Bernaards, C., et al. (2000). Time course of effects of testosterone administration on sexual arousal in women. *Archives of General Psychiatry, 57*(2), 149–153.

Turnquist, K. (1993). Second-trimester markers of fetal size in schizophrenia. *American Journal of Psychiatry, 150*(10), 1571–1572.

Tylor, E. B. (1958). *Primitive culture.* New York: Harper.

U

Ullman, S. E., & Filipas, H. H. (2001). Predictors of PTSD symptom severity and social reactions in sexual assault victims. *Journal of Traumatic Stress, 14*, 369–389.

Ullrich, P. M., & Lutgendorf, S. K. (2002). Journaling about stressful events: Effects of cognitive processing and emotional expression. *Annals of Behavioral Medicine, 24*(3), 244–250.

Ulrich, R. F., & Patten, B. M. (1991). The rise, decline, and fall of LSD. *Perspectives in Biology & Medicine, 34*(4), 561–578.

Unis, A. S., & Rose, J. C. (1996). Psychotropic toxicity. *Journal of the American Academy of Child & Adolescent Psychiatry, 35*(10), 1261–1262.

Upton, M. W. M., & Hoogkamer, R. A. (1994). The strength of the genetic effect: Is there room for an environmental influence in the aetiology of schizophrenia? [Comment]. *British Journal of Psychiatry, 165*(3), 409.

Urakubo, A., Jarskog, L. F., Lieberman, J. A., & Gilmore, J. H. (2001). Prenatal exposure to maternal infection alters cytokine expression in the placenta, amniotic fluid and fetal brain. *Schizophrenia Research, 47*(1), 27–36.

V

Vaillant, G. V. (1988). What can long-term follow up teach us about relapse and prevention of relapse in addiction? *British Journal of Addiction, 83*(10), 1147–1157.

Valenstein, E. (1980). Causes and treatments of mental disorders. In E. Valenstein (Ed.), *The psychsurgery debate: Scientific, legal & ethical perspectives.* San Francisco: W. H. Freeman & Co.

Valenstein, E. (1986). *Great and desperate cures: The rise and decline of psychosurgery and other radical treatments for mental illness.* New York: Basic Books.

Valenstein, E. S. (1998). *Blaming the brain: The truth about drugs and mental health.* New York: Free Press.

Van der Kolk, B. A. (1996). Trauma and memory. In B. A. van der Kolk, A. C. McFarlane, & L. Weisaeth (Eds.), *Traumatic stress: The effects of overwhelming experience on mind, body and society.* New York: Guilford Press.

van Dixhoorn, J. (1998). Cardiorespiratory effects of breathing and relaxation instruction in myocardial infarction patients. *Biological Psychology, 49*, 123–135.

Vance, A., Velakuolis, D., Maruff, P., Wood, S., et al. (2000). Magnetic resonance spectroscopy and schizophrenia: What have we learnt? *Australian and New Zealand Journal of Psychiatary, 34*, 14–25.

VandenBos, G. R., & Leon, P. H. (1988). The use of psychotherapy to improve physical health. *Psychotherapy, 25*, 335–343.

Verhofstadt-Deneve, L. (2000). *Theory and practice of action and drama techniques: Developmental psychotherapy from an existential-dialectical viewpoint* (p. 352). Bristol, PA: Jessica Kingsley Publishers, Ltd.

Vermetten, Y. J., Lodewijks, H. G., & Vermunt, J. D. (2001). The role of personality traits and goal orientations in strategy use. *Contemporary Educational Psychology: Special Issue, 26*(2), 149–170.

Vernon, L. T., Fuller, M. A., Hattab, H., & Varnes, K. M. (2000). Olanzapine-induced urinary incontinence: Treatment with ephedrine. *Journal of Clinical Psychiatry, 61*(8), 601–602.

Viinamaeki, H., Koskela, K., & Niskanen, L. (1996). Rapidly declining mental well-being during unemployment. *European Journal of Psychiatry, 10*, 215–221.

Vinluan, F. (1996). The trouble with hemp. *Governing, 10*, 43–44.

Vocisano, C., Klein, D. N., Keefe, R. S. E., Dienst, E. R., et al. (1996). Demographics, family history, premorbid functioning, developmental characteristics, and course of patients with deteriorated affective disorder. *American Journal of Psychiatry, 153*(2), 248–255.

Volkmar, F., Klin, A., Marans, W., & Cohen, D. (1997). Childhood disintegrative disorder. In D. J. Cohen & F. R. Volkmar (Eds.),

Handbook of autism and pervasive developmental disorders. New York: John Wiley & Sons.

Vollenweier, F. X. (1998). Advances and pathophysiological models of hallucinogenic rug actions in humans: A preamble to schizophrenia research. *Pharmacopsychiatry, 31*(2), S92–S103.

Von Os, J., & Marcelis, M. (1998). The ecogenetics of schizophrenia: A review. *Schizophrenia Research, 32*, 127–135.

Vonnegut, M. (1975). *The Eden express.* New York: Praeger.

W

Wade, N. (2002, July 4). Schizophrenia may be tied to 2 genes, research finds. *The New York Times.*

Wagner, A. R., & Brandon, S. E. (2001). A componential theory of Pavlovian conditioning. In R. R. Mowrer (Ed.). *Handbook of contemporary learning theories* (pp. x, 622, 23–64). Mahwah, NJ: Lawrence Erlbaum Associates, Inc.

Wahlberg, K-E., Wynne, L. C., Oja, H., Keskitalo, P., et al. (1997). Gene-environment interaction in vulnerability to schizophrenia: Findings from the Finnish Family Study of Schizophrenia. *American Journal of Psychiatry, 154*(3), 355–362.

Wakefield, J. C. (1992). Disorder as harmful dysfunction: A conceptual critique of DSM-III-R's definition of mental disorder. *Psychological Review, 99*(2), 232–247.

Wakefield, J. C. (1997). When is development disordered? Developmental psychopathology and the harmful dysfunction analysis of mental disorder. *Development & Psychopathology, 9*(2), 269–290.

Wakefield, J. C. (1999). Evolutionary versus prototype analyses of the concept of disorder. *Journal of Abnormal Psychology, 108*(3), 374–399.

Wakschlag, L. S., Pickett, K. E., Cook, E., Jr., Benowitz, N. L., et al. (2002). Maternal smoking during pregnancy and severe antisocial behavior in offspring: A review. *American Journal of Public Health, 92*(6), 966–974.

Walker, E. F., Logan, C. B., & Walder, D. (1999). Indicators of neurodevelopmental abnormality in schizotypal personality disorder. *Psychiatric Annals, 29*, 132–136.

Walker, L. E. A. (1987). Inadequacies of the masochistic personality disorder diagnosis for women. *Journal of Personality Disorders, 1*, 183–189.

Wallace, J. M. (1999). The social ecology of addiction: Race, risk, and resilience. *Pediatrics, 103*, 1122–1127.

Wallace, J. M., Jr. (1999). The epidemiology of alcohol, tobacco and other drug use among Black youth. *Journal of Studies on Alcohol, 60*(6), 800–809.

Walsh, B. T., Agras, W. S., Devlin, M. J., Fairburn, C. G., et al. (2000). Fluoxetine for bulimia nervosa following poor response to psychotherapy. *American Journal of Psychiatry, 157,* 1332–1334.

Walsh, B. T., Wilson, G. T., Loeb, K. L., Devlin, M. J., et al. (1997). Medication and psychotherapy in the treatment of bulimia nervosa. *American Journal of Psychiatry, 154,* 523–531.

Walsh, T. (1999). Psychopathic and nonpsychopathic violence among alcoholic offenders. *International Journal of Offender Therapy & Comparative Criminology, 43*(1), 34–48.

Wardle, J., Steptoe, A., Oliver, G., & Lipsey, Z. (2000). Stress, dietary restraint and food intake. *Journal of Psychosomatic Research, 48,* 195–202.

Warner, B. S., & Weist, M. D. (1996). Urban youth as witnesses to violence: Beginning assessment and treatment efforts. *Journal of Youth and Adolescence, 25,* 361–377.

Warner, L. A., Kessler, R. C., Hughes, M., Anthony, J. C., & Nelson, C. B. (1995). Prevalence and correlates of drug use and dependence in the United States. Results from the National Comorbidity Survey. *Archives of General Psychiatry, 52,* 219–229.

Warnock, J., Bundren, J., & Morris, D. (1997). Female hypoactive sexual Disorder: case studies of physiologic androgen replacement. *Journal of Sex and Marriage Therapy, 25,* 175–182.

Warwick, H. M. C., & Salkovskis, P. M. (1990). Hypochondriasis. *Behavior Research and Therapy, 28,* 105–117.

Watson, C. G., Felling, J., & Maceachern, D. G. (1967). Objective Draw-A-Person scales: An attempted cross-validation. *Journal of Clinical Psychology, 23*(3), 382–386.

Watson, H. E. (1999). Problem drinkers in acute care settings: Validation of an assessment instrument. *International Journal of Nursing Studies, 36*(5), 415–423.

Watson, J. (1914). *Behavior: An introduction to comparative psychology.* New York: H. Holt & Co.

Watson, J., & Rayner, R. (1920). Conditioned emotional reactions. *Journal of Experimental Psychology, 3,* 1–14.

Watson, J. B. (1970). *Behaviorism.* New York: W. W. Norton. (Original work published 1925)

Watson, J. B., & Rayner, R. (1920). Conditioned emotional reactions. *Journal of Experimental Psychology, 3,* 1–14.

Waxler-Morrison, N., Hislop, T. G., Mears, B., & Kan, L. (1991). Effects of social relationships on survival for women with breast cancer: A prospective study. *Social Science and Medicine, 33,* 177–183.

Weaver, H. N. (2001). Native Americans and substance abuse. In S. L. A. Straussner (Ed.), *Ethnocultural factors in substance abuse treatment* (pp. 77–96). New York: Guilford Press.

Wechsler, D. (1989). *Wechsler Preschool and Primary Scale of Intelligence–Revised.* San Antonio, TX: Psychological Corporation.

Wechsler, D. (1991). *Wechsler Intelligence Scale for Children–Third Edition.* San Antonio, TX: Psychological Corporation.

Wechsler, D. (1992). *Wechsler Individual Achievement Test.* San Antonio, TX: Psychological Corporation.

Wechsler, D. (1997). *Wechsler Adult Intelligence Scale–Third Edition.* San Antonio, TX: Psychological Corporation.

Weinberger, D. R. (1997). The biological basis of schizophrenia: New directions. *Journal of Clinical Psychiatry, 58*(10), S22–S27.

Weiner, D., & Rosen, R. (1999). Sexual dysfunctions and disorders, *Oxford textbook of psychopathology* (Vol. 414, pp. 410–443). New York: Oxford University Press.

Weiner, I. B. (1998). *Principles of Rorschach interpretation.* Mahwah, NJ: Lawrence Erlbaum.

Weiner, M. F. (1991). *The dementias: Diagnosis and management.* Washington, DC: American Psychiatric Press.

Weinstock, L. S. (1999). Gender differences in the presentation and management of social anxiety disorder. *Journal of Clinical Psychiatry: Special Issue: New frontiers in the management of social anxiety disorder: Diagnosis, treatment, and clinical course,* 60(suppl 9), 9–13.

Weintraub, E., Weintraub, D., Dixon, L., Delahanty, J., Gandhi, D., Cohen, A., & Hirsch, M. (2002). Geriatric patients on a substance abuse consultation service. *American Journal of Psychiatry, 10,* 337–342.

Weisberg, R., Brown, T., Wincze, J., & Barlow, D. (2001). Causal attributions and male sexual arousal: The impact of attributions for a bogus erectile difficulty on sexual arousal, cognition and affect. *Journal of Abnormal Psychology, 110*(2), 324–334.

Weiss, D. S., Marmar, C. R., Schlenger, W. E., Fairback, J. A., et al. (1992). The prevalence of lifetime and partial posttraumatic stress disorder in Vietnam theater veterans. *Journal of Traumatic Stress, 5*(3), 365–376.

Weiss, H. (2001). Melanie Klein and Wilfred Bion. On the relationship between some theoretical concepts in the work of Melanie Klein and Wilfred Bion. *Psyche: Zeitschrift fuer Psychoanalyse and ihre Anwendungen, 55*(2), 159–180.

Weissman, M. M., Bruce, M., Leaf, P., Florio, L., et al. (1991). Affective disorders. In L. Robins & E. Reigier (Eds.), *Psychiatric disorders in America* (pp. 53–80). New York: Free Press.

Weitzman, E. A., & Wechsler, H. (2000). Alcohol use, abuse and related problems among children of problem drinkers: Findings from a national survey of college alcohol use. *Journal of Nervous & Mental Disease, 188*(3), 148–154.

Welin, L., Larsson, B., Svardsudd, K., Tibblin, B., et al. (1992). Social network and activities in relation to mortality from cardiovascular disease, cancer and other causes: A 12-year follow-up study of men born in 1913 and 1923. *Journal of Epidemiology and Community Health, 46,* 217–232.

Wells, A. (1997). *Cognitive therapy of anxiety disorders: A practice manual and conceptual guide.* New York: John Wiley & Sons.

Wenar, C., & Kerig, P. (2000). *Developmental psychopathology: From infancy through adolescence.* Boston: McGraw-Hill.

Wender, H., Kety, S. S., Rosenthal, D., Schulsinger, F., et al. (1986). Psychiatric disorders in the biological and adoptive families of individuals with affective disorders. *Archives of General Psychiatry, 43,* 923–929.

West, C. (1999). *First person plural: My life as a multiple.* New York: Hyperion.

West, R. (2001). Theories of addiction. *Addiction, 96*(1), 3–13.

Westen, D., Lohr, N., Silk, K., & Kerber, K. (1994). Measuring object relations and social cognition using the TAT. *Journal of Personality Assessment, 56,* 56–74.

Westen, D., Ludolph, P., Misle, B., Ruffins, S., et al. (1990). Physical and sexual abuse in adolescent girls with borderline personality disorder. *American Journal of Orthopsychiatry, 61,* 55–66.

Westen, D., & Morrison, K. (2001). A multidimensional meta-analysis of treatments for depression, panic, and generalized anxiety disorder: An empirical examination of the status of empirically supported therapies. *Journal of Consulting and Clinical Psychology, 69*(6), 875–899.

Wichstrom, L., & Pedersen, W. (2001). Use of anabolic-androgenic steroids in adolescence: Winning, looking good or being bad? *Journal of Studies on Alcohol, 62*(1), 5–13.

Wicks-Nelson, R., & Israel, A. C. (2000). *Behavior disorders of childhood.* Englewood Cliffs, NJ: Prentice Hall.

Widiger, T. A. (1993). The DSM-III-R categorical personality disorder diagnoses: A critique and an alternative. *Psychological Inquiry, 4*(2), 75–90.

Widiger, T. A., & Costa, P. T. (1994). Personality and the personality disorders. *Journal of Abnormal Psychology, 103,* 78–91.

Widiger, T. A., Frances, A. J., Pincus, H. A., First, M. B., et al. (Eds.). (1994). *DSM-IV sourcebook* (Vol. 1). Washington, DC: American Psychiatric Association.

Widiger, T. A., Frances, A. J., Pincus, H. A., Ross, R., et al. (Eds.). (1998). *DSM-IV sourcebook* (Vol. 4). Washington, DC: American Psychiatric Association.

Widiger, T. A., & Trull, T. J. (1991). Diagnosis and clinical assessment. *Annual Review of Psychology, 42,* 109–133.

Wiederman, M. W., & Pryor, T. (1996). Substance use among women with eating disorders. *International Journal of Eating Disorders, 20,* 163–168.

Wiens, A. N. (1976). The assessment interview. In I. B. Weiner (Ed.), *Clinical methods in psychology.* New York: John Wiley & Sons.

Wilcox, K., Rowlett, J., Paul, I., Ordway, G., & Woolverton, W. (2000). On the relationship between the dopamine transporter and the reinforcing effects of local anesthetics in rhesus monkeys: Practical and theoretical concerns. *Psychopharmacology (Special Issue: Drug Reinforcement), 153*(1), 139–147.

Wilensky, A. S. (1999). *Passing for normal: A memoir of compulsion.* New York: Broadway Books.

Wilkins, P. (2000). Unconditional positive regard reconsidered. *British Journal of Guidance & Counselling, 28*(1), 23–36.

Wilkinson, D. (1993). ECT in the elderly. In R. Levy (Ed.). *Treatment and care in old age psychiatry.* Petersfield, England: Wrights on Biomedical Publishing, 169–181.

Willerman, L., & Cohen, D. (1990). *Psychopathology.* New York: McGraw-Hill.

Williams, B., & Knight, S. (1995). *Healthy for life: Brief version.* Pacific Grove, CA: Brooks/Cole.

Williams, J. M. G., & Brewin, C. R. (1984). Cognitive mediators of reactions to a minor life-event: The British driving test. *British Journal of Social Psychology, 23,* 41–49.

Williams, L. M. (1994). Recall of childhood trauma: A prospective study of women's memories of child sexual abuse. *Journal of Consulting & Clinical Psychology, 62,* 1167–1176.

Willis, D. J., & Walker, C. E. (1989). Etiology. *Handbook of child psychopathology* (2nd ed., pp. 29–51). New York: Plenum Press.

Wills, T. A., & Filer Fegan, M. (2001). Social networks and social support. In A. Baum, T. A. Revenson, & J. E. Singer (Eds.), *Handbook of health psychology* (pp. 209–234). Mahwah, NJ: Lawrence Erlbaum.

Wilson, G. T. (1989). The treatment of bulimia nervosa: A cognitive-social learning analysis. In A. J. Stunkard & A. Baum (Eds.). *Perspectives in behavioral medicine: Eating, sleeping and sex* (pp. 73–98). Hillsdale, NJ: Lawrence Erlbaum.

Wilson, G. T. (2000). Behavior therapy. In R. Corsini & D. Wedding (Eds.), *Current psychotherapies* (6th ed.). Itasca, IL: Peacock Publishers.

Wilson, G. T., & Fairburn, C. G. (2002). Treatments for eating disorders. In P. E. Nathan & J. M. Gorman (Eds.), *A guide to treatments that work* (2nd ed., pp. 559–592). London: Oxford University Press.

Wilson, H. T. (Ed.). (2000). *Annual editions: Drugs, society, and behavior 2000/2001* (15th ed.). Guilford, CT: Dushkin/McGraw-Hill.

Wincze, J. P., & Lange, J. D. (1981). Assessment of sexual behavior. In D. H. Barlow (Ed.), *Behavioral assessment of adult disorders*. New York: Guilford Press.

Windle, M., & Welch, K. (1995). The prevalence and prospective predictors of cocaine use among a national U.S. sample of young adults. *Addiction Research, 3*(1), 39–47.

Wing, C., & Sartorius, N. (1974). *The description and classification of psychiatric symptoms* (pp. 174). Cambridge, England: Cambridge University Press.

Wing, J., Cooper, J., & Sartorius, N. (1974). *Measurement and classification of psychiatric symptoms: An instruction manual for the PSE and Catego Program*. London: Cambridge University Press.

Wing, J. K., & Brown, G. (1970). *Institutionalism and schizophrenia: A comparative study of three mental hospitals*. Cambridge, England: Cambridge University Press.

Wing, J. K., & Brown, G. W. (1961). Social treatment of chronic schizophrenia: A comparative survey of three mental hospitals. *Journal of Mental Science, 107*, 847–861.

Winnicott, D. W. (1965). *The maturational processes and the facilitating environment: Studies in the theory of emotional development*. New York: International Universities Press.

Winokur, G., Coryell, W., Keller, M., Endicott, J., et al. (1995). A family study of manic-depressive (bipolar I) disease: Is it a distinct illness separable from primary unipolar depression? *Archives of General Psychiatry, 52*(5), 367–373.

Winthrop, H. (1964). Word-magic: The dehumanization of clinical diagnosis. *Journal of Humanistic Psychology, 4*(2), 165–175.

Wise, R. A. (1988). The neurobiology of craving: Implications for the understanding and treatment of addiction. *Journal of Abnormal Psychology, 97*, 118–132.

Wise, T. (1999). Psychosocial side effects of sildenafil therapy for erectile dysfunction. *Journal of Sex & Marital Therapy, 25*(2), 145–150.

Wise, T., & Kalyanam, R. (2000). Amputee fetishism and genital mutilation: Case report and literature review. *Journal of Sex & Marital Therapy, 26*(4), 339–344.

Wittchen, H. U., Zhao, S., Kessler, R. C., & Eaton, W. W. (1994). DSM III-R generalized anxiety disorder in the National Comorbidity Survey. *Archives of General Psychiatry, 51*, 355–364.

Wolf, N. (1990). *The beauty myth: How images of beauty are used against women*. New York: W. Morrow.

Wolfe, J. L., & Russianoff, P. (1997). Overcoming self-negation in women. *Journal of Rational-Emotive and Cognitive-Behavioral Therapy, 15*(1), 81–92.

Wolfradt, U., & Neumann, K. (2001). Depersonalization, self-esteem and body image in male-to-female transsexuals compared to male and female controls. *Archives of Sexual Behavior (Special Issue), 30*(3), 301–310.

Wolpe, J. (1958). *Psychotherapy by reciprocal inhibition*. Stanford, CA: Stanford University Press.

Wolpe, J. (1969). *The practice of behavior therapy*. Oxford, England: Pergamon Press.

Wolpe, J. (1990). *The practice of behavior therapy* (4th ed.). New York: Pergamon Press.

Wolpe, J., & Reyna, L. J. (1976). *Behavior therapy in psychiatric patients: The use of behavioral procedures by psychiatrists*. New York: Pergamon Press.

Wonderlich, S., & Mitchell, J. E. (2001). The role of personality in the onset of eating disorders and treatment implications. *Psychiatric Clinics of North America, 24*, 249–258.

Wong, C. M., & Yehuda, R. (2002). Sex differences in posttraumatic stress disorder. In F. Lewis-Hall, T. S. Williams, J. A. Panetta, & J. M. Herrera (Eds.), *Psychiatric illness in women: Emerging treatments and research* (pp. 57–96). Washington, DC: American Psychiatric Publishing.

Wood, J., Nezworski, T., Lilienfeld, S., & Garb, H. (2003). *What's wrong with the Rorschach? Science confronts the controversial inkblot test*. Hoboken, NJ: Jossey-Bass.

Wood, R., Grossman, L., & Fichtner, C. (2000). Psychological assessment, treatment, and outcome with sex offenders. *Behavioral Sciences & the Law, 18*(1), 23–41.

Woodcock, R. W. (1977). *Woodcock-Johnson Psycho-Educational Battery: Technical report*. Allen, TX: DLM Teaching Resources.

Woodside, D. B., Bulik, C. M., Halmi, K. A., Fichter, M. M., et al. (2002). Personality, perfectionism, and attitudes towards eating in parents of individuals with eating disorders. *International Journal of Eating Disorders, 31*, 290–299.

Wool, C. A., & Barsky, A. J. (1994). Do women somatize more than men? Gender differences in somatization. *Psychosomatics, 35*, 445–452.

Worden, J. W. (1991). *Grief counseling and grief therapy: A handbook for the mental health practitioner*. New York: Springer Publishing Co.

Wright, L. B., Treiber, F. A., Davis, H., & Strong, W. B. (1996). Relationship of John Henryism to cardiovascular functioning at rest and during stress in youth. *Annals of Behavioral Medicine, 18*, 146–150.

Wyatt, R. (2001). Diagnosing schizophrenia. In J. Lieberman & R. Murray (Eds.), *Comprehensive care of schizophrenia*. London: Martin Dunitz.

Wylie, K. (1997). Treatment outcome of brief couple therapy in psychogenic male erectile disorder. *Archives of Sexual Behavior, 26*(5), 527–545.

X

Xu, X., Yang, D., Wyss-Coray, T., Yan, J., Gan, L., et al. (1999). Wild-type but not Alzheimer-mutant amyloid precursor protein confers resistance against p53-mediated apoptosis. *Proceedings of the National Academy of Sciences, 96*, 537–552.

Y

Yalom, V. E. (1967). *Psychotherapy and existentialism; selected papers on logotherapy.* New York: Simon & Schuster.

Yamamoto, J., Silva, J. A., Ferrari, M., & Nukariya, K. (1997). *Culture and psychopathology.* In G. Johnson-Powell, J. Yamamoto, G. E. Wyatt, & W. Arroyo (Eds.), *Transcultural child development.* New York: John Wiley & Sons.

Yehuda, R., Marshall, R., Penkower, A., & Wong, C. M. (2002). Pharmocological treatments for posttraumatic stress disorder. In P. E. Nathan & J. M. Gorman (Eds.), *A guide to treatments that work* (2nd Ed., pp. 411–445). New York: Oxford University Press.

Yeschin, N. (2000). A new understanding of attention deficit hyperactivity disorder: Alternate concepts and interventions. *Journal of Child and Adolescent Social Work, 17,* 227–245.

Yonkers, K. A., & Gurguis, G. (1995). Gender differences in the prevalence and expression of anxiety disorders. In I. Al-Issa (Ed.), *Gender and psychopathology.* Washington, DC: American Psychiatric Press, Inc.

York, J., Nicholson, T., Minors, P., & Duncan, D. F. (1998). Stressful life events and loss of hair among adult women: A case-control study. *Psychological Reports, 82,* 1044–1046.

Young, D. A., Zakzanis, K, K., Bailey, C., Davila, R., et al. (1998). Further parameters of insight and neuropsychological deficit in schizophrenia and other chronic mental disease. *Journal of Nervous & Mental Disease, 186*(1), 44–50.

Young, J. E. (1990). *Cognitive therapy for personality disorders: A schema-focused approach.* Sarasota, FL: Practitioner's Resource Series, Professional Resource Exchange.

Young, R. M. (2001). Locating and relocating psychoanalytic ideas of sexuality. In C. Harding (Ed.), *Sexuality: Psychoanalytic perspectives* (p. ix, 201, 18–34). Philadelphia: Brunner-Routledge.

Young-Bruehl, E. (1996). *The anatomy of prejudice.* Cambridge: Harvard University Press.

Yuker, H., & Allison, D. (1994). Obesity: Sociocultural perspectives. In L. Alexander & D. Mott (Eds.), *Understanding eating disorders* (pp. 243–270). Washington, DC: Taylor & Francis.

Z

Zahn, T. P., Moraga, R., & Ray, W. J. (1996). Psychophysiological assessment of dissociative disorders. In L. K. Michelson & W. J. Ray (Eds.), *Handbook of dissociation: Theoretical, empirical, and clinical perspectives* (pp. 269–287). New York: Plenum Press.

Zahniser, J. H., Coursey, R. D., & Hershberger, K. (1991). Individual psychotherapy with schizophrenic outpatients in the public mental health system. *Hospital & Community Psychiatry, 42*(9), 906–913.

Zakzanis, K. K., & Hansen, K. T. (1998). Dopamine D$_2$ densities and the schizophrenic brain. *Schizophrenia Research, 32*(3), 201–206.

Zakzanis, K. K., Poulin, P., Hansen, K. T., & Jolic, D. (2000). Searching the schizophrenic brain for temporal lobe deficits: A systemic review and meta-analysis. *Psychological Medicine, 30*(3), 491–504.

Zakzanis, K. K., Troyer, A. K., Rich, J. B., & Heinrichs, W. (2000). Component analysis of verbal fluency in patients with schizophrenia. *Neuropsychiatry, Neuropsychology, & Behavioral Neurology: (Special Issue), 13*(4), 239–245.

Zaleman, S. (Ed.). (1995). Neural basis of psychopathology. In S. H. Koslow, D. L. Meinecke, I. I. Lederhendler, H. Khachaturian, et al. (Eds.), *The neuroscience of mental health: II—A report on neuroscience research—Status and potential for mental health and mental illness.* Rockville, MD: National Institute of Health, National Institute of Mental Health.

Zarate, R. (1999). Comorbidity between schizophrenia and anxiety disorders. *Dissertation Abstracts International: Section B: The Sciences & Engineering, 60*(6-B). Ann Arbor, MI: University Microfilms International.

Zaubler, T. S., & Katon, W. (1996). Panic disorder and medical comorbidity: A review of the medical and psychiatric literature. *Bulletin of the Menninger Clinic, 60*(2, suppl A), A12–A38.

Zerbe, K. J. (2001). The crucial role of psychodynamic understanding in the treatment of eating disorders. *Psychiatric Clinics of North America, 24,* 305–313.

Zernig, G., Saria, A., Kurz, M., & O'Malley, S. S. (Eds.). (2000). *Handbook of alcoholism.* Boca Raton, FL: CRC Press.

Zhimin, L., Weihua, Z., Zhi, L., Yue, M., et al. (2001). The use of psychoactive substances among adolescent students in an area in the south-west of China. *Addiction, 96*(2), 247–250.

Zhou, J. N., Hofman, M. A., Gooren, L. J. G., & Swaab, D. F. (1997). A sex difference in the human brain and its relation to transsexuality. *International Journal of Transgenderism (Special Issue) 1*(1).

Zigler, E., Styfco, J. C., & Gilman, E. (1993). The national Head Start program for disadvantaged preschoolers. In E. Zigler & S. J. Styfco (Eds.), *Head Start and beyond: A national plan for extended childhood intervention* (pp. 1–41). New Haven, CT: Yale University Press.

Zigler, R., & Holden, L. (1988). Family therapy for learning disabled and attention-deficit disordered children. *American Journal of Orthopsychiatry, 58,* 196–210.

Zigmond, A. (1999). Mental health legislation. *Psychiatric Bulletin, 23*(12), 750.

Zimmerman, M., & Coryell, W. (1989). The reliability of personality disorder diagnosis in a nonpatient sample. *Archives of General Psychiatry, 46,* 682–689.

Zucker, K. (1990). Gender identity disorders in children: Clinical descriptions and natural history. In *Clinical management of gender identity disorders in children and adults* The clinical practice series (pp. 3–23) Vol. 14. Washington, DC: American Psychiatric Press.

Zucker, K., & Blanchard, R. (1997). Transvestic fetishism: Psychopathology and theory. In D. Laws & W. O'Donohue (Eds.), *Sexual deviance: Theory, assessment, and treatment* (pp. 253–279). New York: Guilford Press.

Zucker, K., & Bradley, S. (1995). *Gender identity disorder and psychosexual problems in children and adolescents.* New York: Guilford Press.

Zucker, K., & Bradley, S. (2000). Gender identity disorder. In *Handbook of infant mental health* (2nd ed., pp. 412–424). New York: Guilford Press.

Zucker, K., Bradley, S., & Sanikhani, M. (1997). Sex differences in referral rates of children with gender identity disorder: Some hypotheses. *Journal of Abnormal Child Psychology, 25*(3), 217–227.

Zucker, R. A., Chermack, S. T., & Curran, G. M. (2000). Alcoholism: A life span perspective on etiology and course. *Handbook of developmental psychopathology* (2nd ed., pp. 569–587). New York: Kluwer Academic/Plenum Publishers.

Zucker, R. A., Kincaid, S. B., Fitzgerald, H. E., & Bingham, C. R. (1995). Alcohol schema acquisition in preschoolers: Differences between children of alcoholics and children of non-alcoholics. *Alcoholism: Clinical and Experimental Research, 19,* 1011–1017.

Zuckerman, M. (1991). One person's stress is another person's pleasure. In C. D. Spielberger, I. G. Sarason, Z. Kulczar, & G. L. Vantteck (Eds.). *Stress and emotion: Anxiety, anger and curiosity* (Vol. 14). New York: Hemisphere Publishing.

Zywiak, W., Longabaugh, R., & Wirtz, P. (2002). Decomposing the relationships between pretreatment social network characteristics and alcohol treatment outcome. *Journal of Studies on Alcohol, 63*(1), 114–121.

PHOTO CREDITS

Chapter 1

Opener (top): Alice Neel, "Mrs. Paul Gardner and Sam," 1967. ©Estate of Alice Neel. Courtesy Robert Miller Gallery, New York. Opener (bottom): Cynthia Macadams/Time Life Pictures/Getty Images. Page 4 (top): Cynthia Macadams/Time Life Pictures/Getty Images. Page 4 (center): Gene Shaw/TimePix/Getty Images. Page 4 (bottom left & right): ©AP/Wide World Photos. Page 8 (top): Corbis-Bettmann. Page 8 (bottom): Corbis Images. Page 9: Cameron/Corbis Images.

Chapter 2

Opener (top): Emil Nolde, "Still Life With Masks," 1911 ©Private Collection/Bridgeman Art Library International Ltd.. Opener (bottom): Gjon Lili/Time Life Pictures/Getty Images. Page 12: Gjon Lili/Time Life Pictures/Getty Images. Page 13: ©AP/Wide World Photos. Page 15 (left & right): Corbis-Bettmann. Page 16 (top): Courtesy Dr. Thomas Szasz. Page 16 (bottom): ©AP/Wide World Photos. Page 17: Photofest. Page 25: Courtesy of Jerome Wakfield, Ph.D.

Chapter 3

Opener (top): Arshile Gorky, "The Artist and His Mother," ca. 1926-1936. Oil on canvas (60x50 in.). Photo by Geoffrey Clement. Gift of Julien Levy for Maro and Natasha Gorky in memory of their father. ©1998: Whitney Museum of American Art, New York. ©2004 Artists Rights Society (ARS), New York. Opener (bottom): Gjon Mili/Time Warner Inc. Page 30 (top): Gjon Mili/Time Warner Inc. Page 30 (bottom): ©Science Museum/Heritage/The Image Works. Page 31: Corbis Images. Page 32 (left): ©Science Photo Library/Photo Researchers. Page 32 (right): Michal Heron/Corbis Images. Page 33 (left): Corbis-Bettmann. Page 33 (right): Erich Lessing/Art Resource. Page 34: Erich Lessing/Art Resource. Page 35: Courtesy of Elaine Showalter, Ph.D. Page 36: Jim WIlson/New York Times Pictures. Page 37: Steve Jennings/Corbis Images. Page 45: Bill Aron/PhotoEdit. Page 47: Myrleen Ferguson Cate/PhotoEdit. Page 51: ©AP/Wide World Photos. Page 53: Lief Skoogfors/Woodfin Camp & Associates. Page 58: ©AP/Wide World Photos. Page 60: Steve Rubin/The Image Works. Page 62: Frank Pedrick/The Image Works. Page 65: Pete Saloutos/Corbis Images. Page 68: Spencer Grant/PhotoEdit.

Chapter 4

Opener (top): Gabrielle Munter, "Sinnende," 1917. Courtesy Städtische Galerie im Lenbachhaus, Munich. Opener (bottom): ©Gabriele Münter- und Johannes Eichner-Stiftung, Munich. Courtesy Lenbachhaus, Munich. Page 74: ©Gabriele Münter- und Johannes Eichner-Stiftung, Munich. Courtesy Lenbachhaus, Munich. Page 75: Courtesy Jerry Marshall. Page 76 (top): AFP/Corbis Images. Page 76 (bottom): Richard T. Nowitz/Photo Researchers. Page 77: Corbis-Bettmann. Page 87: ©AP/Wide World Photos. Page 91: Science Photo Library/Photo Researchers. Pages 95 & 97: Laura Dwight Photography. Page 99: William Strode/Woodfin Camp & Associates, Inc. DC. Page 100: ©D. Silbersweig/Photo Researchers. Page 101: Dan McCoy/Rainbow/PictureQuest.

Chapter 5

Opener (top): Edvard Munch, "Seascape," 1899. ©Francis G. Meyer/Corbis ©2004 The Munch Museum/The Munch-Ellingston Group/Artists Rights Society (ARS), New York. Opener 110 (bottom): Roger Viollet/Getty Images News and Sport Services. Page 112: Roger Viollet/Getty Images News and Sport Services. Page 113 (top): David McNew/Newsmakers/Getty Images News and Sport Services. Page 113 (bottom): The Image Bank/Getty Images. Page 114: ©Monica Dalmasso/Photographer's Choice/Getty Images. Page 117: ©AP/Wide World Photos. Page 118: Kevin Vandivier/Stockphoto.com. Page 119: Photofest. Page 120: ©Pierre Perrin/Corbis Sygma. Page 122: ©AP/Wide World Photos. Page 124 (top): Ciniglio Lorenzo/Corbis Sygma. Page 124 (bottom): Stephen Jaffe/The Image Works. Page 128: Jeffrey Reed/Stockphoto.com. Page 129: ©Robert J. Ellison/Black Star Publishing/PictureQuest. Page 135: ©Michael Newman/PhotoEdit. Page 139: ©Bob Daemmrich/The Image Works. Page 141: George D. Lepp/Corbis Images. Page 144: ©Bill Aron/PhotoEdit.

Chapter 6

Opener (top): Emily Carr, "Forest, British Columbia," 1932, oil on canvas, Vancouver Art Gallery, Emily Carr Trust, VAG 42.3.9 (Photo: Trevor Mills). Opener (bottom): British Colombia Archives F-01220. Page 154 (top): Royal British Columbia Museum F-01220. Page 154 (bottom left): Jeff Greenberg/PhotoEdit. Page 154 (bottom right): ©Alan Oddie/PhotoEdit. Page 157: Corbis-Bettmann. Page 161 (top): ©AP/Wide World Photos. Page 161 (bottom): Photofest. Page 162: Robert Sherbow/Time Life Pictures/Getty Images. Page 163: Photofest. Page 165 (left): ©Les Stone/The Image Works. Page 165 (right): ©AP/Wide World Photos. Page 167: Corbis-Bettmann. Page 170 (top): ©Oscar Burriel/Science Photo Library/Photo Researchers,

Inc. Page 170 (bottom): ©Michael Newman/PhotoEdit. Page 171: ©Rob Crandall/The Image Works. Page 173: ©John Olschowka/Phototake. Page 175 (top): Walsall Art Gallery/Bridgeman Art Library/London. Page 175 (bottom left): ©Topham/The Image Works. Page 175 (bottom center): ©Corbis. Page 175 (bottom right): ©Rudolph Burckhardt/Corbis Sygma. Page 176: ©Bill Aron/PhotEdit. Page 177: ©James Wilson/Woodfin Camp & Associates. Page 179: ©Bill Aron/PhotoEdit. Page 183: ©Michael P. Gadomski/Photo Researchers, Inc. Page 188: ©G. Veggi/Photo Researchers, Inc.

Chapter 7

Opener (top): Joan Miro, "La Nuit", 1953. ©Marlborough Graphics, London, UK/Bridgeman Art Library International Ltd. ©2004 Successio Miro/Artists Rights Society (ARS), New York. Opener (bottom): Herbert List/Magnum Photos, Inc. Page 196 (top): Herbert List/Magnum Photos, Inc. Page 196 (bottom left): Roy Philippe/Photo Researchers. Page 196 (bottom right): Gilbert Iundt; TempSport/Corbis Images. Page 199: ©Photothé que R. Magritte-ADAGP/Art Resource. Page 200: Peter Sorel/Photofest. Page 201: Getty Images News and Sport Services. Page 202: Photofest. Page 203: ©AP/Wide World Photos. Page 204: Corbis-Bettmann. Page 205: From Cameron West, *First Person Plural: My Life as a Multiple, Hyperion,* 1999, p. 51. Page 207: Andrew Lichtenstein/Aurora Photos. Page 210: Robert Brenner/PhotoEdit. Page 211: ©AP/Wide World Photos. Page 213: Photofest. Page 214: Kathy Sloane/Photo Researchers. Page 217: Jonathan Nourok/PhotoEdit. Page 219: Corbis Images.

Chapter 8

Opener (top): Van Gogh, "Interiuer d'un Restaurant," 1887. ©Christie's Images. Opener (bottom): Topham/The Image Works. Page 226 (top): Topham/The Image Works. Page 226 (bottom left): ©Chet Gordon/The Image Works. Page 226 (bottom right): ©Anthony Edgeworth/Corbis. Pages 228 & 229: ©AP/Wide World Photos. Page 230: Custom Medical Stock Photo, Inc. Page 231: ©Reuters/Landov. Page 232: ©Keri Pickett/Time Life Pictures/Getty Images. Page 234: ©SW Production/Index Stock Imagery/PictureQuest. Page 235: ©Catherine Karnow/Woodfin Camp & Assocs. Page 237: ©AP/Wide World Photos. Page 238: ©Ian Osborne/Stone/Getty Images. Page 239 (top): ©A. Ramey/Woodfin Camp & Assocs. Page 242: ©David Young-Wolff/PhotoEdit. Page 248 (top left): ©Burstein Collection/Corbis. Page 248 (top center): Corbis-Bettmann. Page 248 (top right): ©Mitchell Garber/Corbis. Page 248 (bottom): ©Rachel Epstein/PhotoEdit. Page 249 (top & bottom): From Claude-Pierre, *The Secret Life of Eating Disorders,* Vintage Books, NY 1999, p. 64.

Chapter 9

Opener (top): Jean-Michel Basquiat, "Furious Man," 1982. Christie's Images. ©2004 Artists Rights Society (ARS), New York/ADAGP, Paris. Opener (bottom): Allen Ginsberg/Corbis Images. Page 256 (top): Allen Ginsberg/Corbis Images. Page 256 (bottom): ©AP/Wide World Photos. Page 257: ©AP/Wide World Photos. Page 258: ©George Ruhe/New York Times Pictures. Pages 259 & 261: ©David Young-Wolff/PhotoEdit. Page 265: ©Roger Ressmeyer/Corbis Images. Page 266: ©Kelly-Mooney Photography/Corbis. Page 268 (left): ©SPL/Photo Researchers, Inc. Page 268 (right): ©PhotoEdit. Page 269: ©Ted Wood/Stockphoto.com. Page 271: ©Sean Sexton Col-

lection/Corbis. Page 272: ©Bettmann/Corbis. Page 274: ©AP/Wide World Photos. Page 276: ©James Wilson/Woodfin Camp & Associates. Page 280: Minnie Evans (1892-1987)/Art Resource, ©Smithsonian American Art Museum, Washington, DC. Page 282: ©AP/Wide World Photos. Page 283: ©Topham/The Image Works. Page 284: ©Scott Barbour/Getty Images. Page 291: ©Tatiana Markow/Corbis Sygma. Page 293: ©A. Ramey/PhotoEdit. Page 294: ©James Leynse/Corbis SABA. Page 297: ©JohnBoykin/PhotoEdit.

Chapter 10

Opener (top): Duchamp, "Nude Descending a Staircase No. 2", 1912. ©Philadelphia Museum of Art, Philadelphia, PA/Bridgeman Art Library International, Ltd . ©2004 Artists Rights Society (ARS), New York/ADAGP, Paris/Succession Marcel Duchamp. Opener (bottom): Hulton Archive/Getty Images. Page 308: Hulton Archive/Getty Images. Page 310 (top): ©AP/Wide World Photos. Page 310 (bottom): ©Peter Yates/Corbis. Page 311: ©Réunion des Musées Nationaux/Art Resource/NY. Page 314 (bottom): ©Erich Lessing/Art Resource, NY. Page 319: ©Chuck Kennedy/Getty Images. Page 321: © Stephanie Welsh/Getty Images. Page 325: Tintoretto, "Susanna Bathing" (after 1560) ©Erich Lessing/Art Resource, NY. Page 326: ©Bill Aron/Photo Researchers, Inc. Page 327: ©AP/Wide World Photos. Page 328: ©Kerin Rochill/Stockphoto.com. Page 330: Robert Brenner/PhotoEdit. Page 337 (top): ©Michael Keller/Corbis. Page 337 (bottom left): ©AP/Wide World Photos. Page 337 (bottom right): ©Gaffney/Liaison/Getty Images. Page 338: ©George Tidemann/Time Life Pictures/Getty Images. 341 (top & bottom): Zucker, K. & Bradley, S. (1995). *Gender Identity disorder and psychosexual problems in children and adolescents.* New York: Guilford Press.

Chapter 11

Opener (top): Salvador Dali, "The Triangular House", 1933. ©Private Collection/Art Resource, NY. ©2003 Salvador Dali, Gala-Salvador Dali Foundation/Artists Rights Society (ARS), New York. Opener (bottom): ©George Karger/Time Life Pictures/Getty Images. Page 352: ©George Karger/Time Life Pictures/Getty Images. Page 353: ©Scott Roper/Corbis Images. Page 354: Dennis Brack/Stockphoto.com. Page 361: S. Grandadam/Alamy Images. Page 363 (top): ©AP/Wide World Photos. Page 363 (bottom): Tyrone Turner/Stockphoto.com. Pages 364, 367 & 370: Photofest. Page 371: Mimmo Jodice/Corbis Images. Page 372: ©Andrew Lichenstein/The Image Works. Page 373: Robert Landau/Corbis Images. Page 375: Bill Aron/PhotoEdit. Page 377: Touchstone/The Kobal Collection//The Picture Desk. Page 385 (top): ©Rudi Von Briel/PhotoEdit. Page 385 (bottom): Corbis Images. Page 386: ©AP/Wide World Photos. Page 387 (top): ©Chris Lisle/Corbis. Page 387 (bottom): Photofest. Page 389: ©AP/Wide World Photos.

Chapter 12

Opener (top): Henry Darger, "After M. Whurther Run Glandelinians Attack and Blow up Train Carrying Children to Refuge." Collection of the American Folk Art Museum, New York. Gift of Sam and Betsey Farber. ©Kiyoko Lerner. Photo by Gavin Ashworth, New York. P10.2000.1b. Opener (bottom): Karen Heyt, Techsetters, Inc. Page 394: Karen Heyt, Techsetters, Inc. Page 401: ©Burstein Collection/Corbis Images. Page 403 (top): Rene Magritte, "The False

Mirror," 1928. ©The Museum of Modern Art/Licensed by SCALA/Art Resource, NY. Page 403 (center): From S. Arietti, *Interpretation of Schizophrenia*, 2e, Basic Books, 1974. Page 403 (bottom): Pablo Picasso, "Violin and Fruit," 1913. The Philadelphia Museum of Art, The A. E. Gallatin Collection. ©2003 Estate of Pablo Picasso/Artists Rights Society (ARS), New York. Page 404: ©Michael Newman/PhotoEdit/PictureQuest. Page 405: ©Grunnitus Studios/Photo Researchers, Inc. Page 409: Alamy Images. Page 410: ©AP/Wide World Photos. Page 411: Jerry Cooke/Photo Researchers. Page 414: From Lieberman et al, *The American Journal of Psychiatry*, 1992, Copyright 1998, The American Psychiatric Association. Reprinted by permission. Page 416 (left): ©AP/Wide World Photos. Page 416 (right): ©Rudi Von Briel/Photoedit. Page 418: Courtesy of Monte S. Buchsbaum, M.D. Page 425 (left): ©AP/Wide World Photos. Page 425 (center): ©Bettmann/Corbis. Page 425 (right): ©Ronald Siemoneit/Corbis Sygma. Page 430: Photofest.

Chapter 13

Opener (top): Willem de Kooning, "Untitled, " 1950. ©Bridgeman Art Library International Ltd. ©2004 The Willem de Kooning Foundation/Artists Rights Society (ARS), New York. Opener (bottom): Christopher Felver/Corbis Images. Page 436 (top): Christopher Felver/Corbis Images. Page 436 (bottom): Austrian Archives/Corbis Images. Page 437 (left): Mary Kate Denny/PhotoEdit. Page 437 (right): Michael Newman/PhotoEdit. Page 438: Corbis-Bettmann. Page 439: Hulton Archive/Getty Images. Page 440: Elizabeth Crews/The Image Works. Page 441: Archives Charmet/Bridgeman Art Library/ London. Page 442: Laura Dwight/Laura Dwight Photography. Page 443: ©L. Willatt/East Anglian Regional Genetics Service/Photo

Researchers. Page 444: Stuart Cohen/The Image Works. Page 451: ©AP/Wide World Photos. Page 455: David Young-Wolff/PhotoEdit. Page 457: Myrleen Ferguson Cate/PhotoEdit. Page 468: Dennis MacDonald/PhotoEdit. Page 469: Michael Newman/PhotoEdit. Page 478: ©Laura Dwight Photography. Page 480 (bottom): ISM/Phototake. Pages 481 & 482: ©AP/Wide World Photos. Page 482: ©AP/Wide World Photos. Page 483 (bottom): Acey Harper/Time Inc. Picture Collection.

Chapter 14

Opener (top): Picasso, "Melancholy Woman", 1902. Bridgeman Art Library/ London. ©2004 Estate of Pablo Picasso/Artists Rights Society (ARS), New York. Opener (bottom): Hulton-Deutch Collection/Corbis Images. Page 488 (top): Hulton-Deutch Collection/Corbis Images. Page 488 (bottom): ©AP/Wide World Photos. Page 491 (top left): Hattie Young/Photo Researchers. Page 491 (top right): Michael Newman/PhotoEdit. Page 491 (bottom): ©AP/Wide World Photos. Page 492 (top): Steven Rubin/The Image Works. Page 492 (bottom): ©AP/Wide World Photos. Page 496: Jean Claude Revy/Phototake. Page 499 (left): Kathy McLaughlin/The Image Works. Page 499 (right): Palmer Hayden, "He Laid Down His Hammer and Cried," 1944-1947. Museum of African American Art. Page 500: Jose Luis Pelaez/Corbis Images. Page 502: Jeff Greenberg/PhotoEdit. Page 503 (left): Courtesy of James Pannebaker, Ph.D. Page 503 (right): Courtesy of Joshua Smyth, Ph.D. Page 504: Tom McCarthy/PhotoEdit. Page 505: Photofest. Page 507: Mary Evans Picture Library. Page 509: REX USA Ltd. Pages 514 & 516: ©AP/Wide World Photos. Page 519: Tom McCarthy/Unicorn Stock Photos.

QUOTATION AND ILLUSTRATION CREDITS

Chapter 2

Table 2.2, pp. 20–21, adapted from DSM-IV by *The New York Times,* December 6, 1995. Reprinted with permission from the *Diagnostic and Statistical Manual of Mental Disorders, Fourth Edition, Text Revision.* Copyright 2000, American Psychiatric Association. Also copyright © 1995 by The New York Times Co. Reprinted with permission.

Excerpts, p. 24, reprinted with permission from pp. xxx, xxxi of the *Diagnostic and Statistical Manual of Mental Disorders, Fourth Edition, Text Revision.* Copyright 2000, American Psychiatric Association.

Figure 2.1, p. 26, from Kessler, R. C., McGonagle, K. A., Zhao, S., Nelson, C. B. et al. (1994). Lifetime and 12-month prevalence of DSM-III psychiatric disorders in the United States: Results from the National Comorbitidy Study. *Archives of General Psychiatry, 51*(1), 8–19. Copyrighted 1994, American Medical Association. Reprinted by permission.

Chapter 3

Table 3.2, p. 47, adapted from Plante, T. (1999). *Contemporary clinical psychology* (p. 63). Copyright © 1999 by John Wiley & Sons. This material is used by permission of John Wiley & Sons.

Box 3.4, p. 48, from Raskin, N., & Rogers, C. (2000). Person centered therapy. In R. Corsini & D. Wedding (Eds.), *Current psychotherapies* (6th ed., pp. 149–150). Itasca, IL: Peacock Publishers. © 2000. Reprinted with permission of Wadsworth, a division of Thomson Learning: www.thomsonrights.com. Fax 800-730-2215.

Box 3.5, p. 55, quotation from Clark, D. M. (1989). Anxiety states. In K. Hawton, P. M. Salkovskis, J. Kirk, & D. M. Clark (Eds.), *Cognitive behaviour therapy for psychiatric problems* (pp. 76–77). New York: Oxford Medical Publications. By permission of Oxford University Press.

Figure 3.3, p. 56, © Windy Dryden & Jane Walker, 1992; revised by Albert Ellis, 1996. Reprinted by permission of Professor Dryden.

Table 3.3, p. 61, adapted from Plante, T. (1999). *Contemporary clinical psychology* (p. 66). Copyright © 1999 by John Wiley & Sons. This material is used by permission of John Wiley & Sons.

Figure 3.4, p. 62, from Kaslow, N., & Celano, M. (1995). The family therapies. In A. Gurman & S. Messer, *Essential psychotherapies* (p. 369). Reprinted by permission of Guilford Publications, Inc.

Chapter 4

Box 4.2, p. 79, excerpted from McHugh, P. R. (1999, December). How psychiatry lost its way. *Commentary, 108*(5), 32–33. Reprinted from *Commentary,* December 1999, by permission of the publisher and the author; all rights reserved.

Table 4.3, p. 80, reprinted with permission from the *Diagnostic and Statistical Manual of Mental Disorders, Third Edition.* Copyright 1980, American Psychiatric Association.

Table 4.4, p. 81, reprinted with permission from the *Diagnostic and Statistical Manual of Mental Disorders, Fourth Edition, Text Revision.* Copyright 2000, American Psychiatric Association.

Table 4.5, p. 82, reprinted with permission from the *Diagnostic and Statistical Manual of Mental Disorders, Third Edition*, pp. 470–471. Copyright 1980, American Psychiatric Association.

Box 4.3, p. 84, from McWilliams, N. (1994). *Psychoanalytic diagnosis: Understanding personality structure in the clinical process* (p. 92). Reprinted by permission of Guilford Publications, Inc.

Table 4.7, p. 88, reprinted with permission from the *Diagnostic and Statistical Manual of Mental Disorders, Fourth Edition, Text Revision.* Copyright 2000, American Psychiatric Association.

Table 4.8, p. 89, reprinted with permission from the *Diagnostic and Statistical Manual of Mental Disorders, Fourth Edition, Text Revision.* Copyright 2000, American Psychiatric Association.

Table 4.9, p. 93, from *Beck Depression Inventory: Second Edition.* Copyright © 1996 by Aaron T. Beck. Reproduced by permission of the publisher, Harcourt Assessment, Inc. All rights reserved. "Beck Depression Inventory" and "BDI" are trademarks of Harcourt Assessment, Inc., registered in the United States of America and/or other jurisdictions.

Table 4.10, p. 94, from MMPI-2™ (Minnesota Multiphasic Personality Inventory-2)™ Manual for Administration, Scoring, and Interpretation, Revised Edition. Copyright © 2001 by the Regents of the University of Minnesota. Used by permission of the University of Minnesota Press. All rights reserved. "MMPI-2" and "Minnesota Multiphasic Personality-2" are trademarks owned by the Regents of the University of Minnesota.

Box 4.5, p. 100, from Goode, E. (2002, December 11). Brain imaging may detect schizophrenia in early stages. *The New York Times.* Copyright © 2002 by The New York Times Co. Reprinted with permission.

Table 4.11, p. 102, from C. Keith Conners, Ph.D., *Conners' Teacher Rating Scale - Revised (L)*. Copyright © 1997, Multi-Health Systems Inc. All rights reserved. In the USA, P.O. Box 950, North Tonawanda, NY 14120-0950, 1-800-456-3003. In Canada, 3770 Victoria Park Ave., Toronto, ON M2H 3M6, 1-800-268-6011. Internationally, +1-416-492-2627. Fax, +1-416-492-3343. Reproduced with permission.

Chapter 5

Table 5.2, p. 115, adapted with permission from the *Diagnostic and Statistical Manual of Mental Disorders, Fourth Edition, Text Revision*. Copyright 2000, American Psychiatric Association.

Table 5.3, p. 115, adapted with permission from the *Diagnostic and Statistical Manual of Mental Disorders, Fourth Edition, Text Revision*. Copyright 2000, American Psychiatric Association.

Table 5.4, p. 116, adapted with permission from the *Diagnostic and Statistical Manual of Mental Disorders, Fourth Edition, Text Revision*. Copyright 2000, American Psychiatric Association.

Figure 5.1, p. 117, adapted from Wells, A. (1997). *Cognitive therapy of anxiety disorders: A practice manual and conceptual guide* (p. 105). Chichester, UK: Wiley. Copyright 1997, © John Wiley & Sons Limited. Reproduced with permission.

Table 5.5, p. 118, adapted with permission from the *Diagnostic and Statistical Manual of Mental Disorders, Fourth Edition, Text Revision*. Copyright 2000, American Psychiatric Association.

Table 5.6, p. 120, adapted with permission from the *Diagnostic and Statistical Manual of Mental Disorders, Fourth Edition, Text Revision*. Copyright 2000, American Psychiatric Association.

Box 5.3, p. 121, from Wilensky, A. (1999). *Passing for normal: A memoir of compulsion* (pp. 88–91). New York: Broadway Books. Copyright © 1999 by Amy S. Wilensky. Used by permission of Broadway Books, a division of Random House, Inc.

Table 5.7, p. 123, adapted with permission from the *Diagnostic and Statistical Manual of Mental Disorders, Fourth Edition, Text Revision*. Copyright 2000, American Psychiatric Association.

Figure 5.2, p. 125, adapted from Brown, T. A. (1996). Validity of the DSM-III-R and DSM-IV classification systems for anxiety disorders. In R. M. Rapee (Ed.), *Current controversies in the anxiety disorders* (p. 26). Reprinted by permission of Guilford Publications, Inc.

Figure 5.3, p. 130, adapted from Goode, E. (2001, November 20). Treatment can ease the lingering trauma of Sept. 11. *The New York Times* (p. D1). Copyright © 2001 by The New York Times Co. Reprinted with permission.

Excerpt, p. 135, from Goode, E. (2001, November 20). Treatment can ease the lingering trauma of Sept. 11. *The New York Times* (pp. D1, D6). Copyright © 2001 by The New York Times Co. Reprinted with permission.

Table 5.9, p. 138, reprinted by permission of Kluwer Academic Publishers from Freeman, A., Pretzer, B., Fleming, B., & Simon, K. M. (1990). *Clinical applications of cognitive therapy* (p. 5). New York: Plenum Press.

Excerpt, pp. 139–140, from Wells, A. (1997). *Cognitive therapy of anxiety disorders: A practice manual and conceptual guide* (pp.

69–70). Copyright 1997, © John Wiley & Sons Limited. Reproduced with permission.

Excerpts, p. 147, reprinted by permission from Abend, S. M. (1996). Psychoanalytic psychotherapy. In C. Lindemann (Ed.), *Handbook of the treatment of anxiety disorders* (pp. 407–408). Northvale, NJ: Jason Aronson. Jason Aronson is part of the Rowman & Littlefield Publishing Group.

Chapter 6

Table 6.1, p. 157, adapted with permission from the *Diagnostic and Statistical Manual of Mental Disorders, Fourth Edition, Text Revision*. Copyright 2000, American Psychiatric Association.

Table 6.2, p. 158, adapted with permission from the *Diagnostic and Statistical Manual of Mental Disorders, Fourth Edition, Text Revision*. Copyright 2000, American Psychiatric Association.

Figure 6.1, p. 159, from Jamison, K. R. (1999). *Night falls fast: Understanding suicide* (p. 101). New York: Knopf.

Box 6.1, p. 160, excerpts from Jamison, K. R. (1999). *Night falls fast: Understanding suicide* (pp. 94–97). New York: Knopf.

Table 6.3, p. 162, adapted with permission from the *Diagnostic and Statistical Manual of Mental Disorders, Fourth Edition, Text Revision*. Copyright 2000, American Psychiatric Association.

Excerpts, p. 162, from Jamison, K. R. (1995). *An unquiet mind: A memoir of moods and madness* (pp. 71–74). New York: Vintage Books.

Excerpt, p. 163, from Jamison, K. R. (1995). *An unquiet mind: A memoir of moods and madness* (pp. 79–80). New York: Vintage Books.

Table 6.4, p. 163, adapted with permission from the *Diagnostic and Statistical Manual of Mental Disorders, Fourth Edition, Text Revision*. Copyright 2000, American Psychiatric Association.

Table 6.5, p. 164, adapted with permission from the *Diagnostic and Statistical Manual of Mental Disorders, Fourth Edition, Text Revision*. Copyright 2000, American Psychiatric Association.

Table 6.6, p. 166, adapted with permission from the *Diagnostic and Statistical Manual of Mental Disorders, Fourth Edition, Text Revision*. Copyright 2000, American Psychiatric Association.

Figure 6.3, p. 183, adapted from Lewinsohn, P. M., Gotlib, I. H., & Hautzinger, M. (1998). Behavioral treatment of unipolar depression. In V. E. Caballo (Ed.), *International handbook of cognitive and behavioural treatments for psychological disorders* (p. 445). Oxford: Elsevier Science. Copyright 1998, with permission from Elsevier. Also Lewinsohn, P. M., Hoberman, H., Teri, L., & Hautzinger, M. (1985). An integrative theory of depression. In S. Reiss and R. Bootzin (Eds.), *Theoretical issues in behavior therapy*. New York: Academic Press.

Table 6.13, p. 190, adapted from Basco, M. R., & Thase, M. E. (1998). Cognitive-behavioral treatment of bipolar disorder. In V. E. Caballo (Ed.), *International handbook of cognitive and behavioural treatments for psychological disorders* (p. 537). Oxford: Elsevier Science. Copyright 1998, with permission from Elsevier. Also adapted from Basco, M. R., & Rush, A. J. (1996). *Cognitive-behavioral therapy for bipolar disorder*. Reprinted by permission of Guilford Publications, Inc.

Chapter 7

Table 7.1, p. 198, adapted with permission from the *Diagnostic and Statistical Manual of Mental Disorders, Fourth Edition, Text Revision.* Copyright 2000, American Psychiatric Association. Prevalence data from Ross, C. A. (1996). History, phenomenology, and epidemiology of dissociation. In L. K. Michelson & W. J. Ray (Eds.), *Handbook of dissociation: Theoretical, empirical, and clinical perspectives* (pp. 3–24). New York: Plenum Press.

Table 7.2, p. 199, adapted with permission from the *Diagnostic and Statistical Manual of Mental Disorders, Fourth Edition, Text Revision.* Copyright 2000, American Psychiatric Association.

Table 7.3, p. 199, adapted with permission from the *Diagnostic and Statistical Manual of Mental Disorders, Fourth Edition, Text Revision.* Copyright 2000, American Psychiatric Association.

Table 7.4, p. 200, adapted by permission of Kluwer Academic Publishers from Loewenstein, R. J. (1996). Dissociative amnesia and dissociative future. In L. K. Michelson & W. J. Ray (Eds.), *Handbook of dissociation: Theoretical, empirical, and clinical perspectives* (Table 3, p. 310). New York: Plenum Press. Originally from (1) Lowenstein, R. J. (1991a). An office mental status examination for chronic complex dissociative symptoms and multiple personality disorder. *Psychiatric Clinics of North America, 14,* 567–604. (2) Lowenstein, R. J. (1991b). Psychogenic amnesia and psychogenic fugue: A comprehensive review. In A. Tasman & S. Goldfinger (Eds.), *American Psychiatric Press annual review of psychiatry* (Vol. 10, pp. 189–222). Washington, DC: American Psychiatric Press. (3) Steinberg, M. (1993). *The structured clinical interview for DSM-III-R dissociative disorders (SCID-D).* Washington, DC: American Psychiatric Press. (4) Steinberg, M. (1994). *The structured clinical interview for DSM-III-R dissociative disorders-revised (SCID-D-R).* Washington, DC: American Psychiatric Press.

Table 7.5, p. 202, adapted with permission from the *Diagnostic and Statistical Manual of Mental Disorders, Fourth Edition, Text Revision.* Copyright 2000, American Psychiatric Association.

Table 7.6, p. 203, adapted with permission from the *Diagnostic and Statistical Manual of Mental Disorders, Fourth Edition, Text Revision.* Copyright 2000, American Psychiatric Association.

Excerpt, pp. 203–204, from Muller, R. J. (November 1998). A patient with dissociative identity disorder "switches" in the emergency room. *Psychiatric Times, 15,* Issue 11. Copyright © 1998 by CMP Media LLC, 600 Community Drive, Manhasset, NY 11030, USA. Reprinted from *Psychiatric Times* with permission. www.psychiatrictimes.com/p981107.html

Box 7.2, p. 205, from West, C. (1999). *First person plural: My life as a multiple.* New York: Hyperion, pp. vii–viii. Copyright © 1999 Cameron West. Reprinted by permission of Hyperion.

Figure 7.1, p. 206, from Lewis, D. O, Yeager, C. A., Swica, Y, Pincus, J. H., & Lewis, M. (1997). Objective documentation of child abuse and dissociation in 12 murderers with dissociative identity disorder. *American Journal of Psychiatry, 154,* 1706. Reprinted with permission from the *American Journal of Psychiatry.* Copyright 1997, American Psychiatric Association.

Table 7.7, p. 209, adapted from Gleaves, D. H. (1996). The sociocognitive model of dissociative identity disorder: A reexamination of the evidence. *Psychological Bulletin, 120,* 53. Copyright © 1996 by the American Psychological Association. Adapted with permission of the publisher and the author.

Chapter 8

Table 8.1, p. 228, adapted with permission from the *Diagnostic and Statistical Manual of Mental Disorders, Fourth Edition, Text Revision.* Copyright 2000, American Psychiatric Association. Prevalence data from same source and from Shisslak, C.M., Crago, M., & Estes, L.S. (1995). The spectrum of eating disorders. *International Journal of Eating Disorders, 18,* 209–219.

Table 8.2, p. 229, adapted with permission from the *Diagnostic and Statistical Manual of Mental Disorders, Fourth Edition, Text Revision.* Copyright 2000, American Psychiatric Association.

Table 8.3, p. 230, adapted with permission from the *Diagnostic and Statistical Manual of Mental Disorders, Fourth Edition, Text Revision.* Copyright 2000, American Psychiatric Association.

Box 8.1, p. 232, from Hornbacher, M. (1998). *Wasted: A memoir of anorexia and bulimia* (pp. 108–109). New York: HarperCollins. Copyright © 1998 by Marya Hornbacher-Beard. Reprinted by permission of HarperCollins Publishers Inc.

Figure 8.1, p. 233, from Treasure, J. & Szmukler, G. (1995). Medical complications of anorexia nervosa. In G. Szmukler, C. Dare, & J. Treasure (Eds.), *Handbook of eating disorders: Theory, treatment and research* (Figures 11.1 and 11.2, pp. 198, 199). Chichester, UK: Wiley. Copyright 1995, © John Wiley & Sons Limited. Reproduced with permission.

Table 8.5, p. 236, from Johnson, C., Powers, P. S., & Dick, R. (1999). Athletes and eating disorders: The National Collegiate Athletic Association Study. *International Journal of Eating Disorders, 26*(2), Tables 2 and 3, 182. Copyright © 1999 John Wiley & Sons. This material is used by permission of Wiley-Liss, Inc., a subsidiary of John Wiley & Sons, Inc.

Excerpts, pp. 240–241, reprinted from Zerbe, K. J. (2001). The crucial role of psychodynamic understanding in the treatment of eating disorders. *Psychiatric Clinics of North America, 24,* 310–311. Copyright 2001, with permission from Elsevier.

Excerpts, p. 242, from Colahan, M. & Senior, R. (1995). Family patterns in eating disorders: Going round in circles, getting nowhere fast. In G. Szmukler, C. Dare, & J. Treasure (Eds.), *Handbook of eating disorders: Theory, treatment and research* (p. 250). Chichester, UK: Wiley. Copyright 1995, © John Wiley & Sons Limited. Reproduced with permission.

Table 8.6, p. 244, from De Silva, P. (1995). Cognitive-behavioural models of eating disorders. In G. Szmukler, C. Dare, & J. Treasure (Eds.), *Handbook of eating disorders: Theory, treatment and research* (p. 145). Chichester, UK: Wiley. Copyright 1995, © John Wiley & Sons Limited. Reproduced with permission.

Figure 8.2, p. 245, adapted from De Silva, P. (1995). Cognitive-behavioural models of eating disorders. In G. Szmukler, C. Dare, & J. Treasure (Eds.), *Handbook of eating disorders: Theory, treatment and research* (pp. 148–149). Chichester, UK: Wiley. Copyright 1995, © John Wiley & Sons Limited. Reproduced with permission.

Table 8.8, p. 246, adapted from Freeman, C. (1995). Cognitive therapy. In G. Szmukler, C. Dare, & J. Treasure (Eds.), *Handbook of eating disorders: Theory, treatment and research* (p. 321). Chichester, UK: Wiley. Copyright 1995, © John Wiley & Sons Limited. Reproduced with permission.

Chapter 9

Table 9.1, p. 257, adapted from Anthony, J., & Arria, A. (1999). Epidemiology of substance abuse in adulthood. In P. Ott, R. Tarter, & R. Ammerman, *Sourcebook on substance abuse: Etiology, epidemiology, assessment, and treatment* (p. 34). Published by Allyn and Bacon, Boston, MA. Copyright © 1999 by Pearson Education. Adapted by permission of the publisher. Dependence data from Kessler, R. C., McGonagle, K. A., Zhao, S., Nelson, C. B., Hughes, M. Eshleman, S., Wittshen, N. U., & Kendler, K. S. (1994). Lifetime and 12 month prevalence of DSM-III-R psychiatric disorders in the United States results from the National Comorbidity Survey. *Archives of General Psychiatry, 51,* 8–19.

Box 9.1, p. 258, from Flaherty, J. (2001, May 9). At Amherst, the day the urns went dry. *The New York Times.* Copyright © 2001 by The New York Times Co. Reprinted with permission.

Table 9.3, p. 261, adapted with permission from the *Diagnostic and Statistical Manual of Mental Disorders, Fourth Edition, Text Revision.* Copyright 2000, American Psychiatric Association.

Table 9.4, p. 261, adapted with permission from the *Diagnostic and Statistical Manual of Mental Disorders, Fourth Edition, Text Revision.* Copyright 2000, American Psychiatric Association.

Table 9.5, pp. 262–263, from Ray, O. & Ksir, C. (2002). *Drugs, society and human behavior* (9th ed., inside cover). Boston: McGraw-Hill. Reproduced with permission of The McGraw-Hill Companies.

Box 9.2, p. 265, from Davis, P. (2001, May 7). Dope: A love story. *Time* (p. 91). Reprinted by permission of the author, Patti Davis.

Table 9.7, p. 267, from Ray, O. & Ksir, C. (2002). *Drugs, society and human behavior* (9th ed., pp. 254, 255). Boston: McGraw-Hill. Reproduced with permission of The McGraw-Hill Companies.

Table 9.8, p. 268, from Ray, O. & Ksir, C. (2002). *Drugs, society and human behavior* (9th ed., p. 256). Boston: McGraw-Hill. Reproduced with permission of The McGraw-Hill Companies.

Table 9.9, p. 270, from Ray, O. & Ksir, C. (2002). *Drugs, society and human behavior* (9th ed., p. 208). Boston: McGraw-Hill. Reproduced with permission of The McGraw-Hill Companies.

Figure 9.1, p. 272, copyright © 1999. From McDowell, D. & Spitz, H. (1999). *Substance abuse: From principles to practice* (p. 23). Philadelphia: Brunner/Mazel. Reproduced by permission of Routledge/Taylor & Francis Books, Inc.

Table 9.10, p. 273, from Kerfoot, Sakoulas, & Hyman (1996). In L. Friedman, N. Fleming, D. Roberts, & S. E. Hyman (Eds.), *Source book of substance abuse and addiction* (p. 158). Baltimore: Williams & Wilkins. Reprinted by permission of Lippincott Williams & Wilkins.

Figure 9.2, p. 276, from Ray, O. & Ksir, C. (2002). *Drugs, society and human behavior* (9th ed., p. 308). Boston: McGraw-Hill. Reproduced with permission of The McGraw-Hill Companies.

Table 9.11, pp. 277–278, from Ray, O. & Ksir, C. (2002). *Drugs, society and human behavior* (9th ed., pp. 337, 340). Boston: McGraw-Hill. Reproduced with permission of The McGraw-Hill Companies.

Box 9.3, p. 288, from Satel, S. L. (1998, April 4). Don't forget the addict's role in addiction. *The New York Times* (Op-Ed page). Copyright © 1998 by The New York Times Co. Reprinted with permission.

Table 9.12, p. 291, from Robson, P. (1999). *Forbidden drugs* (2nd ed., p. 28). Oxford University Press. Originally from Vaillant, G. V. (1988). What can long-term followup teach us about relapse and prevention of relapse in addiction? *British Journal of Addiction, 83,* 1147–1157. Reprinted by permission of the publisher, Blackwell Publishing Ltd.

Table 9.13, p. 298, is reprinted with permission of Alcoholics Anonymous World Services, Inc. (A.A.W.S.). Permission to reprint the Twelve Steps does not mean that A.A.W.S. has reviewed or approved the contents of this publication, or that A.A.W.S. necessarily agrees with the views expressed herein. A.A. is a program of recovery from alcoholism only—use of the Twelve Steps in connection with programs and activities which are patterned after A.A., but which address other problems, or in any other non-A.A. context, does not imply otherwise.

Excerpt, p. 302–303, quoted in Ray, O. & Ksir, C. (2002). *Drugs, society and human behavior* (9th ed., p. 337). Boston: McGraw-Hill. Reproduced with permission of The McGraw-Hill Companies.

Excerpt, p. 305, from Ray, O. & Ksir, C. (2002). *Drugs, society and human behavior* (9th ed., p. 407). Boston: McGraw-Hill. Reproduced with permission of The McGraw-Hill Companies.

Chapter 10

Box 10.1, p. 312, from Boxer, S. (2001, June 9). Yes, but did anyone ask the animals' opinion? *The New York Times,* Think Tank. Copyright © 2001 by The New York Times Co. Reprinted with permission.

Figure 10.2, p. 316, adapted from Masters, W. H., & Johnson, V. E. (1966). *Human sexual response* (Figures 1-1 and 1-2, p. 5). Boston: Little, Brown. Copyright 1966; reprinted by permission of Lippincott Williams & Wilkins.

Table 10.1, p. 317, adapted with permission from the *Diagnostic and Statistical Manual of Mental Disorders, Fourth Edition, Text Revision.* Copyright 2000, American Psychiatric Association.

Table 10.2, p. 318, adapted from Drugs that can influence sexual dysfunction: An update (1992). *Medical Letter on Drugs and Therapeutics, 34*(876), 74–76. Reproduced with special permission from The Medical Letter.

Table 10.3, p. 322, adapted with permission from the *Diagnostic and Statistical Manual of Mental Disorders, Fourth Edition, Text Revision.* Copyright 2000, American Psychiatric Association.

Box 10.2, p. 327, from Marin, R., with Joseph, N. (1998, January 5). Lick me, flog me, buy me! *Newsweek* (p. 85). © 1998 Newsweek, Inc. All rights reserved. Reprinted by permission.

Box 10.3, p. 329, excerpted by permission of the author from Merkin, D. (1996, February 26 and March 4). Unlikely obsession: Confronting a taboo. *The New Yorker* (pp. 112–113, 115).

Table 10.5, p. 331, adapted from Milner & Dopke (1997). In D. Laws & W. O'Donohue, *Sexual deviance: Theory, assessment and treatment* (p. 398). Reprinted by permission of Guilford Publications, Inc.

Table 10.6, p. 336, from Bradford, J. (1997). Medical interventions in sexual deviance, In D. Laws & W. O'Donohue, *Sexual deviance: Theory, assessment, and treatment* (p. 451). Reprinted by permission of Guilford Publications, Inc.

Table 10.7, p. 337, adapted with permission from the *Diagnostic and Statistical Manual of Mental Disorders, Fourth Edition, Text Revision.* Copyright 2000, American Psychiatric Association.

Box 10.4, pp. 338–339, from El-Bashir, T. (1998, May 17). Auto racing: Driver with sex change finds her career stalled. *The New York Times.* Copyright © 1998 by The New York Times Co. Reprinted with permission.

Table 10.8, p. 340, from Zucker, K., Bradley, S., Sullivan, C., Kuskis, M., Birkenfield-Adams, A., & Mitchell, J. (1993). A gender identity interview for children. *Journal of Personality Assessment 61,* 448. Copyright 1993 by Lawrence Erlbaum Associates. Reprinted by permission.

Box 10.5, p. 346, from Sex-change coverage to San Francisco workers (2001, February 18). *The New York Times.* Reprinted with permission of The Associated Press.

Chapter 11

Table 11.1, p. 354, adapted with permission from the *Diagnostic and Statistical Manual of Mental Disorders, Fourth Edition, Text Revision.* Copyright 2000, American Psychiatric Association. Prevalence data from same source and from Torgersen, S., Kringlen, E., & Cramer, V. (2001). The prevalence of personality disorders in a community sample. *Archives of General Psychiatry, 58,* 590–596.

Table 11.2, p. 355, adapted with permission from the *Diagnostic and Statistical Manual of Mental Disorders, Fourth Edition, Text Revision.* Copyright 2000, American Psychiatric Association.

Figure 11.1, p. 356, adapted by permission of Kluwer Academic Publishers from Freeman, A., Pretzer, J., Fleming, B., & Simon, K. M. (1990). *Clinical applications of cognitive therapy* (p. 161). New York: Plenum Press.

Text excerpt, p. 357, reprinted by permission of Kluwer Academic Publishers from Freeman, A., Pretzer, J., Fleming, B., & Simon, K. M. (1990). *Clinical applications of cognitive therapy* (p. 168). New York: Plenum Press.

Table 11.3, p. 358, adapted with permission from the *Diagnostic and Statistical Manual of Mental Disorders, Fourth Edition, Text Revision.* Copyright 2000, American Psychiatric Association.

Table 11.4, p. 360, adapted with permission from the *Diagnostic and Statistical Manual of Mental Disorders, Fourth Edition, Text Revision.* Copyright 2000, American Psychiatric Association.

Table 11.5, p. 362, adapted with permission from the *Diagnostic and Statistical Manual of Mental Disorders, Fourth Edition, Text Revision.* Copyright 2000, American Psychiatric Association.

Table 11.6, p. 365, adapted with permission from the *Diagnostic and Statistical Manual of Mental Disorders, Fourth Edition, Text Revision.* Copyright 2000, American Psychiatric Association.

Figure 11.2, p. 368, adapted by permission of Kluwer Academic Publishers from Freeman, A., Pretzer, J., Fleming, B., & Simon, K. M. (1990). *Clinical applications of cognitive therapy* (p. 199). New York: Plenum Press.

Table 11.7, p. 370, adapted with permission from the *Diagnostic and Statistical Manual of Mental Disorders, Fourth Edition, Text Revision.* Copyright 2000, American Psychiatric Association.

Table 11.8, p. 372, adapted with permission from the *Diagnostic and Statistical Manual of Mental Disorders, Fourth Edition, Text Revision.* Copyright 2000, American Psychiatric Association.

Table 11.9, p. 374, adapted with permission from the *Diagnostic and Statistical Manual of Mental Disorders, Fourth Edition, Text Revision.* Copyright 2000, American Psychiatric Association.

Table 11.10, p. 376, adapted with permission from the *Diagnostic and Statistical Manual of Mental Disorders, Fourth Edition, Text Revision.* Copyright 2000, American Psychiatric Association.

Table 11.11, p. 379, adapted with permission from the *Diagnostic and Statistical Manual of Mental Disorders, Fourth Edition, Text Revision.* Copyright 2000, American Psychiatric Association.

Excerpt, p. 380, from Beck, A. T., & Freeman, A. F. (1990). *Cognitive therapy of personality disorders* (p. 324). Reprinted by permission of Guilford Publications, Inc.

Table 11.13, p. 383, condensed from Beck, A. T., & Freeman, A. F. (1990). *Cognitive therapy of personality disorders* (pp. 54–55). New York: Guilford Press (with additions from Millon & Davis, 2000). Reprinted by permission of Guilford Publications, Inc.

Table 11.14, p. 384, adapted from Beck, A. T., & Freeman, A. F. (1990). *Cognitive therapy of personality disorders* (p. 12). Reprinted by permission of Guilford Publications, Inc.

Box 11.3, p. 389, excerpted from McFadden, R. D. (1996, May 26). From a child of promise to a Unabom suspect. *The New York Times* (pp. 12–13). Copyright © 1996 by The New York Times Co. Reprinted with permission.

Chapter 12

Excerpt, pp. 395–396, from McKenna, P. (2001). Chronic schizophrenia. In J. Lieberman & R. Murray (Eds.), *Comprehensive care of schizophrenia* (p. 169). Malden, MA: Martin Dunitz. Reprinted by permission of Taylor & Francis.

Box 12.1, p. 396, from Vonnegut, M. (1975). *The Eden Express* (pp. preface, 248, 265, 268, and unknown page number). Copyright © 1975 by Praeger Publishers, Inc. Used by permission of Dell Publishing, a division of Random House, Inc.

Figure 12.1, p. 397, from Gottesman, I. (1991). *Schizophrenia genesis: The origins of madness* (Figure 2, p. 32). New York: Freeman. © 1990 by Irving I. Gottesman. Reprinted by permission of Henry Holt and Company, LLC. Adapted from Kuriansky, J., Deming, E., & Gurland, B. (1974, April). On trends in the diagnosis of schizophrenia. *American Journal of Psychiatry, 131*(4), 403. Reprinted with permission from the *American Journal of Psychiatry.* Copyright 1974, American Psychiatric Association.

Table 12.1, p. 399, adapted with permission from the *Diagnostic and Statistical Manual of Mental Disorders, Fourth Edition, Text Revision.* Copyright 2000, American Psychiatric Association.

Excerpt, pp. 400–401, from McKenna, P. (2001). Chronic schizophrenia. In J. Lieberman & R. Murray (Eds.), *Comprehensive care of schizophrenia* (p. 171). Malden, MA: Martin Dunitz. Reprinted by permission of Taylor & Francis.

Excerpt, p. 401, quoted in Torrey, E. F. (2001). *Surviving schizophrenia* (p. 47). New York: HarperCollins. Copyright © 1983 by E. Fuller Torrey. Reprinted by permission of HarperCollins Publishers Inc.

Table 12.3, p. 402: First excerpt quoted in Torrey, E. F. (2001). *Surviving schizophrenia* (p. 47). New York: HarperCollins. Copyright © 1983 by E. Fuller Torrey. Reprinted by permission of HarperCollins Publishers Inc. Second excerpt "Sylvia Frumkin," quoted in Sheehan, S. (1982). *Is there no place on earth for me?* New York: Vintage. Third excerpt from McKenna, P. (2001). Chronic schizophrenia. In J. Lieberman & R. Murray (Eds.), *Comprehensive care of schizophrenia* (p. 171). Malden, MA: Martin Dunitz. Reprinted by permission of Taylor & Francis.

Box 12.3, p. 403, excerpts from Sass, L. (1992). *Madness and modernism* (pp. 4, 357). New York: Basic Books. Reprinted by permission of Copyright Clearance Center.

Excerpt, p. 404, quoted in Torrey, E. F. (2001). *Surviving schizophrenia* (p. 47). New York: HarperCollins. Copyright © 1983 by E. Fuller Torrey. Reprinted by permission of HarperCollins Publishers Inc.

Table 12.4, p. 404, adapted by permission of Lippincott Williams & Wilkins from Ho, B-C. & Andreason, N. (2001). Positive symptoms, negative symptoms and beyond. In A. Breier et al. (2001). *Current issues in the psychopharmacology of schizophrenia* (p. 411).

Table 12.5, p. 406, adapted with permission from the *Diagnostic and Statistical Manual of Mental Disorders, Fourth Edition, Text Revision.* Copyright 2000, American Psychiatric Association. Adaptation from Wyatt, R. (2001). Diagnosing schizophrenia. In J. Lieberman & R. Murray (Eds.), *Comprehensive care of schizophrenia.* London: Martin Dunitz Ltd.

Table 12.7, p. 409, from Gottesman, I. (1991). *Schizophrenia genesis: The origins of madness* (p. 78). New York: Freeman. © 1990 by Irving I. Gottesman. Reprinted by permission of Henry Holt and Company, LLC. After Goldberg, E., & Morrison, S. (1963). Schizophrenia and social class. *British Journal of Psychiatry, 109,* 787. Reprinted by permission of the Royal College of Psychiatrists.

Box 12.4, p. 412, from Fisher, D. B. (2001, August 19). We've been misled by the drug industry. *The Washington Post* (p. B03). Reprinted by permission of Daniel A. Fisher, Executive Director, National Empowerment Center, www.power2u.org

Table 12.8, p. 413, from Gottesman, I. (1991). *Schizophrenia genesis: The origins of madness* (p. 29). New York: Freeman. © 1990 by Irving I. Gottesman. Reprinted by permission of Henry Holt and Company, LLC.

Excerpt, p. 416, quoted in Torrey, E. F. (2001). *Surviving schizophrenia* (p. 37). New York: HarperCollins. Copyright © 1983 by E. Fuller Torrey. Reprinted by permission of HarperCollins Publishers Inc.

Figure 12.4, p. 418, from Gottesman, I. (1991). *Schizophrenia genesis: The origins of madness* (p. 96). New York: Freeman. © 1990 by Irving I. Gottesman. Reprinted by permission of Henry Holt and Company, LLC.

Figure 12.5, p. 419, adapted from Gottesman, I. (1991). *Schizophrenia genesis: The origins of madness* (p. 85). New York: Freeman. © 1990 by Irving I. Gottesman. Reprinted by permission of Henry Holt and Company, LLC.

Table 12.9, p. 420, adapted from Gottesman, I. (1991). *Schizophrenia genesis: The origins of madness* (p. 138). New York: Freeman. © 1990 by Irving I. Gottesman. Reprinted by permission of Henry Holt and Company, LLC.

Table 12.11, p. 424, adapted from Kemp, R. & David, A. (2001). Patient compliance. In J. Lieberman & R. Murray (Eds.), *Comprehensive care of schizophrenia* (p. 270). Malden, MA: Martin Dunitz. Reprinted by permission of Taylor & Francis.

Excerpt, p. 427, quoted in Torrey, E. F. (2001). *Surviving schizophrenia* (p. 36). New York: HarperCollins. Copyright © 1983 by E. Fuller Torrey. Reprinted by permission of HarperCollins Publishers Inc.

Figure 12.6, p. 429, adapted from Harding, C. M., & Keller, A. B. (1998). Social functioning and family interventions. In K. T. Mueser and N. Tarrier, *Handbook of social functioning in schizophrenia* (Figure 20.2). Published by Allyn and Bacon, Boston, MA. Copyright © 1998 by Pearson Education. Adapted by permission of the publisher.

Chapter 13

Table 13.1, p. 440, adapted with permission from the *Diagnostic and Statistical Manual of Mental Disorders, Fourth Edition, Text Revision.* Copyright 2000, American Psychiatric Association.

Table 13.2, p. 441, adapted with permission from the *Diagnostic and Statistical Manual of Mental Disorders, Fourth Edition, Text Revision.* Copyright 2000, American Psychiatric Association.

Table 13.3, p. 441, adapted with permission from the *Diagnostic and Statistical Manual of Mental Disorders, Fourth Edition, Text Revision.* Copyright 2000, American Psychiatric Association.

Table 13.4, p. 445, adapted with permission from the *Diagnostic and Statistical Manual of Mental Disorders, Fourth Edition, Text Revision.* Copyright 2000, American Psychiatric Association.

Figure 13.1, p. 447, from Gerber, A. (1993). *Language-related learning disabilities: Their nature and treatment* (p. 269). Baltimore: Paul H. Brookes, Inc. Reprinted by permission of the author.

Table 13.5, p.449, adapted with permission from the *Diagnostic and Statistical Manual of Mental Disorders, Fourth Edition, Text Revision.* Copyright 2000, American Psychiatric Association.

Box 13.1, p. 451, from Grandin, T. (1995). *Thinking in pictures and other reports from my life with autism* (pp. 20–36). Copyright © 1995 by Temple Grandin. Used by permission of Doubleday, a division of Random House, Inc.

Table 13.6, p. 455, adapted with permission from the *Diagnostic and Statistical Manual of Mental Disorders, Fourth Edition, Text Revision.* Copyright 2000, American Psychiatric Association.

Table 13.7, p. 459, adapted from *All about ADHD: The complete practical guide for classroom teachers* (p. 103), by L. Pfiffer, Ph.D. Copyright © 1996 by Dr. Linda Pfiffner. Reprinted by permission of Scholastic, Inc.

Table 13.8, p. 461, adapted with permission from the *Diagnostic and Statistical Manual of Mental Disorders, Fourth Edition, Text Revision.* Copyright 2000, American Psychiatric Association.

Table 13.9, p. 462, adapted with permission from the *Diagnostic and Statistical Manual of Mental Disorders, Fourth Edition, Text Revision.* Copyright 2000, American Psychiatric Association.

Table 13.10, p. 463, from Frick, P. J. (1998). Conduct disorders. In T. H. Ollendick & M. Hersen (Eds.), *Handbook of child psychopathology* (p. 224). New York: Plenum Press. Reprinted by permission of Kluwer Academic Publishers. The summary here is based on a review of the research in Frick, P. J. (1993). Childhood conduct problems in a family context. *School Psychology Review, 22*(3), 376–385.

Figure 13.4, p. 465, from Allen, J. P., Philliber, S., Herrling, S., & Kupermin, G. P. (1997). Preventing teen pregnancy and academic failure: Experimental evaluation of a developmentally based approach. *Child Development, 64,* 734 (Figure 1). Reprinted with permission of the Society for Research in Child Development.

Table 13.11, p. 468, adapted with permission from the *Diagnostic and Statistical Manual of Mental Disorders, Fourth Edition, Text Revision.* Copyright 2000, American Psychiatric Association.

Figure 13.5, p. 471, from Achenbach, T. M., & Rescorla, L. A. (2001). *Manual for the ASEBA School-Age Forms and Profiles* (p. 23). Burlington, VT: University of Vermont, Research Center for Children, Youth, and Families. Copyright by T. M. Achenbach. Reproduced by permission.

Table 13.12, p. 476, adapted with permission from the *Diagnostic and Statistical Manual of Mental Disorders, Fourth Edition, Text Revision.* Copyright 2000, American Psychiatric Association.

Table 13.13, p. 477, adapted with permission from the *Diagnostic and Statistical Manual of Mental Disorders, Fourth Edition, Text Revision.* Copyright 2000, American Psychiatric Association.

Box 13.3, p. 482, from Snyder, L. (2000). *Speaking our minds: Personal reflections from individuals with Alzheimer's* (pp. 63–64). New York: Freeman. Reprinted by permission of the author.

Chapter 14

Table 14.1, p. 490, adapted from Holmes, T. H. & Rahe, R. H. (1967). The social readjustment rating scale. *Journal of Psychosomatic Research, 11,* 213–218, copyright 1967, with permission from Elsevier.

Figure 14.2, p. 497, in Hugdahl, K. (1995). *Psychophysiology: The mind-body perspective* (Figure 10.2, p. 202). Cambridge: Harvard University Press. Adapted from Manuck, S. B., Kasprowicz, A. L., & Muldoon, M. (1990). Behaviorally-evoked cardiovascular reactivity and hypertension: Conceptual issues and potential associations.

Annals of Behavioral Medicine, 12(1), 17–29. Copyright 1990 by Lawrence Erlbaum Associates. Reprinted by permission.

Box 14.2, p. 503, excerpted from Murray, B. (2002, June). Writing to heal. *Monitor on Psychology, 33,* 54–55. Copyright © 2002 by the American Psychological Association. Reprinted with permission.

Figure 14.3, p. 504, adapted from Helgeson, V. S., Cohen, S., Schulz, R., Yasko, J. (2001). Group support interventions for people with cancer: Benefits and hazards. In A. Baum & B. L. Andersen (Eds.), *Psychosocial interventions for cancer* (p. 274). Washington, DC: American Psychological Association. Copyright © 2001 by the American Psychological Association. Adapted with permission of the publisher and the author.

Table 14.3, p. 505, from Wills, T. A. & Filer Fegan, M. (2001). Social networks and social support. In A. Baum, T. A. Revenson, & J. E. Singer (Eds.). *Handbook of health psychology* (p. 214). Mahwah, NJ: Lawrence Erlbaum Associates. Copyright 2001 by Lawrence Erlbaum Associates. Reprinted by permission.

Box 14.3, p. 507, excerpted from Seferian, E. G. (1997). Polymicrobial bacteremia: A presentation of Munchaeusen syndrome by proxy. *Clinical Pediatrics, 36,* 419, 420. Reprinted by permission of Westminster Publications.

Table 14.4, p. 508, adapted with permission from the *Diagnostic and Statistical Manual of Mental Disorders, Fourth Edition, Text Revision.* Copyright 2000, American Psychiatric Association.

Table 14.5, p. 509, adapted with permission from the *Diagnostic and Statistical Manual of Mental Disorders, Fourth Edition, Text Revision.* Copyright 2000, American Psychiatric Association.

Table 14.6, p. 510, adapted with permission from the *Diagnostic and Statistical Manual of Mental Disorders, Fourth Edition, Text Revision.* Copyright 2000, American Psychiatric Association.

Table 14.7, p. 512, adapted with permission from the *Diagnostic and Statistical Manual of Mental Disorders, Fourth Edition, Text Revision.* Copyright 2000, American Psychiatric Association.

Table 14.8, p. 512, adapted with permission from the *Diagnostic and Statistical Manual of Mental Disorders, Fourth Edition, Text Revision.* Copyright 2000, American Psychiatric Association.

Table 14.9, p. 513, adapted with permission from the *Diagnostic and Statistical Manual of Mental Disorders, Fourth Edition, Text Revision.* Copyright 2000, American Psychiatric Association.

Figure 14.5, p. 521, adapted from Botella, C. & Narvaes, P. M. (1998). Cognitive behavioral treatment for hypochondriasis. In V.E. Caballo (Ed)., *International handbook of cognitive and behavioural treatments for psychological disorders* (p. 359). Oxford: Elsevier Science. Copyright 1998, with permission from Elsevier.

Endpaper

Back endpaper reprinted with permission from the *Diagnostic and Statistical Manual of Mental Disorders, Fourth Edition, Text Revision.* Copyright 2000, American Psychiatric Association.

NAME INDEX

A

Abalbjarnardottir, S., 259
Abend, S.M., 146, 147
Abernathy, T., 276
Abi-Dargham, A., 414
Abikoff, H.B., 459
Abraham, K., 184, 280
Abrams, R.D., 54
Abramson, L.Y., 180
Achenbach, T.M., 438, 470, 471
Ackerman, B.P., 38
Adams, H., 395
Addington, D., 415
Addington, O., 415
Adler, D., 385
Agras, W.S., 247
Aguayo, J., 44
Ahn, C., 408
Aiken, L.R., 97, 102
Akhtar, S., 121, 207, 364
Alarcon, R.D., 19, 386
Albano, A.M., 126
Albee, G.W., 78
Alcabes, P., 303
Aldridge, 280
Alexander, M., 61
Alison, L., 326
Allebeck, P., 394
Allen, J.G., 295, 297
Allen, J.P., 465
Allison, D., 235
Allison, J., 95
Alloy, L.B., 180
Alpert, M., 405
Althof, S., 316, 319
Amador, X.F., 399, 404, 405
Amato, 463
Ammerman, R.T., 278
an der Heiden, W., 409, 410
Anand, 2000, 174
Andersen, A.E., 235, 237

Andersen, R.E., 235
Anderson, B.L., 500
Anderson, S., 303
Andersson, J., 269
Andreason, N.C., 99, 398, 404, 414, 415
Andreski, P., 128
Andrews, G., 143
Aneshensel, C.S., 124, 128
Anthony, J.C., 256, 257
Anton, R., 292
Antoni, M.H., 65
Apsche, J., 52
Arjonilla, S., 276
Arnold, 234
Arnsten, A.F.T., 275
Aron, L., 44
Aronow, E., 95
Aronson, T.A., 366
Arria, A., 257
Arrington, R., 14
Asbridge, M., 276
Asher, R., 507
Athanasiadis, L., 320, 410
Atre-Vaidya, N., 407
Attie, I., 234
Attkinson, C.C., 96
Axelrod, S., 52
Azima, F.J.C., 375

B

Baer, D.M., 278
Bahnson, 204
Bahramali, H., 416
Baker, C.A., 401
Baker, F.M., 408
Baker, L., 241
Baker, R.W., 91
Balster, R.L., 284
Bandura, A., 52, 56, 293, 295, 334
Bane, F., 422
Barber, J.G., 269, 292

Barber, J.P., 369, 381
Bard, R.A., 8
Bardenstein, K.K., 375, 385
Barendregt, C., 304
Barger, S.D., 501
Bark, N.M., 30
Barkan, H., 215
Barker, C., 91
Barkley, R.A., 98, 456, 457, 458, 459
Barlow, D.H., 126, 129, 133, 147, 323
Barnard, M.U., 187
Barron, J.W., 76, 82, 83, 84
Barrowclough, C., 429
Barsky, A.J., 517
Bartlett, A., 19
Barto, P.E., 415
Basco, M.R., 184, 190
Bass, 464
Bateson, G., 61, 429
Batzer, W., 280
Bauer, K., 40
Bauer, M.E., 491
Baumeister, R., 310, 320
Baxter, L., 149
Bayer, R., 310
Bebbington, P., 479
Beck, A.T., 53, 55, 80, 93, 135, 136, 140, 178, 180, 181, 356, 360, 371, 373, 375, 377, 380, 381, 383, 429
Beck, J., 317
Becker, A.E., 238
Beech, A., 328
Beest, I.V., 498
Belknap, R., 37
Bell, C.C., 408
Bell-Dolan, D.J., 126
Bellack, A.S., 429
Belmaker, R.H., 422
Bemis, C., 500
Ben-Shakhar, G., 76
Ben-Zion, I.Z., 143

DSM-IV-TR CATEGORIES
from the American Psychiatric Association, 2000*

DISORDERS USUALLY FIRST DIAGNOSED IN INFANCY, CHILDHOOD, OR ADOLESCENCE

Mental Retardation
Note: these are coded on Axis II.

Mild
Moderate
Severe
Profound

Learning Disorders
Reading Disorder
Mathematics Disorder
Disorder of Written Expression

Motor Skills Disorder
Developmental Coordination Disorder

Communication Disorders
Expressive Language Disorder
Mixed Receptive-Expressive Language Disorder
Phonological Disorder
Stuttering

Pervasive Developmental Disorders
Autistic Disorder
Rett's Disorder
Childhood Disintegrative Disorders
Asperger's Disorder
Attention Deficit and Disruptive Behavior Disorders
Attention-Deficit/Hyperactivity Disorder
  Combined Type
  Predominantly Inattentive Type
  Predominantly Hyperactive-Impulsive Type
Conduct Disorder
Oppositional Defiant Disorder

Feeding and Eating Disorders of Infancy or Early Childhood
Pica
Rumination Disorder
Feeding Disorder of Infancy or Early Childhood

Tic Disorders
Tourette's Disorder
Chronic Motor or Vocal Tic Disorder
Transient Tic Disorder

Elimination Disorders
Encopresis
Enuresis *(Not due to a General Medical Condition)*

Other Disorders of Infancy, Childhood, or Adolescence
Separation Anxiety Disorder
Selective Mutism
Reactive Attachment Disorder of Infancy or Early Childhood
Stereotypic Movement Disorder

DELIRIUM, DEMENTIA, AND AMNESTIC AND OTHER COGNITIVE DISORDERS

Delirium
Dementia
Dementia of Alzheimer's Type, with Early Onset
Dementia of Alzheimer's Type, with Late Onset
Vascular Dimentia
Dementia Due to HIV Disease
Dementia Due to Head Trauma
Dementia Due to Parkinson's Disease
Dementia Due to Huntington's Disease
Dementia Due to Pick's Disease
Dementia Due to Creutzfeldt-Jakob Disease

Amnestic Disorders

SUBSTANCE-RELATED DISORDERS

Alcohol-Related Disorders
Alcohol Dependence
Alcohol Abuse

Amphetamine- (or Amphetamine-like) Related Disorders

Caffeine-Related Disorders

Cannabis-Related Disorders

Cocaine-Related Disorders

Hallucinogen-Related Disorders

Note: In some major categories, additional diagnoses include: (Disorder) Not Otherwise Specified, (Disorder) Due to General Medical Condition, (Disorder) Substance Induced

Inhalent-Related Disorders
Nicotine-Related Disorders
Opioid-Related Disorders
Phencyclidine-(or Phencyclidine-like) Related Disorders
Sedative-, Hypnotic-, or Anxiolytic-Related Disorders
Polysubstance-Related Disorder

SCHIZOPHRENIA AND OTHER PSYCHOTIC DISORDERS

Schizophrenia
Paranoid Type
Disorganized Type
Catatonic Type
Undifferentiated Type
Residual Type

Schizophreniform Disorder
Schizoaffective Disorder
Delusional Disorder
Brief Psychotic Disorder
Shared Psychotic Disorder

MOOD DISORDERS

Depressive Disorders
Major Depressive Disorder
  Single Episode
  Recurrent
Dystymic Disorder

Bipolar Disorders
Bipolar I Disorder
Bipolar II Disorder
Cyclothymic Disorder

ANXIETY DISORDERS

Panic Disorder without Agoraphobia
Panic Disorder with Agoraphobia
Agoraphobia without History of Panic Disorder
Specific Phobia
Social Phobia
Obsessive-Compulsive Disorder
Posttraumatic Stress Disorder